Adobe Illustrator Photoshop & InDesign CS5

Graphic Design Portfolio

Managing Editor: Ellenn Behoriam
Cover & Interior Design: Erika Kendra
Copy Editor: Angelina Kendra
Printer: Prestige Printers

10 9 8 7 6 5 4 3 2

978-1-936201-07-5

4710 28th Street North, Saint Petersburg, FL 33714
800-256-4ATC • www.againsttheclock.com

Acknowledgements

About Against The Clock

Against The Clock, long recognized as one of the nation's leaders in courseware development, has been publishing high-quality educational materials for the graphic and computer arts industries since 1990. The company has developed a solid and widely-respected approach to teaching people how to effectively utilize graphics applications, while maintaining a disciplined approach to real-world problems.

Having developed the *Against The Clock* and the *Essentials for Design* series with Prentice Hall/Pearson Education, ATC drew from years of professional experience and instructor feedback to develop *The Professional Portfolio Series*, focusing on the Adobe Creative Suite. These books feature step-by-step explanations, detailed foundational information, and advice and tips from industry professionals that offer practical solutions to technical issues.

Against The Clock works closely with all major software developers to create learning solutions that fulfill both the requirements of instructors and the needs of students. Thousands of graphic arts professionals — designers, illustrators, imaging specialists, prepress experts, and production managers — began their educations with Against The Clock training books. These professionals studied at Baker College, Nossi College of Art, Virginia Tech, Appalachian State University, Keiser College, University of South Carolina, Gress Graphic Arts Institute, Hagerstown Community College, Kean University, Southern Polytechnic State University, Brenau University, and many other educational institutions.

About the Author

Erika Kendra holds a BA in History and a BA in English Literature from the University of Pittsburgh. She began her career in the graphic communications industry as an editor at Graphic Arts Technical Foundation before moving to Los Angeles in 2000. Erika is the author or co-author of more than twenty books about Adobe graphic design software. She has also written several books about graphic design concepts such as color reproduction and preflighting, and dozens of articles for online and print journals in the graphics industry. Working with Against The Clock for more than ten years, Erika was a key partner in developing *The Professional Portfolio Series* of software training books.

Contributing Authors, Artists, and Editors

A big thank you to the people whose artwork, comments, and expertise contributed to the success of these books:

- **Randy Anderson**, Oklahoma City Community College
- **Jay Beber**, Roslyn, New York
- **Bill Carberry**, ACI4hire.com
- **Jordan Cox**, Against The Clock
- **John Craft**, Appalachian State University
- **Debbie Davidson**, Sweet Dreams Design
- **Jorge Diaz**, International Academy of Design and Technology
- **Eric Dye,** West Virginia Department of Education
- **Pamela Harris**, University of North Texas Dallas
- **Tim Hubbell**, Tampa, Florida
- **Christopher Kocmoud,** Blinn College
- **Somiah Muslimani,** Virginia Tech
- **Beth Rogers**, Nossi College of Art

Finally, thanks to **Angelina Kendra**, editor, for making sure that we all said what we meant to say.

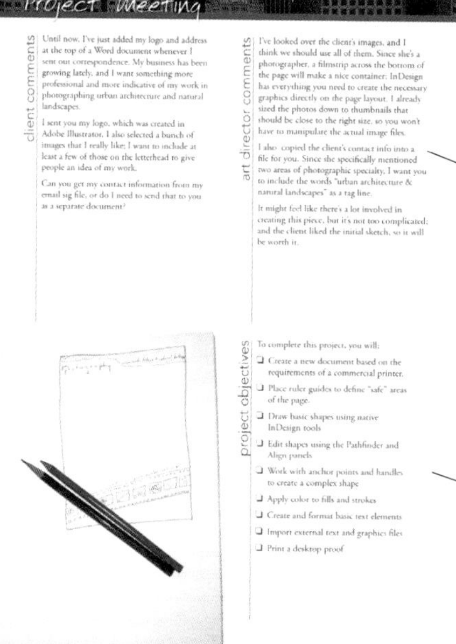

Project Goals

Each project begins with a clear description of the overall concepts that are explained in the project; these goals closely match the different "stages" of the project workflow.

The Project Meeting

Each project includes the client's initial comments, which provide valuable information about the job. The Project Art Director, a vital part of any design workflow, also provides fundamental advice and production requirements.

Project Objectives

Each Project Meeting includes a summary of the specific skills required to complete the project.

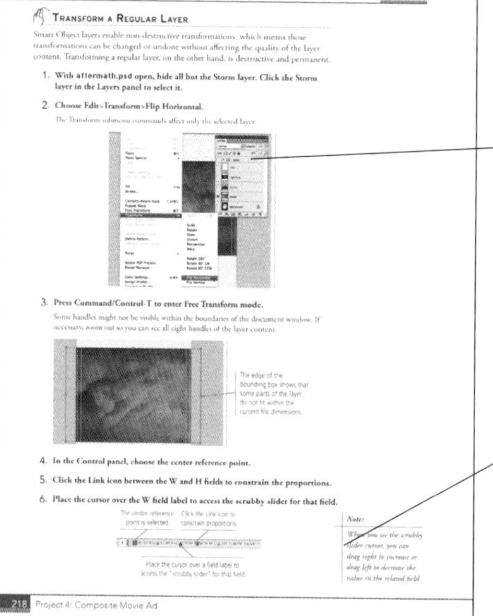

Real-World Workflow

Projects are broken into logical lessons or "stages" of the workflow. Brief introductions at the beginning of each stage provide vital foundational material required to complete the task.

Step-By-Step Exercises

Every stage of the workflow is broken into multiple hands-on, step-by-step exercises.

Visual Explanations

Wherever possible, screen shots are annotated so students can quickly identify important information.

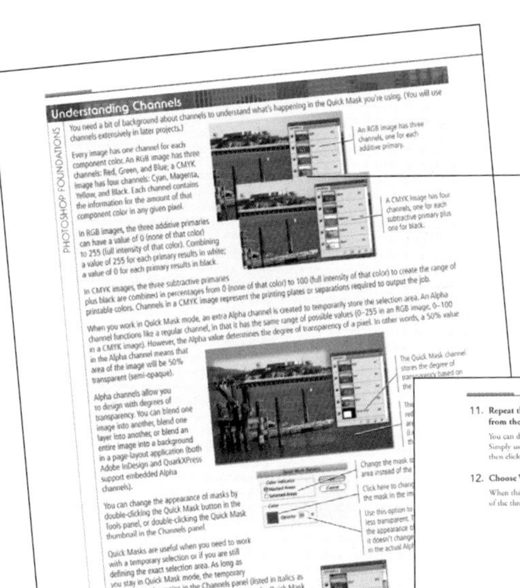

Design Foundations

Additional functionality, related tools, and underlying graphic design concepts are included throughout the book.

Advice and Warnings

Where appropriate, sidebars provide shortcuts, warnings, or tips about the topic at hand.

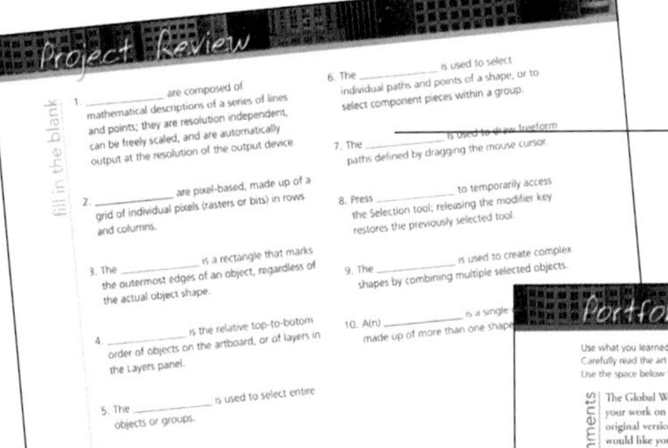

Project Review

After completing each project, students can complete these fill-in-the-blank and short-answer questions to test their understanding of the concepts in the project.

Portfolio Builder Projects

Each step-by-step project is accompanied by a freeform project, allowing students to practice skills and creativity, resulting in an extensive and diverse portfolio of work.

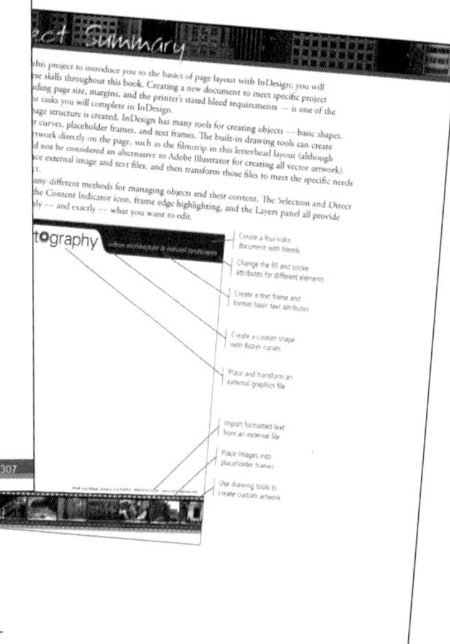

Visual Summary

Using an annotated version of the finished project, students can quickly identify the skills used to complete different aspects of the job.

Projects at a Glance

project 1 — International Symbols

- ❑ Setting up the Workspace
- ❑ Drawing Basic Shapes

project 2 — Balloon Festival Artwork

- ❑ Drawing Complex Artwork
- ❑ Coloring and Painting Artwork
- ❑ Exporting EPS and PDF Files

project 3 — Identity Package

- ❑ Working with Gradient Meshes
- ❑ Working with Type
- ❑ Working with Multiple Artboards
- ❑ Combining Text and Graphics

project 4 — Composite Movie Ad

- ❑ Compositing Images and Artwork
- ❑ Managing Layers
- ❑ Creating Complex Selections
- ❑ Saving Photoshop Files for Print

project 5 — African Wildlife Map

- ❑ Working with Vector Shape Layers
- ❑ Compositing with Smart Objects
- ❑ Using Filters and Adjustments
- ❑ Creating an Artistic Background
- ❑ Creating Variations

project 6 — Menu Image Correction

- ❑ Retouching Damaged Images
- ❑ Correcting Lighting Problems
- ❑ Correcting Color Problems
- ❑ Preparing Images for Print
- ❑ Working with HDR Images

project 7

Letterhead Design

- ❑ Setting up the Workspace
- ❑ Creating Basic Page Elements
- ❑ Placing External Images
- ❑ Creating and Formatting Basic Text
- ❑ Printing InDesign Files

project 10

Combined Brochure

- ❑ Controlling Color for Output
- ❑ Placing and Controlling Images
- ❑ Working with Text
- ❑ Editing Linked Files

project 8

Festival Poster

- ❑ Building Graphic Interest
- ❑ Importing and Formatting Text
- ❑ Graphics as Text and Text as Graphics
- ❑ Outputting the File

project 9

HeartSmart Newsletter

- ❑ Working with Templates
- ❑ Working with Styles
- ❑ Working with Tables
- ❑ Preflighting and Packaging the Job

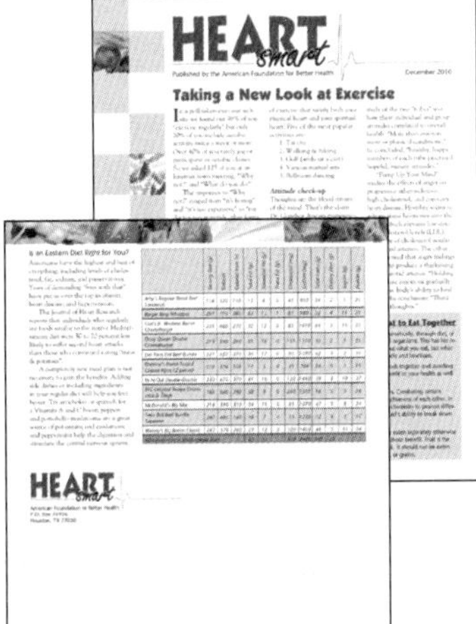

The Against The Clock *Portfolio Series* teaches graphic design software tools and techniques entirely within the framework of real-world projects; we introduce and explain skills where they would naturally fall into a real project workflow.

The project-based approach in *The Professional Portfolio Series* allows you to get in depth with the software beginning in Project 1 — you don't have to read several chapters of introductory material before you can start creating finished artwork.

Our approach also prevents "topic tedium" — in other words, we don't require you to read pages and pages of information about text (for example); instead, we explain text tools and options as part of a larger project.

Clear, easy-to-read, step-by-step instructions walk you through every phase of each job, from creating a new file to saving the finished piece. Wherever logical, we also offer practical advice and tips about underlying concepts and graphic design practices that will benefit students as they enter the job market.

The projects in this book reflect a range of different types of print design jobs using Adobe Illustrator, Photoshop, and InDesign. When you finish the ten projects in this book (and the accompanying Portfolio Builder exercises), you will have a solid foundational knowledge of the three most popular applications in the print design market — and have a substantial body of work that should impress any potential employer.

Contents

Prerequisites

The Professional Portfolio Series is based on the assumption that you have a basic understanding of how to use your computer. You should know how to use your mouse to point and click, as well as how to drag items around the screen. You should be able to resize and arrange windows on your desktop to maximize your available space. You should know how to access drop-down menus, and understand how check boxes and radio buttons work. It also doesn't hurt to have a good understanding of how your operating system organizes files and folders, and how to navigate your way around them. If you're familiar with these fundamental skills, then you know all that's necessary to use *The Professional Portfolio Series*.

Resource Files

All of the files you need to complete the projects in this book — except, of course, the Creative Suite application files — are on the Student Files Web page at www.againsttheclock.com. See the inside back cover of this book for access information.

Each archive (ZIP) file is named according to the related project (e.g., **Print5_RF_Project1.zip**). At the beginning of each project, you must download the archive file for that project and expand that archive to access the resource files that you need to complete the exercises. Detailed instructions for this process are included in the Interface chapter.

Files required for the related Portfolio Builder exercises at the end of each project are also available on the Student Files page; these archives are also named by project (e.g., **Print5_PB_Project1.zip**).

ATC Fonts

You must download and install the ATC fonts from the Student Files Web page to ensure that your exercises and projects will work as described in the book. Specific instructions for installing fonts are provided in the documentation that came with your computer. You should replace older (pre-2004) ATC fonts with the ones on the Student Files Web page.

System Requirements

The Professional Portfolio Series was designed to work on both Macintosh or Windows computers; where differences exist from one platform to another, we include specific instructions relative to each platform. One issue that remains different from Macintosh to Windows is the use of different modifier keys (Control, Shift, etc.) to accomplish the same task. When we present key commands, we follow the Macintosh/Windows format — Macintosh keys are listed first, then a slash, followed by the Windows key command.

Explore the InDesign Interface

Adobe InDesign is a robust desktop-publishing application that — together with Illustrator, Photoshop, and Acrobat — rounds out Adobe's Creative Suite for print applications. InDesign provides the tools you need to design and create effective pages. It allows you to integrate text and graphics from multiple sources to produce files that can be printed to a local or networked printer, taken to a commercial printer or other service provider, or published on the Internet.

The user interface (UI) is what you see when you launch the application. The specific elements that you see — including which panels are open and where they appear on the screen — depend on what was done the last time the application was open. The first time you launch InDesign, you see the default workspace settings defined by Adobe. When you relaunch the application after you or another user has quit, the workspace defaults to the last-used settings.

1. **Create a new empty folder named WIP on any writable disk (where you plan to save your work in progress).**

2. **Download the Print5_RF_Interface.zip archive from the Student Files Web page.**

3. **Macintosh users: Place the ZIP archive in your WIP folder, then double-click the file icon to expand it.**

   This **Interface** folder contains all the files you need to complete this introduction.

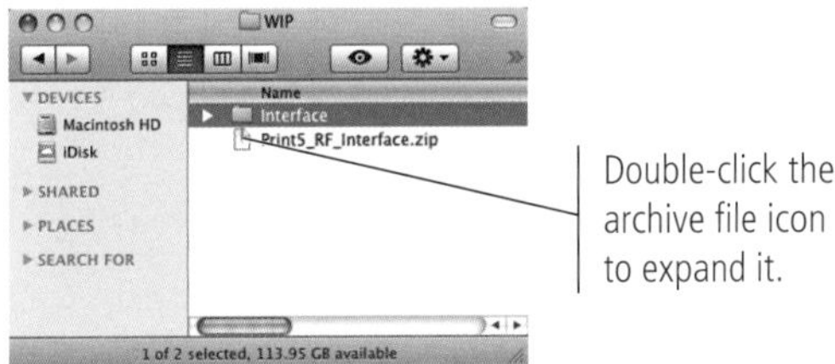

Double-click the archive file icon to expand it.

Windows users: Double-click the ZIP archive file to open it. Click the folder inside the archive and drag it into your primary WIP folder.

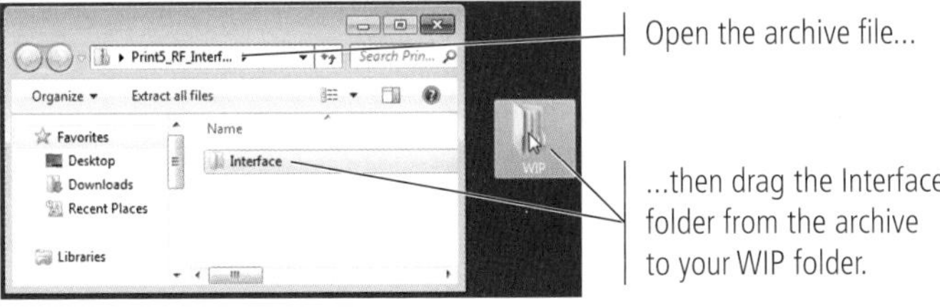

Open the archive file...

...then drag the Interface folder from the archive to your WIP folder.

4. **Macintosh users: While pressing Command-Option-Control-Shift, start InDesign. Click Yes when asked if you want to delete preference files.**

Windows users: Launch InDesign, and then press Control-Alt-Shift. Click Yes when asked if you want to delete preference files.

This step resets InDesign to the preference settings that are defined by Adobe as the application defaults. This helps to ensure that your application functions as we show in our screen shots.

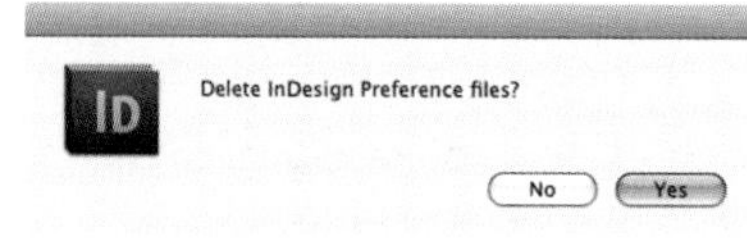

On Windows, each running application is contained within its own frame; all elements of the application — including the Menu bar, panels, tools, and open documents — are contained within the Application frame.

Adobe also offers the Application frame to Macintosh users as an option for controlling your workspace. When you activate the Application frame, the entire workspace shifts into a self-contained area that can be moved around the screen. All elements of the workspace (excluding the Menu bar) move when you move the Application frame.

Note:

Macintosh users have two extra menus. The Apple menu provides access to system-specific commands. The InDesign menu follows the Macintosh system-standard format for all applications; this menu controls basic application operations such as About, Hide, Preferences, and Quit.

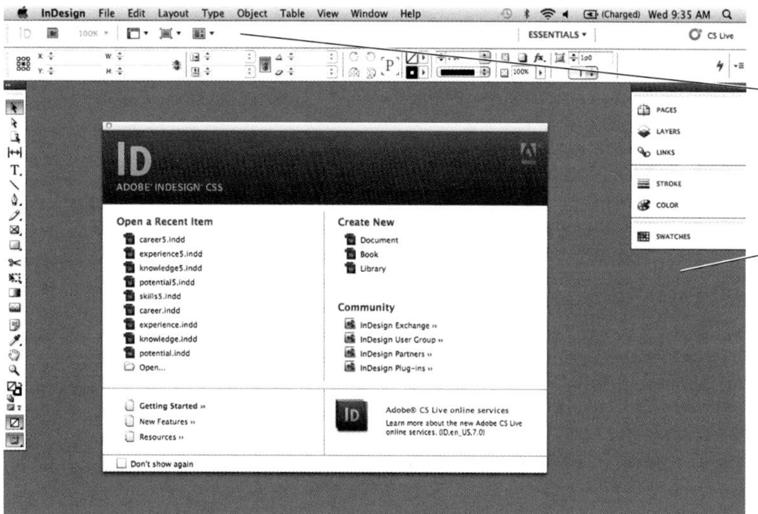

When the Application frame is not active, the Application bar appears below the Menu bar; in this case, the Application bar can be moved or turned off.

When the Application frame is not active, the desktop is visible behind the workspace elements.

Menus in Adobe Applications

If a specific menu command can be accessed with a keyboard shortcut, those shortcuts are listed to the right of the related menu command.

Some menu commands are toggles, which means a feature can be turned on or off, or an option is either visibile or hidden. A checkmark indicates that the command is currently active.

Some menu commands include the "Show" or "Hide" indicator at the beginning of the menu command. When visible, the command appears as "Hide [Option]"; when not already visible, the command appears as "Show [Option]".

Finally, if a specific menu command is grayed out (it can't be selected), that command does not apply in the current context (usually, depending on what is selected in the document).

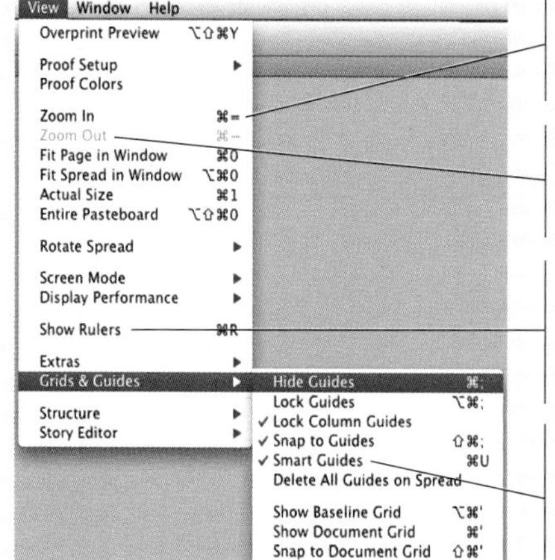

Keyboard shortcuts (if available) are listed on the right side of the menu.

If a menu command is grayed out, it is not available for the current selection.

Some commands appear as Hide [Option] when visible or Show [Option] when not visible.

Many menu commands are toggles; the checkmark indicates that an option is visible or toggled on.

The image here shows the View menu in InDesign CS5. The concepts identified here apply to menus in all Adobe Creative Suite applications.

5. **Macintosh users: Open the Window menu and choose Application Frame to toggle that option on.**

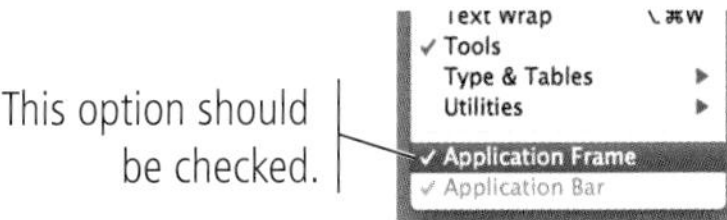

On Macintosh systems, the Application bar includes a number of buttons for accessing different view options. On Windows systems, those same options are available on the right side of the Menu bar.

The default workspace includes the Tools panel on the left side of the screen, the Control panel at the top of the screen, and a set of panels attached to the right side of the screen. (The area where the panels are stored is called the **panel dock**.)

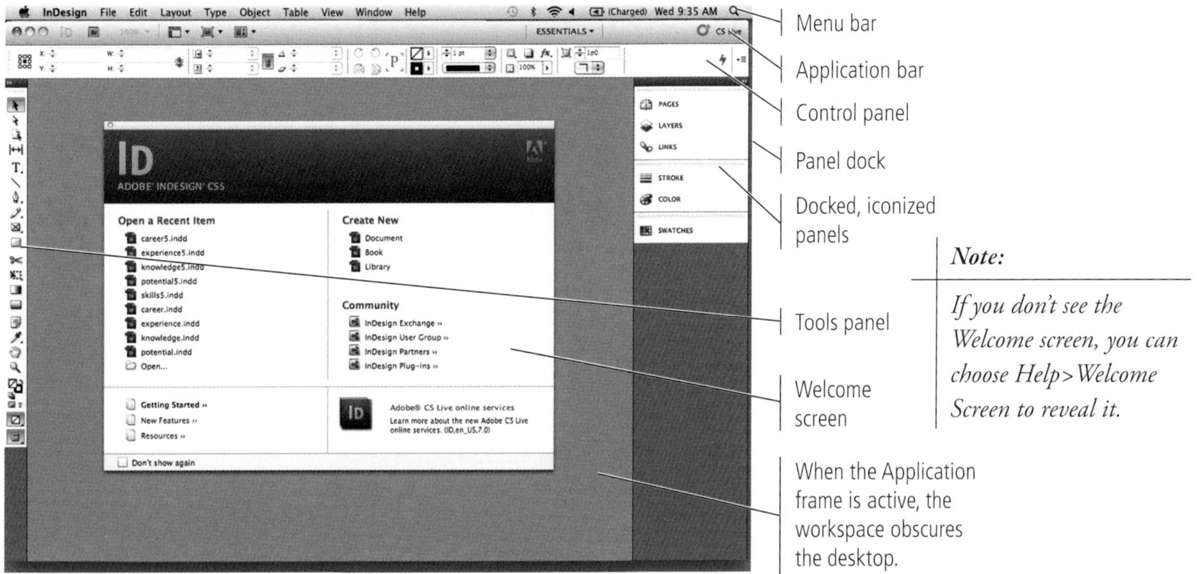

Note:

If you don't see the Welcome screen, you can choose Help>Welcome Screen to reveal it.

On Windows, the right side of the Menu bar provides access to the same options that are in the Macintosh Application bar.

6. **Control/right-click the title bar above the panel dock. Choose Auto-Collapse Iconic Panels in the contextual menu to toggle on that option.**

   As we explained in the Getting Started section, when commands are different for the Macintosh and Windows operating systems, we include the different commands in the Macintosh/Windows format. In this case, Macintosh users who do not have right-click mouse capability can press the Control key and click to access the contextual menu. You do not have to press Control *and* right-click to access the menus.

   (If you're using a Macintosh and don't have a mouse with right-click capability, we highly recommend that you purchase one. They're inexpensive, they're available at almost any retail store, and they save significant amounts of time accessing contextual options.)

   Control/right-clicking a dock title bar opens the dock contextual menu, where you can change the default panel behavior. If you toggle on the Auto-Collapse Iconic Panels option (which is inactive by default), an open panel collapses as soon as you click away from it.

Note:

Most interface functions and behaviors are the same across all three CS5 applications that are discussed in this book (InDesign, Illustrator, and Photoshop). Any significant differences are noted throughout this chapter.

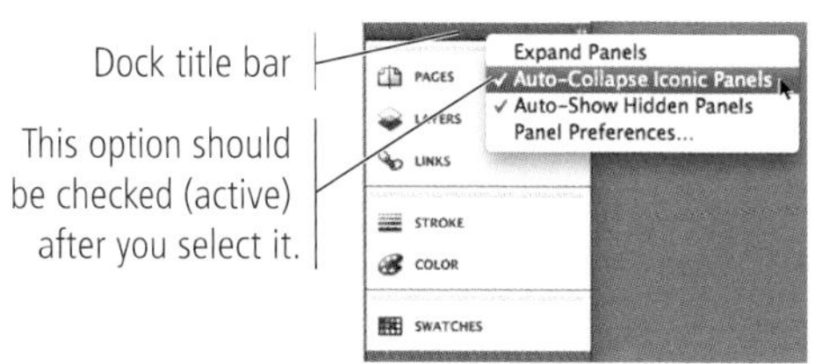

Note:

The Auto-Collapse Iconic Panels option is also available in the User Interface pane of the Preferences dialog box, which you can open directly from the dock contextual menu.

7. **In the panel dock, click the Color button to expand the panel, and then click away from the expanded panel.**

   By default, expanded panels remain open until you manually close them or expand another panel in the same dock column. When Auto-Collapse Iconic Panels is toggled on, the expanded panel collapses as soon as you click away from it.

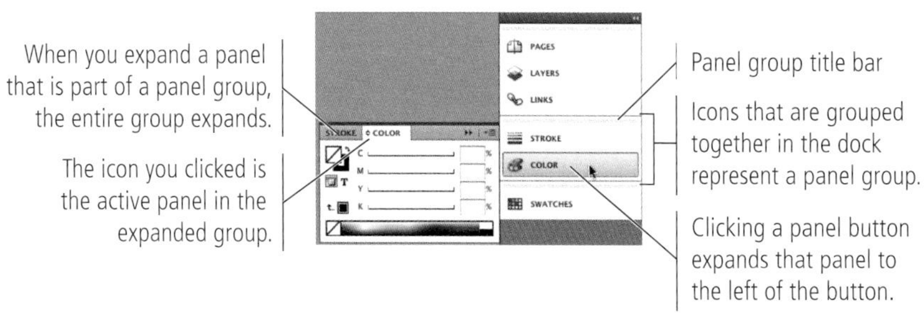

When you expand a panel that is part of a panel group, the entire group expands.
The icon you clicked is the active panel in the expanded group.
Panel group title bar
Icons that are grouped together in the dock represent a panel group.
Clicking a panel button expands that panel to the left of the button.
STROKE
COLOR
PAGES
LAYERS
LINKS
SWATCHES

Note:

*Collapsed panels are referred to as **iconized** or **iconic**.*

8. **Click the left edge of the docked panels and drag right.**

   When panels are iconized, you can reduce the button size to show icons only. Doing so can be particularly useful once you are more familiar with the application and the icons used to symbolize the different panels.

9. **Double-click the title bar above the column of docked panels.**

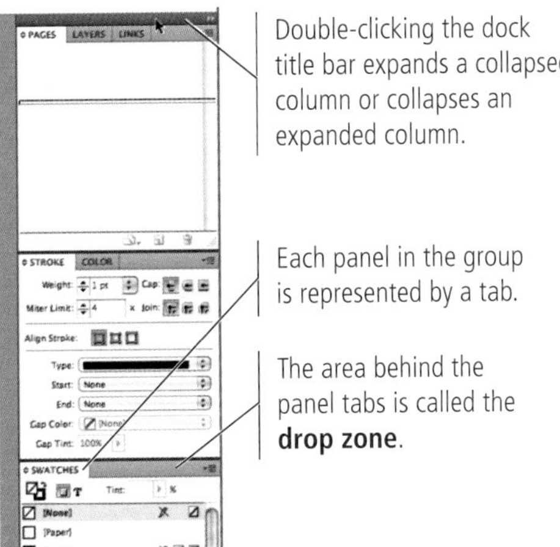

Double-clicking the dock title bar expands a collapsed column or collapses an expanded column.
Each panel in the group is represented by a tab.
The area behind the panel tabs is called the **drop zone**.

10. **On the left side of the workspace, double-click the title bar of the Tools panel.**

The Tools panel can't expand, but it can display as either one or two columns; clicking the Tools panel title bar toggles between the two modes.

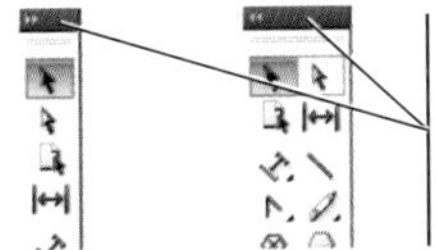

Double-click the Tools panel title bar to toggle between the one-column and two-column layouts.

Deciding whether to use the one- or two-column format is a purely personal choice. The two-column format fits in a smaller vertical space, which is useful if you have a laptop with a widescreen monitor.

The Tools panel can also be floated (moved out of the dock) by clicking its title bar and dragging away from the edge of the screen. To re-dock the floating Tools panel, simply click the panel's title bar and drag back to the left edge of the screen; when a blue line highlights the edge of the workspace, releasing the mouse button places the Tools panel back in the dock.

Note:

If the InDesign Tools panel is floating, you can toggle through three different modes — one-column vertical, one-row horizontal, and two-column vertical.

Photoshop and Illustrator only offer the one- and two-column vertical formats, whether docked or not.

11. **Continue to the next exercise.**

Identifying InDesign Tools

INDESIGN FOUNDATIONS

The following image offers a quick reference of nested tools in InDesign, as well as the keyboard shortcut for each tool (if any). Nested tools are shown indented and in italics.

- Selection tool (V)
- Direct Selection tool (A)
- Page tool (Shift-P)
- Gap tool (U)
- Type tool (T)
  - *Type on a Path tool (Shift-T)*
- Line tool (\)
- Pen tool (P)
  - *Add Anchor Point tool (=)*
  - *Delete Anchor Point tool (-)*
  - *Convert Direction Point tool (Shift-C)*
- Pencil tool (N)
  - *Smooth tool*
  - *Erase tool*
- Rectangle Frame tool (F)
  - *Ellipse Frame tool*
  - *Polygon Frame tool*
- Rectangle tool (M)
  - *Ellipse tool (L)*
  - *Polygon tool*
- Scissors tool (C)
- Free Transform tool (E)
  - *Rotate tool (R)*
  - *Scale tool (S)*
  - *Shear tool (O)*
- Gradient Swatch tool (G)
- Gradient Feather tool (Shift-G)
- Note tool
- Eyedropper tool (I)
  - *Measure tool (K)*
- Hand tool (H)
- Zoom tool (Z)

Accessing Tools in Adobe CS5 Applications

Adobe Creative Suite applications have no shortage of tools; you will learn how to use many of them as you complete the projects in this book. For now, you should simply take the opportunity to identify the tools, and understand how to access the nested variations.

Nested Tools

Any tool with an arrow in the bottom-right corner includes related tools below it. When you click a tool and hold down the mouse button, the **nested tools** appear in a pop-up menu. (In Photoshop and InDesign, you can also Control/right-click a tool to reveal the menu of nested tools.) When you choose one of the nested tools, that variation becomes the default choice in the Tools panel.

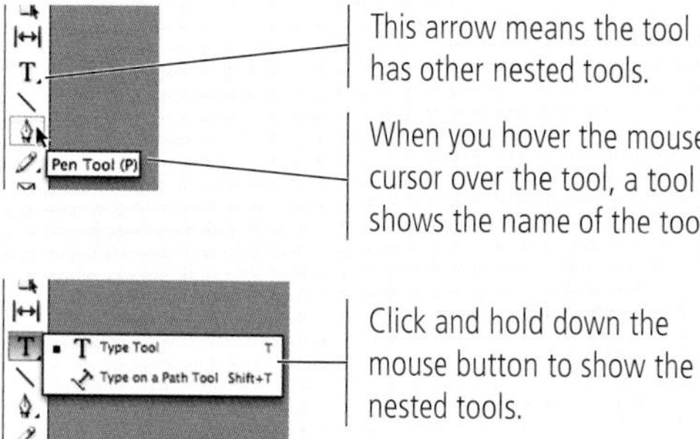
Pen Tool (P)
Type Tool T
Type on a Path Tool Shift+T
This arrow means the tool has other nested tools.
When you hover the mouse cursor over the tool, a tool tip shows the name of the tool.
Click and hold down the mouse button to show the nested tools.

Most of the default tools can be accessed with a keyboard shortcut. When you hover the mouse cursor over a tool, the pop-up **tool tip** shows the name of the tool and a shortcut letter in parentheses. If you don't see tool tips, check the Interface preferences (InDesign and Photoshop) or General preferences (Illustrator); the Show Tool Tips check box should be active.

Keyboard Shortcuts

If a tool has a defined shortcut, pressing that key activates the associated tool. In Photoshop, most nested tools have the same shortcut as the default tool. By default, you have to press Shift plus the shortcut key to access the nested variations. You can change this behavior in the General pane of the Preferences dialog box by unchecking the Use Shift Key for Tool Switch option. When this option is off, you can simply press the shortcut key multiple times to cycle through the variations.

Spring-Loaded Tool Shortcuts

In InDesign and Photoshop, if you press and hold a tool's keyboard shortcut, you can temporarily call the appropriate tool (called **spring-loaded keys**); after releasing the shortcut key, you return to the tool you were using previously. For example, you might use this technique to switch temporarily from the Brush tool to the Eraser tool while painting.

Tool Hints in InDesign

The Tool Hints panel (Window>Utilities>Tool Hints) provides useful tips about the active tool, including a brief description of the tool; an explanation of the tool's behavior when you press one or more modifier keys; and the tool's keyboard shortcut.

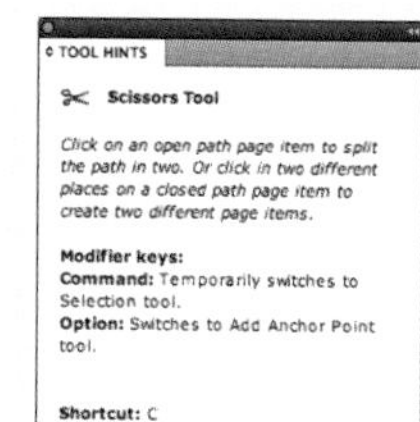
TOOL HINTS
Scissors Tool
Click on an open path page item to split the path in two. Or click in two different places on a closed path page item to create two different page items.
Modifier keys:
Command: Temporarily switches to Selection tool.
Option: Switches to Add Anchor Point tool.
Shortcut: C

Tear-Off Tools in Illustrator

If you drag the mouse cursor to the bar on the right of the nested-tool menu, the nested-tool options separate into their own floating toolboxes so you can more easily access the nested variations. (The primary tool is not removed from the main Tools panel.)

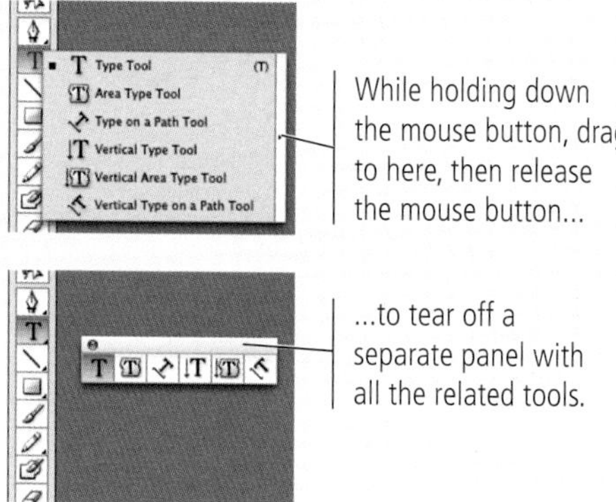
Type Tool (T)
Area Type Tool
Type on a Path Tool
Vertical Type Tool
Vertical Area Type Tool
Vertical Type on a Path Tool
While holding down the mouse button, drag to here, then release the mouse button...
...to tear off a separate panel with all the related tools.

Explore the Arrangement of Application Panels

As you gain experience and familiarity with Adobe applications, you will develop personal artistic and working styles. You will also find that different types of jobs often require different but specific sets of tools. Adobe recognizes this wide range of needs and preferences among users; CS5 applications includes a number of options for arranging and managing the numerous panels so you can customize and personalize the workspace to suit your specific needs.

We designed the following exercise to give you an opportunity to explore different ways of controlling InDesign panels. Because workspace preferences are largely a matter of personal taste, the projects in this book instruct you to use certain tools and panels, but where you place those elements within the interface is up to you. The same techniques apply in Photoshop and Illustrator, so we will not repeat these instructions for each of the applications. In general, all three applications have the same functionality; we do note where differences occur.

1. **With InDesign open, choose Window>Color>Color.**

   All panels can be toggled on and off from the Window menu.

   - If you choose a panel that's already open but iconized, the panel expands to the left of its icon.
   - If you choose a panel that's already open in an expanded group, that panel comes to the front of the group.
   - If you choose a panel that isn't currently open, it opens in the same place as it was when it was last closed.

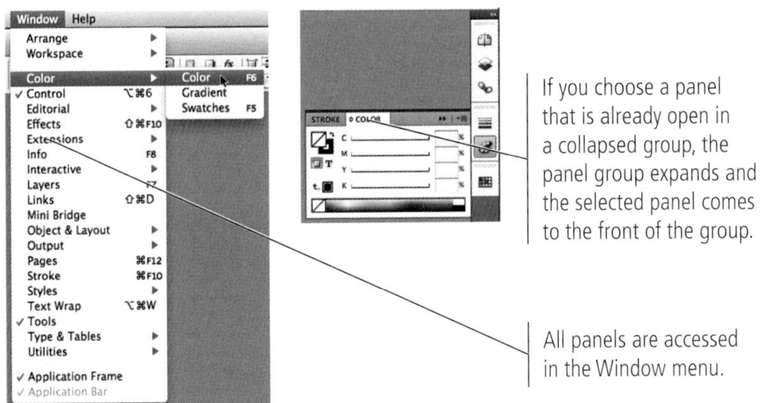

If you choose a panel that is already open in a collapsed group, the panel group expands and the selected panel comes to the front of the group.

All panels are accessed in the Window menu.

2. **Control/right-click the panel group drop zone (to the right of the panel tabs) and choose Close Tab Group from the contextual menu.**

   You can also Control/right-click a panel tab and choose Close to close only one panel in a group.

Note:

You can click and drag a panel group's drop zone to float or move the entire group.

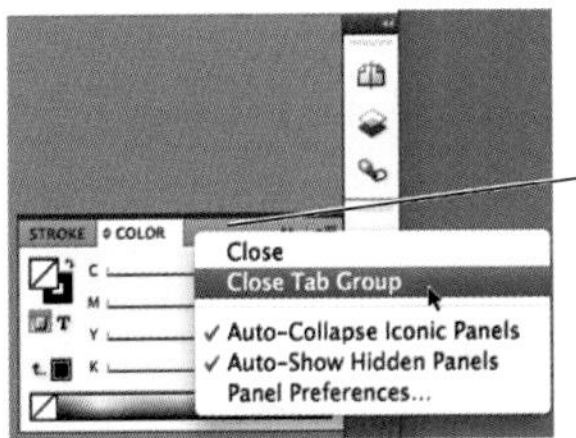

Control/right-click the panel group's drop zone to access the contextual menu.

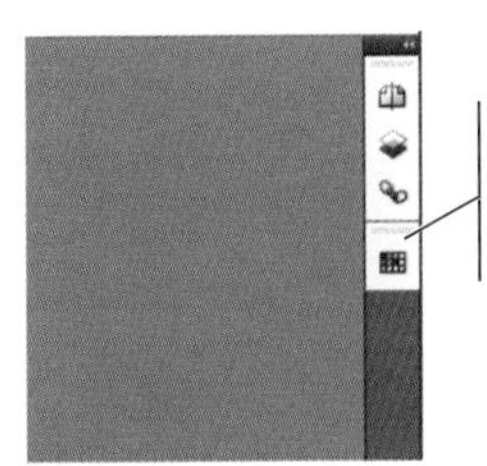

The closed panel group is removed from the panel dock.

3. **Double-click the title bar of the panel dock to expand the dock column.**

4. **Click the Links panel tab in the top panel group and drag away from the panel dock.**

   Panels can be **floated** by clicking a panel tab and dragging away from the dock.

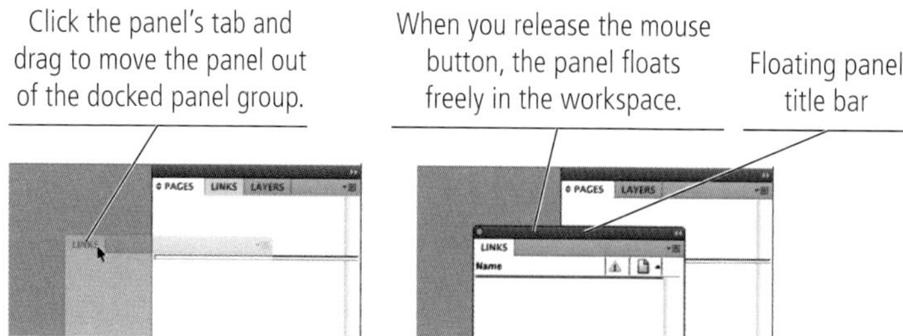

5. **Click the Links panel tab and drag to the dock, between the Pages and Swatches panels. When you see a blue line between the existing docked panels, release the mouse button.**

   Panels and panel groups can be dragged to different locations (including into different groups) by dragging the panel's tab; the target location — where the panel will reside when you release the mouse button — is identified by the blue highlight.

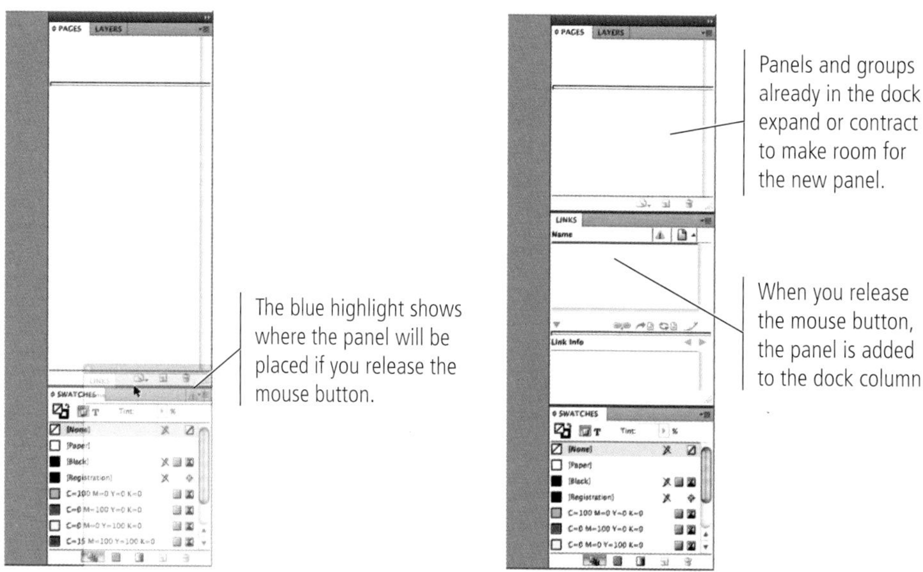

Panels and groups already in the dock expand or contract to make room for the new panel.

6. **Click the Layers panel tab and drag left until the blue highlight shows a second column added to the dock.**

   As we mentioned earlier, you can create multiple columns of panels in the dock. This can be very useful if you need easy access to a large number of panels and have a monitor with enough available screen space.

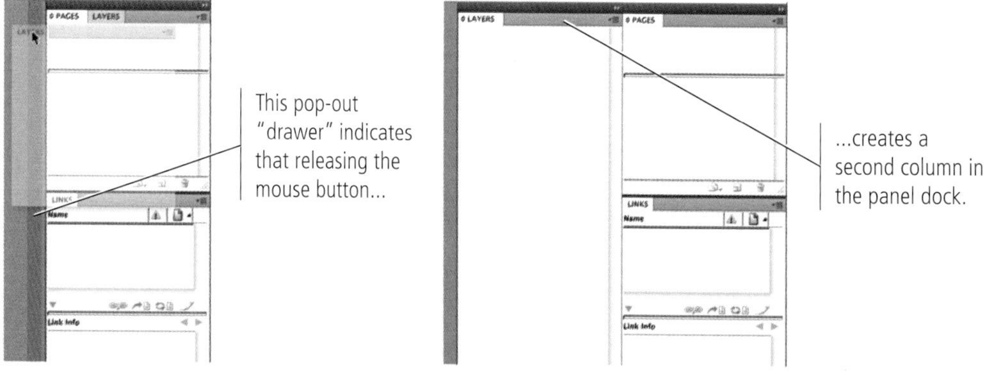

This pop-out "drawer" indicates that releasing the mouse button...
...creates a second column in the panel dock.

7. **Double-click the title bar of the left dock column to iconize that column.**

   You can independently iconize or expand each column of docked panels and each floating panel (group).

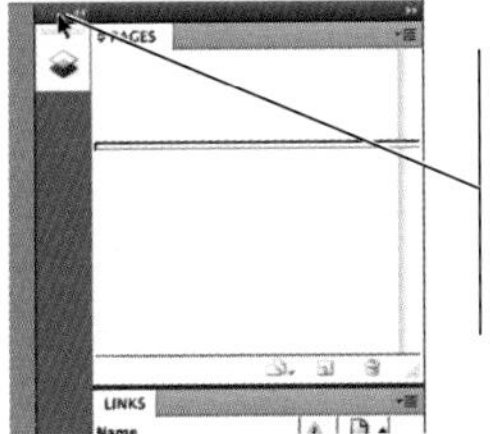

Double-click the title bar at the top of the dock column to collapse or expand it independently of other dock columns.

> *Note:*
>
> *Each dock column, technically considered a separate dock, can be expanded or collapsed independently of other columns.*

8. **Double-click the drop zone behind the Swatches panel tab to collapse the panel group.**

   When a group is collapsed but not iconized, only the panel tabs are visible. Clicking a tab in a collapsed panel group expands the group and makes the selected panel active. You can also expand the group by again double-clicking the drop zone.

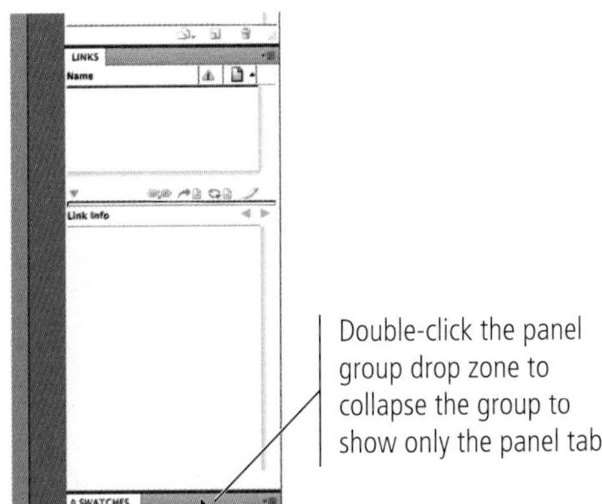

Double-click the panel group drop zone to collapse the group to show only the panel tabs.

> *Note:*
>
> *Each column of the dock can be made wider or narrower by dragging the left edge of the column.*
>
> *Dragging the left edge of a dock column changes the width of all panels in that column.*

9. **In the right dock column, click the bottom edge of the Pages panel group and drag down until the Pages panel occupies approximately half of the vertical dock space.**

   When you drag the bottom edge of a docked group, other panels in the same column expand or contract to fit the available space.

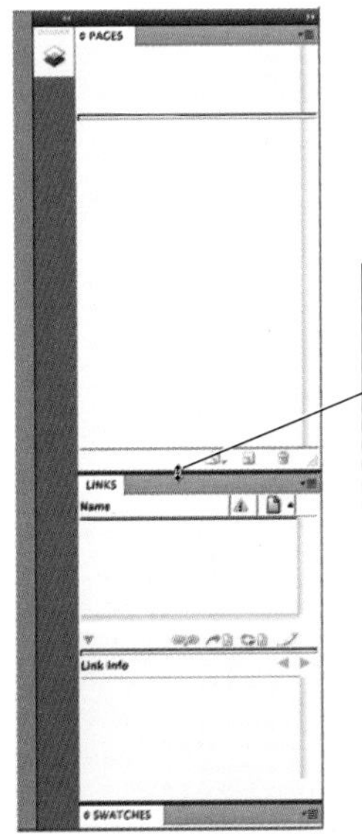

Dragging the bottom edge of a docked panel (or group) changes the height of that panel (or group). Other panels in the same column expand or shrink as necessary to fit the column.

> *Note:*
>
> *Most screen shots in this book show floating panels so we can focus on the most important issue in a particular image. In our production workflow, however, we make heavy use of docked and iconized panels and take full advantage of saved custom workspaces.*

10. **Continue to the next exercise.**

Create a Saved Workspace

By now you should understand that you have extensive control over the appearance of your workspace — what panels are visible, where and how they appear, and even the size of individual panels or panel groups. Over time you will develop personal preferences based on your work habits and project needs. Rather than re-establishing every workspace element each time you return to an application, you can save your custom workspace settings so you can recall them with a single click.

1. **Click the Workspace switcher in the Application/Menu bar and choose New Workspace.**

   Again, keep in mind that we list differing commands in the Macintosh/Windows format. On Macintosh, the Workspace switcher is in the Application bar; on Windows, it's in the Menu bar.

   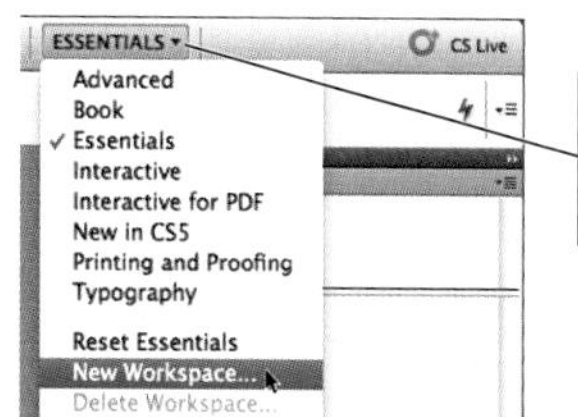

   The Workspace switcher shows the name of the last-called workspace.

2. **In the New Workspace dialog box, type `Portfolio`. Make sure the Panel Locations option is checked and click OK.**

   You didn't define custom menus, so that option is not relevant in this exercise.

   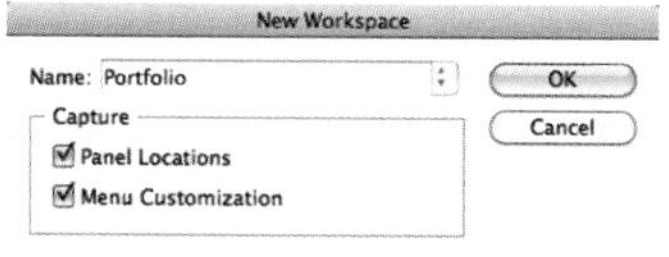

   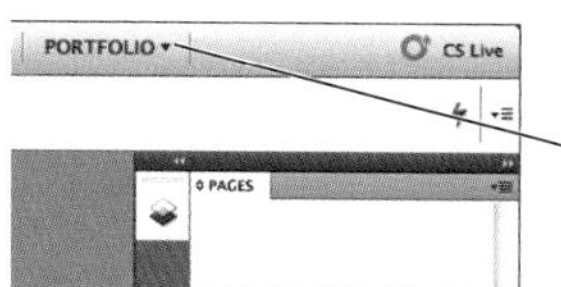

   After saving the current workspace, the Workspace switcher shows the name of the newly saved workspace.

3. **Open the Window menu and choose Workspace>Essentials.**

   Saved workspaces can be accessed in the Window>Workspace submenu as well as the Workspace switcher on the Application/Menu bar.

   Options in this submenu are the same as those in the Workspace switcher.

   Keyboard shortcuts (if available) are listed on the right side of the menu.

   The checkmark indicates that an option is visible or toggled on.

   If an option is grayed out, it is not available for the current selection.

   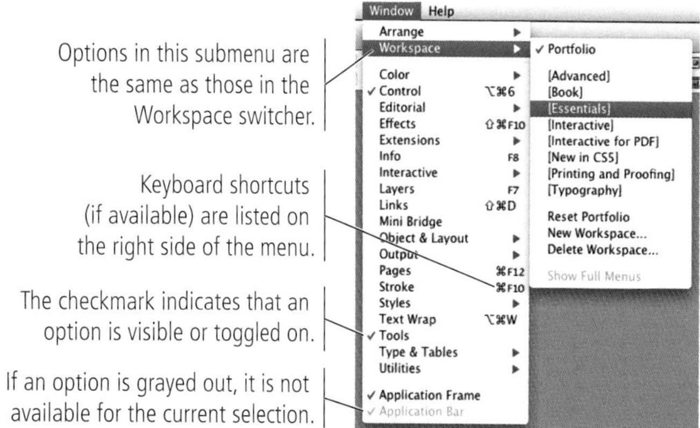

   Calling a saved workspace restores the last-used state of the workspace. You made a number of changes since you launched InDesign with the default Essentials workspace, so calling the Essentials workspace restores the last state of that workspace — in essence, nothing changes from the saved Portfolio workspace.

   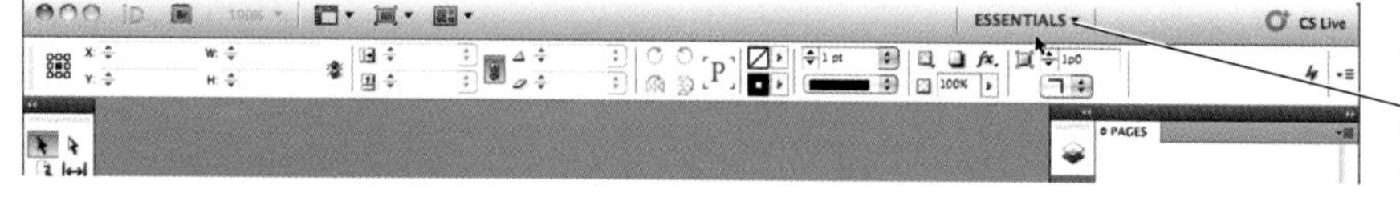

   The only apparent difference is the active workspace name.

> *Note:*
>
> *In Illustrator, the Save Workspace command accomplishes the same function as the New Workspace command in InDesign and Photoshop*

> *Note:*
>
> *The Delete Workspace option opens a dialog box where you can choose a specific user-defined workspace to delete.*

> *Note:*
>
> *If you change anything and quit the application, those changes are remembered even when InDesign is relaunched.*

Customizing Menus and Keyboard Shortcuts

People use Creative Suite applications for many different reasons, sometimes using only a specific, limited set of tools to complete a certain project. CS5 applications have several sophisticated options for customizing the user interface, including the ability to define the available menu options and the keyboard shortcuts associated with various commands.

InDesign & Photoshop

In InDesign and Photoshop, you can choose Edit>Keyboard Shortcuts or Edit>Menus to customize those options. Once you have defined custom shortcuts or menus, you can save your choices as a set so you can access the same choices again without having to redo the work.

If you don't see a specific menu command, it's possible that someone has already modified the visibility of specific menu commands. (Some of the built-in workspaces include limited sets of tools — including menu commands.) When menu commands are hidden, you can choose Show All Menu Items at the bottom of an individual menu to show the hidden commands in that menu.

Illustrator

In Illustrator, you can add to or modify the keyboard shortcuts used for different functions in the application. Choosing Edit>Keyboard Shortcuts opens a dialog box where you can modify the shortcuts for menu commands and tools. If you assign a shortcut that isn't part of the default set, you have to save a custom set of shortcuts (Illustrator won't let you modify the default set of keyboard shortcuts). When more than one set of shortcuts exists (i.e., if you or someone else has added to or changed the default settings), you can switch between the different sets using the menu at the top of the dialog box.

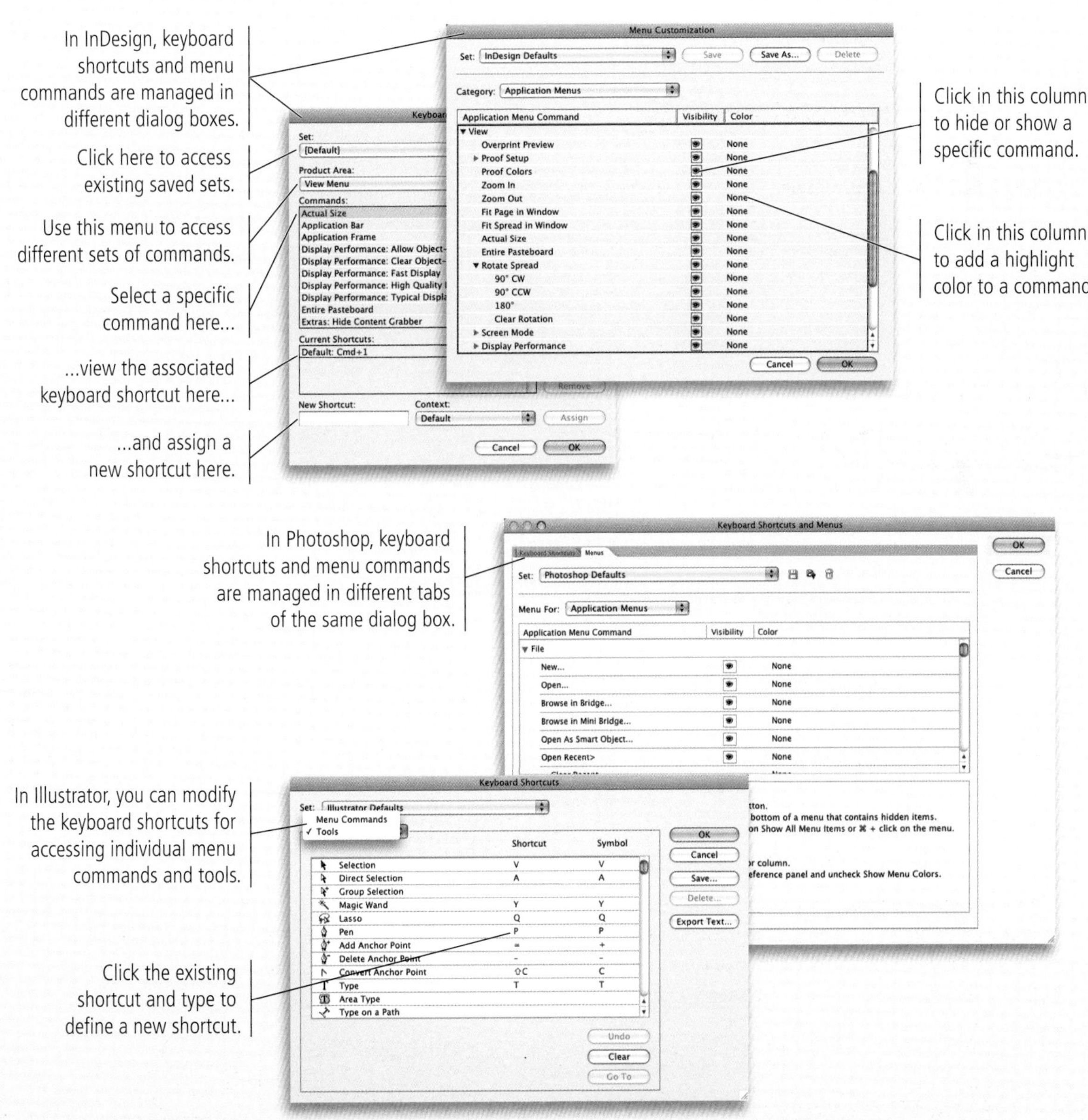

In InDesign, keyboard shortcuts and menu commands are managed in different dialog boxes.
Click here to access existing saved sets.
Use this menu to access different sets of commands.
Select a specific command here...
...view the associated keyboard shortcut here...
...and assign a new shortcut here.
Click in this column to hide or show a specific command.
Click in this column to add a highlight color to a command.
Menu Customization
Keyboard Shortcuts and Menus
In Photoshop, keyboard shortcuts and menu commands are managed in different tabs of the same dialog box.
Keyboard Shortcuts
In Illustrator, you can modify the keyboard shortcuts for accessing individual menu commands and tools.
Click the existing shortcut and type to define a new shortcut.

4. **Choose Window>Workspace>Reset Essentials (or click the Workspace switcher and choose Reset Essentials).**

   Remember: calling a workspace again restores the panels exactly as they were the last time you used that workspace. For example, if you close a panel that is part of a saved workspace, the closed panel will not be reopened the next time you call the same workspace. To restore the saved state of the workspace, including opening closed panels or repositioning moved ones, you have to use the Reset option.

> *Note:*
>
> *Unlike InDesign and Photoshop, calling a workspace in Illustrator recalls the saved version of the workspace and not the last-used version of the workspace. Illustrator does not include the Reset [Workspace] command.*

5. **Continue to the next exercise.**

Application Preferences

CREATIVE SUITE FOUNDATIONS

You can use the Preferences dialog box to customize the behavior of many different program tools and options. On Macintosh, the Preferences dialog box is accessed in the Application menu. Windows users access the Preferences dialog box in the Edit menu.

In InDesign and Photoshop, categories of preferences are listed on the left side of the dialog box; options related to the selected category appear in the right side of the dialog box. In Illustrator, you can use the top menu to review the different categories of preferences.

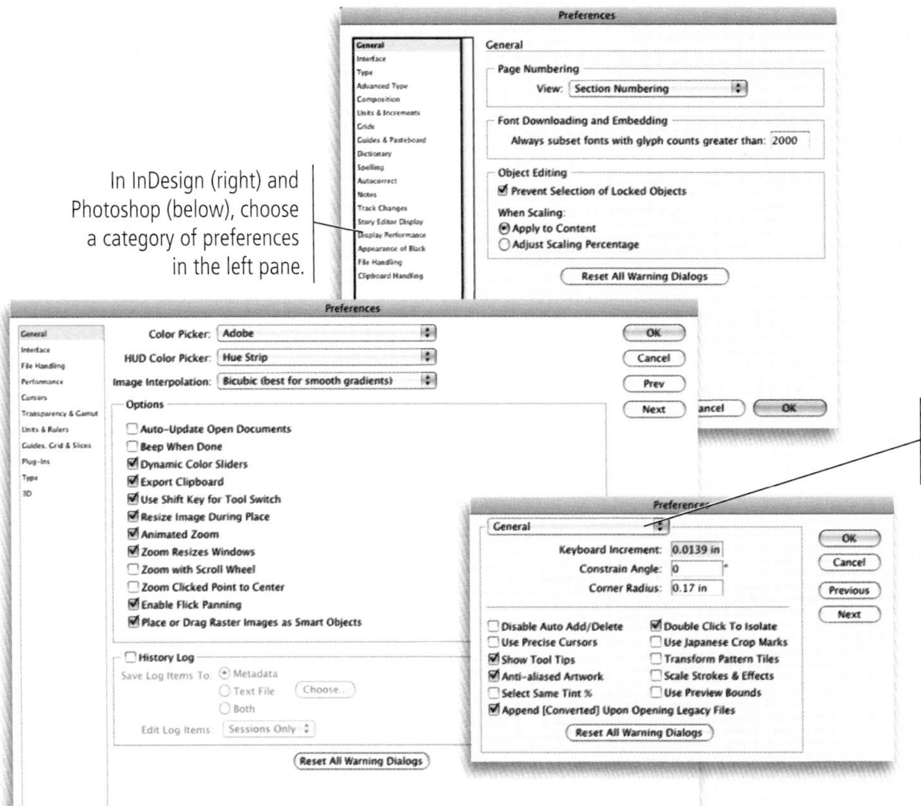

In InDesign (right) and Photoshop (below), choose a category of preferences in the left pane.

In Illustrator, use this menu to view different categories of preferences.

Explore the InDesign Document Views

There is far more to using InDesign than arranging panels around the workspace. What you do with those panels — and even which panels you need — depends on the type of work you are doing in a particular file. In this exercise, you open an InDesign file and explore the interface elements you will use to create documents.

1. **In InDesign, choose File>Open. Navigate to your WIP>Interface folder and select career.indd in the list of available files.**

   The Open dialog box is a system-standard navigation dialog box. This dialog box is one area of significant difference between Macintosh and Windows users.

2. **Press Shift, and then click knowledge.indd in the list of files.**

   Pressing Shift allows you to select multiple contiguous (consecutive) files in the list.

Note:

Press Command/Control-O to access the Open dialog box.

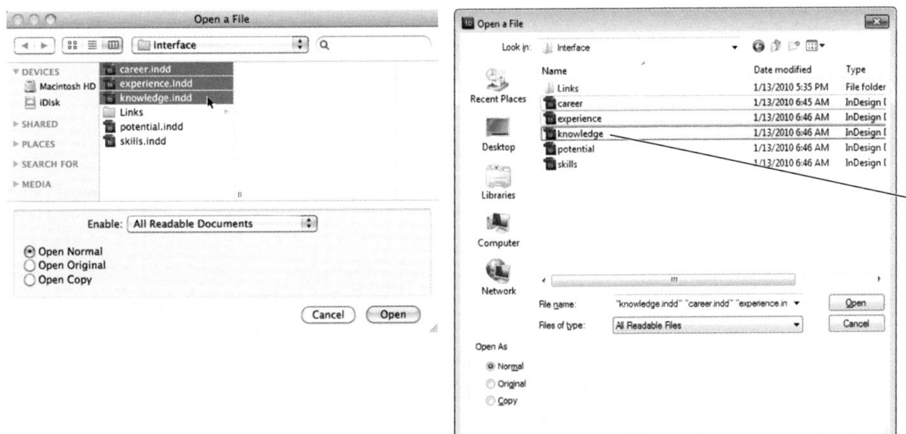

On Windows, the file extensions are not visible in the Open dialog box.

3. **Press Command/Control and click potential.indd and skills.indd to add those files to the active selection.**

   One final reminder: we list differing commands in the Macintosh/Windows format. On Macintosh, you need to press the Command key; on Windows, press the Control key. (We will not repeat this explanation every time different commands are required for the different operating systems.)

   Pressing Command/Control allows you to select and open non-contiguous files. (Depending on how files are sorted in your operating system, folders might be listed before other files — as shown in the Windows screen shot below. If that's the case on your system, you can press Shift or Control to select all five files.)

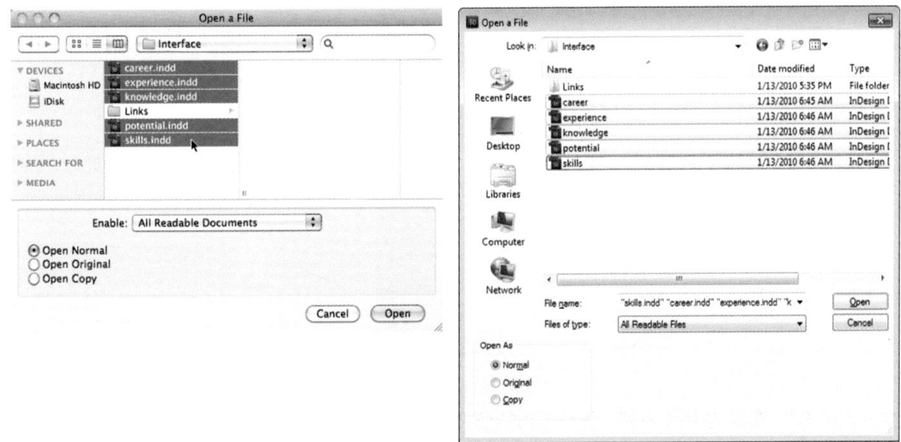

4. **Click Open to open all five selected files.**

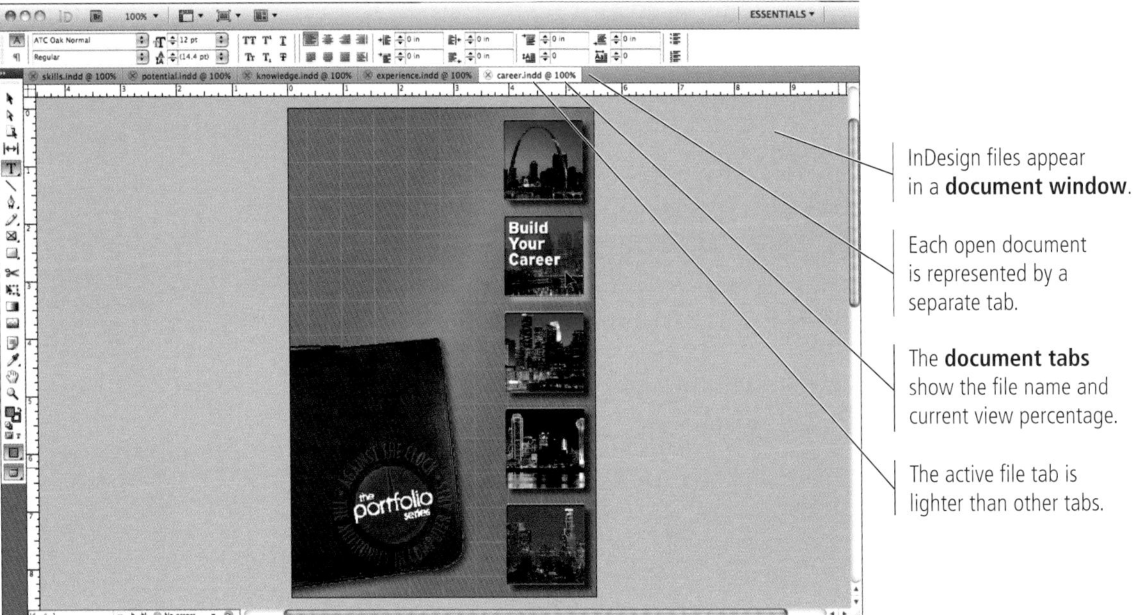

InDesign files appear in a **document window**.
Each open document is represented by a separate tab.
The **document tabs** show the file name and current view percentage.
The active file tab is lighter than other tabs.

5. **Click the experience.indd tab to make that document active.**

6. **Click the Zoom Level field in the Application/Menu bar and change the view percentage to `200`.**

   Different people prefer larger or smaller view percentages, depending on a number of factors (eyesight, monitor size, and so on). As you complete the projects in this book, you'll see our screen shots zoom in or out as necessary to show you the most relevant part of a particular file. In most cases we do not tell you what specific view percentage to use for a particular exercise, unless it is specifically required for the work being done.

Note:

You can set the viewing percentage of an InDesign document to any value from 5% to 4000%.

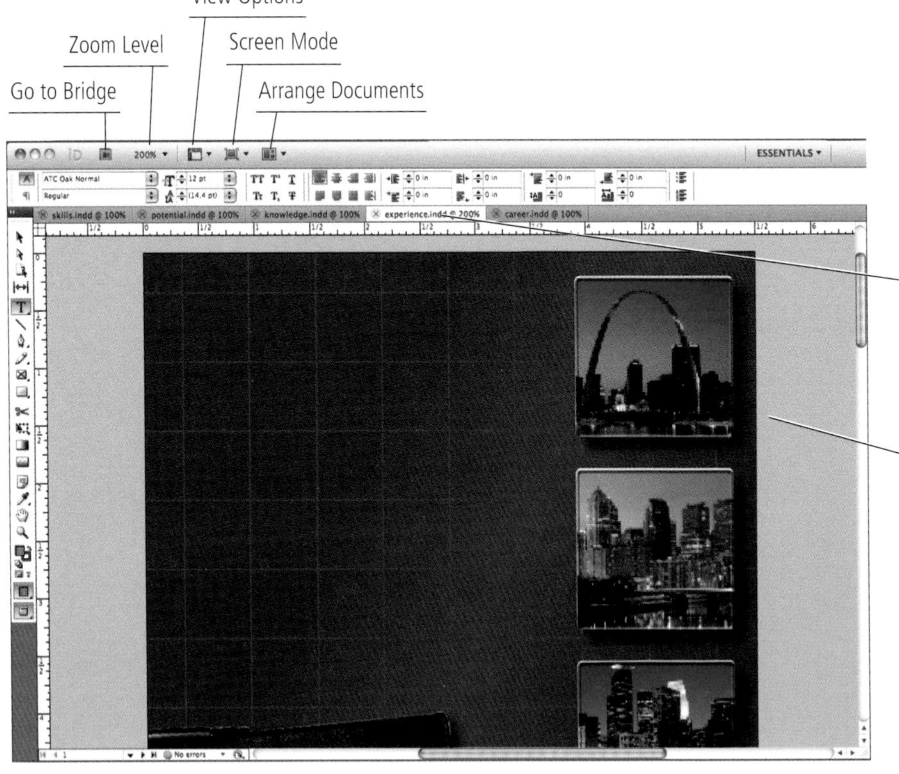

Click the tab to activate a specific file in the document window.

Changing the view percentage of the file does not affect the size of the document window.

7. **Choose View>Fit Page in Window.**

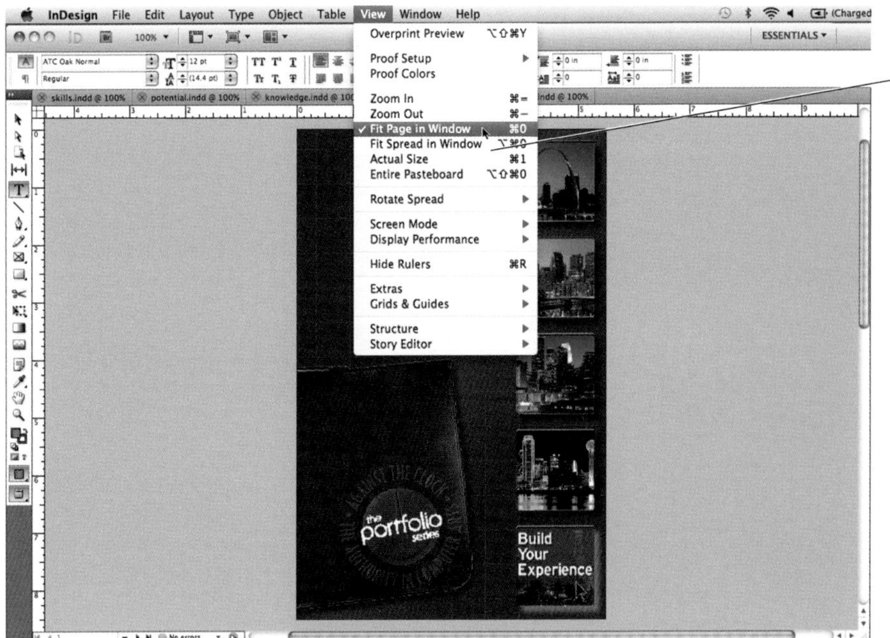

Note:

Fit Page in Window automatically calculates view percentage based on the size of the document window.

Note:

Fit Spread in Window relates to documents that have left- and right-facing pages, such as a magazine or book.

8. **Click the Zoom tool in the Tools panel. Click in the document window and drag a marquee around the logo on the portfolio.**

Dragging a marquee with the Zoom tool enlarges the selected area to fill the document window.

Note:

All open files are listed at the bottom of the Window menu.

✓ *experience.indd @ 12%
career.indd @ 100%
knowledge.indd @ 100%
potential.indd @ 100%
skills.indd @ 100%

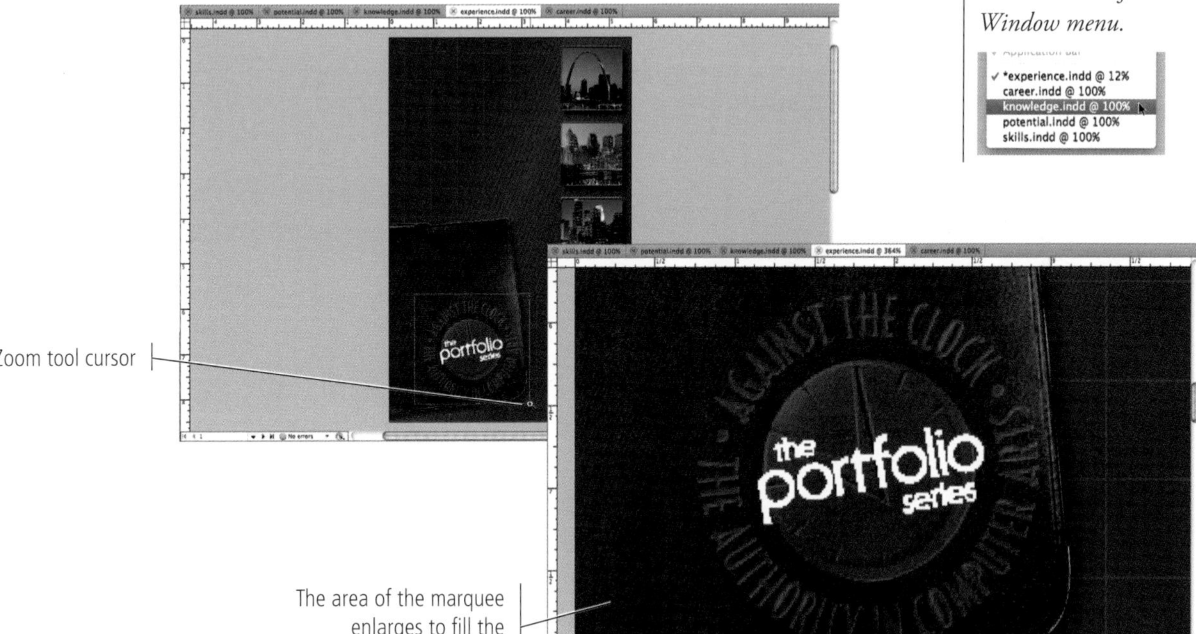

9. **With the Zoom tool selected, Option/Alt-click in the document window.**

Clicking with the Zoom tool enlarges the view percentage in specific, predefined steps. Pressing Option/Alt while clicking with the Zoom tool reduces the view percentage in the reverse sequence of the same percentages.

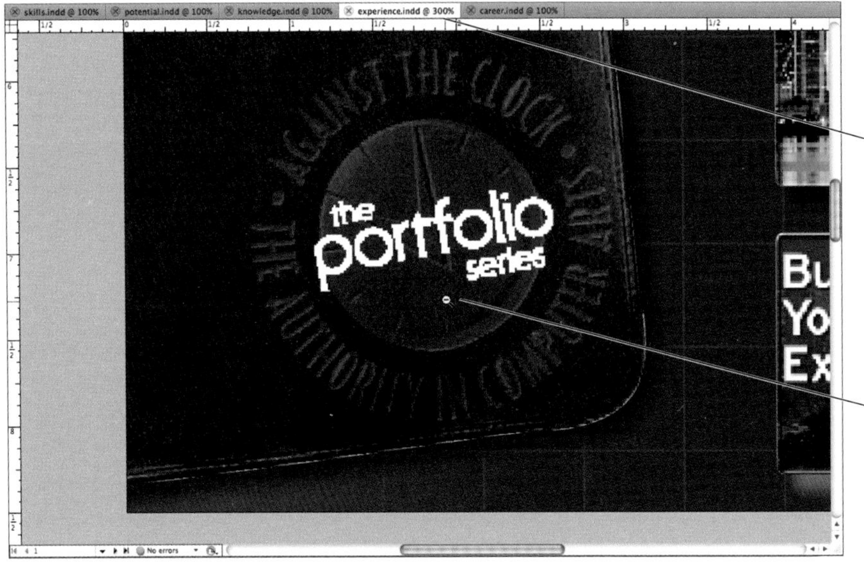

Option/Alt-clicking with the Zoom tool reduces the view percentage in the predefined sequence of percentages.

With the Zoom tool active, pressing Option/Alt changes the cursor to the Zoom Out icon.

Note:

Press the Z key to access the Zoom tool.

Press the H key to access the Hand tool.

10. **Click the Hand tool near the bottom of the Tools panel.**

11. **Click in the document, hold down the mouse button, and drag around.**

The Hand tool is a very easy and convenient option for changing the visible area of an image in the document window.

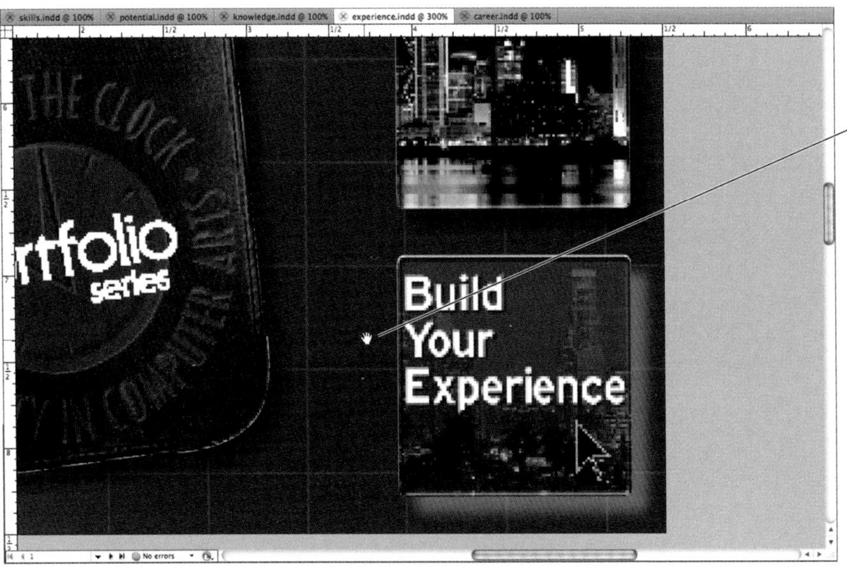

Hand tool cursor

12. Choose View>Display Performance>High Quality Display.

You might have noticed that the images in this file look very bad (they are badly bitmapped). This is even more evident when you zoom in to a high view percentage. By default, InDesign displays a low-resolution preview of placed images to save time when the screen redraws (i.e., every time you change something). Fortunately, however, you have the option to preview the full-resolution images placed in a file.

Note:

The Fast Display option replaces all placed images with a solid medium gray (in other words, no preview image displays).

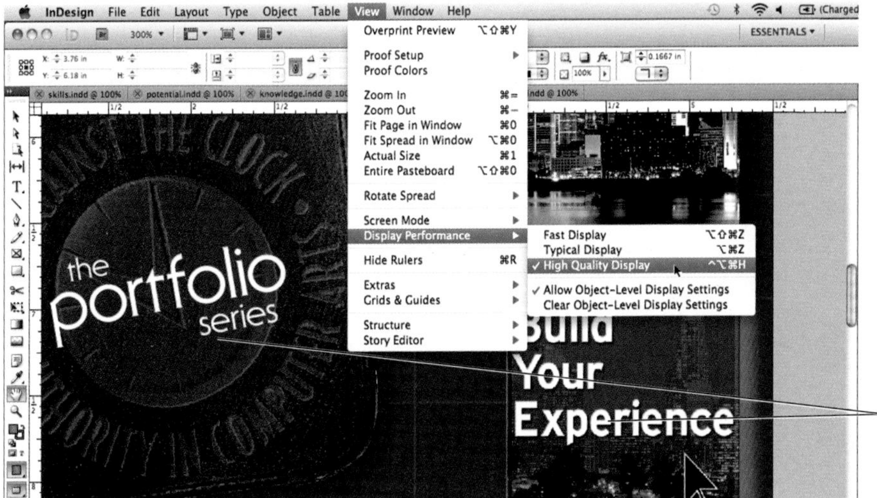

Using the High Quality Display, images do not show the bitmapping of the default low-resolution previews.

13. Using the Selection tool, click the bottom-right image (the one with the text) to select it. Control/right-click the selected image and choose Display Performance>Typical Display from the contextual menu.

In the View menu, the Allow Object-Level Display Settings option is active by default (see the image in the prevous step); this means you can change the display of individual objects on the page.

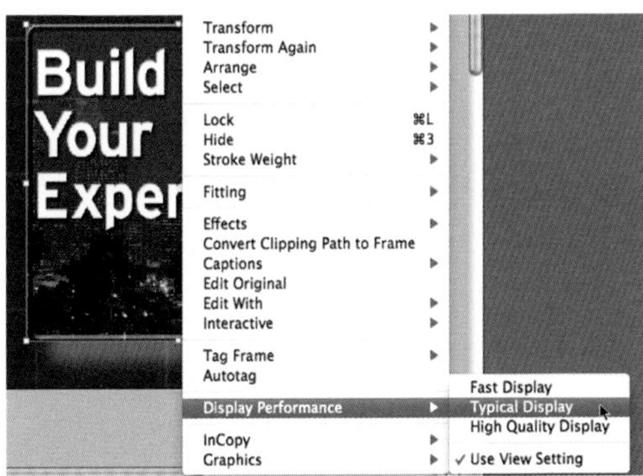

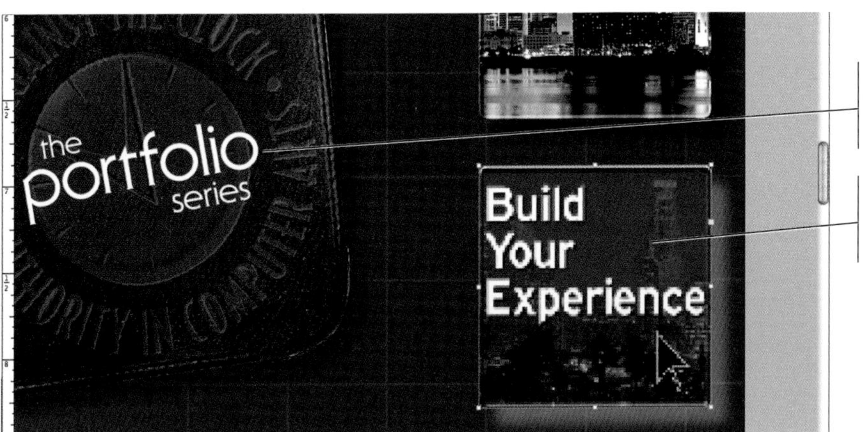

High-Quality Display is especially evident where sharp lines exist.

Typical Display uses a low-resolution preview of placed images.

14. **Choose View>Fit Page in Window to see the entire page.**

15. **Double-click the title bar above the docked panels to expand the panels.**

16. **In the Pages panel, double-click the Page 2 icon to show that page in the document window.**

    The Pages panel is the easiest way to move from one page to another in a multi-page document.

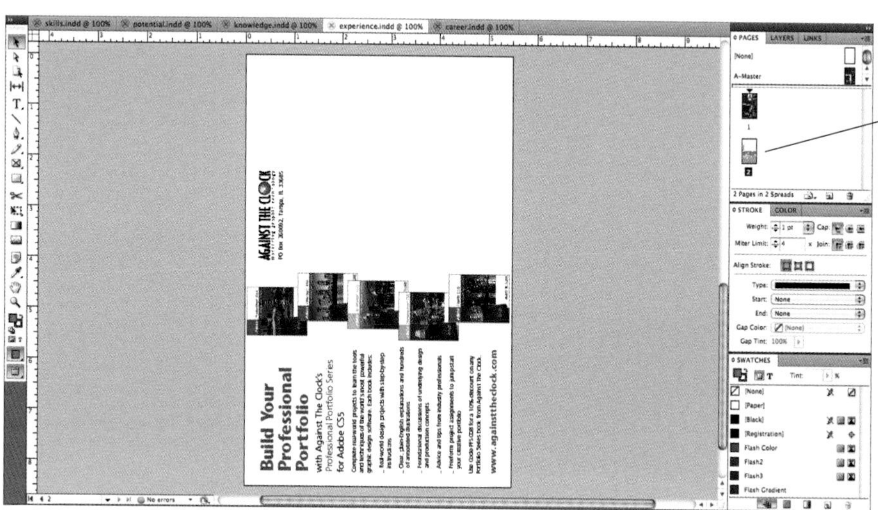

Double-click a page icon to display that page in the document window.

Summing up the InDesign View Options

INDESIGN FOUNDATIONS

Most InDesign projects require some amount of zooming in and out to various view percentages, as well as navigating around the document within its window. As we show you how to complete various stages of the workflow, we usually won't tell you when to change your view percentage because that's largely a matter of personal preference. But you should understand the different options for navigating an InDesign file so you can easily and efficiently get to what you want.

View Menu

The View menu provides options for changing the view percentage. You should also become familiar with the keyboard shortcuts for these commands:

Zoom In	Command/Control-equals (=)
Zoom Out	Command/Control-minus (-)
Fit Page in Window	Command/Control-0 (zero)
Fit Spread in Window	Command-Option-0/Control-Alt-0
Actual Size (100%)	Command/Control-1
Entire Pasteboard	Command-Option-Shift-0/ Control-Alt-Shift-0

Zoom Level Field/Menu

You can use the Zoom Level field in the Application/Menu bar to type a specific view percentage, or you can use the attached menu to choose from the predefined view percentage steps.

Zoom Tool

You can click with the **Zoom tool** to increase the view percentage in specific, predefined intervals (the same intervals you see in the View Percentage menu in the bottom-left corner of the document window). Pressing Option/Alt with the Zoom tool allows you to zoom out in the same predefined percentages. If you drag a marquee with the Zoom tool, you can zoom into a specific location; the area surrounded by the marquee fills the available space in the document window.

Hand Tool

Whatever your view percentage, you can use the **Hand tool** to drag the file around in the document window, including scrolling from one page to another. The Hand tool only changes what is visible in the window; it has no effect on the actual content of the file.

17. **Control/right-click the Page 2 icon in the Pages panel and choose Rotate Spread View>90° CW from the contextual menu.**

Rotating the view only changes the display of the page; the actual page remains unchanged in the file. This option allows you to work more easily on objects or pages that are oriented differently than the overall document. In this example, the front side of the postcard has portrait orientation, but the mailer side has landscape orientation.

Note:

You can also rotate page views using the options in the View>Rotate Spread menu.

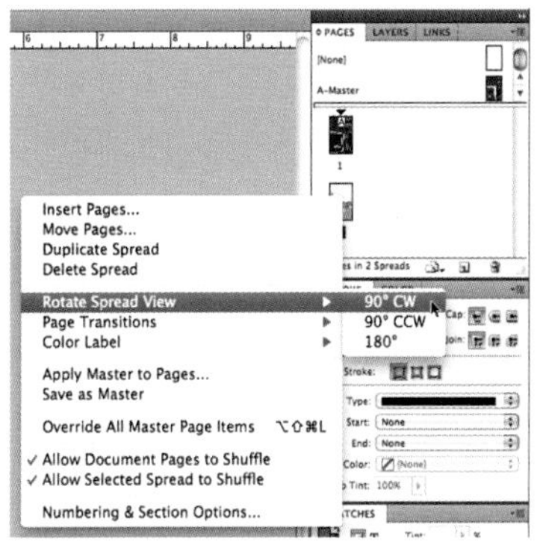

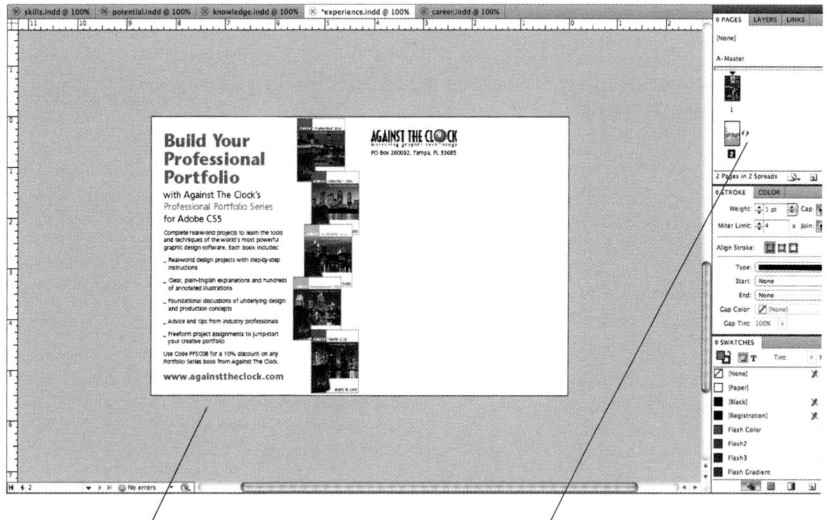

The rotated display makes it easier to work on pages with orientations different from the document definition.

Pages with a rotated view are identified in the Pages panel.

18. **Continue to the next exercise.**

Explore the Arrangement of Multiple Documents

In many cases, you will need to work with more than one layout at the same time. InDesign CS5 incorporates a number of options for arranging multiple documents. We designed the following simple exercise so you can explore these options.

1. **With experience.indd active, choose Window>Arrange>Float in Window.**

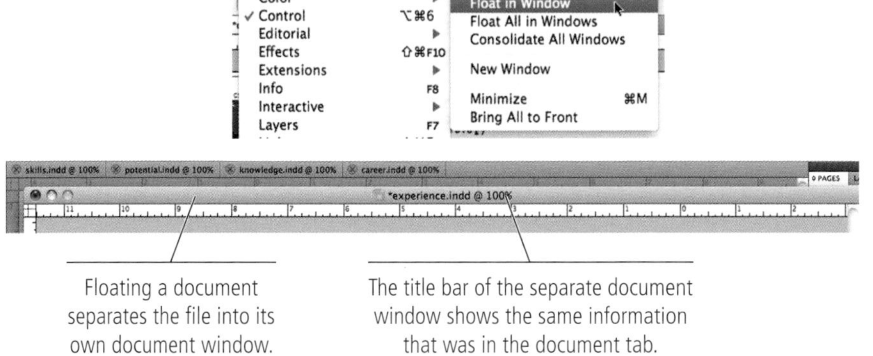

Floating a document separates the file into its own document window.

The title bar of the separate document window shows the same information that was in the document tab.

Note:

When multiple document windows are open, two options in the Window>Arrange menu allow you to cascade or tile the document windows. You can separate all open files by choosing Window>Arrange>Float All in Windows.

2. **In the Application/Menu bar, click the Arrange Documents button to open the panel of defined arrangements.**

3. **Click the 2 Up button in the Arrange Documents panel.**

   The defined arrangements provide a number of options for tiling multiple open files within the available workspace; these arrangements manage all open files, including those in floating windows.

   The Consolidate All button (top left) restores all floating documents into a single tabbed document window. The remaining buttons in the top row separate all open files into separate document windows and then arrange the different windows as indicated.

   The lower options use a specific number of floating documents (2-Up, 3-Up, etc.); if more files are open than an option indicates, the extra files are consolidated as tabs in the first document window.

The Arrange Documents panel includes a number of tiling options for arranging multiple open files in the workspace.

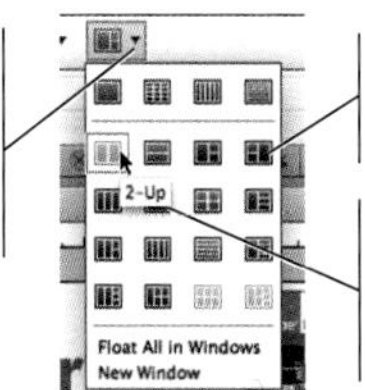

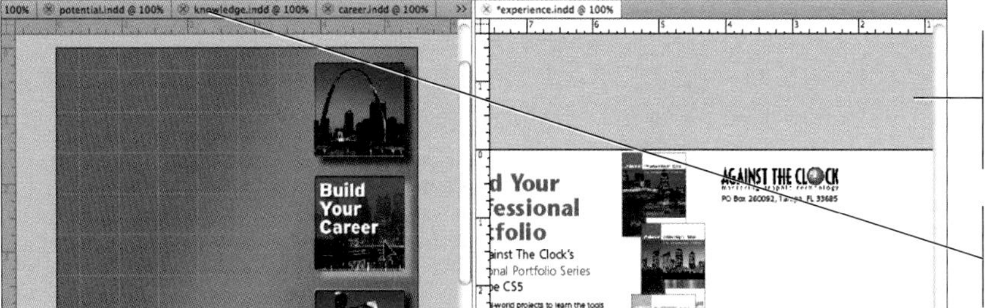

The appearance of each icon suggests the result of that option.
Rolling your mouse cursor over an icon shows the arrangement name in a tool tip.

The 2-Up arrangement divides the document window in half, as indicated by the button icon.
Extra documents remain as tabs in the left document window.

4. **Click the experience.indd document tab and drag left until a blue highlight appears around the document tabs in the other panel.**

   When you release the mouse button, all of the open files are again part of the same document window.

5. **Using the Pages panel, navigate to Page 1 of the file. Choose View>Fit Page in Window to show the entire page.**

   The files you explored in this project were saved in Preview screen mode, which surrounds the page with a neutral gray background. Page guides, frame edges, and other non-printing areas are not visible in the Preview mode.

Note:

On a Macintosh, the Application bar must be visible to access the Arrange Documents button.

6. **Click the Screen Mode button in the Application/Menu bar and choose Bleed.**

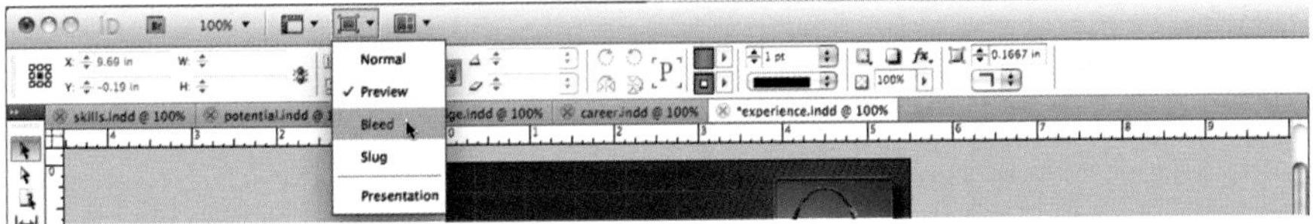
Normal
✓ Preview
Bleed
Slug
Presentation

The Bleed screen mode is an extension of the Preview mode; it shows an extra area (which was defined when the document was originally set up) around the page edge. This bleed area is a required part of print document design — objects that are supposed to print right up to the edge of the page must extend past the page edge, usually 1/8″.

Page edge
In Bleed mode, you can see a defined amount of space around the page edge.

7. **Click the Screen Mode button at the bottom of the Tools panel and choose Normal from the pop-up menu.**

This menu has the same options as the button in the Application/Menu bar. As you will learn throughout this book, there is almost always more than one way to accomplish a particular goal in InDesign.

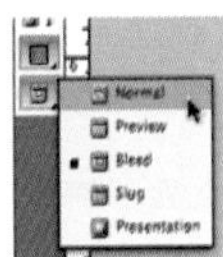

In Normal mode, you can see all non-printing elements, including guides and frame edges (if those are toggled on). You can now also see the white pasteboard surrounding the defined page area; your development work is not limited by the defined page size.

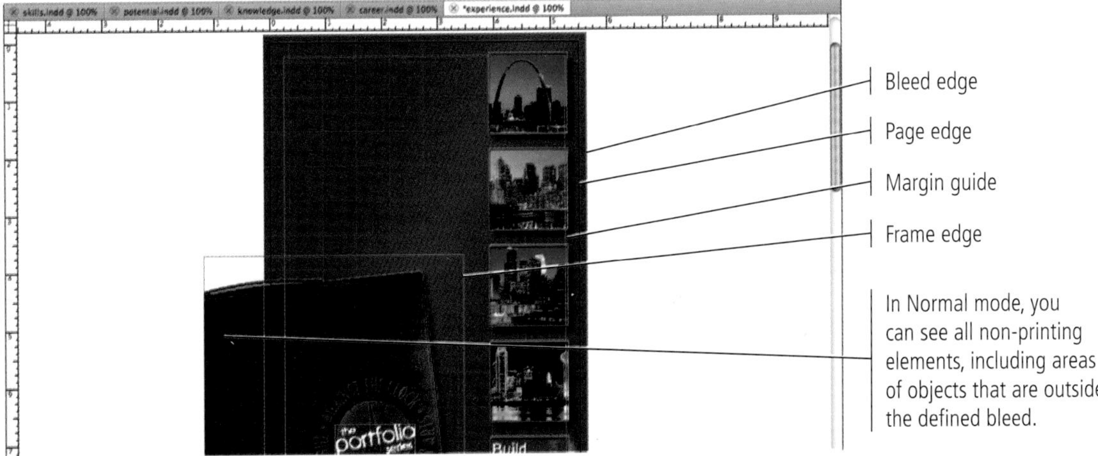
Bleed edge
Page edge
Margin guide
Frame edge
In Normal mode, you can see all non-printing elements, including areas of objects that are outside the defined bleed.

8. **Using either Screen Mode button, choose the Presentation mode.**

   Presentation mode fills the entire screen with the active spread. By default, the area around the page is solid black; you can press W to change the surround to white or press G to change it to neutral gray. In Presentation mode, clicking anywhere on the screen shows the next spread; Shift-clicking shows the previous spread.

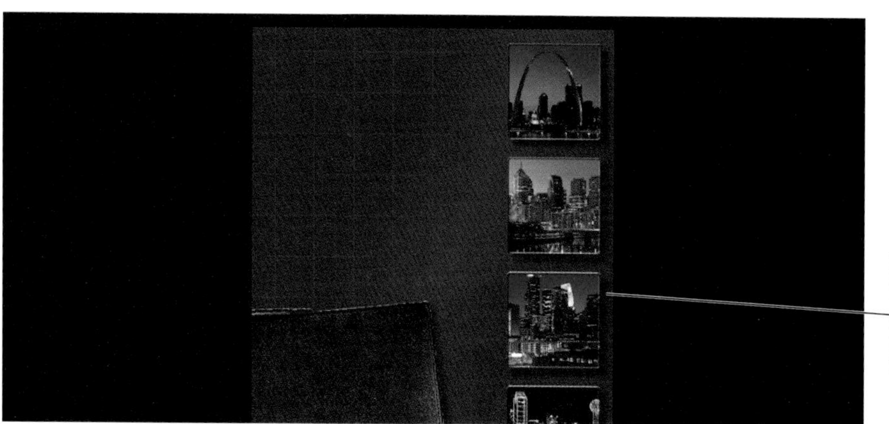

In Presentation mode, the page, surrounded by solid black, fills the entire screen.

9. **Press ESC to exit Presentation mode.**

10. **Click the Close button on the active document tab.**

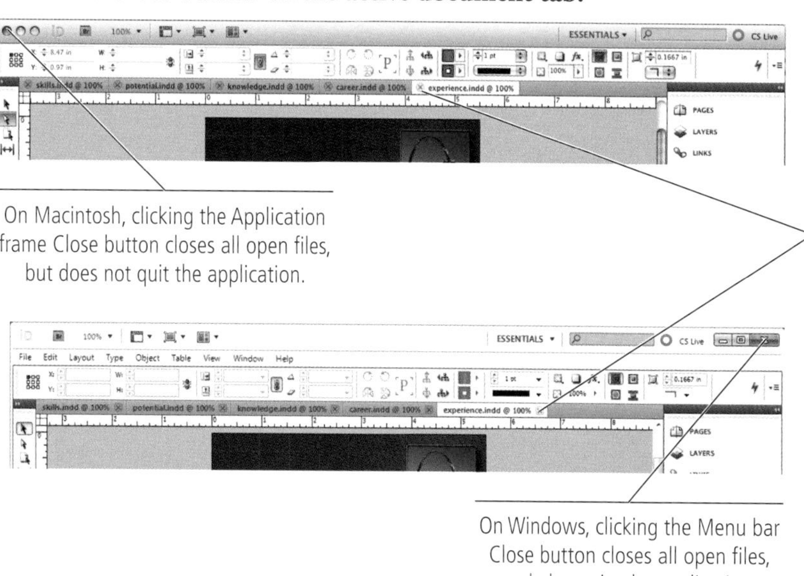

On Macintosh, clicking the Application frame Close button closes all open files, but does not quit the application.

When multiple files are open, clicking the close button on a document tab closes only that file.

On Windows, clicking the Menu bar Close button closes all open files, and also quits the application.

11. **Click Don't Save when asked if you want to save changes to experience.indd.**

    By rotating the spread view on Page 2, the file has technically been changed. InDesign automatically asks if you want to save any file that has been changed before closing it.

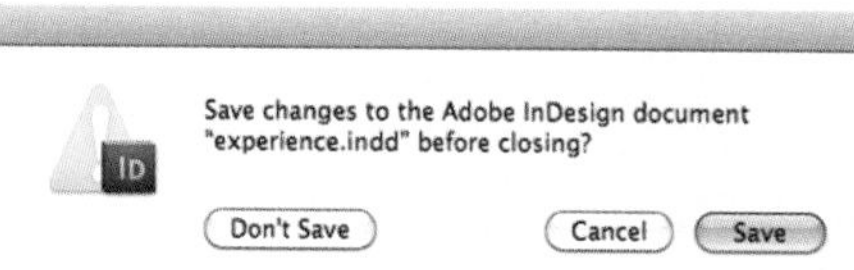

Note:

Closing the Macintosh Application frame closes all open files but does not quit the application. Clicking the Close button on the Windows Menu bar closes all open files and quits the application; to close open files without quitting, you have to manually close each open file.

12. **Close (without saving) all but the skills.indd file.**

13. **Continue to the next exercise.**

Explore the Illustrator User Interface

Illustration is a very broad career path, with potential applications in virtually any industry. In other words, mastering the tools and techniques of Adobe Illustrator can significantly improve your range of career options. Within the general category of illustration, many Illustrator experts specialize in certain types of work: logo design, technical drawing, and editorial illustration are only a few subcategories of artwork you can create with Illustrator.

Adobe Illustrator is the industry-standard application for creating digital drawings or **vector images** (graphics composed of mathematically defined lines instead of pixels). Although not intended as a page-layout application, you can also use the tools in Illustrator to combine type, graphics, and images into a single cohesive design. Many people create flyers, posters, and other one-page projects entirely within Illustrator. With the multiple-artboard capability added to CS5 (explained in Project 3) we will likely see more of this type of Illustrator work in the future.

1. **With skills.indd open (from your WIP>Interface folder), use the Selection tool to select the "the portfolio series" graphic on Page 1.**

2. **Control/right-click the selected object and choose Edit Original from the contextual menu.**

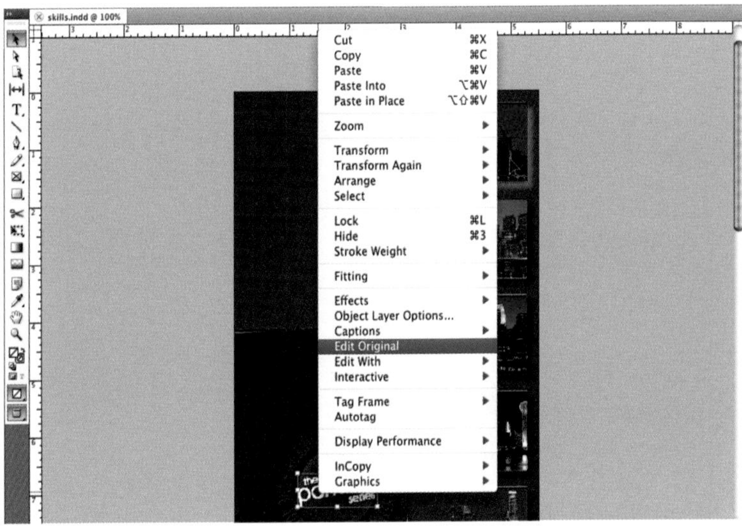

Choosing Edit Original opens the placed file in its native application. This graphic is a native Adobe Illustrator file (with the extension ".ai"), so it opens in the latest possible version of Adobe Illustrator.

If Adobe Illustrator is not already running on your computer, it might take a moment while the application launches. If you have multiple versions of Illustrator running on your computer, the placed graphic will open in the first available version. If CS4 is already launched, for example, the graphic opens in that version instead of launching Illustrator CS5.

3. **Macintosh users: Open the Window menu in Illustrator. If Application Frame is not checked (active), choose that command in the menu.**

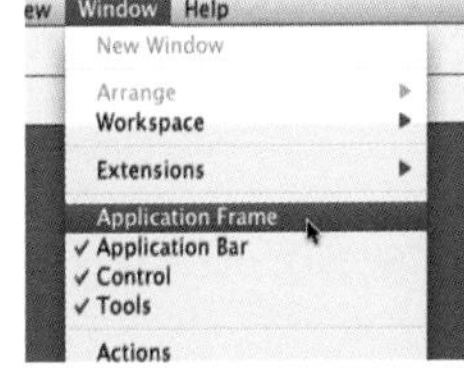

4. Choose Essentials in the Workspace switcher.

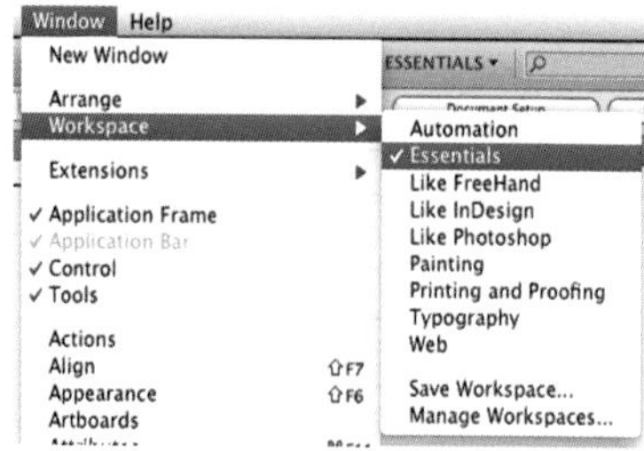

Illustrator panels are arranged and accessed using the same techniques you already learned, and saved workspaces in Illustrator serve the same function as in InDesign. The Essentials workspace includes the two-column Tools panel on the left of the screen, the Control panel at the top, and a set of iconized and docked panels on the right.

> ***Note:***
>
> *The Manage Workspaces option opens a dialog box where you can rename or delete user-defined custom workspaces. You can't alter the default workspaces that come with the application.*

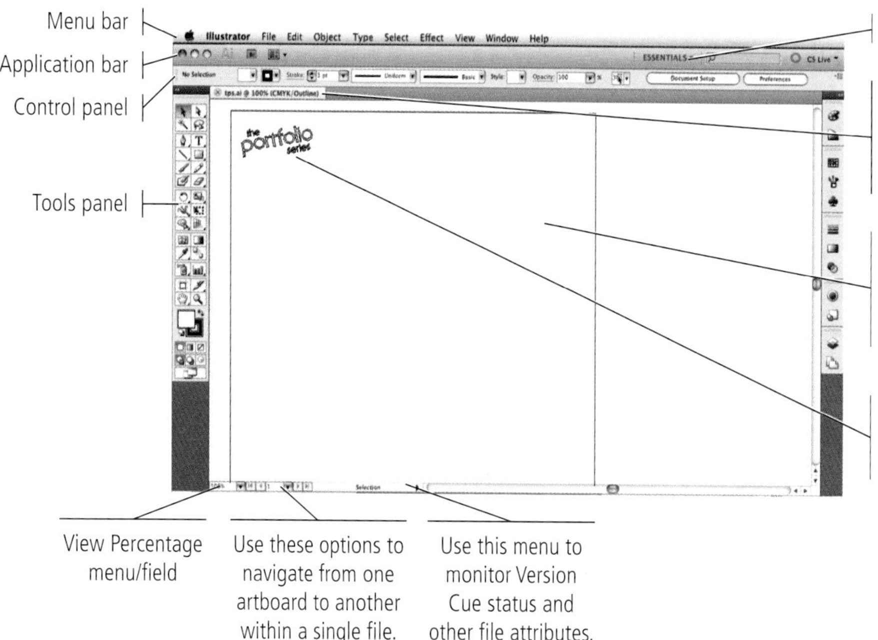

Menu bar
Application bar
Control panel
Tools panel
Workspace switcher
The document tab shows the active file name, view percentage, color space, and current viewing mode.
The **artboard** is essentially the digital page, or the area where artwork should be created or placed.
In Outline viewing mode, only the object's wireframe is visible.
View Percentage menu/field
Use these options to navigate from one artboard to another within a single file.
Use this menu to monitor Version Cue status and other file attributes.

> ***Note:***
>
> *You can zoom an Illustrator document from 3.13% to 6400%.*

Recall that in InDesign, calling a workspace restores the workspace to its last-used state; to restore the saved state of a workspace in InDesign, you have to choose Reset [Workspace] in the Workspace switcher. In Illustrator, however, calling a specific workspace automatically restores the workspace to the saved state; there is no "Reset" option.

5. With nothing selected in the open file, review the options in the Control panel.

We will not discuss all 30+ Illustrator panels here, but the Control panel deserves mention. This panel appears by default at the top of the workspace below the Menu bar (and the Application bar on Macintosh systems). It is context sensitive, which means it provides access to different options depending on which tool is active and what is selected in the document.

When nothing is selected in the file, the most important Control panel options open the Document Setup dialog box and the Preferences dialog box (more about these specific elements in the projects).

> ***Note:***
>
> *For now, don't worry about the specific options that are available. You only need to realize that the Control panel changes depending on what is selected.*

6. **With the tps.ai file open, choose File>Open.**

In many cases, you will open Illustrator files from directly within an InDesign file (as you did for the tps.ai file). Of course, you can also simply open a file from directly within Illustrator. How you open a file does affect what happens to instances that are placed in an InDesign layout. In Project 10 you will see how opening a file from within an InDesign layout offers distinct advantages in an integrated workflow.

7. **Navigate to the WIP>Interface>Links folder. Click atc.ai to select that file, and then click Open.**

This file was saved in Preview mode, which shows the artwork in color.

Note:

Macintosh users: If you turn off the Application frame, the new document will have its own title bar.

Each open file is represented by a tab at the top of the document window.

In Preview mode, you can see the fill and stroke attributes of objects in the file.

8. **Click the Selection tool at the top of the Tools panel to make sure that tool is active.**

The Selection tool (the solid arrow) is used to select entire objects in the file.

9. **Click any of the black letter shapes in the word "Against", then review the options in the Control panel.**

When an object is selected in the file, the Control panel shows the attributes of the selected object. In this case, the entire set of black letter shapes is a group, so the Control panel shows options related to groups.

Selection tool

The Control panel shows options and attributes of the selected object (in this case, a group of shapes).

Selected object (indicated by **bounding box handles** on all four sides of the object)

10. **Click the orange circle to select the clock object.**

The selected object is a single path (not part of a group). The Control panel changes to show options related to paths.

The Control panel shows options related to the selected object (in this case, a filled path).

Selected object

11. **Click the button at the bottom of the Tools panel to show the screen mode options.**

Illustrator has three different **screen modes**, which change the way the document window displays on the screen. The default mode, which you saw when you opened these three files, is called Normal Screen Mode.

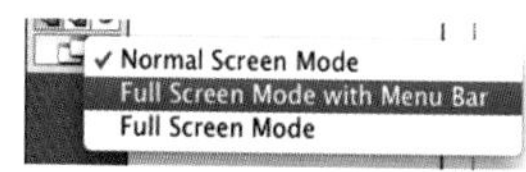

Identifying Illustrator Tools

The chart below offers a quick reference of nested tools, as well as the keyboard shortcut for each tool (if any). Nested tools are shown indented and in italics.

- Selection tool (V)
- Direct Selection tool (A)
  - *Group Selection tool*
- Magic Wand tool (Y)
- Lasso tool (L)
- Pen tool (P)
  - *Add Anchor Point tool (+)*
  - *Delete Anchor Point tool (-)*
  - *Convert Anchor Point tool (Shift-C)*
- Type tool (T)
  - *Area Type tool*
  - *Type on a Path tool*
  - *Vertical Type tool*
  - *Vertical Area Type tool*
  - *Vertical Type on a Path tool*
- Line Segment tool (\)
  - *Arc tool*
  - *Spiral tool*
  - *Rectangular Grid tool*
  - *Polar Grid tool*
- Rectangle tool (M)
  - *Rounded Rectangle tool*
  - *Ellipse tool (L)*
  - *Polygon tool*
  - *Star tool*
  - *Flare tool*
- Paintbrush tool (B)
- Pencil tool (N)
  - *Smooth tool*
  - *Path Eraser tool*
- Blob Brush tool (Shift-B)
- Eraser tool (Shift-E)
  - *Scissors tool (C)*
  - *Knife tool*
- Rotate tool (R)
  - *Reflect tool (O)*
- Scale tool (S)
  - *Shear tool*
  - *Reshape tool*
- Width tool (Shift-W)
  - *Warp tool (Shift-R)*
  - *Twirl tool*
  - *Pucker tool*
  - *Bloat tool*
  - *Scallop tool*
  - *Crystallize tool*
  - *Wrinkle tool*
- Free Transform tool (E)
- Shape Builder tool (Shift-M)
  - *Live Paint Bucket tool (K)*
  - *Live Paint Selection tool (Shift-L)*
- Perspective Grid tool (Shift-P)
  - *Perspective Selection tool (Shift-V)*
- Mesh tool (U)
- Gradient tool (G)
- Eyedropper tool (I)
  - *Measure tool*
- Blend tool (W)
- Symbol Sprayer tool (Shift-S)
  - *Symbol Shifter tool*
  - *Symbol Scruncher tool*
  - *Symbol Sizer tool*
  - *Symbol Spinner tool*
  - *Symbol Stainer tool*
  - *Symbol Screener tool*
  - *Symbol Styler tool*
- Column Graph tool (J)
  - *Stacked Column Graph tool*
  - *Bar Graph tool*
  - *Stacked Bar Graph tool*
  - *Line Graph tool*
  - *Area Graph tool*
  - *Scatter Graph tool*
  - *Pie Graph tool*
  - *Radar Graph tool*
- Artboard tool (Shift-O)
- Slice tool (Shift-K)
  - *Slice Select tool*
- Hand tool (H)
  - *Print Tiling tool*
- Zoom tool (Z)

12. **Choose Full Screen Mode with Menu Bar from the Screen Mode menu.**

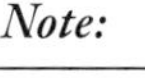

> *Note:*
>
> *Press F to switch between screen modes.*

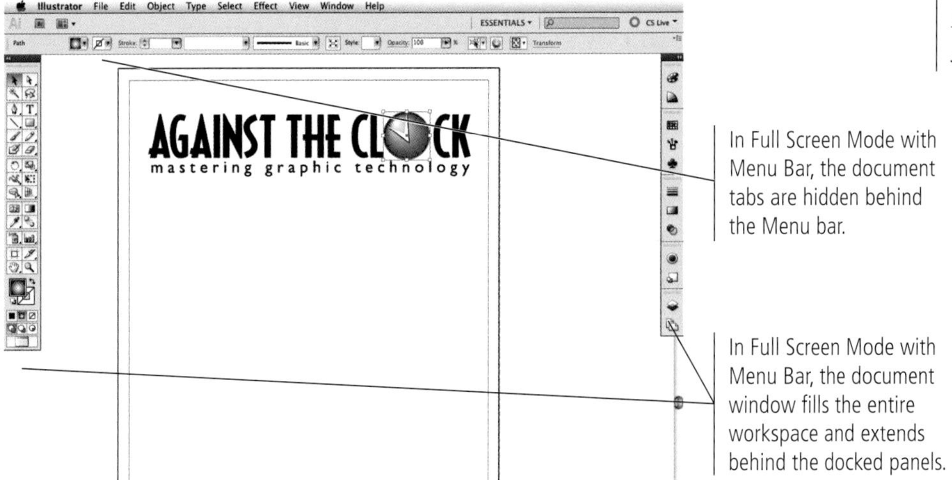

Illustrator File Edit Object Type Select Effect View Window Help
ESSENTIALS
AGAINST THE CLOCK
mastering graphic technology
In Full Screen Mode with Menu Bar, the document tabs are hidden behind the Menu bar.
In Full Screen Mode with Menu Bar, the document window fills the entire workspace and extends behind the docked panels.

13. **Click the Screen Mode button at the bottom of the Tools panel and choose Full Screen Mode.**

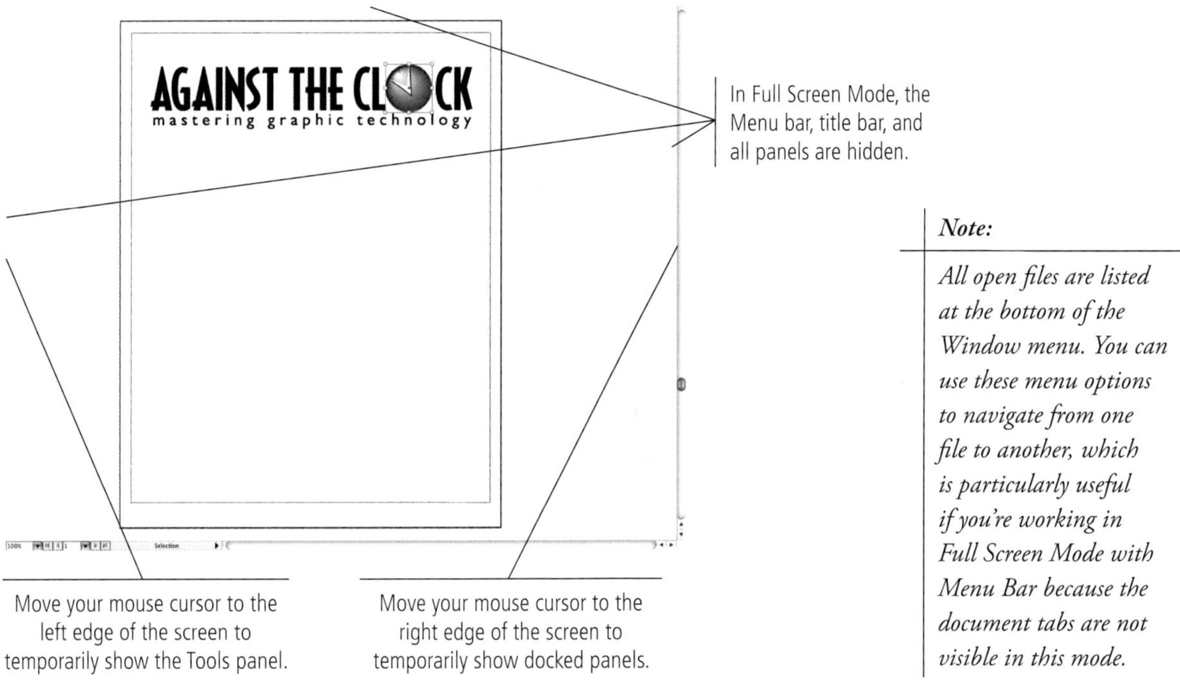

AGAINST THE CLOCK
mastering graphic technology
In Full Screen Mode, the Menu bar, title bar, and all panels are hidden.
Move your mouse cursor to the left edge of the screen to temporarily show the Tools panel.
Move your mouse cursor to the right edge of the screen to temporarily show docked panels.

> *Note:*
>
> *All open files are listed at the bottom of the Window menu. You can use these menu options to navigate from one file to another, which is particularly useful if you're working in Full Screen Mode with Menu Bar because the document tabs are not visible in this mode.*

14. **Press the Escape key to exit Full Screen Mode and return to Normal Screen Mode.**

15. **Click the Close button on the tps.ai tab to close that file.**

    As in InDesign, all open Illustrator files can be accessed and closed using the document tabs at the top of the document window. A file does not need to be active before you close it using the document tab.

16. **Click the Close button on the atc.ai document tab. If asked to save changes, click Don't Save in the warning message.**

17. **Return to the open InDesign file (skills.indd) and then continue to the next exercise.**

Summing up the Illustrator View Options

Most Illustrator projects require some amount of zooming in and out to various view percentages, as well as navigating around the document within its window.

To change the view percentage, you can type a specific percent in the **View Percentage field** of the document window or choose from the predefined options in the related menu.

You can also click with the **Zoom tool** to increase the view percentage in specific, predefined intervals (the same intervals you see in the View Percentage menu in the bottom-left corner of the document window). Pressing Option/Alt with the Zoom tool allows you to zoom out in the same defined percentages. If you drag a marquee with the Zoom tool, you can zoom into a specific location; the area surrounded by the marquee fills the available space in the document window.

The **View menu** also provides options for changing view percentage. (The Zoom In and Zoom Out options step through the same predefined view percentages as clicking with the Zoom tool.)

Zoom In	Command/Control-plus (+)
Zoom Out	Command/Control-minus (-)
Fit Artboard in Window	Command/Control-0 (zero)
Fit All in Window	Command-Option-0/ Control-Alt-0 (zero)
Actual Size (100%)	Command/Control-1

Whatever your view percentage, you can use the **Hand tool** to drag the file around in the document window. The Hand tool changes what is visible in the window; it has no effect on the actual content of the image.

The Navigator Panel

The **Navigator panel** (Window>Navigator) is another method of adjusting what you see, including the view percentage and the specific area that is visible in the document window. The Navigator panel shows a thumbnail of the active file; a red rectangle represents exactly how much of the document shows in the document window.

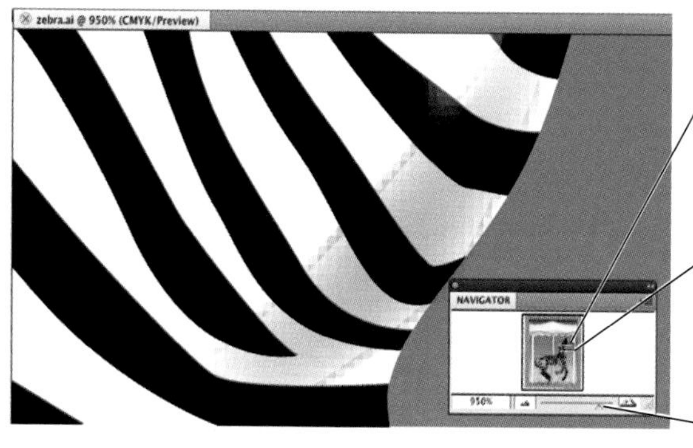

The red rectangle shows the area of the file that is visible in the document window.

Drag the red rectangle to change the visible portion of the file.

Use the slider and field at the bottom of the panel to change the view percentage.

Saved Views

Named views can be helpful if you repeatedly return to the same area and view percentage. By choosing View>New View, you can save the current view with a specific name.

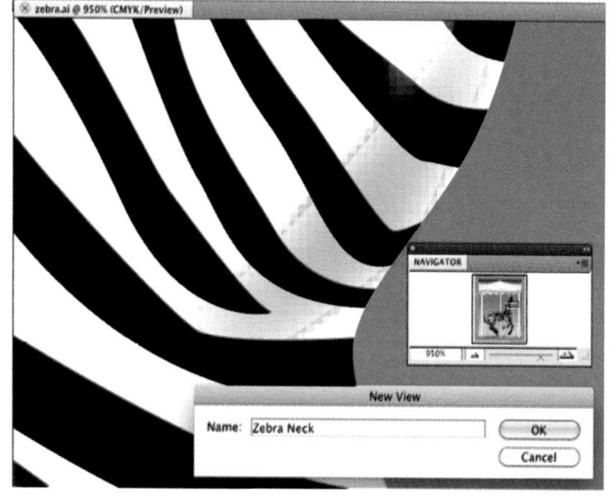

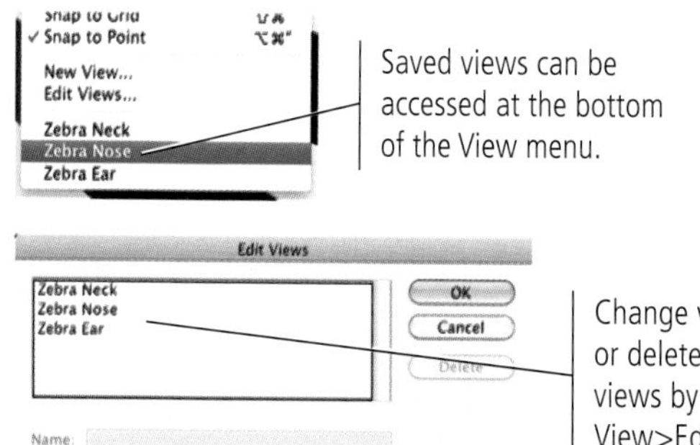

Saved views can be accessed at the bottom of the View menu.

Change view names or delete specific views by choosing View>Edit Views.

Explore the Photoshop User Interface

Adobe Photoshop is the industry-standard application for working with pixels — both manipulating existing ones and creating new ones. Many Photoshop experts specialize in certain types of work. Photo retouching, artistic painting, image compositing, color correction, and Web site design are only a few subcategories of work you can create with Photoshop. Our goal in this book is to teach you how to use the available tools to create different types of work that you might encounter in your professional career.

Although not intended as a layout-design application, you can also use the Photoshop tools to combine type, graphics, and images into a finished design; many people create advertisements, book covers, and other projects entirely in Photoshop. Others argue that Photoshop should never be used for layout design, maintaining that InDesign is the preferred page-layout application.

Projects 4 and 5 result in finished composite designs. We do not advocate doing *all* or even *most* layout composite work in Photoshop. But because many people use the application to create composite designs, we feel the projects in this book portray a realistic workflow. Project 6 focuses specifically on image manipulation or creation — which is the true heart of the application.

As you move forward in your career, it will be your choice to determine which application is appropriate for which task; it is our job to teach you how to use the tools so you can make the best possible decision when that need arises.

1. **With skills.indd open in InDesign, use the Selection tool (the solid arrow) to select the portfolio image in the bottom-left corner of Page 1.**

2. **Control/right-click the selected image and choose Edit With>Adobe Photoshop CS5 in the contextual menu.**

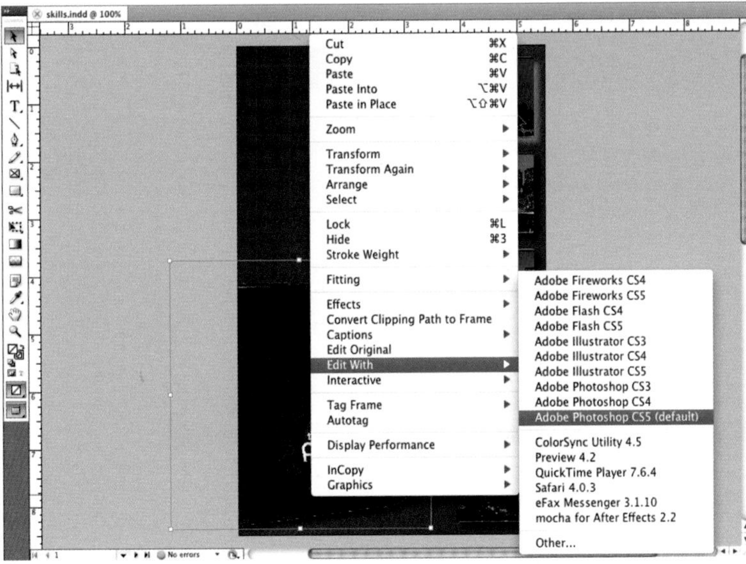

3. **Macintosh users: Open the Window menu. If Application Frame is not checked (active), choose that command in the menu.**

4. **Choose Essentials in the Workspace switcher, then choose Reset Essentials to restore the deault user interface settings.**

Photoshop panels are arranged and accessed using the same techniques you already learned, and saved workspaces in Photoshop serve the same function as in InDesign. Also like InDesign, calling a saved workspace calls the last-used version of the workspace; you have to use the Reset option to call the saved version of the workspace.

On Macintosh systems, the Application bar includes a number of buttons for accessing different view options. On Windows systems, those same options are available on the right side of the Menu bar.

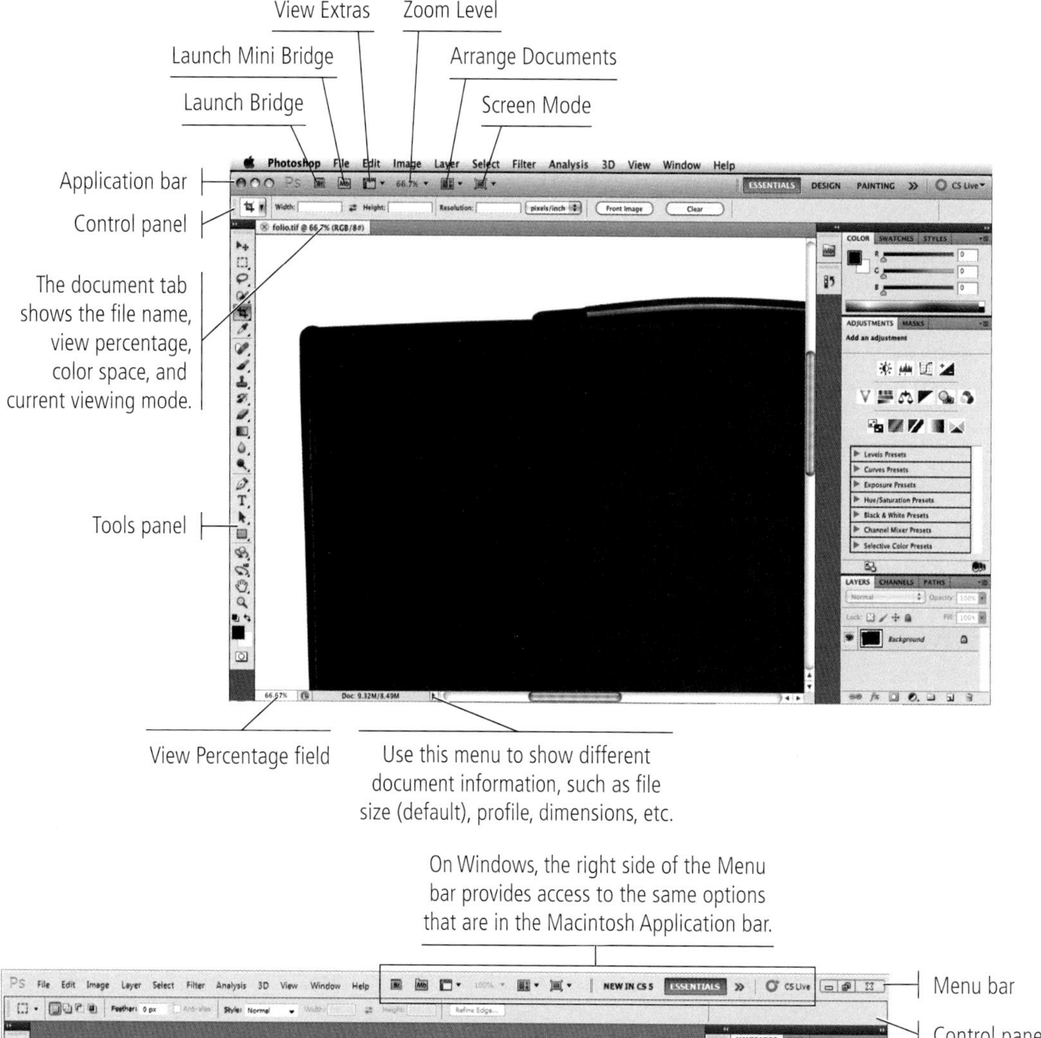

On Windows, the right side of the Menu bar provides access to the same options that are in the Macintosh Application bar.

Menu bar

Control panel

5. **Click the Zoom tool in the Tools panel, and then review the options in the Control panel.**

As in Illustrator, the Control panel is context sensitive. (The Control panel is also called the Options bar in Photoshop, and is turned on or off by choosing Window>Options. For the sake of consistency, we refer to it as the Control panel throughout this book.)

6. **In the Control panel, click the Fit Screen button.**

   The Fit Screen command resizes the document view percentage to fit in the available document window space.

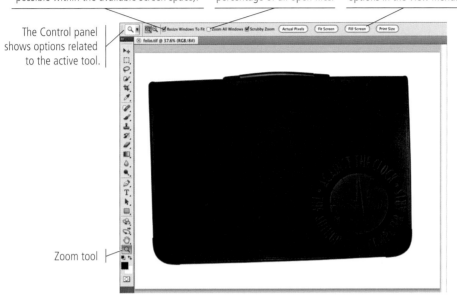

7. **In the Control panel, click the Actual Pixels button.**

   This option, the same as the Actual Pixels command in the View menu, changes the image view to 100%.

8. **Using the Zoom tool, press Option/Alt, and then click three times anywhere in the document window.**

   Clicking with the Zoom tool enlarges the view percentage in specific, predefined percentage steps. Pressing Option/Alt while clicking with the Zoom tool reduces the view percentage in the reverse sequence of the same percentages.

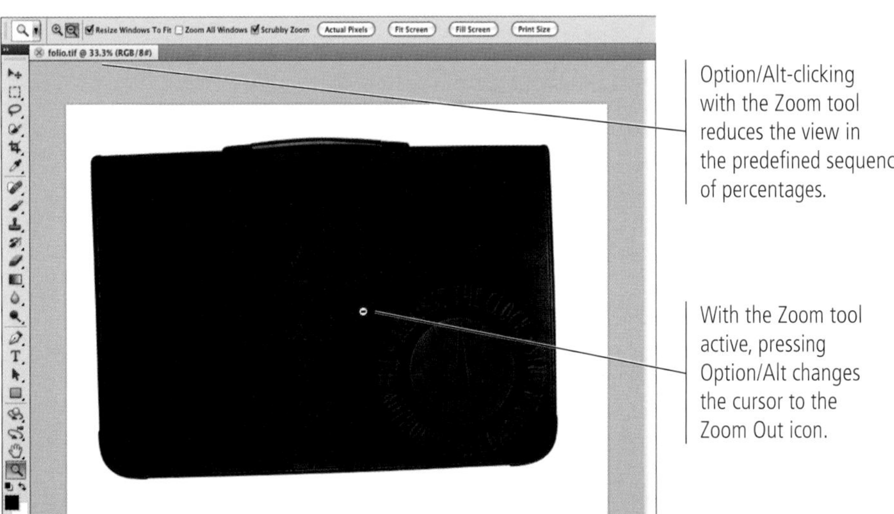

Option/Alt-clicking with the Zoom tool reduces the view in the predefined sequence of percentages.
With the Zoom tool active, pressing Option/Alt changes the cursor to the Zoom Out icon.

Note:

In Photoshop, you can zoom a document between approximately 0.098% and 3200%. We say "approximately" because the actual smallest size depends on the original image size; you can zoom out far enough to "show" the image as a single tiny square, whatever that percentage of the image.

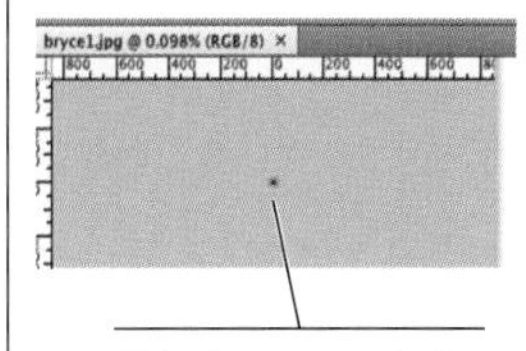

This tiny square is the entire image, zoomed out as far as possible.

Identifying Photoshop Tools

The following chart offers a quick reference of nested tools, as well as the shortcut for each tool (if any). Nested tools are shown indented and in italics.

- Move tool (V)
- Rectangular Marquee tool (M)
  - *Elliptical Marquee tool* (M)
  - *Single Row Marquee tool*
  - *Single Column Marquee tool*
- Lasso tool (L)
  - *Polygonal Lasso tool* (L)
  - *Magnetic Lasso tool* (L)
- Quick Selection tool (W)
  - *Magic Wand tool* (W)
- Crop tool (C)
  - *Slice tool* (C)
  - *Slice Select tool* (C)
- Eyedropper tool (I)
  - *Color Sampler tool* (I)
  - *Ruler tool* (I)
  - *Note tool* (I)
  - *Count tool* (I)
- Spot Healing Brush tool (J)
  - *Healing Brush tool* (J)
  - *Patch tool* (J)
  - *Red Eye tool* (J)
- Brush tool (B)
  - *Pencil tool* (B)
  - *Color Replacement tool* (B)
  - *Mixer Brush tool* (B)
- Clone Stamp tool (S)
  - *Pattern Stamp tool* (S)
- History Brush tool (Y)
  - *Art History Brush tool* (Y)
- Eraser tool (E)
  - *Background Eraser tool* (E)
  - *Magic Eraser tool* (E)
- Gradient tool (G)
  - *Paint Bucket tool* (G)
- Blur tool
  - *Sharpen tool*
  - *Smudge tool*
- Dodge tool (O)
  - *Burn tool* (O)
  - *Sponge tool* (O)
- Pen tool (P)
  - *Freeform Pen tool* (P)
  - *Add Anchor Point tool*
  - *Delete Anchor Point tool*
  - *Convert Point tool*
- Horizontal Type tool (T)
  - *Vertical Type tool* (T)
  - *Horizontal Type Mask tool* (T)
  - *Vertical Type Mask tool* (T)
- Path Selection tool (A)
  - *Direct Selection tool* (A)
- Rectangle tool (U)
  - *Rounded Rectangle tool* (U)
  - *Ellipse tool* (U)
  - *Polygon tool* (U)
  - *Line tool* (U)
  - *Custom Shape tool* (U)
- 3D Object Rotate tool (K)
  - *3D Object Roll tool* (K)
  - *3D Object Pan tool* (K)
  - *3D Object Slide tool* (K)
  - *3D Object Scale tool* (K)
- 3D Rotate Camera tool (N)
  - *3D Roll Camera tool* (N)
  - *3D Pan Camera tool* (N)
  - *3D Walk Camera tool* (N)
  - *3D Zoom Camera tool* (N)
- Hand tool (H)
  - *Rotate View tool* (R)
- Zoom tool (Z)

9. **In the Tools panel, Control/right-click the Hand tool and choose the Rotate View tool from the list of nested tools. Click in the document window and drag right to turn the document clockwise.**

The Rotate View tool turns an image without permanently altering the orientation of the file; the actual image data remains unchanged. This tool allows you to more easily work on objects or elements that are not oriented horizontally (for example, text that appears on an angle in the final image).

If you are unable to rotate the image view, open the Performance pane of the Preferences dialog box and make sure Enable OpenGL Drawing is checked. You will have to close the file and reopen it after enabling OpenGL Drawing for the change to take effect.

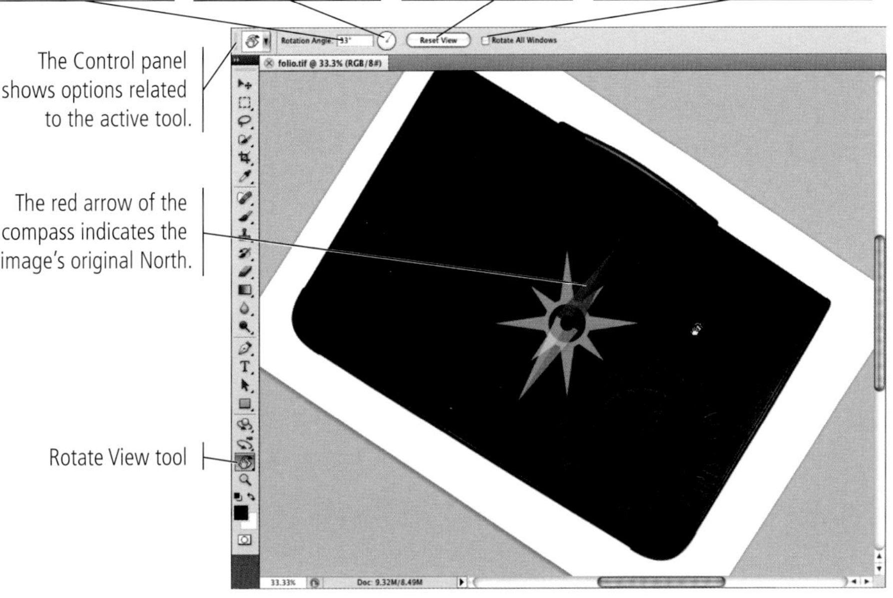

Type a specific angle in this field to rotate the image view.
Click and drag around this icon to rotate the image view.
Clicking Reset View restores the original image orientation.
If Rotate All Windows is checked, dragging in one window affects the view angle of all open files.
The Control panel shows options related to the active tool.
The red arrow of the compass indicates the image's original North.
Rotate View tool

Note:

The Hand tool in Photoshop and Illustrator serves the same purpose as the Hand tool in InDesign. Simply click and drag to reposition the document within the document window.

Note:

OpenGL is a hardware/software combination that makes it possible to work with complex files such as 3D. If this option is not available (grayed out) on your computer, your video card and/or driver does not support OpenGL. You will not be able to rotate the image view.

10. **In the Control panel, click the Reset View button.**

As we said, the Rotate View tool is non-destructive. You can easily use the tool's options to define a specific view angle or to restore an image to its original orientation.

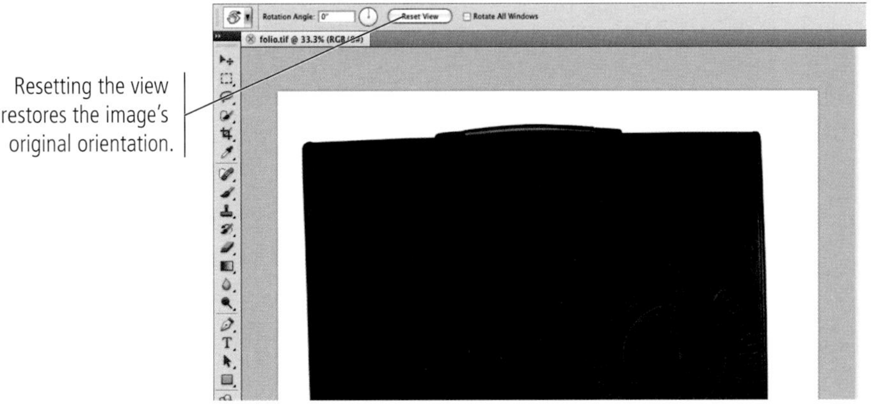

Resetting the view restores the image's original orientation.

Note:

Like Illustrator, Photoshop has three ***screen modes*** *that change the way the document window displays on the screen. In Photoshop, you can access these options using the Screen Mode button in the Application/Menu bar.*

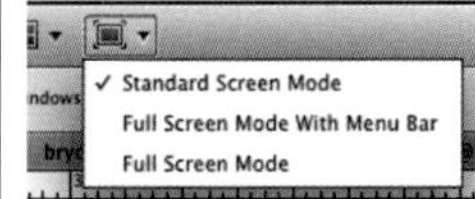

11. **Click the Close button on the folio.tif tab.**

12. **Return to InDesign. Close the skills.indd file without saving, and then continue to Project 1.**

Summing up the Photoshop View Options

Most Photoshop projects require some amount of zooming in and out to various view percentages, as well as navigating around the document within its window.

Zoom Level Field/Menu

In the Application/Menu bar, you can type a specific view percentage in the Zoom Level field, or choose one of the defined percentages in the attached menu. You can also type a specific percentage in the View Percentage field in the bottom-left corner of the document window.

View Menu

The View menu also provides options for changing the view percentage, including the associated keyboard shortcuts. (The Zoom In and Zoom Out options step through the same predefined view percentages that the Zoom tool uses.)

Zoom In	Command/Control-plus (+)
Zoom Out	Command/Control-minus (-)
Fit On Screen	Command/Control-0 (zero)
Actual Pixels (100%)	Command/Control-1

Zoom Tool

You can click with the **Zoom tool** to increase the view percentage in specific, predefined intervals. Pressing Option/Alt with the Zoom tool allows you to zoom out in the same predefined percentages. If you drag a marquee with the Zoom tool, you can zoom into a specific location; the area surrounded by the marquee fills the available space in the document window.

When the Zoom tool is active, you can also activate the Scrubby Zoom option in the Control panel. This allows you to click and drag left to reduce the view percentage, or drag right to increase the view percentage; in this case, the tool does not follow predefined stepped percentages.

Hand Tool

Whatever your view percentage, you can use the **Hand tool** to drag the file around in the document window. The Hand tool changes only what is visible in the window; it has no effect on the actual pixels in the image.

Mouse Scroll Wheel

If your mouse has a scroll wheel, rolling the scroll wheel up or down moves the image up or down within the document window. If you press Command/Control and scroll the wheel, you can move the image left (scroll up) or right (scroll down) within the document window. You can also press Option/Alt and scroll the wheel up to zoom in or scroll the wheel down to zoom out.

(In the General pane of the Preferences dialog box, the Zoom with Scroll Wheel option is unchecked by default. If you check this option, scrolling up or down with no modifier key zooms in or out and does not move the image within the document window.)

Application/Menu Bar

The Application/Menu bar consolidates many of the view-related tools and options into a single location, which is always visible at the top of the workspace (unless you're on a Macintosh and have turned off the Application frame and Application bar).

Navigator Panel

The **Navigator panel** is another method of adjusting how close your viewpoint is and what part of the page you're currently viewing (if you're zoomed in close enough so you can see only a portion of the page). The Navigator panel shows a thumbnail of the active file; a red rectangle represents exactly how much of the document shows in the document window.

The red rectangle shows the area of the file that is visible in the document window.

Drag the red rectangle to change the visible portion of the file.

Use the slider and field at the bottom of the panel to change the view percentage.

project 1

International Symbols

Biotech Services manages large-scale manufacturing facilities specializing in everything from digital photographic equipment to large earth-moving machines used to build new roads. The company builds plants all over the world that in many cases handle dangerous chemicals and undertake dangerous tasks — which means they must prominently display appropriate warnings. Biotech Services hired you to create a digital collection of universal symbols that they can use to create signs, print on the side of large machines, place as icons on their Web sites, and embroider onto employee uniforms.

This project incorporates the following skills:

- ❑ Placing raster images into an Illustrator file to use as drawing templates
- ❑ Creating and managing simple shapes and lines
- ❑ Using various tools and panels to transform objects' color, position, and shape
- ❑ Cloning objects to minimize repetitive tasks
- ❑ Using layers to organize and manage complex artwork
- ❑ Drawing complex shapes by combining simple shapes

Project Meeting

client comments

We have a set of universal warning symbols on our Web site, but we need to use those same icons in other places as well. Our printer told us that the symbols on our Web site are "low res," so they can't be used for print projects. The printer also said he needs vector graphics that will scale larger and still look good. The printer suggested we hire a designer to create digital versions of the icons so we can use them for a wide variety of purposes, from large machinery signs to small plastic cards to anything else that might come up. We need you to help us figure out exactly what we need and then create the icons for us.

art director comments

Basically, we have the icons, but they're low-resolution raster images, so they only work for the Web, and they can't be enlarged. The good news is that you can use the existing icons as templates and more or less trace them to create the new icons.

The client needs files that can be printed cleanly and scaled from a couple of inches up to several feet. Illustrator vector files are perfect for this type of job. In fact, vector graphics get their resolution from the printer being used for a specific job, so you can scale them to any size you want without losing quality.

project objectives

To complete this project, you will:

- ❑ Create a grid that will eventually hold all icons in one document
- ❑ Control objects' stroke, fill, and transparency attributes
- ❑ Import and use the client's raster images as templates, which you can then trace
- ❑ Use layers to manage complex artwork
- ❑ Use the Line Segment tool to create a complex object from a set of straight lines
- ❑ Lock, unlock, hide, and show objects to navigate the objects' stacking order
- ❑ Rotate and reflect objects to create complex artwork from simple shapes
- ❑ Use the Pathfinder to combine simple shapes into a single complex object

Stage 1 Setting up the Workspace

There are two primary types of digital artwork: raster images and vector graphics. (**Line art**, sometimes categorized as a third type of image, is actually a type of raster image.)

Raster images are pixel-based, made up of a grid of individual **pixels** (**rasters** or **bits**) in rows and columns (called a **bitmap**). Raster files are **resolution dependent**; their resolution is determined when you scan, photograph, or create the file. As a professional graphic designer, you should have a basic understanding of the following terms and concepts:

- **Pixels per inch (ppi)** is the number of pixels in one horizontal or vertical inch of a digital raster file.
- **Lines per inch (lpi)** is the number of halftone dots produced in a linear inch by a high-resolution imagesetter, which simulates the appearance of continuous-tone color.
- **Dots per inch (dpi)** or **spots per inch (spi)** is the number of dots produced by an output device in a single line of output.

Drawing objects that you create in Illustrator are **vector graphics**, which are composed of mathematical descriptions of a series of lines and points. Vector graphics are **resolution independent**; they can be freely scaled and are automatically output at the resolution of the output device.

Create a New Document

In this project, you work with the basics of creating vector graphics in Illustrator using a number of different drawing tools, adding color, and managing various aspects of your artwork. The first step is to create a new document for building your artwork.

1. **Download `Print5_RF_Project1.zip` from the Student Files Web page.**
2. **Expand the ZIP archive in your WIP folder (Macintosh) or copy the archive contents into your WIP folder (Windows).**

   This results in a folder named **Symbols**, which contains all of the files you need for this project. You should also use this folder to save the files you create in this project.

   If necessary, refer to Page 1 of the Interface chapter for specific information on expanding or accessing the required resource files.
3. **In Illustrator, choose File>New.**
4. **In the resulting New Document dialog box, type `icons` in the Name field.**

   The New Document dialog box defaults to the last-used settings.
5. **Choose Print in the New Document Profile menu, and make sure the Number of Artboards field is set to 1.**

   Illustrator CS5 includes the ability to create multiple **artboards** (basically, Illustrator's version of "pages"). You will work with multiple artboards in Projects 3 and 5.
6. **Choose Letter in the Size menu, choose Points in the Units menu, and choose the Portrait Orientation option.**

   The **point** is a standard unit of measurement for graphic designers. There are 72 points in an inch. As you complete this project, you will work with other units of measurement; you will convert the units later.

7. **Set all four bleed values to `0`.**

   Bleed is the amount an object needs to extend past the edge of the artboard or page to meet the mechanical requirements of commercial printing.

> *Note:*
>
> *You learn more about bleeds in Project 3.*

8. **If the Advanced options aren't visible, click the arrow button to the left of the word Advanced.**

9. **Make sure the Color Mode is set to CMYK and the Preview Mode is set to Default.**

   CMYK is the standard color mode for printing, and RGB is the standard color mode for digital distribution. You learn much more about color and color modes in Project 2.

   Don't worry about the other Advanced options for now. You will learn about those in later projects when they are more relevant.

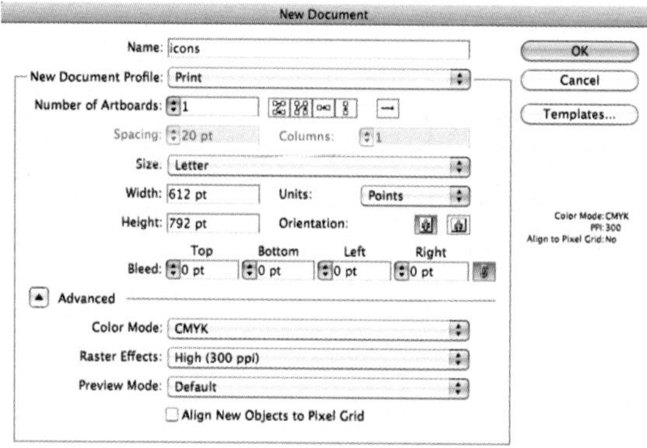

10. **Click OK to create the new file.**

    In the resulting document window, the letter-size "page" (or artboard) is represented by a dark black line. The artboard concept will be important in the final stage of this project, when you save the icon files for use in other applications.

    As we explained in the Interface chapter, the panels you see depend on what was done the last time you (or someone else) used the application. Because workspace arrangement is such a personal preference, we tell you what panels you need to use, but we don't tell you where to place them. (Remember that panels can be accessed in the Window menu.)

    In our screen shots, we typically float panels over the relevant area of the document so we can focus the images on the most important part of the file at any particular point. As you complete the projects in this book, feel free to dock the panels, grouped or ungrouped, iconized or expanded, however you prefer.

> *Note:*
>
> *Our screen shots show the Macintosh operating system using the Application frame. If you're on a Macintosh system and your screen doesn't look like our screen shots, choose Window>Application Frame to toggle on that option.*

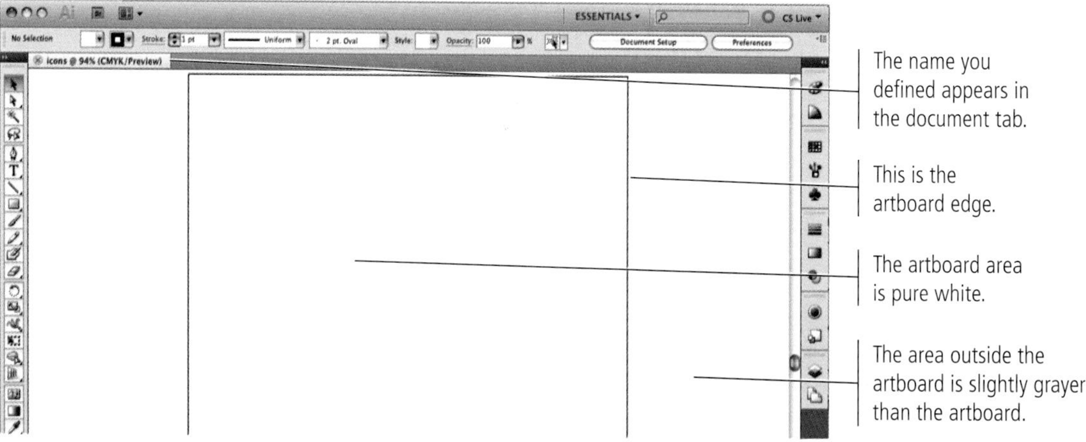

11. Choose File>Save As and navigate to your WIP>Symbols folder.

If you assign a name in the New Document dialog box (as you did in Step 4), that name becomes the default file name in the Save As dialog box.

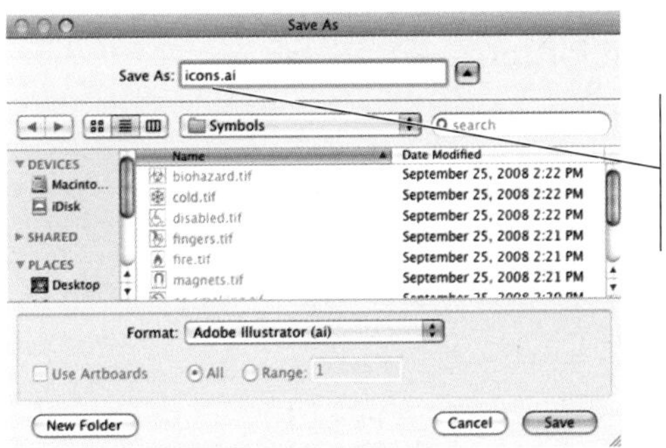

The file name defaults to the name you defined when you created the file, including the ".ai" extension.

> ***Note:***
>
> *Press Command/Control-S to save a document, or press Command/Control-Shift-S to open the Save As dialog box.*

12. Click Save in the Save As dialog box. Review the options in the resulting Illustrator Options dialog box.

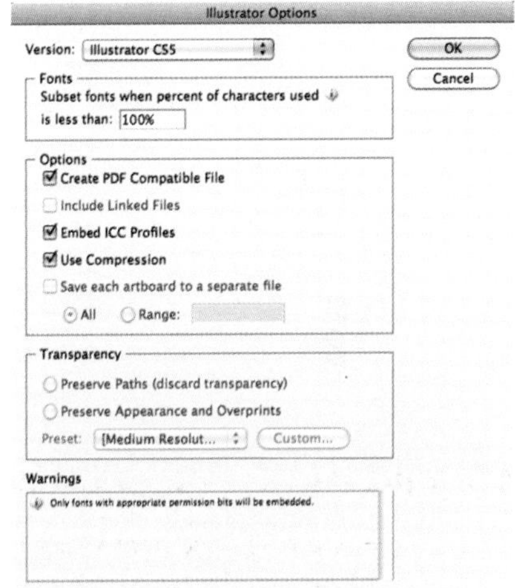

This dialog box determines what is stored in the resulting file (the default options are adequate for most files).

- Use the **Version** menu to save files to be compatible with earlier versions of the software. (Keep in mind that many features are not supported by earlier versions; if you save a file for an earlier version, some file information will probably be lost.)
- **Subset Embedded Fonts when Percent of Characters Used Is Less Than** determines when to embed an entire font instead of just the characters that are used in the file. (Embedding the entire font can significantly increase file size.)
- Make sure **Create PDF Compatible File** is checked if you want to use the file with other Adobe applications (such as placing it into an InDesign layout).
- **Include Linked Files** embeds files that are linked to the artwork. (You will learn about linked and embedded files in Project 5.)
- **Embed ICC Profiles** stores color information inside the file for use in a color-managed workflow.
- **Use Compression** compresses PDF data in the Illustrator file.
- **Save Each Artboard to a Separate File** saves each artboard as a separate file; a separate master file with all artboards is also created.
- **Transparency** options determine what happens to transparent objects when you save a file for Illustrator 9.0 or earlier. Preserve Paths discards transparency effects and resets transparent artwork to 100% opacity and Normal blending mode. Preserve Appearance and Overprints preserves overprints that don't interact with transparent objects; overprints that interact with transparent objects are flattened.

13. Click OK to save the file, and then continue to the next exercise.

Define Smart Guide Preferences

Adobe Illustrator provides many tools to help you create precise lines and shapes. **Smart Guides** are temporary snap-to guides that help you create, align, and transform objects. Smart Guides also show you when the cursor is at a precise angle relative to the original position of the object or point you're moving. In this exercise, you will make sure the correct Smart Guides are active.

1. **With `icons.ai` open and nothing selected in the file, click the Preferences button in the Control panel.**

> *Note:*
>
> *When nothing is selected in the file, you can access the Preferences dialog box directly from the Control panel.*
>
> *If something is selected in the file, you have to choose Illustrator>Preferences on Macintosh or Edit>Preferences on Windows.*

2. **Choose Smart Guides in the menu at the top of the Preferences dialog box.**
3. **Make sure the Alignment Guides, Object Highlighting, Anchor/Path Labels, and Measurement Labels options are selected and click OK.**

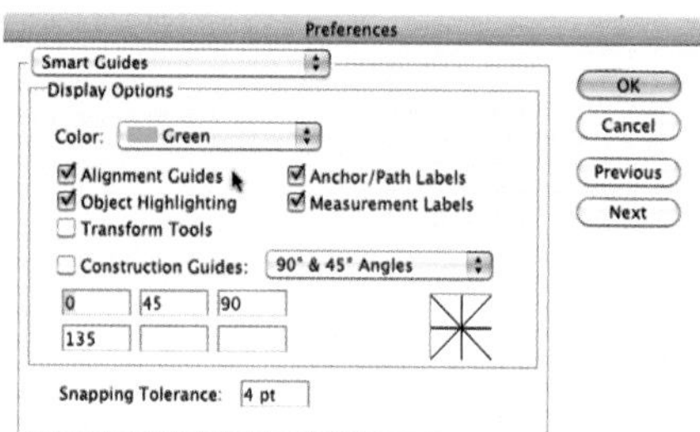

4. **Choose View>Smart Guides to make sure that option is toggled on (checked).**

   If the option is already checked, simply move your mouse away from the menu and click to dismiss the menu without changing the active option.

5. **Continue to the next exercise.**

Using Smart Guides

ILLUSTRATOR FOUNDATIONS

You can change the appearance and behavior of Smart Guides in the Preferences dialog box. The Display options determine what is visible when Smart Guides are active:

This anchor is being dragged with the Direct Selection tool.

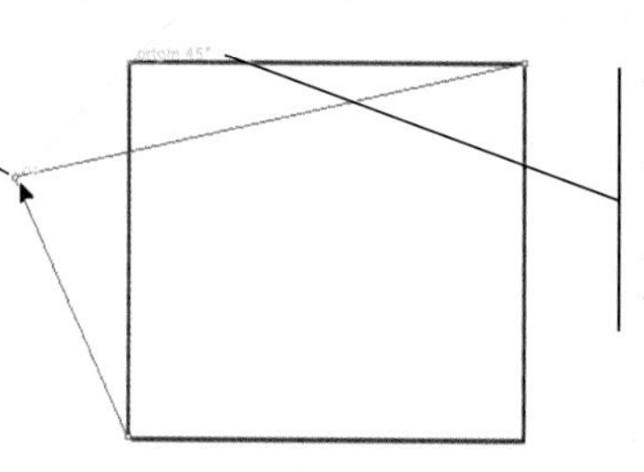

The Smart Guide shows that the anchor is being moved at a 45-degree angle from the original position.

- When **Alignment Guides** is active, Smart Guides show when a new or moved object aligns to the center or edge of a nearby object.
- When **Object Highlighting** is active, moving the mouse over any part of an unselected object shows the anchors and paths that make up that object.
- When **Transform Tools** is active, Smart Guides display when you scale, rotate, or shear objects.
- When **Anchor/Path Labels** is active, Smart Guides include labels that show the type of element (path or anchor) under the cursor.
- When **Measurement Labels** is active, Smart Guides show the distance and angle of movement.
- When **Construction Guides** is active, Smart Guides appear when you move objects in the file at or near defined angles (0°, 45°, 90°, and 135° are the default angles). A number of common angle options are built into the related menu, or you can type up to six specific angles in the available fields.

Draw Basic Shapes

Now that you have a place to draw (the artboard), you're ready to start creating the icon artwork. The first step of this project requires a set of background shapes — simple rectangles with rounded corners — to contain each icon. Illustrator includes a number of shape tools that make it easy to create this kind of basic shape — rectangles (or squares), ellipses (or circles), and so on.

1. **With icons.ai open, click the Rectangle tool in the Tools panel and hold down the mouse button until the nested tools appear. Choose the Rounded Rectangle tool from the list of nested tools.**

> *Note:*
>
> *A point is a unit of measurement that comes from the traditional typesetting industry; there are 72 points in an inch.*

2. **Click the Default Fill and Stroke button at the bottom of the Tools panel.**

   In Illustrator, the default fill is white and the default stroke is 1-pt black.

   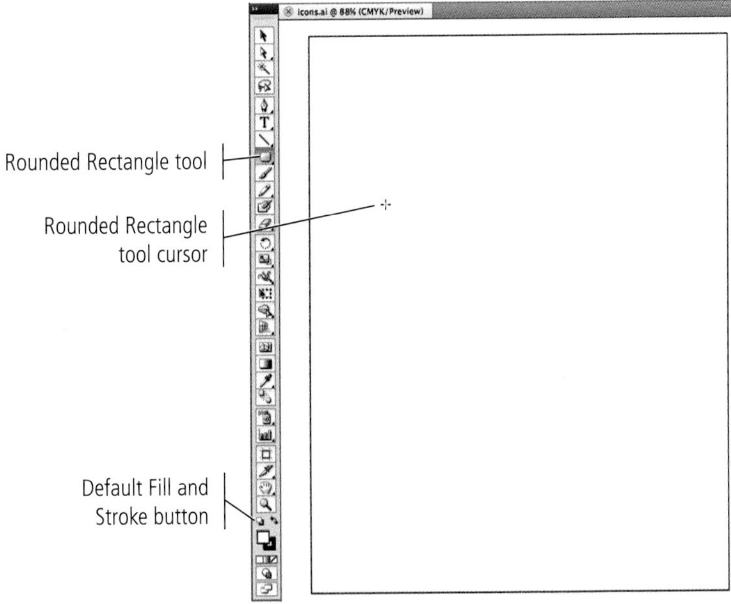

3. **Click the Rounded Rectangle tool anywhere on the artboard.**

   The resulting dialog box asks how big you want to make the new rectangle, defaulting to the last-used measurements. The default application measurement system is points; however, it is possible to change the default units, so you might see inches, millimeters, or some other unit on your screen (i.e., if someone changed the default settings).

   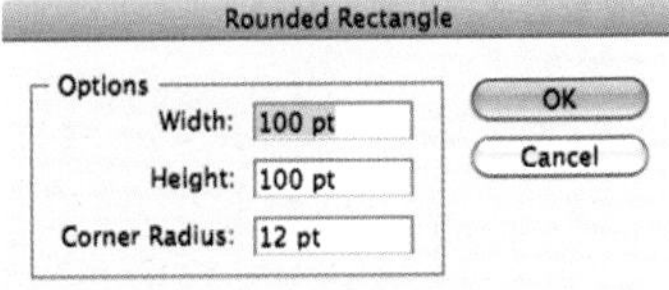

> *Note:*
>
> *If you Option/Alt-click with any of the shape tools, the place where you click becomes the center of the new shape.*

4. **Type 1.5" in the Width field and then press Tab to move to the Height field.**

   Regardless of what unit you see in the dialog box, you can enter values in whatever system you prefer, as long as you remember to type the correct unit in the dialog box fields (use " for inches, mm for millimeters, and pt for points; there are a few others, but they are rarely used). Illustrator automatically translates one unit of measurement to another.

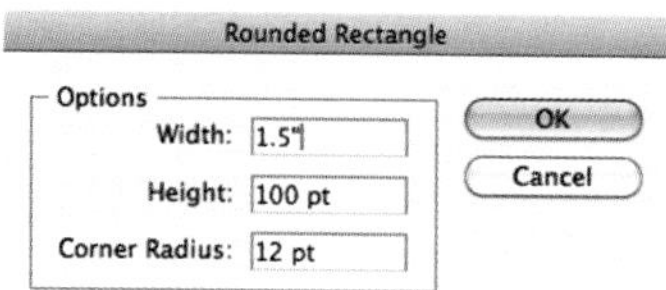

   When you move to the next field, Illustrator calculates the conversion of 1.5 inches (the value you placed in the Width field) to 108 pt (the value that automatically appears in the Width field after you move to the Height field).

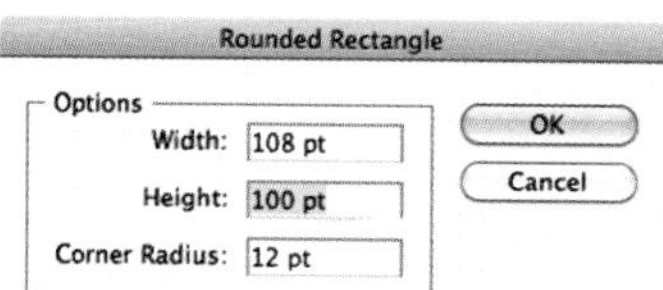

5. **Type 1.5" in the Height field. Set the Corner Radius field to 12 pt, and then click OK.**

   A shape appears on the artboard with its top-left corner exactly where you clicked the Rounded Rectangle tool.

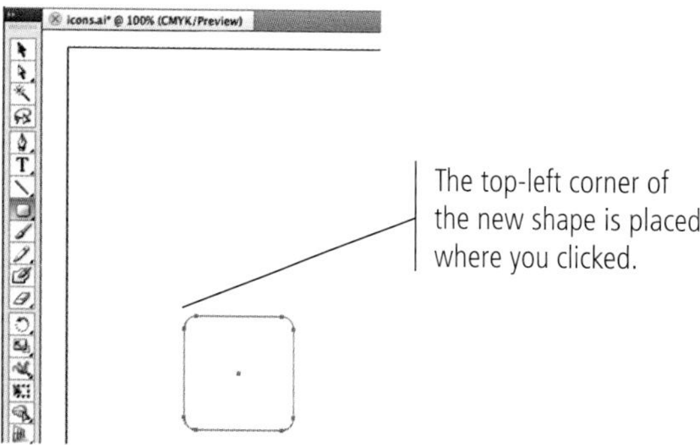

Note:

A rounded-corner rectangle is simply a rectangle with the corners cut at a specific distance from the end (the corner radius). The two sides are connected with one-fourth of a circle, which has a radius equal to the amount of the rounding.

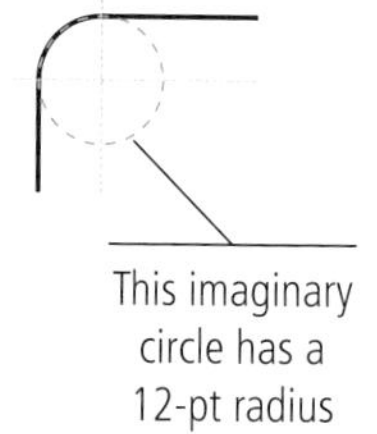

This imaginary circle has a 12-pt radius

6. **Click the Selection tool in the Tools panel and zoom in to 200%.**

   When the object is selected, the **bounding box** marks the outermost edges of the shape. **Bounding box handles** mark the corners and exact horizontal and vertical center of the shape. If you don't see the bounding box, choose View>Show Bounding Box.

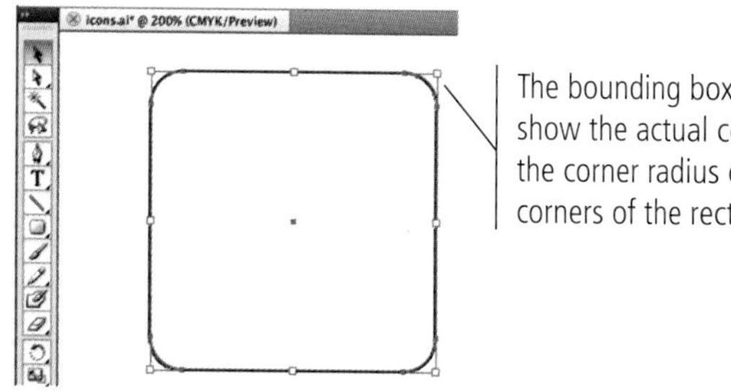

The bounding box handles show the actual corners, where the corner radius cut off the corners of the rectangle.

Note:

As a rule, we don't tell you what view percentage to use unless we want to highlight a specific issue. As you work through the projects in this book, we encourage you to zoom in and out as necessary to meet your specific needs.

7. **Select the Rounded Rectangle tool in the Tools panel.**

   When you choose a nested tool, that variation becomes the default option in the Tools panel. You don't need to access the nested menu to select the Rounded Rectangle tool again.

8. **Move the cursor to the right of the top edge of the existing shape.**

9. **When you see a green line connected to the top edge of the first shape, click, hold down the mouse button, and drag down and right to begin creating a second shape. Do not release the mouse button.**

   The green line is a function of the Smart Guides feature, which provides instant feedback while you draw. As you drag, notice the cursor feedback showing the size of the new shape. Also notice that as you drag near the bottom edge of the first shape, a Smart Guide appears to indicate your position.

Note:

Cursor feedback and Smart Guides provide precise control over what you're creating — as individual objects and in relation to other objects on the artboard.

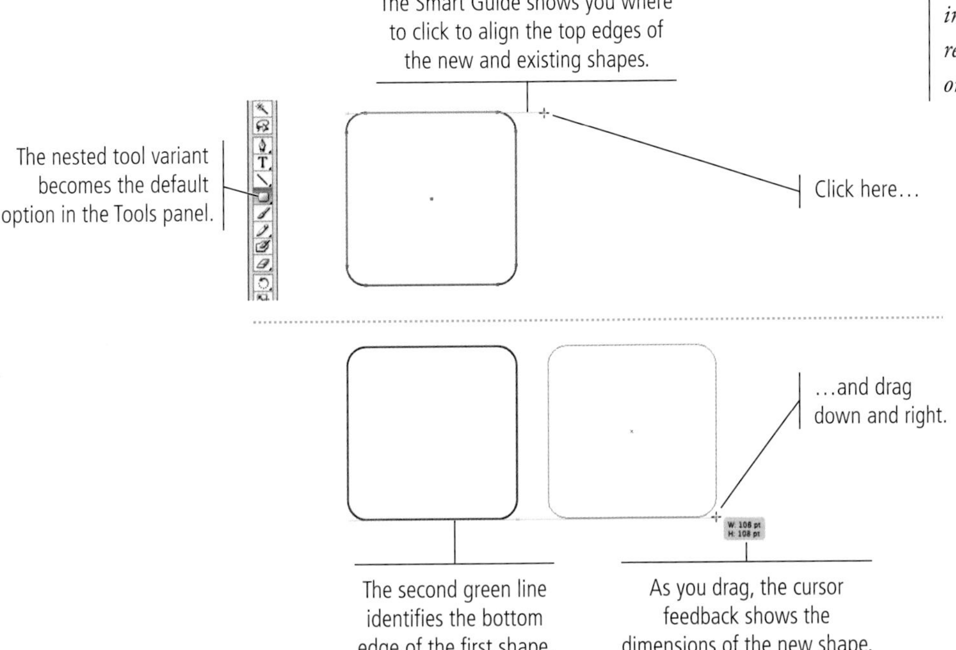

The Smart Guide shows you where to click to align the top edges of the new and existing shapes.
The nested tool variant becomes the default option in the Tools panel.
Click here...
...and drag down and right.
W: 108 pt
H: 108 pt
The second green line identifies the bottom edge of the first shape.
As you drag, the cursor feedback shows the dimensions of the new shape.

10. **While still holding down the mouse button, press the Shift key. When the cursor feedback shows both Width and Height values of 108 pt, release the mouse button to create the second shape.**

    Pressing Shift **constrains** the shape to equal height and width. Although you can accomplish the same result by carefully monitoring the cursor feedback, pressing the Shift key makes the process faster and easier.

Note:

If you do something wrong, or aren't happy with your results, press Command/Control-Z to undo the last action you took.

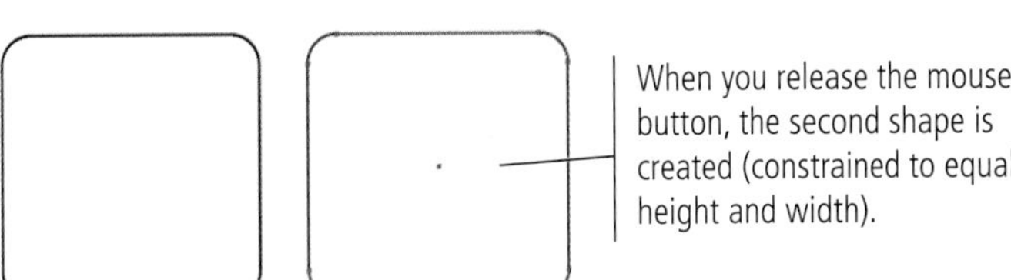

When you release the mouse button, the second shape is created (constrained to equal height and width).

Selection Basics

Most Illustrator objects (including shapes like rounded-corner rectangles) contain two basic building blocks: anchor points and paths. In fact, these building blocks are the heart of vector graphics. Fortunately, you don't really need to worry about the geometric specifics of vectors because Illustrator manages them for you. But you do need to understand the basic concept of how Illustrator works with anchor points and paths. You should also understand how to access those building blocks so you can do more than create basic shapes.

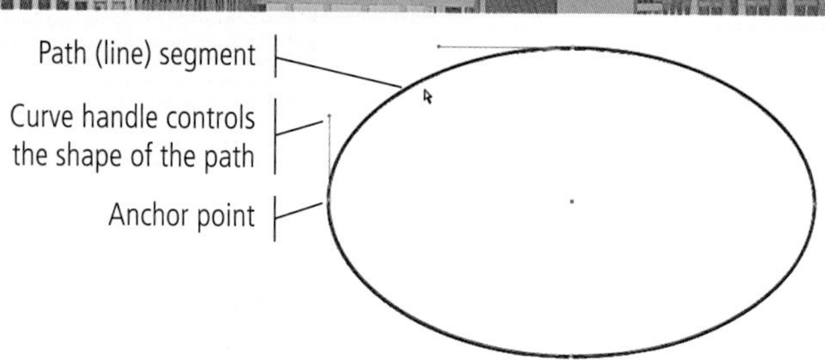

When you select an object with the **Selection tool** (the solid arrow), you can see the bounding box that identifies the outermost dimensions of the shape. Around the edges of the bounding box you see the bounding box handles, which you can use to resize the shape. (Press Command/Control-Shift-B to show or hide the bounding box of selected objects.)

When you select an object with the **Direct Selection tool** (the hollow arrow), you can see the anchor points and paths that make up the selected object rather than the object's bounding box. As you work with Illustrator, keep this distinction in mind: use the Selection tool to select an entire object; use the Direct Selection tool to edit the points and paths of an object.

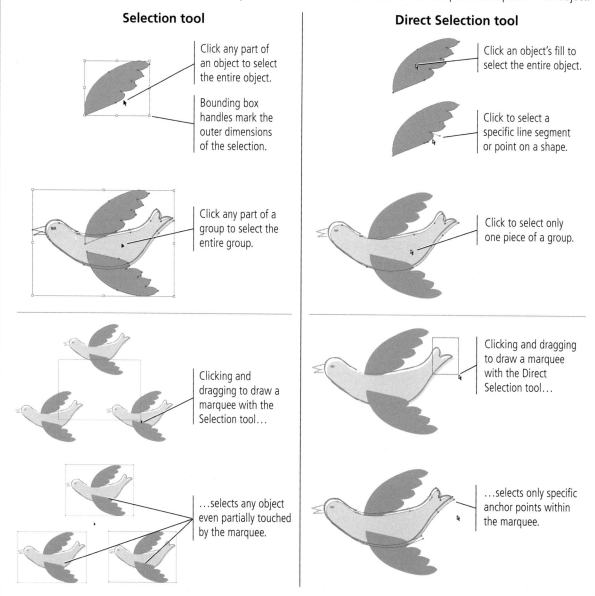

Selection tool

Click any part of an object to select the entire object.

Bounding box handles mark the outer dimensions of the selection.

Click any part of a group to select the entire group.

Clicking and dragging to draw a marquee with the Selection tool…

…selects any object even partially touched by the marquee.

Direct Selection tool

Click an object's fill to select the entire object.

Click to select a specific line segment or point on a shape.

Click to select only one piece of a group.

Clicking and dragging to draw a marquee with the Direct Selection tool…

…selects only specific anchor points within the marquee.

11. **Move the cursor to the right until a green line connects to the center of the second shape. Click, press Option/Alt-Shift, and drag down and right until a green line connects to the bottom of the second shape.**

    Pressing the Option/Alt key allows you to create a shape from the center out; in other words, the point where you click will be the exact center of the resulting shape.

    Pressing Shift as well constrains the new shape to equal height and width, growing out from the center point where you first clicked.

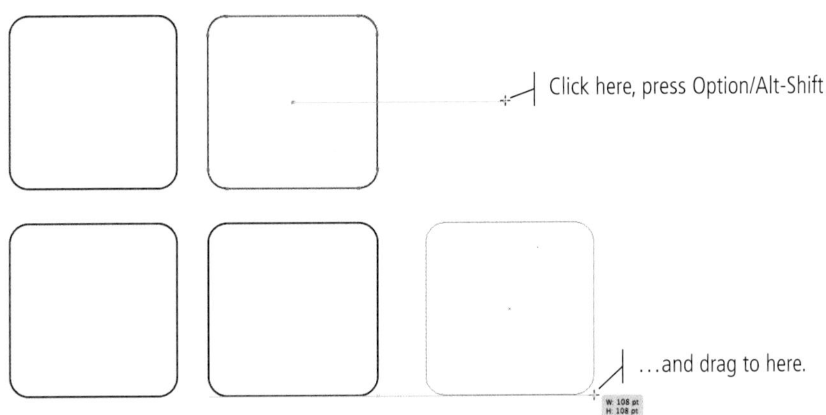

Note:

Don't worry about the spaces between the objects. You'll adjust the object spacing in a later exercise.

12. **When the cursor feedback shows both Width and Height values of 108 pt, release the mouse button.**

13. **Save the file and continue to the next exercise.**

 Control Fill and Stroke Attributes

At the beginning of the previous exercise, you clicked the Default Fill and Stroke button in the Tools panel to apply a white fill and 1-pt black stroke to the objects you created. Obviously, most artwork requires more than these basic attributes. Illustrator gives you almost unlimited control over the fill and stroke attributes of objects on the artboard.

As you complete the projects in this book, you will learn about styles, patterns, gradients, effects, and other attributes that can take an illustration from flat to fabulous. In this exercise, you learn about a number of options for changing the basic fill, stroke, and color attributes for objects on the page.

1. **With icons.ai open, choose the Selection tool at the top of the Tools panel. Click the left rectangle on the artboard to select it.**

    The Selection tool is used to select entire objects.

2. **Open the Swatches panel.**

    The Swatches panel includes a number of predefined and saved colors, which you can use to change the color of the fill and stroke of an object. You can also save custom swatches, which you will learn about in Project 2.

Note:

Remember, panels can always be accessed in the Window menu.

3. **Near the bottom of the Tools panel, click the Stroke icon to bring it to the front of the stack.**

The Fill and Stroke icons in the Tools panel are used to change the color of the related attributes. Clicking one of these buttons brings it to the front of the stack (makes it active) so you can change the color of that attribute.

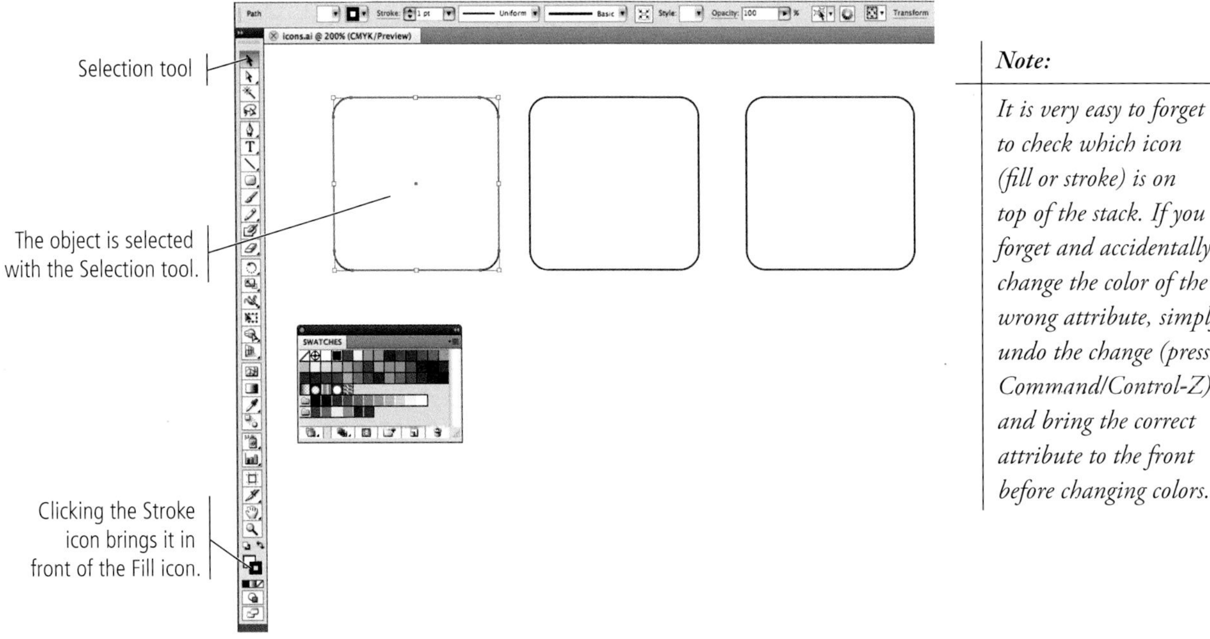

Selection tool
The object is selected with the Selection tool.
Clicking the Stroke icon brings it in front of the Fill icon.

> *Note:*
>
> *It is very easy to forget to check which icon (fill or stroke) is on top of the stack. If you forget and accidentally change the color of the wrong attribute, simply undo the change (press Command/Control-Z) and bring the correct attribute to the front before changing colors.*

4. **In the Swatches panel, click the gold swatch at the beginning of the second row.**

Because the Stroke icon is active in the Tools panel, the color of the selected object's stroke (border) changes to gold.

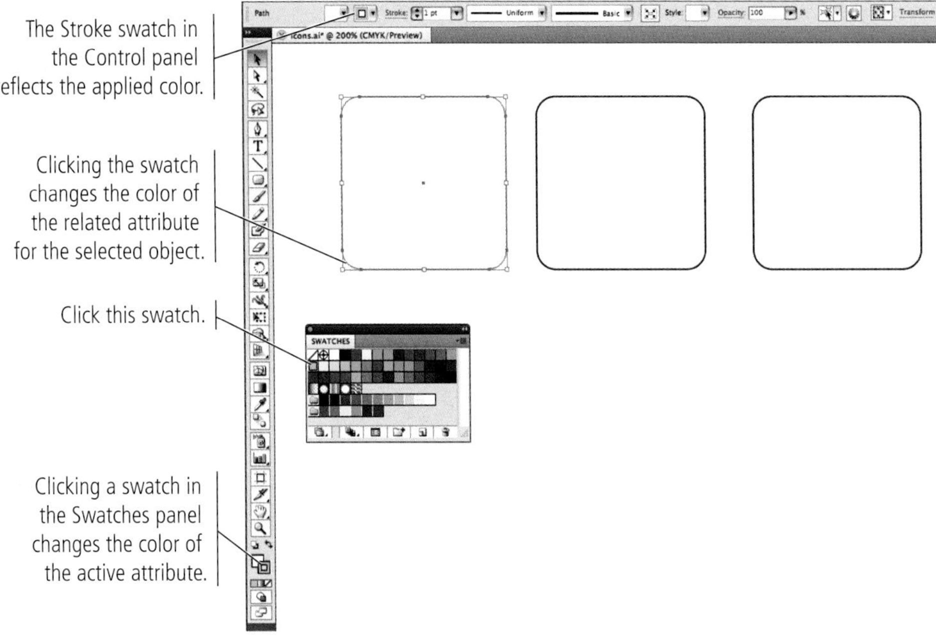

5. **In the Tools panel, click the Fill icon to bring it to the front of the stack.**

6. **In the Swatches panel, click the black swatch in the first row.**

   Because the Fill icon is active in the Tools panel, clicking the black color swatch changes the fill color of the selected object.

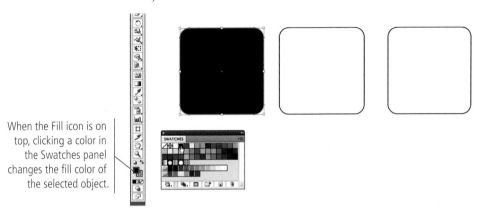

When the Fill icon is on top, clicking a color in the Swatches panel changes the fill color of the selected object.

Transforming Objects with the Bounding Box

ILLUSTRATOR FOUNDATIONS

Bounding box handles make it easy to transform an object on the artboard. You can resize an object by dragging any handle, and even rotate an object by placing the cursor directly outside a corner handle. (If Smart Guides are active, cursor feedback helps if you want to make specific transformations, or you can work freestyle and drag handles until you're satisfied with the results.)

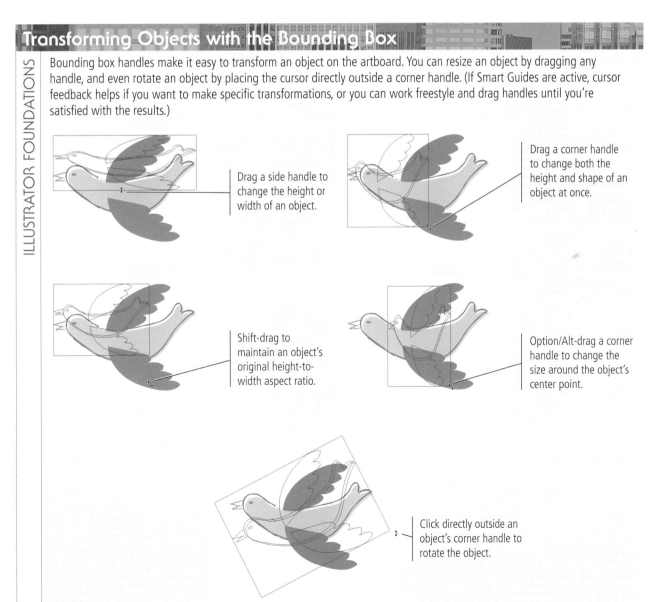

Drag a side handle to change the height or width of an object.

Drag a corner handle to change both the height and shape of an object at once.

Shift-drag to maintain an object's original height-to-width aspect ratio.

Option/Alt-drag a corner handle to change the size around the object's center point.

Click directly outside an object's corner handle to rotate the object.

Free Transform Options

The Free Transform tool allows you to change the shape of selected objects by dragging the bounding box handles. Depending on where you click and whether you press a modifier key, you can use this tool to stretch, shrink, rotate, distort, or skew a selection.

Click a center handle to stretch or shrink the selection in one direction.

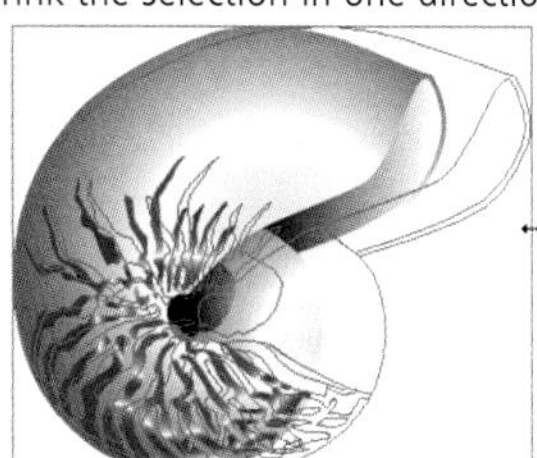

Click a corner handle to stretch or shrink the selection horizontally and vertically at the same time.

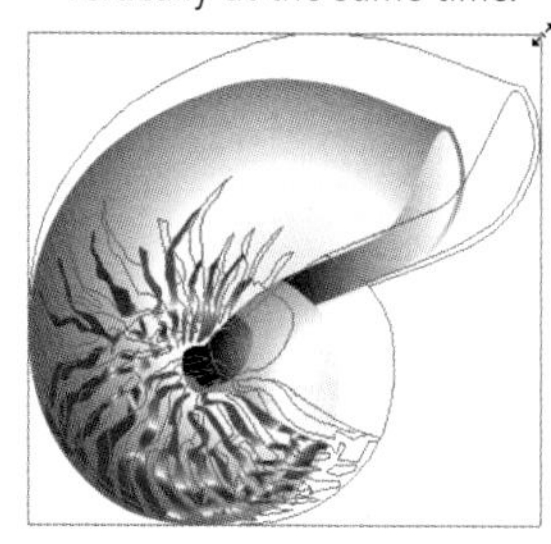

Click slightly outside a corner handle to rotate the selection.

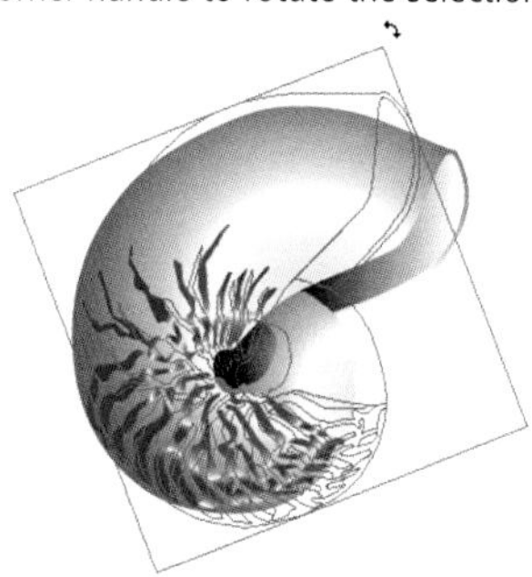

Click a center handle, then press Command/Control to skew the selection.

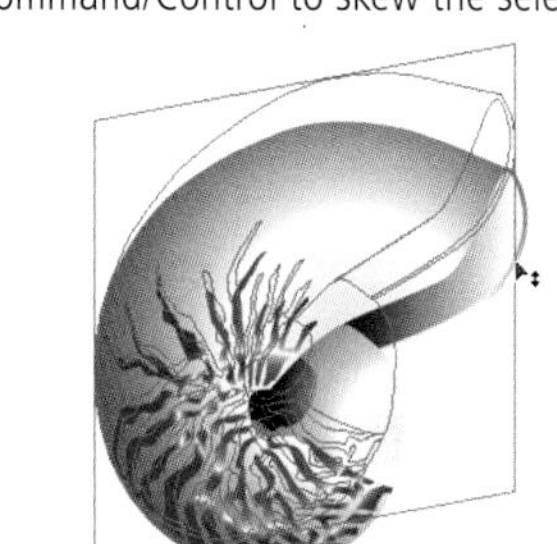

Click a corner handle, then press Command/Control to distort the selection.

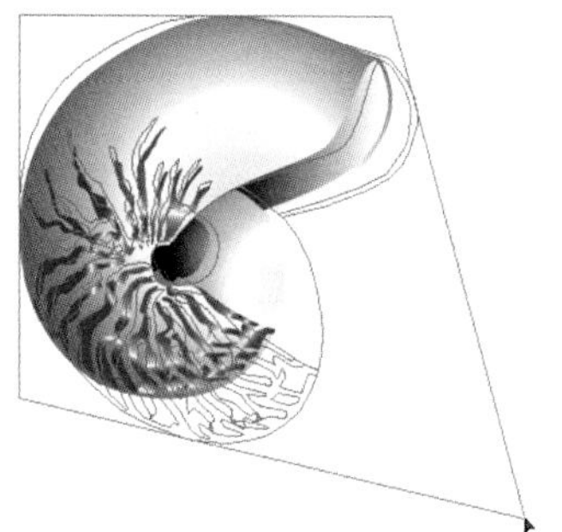

Click a corner handle, then press Command-Option-Shift/Control-Alt-Shift to alter the perspective of the selection.

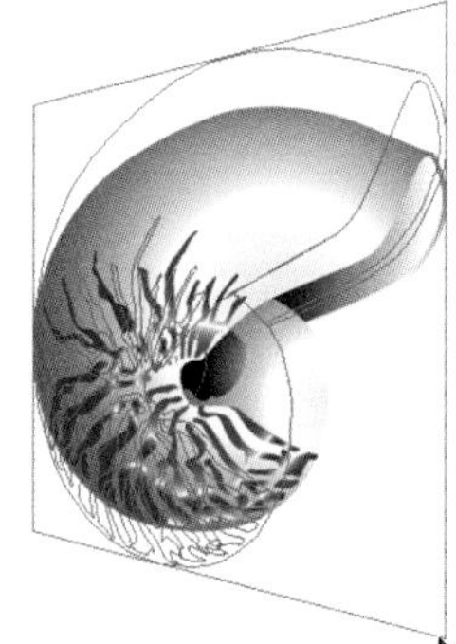

Press Option/Alt while making any free transformation to apply it equally on both sides of the selection center.

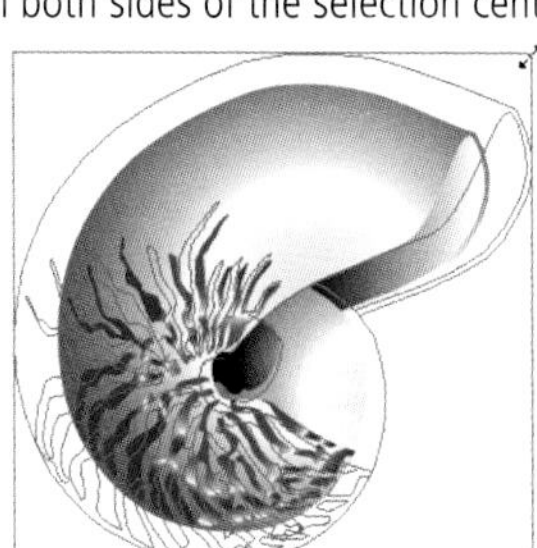

Press Shift and drag a handle to constrain the related transformation. For example, press Shift while dragging a corner handle to scale the selection at the same proportional height and width (below left) rather than scaling disproportionately (below right).

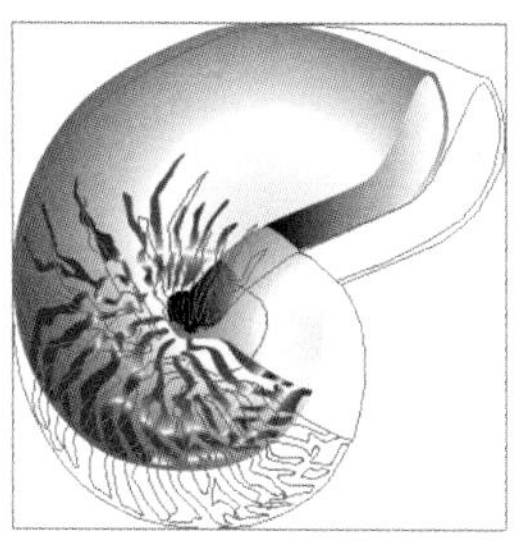

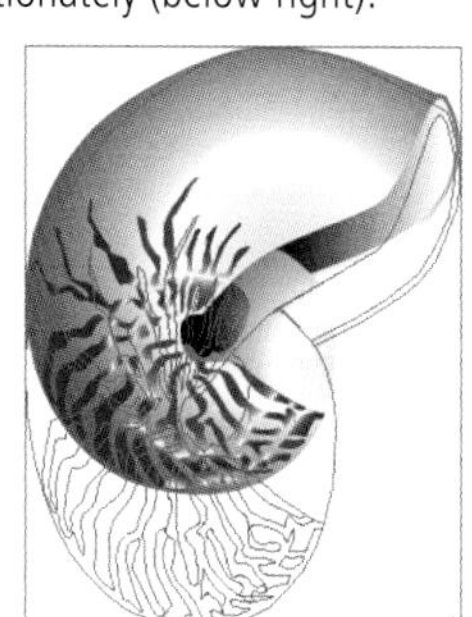

7. **Open the Stroke panel. With the rounded rectangle still selected on the artboard, change the Stroke Weight to `3 pt`.**

The Stroke icon in the Tools panel does not need to be active to change the stroke weight. The Tools panel icon relates to the stroke color only.

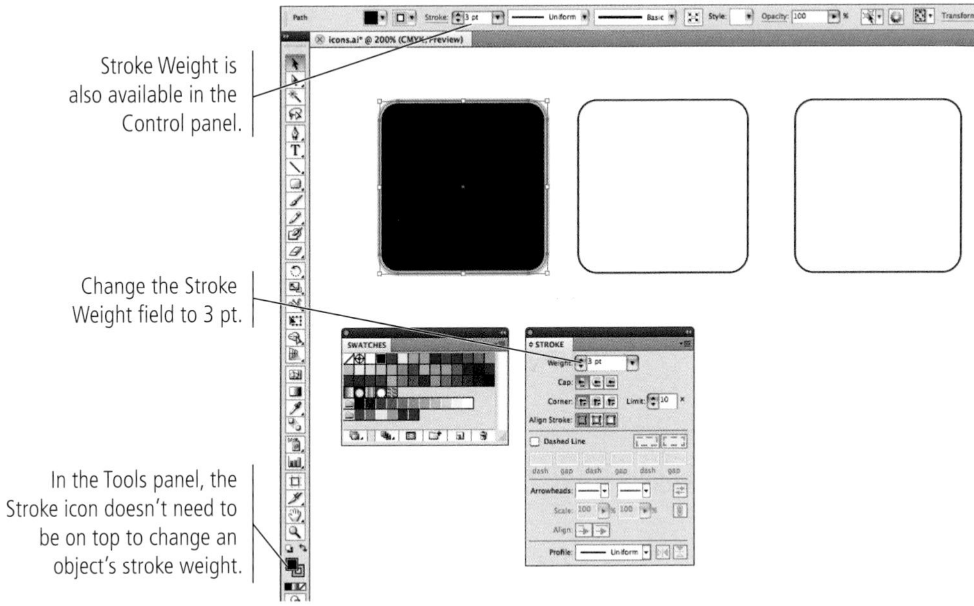

8. **With the rectangle still selected, click the Swap Fill and Stroke button in the Tools panel.**

This button makes it easy to reverse the fill and stroke colors of an object; the stroke weight remains unaffected when you swap the colors.

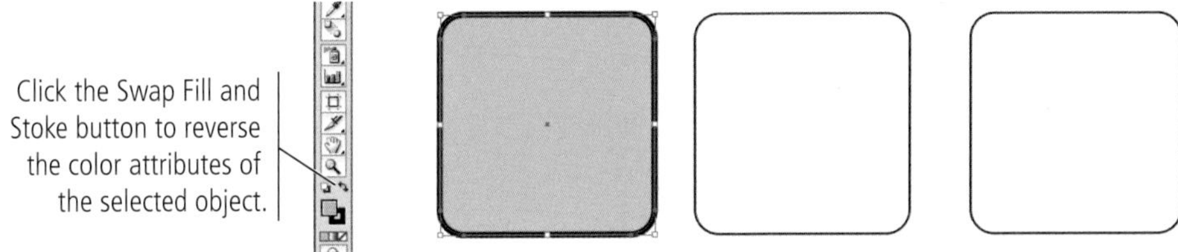

Click the Swap Fill and Stoke button to reverse the color attributes of the selected object.

9. **Using the Selection tool, click the second rectangle on the artboard.**

The Fill and Stroke icons change to reflect the colors of the selected objects.

10. **Click the Fill color swatch in the Control panel. Choose the gold swatch in the second row to change the fill color for the selected object.**

When an object is selected with the Selection tool, the Control panel provides quick access to the stroke and fill attributes of the selected object.

Clicking the Fill color swatch opens an attached Swatches panel so you can change the fill for the selected object without opening the separate Swatches panel.

Note:

When you use the Control panel options, you don't need to worry about which icon is active in the Tools panel.

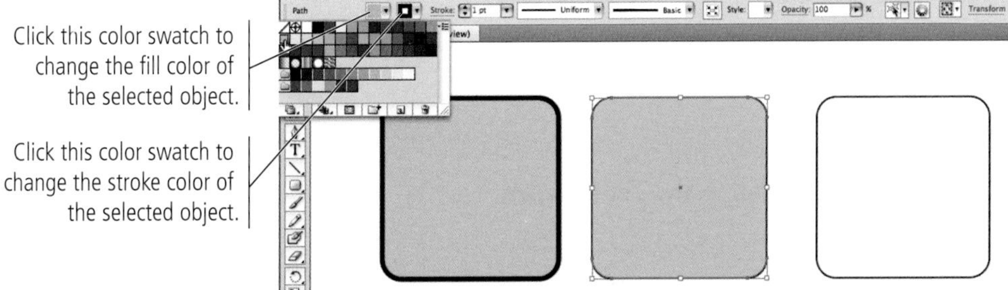

Click this color swatch to change the fill color of the selected object.
Click this color swatch to change the stroke color of the selected object.

11. **In the Control panel, change the Stroke Weight value to `3 pt`.**

Again, the Control panel options allow you to change the attribute value without opening the Stroke panel. The Control panel can be a significant time-saver for common operations such as changing stroke and fill attributes.

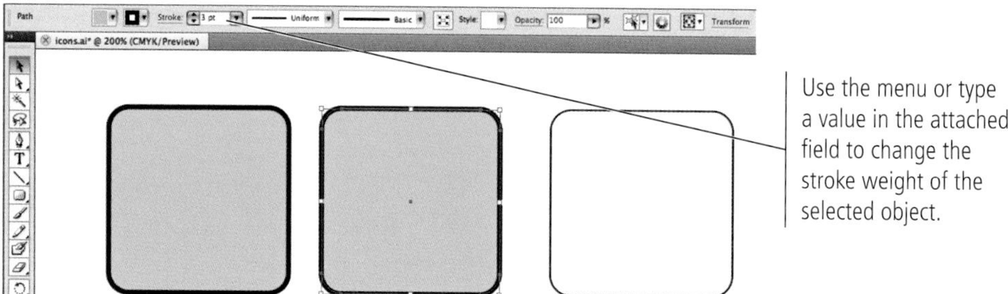

12. **Using the Selection tool, click the third rectangle on the artboard.**

Again, the Fill and Stroke icons in the Tools panel change to reflect the colors of the selected object.

13. **Select the Eyedropper tool in the Tools panel, and then click the first or second rectangle on the artboard.**

The Eyedropper tool copies fill and stroke attributes from one object (the one you click) to another (the one you first selected).

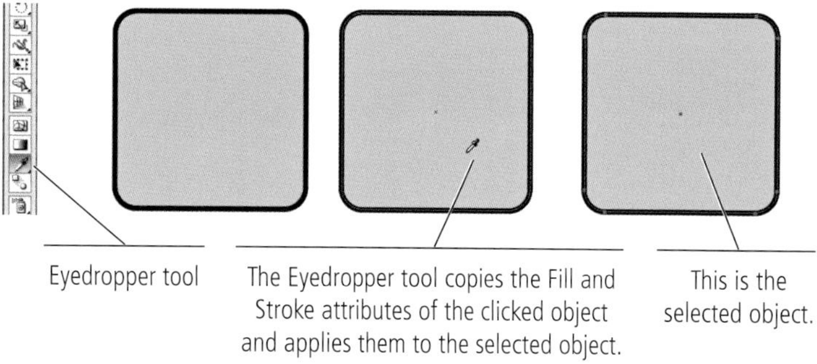

Eyedropper tool
The Eyedropper tool copies the Fill and Stroke attributes of the clicked object and applies them to the selected object.
This is the selected object.

14. **Press Command/Control and click anywhere on the artboard away from the three rectangles.**

Pressing Command/Control temporarily switches to the Selection tool. By clicking on the empty artboard area, you can quickly deselect the selected object(s). When you release the Command/Control key, the tool reverts to the one you last used.

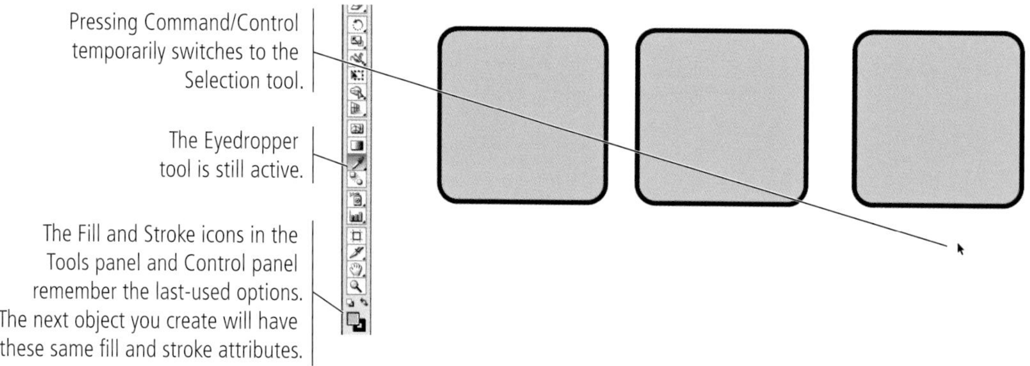

15. **Choose the Rounded Rectangle tool in the Tools panel.**

16. **To the right of the third shape on the artboard, use any method you learned in the previous exercise to draw a fourth rounded rectangle that is 108 pt square.**

    The new rectangle has the same heavy black stroke and gold fill as the others.

17. **Save the file (File>Save or Command/Control-S) and continue to the next exercise.**

Control Object Positioning

The ability to move objects around on the artboard is one of the advantages of digital drawing. On paper, you have to manually erase items and then redraw them in their new locations. Illustrator offers a number of tools that make it easy to move existing objects around the artboard, either as isolated objects or in relation to other elements on the page. In this exercise, you learn several techniques for moving objects around on the artboard.

1. **With `icons.ai` open, change your zoom percentage so you can see the entire top of the artboard.**

2. **Choose the Selection tool from the top of the Tools panel. Click the left rectangle on the artboard to select it.**

3. **Choose View>Rulers>Show Rulers to show the rulers at the top and left edges of the document window.**

   Because you created this file using points as the default unit of measurement, the rulers — and fields in dialog boxes and panels — show measurements in points.

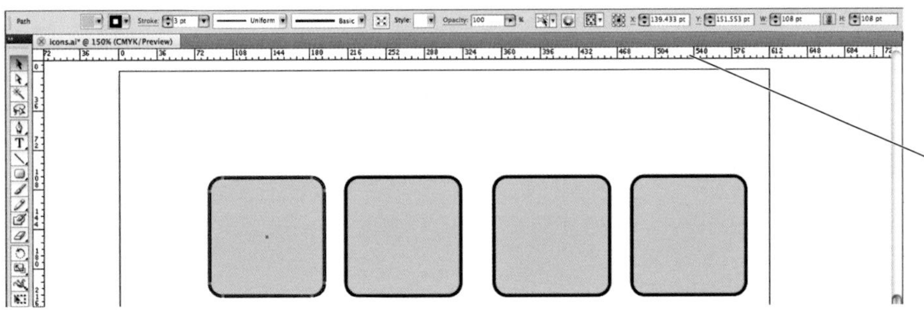

Rulers on the top and left edges show measurements in the default units of measurement.

4. **Control/right-click the top ruler and choose Inches from the contextual menu.**

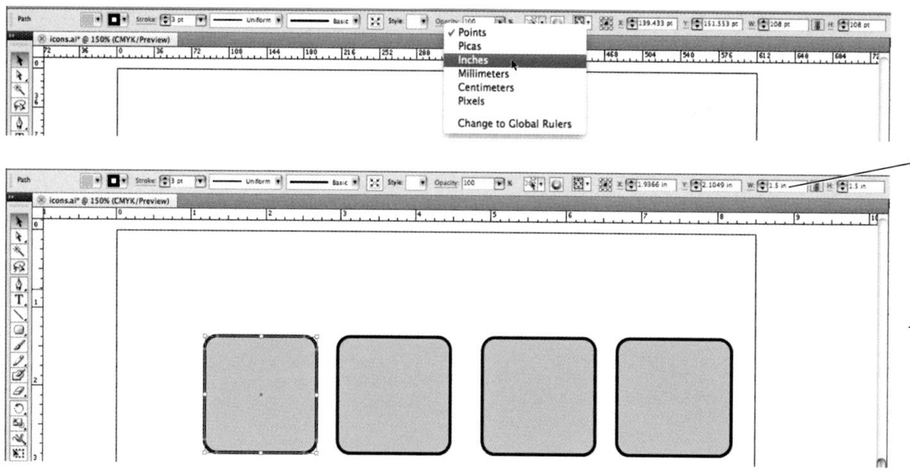

By changing the rulers to inches, measurements in the Control panel and other areas now appear in terms you are probably more familiar with.

> ***Note:***
>
> *The Change to Global Rulers option is only relevant when you work with multiple artboards. You will explore this in Projects 3 and 5.*

5. **With the left rectangle selected, look at the right side of the Control panel.**

The reference points correspond to the bounding box handles of the selected object. The selected square in this icon identifies which point of the object is being measured.

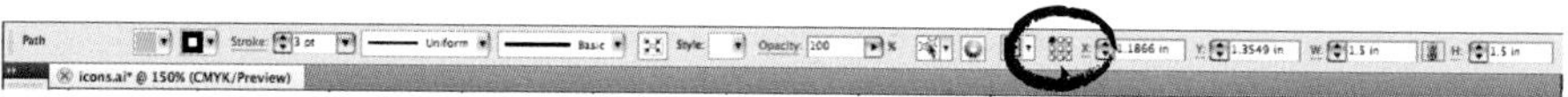

If you don't see the X, Y, W, and H fields in the Control panel, you must click the Transform hot-text link to open the pop-up Transform panel, where you can make changes to the object's position, size, angle, or skew. If you use the panel to resize an object, you can constrain the object's height-to-width aspect ratio by clicking the chain icon. (The same options are available in the Control panel between the W and H fields.)

If you have a small monitor (or have reduced the Application frame width), the X, Y, W, and H options are replaced by a hot-text link that opens the Transform panel.

In Illustrator, the default **zero point** (the source of measurements) is the top-left corner of the artboard; the X and Y positions of an object are measured relative to that location. (The X axis is the horizontal value and the Y axis is the vertical value.)

Keep these ideas in mind when you move something in an Illustrator file:

- Moving something up requires subtracting from the Y value.
- Moving something down requires adding to the Y value.
- Moving something left requires subtracting from the X value.
- Moving something right requires adding to the X value.

You can change the zero point by clicking where the horizontal and vertical rulers meet and dragging to a new position.

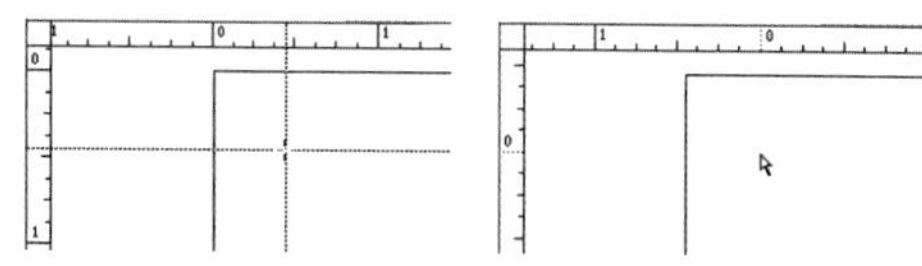

> ***Note:***
>
> *The default zero point in Illustrator CS5 is the top-left corner of the artboard. This is a significant change if you have used previous versions of Illustrator.*

6. **Click the top-left reference point (if it's not already selected).**

   The X and Y fields now show the exact position of the top-left bounding box handle for the selected object.

> *Note:*
>
> *As with dialog boxes, you can enter values in a unit of measurement other than the default, as long as you remember to type the unit abbreviation.*

7. **Highlight the X field in the Control panel and type** .5. **Press Return/Enter to apply the change.**

   You don't need to type the measurement unit ("), or the preceding "0". Because the rulers are showing inches, Illustrator automatically applies inches as the unit of value.

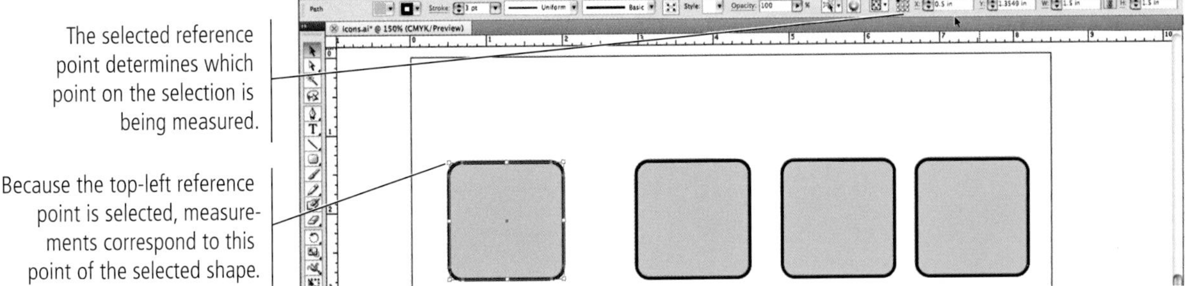

The selected reference point determines which point on the selection is being measured.
Because the top-left reference point is selected, measurements correspond to this point of the selected shape.

8. **Highlight the Y field and type** .5, **then press Return/Enter to apply the change.**

   The top-left handle of the selected object is now 1/2" from the top and left edges. The numbers you typed correspond to the measurements you see on the rulers.

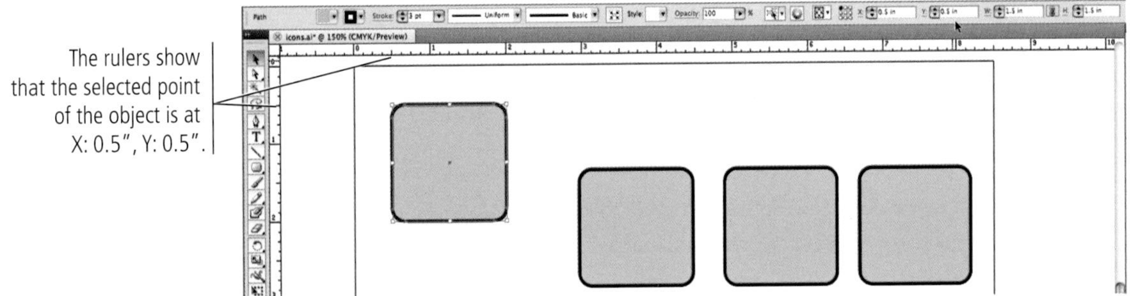

9. **Using the Selection tool, click the second rectangle on the artboard and drag until a green line appears, connecting the center points of the first and second shapes.**

   As you drag the cursor, feedback shows the relative position of the object. In other words, you can see the change (difference) in the object's position, both horizontally (X) and vertically (Y) — hence the "dX" and "dY" values.

   In addition to providing cursor feedback, Smart Guides can be very useful for aligning objects on the artboard. As you drag, Illustrator identifies and highlights relative alignment, and snaps objects to those alignment points as you drag.

> *Note:*
>
> *Remember, moving left decreases the X value and moving up decreases the Y value.*

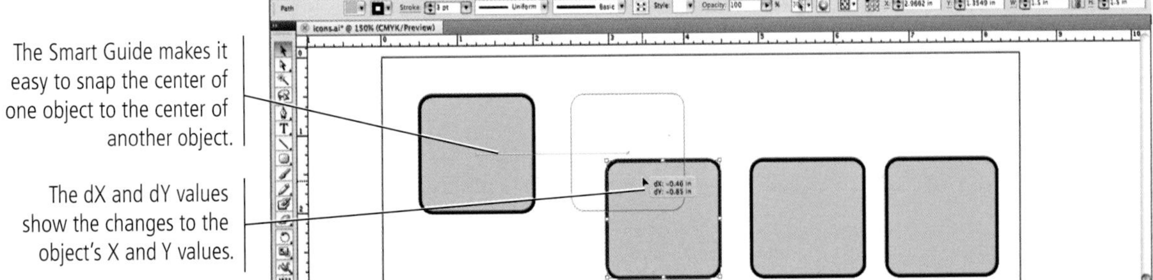

The Smart Guide makes it easy to snap the center of one object to the center of another object.

10. **Release the mouse button while the center Smart Guide is visible.**

    If you don't see the alignment guides as you drag, make sure that option is checked in the Smart Guides preferences.

11. **Click the fourth shape on the page. In the Control panel, select the top-right reference point, type 8 in the X field, and type .5 in the Y field.**

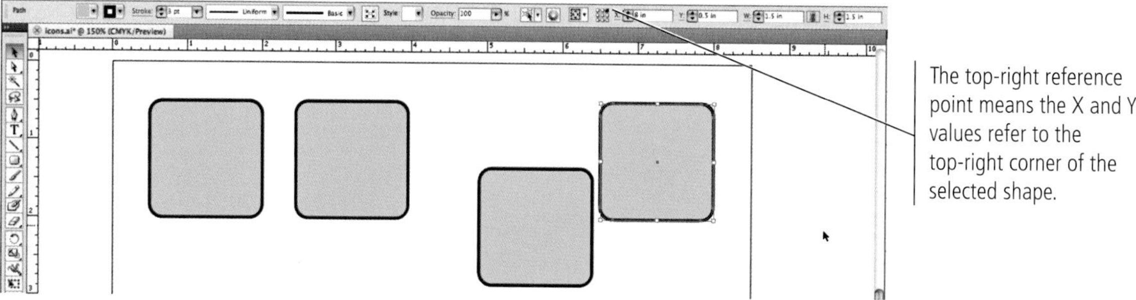

The top-right reference point means the X and Y values refer to the top-right corner of the selected shape.

Because you changed the reference point, you defined the X/Y position for the top-right bounding box handle of the fourth rectangle.

12. **Save the file and continue to the next exercise.**

Align and Distribute Objects

In addition to dragging objects around the artboard, the Illustrator Align panel makes it very easy to align and distribute selected objects relative to one another, to a specific key object in the file, or to the overall artboard. In this exercise, you learn how to use the Align panel to align shapes.

1. **With icons.ai open, use the Selection tool to drag a marquee that touches some part of all four objects on the artboard.**

    The Selection tool selects objects, so the selection marquee only needs to touch the objects you want to select. The marquee doesn't need to surround the objects entirely.

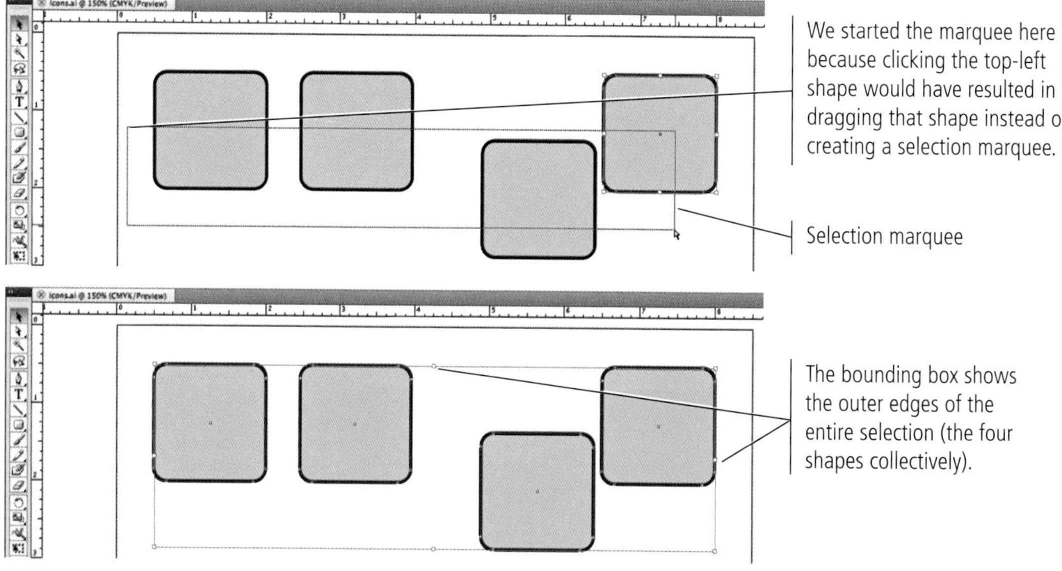

We started the marquee here because clicking the top-left shape would have resulted in dragging that shape instead of creating a selection marquee.

Selection marquee

The bounding box shows the outer edges of the entire selection (the four shapes collectively).

2. **Open the Align panel (Window>Align) and click the Vertical Align Top button.**

   By default, alignment and distribution functions occur relative to the selected objects. In other words, when you click the Vertical Align Top button, Illustrator determines the topmost edge of the selected objects, and then moves the top edges of all other selected objects to that position.

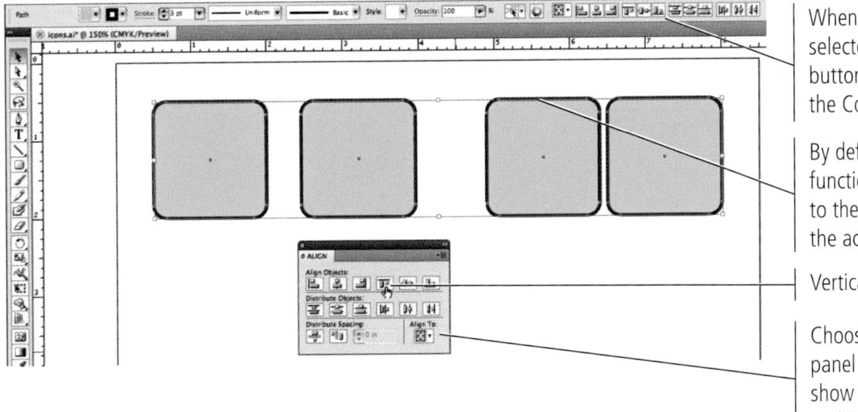

When multiple objects are selected, Align and Distribute buttons are also available in the Control panel.
By default, alignment functions move all objects to the outermost edge of the active selection.
Vertical Align Top button
Choose Show Options in the panel Options menu to show the Distribute Spacing and Align To options.

3. **With all four objects selected, click the Horizontal Distribute Center button.**

   By default, the distribution functions create equal distance between the selected point of the selected objects. In this case, Illustrator distributed the center points along the horizontal axis. Illustrator determined the center-point positions of the outermost selected objects, and then moved the middle two objects to create equal distance between the center points of all four selected objects; the positions of the two outer objects remained unchanged.

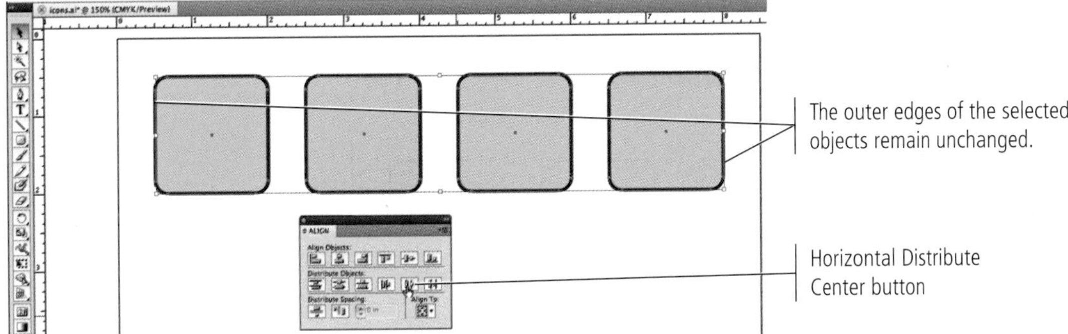

4. **With all four objects selected, choose Object>Group.**

   When you group multiple objects, the group is essentially treated as a single object. A single bounding box surrounds all objects within the group.

5. **Click inside any of the grouped objects, press the Option/Alt key, and drag down.**

Note:

Press Command/Control-G to group selected objects. Press Command/Control-Shift-G to ungroup grouped objects.

6. **Use the Smart Guides and cursor feedback to drag exactly vertical (the dX value should be 0). When the dY value in the cursor feedback is 2 in, release the mouse button.**

   Pressing Option/Alt while you drag makes a copy of the original selection. This technique, called **cloning**, can save significant amounts of time when you build illustrations that contain numerous repetitive elements.

Note:

There is almost always more than one way to accomplish a specific task. The Align panel is useful for certain functions (especially distribution), but Smart Guides make object-to-object alignment very easy.

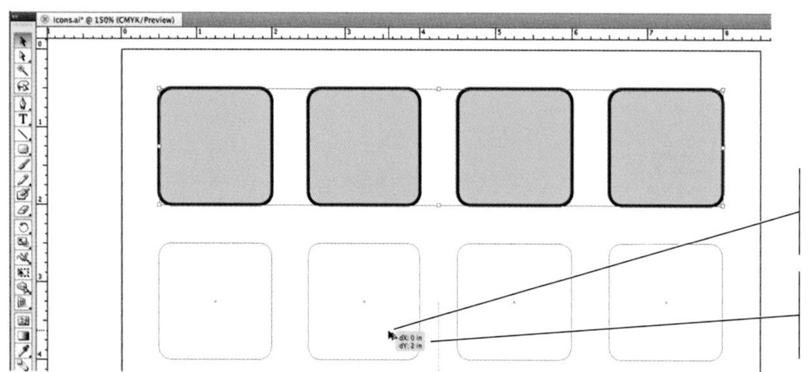

The cursor icon shows that you are cloning instead of simply dragging.

Cursor feedback makes it easy to move something to precise locations.

7. **With the second group of rectangles selected, choose Object>Transform>Transform Again.**

   This command repeats the last-used transformation. In this case, the last transformation was the cloning movement, so it creates the third row of rectangles.

Note:

Press Command/Control-D to repeat the last-used transformation.

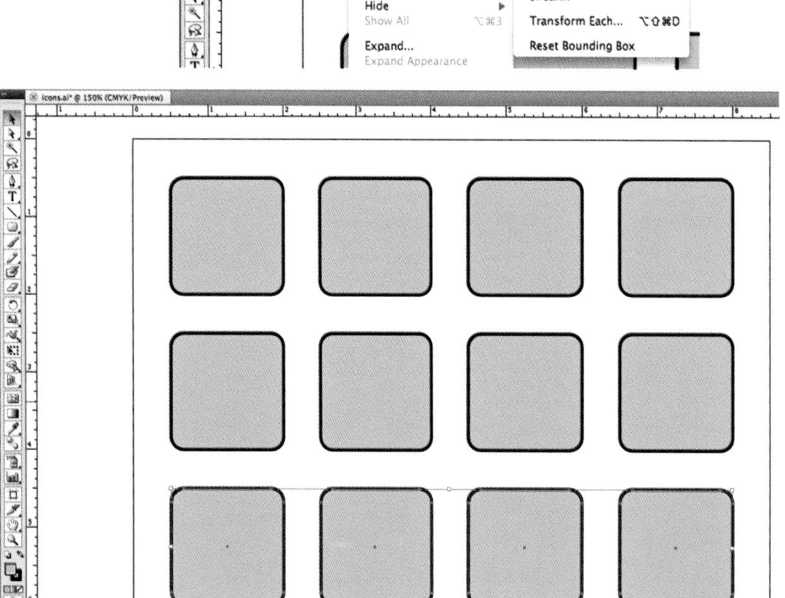

8. **Click anywhere outside the rectangle shapes to deselect all objects and groups.**

9. **Save the file and continue to the next exercise.**

Edit Individual Grouped Elements

The client in this project requested only ten icons, so you don't need two of the rectangles in the third row. As you know, the Selection tool selects entire objects on the page. You also know that grouped objects are treated as a single object — which means you can't use the Selection tool to select part of a group. In this exercise, you use two techniques to work with component pieces of a group.

Note:

Think carefully about your ultimate goal when you group objects, especially for alignment purposes. If the objects in a group don't need to stay together, it's often a good idea to ungroup them.

1. **With `icons.ai` open, use the Selection tool to click the fourth rectangle in the third row.**

   Because the four objects are grouped, the Selection tool selects the entire group. You need to use a different method to select certain elements within the group.

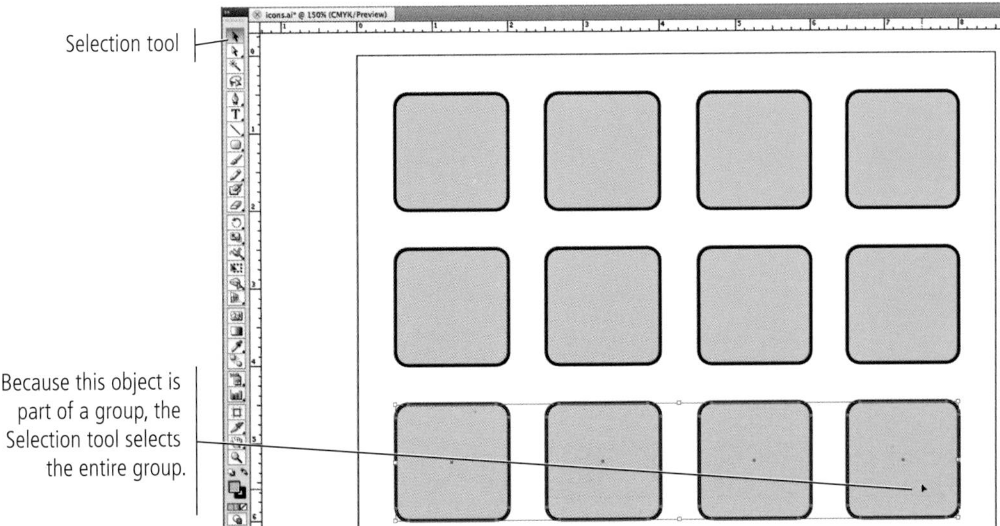

Selection tool
Because this object is part of a group, the Selection tool selects the entire group.

2. **Click anywhere outside the rectangle shapes to deselect the group, then choose the Direct Selection tool in the Tools panel.**

   The Direct Selection tool selects pieces of an object — specific paths, anchor points, or individual elements in a grouped object.

3. **Click the gold fill of the fourth rectangle in the third row.**

   Because you clicked the fill, you selected the entire object. If you had clicked along the object's stroke, you would have selected that particular segment of the shape's edge.

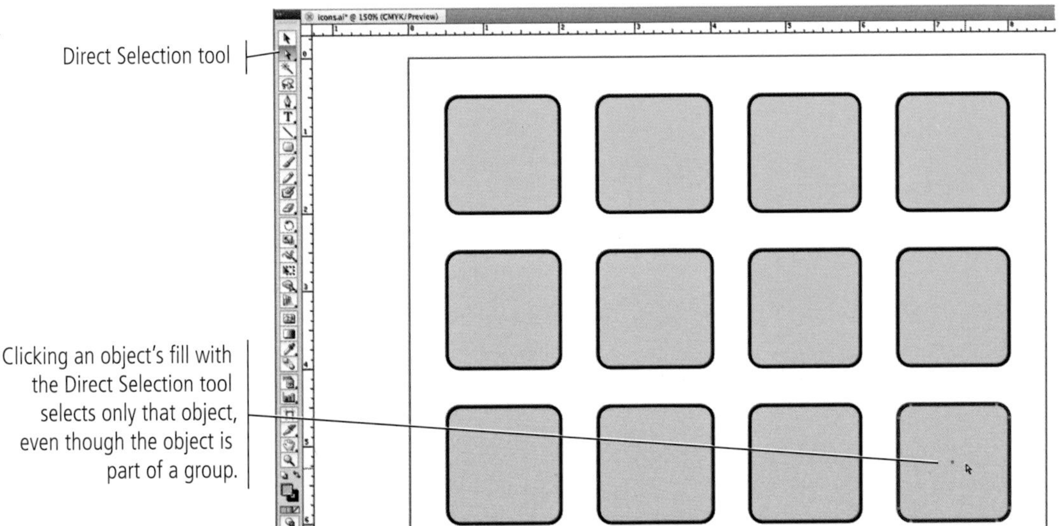

Direct Selection tool
Clicking an object's fill with the Direct Selection tool selects only that object, even though the object is part of a group.

4. **Press Delete to remove the selected object.**

   Easy enough, especially because this is a very simple group of objects that don't overlap. When you start working with complex files that have multiple levels of grouping, however, it can be challenging to manipulate objects within a group using only the Direct Selection tool.

5. **Choose the Selection tool in the Tools panel, and then double-click the third rectangle in the third row.**

   Double-clicking a group enters into Isolation mode, where only objects within the selected group are available. Basically, Isolation mode provides access to objects in the group without ungrouping the objects on the main artboard.

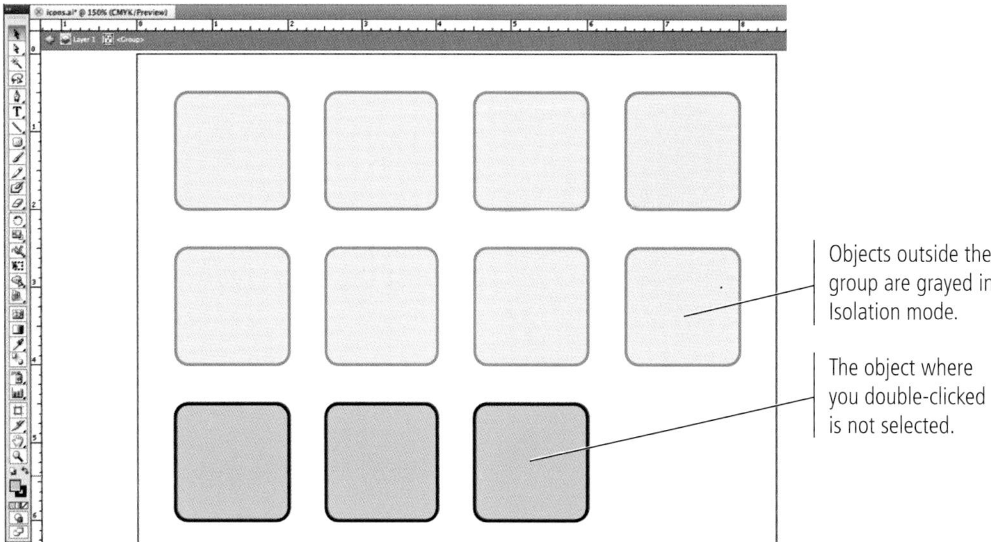

Objects outside the group are grayed in Isolation mode.

The object where you double-clicked is not selected.

6. **Using the Selection tool, click the third rectangle in the third row to select it, and then press Delete.**

   Because you created only a single level of grouping, you can now use the Selection tool to select individual objects.

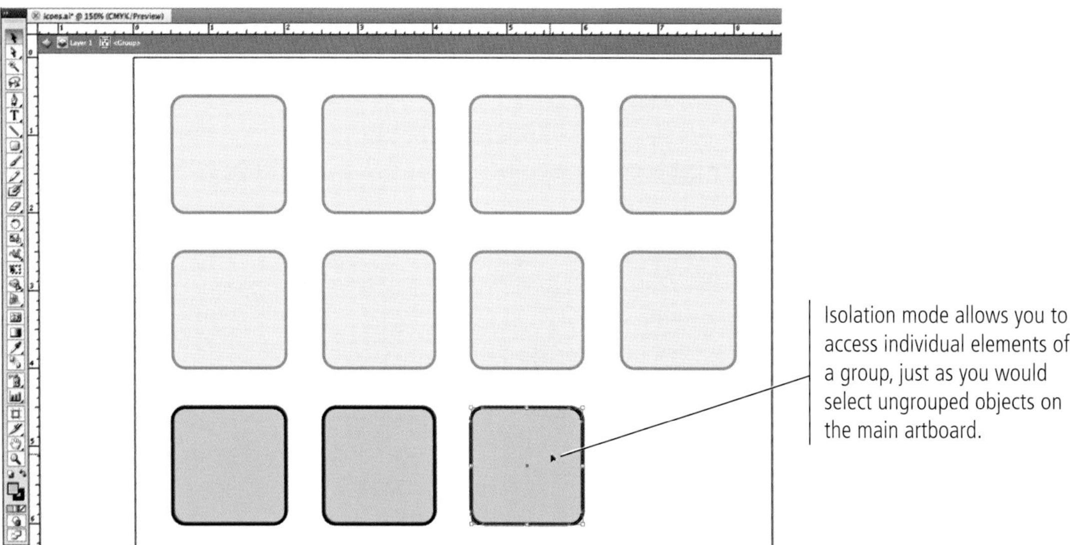

Isolation mode allows you to access individual elements of a group, just as you would select ungrouped objects on the main artboard.

7. **At the top of the document window, click the Arrow button twice to return to the main artboard.**

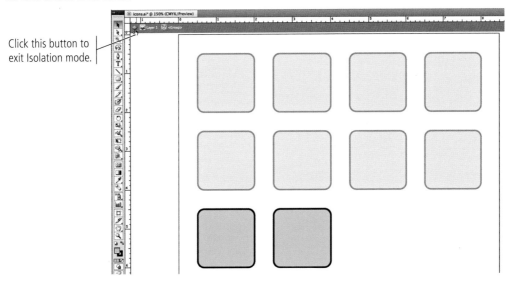

The third row, now with two rectangles, is still a single group on the main artboard.

8. **Save the file and continue to the next exercise.**

Import Template Images

Many Illustrator projects require you to start with something that has already been captured — a sketch, photograph, or low-resolution image (which is the case in this project). Illustrator makes it easy to place existing digital files to use as templates for your new artwork. You will use this feature in this exercise.

1. **With `icons.ai` open, choose File>Place. Navigate to your WIP>Symbols folder and click `cold.tif` to select that file.**

2. **At the bottom of the Place dialog box, make sure the Link option is unchecked.**

   If you check the Link option, the placed file does not become a part of the actual file where you're working; for the file to output properly, Illustrator must be able to locate the linked file in the same location (hard drive, CD, etc.) as when you placed it. If the Link option is *not* checked, the placed file is **embedded** — it becomes part of the file where it's placed; the original external file is not necessary for the artwork to output properly. We will explore the details of placed files in later projects.

3. **Check the Template option.**

   When you place an object as a template, it's added to the file on a separate, non-printing layer that is partially grayed, making it easier to work with.

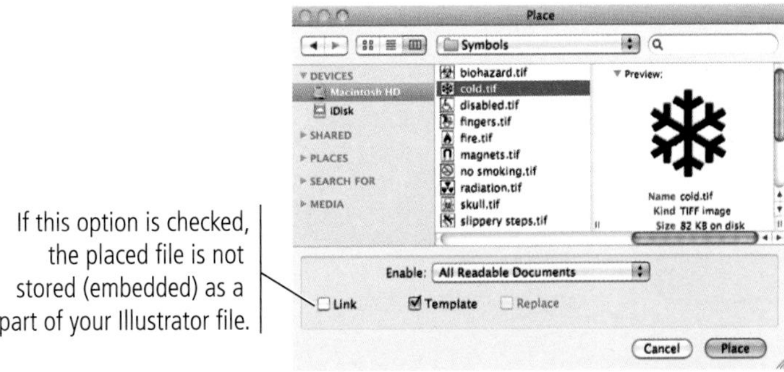

4. **Click Place.**

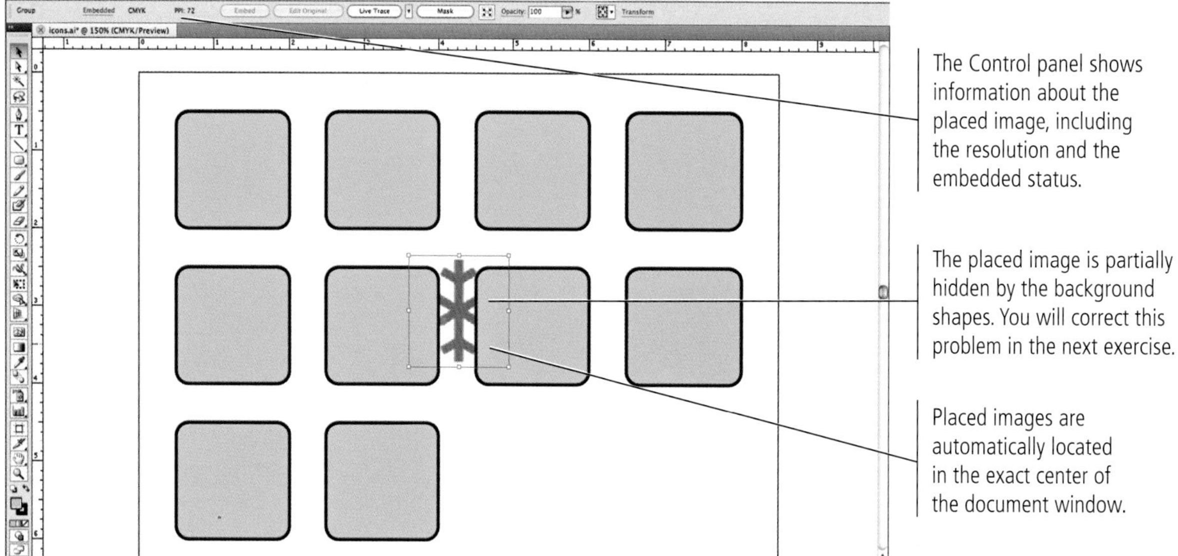

The Control panel shows information about the placed image, including the resolution and the embedded status.

The placed image is partially hidden by the background shapes. You will correct this problem in the next exercise.

Placed images are automatically located in the exact center of the document window.

5. **Choose File>Place a second time. Select `radiation.tif` in the list, check the Template option, and click Place.**

The Place dialog box remembers the last-used location, so you don't have to re-navigate to the Symbols folder. The Link option also remembers the last-used settings. The Template option, however, always defaults to off, so you have to manually check this box for each template object.

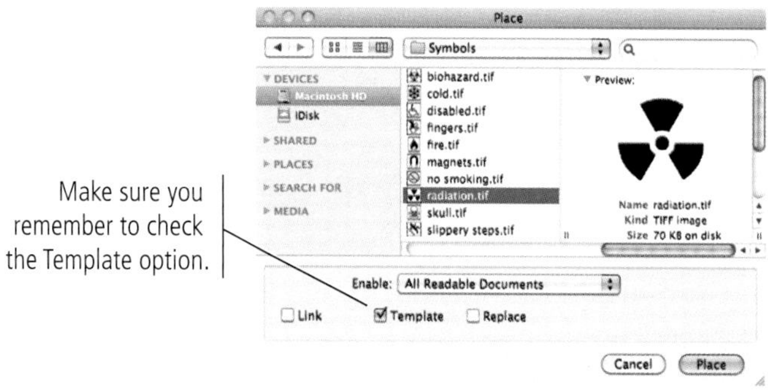

Make sure you remember to check the Template option.

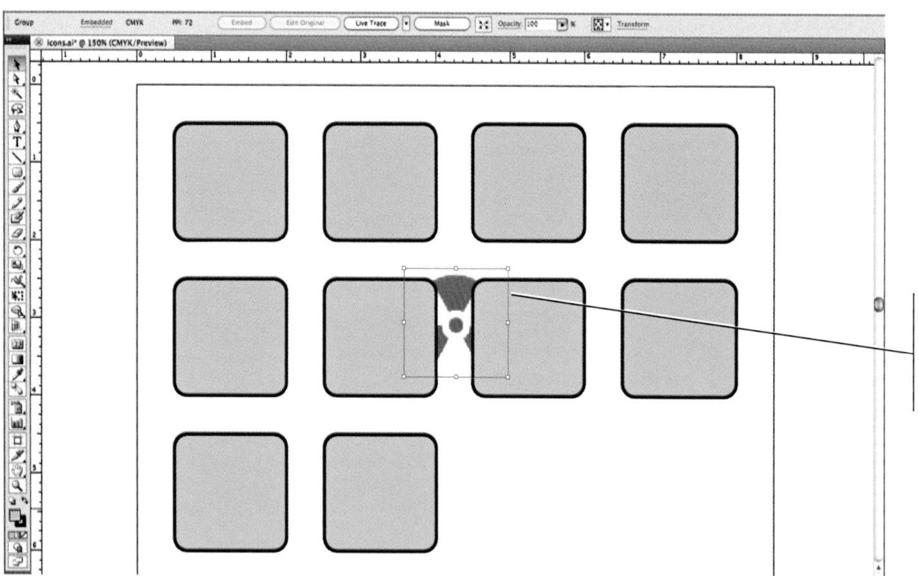

This image is also placed in the center of the document window, directly on top of the first placed image.

6. **Repeat Step 5 to place `fire.tif` into your file as a template image.**

7. **Save the file and continue to the next exercise.**

Manage Multiple Layers

When you create digital artwork in Illustrator, you almost always end up with more than one object on the artboard. In many cases, a completed file has dozens or hundreds of objects, arranged in specific order on top of one another. As files become more and more complex, it can be difficult to find and work with exactly the pieces you need. Illustrator layers are one of the most powerful tools available for solving this organizational problem.

1. **In the open `icons.ai` file, open the Layers panel.**

   By default, all files have a single layer, named Layer 1. Your file has three additional layers — the template layers — below Layer 1. Template layers are locked by default, which means you can't select or modify objects on those layers.

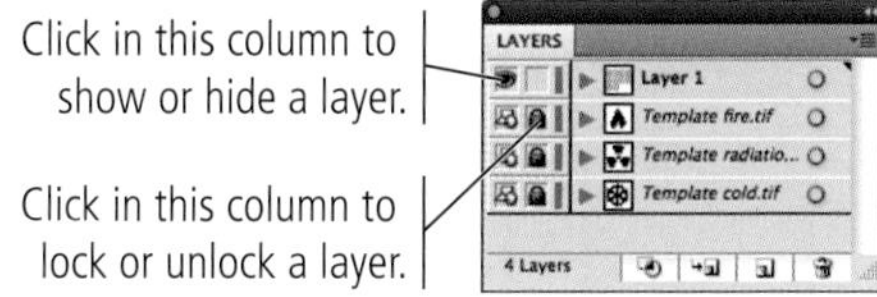
Click in this column to show or hide a layer.
Click in this column to lock or unlock a layer.
LAYERS
Layer 1
Template fire.tif
Template radiatio...
Template cold.tif
4 Layers

2. **In the Layers panel, click the Layer 1 name and drag it below all three template layers in the stack.**

   The top-to-bottom position of objects or layers is called the **stacking order**. Objects and layers typically appear in the stack based on the order in which they are created — the first-created is at the bottom, the last-created is at the top, and so on in between.

   Placed template objects are the exception; these layers are placed *below* the currently selected layer (i.e., lower in the stacking order). In this case, the rectangle shapes are filled with a color, which obscures the template images on the underlying layers. To see the template images, you need to move the template object layers above the layer containing the background shapes. Rather than moving three layers above Layer 1, you can save a few clicks by moving Layer 1 below all of the template layers.

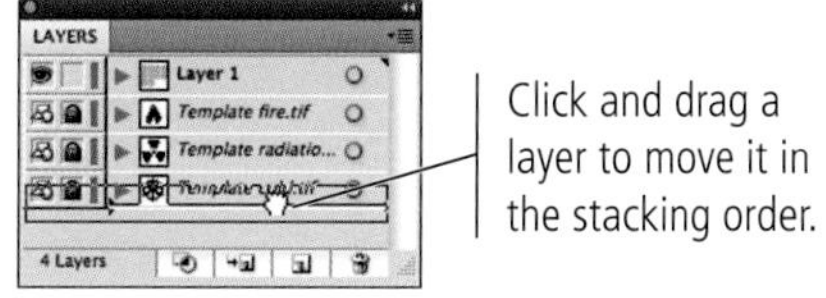
LAYERS
Layer 1
Template fire.tif
Template radiatio...
4 Layers
Click and drag a layer to move it in the stacking order.

3. **Using the Selection tool, click the top-left rounded rectangle to select it.**

   Remember, this object is grouped with the other rectangles in the same row. You need to align the placed object to only the first rectangle, which means you need to be able to select only that object.

   As you saw in an earlier exercise, you can use Isolation mode to access a single element of a group. However, each rectangle shape is ultimately going to be a separate icon; you're simply creating them all in the same workspace. The best choice here is to simply ungroup the rectangles, returning them to individual objects.

4. **With the top-row group selected, choose Object>Ungroup.**

> *Note:*
>
> *Press Command/Control-Shift-G to ungroup objects in a group.*

5. **Click away from the selected objects to deselect them, and then click the top-left rectangle to select that object only.**

6. **In the Layers panel, click the Lock icon for the Template cold.tif layer.**

   Because you need to move the placed template object into the correct position, you first need to unlock the layer.

7. **With the Selection tool still active, press Shift and click anywhere inside the area where the template images are placed.**

   Pressing Shift allows you to add objects to the current selection. The first rectangle and the image should both be selected.

8. **With both objects selected, click the Align To button in the Control panel.**

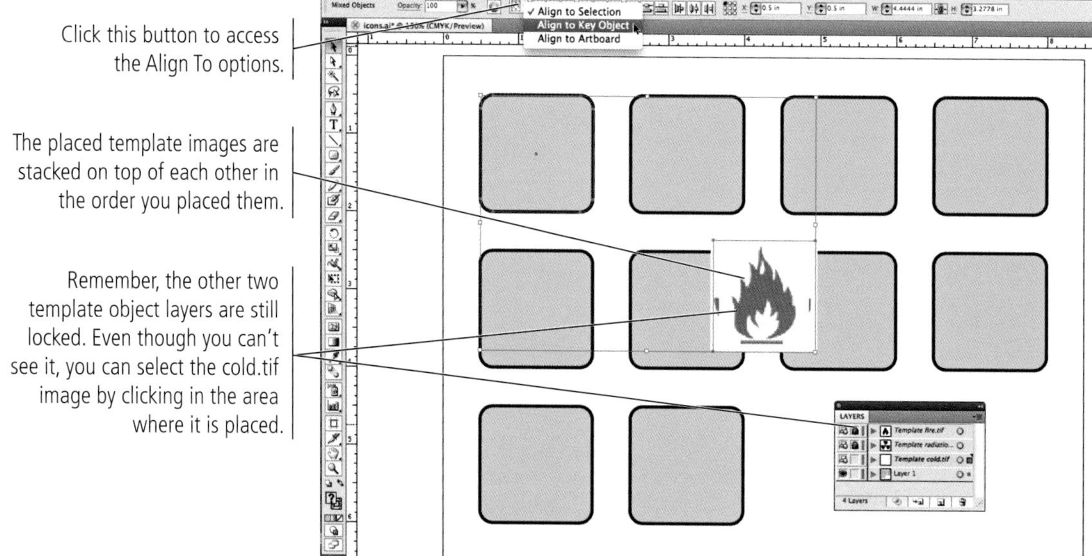

Click this button to access the Align To options.
The placed template images are stacked on top of each other in the order you placed them.
Remember, the other two template object layers are still locked. Even though you can't see it, you can select the cold.tif image by clicking in the area where it is placed.
✓ Align to Selection
Align to Key Object
Align to Artboard
LAYERS

9. **Choose Align to Key Object in the menu.**

The Align and Distribute options in the Control panel are the same as the options in the Align panel.
The default key object is identified with a heavy border.

10. **Click the selected rounded rectangle on the artboard.**

Key Object alignment allows you to define where you want other objects to align. By selecting the key object, you're telling Illustrator which object to use as the basis for alignment.

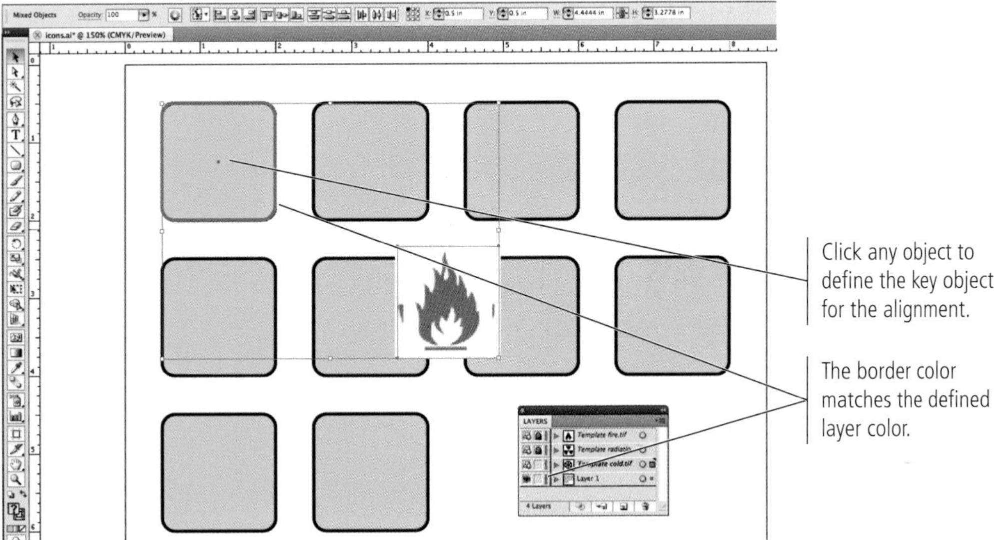

Click any object to define the key object for the alignment.
The border color matches the defined layer color.

11. **Click the Horizontal Align Center and Vertical Align Center buttons in the Control panel.**

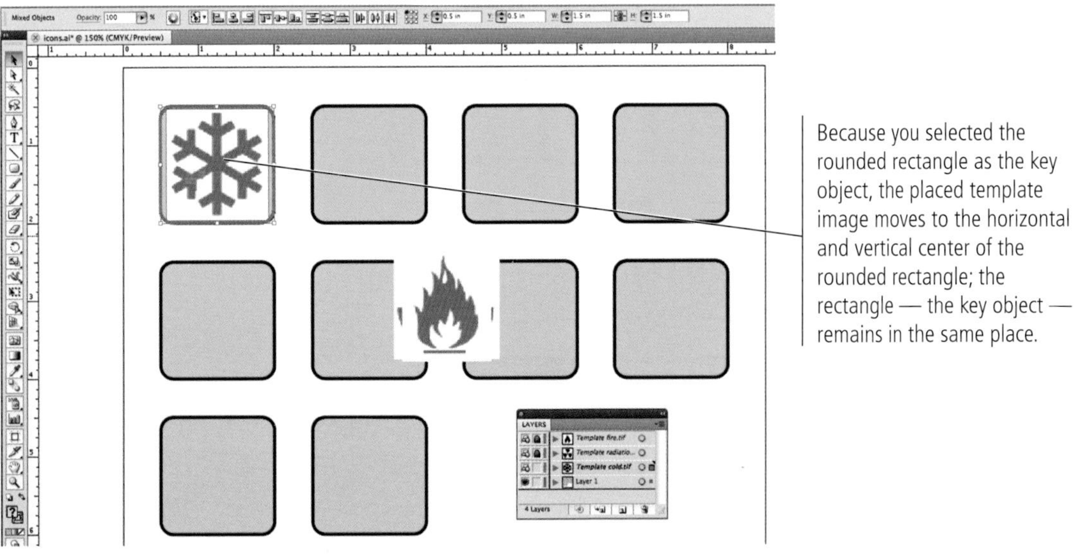

Because you selected the rounded rectangle as the key object, the placed template image moves to the horizontal and vertical center of the rounded rectangle; the rectangle — the key object — remains in the same place.

12. **In the Layers panel, click the empty space to the left of the Template cold.tif layer to relock that layer.**

    Now that the template object is in place, it's a good idea to lock it again so you don't accidentally move the object.

13. **Double-click the name of the Template cold.tif layer.**

    Double-clicking a layer name opens the Layer Options dialog box for that layer, where you can change a number of attributes for the selected layer.

14. **Change the Dim Images To field to `30`, and then click OK to close the Layer Options dialog box.**

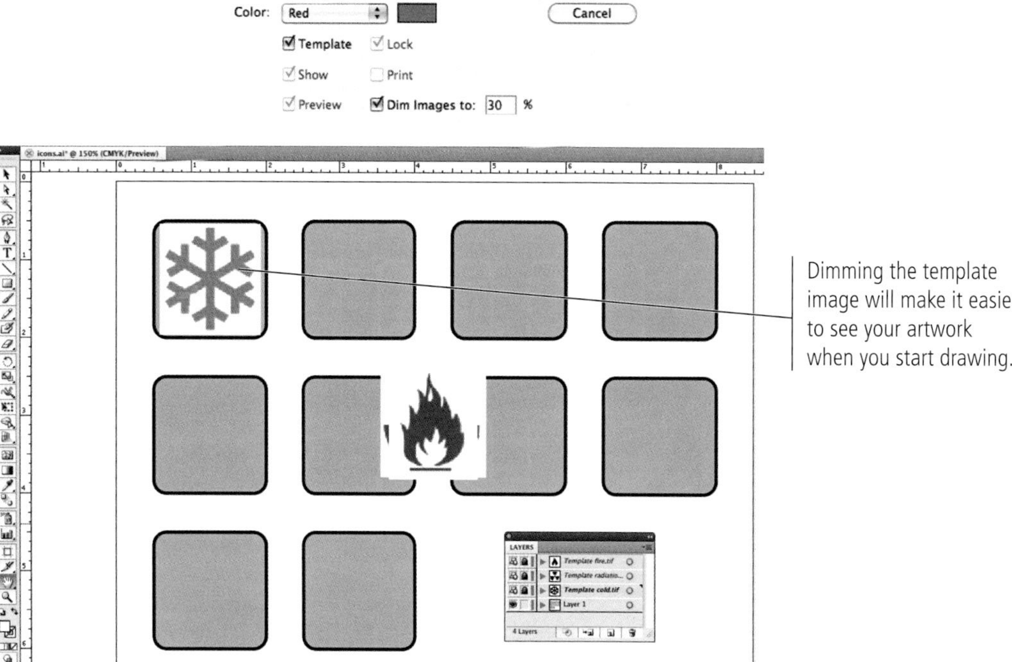

15. **Repeat Steps 6–14 to position the other two template images in the first-row rectangles (as shown in the following image).**

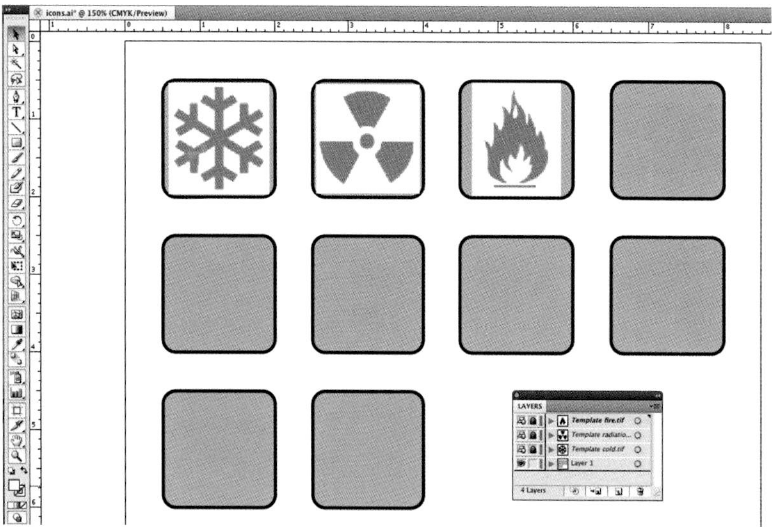

16. **In the Layers panel, double-click the Layer 1 name to open the Layer Options dialog box. Change the Layer Name field to `Background Shapes` and click OK.**

    Whenever you have more than one working layer, it's a good idea to use names that tell you what is on each layer. Doing so prevents confusion later when you or someone else needs to change a particular item.

17. **In the Layers panel, click the empty space immediately left of the Background Shapes layer.**

    This step — locking the Background Shapes layer — is simply a safeguard to avoid accidentally changing the background rectangles while you're drawing the icon artwork.

18. **In the Layers panel, click the New Layer button at the bottom of the panel.**

    In the next stage of the project, you will start tracing the object in the template. The completed icon will be a black icon on top of the rounded rectangle with the gold background color.

    At this point, most of the gold color in the background shapes is obscured by the placed images, because the template layers are above the layer containing the rectangles. If you tried to draw the icon shapes on the existing non-template layer, you would be drawing *behind* the template — in other words, you wouldn't be able to see what you were drawing. Instead, you need a layer above the template layers, where you can create the icon artwork.

19. **In the Layers panel, drag Layer 5 to the top of the layer stack.**

    New layers are automatically placed immediately above the selected layer. You need this new layer to be above the template layers so you can see what you're drawing.

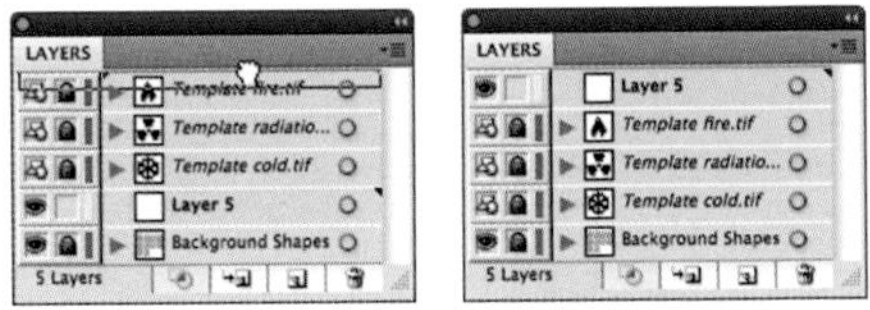

20. **Double-click the Layer 5 name in the Layers panel. Change the layer name to `Icon Art`. Choose Dark Green from the Color menu and click OK.**

    The Color option determines the color of bounding box handles and other visual indicators for objects on a layer. (The default for Layer 5, Yellow, can be very difficult to see. We chose Dark Green because it shows better in our screen shots.)

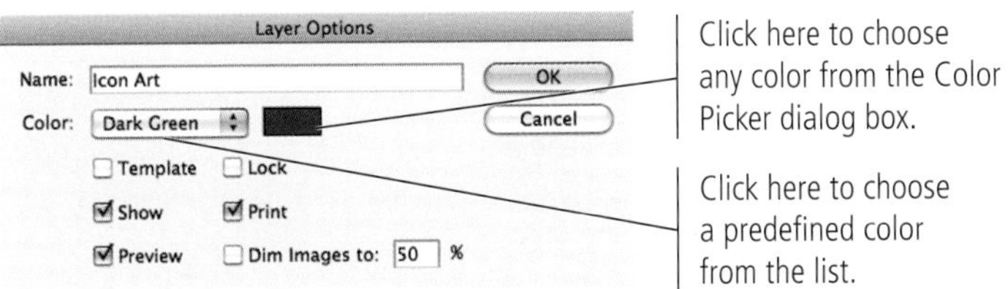

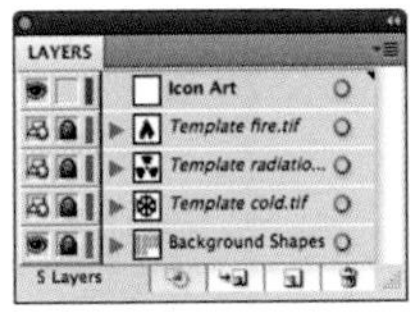

21. **Save the file and continue to the next stage of the project.**

Stage 2 Drawing Basic Shapes

If you remember from the client meeting, the client's bitmap icons work fine on the Web, but they look terrible in print. After you redraw the icons in Illustrator, the client will be able to print them anywhere, with no loss in quality — which is the primary advantage of vector-based artwork vs. raster-based images. A number of tools and utilities can be used to create complex Illustrator artwork. Creating the icons in this project gives you an opportunity to experiment with some of these options. As you complete the other projects in this book, you will delve deeper into complex drawing techniques.

Create Artwork with Lines

The snowflake icon is really nothing more than a series of straight lines — which makes it an ideal image to introduce the Illustrator Line Segment tool. In this exercise, you create simple lines, and then use some basic modification techniques to create the final icon.

1. **With icons.ai open, make sure the Icon Art layer is selected. Zoom in to the top-left rectangle (with the snowflake image).**

2. **In the Tools panel, select the Line Segment tool, and then click the Default Fill and Stroke button.**

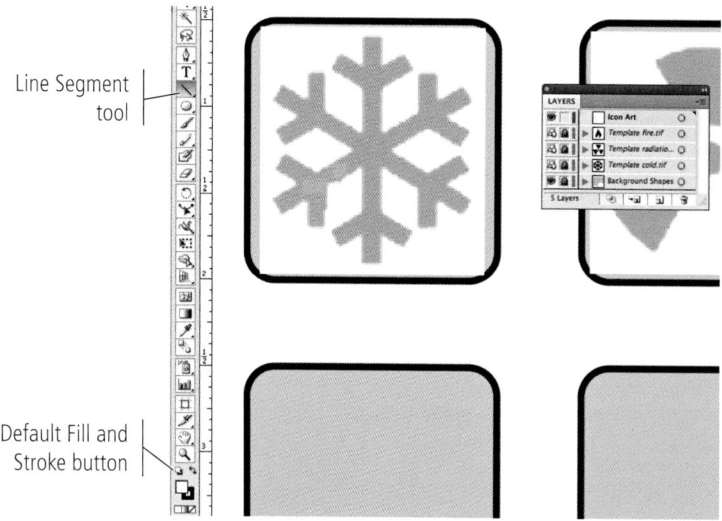

3. **Click at the bottom of the vertical line in the snowflake image, and then drag up to the top of the snowflake image. Release the mouse button while the cursor feedback shows the line at 90°.**

   As you drag, the cursor feedback shows the length and — more importantly in this case — the angle of the line you're drawing. If you don't see the cursor feedback, choose View>Smart Guides to toggle on that option.

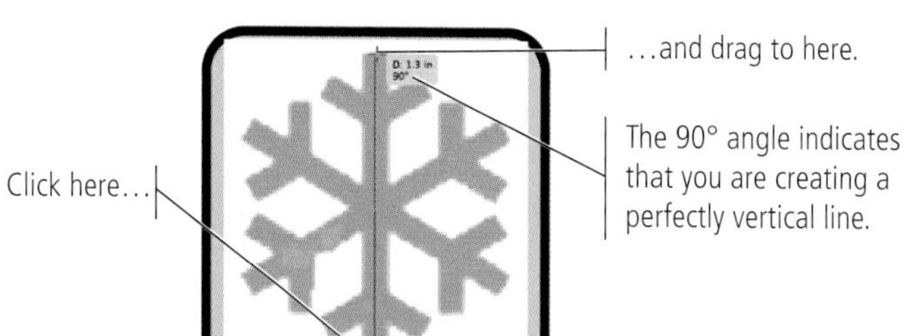

...and drag to here.
The 90° angle indicates that you are creating a perfectly vertical line.
Click here...

> *Note:*
>
> *You can also press Shift to constrain a line to increments of 45°.*

4. **With the Line Segment tool still active, click the cursor on the top of the left flake branch in the template image. Hold down the mouse button, drag down and right until you see the word "path" appear near the cursor, then release the mouse button.**

   The word "path" is another function of Illustrator's Smart Guides; when you drag near an existing path, Illustrator identifies the path so you can place a point exactly on top of the existing path.

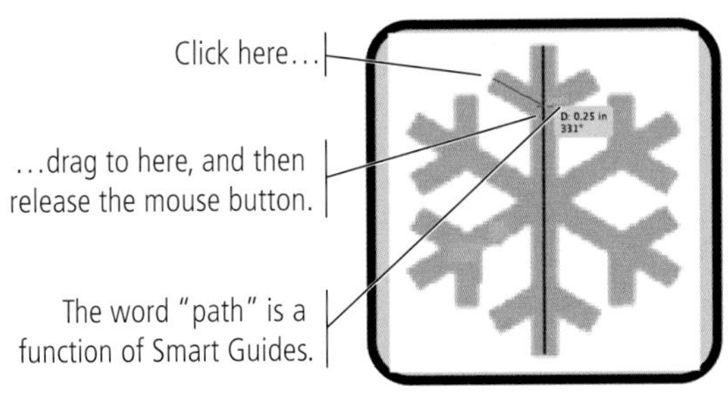

5. **Move the cursor to the top of the right flake branch until you see a green line connecting to the top of the left branch that you drew in Step 4.**

6. **Click the mouse button, drag down and left until the word "anchor" appears next to the cursor, and then release the mouse button.**

   The "anchor" label indicates that you have dragged to the position of an existing anchor point (in this case, the endpoint of the left flake branch). As you can see, Illustrator makes it easy to create precise lines and shapes in relation to other objects on the page.

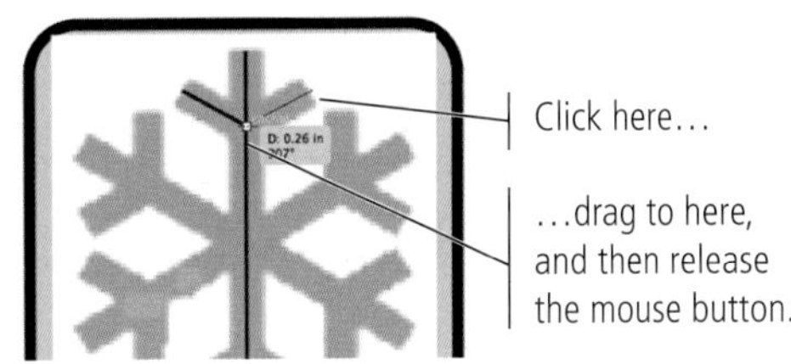

7. **Choose the Selection tool from the Tools panel, and then click the vertical line you drew in Step 3. Choose Object>Lock>Selection.**

   When an object is locked, you can't select or change it — just as locking a template layer protects the template object from being moved. In the next few steps, you select and join the endpoints of the two angled lines, which is much easier if the vertical line can't be selected (you want the vertical line to remain unchanged).

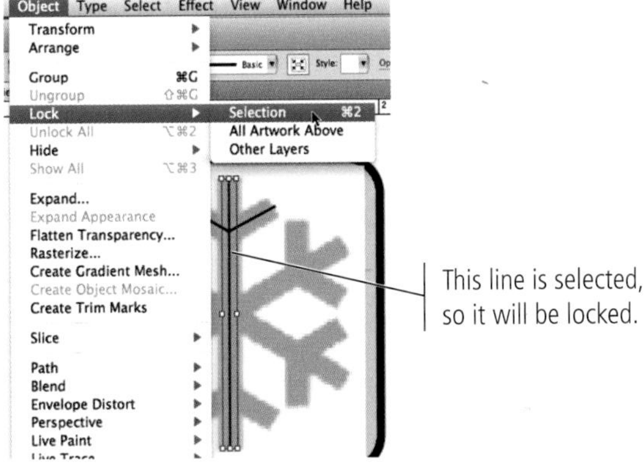

8. **Using the Direct Selection tool, drag a marquee around the bottom points of both angled lines.**

   You want to join the lines' endpoints, so you need to select only those specific points (instead of the entire lines). As mentioned earlier, you need the Direct Selection tool to select specific points on a path.

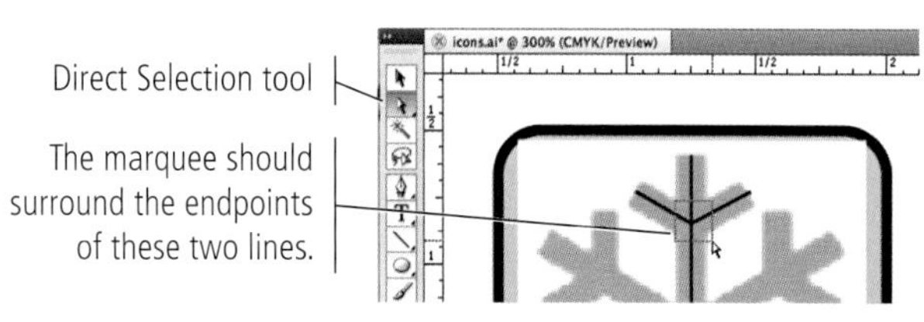

Direct Selection tool
The marquee should surround the endpoints of these two lines.

These anchor points are hollow, which means they are not selected.
These anchor points are solid, which means they are selected.

9. **Choose Object>Path>Join.**

   This command connects any two selected open endpoints. If the selected points overlap, as in this exercise, the two points are simply combined into a single corner endpoint. If the two selected points do not overlap, Illustrator automatically connects them with a straight line segment.

10. **Choose the Selection tool to reveal the bounding box for the selected object.**

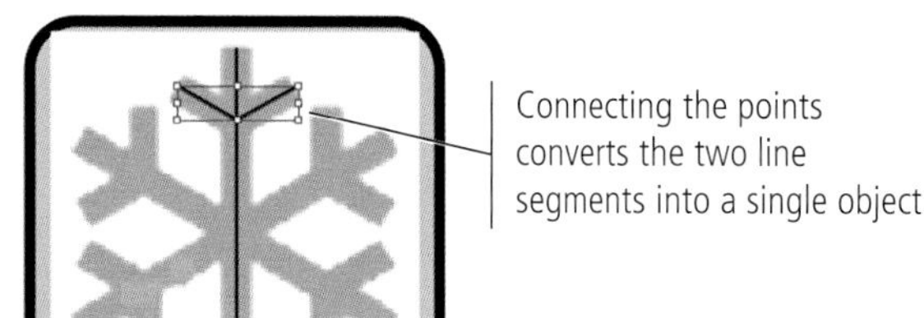

11. **Save the file and continue to the next exercise.**

Reflect Drawing Objects

Illustrator includes four important transformation tools — Rotate, Reflect, Scale, and Shear. Each of these transformations can be applied by hand using the related tool in the Tools panel, as well as numerically using the appropriate dialog box from the Object>Transform menu.

Much of the work you do in Illustrator requires changing objects that already exist. In this exercise, you use reflection to create additional sections of the snowflake icon.

1. **With icons.ai open, choose the Selection tool in the Tools panel. Make sure the angled-branch object is selected on the artboard.**

   Because the Selection tool is active, you can now see the bounding box of the selected object — both angled lines, which have been joined into a single object.

2. **Choose Object>Transform>Reflect.**

   You can reflect objects around the vertical or horizontal axis at specific degrees. In this case, you want to make the braches at the bottom of the snowflake, so you need to reflect the object around the horizontal axis.

3. **In the Reflect dialog box, make sure the Preview check box is active.**

   The Preview option, which is available in all of the Illustrator transformation dialog boxes, allows you to see the effects of your changes before you commit them.

4. **Choose the Horizontal option and click Copy.**

   If you click OK in any of the transformation dialog boxes, the transformation directly affects the selected object. Because you want another branch for the bottom of the flake, you are using the Copy function instead of simply clicking OK.

When Preview is checked, you can see the result of clicking OK.

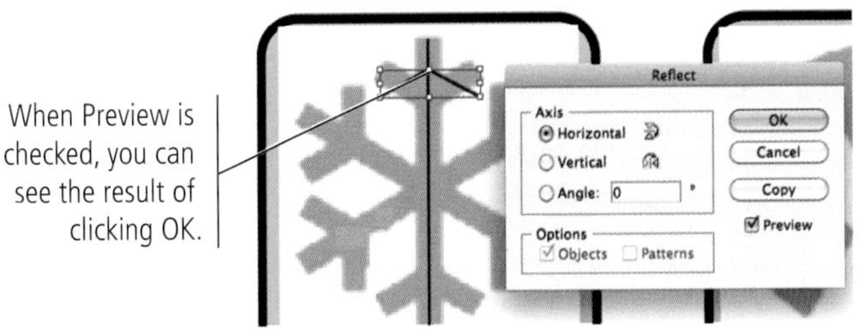

The original object remains in position.

The Copy option reflects the new object.

5. **With the Selection tool still active, click the reflected branches and drag them to the bottom of the flake and place the object appropriately. Use the template image as a guide.**

   Again, the Smart Guides function helps you place the object; the green line and cursor feedback show the angle at which you're moving the selected object, so you can more easily maintain the same horizontal position.

> *Note:*
>
> *Reflecting on the horizontal axis flips the object top over bottom. Reflecting around the vertical axis flips the object left to right.*

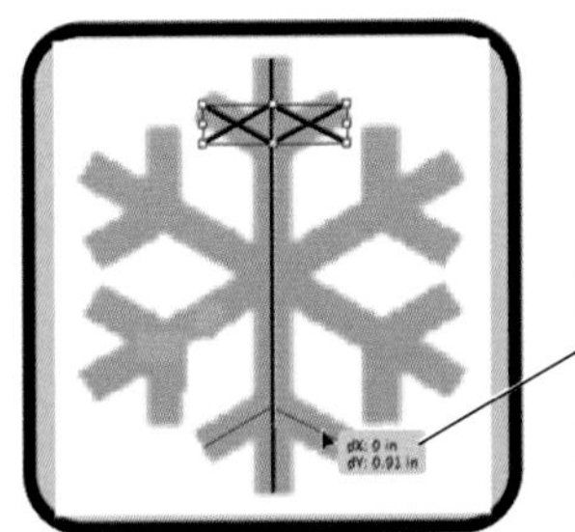

Use cursor feedback to move the shape to the exact horizontal position (dX = 0).

6. **Choose Object>Unlock All.**

   Remember, you locked the original vertical line to protect it while you worked with the endpoints of the angled branches. Now that you have one complete set of branches, you can use the existing objects to create the remaining icon elements — which means you need to unlock the vertical line so you can access and copy it.

7. **Choose Select>All.**

   All three objects — the vertical line and the two branch objects — are now selected.

8. **In the Control panel, change the stroke width to 7 pt.**

9. **Choose Object>Group.**

   Because these three objects are basically a single entity in the icon, it's a good idea to treat them as a single object.

10. **Save the file and continue to the next exercise.**

Rotate Drawing Objects

Very few projects are entirely horizontal, making rotating objects a foundational Illustrator skill. In this exercise, you use several rotation techniques to create the rest of the snowflake artwork.

1. **With `icons.ai` open, make sure the grouped object is selected.**

2. **Activate the Rotate tool in the Tools panel.**

   When you select the Rotate tool, an **origin point** appears by default at the center of the selected object. This origin point is the point around which rotation occurs. If you want to rotate an object around some other point, you can single-click anywhere to define a different origin point.

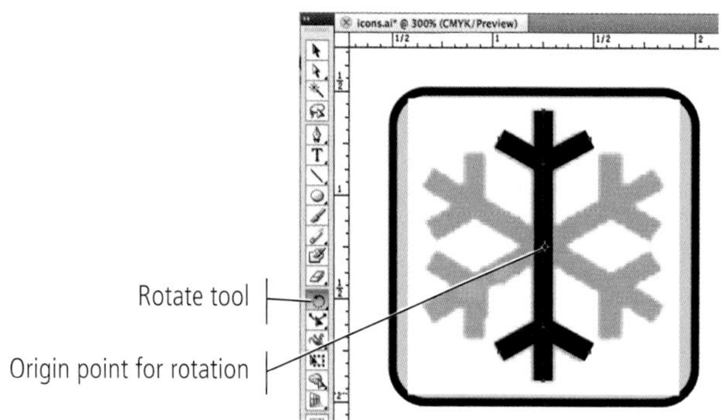

Note:

The Illustrator transformation tools all use this same origin point concept as the basis for transformations. You can click without dragging to reposition the origin point before applying the transformation.

3. **Click near the top of the vertical line, hold down the mouse button, and then drag left and down until the line appears over the next branch in the snowflake. Note the angle in the cursor feedback, and then release the mouse button.**

   As you can see, the rotation moved the selected objects around the origin point. Unfortunately, the vertical line is no longer there because you just rotated it.

When you drag with the Rotate tool, the cursor feedback shows the angle of rotation.

When you release the mouse button, the original object rotates.

4. **Press Command/Control-Z to undo the rotation.**

5. **With the group still selected, double-click the Rotate tool to open the Rotate dialog box.**

   This dialog box is the same one you would see by choosing Object>Transform>Rotate. Transformation dialog boxes, which default to the last-used settings for that transformation, make it easy to apply very specific numeric transformations to selected objects.

6. **Type 60 in the Rotate field, and then click Copy.**

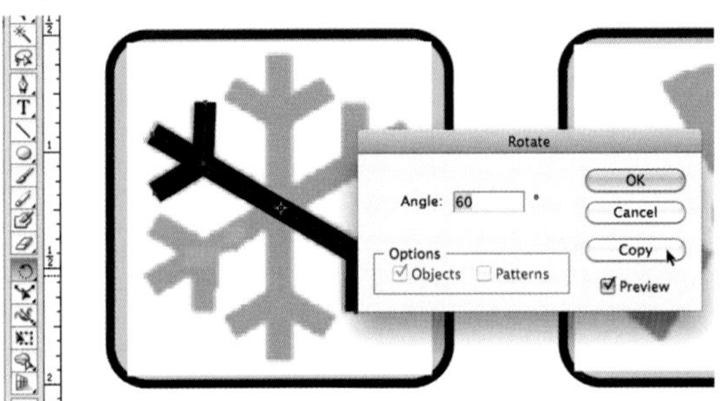

> *Note:*
>
> *The Transform Again command applies the last-used transformation of any type to a selected object without opening a dialog box. This command might result in movement, rotation, reflection, shear, or scale, depending on the last transformation you applied.*

7. **Choose Object>Transform>Transform Again to create the third branch of the snowflake icon.**

   As before, the Transform Again command repeats the last-used transformation — in this case, the copy-rotate transformation from Step 6.

8. **Choose Select>All. Using the Control panel, click the Vertical Align Center and Horizontal Align Center buttons.**

   Because each "branch" is a group, the alignment functions work as you would expect. The three sets of branches are now exactly centered in both directions.

   This step might not cause a noticeable change, depending on how precisely you placed the lines, but it's a good idea to be certain that the groups align properly.

> *Note:*
>
> *You can Option/Alt-click and drag to clone an object while you transform it. In other words, if you press Option/Alt while dragging with the Rotate tool, you can create a rotated copy.*

9. **With all snowflake objects selected, choose Object>Lock>Selection.**

10. **In the Layers panel, select the Template cold.tif layer and click the Delete Selection button at the bottom of the panel. Click Yes in the confirmation message.**

    Since the snowflake drawing is complete, you no longer need the template image.

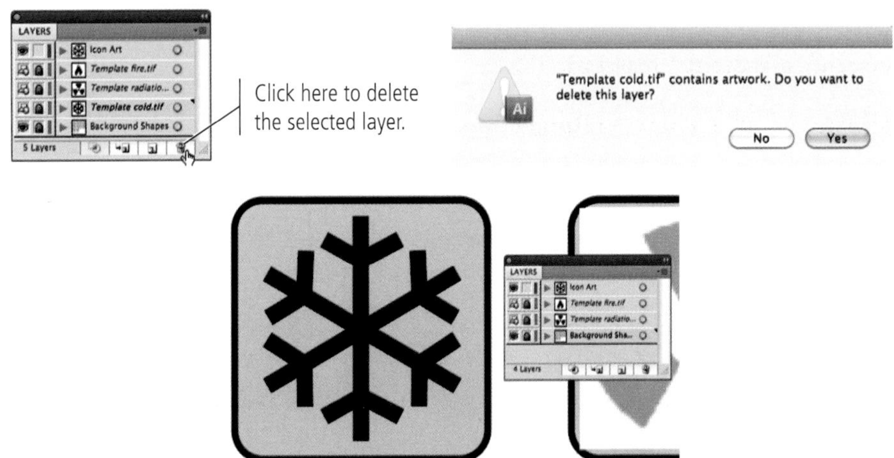

11. **Save the file and continue to the next exercise.**

Divide Basic Shapes into Component Pieces

Using the Illustrator Pathfinder panel, you can combine multiple shapes in a variety of ways, or you can use one object as a "cookie cutter" to remove or separate one shape from another. As you work with more complicated artwork in Illustrator, you will find many different ways to use the Pathfinder functions, either alone or in combination.

1. **With `icons.ai` open, make sure the Icon Art layer is selected in the Layers panel. Zoom into the second rectangle in the first row of background shapes.**

2. **Select the Ellipse tool (nested under the Rounded Rectangle tool) in the Tools panel. Set the fill color to black and the stroke color to None.**

We used the Control panel to set the Fill and Stroke colors.

Ellipse tool

The Icon Art layer is selected (active).

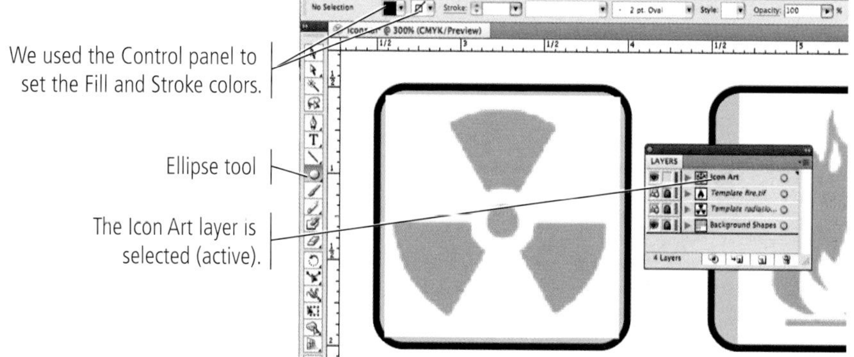

3. **Click in the center of the biohazard icon, press Option/Alt-Shift, and then drag to create a circle that covers the entire biohazard icon.**

   Remember, pressing Option/Alt allows you to draw a shape from the center out. Pressing Shift constrains the shape to equal height and width.

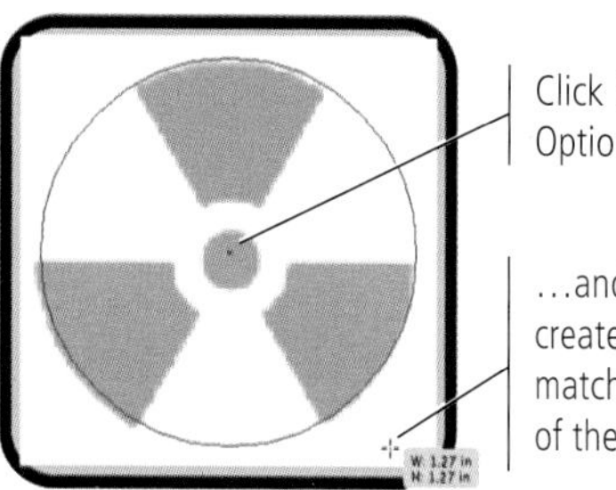

Click here, press Option/Alt-Shift…

…and drag out to create a circle that matches the outer edge of the icon image.

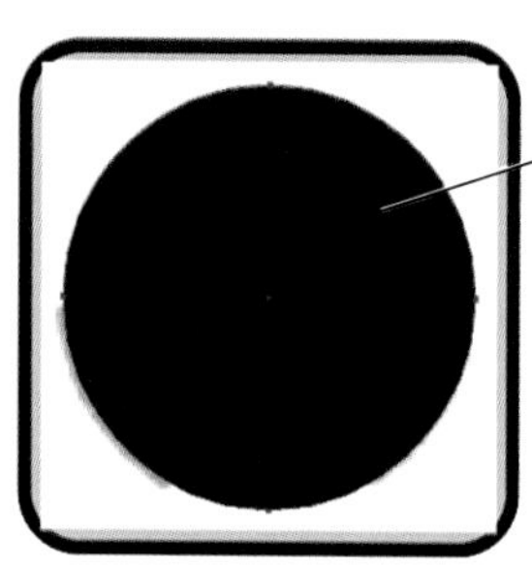

The fill color appears when you release the mouse button.

> *Note:*
>
> *The fill color does not appear until you release the mouse button.*

4. **With the new circle selected, change the Opacity field in the Control panel to `50`.**

   Opacity defines the transparency of the selected object. In this case, you're reducing the opacity from 100% (entirely solid or opaque) so you can see the template image behind the circle you just drew.

> *Note:*
>
> *You can also use the Transparency panel to change an object's opacity.*

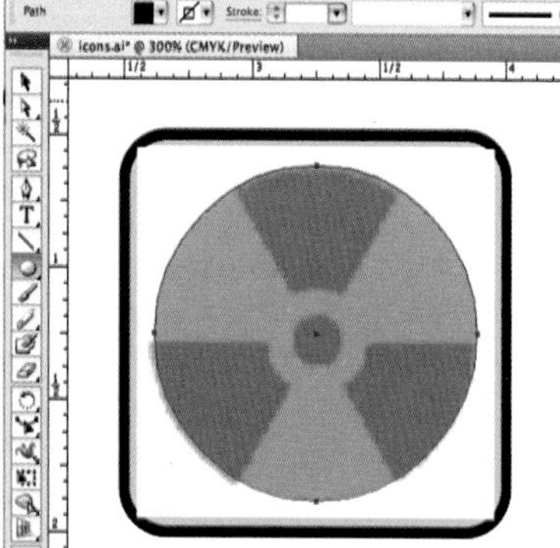

Change the shape's Opacity value so you can see the underlying template image.

> *Note:*
>
> *You'll work with opacity as a design element in Project 6.*

5. **Using the Ellipse tool, click again in the center of the template image, press Option/Alt-Shift, and drag to create the smaller circle in the center of the shape.**

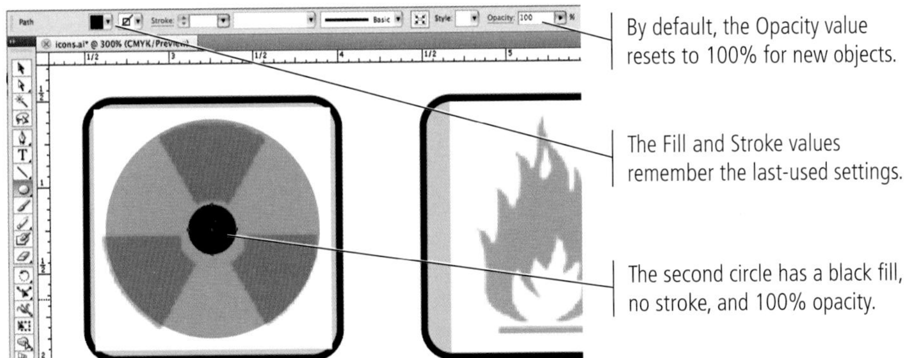

By default, the Opacity value resets to 100% for new objects.

The Fill and Stroke values remember the last-used settings.

The second circle has a black fill, no stroke, and 100% opacity.

6. **With the smaller circle selected, change the fill color to None and the stroke color to white. Change the stroke weight to `5 pt`.**

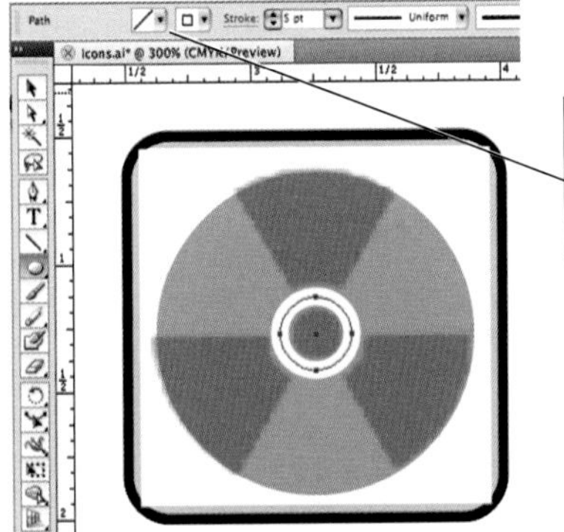

Again, we used the Control panel to change the Fill and Stroke attributes for the selected object.

7. **Press Command/Control to temporarily access the Selection tool, and click away from the existing shapes to deselect them.**

   If you don't deselect the circle, changing the Fill and Stroke attributes in the next step will change the attributes of the selected shape.

8. **Choose the Line Segment tool in the Tools panel, and then click the Default Fill and Stroke button at the bottom of the Tools panel.**

9. **Move the cursor below the circles you created until you see the Smart Guide connecting to the existing shape's center point. Click and drag up to create a vertical line that extends past the top edge of the outer circle.**

   Although none of the icon wedges have a vertical line, it's easier to start at vertical and rotate the objects as necessary.

Note:

To create the vertical line, use the cursor feedback to drag a 90° line, or press Shift to automatically constrain the line to 90°.

Clicking the Default Fill and Stroke button in the Tools panel resets the options in the Control panel.

Line Segment tool

Smart Guides indicate when you are in line with the center of the existing circles.

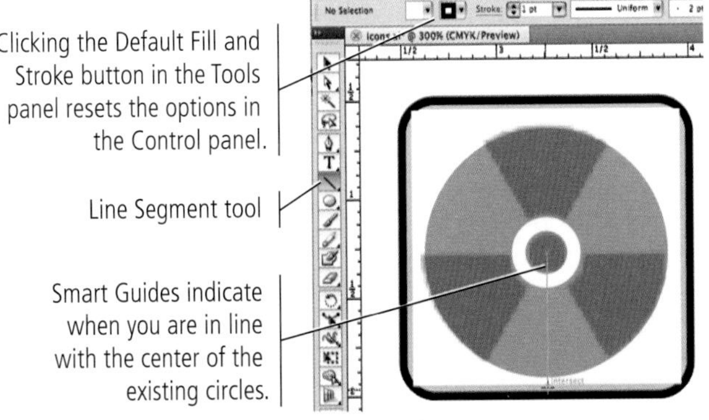

Extend the line past the top of the outer circle.

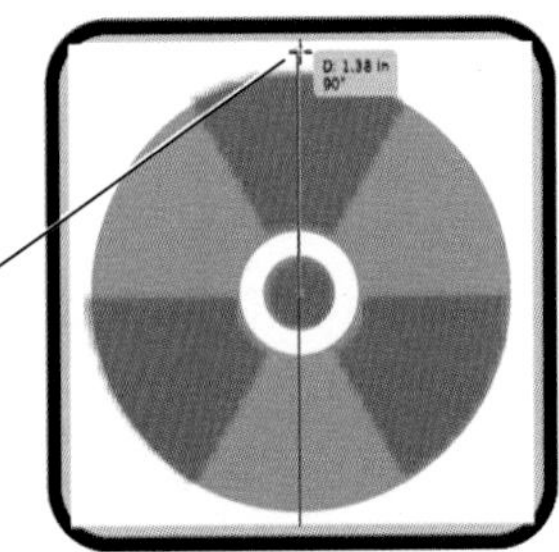

10. **Using the Selection tool, draw a marquee around the three objects that you have created to select them all. Use the options in the Control panel to align the selected objects horizontally and vertically.**

Alignment functions default to Align to Selection mode.

11. **Click away from the selected objects, and then select only the vertical line.**

The icon has six wedges, which means each half of the circle needs to be divided into three pieces. To accomplish this, you use precise rotation to slice the larger circle into the necessary parts.

12. **With the vertical line selected, choose Object>Transform>Rotate. Type `60` in the Angle field and click Copy.**

This menu command has the same result as double-clicking the Rotate tool, but you don't have to switch tools.

A full circle has 360 degrees. You're cutting the circle into six equal pieces; one sixth of 360° is 60°, so this is the exact angle that you need to create the correct number of pieces.

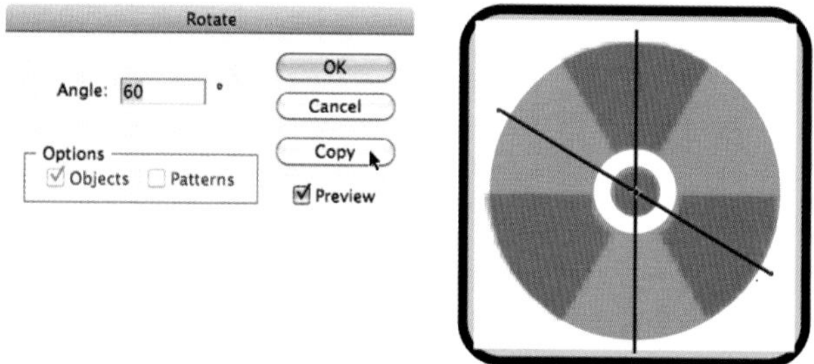

13. **Choose Object>Transform>Transform Again to make a third line.**

The Transform Again command applies the last-used transformation of any type to a selected object without opening a dialog box. Because you used the Rotate dialog box with the Copy button in the previous step, the Transform Again command copies the current selection and rotates it by the same angle you used in Step 12.

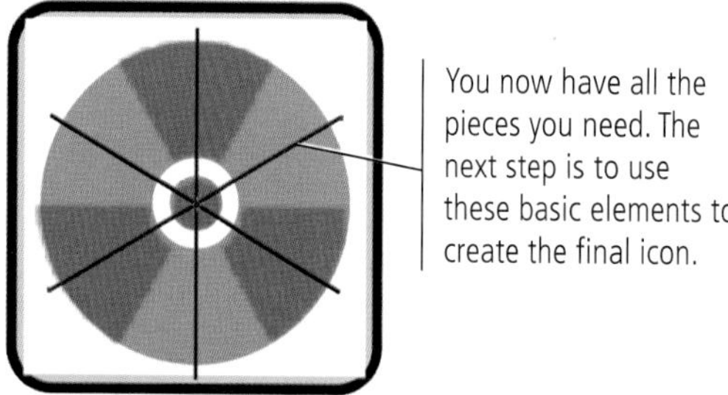

You now have all the pieces you need. The next step is to use these basic elements to create the final icon.

14. Using the Selection tool, select the smaller circle only and choose Object>Path>Outline Stroke.

This command changes the object stroke to a filled object. You drew the white circle to "cut out" the smaller black circle from the wedges. The Pathfinder functions recognize strokes for cutting apart shapes, but the stroke weight is not considered when the new paths are generated. To create the thick white space in the actual icon, you need to convert the heavy stroke to a filled shape.

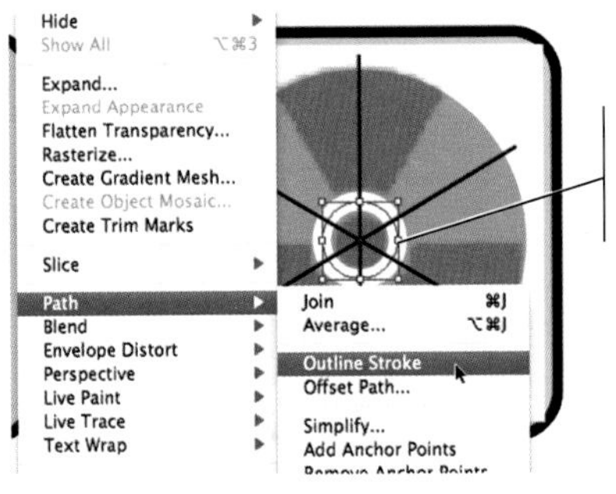

The original object had a 5-pt stroke weight.

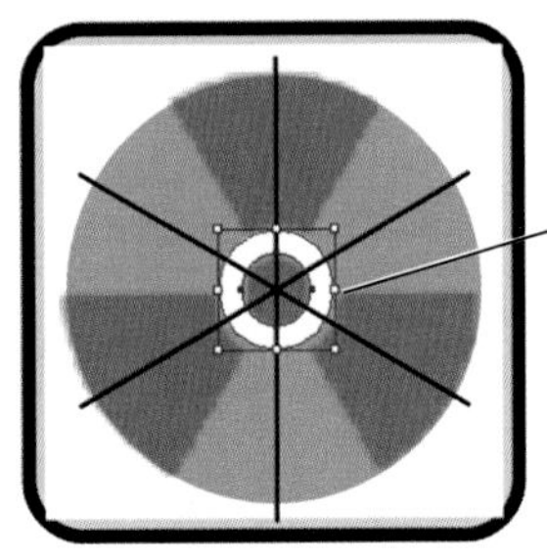

The Outline Stroke command changes the selected object to a filled shape with no visible stroke attributes.

15. Select all the objects in the icon, and then open the Pathfinder panel (Window>Pathfinder).

You can drag a marquee with the Selection tool, or choose Select>All. Because you locked the snowflake artwork in the first icon, those objects are not selected.

Note:

Press Command/Control-A to select all unlocked objects on the artboard.

The Pathfinder Panel in Depth

In the Pathfinder panel, the top row of buttons — the Shape Modes — create complex shapes by combining the originally selected shapes. (You can press Option/Alt and click a Shape Mode to maintain the paths from the original objects.)

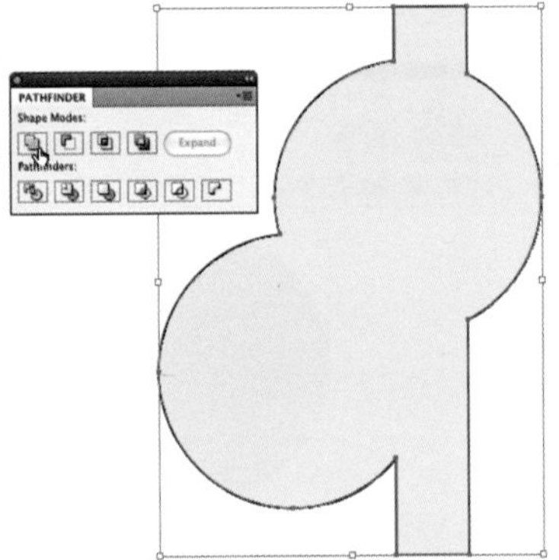

Unite combines all selected objects into a single shape.

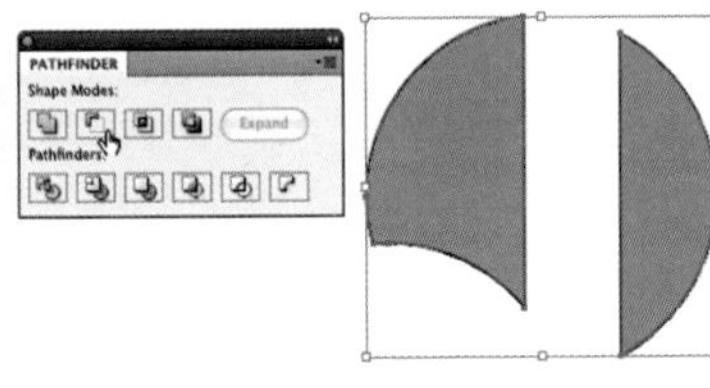

Minus Front removes overlapping areas from the backmost shape in the selection.

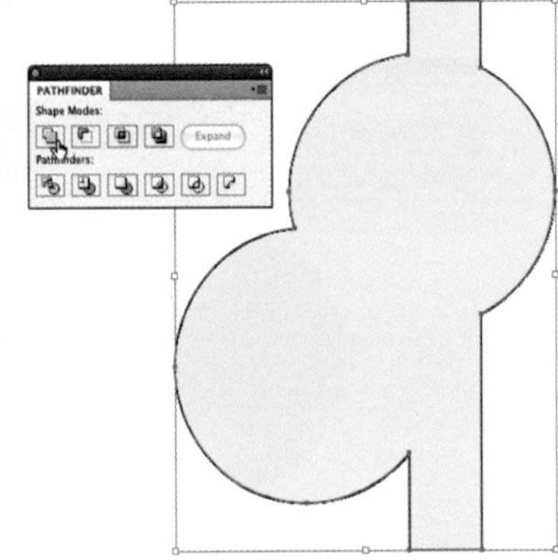

By default, the Shape options result in a single new object.

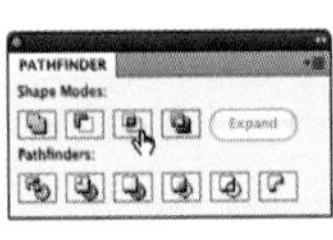

Intersect creates a shape of only areas where selected objects overlap.

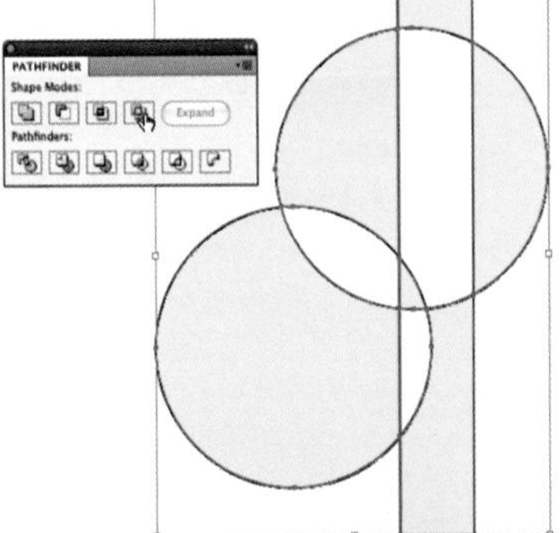

Exclude removes any areas where two objects overlap.

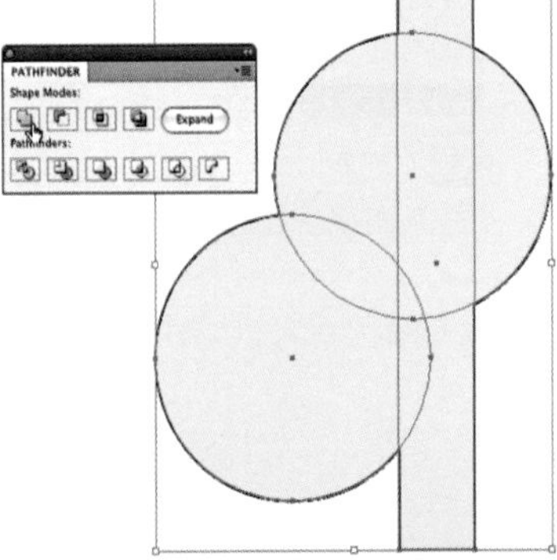

If you Option/Alt-click a shape mode button, the result maintains the original paths unless you manually expand it.

16. In the Pathfinder panel, click the Divide button.

Options in the Pathfinder panel allow you to cut shapes out of other shapes and merge multiple shapes into a single shape.

It's important to realize that many Pathfinder options can be applied in more than one way. We're using the Divide and Unite options in this exercise to give you an idea of what you can accomplish with Pathfinder.

Divide button

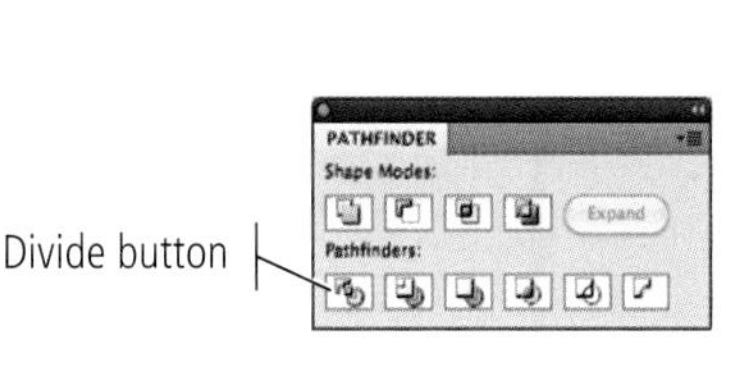

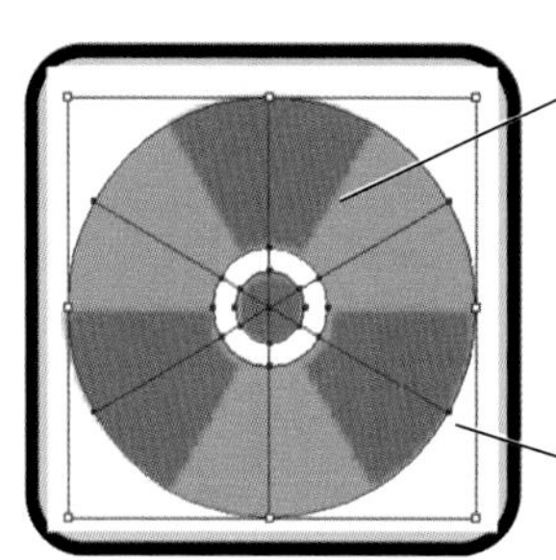

The Divide function slices apart all possible shapes of the selected objects. Everywhere two objects overlap, a new shape is created.

Because the straight lines are open shapes, they divide the circles into sixths, but the open ends of the lines (outside the area of the larger circle) are removed.

17. Save the file and continue to the next exercise.

The Pathfinder Panel in Depth (continued)

The second row of options — the Pathfinders — do exactly that. The resulting shapes are some combination of the paths that made up the originally selected objects.

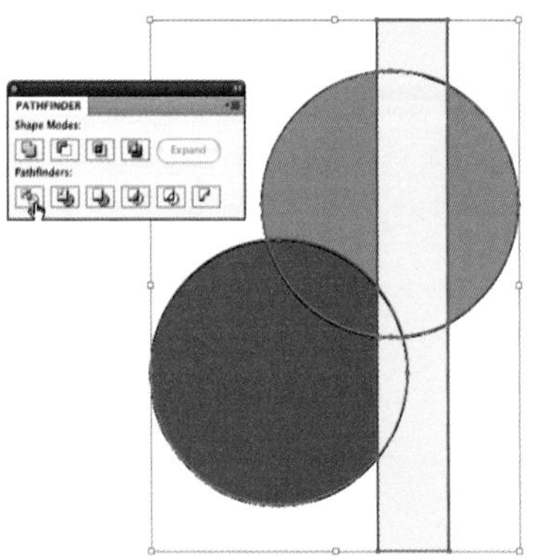

Divide creates separate shapes from all overlapping areas of selected objects.

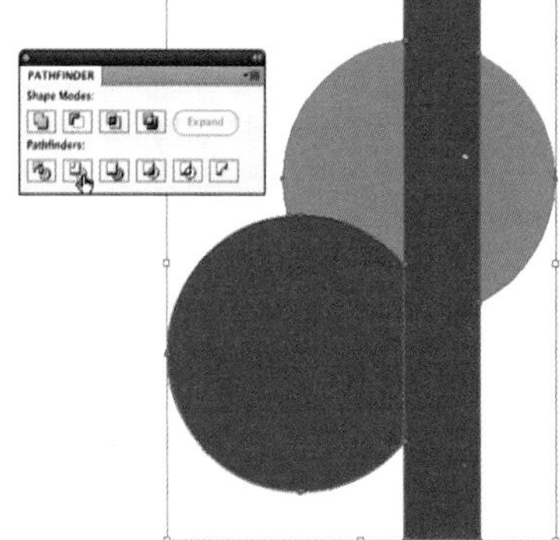

Trim removes underlying areas of overlapping objects. Objects of the same fill color are not combined.

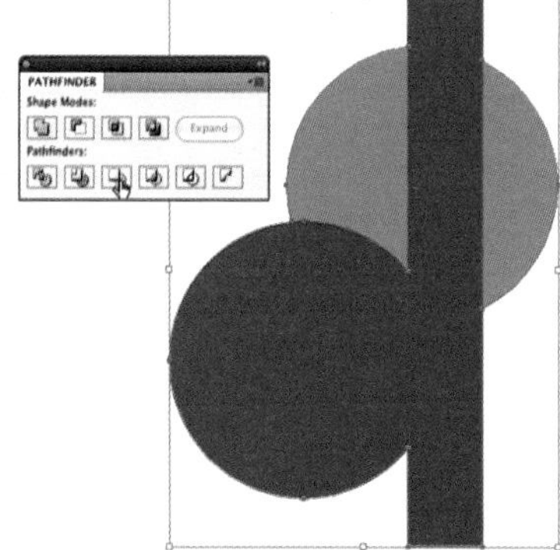

Merge removes underlying areas of overlapping objects. Objects of the same fill color are combined.

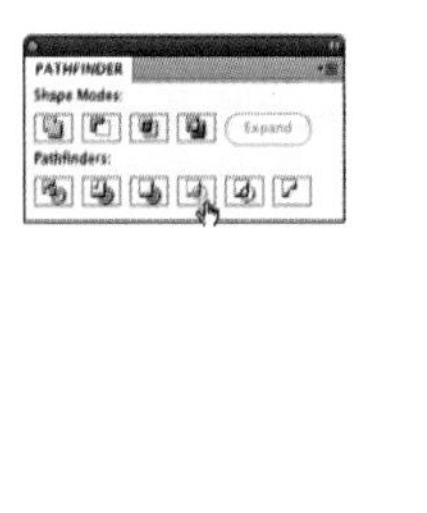

Crop returns the areas of underlying objects that are within the boundary of the topmost object.

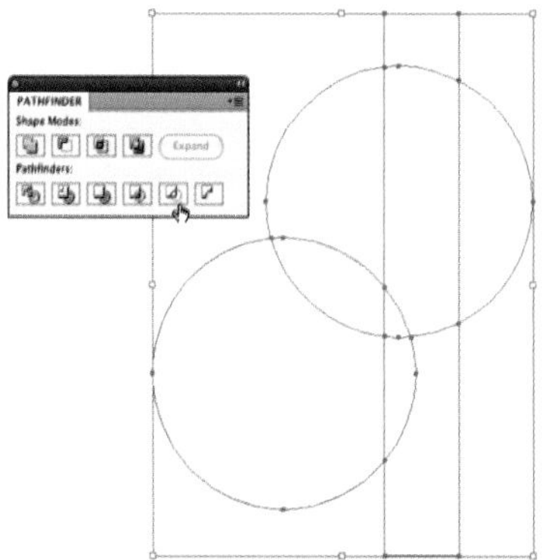

Outline divides the selected objects, then returns unfilled, open paths.

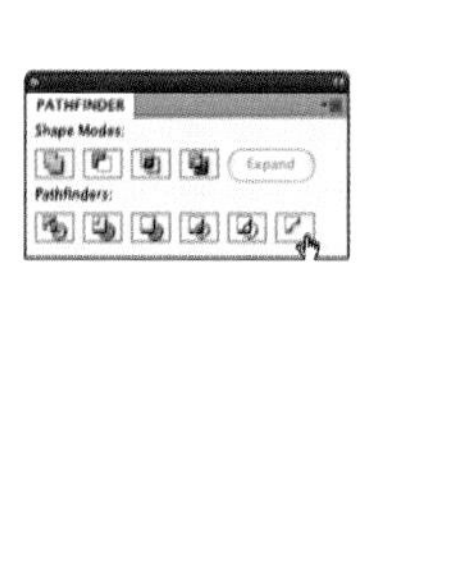

Minus Back removes the area of underlying objects from the front object.

Work in Isolation Mode

Groups can be invaluable when you need to treat multiple items as a single object. When items are grouped, it is easy to move and manipulate the entire group as a single object. In many cases, however, you will need to make changes to only part of a group. Depending on the complexity of the file, this can be very difficult without first breaking apart the group ("ungrouping"). Illustrator's Isolation mode offers a convenient workspace, where you can work with grouped objects as if they were stand-alone objects.

1. **With icons.ai open, use the Selection tool to double-click any of the shapes in the biohazard icon to enter Isolation mode.**

   When you use the Pathfinder panel, the resulting shapes are automatically grouped. Because all of these shapes make up the icon artwork, it's a good idea to leave them grouped. Isolation mode allows you to work with the constituent objects without ungrouping.

2. **Using the Selection tool, click the wedge shape in the top-left area of the icon, and then press Delete.**

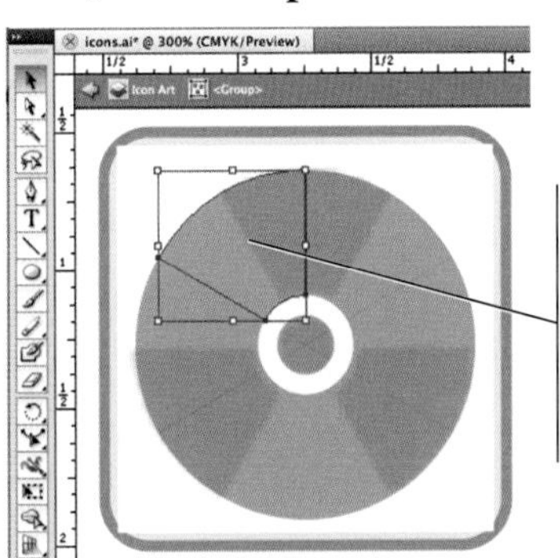

Because you're working in Isolation mode, you can use the Selection tool to select one object, even though the object is part of a group on the main artboard.

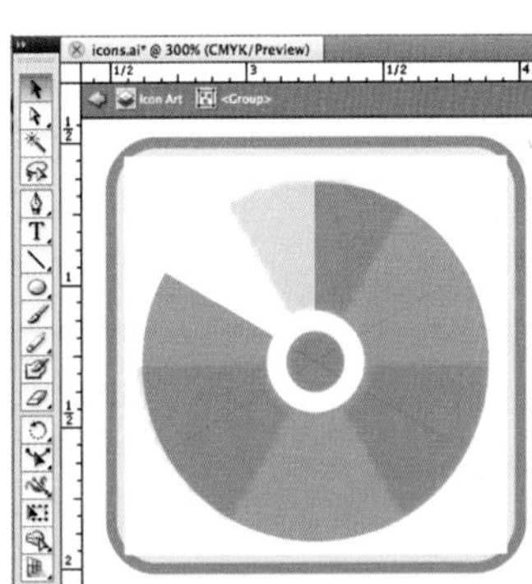

3. **Select and delete every other wedge in the outside area of the group.**

4. **Choose View>Outline.**

   Outline mode allows you to see and work with the basic shapes only. This way, object fills don't obscure the shapes that you need to see clearly.

5. **Click in the center set of wedges and drag a marquee that encompasses the center points of all six center wedges.**

   If you tried to do this in Preview mode, clicking one of the filled shapes and dragging would actually move the shape you clicked. Because the fills are not technically present in Outline mode, you can use the click-drag method to select all six shapes instead of Shift-clicking each one individually.

   Be sure you don't click on any actual line when you begin to draw the selection marquee. If necessary, zoom in so you can clearly see the empty spaces in the small wedge shapes.

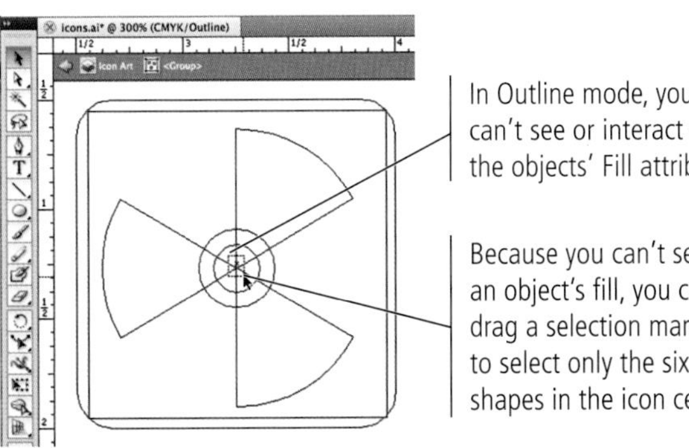

In Outline mode, you can't see or interact with the objects' Fill attributes.

Because you can't select an object's fill, you can drag a selection marquee to select only the six small shapes in the icon center.

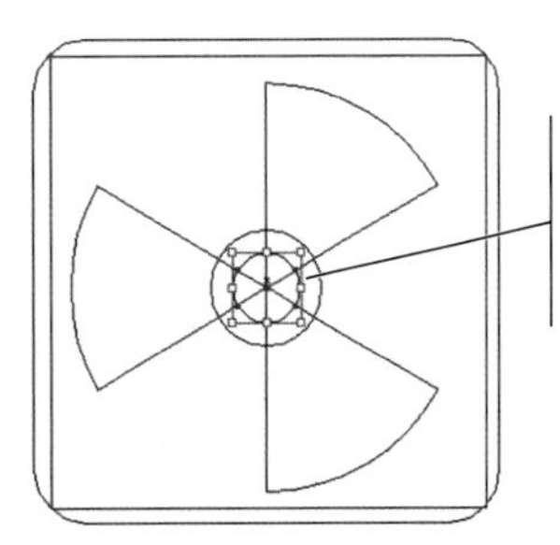

When you release the mouse button, you can see that all six objects are selected.

6. **In the Pathfinder panel, click the Unite button.**

   This function merges the selected shapes into a single object.

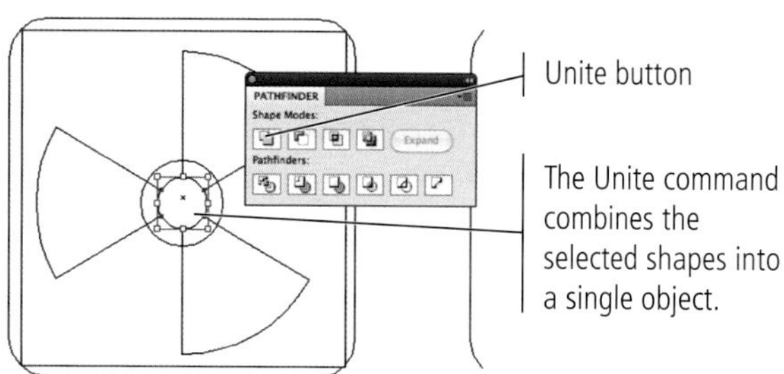

7. **Choose View>Preview to exit Outline mode and display the normal artwork.**

8. **Using the Selection tool, click to select any one of the black (partially transparent) objects.**

9. **In the Control panel, click the Select Similar Objects button and choose Opacity from the menu.**

   The options in this menu (and in the Select>Same menu) are very useful for finding objects that share specific attributes.

Note:

The Select Similar functions can also be accessed in the Select>Same menu.

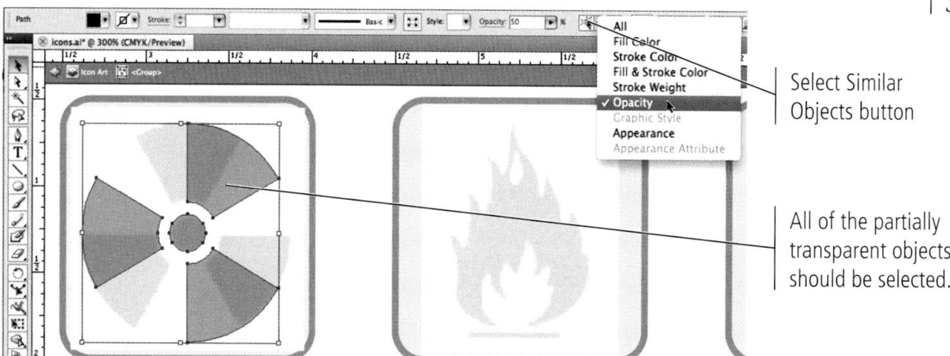

10. **Change the Opacity value (in the Control panel) to `100` for the selected objects.**

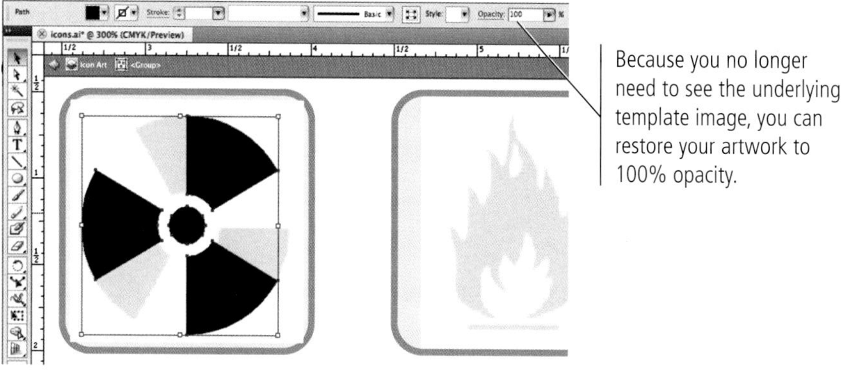

Because you no longer need to see the underlying template image, you can restore your artwork to 100% opacity.

11. **At the top of the document window, click the arrow button twice to return to the main artboard.**

    Your icon is almost complete; you only need to rotate the shape to match the image.

12. **Save the file and continue to the next exercise.**

Use Measurements to Adjust Your Artwork

Depending on the type of work you do, Illustrator drawings can be entirely freeform, precisely measured, or a combination of the two (as in this case). You have already used a number of tools that help you create exactly what you need where you need it — Smart Guides, document rulers, the Transform panel, and even the Control panel all offer ways to precisely move and size objects on the artboard.

You can also use the Measure tool, which evaluates different dimensional attributes of objects on the page. As you might expect from the name, the Measure tool acts like a digital tape measure. In addition to sizes and positions, the tool also measures angles — an important feature for technical drawing that requires precise detail.

1. **With `icons.ai` open, choose the Measure tool in the Tools panel (nested under the Eyedropper tool).**

2. **Click at the outside corner of the left wedge, and then drag down and right along the shape edge (as shown in the following image).**

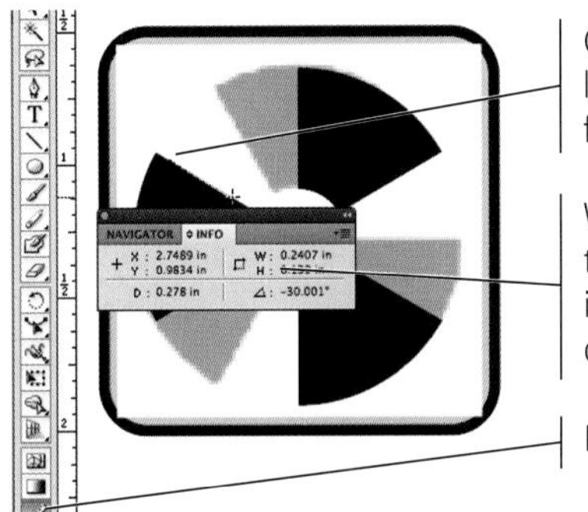

Click and drag along this line (down and right) to find the angle of the line.

When you use the Measure tool, measurements appear in the Info panel (which opens automatically).

Measure tool

The Measure tool tells you that the angle of this line is –30°. You need it to be 180° (horizontal), which means you need to rotate the shape by 30°.

> ***Note:***
>
> *If you drag from the inside out, the Info panel shows an angle of 150°. This provides the same information, because 180° — your goal — minus 150° equals 30°.*

3. **Select the group with the Selection tool, and then choose Object>Transform>Rotate.**

4. **Change the Angle field to `30` and click OK.**

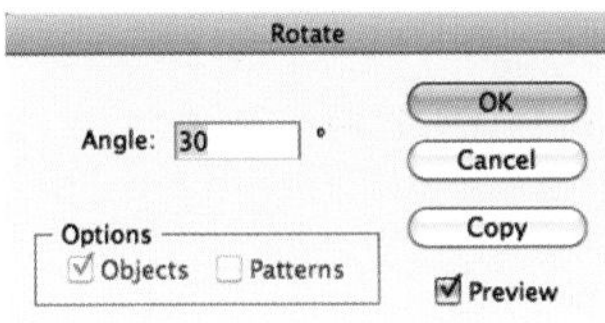

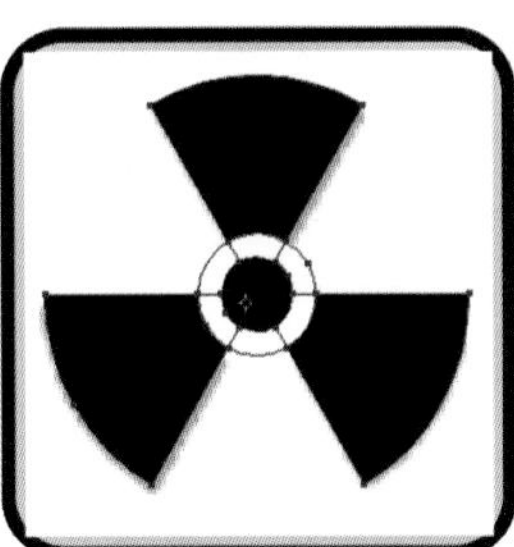

5. **In the Layers panel, select and delete the Template radiation.tif layer.**

After you remove the template image, you can see the remaining problem — the Divide Pathfinder function left a white ring in the shape. You need to remove these white objects.

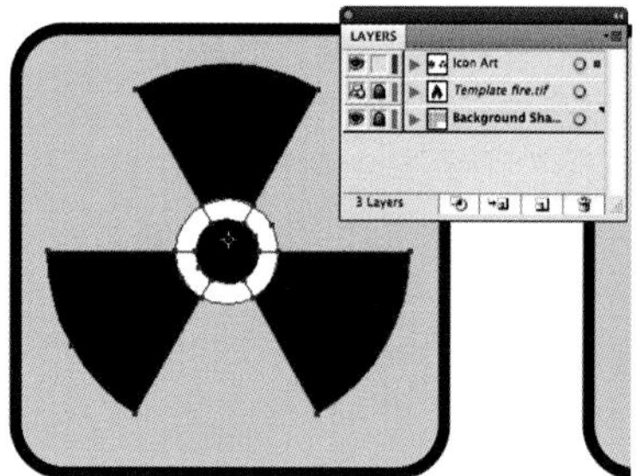

6. **Click away from all objects to deselect the icon artwork.**

7. **Using the Direct Selection tool, click the fill of one of the white shapes to select it.**

Remember, all of the constituent shapes are part of a group — the result of the Pathfinder Divide function — so you can't use the Selection tool. The irregular position of these small shapes also makes it difficult to individually select the six objects with the Direct Selection tool.

Note:

Be careful when you use the Select Similar functions. They select all similar unlocked objects on the entire artboard. If the art for another icon had a white fill, for example, it would also be selected.

8. **In the Control panel, click the Select Similar Objects button and choose Fill Color from the menu.**

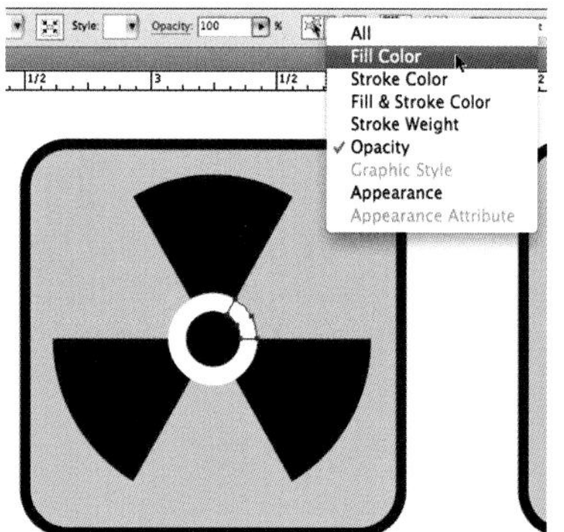

All six white-filled objects are selected because the original selection had a white fill.

9. **With all six white shapes in the icon selected, press Delete.**

10. **Select all objects in the radiation icon art and choose Object>Lock>Selection.**

This step protects the completed icon artwork from being inadvertently changed while you work on the rest of this project.

11. **Save the file and continue to the next exercise.**

Draw with the Pencil Tool

At this point, you have used a number of basic shapes to create finished icon artwork. As you might already realize, however, not all artwork can be created from basic shapes and lines. Illustrator includes everything you need to create artwork in any form, from a basic square to irregular shapes without a single visible straight edge. The Pencil tool is one method for creating custom shapes. Like a regular pencil on a piece of paper, the Pencil tool creates lines that follow the path of your cursor. (If you have a digital drawing tablet, the Pencil tool can be particularly useful for drawing custom artwork.)

Note:

In Project 2, you will learn how to use the Pen tool to control every point and path of your Illustrator drawings.

1. **With `icons.ai` open, make sure the Icon Art layer is selected in the Layers panel. Zoom in to the third rectangle in the first row of background shapes.**

2. **Choose the Pencil tool and click the Default Fill and Stroke button in the Tools panel.**

3. **Double-click the Pencil tool in the Tools panel.**

   Double-clicking certain tools in the Tools panel opens an Options dialog box, where you can control the default behavior for the selected tool. The Pencil tool options include:

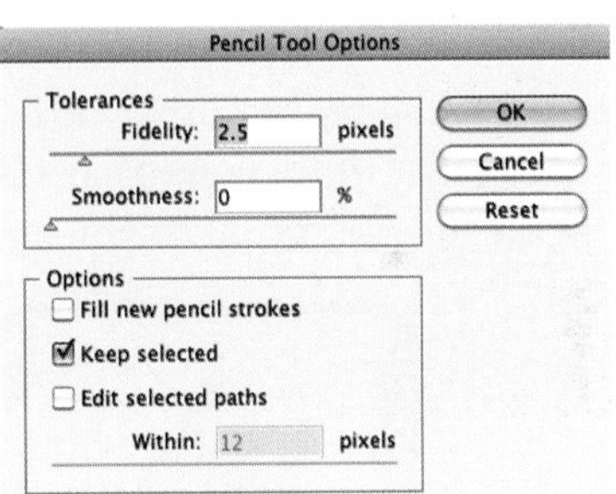

   - **Fidelity.** This option determines how far apart anchor points are added as you drag. Higher values result in fewer points and smoother lines; lower values result in more anchor points, which can make the lines appear choppy.
   - **Smoothness.** This option determines how closely a path follows the path of your cursor. Lower values result in more anchor points, especially if your cursor movement is choppy.
   - **Fill New Pencil Strokes.** By default, pencil paths are not filled regardless of the fill color defined in the Tools panel.
   - **Keep Selected.** If this option is checked, the line you draw is automatically selected when you release the mouse button.
   - **Edit Selected Paths.** If this option is checked, drawing near a selected path can change the existing path. This is an important distinction (especially when Keep Selected is checked) because you can accidentally edit the first path instead of creating a second shape.

4. **Set the Fidelity value to `2.5` pixels and Smoothness to `0`%.**

   To draw this icon, you must make many fine movements and change direction often. Even though this icon artwork doesn't have to be exact to communicate the necessary message ("fire"), you should try to match the template as closely as possible.

5. **Make sure the Fill New Pencil Strokes and Edit Selected Paths options are unchecked, and then click OK.**

6. **Click at the bottom-left point of the fire icon, hold down the mouse button, and begin dragging around the shape of the fire. When you get near your original starting point, press Option/Alt and release the mouse button.**

   As you drag, a colored line indicates the path you're drawing. Don't worry if the path isn't perfect; when you release the mouse button, Illustrator automatically smoothes the path.

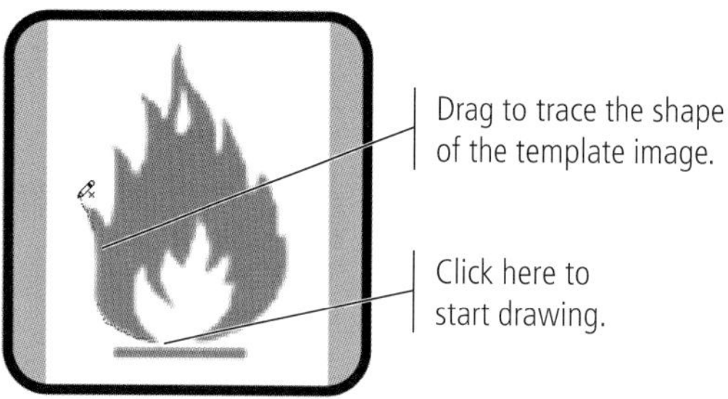

Drag to trace the shape of the template image.

Click here to start drawing.

The Pencil tool creates open-ended lines. To create a closed shape with your path, press Option/Alt before releasing the mouse button at your original starting point.

The hollow circle in the cursor icon indicates that releasing the mouse button will create a closed shape.

When you release the mouse button, the shape shows the defined stroke color but not the fill color.

7. **Click near the top point of the white flame area (inside the first path) and drag to create the white inner shape in the fire icon. Press Option/Alt before releasing the mouse button so you end up with a closed shape.**

Use the Pencil tool to draw this shape. Press Option/Alt before releasing the mouse button to create a closed shape.

8. **Using the Rectangle tool, draw the shape below the fire in the template image.**

9. **In the Layers panel, delete the Template fire.tif layer.**

10. **Use the Selection tool to select all three shapes of the icon art. Change the fill color to black and the stroke color to None.**

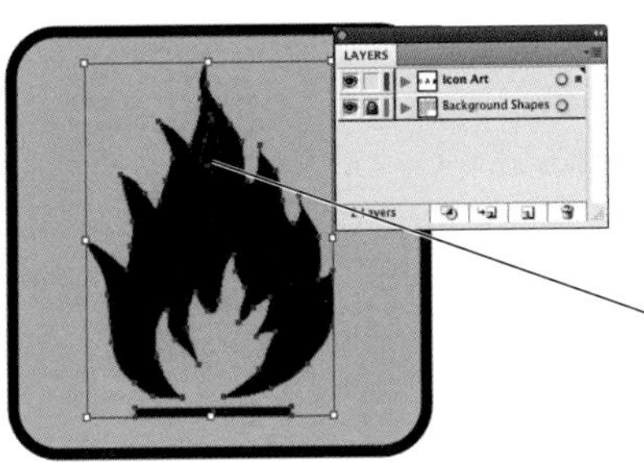

When all three objects are filled, you can't see the inner shape at the top of the flame.

> *Note:*
>
> *A **compound path** is a single shape made up of more than one path. Compound paths usually have inner "empty" areas, such as the letter O or Q.*

11. **Choose Object>Compound Path>Make.**

This option combines all three selected shapes into a single shape; the area of the smaller shape is removed from the larger shape behind it.

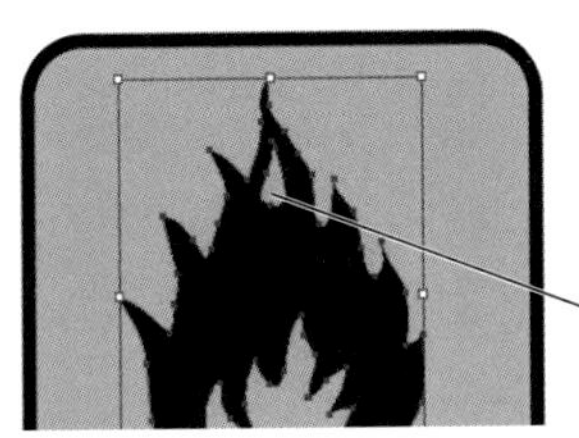

As a compound path, the inner shape is removed from the outer shape.

12. **Save the file and close it.**

Using Live Trace to Create Artwork from Images

ILLUSTRATOR FOUNDATIONS

In many cases, the basic drawing tools are often not enough to efficiently create the artwork you need. When you need to create artwork from a placed image — as in the case of the low-resolution icons that you're using in this project — you can also use the Live Trace function to create vector graphics from placed bitmap images. (Be sure you don't place the image using the Template option.)

When an image is selected, choose Object>Live Trace>Tracing Options to open the Tracing Options dialog box. (A number of defined presets are also available in the Live Trace menu.)

When you use the Live Trace function, the result is a special type of object, which you can edit by changing the settings in the Live Trace dialog box. To access the individual paths and anchor points of the traced shape, you first have to expand the Live Trace object by choosing Object>Expand.

(Our goal in this project is to teach you the basics of drawing in Illustrator, so we don't include a complete exercise on Live Trace here. However, feel free to experiment with the different options; a number of additional icon files are provided in the WIP>Symbols folder.)

Original placed image

Result using the built-in Black and White Logo preset

Result using the custom settings shown at right

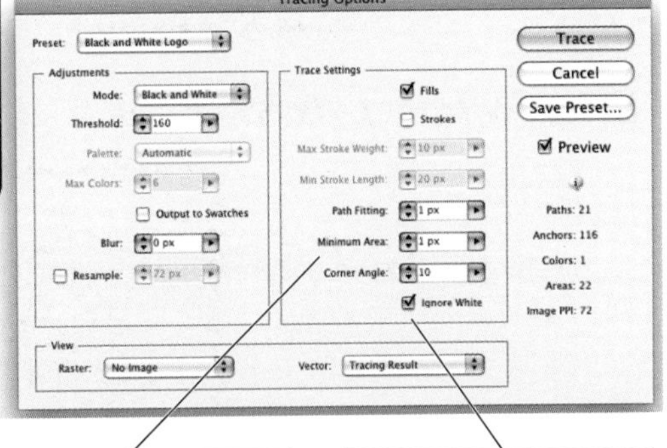

With Preview active, we adjusted the various settings to fine-tune the result.

Checking Ignore White removes the white areas of the placed image.

Project Review

fill in the blank

1. _______________ are composed of mathematical descriptions of a series of lines and points; they are resolution independent, can be freely scaled, and are automatically output at the resolution of the output device.

2. _______________ are pixel-based, made up of a grid of individual pixels (rasters or bits) in rows and columns.

3. The _______________ is a rectangle that marks the outermost edges of an object, regardless of the actual object shape.

4. _______________ is the relative top-to-botom order of objects on the artboard, or of layers in the Layers panel.

5. The _______________ is used to select entire objects or groups.

6. The _______________ is used to select individual paths and points of a shape, or to select component pieces within a group.

7. The _______________ is used to draw freeform paths defined by dragging the mouse cursor.

8. Press _______________ to temporarily access the Selection tool; releasing the modifier key restores the previously selected tool.

9. The _______________ is used to create complex shapes by combining multiple selected objects.

10. A(n) _______________ is a single object that is made up of more than one shape.

short answer

1. Briefly explain the difference between vector graphics and raster images.

2. Briefly explain the difference between the Selection tool and the Direct Selection tool.

3. Briefly explain the difference between Shape Mode and Pathfinder operations in the Pathfinder panel.

Portfolio Builder Project

Use what you learned in this project to complete the following freeform exercise.
Carefully read the art director and client comments, then create your own design to meet the needs of the project.
Use the space below to sketch ideas; when finished, write a brief explanation of your reasoning behind your final design.

art director comments

The client is pleased with the first three icons, and they want you to complete the rest of the warning icons. They also want you to create an additional set of icons for travel and outdoor activities that they offer as benefits during their international corporate conferences.

To complete this project, you should:

- ❑ Complete the remaining international warning icons. The bitmap versions are in your WIP>Symbols folder.
- ❑ Carefully consider the best approach for each icon and use whichever tool (or tools) you feel is most appropriate.
- ❑ Create a second Illustrator file for the six new recreation icons.

client comments

We host a number of large, international conventions and conferences every year, and many attendees bring their families along for a working vacation. To keep everyone happy, we have started offering different outdoor activities for the families while their spouses are attending sessions, but the international crowd means that many people need visual help getting to the right place.

Since you did such a good job on the first three icons, we would like you to finish those. But first, we want you to create icons for horseback riding, sailing, swimming, hiking, rock climbing, and nature walks.

We don't have the images for these ones, so we would like you to come up with something. Remember, icons need to be easily recognizable, so they should very clearly convey visually what each one is for.

project justification

Project Summary

The skills that you learned in this project will serve as the foundation for most work you create in Illustrator. You learned how to place raster images as templates, from which you created scalable vector graphics that will work in virtually any printed application. You learned a number of techniques for selecting objects and component pieces of objects, as well as various options for aligning objects relative to one another and to the artboard.

You learned how to draw primitive geometric shapes, and how to control the color of objects' fill and stroke attributes. You used a number of transformation options, including cloning methods to copy existing objects. Finally, you learned how to draw freeform shapes to suit more complex needs. As you move forward in this book, you will build on the basic skills you learned in this project to create increasingly complex artwork.

Create and transform basic rectangles with rounded corners
Control object fill and stroke color
Clone, rotate, and mirror basic lines

Use various techniques to select objects, groups, and the component pieces of those objects and groups
Use the Pathfinder to combine basic shapes into complex artwork

Use a variety of methods to place objects relative to one another
Use the Pencil tool and compound paths to draw complex shapes

Balloon Festival Artwork

Your client is the marketing director for the Temecula Hot Air Balloon Festival, which attracts thousands of tourists to the desert community throughout the three-day event. You have been hired to create the primary artwork for this year's event, which will be used in a variety of different products (ads, souvenirs, etc.).

This project incorporates the following skills:

- ❑ Drawing complex custom shapes with the Pen tool
- ❑ Editing anchor points and handles to control the precise position of vector paths
- ❑ Drawing irregular shape outlines by painting with the Blob Brush tool
- ❑ Creating a custom color scheme using saved swatches
- ❑ Adding interest and depth with color gradients
- ❑ Adjusting color, both globally and in specific selections
- ❑ Saving multiple file versions for various print applications

Project Meeting

client comments

Although the festival is popular, it's an aging crowd; we hope to bring in more families so we can get more younger people interested in ballooning as a hobby. This year is the 25th anniversary of the festival, and we've added a range of entertainment and educational options for younger children.

We want this year's artwork to be very bright and colorful; we also want a "cartoon-y" look that might appeal to young kids. It will be used on everything from festival programs to glassware — we're even planning on a teddy bear who is wearing a t-shirt with the artwork silk-screened on the back.

art director comments

I sketched a mock-up of a hot air balloon that you can use as the basis for the artwork. You should use the Pen tool to draw the balloon because simple shapes won't work and the Pencil tool doesn't provide fine enough control to efficiently achieve what you need.

Temecula is on the edge of the desert in southern California, so I'm going to have your partner create a desert panorama scene to put behind the balloons.

Rather than just one balloon floating over the desert, the finished piece should create the effect of a whole fleet of balloons. You can just clone the first balloon a couple of times, but make sure you change the color scheme in each one so they are all a bit different.

This is going to be a complex piece of artwork, so I recommend using layers to organize the various pieces. That will make it far easier to edit specific components as necessary if the client decides to make changes.

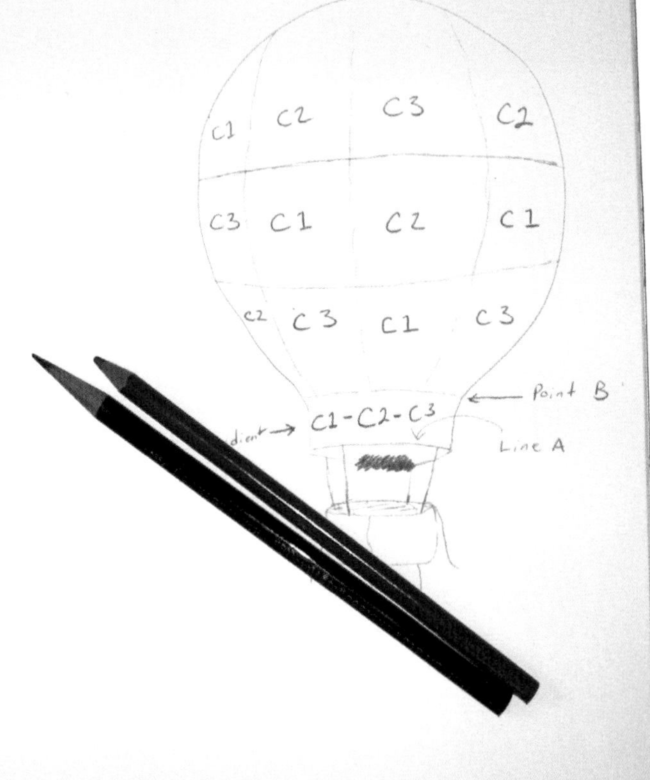

project objectives

To complete this project, you will:

- ❑ Use the Pen tool to draw precise curves
- ❑ Adjust anchor points and handles to precisely control the shape of vector objects
- ❑ Use the Blob Brush tool to "paint" the area of vector shapes
- ❑ Define custom color swatches to allow easy universal changes
- ❑ Create color gradients to blend multiple colors in a single object
- ❑ Adjust gradients in context on the artboard
- ❑ Change colors in specific selected objects
- ❑ Save multiple file versions for use in various design applications

Stage 1 Drawing Complex Artwork

In Project 1, you used a number of techniques to create finished artwork from basic shapes. Of course, much of the artwork you create will require far more complexity than simple lines and geometric shapes. When you need to produce custom artwork — whether from scratch or by tracing a hand-drawn sketch or photo — Illustrator includes a powerful set of tools to create and manipulate every point and path in the illustration. In the first stage of this project, you begin exploring the Pen tool, as well as other options for building and controlling custom shapes.

Prepare the Drawing Workspace

As with any project, setting up the workspace is an important first step. This project requires a single artboard to contain the entire illustration.

1. **Download `Print5_RF_Project2.zip` from the Student Files Web page.**

2. **Expand the ZIP archive in your WIP folder (Macintosh) or copy the archive contents into your WIP folder (Windows).**

   This results in a folder named **Festival**, which contains the files you need for this project. You should also use this folder to save the files you create in this project.

   Note:

   If you use the Welcome Screen instead of the menu command to make the new file, click the Create New Print Document link.

3. **In Illustrator, choose File>New. Type `balloons` in the Name field, choose Letter in the Size menu, and choose Inches in the Units menu.**

4. **If the Advanced options are not visible, click the down-arrow button to show those options. Choose CMYK in the Color Mode menu and choose High (300 PPI) in the Raster Effects menu.**

   This illustration will be printed in various documents, so you should design the job in the CMYK color mode. Some Illustrator functions, such as effects and gradient meshes, will be rasterized for commercial output; the High (300 PPI) raster effects setting results in sufficient resolution for those elements.

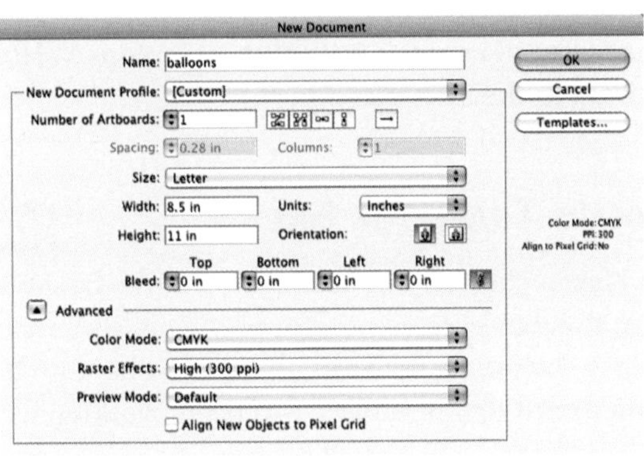

5. **Click OK to create the file.**

6. **Choose File>Place. Navigate to the file `sketch.jpg` in your WIP>Festival folder. Make sure the Link option is not checked and the Template option is checked, and then click Place.**

   You will use this client-supplied sketch to create the primary artwork for this illustration.

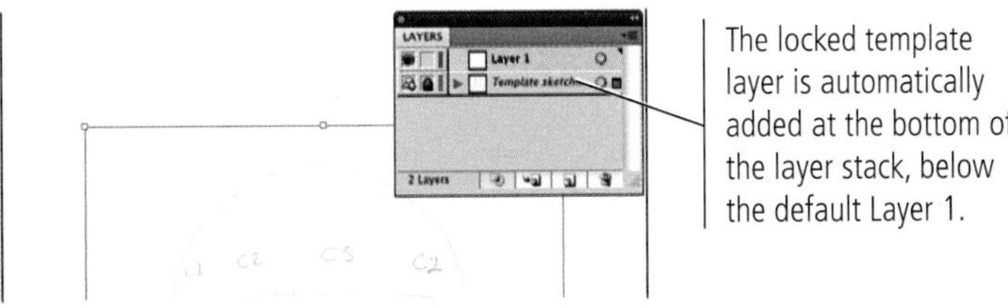

The locked template layer is automatically added at the bottom of the layer stack, below the default Layer 1.

7. **Double-click the template layer in the Layers panel to open the Layer Options dialog box. Uncheck the Dim Images option and click OK.**

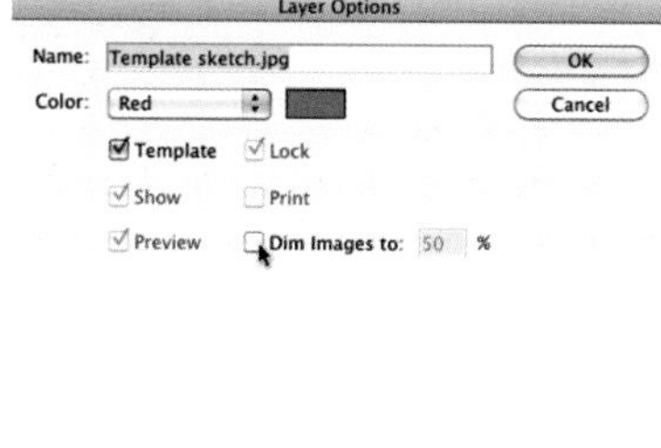

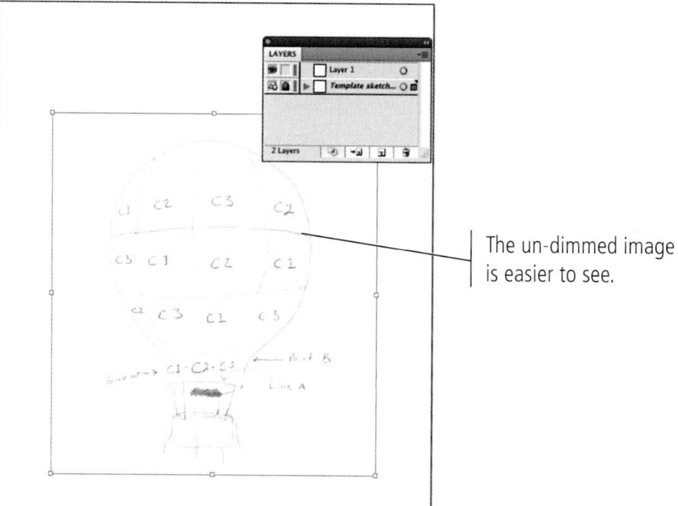

The un-dimmed image is easier to see.

8. **Double-click Layer 1 to open the Layer Options dialog box. Rename the layer** Balloon 1 **and click OK.**

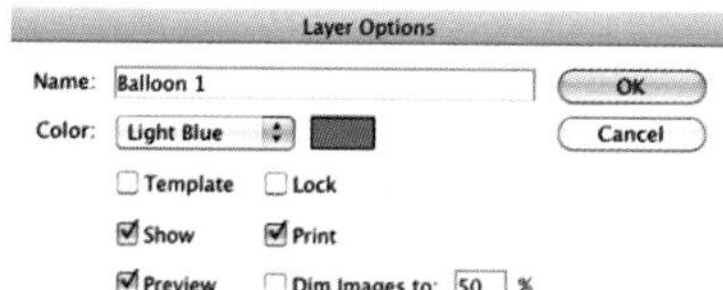

9. **Click away from the placed sketch image to deselect it.**

10. **Save the file as an Illustrator file named** balloons.ai **in your WIP>Festival folder, and then continue to the next exercise.**

Use the Pen Tool to Trace the Sketch

As you discovered in Project 1, many objects can be drawn with the basic shape tools. The true power of Illustrator, however, comes from being able to draw just as you would on a piece of paper — including freeform objects that have no basis in geometric shapes. You used the Pencil tool in Project 1 to begin working with custom artwork. In this project, you use the Pen tool, which provides far more power to control the precise position of every line in a drawing. In fact, many believe the Pen tool is the most powerful and important tool in the Illustrator Tools panel.

When you draw with the Pen tool, an anchor point marks the end of a line segment, and the point handles determine the shape of that segment. That's the basic definition of a geometric vector. Fortunately, you don't need to be a mathematician to master the Pen tool because Illustrator handles the underlying geometry for you.

Each segment in a path has two anchoring end points and two associated handles. In the following image, we first clicked to create Point A and dragged to the right (without releasing the mouse button) to create Handle A1. We then clicked and dragged to create Point B and Handle B1; Handle B2 was automatically created as a reflection of B1 (Point B is a smooth symmetrical point).

> **Note:**
>
> *The lines you create by connecting anchor points and pulling handles are called* ***Bézier curves****.*

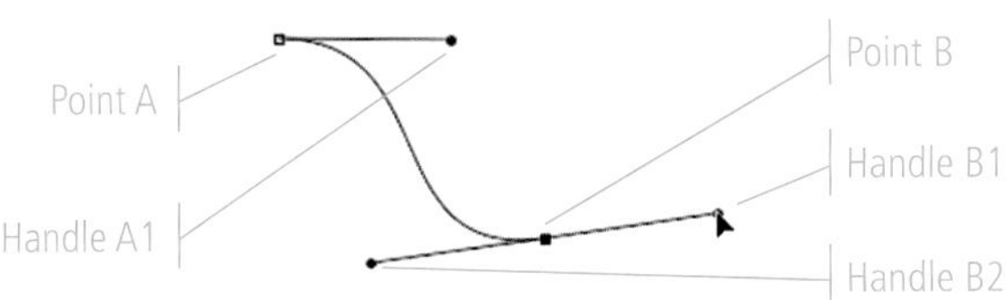

The following image shows the result of dragging Handle B1 to the left instead of to the right. Notice the difference in the curve, as compared to the curve above. When you drag the handle, the segment arcs away from the direction of the handle.

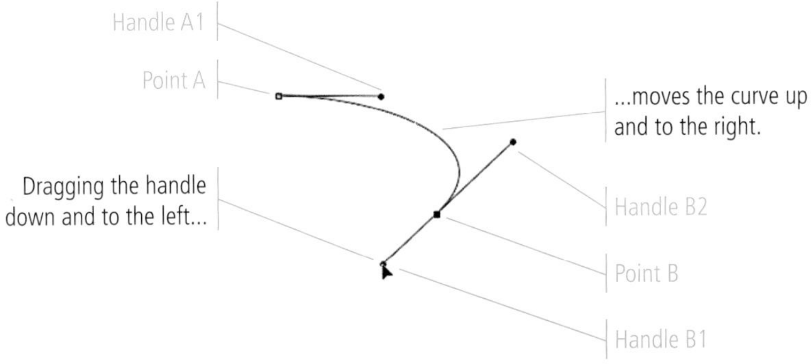

It's important to understand that every curved segment is connected to two handles. In this image, dragging the handle to the right pulls out the arc of the connected segment. You could change the shape of Segment A by dragging either Handle A1 or B2.

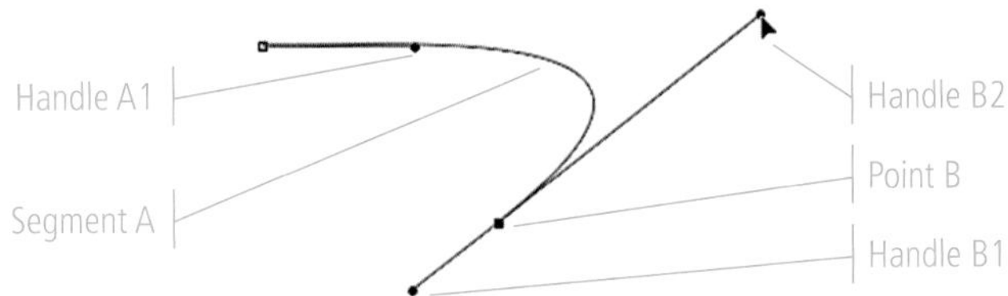

The final concept you should understand about anchors and handles (for now, at least) is that clicking and dragging to create a point creates a smooth symmetrical point. Dragging one handle of a smooth point also changes the other handle of that point. In the image shown below, dragging Handle B1 also moves Handle B2, which affects the shape of Segment A.

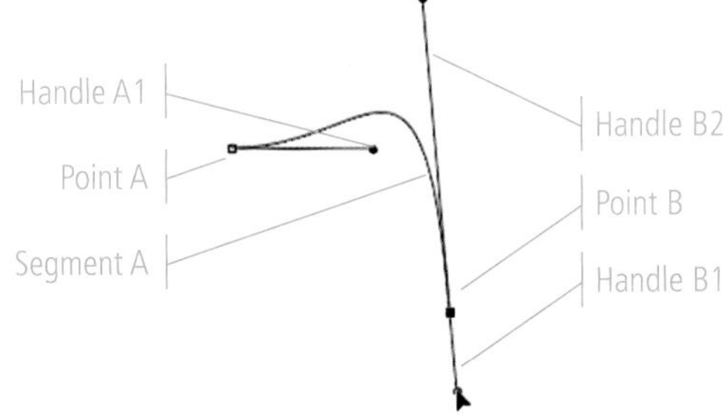

You can create corner points by simply clicking with the Pen tool instead of clicking and dragging. Corner points do not have their own handles; the connected segments are controlled by the handles of the other associated anchor points.

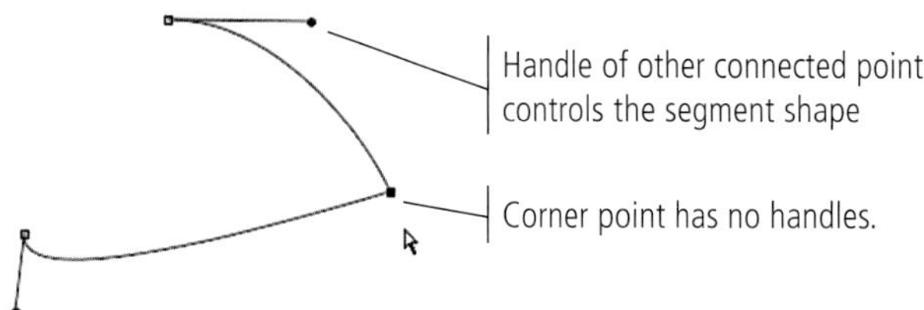

Handle of other connected point controls the segment shape
Corner point has no handles.

You can convert a symmetrical point into a smooth point by clicking the point with the Convert Anchor Point tool (nested under the Pen tool), or click and drag a corner point to convert it to a smooth point. If you click and drag a specific handle with the Convert Anchor Point tool, you can move one handle without affecting the opposing handle of the same point.

1. **With balloons.ai open, choose the Pen tool in the Tools panel.**

2. **Using the Control panel, set the stroke to 1-pt black and the fill to None.**

3. **Click with the Pen tool to place the first anchor point on the left side of the balloon where the round part meets the flat base.**

   We typically find it easier to start drawing at a corner (if one exists).

Note:

As you draw, zoom in as necessary to view different parts of the sketch.

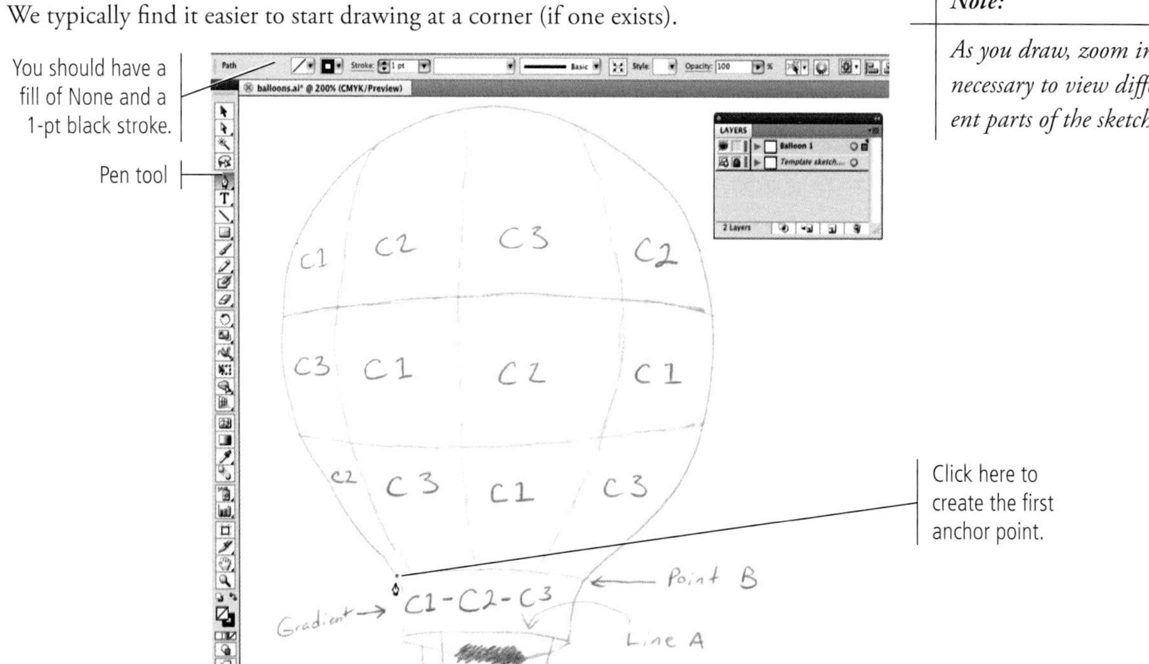

You should have a fill of None and a 1-pt black stroke.
Pen tool
Click here to create the first anchor point.
C1
C2
C3
C2
C3
C1
C2
C1
C2
C3
C1
C3
Point B
Gradient
C1-C2-C3
Line A

4. **Click the right side of the balloon (at Point B in the sketch) and immediately drag right and slightly down to create handles for the second point. When the segment between the two points matches the line in the sketch, release the mouse button.**

   When you click and drag without releasing the mouse button, you create handles, which determine the shape of the segment that connects the two points.

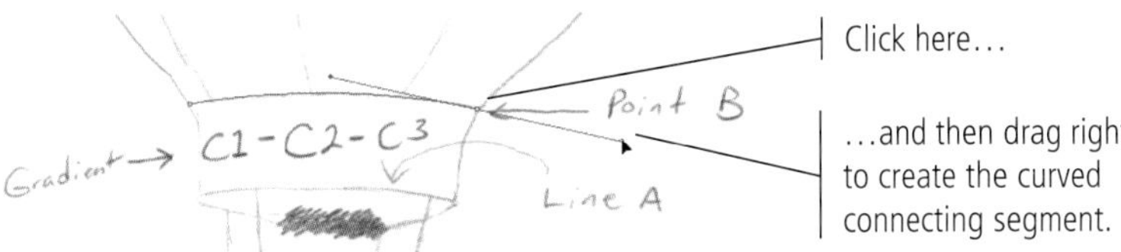

5. **Click again on the second anchor point and release the mouse button without dragging.**

   Clicking a smooth point as you draw converts it to a corner point, removing the outside handle from the point; the inside handle that defines the shape of the connecting segment remains in place. This allows you to change direction as you draw.

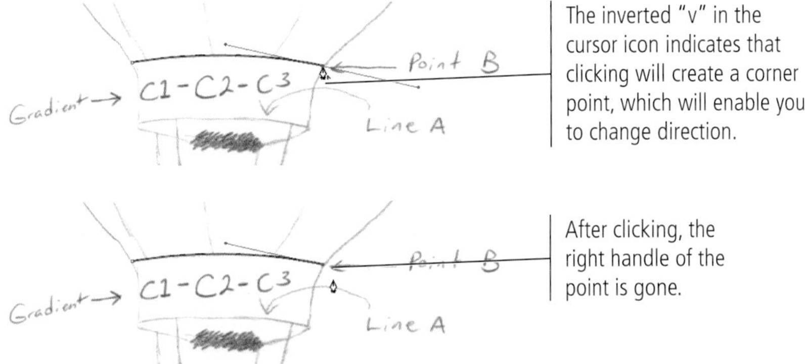

Gradient →
C1-C2-C3
Point B
Line A
The inverted "v" in the cursor icon indicates that clicking will create a corner point, which will enable you to change direction.
Gradient →
C1-C2-C3
Point B
Line A
After clicking, the right handle of the point is gone.

Note:

If you're editing an existing path, you can click a point with the Convert Anchor Point tool (nested under the Pen tool) to change a smooth point to a corner point. You can also click and drag to change an existing corner point to a smooth point.

6. **Option/Alt-click the second anchor point, hold down the mouse button, and pull slightly up and right to generate a new handle for the right side of the anchor point.**

   Pulling the new handle determines the direction of the next segment you create. The curve will bend in the direction of the new handle.

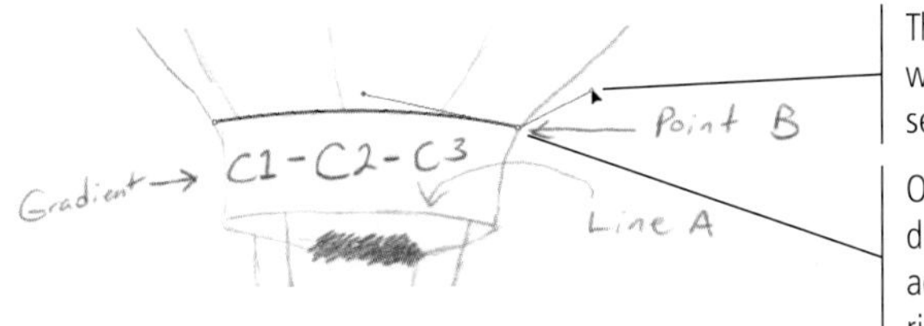

The handle you drag will define the next segment shape.

Option/Alt-click and drag from this point to add a handle on the right side of the point.

7. **Click and drag to create a new point (with handles) on the outside edge of the balloon where the C3 section meets the C1 section.**

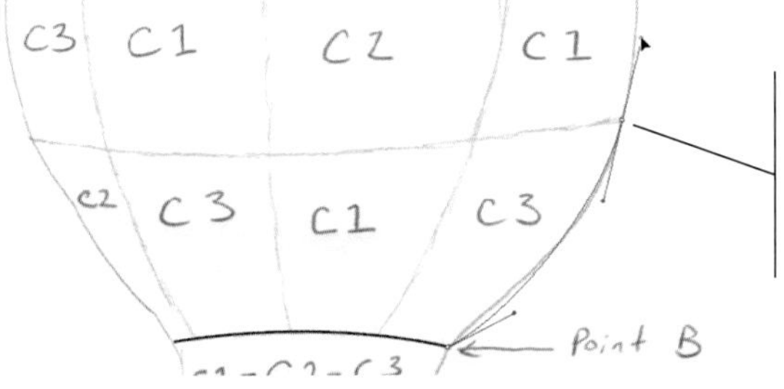

Click here and immediately drag up and right until the connecting segment matches the shape of the sketched line.

Note:

When we say "click and drag", you should hold down the mouse button until the end of the step.

8. **Continue adding points and handles to outline the entire outside edge of the balloon.**

9. **Click the original point without dragging to close the shape.**

   When you return to the original point, the cursor shows a small hollow circle. This indicates that clicking the existing point will close the shape.

> *Note:*
>
> *As a general rule, use as few points as necessary to create a shape with the Pen tool.*

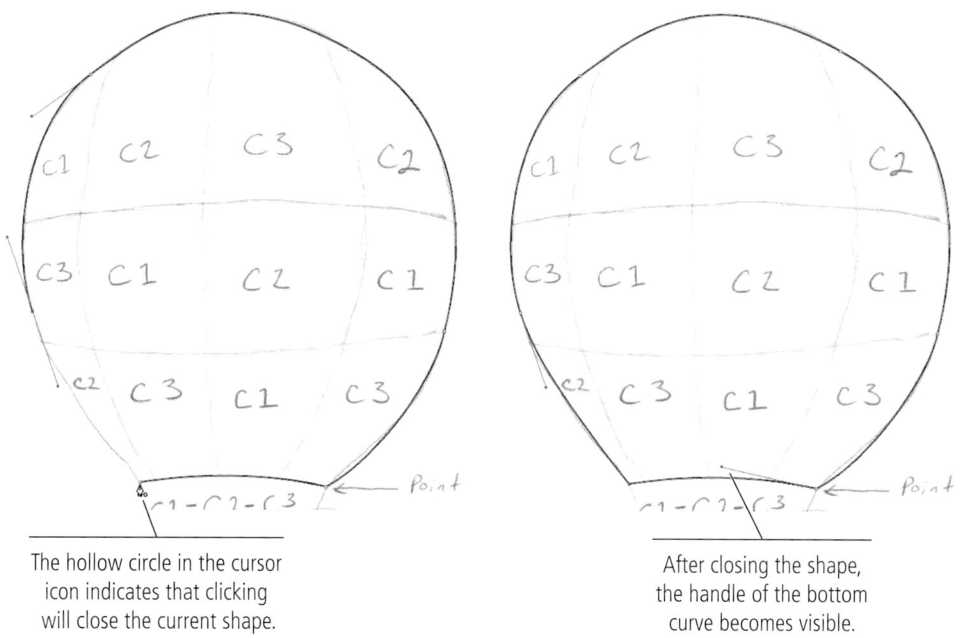

The hollow circle in the cursor icon indicates that clicking will close the current shape.

After closing the shape, the handle of the bottom curve becomes visible.

10. **Using the Direct Selection tool, click Point B to select that anchor point.**

    Depending on your precision when you dragged the handles, some curves might not match the sketch. When tracing a hand-drawn sketch, however, your shape doesn't need to be exact — but it should be close. You can use the Direct Selection tool to edit any specific anchor point or segment.

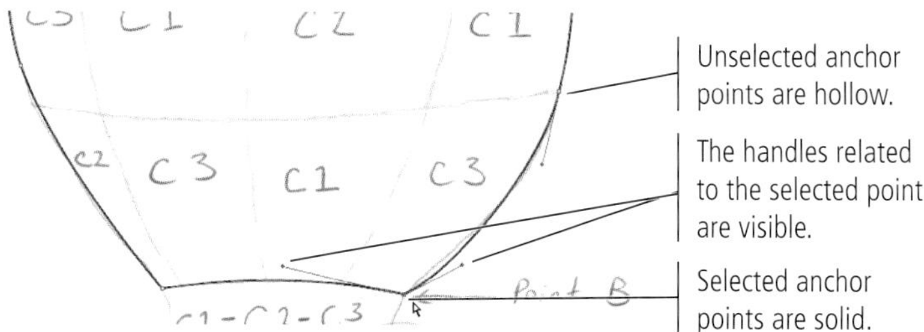

Unselected anchor points are hollow.

The handles related to the selected point are visible.

Selected anchor points are solid.

11. **Use the Direct Selection tool to make any adjustments you feel necessary. You can move specific anchor points by dragging them to a new position, and/or drag handles to adjust curve segments that connect two anchor points.**

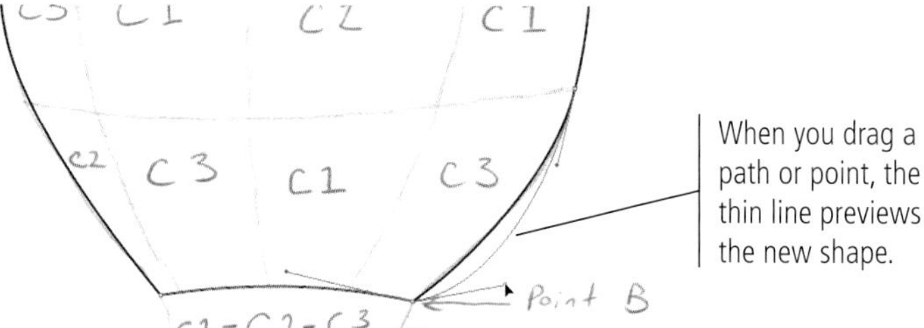

When you drag a path or point, the thin line previews the new shape.

12. **Save the file and continue to the next exercise.**

Select and Edit Complex Paths

In Illustrator, you can manipulate and change your drawings until they precisely match your vision for the artwork. You can use numerous options to select and modify shapes — or parts of shapes — so you can create exactly what you need, regardless of what is already on the artboard.

1. **With `balloons.ai` open, choose the Direct Selection tool.**

2. **With nothing selected, click the horizontal segment that represents the bottom of the balloon shape.**

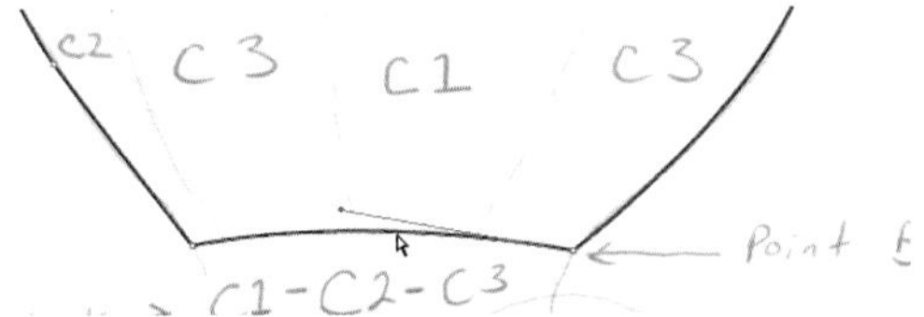

3. **Choose Edit>Copy to copy the selected segment.**

4. **Choose Object>Hide>Selection.**

   The Hide command affects only the selected object(s). The object is still on the artboard but not visible, and the layer is still visible.

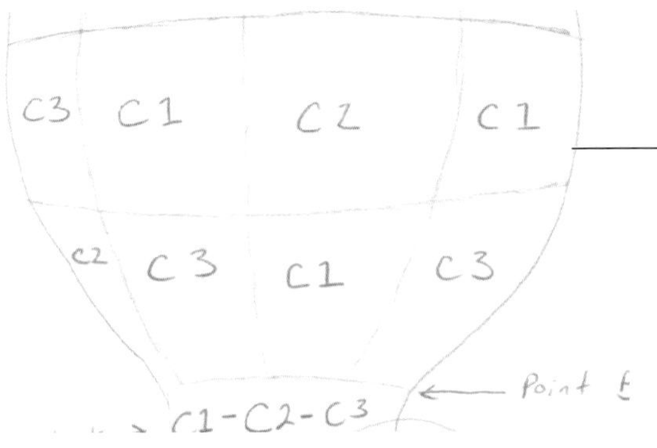

Even though you selected only the bottom segment of the balloon shape, the entire balloon shape is now hidden; you can't hide a single segment of a shape.

5. **Choose Edit>Paste in Front.**

   The segment you copied is pasted in exactly the same place as the original. Because you selected the segment with the Direct Selection tool, only that segment (not the entire object) was copied and pasted.

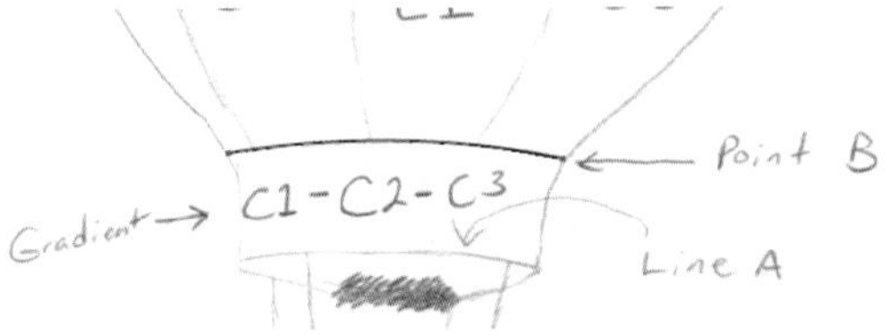

6. **Choose the Pen tool in the Tools panel and move the cursor over the right open endpoint.**

   The diagonal line in the cursor indicates that clicking will connect to the existing opening endpoint.

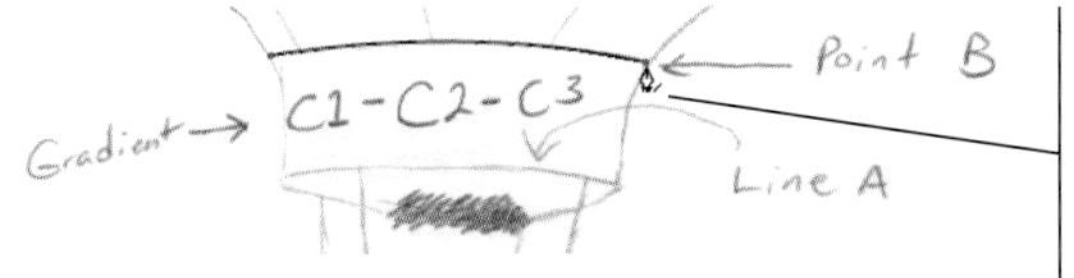

A diagonal line in the cursor icon indicates that clicking will connect to the open endpoint so you can continue drawing the shape.

> ***Note:***
>
> *If you turn on Smart Guides (View>Smart Guides), the cursor shows the word "anchor" when the cursor is over an existing anchor point. This can be helpful if you are trying to connect to an open endpoint of an existing line (as in Step 6).*

7. **Click to resume working from the open endpoint.**

8. **Click and drag to create the bottom-right point of the balloon shape. Drag the handle down and right until the connecting curve matches the shape of the line in the sketch.**

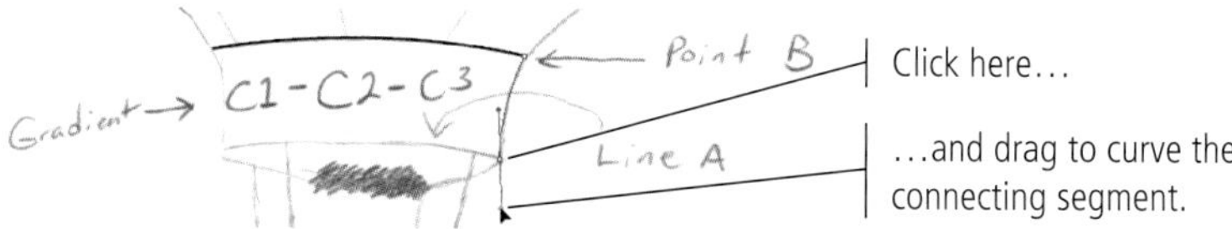

9. **Click the point from Step 8 to remove the handle from the outside of the point, and then click and drag again to create the bottom-left point.**

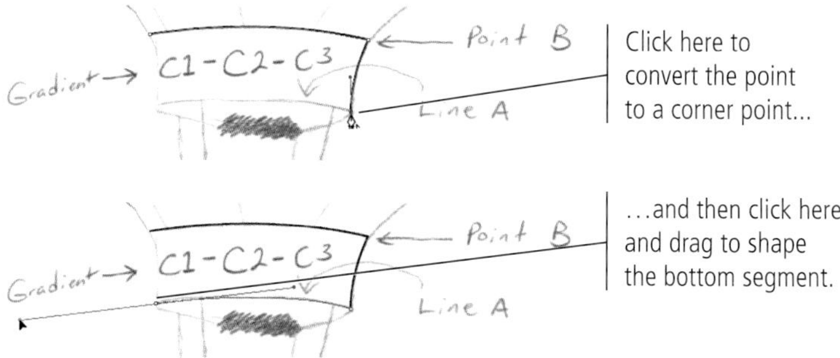

10. **Move the cursor over the open left endpoint of the top segment and click to close the shape.**

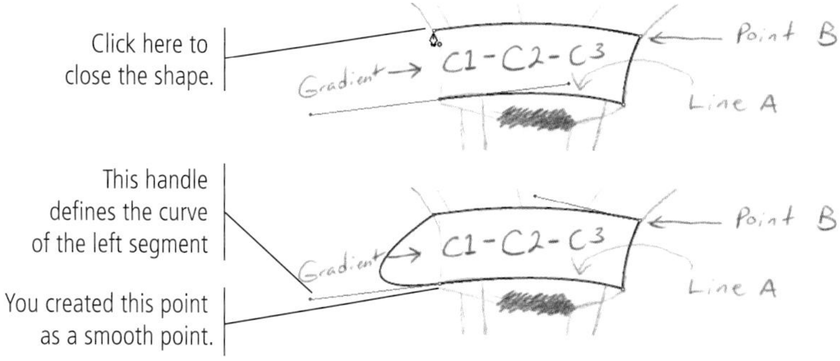

11. **Choose the Direct Selection tool in the Tools panel. Press Option/Alt, and then click and drag the outside handle of the bottom-left point. Drag the handle right until the left segment matches the shape of the line in the sketch.**

    Remember, the Direct Selection tool allows you to adjust individual anchor points and handles. Option/Alt-dragging one handle of a smooth point converts the point to a corner point, but leaves both handles in place. This method allows you to change the direction of an existing point, but leave the opposite curve intact.

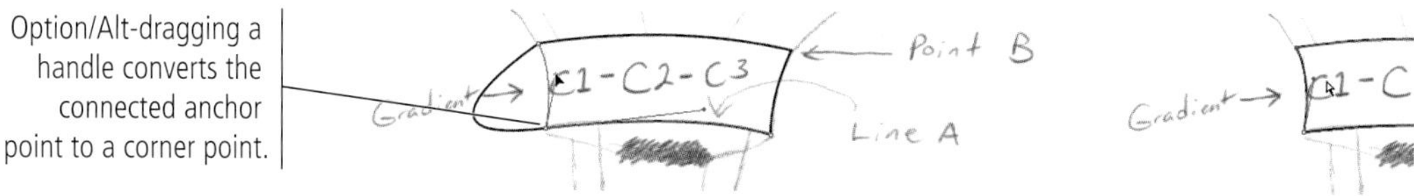

12. **Save the file and continue to the next exercise.**

Build Shapes from Overlapping Paths

The Shape Builder tool, new in Illustrator CS5, makes it very easy to break apart overlapping objects into component pieces. This tool offers similar functionality to the Pathfinder, but on a piece-by-piece basis rather than for entire selected shapes. In this exercise, you will use the Shape Builder tool to break up the balloon into the individual patches that are shown on the sketch.

1. **With balloons.ai open, choose Object>Show All.**

   Although the Hide command affects only selected objects, the Show All command is not selective; all hidden objects become visible.

2. **Using either the Selection or Direct Selection tool, select only the bottom shape and choose Object>Lock>Selection.**

   Because the lower shape is now locked, you can't select it.

   You can't lock only part of an object, so the entire object is locked even if you only select one of the segments or anchor points using the Direct Selection tool.

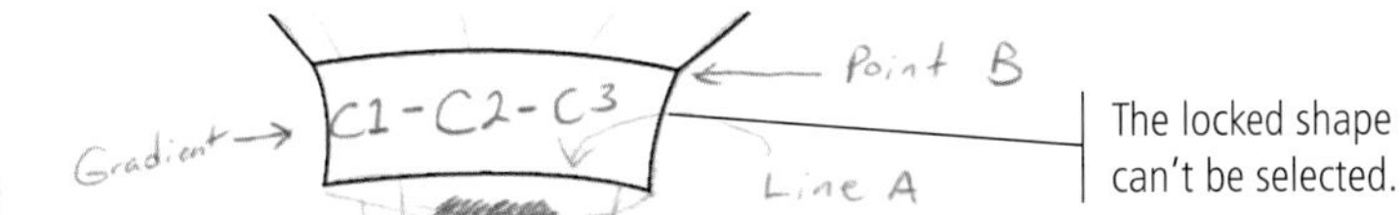

3. **Using the sketch as a guide, use the Pen tool to create the leftmost vertical line in the balloon, starting and stopping past the edges of the balloon shape (as shown in the following image).**

   You are going to use the Shape Builder tool to divide the balloon into the necessary shapes. For this process to work properly, the dividing lines need to be at least on top of the outside shape; to be sure, you need to extend the lines farther than they need to be.

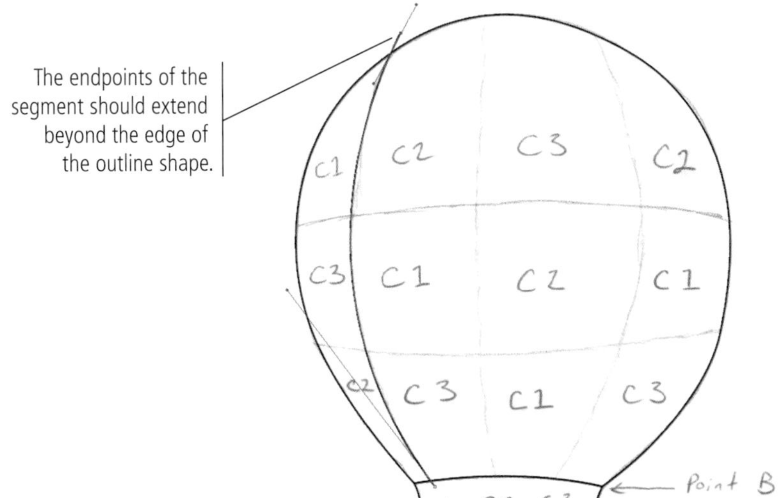

4. **While the Pen tool is still active, press Command/Control to temporarily access the Selection tool and click away from the line to deselect it.**

   When you release the mouse button, you return to the Pen tool. This technique allows you to easily deselect the current path and then continue to draw the next, unconnected path.

Note:

Remember, simply click away from an object with the Selection or Direct Selection tool to deselect it.

You can also press Command/Control-Shift-A to deselect the current selection.

5. **Repeat Steps 3–4 to create the remaining vertical and horizontal lines of the balloon.**

   If you don't deselect the path from Step 3 before clicking to draw the next line, the third click would create a segment that is connected to the last place you clicked (on the first line). In the context of this exercise, a single line with multiple anchor points is much more difficult to control than two separate lines with open endpoints.

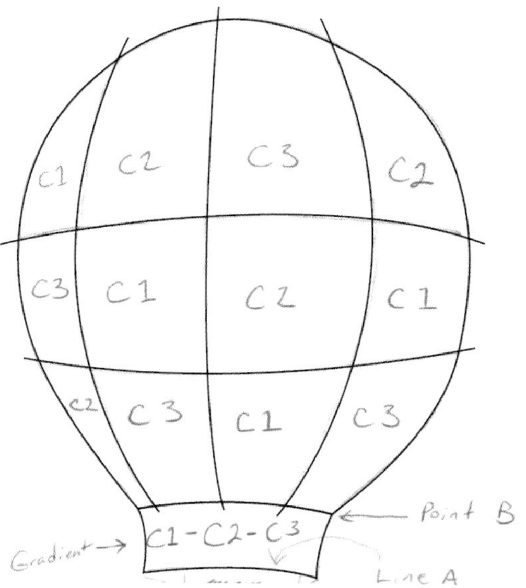

Note:

If necessary, use the Direct Selection tool to adjust the anchor points and handles of the line until they match the sketch.

6. **Choose the Selection tool in the Tools panel, and then choose Select>All.**

   Because the bottom shape is locked, it is not included in the selection.

Note:

Press Command/Control-A to select everything in the drawing space that is not locked.

7. **Choose the Shape Builder tool in the Tools panel, and then reset the default fill and stroke colors.**

8. **Move the cursor over the top-left section of the balloon (C1 in the sketch).**

   The Shape Builder tool identifies overlapping areas of selected objects, which is why you had to select the pieces in Step 6.

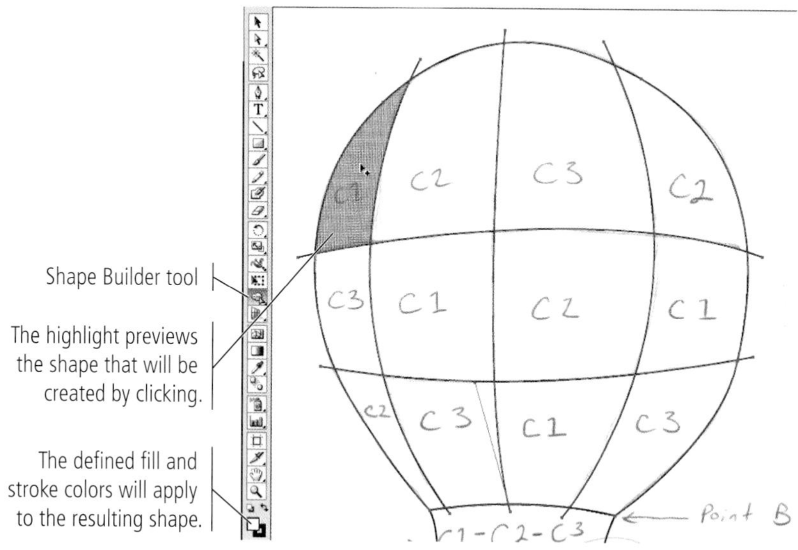

9. **Click the highlighted area to create the new shape.**

   Because you set the Fill color to white, the resulting shape obscures the sketch behind it. This helps to identify which pieces you have already created.

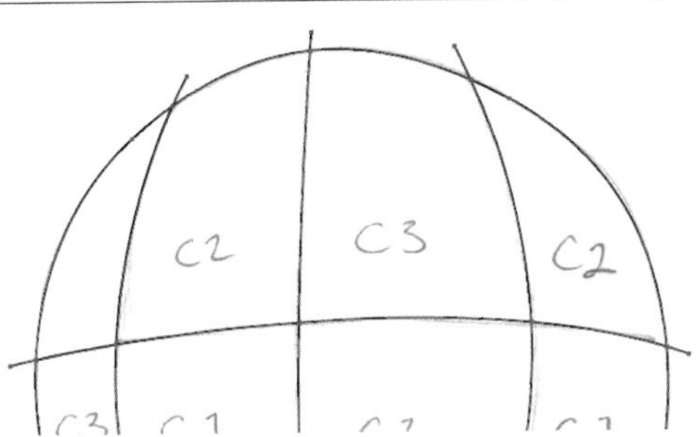

10. **Repeat Steps 8–9 for the remaining 11 pieces of the balloon.**

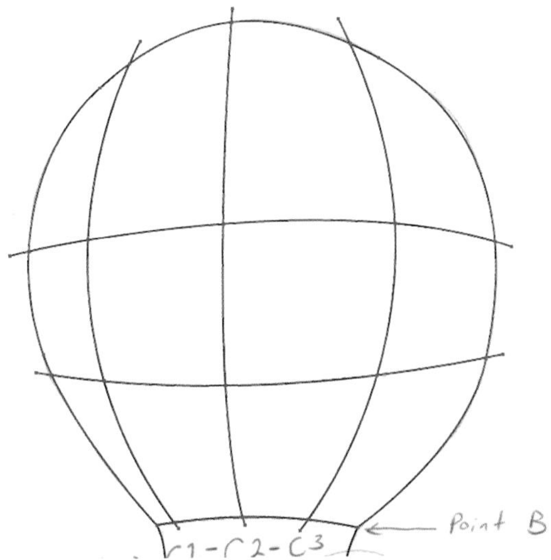

11. **Press Option/Alt, and move the cursor over the first line segment outside the right balloon edge. When the line segment is highlighted and the cursor shows a minus sign in the icon, click the segment to remove it.**

    The Shape Builder tool can be used to both create and remove shapes. Pressing Option/Alt switches the tool into Erase mode so you can remove paths or shapes.

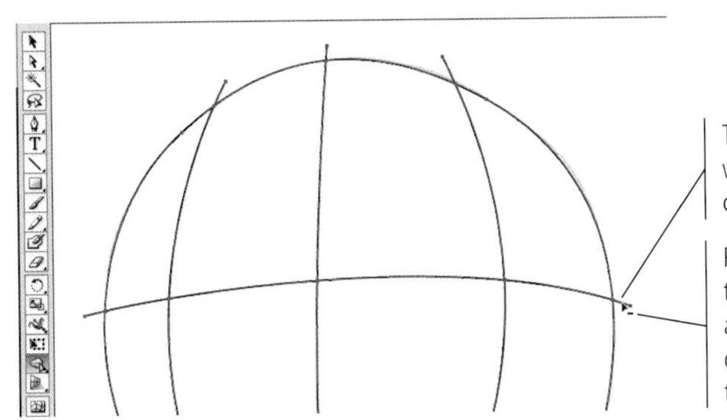

The area or path that will be affected by clicking is highlighted.

Pressing Option/Alt with the Shape Builder tool allows you to remove areas or paths, as indicated by the "–" in the cursor icon.

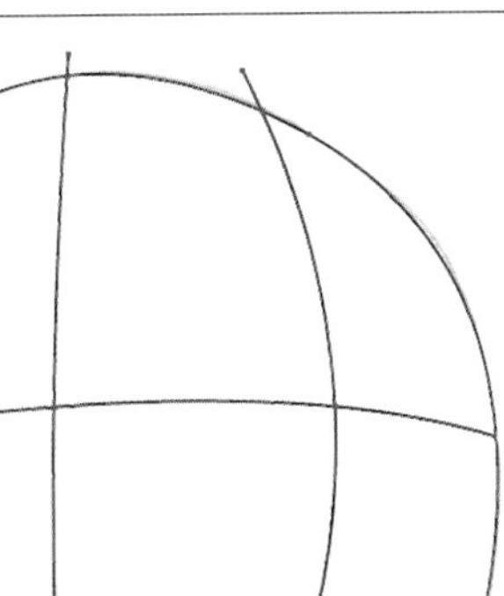

12. **Repeat Step 11 to remove the remaining extraneous line segments.**

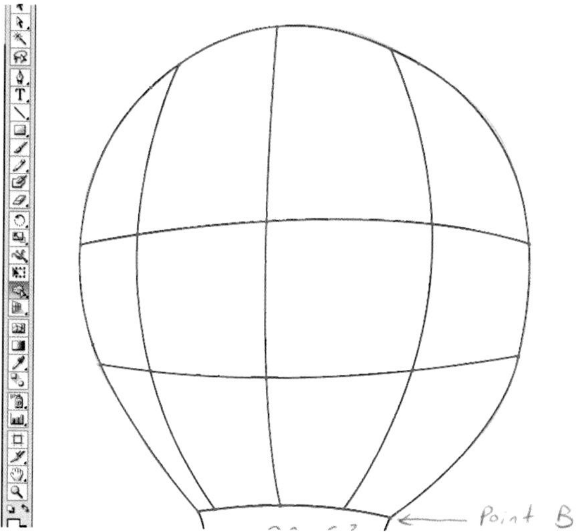

13. **Save the file and continue to the next exercise.**

More on the Shape Builder Tool

ILLUSTRATOR FOUNDATIONS

As you just saw, the Shape Builder tool makes it very easy to cut apart overlapping objects into pieces. The tool offers a number of options that can significantly enhance your ability to create complex, sophisticated artwork.

If a small opening exists in a path, you can activate **Gap Detection** settings to overlook small, medium, large, or custom-sized gaps in the open paths. This option is especially useful if the Consider Open Filled Paths as Closed option is not checked.

The **Pick Color From** menu determines whether the tool recognizes all swatches in the file or only colors that are actually used in the artwork.

You can also use the **Highlight** options to determine what, if anything, is highlighted when you move the tool cursor over a shape.

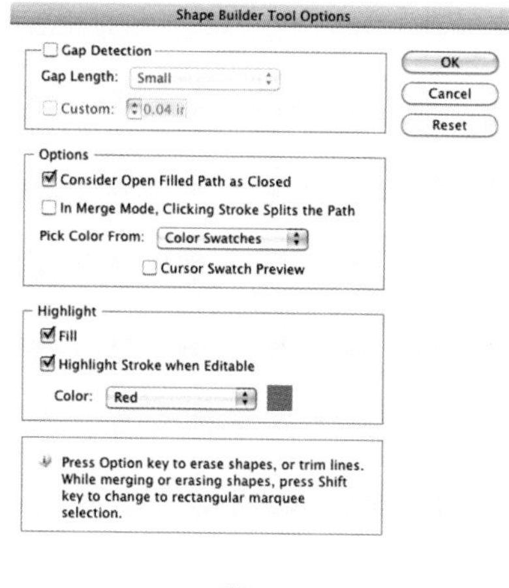

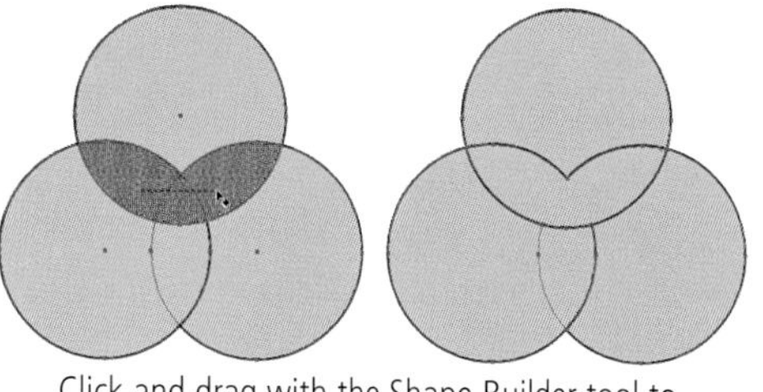

Click and drag with the Shape Builder tool to combine multiple pieces into a single shape.

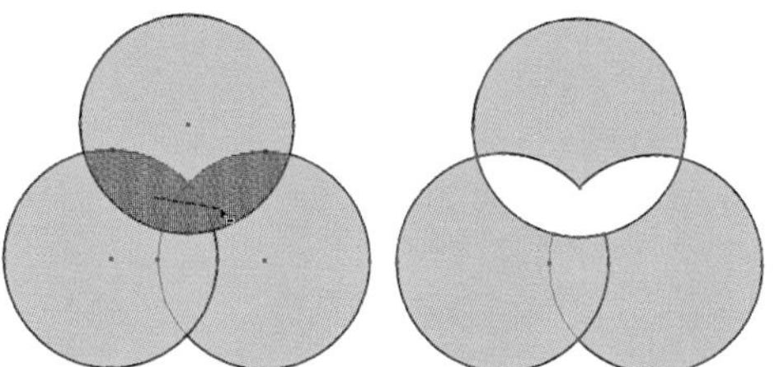

Option/Alt-click and drag with the Shape Builder tool to remove multiple pieces at the same time.

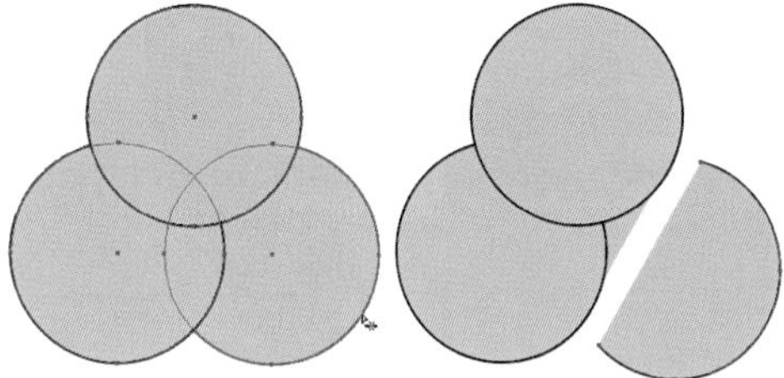

When In Merge Mode, Clicking Stroke Splits the Path is checked in the tool options dialog box, click a path to cut apart the path at the nearest anchor points.

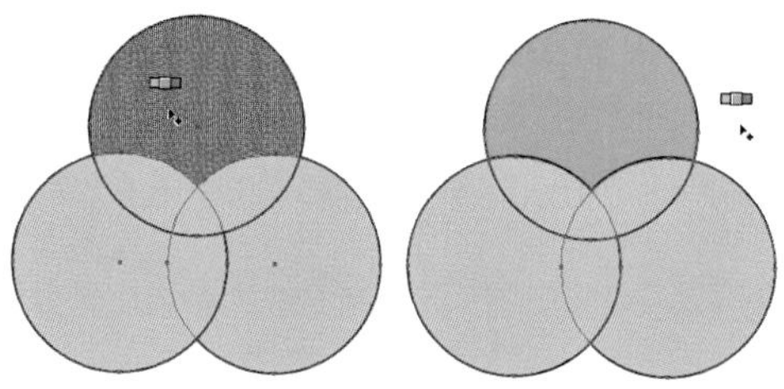

When Cursor Swatch Preview is checked in the tool options dialog box, three swatches appear above the tool cursor. You can use the Left and Right Arrow keys to move through the available color swatches.

Adjust Anchor Points and Handles

Practice is the best way to master Bézier curves. In this exercise, you use the techniques you have already learned to adjust and fine-tune the filled shapes created in the previous exercise.

1. **With balloons.ai open, choose the Direct Selection tool.**

2. **Deselect all objects by clicking away from the current selection, then click the top-left segment of the balloon's outer edge (labeled C1 in the sketch).**

   Remember, clicking a segment with the Direct Selection tool reveals the handles that define the shape of the segment.

3. **If your segment includes an extra anchor point, place the Pen tool cursor over the point and click to delete it.**

   Your original points might have been in different places, depending on where you clicked to create the initial outline shape. When the Shape Builder tool divides the objects into separate shapes, it creates anchor points as necessary at the intersections, but also maintains the original points — which are not always necessary.

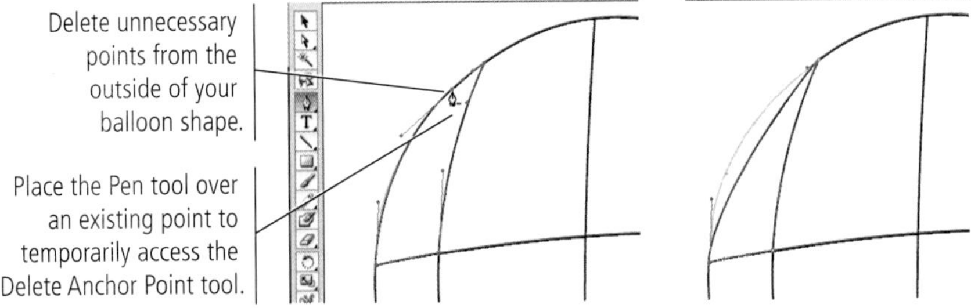

Delete unnecessary points from the outside of your balloon shape.
Place the Pen tool over an existing point to temporarily access the Delete Anchor Point tool.

4. **Using the Direct Selection tool, click the top handle of the selected segment and drag up and left.**

   By adjusting the segment, you can create the "pillow" appearance of the panels of a hot air balloon. The point where the two shapes meet is unaffected by dragging the point handle.

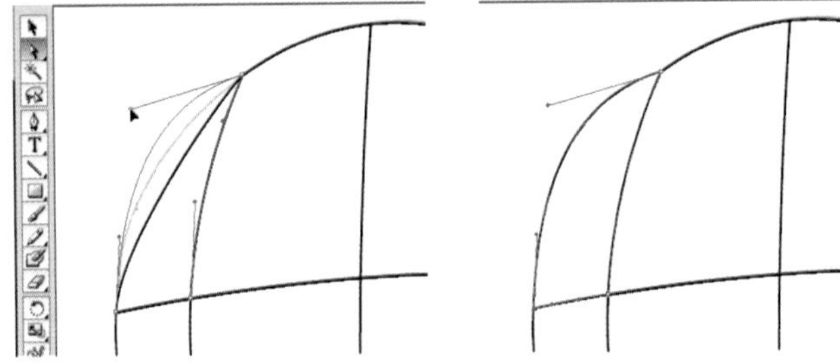

5. **Repeat Steps 2–4 to adjust the top edges of the other three top shapes to remove unnecessary anchor points and create a similar "pillow" effect on the four top pieces of the balloon.**

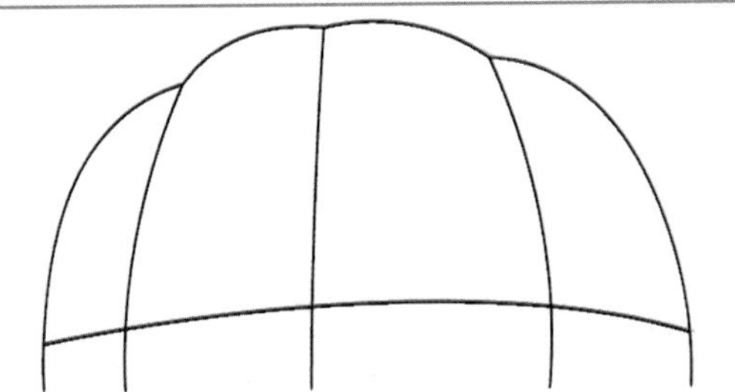

6. **Choose Object>Unlock All.**

   As with the Show All command, the Unlock All command affects all individually locked objects, regardless of when the Lock command was applied.

7. **Select the now-unlocked shape that makes up the band around the bottom of the balloon and change its fill to white.**

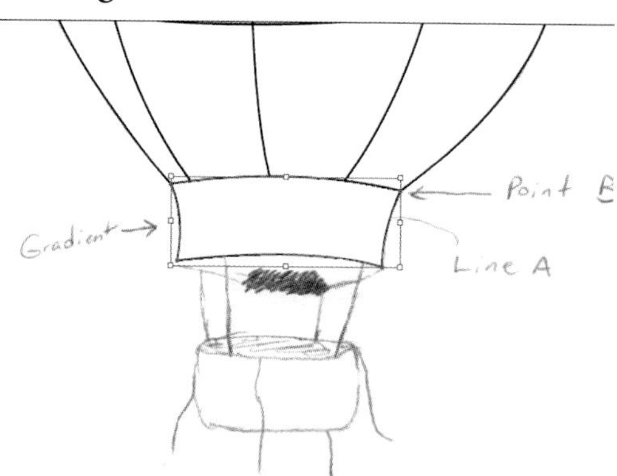

8. **Save the file and continue to the next exercise.**

Understanding Anchor Point and Bézier Curve Tools

Keep the following points in mind as you work with the Pen tool (and its four nested variations) and Bézier curves.

Using the Direct Selection tool...

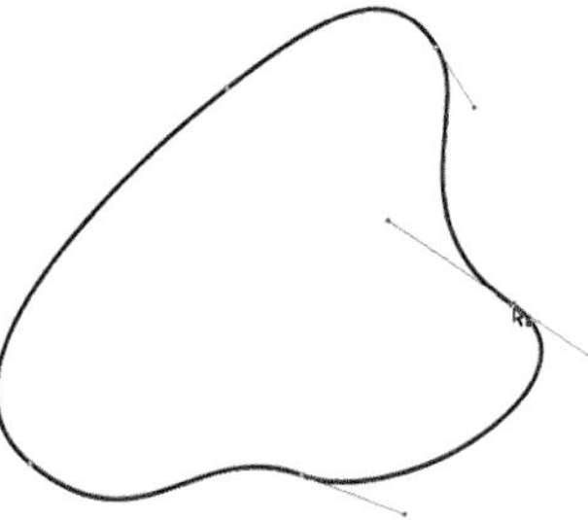

Click a specific anchor point to select it and show all handles that relate to that point.

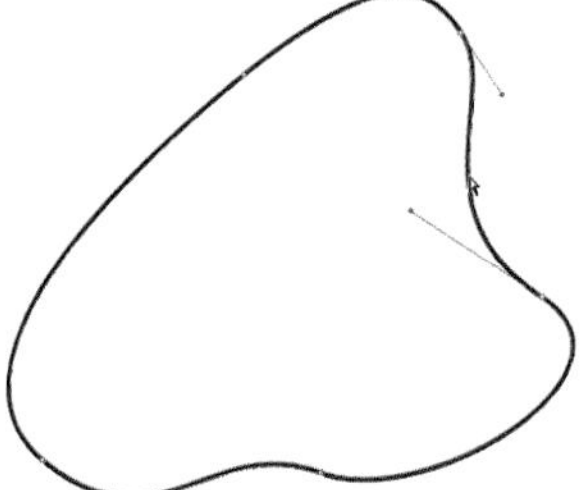

Click a specific segment to select it and show all handles that relate to that segment.

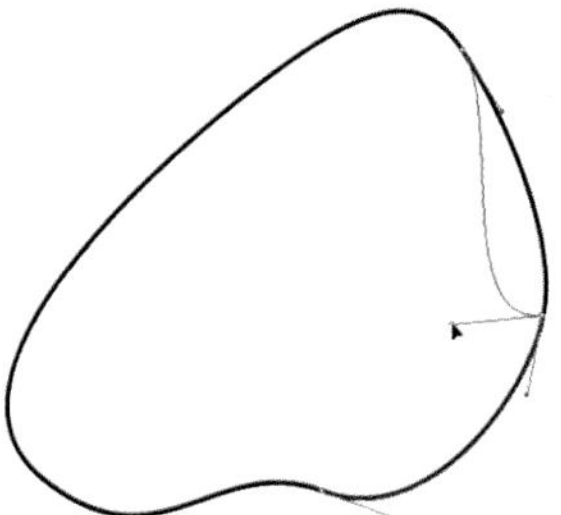

Option/Alt drag a handle of a smooth point to convert it to a corner point.

Using the Pen tool...

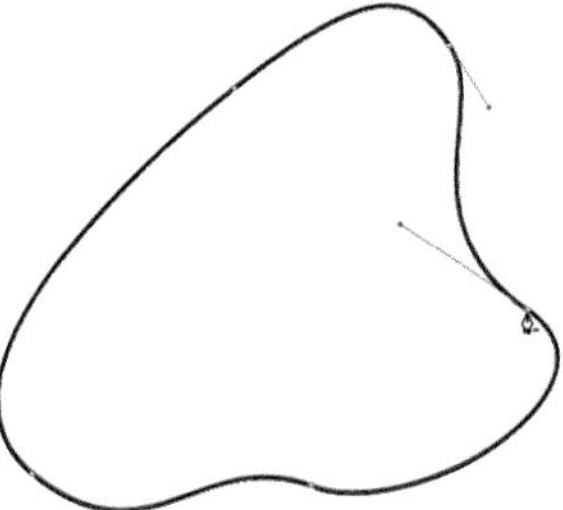

Place the cursor over an existing point to temporarily access the Delete Anchor Point tool.

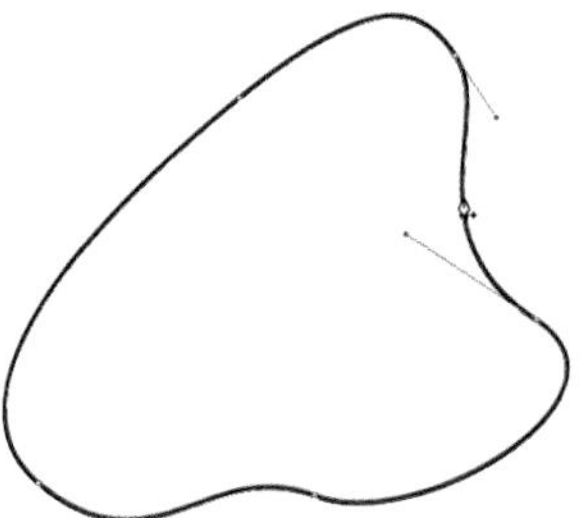

Place the cursor over an existing segment to temporarily access the Add Anchor Point tool.

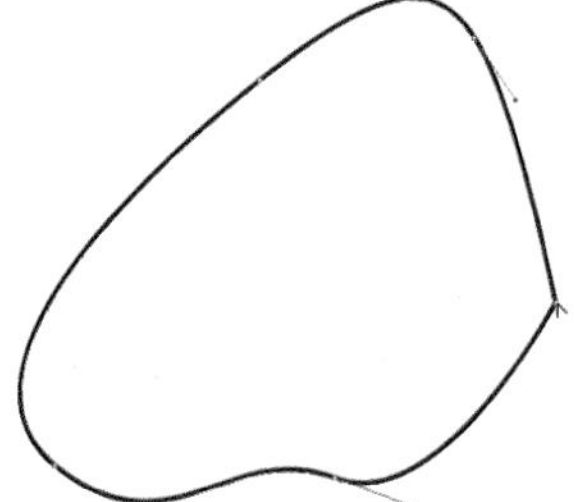

Press Option/Alt and place the cursor over an existing point to temporarily access the Convert Anchor Point tool.

Add Detail with the Pencil and Line Segment Tools

Drawing with the Pencil tool is similar to sketching with a pencil and paper. The Pencil tool is a good choice if you want to create an object that appears sketchy or hand-drawn. Illustrator adds anchor points and handles as necessary to create the path you draw; you don't have control over where the anchor points are placed, but you can edit the path however you prefer.

1. **With balloons.ai open, select the Pencil tool in the Tools panel. Set the fill to white and the stroke to 1-pt black.**

2. **Double-click the Pencil tool in the Tools panel to open the Pencil Tool Options dialog box.**

3. **Set the Fidelity value to 2 pixels and Smoothness to 1%. Make sure Keep Selected is checked and Edit Selected Paths is not checked, and then click OK.**

   Low Fidelity and Smoothness settings result in fewer anchor points, which makes it easier to edit later (especially when working with small shapes).

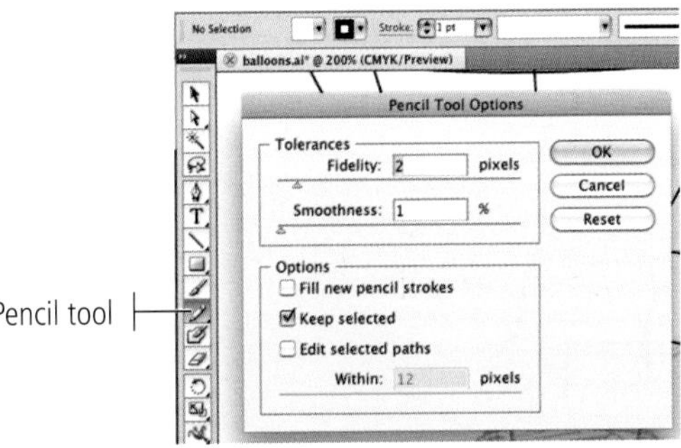

Editing Anchor Points with the Control Panel

ILLUSTRATOR FOUNDATIONS

When you are working with Bézier paths, the Control panel provides a number of options for editing selected anchor points.

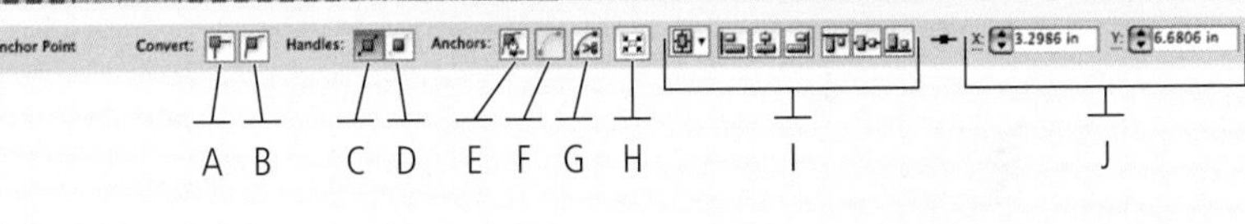

A Convert Selected Anchor Points to Corner. This button removes the direction handles from both sides of the selected point(s).

B Convert Selected Anchor Points to Smooth. This button adds symmetrical direction handles to both sides of the selected point(s).

C Show Handles for Multiple Selected Anchor Points. If this option is toggled on, direction handles display for all selected points.

D Hide Handles for Multiple Selected Anchor Points. If this option is toggled on, direction handles are not visible when more than one point is selected.

E Remove Selected Anchor Points. This button removes the selected point from the path. If the removed point was between two other points, the connecting segment is not removed.

F Connect Selected End Points. This button has the same effect as the Object>Path>Join command.

G Cut Path at Selected Anchor Points. This button results in two overlapping, open endpoints where the selected point was previously a single point.

H Isolate Selected Object. This button enters isolation mode with the object containing the selected anchor point(s). If points are selected on more than one object, this button is not available.

I Align Options. When only one point is selected, you can use the Align to Artboard option to position the point. If multiple points are selected, you can use these options relative to each other (for example, aligning them both horizontally and vertically to move two points to the same exact position).

J Point Position. Use the X and Y fields to define a specific position for the selected point. You can also use mathematical operations to move a point relative to its current position (e.g., move it left by typing "-1" after the current X value).

4. **Starting at the top-right corner, carefully trace the outline of the basket. As you approach the starting point, press Option/Alt and release the mouse button to close the basket shape.**

   As you drag the Pencil tool, a dotted line shows the path you traced (and thus, the shape you created). Don't worry if the shape isn't perfect; you will clean up the path in the next step.

5. **Adjust the anchor points and handles of the resulting shape until you are satisfied with the result.**

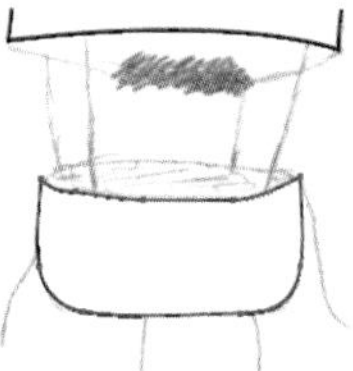

6. **Deselect the basket shape. Activate the Pencil tool, change the fill color to None, and change the stroke weight to 2 pt.**

7. **Trace the rope lines hanging from the basket. Select the two lines that appear to be behind the basket and choose Object>Arrange>Send to back.**

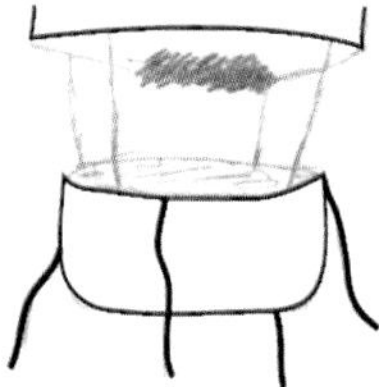

8. **Use the Line Segment tool to draw the lines that connect the basket shapes to the balloon shapes.**

   Using the Line Segment tool, you don't need to deselect after each line. The Line Segment tool also makes it much easier to create straight lines.

   These lines don't need to be perfect, because the ends will be covered by the shapes you will create in the next exercise.

9. **Change the Line Segment tool stroke weight to 1 pt, and then draw crossing diagonal lines to represent a "basket weave" texture (using the following image as a guide).**

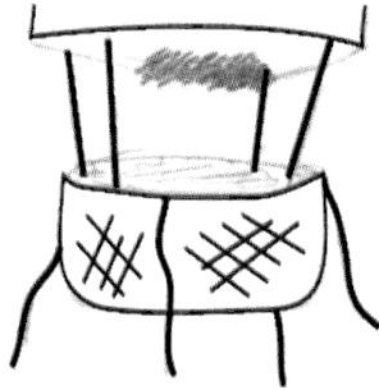

10. **Save the file and continue to the next exercise.**

Create Shapes with the Blob Brush Tool

The Blob Brush tool is used to paint filled shapes, which you can manipulate just as you would any other shape made up of anchor points and handles. In this exercise, you use the Blob Brush tool to quickly create the shapes of the inside areas of the balloon and basket.

> *Note:*
>
> *Press Command/Control-A to select all objects in the file.*

1. **With balloons.ai open, select everything on the artboard (Select>All), and lock the selection (Object>Lock>Selection).**

2. **Double-click the Blob Brush tool in the Tools panel to open the Blob Brush Tool Options dialog box.**

3. **Make sure Keep Selected is checked. Set the Fidelity value to 4 pixels and Smoothness value to 9%. In the Default Brush Options area, define a 10-pt brush size with a 0° angle and 100% Roundness. Click OK to apply the settings.**

   Like the Pencil tool, the Blob Brush tool Tolerance options determine the accuracy of the resulting shape. Higher Fidelity and Smoothness values result in finer precision, but also more anchor points on the shape. The lower half of the dialog box defines the size, angle, and roundness of the brush cursor.

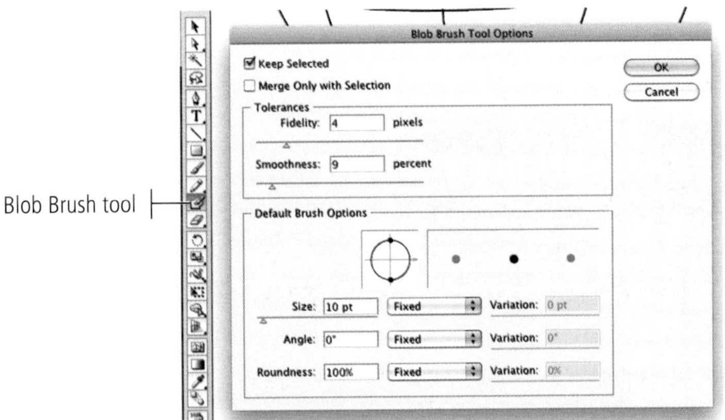

> *Note:*
>
> *Press the right bracket key ( ]) to increase the brush size by 1 point. Press the left bracket key ([ ) to reduce the brush size by 1 point.*

4. **Set the fill color to Black and the stroke to None.**

5. **At the bottom of the Tools panel, choose the choose Draw Behind option.**

   If your Tools panel is in one-column mode, the Drawing Mode options are available in a pop-up menu.

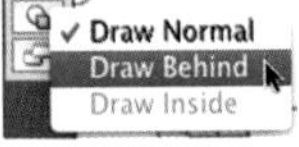

   If your Tools panel is in two-column mode, the Drawing Mode options are presented as three buttons (from left to right: Draw Normal, Draw Behind, and Draw Inside).

   When you use the Draw Behind mode, new objects are automatically placed behind the selected object(s), or at the bottom of the stacking order if nothing is selected.

> *Note:*
>
> *You can always rearrange the stacking order of objects on the same layer by using the options in the Object>Arrange menu.*

6. **Click at the right side of the balloon base and drag an arc that flows down and to the left, as shown in the following illustration.**

   When you release the mouse button, the result is a single shape that fills the entire area where you drew; overlapping areas of the shape you paint combine to make one shape.

   As you paint, the path might look a bit sketchy; however, the resulting path is smoothed based on the Smoothness option defined in the Blob Brush Tool Options dialog box.

When you draw with the Blob Brush tool, the cursor shows the size and shape of the defined brush.

Click and drag left, following this line in the sketch.

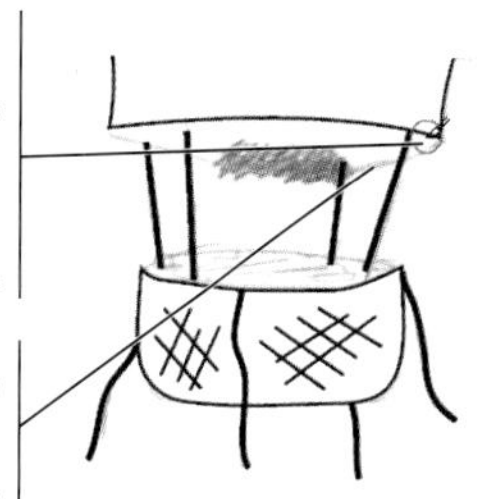

When you release the mouse button, the result is a filled shape based on where you dragged the brush cursor.

Anchor points are automatically created to define the outside edge of the shape.

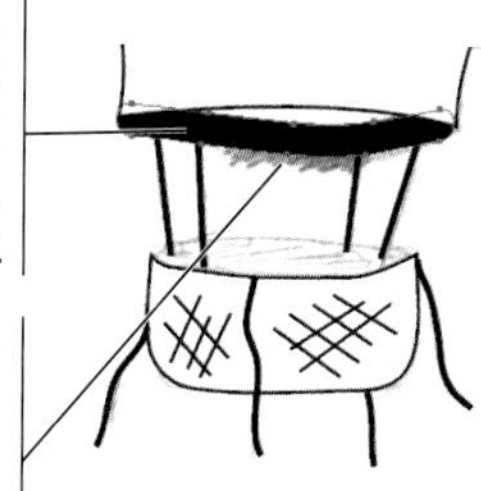

7. **With the new shape still selected, click again near the left edge and drag right to fill in the entire area inside the balloon. Continue dragging until the entire area is painted, and then release the mouse button**

Start here...

...and drag to here to fill in the entire area.

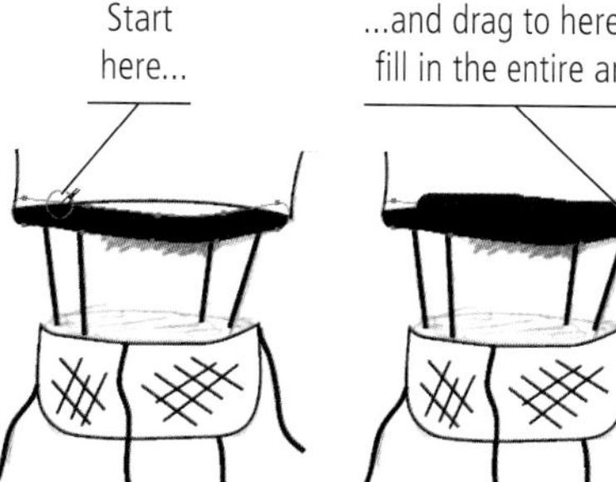

The new shape is automatically merged with the selected shape.

Because you are using the Draw Behind mode, areas behind the existing shapes are not visible.

> *Note:*
>
> *If the Merge Only with Selection option is checked in the Blob Brush Tool Options dialog box, Blob Brush shapes only automatically merge with existing, selected brush strokes. To create separate shapes from the blob paths, deselect any previously drawn shapes.*

Using the Draw Inside Mode

ILLUSTRATOR FOUNDATIONS

The Draw Inside mode, which is only available when an existing object is already selected, is an easy way to create new objects inside a **clipping path** (a shape that defines areas of other objects that will be visible; anything outside the area of the clipping path is not visible).

If you select the clipped object with the Selection tool, you can use the Edit Clipping Path and Edit Contents buttons in the Control panel to edit either shape without ungrouping and without entering isolation mode.

With the Blue rectangle selected, we switched to Draw Inside mode and drew the oval...

...then changed the oval's fill color to green.

Areas outside the originally selected shape are not visible.

These dashed lines indicate that the object is a clipping path.

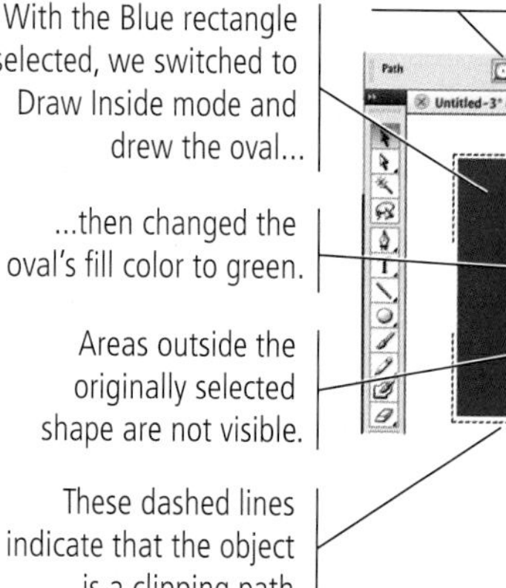

Edit Clipping Path

Edit Contents

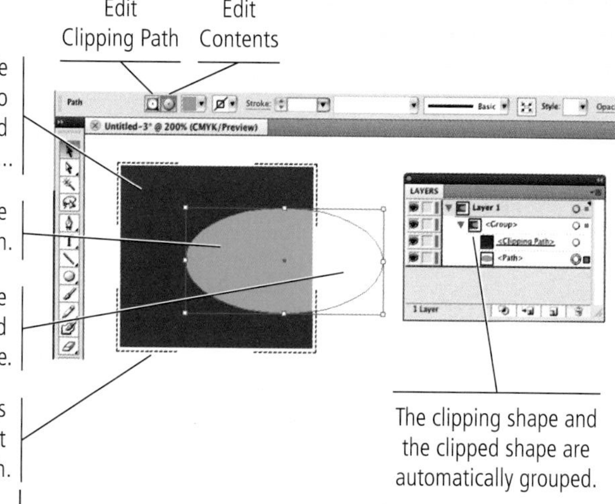

The clipping shape and the clipped shape are automatically grouped.

8. **Repeat this process to create a shape that represents the inside of the balloon basket, as shown below.**

9. **If necessary, adjust the anchor points of the two new shapes until you are satisfied with the results.**

10. **In the Tools panel, click the Drawing Mode button and choose Draw Normal.**

    The drawing mode remains at the last-used setting. Although it isn't exactly necessary to do this right now, it is very easy to forget and later accidentally draw in the wrong mode — which means you would have to undo your work in one way or another.

11. **Save the file and continue to the next stage of the project.**

Stage 2 Coloring and Painting Artwork

The CMYK color model, also called "process color," recreates the range of printable colors by overlapping layers of cyan, magenta, yellow, and black inks in varying percentages from 0–100.

Using theoretically pure pigments, a mixture of equal parts of cyan, magenta, and yellow would produce black. Real pigments, however, are not pure; the actual result of mixing these three colors usually appears as a muddy brown. The fourth color, black (K), is added to cyan, magenta, and yellow to extend the range of printable colors and allow much purer blacks to be printed. (Black is abbreviated as "K" because it is the "key" color to which others are aligned on the printing press. Using K for black also avoids confusion with blue in the RGB color model, which is used for digitally distributed files.)

In process-color printing, each of the four process colors — cyan, magenta, yellow, and black — is imaged, or separated, onto an individual printing plate. Each color separation is printed on a separate unit of a printing press. When printed on top of each other in varying percentages, the semi-transparent inks produce the range of colors in the CMYK **gamut**. Other special colors (called spot colors) are printed using specifically formulated inks as additional color separations.

 +  +  +  = 

Different color models have different ranges or gamuts of possible colors. A normal human visual system is capable of distinguishing approximately 16.7 million different colors; color reproduction systems, however, are far more limited. The RGB model has the largest gamut of the output models. The CMYK gamut is much more limited; many of the brightest and most saturated colors that can be reproduced using light (in the RGB model) cannot be reproduced using CMYK inks.

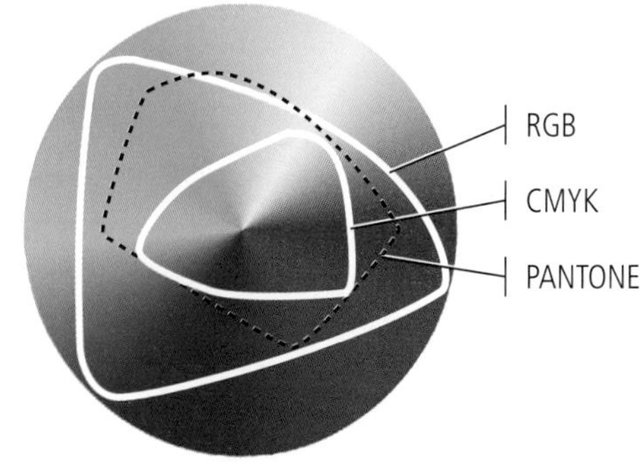

Use the Color Panel to Define Custom Swatches

As you saw in the original sketch, the balloon in this project will be filled using three different colors (indicated as C1, C2, and C3). In the next two exercises, you will use the Color panel to create the colors you need, and then save those colors as custom swatches.

1. **With balloons.ai open, choose Object>Unlock All.**

   You need to be able to select an object before you can change its color attributes. Remember, the Unlock All command unlocks all locked objects on the artboard; it does not, however, affect layers that have been locked in the Layers panel.

2. **Deselect everything, then open the Color and Swatches panels.**

   Because you defined CMYK as the color mode for this document, the Color panel sliders show inks for those four primary colors.

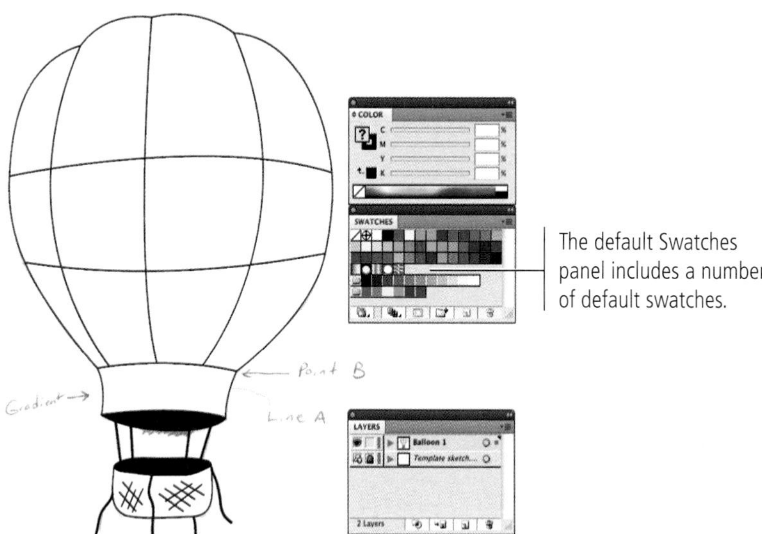

Note:

We dragged both panels out of the panel dock so we could work with both panels at once.

Note:

The default swatches appear in every new file you create, even if you delete them from a specific file.

3. **Select only the basket shape. In the Color panel, make sure the Fill icon is on top of the Stroke icon.**

   Like the options in the Tools panel, the Fill and Stroke icons determine which attribute you are currently changing. Whichever icon is on top will be affected by changes to the color values.

4. **Highlight the C (cyan) field and type 15. Press Tab to highlight the M (magenta) field and type 25. Press Tab again and change the Y (yellow) field to 45. Press Tab again and change the K (black) field to 0.**

   The selected object dynamically reflects the new color as you change the color values.

The Fill and Stroke icons serve the same purpose here as they do in the Tools panel.
Type directly in these fields to enter specific values.
You can also drag these sliders to adjust the component color percentages.
Or you can click in the spectrum to select a color.

Note:

Press Shift while dragging any of the sliders in the Color panel to drag all four sliders at once. Their relative relationship to each other remains the same while you drag.

5. **With the basket shape still selected, make sure the Fill icon is active in the Color panel, and then click the New Swatch button at the bottom of the Swatches panel.**

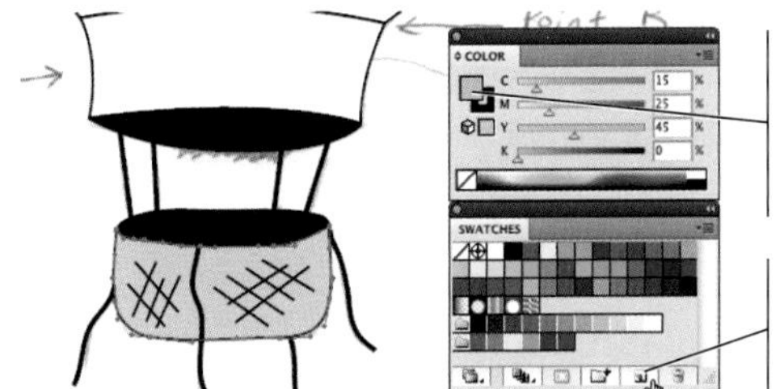

Because the Fill icon is active, the fill color is the one that will be stored in the new swatch.

Click this button to make a new swatch from the currently active color.

6. **Click OK to accept the default options in the New Swatch dialog box.**

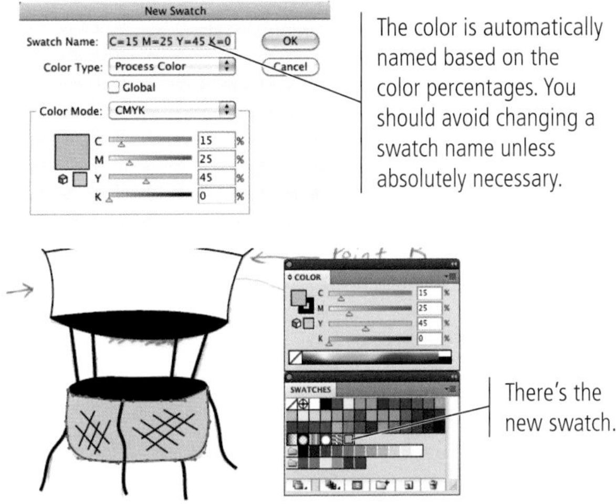

The color is automatically named based on the color percentages. You should avoid changing a swatch name unless absolutely necessary.

There's the new swatch.

7. **Open the Swatches panel Options menu and choose Select All Unused.**

The default Swatches panel includes a number of basic swatches that provide a good starting point for some artwork; however, because you are creating your own swatches for this project, the built-in ones are unnecessary. When you build custom swatches, it's a good idea to delete any default swatches that you don't need.

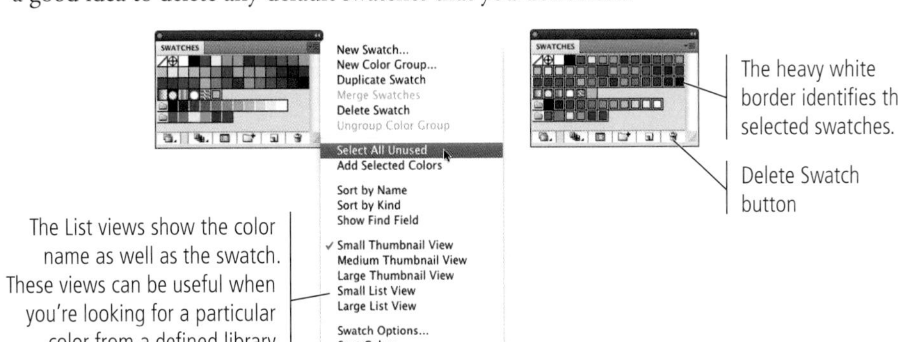

The List views show the color name as well as the swatch. These views can be useful when you're looking for a particular color from a defined library (e.g., a specific Pantone color).

The heavy white border identifies the selected swatches.

Delete Swatch button

> ***Note:***
>
> *If you delete a swatch that you applied to objects in a project, there is no effect on the existing objects; you simply can't apply that color to any new objects in the project.*

8. **Click the Swatches panel Delete button, and then click Yes in the resulting warning dialog box.**

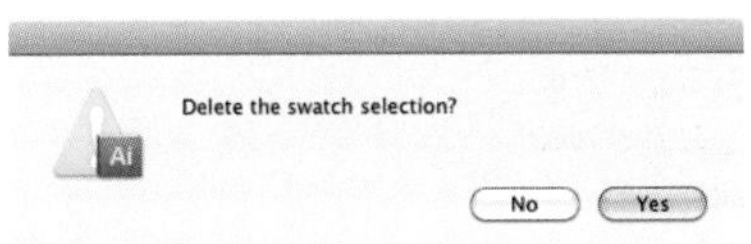

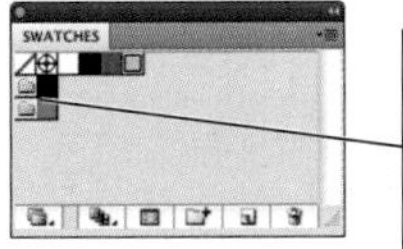

Illustrator sometimes maintains extra swatches, even if they are not used.

> ***Note:***
>
> *The extra three swatches that remain are likely the result of a bug in the software. You know they are not used in the file, but Illustrator does not identify them as "unused."*

9. **Save the file and continue to the next exercise.**

Create Global Swatches

The basket shape is now filled with a custom swatch, which is stored in the Swatches panel for the open document. You also need three more colors to fill the various sections of the balloon. You are going to use a different method to create these colors, and then save them as swatches that can be changed at any time to dynamically modify the colors in the artwork.

1. **With balloons.ai open, select all of the white-filled objects and change their fill to 50% opacity.**

   You can either draw a marquee to select the white-filled objects, or use the Select Similar Objects options. Changing the objects' opacity allows you to see the color indicators on the original sketch.

2. **Deselect everything, and then select only the top-left section of the balloon (labeled C1 in the sketch).**

3. **Press Shift and click the other three C1 shapes to add them to the selection.**

   By pressing Shift, you can click to add other objects to the current selection. Shift-clicking an object that is already selected removes it from the active selection.

4. **In the Color panel, click a green area in the color spectrum bar.**

   All four selected objects fill with the green color you clicked. They seem lighter because they are still semi-transparent.

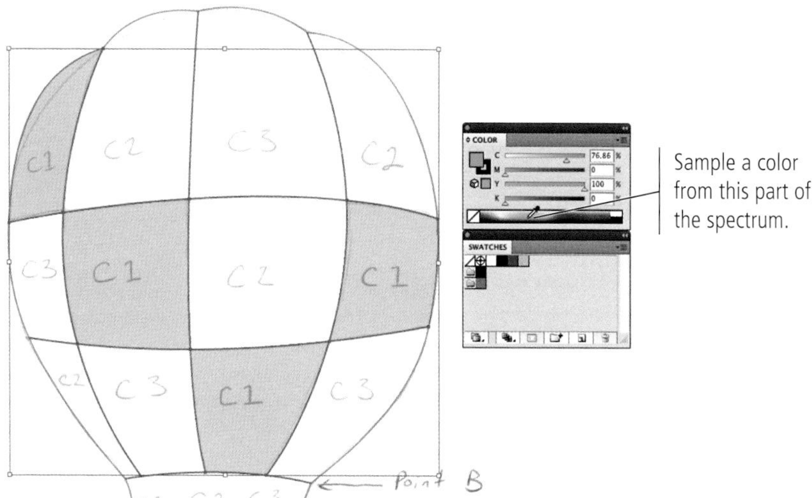

5. **With the Fill icon still active, click the New Swatch button in the Swatches panel.**

6. **Check the Global option in the New Swatch dialog box and click OK.**

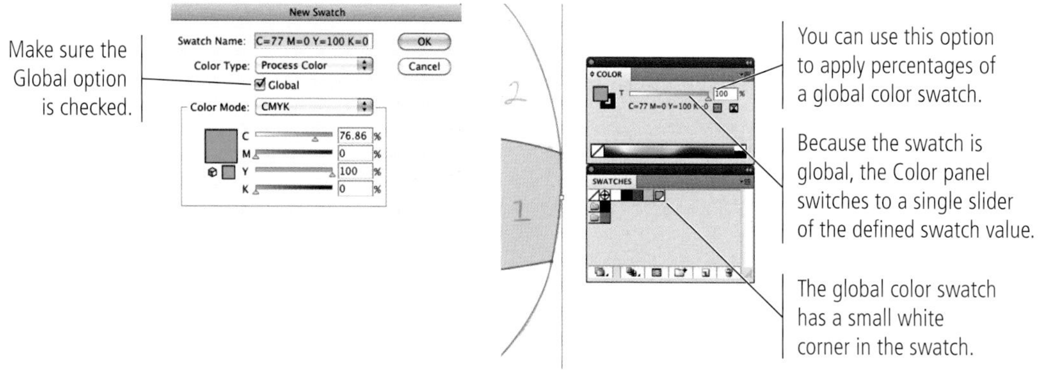

7. **Select the four shapes marked C2 in the sketch.**

8. **Repeat the process from Steps 4–6 to fill the C2 shapes with a blue color and then create a global swatch from the color.**

9. **Select the four shapes marked C3 in the sketch, fill them with a purple color, and then create a third global swatch from the color.**

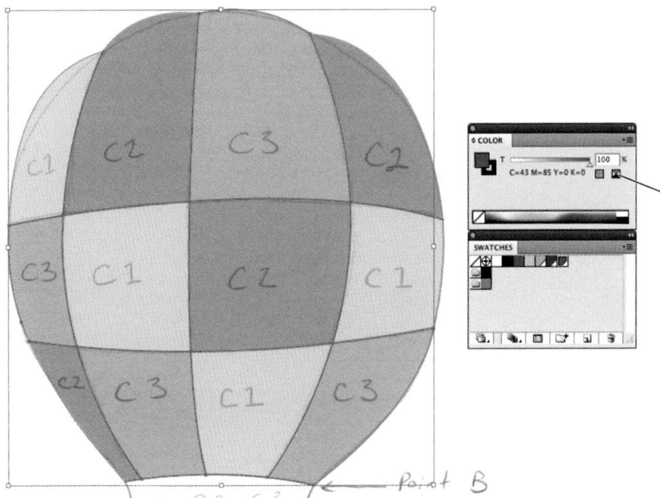

When an object is filled with a global swatch, click this button to convert it to the component color percentages (i.e., breaking the link to the global swatch).

10. **With the purple shapes still selected, choose Select>Same>Opacity. Return the selected objects' opacity to 100%.**

    You no longer need to see the color markers on the sketch, so you can return these objects to full opacity.

11. **Deselect all objects in the file, then save the file and continue to the next exercise.**

Add a Color Gradient

The original sketch shows that the bottom of the balloon needs to be a gradient of the three colors in the balloon sections. Illustrator's Gradient tool makes it easy to create this gradient based on the three custom swatches you defined in the previous exercise.

1. **With balloons.ai open, select the shape that represents the bottom edge of the balloon by clicking the path with the Selection tool.**

2. **Open the Gradient panel (Window>Gradient) and click the swatch in the top-left corner.**

   Clicking the swatch applies the linear gradient to the selected object.

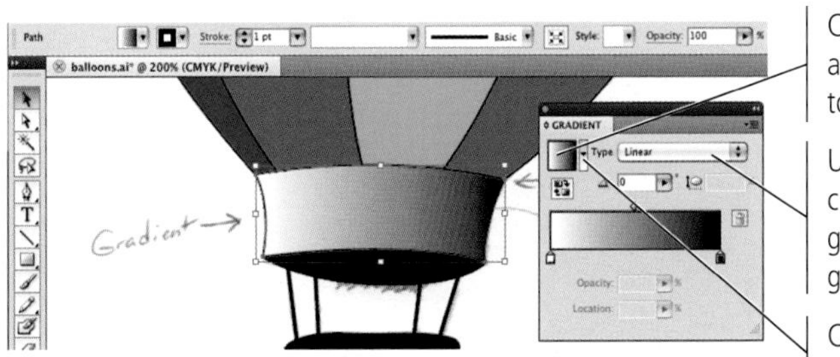

Click this swatch to apply a linear gradient to the selected object.

Use this menu to change from a linear gradient to a radial gradient (or vice versa).

Call a stored gradient swatch in this menu.

Note:

Gradients can only be applied to an object's fill, so in this instance, it doesn't matter whether the Fill icon is active in the Tools panel or Color panel.

3. **In the Gradient panel, double-click the left gradient stop on the gradient ramp.**

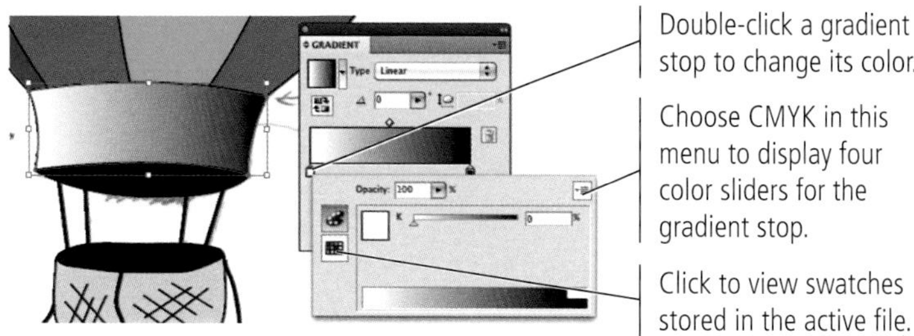

4. **In the pop-up panel, click the Swatches button to display the swatches stored in the current document.**

5. **Click the blue global swatch you created in the previous exercise, and then press Return/Enter to close the pop-up panel.**

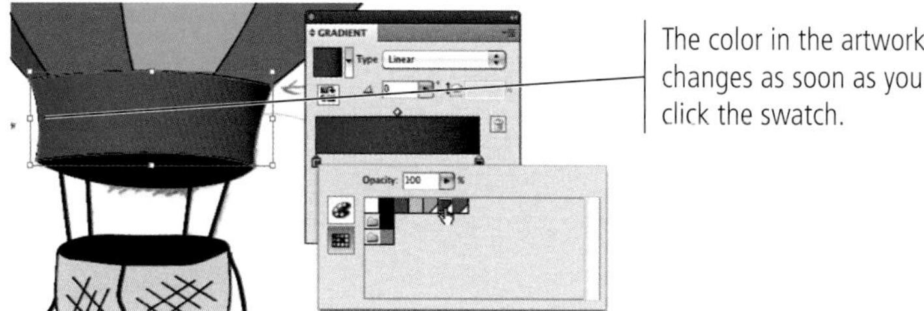

The color in the artwork changes as soon as you click the swatch.

6. **Double-click the right gradient stop to open the pop-up panel. Apply the purple custom swatch to this stop.**

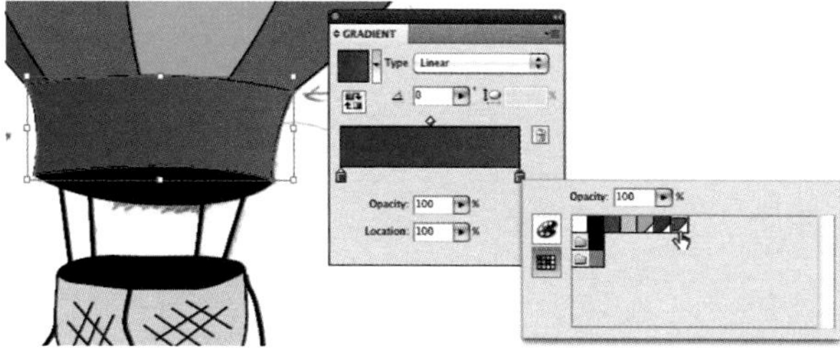

> *Note:*
>
> *You can also drag a swatch from the Swatches panel onto a particular gradient stop to change the color of that stop.*

> *Note:*
>
> *You can remove a stop by dragging it down and off the gradient ramp.*

7. **Click once below the gradient ramp to add another stop to the gradient. With the new stop selected, type `50` in the Location field.**

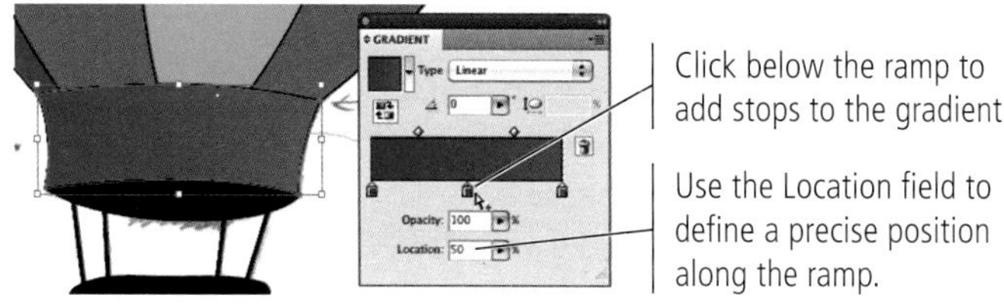

Click below the ramp to add stops to the gradient.
Use the Location field to define a precise position along the ramp.

8. **Double-click the middle stop and apply the green swatch.**

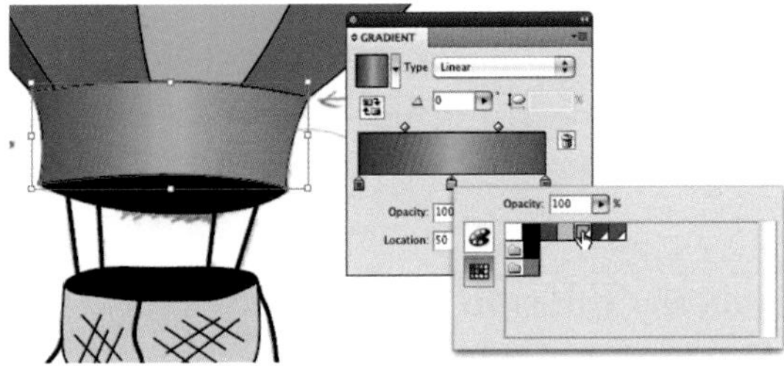

9. **Click the left gradient stop and drag right until the Location field shows approximately 10%.**

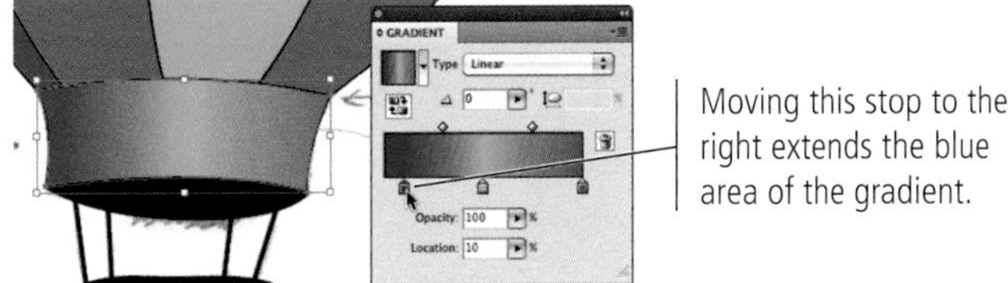

Moving this stop to the right extends the blue area of the gradient.

10. **Click the right gradient stop and drag left until the Location field shows approximately 90%.**

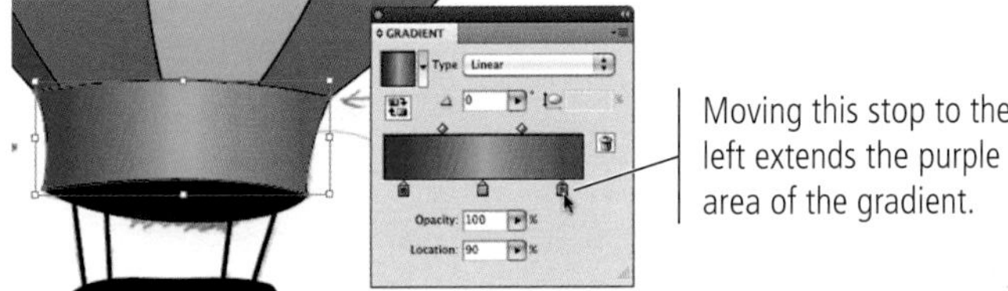

Moving this stop to the left extends the purple area of the gradient.

11. **Click the marker above the gradient ramp between the left and middle stops. Drag left until the Location field shows approximately 40%.**

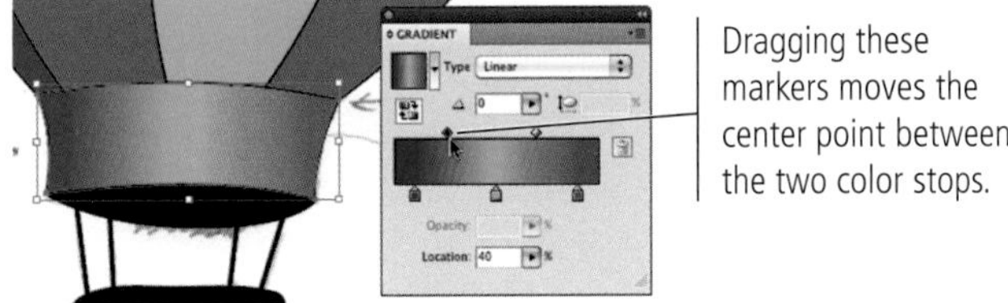

Dragging these markers moves the center point between the two color stops.

12. **Click the marker above the gradient ramp between the middle and right stops. Drag right until the Location field shows approximately 60%.**

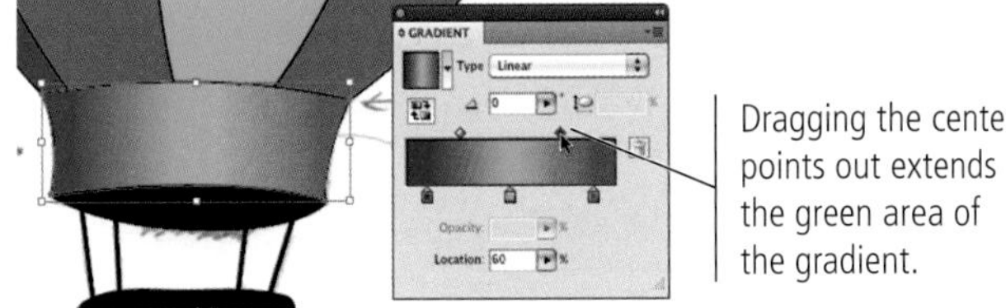

Dragging the center points out extends the green area of the gradient.

13. **Save the file and continue to the next exercise.**

Edit Global Color Swatches

Global swatches offer a particular advantage when you need to change the colors used in your artwork. In the case of this project, the client requested a red-orange-yellow scheme for the balloon, so you need to change the custom swatches you created in the previous exercise.

1. **With balloons.ai open, deselect all objects on the artboard.**

2. **In the Swatches panel, double-click the blue custom swatch.**

3. **In the resulting Swatch Options dialog box, make sure the Preview option is checked.**

4. **Change the color values to C=0 M=100 Y=100 K=0, and then click OK to change the swatch definition.**

   Because this is a global color swatch, any objects that use the color — including the gradient — reflect the new swatch definition. Locked objects are also affected by the change.

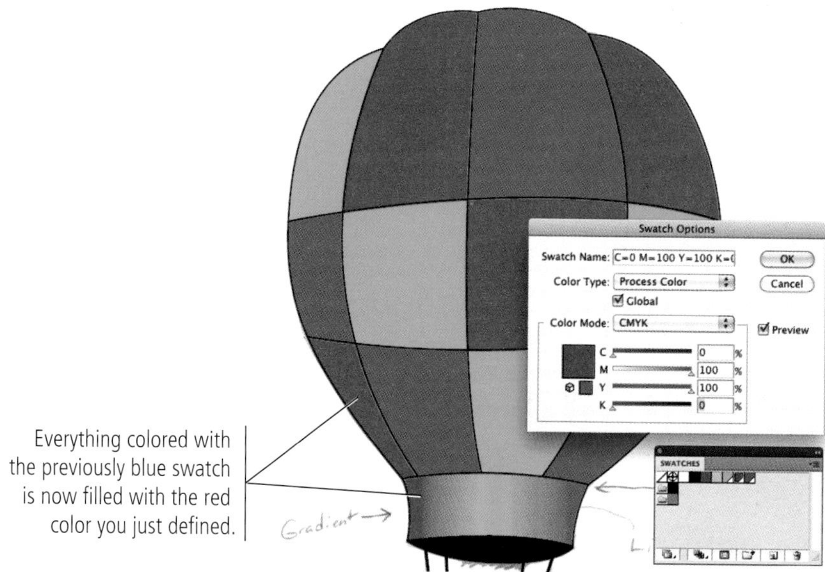

Everything colored with the previously blue swatch is now filled with the red color you just defined.

5. **Repeat Steps 2–4 to change the green swatch definition to C=0 M=10 Y=100 K=0.**

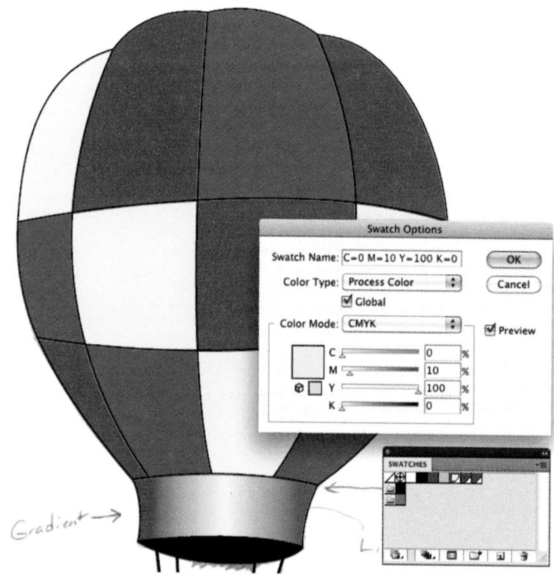

6. **Repeat Steps 2–4 to change the purple swatch definition to C=0 M=60 Y=100 K=0.**

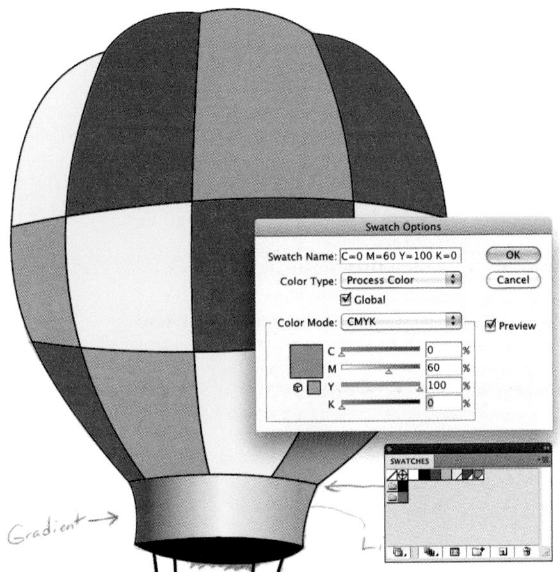

7. **Select all the objects on the Balloon layer and group them (Object>Group).**

8. **Save the file and continue to the next exercise.**

Use the Gradient Tool

In addition to simply applying a gradient with the Gradient panel, you can also use the Gradient tool to define the gradient directly in the context of the artwork.

1. **Open the file `desert.ai` from your WIP>Festival folder.**

2. **Select the front dune shape, then fill it with the default black-to-white linear gradient in the Gradient panel.**

3. **Choose the Gradient tool in the Tools panel.**

   When a selected object is filled with a gradient, choosing the Gradient tool reveals the Gradient Annotator for that shape. The Gradient Annotator is simply a visual tool for applying most of the same options that are available in the Gradient panel.

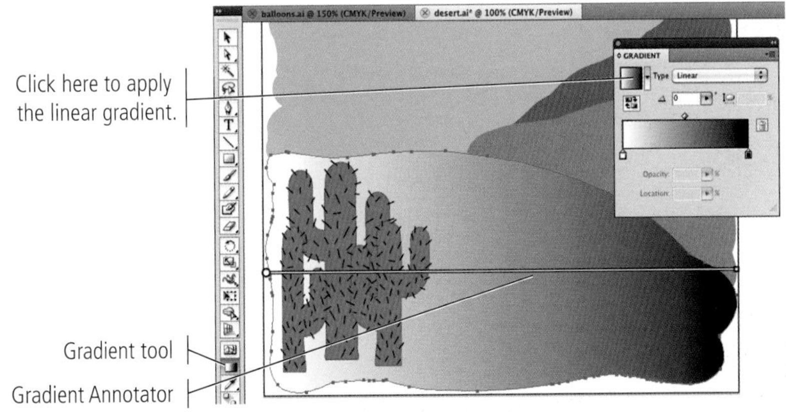

Note:

You can turn off the Gradient Annotator in the View menu (View>Hide Gradient Annotator).

4. **Move your cursor over the Gradient Annotator to show the associated stops.**

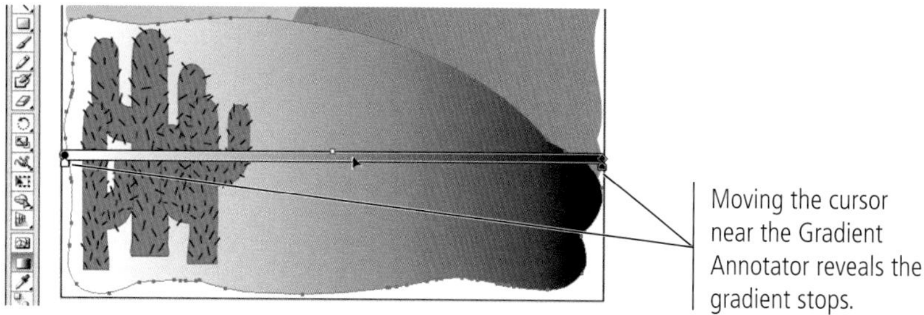

Moving the cursor near the Gradient Annotator reveals the gradient stops.

5. **On the Gradient Annotator, click the white stop and drag to about the halfway point of the gradient.**

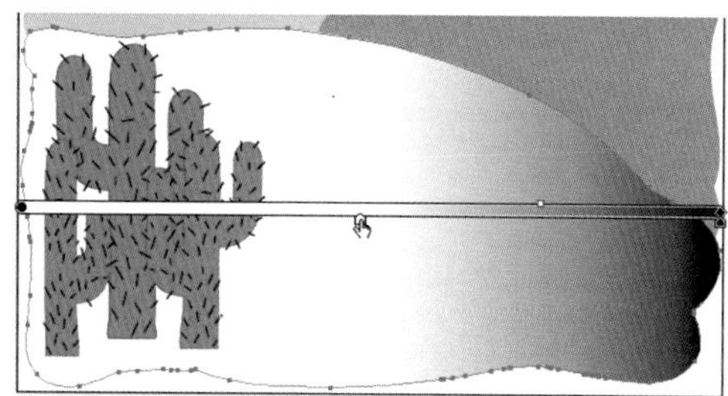

6. **Place the cursor directly below the left end of the Gradient Annotator. When you see a plus sign (+) in the cursor, click to add a new stop to the gradient.**

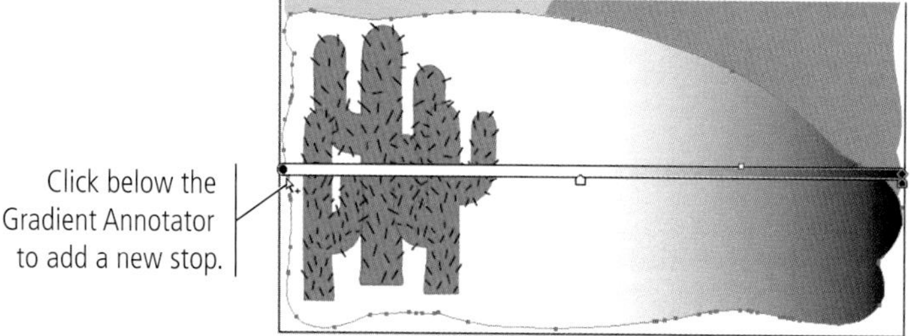

Click below the Gradient Annotator to add a new stop.

7. **Double-click the new stop to open the pop-up panel. Change the stop color to the available orange swatch.**

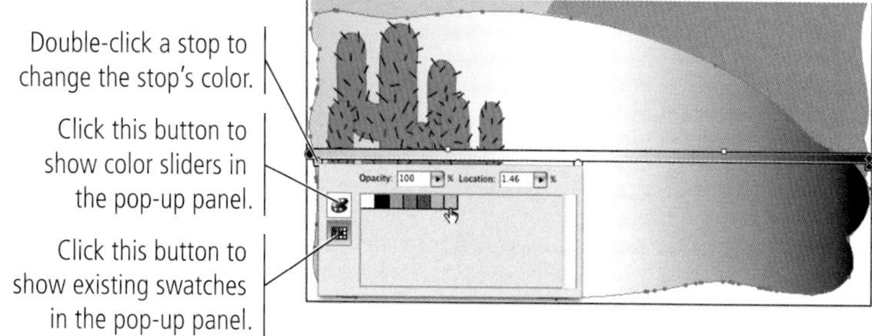

Click this button to show color sliders in the pop-up panel.
Click this button to show existing swatches in the pop-up panel.

8. **Repeat Step 7 to apply the same orange swatch to the right gradient stop.**

> ***Note:***
>
> *If the current selection is part of a group, selecting the Gradient tool does not reveal the Gradient Annotator. You have to first deselect the active group, and then click a specific object with the Gradient tool to show the Gradient Annotator for the object.*

9. **Click the right end of the annotator and drag left (toward the center of the artboard), until the Annotator is about two-thirds the width of the selected object.**

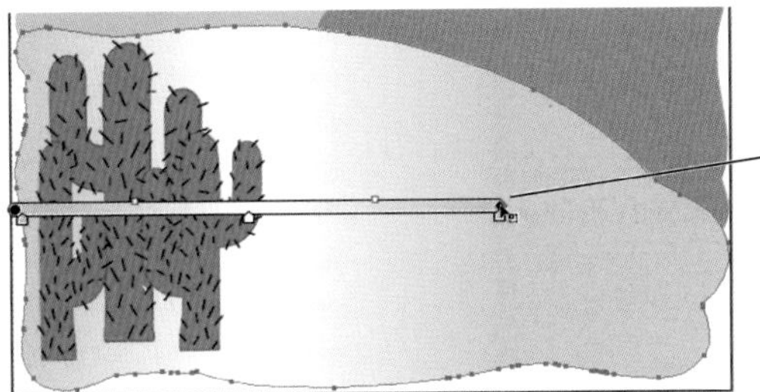

Drag the right end of the annotator to shorten or lengthen the gradient within the shape.

10. **Place the cursor near the right end of the Gradient Annotator. When the cursor changes to a rotation symbol, click and drag down to rotate the gradient clockwise.**

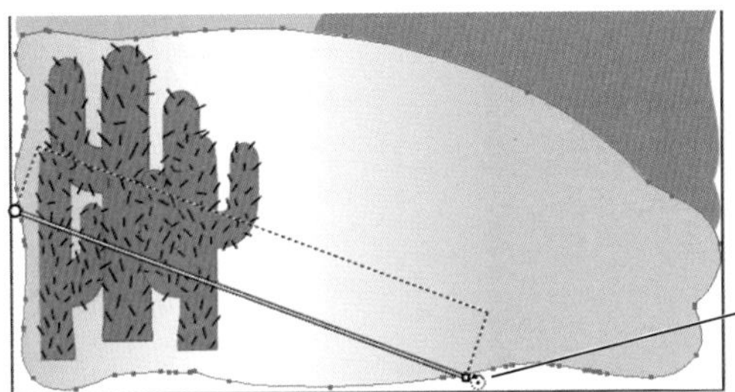

Rotate the gradient by clicking directly outside the right end of the gradient.

Note:

After you rotate the Gradient Annotator, it snaps back to the center of the object.

11. **Select the second dune shape, and then click the gradient swatch in the Gradient panel.**

The Gradient panel remembers the last-used gradient, so you can simply click the sample to apply the gradient to the new object.

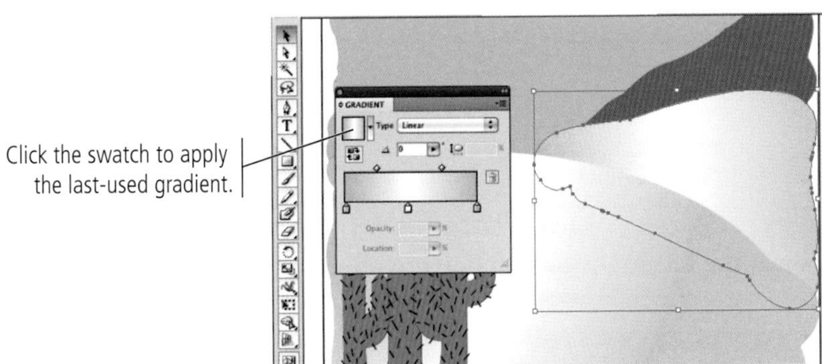

Click the swatch to apply the last-used gradient.

12. **Using the Gradient tool, click near the left edge of the selected shape and drag close to the right edge of the selected shape.**

Rather than dragging the Annotator bar, you can also click and drag with the Gradient tool to define the direction and position of the gradient within a selected object.

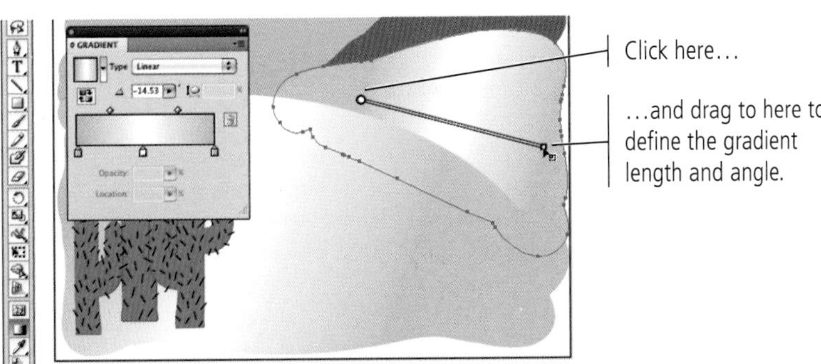

Click here…

…and drag to here to define the gradient length and angle.

13. **Use the same method from Steps 11–12 to apply the gradient to the third dune shape. Drag this gradient from the bottom-left area to the top-right area of the selected shape.**

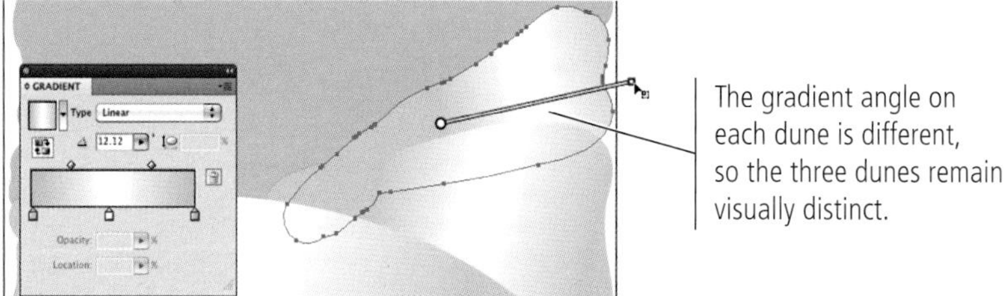

The gradient angle on each dune is different, so the three dunes remain visually distinct.

14. **Save the file as** `poster.ai` **in your WIP>Festival folder and continue to the next exercise.**

Manage Artwork with Layers

The next step in the process is to place your finished balloon in the background illustration; you can then duplicate the balloon artwork to create a small fleet of different-colored balloons floating over the desert.

You created the entire balloon artwork on a single layer. In this exercise, you add multiple layers so you can organize and manage the additional balloon objects.

1. **With** `poster.ai` **open, Shift-click to select all three layers in the Layers panel.**

2. **Choose Merge Selected in the Layers panel Options menu.**

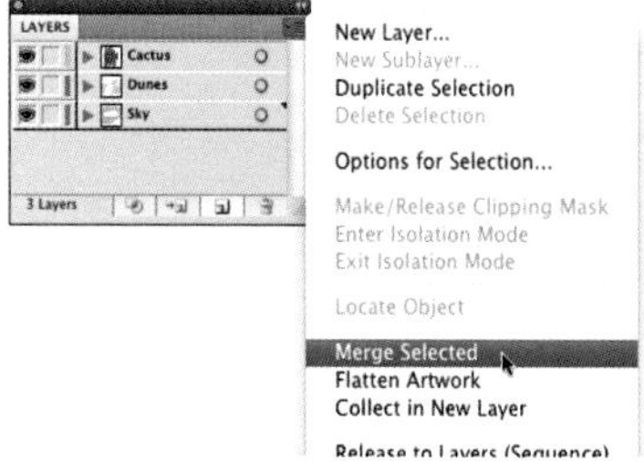

3. **Double-click the new layer to open the Layer Options dialog box. Rename the layer** `Desert` **and click OK.**

4. **Activate (or open, if necessary) the `balloons.ai` file.**

5. **Select the sketch layer in the Layers panel and drag it to the panel's Delete button.**

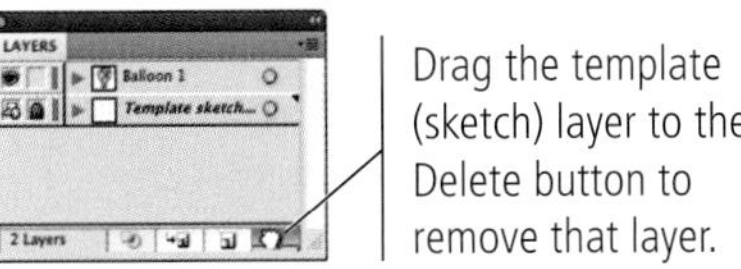

Drag the template (sketch) layer to the Delete button to remove that layer.

> *Note:*
>
> *If you delete a non-template layer that contains artwork, Illustrator asks you to confirm that you want to delete the layer (and all artwork on the layer).*

6. **Select everything on the artboard, choose Edit>Copy, save the `balloons.ai` file, and then close it.**

7. **With `poster.ai` active, click the New Layer button in the Layers panel. Double-click the new layer, name it `Balloon 1`, and then click OK.**

8. **Make sure the Balloon 1 layer is active in the Layers panel and choose Edit>Paste. Drag the pasted artwork to the approximate center of the artboard.**

9. **Click the Balloon 1 layer and drag it to the New Layer button at the bottom of the Layers panel.**

   You now have a copy of the layer you dragged. You see no difference on the artboard because the copy is in the same position as the original layer.

Drag an existing layer to the New Layer button to make an exact copy of the layer.

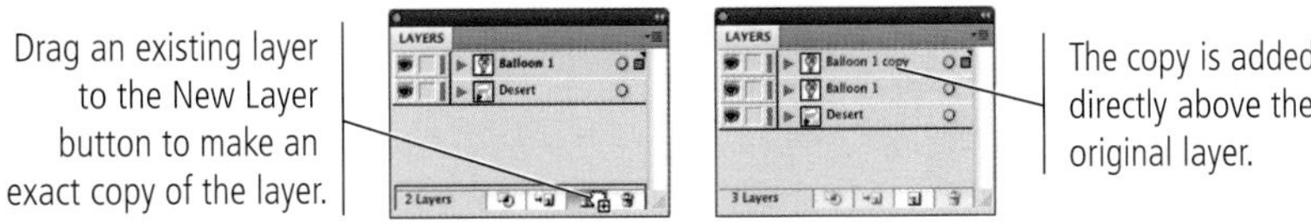

The copy is added directly above the original layer.

10. **Rename the Balloon 1 copy layer as `Balloon 2`.**

11. **Drag the Balloon 2 layer to the New Layer button. Rename this layer `Balloon 3`.**

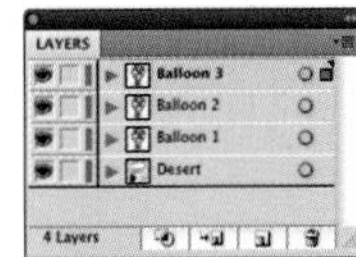

12. Lock all but the Balloon 3 layer, and then choose Select>All.

Because all the other layers are locked, you selected only the artwork on the Balloon 3 layer. The difference between locking objects and locking layers depends on what you need to accomplish. In this case, it's best to place each piece of artwork on its own layer, so you can lock the layers you want to protect from change.

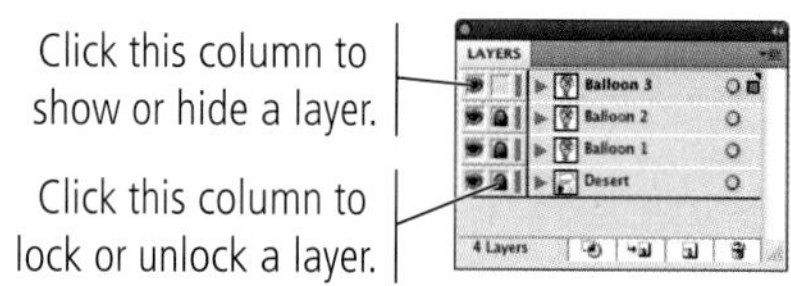

> *Note:*
>
> *You can also select all objects on a specific layer by clicking the space at the right edge of the Layers panel (to the right of the round Target icon).*

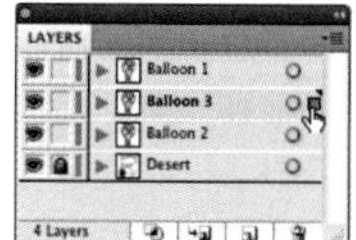

13. Choose Object>Transform>Scale. In the Scale dialog box, type 75% in the Uniform Scale field. Make sure the Scale Strokes & Effects option is checked, and then click OK.

If Scale Strokes & Effects is not checked, a 2-pt stroke will remain a 2-pt stroke, even if you reduce the selected object to 10% of its original size. With the Scale Strokes & Effects option checked, a 2-pt stroke scaled to 75% becomes a 1.5-pt stroke.

14. Drag the scaled artwork left.

15. Lock the Balloon 3 layer and unlock the Balloon 2 layer.

16. Repeat Steps 12–14 for the artwork on Balloon 2 layer. Scale it to 50%, and then move it right and up to make it seem farthest back in the fleet.

The different scaling, position, and stacking order of the three balloons creates the illusion of depth within the illustration.

17. **Unlock all three Balloon layers. In the Layers panel, click the Balloon 1 layer and drag it to the top of the layer stack.**

18. **Adjust the position and scale of each balloon until you are satisfied with the overall result.**

19. **Save the file and continue to the next exercise.**

Recolor Artwork

Your illustration is nearly complete. The only work left to do is to change the colors of the two new balloons. Although you could manually select the shapes and apply different ink percentages, Illustrator includes a sophisticated tool that makes it easy to experiment with and change all colors in a selection.

1. **With poster.ai open, click the empty space to the right of the Balloon 3 layer name to select all objects on that layer.**

2. **Click the Recolor Artwork button in the Control panel.**

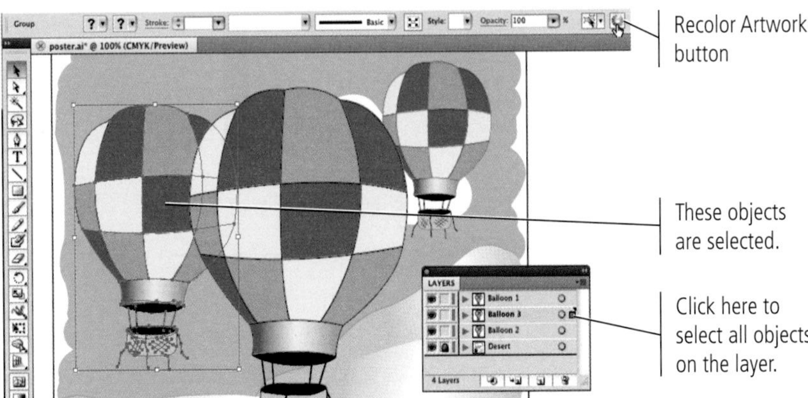
Recolor Artwork button
These objects are selected.
Click here to select all objects on the layer.

Note:

You can also choose Edit>Edit Colors>Recolor Artwork to open the dialog box.

Understanding Color Terms

Many vague and technical-sounding terms are mentioned when discussing color. Is hue the same as color? The same as value? As tone? What's the difference between lightness and brightness? What is chroma? And where does saturation fit in?

This problem has resulted in several attempts to normalize color communication. A number of systems have been developed to define color according to specific criteria, including Hue, Saturation, and Brightness (HSB); Hue, Saturation, and Lightness (HSL); Hue, Saturation, and Value (HSV); and Lightness, Chroma, and Hue (LCH). Each of these models or systems plots color on a three-dimensional diagram, based on the elements of human color perception — hue, colorfulness, and brightness.

Hue is what most people think of as color — red, green, purple, and so on. Hue is defined according to a color's position on a color wheel, beginning from red (0°) and traveling counterclockwise around the wheel.

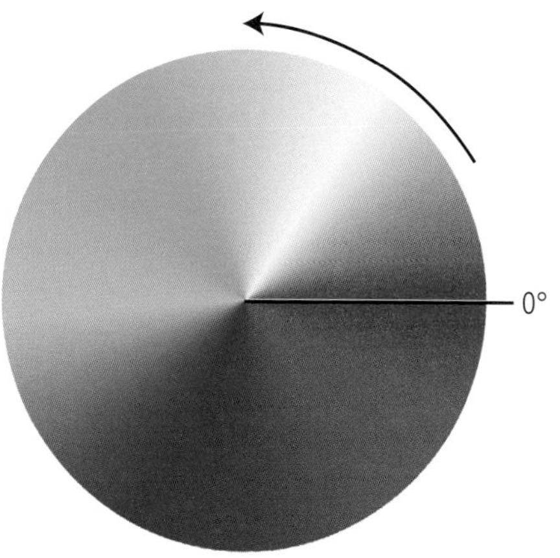

Saturation (also called "intensity") refers to the color's difference from neutral gray. Highly saturated colors are more vivid than those with low saturation. Saturation is plotted from the center of the color wheel. Color at the center is neutral gray and has a saturation value of 0; color at the edge of the wheel is the most intense value of the corresponding hue and has a saturation value of 100.

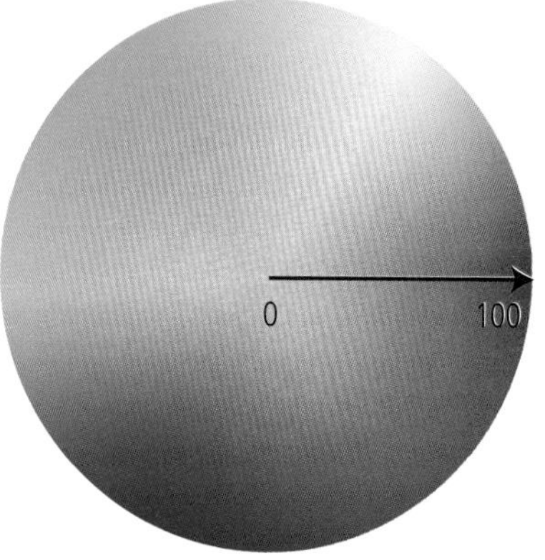

If you bisect the color wheel with a straight line, the line creates a saturation axis for two complementary colors. A color is dulled by the introduction of its complement. Red, for example, is neutralized by the addition of cyan (blue and green). Near the center of the axis, the result is neutral gray.

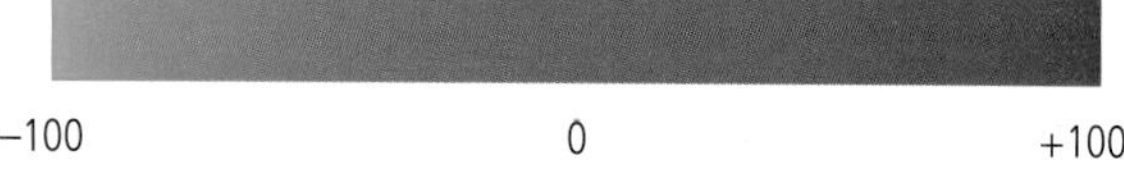

Chroma is similar to saturation, but chroma factors in a reference white. In any viewing situation, colors appear less vivid as the light source dims. The process of chromatic adaptation, however, allows the human visual system to adjust to changes in light and still differentiate colors according to the relative saturation.

Brightness is the amount of light reflected off an object. As an element of color reproduction, brightness is typically judged by comparing the color to the lightest nearby object (such as an unprinted area of white paper).

Lightness is the amount of white or black added to the pure color. Lightness (also called "luminance" or "value") is the relative brightness based purely on the black-white value of a color. A lightness value of 0 means there is no addition of white or black. Lightness of +100 is pure white; lightness of –100 is pure black.

All hues are affected equally by changes in lightness.

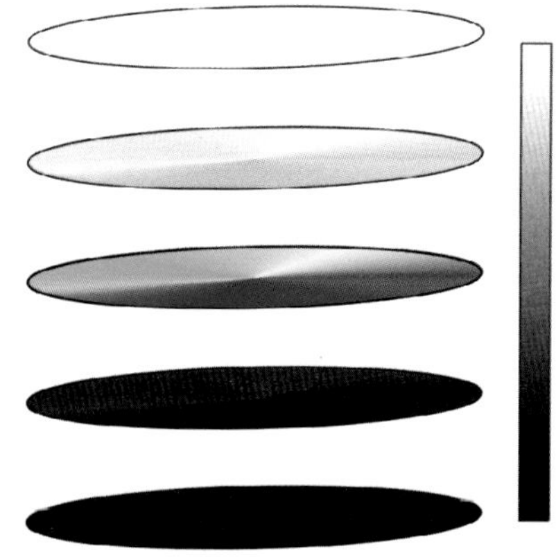

The Recolor Artwork dialog box shows all colors used in the selection. You can edit or replace individual colors, or you can apply global changes that affect the entire selection.

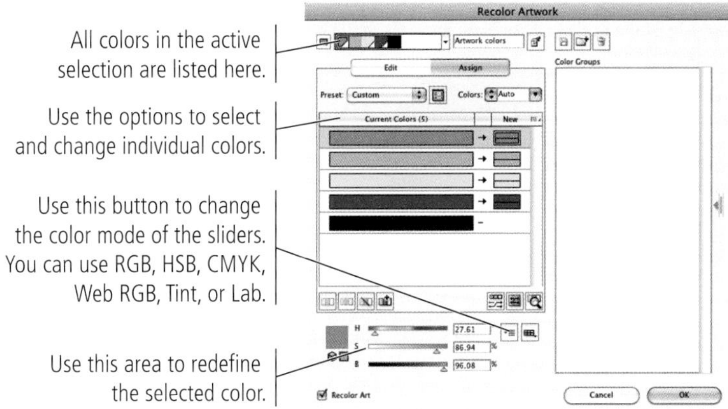
All colors in the active selection are listed here.
Use the options to select and change individual colors.
Use this button to change the color mode of the sliders. You can use RGB, HSB, CMYK, Web RGB, Tint, or Lab.
Use this area to redefine the selected color.
Recolor Artwork
Artwork colors
Color Groups
Edit
Assign
Preset: Custom
Colors: Auto
Current Colors (5)
New
27.61
86.94
96.08
Recolor Art
Cancel
OK

3. **Click the Edit button to show the active colors on a color wheel.**

4. **Click the button to the right of the color sliders and choose CMYK from the menu.**

5. **Make sure the Recolor Art option is checked, and then click the Display Segmented Color Wheel button.**

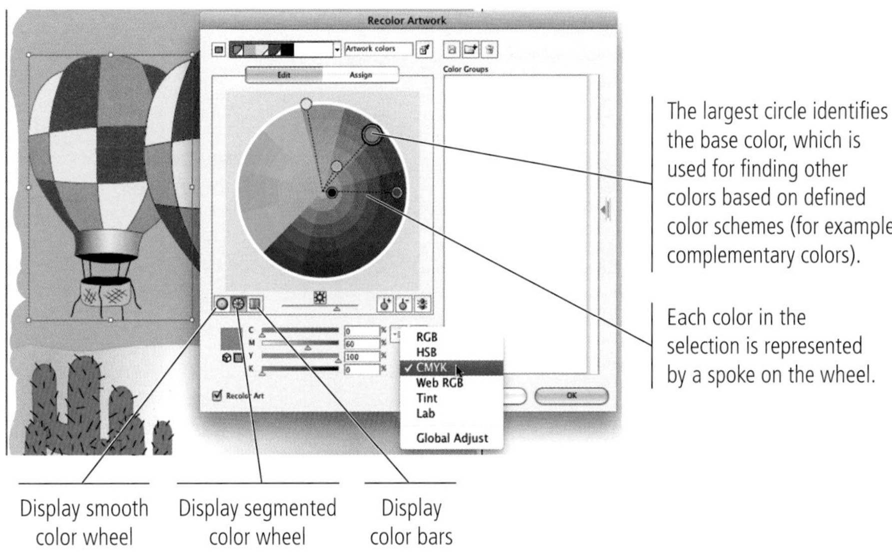
Recolor Artwork
Artwork colors
Color Groups
Edit
Assign
The largest circle identifies the base color, which is used for finding other colors based on defined color schemes (for example, complementary colors).
Each color in the selection is represented by a spoke on the wheel.
RGB
HSB
✓ CMYK
Web RGB
Tint
Lab
Global Adjust
OK
Display smooth color wheel
Display segmented color wheel
Display color bars

6. **Click the orange circle and drag it to a middle-blue area on the color wheel.**

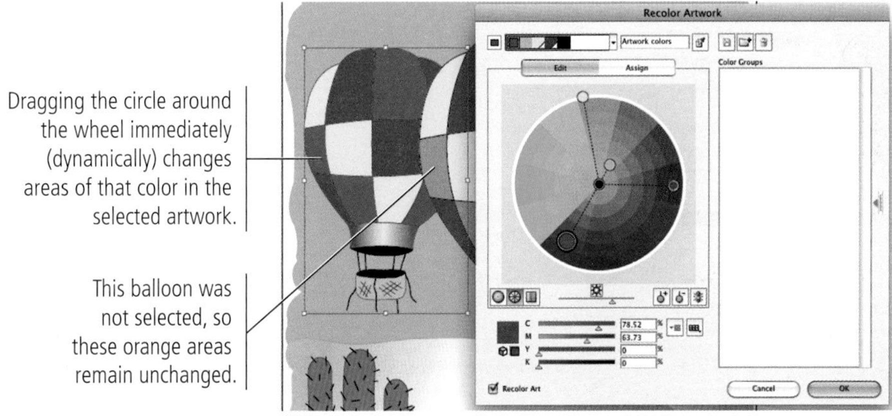
Dragging the circle around the wheel immediately (dynamically) changes areas of that color in the selected artwork.
This balloon was not selected, so these orange areas remain unchanged.
Recolor Artwork
Artwork colors
Color Groups
Edit
Assign
78.52
63.73
0
0
Recolor Art
Cancel
OK

7. **Click the yellow circle and drag it to a medium-dark green.**

8. **Click the red circle and drag it to a medium-dark purple.**

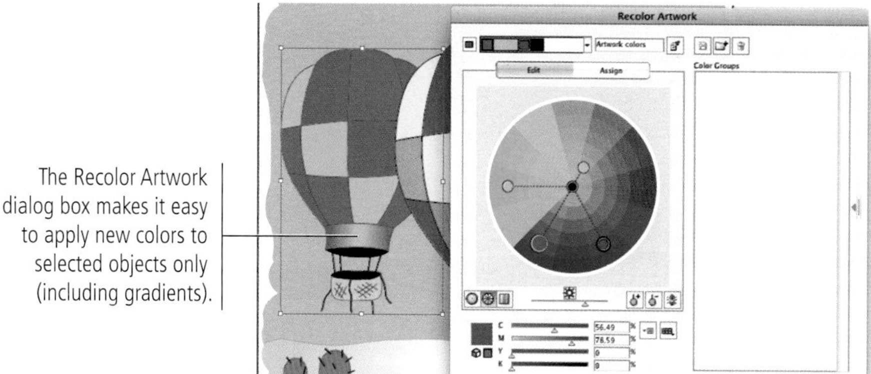

9. **Click OK to return to the artboard.**

10. **Select everything on the Balloon 2 layer, and then click the Recolor Artwork button in the Control panel.**

11. **With the dialog box in Assign mode, make sure the first color is selected in the list.**

12. **Click the button to the right of the color sliders and choose CMYK from the menu.**

13. **Use the sliders to change the color definition to C=0 M=100 Y=0 K=0.**

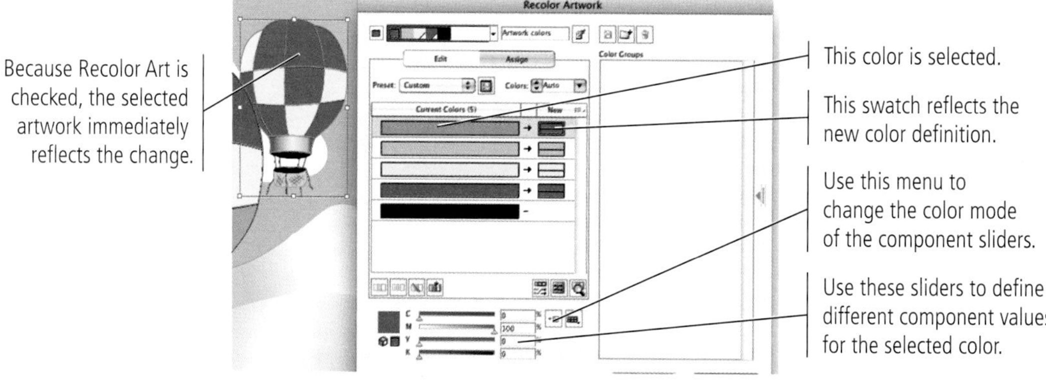

Because Recolor Art is checked, the selected artwork immediately reflects the change.
Recolor Artwork
This color is selected.
This swatch reflects the new color definition.
Use this menu to change the color mode of the component sliders.
Use these sliders to define different component values for the selected color.

14. **Click the red color in the Current Colors list, and then use the sliders to change the color definition to C=100 M=0 Y=15 K=0.**

15. **Click the yellow color in the Current Colors list, and then use the sliders to change the color definition to C=0 M=0 Y=60 K=0.**

Note:

If you are working with global color swatches, you can also use the Tint slider you saw earlier when you worked with the global color swatches.

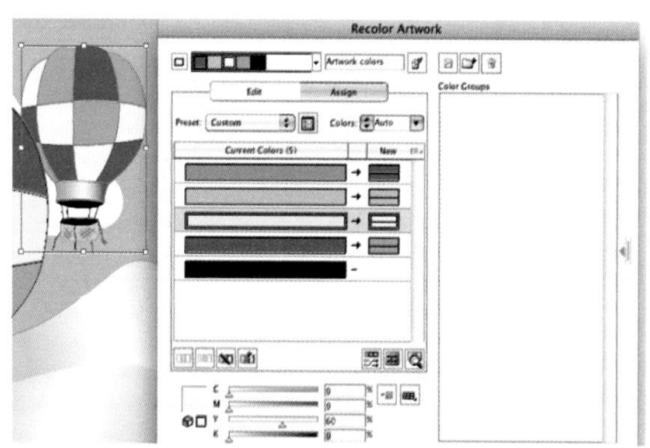

16. **Click OK to return to the artboard.**

17. **Save the file and continue to the final stage of the project.**

Recoloring Options

The Recolor Artwork dialog box has dozens of options for changing colors, and the sheer number of choices can be intimidating. However, you already used two of the most important options in this dialog box, so you should feel confident in your ability to use it — especially when experimenting with colors to use in a particular piece of artwork. In addition to the functions you already used, the Recolor Artwork dialog box also enables global color changes.

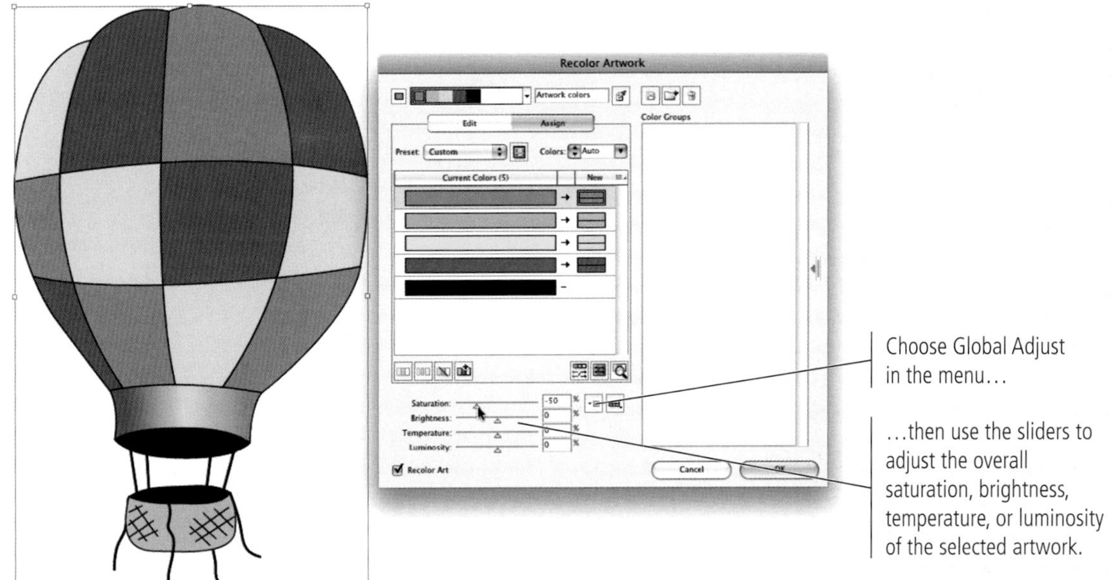

Recolor Artwork
Choose Global Adjust in the menu...
...then use the sliders to adjust the overall saturation, brightness, temperature, or luminosity of the selected artwork.

You should also understand that you aren't required to do a 1-to-1 replacement. You can replace multiple colors with the same new color by simply dragging one current color onto another. (This is especially useful if you are converting four-color artwork to a two-color or one-color job.)

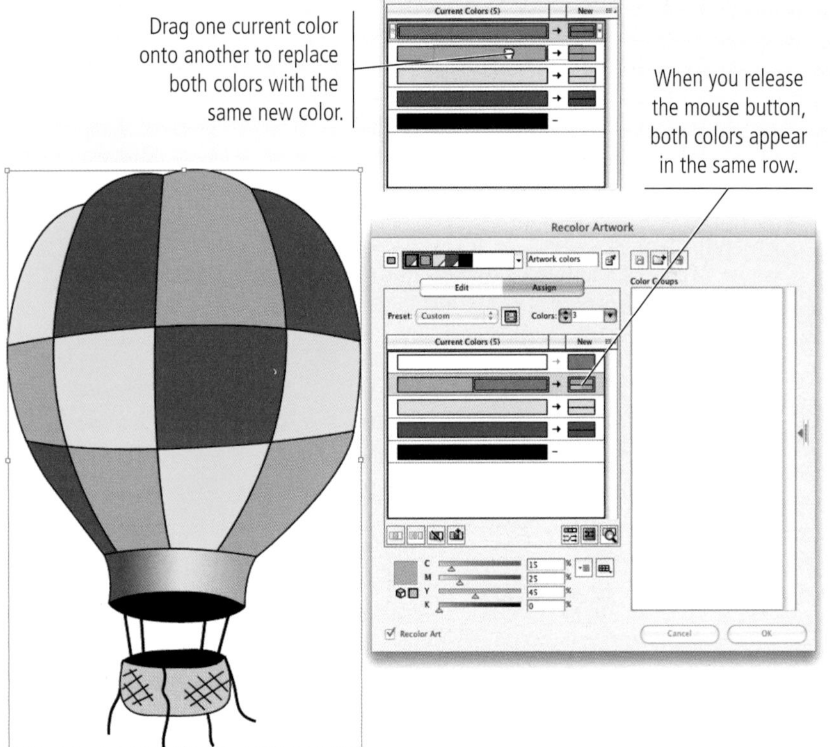

Stage 3 Exporting EPS and PDF Files

Although most current versions of page-layout software can manage the native Illustrator file format, some older applications that are still in common use can't interpret Illustrator files. For those applications, you need to save files in formats that can be used — namely, EPS and PDF.

Save an EPS File

The EPS (Encapsulated PostScript) file format was designed for high-quality print applications. The format can store both raster and vector elements, and it supports transparency. Before page-layout applications were able to support native Illustrator files (or PDF), EPS was the most common format used for files created in Illustrator.

1. **With poster.ai open, choose File>Save As and navigate to your WIP>Festival folder as the target location.**

2. **Choose Illustrator EPS in the Format/Save As Type menu.**

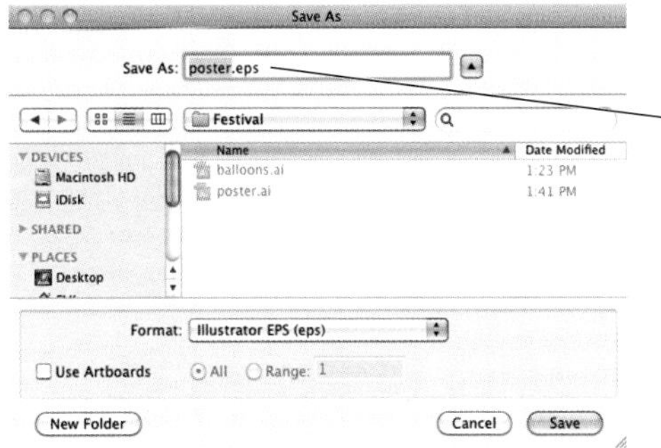

The file name automatically changes to show the correct extension (.eps).

> *Note:*
>
> *If you have more than one artboard in a file, you can check the Use Artboards option to export each artboard as a separate EPS file.*

EPS Options

ILLUSTRATOR FOUNDATIONS

When you save a file in the EPS format, you can define a number of format-specific options.

Version allows you to save a file to be compatible with earlier versions of Illustrator. Be aware that features not available in earlier versions will be lost in the saved file.

Format defines the type of preview that will be saved in the file (these previews are used for applications that can't directly read the EPS file format). Be aware that Windows users cannot access Macintosh-format previews; if you're working in a Windows-based or cross-platform environment, use one of the TIFF preview options.

Another advantage of the TIFF preview is the ability to save the preview with a transparent background or opaque background. When you choose TIFF (8-bit Color) in the Preview menu, you can choose the **Transparent** option to save a preview that will show background objects through the empty areas of the artwork; the **Opaque** option creates the preview with a solid white background.

Transparency options control the output settings for transparent and semi-transparent objects, including drop shadows and other effects. (These options will be explained in depth in Project 6.)

Embed Fonts (for other applications) embeds used fonts into the EPS file. This ensures that the type appears properly when the file is placed into another application.

Include Linked Files embeds linked files.

Include Document Thumbnails creates a thumbnail image of the artwork that displays in the Illustrator Open and Place dialog boxes.

Include CMYK PostScript in RGB Files allows RGB color documents to be printed from applications that do not support RGB output. When the EPS file is reopened in Illustrator, the RGB colors are preserved.

Compatible Gradient and Gradient Mesh Printing is necessary for older printers and PostScript devices to print gradients and gradient meshes; those elements (explained in Project 3) are converted to the JPEG format.

Adobe PostScript® determines what level of PostScript is used to save the artwork. PostScript Level 2 represents color as well as grayscale vector and bitmap images. PostScript Level 3 includes the ability to print mesh objects when printing to a PostScript 3 printer.

3. **Click Save.**

4. **In the resulting EPS Options dialog box, choose TIFF (8-bit Color) in the Format menu and click the Transparent radio button. Make sure Embed Fonts is checked.**

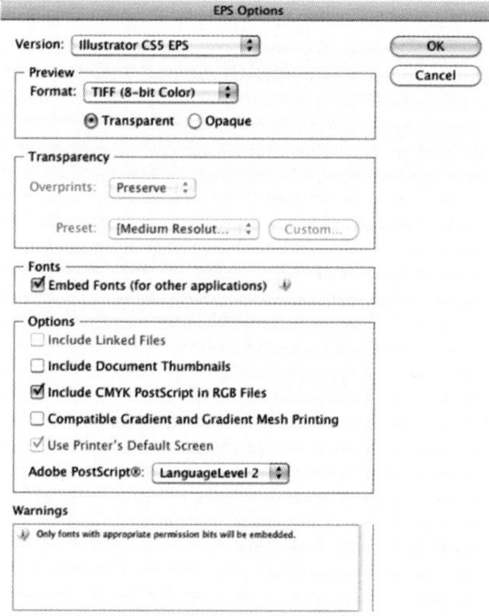

5. **Click OK to create the EPS file.**

6. **Close the EPS file and continue to the next exercise.**

Save a File as PDF

Adobe PDF (or simply PDF, for Portable Document Format) has become a universal method of moving files to virtually any digital destination. One of the most important uses for the PDF format is the ability to create perfectly formatted digital documents, exactly as they would appear if printed on paper. You can embed fonts, images, drawings, and other elements into the file so all the required bits are available on any computer. The PDF format can be used to move your artwork to the Web as a low-resolution RGB file or to a commercial printer as a high-resolution CMYK file.

1. **Open poster.ai from your WIP>Festival folder, then choose File>Save As. If necessary, navigate to your WIP>Festival folder as the target location.**

2. **Choose Adobe PDF in the Format/Save As Type menu and click Save.**

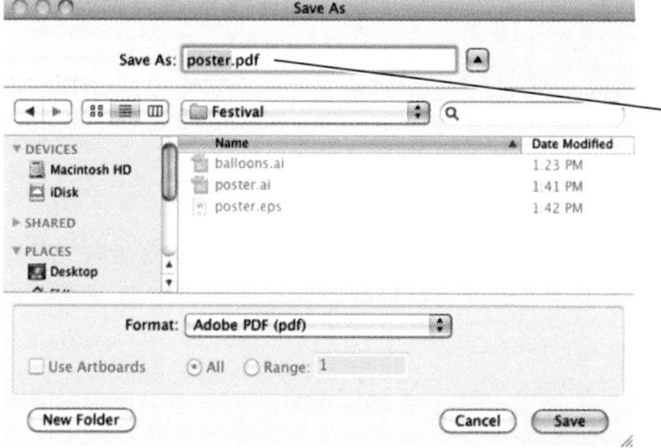

Again, the extension automatically changes to reflect the selected format (.pdf).

3. **Review the options in the General pane.**

Read the description area to see what Adobe has to say about these options.

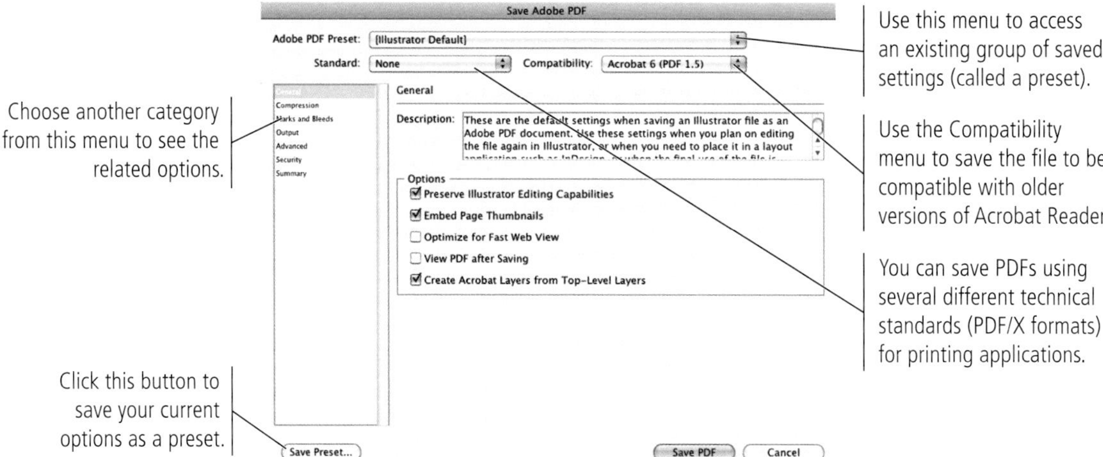

4. **Choose Illustrator Default in the Adobe PDF Preset menu.**

5. **Click Compression in the list of categories on the left and review the options.**

These options allow you to reduce the resulting file size by compressing color, grayscale, and/or monochrome bitmap (raster) images. You can also compress text and line art by clicking the check box at the bottom.

> *Note:*
>
> *The other categories of options are explained in later projects that discuss transparency and color management.*

6. **Review the Marks and Bleeds options.**

These options add different marks to the output page:

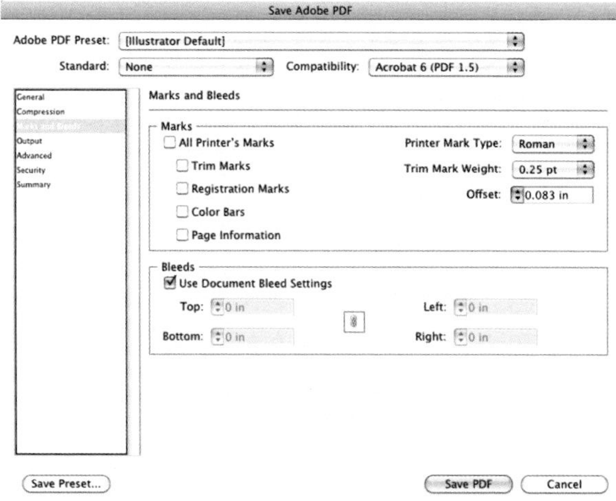

- **Trim marks** indicate the edge of the page, where a page printed on a larger sheet will be cut down to its final size. You can also define the thickness (weight) of the trim marks, as well as how far from the page edge the lines should appear (offset).
- **Registration marks** resemble a small crosshair. These marks are added to each ink unit on a printing press to make sure the different inks are properly aligned to one another.
- **Color bars** are rows of small squares across the sheet, used to verify press settings for accurate color reproduction.
- **Page information** adds the file name, date, and time of output.
- **Bleeds** define how much of elements outside the page boundaries will be included in the final output. Most printers require at least a 0.125″ bleed on each side, but you should always ask before you create the final file.

> *Note:*
>
> *Most printers require trim marks to be created outside the bleed area. Always check with your service provider when saving a PDF for commercial output.*

7. **Click Save PDF.**

8. **Close the Illustrator file.**

Project Review

fill in the blank

1. The ______________ tool is used to place anchor points that are connected by line segments.

2. The ______________ tool is used to change a smooth anchor point to a corner anchor point (and vice versa).

3. The ______________ tool is used to edit individual anchor points (and their related handles) on a vector path.

4. ______________ is the range of possible colors within a specific color model.

5. ______________________________ are the four component colors in process-color output.

6. The ______________ panel includes value sliders for each component in the defined color model.

7. The ______________ is used to paint shapes of solid color based on the defined brush size and the area you drag with a single mouse click.

8. The ______________ appears over a gradient-filled object when selected with the Gradient tool; you can use it to control the position and direction of color in the gradient-filled object.

9. Changes made to a ______________ color swatch are reflected in all elements where that color is applied.

10. The ______________ dialog box can be used to change individual colors in an entire file, or to make global changes to all colors in the file.

short answer

1. Describe three ways to deselect the current selection on the artboard.

2. Briefly explain the significance of "process color" related to Illustrator artwork.

3. Briefly explain three advantages of using the PDF format for creating printable files.

Portfolio Builder Project

Use what you learned in this project to complete the following freeform exercise.
Carefully read the art director and client comments, then create your own design to meet the needs of the project.
Use the space below to sketch ideas; when finished, write a brief explanation of your reasoning behind your final design.

art director comments

The former marketing director for the Temecula Balloon Festival recently moved to Florida to be the director of the annual Miami Jazzfest. She was pleased with your work on the balloon festival project, and would like to hire you to create the advertising for next year's jazz festival event.

To complete this project, you should:

❏ Develop artwork that will be the primary image for posters and print advertisements, as well as shirts and other souvenirs.

❏ Create the primary artwork to fit onto the festival program cover, which is 8×10″.

client comments

Jazzfest is one of the longest running and well-known music festivals in the southeastern United States. In addition to the music, the festival also features food from prominent restaurants; the food is almost as big an attraction as the music — maybe even moreso for some people.

We want artwork that appeals to a 40-something, middle- and upper-class audience; tickets to this event are fairly expensive, but we always have some very well-known acts that make it worth the price.

Finally, we want the artwork to be an appealing aspect of our ad campaign, but we want it to be artwork in its own right as well. The artwork gets printed as posters that are hung in some very exclusive establishments around the Miami area, and they weren't happy with the cartoon style of art used in previous years.

project justification

Project Summary

This project built on the skills you learned in Project 1, incorporating more advanced drawing techniques that allow you to exercise precise control over every point and path in a file. The Pen tool is arguably one of the most important tools you will use throughout your career as an illustrator; although it can be difficult at first, practice is the best way to master this skill.

The second half of this project explored color in Illustrator: applying color, saving global color swatches to make changes more efficiently, using gradients to add visual interest, and making changes to specific colors throughout a selection.

Finally, you created files in two different formats that are commonly used to share Illustrator artwork with other applications. EPS and PDF formats are invaluable parts of design workflows using software applications that can't import native Illustrator files.

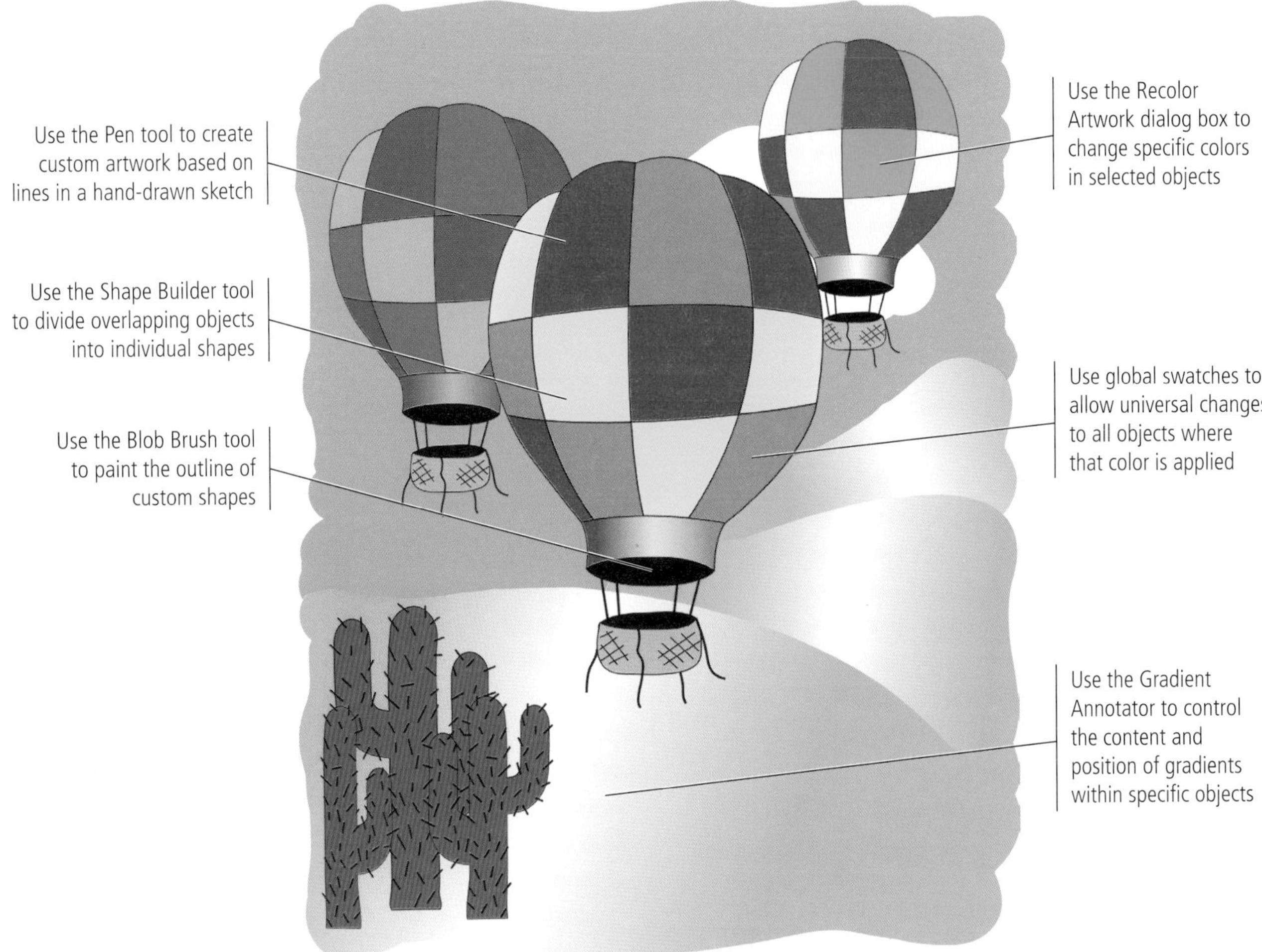
Use the Pen tool to create custom artwork based on lines in a hand-drawn sketch
Use the Shape Builder tool to divide overlapping objects into individual shapes
Use the Blob Brush tool to paint the outline of custom shapes
Use the Recolor Artwork dialog box to change specific colors in selected objects
Use global swatches to allow universal changes to all objects where that color is applied
Use the Gradient Annotator to control the content and position of gradients within specific objects

project 3

Identity Package

Your client, Graham Apple, owns an organic orchard in Central Florida. He hired you to create a corporate identity package so he can begin branding his products to reach a larger consumer base in gourmet groceries throughout the Southeast. He asked you to develop a logo, and then create the standard identity pieces (letterhead and envelope) that he will use for business promotion and correspondence.

This project incorporates the following skills:

- ❑ Developing custom logo artwork based on an object in a photograph
- ❑ Using a gradient mesh to create realistic color blends
- ❑ Converting type to outlines and manipulating letter shapes to create a finished logotype
- ❑ Using layers to easily manage complex artwork
- ❑ Creating multiple artboards to contain specific projects and layouts
- ❑ Building various logo versions to meet specific output requirements
- ❑ Saving EPS files for maximum flexibility
- ❑ Printing desktop proofs of individual artboards

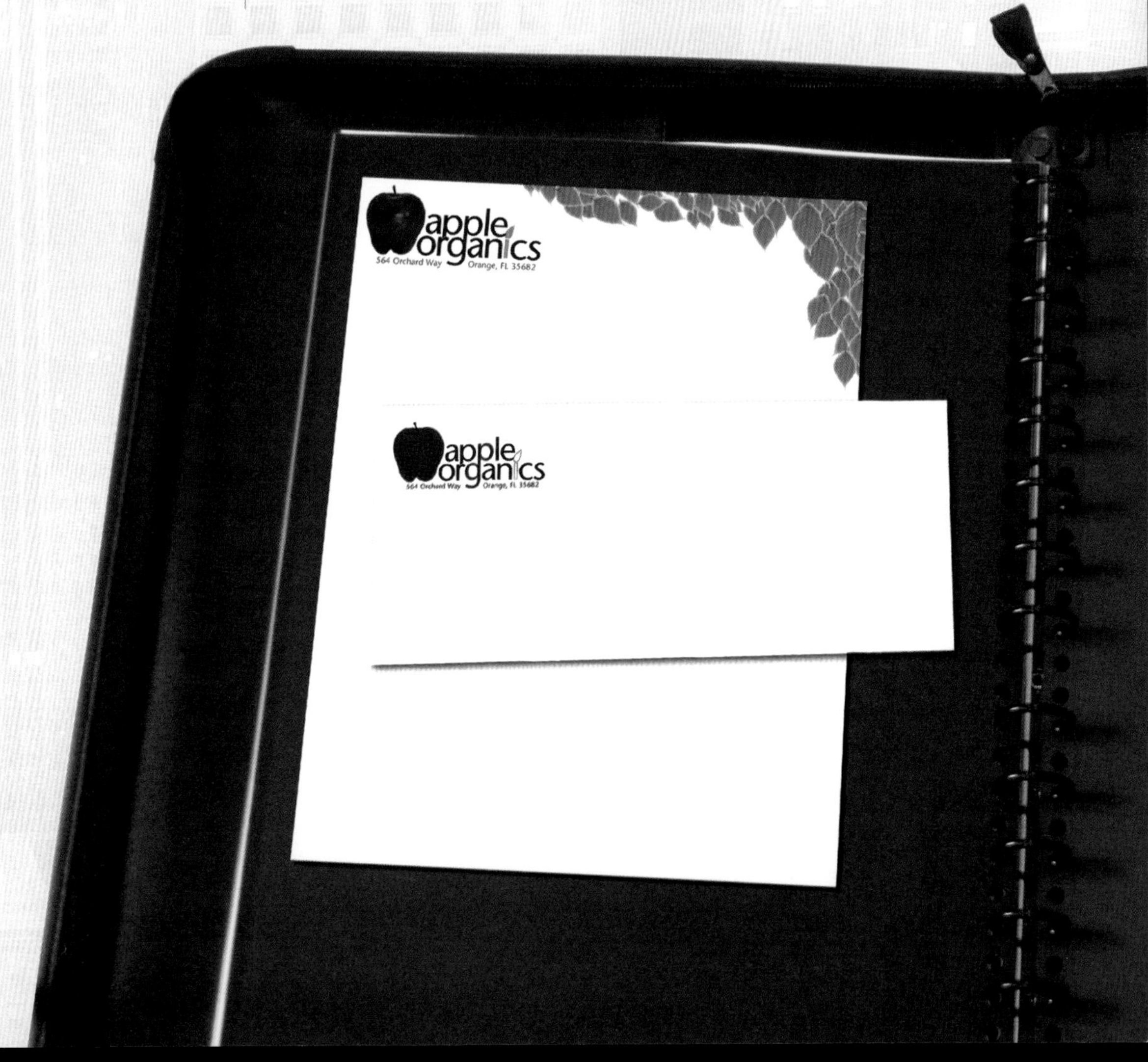

Project Meeting

client comments

It's just a coincidence that my last name is Apple and I own an organic orchard, but I might as well take advantage where I can. I want my logo to be — surprise! — an apple, with some creative type treatment for the name of the farm (Apple Organics).

Once the logo is complete, I want you to use it to create letterhead and envelopes that I will have preprinted; I want a more professional feel than I can create using my laser printer. The printer I spoke with said I could do this for less money if I go "4-color" for the letterhead, but "2-color" for the envelope; I really don't know what that means — I'm hoping you do.

art director comments

The logo is the first part of this project because you will use it on the other two pieces. The client told you exactly what he wants, so that part is taken care of. I had our photographer take a good apple picture; use that as the basis for the one you draw in the logo art.

The client wants to print the letterhead in four-color and the envelope in two-color, so you will have to create two different versions of the logo. Since logos are used on far more than just these two jobs in this one application, you should also create a one-color version because the client will inevitably ask for it at some point.

project objectives

To complete this project, you will:

- ❑ Use the Pen tool to trace the outline of a photograph
- ❑ Create a gradient mesh
- ❑ Use Smart Guides to manage a gradient mesh
- ❑ Use effects to add object highlights
- ❑ Create and control point-type objects
- ❑ Convert text to outlines so you can manipulate the letter shapes
- ❑ Use the Appearance panel to revert gradient mesh objects back to regular paths
- ❑ Apply spot-color inks for special printing applications
- ❑ Create versions of the final logo for 1-color, 2-color, and 4-color printing
- ❑ Print desktop proofs of the completed identity pieces

Stage 1 Working with Gradient Meshes

There are several important points to keep in mind when you design a logo.

First, logos need to be scalable. A company might place its logo on the head of a golf tee or on the side of a building. This is a strong argument for using the simpler line-art approach instead of photography. Vector graphics — the kind you typically create in Illustrator — can be scaled as large or small as necessary without losing quality; photographs are raster images, and they can't be greatly enlarged or reduced without losing quality. That's why you're converting a photograph (a raster image) into a vector graphic in this project.

Second, you almost always need more than one version of any given logo — very often in more than one file format. Different kinds of output require different formats (specifically, one set of files for print and one for the Web), and some types of jobs require special options saved in the files — such as the 4-color, 2-color, and 1-color versions of the logo that you will create in this project.

Set up the Workspace

Your client needs several versions of a new logo, including one with realistic color. Illustrator includes a number of tools ideally suited for creating lifelike illustrations. In this project, you will work from a photograph to create a vector-based apple graphic that will be part of your client's logo. You will start with the full-color version, and then work from there to create the other variations that are part of a typical logo package.

1. **Download Print5_RF_Project3.zip from the Student Files Web page.**

2. **Expand the ZIP archive in your WIP folder (Macintosh) or copy the archive contents into your WIP folder (Windows).**

   This results in a folder named **Organics**, which contains the files you need for this project. You should also use this folder to save the files you create in this project.

3. **In Illustrator, choose File>New.**

4. **Type apple in the Name field, choose Letter as the page size, and choose Inches as the unit of measurement.**

   At this point, you are simply using the artboard as a drawing space, so you only need to make it large enough to draw. Later, you will adjust the artboard to meet the specific needs of the finished logo.

5. **Make sure the Number of Artboards field is set to 1.**

   Later in this project, you will add multiple artboards to hold various versions of the logo. For now, you only need one artboard, which will serve as a drawing board.

6. **In the Advanced options, choose CMYK in the Color Mode menu and choose High (300 ppi) in the Raster Effects menu.**

   Because the CMYK gamut is smaller than the RGB gamut, you are starting with the smaller gamut to avoid the color shift that could occur if you started with RGB and converted the colors to CMYK. You are also creating the file to meet the high-resolution requirements of commercial printing. While not part of this project, you can easily use the Save For Web & Devices utility to export low-resolution RGB versions of the file for digital media.

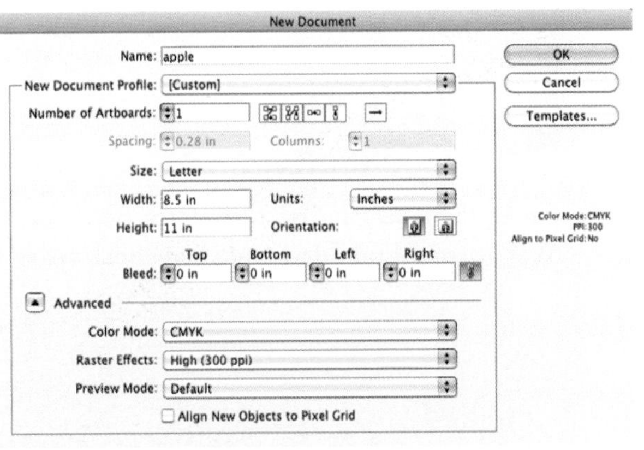

7. **Click OK to create the new file.**

8. **Choose File>Place. Navigate to apple.jpg in your WIP>Organics folder. Make sure the Link and Template options are not checked, and click Place.**

   Choosing the Template option places an image onto a template layer that is automatically dimmed. That's not what you want to do here; you want the photograph to remain at full visibility so you can extract colors from the photo.

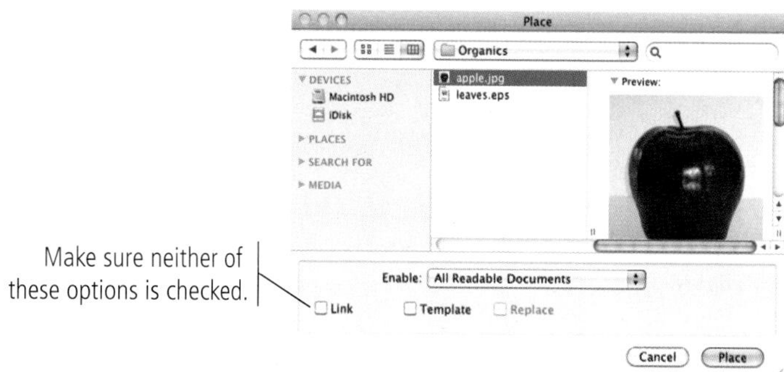

Make sure neither of these options is checked.

9. **Center the photo to the horizontal and vertical center of the artboard.**

10. **Rename Layer 1 Apple Photo, and then lock the layer.**

    For most of the drawing process, you will use the Apple Photo layer as the basis of your artwork. You will draw on other layers, and then delete the photo layer when your apple graphic is complete.

Lock the Apple Photo layer to protect it.

You're starting with a letter-size Artboard. After you finish the logo graphic, you will resize the Artboard to fit the artwork.

11. **Save the file as a native Illustrator file named apple.ai in your WIP>Organics folder, and then continue to the next exercise.**

DRAW THE APPLE SHAPES

In Project 2, you used the Pen tool to create custom shapes using a hand-drawn sketch as your template. The apple shape in this logo is another example of a custom shape composed of lines and paths. In this project you will be using a photograph as your guide. The first step is to determine what shapes you need to create.

1. **With `apple.ai` open, create a new layer at the top of the layer stack and rename it `Apple Front`.**

2. **Using the Pen tool with a 1-pt black stroke and no fill, draw the outline of the front part of the apple. Follow the shape of the apple as it curves in front of the stem.**

   We started our contour line at the bottom part of the apple where there is a sharp corner because starting a contour line on a curve often creates less than perfect results. Use our image as a rough guide for where to place the anchor points; yours doesn't have to match exactly, but it should come close.

Pen tool
Skip over the area that wraps behind the stem.
We started drawing here (at a corner).
LAYERS
Apple Front
Apple Photo
2 Layers

> ***Note:***
>
> *Refer back to Project 2 for details about drawing and editing Bézier curves.*

3. **If necessary, use the Direct Selection tool to adjust the anchor points and handles until the outline matches the shape of the apple.**

4. **Create another new layer and rename it `Apple Back`. In the Layers panel, drag this layer below the Apple Front layer.**

5. **On the Apple Back layer, use the Pen tool to draw the shape of the back part of the apple (where the apple curves behind the stem).**

   Be sure to overlap this shape with the Apple Front shape so no blank space will show between the two elements later.

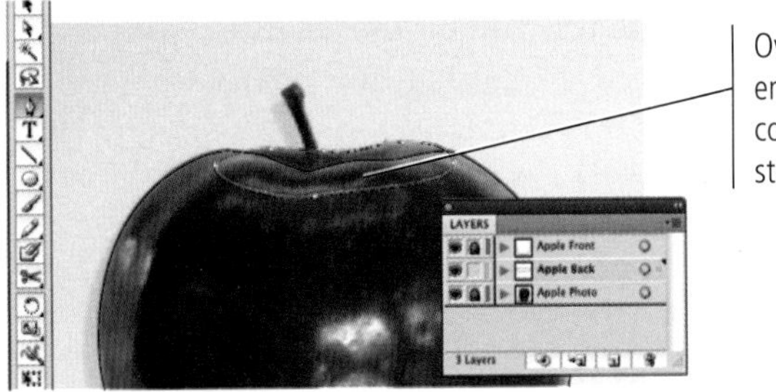
Overlap this line to ensure complete coverage when you start adding color.
LAYERS
Apple Front
Apple Back
Apple Photo
3 Layers

6. **Create a new layer and rename it `Stem`.**

   Since you were just working on the Apple Back layer, the new Stem layer should automatically reside between the Apple Front and Apple Back layers in the Layers panel (which is where you want it to reside). If not, drag the Stem layer to the correct position before continuing.

7. **Draw the outline of the stem on the active Stem layer. Again, overlap the bottom of the Stem shape with the Apple Front shape.**

   You now have all the outlines for the apple, with each outline on its own layer. When you start adding gradient meshes in the next stage of the project, you will see how important it is to use a different layer for each element.

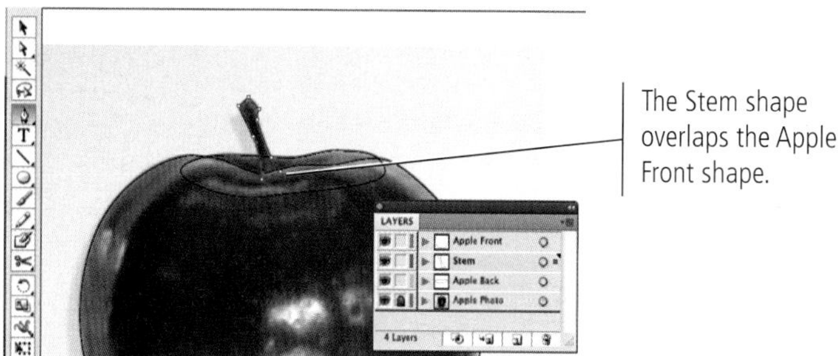
LAYERS
Apple Front
Stem
Apple Back
Apple Photo
4 Layers

The Stem shape overlaps the Apple Front shape.

8. **Save the file and continue to the next exercise.**

Create a Gradient Mesh

A gradient mesh is basically a special type of fill. Each point in the mesh can have a different color value; the colors of adjacent mesh points determine the colors in the gradient between the two points. When you paint objects with a mesh, it's similar to painting with ink or watercolor. It takes considerable practice to become proficient with gradient meshes.

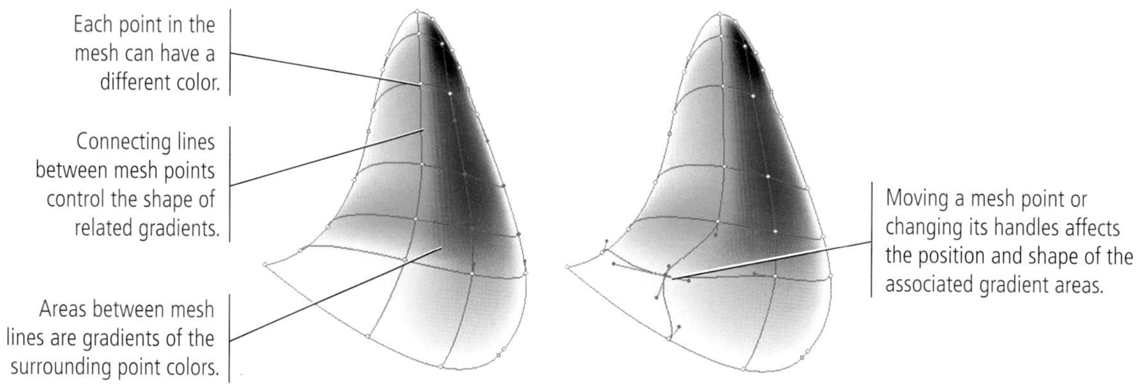
Each point in the mesh can have a different color.
Connecting lines between mesh points control the shape of related gradients.
Areas between mesh lines are gradients of the surrounding point colors.
Moving a mesh point or changing its handles affects the position and shape of the associated gradient areas.

One of the techniques you apply in this project is Illustrator's Outline mode. Outline mode allows you to see the points and paths of an object without the colors and fills. This viewing mode can be very useful when you need to adjust anchor points of one shape while viewing the underlying objects.

1. **With `apple.ai` open, click the eye icons in the Layers panel to hide the Apple Back and Stem layers, and then select the Apple Front layer.**

2. **Using the Selection tool, select the outline shape on the Apple Front layer.**

3. **Using the Eyedropper tool, click a medium-red color in the apple image to fill the selected apple shape with the sampled color.**

   You can add a gradient mesh to a path without filling it with color first, but if you don't choose a color, the mesh will automatically fill with white. It's easier to create a good mesh if you start with a fill that colors most of the object.

4. **Choose Object>Create Gradient Mesh and make sure the Preview option is checked.**

5. **In the Create Gradient Mesh dialog box, set the Rows value to 8 and the Columns value to 9, and make sure the Appearance menu is set to Flat.**

Note:

When you convert a path to a mesh, the shape is no longer a path. You cannot apply a stroke attribute to a gradient mesh object.

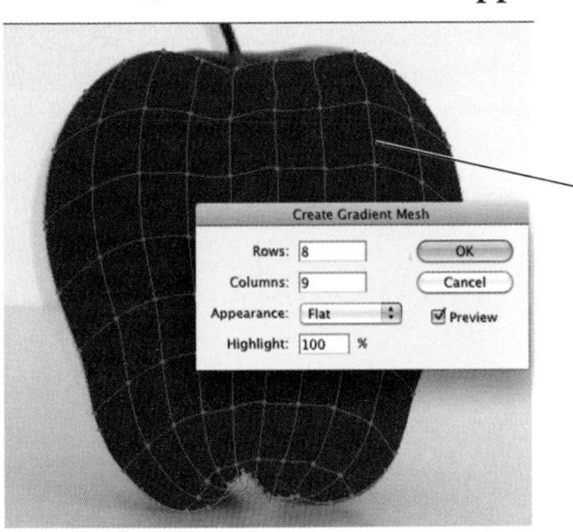

The Rows and Columns settings determine how many lines will make up the resulting mesh.

6. **Click OK to create the mesh.**

7. **Choose View>Outline.**

   In Outline mode, you see only the edges or **wireframes** of the objects in the file. (Your mesh might appear different than ours, based on where you placed your anchor points on the shape edges. Don't worry — you will still be able to achieve the same overall effect as what you see in our examples.)

Note:

In our screen shots, we have the bounding box turned off to better show only the mesh points. You can turn off the bounding box by choosing View>Hide Bounding Box.

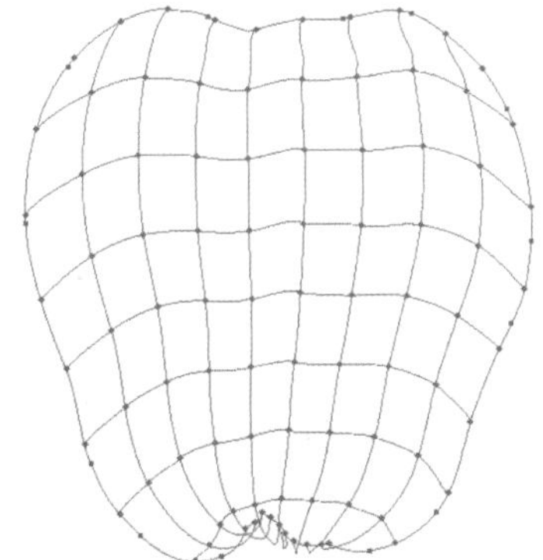

8. **Command/Control-click the eye icon next to the Apple Photo layer to return it to Preview viewing mode.**

You can now see the mesh wireframe and the actual pixels of the apple image, enabling you to sample colors directly from the apple image, and then use those colors to paint the mesh points.

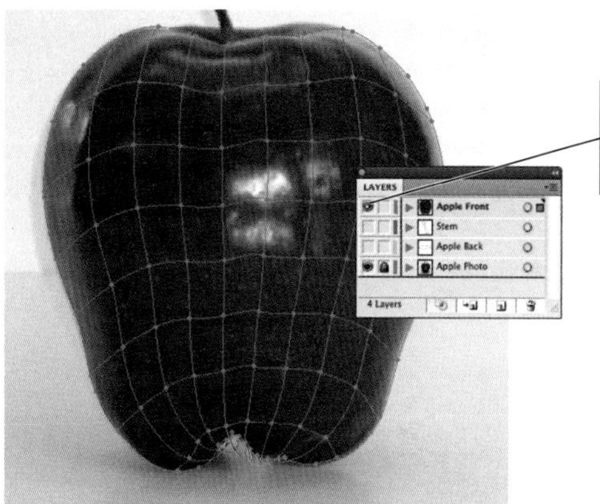

The iris in the icon is hollow when a layer displays in Outline mode.

Note:

When working in Outline mode, Command/Control-clicking a layer's visibility icon (the eye icon) returns only that layer to Preview mode.

9. **Using the Direct Selection tool, click the top-left point on the inside of the mesh object to select only that mesh point.**

Don't select one of the mesh points on the outside edge of the shape.

Gradient Mesh Options

ILLUSTRATOR FOUNDATIONS

When creating a gradient mesh, the number of rows and columns you create depends on the size and shape of the object you want to create. You might want to experiment with these settings before you click OK and create the mesh. If you add too many mesh points, the colors blend incorrectly and take a long time to paint; if you add too few mesh lines, it can be difficult — if not impossible — to add enough depth to the illustration. (Even though you can use the Mesh tool to add and delete mesh lines later, it's more efficient to create a mesh as close as possible to what you need as the final result.)

The Appearance option in the Create Gradient Mesh dialog box determines how colors affect the mesh you create:

- The **Flat** option, which you used in this exercise, spreads a single color to all points in the mesh. If you don't fill the shape with a color before creating the mesh, the mesh object will fill with solid white.
- The **To Center** option (upper right) creates a white highlight at the center of the mesh and gradually spreads the highlight color outward toward the edges of the object. The Highlight (%) field controls the strength of the white highlight in the resulting mesh.
- The **To Edge** option (lower right) is essentially the opposite of the To Center option; the white highlight appears around the edges of the mesh, blending to the solid color in the center of the mesh object.

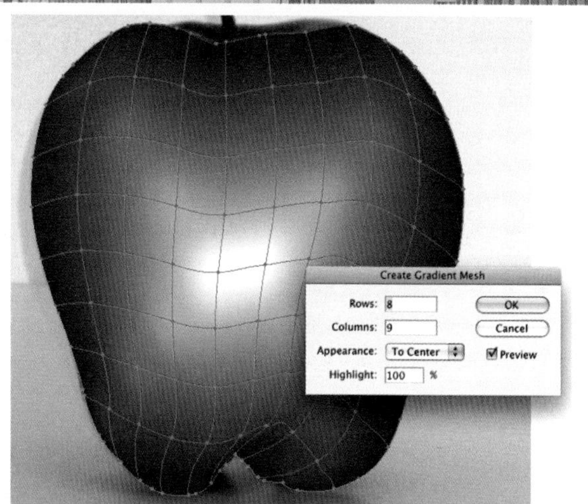

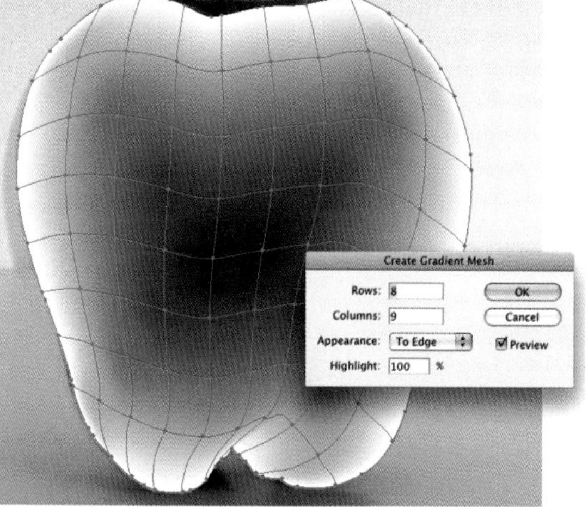

10. **With the mesh point selected, choose the Eyedropper tool in the Tools panel, and then click next to the selected mesh point to sample the color from the apple photo.**

    Because the mesh object is still displayed in Outline mode, you can't see the effect of the color sampling.

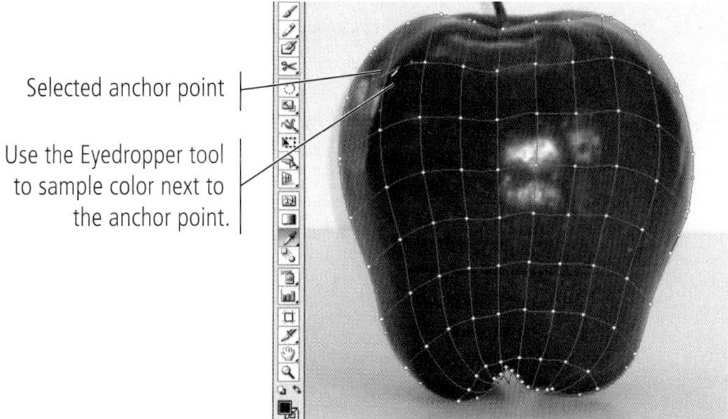

Selected anchor point
Use the Eyedropper tool to sample color next to the anchor point.

11. **Press Command/Control to temporarily access the Direct Selection tool, and then click the next mesh point on the same vertical mesh line.**

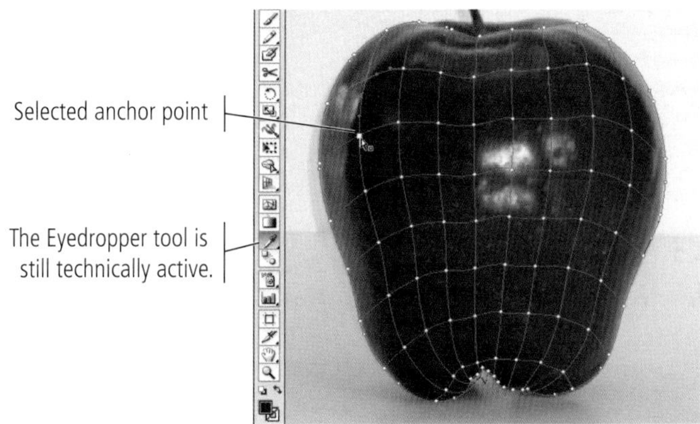

Selected anchor point
The Eyedropper tool is still technically active.

> *Note:*
>
> *You can use the Opacity field in the Control panel to define a different opacity for every point in a gradient mesh.*

12. **Release the Command/Control key to return to the Eyedropper tool, and then click to sample the color next to the selected mesh point.**

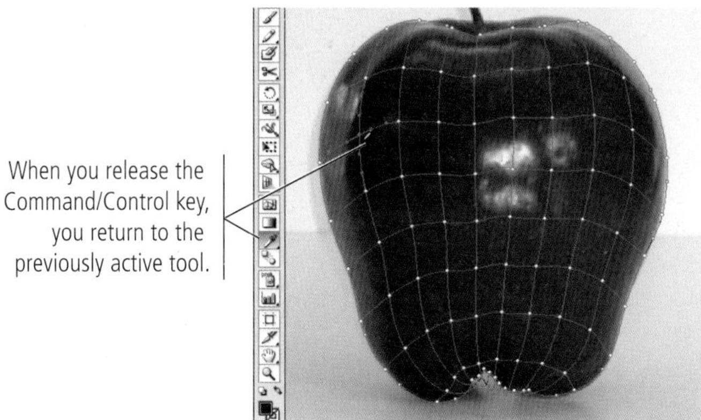

13. **Continue this process to change the color of the mesh points in the first three columns of the mesh.**

14. **Choose View>Preview to see the actual content of the visible layers.**

15. **Deselect everything on the page and review your progress.**

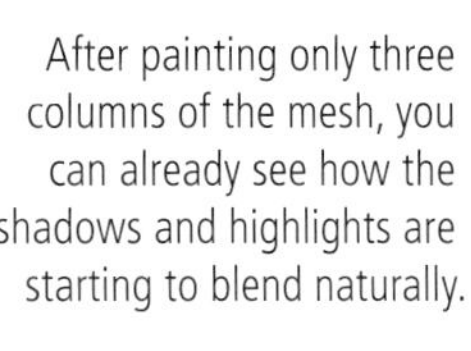

After painting only three columns of the mesh, you can already see how the shadows and highlights are starting to blend naturally.

16. **Command/Control-click the eye icon for the Apple Front layer to change only that layer back to Outline mode.**

17. **Using the same technique from the previous steps, finish painting all the mesh points in the mesh object.**

Ignore the bright highlights for now; you will add the proper highlights later.

This task might seem tedious because there are so many points in the mesh, but with this process, you can create realistic depth in a flat vector object in a matter of minutes. To accomplish the same result using manual techniques would require many hours of time and a high degree of artistic skill.

18. **Command/Control-click the Apple Front layer eye icon to return the layer to Preview mode, and then deselect the mesh object and review your results.**

19. **Save the file and continue to the next exercise.**

Work with a Mesh Using Smart Guides

It can be difficult to select and manipulate points in a mesh in Preview mode because you can't see the actual mesh lines and points until the mesh object is selected. You could move your cursor around until you locate the exact mesh point you want to work with; or you could continue switching back and forth between Preview and Outline modes. Both methods, however, can be time consuming (and frustrating).

Fortunately, Smart Guides solve this problem. Using Smart Guides, you can see the entire mesh wireframe as soon as your cursor touches any part of the object — providing a temporary outline/preview combination.

> *Note:*
>
> *When using Smart Guides, make sure the Snap to Point option is toggled off. If Snap to Point is active, Smart Guides will not work (even if you have the command selected in the menu).*

1. **With apple.ai open, choose View>Smart Guides to make sure that option is turned on.**

2. **Make sure the Snap to Point option is toggled off in the View menu.**

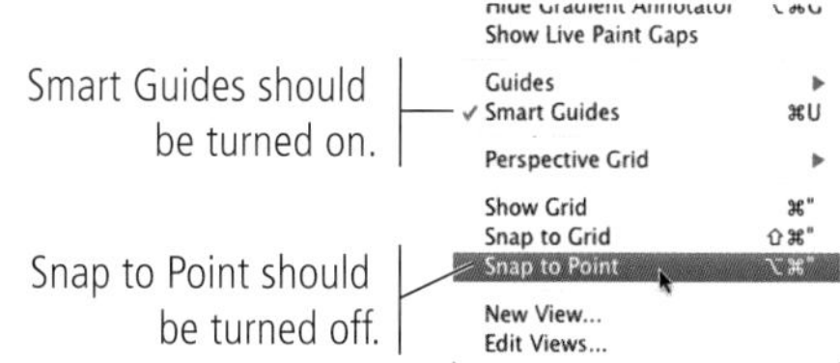

Snap to Point should be turned off.

3. **Make sure everything in the file is deselected, and then roll the Direct Selection tool over the apple shape.**

   You can now see the mesh points and lines, as well as the precise location of the Direct Selection tool.

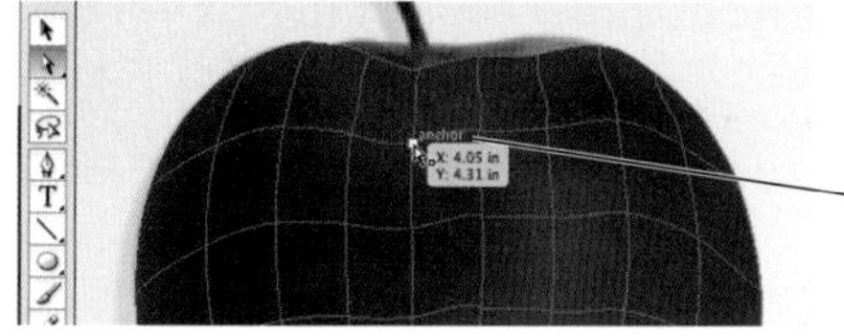

With Smart Guides turned on, you can easily view and select specific anchors in the mesh.

4. **Command/Control-click the visibility icon for the Apple Front layer so you can see the photo behind the mesh object.**

5. **Using the Eyedropper tool, sample the highlight color on the top-left side of the apple shape.**

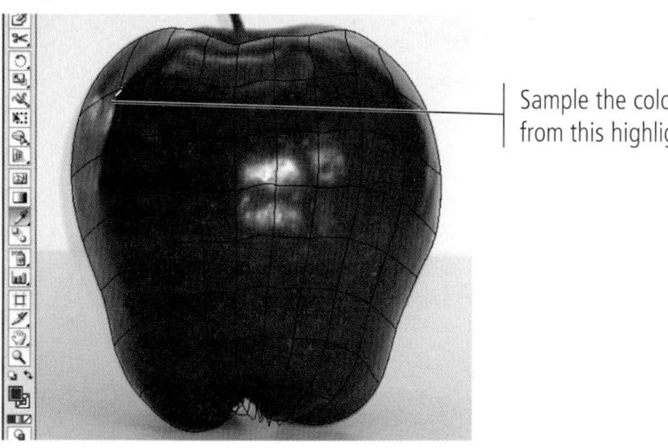

Sample the color from this highlight.

6. **Command/Control-click the visibility icon for the Apple Front layer to restore that layer to Preview mode.**

7. **Choose the Mesh tool from the Tools panel.**

   The Mesh tool adds new gridlines to an existing mesh, or it creates a mesh if you click inside a basic shape that doesn't currently have a mesh.

8. **Click the third horizontal mesh line, between the first and second vertical mesh lines, to create a new vertical mesh line (as shown in the following image).**

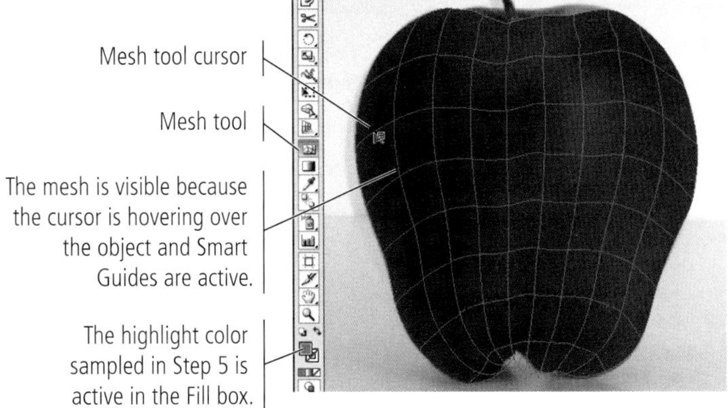

Mesh tool cursor
Mesh tool
The mesh is visible because the cursor is hovering over the object and Smart Guides are active.
The highlight color sampled in Step 5 is active in the Fill box.

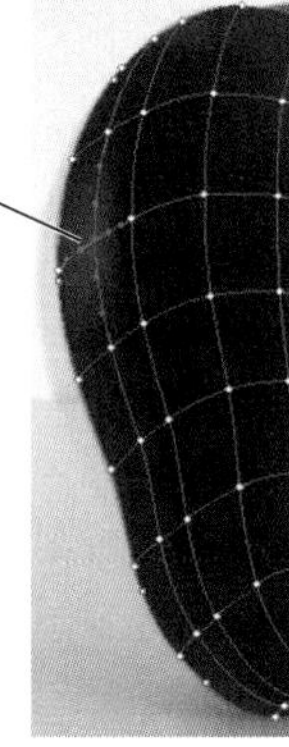

Clicking this horizontal mesh line with the Mesh tool adds a new vertical mesh line, colored with the highlight color you sampled in the previous step.

9. **Press Command/Control and click away from the mesh object to deselect it.**

10. **Change the Apple Front layer to Outline mode.**

11. **Select the Mesh tool. Click twice along the vertical mesh line directly below the stem to add two horizontal mesh lines between the first two rows of the existing mesh.**

    It isn't necessary to return the layer to Preview mode before adding lines to the mesh.

Click this vertical mesh line twice to add two horizontal mesh lines.

12. **Using the Direct Selection tool, select the point on the (now) second horizontal mesh line, directly below the stem.**

    This is one of the mesh lines you created with the Mesh tool in the previous step.

Note:

Clicking a horizontal mesh line with the Mesh tool creates a new vertical mesh line. To add a horizontal mesh line, click the Mesh tool on a vertical mesh line.

Note:

It might be helpful to deselect the mesh after adding the first new mesh line, and then click again to add the second mesh line.

13. **With the mesh point selected, use the Eyedropper tool to sample the light red of the apple's highlight to change the color of the point.**

When you change the color of a mesh point, you change the way surrounding colors blend into that point's color. By changing this point to a medium red, you reduce the distance over which the highlight color (in the lower point) can blend — effectively shortening the highlight area.

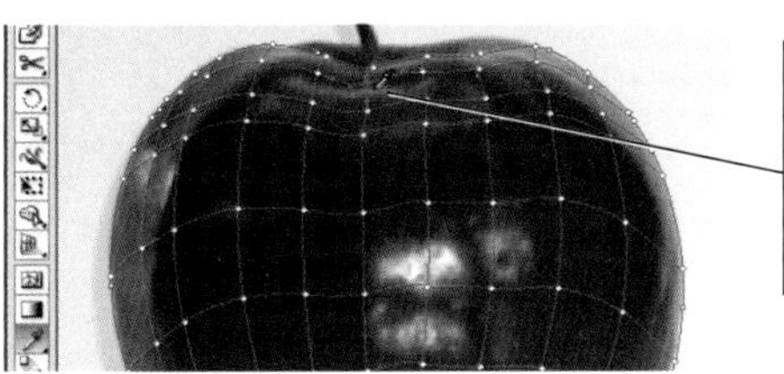

Changing this anchor point to a lighter red adds a highlight to the apple graphic, more closely matching the highlight in the original image.

Note:

Remember, pressing Command/Control with another tool selected temporarily accesses the Direct Selection tool.

14. **Command/Control-click to select the mesh point to the immediate left of the point where you placed the highlight.**

15. **Release the mouse button to return to the Eyedropper tool, and then sample the highlight color again to spread the highlight horizontally across the apple.**

16. **Repeat Steps 14–15 for the point to the right of the one you changed in Step 13.**

By filling these two anchors with the highlight color, you extend the highlight horizontally along the mesh line.

17. **Deselect the mesh object, return the Apple Front layer to Preview mode, and review your work.**

The highlight adds depth, but it spreads a bit too far down (compared to the original image).

18. **Using the Direct Selection tool, drag up the three mesh points immediately below the highlight points.**

Reducing the distance between the points shortens the distance of the blended highlight-colored area.

Moving the anchors below the highlight shortens the height of the blended highlight.

As soon as you move the cursor over the object, the mesh lines become visible.

19. **Continue adjusting the positions and colors of the mesh points until you are satisfied with the result.**

20. **Choose View>Smart Guides to toggle off the Smart Guides.**

21. **Save the file and continue to the next exercise.**

Color the Remaining Objects

Building and coloring the shape for the apple's front should have given you a good idea of how mesh points control color blending from one point to another. Because you set up the file using layers for the individual shapes that make up the apple, it will be fairly easy to create additional meshes for the remaining pieces of the apple.

1. **With apple.ai open, hide the Apple Front layer and then show the Apple Back layer.**

2. **Using the Selection tool, select the shape on the Apple Back layer.**

3. **Using the Eyedropper tool, click a darker part of the apple to fill the selected shape with the sampled color.**

4. **Choose Object>Create Gradient Mesh and add a 3-row, 5-column mesh with the Appearance menu set to Flat.**

5. **Use the same method you learned in the previous exercise to color the mesh points for the Apple Back shape.**

   Switch the Apple Back layer to Outline mode, and then use the Eyedropper tool to sample colors from the photo for each point in the mesh.

6. **Show the Apple Front layer and review your work.**

7. **Lock the Apple Back layer, and then show the Stem layer.**

8. **Select the stem shape and fill it with a color sampled from the lightest color near the top of the stem.**

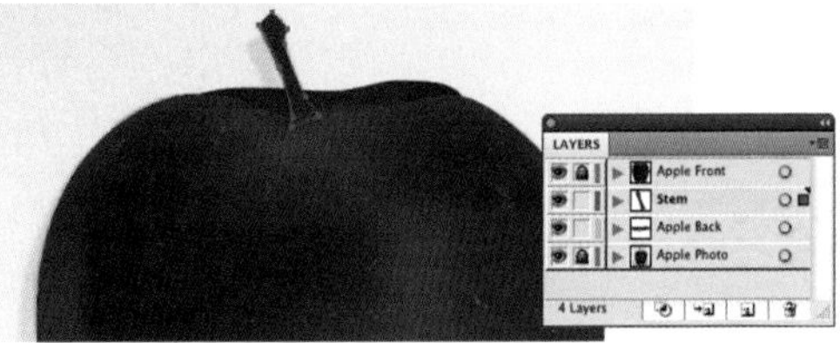

9. **Change the Stem layer to Outline mode.**

10. **Deselect all objects, and then use the Eyedropper tool to sample the dark color of the stem.**

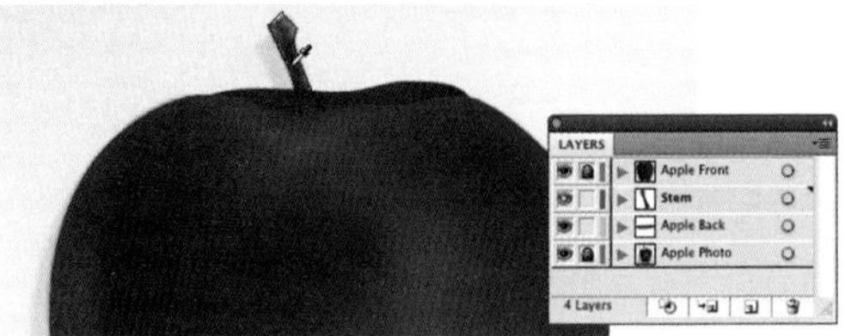

11. **Return the Stem layer to Preview mode.**

12. **Using the Mesh tool, click in the middle of the stem shape to create a mesh.**

    The stem shape is converted to a mesh, and a new mesh point (with the color you sampled in Step 10) is added where you click.

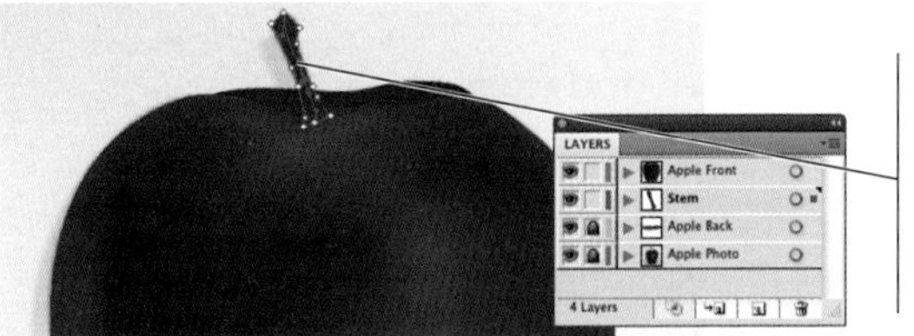

Clicking with the Mesh tool converts the stem shape to a mesh object and adds a point (and the associated lines) where you click.

13. **Deselect everything, and then hide the Apple Photo layer to review your work.**

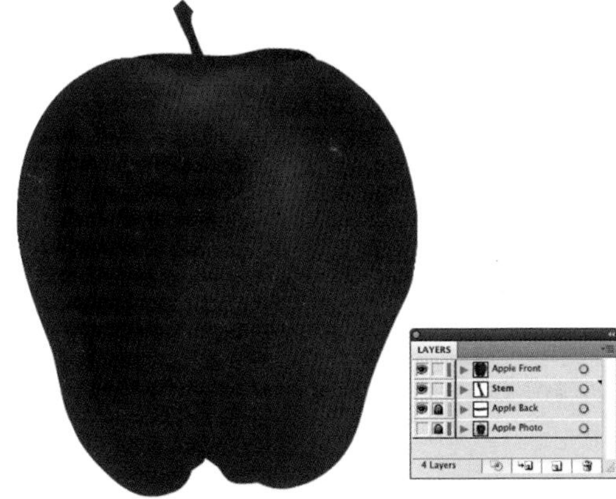

14. **Show the Apple Photo layer again, save the file, and then continue to the next exercise.**

 Use Filters to Add Object Highlights

As with any illustration, painting, or drawing, the details separate good work from great work. In this exercise, you add the highlights on the front and left sides of the apple to finish the illustration.

1. **With apple.ai open, hide the Apple Front, Apple Back, and Stem layers.**

2. **Create a new layer named Highlights and move this layer to the top of the stack in the Layers panel.**

3. **Using the Pen tool with a 1-pt black stroke and no fill, create the shapes of the highlights on the front of the apple.**

4. **Select all the highlight shapes you drew in Step 3 and fill them with a color sampled from the highlights in the photo.**

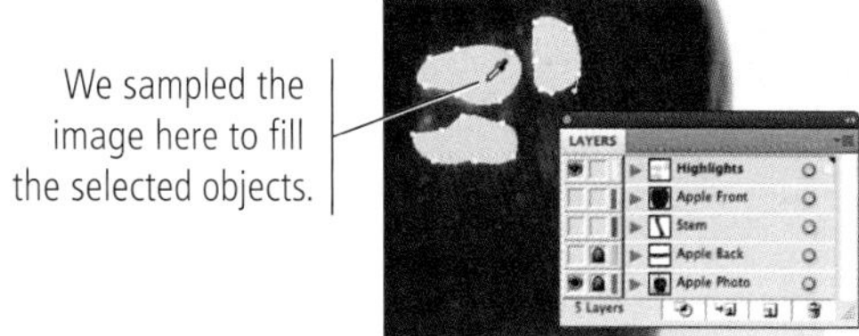

We sampled the image here to fill the selected objects.

5. **Deselect all objects. Select one of the larger highlight shapes and choose Effect>Stylize>Feather.**

   Make sure you choose from the Illustrator Effects list (at the top of the menu) and not the Photoshop Effects list. (You will learn more about these effects, including the difference between the two sets, in Project 6.)

6. **Activate the Preview option in the Feather dialog box, and then set the Feather Radius to 0.2″.**

   The Feather effect softens the edges of the shape, blending from fully opaque to fully transparent. A higher Feather Radius value extends the distance from opaque to transparent color in the effect.

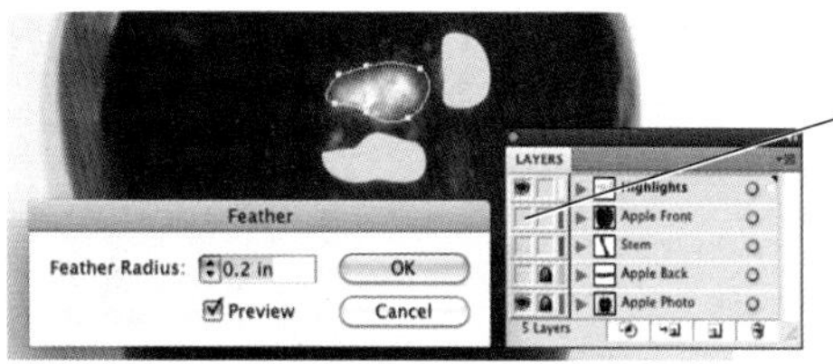

It is difficult to evaluate the actual results while the Apple Front layer is hidden.

7. **Click OK, and then show the Apple Front layer.**

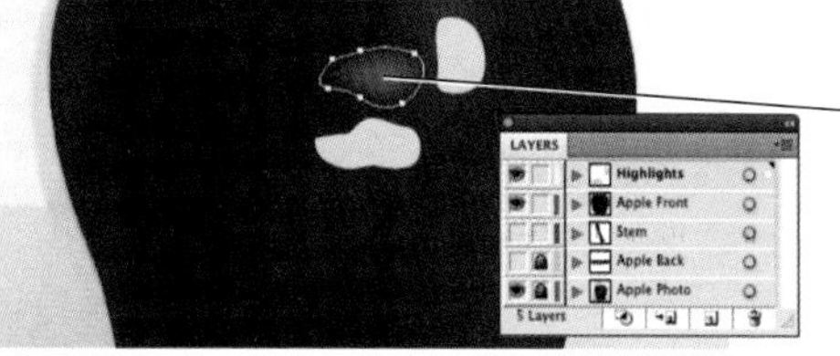

With the Apple Front layer showing, the large feather radius appears weak.

8. **With the feathered object selected, open the Appearance panel.**

   Effects in Illustrator are non-destructive attributes, which means they do not permanently change the object being styled. Because these effects are stored as object attributes, you can change the settings for any effect at any time.

9. **In the Appearance panel, click the Feather hot text to open the dialog box for that appearance attribute.**

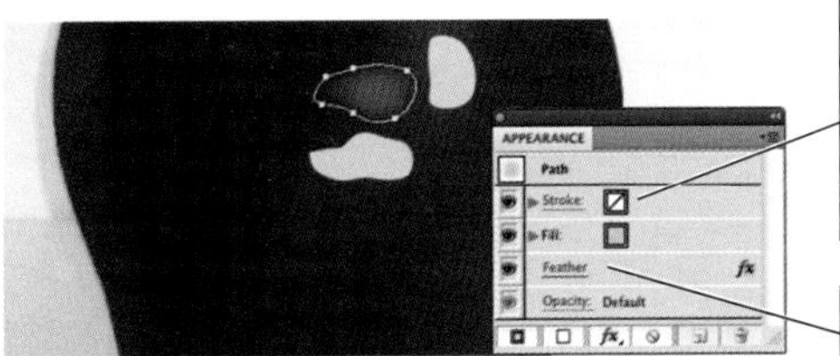

The Appearance panel shows the attributes — including stroke, fill, and applied effects — defined for the selected object.

Click the Feather hot text to open that dialog box.

Note:

"Hot text" is any text in the user interface that appears blue and underlined. Clicking these hot-text links opens a panel or dialog box where you can change related settings.

10. **Make sure the Preview option is checked, and then experiment with the Feather Radius setting until you are satisfied with the highlight.**

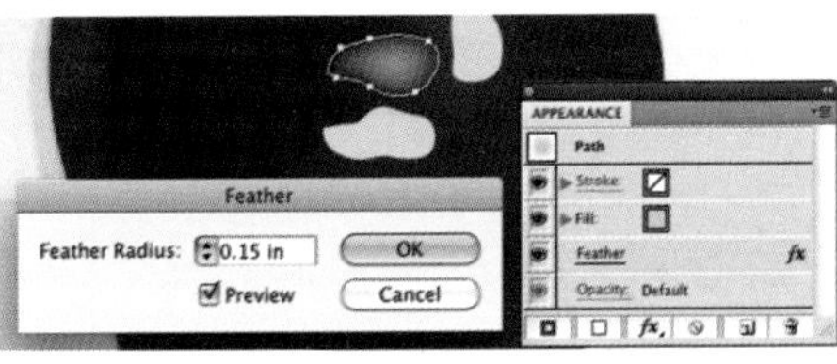

11. **Apply the Feather effect to all highlight areas, changing the Feather Radius value as appropriate for each object.**

12. **Delete the Apple Photo layer, and then show and unlock all remaining layers.**

The Appearance Panel in Depth

ILLUSTRATOR FOUNDATIONS

The Appearance panel allows you to review and change the appearance attributes of objects, including stroke, fill, transparency, and applied effects.

As you know, the last-used settings for fill color, stroke color, and stroke weight are applied to new objects. Other attributes, such as the applied brush or effects, are not automatically applied to new objects. If you need to create a series of objects with the same overall appearance, you can turn off the **New Art Has Basic Appearance** option in the Appearance panel Options menu.

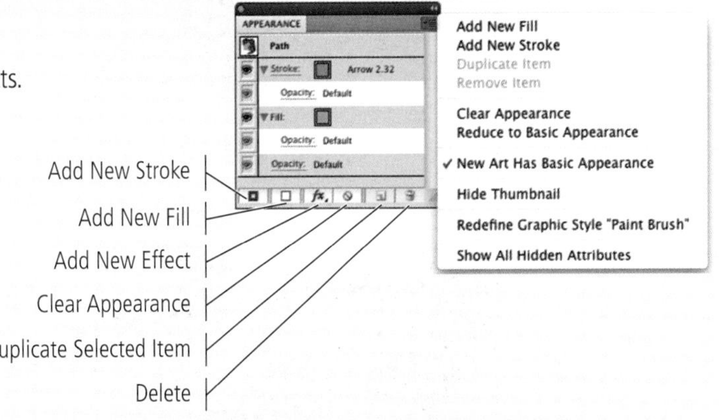

Add New Stroke

Add New Fill

Add New Effect

Clear Appearance

Duplicate Selected Item

Delete

Clicking the **Clear Appearance** button reduces the selected object to a fill and stroke of None. Choosing **Reduce to Basic Appearance** in the panel Options menu resets an object to only basic fill and stroke attributes; fill color and stroke weight and color are maintained, but all other attributes are removed.

You can use the **Duplicate Selected Item** button to create multiple versions of the same attribute for an object, such as two stroke weights/colors — allowing you to compound the effect without layering multiple objects. If you want to remove a specific attribute, simply select that item and click the panel's **Delete** button.

13. **Select everything on the artboard. Use the Control panel or Transform panel to position the top-left corner of the selection at X: 0.1″, Y: 0.1″.**

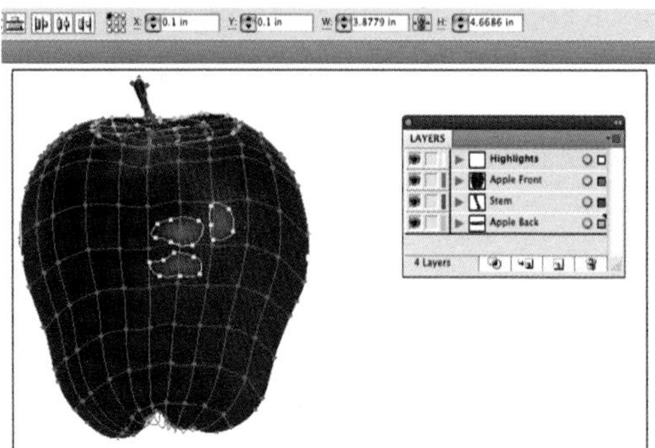

14. **Lock all layers, save the file, and continue to the next stage of the project.**

Type Terminology

ILLUSTRATOR FOUNDATIONS

Before you begin the exercises in the second stage of this project, you should understand the terms that are commonly used when people talk about type. Keep the following terms in mind as you work through the following exercises.

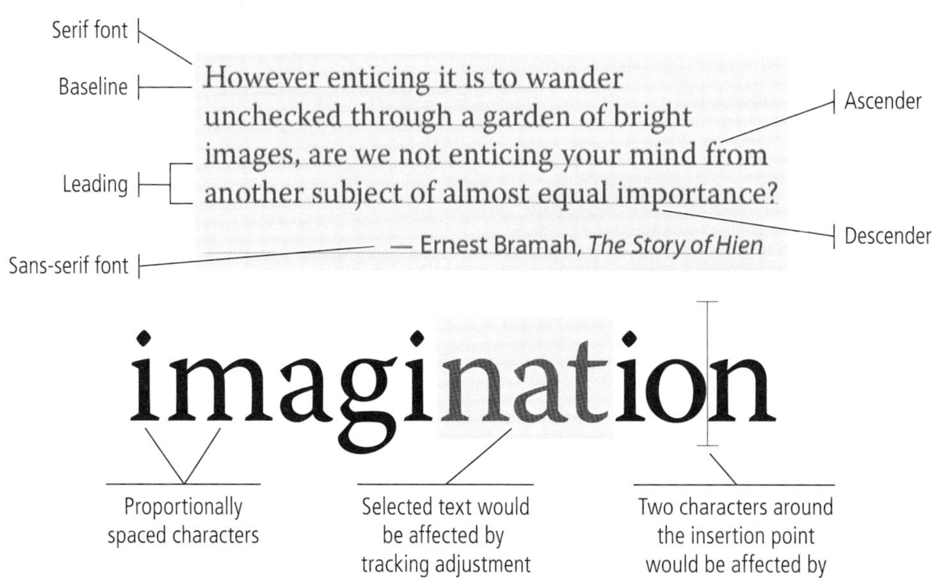

Type is typically divided into two basic categories: serif and sans serif. **Serif type** has small flourishes on the ends of the letterforms; **sans-serif** has no such decorations (sans is French for "without"). There are other categories of special or decorative fonts, including script, symbol, dingbat, decorative, and image fonts.

The actual shape of letters is determined by the specific **font** you use; each character in a font is referred to as a **glyph**. Fonts can be monospaced or proportionally spaced. In a monospace font, each character takes up the same amount of space on a line; in other words, a lowercase i and m occupy the same horizontal space. In a proportionally spaced font, different characters occupy different amounts of horizontal space as necessary.

The **x-height** of type is the height of the lowercase letter x. Elements that extend below the baseline are called **descenders** (as in g, j, and p); elements that extend above the x-height are called **ascenders** (as in b, d, and k).

The size of type is usually measured in **points** (there are approximately 72 points in an inch). When you define a type size, you determine the distance from the bottom of the descenders to the top of the ascenders (plus a small extra space above the ascenders called the **body clearance**).

When you set type in a digital application, it rests on a non-printing line called the **baseline**. If a type element has more than one line in a single paragraph, the distance from one baseline to the next is called **leading** (pronounced "ledding"). Most applications set the default leading as 120% of the type size.

Stage 2 Working with Type

To create a complete logo, you pair logo artwork with text that makes up the corporate brand (the company name and tagline, if there is one). Illustrator includes sophisticated tools for controlling type — from changing the font and size to controlling the appearance of quotes and using styles to format long blocks of text.

In this stage of the project, you will use some of the basic type formatting options to set your client's company name. You will also use illustration techniques to manipulate the individual letter shapes in the company name to create the finished logotype.

Create Point-Type Objects

Creating type in Illustrator is fairly simple; simply click with the Type tool and begin typing. Many advanced options are also available, such as importing type from an external file, using type areas to control long blocks of text, and so on. In this project, you concentrate on the basic type formatting controls.

1. **With apple.ai open (from your WIP>Organics folder), create a new layer named Logotype at the top of the layer stack.**

2. **Choose the Type tool in the Tools panel, and then click the empty area of the artboard to the right of the apple graphic.**

   You can create two basic kinds of type (or text) objects in Illustrator: **point-type objects** (also called **path type**), where the text usually resides on a single line or path; and **area-type objects,** where the text fills a specific shape (usually a rectangle).

   When you single-click with the Type tool, you create **point type**. You will see a flashing **insertion point** where text will appear when you begin typing.

3. **With the insertion point flashing, type apple.**

   When you add a new type object (either point type or area type) without changing anything in Illustrator, the type is automatically set in the last-used font and type settings, which will probably be different from one computer to the next.

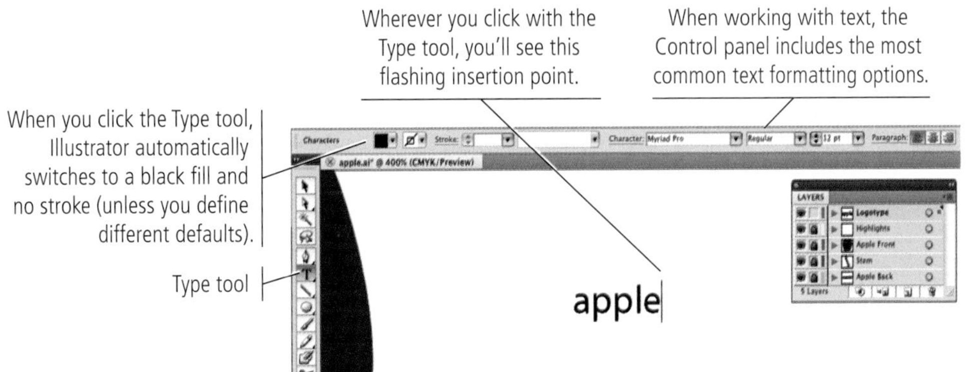

4. **Choose the Direct Selection tool in the Tools panel.**

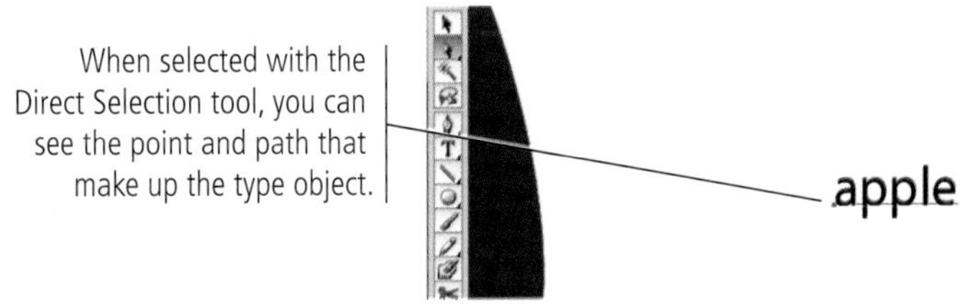

When selected with the Direct Selection tool, you can see the point and path that make up the type object.
apple

Note:

If you want to add another type object, you have to first deselect the one where the insertion point is flashing. To accomplish this, you can Command/Control-click away from the currently active type object. Remember, pressing Command/Control temporarily switches to the Selection or Direct Selection tool (whichever was last used); when you release the Command/Control key, you return to the previously active tool — in this case, the Type tool.

You can also choose Select>Deselect, and then click again with the Type tool to create a new type object.

5. **With the type object selected, click the Paragraph Align Center button in the Control panel.**

Individual characters do not need to be selected to change text formatting. Changes made while a type *object* is selected apply to all text in that type object.

> *Note:*
>
> *If the Paragraph Align buttons are not available in the Control panel, you can find the same option in the Paragraph panel (Window>Type>Paragraph).*

6. **Click the arrow to the right of the Font menu. Scroll through the list of available fonts and choose ATC Oak Normal.**

If your Control panel does not include the Font menu, click the Character hot-text link to open the Character panel, and then apply the ATC Oak Normal font.

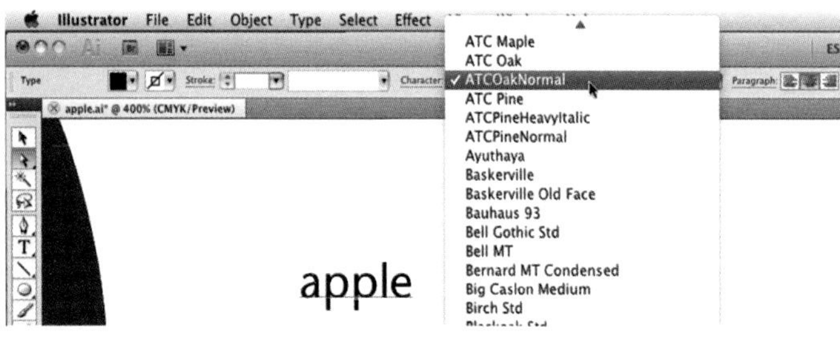

> *Note:*
>
> *You can simply type in the Font field to find a specific font. As you type in the field, Illustrator skips to the first available font with the characters you type (for example, typing "Aar" would automatically find an installed font named Aardvark).*

7. **Click the Selection tool in the Tools panel.**

When the Selection tool is active, you can see the bounding box of the type object. Like any other object, you can use the bounding box handles to stretch, scale, or rotate the type object (including the characters in the type object). If you don't see the bounding box, choose View>Show Bounding Box to toggle on that option.

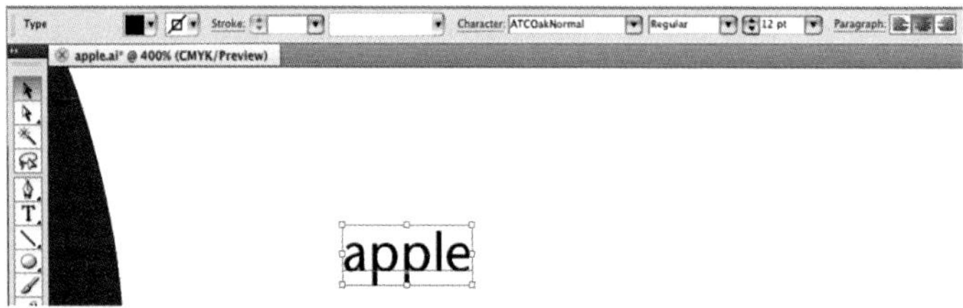

8. **Click any of the type object's corner handles and drag out to make the type larger.**

When you resize a type object with the Selection tool, you'll probably notice that the baseline of the letters moves when you drag the top-right handle. You might need to reposition the type object and resize it a couple of times to achieve the desired result. Guides can be very helpful in this process, depending on what you want to accomplish.

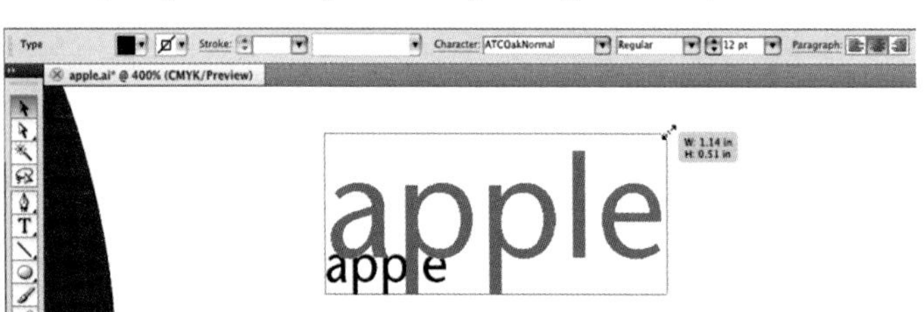

> *Note:*
>
> *You can press Shift to constrain the object's original proportions.*

> *Note:*
>
> *We turned Smart Guides on (View>Smart Guides) to show the cursor feedback in our screen shots.*

9. **In the Control panel, click the Character hot text to open the Character panel directly below the hot text.**

   In addition to the font and size values in the main Control panel, the Character panel provides access to all the character formatting options that can be applied in Illustrator.

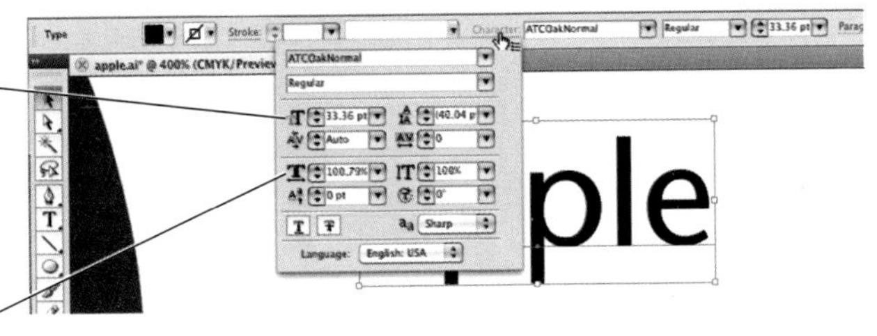

The Size menu shows the new size that results from resizing the object by dragging its bounding box handles.

If you do not constrain the resizing process, you might have a horizontal or vertical scale other than 100% of the font size.

   Some argue that you should never artificially scale type horizontally or vertically (as you did in Step 8) because it distorts the spacing and shape of characters, and requires more processing time for an output device to accurately output the non-standard type sizes.

   However, this type will eventually be converted to vector outlines so artificially scaling the type will cause no problems.

Note:

You can also open the regular Character panel by choosing Window>Type>Character.

10. **In the Character panel, change the Size field to 72. Make sure both the horizontal and vertical scale values are set to 100%.**

   Pressing Tab moves through the panel fields; as soon as you move to a new field, your changes in the previous field are reflected in the document. You can also press Return/Enter to apply a change and collapse the Character panel back into the Control panel.

Note:

Deselecting the selected object applies changes that you defined in the Character panel while the object was selected.

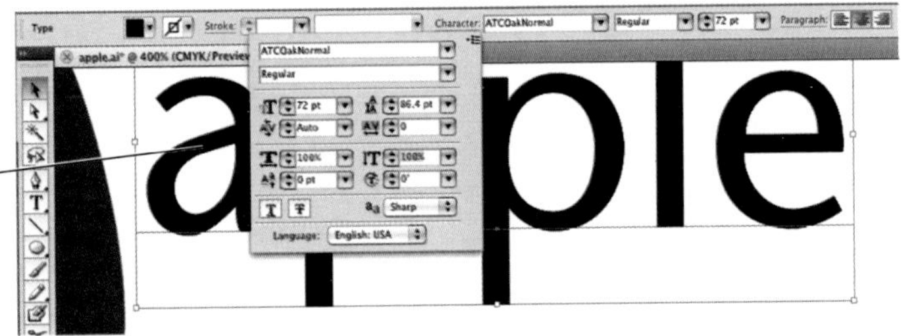

Changes in the panel dynamically reflect in the selected object.

11. **Using the Type tool, double-click the word "apple" to select all the letters in the word, and then open the Character panel (from the Control panel or the Window menu).**

   Tracking and kerning are two terms related to the horizontal spacing between characters in a line of text. **Kerning** is the spacing between two specific characters; **tracking** refers to the spacing between all characters in a selection.

   Most industrial-quality font families come with built-in kern and track values. Smaller type does not usually pose tracking and kerning problems; when type is very large, however, spacing often becomes an issue. To fix spacing problems, you need to adjust the kerning and/or tracking values.

Note:

Kerning and tracking are largely matters of personal preference. Some people prefer much tighter spacing than others.

12. **Change the Tracking field to –25 to tighten the space between all selected letters.**

You can change the field manually, choose a pre-defined value from the Tracking menu, or click the up- or down-arrow button to change the tracking by 1 unit with each click.

The Kern (Pair) value remains set to "Auto," which is the default setting built into this particular typeface.

The Tracking field icon has an arrow below the two letters.

Note:

If you use the panel's arrow buttons or menus to make changes, you don't need to press Return/Enter to apply the change.

The Character Panel in Depth

ILLUSTRATOR FOUNDATIONS

The Character panel, accessed either from the Control panel hot text or as an independent panel by choosing Window>Type>Character, includes all the options you can use to change the appearance of selected text characters.

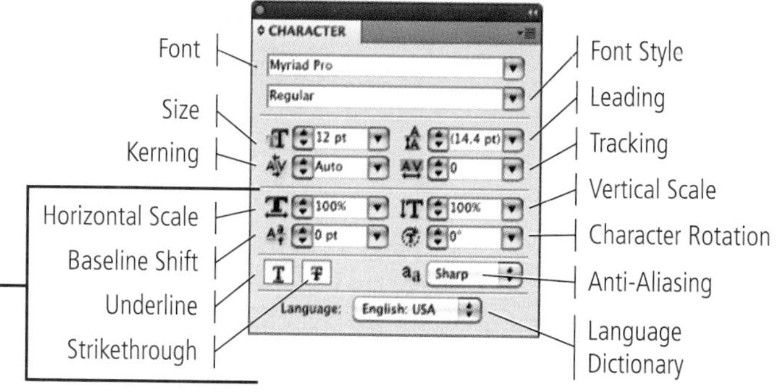

If these options are not visible, choose Show Options in the panel Options menu.

- **Leading** is the distance from one baseline to the next. Adobe applications treat leading as a character attribute, even though leading controls the space between lines of an individual paragraph. (Space between paragraphs is controlled using the Space Before option in the Paragraph panel.) To change leading for an entire paragraph, you must first select the entire paragraph. This approach means you can change the leading for a single line of a paragraph by selecting any character(s) in that line; however, changing the leading for any character in a line applies the same change to the entire line that contains those characters.
- **Kerning** increases or decreases the space between pairs of letters. Kerning is used in cases where particular letters in specific fonts need to be manually spread apart or brought together to eliminate a too-tight or too-spread-out appearance. Manual kerning is usually necessary in headlines or other large type elements. (Many commercial fonts have built-in kerning pairs, so you won't need to apply much hands-on intervention with kerning. Adobe applications default to the kerning values stored in the **font metrics**.)
- **Tracking**, also known as "range kerning," refers to the overall tightness or looseness across a range of characters. Tracking and kerning are applied in thousandths of an **em** (or the amount of space occupied by an uppercase "M," which is usually the widest character in a typeface).
- **Vertical Scale** and **Horizontal Scale** artificially stretch or contract the selected characters. This scaling is a quick way of achieving condensed or expanded type if those variations of a font don't exist. (Type that has been artificially condensed or expanded too much looks bad because the scaling destroys the type's metrics; if possible, use a condensed or expanded version of a font before resorting to horizontal or vertical scaling.)
- **Baseline Shift** moves the selected type above or below the baseline by a specific number of points. Positive numbers move the characters up; negative values move the characters down.
- **Character Rotation** rotates only selected letters, rather than rotating the entire type object.
- **Underline** places a line below the selected characters.
- **Strikethrough** places a line through the middle of selected characters.
- **Anti-Aliasing** can be used to help smooth the apparent edges of type that is exported to a bitmap format that does not support vector information.
- In addition to these options, several artificial type styles (**All Caps**, **Small Caps**, **Superscript**, and **Subscript**) can be applied using the panel Options menu.

13. **Click with the Type tool to place the insertion point between the "a" and the "p".**

This is a good example of a **kern pair** that needs adjustment. The Auto setting built into the font leaves a little too much space between the two characters — even after you have tightened the tracking considerably.

14. **Change the Kerning value to –20.**

Like tracking, you can change this value manually, choose a value from the pop-up menu, or use the Kerning field buttons to change kerning by 1 unit.

The Kerning field icon shows a slash between the two letters.
The insertion point is placed between these two letters.
apple

15. **Save the file and continue to the next exercise.**

Note:

These slight modifications to tracking and kerning improve the overall appearance and readability of the logo. Later in the project, you will use a different technique to adjust letter spacing. For now, however, you should become familiar with making this type of manual adjustment.

Manipulate Type Objects

When you work with type in Illustrator, you need to be aware of a few special issues that can affect the way you interact with the application. This exercise explores some common problems that can arise when you work with type, as well as some tricks you can use to work around them.

1. **With apple.ai open, select the Type tool in the Tools panel. Click at the end of the existing type object to place the insertion point.**

Note:

When the insertion point is flashing in a type object, you can't use the keyboard shortcuts to access tools; instead, pressing a key adds that letter to the current type object, at the location of the insertion point.

2. **Move the Type tool cursor below the existing type object and click.**

When the insertion point is already flashing, you can't click with the Type tool to create a new point-type object.

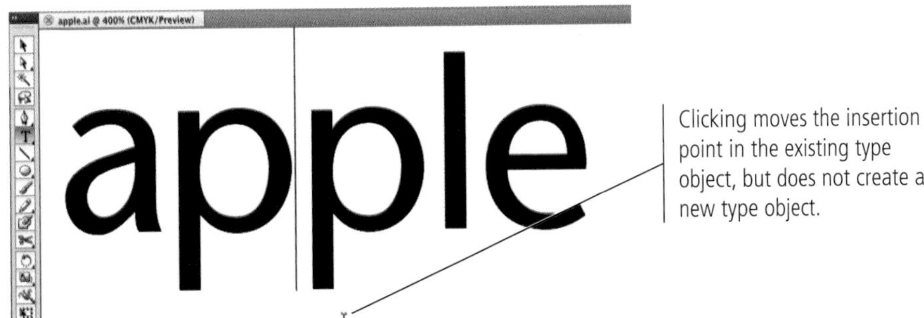

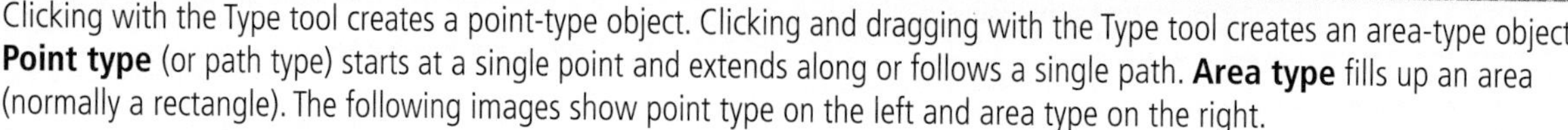

Point Type vs. Area Type

ILLUSTRATOR FOUNDATIONS

Clicking with the Type tool creates a point-type object. Clicking and dragging with the Type tool creates an area-type object. **Point type** (or path type) starts at a single point and extends along or follows a single path. **Area type** fills up an area (normally a rectangle). The following images show point type on the left and area type on the right.

The difference between the two kinds of type becomes obvious when you try to resize them or otherwise modify their shapes using the Selection tool. Area type is contained within an area. If you resize that area, the type doesn't resize; it remains within the area but simply flows (or wraps) differently. If you scale or resize point type by dragging a bounding box handle, the type within the object resizes accordingly.

This point-type object is selected with the Direct Selection tool. You can see the paths that make up the single type object.

This is a point type object, which is created by clicking once with the Type tool.

This is an area type object, which is created by clicking and dragging with the Type tool.

This area-type object is selected with the Direct Selection tool. You can see the edges of the type object, but no bounding box handles appear.

The object is selected with the Selection tool. You can now see the object's bounding box handles.

This is a point type object, which is created by clicking once with the Type tool.

This is an area type object, which is created by clicking and dragging with the Type tool.

The object is selected with the Selection tool. You can see the edges of the type object, as well as the object's bounding box handles.

Resizing the bounding box with the Selection tool resizes the text in the point-type object.

Resizing the bounding box with the Selection tool resizes the object; the text rewraps inside the new object dimensions.

Another consideration is where the "point" sits on the type path. When you change the paragraph alignment of point type, the point remains in the same position; the text on the point moves to the appropriate position, relative to the fixed point.

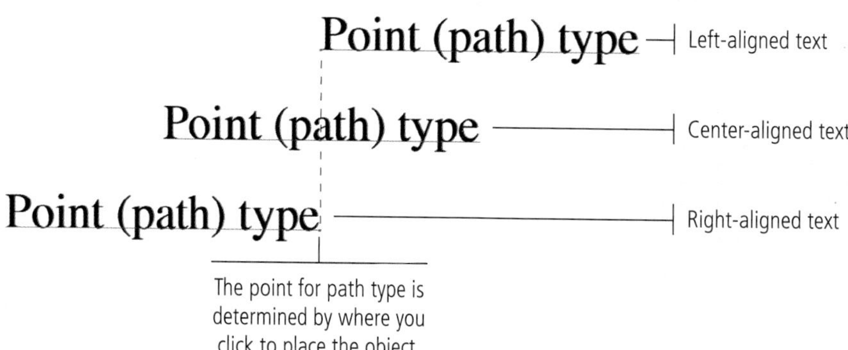

The point for path type is determined by where you click to place the object.

When you're working with type, it can be easier — at least at first — to work with bounding boxes turned off. You can turn off the bounding boxes for all objects — including type objects — by choosing View>Hide Bounding Box.

3. **With the insertion point flashing, press Command/Control.**

   As you know, this modifier key temporarily switches the active tool to the Selection tool. The bounding box of the type object remains visible as long as you hold down the Command/Control key.

4. **While still holding down the Command/Control key, click within the bounding box of the type object.**

   When you click, you select the actual type object. The point and path become active, and the insertion point no longer flashes. You can use this method to move or modify a type object without switching away from the Type tool.

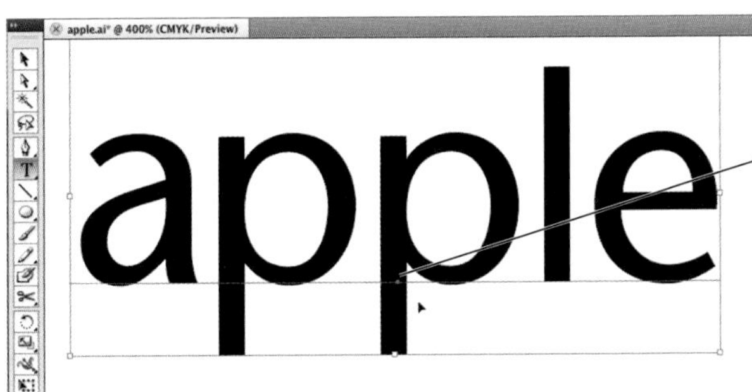

Clicking to select the type object reveals the type path and alignment point.

5. **Release the Command/Control key to return to the Type tool.**

6. **Click below the existing type object to create a new type object.**

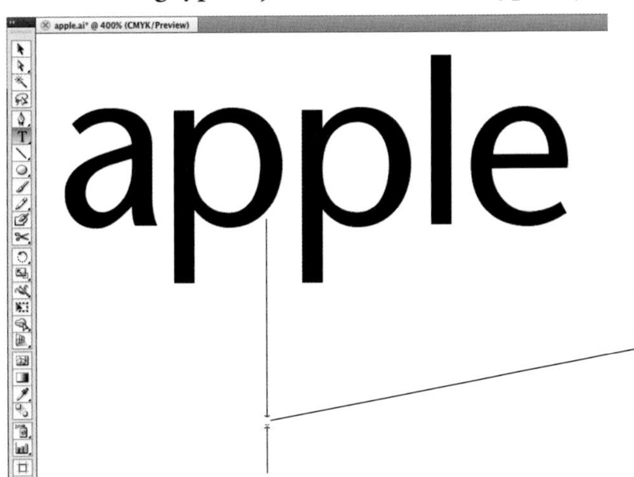

Because the insertion point was not flashing, you can click with the Type tool to create a new type object.

Note:

While working in a type object, you can simply Command/Control-click away from the object to deselect it (and effectively turn off the insertion point). You can then release the Command/Control key to return to the Type tool, and then click the artboard to create a new type object.

7. **Type organics.**

   When you add a new type object, the type is automatically set using the last-used formatting options.

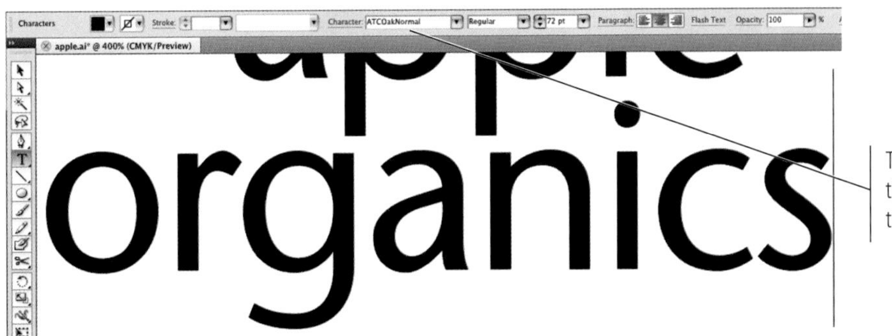

The new type object has the same formatting as the last-used settings.

8. **Press Command/Control. Click the new type object and drag it up until the descender of the second "p" in apple aligns with the stem of the "g" in the word "organics."**

   Leave approximately 0.125″ between the baseline of "apple" and the x-height of the letters in "organic."

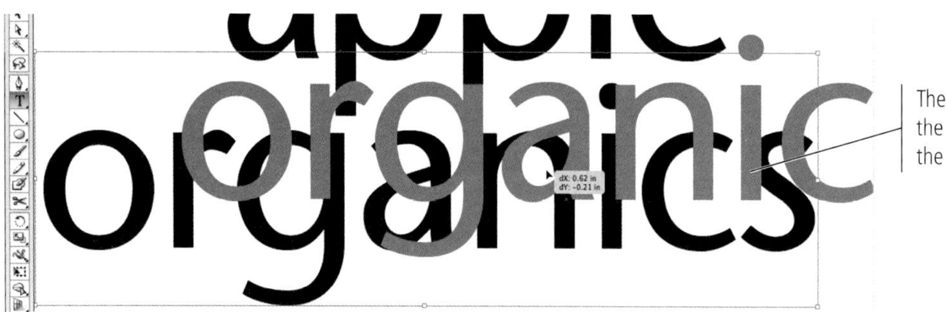

The layer color shows the new position of the type object.

9. **Release the mouse button to reposition the type object, and then release the Command/Control key to return to the Type tool.**

10. **Save the file and continue to the next exercise.**

Convert Type to Outlines

In Illustrator, fonts — and the characters that compose them — are like any other vector objects. They are made up of anchors and paths, which you can modify just as you would any other vector object. To access the anchor points, however, you must first convert the text to outlines.

1. **With apple.ai open, use the Selection tool to select both type objects in the file.**

2. **Choose Type>Create Outlines.**

   When you convert the type to outlines, the anchor points and paths that make up the letter shapes appear. Each type object (in this case, one for "apple" and and one for "organics") is a separate group of letter shapes.

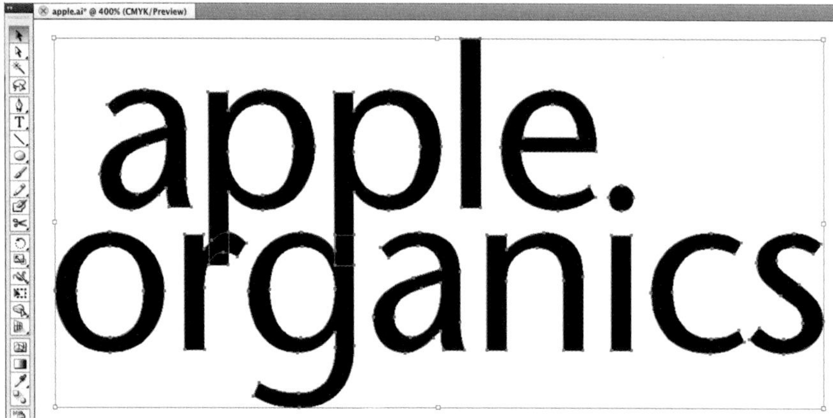

3. **Click away from the objects to deselect them, and then click the word "apple."**

4. **In the Layers panel, click the arrow to the left of the Logotype layer name to expand the layer.**

   In addition to arranging layers, you can use the expanded lists in the Layers panel to review and manage the individual objects on each layer (called **sublayers**).

5. **In the Layers panel, expand the apple group.**

6. **Click the Target icon for the first (lowest) "p" to select only that object.**

   By expanding the individual layers, you can use the Layers panel to access and work with individual objects in a group, without ungrouping the objects.

7. **Press the Right Arrow key to nudge the selected object right (narrowing the space between the letter shapes).**

   You could have fine-tuned the letter spacing with the tracking and kerning controls before you converted the letters to outlines. Since you're working with these letters as graphics, however, you are accessing and nudging individual pieces of a group to adjust the spacing in the overall logotype.

8. **Repeat Step 7 to move the "a" shape right, and again to move the "l" and "e" shapes left.**

   As mentioned previously, letter spacing is largely a matter of personal preference. You might prefer more or less space between the letters than what you see in our images.

Note:

*Open the General pane of the Preferences dialog box to change the distance an object moves when you press the arrow keys (called the **keyboard increment**).*

Press Shift and an arrow key to move an object 10 times the default keyboard increment.

9. **In the Layers panel, collapse the apple group and expand the organics group.**

10. **Click the Target icon for the "s" shape, and then Shift-click the Target icons for the "c", "i", "n", and "a" shapes.**

    Just as Shift-clicking objects selects multiple objects, Shift-clicking the Target icons allows you to easily select multiple objects within a group.

11. **Press the Left Arrow key to nudge the selected shapes left.**

12. **In the Layers panel, shift-click the Target icon for the selected "a" letter shape.**

    Shift-clicking a selected object (Target icon) deselects that object only.

13. **Press the Left Arrow key to nudge the remaining selection left.**

14. **Continue selecting and nudging the letter shapes to reduce the spacing between all letters in the word "organics." Use the following image as a guide.**

15. **Save the file and continue to the next exercise.**

Create Custom Graphics from Letter Shapes

The logo text is no longer type, so you can apply your drawing skills to create a unique logotype. Remember, you can use the Add Anchor Point tool to add points to a vector path, use the Delete Anchor Point tool to remove points from a vector path, and use the Convert Anchor Point tool to convert smooth points to corner points (and vice versa). All three of these tools are nested below the Pen tool in the Tools panel.

1. **With apple.ai open, use the Direct Selection tool to adjust the anchor points at the bottom of the "p" to follow the same arch as the lowercase "r".**

   Remember, click directly on an anchor point to select and move only that point. The selected point appears solid, while unselected points appear hollow.

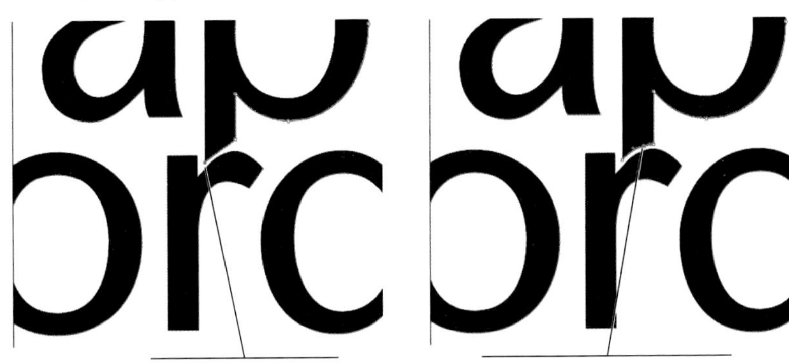

We first moved the bottom anchor points above the "r"...
...added an anchor point to the middle of the path, and then converted the new point to a smooth point.

Note:

It is helpful to zoom in very close to complete this part of the project.

2. **Using the Direct Selection tool, click the second "p" in the word "apple". Press Shift, and then click the "g" in the word "organics".**

3. **Using the Shape Builder tool, click and drag to merge the two shapes that make up the "p" and "g".**

Click and drag with the Shape Builder tool to merge the selected areas into a single shape.
Shape Builder tool
The merged object moves into the lowest group in the stacking order.

4. **Using the Direct Selection tool, click the edge of the dot (above the letter "i") to show the anchor points of that shape. Use what you know about points and handles to change the dot to a leaf shape.**

5. **In the Layers panel, click the Target icon for the "i" shape to select the entire compound path. Change the fill color of the selected object to a medium green from the built-in swatches.**

6. **Select both groups of type shapes and group them.**

7. **Zoom out so you can see the apple artwork and the logotype graphics.**

8. **In the Control panel, click the Transform hot text to open the Transform panel. Make sure the W and H fields are linked, and type `250%` in the W field.**

   When you press Return/Enter (or simply click away from the Transform panel), the logotype group is scaled proportionally to 250% of its original size.

Click the hot-text link in the Control panel to access the related panel.

You can resize this group just as you would any other object.

> *Note:*
>
> *The appearance of the Transform hot text depends on the width of your Application frame; if you have enough vertical screen space, the Transform hot text is replaced by individual X, Y, W, and H fields. In that case, you can click any of those field names to open the Transform panel.*

9. **Drag the logotype group so the "a" and "o" closely align with the outer contour of the apple shape. Use the following image as a guide.**

10. **Save the file and continue to the next stage of the project.**

Stage 3 Working with Multiple Artboards

For all intents and purposes, the Apple Organics logo is now complete. However, you still need to create the alternate versions that can be used in other applications. You need a two-color version for jobs that will be printed with spot colors, and you need a one-color version for jobs that will be printed with black ink only.

In older workflows, creating multiple variations of a logo meant generating multiple files, with each variation residing in a separate file. This process could result in dozens of logo files that needed to be maintained and tracked for a single client. In Illustrator CS5, however, you can streamline the process by creating a single file that includes multiple artboards, with each artboard containing one variation of the logo.

In this stage of the project, you adjust the artboard to fit the completed logo. You then duplicate the artwork on additional artboards, and adjust the colors in each version to meet the specific needs of different color applications.

Adjust the Default Artboard

When you place an Illustrator file into another file (for example, a page-layout file in InDesign or even another Illustrator file) you can decide how to place that file — based on the artwork boundaries (the outermost bounding box), on the artboard boundaries, or on other specific dimensions. To make the logo artwork more placement-friendly, you should adjust the Illustrator artboard to fit the completed logo artwork.

1. **With apple.ai open, make sure all layers are unlocked.**

2. **Select everything on the artboard, and then review the W and H values in the Control panel.**

   You created this file with a letter-size artboard. As you can see, the size is both too narrow and too high for the finished artwork. (Your W and H values might be slightly different than what you see in our screen shots, but they should be in the same general ballpark.)

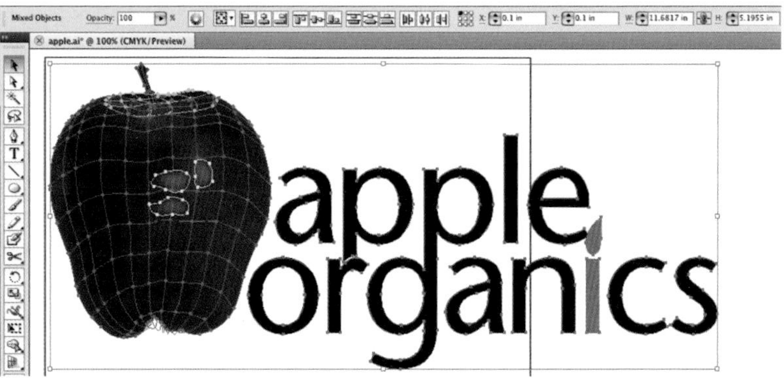

Managing Artboard Options

When the Artboard tool is active, the Control panel presents a number of options for adjusting the active artboard.

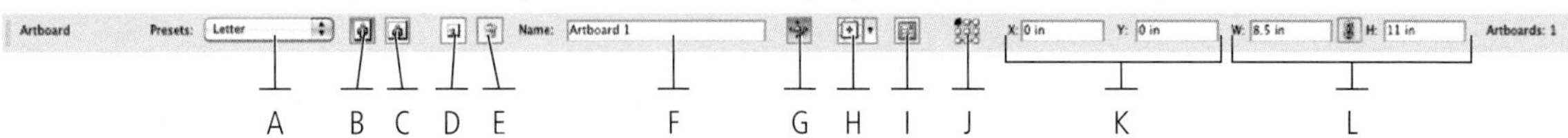

A Use this menu to change the artboard to a predefined size (letter, tabloid, etc.)

B Click to change the artboard to portrait orientation

C Click to change the artboard to landscape orientation

D Click to add a new artboard at the currently defined size. The cursor is "loaded" with the new artboard; you can click to place the new artboard in the workspace.

E Click to delete the active artboard

F Type here to define a name for the active artboard

G Click to toggle the Move/Copy Artwork with Artboard option. When active, objects on the artboard move along with the artboard being moved (or cloned).

H Click to access view options (Show Center Mark, Show Cross Hairs, and Show Video Safe Areas)

I Click to open the Artboard Options dialog box

J Choose a registration point for changes in size or position

K Use these fields to define the position of the artboard. (The first artboard always begins at X: 0, Y: 0.)

L Use these fields to change the size of the artboard. If the link icon is active, the height and width will be constrained.

Clicking the Artboard Options button opens a dialog box where you can further manage and control the selected artboard.

Most of these options (Preset, Width, Height, Orientation, and Position) are the same as those available in the Control panel. The remaining choices are explained here:

- **Constrain Proportions** maintains a consistent aspect ratio (height to width) if you resize the artboard.
- The Display options determine what is visible when the Artboard tool is active. **Show Center Mark** displays a point in the center of the crop area. **Show Cross Hairs** displays lines that extend into the artwork from the center of each edge of the crop area. **Show Video Safe Areas** displays guides that represent the areas that fall inside the viewable area of video.

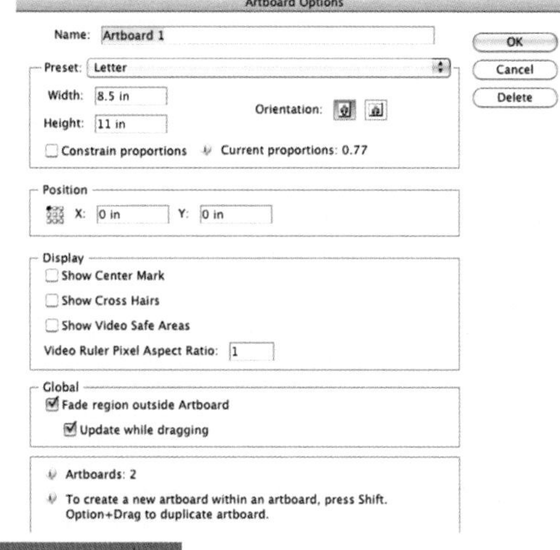

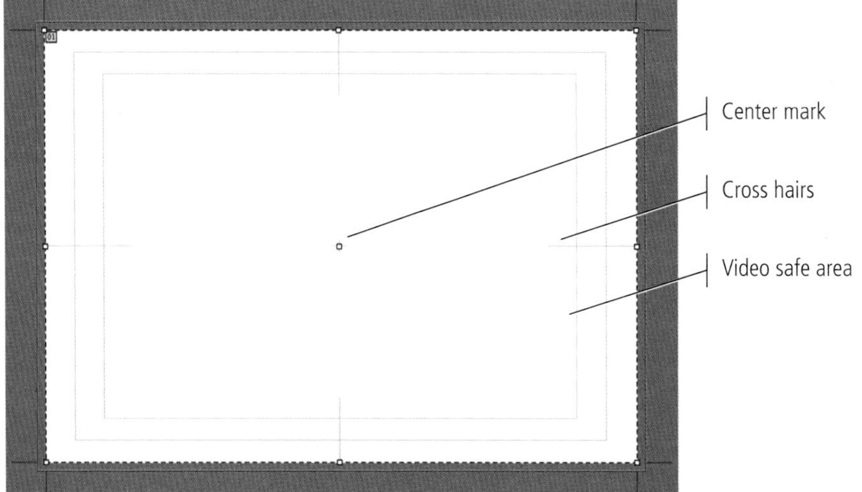

- **Video Ruler Pixel Aspect Ratio** specifies the pixel aspect ratio used for artboard rulers.
- **Fade Region Outside Artboard** displays the area outside the artboard darker than the area inside the artboard.
- **Update While Dragging** keeps the area outside the artboard darker as you move or resize the artboard.

3. **Select the Artboard tool in the Tools panel.**

   When the Artboard tool is active, the artboard edge is surrounded by marching ants; you can drag the side and corner handles to manually resize the artboard in the workspace.

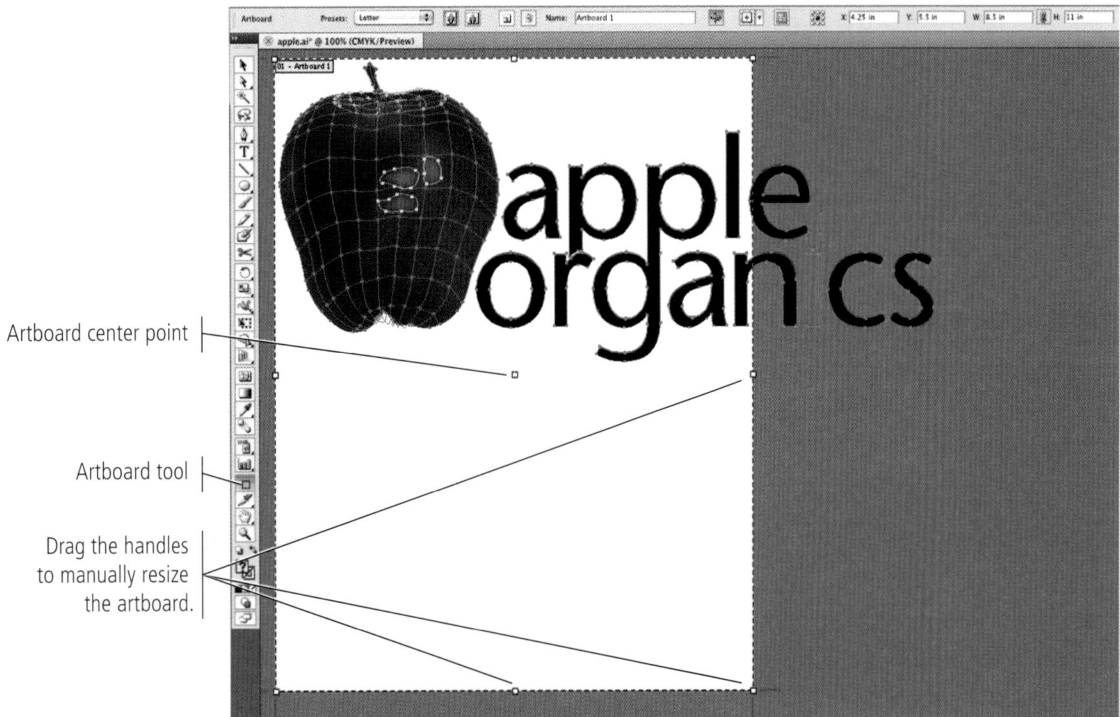

4. **In the Control panel, select the top-left reference point and then change the artboard width to 11.9″ and the height to 5.4″.**

   If your Control panel does not show the W and H fields, click the Artboard Options button in the Control panel and use the Artboard Options dialog box to change the artboard width and height.

   These dimensions are large enough to entirely encompass the logo artwork. If your dimensions are different than ours, use whatever values you need to fit your artwork and leave a bit of white space on all four sides.

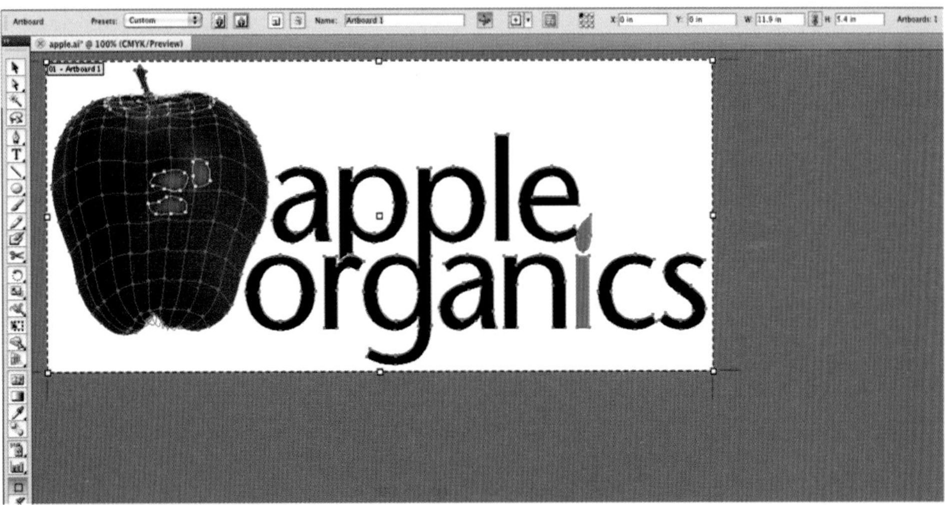

5. **Click the Selection tool to exit the Artboard-editing mode.**

6. **Save the file and continue to the next exercise.**

Use the Layers Panel to Organize Artwork

Your goal is to create three separate versions of the logo — the four-color version that's already done, a two-color version for spot-color applications, and a one-color version that will be used in jobs that are printed black-only.

As you created the artwork, you used five layers to manage the arrangement and stacking order of the various elements. The Apple Back layer is behind the Stem layer, which is behind the Apple Front layer, which is behind the Apple Highlights layer. This precise order produces the effect you need to create a realistic illustration.

Now that the drawing is complete, however, you will use layers for a different purpose — to create, isolate, and manage multiple versions of the logo in a single file.

1. **With apple.ai open, make sure all layers are unlocked in the Layers panel.**

2. **Click the Target icon of the Stem layer to select the objects on that layer.**

3. **Click the Selected Art icon to the right of the Target icon and drag down to the Apple Back layer.**

   Dragging the Selected Art icon is an easy way to move objects from one layer to another without manually cutting and pasting.

Drag the Selected Art icon to a different layer to move selected objects without affecting their position on the artboard.

4. **Expand the Apple Back layer.**

5. **Repeat Steps 2–3 for the Apple Front, Highlights, and Logotype layers.**

6. **Shift-click to select the four empty layers in the Layers panel, and then click the panel's Delete button.**

7. **Rename the Apple Back layer `Four Color`.**

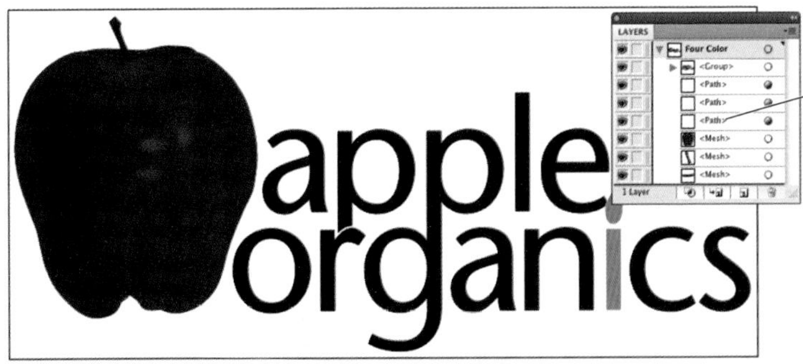

You can access the sublayers, so you can still use the panel to select, arrange, and manage individual objects.

8. **Collapse the Four Color layer to hide the sublayers.**

9. **Save the file and continue to the next exercise.**

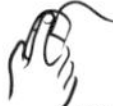

Copy the Artboard and Artwork

Now that all the logo artwork resides on a single layer, the final step is to create the two alternate versions of the logo. This process is largely a matter of cloning the existing artboard and artwork — but you need to complete a few extra steps to convert the mesh objects to standard filled paths.

1. **With `apple.ai` open, choose the Artboard tool in the Tools panel.**

2. **With the only artboard currently active, highlight the contents of the Name field in the Control panel and type `Four Color Apple`.**

3. **Make sure the Move/Copy Artwork with Artboard option is toggled on.**

4. **Place the cursor inside the artboard area. Press Option/Alt-Shift and then click and drag down to clone the existing artboard.**

> *Note:*
>
> *You might want to zoom out so you can see the entire original artboard and the empty space below it.*

The Artboard name appears in the Name field and in the artboard tag.

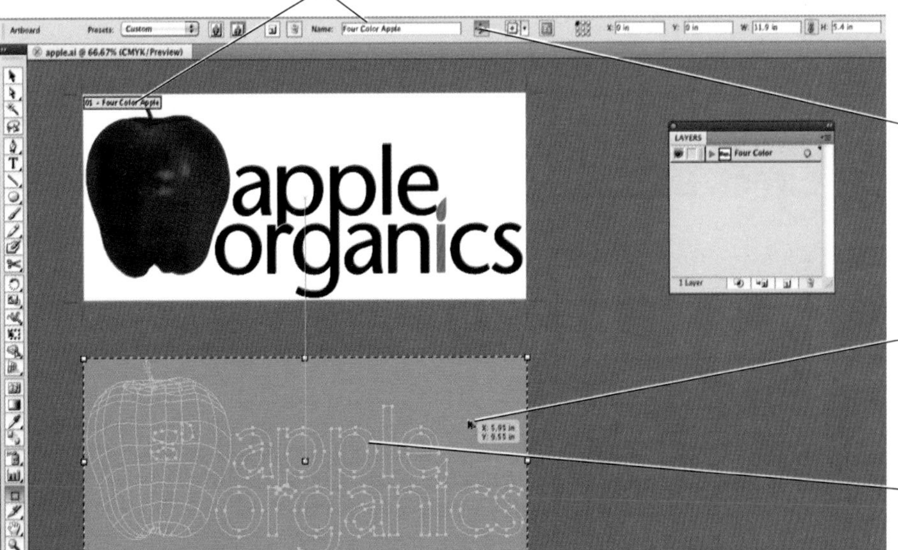

The Move/Copy Artwork with Artboard option should be toggled on.

Pressing Option/Alt allows you to clone the existing artboard, just as you would clone a regular drawing object.

Because the Move/Copy Artwork option is toggled on, the logo artwork and the artboard are both cloned at the same time.

5. **When the new artboard/artwork is entirely outside the boundaries of the first artboard, release the mouse button.**

Because you cloned the first artboard, the second is named "Four Color Apple Copy".

6. **With the second artboard active, change the Name field to** `Two Color Apple`**.**

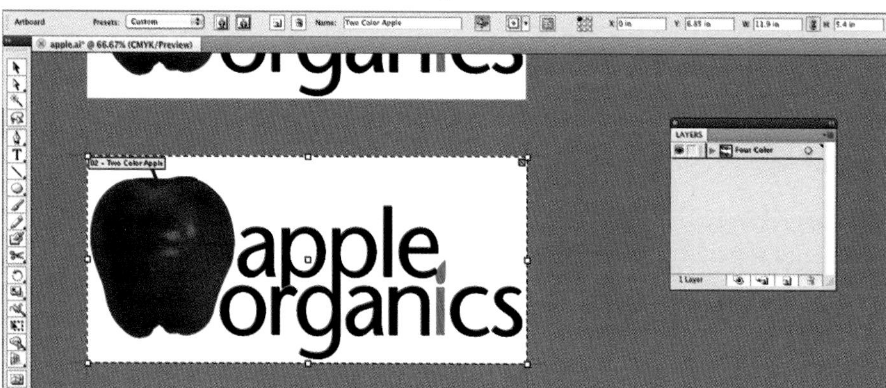

7. **Add a new layer to the file. Change the new layer's name to** `Two Color`**.**

8. **Using the Selection tool, drag a marquee to select all the objects on the second artboard.**

9. **In the Layers panel, drag the Selected Art icon from the Four Color layer to the Two Color layer.**

The second version of the artwork should now be on the Two Color layer.

10. **Save the file and continue to the next exercise.**

Convert Mesh Objects to Regular Paths

When you created the gradient meshes in the first stage of this project, you saw that adding the mesh removed the original path you drew. When you worked on the mesh, you might have noticed that the Control panel showed that the selected object was transformed from a path object to a mesh object.

To create the flat two-color version of the logo, however, you need to access the original paths you drew to create the mesh objects. There is no one-step process to convert the mesh object back to a flat path object, so you need to take a few extra steps to create the flat version of the logo.

1. **With apple.ai open, deselect everything in the file and then open the Artboards panel (Window>Artboards).**

   The Artboards panel can be used to access and arrange the various artboards in a file.

2. **Double-click Two Color Apple in the panel.**

   This forces the selected artboard to fill the space available in the document window.

> *Note:*
>
> *Because the black-only version of the logo is also flat, you are going to create the flat two-color version first, and then clone it. Doing so avoids unnecessary repetition of the process presented in this exercise.*

3. **Expand the Two Color layer in the Layers panel.**

4. **Use the Layers panel to select the mesh object that represents the Front Apple shape, and then open the Appearance panel.**

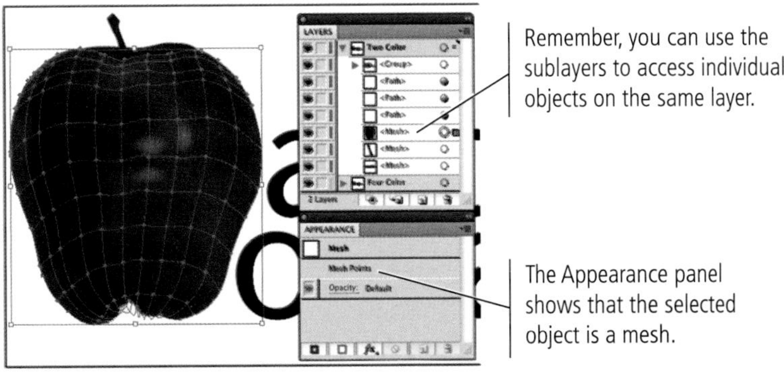

Remember, you can use the sublayers to access individual objects on the same layer.
The Appearance panel shows that the selected object is a mesh.

> *Note:*
>
> *When working with a mesh object, it can be helpful to turn off object bounding boxes (View>Hide Bounding Box).*

5. **With the mesh object selected, click the Add New Stroke button at the bottom of the Appearance panel.**

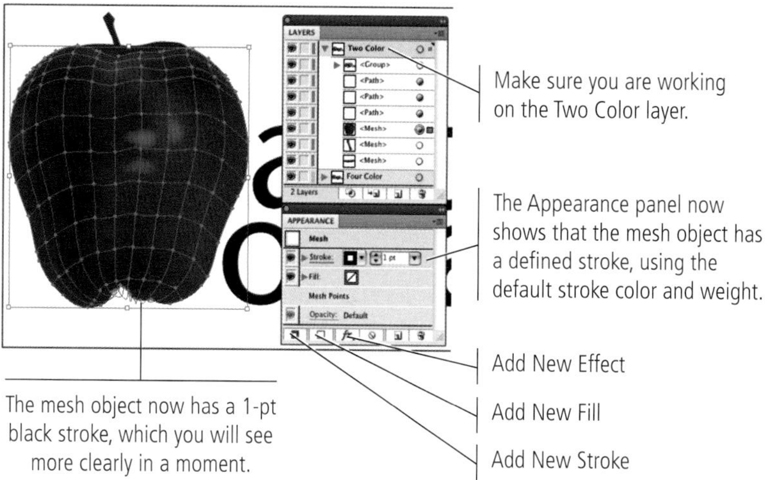

Make sure you are working on the Two Color layer.
The Appearance panel now shows that the mesh object has a defined stroke, using the default stroke color and weight.
Add New Effect
Add New Fill
Add New Stroke
The mesh object now has a 1-pt black stroke, which you will see more clearly in a moment.

Note:

In addition to changing the existing attributes of an object, you can also use the Appearance panel to compound effects and attributes. In other words, you can add a new stroke to any object, including an object that already has a defined stroke.

6. **With the mesh object still selected, choose Object>Expand Appearance.**

   This command converts the selected object into separate constituent objects — one path for the shape's stroke attribute and one for the object's mesh fill — which are automatically grouped together.

7. **In the Layers panel, expand the new group.**

8. **Use the Layers panel to select only the mesh object in the group.**

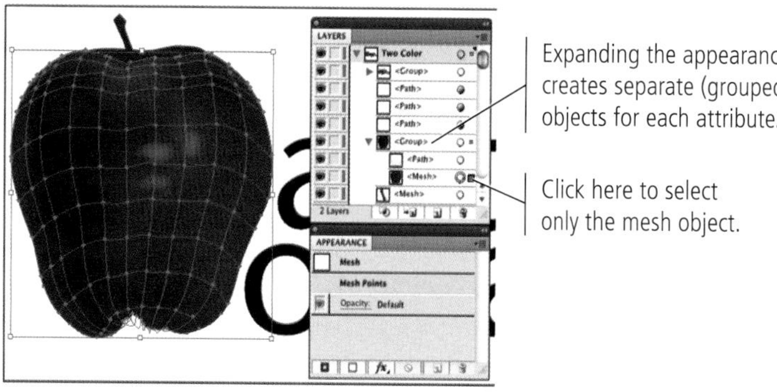

Expanding the appearance creates separate (grouped) objects for each attribute.
Click here to select only the mesh object.

9. **Press Delete/Backspace to remove the selected mesh object.**

   You now have a simple path object that is essentially the Apple Front shape. However, you need to complete one more step because the path is still part of the group that was created by the Expand Appearance command.

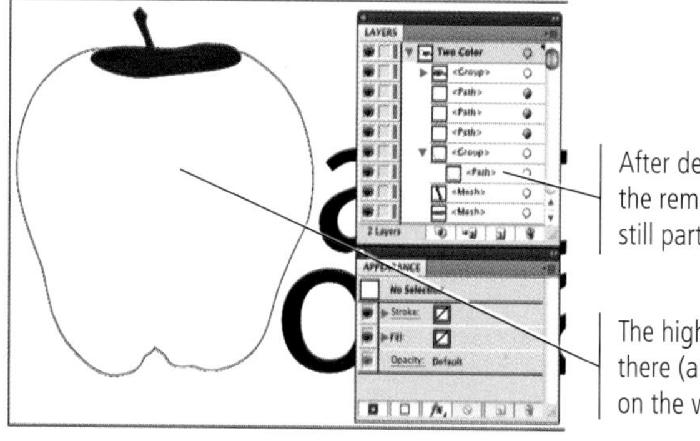

The highlight objects are still there (although difficult to see on the white-filled shape).

10. **Use the Layers panel to select the path in the group, and then choose Object>Ungroup.**

After ungrouping, the selected path is a regular sublayer (it is not grouped).

11. **Repeat this process to convert the other two mesh objects (the Stem shape and the Apple Back shape) back into standard paths with the default stroke attributes.**

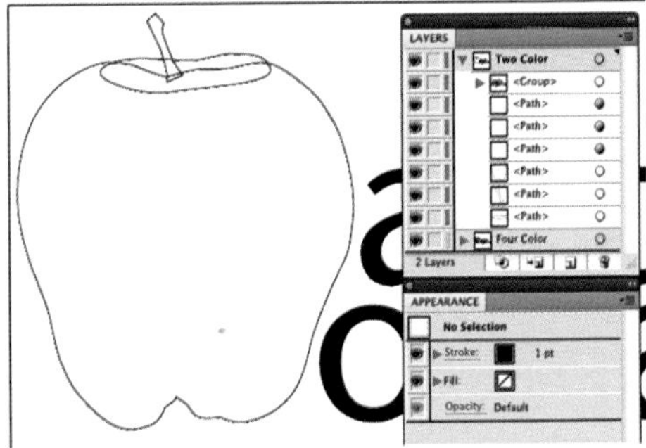

12. **Save the file and continue to the next exercise.**

Add Spot Color to the Two-Color Logo

Spot colors are created with special premixed inks that produce a certain color with one ink layer; spot colors are not built from the standard process inks used in CMYK printing. When you output a job with spot colors, each spot color appears on its own separation. Spot inks are commonly used to reproduce colors you can't get from a CMYK build, in two- and three-color documents, and as additional separations in a process color job when an exact color (such as a corporate color) is needed.

You can choose a spot color directly from the library on your screen, but you should look at a printed swatch book to verify that you're using the color you intend. Special inks exist because many of the colors can't be reproduced with process inks, nor can they be accurately represented on a monitor. If you specify spot colors and then convert them to process colors later, your job probably won't look exactly as you expect.

Note:

In the United States, the most popular collections of spot colors are the Pantone Matching System (PMS) libraries. TruMatch and Focoltone are also used in the United States. Toyo and DICColor (Dainippon Ink & Chemicals) are used primarily in Japan.

1. **With apple.ai open, choose Window>Swatch Libraries>Color Books>Pantone Solid Coated.**

   Illustrator includes swatch libraries of all the common spot-color libraries. You can open any of these libraries to access the various colors available in each collection.

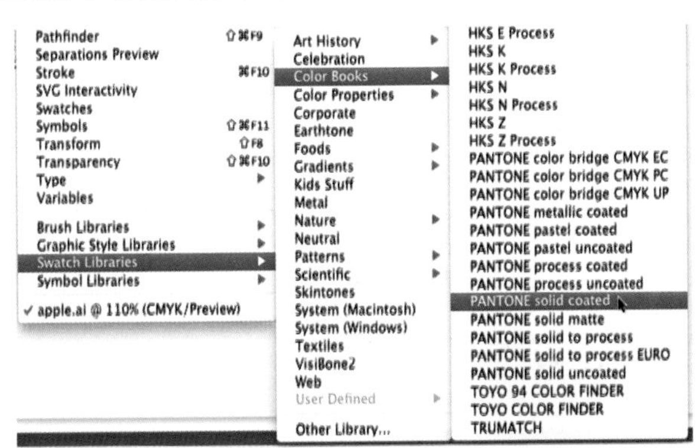

2. **In the Pantone Solid Coated library Options menu, choose Small List View to show the color names for each swatch.**

   It is often easier to view swatches with their names and samples, especially when you need to find a specific swatch (as in this exercise).

> *Note:*
>
> *The View options in the panel Options menu are available for all swatch panels, including colors, patterns, and brushes. You use many types of swatches in Project 4.*

3. **On the Two Color artboard/layer, select the shape that represents the apple front.**

4. **Scroll through the Pantone swatch Library panel until you find Pantone 188 C.**

5. **Make sure the Fill icon is active in the Tools panel, and then click Pantone 188 C in the swatch Library panel.**

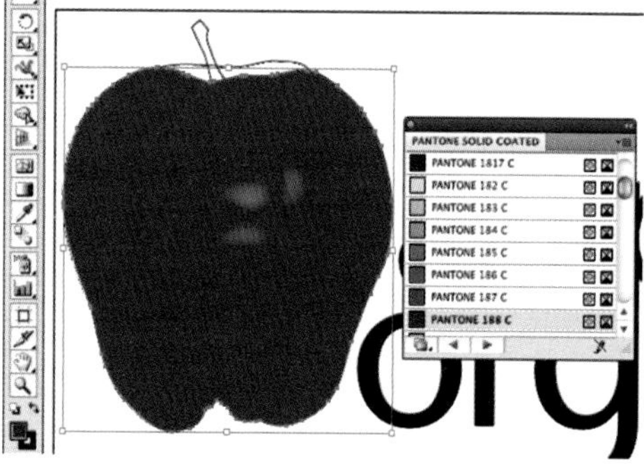

6. **Review the Swatches panel (Window>Swatches).**

   When you apply a color from a swatch library, that swatch is added to the Swatches panel for the open file.

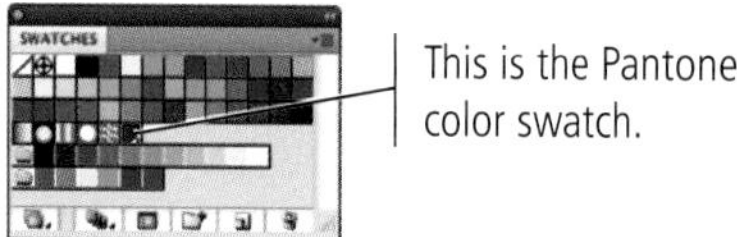

This is the Pantone color swatch.

7. **Using whichever method you prefer, change the stroke color of the selected object to None.**

8. **Select and delete the three highlight shapes.**

   In a flat logo, the highlight shapes are unnecessary. In fact, the technical aspects involved in reproducing the feather effect applied to those shapes can cause output problems.

9. **Select the Apple Back shape. Apply Pantone 188 C as the fill color and None as the stroke color.**

10. **Select the Stem shape. Swap the current stroke and fill colors so the shape is filled with black and has no stroke.**

11. **Select the shape that comprises the "p" and "g" in the logotype and change the fill color to Pantone 188 C.**

    Because this shape is part of a group, you must use the Direct Selection tool or the sublayers in the Layers panel to select only this shape.

12. **Select the "i" shape. Change the fill color to white (not None) and change the stroke to 2-pt Pantone 188 C.**

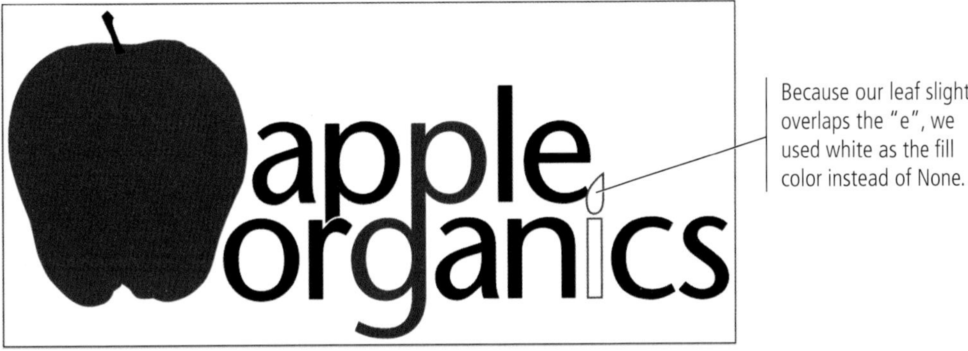

Because our leaf slightly overlaps the "e", we used white as the fill color instead of None.

13. **Choose the Artboard tool. With the Move/Copy Artwork option still active, press Option/Alt-Shift and then click and drag down to clone the flat version. Rename the new artboard `One Color Apple`.**

14. **Move the artwork on the third artboard to a new layer named `One Color`. Change all Pantone 188 C elements in the third version to black.**

Change all Pantone 188 C elements in this version to black.

15. **Save the file, close it, and then continue to the next exercise.**

Export EPS Logo Files

Although the current versions of most graphic-design software can work with native Illustrator files, many older applications — especially page-layout software — require EPS (Encapsulated PostScript) files for vector-based files created in Illustrator. Because logos need to be versatile, you are going to save EPS files in this exercise so the necessary pieces are in place if and when they are needed.

1. **With apple.ai open, choose File>Save As. If necessary, navigate to your WIP>Organics folder as the target location.**

2. **Choose Illustrator EPS in the Format/Save As Type menu. Activate the Use Artboards option and make sure the All radio button is selected.**

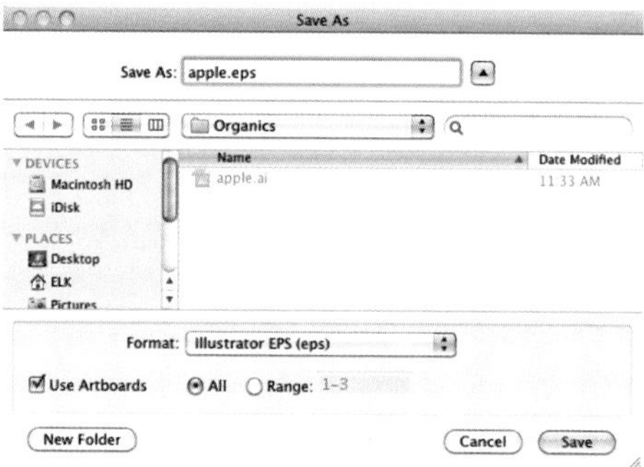

3. **Click Save. Read the resulting warning and then click Continue.**

   Because your file uses a spot-color swatch, the application warns you about potential output problems if you use transparency with gradients. Because you did not use spot colors in any of the transparent elements (this is why you deleted the feathered highlights), you can dismiss this message.

4. **In the resulting EPS Options dialog box, choose High Resolution in the Transparency Presets menu.**

   Both gradient meshes and feather effects require rasterization at some point to properly output the subtle changes in color. The High Resolution option creates high enough resolution for most print applications. (You'll learn more about this issue in Project 6.)

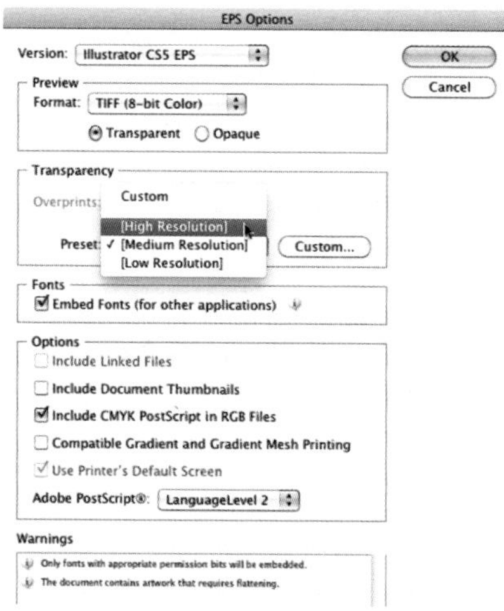

5. **Check the Compatible Gradient and Gradient Mesh Printing option.**

   This option helps older output devices to print gradient meshes.

6. **Click OK to generate the EPS files. When the Parsing process is complete, close the open file.**

7. **On your desktop, open your WIP>Organics folder.**

   Because you checked the Use Artboards option, Illustrator generated four separate EPS files: one that contains all three logos with no consideration of the artboard concept, and separate files for each of the three defined artboards.

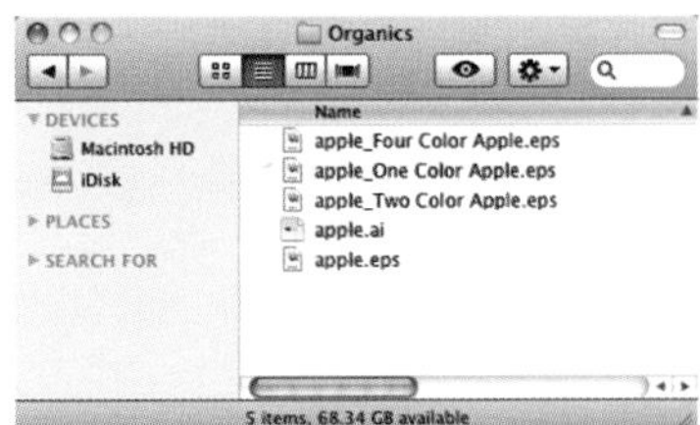

8. **Continue to the next stage of the project.**

Stage 4 Combining Text and Graphics

The final stage of this project requires two additional layouts: a letterhead and a business envelope. Rather than adding more artboards to the logo file, you are going to create a new file that will contain both pieces of stationery. This means you must place the logos from the original apple.ai file, and understand how to work with objects that are placed from external files.

Work with Placed Graphics

Some production-related concerns dictate how you design a letterhead. In general, there are two ways to print a letterhead: commercially in large quantities or one-offs on your desktop laser or inkjet printer. (The second method includes a letterhead template, which you can use to write and print your letters from directly within a page-layout program. While this method is quite common among designers, it is rarely done using Illustrator.)

If your letterhead is being printed commercially, it's probably being printed with multiple copies on a large press sheet, from which the individual letterhead sheets will be cut. (In fact, most commercial printing happens this way.) This type of printing typically means that design elements can run right off the edge of the sheet, called **bleeding**. If you're using a commercial printer, always ask the output provider whether it's safe (and cost-effective) to design with bleeds, and find out how much bleed allowance to include.

If you're designing for a printer that can only run letter-size paper, you need to allow enough of a margin area for your printer to hold the paper as it moves through the device (called the **gripper margin**); in this case, you can't design with bleeds.

Note:

Older desktop printers typically have a larger minimum gripper margin; you're usually safe with 3/8" margins. Newer inkjet printers often have the capability to print 8.5 × 11" sheets with full bleed. In either case, consult your printer documentation before you design your document.

1. **Open the New Document dialog box (File>New). Name the new file `stationery`, with 1 artboard that is letter-size in portrait orientation. Define 0.125″ bleeds on all four sides, CMYK color mode, and 300 PPI raster effects.**

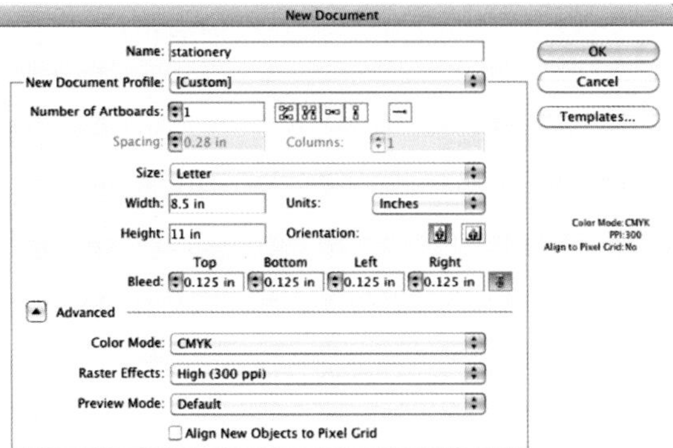

> *Note:*
>
> *When you create a new file, the Raster Effects setting determines the resolution of raster objects that are created by Illustrator to output effects like gradient meshes and feathering.*

2. **Click OK to create the new file.**

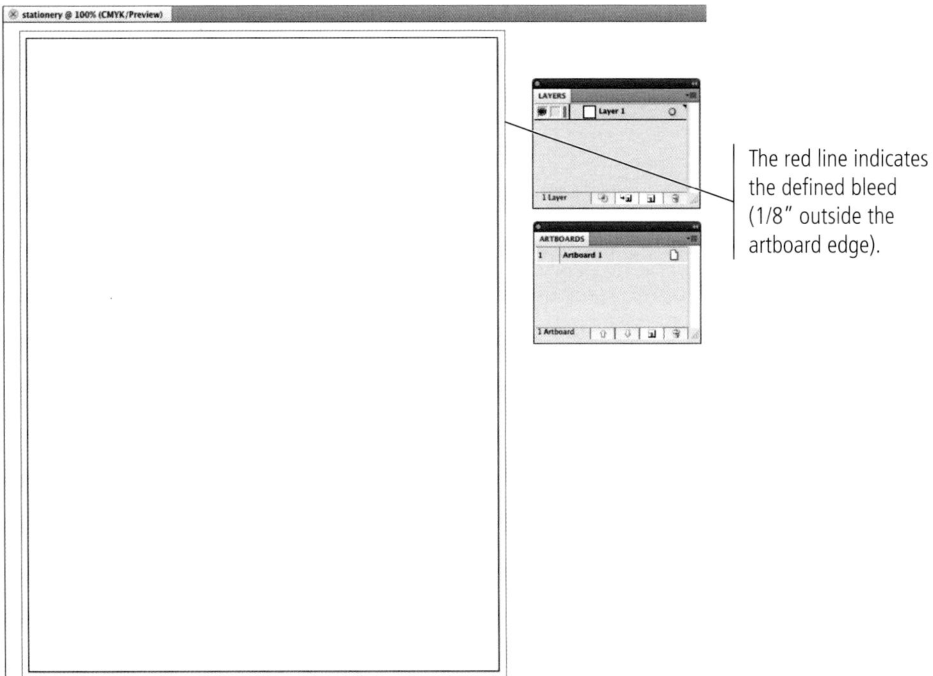

The red line indicates the defined bleed (1/8″ outside the artboard edge).

3. **Choose File>Place. Navigate to the file `apple.ai` in your WIP>Organics folder, make sure Link and Template are both unchecked, and then click Place.**

Until now, you have placed raster images in the JPEG format. Different types of files, however, have different options that determine what is imported into your Illustrator file.

4. Review the options in the Place dialog box.

Although you're placing a native Illustrator (.ai) file, the dialog box shows options for placing PDF files. Illustrator files use PDF as the underlying structure (which is what enables multiple artboard capability), so the options are the same as the ones you would see if you were placing a PDF file.

5. Choose Art in the Crop To menu, and then click OK to place the four-color logo.

6. If you get a warning about an unknown image construct, click OK to dismiss it.

For some reason, gradient mesh objects *created in Illustrator* are unrecognized *by Illustrator* when the logo file is placed into another Illustrator file. Gradient meshes are imported into the new file as "non-native art" objects that can't be edited in the new file unless you use the Flatten Transparency command to turn them into embedded raster objects.

7. Open the General pane of the Preferences dialog box. Make sure the Scale Strokes & Effects option is checked, and then click OK.

If this option is checked, scaling an object also scales the applied strokes and effects (including the Feather effect you used to create the front highlight objects) proportionally to the new object size. For example, reducing an object by 50% changes a 1-pt stroke to a 0.5-pt stroke. If this option is unchecked, a 1-pt stroke remains a 1-pt stroke, regardless of how much you reduce or enlarge the object.

Note:

On Macintosh, open the Preferences dialog box in the Illustrator menu. On Windows, open the Preferences dialog box in the Edit menu.

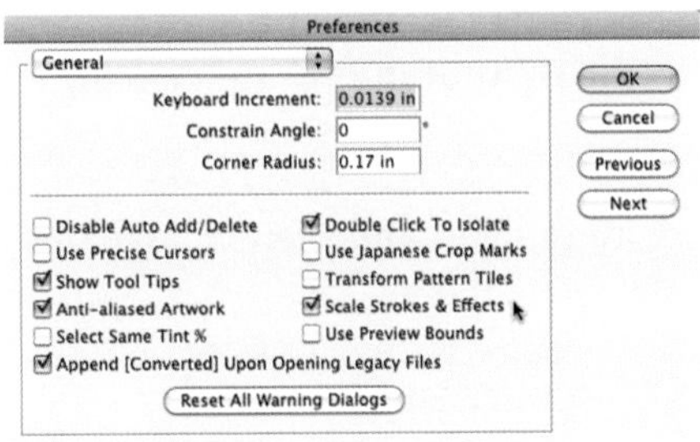

Understanding Placed-Image Bounding Boxes

ILLUSTRATOR FOUNDATIONS

The **Crop To** option determines exactly what is placed into an Illustrator file. (If you are placing an Illustrator file, many of these options produce the same result.)

- The **Bounding Box** setting places the file's bounding box, or the minimum area that encloses the objects on the page or artboard.
- The **Art** setting crops incoming files relative to the size and position of any objects selected at the time of the cropping. For example, you can create a frame and use it to crop an incoming piece of artwork.
- Use the **Crop** setting when you want the position of the placed file to be determined by the location of a crop region drawn on the page (when placing an Illustrator file, this refers to the defined artboard).
- The **Trim** setting identifies where the page will be physically cut in the production process, if trim marks are present.
- The **Bleed** setting places only the area within bleed margins (if a bleed area is defined). This is useful if the page is being output in a production environment. (The printed page might include page marks that fall outside the bleed area.)
- The **Media** setting places the area that represents the physical paper size of the original PDF document (for example, the dimensions of an A4 sheet of paper), including printers' marks.

8. **With the placed artwork selected, use the Transform panel to scale the artwork to 3″ wide (constrained). Using the top-left reference point, position the artwork 1/8″ from the top and left edges (as shown in the following image).**

Constrain the width and height before changing the object size.

Use the Transform panel to scale to image to 3″ wide and position the group at X: 0.125″, Y: 0.125″.

Note:

Remember, your original artwork might be a slightly different size than ours, so your resized height might also be slightly different than what is shown here.

9. **Using the Type tool, click to create a new point-type object. Type** 564 Orchard Way**. Format the type as 10-pt ATC Oak Normal with right paragraph alignment. Apply a medium-red swatch as the type fill color and define no stroke color.**

10. **Using the Selection tool, position the type object directly to the left of the "g" descender (use the following image as a guide).**

11. **Option/Alt-click-drag the type object to clone it to the right. Press the Shift key after you begin dragging to constrain the clone's movement to exactly horizontal. Move the clone immediately to the right of the "g" descender, and then release the mouse button.**

12. **Change the cloned object to left paragraph alignment, and then change the type to** Orange, FL 35682**.**

13. **Activate the Selection tool, then choose File>Place. Navigate to the file** leaves.eps **in your WIP>Organics folder and click Place.**

This format, which you used to create alternate versions of the apple logos in the previous exercise, is commonly used for vector-based images — especially when saving files for older page-layout applications that do not support the native Illustrator format. When you place an EPS file into Illustrator, you do not have additional options when you place the file into Illustrator; it is **parsed** (processed) and placed onto the Illustrator artboard.

14. **Drag the placed graphic so the edges of the artwork bleed past the edge of the artboard area. Use the following image as a guide.**

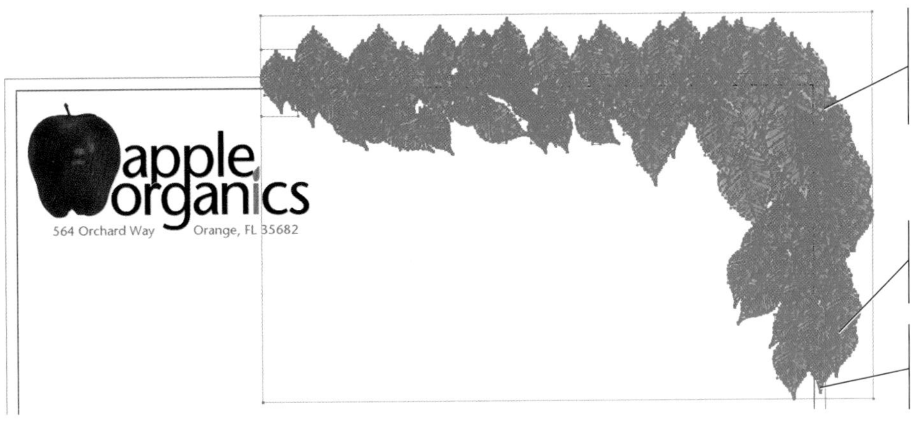

When processed and placed, vector artwork in the file becomes accessible.

Areas outside the bleed guide will not be included in the output.

Areas outside the artboard edge will be trimmed from the press sheet.

15. **Save the file as an Illustrator file named `stationery.ai` in your WIP>Organics folder, and then continue to the next exercise.**

Create the Envelope Layout

In general, printed envelopes can be created in two ways. You can create and print the design on a flat sheet, which will be specially **die cut** (stamped out of the press sheet), and then folded and glued into the shape of the finished envelope. Alternatively (and usually at less expense), you can print on pre-folded and -glued envelopes.

Both of these methods for envelope design have special printing requirements, such as ensuring no ink is placed where glue will be applied (if you're printing on flat sheets), or printing far enough away from the edge (if you're printing on pre-formed envelopes). Whenever you design an envelope, consult with the output provider that will print the job before you get too far into the project.

In this case, the design will be output on pre-folded #10 business-size envelopes (4-1/8″ by 9-1/2″). The printer requires a 1/4″ gripper margin around the edge of the envelope where you cannot include any ink coverage.

Note:

*The **live area** is the "safe" area inside the page edge, where important design elements should remain. Because printing and trimming are mechanical processes, there will always be some variation, however slight. Elements too close to the page edge run the risk of being accidentally trimmed off.*

1. **With `stationery.ai` open, zoom out until you can see the entire artboard and an equal amount of space to the right.**

2. **Choose the Artboard tool. With the current artboard active, type `Letterhead` in the Name field of the Control panel.**

3. **Place the cursor to the right of the existing artboard, click, and drag to create a new artboard.**

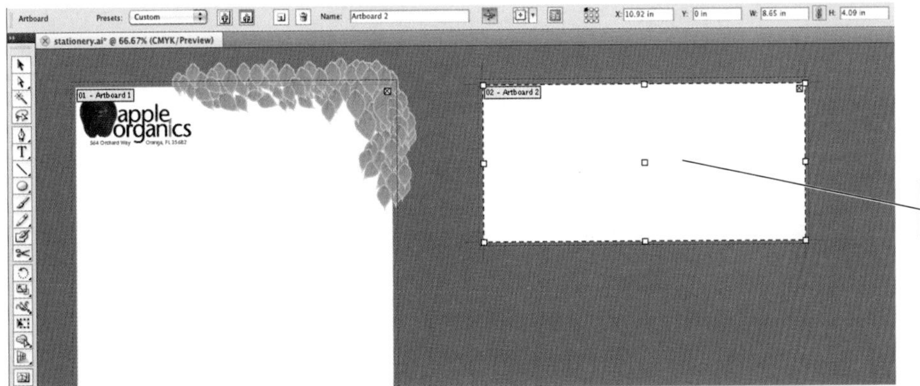

Click and drag to create a new artboard.

4. **With the second artboard active, use the fields in the Control panel to change the artboard dimensions to W: 9.5″, H: 4.13″.**

   If the W and H fields are not visible in your Control panel, click the Artboard Options button in the Control panel and use the resulting dialog box to change the artboard size.

5. **With the second artboard active, type Envelope in the Name field of the Control panel.**

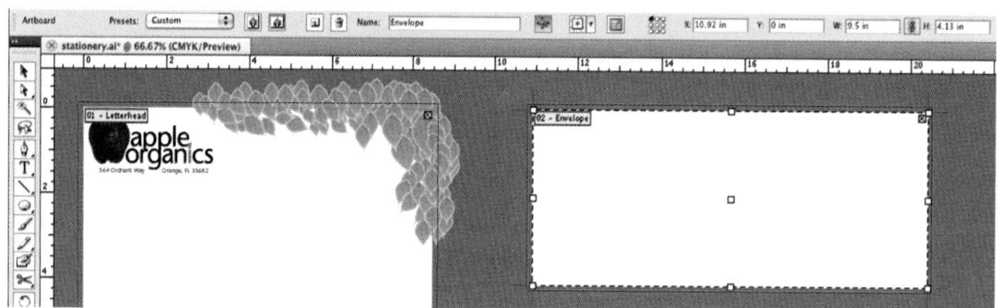

6. **Choose File>Place. Navigate to the file apple.ai in your WIP>Organics folder and click Place.**

7. **In the Place PDF dialog box, click the right-arrow button to show 2 of 3, then click OK.**

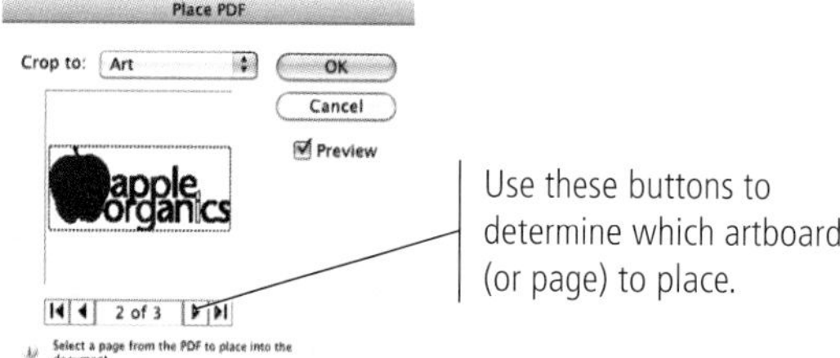

Use these buttons to determine which artboard (or page) to place.

8. **Make the Selection tool active. Choose View>Rulers and make sure the menu option reads "Change to Global Rulers".**

   Artboard rulers show all measurements from the zero-point of the active artboard. Global rulers show all measurements from the zero-point of Artboard 1 (unless you reset the zero-point when a diferent artboard is active).

   When Artboard rulers are active — which you want for this exercise — the menu command reads to "Change to Global Rulers".

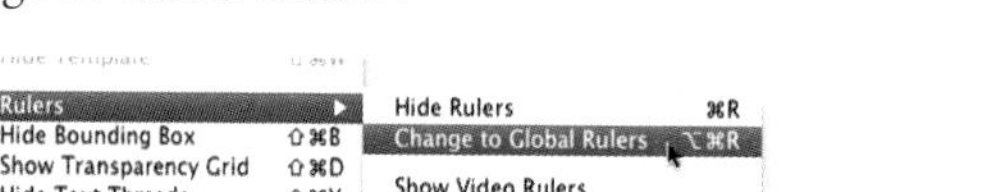

Note:

You can't switch between Artboard and Global rulers while the Artboard tool is active.

9. **Select the placed object with the Selection tool. Scale it to 2.5″ wide (constrained) and place it 0.25″ from the top and left edges of the envelope artboard.**

Because Artboard rulers are active, each artboard has its own zero point.

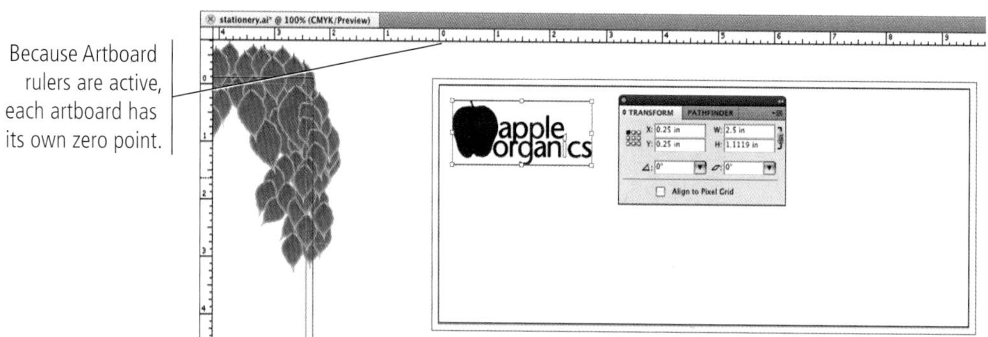

10. **Copy the type objects from the letterhead layout and paste them onto the envelope layout. Change the size of the type in the pasted objects to 8 pt and change the fill to Pantone 188 C (the same color you used in the two-color logo artwork).**

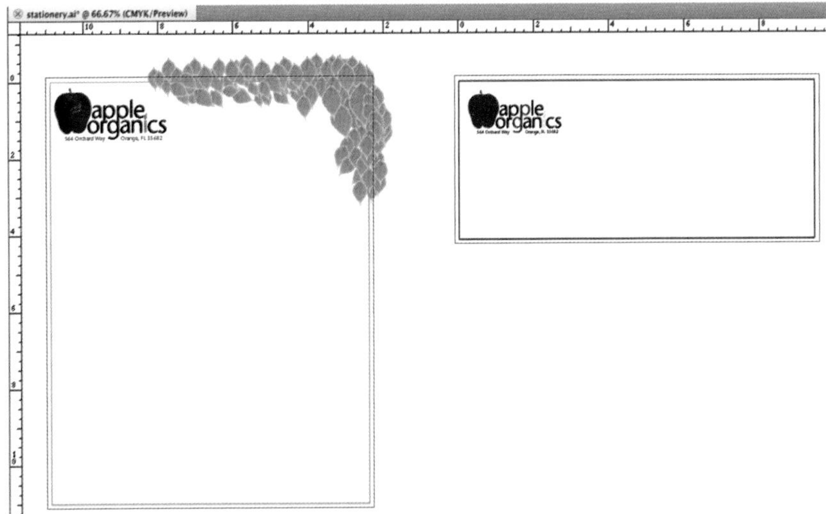

11. **Save the file and continue to the next exercise.**

Print Desktop Proofs of Multiple Artboards

Before you send a file to a commercial output provider, it's a good idea to print a sample to see how the artwork looks on paper. Illustrator provides a large number of options for outputting files, including the ability to define the area of the actual artwork.

There are two important points to remember about using inkjet and laser proofs. First, inkjet printers are usually not PostScript driven; because the commercial output process revolves around the PostScript language, proofs should be created using a PostScript-compatible printer if possible (if not, the proofs might not accurately represent what will appear in final output). Second, inkjet and laser printers typically do not accurately represent color.

> *Note:*
>
> *The most important options you'll select are the Printer and PPD (PostScript printer description) settings, located at the top of the dialog box. Illustrator reads the information in the PPD to determine which of the specific print options are available for the current output.*

1. **With stationery.ai open, choose File>Print.**

   The Print dialog box is divided into eight sections or categories, which display in the window on the left side of the dialog box. Clicking one of the categories in the list shows the associated options in the right side of the dialog box.

2. **In the Printer menu, choose the printer you want to use, and then choose the PPD for that printer in the PPD menu (if possible).**

   If you are using a non-PostScript printer, complete as much of the rest of this exercise as possible based on the limitations of your output device.

3. **With the General options showing, choose the Range radio button and type 1 in the field.**

   By default, all artboards in the file are output when you click Print.

   If your printer can only print letter-size paper, you need to tile the letterhead artboard to multiple sheets so you can output a full-size proof. Tiling is unavailable when printing multiple artboards, so in this exercise you are printing each artboard separately.

> *Note:*
>
> *You can purchase a software RIP (such as the one we use from Birmy Graphics) that allows you to print PostScript information to some inkjet printers. Consult the documentation that came with your printer to see if this option is available.*

4. **In the Options section, make sure the Do Not Scale option is selected.**

As a general rule, proofs — especially final proofs that would be sent to a printer with the job files — should be output at 100%.

5a. **If your printer is capable of printing oversize sheets, choose Tabloid/ A3/11×17 in the Media menu. Choose the Portrait orientation option.**

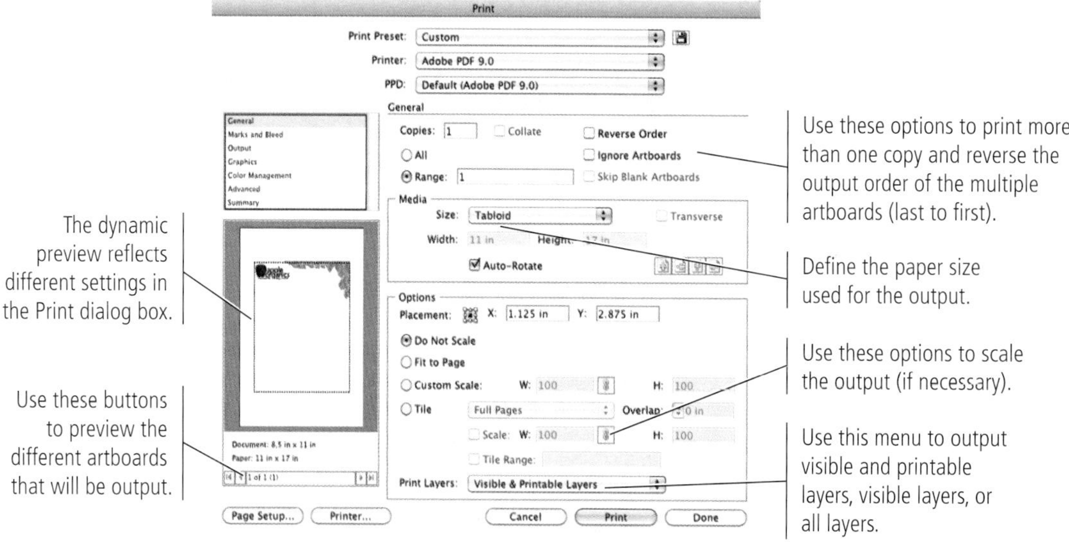

Define the paper size used for the output.

Use this menu to output visible and printable layers, visible layers, or all layers.

5b. **If you can only print to letter-size paper, turn off the Auto-Rotate option and choose the Landscape orientation option. Activate the Tile option and define a 0.5″ Overlap.**

To output a letter-size page at 100% on letter-size paper, you have to tile to multiple sheets of paper; using the landscape paper orientation allows you to tile to 2 sheets instead of 4 (as shown in the preview area).

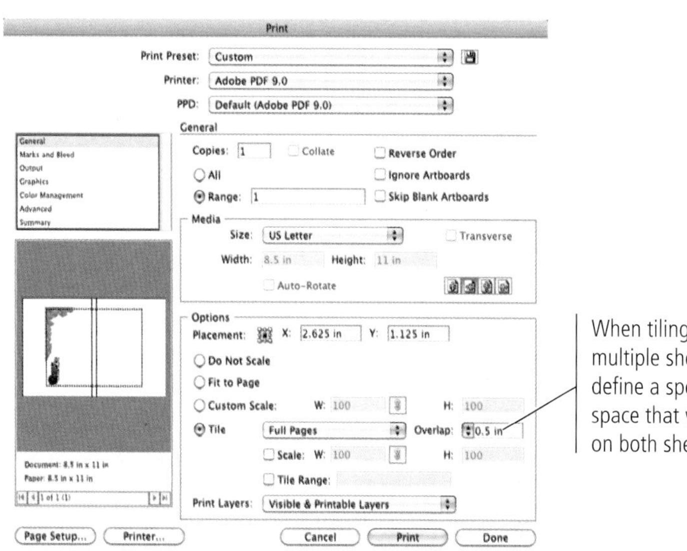

When tiling a page to multiple sheets, you can define a specific amount of space that will be included on both sheets.

Note:

A print preset is a way to store many different settings in a single menu choice. You can create a print preset by making your choices in the Print dialog box, and then clicking the Save Preset button.

Note:

The Tile options are not available if you are printing multiple artboards at one time.

Note:

The Auto-Rotate option is useful if you are printing multiple artboards; when this option is active, the application automatically positions each artboard to take best advantage of the available paper.

6. **Click the Marks and Bleed option in the list of categories on the left. Activate the All Printer's Marks option, and then change the Offset value to 0.125″.**

7. **In the Bleeds section, check the Use Document Bleed Settings option.**

   When you created the stationery file, you defined 1/8″ bleeds on all four sides of the artboard. Checking this box in the Print dialog box includes that same 1/8″ extra on all four sides of the output.

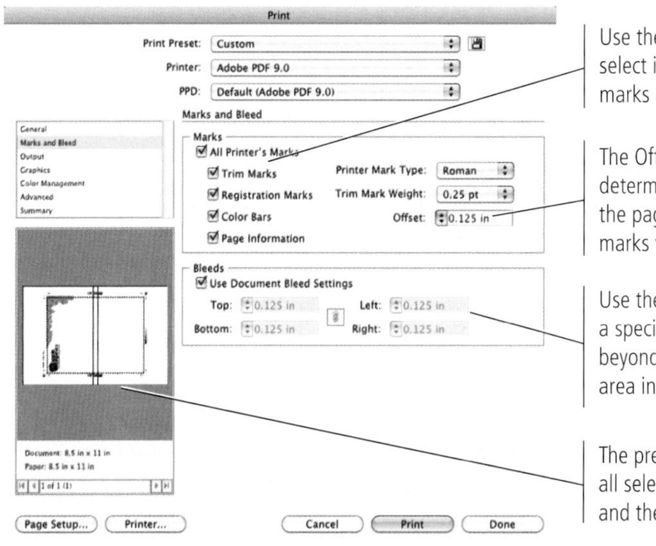

Use these options to select individual printer's marks or print all marks.

The Offset value determines how far from the page edge the printer's marks will be placed.

Use these fields to include a specific amount of space beyond the defined crop area in the output.

The preview now includes all selected printer's marks and the defined bleed area.

Note:

Some printers require printer's marks to stay outside the bleed area, which means the offset should be at least the same as or greater than the defined bleed area.

8. **Click the Output option in the list of categories on the left. Choose Composite in the Mode menu.**

   You can print all colors to a single sheet by choosing Composite, or you can print each color to an individual sheet by choosing Separations (Host-based). The third option — In-RIP Separation — allows the file data to be separated by the output device instead of by the software.

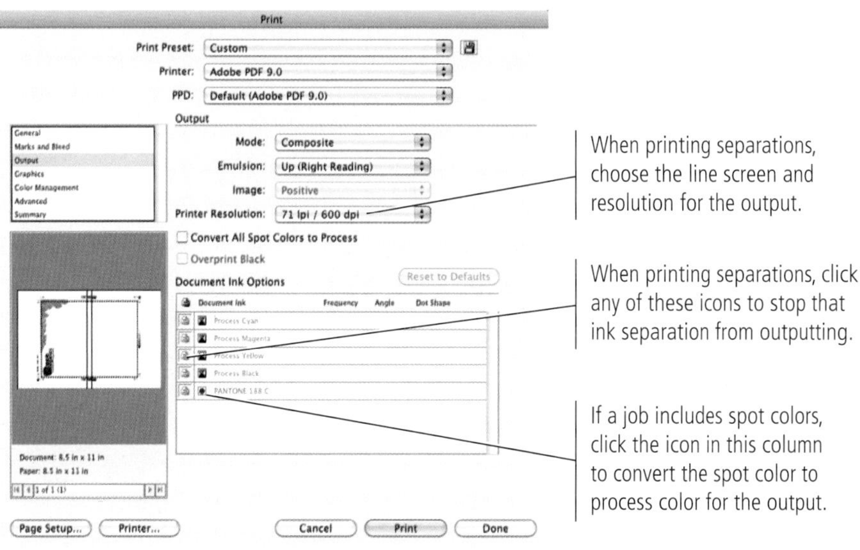

When printing separations, choose the line screen and resolution for the output.

When printing separations, click any of these icons to stop that ink separation from outputting.

If a job includes spot colors, click the icon in this column to convert the spot color to process color for the output.

Note:

The other options in this dialog box (Emulsion and Image) are reserved for high-end commercial output to a filmsetter or imagesetter.

9. **Click Print to output the artwork.**

10. **Choose File>Print again. Choose the Range radio button and type 2 in the field to print the envelope layout.**

11. **Choose Letter/US Letter in the Size menu and choose the Landscape orientation option. Make sure the Do Not Scale option is checked.**

    In this case, a letter-size sheet is large enough to print the envelope artboard without scaling. (Some of the printer's marks might be cut off by the printer's gripper margin, but that is fine for the purpose of a desktop proof.

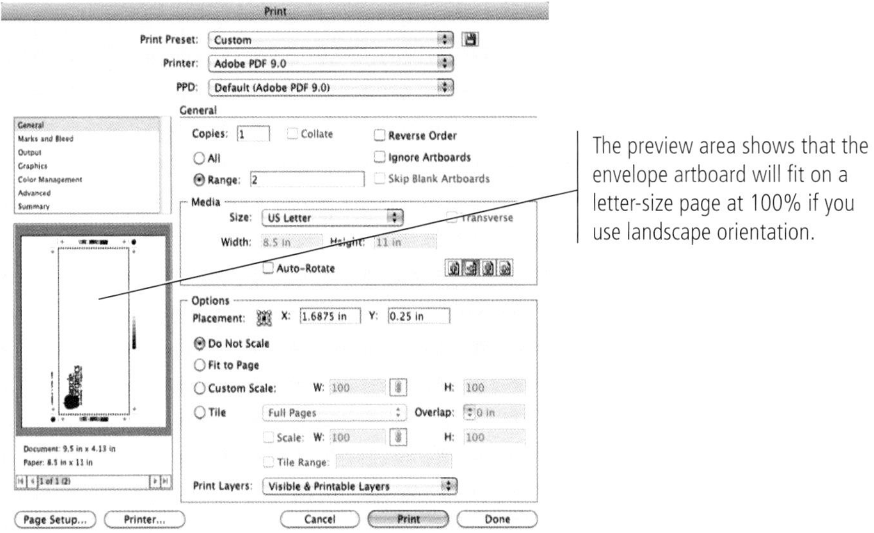

The preview area shows that the envelope artboard will fit on a letter-size page at 100% if you use landscape orientation.

12. **Click Print to output the envelope proof.**

13. **When the document comes back into focus, save and close it.**

Project Review

fill in the blank

1. The _______________ can be used to draw a new artboard in the current file.

2. Press _______________ and click the eye icon on a specific layer to switch only that layer between Preview and Outline mode.

3. When _______________ are active, moving your cursor over an unselected object reveals the paths that make up that object.

4. The _______________ tool is used to sample colors from an object already placed in the file.

5. The _______________ is used to monitor and change the individual attributes (fill, stroke, etc.) of the selected object.

6. The _______________ is the imaginary line on which the bottoms of letters rest.

7. _______________ is the spacing between specific pairs of letters (where the insertion point is placed).

8. The _______________ command makes the vector shapes of letters accessible to the Direct Selection tool.

9. A _______________ is a special ink used to reproduce a specific color, typically used for one- or two-color jobs.

10. Click the _______________ in the Layers panel to select a specific sublayer.

short answer

1. Explain the advantages of using a gradient mesh, compared to a regular gradient.

2. Briefly explain two primary differences between point-type objects and area-type objects.

3. Explain the potential benefits of using multiple artboards rather than different files for different pieces.

Portfolio Builder Project

Use what you learned in this project to complete the following freeform exercise.
Carefully read the art director and client comments, then create your own design to meet the needs of the project.
Use the space below to sketch ideas; when finished, write a brief explanation of your reasoning behind your final design.

art director comments

Your client, Tracey Dillon, is a local architect. She has hired you to create a corporate identity package so she can begin marketing her services to local land development companies. She has asked you first to develop a logo, and then to create the standard identity pieces that she can use for business promotion and correspondence.

To complete this project, you should:

- ❑ Develop a compelling logo that suggests the agency's purpose (architectural services).
- ❑ Incorporate the agency's name (TD Associates) into the logo.
- ❑ Build the letterhead and envelope with the same technical specs that you used to design the Apple Organics pieces.
- ❑ Build the business card layout to the standard 3.5 × 2″ size.

client comments

I've decided to open my own architectural services firm, and I need to start advertising. That means I need to brand my business so companies who need an architect will recognize and remember my name. I'm calling my business TD Associates.

I want a logo that really says 'architect', and I want the central color in my logo to be blue — like the blue you'd see on a blueprint.

Once the logo is finished, I need you to use the logo on business cards, letterhead, and envelopes that I will have preprinted; I want a more professional feel than I can create using my laser printer. The printer I spoke with said I could do this for less money if I go 4-color for the letterhead, but 2-color for the envelope.

Eventually, I'll be incorporating my logo into all kinds of advertising — newspaper, local magazines, and even the Internet; I'd like you to create whatever versions you think I'll need for any purpose.

project justification

Project Summary

Logos are one of the most common types of artwork that you will create in Illustrator. These can be as simple as text converted to outlines, or as complex as a line drawing based on an object in a photograph. Most logos will actually be some combination of drawing and text-based elements. As you learned throughout this project, one of the most important qualities of a logo is versatility — the ability to use it in many different types of projects and output it in many different types of print processes. To accomplish this goal, logos should work equally well in grayscale, four-color, and spot-color printing.

By completing this project, you worked with complex gradients to draw a realistic apple, then added creative type treatment to build the finished logotype. After completing the initial logo, you converted it to other variants that will work with different output processes (two-color and one-color). Finally, you incorporated the logo artwork into completed stationery to help solve your client's communication needs as he expands his business.

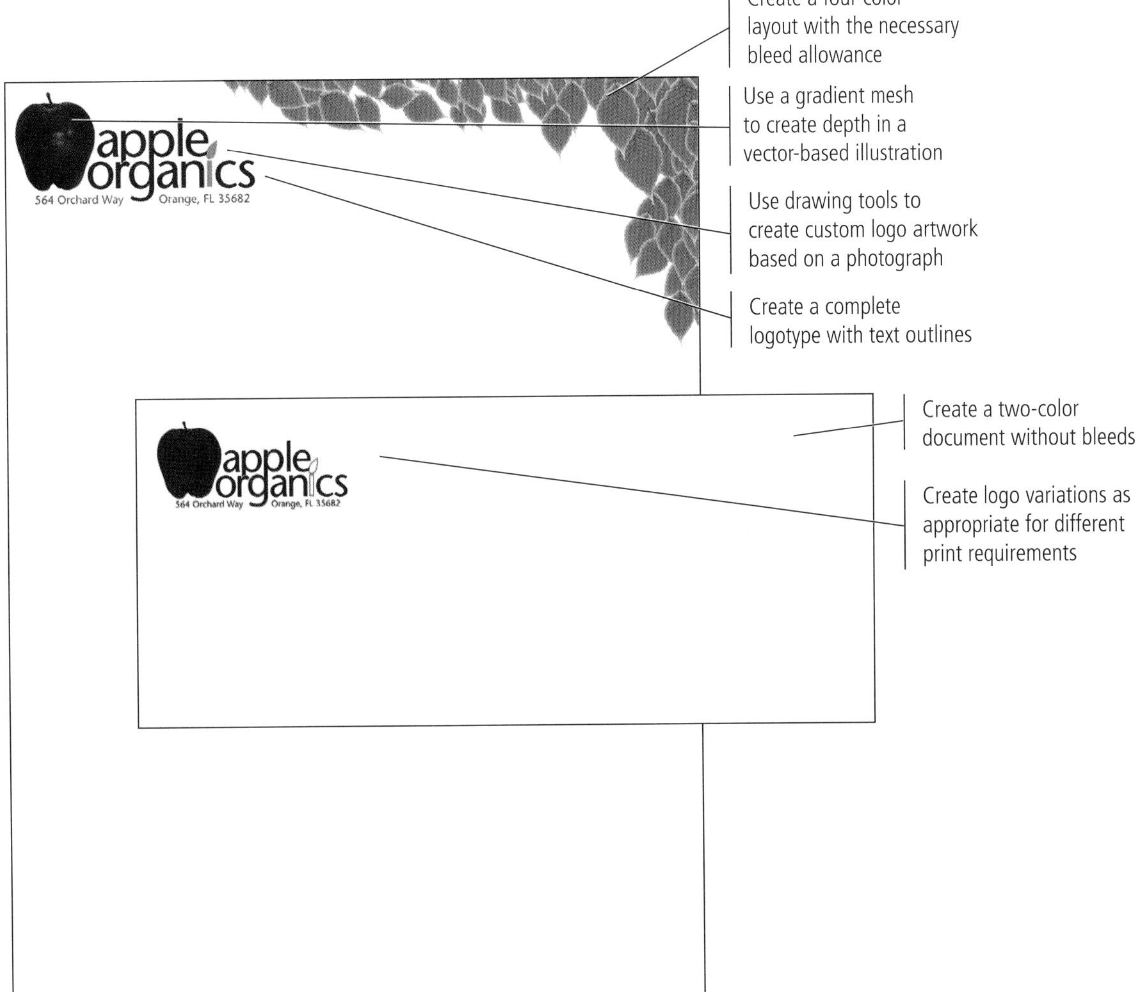
apple organics
564 Orchard Way
Orange, FL 35682
apple organics
564 Orchard Way
Orange, FL 35682
Create a four-color layout with the necessary bleed allowance
Use a gradient mesh to create depth in a vector-based illustration
Use drawing tools to create custom logo artwork based on a photograph
Create a complete logotype with text outlines
Create a two-color document without bleeds
Create logo variations as appropriate for different print requirements

project 4

Composite Movie Ad

Tantamount Studios, one of the largest film production companies in Hollywood, is developing a new movie called "Aftermath." You have been hired to develop an advertisement that will be used to announce the movie in several different trade magazines.

This project incorporates the following skills:

- ❑ Creating a single composite ad from multiple supplied images
- ❑ Compositing multiple photographs, using various techniques to silhouette the focal object in each image
- ❑ Incorporating vector graphics as rasterized layers and Smart Object layers
- ❑ Scaling and aligning different objects in relation to the page and to each other
- ❑ Managing individual layout elements using layers and layer groups
- ❑ Saving multiple versions of a file to meet different output requirements

Project Meeting

client comments

Here's a basic synopsis of the movie:

> *A massive hurricane, unlike anything ever seen on the West Coast of the United States, takes aim at San Francisco. The category 6 hurricane sparks tidal waves, fires, floods — the resulting destruction dwarfs even the earthquake and fire of 1906. The movie follows the storm survivors through the process of rebuilding, both personally and politically.*

This movie is going to be one of our summer blockbusters, and we're throwing a lot of resources behind it. We'll be putting the same ad in multiple magazines, and they all use different software to create the magazine layouts. We need the ad to work for all of our placements, regardless of what software is being used by the magazine publishers.

art director comments

The client loved the initial concept sketch I submitted last week, so we're ready to start building the files. I've had the photographer prepare the images we need, and the client has provided the studio and rating logo files. They also sent me the first two magazines' specs:

Magazine 1

- Bleed size: 8.75 × 11.25″
- Trim size: 8.5 × 11″
- Live area: 8 × 10.5″
- Files should be submitted as native layout files or layered TIFF

Magazine 2

- Sizes are the same as Magazine 1
- Files should be submitted as flattened TIFF or PDF

project objectives

To complete this project, you will:

- ❑ Resize a raster image to change resolution
- ❑ Composite multiple images into a single background file
- ❑ Incorporate both raster and vector elements into the same design
- ❑ Transform and arrange individual layers to create a cohesive design
- ❑ Create layer groups to easily manage related layer content
- ❑ Use selection techniques to isolate images from their backgrounds
- ❑ Save two different types of TIFF files for different ad requirements

Stage 1 Compositing Images and Artwork

Technically speaking, **compositing** is the process of combining any two or more objects (images, text, illustrations, etc.) into an overall design. When we talk about compositing in Photoshop, we're typically referring to the process of combining multiple images into a single cohesive image. Image compositing might be as simple as placing two images into different areas of a background file; or it could be as complex as placing a person into a group photo, carefully clipping out the individual's background, and adjusting the shadows to match the lighting in the group.

Note:

The ad you're building in this project requires compositing four digital photographs. You will also incorporate title treatment and logo files that were created in Adobe Illustrator by other members of your creative team. The various elements that make up the ad are fairly representative of the type of work you can (and probably will) create in Photoshop.

Types of Images

There are two primary types of digital artwork: vector graphics and raster images.

Vector graphics are composed of mathematical descriptions of a series of lines and shapes. Vector graphics are **resolution independent**; they can be freely enlarged or reduced, and they are automatically output at the resolution of the output device. The shapes that you create in Adobe InDesign, or in drawing applications such as Adobe Illustrator, are vector graphics.

Raster images, such as photographs or files created in Adobe Photoshop, are made up of a grid of independent pixels (rasters or bits) in rows and columns (called a **bitmap**). Raster files are **resolution dependent** — their resolution is fixed, determined when you scan, photograph, or otherwise create the file. You can typically reduce raster images, but you cannot enlarge them without losing image quality.

Line art is a type of raster image that it made up entirely of 100% solid areas; the pixels in a line-art image have only two options: they can be all black or all white. Examples of line art are UPC bar codes or pen-and-ink drawings.

Screen Ruling

The ad that you will be building in this project is intended to be placed in print magazines, so you have to build the new file with the appropriate settings for commercial printing. When reproducing a photograph on a printing press, the image must be converted into a set of printable dots that fool the eye into believing it sees continuous tones. Prior to image-editing software, pictures that were being prepared for printing on a press were photographed through a screen to create a grid of halftone dots. The result of this conversion is a halftone image; the dots used to simulate continuous tone are called **halftone dots**. Light tones in a photograph are represented as small halftone dots; dark tones become large halftone dots.

Note:

Despite their origins in pre-digital print workflows, these terms persist in the digital environment.

The screens used to create the halftone images had a finite number of available dots in a horizontal or vertical inch. That number was the **screen ruling**, or **lines per inch (lpi)** of the halftone. A screen ruling of 133 lpi means that in a square inch there are 133 × 133 (17,689) possible locations for a halftone dot. If the screen ruling is decreased, there are fewer total halftone dots, producing a grainier image; if the screen ruling is increased, there are more halftone dots, producing a clearer image.

Line screen is a finite number based on a combination of the intended output device and paper. You can't randomly select a line screen. Ask your printer what line screen will be used before you begin creating your images.

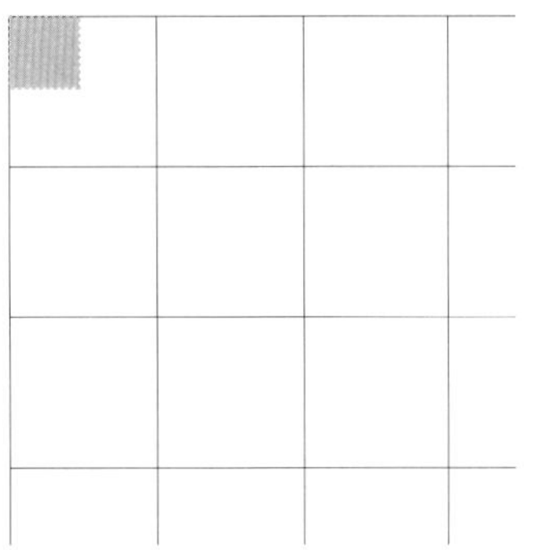

72 ppi

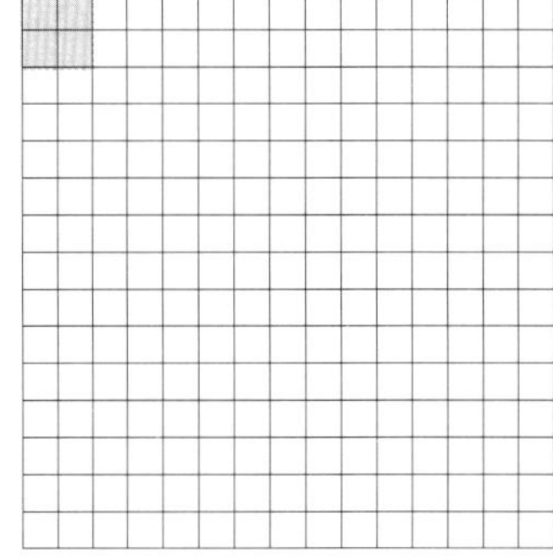

300 ppi

Each white square represents a pixel. The highlighted area shows the pixel information used to generate a halftone dot. If an image only has 72 pixels per inch, the output device has to generate four halftone dots per pixel, resulting in poor printed quality.

If you can't find out ahead of time, or if you're unsure, follow these general guidelines:

- Newspaper or newsprint: 85–100 lpi
- Magazine or general commercial printing: 133–150 lpi
- Premium-quality-paper jobs (such as art books or annual reports): 150–175 lpi; some specialty jobs might use 200 lpi or more

Image Resolution

When a printer creates halftone dots, it calculates the average value of a group of pixels in the raster image and generates a spot of appropriate size. A raster image's resolution — measured in **pixels per inch (ppi)** — determines the quantity of pixel data the printer can read. Regardless of their source — camera, scanner, or files created in Photoshop — images need to have sufficient resolution so the output device can generate enough halftone dots to create the appearance of continuous tone. In the images to the right, the same raster image is reproduced at 300 ppi (top) and 72 ppi (bottom); notice the obvious degradation in quality in the 72-ppi version.

Ideally, the printer will have four pixels for each halftone dot created. The relationship between pixels and halftone dots defines the rule of resolution for raster-based images — the resolution of a raster image (ppi) should be two times the screen ruling (lpi) that will be used for printing.

For line art, the general rule is to scan the image at the same resolution as the output device. Many laser printers today image at 600–1200 dots per inch (dpi), but imagesetters typically output at much higher resolution, possibly 2400 dpi or more.

Open a File from Adobe Bridge

Adobe Bridge is a stand-alone application that ships and installs along with Photoshop. This asset-management tool enables you to navigate, browse, and manage files anywhere on your system. If you have the entire Adobe Creative Suite, Bridge can also help streamline the workflow as you flip from one application to another to complete a project.

> *Note:*
>
> *Adobe Bridge is a complete stand-alone application. However, this is a book about Photoshop, not Bridge. We're simply introducing you to the Bridge interface and showing you how to use Bridge to navigate and access files. We encourage you to read the Bridge documentation (accessed in the Help menu when you are in the Bridge application).*

1. **Download Print5_RF_Project4.zip from the Student Files Web page.**
2. **Expand the ZIP archive in your WIP folder (Macintosh) or copy the archive contents into your WIP folder (Windows).**

   This results in a folder named **Movie**, which contains all of the files you need for this project. You should also use this folder to save the files you create in this project.

   If necessary, refer to Page 1 of the Interface chapter for specific information on expanding or accessing the required resource files.
3. **In Photoshop, click the Launch Bridge button in the Application/Menu bar.**

   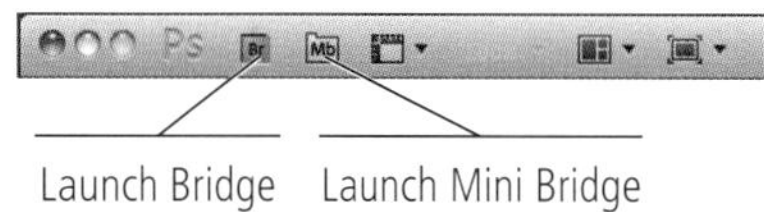

4. **In Bridge, use the Folders panel to navigate to your WIP>Movie folder.**

   Bridge is primarily a file manager, so you can think of it as a media browser. If some panels aren't visible, you can access them in the Bridge Window menu.

5. **Click the `bricks.jpg` thumbnail in the Content panel to select it.**

6. **If you don't see the Metadata panel, choose Window>Metadata. Review the File Properties of the selected image.**

   The most important information in File Properties is the resolution and color mode. This image was photographed at 72 ppi in the RGB color mode.

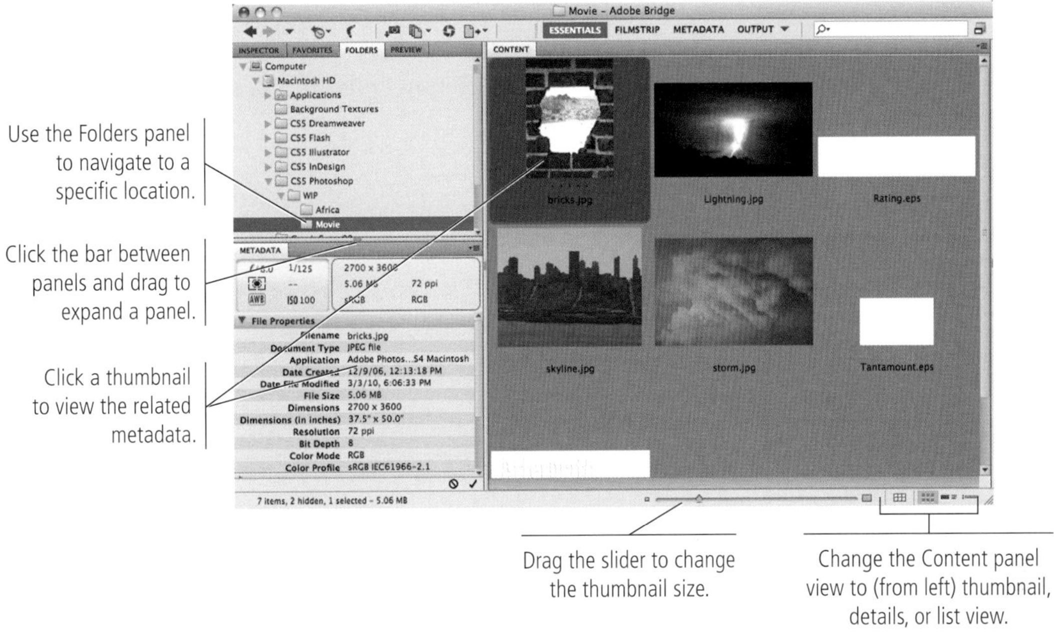

Use the Folders panel to navigate to a specific location.
Click the bar between panels and drag to expand a panel.
Click a thumbnail to view the related metadata.
Drag the slider to change the thumbnail size.
Change the Content panel view to (from left) thumbnail, details, or list view.

7. **Double-click the `bricks.jpg` thumbnail to open that file in Photoshop.**

   In this case, Bridge is an alternative to the File>Open method for opening files in Photoshop. The Bridge method can be useful because it provides more information than Photoshop's Open dialog box.

8. **If the rulers are not visible on the top and left edges, choose View>Rulers.**

   As you can see in the rulers, this image has a very large physical size. As you saw in the image metadata (in Bridge), however, the current image is only 72 ppi; for commercial printing, you need at least 300 ppi. You can use the principle of **effective resolution** to change the file to a high enough resolution for printing.

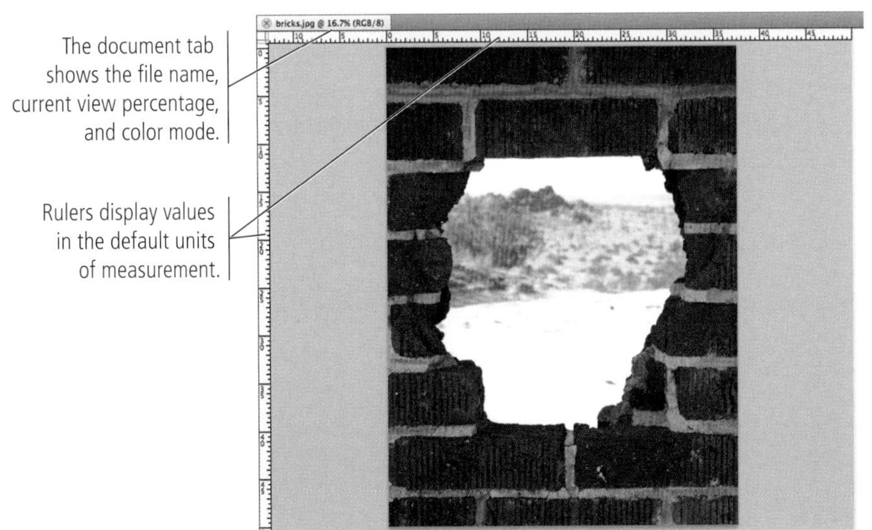

The document tab shows the file name, current view percentage, and color mode.
Rulers display values in the default units of measurement.

Note:

Although designers trained in traditional (non-digital) methods are sometimes comfortable talking about picas or ciceros, most people use inches as the standard unit of measurement in the U.S.

You can change the default unit of measurement in the Units & Rulers pane of the Preferences dialog box. (Double-clicking either ruler opens the appropriate pane of the Preferences dialog box.)

9. **Choose File>Save As. If necessary, navigate to your WIP>Movie folder as the target location. Change the file name (in the Save As field) to aftermath.**

   Since this is a basic image file with only one layer (so far), most of the other options in the Save As dialog box are grayed out (not available).

10. **Choose Photoshop in the Format menu and then click Save.**

    You can save a Photoshop file in a number of different formats, all of which have specific capabilities, limitations, and purposes. While you are still working on a file, it's best to keep it as a native Photoshop (PSD) file. When you choose a different format, the correct extension is automatically added to the file name.

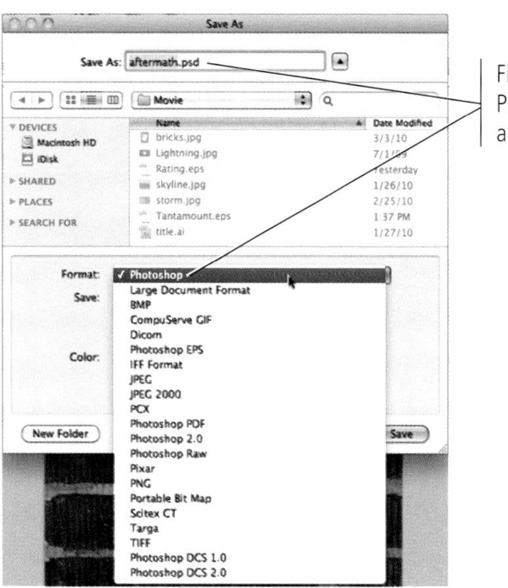

Files saved in the native Photoshop format display a ".psd" extension.

Note:

Also called "native", the PSD format is the most flexible format to use while building files in Photoshop.

11. **Continue to the next exercise.**

Resize the Image

Every raster image has a defined, specific resolution that is established when the image is created. If you scan an image to be 3″ high by 3″ wide at 150 ppi, that image has 450 pixels in each vertical column and 450 pixels in each horizontal row. Simply resizing the image stretches or compresses those pixels into a different physical space, but does not add or remove pixel information. If you resize the 3 × 3″ image to 6 × 6″ (200% of the original), the 450 pixels in each column or row are forced to extend across 6″ instead of 3, causing a marked loss of quality.

The **effective resolution** of an image is the resolution calculated after any scaling is taken into account. This number is equally important as the original image resolution — and perhaps moreso. The effective resolution can be calculated with a fairly simple equation:

Original resolution ÷ (% magnification ÷ 100) = Effective resolution

If a 300-ppi image is magnified 150%, the effective resolution is:

300 ppi ÷ 1.5 = 200 ppi

In other words, the more you enlarge a raster image, the lower its effective resolution becomes. In general, you can make an image 10% or 15% larger without significant adverse effects; the more you enlarge an image, however, the worse the results. Even Photoshop, which offers very sophisticated formulas (called "algorithms") for sizing images, cannot guarantee perfect results.

Effective resolution can be a very important consideration when working with client-supplied images, especially those that come from consumer-level digital cameras. Many of those devices capture images with a specific number of pixels rather than a number of pixels per inch (ppi). In this exercise, you will explore the effective resolution of an image to see if it can be used for a full-page printed magazine ad.

1. **With aftermath.psd open, choose Image>Image Size.**

   The Image Size dialog box shows the number of pixels in the image, as well as the image dimensions and current resolution. You can change any value in this dialog box, but you should understand what those changes mean before you do so.

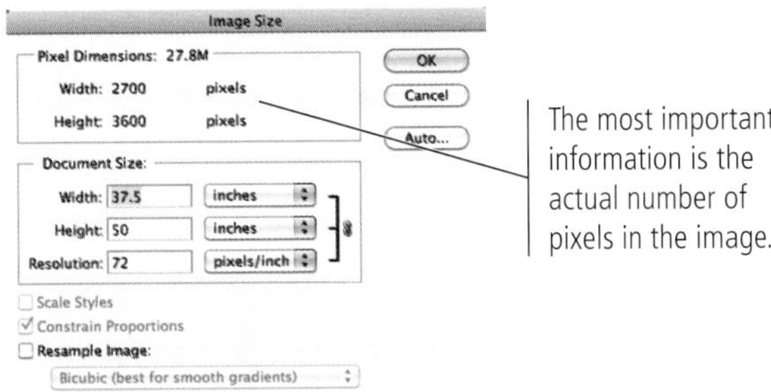

The most important information is the actual number of pixels in the image.

2. **Check the Resample Image option at the bottom of the dialog box.**

   The options in this dialog box remember the last-used choices. The Resample options might already be checked in your dialog box.

   Resampling means maintaining the existing resolution in the new image dimensions; in other words, you are either adding or deleting pixels to the existing image. When this option is turned on, you can change the dimensions of an image without affecting the resolution, or you can change the resolution of an image (useful for removing excess resolution or **downsampling**) without affecting the image size.

3. **Change the Resolution field to 300 pixels/inch.**

   When you change the resolution with resampling turned on, you do not change the file's physical size. To achieve 300-ppi resolution at the new size, Photoshop needs to add a huge number of pixels to the image. You can see at the top of the dialog box that this change would increase the total number of pixels from 2700 × 3600 to 11250 × 15000.

   You can also see that changing the resolution of an image without affecting its physical dimensions would have a significant impact on the file size. Changing the resolution to 300 ppi at the current size would increase the file size to nearly 483 megabytes.

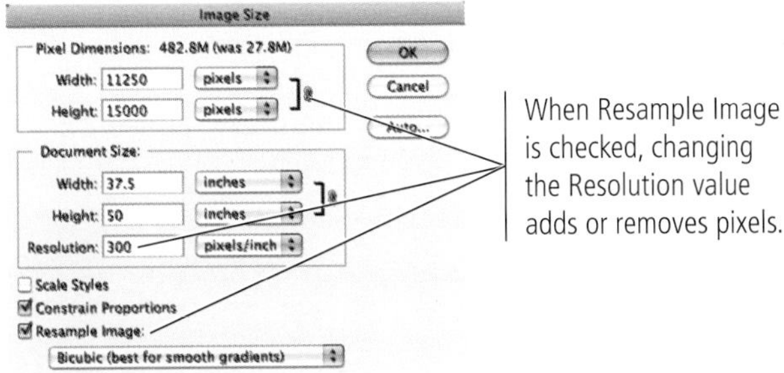

When Resample Image is checked, changing the Resolution value adds or removes pixels.

4. **Press Option/Alt and click the Reset button to restore the original image dimensions in the dialog box.**

   In many Photoshop dialog boxes, pressing the Option/Alt key changes the Cancel button to Reset. You can click the Reset button to restore the original values that existed when you opened the dialog box.

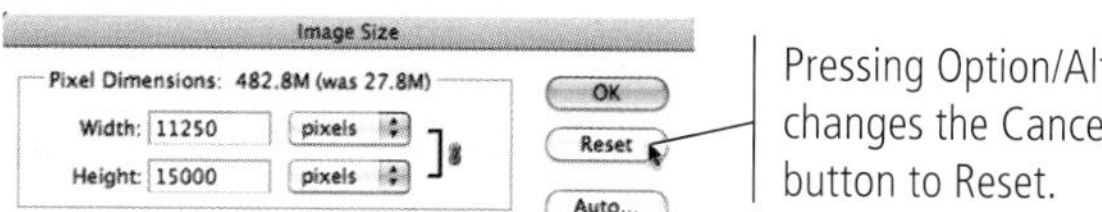

Pressing Option/Alt changes the Cancel button to Reset.

5. **Uncheck the Resample Image option at the bottom of the dialog box.**

6. **Change the Resolution field to `300` pixels/inch.**

   Resizing *without* resampling basically means dividing the same number of pixels over a different area. When you resize an image without resampling, you do not change the number of pixels in the image. (In fact, those fields in the dialog box become simple text; the fields are unavailable and you cannot change the number of pixels in the image.)

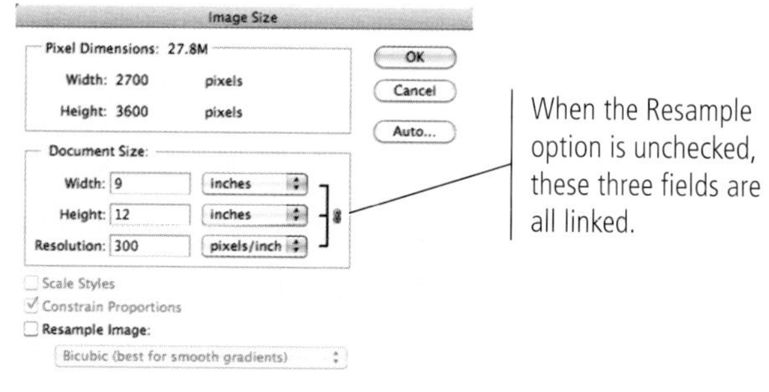

When the Resample option is unchecked, these three fields are all linked.

   You can see how changing one of the linked fields (Resolution) directly affects the other linked fields (Width and Height). By resizing the image to be 300 ppi — enough for commercial print quality — you now have an image that is 9″ × 12″.

More on Resolution and Resampling

PHOTOSHOP FOUNDATIONS

Discarding Pixels

Higher resolution means larger file sizes, which translates to longer processing time for printing or longer download time over the Internet. When you scale an image to a smaller size, simply resizing can produce files with far greater effective resolution than you need. Resampling allows you to reduce the physical size of an image without increasing the resolution, resulting in a smaller file size.

The caveat here is that once you discard (delete) pixels, they are gone. If you later try to re-enlarge the smaller image, you will not achieve the same quality as the original (before it was reduced). You should always save reduced images as copies instead of overwriting the originals.

Resampling

In general, you should always scan images to the size you will use in your final job. If you absolutely must resize a digital image, you can use resampling to achieve better results than simply changing the image size. Photoshop offers five types of resampling algorithms to generate extra pixel data (when increasing the image size) or to determine which pixels to discard (when reducing the image size).

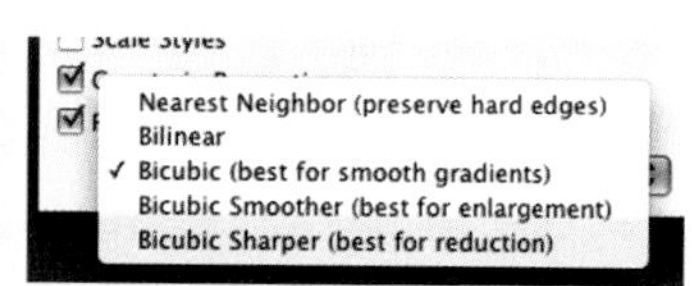

- **Nearest Neighbor** is a low-quality but quick method. Nearest neighbor interpolates new pixel information based on only one of the squares in the grid of pixels, usually resulting in an image with a blocky appearance.
- **Bilinear** is a medium-quality resampling method. Bilinear resampling averages adjacent pixels to create new information.
- **Bicubic** creates the most accurate pixel information for continuous-tone images; it also takes the longest to process and produces a softer image. To understand how this option works, think of a square bisected both horizontally and vertically — bicubic resampling averages the value of all four of those squares (pixels) to interpolate the new information.
- **Bicubic Smoother** is useful for enlarging images with smoother results than basic bicubic resampling.
- **Bicubic Sharper** is useful for reducing the size of an image and maintaining sharp detail.

7. **Click OK to apply the change and return to the document window.**

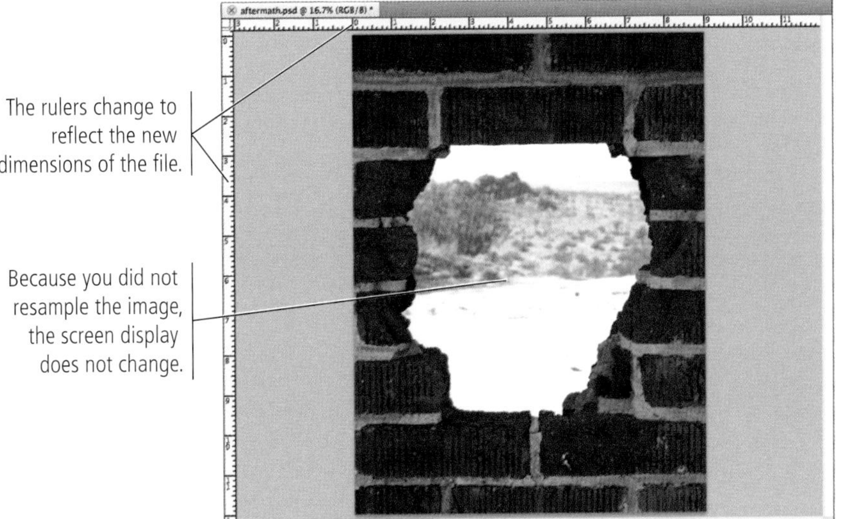

The rulers change to reflect the new dimensions of the file.
Because you did not resample the image, the screen display does not change.

Note:

Although many magazines are printed at 133 lpi, some are printed at 150 lpi. By setting the resolution to 300, your file will work for any magazine that prints at 133 or 150 lpi.

8. **Save the file and continue to the next exercise.**

   Because you have already saved this working file with a new name, you can simply choose File>Save, or press Command/Control-S to save without opening a dialog box. If you want to change the file name, you can always choose File>Save As.

Crop the Canvas and Place Ruler Guides

The final step in preparing the workspace is defining the live area of the page. **Trim size** is the actual size of a page once it has been cut out of the press sheet. According to your client, the magazine has a trim size of 8.5″ × 11″.

Any elements that print right to the edge of a page (called **bleeding**) must actually extend beyond the defined trim size. The **bleed allowance** is the amount of extra space that should be included for these bleed objects; most applications require at least 1/8″ bleed allowance on any bleed edge.

Because of inherent variation in the mechanical printing and trimming processes, most magazines also define a safe or **live area**; all important design elements (especially text) should stay within this live area. The live area for this project is 8 × 10.5″.

Note:

You should familiarize yourself with the most common fraction-to-decimal equivalents:

1/8 = 0.125

1/4 = 0.25

3/8 = 0.375

1/2 = 0.5

5/8 = 0.625

3/4 = 0.75

7/8 = 0.875

1. **With aftermath.psd open, choose the Crop tool in the Tools panel.**

2. **Click in the image window and drag a marquee with the Crop tool.**

   The crop marquee has eight handles, which you can drag to change the size of the cropped area. When you draw a marquee with the Crop tool, the area outside the marquee is "shielded" by a darkened overlay so you can get an idea of what will remain after you finalize the crop. You can turn off this preview by unchecking the Shield box on the Control panel.

3. **Choose None in the Crop Guide Overlay menu.**

   Because you're simply cropping to a known size before you define the overall composition, neither grid is useful for this project.

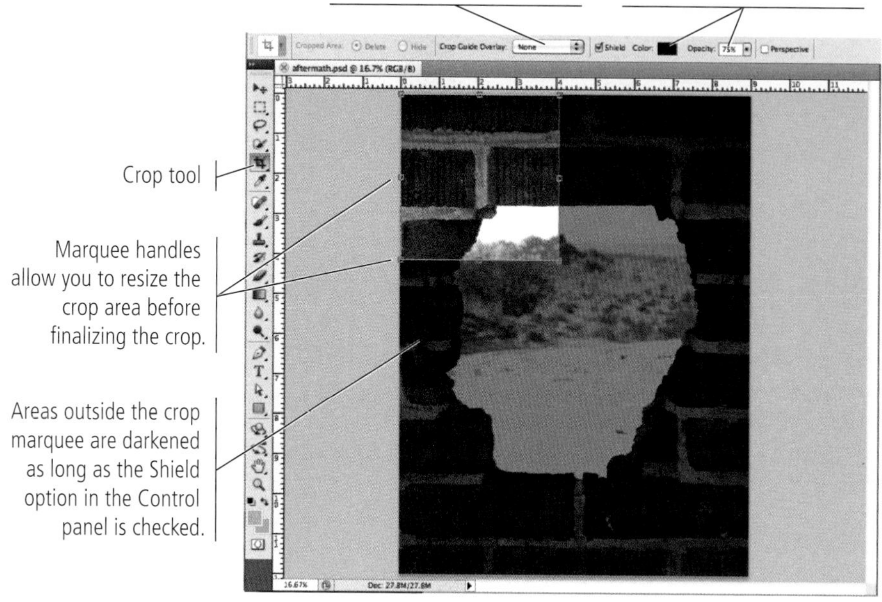

Use this menu to display a standard grid or rule-of-thirds grid inside the crop area.
Use these options to change the color and opacity of the area outside the crop area.
Crop tool
Marquee handles allow you to resize the crop area before finalizing the crop.
Areas outside the crop marquee are darkened as long as the Shield option in the Control panel is checked.

4. **Using the rulers as a guide, change the marquee to 8.75″ wide × 11.25″ high.**

   Remember, the defined trim size for this ad is 8.5″ × 11″. Anything that runs to the page edge has to incorporate a 0.125″ bleed allowance, so the actual canvas size must be large enough to accommodate the bleed allowance on all edges:

   [Width] 8.5″ + 0.125″ + 0.125″ = 8.75

   [Height] 11″ + 0.125″ + 0.125″ = 11.25

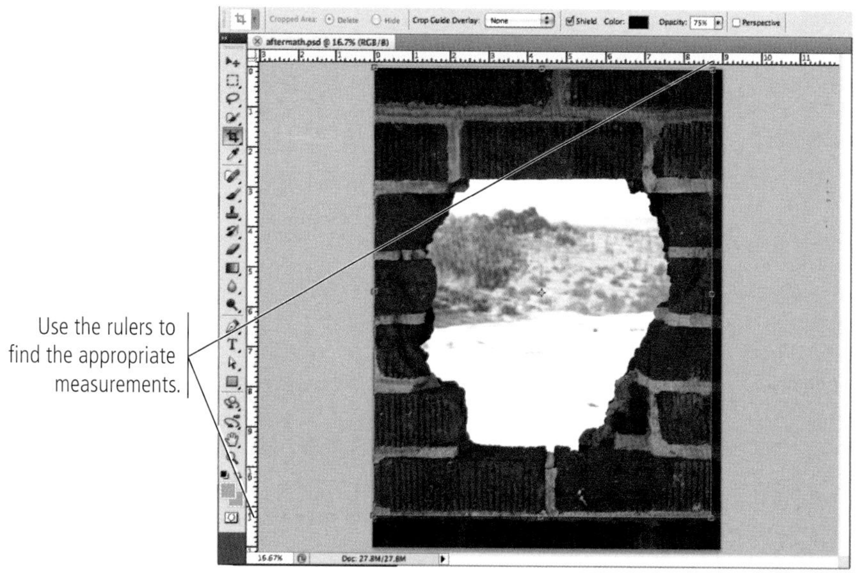

Use the rulers to find the appropriate measurements.

Note:

If rulers are not still visible, choose View>Rulers or press Command/Control-R.

Note:

You can press the Escape key to cancel the crop marquee and return to the uncropped image.

Note:

You can rotate a crop marquee by placing the cursor slightly away from a corner handle.

5. **Click inside the crop area and drag to position it in the approximate middle of the image window.**

   It might be helpful to toggle off the Snap feature (View>Snap), which causes certain file elements to act as magnets when you move a marquee or drag a selection.

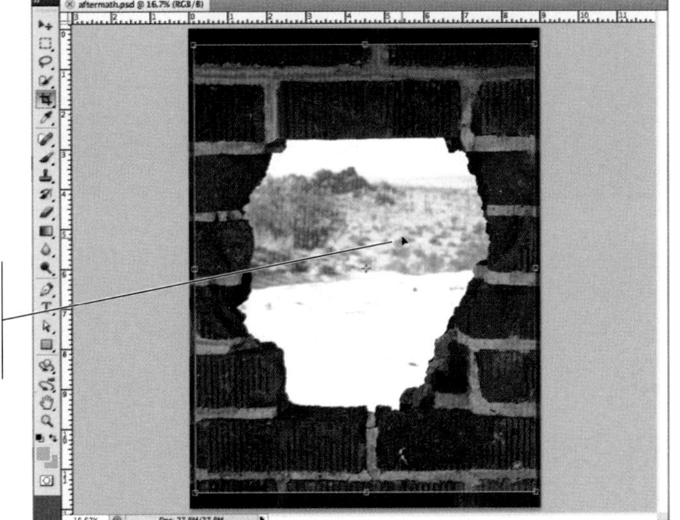

You can click inside the crop area to drag the area without changing its size.

Note:

You can use the Arrow keys on your keyboard to nudge the marquee one pixel at a time in a specific direction.

6. **Press Return/Enter to finalize the crop.**

7. **Choose the Move tool, and then open the Info panel (Window>Info).**

   As we explained in the Interface chapter, the panels you see depend on what was done the last time you (or someone else) used the Photoshop application. Because workspace arrangement is such a personal preference, we tell you what panels you need to use but we don't tell you where to put them.

Note:

Remember: panels can always be accessed in the Window menu.

8. **Click the horizontal page ruler at the top of the page and drag down to create a guide positioned at the 1/8″ (0.125″) mark.**

   If you watch the vertical ruler, you can see a marker indicating the position of the cursor. The Info panel also shows the precise numeric position of the guide you are dragging.

   It helps to zoom in to a higher view percentage if you want to precisely place guides. We found it necessary to use at least 66.7% view before the Info panel reflected exactly the 0.125″position. If you zoom in, you can press the Spacebar to temporarily access the Hand tool to reposition the image so you can see the top-left corner.

Click and drag from the horizontal ruler to add a horizontal guide.

The gray line indicates the location of the guide you're dragging.

Watch the ruler to see the location of the guide you're dragging.

The Info panel shows the exact Y location of the guide you are dragging.

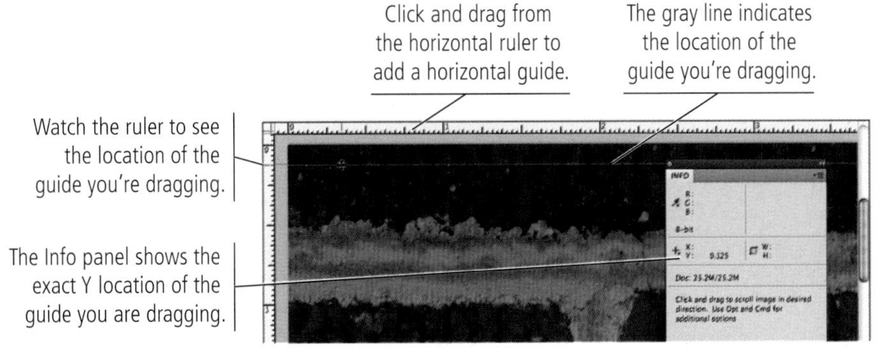

Note:

The X coordinate refers to an object's horizontal position and Y refers to the vertical position.

9. **Click the vertical ruler at the left and drag right to place a guide at the 0.125″ mark.**

Watch the marker on the horizontal ruler to judge the guide's position.

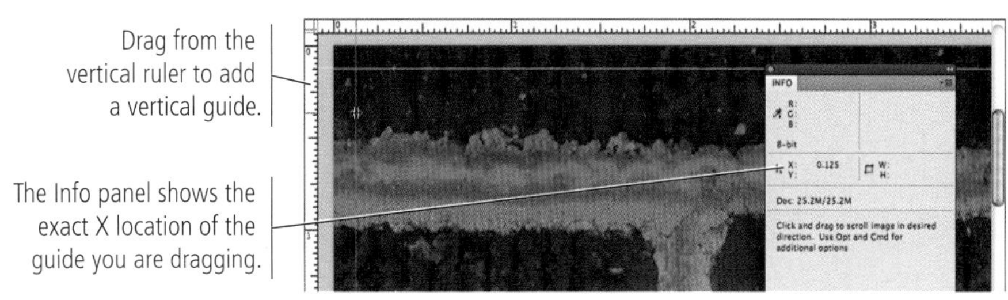

10. **Choose View>New Guide. In the resulting dialog box, choose the Vertical option and type `8.625` in the field and click OK.**

You don't need to type the unit of measurement because the default unit for this file is already inches. Photoshop automatically assumes the value you type is in the default unit of measurement.

11. **Choose View>New Guide again. Choose the Horizontal option and type `11.625` in the field. Click OK.**

At this point you should have four guides – two vertical and two horizontal, each 1/8″ from the file edges. Thee mark the trim size of your final 8.5 × 11″ file.

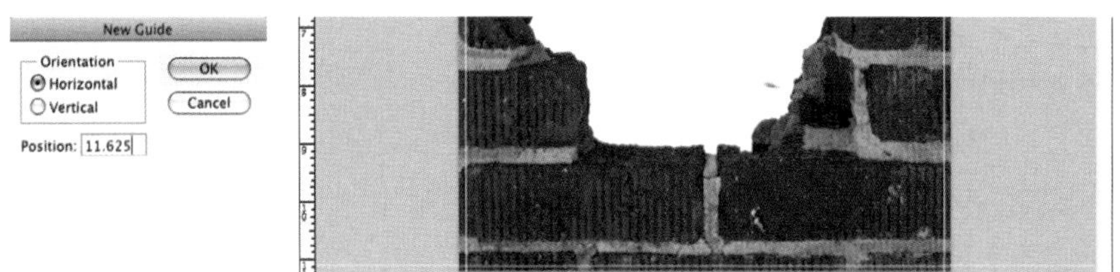

12. **In the top-left corner of the document window, click the zero-point crosshairs and drag to the top-left intersection of the guides.**

You can reposition the zero point to the top-left corner of the bleed allowance by double-clicking the zero-point crosshairs.

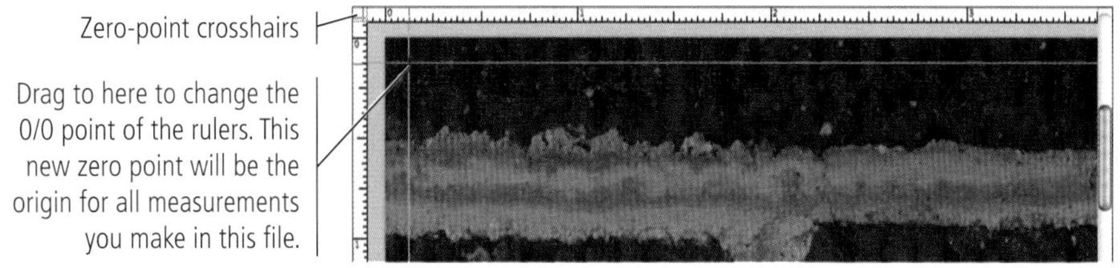

Zero-point crosshairs
Drag to here to change the 0/0 point of the rulers. This new zero point will be the origin for all measurements you make in this file.

13. **Drag new guides 0.25″ inside each trim guide to mark the live area of the page.**

These guides mark the defined live area of the ad (8 × 10.5″). This is how we determined where to put these guides:

[Width] 8.5″ – 8.0″ = 0.5 ÷ 2 = 0.25″

[Height] 11″ – 10.5″ = 0.5″ ÷ 2 = 0.25″

Note:

Use the Move tool to reposition placed guides. Remove individual guides by dragging them back onto the ruler.

If you try to reposition a guide and can't, choose View>Lock Guides. If this option is checked, guides are locked; you can't move them until you toggle this option off.

Note:

Press Option/Alt and click a guide to change it from vertical to horizontal (or vice versa). The guide rotates around the point where you click, which can be useful if you need to find a corner based on the position of an existing guide.

14. **Click the View menu and make sure a checkmark appears to the left of Lock Guides. If no checkmark is there, choose Lock Guides to toggle on that option.**

After you carefully position specific guides, it's a good idea to lock them so you don't accidentally move or delete them later. If you need to move a guide at any point, simply choose View>Lock Guides to toggle off the option temporarily.

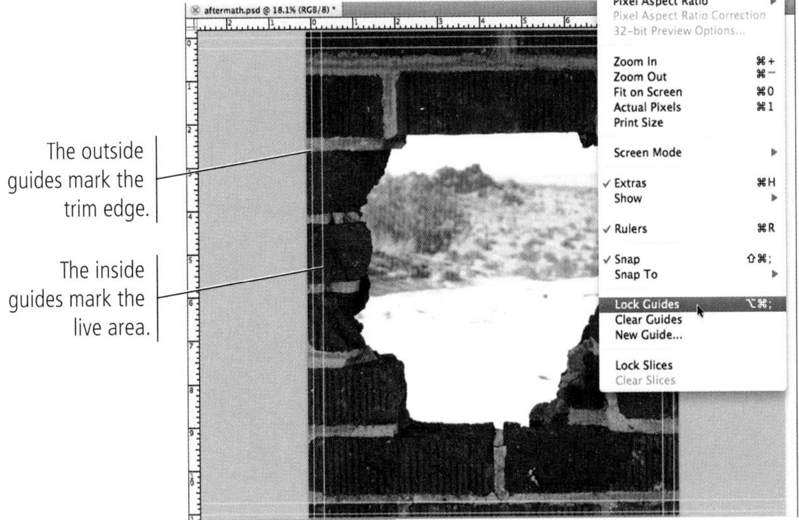

Note:

You can press Command/Control-; to toggle the visibility of page guides.

15. **Save the file and continue to the next exercise.**

Drag a File to Composite Images

Compositing multiple images in Photoshop is a fairly simple process — or at least, it starts out that way. But there are a number of technical and aesthetic issues that you must resolve when you combine multiple images in a single design.

1. **With aftermath.psd open, click the Launch Bridge button at the top of the Photoshop interface to return to that application.**

2. **Click the storm.jpg thumbnail, then review the metadata for that file.**

   This image is only 180 ppi, but it has a physical size much larger than the defined ad size. The principle of effective resolution might make this image usable in the composite ad.

Note:

When you created the background file for this project, you created a raster image that contains pixels (Photoshop files are almost always pixel-based). Digital photographs and scans are also pixel-based, which is why you use Photoshop to edit and manipulate those types of files.

3. **Double-click the `storm.jpg` thumbnail to open that file in Photoshop.**

4. **Use the Arrange Documents panel in the Application/Menu bar to show both open files at one time.**

   As you saw in the Interface chapter, these options are useful for arranging and viewing multiple open files within your workspace.

5. **Choose the Move tool in the Tools panel.**

6. **Click in the storm.jpg image window and drag into the aftermath.psd image window, then release the mouse button.**

   Basic compositing can be as simple as dragging a selection from one file to another. If no active selection appears in the source document, this action moves the entire active layer from the source document.

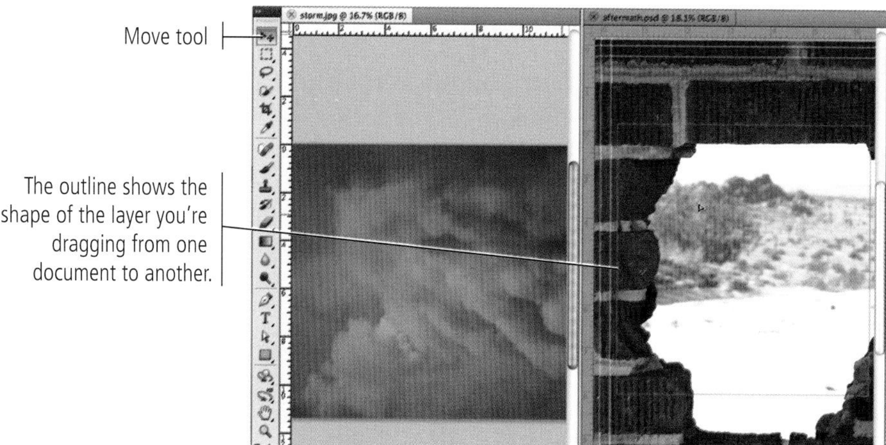

Move tool
The outline shows the shape of the layer you're dragging from one document to another.

7. **Click the Close button on the storm.jpg document tab to close that file.**

   After closing the storm file, the aftermath.psd document window expands to fill the available space.

   If you remember from the Bridge metadata, the storm image was 17.1″ × 11.4″ at 180 ppi. Photoshop cannot maintain multiple resolutions in a single file. When you move the image content into the aftermath file, it adopts the resolution of the target file (in this case, 300 ppi). The concept of effective resolution transforms the storm image/layer to approximately 10.25″ × 6.825″ at 300 ppi.

8. **Open the Layers panel (Window>Layers).**

   The original aftermath.psd file had only one layer — Background. Before editing, every scan and digital photograph has this characteristic. When you copy or drag content from one file into another, it is automatically placed on a new layer with the default name "Layer *n*", where "n" is a sequential number.

When a file contains more than one layer, the document tab shows the name of the active layer.

A new layer (Layer 1) is automatically added to contain the contents that you dragged from the storm.jpg file.

The Background layer contains the original bricks file content.

9. **Choose File>Save, and read the resulting message.**

   Because this is the first time you have saved the file after adding new layers, you should see the Photoshop Format Options dialog box, with the Maximize Compatibility check box already activated. It's a good idea to leave this check box selected so your files will be compatible with other CS5 applications and other versions of Photoshop.

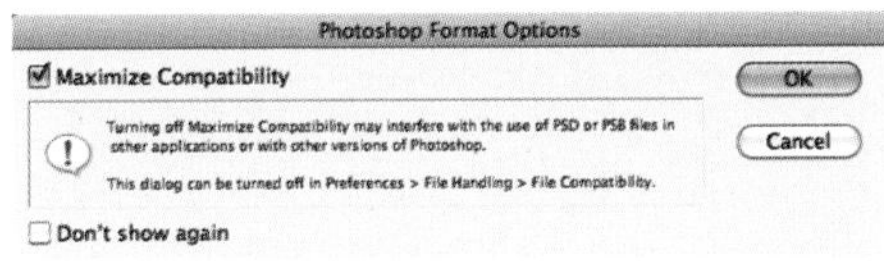

10. **Make sure the Maximize Compatibility check box is selected and click OK.**

11. **Continue to the next exercise.**

> ***Note:***
>
> *If you don't see this warning, check the File Handling pane of the Preferences dialog box. You can set the Maximize PSD and PSB File Compatibility menu to Always, Never, or Ask.*

Open Files with Mini Bridge

Mini Bridge provides access to certain file-management operations of the full Bridge application, from a panel directly within Photoshop. If Bridge is not already running on your computer, it might take a while for the Mini Bridge panel to show anything.

1. **With aftermath.psd open, choose View>Fit on Screen to show the entire image centered in the document window.**

2. **Click the Launch Mini Bridge button in the Application/Menu bar.**

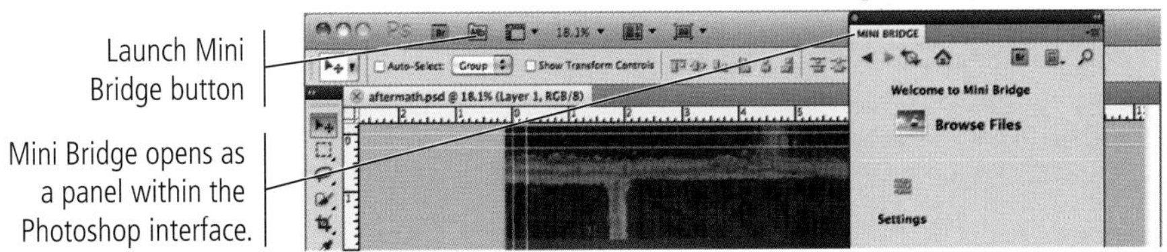

3. **If the Mini Bridge panel does not show the thumbnails in the WIP>Movie folder, click the Browse Files button.**

   Mini Bridge defaults to the location of the currently opened file. You should see thumbnails of all the files in the WIP>Movie folder.

4. **Click the View button at the bottom of the panel and choose As Thumbnails.**

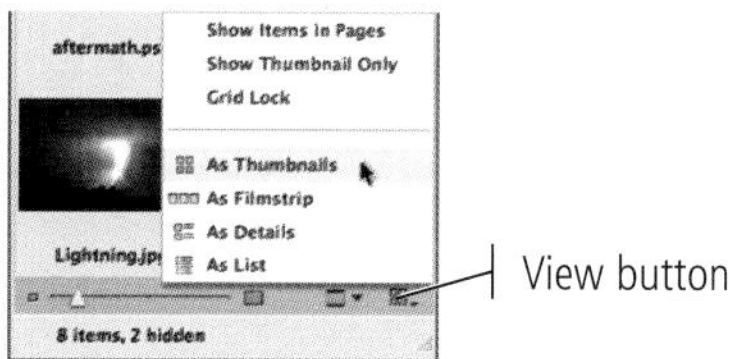

5. **Scroll through the thumbnails (if necessary), and double-click the skyline.jpg image thumbnail to open that file.**

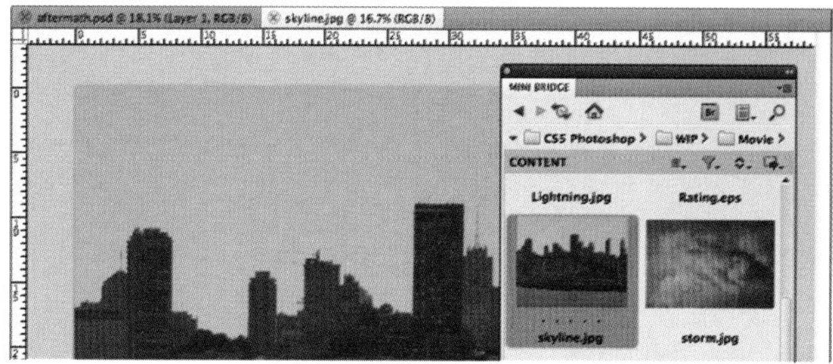

Note:

As in the full Bridge application, double-clicking a file in the Mini Bridge panel opens that file in a separate document window.

6. **Open the Image Size dialog box (Image>Image Size). Make sure the Resample Image option is not checked and change the Resolution field to 300 ppi. Click OK to return to the document window.**

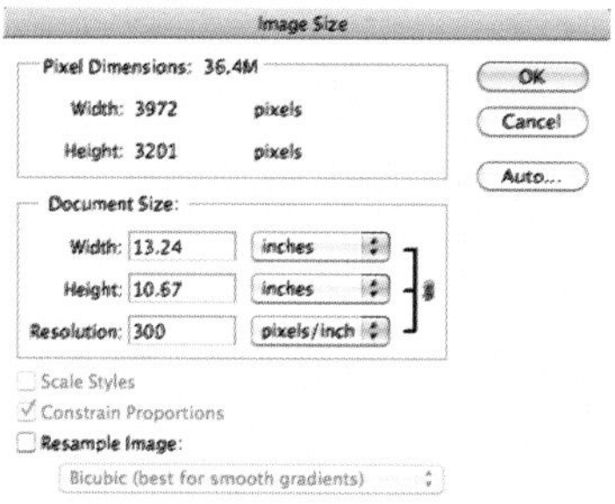

7. **Choose the Rectangular Marquee tool in the Tools panel and review the options in the Control panel.**

   By default, dragging with a marquee tool creates a new selection. You can use the buttons on the left end of the Control panel to add to the current selection, subtract from the current selection, or intersect with the current selection.

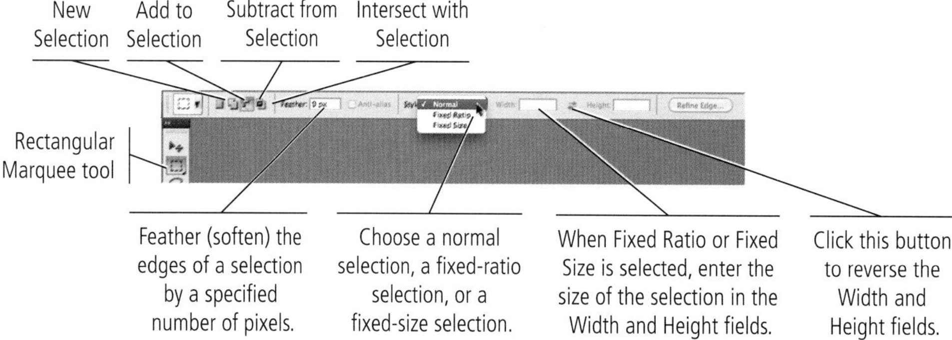

8. **Choose the New Selection option in the Control panel. Click outside of the top-left corner, drag down past the bottom edge of the image, and drag right to the 8.5″ mark on the horizontal ruler.**

   You can't select an area larger than the current canvas, so the top, left, and bottom edges of the selection snap to the canvas edges.

   The edges of this image will be hidden by the bricks, so you don't need the full 8.75″ width of the overall ad.

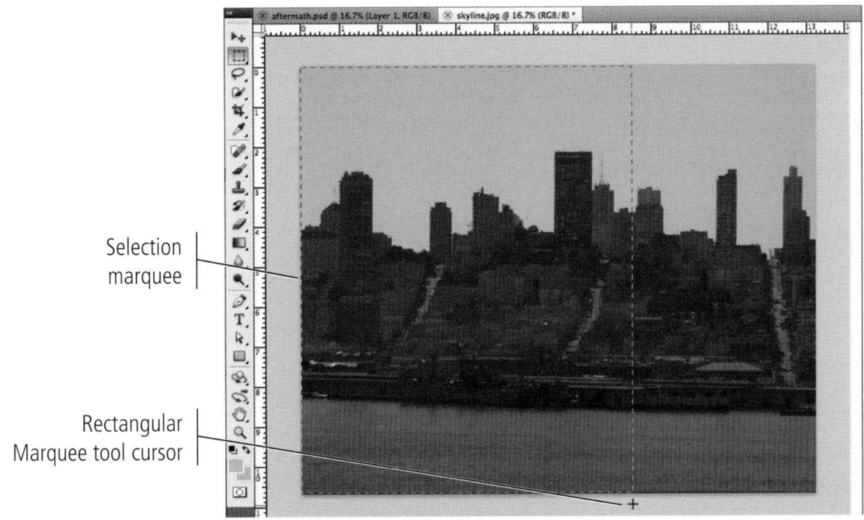
Selection marquee
Rectangular Marquee tool cursor

> *Note:*
>
> *Use the marquee tools to create simple-shape selections such as rectangular, elliptical, single row of pixels, or a single column of pixels.*

> *Note:*
>
> *Press Shift while dragging a new marquee to constrain the selection to a square (using the Rectangular Marquee tool) or circle (using the Elliptical Marquee tool).*

9. **Click inside the selection marquee and drag it to the approximate center of the image.**

   You can move a selection marquee by clicking inside the selected area with the Marquee tool and dragging to the desired area of the image.

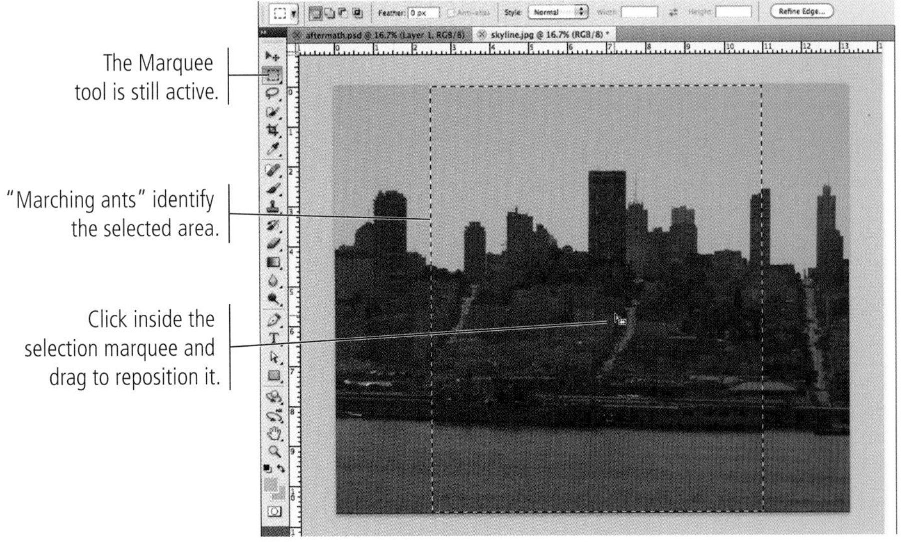
The Marquee tool is still active.
"Marching ants" identify the selected area.
Click inside the selection marquee and drag to reposition it.

> *Note:*
>
> *If you want to move a marquee, make sure the Marquee tool is still selected. If the Move tool is active, clicking inside the marquee and dragging will actually move the contents within the selection area.*

10. **In the Control panel, choose the Subtract from Selection option.**

11. **Click near the waterline at the left edge of the existing selection, drag down past the bottom edge of the image, and right past the right edge of the existing selection.**

Subtract from Selection is active.
Click here...
...and drag to here.
The cursor shows a minus sign because you are subtracting from the existing selection.

You only want the city to appear in the ad, so you don't need the water area of this image. When you release the mouse button, the selection is the area of the first marquee, minus the area of the second marquee. (This two-step process isn't particularly necessary in this case, but you should know how to add to and subtract from selections.)

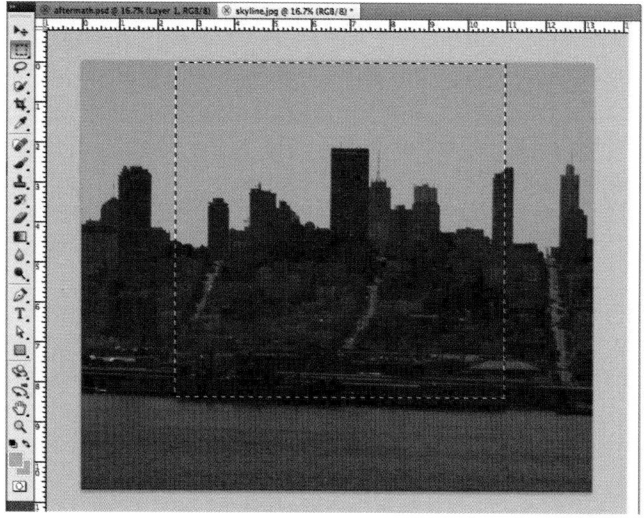

Note:

Press Shift to add to the current selection or press Option/Alt to subtract from the current selection.

12. **Choose Edit>Copy.**

The standard Cut, Copy, and Paste options are available in Photoshop, just as they are in most applications. Whatever you have selected will be copied to the Clipboard, and whatever is in the Clipboard will be pasted.

13. **Click the Close button on the skyline.jpg document tab to close the file. When asked, click Don't Save.**

Although the city would have adopted the resolution of the composite file, you manually resized the image so you could see the appropriate measurements for making your selection. You don't need to save this change.

14. **With the aftermath.psd file active, choose Edit>Paste.**

The copied selection is pasted in the center of the document window. Because you used the Fit on Screen option at the beginning of this exercise, the pasted image is centered in the document. Another new layer is automatically created to store the pasted content.

15. **Save the file and continue to the next exercise.**

 Place a File from Mini Bridge

In addition to opening new files, you can also use the Mini Bridge panel to place content directly into an open file. This removes a few steps from the process of compositing multiple images.

1. **With aftermath.psd open, choose View>Fit on Screen.**
2. **Click the Launch Mini Bridge button in the Application/Menu bar to open that panel (if it is not still open).**
3. **Click the Lightning.jpg thumbnail in the panel and drag it to the aftermath.psd document window.**

   The placed file appears with bounding box handles and crossed diagonal lines. The placement isn't final until you press Return/Enter; if you press the Escape key, the file will not be placed.

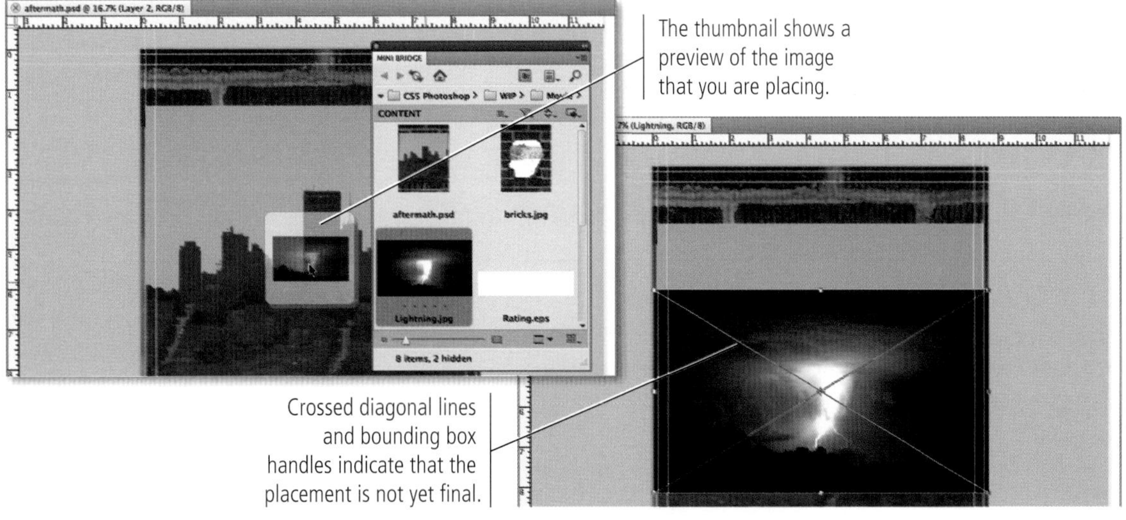

The thumbnail shows a preview of the image that you are placing.
Crossed diagonal lines and bounding box handles indicate that the placement is not yet final.

4. **Press Return/Enter to finalize the placement.**

   After you finalize the placement, the bounding box handles and crossed diagonal lines disappear. In the Layers panel, the placed file has its own layer (just as the copied layers do). This layer, however, is automatically named, based on the name of the placed file.

   The layer's thumbnail indicates that this layer is a **Smart Object** — it is linked to the file that you placed. Changes in the original file will also be reflected in the file where the original is placed. (You will work extensively with Smart Objects in Project 5.)

Note:

You can place either raster or vector files as Smart Objects. If you place a raster file as a Smart Object, double-clicking the thumbnail opens the placed raster file in another Photoshop window.

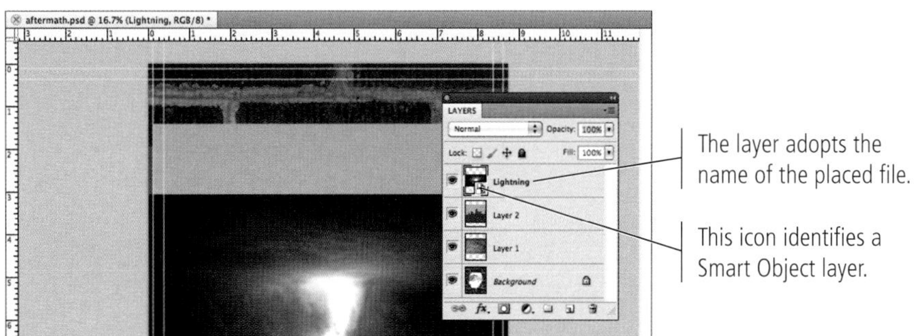

The layer adopts the name of the placed file.
This icon identifies a Smart Object layer.

5. **Control/right-click the Smart Object layer name and choose Rasterize Layer.**

   You don't need to maintain a link to the original file, so this step converts the Smart Object layer to a regular layer.

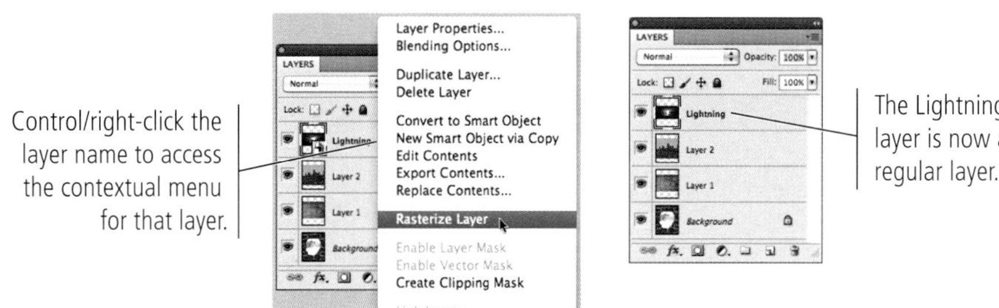

6. **Save the file and continue to the next exercise.**

Rasterize a Vector File

As you learned earlier, vector graphics are based on a series of mathematical descriptions that tell the computer processor where to draw lines. Logos and title treatments — such as the ones you will use in this project — are commonly created as vector graphics. Although Photoshop is typically a "paint" (pixel-based) application, you can also open and work with vector graphics created in illustration programs like Adobe Illustrator.

1. **With aftermath.psd open, choose File>Open and navigate to your WIP>Movie folder.**

2. **Select title.ai in the list of files and then click Open.**

   This is an Adobe Illustrator file of the movie title text treatment. The Format menu defaults to Photoshop PDF because Illustrator uses PDF as its underlying file structure.

   When you open a vector file (Illustrator, EPS, or PDF) in Photoshop, it is rasterized (converted to a raster graphic). The Import PDF dialog box allows you to determine exactly what and how to rasterize the file. The default values in this box are defined by the contents of the file you're opening.

Note:

If you double-clicked title.ai in Adobe Bridge, it would default to open in Adobe Illustrator — its native application, or the application in which it was created. You could, however, Control/right-click the thumbnail in Bridge and choose Open With>Adobe Photoshop CS5 from the contextual menu.

The Crop To options determine the size of the opened file. Depending on how the file was created, some of these values might be the same as others:

- **Bounding Box** is the outermost edges of the artwork in the file.
- **Media Box** is the size of the paper as defined in the file.
- **Crop Box** is the size of the page including printer's marks.
- **Bleed Box** is the trim size plus any defined bleed allowance.
- **Trim Box** is the trim size as defined in the file.
- **Art Box** is the area of the page as defined in the file.

Note:

The Image Size fields default to the settings of the bounding box you select. You can change the size, resolution, color mode, and bit depth by entering new values.

3. **Highlight the Width field and type 8, and make sure the Resolution field is set to 300 pixels/inch.**

   You know the live area of the ad you're building is 8″ wide, so you can import this file at a size small enough to fit into that space. Because the Constrain Proportions option is checked by default, the height changes proportionally to match the new width.

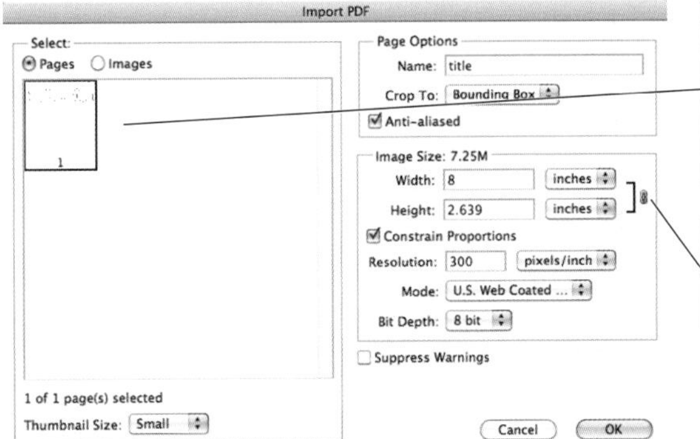

If you're opening a multi-page PDF or an Illustrator file with more than one Artboard, this window shows previews of each "page" in the file.

When this chain icon appears, the width and height are constrained.

4. **Click OK.**

   The title treatment file opens in Photoshop. The checkered area behind the text indicates that the background is transparent. If you look at the Layers panel, you will see that Layer 1 isn't locked; because it's transparent, it is not considered a background layer.

5. **Choose Select>All.**

   This command creates a marquee for the entire canvas.

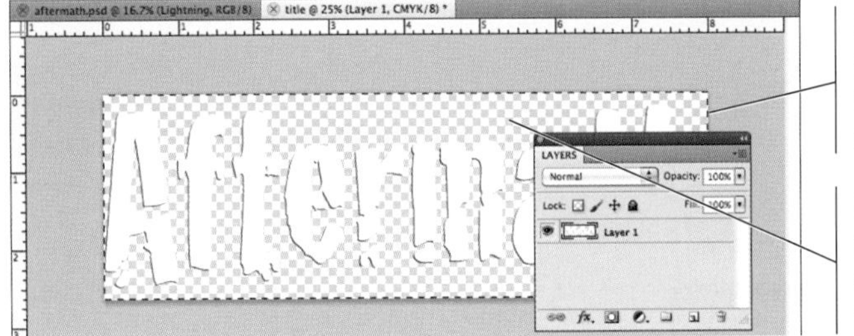

Using the Select>All command surrounds the entire canvas in a selection marquee.

The gray-and-white checked pattern identifies areas of transparency in the layer content.

Note:

Command/Control-clicking a layer thumbnail results in a selection around the contents of that layer.

6. **Choose Edit>Copy, then click the Close button on the title document tab to close that file. Click Don't Save when asked.**

7. **With the aftermath.psd file active, choose Edit>Paste.**

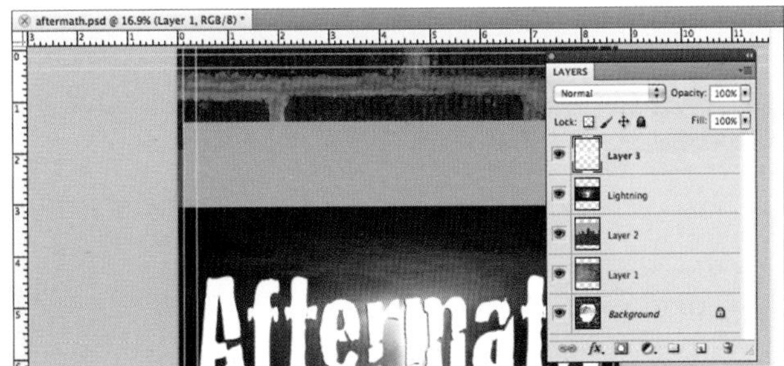

8. **Save aftermath.psd and continue to the next exercise.**

Place Multiple EPS Graphics

Vector graphics offer several advantages over raster images, including sharper edges and free scaling without deteriorating image quality. To take advantage of these benefits, you might want to maintain vector files as vector objects instead of rasterizing them. Photoshop CS5 gives you the option to do exactly that — maintaining vector information and raster information in the same file.

1. **With aftermath.psd open, click the Launch Mini Bridge button if the panel is not already open.**

2. **Click the Rating.eps thumbnail to select it.**

3. **Press Command/Control and then click the Tantamount.eps file to add it to the active selection.**

   These vector graphics were created in Adobe Illustrator and saved as EPS files. (The EPS format supports both raster and vector information, however, so don't assume that an EPS file always contains only vector information.

4. **Click either of the selected thumbnails and drag into the aftermath.psd image window to place both files.**

   Unlike opening or placing a native Illustrator file, there are no further options when you place an EPS file.

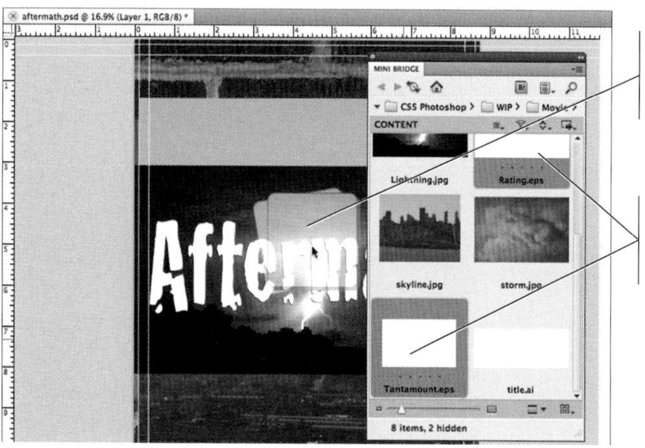

The cursor icon shows how many files are being placed.

Press Command/Control to select non-contiguous files in the panel.

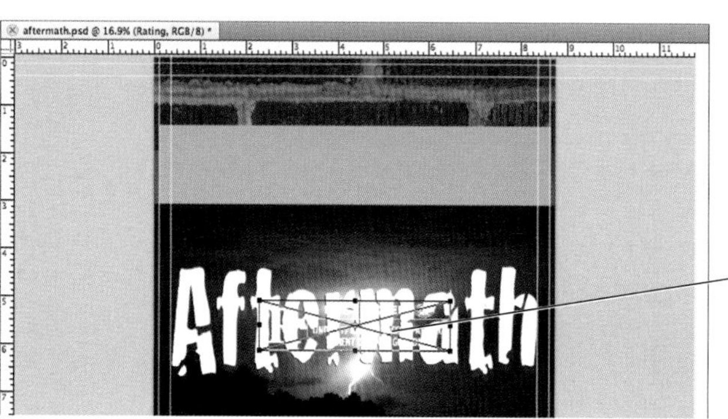

After releasing the mouse button, the first selected file appears with crossed diagonal lines (not yet finalized).

Note:

If you place a native Illustrator file from the Mini Bridge panel, you can define the Crop To area for the placement, but you can't access any of the other options that are available when you open an Illustrator file.

The Mini Bridge Panel in Depth

PHOTOSHOP FOUNDATIONS

The Mini Bridge panel provides access to a number of file management options, directly within the Photoshop interface.

The **Path bar** shows the list of folders that is the "address" of the files currently displayed in the Content pod.

The **Content pod** (which is always visible) shows the files in the selected folder.

The **Navigation pod** shows a standard file navigation structure, which you can use to find a location on your computer.

The **Preview pod** shows a larger version of the selected thumbnails (in the Content pod).

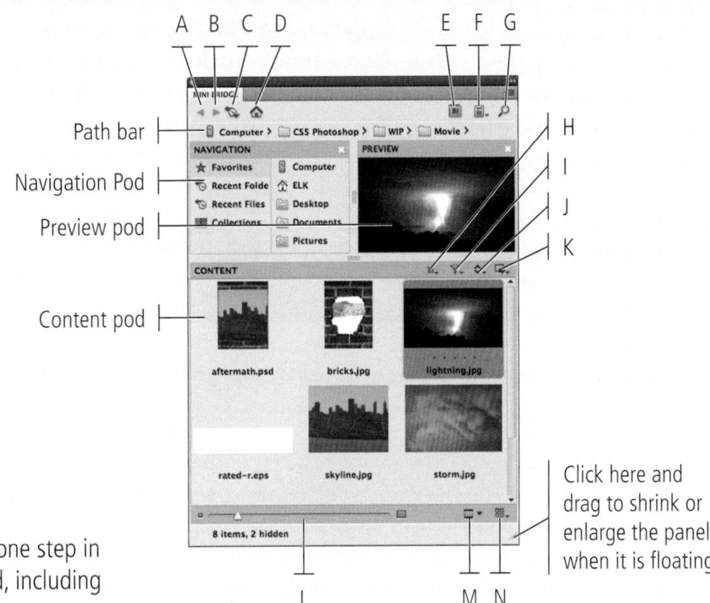

Click here and drag to shrink or enlarge the panel when it is floating.

A Use the **Go Back** button to navigate back one step in the panel's history (which folder you viewed, including the panel's Home Page).

B Use the **Go Forward** button to navigate forward one step in the panel's history.

C Use the **Go to Parent, Recent Items,** or **Favorites** button to access a menu of the relevant folders on your computer.

D Use the **Home Page** button to restore the panel to its default interface, with buttons to browse files and change the panel's settings.

E Use the **Go to Adobe Bridge** button to switch to the full Bridge application.

F Use the **Panel View** button to show or hide the Path bar, Navigation pod, and Preview pod in the panel.

G Use the **Search** button to find specific files anywhere on your computer.

H Use the **Select** button to show or hide rejected files, hidden files, and folders. This menu also includes commands to select all files in the current folder, deselect all selected files, or invert the current selection (select only the unselected files).

I Use the **Filter Items** button to show only certain items in the panel's Content pod, based on user-defined ratings for each file (see below).

J Use the **Sort** button to change the order of files in the panel's Content pod, based on specific criteria such as file name, type, or date created or modified.

K Use the **Tools** button to access options for placing the selected file in InDesign or Photoshop, as well as access a number of other Photoshop-specific options (such as loading all selected files into Photoshop layers).

L Use the **Thumbnail Size** slider to change the size of thumbnails in the panel's Content pod.

M Click the **Preview** button to show a larger version of the selected thumbnail. If you click the arrow to the right of the button, you can view selected files as a slideshow, enter Review mode, or view full-screen previews.

N Click the **View** button to change the appearance of items in the panel's Content pod.

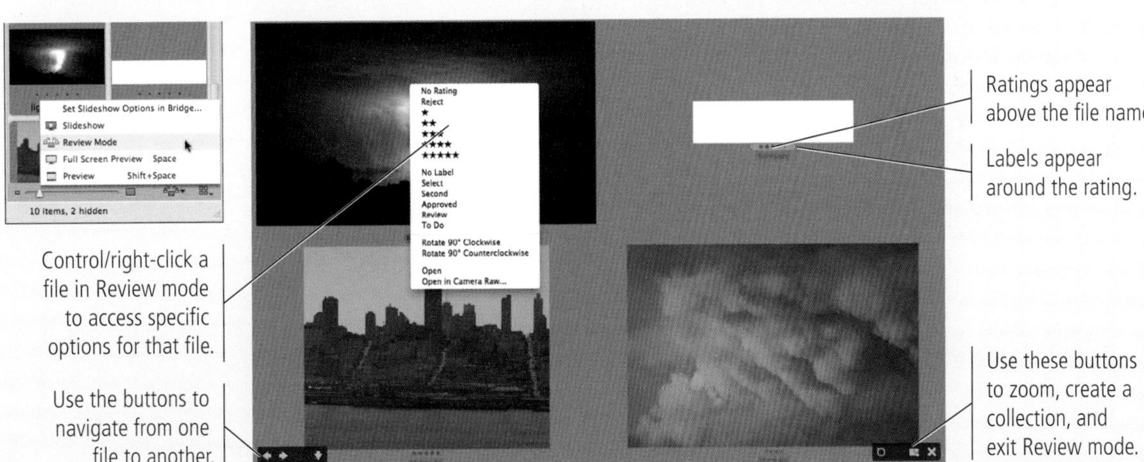

Control/right-click a file in Review mode to access specific options for that file.
Use the buttons to navigate from one file to another.
Ratings appear above the file name.
Labels appear around the rating.
Use these buttons to zoom, create a collection, and exit Review mode.

5. **Press Return/Enter to finalize the placement of the first file.**

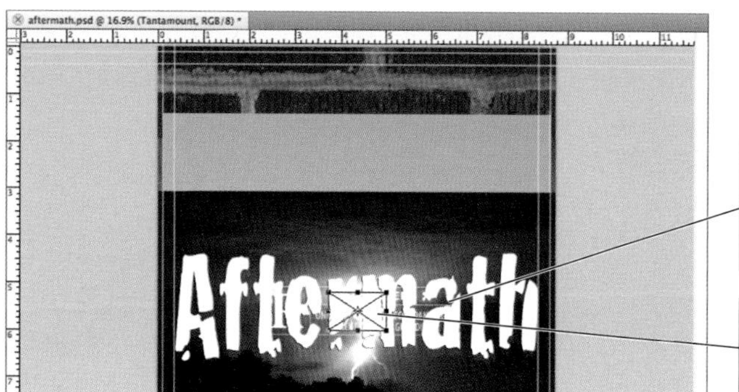

After finalizing, the first file no longer shows the bounding box handles.

The second file automatically appears, ready to be finalized.

6. **Press Return/Enter again to finalize the placement of the second file.**

The two placed files are stored on layers named based on the placed file names.

The placed files are Smart Object layers.

> *Note:*
>
> *If you have the entire Adobe Creative Suite, Smart Objects provide extremely tight integration between Adobe Photoshop and Adobe Illustrator. You can take advantage of the sophisticated vector-editing features in Adobe Illustrator, and then place those files into Photoshop without losing the ability to edit the vector information.*

7. **Save the file and continue to the next stage of the project.**

   Right now, you have a fairly incomprehensible mess of four raster images and two vector objects all piled on top of one another. You will start to make sense of these files in the next stage.

Stage 2 Managing Layers

Your ad file now has most of the necessary pieces, but it's still not an actual design — just a pile of images. When you composite images into a cohesive design, you almost certainly need to manipulate and transform some of the layers to make all of the pieces work together.

Photoshop includes a number of options for managing layers: naming layers for easier recognition, creating layer groups so multiple layers can be manipulated at once, moving layers around on the canvas, transforming layers both destructively and non-destructively, controlling individual layer visibility, and arranging the top-to-bottom stacking order of layers to determine exactly what is visible. You will use all of these options in this stage of the project.

 Name Layers and Layer Groups

It's always a good idea to name your layers because it makes managing the file much easier — especially when you work with files that include dozens of layers. Even with only four unnamed layers in this file (counting the Background layer), it would be tedious to have to toggle each layer on to find the one you want.

1. **With aftermath.psd open, review the Layers panel.**

2. **Click the eye icons to hide all but Layer 1.**

   Toggling layer visibility is an easy way to see only what you want to see at any given stage in a project.

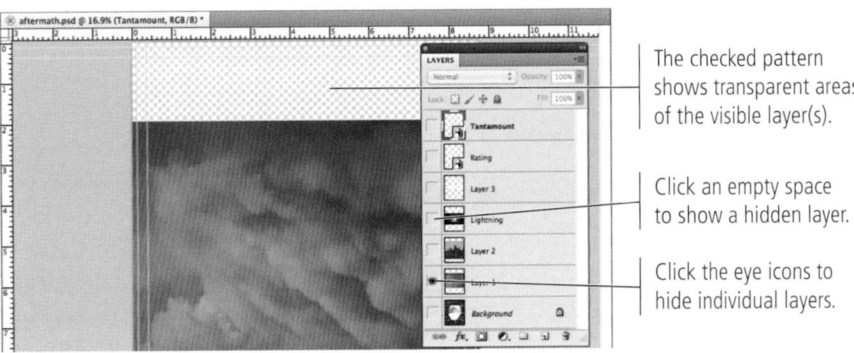

The checked pattern shows transparent areas of the visible layer(s).

> *Note:*
>
> *To show or hide a series of contiguous layers, click the visibility icon (or empty space) for the first layer you want to affect, hold down the mouse button, and drag down to the last layer you want to show or hide.*

3. **Double-click the Layer 1 layer name, and then type `Storm`.**

   You can rename any layer by simply double-clicking the name and typing.

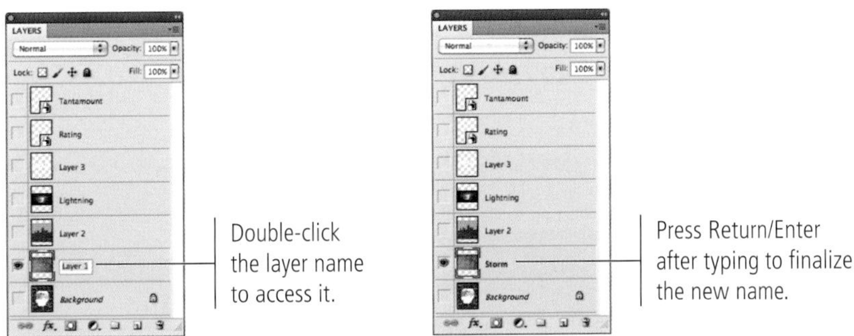

Double-click the layer name to access it.
Press Return/Enter after typing to finalize the new name.

4. **Click the eye icon to hide the renamed Storm layer, and then click the empty space to the left of Layer 2 to show only that layer.**

5. **Double-click the Layer 2 name and then type `Skyline` to rename the layer.**

6. **Repeat Steps 4–5 to rename Layer 3 as `Title`.**

7. **Click the spaces on the left side of the Layers panel to show all hidden layers.**

8. **In the Layers panel, click the Tantamount layer to select it.**

9. **Press Shift and click the Rating layer to select that layer as well.**

   Since the Tantamount layer was already selected, the Rating layer should now be a second selected (highlighted) layer.

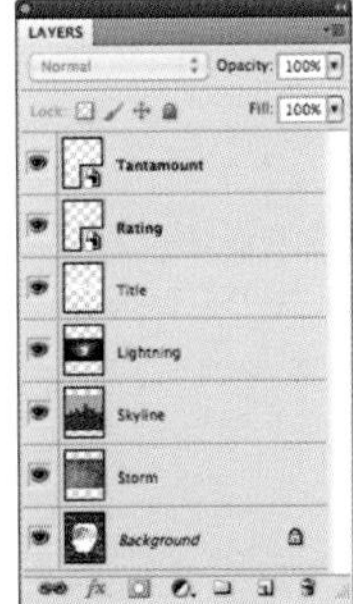

> *Note:*
>
> *Press Shift and click to select contiguous layers in the Layers panel.*
>
> *Press Command/Control and click to select non-contiguous layers in the Layers panel.*

10. **Click the button in the top-right corner of the panel to open the Layers panel Options menu. Choose New Group from Layers.**

This option creates a group that automatically contains the selected layers. You can also create an empty group by choosing New Group (this option is available even when no layer is selected) or by clicking the New Group button at the bottom of the panel.

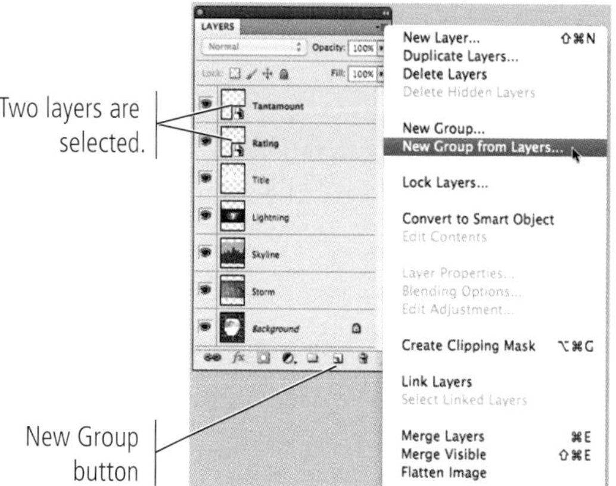

> ***Note:***
>
> *You can create a group from selected layers by dragging the selected layers onto the New Group button at the bottom of the panel. In this case, the new group is automatically named "Group N" (N is a placeholder for a sequential number); of course, you can rename a layer group just as easily as you can rename a layer.*

11. **In the New Group from Layers dialog box, type `Logos` in the Name field and click OK.**

As with any other layer, you should name groups based on what they contain so you can easily identify them later.

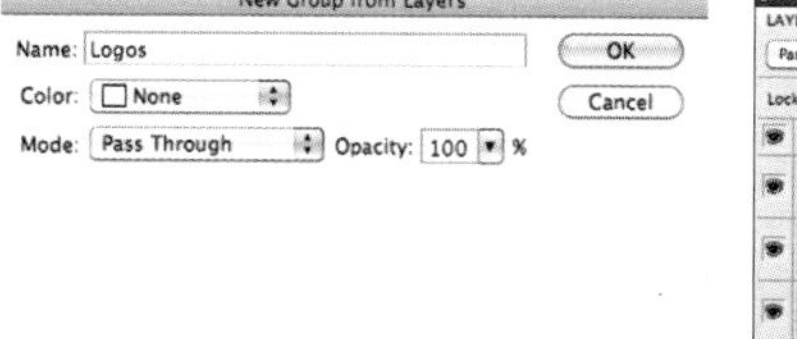

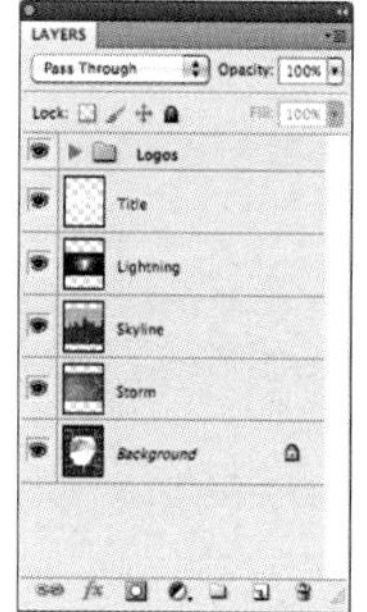

> ***Note:***
>
> *You can create up to ten levels of nested layer groups, or groups inside of other groups.*

12. **Click the arrow to the left of the Logos group name to expand the layer group.**

You have to expand the layer group to be able to access and edit individual layers in the group. If you select the entire layer group, you can move all layers within the group at the same time. Layers in the group maintain their position relative to one another.

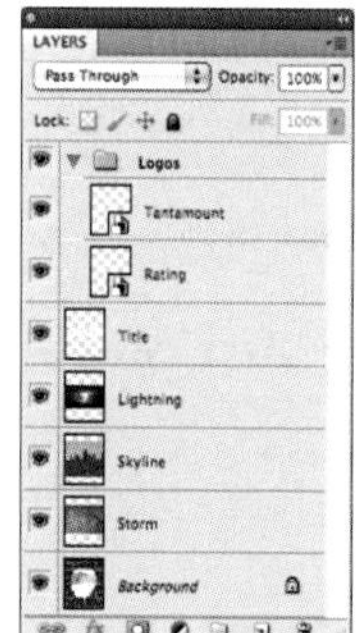

> ***Note:***
>
> *You can click the eye icon for a layer folder to hide the entire layer group (and all layers inside the folder).*

13. **Save the file and continue to the next exercise.**

Move and Transform Smart Object Layers

Photoshop makes scaling, rotating, and other transformations fairly easy to implement, but it is important to realize the potential impact of your transformations.

1. **With aftermath.psd open, click the Tantamount layer (in the Logos folder) in the Layers panel to select only that layer.**

2. **Choose the Move tool in the Tools panel.**

   As the name suggests, the Move tool is used to move a selection around on the canvas. You can select a specific area, and then click and drag to move only the selection on the active layer. If there is no active selection area, you can click and drag to move the contents of the entire active layer.

3. **In the Control panel, make sure the Auto-Select option is not checked.**

   When Auto-Select is checked, you can click in the image window and drag to move the contents of the layer containing the pixels where you click; you do not need to first select the layer in the Layers panel before moving the layer content. This is very useful in some cases, as you will see later in this project. However, the Auto-Select option is *not* very useful when the contents of multiple layers are stacked on top of each other (as is the case in your file as it exists now).

Note:

Deselect all layers by clicking in the empty area at the bottom of the Layers panel.

4. **Click in the image window and drag until the Tantamount layer content snaps to the bottom-right live-area guides.**

   If you toggled off the Snap feature when you used the Crop tool, you should turn it back on now by choosing View>Snap.

This option should not be checked.
Move tool
With no marching ants in the image window, select the layer you want to move, then click and drag to move the layer's contents.

5. **Click the Rating layer in the Layers panel to select that layer.**

6. **Click in the image window and drag until the Rating layer content snaps to the bottom-left live-area guides.**

7. **With the Rating layer still active, choose Edit>Free Transform.**

   When you use the transform options, bounding box handles surround the selection.

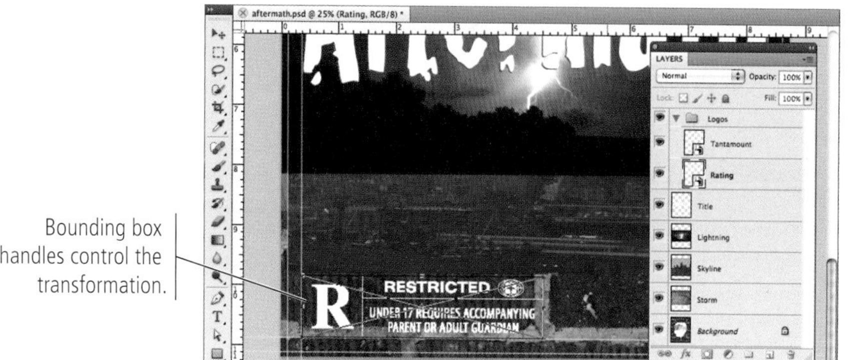

Bounding box handles control the transformation.
RESTRICTED

Note:

You can also use the Edit>Transform submenu to apply specific transformations to a layer or selection.

8. **Press Shift, click the top-right bounding box handle, and then drag down and left until the layer content is approximately two-thirds the original size.**

   The selection (in this case, the entire Rating layer) dynamically changes as you scale the layer. Pressing Shift while you drag a handle constrains the image proportions as you resize it. When you release the mouse button, the handles remain in place until you finalize ("commit") the transformation.

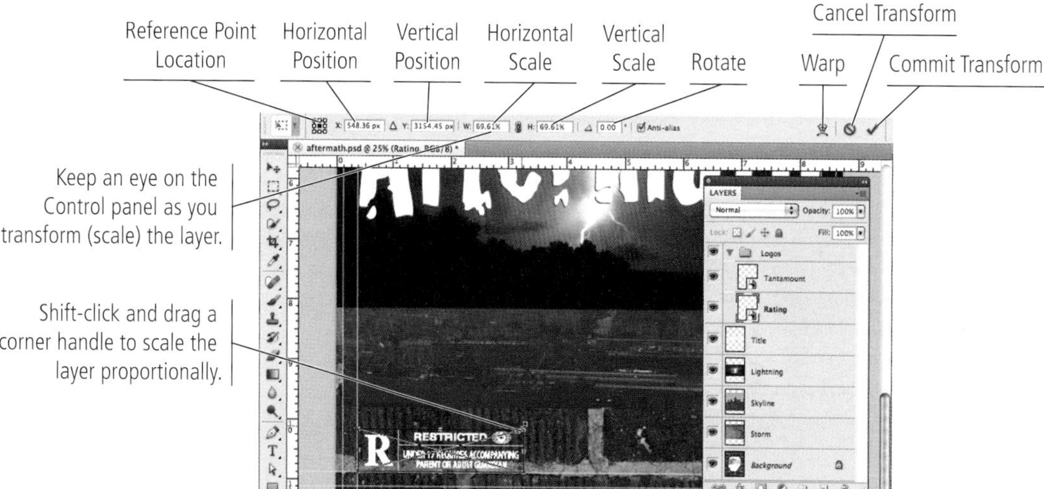

Reference Point Location
Horizontal Position
Vertical Position
Horizontal Scale
Vertical Scale
Rotate
Warp
Cancel Transform
Commit Transform
Keep an eye on the Control panel as you transform (scale) the layer.
Shift-click and drag a corner handle to scale the layer proportionally.

   While you're manually transforming a layer or selection, the Control panel shows the specifics. You can also type into these fields to apply specific numeric transformations.

9. **Press Return/Enter to finalize the transformation.**

10. **With the Rating layer still active, press Command/Control-T to enter Free Transform mode again and look at the Control panel.**

    Because the rating layer is a Smart Object layer, the W and H fields still show the scaling percentage based on the original.

11. **In the Control panel, choose the bottom-left reference point location.**

12. **Click the Link icon between the W and H fields to constrain proportions during the transformation.**

13. **Type `50` in the Control panel W field.**

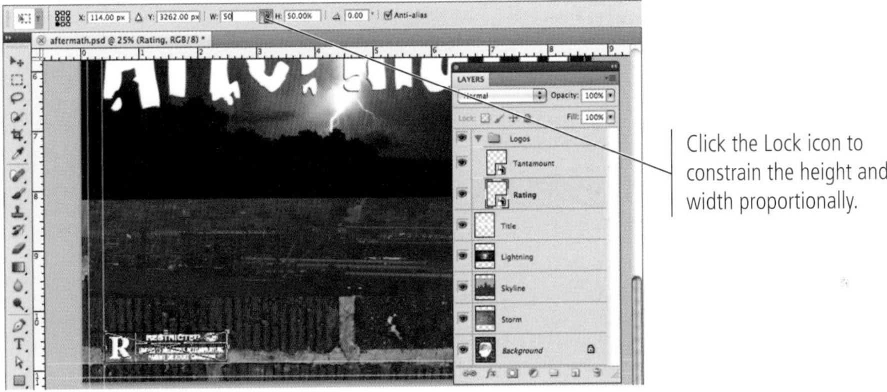

Click the Lock icon to constrain the height and width proportionally.

14. **Click the Commit Transform button on the Control panel (or press Return/Enter) to finalize the transformation.**

15. **Collapse the layer group by clicking the arrow at the left of the group name.**

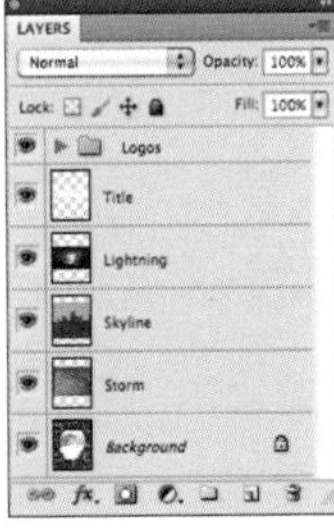

16. **Save the file and continue to the next exercise.**

Transform a Regular Layer

Smart Object layers enable non-destructive transformations, which means those transformations can be changed or undone without affecting the quality of the layer content. Transforming a regular layer, on the other hand, is destructive and permanent.

1. **With `aftermath.psd` open, hide all but the Storm layer. Click the Storm layer in the Layers panel to select it.**

2. **Choose Edit>Transform>Flip Horizontal.**

   The Transform submenu commands affect only the selected layer.

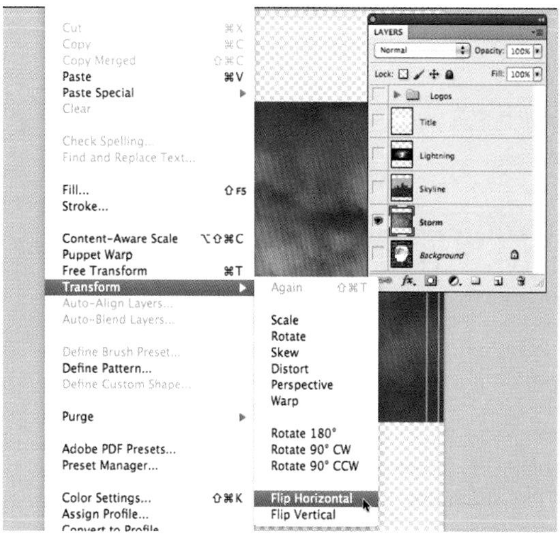

3. **Press Command/Control-T to enter Free Transform mode.**

   Some handles might not be visible within the boundaries of the document window. If necessary, zoom out so you can see all eight handles of the layer content.

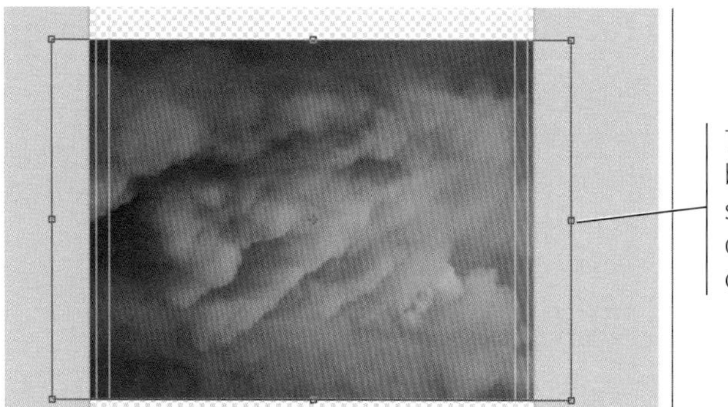

The edge of the bounding box shows that some parts of the layer do not fit within the current file dimensions.

4. **In the Control panel, choose the center reference point.**

5. **Click the Link icon between the W and H fields to constrain the proportions.**

6. **Place the cursor over the W field label to access the scrubby slider for that field.**

The center reference point is selected.

Click the Link icon to constrain proportions.

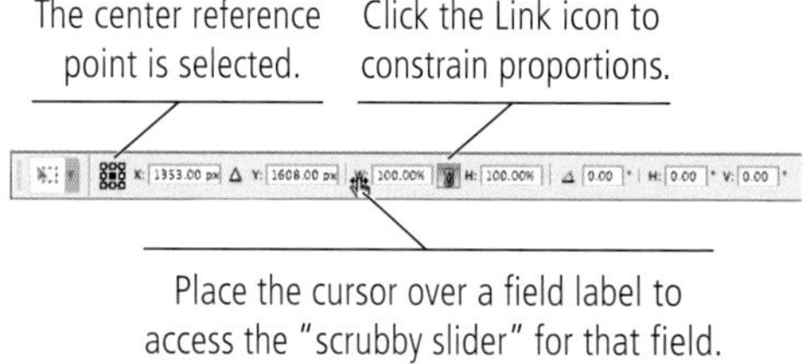

Place the cursor over a field label to access the "scrubby slider" for that field.

> ***Note:***
>
> *When you see the scrubby slider cursor, you can drag right to increase or drag left to decrease the value in the related field.*

7. **Click and drag left until the W field shows 90%.**

8. **Press Return/Enter to finalize the transformation.**

9. **With the Storm layer still active, press Command/Control-T to re-enter Free Transform mode.**

   Once you commit the transformation on a regular layer, the transformation is final. Looking at the Control panel now, you can see that it shows the layer at 100% instead of the 90% from Step 7.

Re-entering Free Transform mode shows that the regular layer is again 100%, even after scaling.

Note:

If you transform a Smart Object layer, the scale percentage is maintained even after you finalize the change (unlike scaling a regular layer, where the layer re-calibrates so the new size is considered 100% once you finalize the scaling).

10. **Press Esc to exit Free Transform mode without changing anything.**

11. **Save the file and continue to the next exercise.**

Transform the Background Layer

Your file currently has a number of layers, most of which were created by pasting or placing external files into the original file. Because every photograph and scan (and some images that you create from scratch in Photoshop) begins with a default locked Background layer, it is important to understand the special characteristics of that layer:

- You can't apply layer transformations, styles, or masks to the Background layer.
- You can't move the contents of the Background layer around in the document.
- If you delete pixels from the Background layer, the removed pixels will automatically be filled with the current background color.
- The Background layer cannot include transparent pixels, which are necessary for underlying layers to be visible.
- The Background layer is always the bottom layer in the stacking order; you can't add or move layers lower than the Background layer.

In the final composite file for this project, you need to flip the bricks image from top to bottom, remove the desert area from the hole in the bricks, and place the other photographs to appear through the hole in the wall. For any of these options to work properly, you need to convert the default Background layer to a regular layer.

Note:

Although the Background layer exists by default in many files, it is not a required component.

1. **With aftermath.psd open, hide the Storm layer and then show the Background layer.**

2. **Click the Background layer to select it and then choose Edit>Transform.**

   The Transform submenu commands are not available for the locked Background layer.

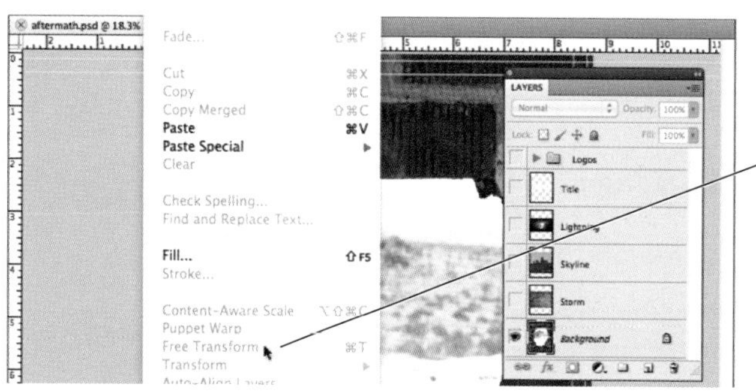

Many commands are not available because the Background layer is locked.

3. **With the Background layer still selected, choose Image>Image Rotation> Flip Canvas Vertical.**

   To affect the locked background layer, you have to flip the actual canvas.

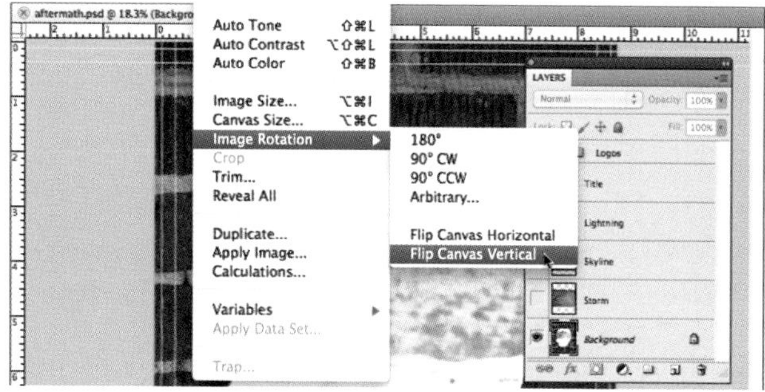

4. **Show the Logos layer group.**

   Because you flipped the canvas, the Tantamount and Ratings layers are also flipped upside-down. Rotating or flipping the entire canvas affects all layers in the file; this is obviously not what you want to happen.

Because you flipped the canvas, the logos are now upside-down.
Showing the layer group shows all layers in that group.

5. **Choose Edit>Undo to restore the canvas back to its original orientation.**

The Undo command affects the last action you performed. Showing or hiding a layer is not considered an "action," so the Undo command simply un-flips the canvas. As you can see, though, the Logos group is again hidden, as it was when you flipped the canvas in Step 3.

Note:

The Undo menu command changes to reflect the action that will be affected. In this case, the actual command is Edit>Undo Flip Canvas Vertical.

6. **In the Layers panel, double-click the Background layer.**

7. **In the resulting New Layer dialog box, type `Bricks` in the Name field, then click OK.**

Renaming the Background layer automatically unlocks and converts it to a regular layer.

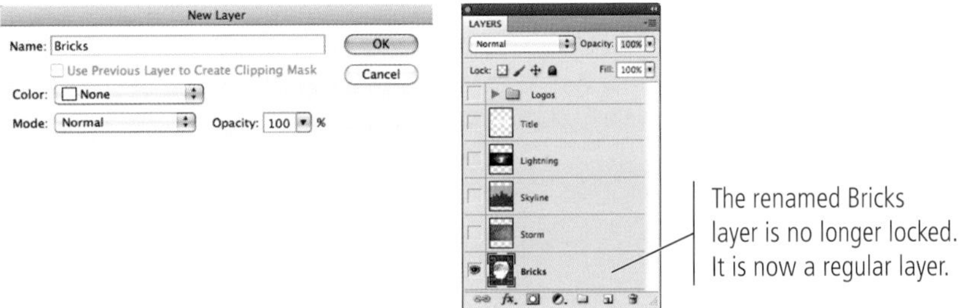

The renamed Bricks layer is no longer locked. It is now a regular layer.

8. **With the Bricks layer selected in the panel, choose Edit>Transform>Flip Vertical.**

Because the layer is no longer locked, you can now access and apply the transform commands that affect only the selected layer.

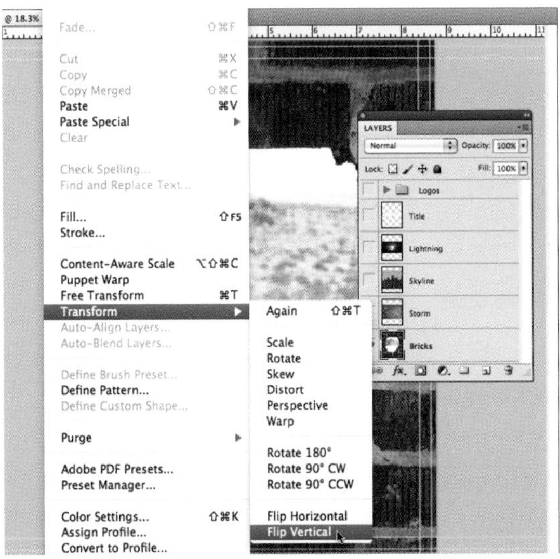

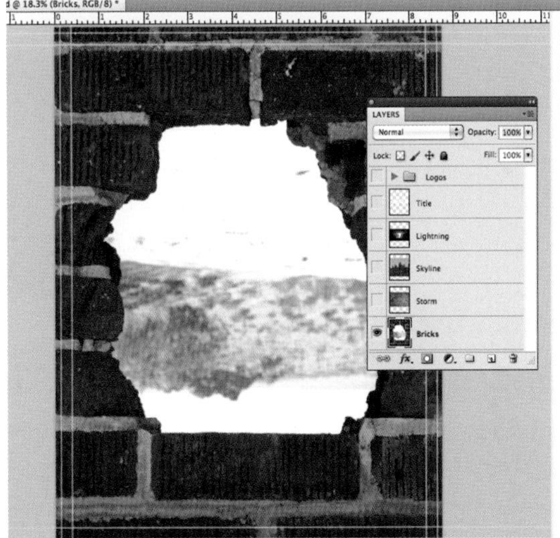

9. **Show all layers in the file.**

10. **Save the file and continue to the next stage of the project.**

Stage 3 Creating Complex Selections

At this stage of the project, you still have a few issues to resolve: some of the images are still randomly stacked on top of one another, and some images have areas that are hiding other images (the blue sky in the Skyline layer, for example). In this stage, you start fixing these problems.

Virtually any Photoshop project involves making some kind of selection. Making selections is so important, in fact, that there are no fewer than nine tools dedicated specifically to this goal, as well as a whole Select menu and a few other options for making and refining selections.

In an earlier lesson you learned how to use the Rectangular Marquee tool to draw selections. In the next series of exercises, you use several other selection methods to isolate pixels from their backgrounds (called **silhouetting**).

Make a Feathered Selection

1. **With aftermath.psd open, hide all but the Lightning layer. Click the Lightning layer to make it active.**

2. **Select the Lasso tool in the Tools panel.**

3. **Drag a rough shape around the lightning in the photo.**

   The lasso tools allow you to make irregular selections — in other words, selections that aren't just rectangular or elliptical. When you release the mouse button, the end point automatically connects to the beginning point of the selection.

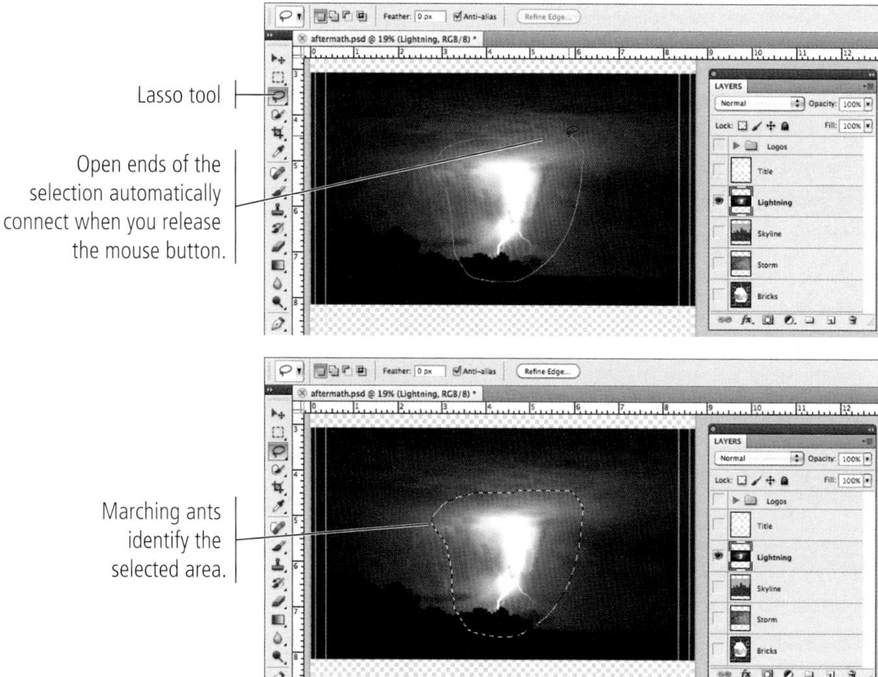

4. **With the marching ants active, choose Select>Modify>Feather.**

   Feathering means to soften the edge of a selection so the image blends into the background instead of showing a sharp line around the edge. The Smooth, Expand, and Contract options in the Select>Modify submenu are self-explanatory; the Border option creates a specific number of pixels around the active selection (like the stroke/border that surrounds a shape in an illustration program).

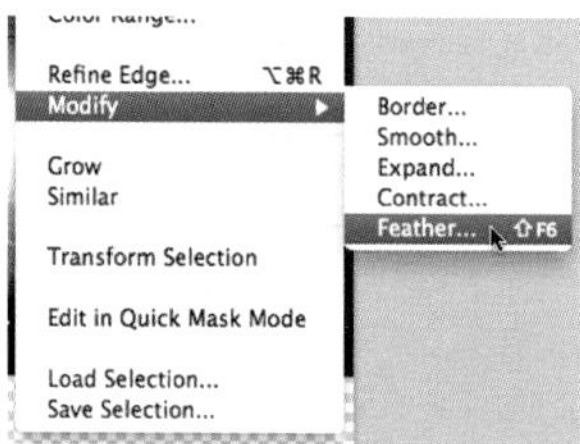

5. **In the resulting dialog box, type 35 in the Feather Radius field. Click OK to return to the image window.**

Feather Selection
Feather Radius: 35 pixels
OK
Cancel

The Feather Radius defines the distance from solid to transparent. In the image window, there's no apparent difference in the selection because the marching ants can't show shades of a selection.

6. **Click the Quick Mask button at the bottom of the Tools panel to toggle into Quick Mask mode.**

This mode creates a temporary red overlay (called an Alpha channel) that shows the graded selection. By default, the overlay is semi-transparent, which allows you to see the underlying image.

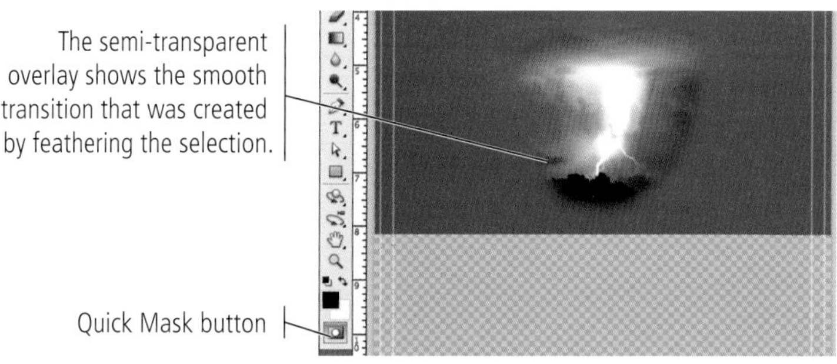

The semi-transparent overlay shows the smooth transition that was created by feathering the selection.
Quick Mask button

The Lasso Tools

PHOTOSHOP FOUNDATIONS

The basic **Lasso tool** works like a pencil, following the path where you drag the mouse.

The **Polygonal Lasso tool** creates selections with straight lines, anchoring a line each time you click the mouse. To close a selection area, you must click the first point in the selection.

The **Magnetic Lasso tool** snaps to edges of high contrast; you can use the Control panel to control the way Photoshop detects the edges of an image. **Width** is the distance away from the edge the cursor can be and still detect the edge; if you set this value higher, you can move the cursor farther from the edge. **Contrast** is how different the foreground can be from the background and still be detected; if there is a very sharp distinction between the foreground and background (as in the case of the white quill against the blue background in these sample images), you can set this value higher. **Frequency** is the number of points that will be created to make the selection; setting this number higher creates finer selections, while setting it lower creates smoother edges.

It isn't uncommon for a mouse to unexpectedly jump when you don't want it to — which can be particularly troublesome if you're drawing a selection with the Polygonal or Magnetic Lasso tools. If you aren't happy with your Polygonal or Magnetic Lasso selection, press Escape to clear the selection and then try again.

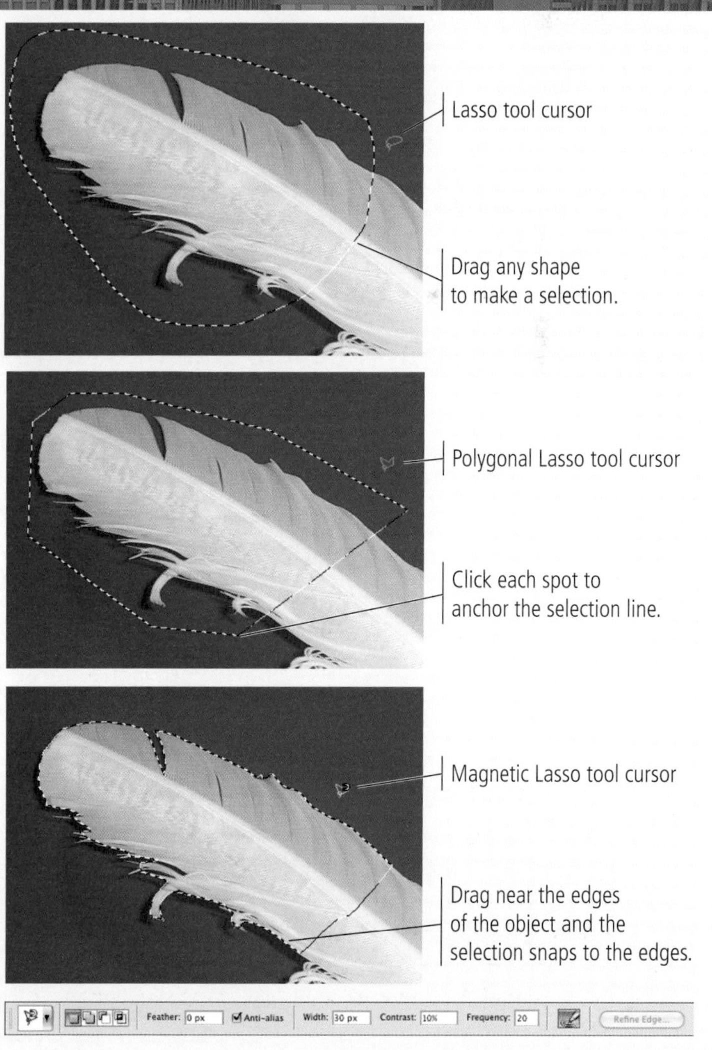

Drag near the edges of the object and the selection snaps to the edges.

7. **Click the Quick Mask button at the bottom of the Tools panel to toggle off the Quick Mask.**

8. **Choose Select>Inverse.**

   You want to remove the area around the lightning, so you have to select everything *other than* what you originally selected — in other words, the inverse of the previous selection.

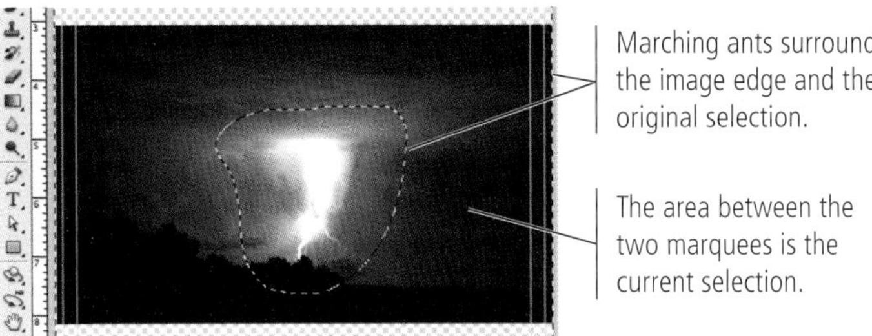

Marching ants surround the image edge and the original selection.

The area between the two marquees is the current selection.

9. **With the Lightning layer selected in the Layers panel, press Delete/Backspace.**

   Selection marquees are not particular to a specific layer. You have to make sure the correct layer is active before you use the selection to perform some action.

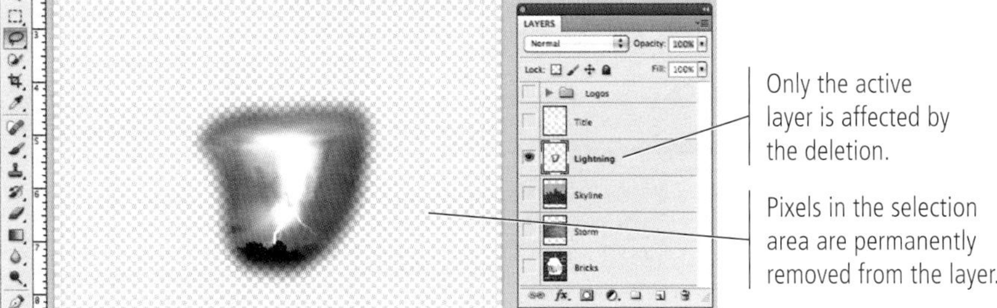

Only the active layer is affected by the deletion.

Pixels in the selection area are permanently removed from the layer.

10. **Choose Select>Deselect to turn off the active selection (marching ants).**

11. **Save the file and continue to the next exercise.**

Note:

Pressing Command/Control-D deselects the active selection.

Select a Color Range and Create a Layer Mask

As we said earlier, there are many selection options in Photoshop CS5, each with its own advantages and disadvantages. You have already used the marquee tools and lasso tools to select general areas of images.

Many images have both hard and soft edges, and/or very fine detail that needs to be isolated from its background (think of a model's blowing hair overlapping the title on the cover of a magazine). In this type of image, other tools can be used to create a very detailed selection based on the color in the image.

Rather than simply deleting pixels, as you did for the lightning image, another option for isolating an object with a path is to create a **layer mask** that hides unwanted pixels. Areas outside the mask are hidden but not deleted, so you can later edit the mask to change the visible part of the image.

1. **With `aftermath.psd` open, hide all but the Skyline layer. Click the Skyline layer to make it active.**

2. **Choose the Magic Wand tool (under the Quick Selection tool). In the Control panel, make sure the New Selection button is active and set the Tolerance field to 32.**

The Magic Wand tool is an easy way to select large areas of solid color. The first four options in the Control panel are the same as those for the Marquee tools (New Selection, Add to Selection, Subtract from Selection, and Intersect with Selection).

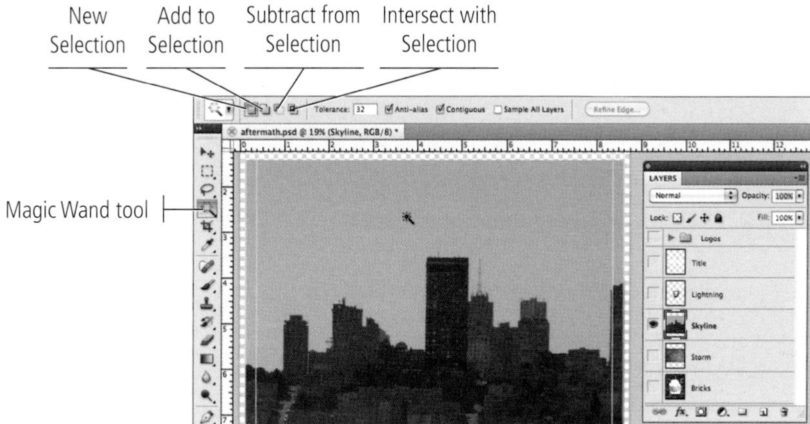

Tolerance is the degree of variation between the color you click and the colors Photoshop will select; higher tolerance values select a larger range based on the color you click. If you're trying to select a very mottled background (for example), you should increase the tolerance; be careful, however, because increasing the tolerance might select too large a range of colors if parts of the foreground object fall within the tolerance range.

The **Anti-alias** check box, selected by default, allows edges to blend more smoothly into the background, preventing a jagged, stair-stepped appearance.

When **Contiguous** is selected, the Magic Wand tool only selects adjacent areas of the color; unchecking this option allows you to select all pixels within the color tolerance, even if some pixels are non-contiguous (for example, inside the shape of the letter Q).

By default, selections relate to the active layer only. You can check **Sample All Layers** to make a selection of all layers in the file.

The **Refine Edge** button opens a dialog box where you can use a number of tools to fine-tune the selection edge.

Note:

***Anti-aliasing** is the process of blending shades of pixels to create the illusion of sharp lines in a raster image.*

3. **Click anywhere in the blue sky area of the image.**

Marching ants indicate the selection area.
Fine areas of detail can't be distinguished by the marching ants, so you don't know if they're selected.

4. **Choose Select>Deselect to turn off the current selection.**

Although you could keep adding to the selection with the Magic Wand tool, the marching ants can't really show the fine detail.

5. **Choose Select>Color Range.**

6. **Make sure the Localized Color Clusters option is unchecked.**

7. **Choose White Matte in the Selection Preview menu (if it is not already).**

   By changing the Selection Preview, you can more easily determine exactly what is selected. You can preview color range selections in the image window as:

   - **None** shows the normal image in the document window.
   - **Grayscale** shows the entire image in shades of gray; selected areas are solid white and unselected areas are solid black.
   - **Black Matte** shows unselected areas in solid black; selected areas appear in color.
   - **White Matte** shows unselected areas in solid white; selected areas appear in color.
   - **Quick Mask** adds a partially transparent overlay to unselected areas.

8. **Set the Fuzziness value to 25 and click anywhere in the blue sky (in the document window).**

   Fuzziness is similar to the Tolerance setting for the Magic Wand tool. Higher Fuzziness values allow you to select more variation from the color you click.

Note:

Because the dialog box preview is so small, we prefer to rely on the preview in the document window, which is controlled in the Selection Preview menu at the bottom of the dialog box.

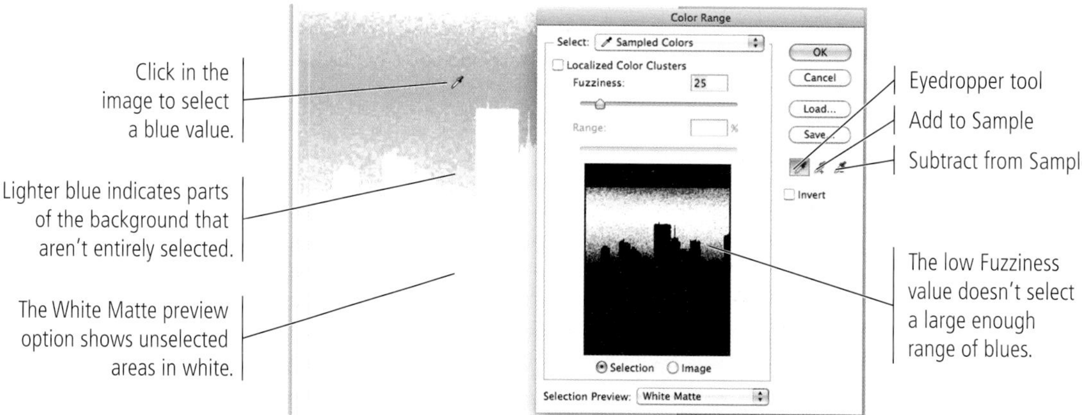

Click in the image to select a blue value.
Lighter blue indicates parts of the background that aren't entirely selected.
The White Matte preview option shows unselected areas in white.
Color Range
Select: Sampled Colors
Localized Color Clusters
Fuzziness: 25
Range: %
OK
Cancel
Load...
Save...
Invert
Selection
Image
Selection Preview: White Matte
Eyedropper tool
Add to Sample
Subtract from Sample
The low Fuzziness value doesn't select a large enough range of blues.

Selecting Localized Color Clusters

The Localized Color Clusters option in the Color Range dialog box can be used to select specific areas of a selected color. When this option is checked, the Range slider defines how far away (in physical distance) a color can be located from the point you click and still be included in the selection.

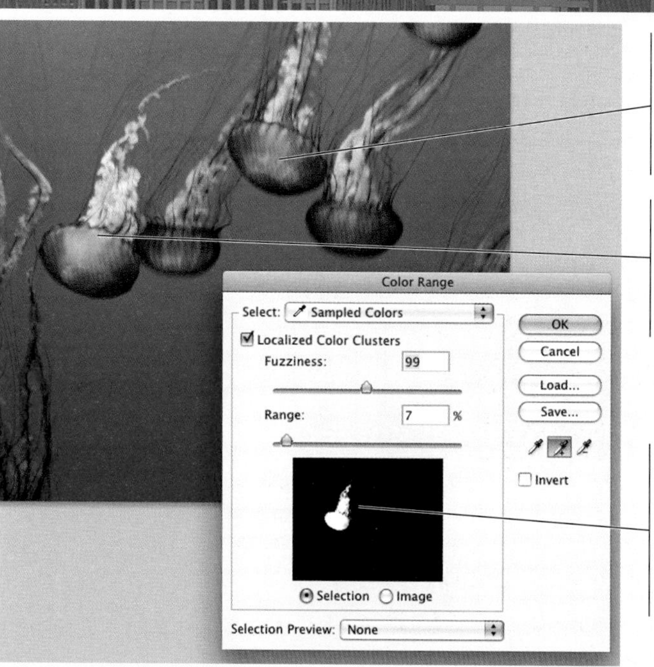

Color Range
Select: Sampled Colors
Localized Color Clusters
Fuzziness: 99
Range: 7 %
OK
Cancel
Load...
Save...
Invert
Selection
Image
Selection Preview: None
The same colors in other jellyfish are not selected because they are outside the reduced Range value.
We used a number of clicks with different Fuzziness values to sample the colors in this jellyfish.
Using Localized Color Clusters and a reduced Range value, we were able to isolate this jellyfish from its school.

9. **Change the Fuzziness value to `80` and watch the effect on the dialog box preview.**

   Changing the Fuzziness value expands (higher numbers) or contracts (lower numbers) the selection. Be careful, though, since higher fuzziness values can eliminate fine lines and detail.

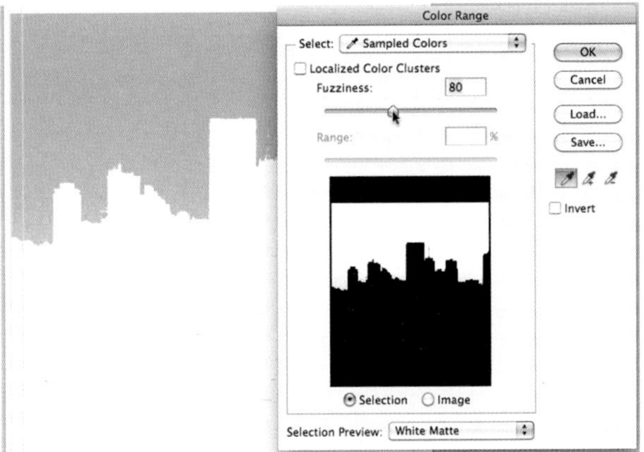

> *Note:*
>
> *Depending on where you clicked, your selection might not exactly match what you see in our screen shot. For now, the important point is to know that the visible areas indicate the current selection.*

10. **Click the Add to Sample eyedropper and click in the image where parts of the blue sky are not shown in full strength.**

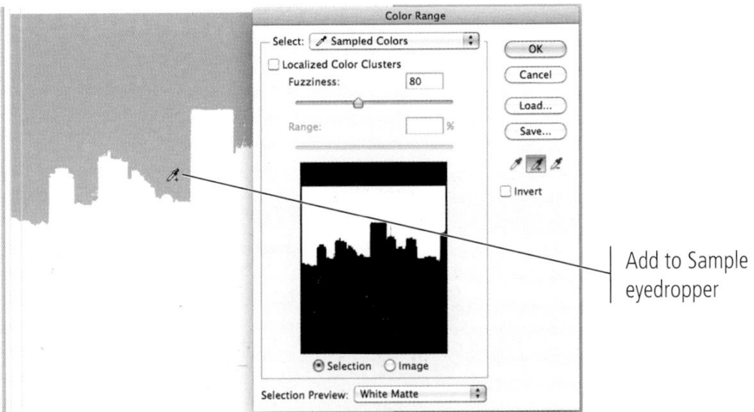

11. **Check the Invert box in the Color Range dialog box.**

    Because your goal is to isolate the city and not the sky, it helps to look at what you want to keep instead of what you want to remove.

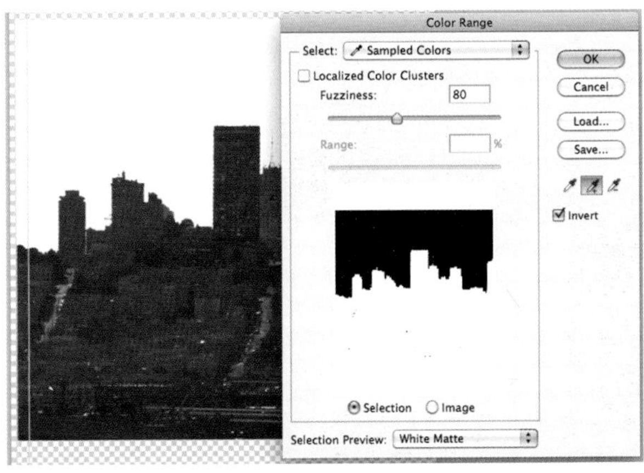

> *Note:*
>
> *When the Color Range dialog box is open, you can press Command/Control to switch between the Selection and Image previews within the dialog box.*

12. **Continue adding to (or subtracting from, if necessary) your selection until you are satisfied that all the blue sky is gone.**

    You can also adjust the Fuzziness slider if necessary, but be sure you don't adjust it too far to include areas of the city.

13. Click OK when you're satisfied with your selection.

When you return to the image window, the marching ants indicate the current selection. In the Color Range dialog box, you selected the blue and inverted the selection — in other words, your selection is everything that isn't blue.

If you zoom out to see the entire file, you will see the marching ants surround the file as well as the blue sky. Since the transparent area is not blue, it is included in the selection.

Marching ants surround the image edge.

> ***Note:***
>
> *For the purposes of this exercise, don't worry if you have small unselected areas in the sky area. In Project 5 you will learn how to paint on a mask to clean up specific areas such as the artifacts you might see in your sky.*

14. Choose the Magic Wand tool in the Tools panel and choose the Subtract from Selection option on the Control panel.

15. Click anywhere in the transparent area (the gray-and-white checkerboard) to remove that area from the selection.

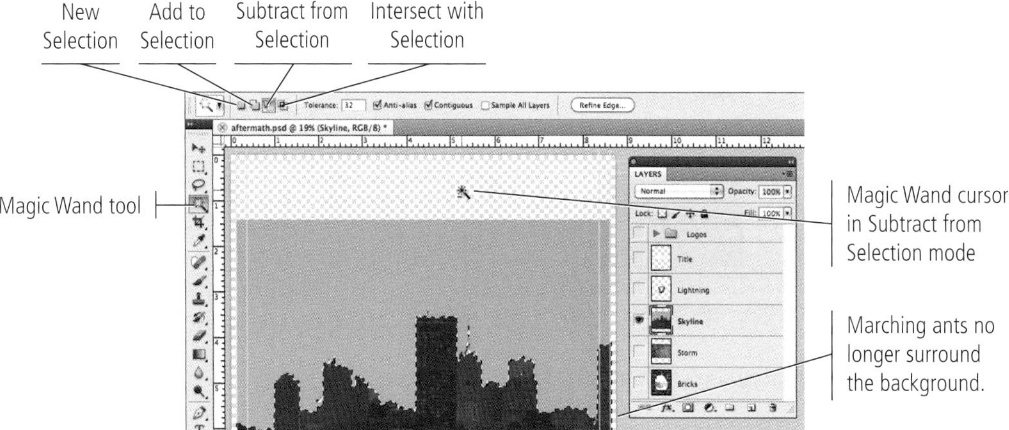

16. In the Layers panel, click the Add Layer Mask button.

A **layer mask** is a map of areas that will be visible in the selected layer. The mask you just created is a raster-based pixel mask, based on the active selection when you created the mask. This is a non-destructive way to hide certain elements of a layer without permanently deleting pixels; you can edit or disable the layer mask at any time.

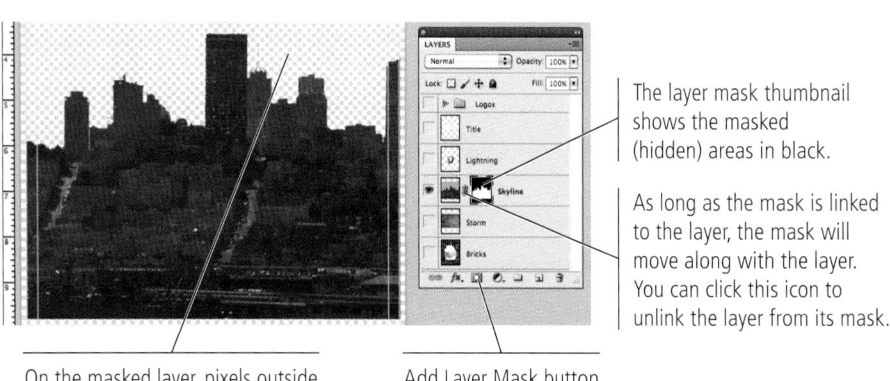

The layer mask thumbnail shows the masked (hidden) areas in black.
As long as the mask is linked to the layer, the mask will move along with the layer. You can click this icon to unlink the layer from its mask.
On the masked layer, pixels outside the original selection are hidden.
Add Layer Mask button

> ***Note:***
>
> *Creating selections, reversing them, and then deleting the pixels surrounding an object is a common method for creating silhouettes — but not necessarily the best method. Masks protect the original pixels while providing exactly the same result.*

17. **Control/right-click the mask thumbnail and choose Disable Layer Mask from the contextual menu.**

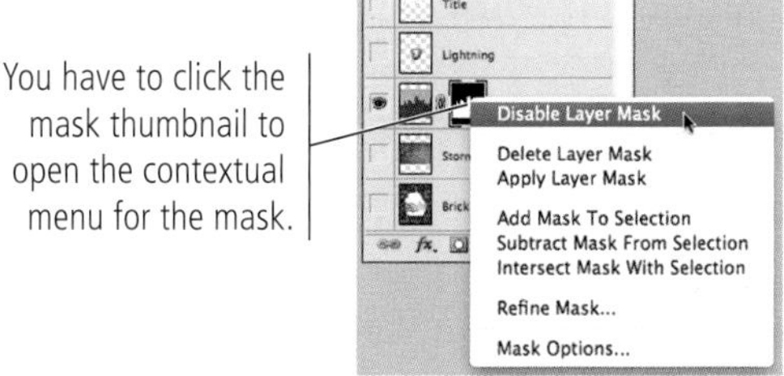

> *Note:*
>
> *You can also create a vector mask based on a path created with the Pen tool.*

When you disable the mask, the background pixels are again visible. This is one of the advantages of using masks — the background pixels are not permanently removed, they are simply hidden.

When the mask is disabled, the masked pixels are visible.
A red X indicates that the mask is disabled.

18. **Control/right-click the mask thumbnail and choose Apply Layer Mask from the contextual menu.**

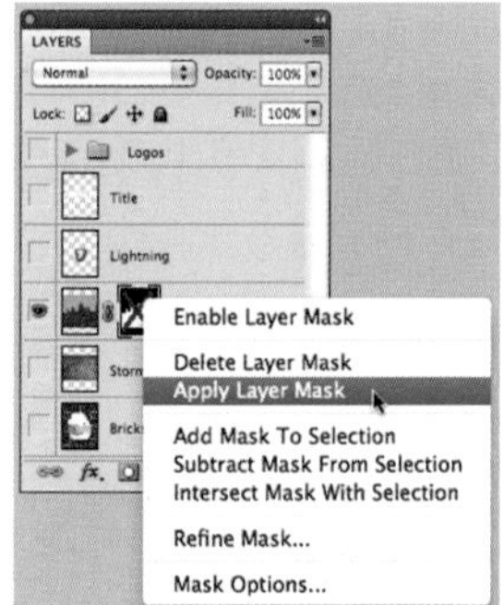

This option applies the mask to the attached layer, permanently removing the masked pixels from the layer.

The masked pixels are permanently removed from the layer.
The mask is removed from the layer.

19. **Choose Edit>Undo to restore the layer mask.**

As you saw in the previous step, applying a mask permanently removes the masked pixels. This essentially defeats the purpose of a mask, so you are restoring it in this step.

20. **Control/right-click the mask thumbnail and choose Enable Layer Mask from the contextual menu.**

21. **Save the file and continue to the next exercise.**

Make and Refine a Quick Selection

As you just saw, you can make selections based on the color in an image. This technique is especially useful when you want to select large areas of solid color, or in photos with significant contrast between the foreground and background. When the area you want to select has a complex edge, refining the selection edge can produce very detailed results.

1. **With `aftermath.psd` open, hide all but the Bricks layer. Click the Bricks layer to select it as the active layer.**

2. **Choose the Quick Selection tool (nested under the Magic Wand tool).**

3. **In the Control panel, make sure the Sample All Layers option is not checked.**

   You only want to select the area in the bricks layer (the hole in the wall), so you do not want to make a selection based on the content of other layers in the file.

4. **Click at the top area of the hole in the wall and drag down to the bottom edge of the hole.**

   The Quick Selection tool essentially allows you to "paint" a selection. As you drag, the selection expands and automatically finds the edges in the image.

Note:

If you stop dragging and then click in a nearby area, the selection grows to include the new area.

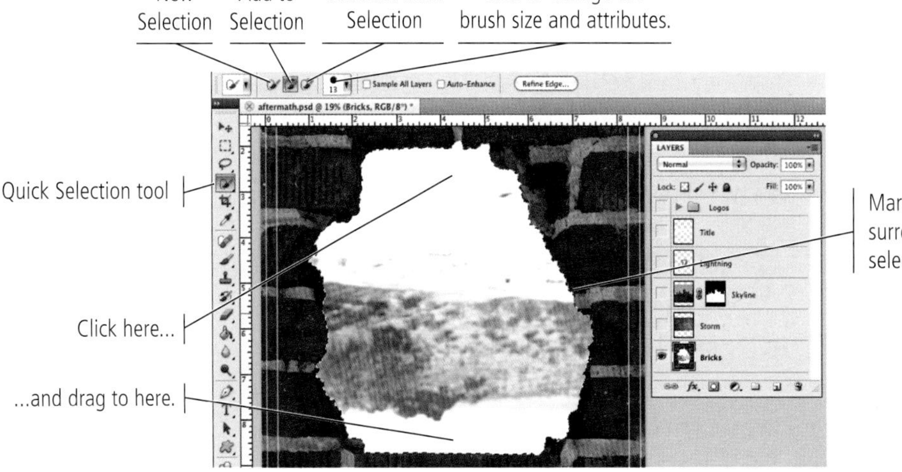

5. **Click the Refine Edge button in the Control panel.**

6. **Click the View button. Choose the On White option from the menu if it is not already selected.**

   The preview options allow you to change the way your image appears in the document window while you refine the edges within the dialog box.

   - **Marching Ants** shows the basic standard selection.
   - **Overlay** shows the unselected areas with a Quick Mask overlay.
   - **On Black** shows the selection in color against a black background.
   - **On White** shows the selection in color against a white background.
   - **Black & White** shows the selection area in white and the unselected area in black.
   - **On Layers** shows only the selected area; unselected areas are hidden.
   - **Reveal Layer** shows the entire layer, with no visual indication of the selection.

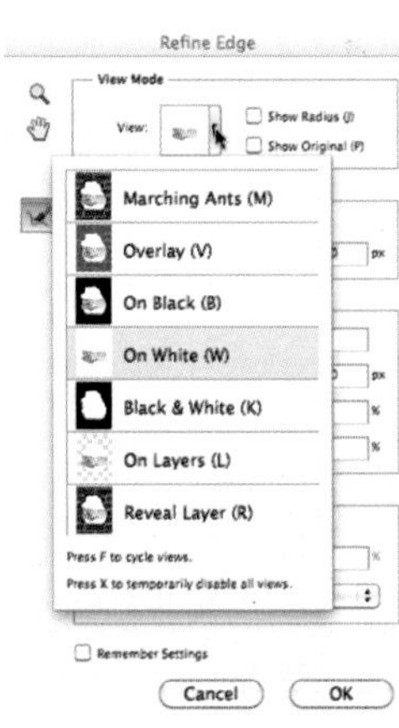

7. **Experiment with the adjustments until you're satisfied with the selection edge.**

You want to include a small amount of darkness around the edge so that, when you invert the selection to remove the hole in the wall, there is no light halo effect left by the selection edge. We used the Shift Edge slider to slightly expand the selection edge.

- **Radius** is the number of pixels around the edge that are affected. Higher radius values (up to 250 pixels) improve the edge in areas of fine detail.
- **Smooth** reduces the number of points that make up your selection and, as the name suggests, makes a smoother edge. You can set smoothness from 0 (very detailed selection) to 100 (very smooth selection).
- **Feather** softens the selection edge, resulting in a transition that does not have a hard edge (in other words, blends into the background). You can feather the selection up to 250 pixels.
- **Contrast** is the degree of variation allowed in the selection edge. Higher Contrast values (up to 100%) mean sharper selection edges.
- **Shift Edge** shrinks or grows the selection edge by the defined percentage (from –100% to 100%).
- **Decontaminate Colors** can be checked to remove a certain percentage of color from the edge of a selection.

Note:

It might help to work with a closer view while you refine edges. You can use the Zoom and Hand tools in the Refine Edge dialog box to change the image view behind the open dialog box.

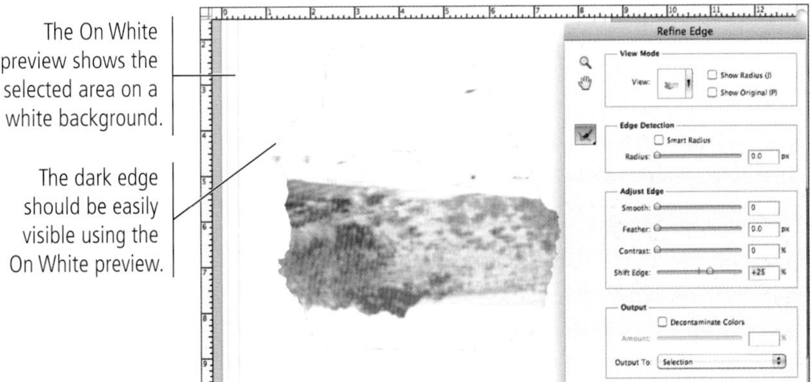

The On White preview shows the selected area on a white background.

The dark edge should be easily visible using the On White preview.

8. **At the bottom of the dialog box, choose the Layer Mask option in the Output To menu.**

This menu can be used to create a new layer or file (with or without a mask) from the selection. You want to mask the existing layer, so you are using the Layer Mask option.

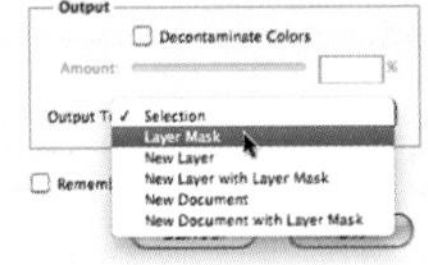

9. **Click OK to accept your refined selection.**

The resulting layer mask hides areas that were not selected.

10. **Click the mask thumbnail in the Layers panel to select only the mask, and then open the Masks panel (Window>Masks).**

    As you know, you want to remove the hole in the wall and not the wall. You selected the area in the hole to create the mask, but you now need to invert the mask.

11. **In the Masks panel, click the Invert button.**

    This button reverses the mask, so now only the bricks are visible.

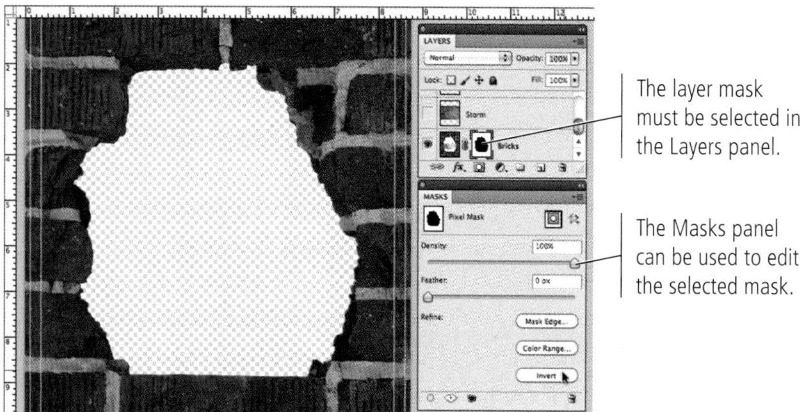
The layer mask must be selected in the Layers panel.
The Masks panel can be used to edit the selected mask.

12. **Save the file and continue to the next exercise.**

Arrange Layer Position and Stacking Order

The ad is almost final, but a few pieces are still not quite in position. You already know you can use the Move tool to move the contents of a layer around on the canvas. You can move a layer to any position in the **stacking order** (the top-to-bottom position of a layer) by simply dragging it to a new position in the Layers panel.

1. **With `aftermath.psd` open, make all layers visible.**

2. **Click the Bricks layer in the Layers panel and drag up. When a heavy black bar appears below the Title layer, release the mouse button.**

The heavy line indicates where the layer will be positioned when you release the mouse button.

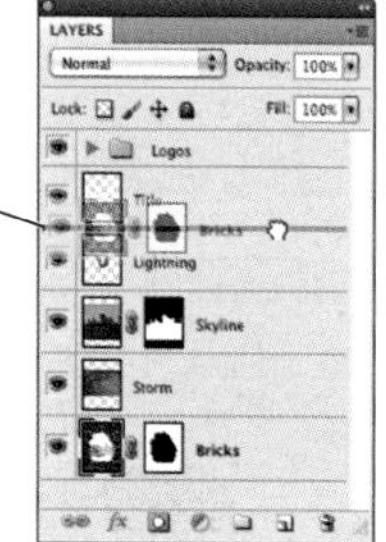

Note:

If the black border appears around a layer group, releasing the mouse button would place the dragged layer inside of the group.

3. **With the Move tool active, check the Auto-Select option in the Control panel. Open the attached menu and choose Layer.**

    When Layer is selected in the Auto-Select menu, only the relevant layer will move even if it is part of a layer group. If you want all layers in a group containing the selected layer to move, you can choose Group in the menu.

4. **In the document window, click any pixel in the storm image, and drag until the image fills the top of the hole in the bricks.**

   Make sure you click an area where no pixels from another layer are visible. (Because the layer mask on the Bricks layer hides the inner pixels, you can click within the mask shape to select the underlying layers.)

Aftermath
Check the Auto-Select option and choose Layer in the menu.
Click any pixel in the storm image and drag to move that layer's content.
Be careful to not click an area where a different layer is visible.
You don't have to first select a specific layer to move that layer's content.

5. **In the document window, click any pixel in the city image and drag until you are happy with the position of the layer content.**

6. **In the Layers panel, click the Lightning layer and drag it below the Skyline layer.**

7. **In the document window, click any pixel of the lightning image and drag to position the layer content so the lightning appears to strike one of the buildings.**

8. **In the document window, click any pixel in the title treatment and drag down so the title appears in the bottom half of the canvas.**

   Your layers should appear in the same order as shown in the following image, with the Logos layer group at the top of the layer stack.

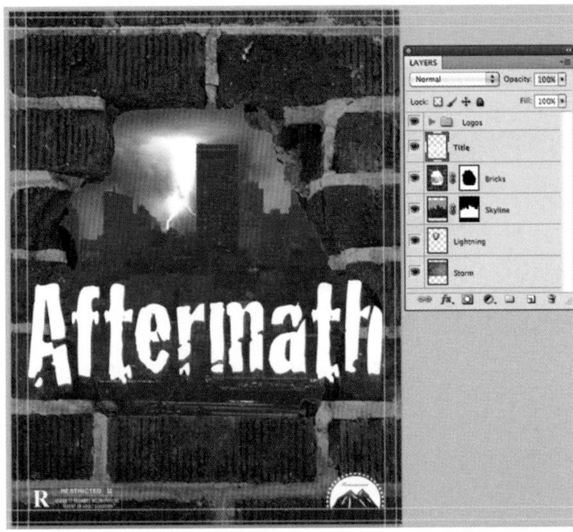

Note:

When the Move tool is active, you can move the selected object or layer 1 pixel by pressing the Arrow keys. Pressing Shift with any of the Arrow keys moves the selected object/layer by 10 pixels.

9. **Save the file and continue to the next stage of the project.**

Stage 4 Saving Photoshop Files for Print

At the beginning of the project, you saved this file in Photoshop's native format (PSD). However, many Photoshop projects require saving the completed file in at least one other format. Many artists prefer to leave all files in the PSD format since there is only one file to track. Others prefer to send only flattened TIFF files of their artwork because the individual elements can't be changed. Ultimately, the format (or formats, if the file is being used in multiple places) you use will depend on where and how the file is being placed.

Many Photoshop projects are pieces of a larger composition; the overall project defines the format you need to use when you save a complete project. The ad you just created, for example, will be placed in magazine layouts, which will be built in a page-layout application such as Adobe InDesign or QuarkXPress.

Although the current versions of both industry-standard page-layout applications can support native layered PSD files, older versions can't import those native files. If a magazine is being designed in QuarkXPress 4, for example (and many still are), you can't place a layered PSD file into that layout. As the Photoshop artist, you would have to save your work in a format that is compatible with the magazine layout.

As you know, the ad you created will be placed in multiple magazines, and different publishers have provided different file requirements. You need to save two different versions of the ad to meet those requirements.

Save a Layered TIFF File

Some software that can't use native PSD files can use layered TIFF files, which allow you to maintain as much of the native information as possible in the resulting file.

1. **With aftermath.psd open, choose File>Save As.**
2. **If necessary, navigate to your WIP>Movie folder as the target location.**

   The Save As dialog box defaults to the last-used location. If you continued the entire way through this project without stopping, you won't have to navigate.

3. **In the Save As field, type _layered at the end of the current file name (before the .psd extension).**

Common File Formats

PHOTOSHOP FOUNDATIONS

Photoshop, with the extension PSD, is the native format.

Photoshop EPS can maintain vector and raster information in the same file, and can maintain spot-color channels.

JPEG is a lossy compressed file format that does not support transparency.

Large Document Format, using the extension PSB, is used for images larger than 2 GB (the limit for PSD files); this format supports all Photoshop features including transparency and layers.

Photoshop PDF can contain all required font and image information in a single file, which can be compressed to reduce file size.

Photoshop 2.0 saves a flattened file that can be opened in Photoshop 2.0; all layer information is discarded.

Photoshop Raw supports CMYK, RGB, and grayscale images with alpha channels, and multichannel and LAB images without alpha channels; this format does not support layers.

Scitex CT is used for high-end image processing on proprietary Scitex computers. (Although rarely used today, this format is still used occasionally, so we include it here.)

TIFF is a raster-based image format that supports layers, alpha channels, and file compression.

Photoshop DCS 1.0 creates a separate file for each color channel in a CMYK image, plus a fifth composite file that can be used for placement.

Photoshop DCS 2.0 is a later variation of DCS 1.0; version 2 supports spot-color channels, and can be saved as multiple files (one for each channel) or as a single file.

4. **Click the Format menu and choose TIFF.**

5. **Make sure the Layers check box is selected in the lower half of the dialog box.**

   Because this file contains layers, this option is probably checked by default. If your file contained alpha channels, annotations, or spot colors, those check boxes would also be available. The As a Copy check box can be used if you want to save multiple versions of the same file with different options (which you will do in the next exercise).

Choosing a different format automatically changes the file's extension.

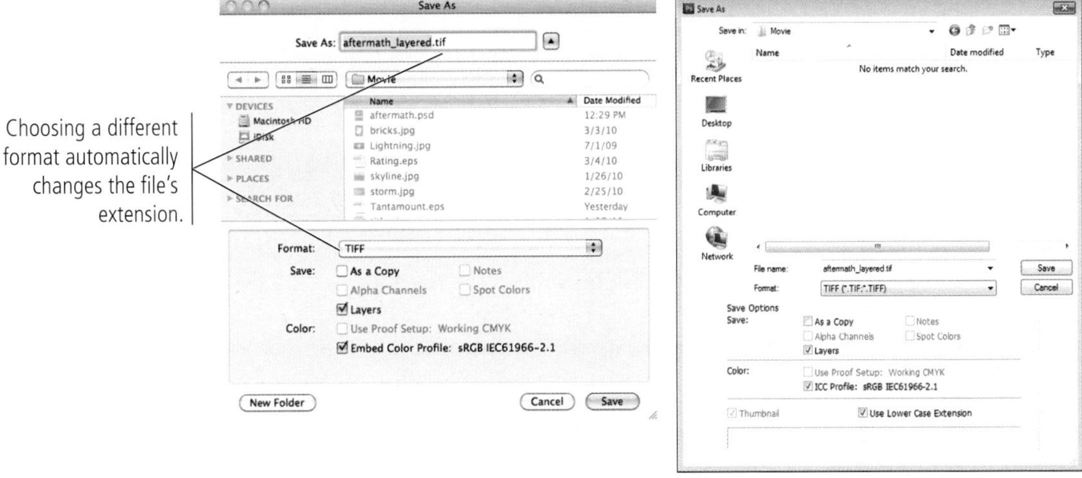

6. **Leave the remaining options at their default values and click Save.**

7. **In the resulting TIFF Options dialog box, make sure the None image compression option is selected.**

   TIFF files can be compressed (made smaller) using one of three methods:

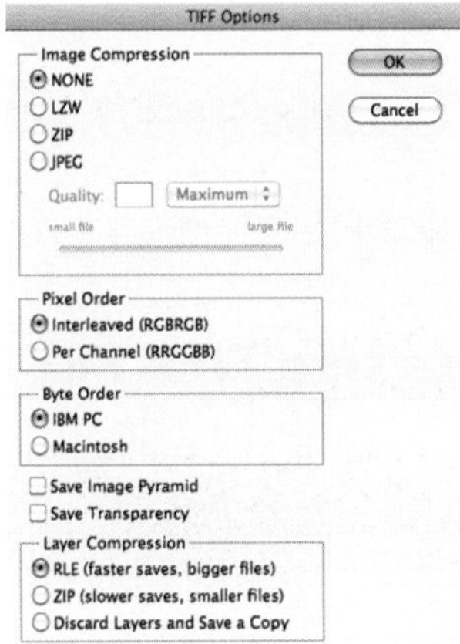

   - **None** (as the name implies) applies no compression to the file. This option is safe if file size is not an issue, but digital file transmission often requires files to be smaller than a full-page, multi-layered Photoshop file.
   - **LZW** (Lempel-Ziv-Welch) compression is **lossless**, which means all file data is maintained in the compressed file.
   - **ZIP** compression is also lossless, but is not supported by all desktop-publishing software (especially older versions).
   - **JPEG** is a **lossy** compression scheme, which means some data will be thrown away to reduce the file size. If you choose JPEG compression, the Quality options determine how much data can be discarded. Maximum quality means less data is thrown out and the file is larger. Minimum quality discards the most data and results in a smaller file size.

8. **Leave the Pixel Order radio button at the default value, and choose the Byte Order option for your operating system.**

   Pixel Order determines how channel data is encoded. The Interleaved (RGBRGB) option is the default; Per Channel (RRGGBB) is called "planar" order.

   Byte Order determines which platform can use the file, although this is somewhat deceptive. On older versions of most desktop-publishing software, Macintosh systems can read the PC byte order but Windows couldn't read the Macintosh byte order — which is why even the Macintosh system defaults to the IBM PC option. This option is becoming obsolete because most newer software can read either byte order. Nonetheless, some experts argue that choosing the order for your system can improve print quality, especially on desktop output devices.

   Save Image Pyramid creates a tiered file with multiple resolution versions; this isn't widely used or supported by other applications, so you can typically leave it unchecked.

   If your file contains transparency, the Save Transparency check box will be available. If you don't choose this option, transparent areas will be white in the saved file.

9. **In the Layer Compression area, make sure the RLE option is selected.**

   These three options explain — right in the dialog box — what they do.

10. **Click OK to save the file.**

    Photoshop warns you that including layers will increase the file size.

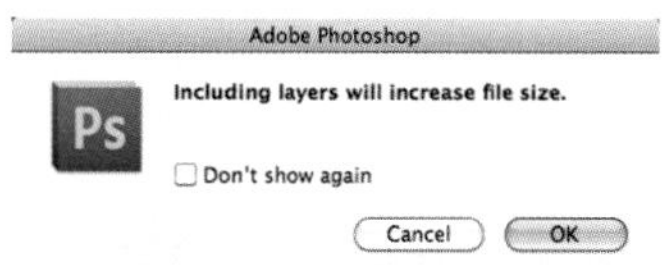

11. **Click OK to dismiss the warning and save the file.**

12. **Continue to the next exercise.**

Note:

If you don't see the warning, it's possible that someone checked the Don't Show Again check box. If you want to make sure that you see all warnings and messages, click Reset All Warning Dialogs in the General pane of the Preferences dialog box.

Save a Flattened TIFF File

Magazines using older page-layout applications need files that no longer maintain the layer information — called **flattened** files. You can flatten a file's layers manually using the Layers panel Options menu, or simply flatten the file during the Save As process.

1. **With aftermath_layered.tif open in Photoshop, choose File>Save As.**

   If you continued directly from the previous exercise, this is the version you just saved. If you quit before you began this exercise, make sure you open the TIFF version and not the PSD version from your WIP>Movie folder.

   Assuming that you started this exercise with the TIFF file from the previous exercise, the format and file name extension already reflect the TIFF options.

2. **Uncheck the Layers check box.**

   The As a Copy box is now selected by default. A warning shows that the file must be saved as a copy when the Layers option is unchecked. This is basically a failsafe built into Photoshop that prevents you from overwriting your layered file with a flattened version.

Note:

You can manually flatten a file by choosing Layer>Flatten Image.

3. **In the Save As field, highlight the words "layered copy" and type flat.**

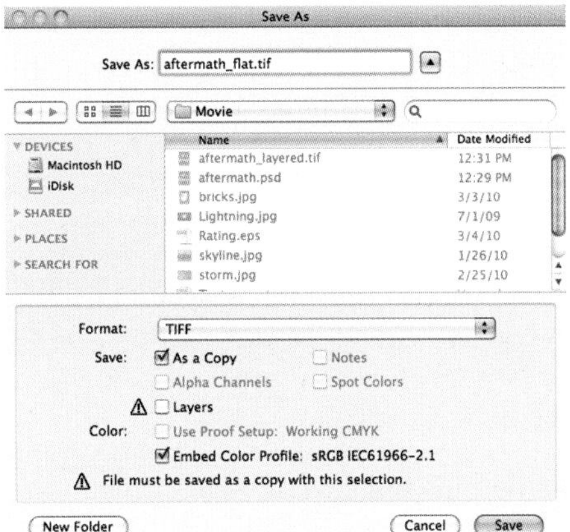

Note:

Older desktop-publishing software doesn't always support compressed TIFF files. When saving for those workflows, you might have to save the file without compression, regardless of the resulting file size.

4. **Click Save. In the resulting TIFF Options dialog box, make sure the None compression option is selected and the Byte Order is set to IBM PC. At the bottom of the dialog box, make sure the Discard Layers and Save a Copy option is checked.**

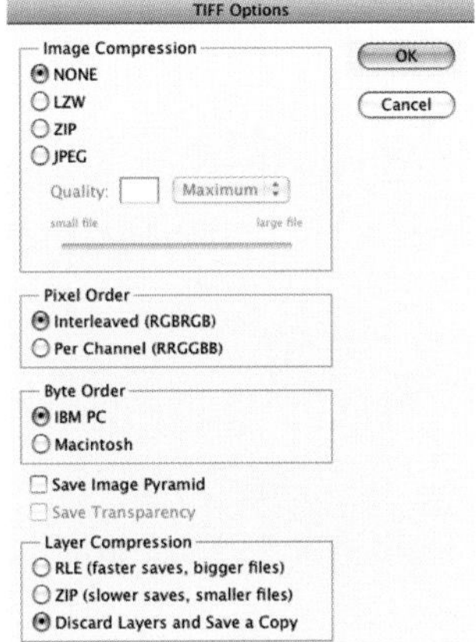

5. **Click OK to save the second version of the file.**

6. **When the save is complete, choose File>Close. Click Don't Save when asked.**

Project Review

fill in the blank

1. _______________ is likely to cause degradation of a raster image when it's reproduced on a printing press.

2. A _______________ is a linked file that you placed into another Photoshop document.

3. The _______________ is context sensitive, providing access to different functions depending on what tool is active.

4. The _______________ is the final size of a printed page.

5. The _______________ tool is used to draw irregular-shaped selection marquees.

6. The _______________ tool is used to select areas of similar color by clicking and dragging in the image window.

7. The _______________ tool can be used to drag layer contents to another position within the image, or into another open document.

8. When selecting color ranges, the _______________ value determines how much of the current color range falls into the selection.

9. A _______________ can be used to non-destructively hide certain areas of a layer.

10. _______________ is a lossy compression method that is best used when large file size might be a problem.

short answer

1. Briefly describe the difference between raster images and vector graphics.

2. Briefly explain three separate methods for isolating an image from its background.

3. Briefly explain the concept of a layer mask.

Portfolio Builder Project

Use what you learned in this project to complete the following freeform exercise.
Carefully read the art director and client comments, then create your design to meet the needs of the project.
Use the space below to sketch ideas; when finished, write a brief explanation of the reasoning behind your design.

art director comments

Tantamount Studios is pleased with your work on the *Aftermath* ad, and they would like to hire you again to create the ad concept and final files for another movie that they're releasing early next year.

To complete this project, you should:

- ❑ Download the **Print5_PB_Project4.zip** archive from the Student Files Web page to access the client-supplied title artwork and rating placeholder file.
- ❑ Find appropriate background and foreground images for the movie theme (see the client's comments at right).
- ❑ Incorporate the title artwork, logos, and rating placeholder that the client provided.
- ❑ Composite the different elements into a single completed file; save both a layered version and a flattened version.

client comments

The movie is titled *Above and Beyond.* Although the story is fictionalized, it will focus on the men who led the first U.S. Airborne unit (the 501st), which suffered more than 2000 casualties in the European theater of World War II.

We don't have any other images in mind, but the final ad should reflect the time period (the 1940s) of the movie. The 501st Airborne was trained to parachute into battle, so you should probably incorporate some kind of parachute image.

This movie is a joint venture between Sun and Tantamount, so both logos need to be included in the new ad. It isn't rated yet, so please use the "This Movie Is Not Yet Rated" artwork as a placeholder.

Create this ad big enough to fit on an 8.5 × 11″ page, but keep the live area an inch inside the trim so the ad can be used in different-sized magazines.

project justification

Project Summary

Making selections is one of the most basic, and most important, skills that you will learn in Photoshop. Selections are so important that Photoshop dedicates an entire menu to the process.

As you created the movie ad in this project, you used a number of skills and techniques that you will apply in many (if not all) projects you build in Photoshop. You learned a number of ways to make both simple and complex selections — and you will learn additional methods in later projects. You also learned how to work with multiple layers, which will be an important part of virtually every Photoshop project you create, both in this book and throughout your career.

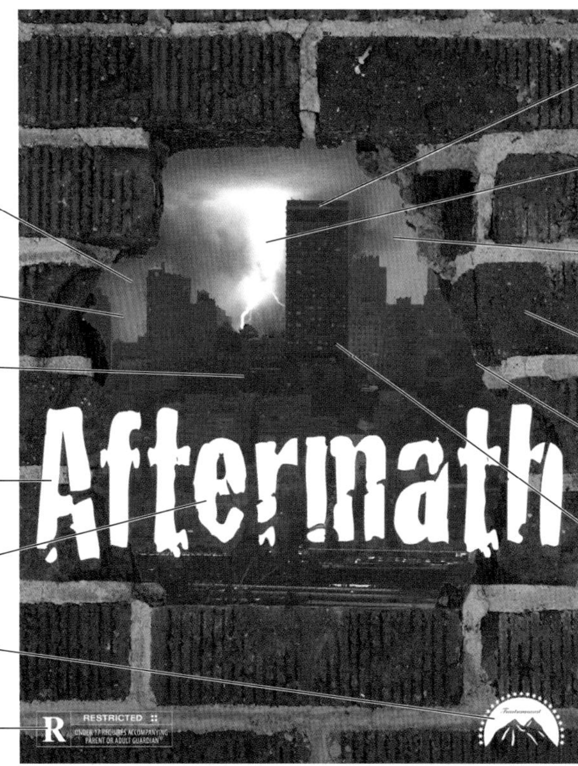

Composite images by dragging from one document to another

Transform a regular layer

Composite images by copying and pasting

Incorporate vector graphics into a raster image

Move layer content around on the canvas

Composite images by placing from Mini Bridge

Transform a Smart Object layer

Make a basic selection with a Marquee tool

Create a feathered selection to blend one layer into another

Create a silhouette using the Select Color Range utility

Create a silhouette using the Quick Selection tool

Refine a selection using the Refine Edges utility

Use a layer mask to hide pixels on a layer

project 5

African Wildlife Map

Your client, the Global Wildlife Fund (GWF), is a not-for-profit organization dedicated to preserving wildlife resources around the world. Every year GWF does a direct-mail fundraising drive, offering premiums for certain levels of membership donations. This year they want to offer a series of limited-edition art prints. Anyone who donates at least $100 will be allowed to pick one of the prints; people who donate over $1000 will receive the entire set of six prints. Your job is to create the first piece in the series as a sample.

This project incorporates the following skills:

- ❑ Using a small, low-resolution image as a drawing template
- ❑ Creating complex, scalable vector shape layers
- ❑ Compositing images as Smart Objects
- ❑ Creating and modifying selections and layer masks
- ❑ Applying filters and adjustments to create artistic effects
- ❑ Developing custom artistic backgrounds
- ❑ Presenting multiple layout variations using layer comps

Project Meeting

client comments

This is our 25th anniversary, and we want our fundraising drive to set records. In the past, we've sent out address labels, note pads, and even beanie animals as incentives for donating. This year we want to commission a series of paintings that we could reproduce as limited-edition prints for people who contribute a certain amount of money.

We're a not-for-profit organization, and we try to keep most of our finances dedicated to conservation activities. A colleague suggested that we might be able to find someone who can do what we want with Photoshop, and probably do it much faster and for far less money than a traditional artist.

Here's what we have in mind: we thought each piece in the series could be the shape of a different continent with various indigenous animals inside each continent. We're going to skip Antarctica because there isn't much wildlife there. You can start with Africa, because we've already gathered up a collection of images for that poster. We'd rather not have to pay for stock images when we already have so many of our own images in-house.

art director comments

I downloaded a comp image with a map of Africa that we can use to get the shape right, and then we can incorporate their photos into the map outline. I think the ideal size for the final piece is 10 × 12″.

Photoshop is ideal for this type of job; there are dozens of filters for making photographs look like artwork. You're going to have to be creative with the background; Africa is surrounded by water, and we don't want to give them a plain, flat blue background.

Since we're creating this artwork digitally, we have options that traditional painters don't have. I want you to use different filters and options to try a couple of variations, so the client can choose which one they prefer.

project objectives

To complete this project, you will:

- ❑ Create a compound shape layer using variations of the Pen tool
- ❑ Composite and work with multiple images as Smart Objects
- ❑ Modify selections to create soft-edge layer masks
- ❑ Use the brush tools to refine a layer mask
- ❑ Create a clipping mask from a vector shape layer
- ❑ Apply artistic filters using the Filter Gallery
- ❑ Define a custom gradient
- ❑ Use patterns, blending modes, and filters to create a custom background
- ❑ Use layer comps to present multiple options to your client

Stage 1 Working with Vector Shape Layers

Any project that you build in Photoshop — especially an oversize project like this map — requires some amount of zooming in and out to various view percentages, as well as navigating around the document within its window. As we show you how to complete different stages of the workflow, we usually won't tell you when to change your view percentage because that's largely a matter of personal preference. But you should understand the different options for navigating around a Photoshop file so you can easily and efficiently get to what you want, when you want to get there.

To review information from the Interface chapter, keep in mind that you have a number of options for navigating around a document:

- Click with the Hand tool to drag the image around in the document window.
- Click with the Zoom tool to zoom in; Option/Alt-click to zoom out.
- Use the Zoom Level field/menu on the Application/Menu bar.
- Use the options in the View menu (or the corresponding keyboard shortcuts).
- Use the Navigator panel.

Note:

As you complete the exercises in this project, use any of these methods to zoom in or out on different areas of the file.

Review and Resample the Existing Source Image

This project — like many others you will build throughout your career — starts with an existing image, which you will open and use as the basis for the rest of the project. Whenever you start with an existing file, it's best to evaluate what you already have before you make any changes.

1. **Download Print5_RF_Project5.zip from the Student Files Web page.**

2. **Expand the ZIP archive in your WIP folder (Macintosh) or copy the archive contents into your WIP folder (Windows).**

   This results in a folder named **Africa**, which contains the files you need for this project. You should also use this folder to save the files you create in this project.

3. **In Photoshop, choose File>Open. Navigate to the file africa.jpg in the WIP>Africa folder and click Open.**

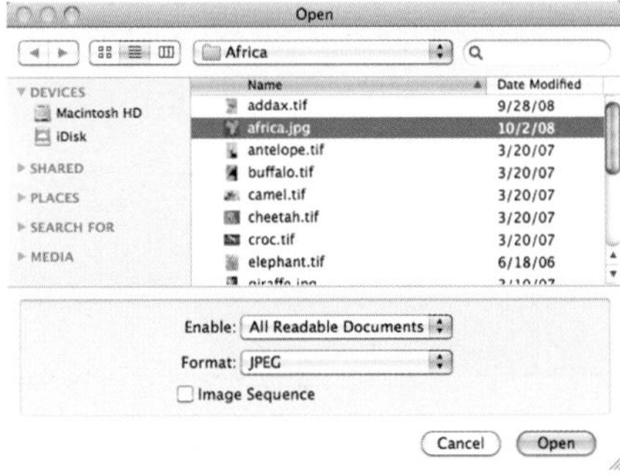

4. **Make sure your image displays at 100% and the rulers are visible, and then choose Image>Image Size.**

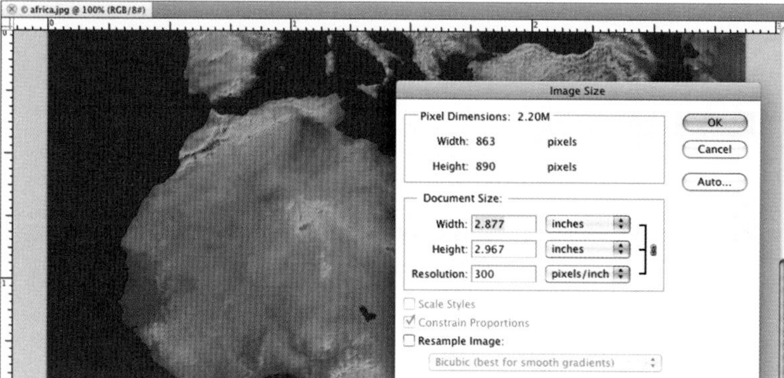

The africa.jpg file is slightly less than 3″ wide by 3″ high, with a resolution of 300 dpi. In Project 4, you learned that commercial printing typically requires 300 dpi, so this image would be considered "print quality" at its current size; however, you need to build the final artwork at 10 × 12″ — nearly 4 times the current size.

5. **Check the Resample Image option at the bottom of the dialog box.**

6. **Highlight the Height field and type** 12.

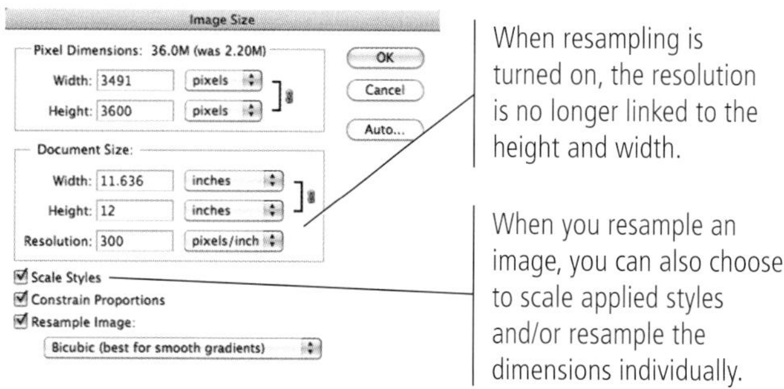

> ***Note:***
>
> *You can also see the effect of more pixels on file size — more pixels at larger sizes means much larger (potentially huge) file sizes.*

7. **Click OK to return to the document window.**

The map image, which was originally crisp and clear, is now blurry and pixelated. You no longer have clean lines to use as the basis for the map outline.

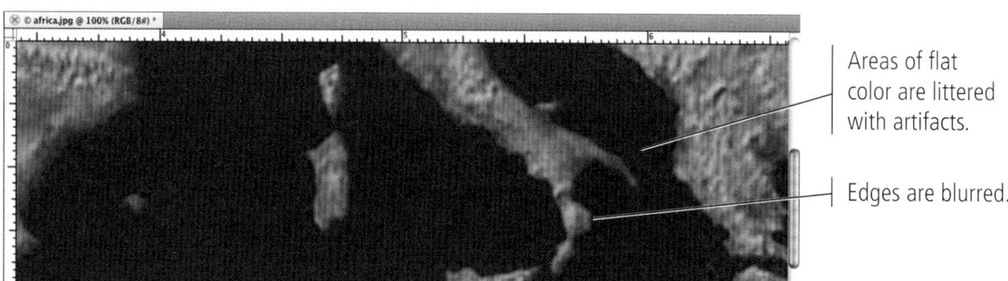

8. **Choose Edit>Undo Image Size to return the file to its original size.**

The Photoshop Undo command is a single-action toggle; after you use the command, it becomes Redo for the same action. To move back through more than one action, you must use the Step Backward command or the History panel.

9. **Choose View>Rulers to toggle them off.**

10. **Save the file as a Photoshop file named** `africa_working.psd` **in your WIP>Africa folder, and then continue to the next exercise.**

> ***Note:***
>
> *Press Command/Control-Z to undo the previous action.*
>
> *Press Command-Option-Z/Control-Alt-Z to step backward one action at a time through the file history.*

Create a Vector Shape Layer

If you completed Project 4, you learned that one of the disadvantages of raster images is that their size and resolution are fixed at the time they are created. Photoshop is very powerful, but it simply can't create enough pixels to generate a high-quality 14″ image from a 4″ image.

Vector graphics, on the other hand, are based on mathematically defined lines and points instead of pixels. When you output a vector file, the output device calculates the relative position of those lines and points as necessary to create the final version at whatever size you need. Because of this, vectors can be resized as large as you need without any loss of quality.

To work around the problem of low resolution in the original map image, you're going to create a vector shape layer using the original map as a guide.

1. **With africa_working.psd open, choose the Pen tool in the Tools panel.**

   The Pen tool can be used to create precise vector paths called **Bézier curves**, defined by the position of anchor points and the length and angle of handles that are connected to those anchor points. You can use the regular Pen tool to place individual anchor points and drag handles, precisely controlling the shape of the resulting paths (see Photoshop Foundations: Understanding Anchor Points and Handles on Page 246).

   For this project, your ultimate goal is an artistic rendering — which means you don't have to precisely match the individual points and curves of the continental shape. Rather than individually creating every anchor point and precisely pulling every curve, you can use the Freeform Pen tool to draw as you would with a pencil.

2. **In the Control panel, choose the Shape Layers option and click the Freeform Pen tool icon.**

   The Pen tool can be used to create shape layers or paths. Shape layers are vector-based, which means they have mathematically defined edges and can be filled with colors or pixel-based images. Paths are also vector-based, but they do not create their own layers and cannot be directly filled; instead, paths are most commonly used to isolate certain portions of an image.

   You can use the Control panel to determine what type of path you want to create. The Pen tool defaults to create a shape layer. Regardless of which option is selected, you can select any of the vector drawing tools from the group of eight buttons; you see the same buttons when you choose one of the Pen or Shape tools directly from the Tools panel.

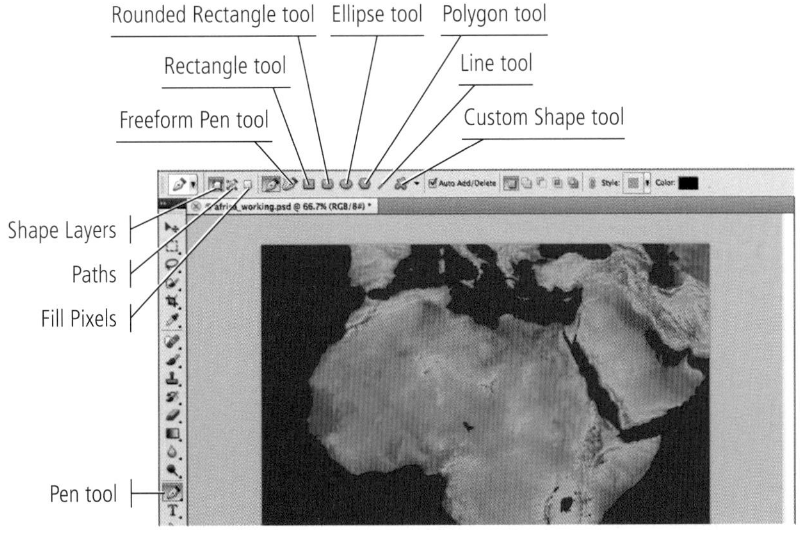

Note:

Choosing one of the tool variations in the Control panel is the same as choosing the alternate tool in the Tools panel.

Note:

The Auto Add/Delete option, active by default, allows you to add or remove points on an active path without manually switching to the Add Anchor Point or Delete Anchor Point tool (both of which are nested under the Pen tool).

Understanding Anchor Points and Handles

PHOTOSHOP FOUNDATIONS

An **anchor point** marks the end of a line **segment**, and the point **handles** determine the shape of that segment. That's the basic definition of a vector, but there is a bit more to it than that. (The Photoshop Help files refer to handles as direction lines, and distinguishes different types of points with different names. Our aim here is to explain the overall concept of vector paths, so we use the generic industry-standard terms. For more information on Adobe's terminology, refer to the Photoshop CS5 Help files.)

Each segment in a path has two anchor points and two associated handles. We first clicked to create Point A and dragged (without releasing the mouse button) to create Handle A1. We then clicked and dragged to create Point B and Handle B1; Handle B2 is automatically created as a reflection of B1 (Point B is a **symmetrical point**).

Point A
Handle A1
Segment A
Point B
Handle B1
Handle B2

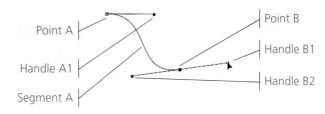

This image shows the result of dragging Handle B1 to the left instead of to the right when we created the initial curve. Notice the difference in the curve here, compared to the curve above. When you drag a handle, the connecting segment arcs away from the direction of the handle you drag.

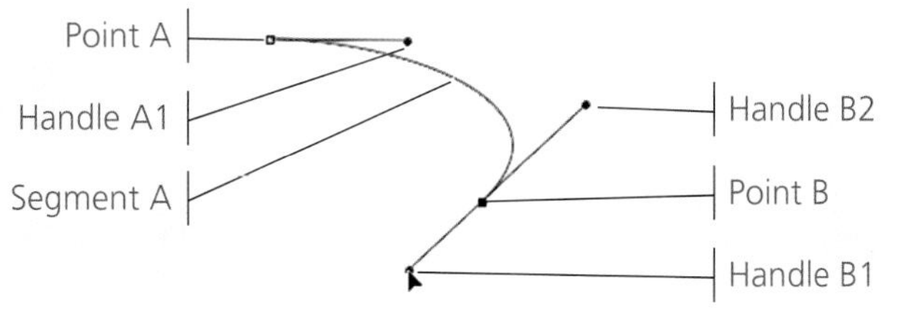

It's important to understand that every line segment is connected to two handles. In this example, Handle A1 and Handle B2 determine the shape of Segment A. Dragging either handle affects the shape of the connected segment.

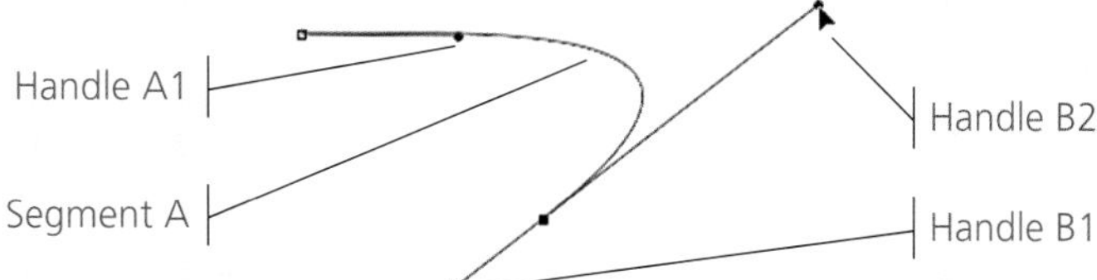

Clicking and dragging a point creates a symmetrical (smooth) point; both handles start out at equal length, directly opposite one another. Changing the angle of one handle of a symmetrical point also changes the opposing handle of that point. In the example here, repositioning Handle B1 also moves Handle B2, which affects the shape of Segment A. (You can, however, change the length of one handle without affecting the length of the other handle.)

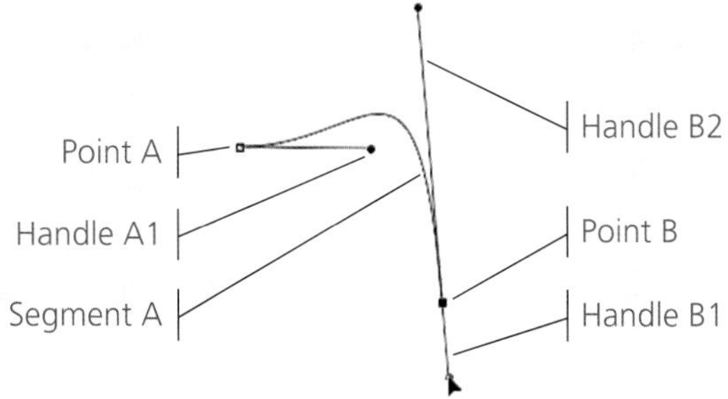

You can create corner points by simply clicking with the Pen tool instead of clicking and dragging. Corner points do not have their own handles; the connected segments are controlled by the handles of the other associated points.

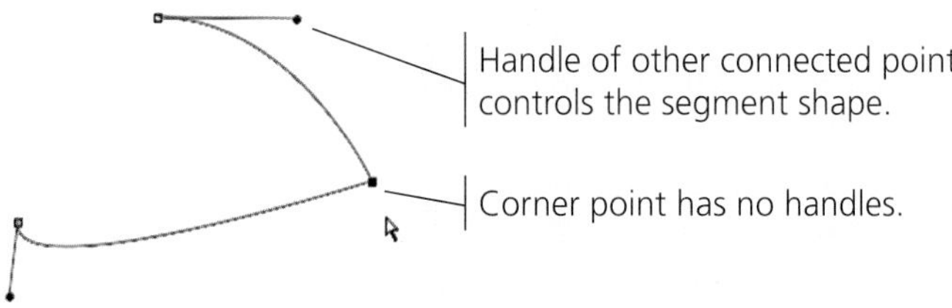

You can convert a symmetrical point into a corner point by clicking the point with the Convert Point tool [ ] (nested under the Pen tool). You can also add a handle to only one side of an anchor point by Option/Alt-clicking a point with the Convert Direction Point tool and dragging.

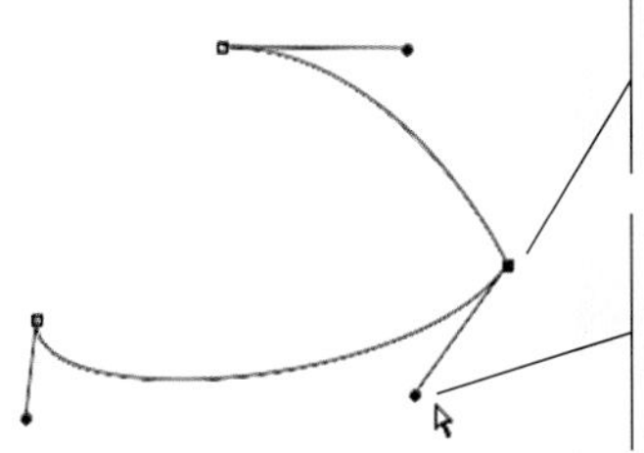

Option/Alt-click this point with the Convert Direction Point tool and drag to create only one handle.

This handle controls the connected segment; the handle is not reflected on the other side of the point.

3. **In the Control panel, click the arrow button to the right of the tool variations to access the options for the Freeform Pen tool.**

   The Curve Fit field determines how closely the resulting curve will match the path you drag with the tool. Lower values (minimum 0.5 pixels) result in more anchor points and curves that more closely match the path you draw; higher values (up to 10 pixels) create fewer anchor points and smoother curves with greater variation from the path you draw.

4. **Set the Curve Fit field to `2 px` and press Return/Enter to close the options dialog box.**

   This field remembers the last-used value; 2 px is the application default value, but this setting might have been changed by another user.

5. **In the Control panel, click the Style button and choose the No Style option.**

   Both the Style and Color options maintain the last-used settings. You're simply making sure no style is automatically applied to the new shape. We'll return to the idea of styles later in this project.

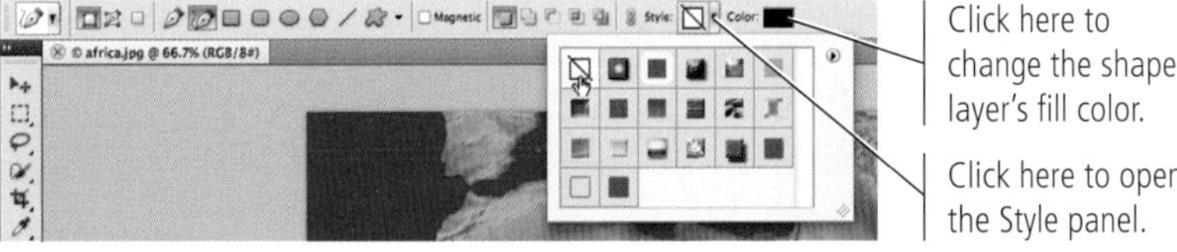

Click here to change the shape layer's fill color.
Click here to open the Style panel.

6. **Click the Color swatch to open the Color Picker. In the resulting Color Picker dialog box, select a color that will be visible against the background map image, and then click OK.**

   This step determines the color that will fill the shape you are about to create. We used a light blue, which will stand out well against the background image.

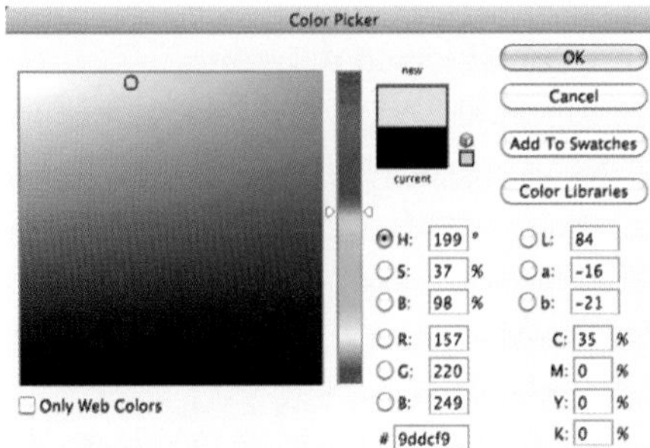

7. **Zoom in to Madagascar (the island east of the main African continent).**

8. **With the Freeform Pen tool active, click near the top of Madagascar to establish the starting point, hold down the mouse button, and then drag to trace the outside edge of the island.**

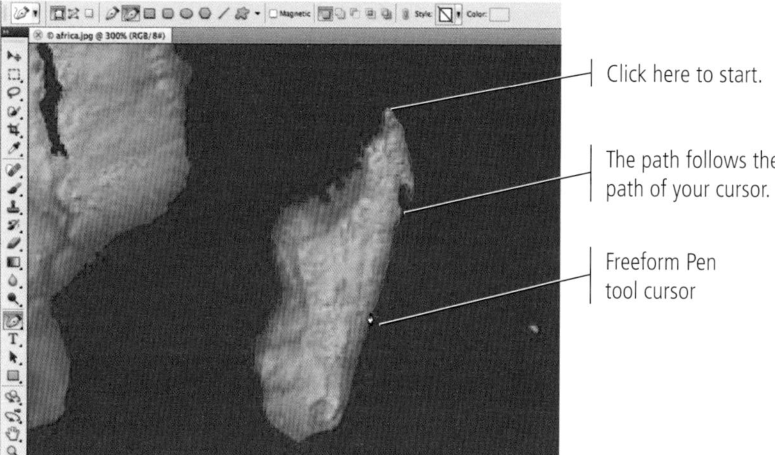

Click here to start.
The path follows the path of your cursor.
Freeform Pen tool cursor

9. **Release the mouse button about halfway down the east side of the island.**

   When you release the mouse button, the shape you drew fills with whatever color is visible in the Color swatch on the Control panel. This happens even when you draw a shape that isn't a closed path.

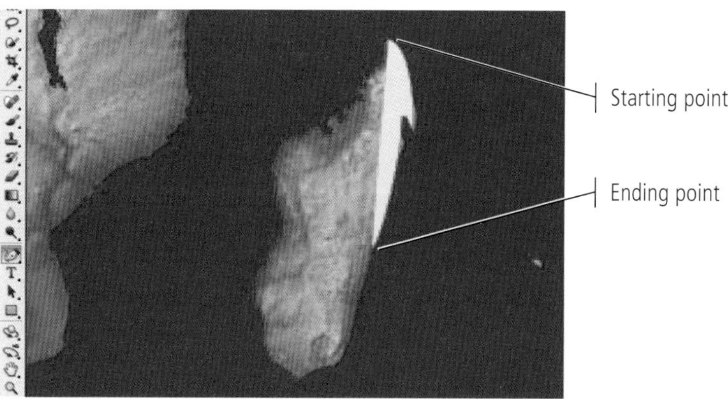

10. **Place the mouse cursor over the point where you stopped dragging.**

   When the Pen tool cursor is over the end of an open path, the small slash in the icon indicates that you can click to continue drawing the same path.

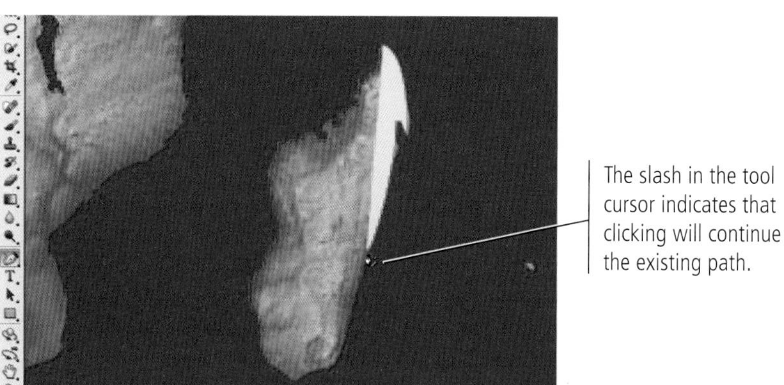

Note:

When you draw by holding down a button (mouse button or the button on a graphics tablet/pen) it is not uncommon for the line to "jump" where you don't want it to jump. If this happens, press Esc to remove your selection or path and start drawing again.

11. **Click over the open end point and continue tracing the outline of the island.**

When you return to the original starting point, a small circle in the tool cursor indicates that you are closing the shape. If you release the mouse button when you see the circle, the entire island shape will fill with the shape color.

The tool cursor shows that releasing the mouse button here will close the shape.

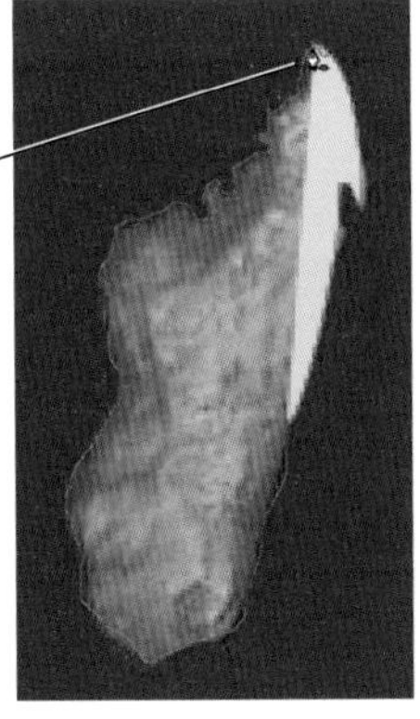

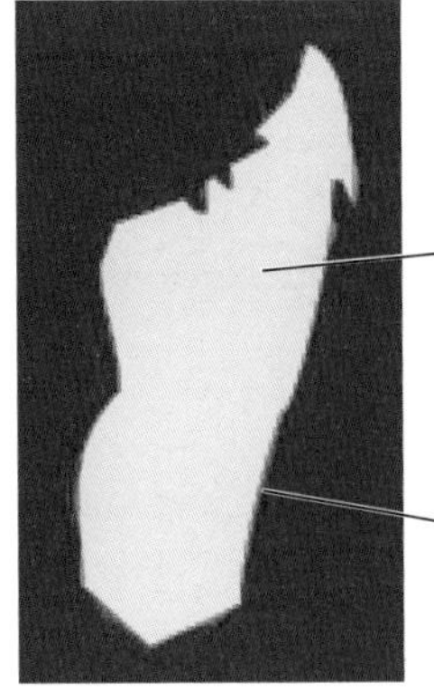

Releasing the mouse button fills the entire shape with the color you selected in the Color Picker.

The resulting path can be edited with the Direct Selection tool (nested under the Path Selection tool).

12. **Look at the Layers panel.**

When you draw with a Pen tool in Shape Layer mode, the resulting vector shape exists on its own layer.

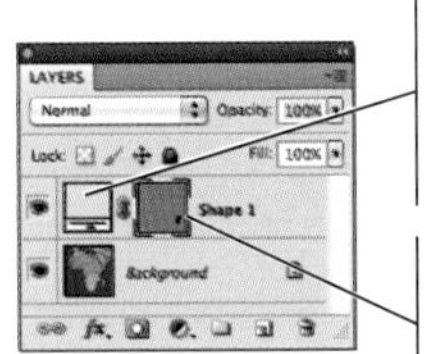

This is the layer fill color. This color is visible within the area of the vector mask.

This is the vector mask that you drew with the Freeform Pen tool.

13. **Save the file and continue to the next exercise. If you get a warning about maximizing capability, click OK.**

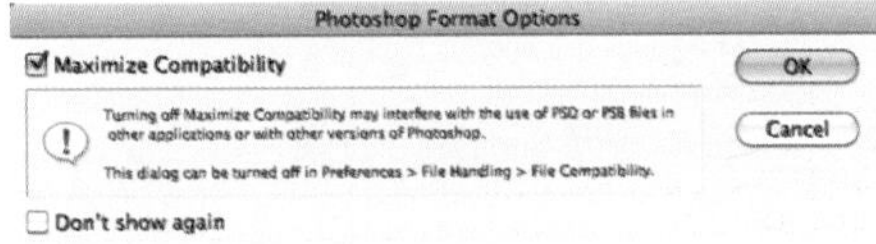

> *Note:*
>
> *The underlying map image is simply a guide for you to create the necessary map. Your shapes do not need to be perfect — although they should be close.*

Add to an Existing Shape Layer

The Freeform Pen tool is very useful for drawing custom vector shapes, whether you're tracing a map or drawing original freeform art. When using this tool, however, you must hold down the mouse button the entire time you draw (unless you have a graphics tablet).

In the case of this artwork, you have a better option because you don't need to precisely match the shape of the continent. The Freeform Pen tool has a Magnetic mode that snaps to edges of high-contrast pixel values in the image. Using this method will make it far easier to complete the outline you need.

1. **With africa_working.psd open, zoom out so you can see the entire image.**

2. **Make sure the shape layer is selected in the Layers panel.**

3. **With the Freeform Pen tool active, check the Magnetic option in the Control panel.**

4. **In the Control panel to the right of the Magnetic check box, choose the Add to Shape Area option.**

   You want to create a single shape layer with all the land masses, so you must make sure each new disconnected shape is added to the previous shapes.

   An object that is made up of multiple, separate pieces is called a **compound path**. Compound paths can also be used to remove inner areas from a shape, such as the interior of the letter A or the number 9.

5. **Click the Geometry Options button (to the right of the tool variations).**

   You can still define the Curve Fit option when drawing in Magnetic mode. You also have three new options:

   - **Width** determines how far from an edge you have to drag (1–256 pixels) for Photoshop to still find the edge.
   - **Contrast** determines how much variation (1–100%) must exist between pixels for Photoshop to define an edge.
   - **Frequency** determines the rate at which Photoshop places anchor points. Higher values (up to 100) create anchor points faster than lower values (down to 0).

Note:

The Pen Pressure option only applies if you have a pressure-sensitive graphics tablet. When this option is turned on, higher pressure decreases the Width tolerance.

6. **Set the Width to `40`, the Contrast to `20%`, and the Frequency to `25`.**

   This image has very high contrast between the land and the water, so you can use a lower contrast value and still find the edges.

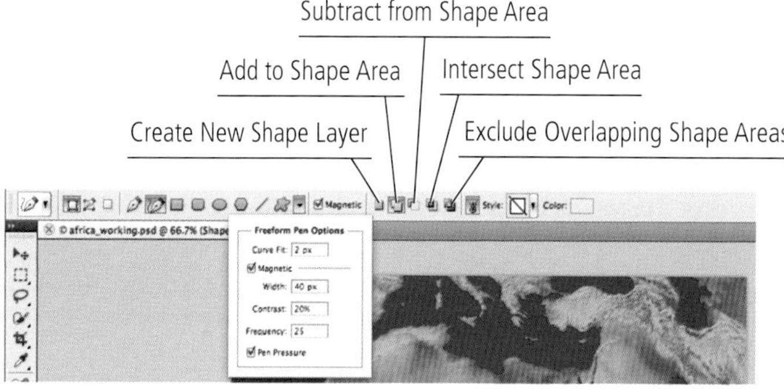

7. **Click at the northeast point of Somalia to place the first anchor point, release the mouse button, and then drag around the shape of the African continent.**

   You don't have to hold down the mouse button when you draw with the Freeform Pen tool in Magnetic mode. Although you can click specific points while you draw to manually place anchor points along the way, Photoshop automatically draws the path and points as necessary to create the shape.

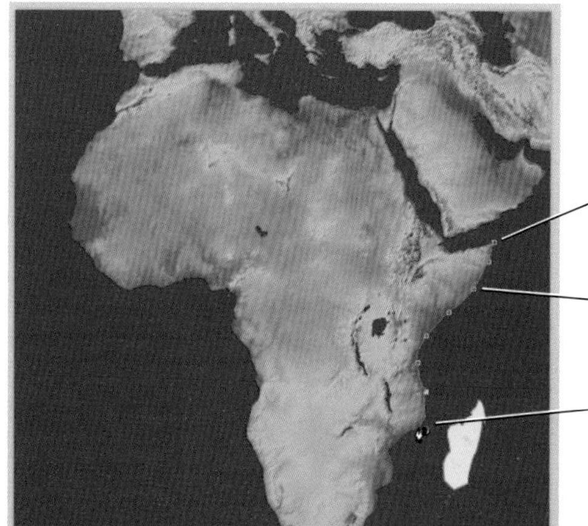

Note:

Manually clicking while using the Magnetic Freeform Pen tool option is a good way to make sharp turns along thin areas, which you will see shortly.

8. **When you get to the point where Africa meets the Arabian Peninsula, drag across the Suez Canal. Photoshop will find and recognize the edge where Africa meets the Red Sea.**

9. **Drag around to the original starting point and click to close the shape.**

> *Note:*
>
> *Even if the cursor is not directly over the open endpoint, you can double-click with the Freeform Pen tool in Magnetic mode to close the shape.*

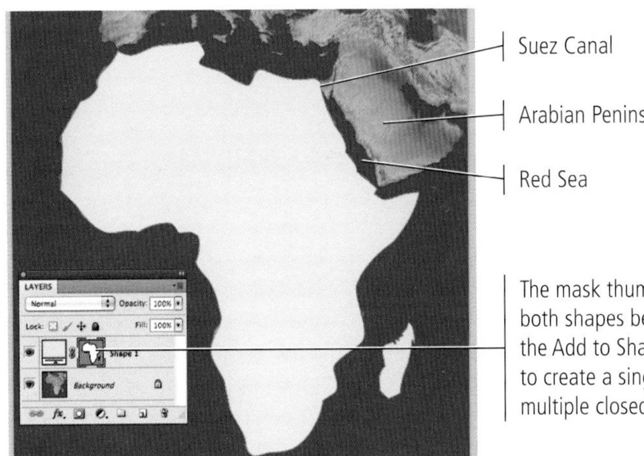
Suez Canal
Arabian Peninsula
Red Sea
The mask thumbnail shows both shapes because you used the Add to Shape Area option to create a single shape of multiple closed paths.

10. **Save the file and continue to the next exercise.**

Control and Edit a Shape Layer

When you outlined the shape of Africa, the Magnetic mode of the Freeform Pen tool made the work much easier than manually tracing the shape — but the path is not perfectly matched to the original. In this case, the result is acceptable because you don't need precision to achieve your ultimate goal.

In many cases, however, the path you first draw will be a good starting point, but will need some (if not significant) refinement before you can call it complete. You will probably need to edit at least one or two points or segments, move existing points, or even add or delete points before your path exactly matches the shape you're outlining. As you complete this exercise, we show you how to correct the path in our screen shots. You should follow the general directions to correct the path that you drew in the previous exercise as necessary.

1. **In the open `africa_working.psd` file, zoom in to the southern part of Europe at the top of the image. Make sure the shape layer is selected in the Layers panel.**

2. **Using the Freeform Pen tool in Magnetic mode and adding to the existing shape layer, click to anchor the path where Italy meets the top edge of the image.**

3. **Drag around Italy to create the path.**

   When you drag around the tip of the "boot," the area is too narrow for Photoshop to accurately create the outline.

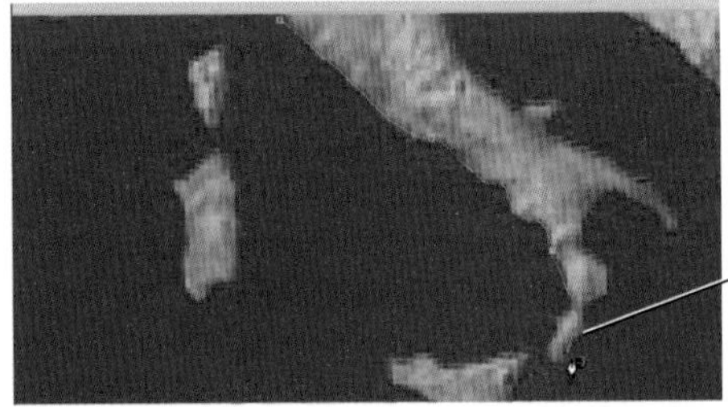
The path can't accurately snap to the tip of the boot.

4. **Drag back to the tip of the boot and click to manually place an anchor point, and then continue dragging around the outline. Anywhere the path doesn't accurately snap to the edge, click to manually create a point.**

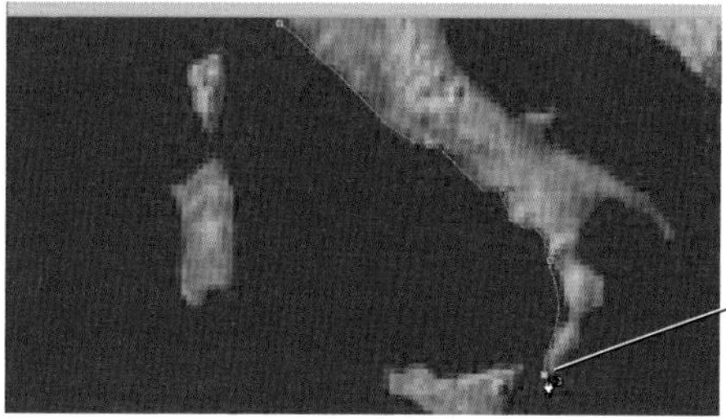

Click to manually anchor a point while drawing with the Freeform Pen tool in Magnetic mode.

5. **Click over the original starting point to close the shape.**

   When you close the shape, you can probably see that it needs some help.

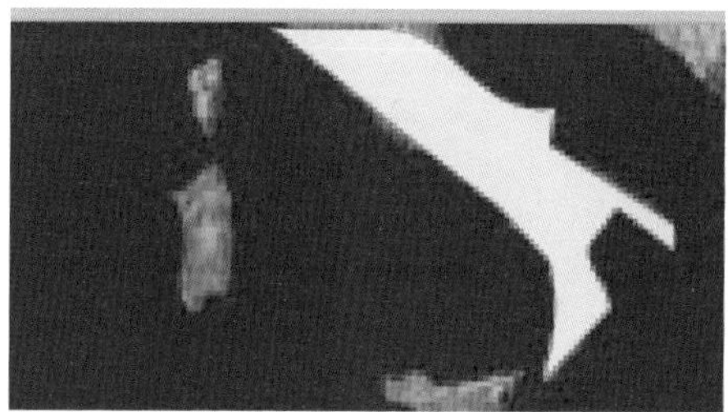

6. **Use the following information to fine-tune your outline of Italy.**

   This is one place where we can't give you specific instructions because everyone's path will be a bit different. Keep the following points in mind as you refine your shape.

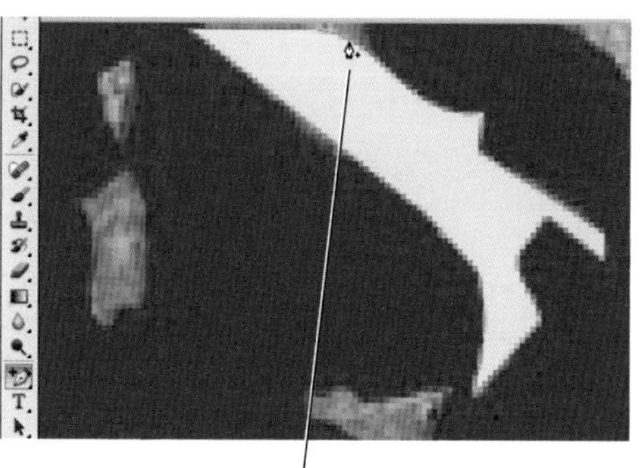

Use the Add Anchor Point tool to add a point to a path.

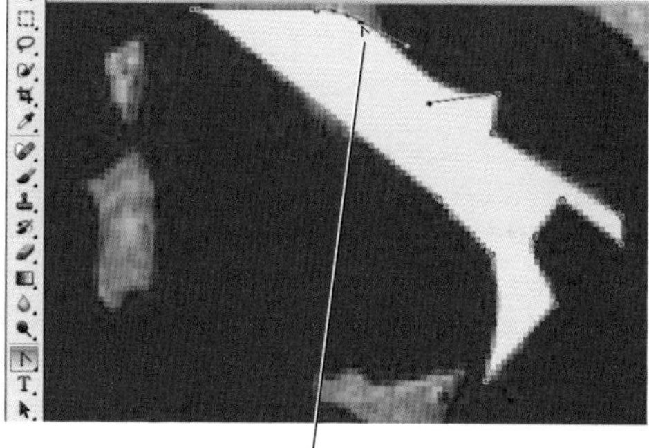

Use the Convert Anchor Point tool to change a smooth point to a corner point (and vice versa).

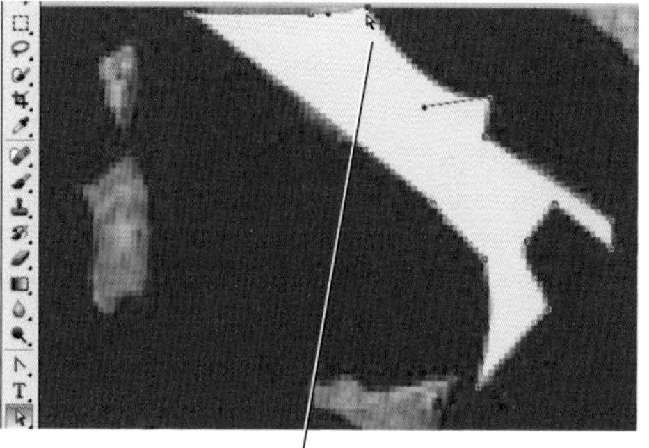

Use the Direct Selection tool to select and edit individual anchor points and their handles.

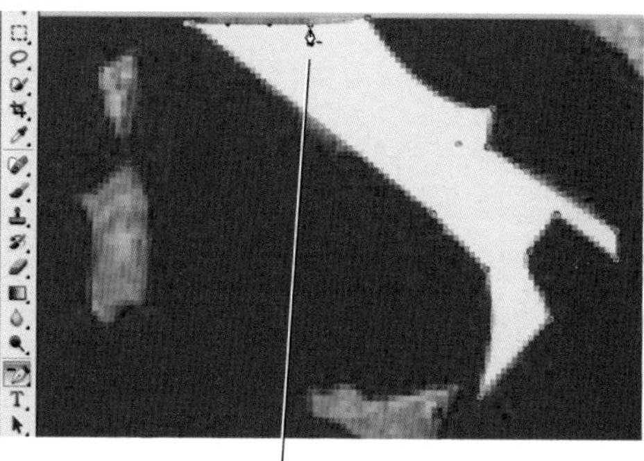

Use the Delete Anchor Point tool to delete a point from the path.

This is our final result:

7. **Save the file and continue to the next exercise.**

Subtract from a Shape Layer

You now have a single shape layer consisting of three different shapes. The final step of creating the continent shape layer is to outline the remaining land areas, and then remove the areas of large bodies of water from the shape.

1. **With africa_working.psd open, use what you have learned about drawing shape layers to add the remaining land areas to the existing shape layer. Use the following guidelines as you create the shapes:**
   - Make sure the shape layer is selected in the Layers panel and the Add to Shape option is selected in the Control panel.
   - Make sure all the points that touch the image edges are corner points, with no extraneous points on the segments that touch the image edge.
   - Include the larger islands in the Mediterranean Sea (Sicily, Corsica, Sardinia, Crete, and Cyprus).
   - For now, don't worry about tracing the Black and Caspian Seas above the Arabian Peninsula. You will remove those in the next few steps.

   When you have finished drawing the outlines, you're almost done — except that you covered two large seas and at least five major lakes within the African continent. You will fix that problem next.

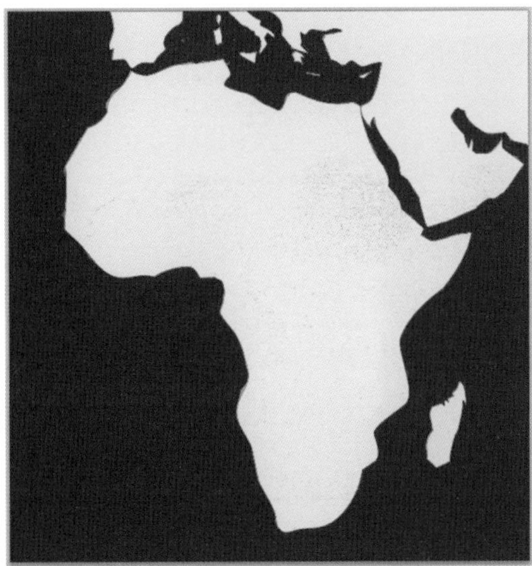

Note:

We used the Freeform Pen tool without the Magnetic option because we prefer the control of the line exactly following the mouse cursor. This decision is entirely up to you, especially since the shape you're drawing doesn't have to be perfect.

2. **In the Layers panel, change the Shape Layer opacity to 50%.**

   You can change the opacity of any layer, including a shape layer. By reducing the layer opacity, you can see the underlying layers enough to trace the seas and lakes.

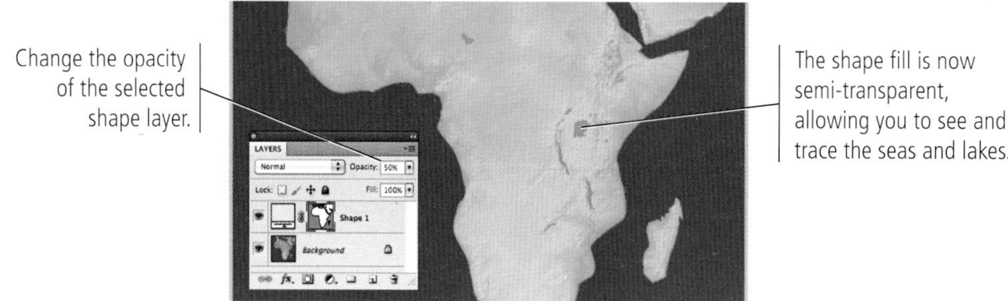

Change the opacity of the selected shape layer.
The shape fill is now semi-transparent, allowing you to see and trace the seas and lakes.

3. **With the Freeform Pen tool active (with or without Magnetic mode), click the Subtract from Shape Area option in the Control panel.**

4. **Using the same techniques you used to create the existing shape layer, trace the outline of the Caspian Sea.**

   Refer to the image at the bottom of the page if your geography is a bit rusty.

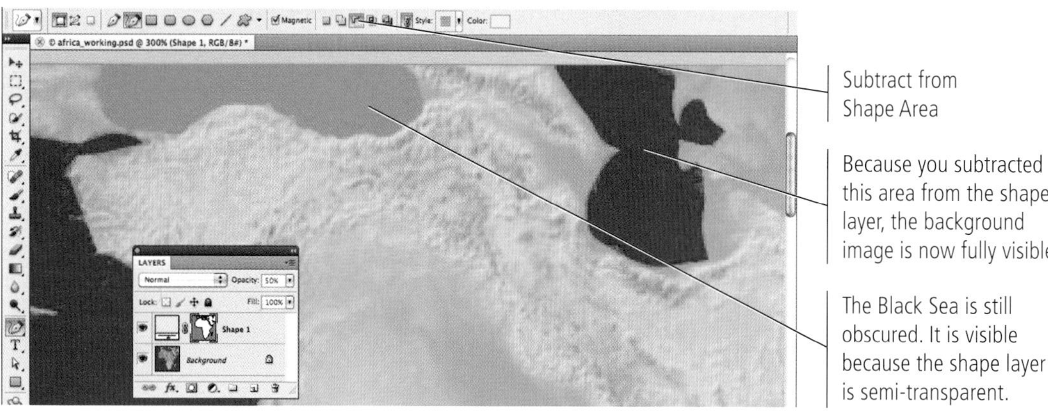

5. **Continue removing the areas of any large bodies of water from the shape layer. Make sure you exclude the larger African lakes identified in the following image.**

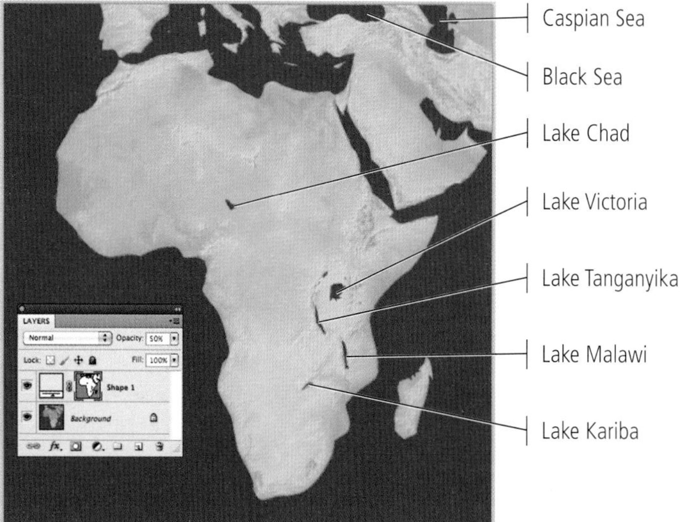

6. **Save the file and continue to the next exercise.**

The Paths Panel in Depth

If you use the Pen tool in Paths mode, the vector path that you create is stored in the Paths panel rather than attached to a specific layer.

When you first create a path, it is stored as the work path. If you use the Add to Path option in the Control panel, drawing another shape adds to the current work path, which is stored temporarily until you deselect the path.

If you want to be able to access a path later in your work, you can save the work path with a user-defined name. Saved paths are stored in the Paths panel until you intentionally delete them.

Paths mode

The work path is only temporary.

Click here to open the panel Options menu.

If you click a path name in the panel, the path becomes visible in the document window. You can then use use the Direct Selection tool to access individual anchor points and handles, use the Path Selection tool to select and move the entire path, or use the Pen tool (and its variants) to edit the path.

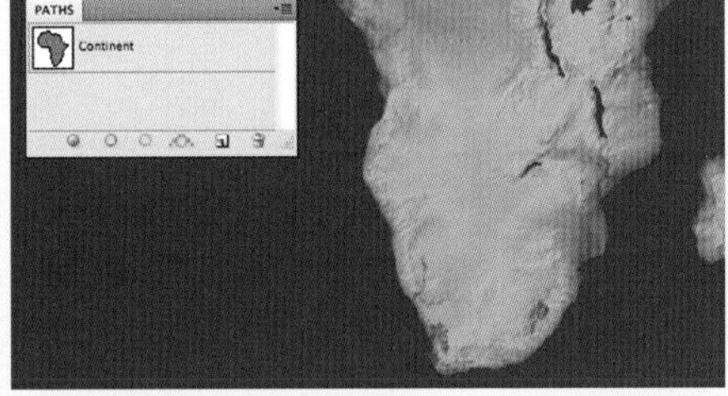

Click the empty area of the panel to deselect the active path and hide it in the document window.

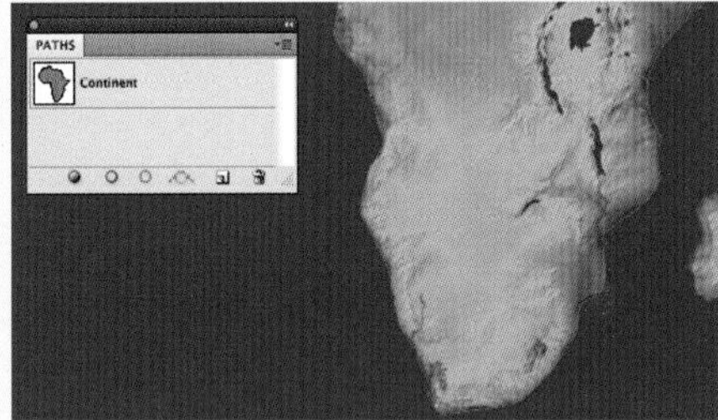

Click a saved path to select it and reveal the path in the document window.

You can choose **Make Selection** in the panel Options menu to make a marching-ants selection based on the path shape. You can use the resulting dialog box to define the details of the selection.

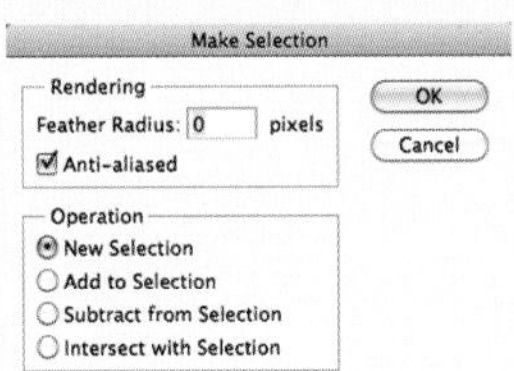

If you choose **Fill Path** in the Options menu, you can use the resulting dialog box to determine how the fill will be created. You can choose the color or pattern, the blending mode and opacity, and whether to feather the edge of the resulting fill so it blends smoothly into underlying layers.

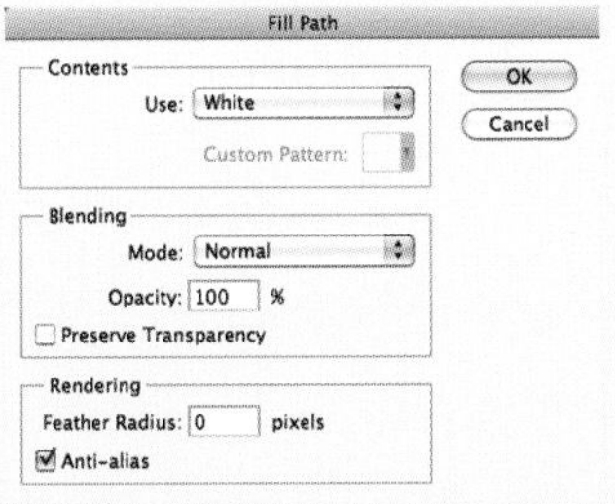

If you choose the **Stroke Path** option, you must also choose which tool will create the stroke; the applied stroke will have the last-used settings for the selected tool. In other words, you have to define the tool options (brush size, hardness, etc.) that you want before using this option.

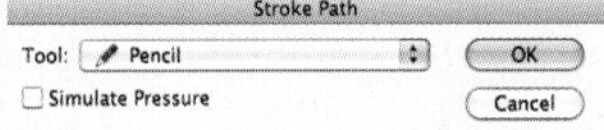

The Fill Path and Stroke Path options add the resulting pixels to the currently active layer — an important distinction from the Shape Layer option, which automatically creates a new layer when you begin drawing the vector path. It is also important to remember that, although the path remains a vector path, color that is applied to the fill or stroke of the path is raster or pixel-based; it does not have the same scalability as a vector shape layer.

If you choose the **Clipping Path** option, the selected path will become a clipping path, which is essentially a vector mask that defines the visible area of an image if the file is placed into a page-layout application such as Adobe InDesign. (The white area in the path thumbnail defines what areas will be visible in the image.)

Resample the Shape Layer and Change the Canvas Size

You now have a complete compound shape layer that outlines all the land areas in the original image. The file, however, is still only about 4″ wide. Before you add the animal images, you need to convert the file to the appropriate size so the placed animal pictures are not resampled when you enlarge the image.

1. **With `africa_working.psd` open, choose Image>Image Size.**

2. **In the Image Size dialog box, make sure the Resample Image option is active.**

3. **Change the Height field to 12 [inches] and click OK.**

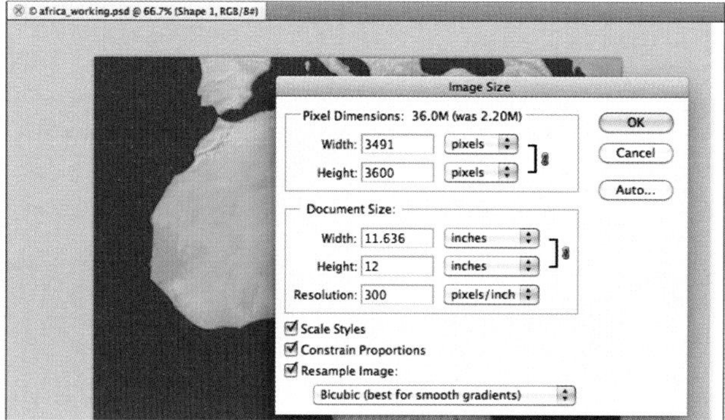

You're adding a sizeable amount of information to this file, so the resampling process might take a few minutes. Depending on the power and speed of your computer, you might see a progress bar as the image size is remapped.

4. **When the Progress bar disappears, zoom in so you can clearly see the shape layer edges.**

5. **In the Layers panel, click away from the shape layer to turn off the vector path in the document window.**

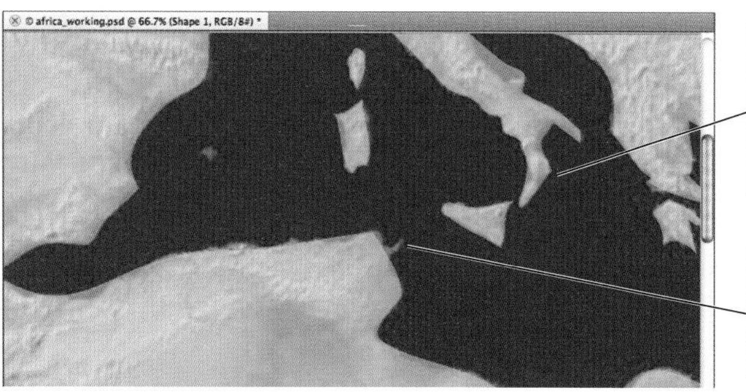

The vector edge of the shape layer is still just as sharp as it was when you created it at the original size.

The background image is still badly pixelated, just as it was when you resized it earlier.

Note:

Clicking the empty area at the bottom of the Layers panel is the best option to deselect the shape layer.

6. **Change your view to fit the entire image in the document window.**

7. **Choose Image>Canvas Size.**

When you resampled the image to 12″ high, you might have noticed that the width was proportionally changed to 11.636″. That's slightly larger than the 10″ you want, so you need to crop the image to the correct dimensions.

In Project 4, you used the Crop tool to crop a file to a specific size. If you know the exact size you need, you can change the size of the canvas to change the size of an image.

The Anchor area shows the reference point around which the canvas will be enlarged or cropped. If the center point is selected, for example, reducing the width by 1″ would remove 0.5″ from the left and right edges of the image.

8. **Change the Width field to 10 [inches] and click OK.**

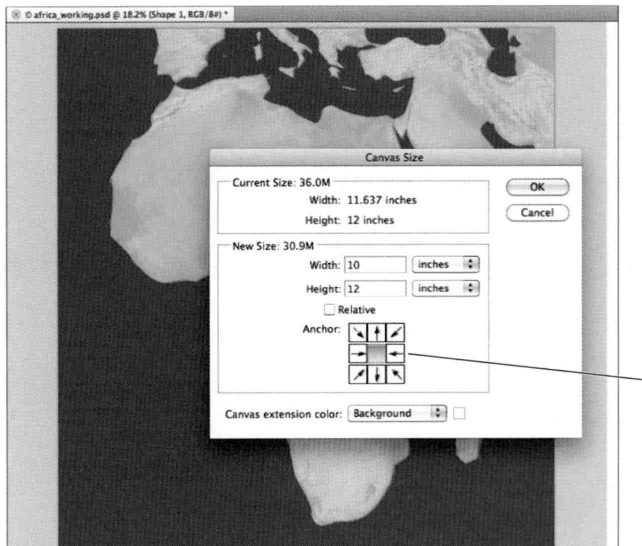

The inward-pointing arrows show that space will be removed from the left and right of the image.

Note:

If you are enlarging the canvas, you can define the color that will be used in the new area outside the existing image size. Your choices are Foreground, Background, Black, White, Gray, or a custom color.

When you reduce a canvas size, you're warned that elements outside the new dimensions will be clipped (removed).

Note:

If you activate the Relative check box, you can define how much you want to add or subtract instead of defining a specific height and width. For example, you can reduce the height by 1" by typing –1 in the height field.

9. **Click Proceed to crop the canvas to 10" wide.**

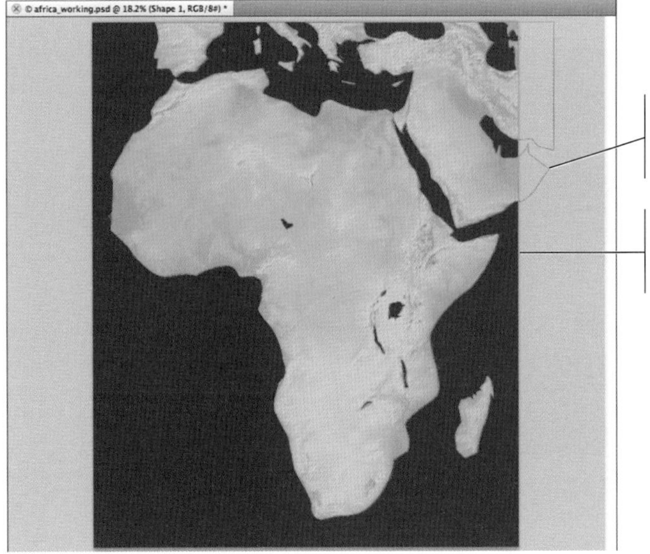

The shape layer path is not clipped to the new canvas edge.

The image canvas is clipped to the new dimensions.

10. **Save the file and continue to the next exercise.**

Add Color and Texture to the Shape Layer

Aside from their usefulness as scalable vector paths, shape layers can be filled with solid colors (as yours is now), with styles or patterns (which you will add in this exercise), or even with other images (which you will do later).

Most of the shape layer in this file is going to be filled with pictures of animals, but some areas will remain visible. Adding a texture to the whole shape layer will create an effective background in areas where the animal pictures don't completely fill in the shape layer.

1. **With `africa_working.psd` open, click the eye icon of the shape layer to hide that layer.**

   You're going to pull a color from the placed image to use as the layer's fill color. To do that, you must be able to see the underlying layer.

2. **In the Layers panel, double-click the Color icon to the left of the (hidden) shape layer.**

   In the Color Picker dialog box, you can choose a color to apply using three different techniques:

   - Numerically define a color in any of the available color modes.
   - Click in the Color Picker window.
   - Move the cursor over the image window to access the Eyedropper tool, then click in the image window and sample a color from the image.

3. **Click the eyedropper cursor in one of the gold areas of the image.**

   We sampled a color in the lower left part of the main African continent.

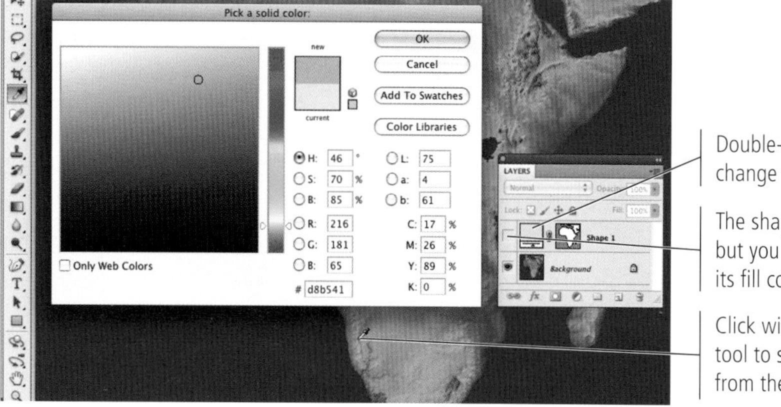

Double-click this icon to change the fill color.

The shape layer is hidden, but you can still modify its fill color.

Click with the Eyedropper tool to sample a color from the existing image.

4. **Click OK to close the Color Picker.**

   The shape layer fill changes as soon as you choose a color in the Color Picker dialog box; however, you can't see this effect while the layer is hidden.

5. Show the shape layer, and change its opacity back to 100%.

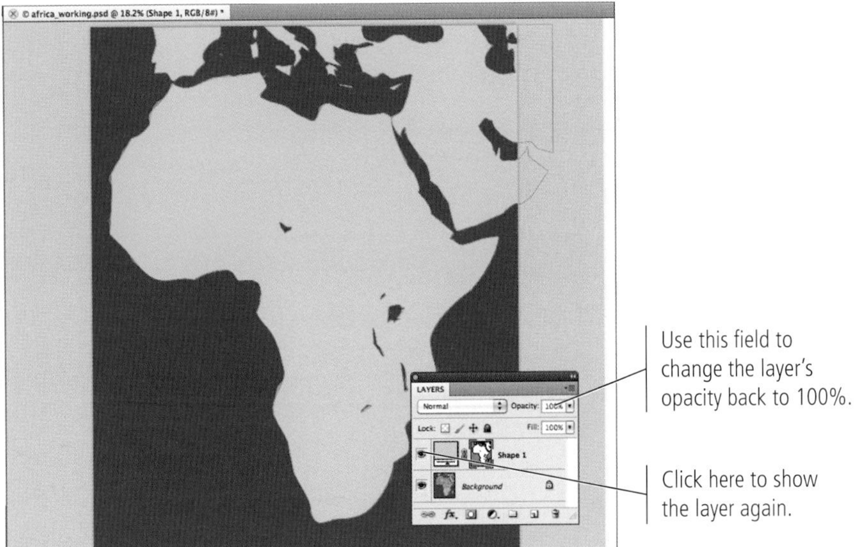

Use this field to change the layer's opacity back to 100%.

Click here to show the layer again.

6. Choose Window>Styles to open the Styles panel.

This panel shows the predefined styles that can be applied to a shape layer. The icons give you an idea of what the styles do, but these small squares can be cryptic.

> *Note:*
>
> *The same style options can also be accessed and applied in the Styles panel that is accessed in the Control panel when the Pen tool is active.*

7. Click the arrow in the top-right corner of the Styles panel and choose Large List from the Options menu.

We prefer the list view because the style names provide a better idea of what the styles do. The Large List option displays a bigger style thumbnail than the Small List view.

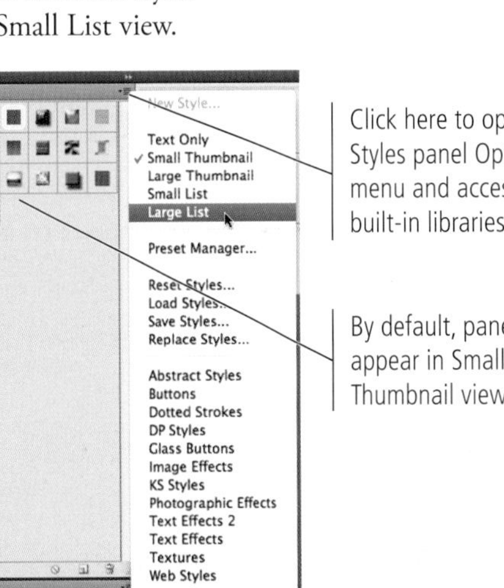

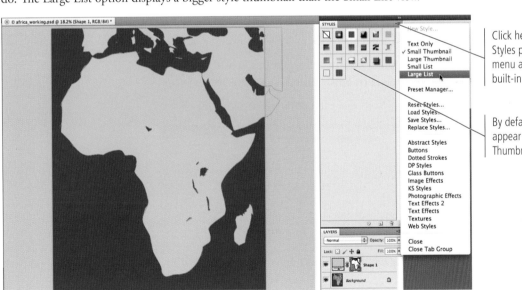

Click here to open the Styles panel Options menu and access the built-in libraries of styles.

By default, panels appear in Small Thumbnail view.

8. **Open the Styles panel Options menu again and choose Textures near the bottom of the list.**

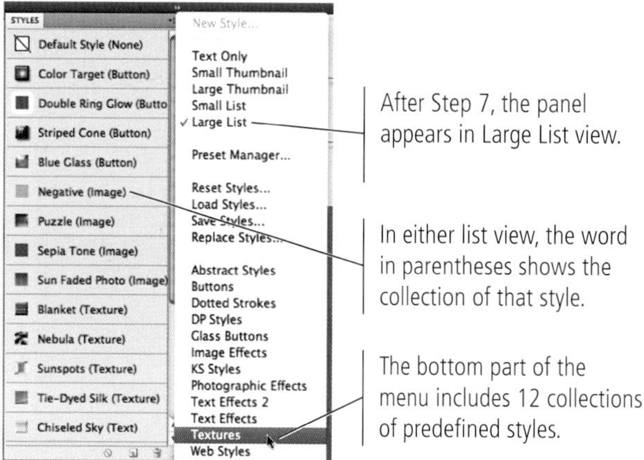

After Step 7, the panel appears in Large List view.

In either list view, the word in parentheses shows the collection of that style.

The bottom part of the menu includes 12 collections of predefined styles.

9. **Click OK to replace the current set with the Textures set.**

When you call a new set of styles, Photoshop asks if you want to replace the current set or append the new set to the existing set(s).

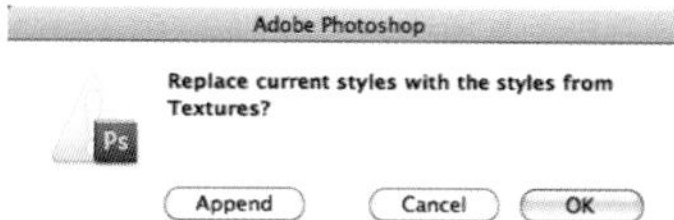

If you select Append, the new styles will be added to the existing ones. This can result in a very long list, which makes it difficult to find what you want. By replacing the current set, you will only see the styles in the texture set. This does not delete the previous styles, it only removes them from the panel; you can recall the previous styles by choosing Reset Styles in the panel Options menu.

10. **Make sure the shape layer is selected in the Layers panel and then click Ancient Stone in the Styles panel to apply the style to the shape layer.**

A **style** is simply a saved group of effects that can be applied with a single click.

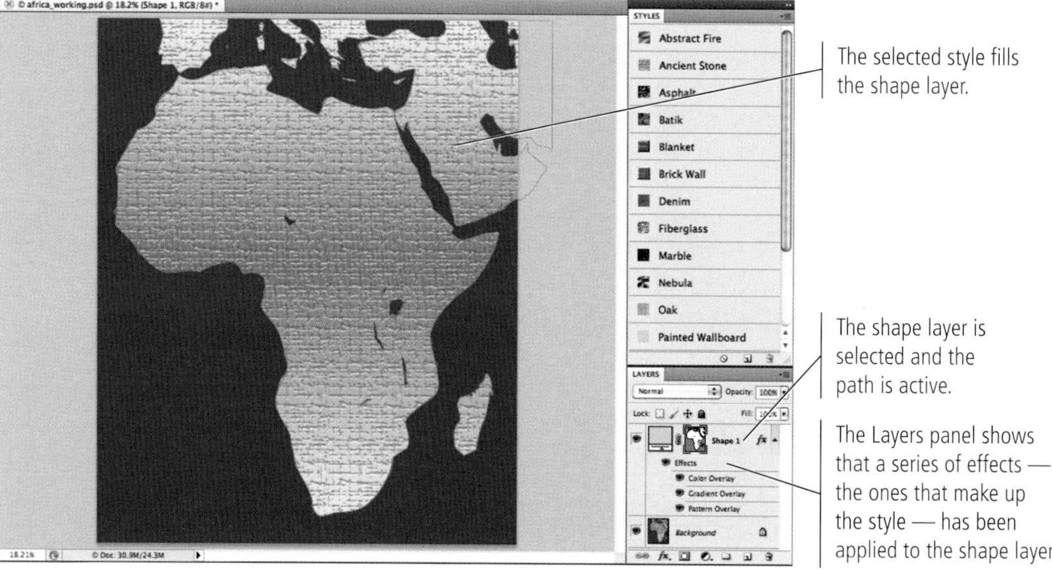

The selected style fills the shape layer.

The shape layer is selected and the path is active.

The Layers panel shows that a series of effects — the ones that make up the style — has been applied to the shape layer.

11. **Save the file and continue to the next stage of the project.**

Stage 2 Compositing with Smart Objects

Your client provided a number of animal pictures that you can use in the finished artwork. In Project 4, you learned several basic methods for compositing files into another file — copying and pasting (or dragging), and placing a file as a Smart Object. Your ultimate goal determines which of these methods is most appropriate for a specific job.

When you apply tranformations or filters to a regular layer, the pixels on the layer are permanently affected (unless you undo the filter or step back through the History panel). Smart Objects are layers that preserve source content, which means you can apply **non-destructive** edits to the layer. Those transformations do not alter the actual image data of a smart object; you can restore the original image content, or make changes to the transformations that you apply, without negatively affecting quality.

Note:

In addition to placing files as Smart Objects, you can also open a file as a Smart Object in the File menu.

Compare Smart Object Layers to Normal Layers

In this stage of the project, you will apply layer masks and filters to the client's animal pictures. However, you don't want to modify the actual photo files, and you need to be able to change the filter settings if the client doesn't like the initial results. In this exercise, you will place two of the animal images as Smart Object layers and paste two of the animal images as regular layers, so we can point out the differences between the two types of layers.

1. **With `africa_working.psd` open, choose File>Place.**

   The File>Place command has the same effect as dragging a thumbnail from the Mini Bridge panel into an open image.

2. **Navigate to `addax.tif` in your `WIP>Africa` folder, click Place, and then press Return/Enter to finalize the placement in the document window.**

3. **Repeat Step 2 to place `lion.tif` into your working file.**

4. **Choose File>Open. Select `giraffe.jpg` and `gorilla.tif` and click Open.**

5. **Use the Arrange Documents panel in the Applications/Menu bar to show all three documents at once within the workspace.**

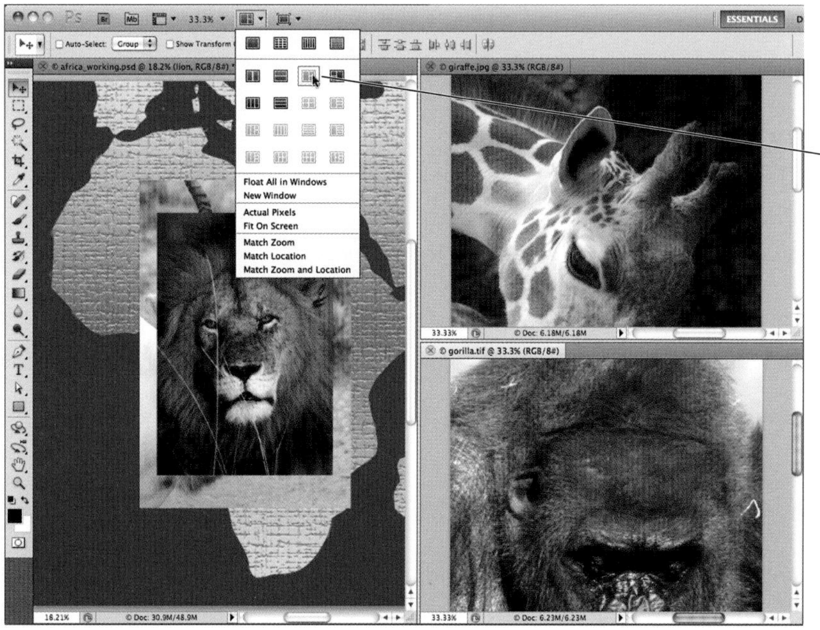

We used the 3-Up arrangement in the Arrange Documents panel.

6. **Choose the Move tool in the Tools panel.**

7. **Click the Giraffe window to activate that file, and then drag the giraffe image into your working map file. Close the giraffe file.**

8. **Repeat Step 7 for the gorilla file.**

9. **Fit the entire working file into the document window, and then review the Layers panel.**

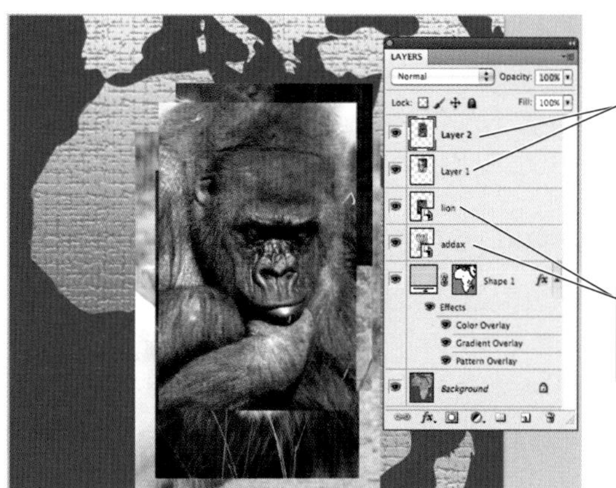

The giraffe layer (Layer 1) and gorilla layer (Layer 2) are regular Photoshop layers. They are not linked to external files.

The lion and addax layers are Smart Object layers; the layer names are defined by the names of the files you placed.

> *Note:*
>
> *In a later exercise, you will explore the different ways in which Photoshop manages masks for regular layers compared to Smart Object layers.*

10. **Rename the two regular layers to reflect which animals reside on those layers.**

    Remember, to rename a layer, simply double-click the layer name in the Layers panel and then type the new name.

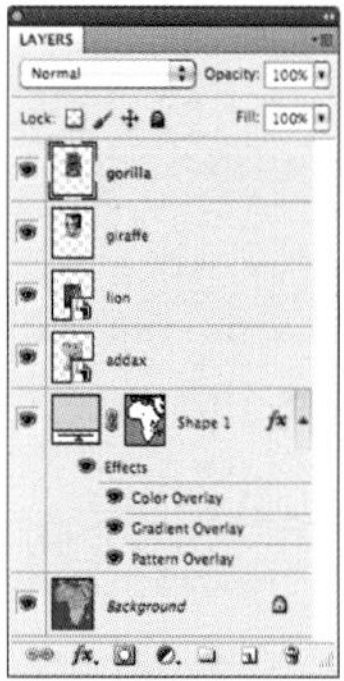

11. **Save the file and continue to the next exercise.**

 Work with Feathered Selections in Quick Mask Mode

In the Interface chapter, we said that making selections is so important that Photoshop has an entire menu dedicated to that task. In Project 4, you learned several methods for creating selections. To complete the map in this project, you will expand on those skills to create soft-edge layer masks that blend the edges of the animal pictures into the background.

1. **With `africa_working.psd` open, hide all the layers except the background and the lion.**

2. **Click the lion layer in the Layers panel to select that layer.**

3. **Choose the Elliptical Marquee tool (nested under the Rectangular Marquee tool) in the Tools panel.**

Understanding Channels

You need a bit of background about channels to understand what's happening in the Quick Mask you're using. (You will use channels extensively in later projects.)

Every image has one channel for each component color. An RGB image has three channels: Red, Green, and Blue; a CMYK image has four channels: Cyan, Magenta, Yellow, and Black. Each channel contains the information for the amount of that component color in any given pixel.

An RGB image has three channels, one for each additive primary.

A CMYK image has four channels, one for each subtractive primary plus one for black.

In RGB images, the three additive primaries can have a value of 0 (none of that color) to 255 (full intensity of that color). Combining a value of 255 for each primary results in white; a value of 0 for each primary results in black.

In CMYK images, the three subtractive primaries plus black are combined in percentages from 0 (none of that color) to 100 (full intensity of that color) to create the range of printable colors. Channels in a CMYK image represent the printing plates or separations required to output the job.

When you work in Quick Mask mode, an extra Alpha channel is created to temporarily store the selection area. An Alpha channel functions like a regular channel, in that it has the same range of possible values (0–255 in an RGB image, 0–100 in a CMYK image). However, the Alpha value determines the degree of transparency of a pixel. In other words, a 50% value in the Alpha channel means that area of the image will be 50% transparent (semi-opaque).

Alpha channels allow you to design with degrees of transparency. You can blend one image into another, blend one layer into another, or blend an entire image into a background in a page-layout application (both Adobe InDesign and QuarkXPress support embedded Alpha channels).

The Quick Mask channel stores the degree of transparency based on the current selection.

The semi-transparent red overlay shows areas being masked (i.e., the areas outside the current selection).

You can change the appearance of masks by double-clicking the Quick Mask button in the Tools panel, or double-clicking the Quick Mask thumbnail in the Channels panel.

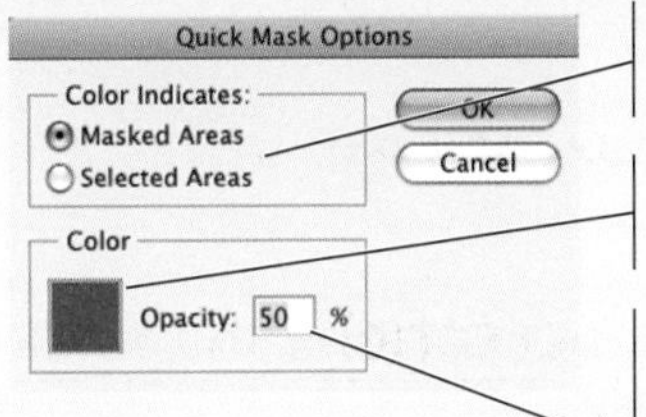

Change the mask to overlay the masked area instead of the selected area.

Click here to change the color of the mask in the image window.

Use this option to make the mask more or less transparent. This setting only affects the appearance of the mask in Photoshop; it doesn't change the transparency values in the actual Alpha channel.

Quick Masks are useful when you need to work with a temporary selection or if you are still defining the exact selection area. As long as you stay in Quick Mask mode, the temporary Alpha channel remains in the Channels panel (listed in italics as "Quick Mask"). If you return to Standard mode, the Quick Mask disappears from the window and the panel.

Once you have created a complex selection, you can save it as a permanent Alpha channel by dragging the Quick Mask channel onto the New Channel button at the bottom of the Channels panel. Doing so adds a channel named "Quick Mask copy" (not in italics), which will be a permanent part of the file even if you exit Quick Mask mode.

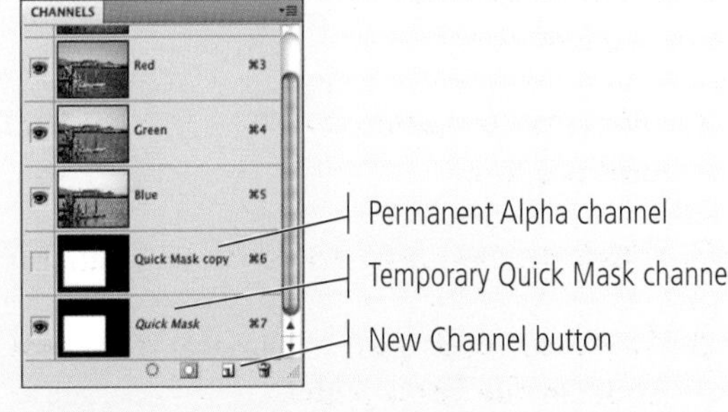

Permanent Alpha channel

Temporary Quick Mask channel

New Channel button

4. **Press Option/Alt, then click the middle of the lion's nose and drag out to create a selection with the center point where you first clicked.**

   Pressing Option/Alt places the center of the selection marquee at the point where you click; when you drag out, the marquee is created around that point.

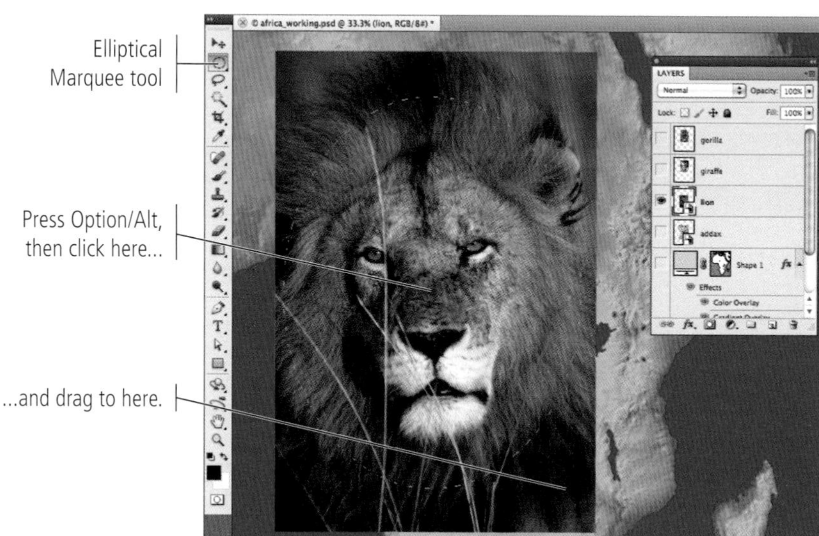

> *Note:*
>
> *If you choose Transform Selection in the Select menu, the selection marquee shows bounding box handles, which you can use to transform the marquee just as you would transform a layer.*

> *Note:*
>
> *When a marquee is visible and the Marquee tool is active, you can click inside the marquee area and drag to reposition the selection area in the image.*

5. **Choose Select>Modify>Feather.**

6. **In the Feather Selection dialog box, type 25 in the Feather Radius field.**

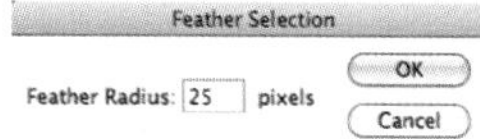

7. **Click OK to return to the image window.**

8. **Click the Quick Mask button at the bottom of the Tools panel to toggle into Quick Mask mode.**

   This mode creates a temporary Alpha channel that shows the feathered selection.

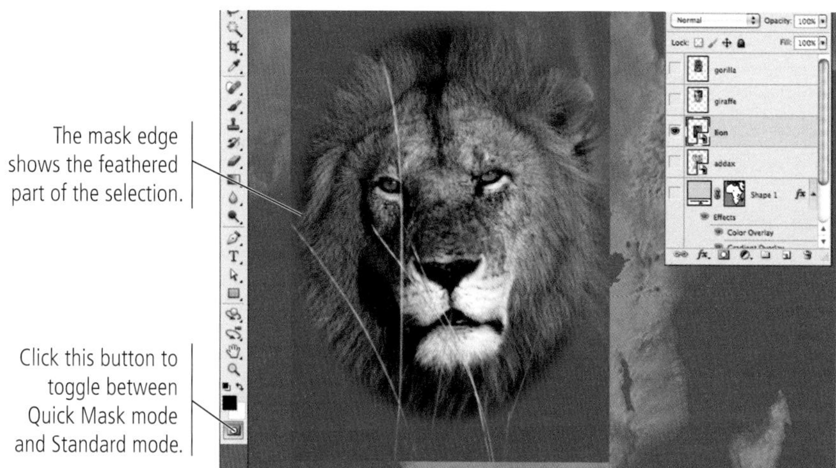

The mask edge shows the feathered part of the selection.
Click this button to toggle between Quick Mask mode and Standard mode.

9. **Click the Quick Mask button at the bottom of the Tools panel to toggle off the Quick Mask.**

   If you don't turn off the Quick Mask mode, Step 10 will create an empty layer mask.

10. **In the Layers panel, click the Add Layer Mask button.**

    A layer mask is basically an Alpha channel connected to a specific layer.

The layer mask is linked to the selected layer.

Add Layer Mask button

The feathered-selection-turned-layer-mask allows the lion image to blend into the background instead of ending abruptly.

> *Note:*
>
> *Alternatively, you could Command/Control-click the Quick Mask in the Channels panel to show the marching ants, and then click the Add Layer Mask button in the Layers panel.*

11. **Hide the lion layer and show the gorilla layer. Click the gorilla layer in the Layers panel to make that the active layer.**

12. **Use the same basic technique from Steps 4–10 to create a feathered mask around the gorilla's face.**

    Even though one of these layers is a Smart Object and one is a regular layer, the technique and the result are basically the same. Both layers show the appropriate layer mask in the Layers panel.

> *Note:*
>
> *When a masked layer is selected in the Layers panel, the layer mask appears in the Channels panel as a temporary Alpha channel.*

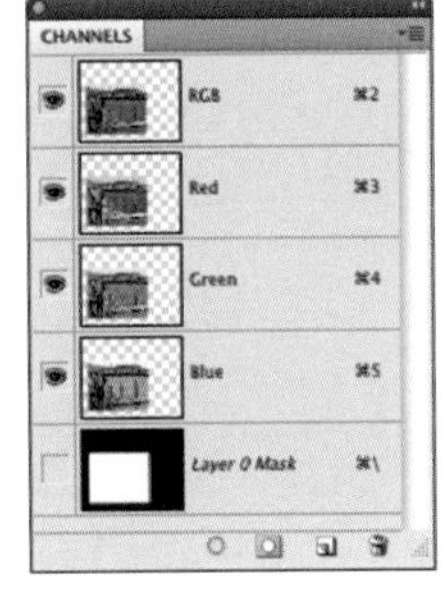

13. **Hide the gorilla layer, save the file, and continue to the next exercise.**

Apply a Layer Mask to a Smart Object Layer

In the previous exercise, you created a feathered layer mask for a Smart Object layer; you added the layer mask within the main africa_working Layers panel, so the layer mask did not affect the original file. Depending on the project you're building, you might want to create a layer mask once and have it affect all instances of that Smart Object. In this case, you should edit the actual Smart Object file instead of affecting only a single placed instance.

1. **In africa_working.psd, show only the addax layer.**

Double-click this icon to open the Smart Object file.

2. **Double-click the layer thumbnail to open the Smart Object file in its own window. If you see a warning message, click OK.**

   This message tells you that you must save the Smart Object with the same name for the changes to reflect in the africa_working file. You can't use the Save As function to save the file with a different name or in a different location.

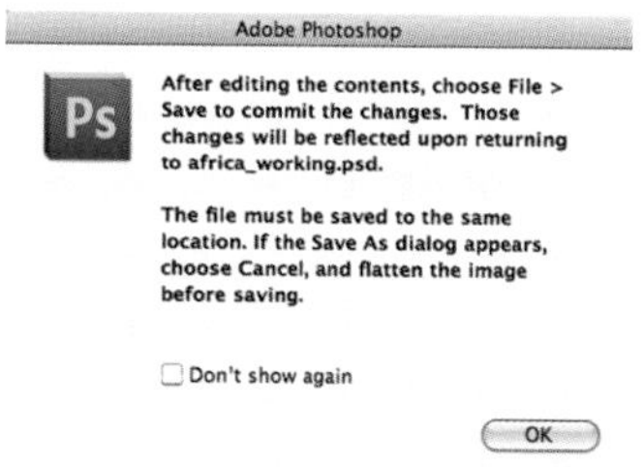

   The addax file opens separately, appearing by default as a separate tab at the top of the document window.

3. **Using the Rectangular Marquee tool, drag a selection around the addax's head, and then feather the selection by 25 pixels.**

   In the Layers panel, the Add Layer Mask option is not available because the file has only one layer — Background. You can't apply a layer mask to the Background layer of a file.

> *Note:*
>
> *If you don't see this message, you can open the General pane of the Preferences dialog box and click the Reset All Warning Dialogs button.*

4. **In the Layers panel, double-click the Background layer to see your options.**

   The addax image is a flat image, which means it has only a Background layer that is locked. You can't apply a layer mask to the locked Background layer, so you first have to convert the Background layer to a regular layer.

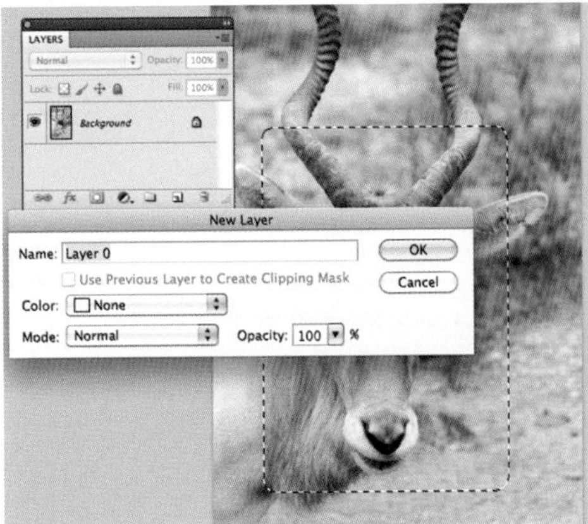

5. **In the New Layer dialog box, leave the options at their default values and click OK.**

   The former Background layer is now a regular unlocked layer named Layer 0. You could have renamed it, but that is unnecessary for this exercise.

6. **With the feathered selection still active, click the Add Layer Mask button at the bottom of the Layers panel.**

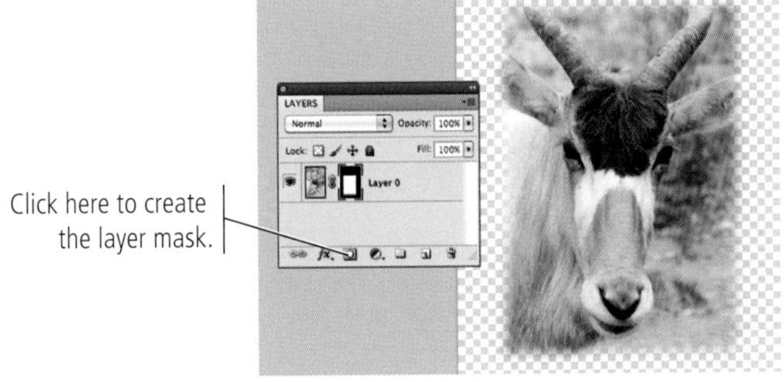

7. **Choose File>Save (or press Command/Control-S).**

   The TIFF Options dialog box appears because your file now has new layer information. Even though the file has only one layer, that layer is partially transparent.

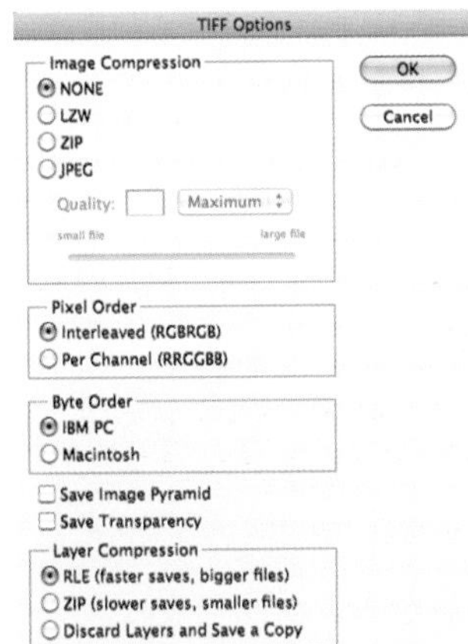

Note:

This technique wouldn't work if you placed a JPEG file as a Smart Object. To save a JPEG file with layer information, you must save the file as a copy — and you would see a related warning if you tried to do so. Saving as a copy means saving under a different file name, which would defeat the purpose and function of Smart Objects.

8. **Leave the TIFF options at their default values and click OK. If you see a warning about including layers, click OK again.**

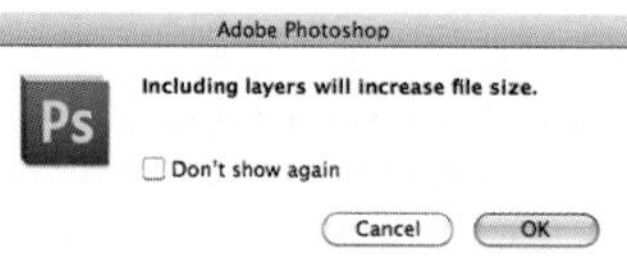

9. **Close the addax.tif file.**

   When you look at the africa_working file, you can see that the layer mask has been applied to the addax image, but the Layers panel doesn't show the layer mask thumbnail. That's because the mask is applied in the Smart Object, not in the main file.

The addax layer has no applied layer mask; the mask exists only in the Smart Object file.

10. **Save the file, clicking OK to the warning about maximizing layer compatibility. Continue to the next exercise.**

Edit a Layer Mask

Creating a layer mask from a selection is easy enough, and it's sometimes sufficient for a particular job (as was the case for the lion). But in other cases, you may want to create a mask that is beyond what you can easily accomplish with the basic selection tools. If necessary, you can paint directly on a layer mask to achieve virtually any effect — such as a mask that better outlines the addax in the map you're building.

1. **With `africa_working.psd` open, double-click the addax layer thumbnail to open the Smart Object file.**

2. **In the Layers panel, click the layer mask thumbnail to select it.**

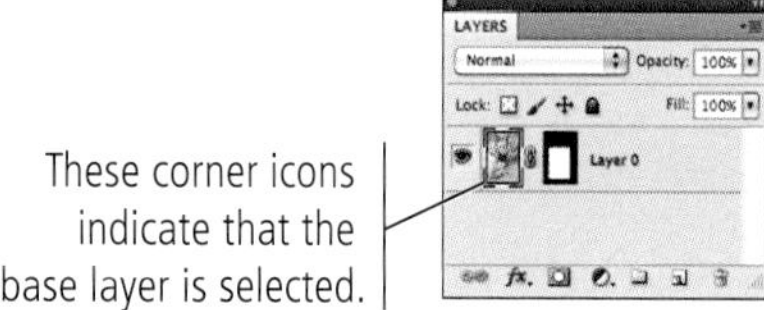

These corner icons indicate that the base layer is selected.

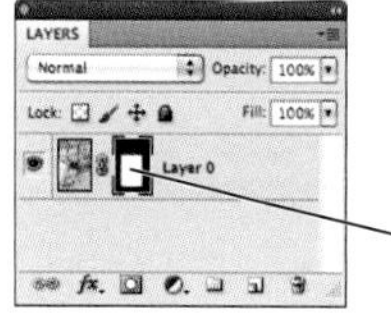

Clicking the layer mask thumbnail selects the mask so you can edit it.

3. **In the Channels panel (Window>Channel), make sure the Layer 0 Mask channel is visible.**

   Layer masks are not visible by default; you have to turn them on in the Channels panel to see them. This isn't strictly necessary, since you can paint a mask without seeing it, but we find it easier (at least when you're first learning) to be able to see what you're painting. By painting on a layer mask, you're not really "painting" anything; instead, you're actually "painting" the visibility of the associated layer.

Making the mask channel visible allows you to see the red overlay in the image.

4. **Double-click the Layer 0 Mask channel thumbnail, and then change the Opacity value to 100% in the Layer Mask Display Options dialog box.**

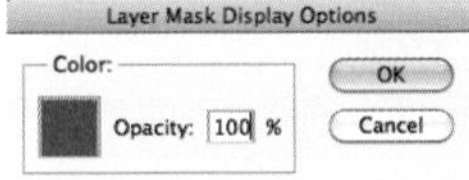

5. **Click OK to return to the image window.**

   Remember, this change only affects the transparency of the mask, not the degree of transparency applied to the layer. By setting the mask opacity to 100%, you know that anything solid red will be hidden and anything with no red will be visible.

6. **Choose the Brush tool in the Tools panel, and then click the Default Foreground and Background Colors button at the bottom of the Tools panel.**

   If you look at the layer mask thumbnail for the layer, you can see it's just a black-and-white shape. White areas of the thumbnail show which parts of the layer are visible in the main document; the black parts of the mask hide the associated areas of the layer. This is an important distinction: painting with black on a layer mask hides those areas; painting with white on a layer mask reveals those areas.

Note:

Painting with black on a layer mask hides those areas; painting with white on a layer mask reveals those areas.

Brush tool

Click here to return the foreground to black and the background to white.

7. **In the Control panel, open the Brush Preset picker to access the tool options.**

   This panel shows the different brushes that are included with Photoshop. The default brush set includes a number of specific-diameter hard- and soft-edge brushes, as well as some artistic options. A number below a brush icon shows the size of the brush; if you click a specific brush in the panel, the same number displays in the Size field.

8. **Change the Size value to 200 px and the Hardness value to 0%.**

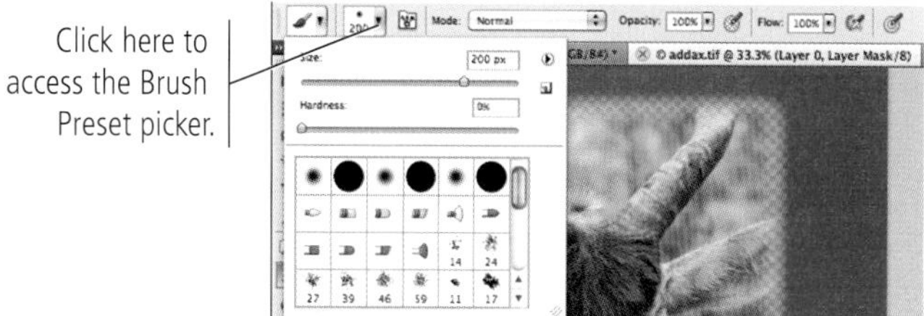

9. **Click once between the addax's horns.**

   The Brush tool paints with whatever is defined as the foreground color, which is black in this case. Because you're using a soft-edge brush, the place where you click blends from solid black to nothing — resulting in a soft edge to the brush stroke (or dot in this case).

Even though you're painting with black, the stroke appears as red because that's the defined mask color.

10. **Using the brush, click and drag to paint the entire area between the horns and to the right of the animal's head.**

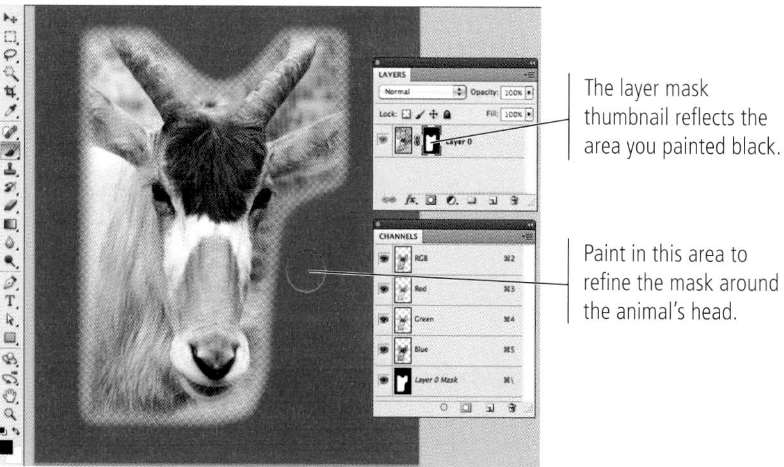

The layer mask thumbnail reflects the area you painted black.
Paint in this area to refine the mask around the animal's head.

11. **Click the Switch Foreground and Background Colors button near the bottom of the Tools panel.**

12. **Paint over the area where the tip of the left ear should be.**

    Because you're now painting with white, you're basically removing area from the mask. You can also use the Eraser tool on a mask. Be careful, though, because erasing an area of the mask when the foreground color is white has the same effect as painting with black — "erasing" on the mask actually adds to the mask.

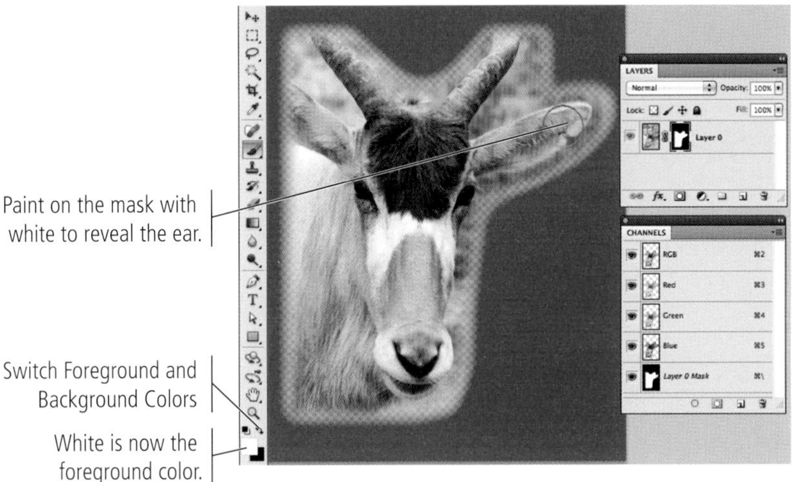

13. **Continue refining the mask to make both horns and ears visible, until you're satisfied with the result.**

    You should have no hard edges around the outside of the image.

14. **Save the addax file and close it.**

    Remember, you're working in a Smart Object file, so don't choose Save As or save the file with a different name. Once the process has updated, the Smart Object layer in the africa_working file shows the results of the refined layer mask.

15. **Save the map file and continue to the next exercise.**

Note:

You can change the Brush tool cursor in the Cursors pane of the Preferences dialog box. Standard shows only the tool icon; Precise shows a crosshair icon; Normal shows the solid-area brush size; Full Size expands the normal brush to include the feathered area. You can also choose to show a crosshair icon in the center of the brush area.

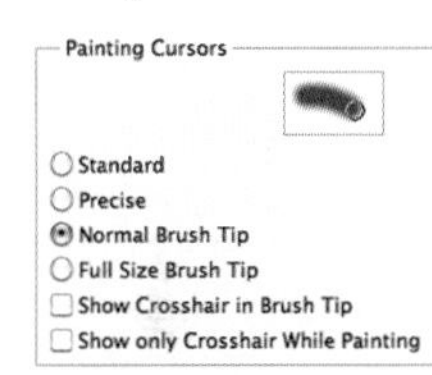

Note:

You can create a layer mask from scratch by adding the mask with nothing selected, and then painting and erasing as necessary to mask the areas you want to hide. You can even use a black-to-white gradient on a layer mask to create unique effects in a non-specific shape.

Accessing Brush Libraries

In the first part of this project, you learned how to access additional sets of built-in styles. You can use the same basic technique to access any of the built-in brush libraries from the Brush Preset panel Options menu. If you call a brush library from the menu, you have the choice of appending the brushes to the current set or replacing the current set with the new library (just as you do with built-in style libraries).

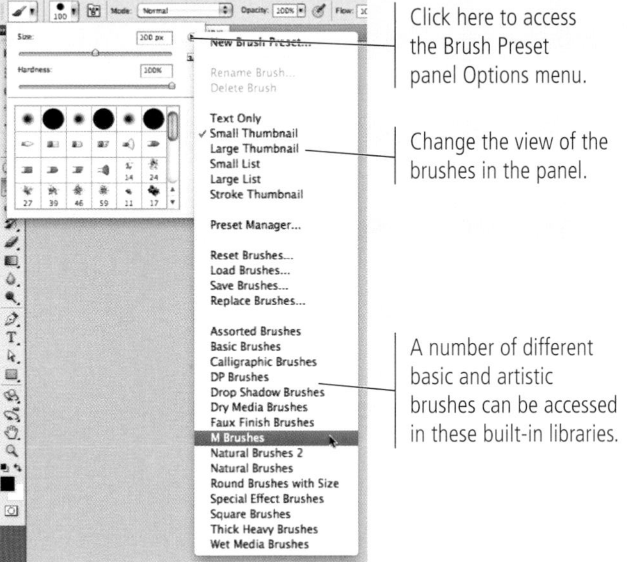

Use the Masks Panel

In the previous exercises, you learned how to create a feathered selection and a layer mask based on that selection. You also learned how to use black and white to paint directly on a layer mask. These same techniques work for both normal layers and Smart Object layers. The Masks panel provides another option for creating and managing layer masks. This panel consolidates mask-related options from multiple locations in a single, convenient interface.

1. **With africa_working.psd open, hide the addax layer and show the giraffe layer. Click the giraffe layer to select it.**

2. **Choose the Lasso tool in the Tools panel. Drag to create a selection roughly matching the shape of the giraffe's head.**

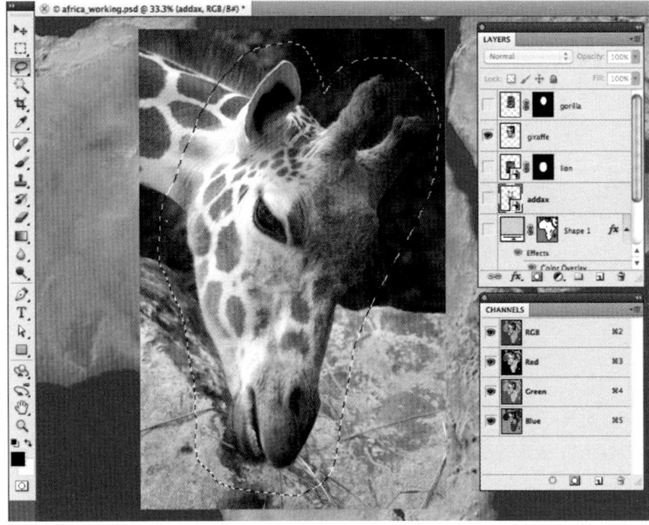

3. **Open the Masks panel (Window>Masks), and then click the Add a Pixel Mask button.**

Clicking this button in the Masks panel is basically the same as clicking the Add Layer Mask button in the Layers panel. The active selection automatically becomes a mask for the selected layer.

> *Note:*
>
> ***Pixel mask** is simply another term for a raster-based layer mask.*

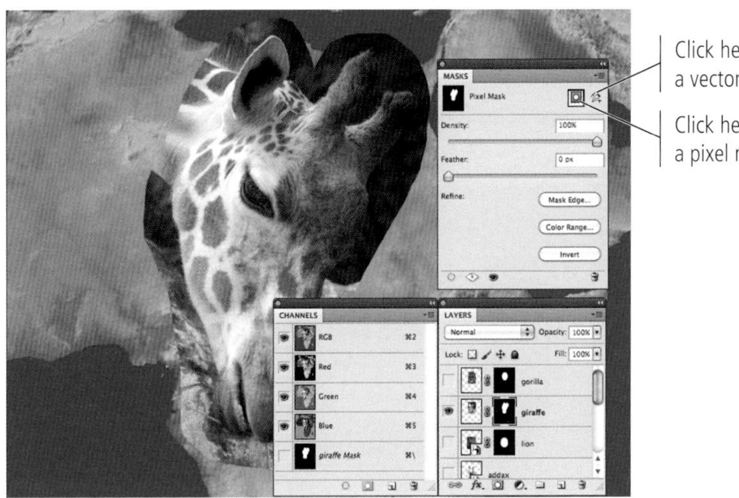
Click here to add a vector mask.
Click here to add a pixel mask.

4. **In the Masks panel, drag the Feather slider until the field shows 25 px.**

When you feather a selection and then make a layer mask from that selection, the feathering becomes a permanent part of the mask (unless you manually paint the mask to remove the feathering).

The Masks panel allows you to adjust the feathering of a hard-edge mask, and then later change or even remove the feathering if necessary, without painting on the mask.

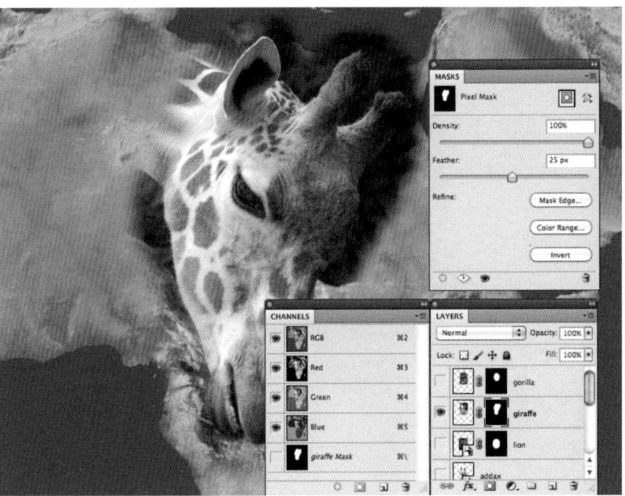

5. **Choose the Brush tool from the Tools panel.**

6. **In the Control panel, open the Brush Preset picker. At the top of the panel, use the slider to change the Size to 100 px, and set the Hardness to 100%.**

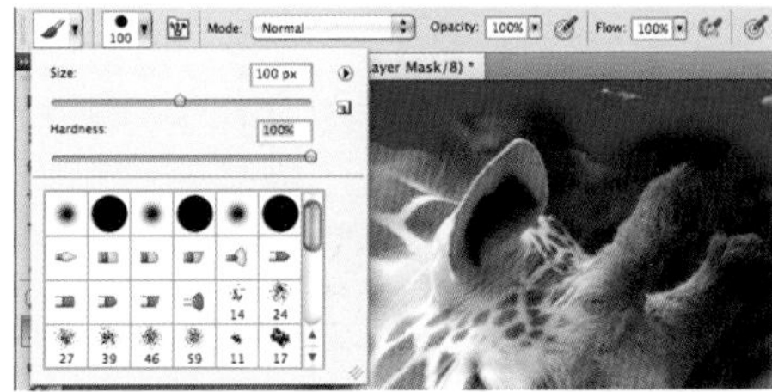

7. **In the Layers panel, click the giraffe layer mask thumbnail to select the layer mask instead of the actual layer.**

8. **Choose black as the foreground color and paint around the edges of the giraffe's horns.**

   The mask should closely follow the shape of the horns. If you paint over part of a horn (or anything else you want to keep), simply change the foreground color to white and paint to remove that area from the mask.

   Although you are painting with a hard-edge brush, the result is a soft edge because the mask is feathered in the Masks panel.

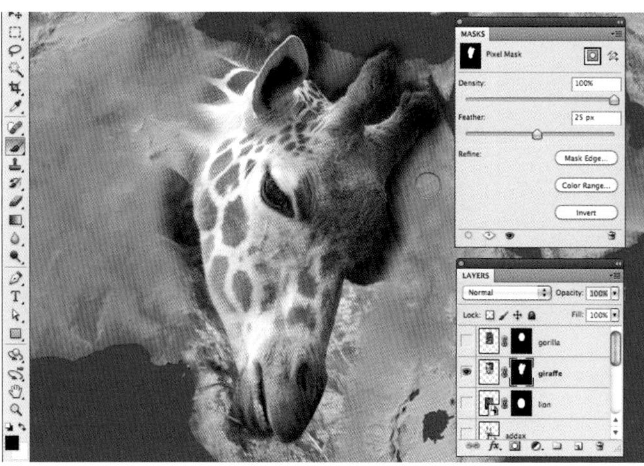

Note:

Press X to switch the current foreground and background colors. This is very useful to remember when you are painting on a mask, because you can reset the default (black and white) colors and switch them as necessary depending on what you want to accomplish.

Note:

You can use the bracket keys to enlarge (]) or reduce ([) the brush size.

Vector Masks vs. Pixel Masks

PHOTOSHOP FOUNDATIONS

Clicking the **Add a Vector Mask** button creates a vector-based mask from the active path (either the current work path or a saved path that is selected in the Paths panel).

You can use the Masks panel to feather the mask edges and adjust the density, but the Refine options are not available for a vector mask; refining a vector mask is performed using the Path Selection tool, Direct Selection tool, and Pen tool.

The Layers panel shows the vector mask thumbnail, and the Paths panel shows a vector mask path that is only visible in the panel when the layer is selected. Nothing is added to the Channels panel because channels are only raster-based.

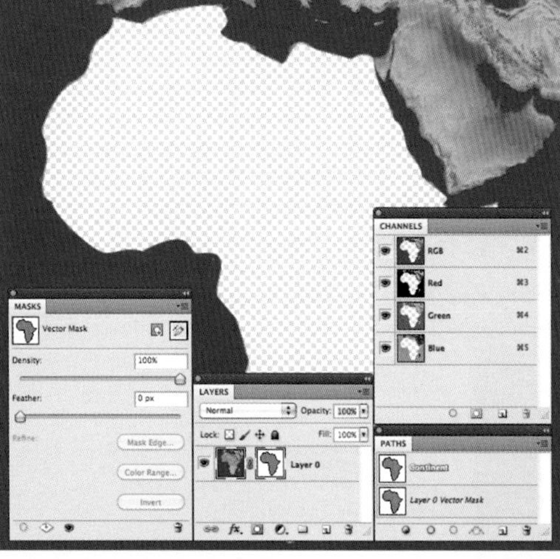

Clicking the **Add a Pixel Mask** button adds a pixel-based mask in the shape of the current selection. This requires the marching-ants selection, and not an active path.

For a pixel-based mask, you can refine the mask edges using the Mask Edge and Color Range buttons. Clicking the Invert button swaps the black-to-white value of pixels in the mask, reversing the visible areas of the masked layer.

A pixel mask is added to the active layer and to the Channels panel, but nothing is added to the Paths panel.

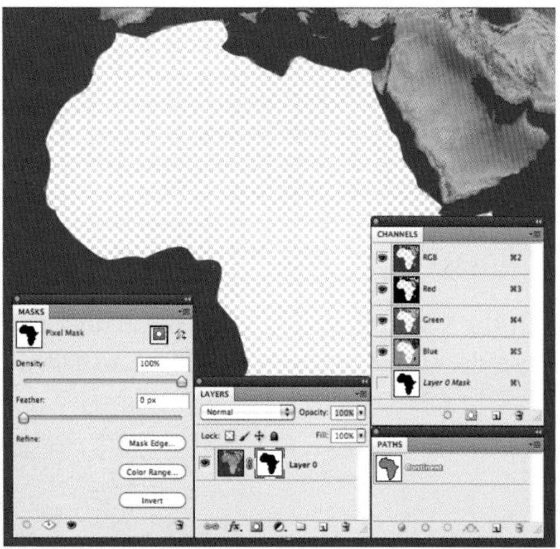

9. **In the Masks panel, change the Feather value to 0 px.**

   Remember, you were painting with a hard-edge brush, so the edges where you painted have a hard edge. Because the Masks panel allows you to change the Feather value, you can easily turn feathering on or off to monitor your progress.

10. **Change the Feather value back to 25 px.**

11. **Save the file and continue to the next exercise.**

Convert Regular Layers to Smart Objects

Your file currently has two layers that you simply copied into the map file. You need to change these layers to Smart Objects before you apply filters. You can convert a regular layer to a Smart Object layer (or vice versa) easily, but it is important to know what to expect before you start converting in either direction.

1. **With africa_working.psd open, Control/right-click the giraffe layer name in the Layers panel.**

   When you Control/right-click a layer name, you see a contextual menu of options that are specific to the selected layer. Different options are available when you Control/right-click the layer thumbnail icons.

2. **Choose Convert to Smart Object in the menu.**

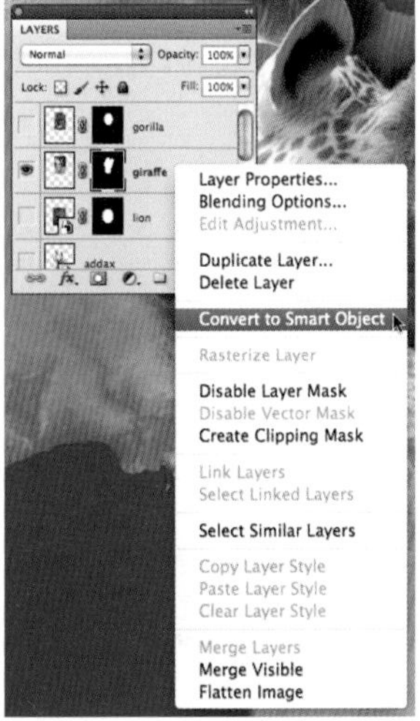

Remember, you copied the giraffe image into the map file, so it was not originally placed as a Smart Object.

Depending on the size of the file and the speed of your computer, this conversion might take a while; a Progress bar might show the Merging Layers message.

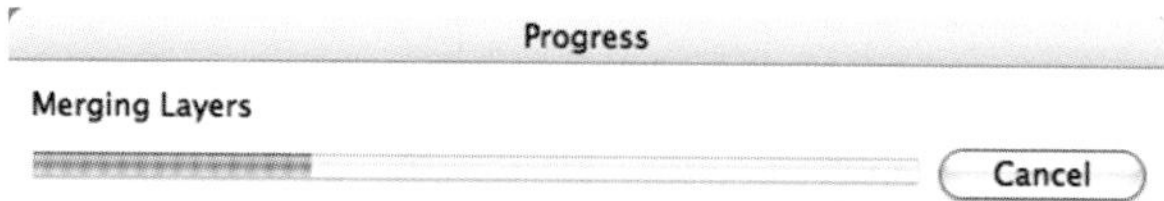

When the process is complete, the Layers panel shows that the giraffe layer is now a Smart Object.

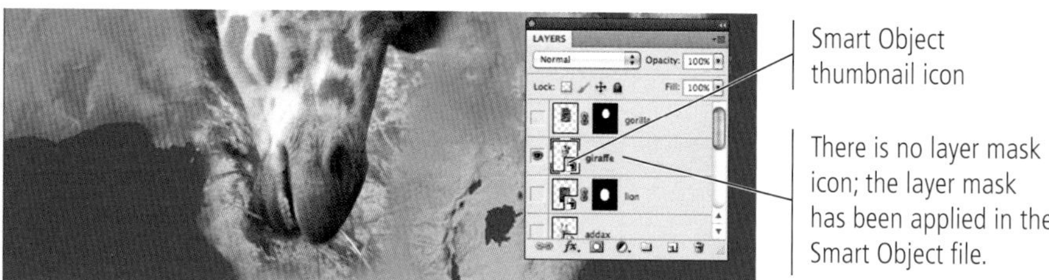

Smart Object thumbnail icon

There is no layer mask icon; the layer mask has been applied in the Smart Object file.

3. **Double-click the giraffe Smart Object thumbnail to open the file; click OK if you see a warning message.**

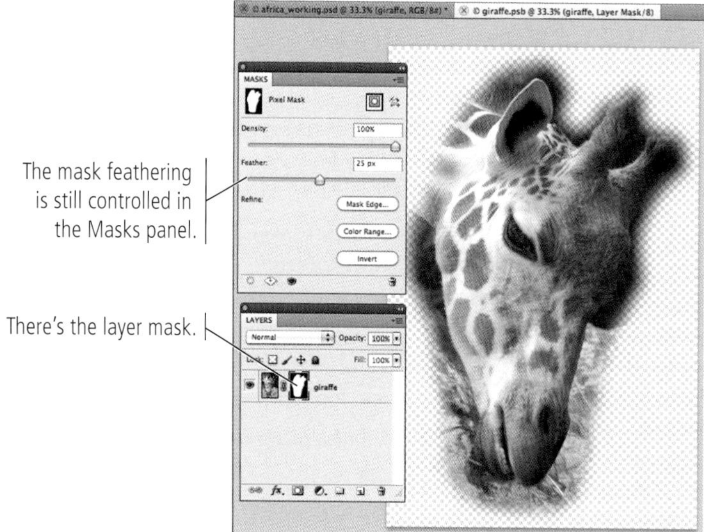

The mask feathering is still controlled in the Masks panel.

There's the layer mask.

4. **Close the giraffe file.**

5. **In the map file, repeat this process to convert the gorilla layer to a Smart Object.**

   You now have four Smart Objects, each with a layer mask. However, one of the layer masks (for the lion) is applied within the map file instead of within the Smart Object file. For the sake of uniformity (and to show you how to do it), you're going to move that layer mask into the Smart Object file.

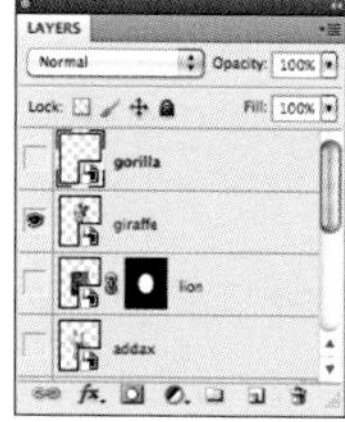

6. **Look closely at the thumbnail of the gorilla layer.**

   You might notice that nothing is visible in the thumbnail. That's because the layer was hidden when you converted it to a Smart Object.

7. **Double-click the gorilla layer thumbnail to open that file.**

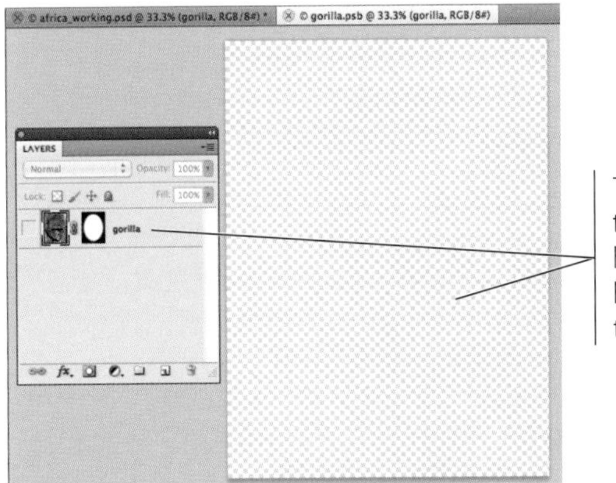

The masked gorilla layer is there, but the layer is hidden because it was hidden when you created the Smart Object in Step 5.

8. **Show the gorilla layer, save the gorilla file, and then close it.**

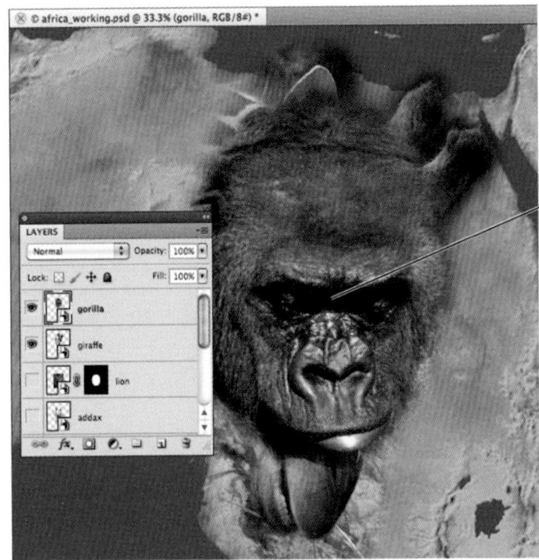

In the main file, the gorilla is now visible because that Smart Object layer is visible and the appropriate layer is now visible within the Smart Object file.

9. **Show the lion layer. Control/right-click the lion layer and choose Convert to Smart Object from the contextual menu.**

   Although the layer is already a Smart Object, you must complete this step to move the existing layer mask from the map file into the Smart Object file.

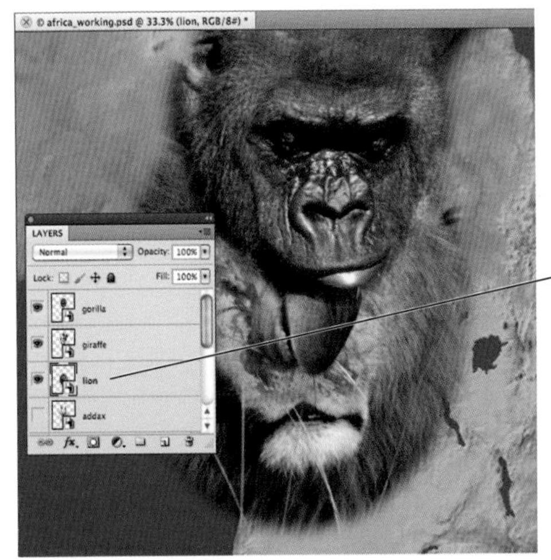

By converting the layer to a Smart Object, the layer mask is removed from the map file layer and placed inside the Smart Object file.

10. **Double-click the lion Smart Object thumbnail to open that file.**

    The file contains the original Smart Object, as well as the layer mask you created. The more Smart Objects you have (including nested ones), the larger your file size. To avoid unnecessary bloating, you can eliminate the nested Smart Object.

11. **In the Layers panel, Control/right-click the area to the right of the layer name for the lion layer. Choose Rasterize Layer from the contextual menu.**

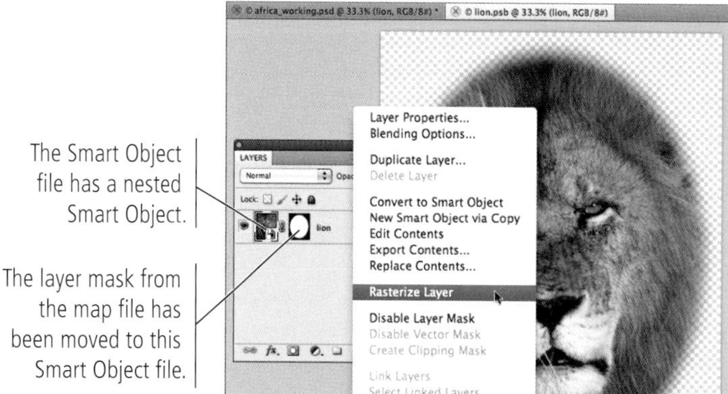

    Rasterizing the Smart Object basically removes the link to any external file, making the Smart Object a part of the file in which it has been placed.

12. **Save the lion file and close it.**

    Other than the missing layer mask thumbnail, there is no apparent change in the map. By completing the last few steps, you reduced the complexity of the file you're building — a good thing since you're going to add more layers later.

13. **Save the map file and continue to the next exercise.**

Rasterizing Smart Objects with Masks

PHOTOSHOP FOUNDATIONS

If a Smart Object file has a layer mask, and you rasterize that Smart Object, the layer mask in the Smart Object will be applied before the file becomes a part of the master file.

In the image to the right, the gorilla Smart Object had a layer mask in the placed file before the Smart Object was rasterized. Rasterizing the gorilla layer converts the Smart Object layer to a regular layer, but the layer mask from the placed file is no longer available or editable.

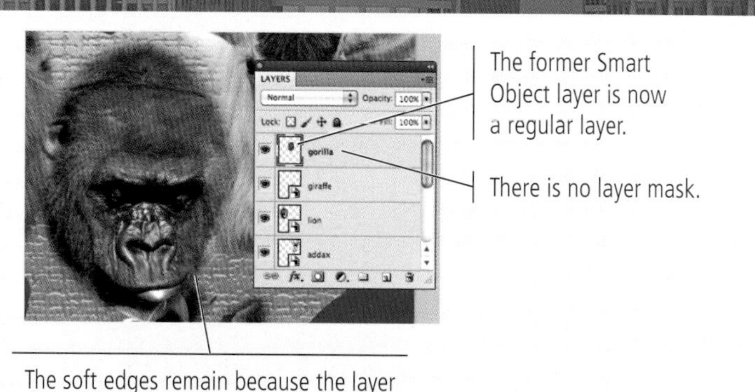

The former Smart Object layer is now a regular layer.
There is no layer mask.

The soft edges remain because the layer mask was applied to the placed file before it was rasterized into a regular layer.

Create a Clipping Mask

You now have four masked animals and the shape of the map, but your client wants the animal pictures to appear *inside* the map shape. You can accomplish this task by using the map shape as a clipping mask. It's relatively easy to create a clipping mask from any layer. As with Smart Objects, however, you should know what to expect when you create a clipping mask. Specifically, you should understand how the different layers will behave and interact with one another.

1. **With africa_working.psd open, make all layers visible.**

2. **Using the Move tool, drag the giraffe to fill the bottom portion of the African continent. Move the lion layer into the top-left area, move the addax so its ear extends into the middle east, and move the gorilla into the space between the lion and the addax.**

Note:

Remember, if the Auto-Select option is checked in the Control panel, you can simply click pixels of the layer you want to move without first selecting the layer.

3. **Control/right-click the gorilla layer and choose Create Clipping Mask from the contextual menu.**

   A clipping mask is another way to show only certain areas of a layer; in this case, using the shape of one layer (giraffe) to show parts of the layer above it (gorilla). Because very little area of the gorilla layer is inside the area of the giraffe layer, most of the gorilla is now hidden.

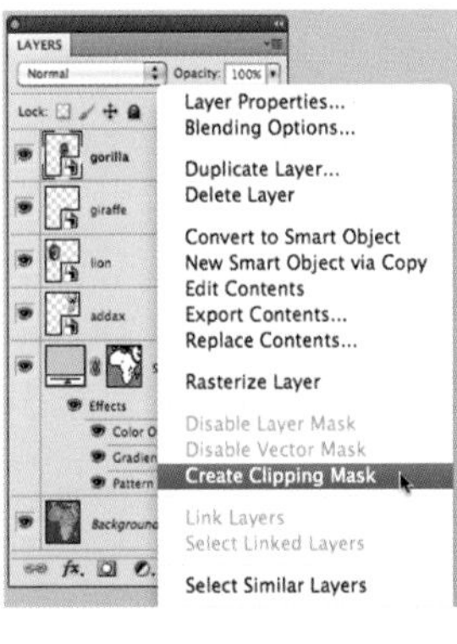

The only visible area is where the gorilla overlaps the giraffe.

The gorilla layer is indented and linked to the giraffe layer.

   Your goal is to put the animals inside the map shape, not inside the shapes of the other animals, so this isn't what you want.

4. **Control/right-click the gorilla layer and choose Release Clipping Mask from the contextual menu.**

   As with layer masks, clipping masks do not permanently modify the pixels in the layer, so you can always hide or remove clipping masks without damaging the masked images.

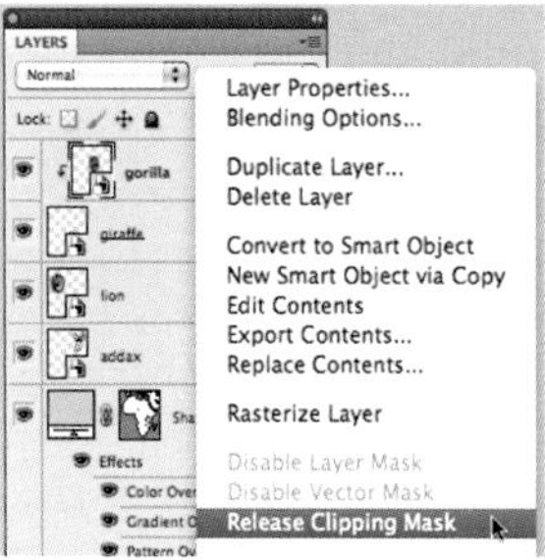

> *Note:*
>
> *Remember, to access the contextual menu for a specific layer, you have to Control/right-click in the area to the right of the layer name.*

5. **Shift-click to select all four animal layers. Control/right-click any of the selected layers and choose Create Clipping Mask from the contextual menu.**

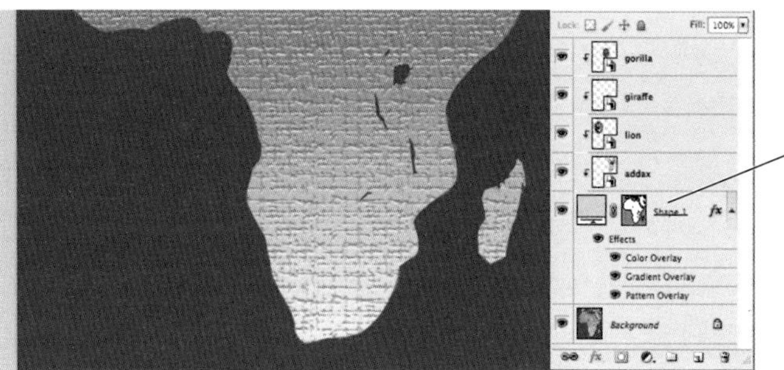

When multiple layers are selected, all the selected layers are clipped by the next-lowest layer.

This highlights a problem that occurs when working with a shape layer filled with a pattern (this shape layer is filled with the Ancient Stone pattern/style). This style includes overlays, which technically overlay the animal layers you placed inside the clipping mask. In other words, the pattern overlay completely obscures the animal layers.

If you don't need or want to maintain the layer style, you can simply clear the layer style using the layer's contextual menu. In this case, however, you want to keep the style but prevent it from overlaying the clipped animal images, so you need to use a different technique.

6. **Click the Shape 1 layer in the Layers panel to select it, and then choose Layer>Layer Style>Create Layers.**

   This command converts each applied effect to a separate layer, all of which are clipped by the original shape layer; only the area within the shape layer is visible.

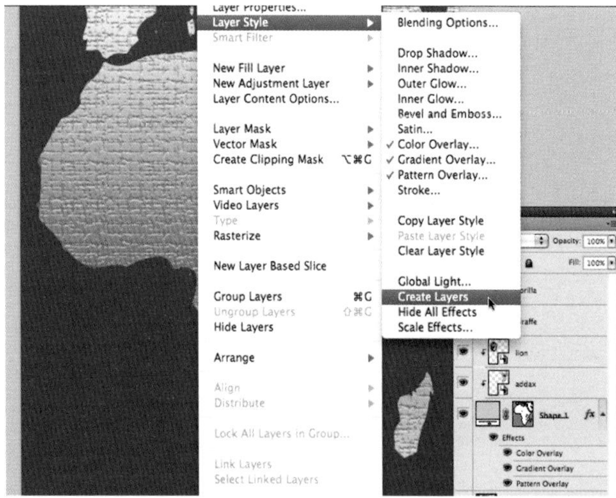

7. **When you see a warning that some effects cannot be reproduced with layers, click OK.**

   This warning is very common, but we prefer to let the conversion happen and review the results before we make a final design decision. If you're not satisfied with the result, you can always undo the conversion and try again.

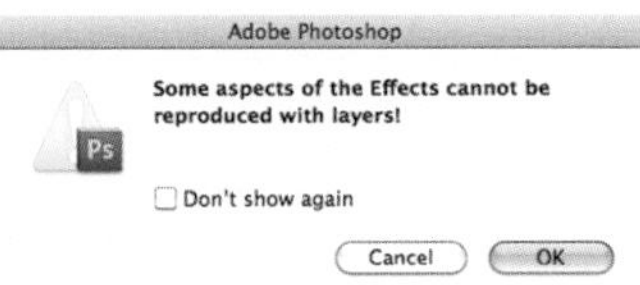

8. **Review the image and the Layers panel.**

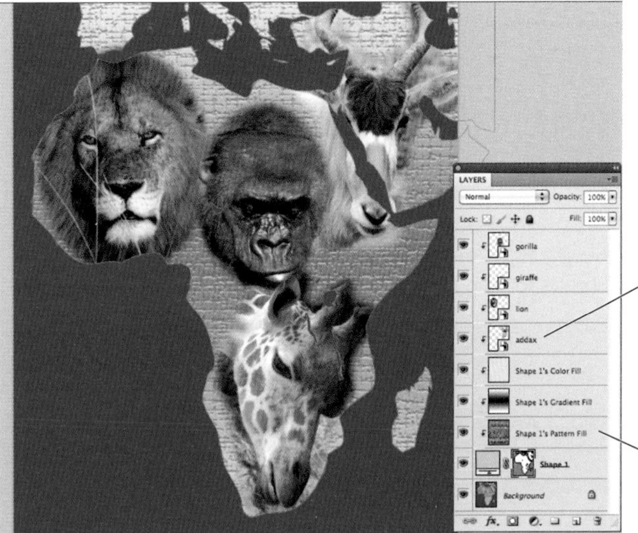

The animals are still clipped by the shape layer, and they are higher than the fill layers created from the effects.

The effects layers are now individual layers, which are also clipped by the shape layer.

> *Note:*
>
> *Now that you can see how the animals appear within the continent shape, it's easier to see where changes might be necessary.*

9. **Use the Move tool to reposition the animal layers as necessary to fill the continent as much as possible. Our solution is shown here.**

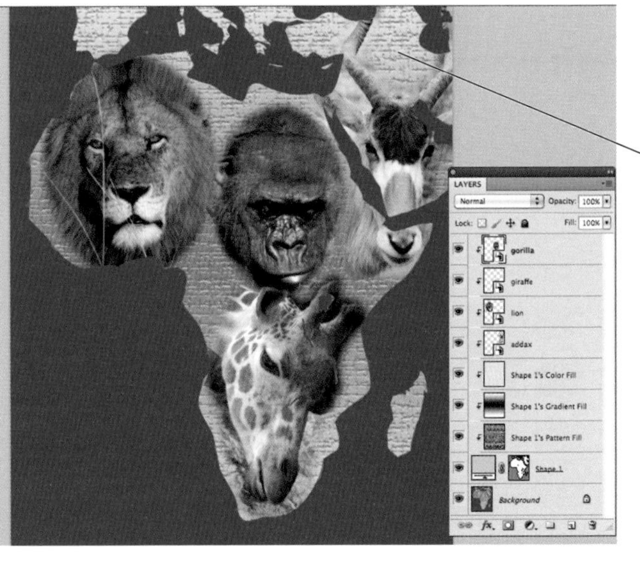

It's okay if some areas aren't filled; that's why you applied the pattern style to the shape layer — to add texture in areas that aren't covered by animal images.

> *Note:*
>
> *The client supplied several other animal photos (in the WIP> Africa folder). Feel free to add more animals to your artwork if you want to experiment further with masking techniques.*

10. **Save the file and continue to the next stage of the project.**

Stage 3 Using Filters and Adjustments

Your client originally wanted a traditional painter to create this job, but decided instead on a digital version to save time and money. The advantage of using Photoshop is that you can easily create an art-like version of existing files using the built-in filters. You can make images look like pencil sketches, paintings, or any of dozens of other options. You can even compound multiple filters to create unique effects that would require extreme skill in traditional art techniques such as oil painting.

Apply Non-Destructive Filters to Smart Objects

Because the animals are placed into the map file as Smart Objects, any filters that you choose to apply do not affect the placed file data. In other words, they are non-destructive. This means you can later change the filter settings, add additional filters, or even delete a filter effect without damaging the placed file.

1. **With `africa_working.psd` open, select the giraffe layer in the Layers panel.**

2. **Choose Filter>Artistic and review the options.**

   Photoshop ships with more than 100 filters divided into 13 categories; some of these are functional while others are purely decorative. You will use some of the art filters in this project and experiment with some of the functional filters in later projects.

Note:

Filters apply to the selected layer, not to the entire file.

Note:

You can choose Filter>Filter Gallery to open the Filter Gallery showing the last-used settings.

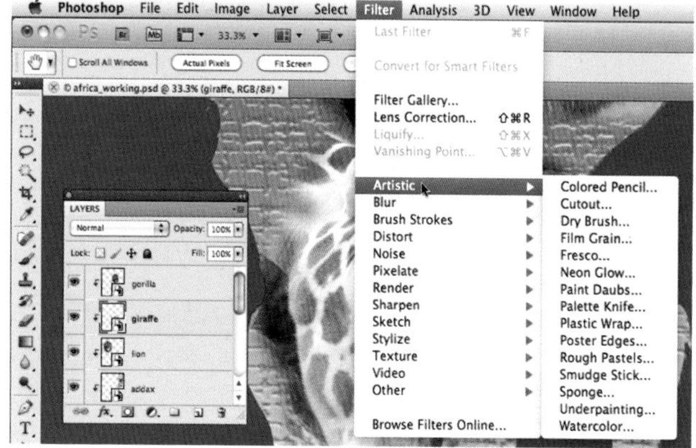

3. **Choose Dry Brush in the Artistic submenu.**

   The "Art" filters are controlled in a separate dialog box called the Filter Gallery. This gallery opens when you choose one of the Artistic, Brush Strokes, Distort, Sketch, Stylize, or Texture filters in the menu.

Note:

You might want to zoom in to get a better idea of the filtering results.

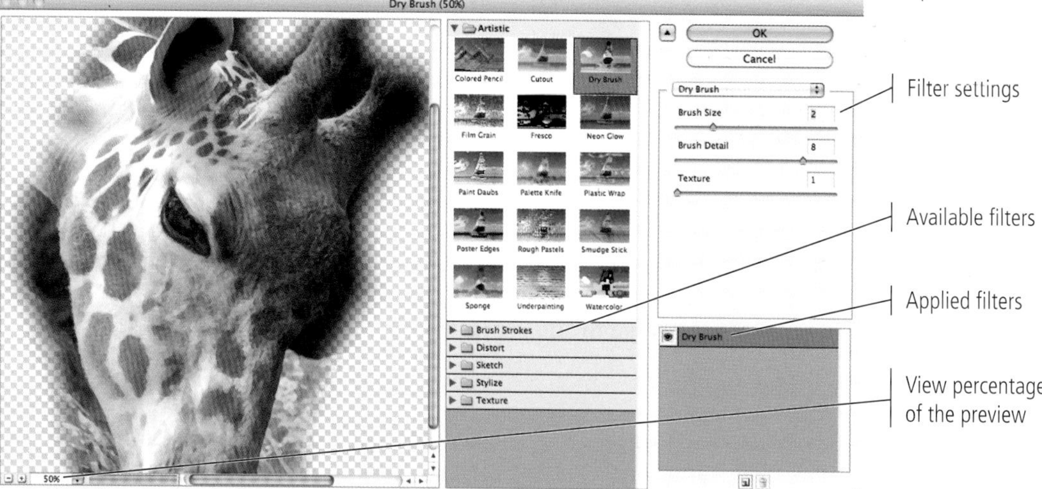

4. **In the filter settings area, change the Brush Size slider to 3, the Brush Detail slider to 6, and the Texture slider to 1.**

   When you change the filter settings, the preview window dynamically changes to show the new options. You can reduce the preview viewing percentage, but it's a good idea to look at your changes at least at 100% to get a good idea of what you're applying.

5. **Click OK to close the Filter Gallery and apply your choices.**

   In the Layers panel, a new icon appears in the giraffe layer, and a Smart Filters layer appears indented below it.

Note:

The filter might not be obvious in the image window, especially if you're viewing the file at a low view percentage (we're using 33% in these screen shots). We recommend previewing at a higher percentage in the Filter Gallery.

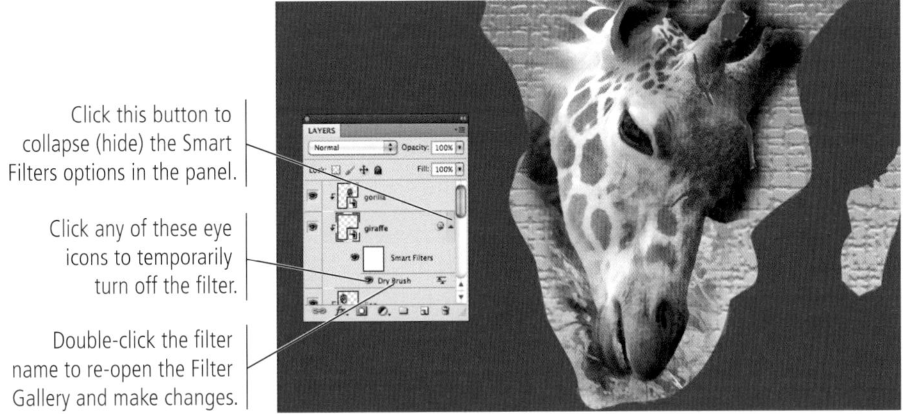

6. **Double-click the Dry Brush item in the Layers panel to reopen the Filter Gallery.**

7. **In the bottom-right corner of the Filter Gallery, click the New Effect Layer button.**

   As we mentioned earlier, you can apply multiple filters to a single layer to create unique effects. When you add a new filter layer, it defaults to the same settings as the previous filter (in this case, Dry Brush). The preview shows the effect of compounding the Dry Brush filter two times.

Note:

You can choose any of the available filters from the menu above the filter settings.

8. **With the bottom Dry Brush layer selected, click the arrow to the left of the Brush Strokes filter set to expand the folder.**

9. **In the Brush Strokes set, click Dark Strokes to apply that filter.**

10. **In the filter settings area, adjust the settings until you are satisfied with the result.**

11. Click OK to close the Filter Gallery and apply your changes.

Since multiple filters are applied, this item now says Filter Gallery instead of Dry Brush.

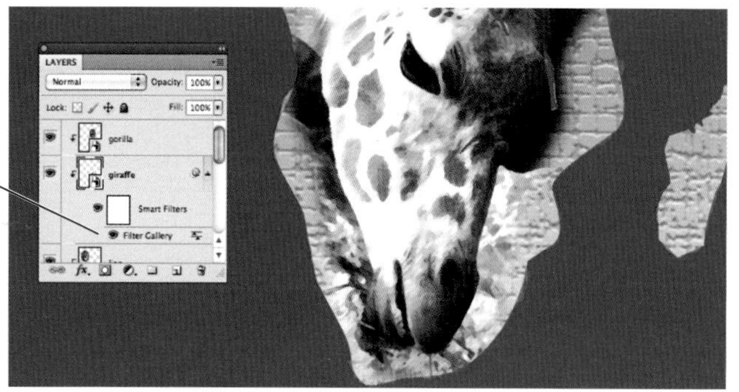

> *Note:*
>
> *You can reorder filter layers in the Layers panel just as you can reorder regular layers. Filters are applied from the bottom up; when you want to create a unique effect, experiment with multiple filters, as well as the order in which they are applied.*

12. Press Option/Alt, then click the Filter Gallery listing under the giraffe layer and drag it to the gorilla layer.

This copies the applied filters, using the exact same settings, to the target layer.

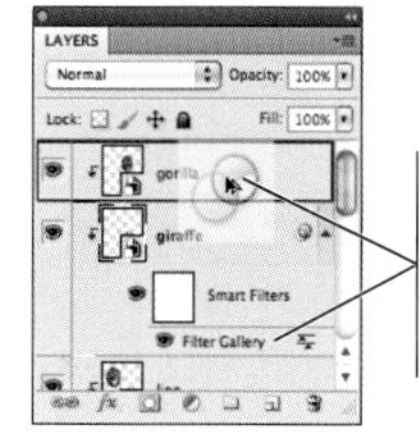

Press Option/Alt, then drag the Filter Gallery item to the gorilla layer to copy the applied effects.

13. In the Layers panel, click the arrow button to the right of the gorilla layer.

Applied smart effects, filters, and styles are listed under the layer name. You can collapse or expand the listings by clicking this button.

Click these arrows to hide or show the Smart Filters information.

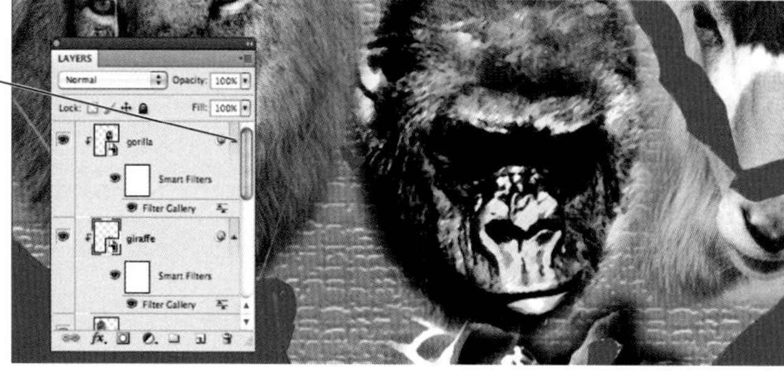

Fading Effects

PHOTOSHOP FOUNDATIONS

The Fade option (Edit>Fade) changes the opacity and blending mode of the last-used filter, painting tool, or color adjustment; you can also fade the effects of using the Liquify filter, and Brush Strokes filters. The following example shows the result of fading the Emboss filter that was applied in the left image.

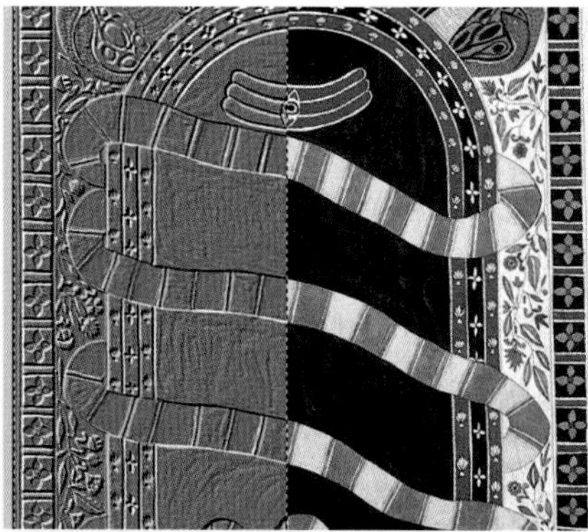

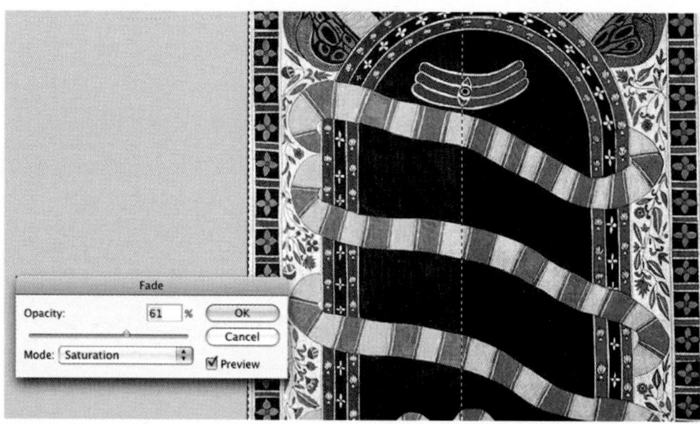

14. **Repeat Step 12 to apply the same filters to the lion and addax layers.**

    Feel free to modify the filter settings as appropriate until you are satisfied with the result for each layer.

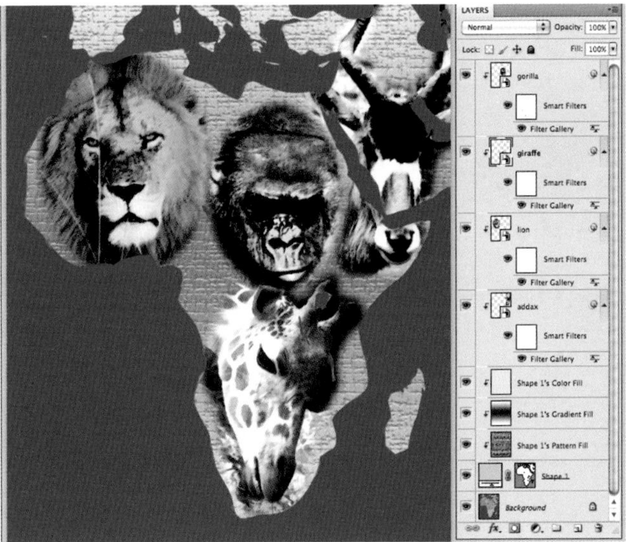

15. **In the Layers panel, collapse the Smart Filter information for each animal layer.**

16. **Save the file and continue.**

Apply Destructive Filters to Regular Layers

The previous exercise highlighted the Filter Gallery, and the benefits of applying non-destructive filters to Smart Objects. If you're working with regular layers, however, filters are destructive; they can't be edited or removed (although they can be undone).

1. **With `africa_working.psd` open, select the Shape 1's Pattern Fill layer.**

   Remember, this layer was created when you converted the shape layer's applied effects to layers. It is currently clipped by the shape layer.

2. **Choose Filter>Distort>Glass. Adjust the filter options until you are satisfied with the result.**

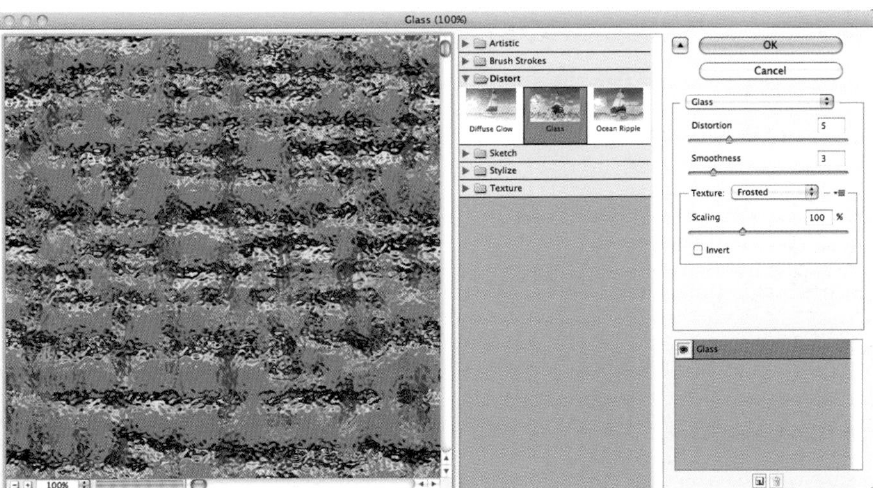

3. Click OK to apply the filter.

In the image, the pattern behind the animals is now much softer and less defined. Filtering the pattern layer helps you achieve the goal of a "painting" effect.

The regular layer shows no Smart Filter; filters applied to regular layers are destructive and permanent.

4. Select the Shape 1 layer and choose Filter>Stylize>Diffuse.

Rather than leaving the sharp, defined edges of the vector shape layer, you are going to use the Diffuse filter to help blend the edges into the other areas of the image.

Functional filters such as Diffuse are not applied in the Filter Gallery; instead, each filter has its own dialog box. However, before you can access the Diffuse dialog box, you have to rasterize the shape layer.

5. Read the resulting warning message.

You can't apply filters to vector shape layers. Photoshop automatically warns you that the layer will be rasterized, which means you will no longer be able to edit the path that created the shape. Depending on your goals, you might want to duplicate the shape layer and hide a copy before you rasterize the shape layer to apply the filter.

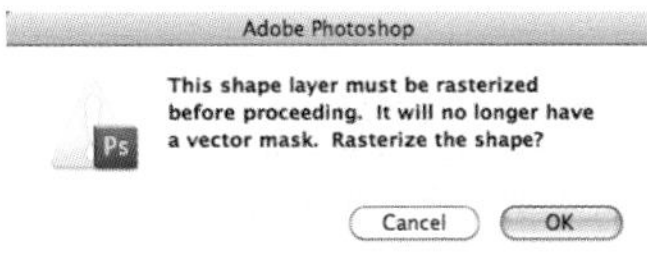

6. Click OK in the warning message to rasterize the shape layer.

The Diffuse dialog box can apply four different types of diffusion:

- **Normal** diffusion scatters pixels randomly.
- **Darken Only** replaces light pixels with dark ones.
- **Lighten Only** replaces dark pixels with light ones.
- **Anisotropic** scatters pixels where there is the least difference in color.

7. While the Diffuse dialog box is open, use the keyboard shortcuts to zoom in on the image in the document window. Use the scroll bars to drag the image until you see an edge of the shape layer.

You can use the keyboard shortcuts to change the view percentage of a file even when a dialog box is open. You can also scroll a document if you have scroll-wheel capabilities on your mouse.

Note:

Webster's dictionary defines diffuse as "to pour, spread out, or disperse in every direction; spread or scatter wildly." The Photoshop Diffuse filter reflects the second half of that definition, scattering the pixels in the selected layer.

The Stylize Filters

In addition to the options in the Filter Gallery, other artistic filters can also be found in the various Filter submenus. The Stylize filters (Filter>Stylize) generate artistic effects, typically referred to as *painted* or *impressionist*.

Keep the following points in mind when you use filters:

- Filters can be applied to the entire selected layer or to an active selection.
- Some filters work only on RGB images; if you are in a different color mode, some or all filter options — including the Filter Gallery — will be unavailable.
- All filters can be applied to 8-bit images; available filter options are limited for 16-bit and 32-bit images (see Project 6).
- If you don't have enough available RAM to process a filter effect, you might get an error message.

Original Image

Diffuse shuffles pixels to soften focus.

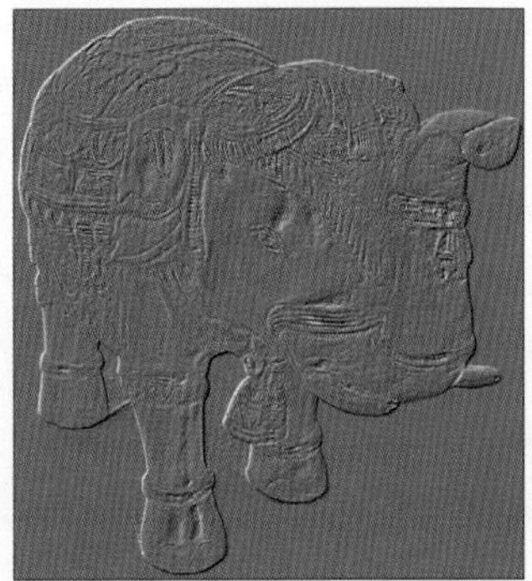

Emboss makes an image look like it was pushed out from (embossed) or into (debossed) the surface.

Extrude creates a 3D texture of raised blocks or pyramids, using a defined or random depth for the resulting grid.

Find Edges identifies areas with significant transitions and emphasizes the edges with dark lines.

Glowing Edges identifies color edges and adds a neon-like glow.

Solarize blends a negative and a positive image version of the image.

Tiles splits an image into a grid, and then offsets the resulting tiles with your choice of "grout" or gap fill.

Trace Contour finds the transitions of major brightness areas and thinly outlines them for each color channel.

Wind adds tiny horizontal lines in the image to create a windblown effect.

The Distortion Filters

Filters can be used for a variety of purposes, from purely aesthetic to technically functional. You can apply filters to specific selections, individual layers, or even individual channels depending on what you need to accomplish. If you combine filters with Smart Objects, you can also apply nondestructive filters and then change the settings or turn off the filters to experiment with different results.

The Distortion filters let you squeeze, stretch, bend, twist, and otherwise distort an image or selection. Some of these filters are controlled in the Filter Gallery, while others have their own dialog boxes.

Original Image

Diffuse Glow adds a haze of the current background color to lighter regions of the image.

Displace distorts an image based on a displacement map (the tone values of which determine the distortion).

Glass simulates the effect of looking through different types of glass.

Ocean Ripple simulates an underwater effect by adding randomly spaced ripples.

Pinch creates the effect of squeezing the edges of the image toward the center.

Polar Coordinates creates the effect of wrapping the image into a cylinder.

Ripple distorts the image. You can only define the amount and size of the effect.

Shear distorts the image as if it were being reflected on an angled mirror.

Spherize simulates the effect of wrapping an image around a three-dimensional sphere.

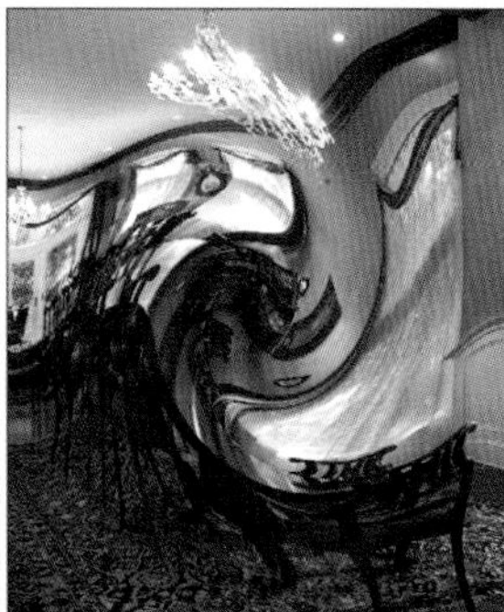

Twirl simulates the effect of placing the image into a whirlpool.

Waves creates a rippled effect with control over wavelength, amplitude, and wave type.

ZigZag distorts pixels diagonally, out from the center, or around the center.

8. **Move the mouse cursor over an edge in the document window. Click an edge of the shape layer to change the preview area of the dialog box.**

   When you see the edges, you can see the effect of the diffusion. (If the shape layer had more than just flat color, you would see the effect right away.) The diffused pixels allow the layer edges to blend into the background instead of ending at an abrupt, sharp edge.

> *Note:*
>
> *You can also click and drag in the preview area of the dialog box to change the visible area in only the preview.*

With the dialog box open, clicking in the image changes the visible area in preview window.

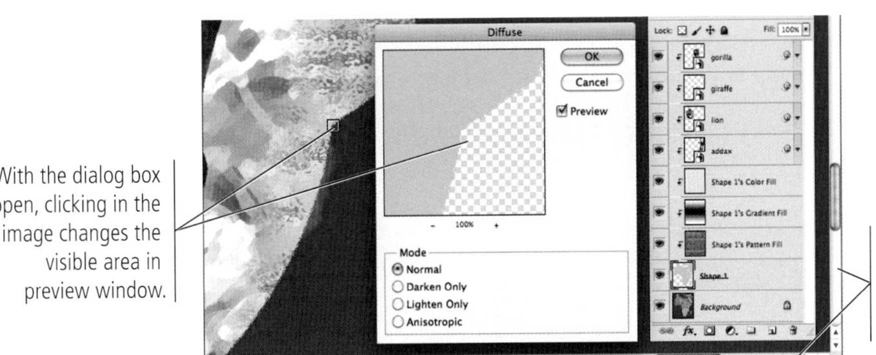

When the dialog box is open, you can use the scroll bars to change the visible part of the image.

9. **Leave the mode set to Normal and click OK.**

10. **Save the file and continue to the next stage of the project.**

Stage 4 Creating an Artistic Background

Since the background image (the original map) is badly deteriorated from resampling, you're going to use several built-in Photoshop tools to create a custom artistic background. Doing so gives you an advantage: you can create any effect you want instead of using the flat blue color in the existing background image. In this series of exercises, you combine Photoshop's filters with a custom gradient and a pattern fill, and then liquify the background to create a watery background to use in place of the low-resolution map image.

 Use the Eyedropper Tool

In Photoshop, there is almost always more than one way to complete a task. In this exercise, you use the Eyedropper tool to change the Foreground and Background colors by sampling from the original map image.

1. **With africa_working.psd open, zoom out to show the entire image in the document window.**

2. **Using the Layers panel, hide all but the background layer.**

   You can hide multiple layers by clicking and dragging over the eye icons of each layer that you want to hide.

Click here and drag down over the layer eye icons to hide multiple layers.

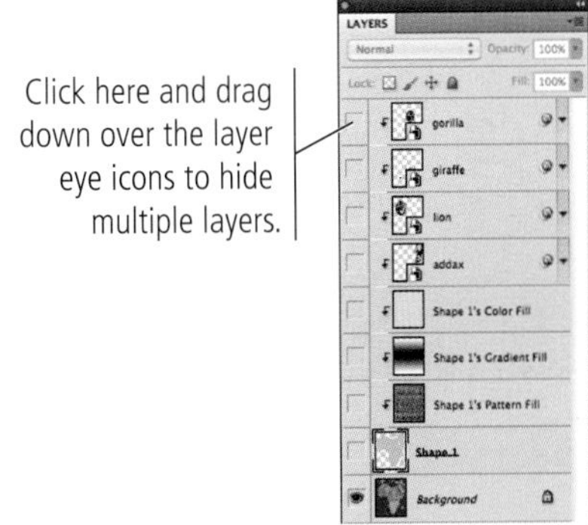

3. **Choose the Eyedropper tool in the Tools panel.**

4. **In the Control panel, choose 5 by 5 Average in the Sample Size menu and choose All Layers in the Sample menu. Make sure the Show Sampling Ring option is checked.**

   The default eyedropper option — Point Sample — selects the color of the single pixel where you click. Using one of the average values avoids the possibility of sampling an errant artifact color because the tool finds the average color in a range of adjacent pixels.

   By default, the sample will be selected from All [visible] Layers. You can choose Current Layer in the Sample menu to choose a color from only the active layer.

5. **Move the cursor over a blue area in the visible image and click to change the foreground color.**

   When you click with the Eyedropper tool, the sampling ring shows the previous foreground color on the bottom and the current sample color on the top half.

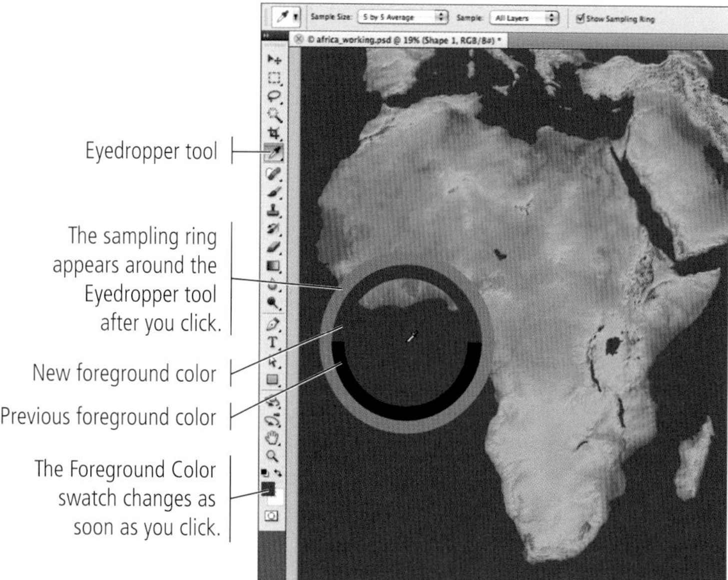
Eyedropper tool
The sampling ring appears around the Eyedropper tool after you click.
New foreground color
Previous foreground color
The Foreground Color swatch changes as soon as you click.

> *Note:*
>
> *While you hold down the mouse button, you can drag around the image to find the color you want. The sampling ring previews what color will be selected if you release the mouse button.*

6. **Move the cursor over a darker green area of the image. Option/Alt-click to change the background color.**

   Pressing Option/Alt while you click with the Eyedropper tool changes the Background color. In this case, the sampling ring shows the previous background color on the bottom and the current selection on the top.

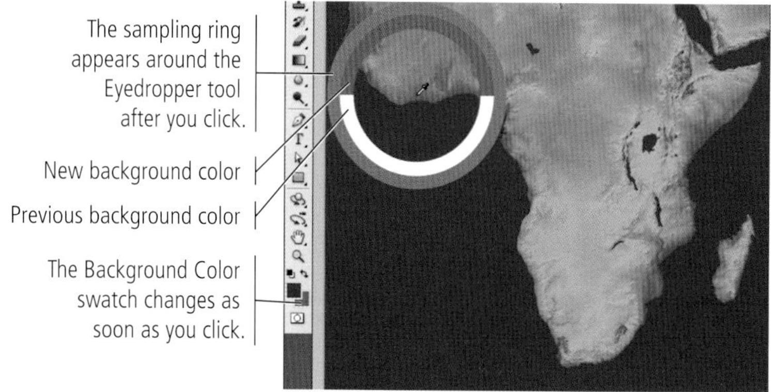
The sampling ring appears around the Eyedropper tool after you click.
New background color
Previous background color
The Background Color swatch changes as soon as you click.

7. **Save the file and continue to the next exercise.**

Create a Custom Gradient

A **gradient** (sometimes called a blend) is a fill that creates a smooth transition from one color to another or across a range of multiple colors. Photoshop can create several different kinds of gradients (linear, radial, etc.) from one color to another, and you can access a number of built-in gradients. You can also create your own custom gradients, which you will do in this exercise.

1. **With africa_working.psd open, choose the Gradient tool in the Tools panel.**

2. **In the Control panel, click the arrow to the right of the gradient sample bar to show the Gradient panel.**

   The Gradient panel shows a set of predefined gradients, including black-to-white, foreground-to-transparent, foreground-to-background, and several other common options. You can also access additional gradient libraries in the panel Options menu.

3. **Open the Gradient panel Options menu and choose Small List view.**

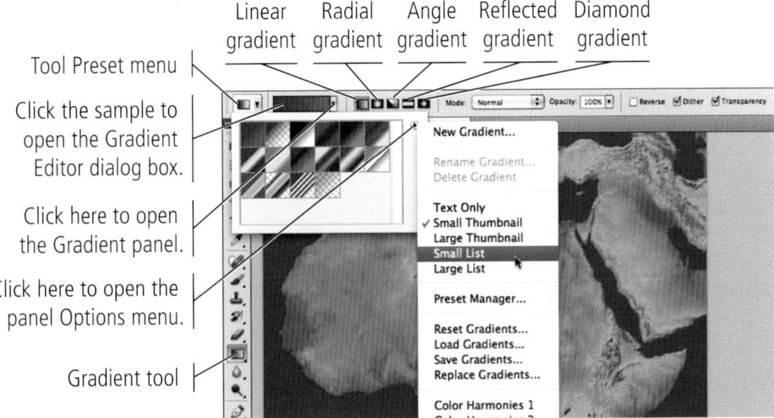

4. **Open the Gradient panel again and choose Foreground to Background from the list of gradients.**

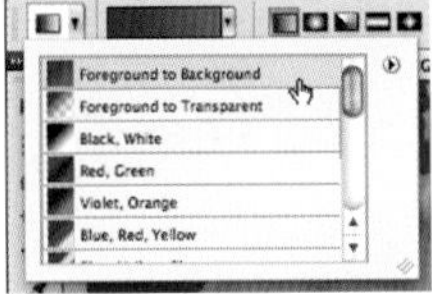

5. **Click the gradient sample in the Control panel to open the Gradient Editor dialog box.**

   You can use this dialog box to edit existing gradients or create new ones.

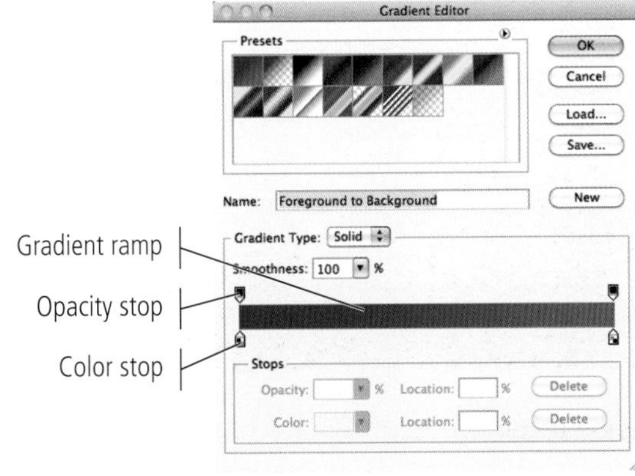

6. **Click the right color stop below the gradient ramp. Drag left until the Location field shows 25%.**

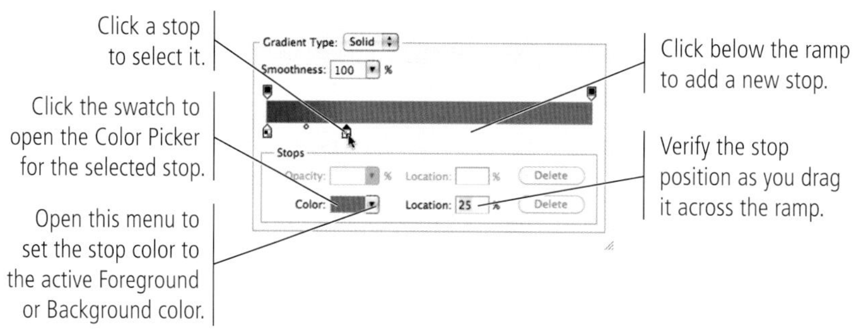

> *Note:*
>
> *As soon as you click the color stop, the name changes to Custom because you're defining a custom gradient.*

7. **Press Option/Alt, then click the left stop and drag to the right end of the gradient ramp.**

   This adds a new stop with the same settings as the one you Option/Alt-dragged. If you click before pressing Option/Alt, you will simply move the existing stop rather than copying it and repositioning the copy.

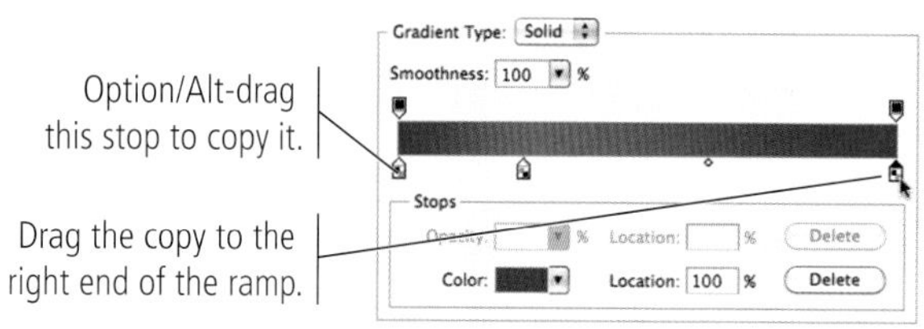

> *Note:*
>
> *You can simply click below the gradient ramp to add a new stop at the location where you click. The new stop adopts a color as necessary, based on the existing gradient.*

8. **Repeat Step 7 to create a third blue stop at a location of 50%.**

9. **Option/Alt-click the green stop and drag right until the location of the new stop is 75%.**

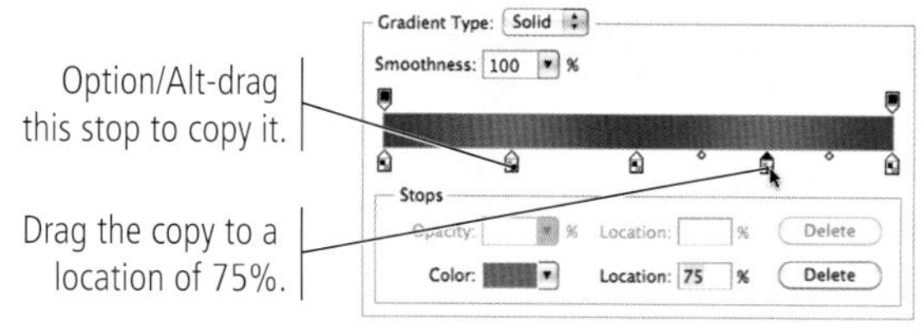

> *Note:*
>
> *Double-click a specific color stop to open the Color Picker where you can change the color of that stop.*

> *Note:*
>
> *Drag a stop off the gradient ramp to remove it from the gradient.*

10. **Type `Ocean Blues` in the Name field and click the New button.**

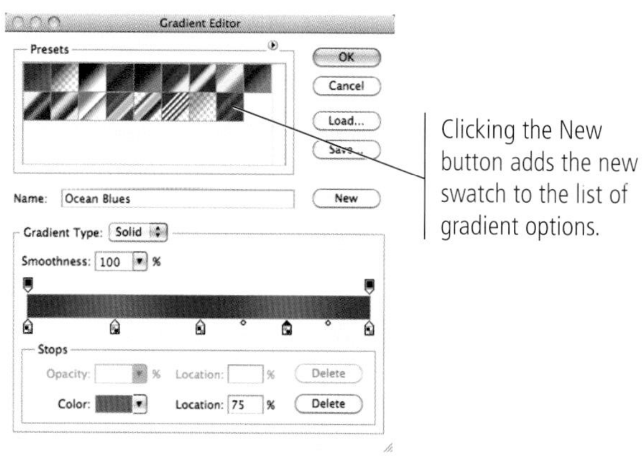

11. **Click OK to close the dialog box.**

12. **Save the file and continue to the next exercise.**

Create a Gradient Fill Layer

Once you have the gradient you want, applying it is fairly easy: add a layer (if necessary), select the type of gradient you want to create, and then click and drag.

> *Note:*
>
> *If you added a new layer between any of the layers in the Shape Layer clipping mask set, the new layer would become the basis of the clipping path for any layers above it.*

1. **With `africa_working.psd` open, show all layers, and then click the Background layer to select it.**
2. **Click the New Layer button at the bottom of the Layers panel. Name the new layer `Ocean`.**

   When you add a new layer, it is automatically added directly above the selected layer.
3. **Make sure the Gradient tool is selected. In the Control panel, make sure the Ocean Blues gradient is selected and the Linear gradient option is active.**
4. **Click in the top-left corner of the image and drag to the bottom-right corner.**

When you release the mouse button, the layer fills with the gradient. Areas before and after the line drawn with the Gradient tool fill with the start and stop colors of the gradient (in this case, they're both the blue color).

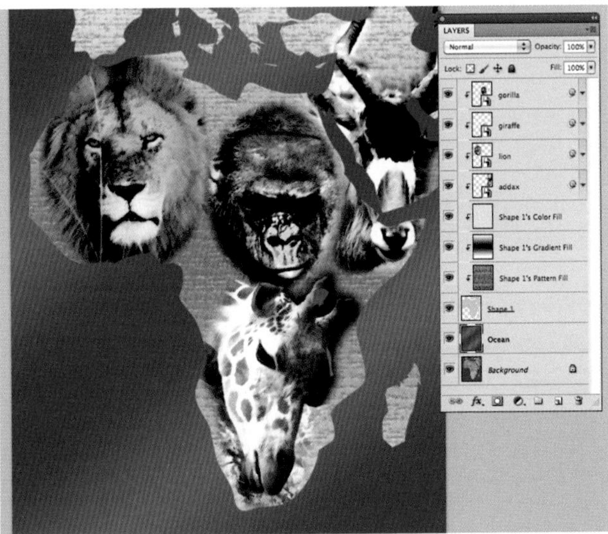

5. **Save the file and continue to the next exercise.**

Create a Pattern Fill Layer

The gradient layer is a good start for your art background, but it needs some texture to look more like a painting. A pattern fill will create the texture you need.

1. **With africa_working.psd open, create a new layer named Waves above the Ocean layer.**

2. **Choose the Paint Bucket tool (nested under the Gradient tool) and review the Control panel.**

   When you click with the Paint Bucket tool, it fills areas of similar color (like the Magic Wand tool you used to make selections in Project 4). You can define the Paint Bucket tool tolerance in the Control panel, just as you did for the Magic Wand tool.

Use this menu to fill with a color or pattern.
Click this button to open the Pattern panel.
Paint Bucket tool

3. **Choose Pattern in the left menu of the Control panel, and then open the Pattern panel.**

4. **In the Pattern panel Options menu, choose Small List to see the names of the various patterns.**

5. **Choose Artist Surfaces in the Options menu to show that set of patterns.**

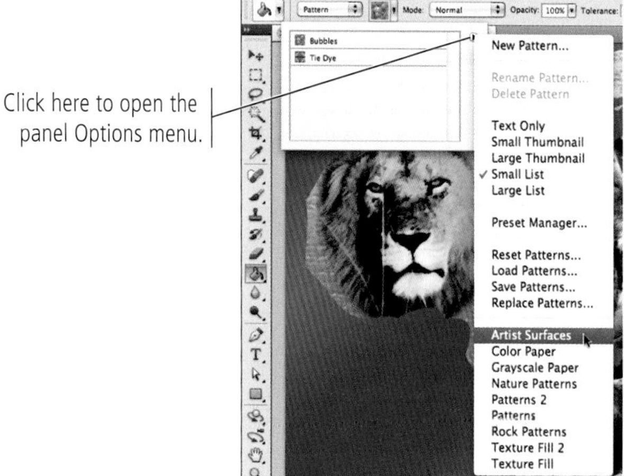

6. **When you see a warning that the patterns will replace the current set, click OK.**

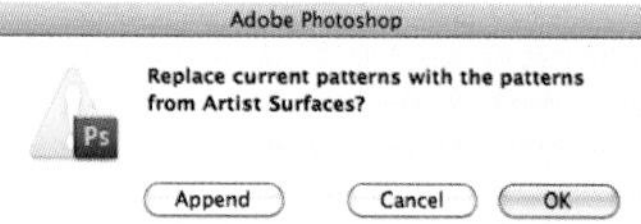

7. **Scroll through the list and click Oil Pastel on Canvas.**

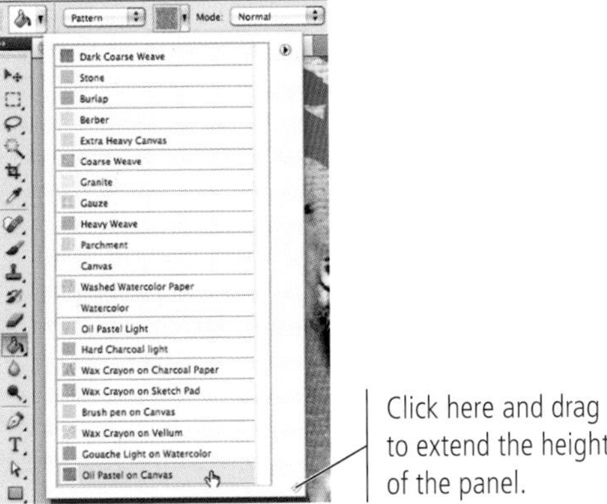

8. **Place the cursor anywhere in the image window and click.**

   Because there is nothing on the currently selected layer, every pixel in the layer is within the tool's tolerance — the entire layer fills with the pattern.

9. **Save the file and continue.**

Adjust Layer Order and Blending Mode

The pattern fill layer is currently on top of the gradient layer. You need to reverse that order, and then blend the two layers together to create the textured, colored ocean background.

1. **With `africa_working.psd` open, drag the Waves layer below the Ocean layer in the Layers panel.**

   Now the gradient obscures the pattern, which isn't right either. To blend the two layers together, you have to change the top layer's blending mode.

2. **Select the Ocean layer, and then click the Blending Mode menu at the top of the Layers panel.**

   Photoshop provides access to 27 different layer blending modes (the default is Normal, or no blending applied).

Distinguishing Photoshop Blending Modes

When working with blending modes, think of the top layer as the "blend" layer and the next lowest layer as the "base".

- **Normal** is the default mode (no blending applied).
- **Dissolve** results in a random scattering of pixels of both the blend and base colors.
- **Darken** returns the darker of the blend or base color. Base pixels that are lighter than the blend color are replaced; base pixels that are darker than the blend color remain unchanged.
- **Multiply** multiplies (hence the name) the base color by the blend color, resulting in a darker color. Multiplying any color with black produces black; multiplying any color with white leaves the color unchanged (think of math — any number times 0 equals 0).
- **Color Burn** darkens the base color by increasing the contrast. Blend colors darker than 50% significantly darken the base color by increasing saturation and reducing brightness; blending with white has no effect.
- **Linear Burn** darkens the base color similar to Color Burn; using Linear Burn, the brightness is reduced about twice as much for blend colors in the mid-tone range.
- **Darker Color** compares the channel values of the blend and base colors, resulting in the lower value.
- **Lighten** returns whichever is the lighter color (base or blend). Base pixels that are darker than the blend color are replaced; base pixels that are lighter than the blend color remain unchanged.
- **Screen** is basically the inverse of Multiply, always returning a lighter color. Screening with black has no effect; screening with white produces white.
- **Color Dodge** brightens the base color. Blend colors lighter than 50% significantly increase brightness; blending with black has no effect.
- **Linear Dodge (Add)** is similar to Color Dodge, but creates smoother transitions from areas of high brightness to areas of low brightness.
- **Lighter Color** compares channel values of the blend and base colors, resulting in the higher value.
- **Overlay** multiplies or screens the blend color to preserve the original lightness or darkness of the base.
- **Soft Light** darkens or lightens base colors depending on the blend color. Blend colors lighter than 50% lighten the base color (as if dodged); blend colors darker than 50% darken the base color (as if burned).
- **Hard Light** combines the Multiply and Screen modes. Blend colors darker than 50% are multiplied, and blend colors lighter than 50% are screened.
- **Vivid Light** combines the Color Dodge and Color Burn modes. Blend colors lighter than 50% lighten the base by decreasing contrast; blend colors darker than 50% darken the base by increasing contrast.
- **Linear Light** combines the Linear Dodge and Linear Burn modes. If the blend color is lighter than 50%, the result is lightened by increasing the base brightness. If the blend color is darker than 50%, the result is darkened by decreasing the base brightness.
- **Pin Light** preserves the brightest and darkest areas of the blend color; blend colors in the mid-tone range have little (if any) effect.
- **Hard Mix** pushes all pixels in the resulting blend to either all or nothing. The base and blend values of each pixel in each channel are added together (e.g., R 45 [blend] + R 230 [base] = R 275). Pixels with totals over 255 are shown at 255; pixels with a total lower than 255 are dropped to 0.
- **Difference** inverts base color values according to the brightness value in the blend layer. Lower brightness values in the blend layer have less of an effect on the result; blending with black has no effect.
- **Exclusion** is very similar to Difference, except that mid-tone values in the base color are completely desaturated.
- **Subtract** removes the blend color from the base color.
- **Divide** looks at the color information in each channel and divides the blend color from the base color.
- **Hue** results in a color with the luminance and saturation of the base color and the hue of the blend color.
- **Saturation** results in a color with the luminance and hue of the base color and the saturation of the blend color.
- **Color** results in a color with the luminance of the base color and the hue and saturation of the blend color.
- **Luminosity** results in a color with the hue and saturation of the base color and the luminance of the blend color (basically the opposite of the Color mode).

3. **Choose Overlay in the Blending Mode menu.**

The texture of the pattern is now visible behind the gradient. The pattern is very obvious, however, which doesn't lend well to the "painting" effect you're trying to create.

4. **Select the Waves layer. Open the Filter menu and choose the Filter Gallery option that is third from the top.**

When you use this command to open the Filter Gallery, the dialog box automatically applies the last-used filter(s). You can then edit the settings or change the specific filters that are applied to the currently selected layer.

The top command in the Filter menu applies the last-used filter without opening the related dialog box. If you used the Filter Gallery before the opening this menu, it would apply the same artistic filters that you last applied.

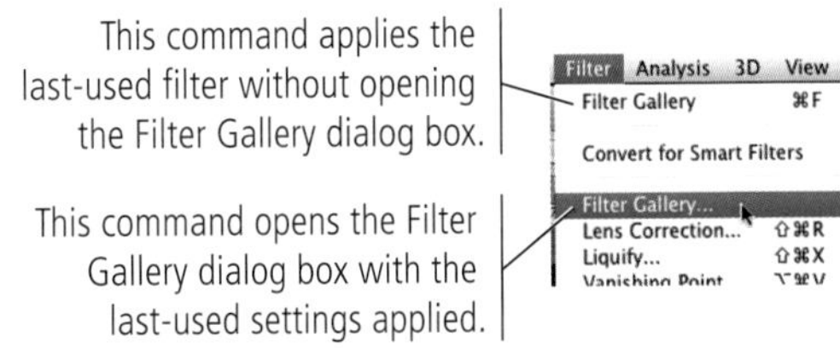

This command applies the last-used filter without opening the Filter Gallery dialog box.
This command opens the Filter Gallery dialog box with the last-used settings applied.
Filter
Analysis
3D
View
Filter Gallery
⌘F
Convert for Smart Filters
Filter Gallery...
Lens Correction...
⇧⌘R
Liquify...
⇧⌘X

5. **In the Filter Gallery window, apply two filters in the following order:**

Top filter:	Smudge Stick (Artistic) Settings: Stroke Length = 2, Highlight Area = 7, Intensity = 10
Bottom filter:	Ocean Ripple (Distort) Settings: Ripple Size = 3, Ripple Magnitude = 9

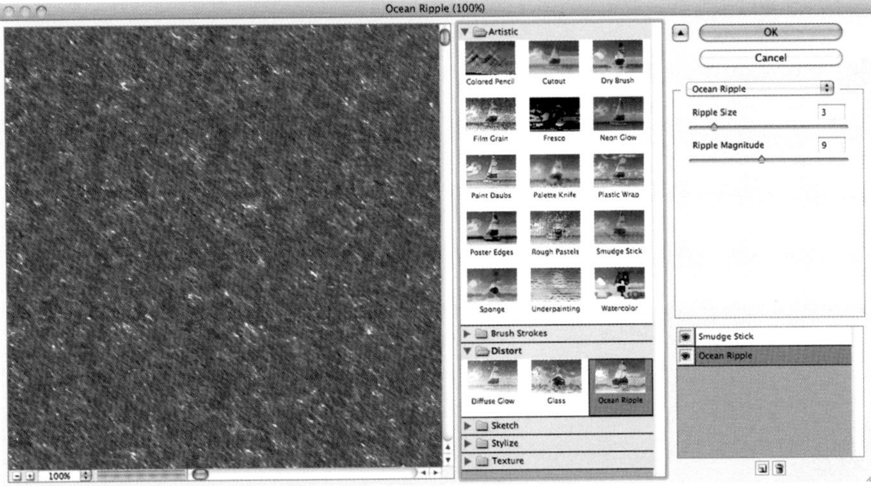

6. **Click OK to close the Filter Gallery.**

The pattern is now less obvious, and the filters have added a much more random texture.

7. **With the Waves layer selected, choose Filter>Blur>Blur.**

   This filter does not have a dialog box interface; it simply blurs the pixels in the selected layer. If you want more control over the blur, you must use one of the more sophisticated blur filters (see Project 6).

Note:

The result of the Blur filter might not be apparent unless you're viewing the image at 100% magnification.

8. **Save the file and continue to the next exercise.**

Liquify a Layer

You're nearly done, but the background layers still have a strong patterned feel — which makes sense, since you created them with a pattern fill. In this exercise, you use the Liquify filter to push around the background layer pixels in a freeform style to create a unique, non-patterned background.

1. **With `africa_working.psd` open, Shift-click the Ocean and Waves layers to select both.**

2. **Control/right click either of the selected layers and choose Merge Layers from the contextual menu.**

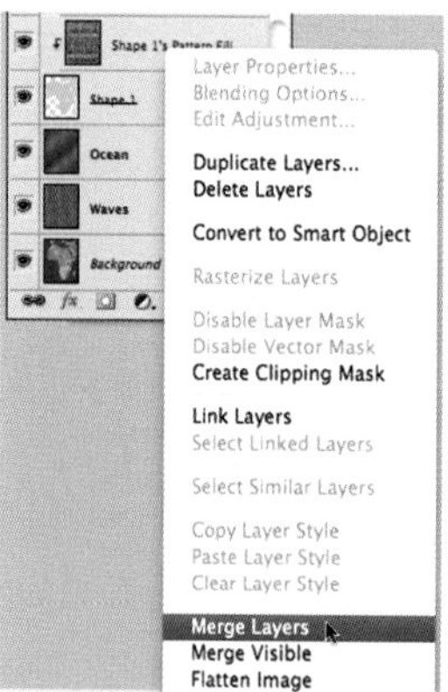

Note:

You can also choose Merge Layers from the Layers panel Options menu.

   When you merge selected layers, the resulting single layer adopts the name of the selected layer that was highest in the stacking order.

3. **With the resulting Ocean layer still selected, choose Filter>Liquify.**

   The Liquify filter has its own interface and tools. Depending on which tool you select, different options become available in the right side of the dialog box.

4. **In the Liquify filter dialog box, use the View Percentage menu to make the entire layer visible.**

5. **Click the Turbulence tool in the top-left corner and review your options in the top-right corner.**

   For any of the distortion tools, you have to define a brush size, density (feathering around the edges), and pressure. Some tools also allow you to define the brush rate (how fast distortions are made); using the Turbulence tool, you can set the Turbulent Jitter (how tightly pixels are scrambled by the effect).

6. **Using the Turbulence tool, select a large brush size, medium density, high pressure, and mid-to-high jitter.**

   Our settings are shown in the screen shot after Step 7.

7. **Drag in the preview where the green blends into the blue, starting at the left side and dragging to the right.**

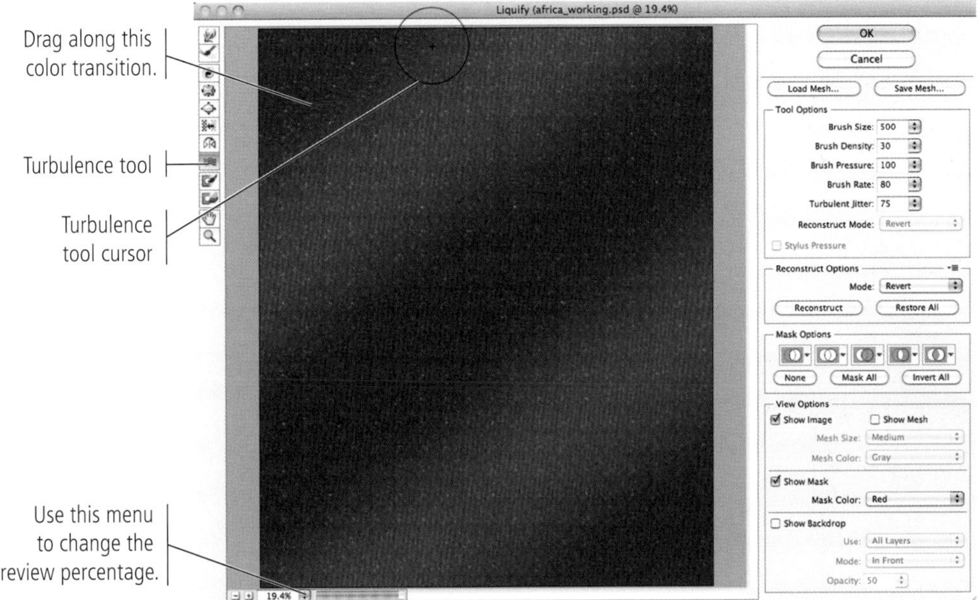

8. **Continue adding turbulence to the blend lines, and then experiment with some of the other tools. Our solution, shown here, made heavy use of the Turbulence and Forward Warp tools to push the pixels around.**

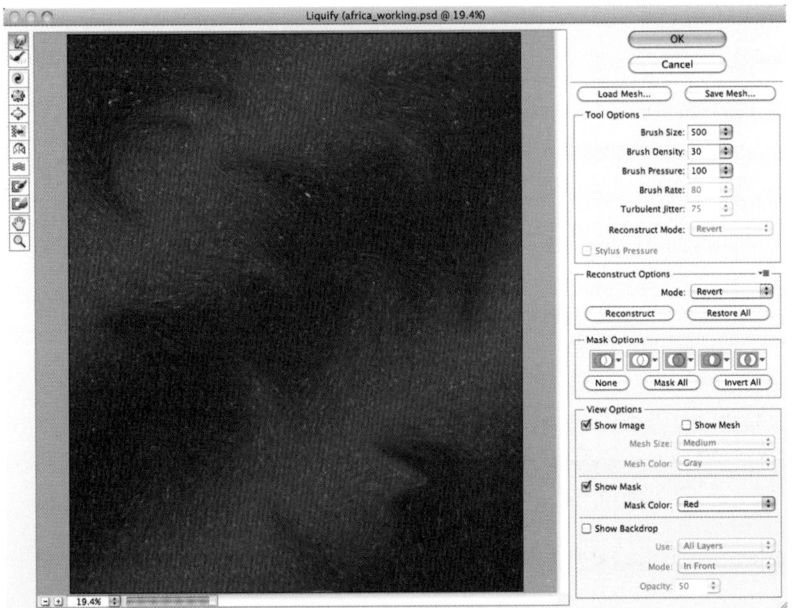

Note:

If necessary, you can press Command/Control-Z to undo your last brush stroke in the Liquify dialog box.

9. **Click OK to return to the image.**

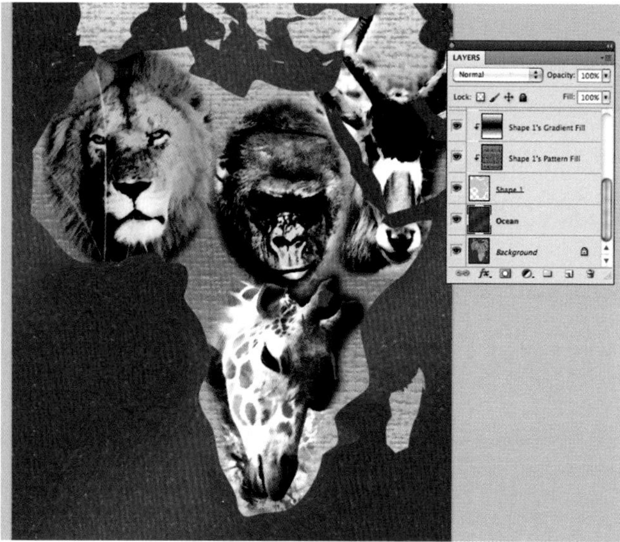

10. **Save the file and continue to the next stage of the project.**

Liquify Filter Tools

PHOTOSHOP FOUNDATIONS

Tools in the Liquify filter distort the brush area when you drag; the distortion is concentrated at the center of the brush area, and the effect intensifies as you hold down the mouse button or repeatedly drag over an area.

A. The **Forward Warp tool** pushes pixels as you drag.

B. The **Reconstruct tool** restores distorted pixels.

C. The **Twirl Clockwise tool** rotates pixels clockwise as you hold down the mouse button or drag. Press Option/Alt to twirl pixels counterclockwise.

D. The **Pucker tool** moves pixels toward the center of the brush, creating a zoomed-out effect if you simply hold down the mouse button without dragging.

E. The **Bloat tool** moves pixels away from the center of the brush, creating a zoomed-in effect.

F. The **Push Left tool** moves pixels left when you drag up, and right when you drag down. You can also drag clockwise around an object to increase its size, or drag counterclockwise to decrease its size.

G. The **Mirror tool** copies pixels to the brush area. Drag to mirror the area perpendicular to the direction of the stroke. Press Option/Alt to mirror the area in the direction opposite the stroke.

H. The **Turbulence tool** scrambles pixels under the brush area.

I. The **Freeze Mask tool** protects areas where you paint.

J. The **Thaw Mask tool** removes the protection created by the Freeze Mask tool.

K. The **Hand** and **Zoom tools** have the same function here as in the main Photoshop interface.

A B C D E F G H I J K L

Using Masks in the Liquify Filter

You can freeze areas in the Liquify preview to protect them from distortion with a mask that looks and behaves like Quick Mask mode in the main interface. You can also use the Mask options to freeze areas based on existing selections, transparent areas, or layer masks in the original image.

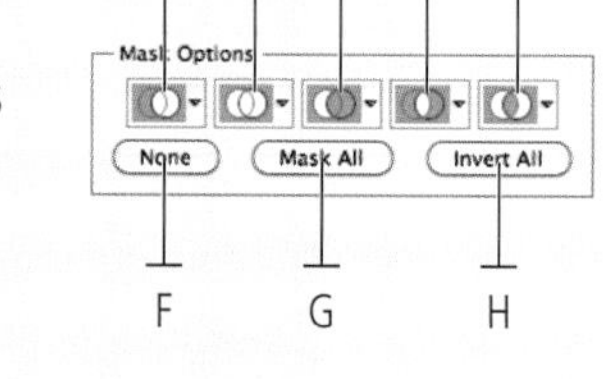

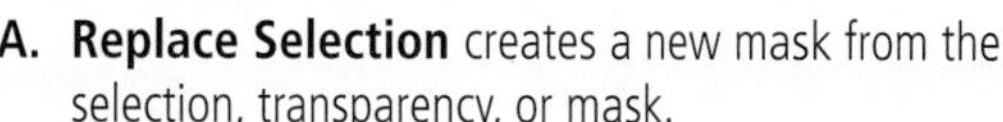

A. **Replace Selection** creates a new mask from the selection, transparency, or mask.

B. **Add to Selection** adds the selection, transparency, or mask to the currently thawed area.

C. **Subtract from Selection** adds the selection, transparency, or mask to the currently frozen area.

D. **Intersect with Selection** creates a mask with areas that are frozen in the preview, and in the selection, transparency, or mask from the original image.

E. **Invert Selection** inverts the mask in the preview image within the boundaries of the selection, transparency, or mask from the original image.

F. Click the **None** button to thaw all masked areas.

G. Click the **Mask All** button to mask the entire image.

H. Click the **Invert All** button to reverse the current mask.

 Stage 5 Creating Variations

The map image is now virtually done, but the colors in the animal layers seem a bit harsh in some areas. In this exercise, you use a color adjustment layer to reduce that harshness, and then give your client two PDF files showing the different options from which to choose.

Unify Effects with a Solid Color Overlay

Each animal image has a unique color range, which doesn't create the feeling of a "whole composition." You can unify the disparate elements within the clipping mask by blending a single color fill into all of the animal images.

1. **With africa_working.psd open, hide all layers except the Background layer.**

2. **Click the Foreground swatch in the Tools panel to open the Color Picker.**

   The eyedropper cursor that appears has the same effect as choosing the Eyedropper tool in the Tools panel. The primary difference is that the open dialog box shows the color values of the location where you click. You can also use this dialog box to manually define color values by typing in the various fields.

Note:

Hiding the clipping mask layer (the Shape 1 layer) hides all layers clipped by that layer.

3. **Click with the eyedropper cursor in a gold area of the original map image to pick up that color as the new foreground color, and then click OK.**

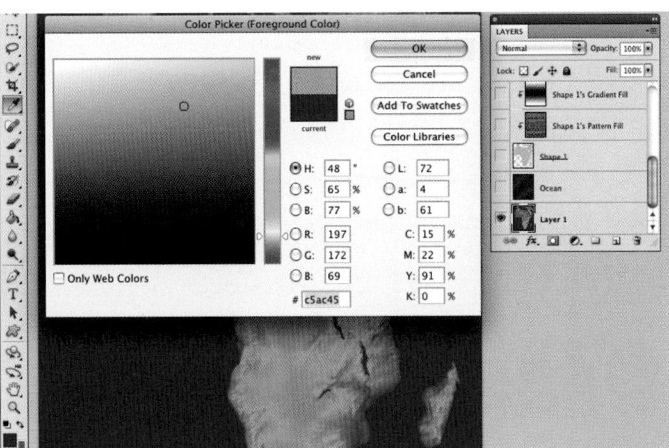

4. **Show all the layers, and then click the highest layer in the Layers panel stack to select it.**

5. **Create a new layer at the top of the stack named Gold Tone.**

6. **With the new layer selected, choose Edit>Fill.**

7. **In the Use menu, choose Foreground Color.**

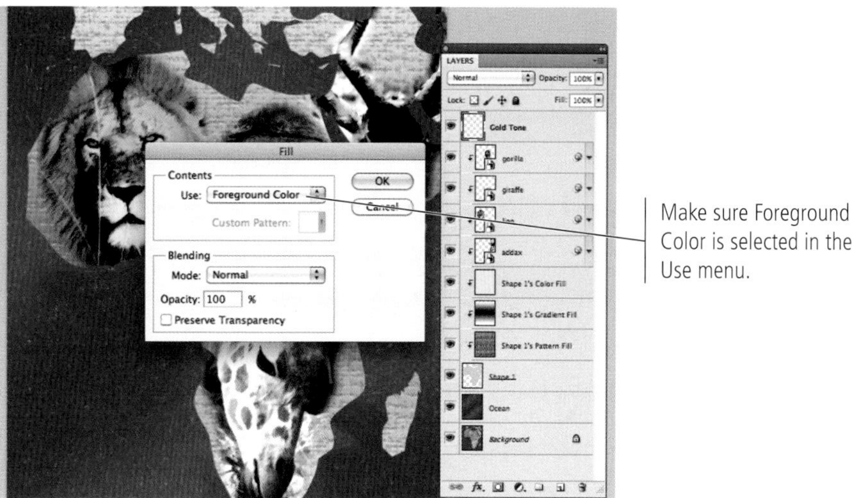

8. **Click OK to fill the selected layer with the solid color.**

9. **In the Layers panel, make sure the Gold Tone layer is selected, and then change the blending mode to Soft Light.**

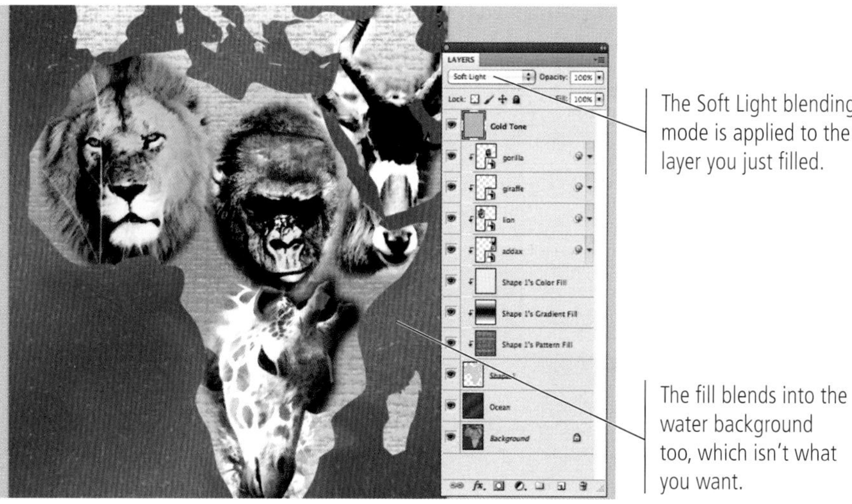

The Soft Light blending mode is applied to the layer you just filled.
The fill blends into the water background too, which isn't what you want.

10. **Control/right-click the Gold Tone layer and choose Create Clipping Mask.**

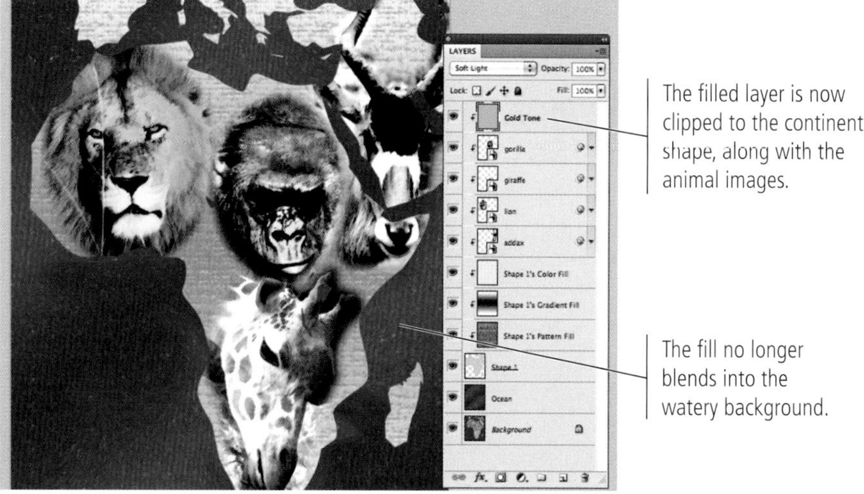

The filled layer is now clipped to the continent shape, along with the animal images.
The fill no longer blends into the watery background.

11. **Click the Background layer in the Layers panel and drag it to the panel's Delete button.**

    This layer is the low-resolution map image from which you drew the shape layer. It is no longer necessary, so you can remove it from the file.

12. **Save the file and continue to the next exercise.**

Create Layer Comps

The Layer Comps feature allows you to save multiple iterations of a file at one time. A layer comp can store the position and visibility of individual layers, as well as any effects applied. This feature is useful when you want to experiment with the position of specific layers, but you want to keep a record of earlier positions of the layers — or, as in this case, when you want to present two versions of a file: one version with a layer visible, and one version with a layer hidden.

It's important to know that layer comps do not store pixel information. Modifying the actual pixel data on a layer will not be undone by reverting to an earlier layer comp. To undo that kind of change, you must use the History panel and snapshots, assuming you haven't closed the file since you created the snapshots.

Note:

Smart Filter settings are not stored in a layer comp.

1. **With africa_working.psd open, open the Layer Comps panel (Window>Layer Comps).**

2. **Without changing anything in the file (the Gold Tone layer should be visible), click the New Layer Comp button.**

3. **In the New Layer Comp dialog box, name the comp Final Golden. Make sure the Visibility option is checked, and then click OK.**

    When you choose the Visibility option, only the currently visible layers (in this case, all of them) will be included in the comp.

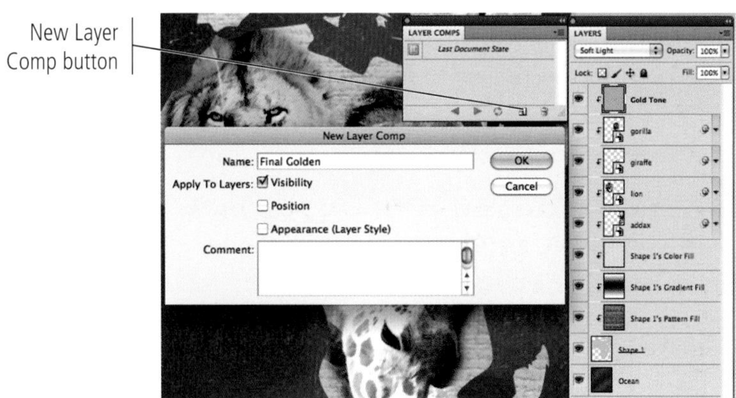

4. **In the Layers panel, hide the Gold Tone layer.**

5. **Create a second layer comp named `Final Plain`, again including only the layer visibility attributes in the comp.**

   Because you hid the Gold Tone layer in Step 4, checking the visibility option prevents that layer from being included in the comp.

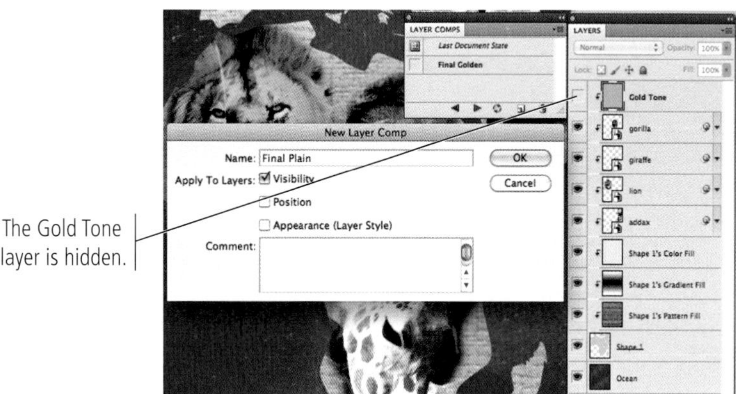

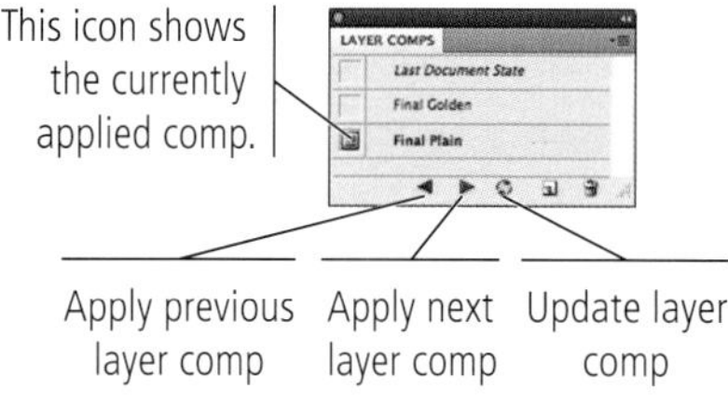

6. **Choose File>Scripts>Layer Comps to Files.**

   This is a common workflow step, which is why Adobe provides a predefined script to make it easy to create multiple comp versions of a file as PDFs in a single pass.

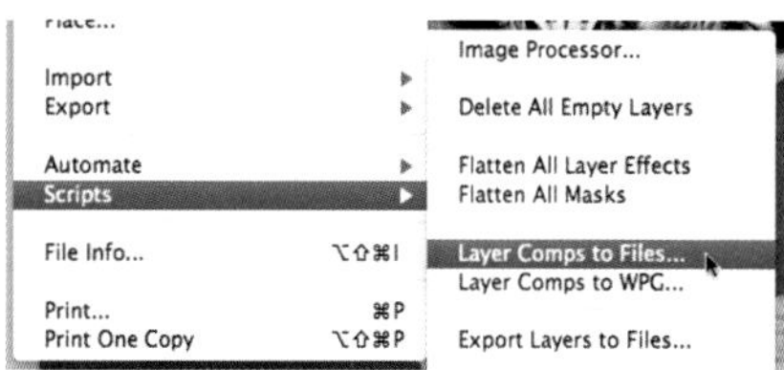

7. **In the Layer Comps to Files dialog box, choose PDF in the File Type menu, and leave the lower options at their default values.**

8. **Type `africa` in the File Name Prefix field.**

   This script creates separate files for each layer comp. The target location defaults to the same location as the working file, and the file name defaults to the current file name. The new file names begin with the text string that you enter in the File Name Prefix field.

9. **Click Run.**

   The process could take a while to complete, since you are exporting two versions of a very large file. Don't panic and don't get impatient. When the file is done, you will see the message shown here.

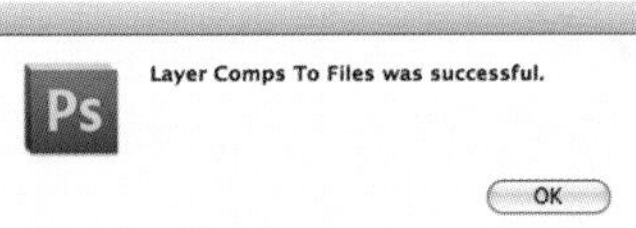

10. **Click OK to close the message, and then save and close the Photoshop file.**

11. **Open the two PDF files (in your WIP>Africa folder) in any PDF reader and review the results.**

12. **Close the PDF files.**

Project Review

fill in the blank

1. You can toggle on _______________ to see the feathered areas of a soft-edge mask.

2. The _______________ tool is used to create vector-based shapes and paths.

3. _______________ control the shape of a curve between two anchor points.

4. In RGB mode, a _______________ value of each color channel results in black.

5. The _______________ tool can be used to fill areas with solid colors or patterns.

6. A _______________ is a smooth transition from one color to another.

7. A _______________ is a resolution-independent, vector-based layer that can be filled with a solid color or pattern.

8. The _______________ command is used to show only areas of one layer that fall within the area of the underlying layer.

9. _______________ are used to store multiple interations of a file at one time, including different visibility and positioning of specific layers in the file.

10. The _______________ allows you to experiment with different filters and filter settings, and compound multiple filters to create unique artistic effects.

short answer

1. Briefly describe the concept of resampling, and how it relates to effective resolution.

2. Briefly describe the advantages and disadvantages of placing files as Smart Objects.

3. Briefly explain the concept of alpha channels.

Portfolio Builder Project

Use what you learned in this project to complete the following freeform exercise.
Carefully read the art director and client comments, then create your design to meet the needs of the project.
Use the space below to sketch ideas; when finished, write a brief explanation of the reasoning behind your design.

art director comments

The Global Wildlife Fund is very happy with your work on the Africa poster. They chose the original version without the color overlay. They would like you to create at least two more of the pieces in the series. If you only have time for two, use North America and Asia.

To complete this project, you should:

- ❑ Search the Internet for maps you can use as templates to create the continent shapes.
- ❑ Download the **Print5_PB_Project5.zip** archive from the Student Files Web page to access the client-supplied animal photos.
- ❑ Save the animal images in the TIFF format if you want to place them as Smart Objects.
- ❑ Create each piece with styles similar to the ones you used in the Africa map.
- ❑ Create each poster at 10 × 12″ for the final size.

client comments

Remember, this is a series of pieces that make up an entire collection, so each piece should be similar. We really like the style you created in the first version, and we want the other pieces to have a similar feel. Use the same style as the Africa artwork (without the overlay) for each of the other pieces.

One thing we do want is a similar-but-different background for each piece. Of course they're all water, but the water isn't exactly the same around the entire globe. Make sure there's some variation from one background to the next — maybe a slightly different color or a different pattern.

We sent some images you can usewe know there aren't enough for most of the continents, so please find other images as necessary to fill out each continent. Just make sure the animals you put into each continent actually live in those areas. Keep in mind, we'd like to avoid a huge stock-image bill.

Our campaign kicks off in a little less than two months; can you complete the work in two weeks?

project justification

Project Summary

This project extended many of the concepts you learned in Project 4, adding new options for compositing multiple images into a single cohesive piece of artwork. Smart Objects, which played a major role in this project, are one of the most significant advances in image compositing technology. They allow you to apply effects and filters without affecting or damaging the original image data. You also learned how to create and edit soft-edge layer masks to smooth the transitions between layer edges, and you learned how to manage those layer masks in regular layers and Smart Objects.

This project also introduced some of the creative tools that can turn photos and flat colors into painting-like artwork. You learned to use the Filter Gallery — with its many options, custom gradients, gradient and pattern fill layers, and blending modes — and the Liquify filter. You will use these options many times in your career as you complete different types of projects in Photoshop.

Create a compound vector shape layer using a low-resolution image as a template

Add a pattern and fill color to the vector shape layer

Composite multiple images using Smart Objects

Create a clipping mask to place images into the vector shape layer

Use soft-edge layer masks to blend one image into another

Apply filters to images to create a "painting" effect

Use gradients and patterns to create a custom background

Liquify pixels to create unique effects

Change blending modes to merge one layer into another

project 6

Menu Image Correction

Your client is the owner of The Chateau, a five-star gourmet restaurant that has been operating in northern Los Angeles County for over five decades. The restaurant changes its menu frequently, so they currently use a chalkboard menu, presented on an easel at each table when guests are seated. The owner recently received a number of comments about the chalkboard menu being difficult to read, so he decided to create printed menus with the standard offerings and use the chalkboard to display the chef's daily specials.

This project incorporates the following skills:

- ❑ Repairing damaged images
- ❑ Understanding the relationship between tonal range and contrast
- ❑ Correcting image lighting and exposure problems
- ❑ Understanding how gray balance affects overall image color
- ❑ Correcting minor and severe image color problems
- ❑ Preparing corrected images for printing
- ❑ Combining exposures into an HDR image

Project Meeting

client comments

The Chateau is a unique destination restaurant that consistently wins awards from local and national food and wine reviewers. The restaurant was first opened in 1952 by Paul and Gina Roseman as a rest stop and diner for travelers along the Sierra Highway. While the restaurant remains in the family, it has evolved from home-style comfort food to more exotic fare such as wild game with a French twist.

The history of the restaurant is important to us. We have a Roseman family portrait — my great-grandparents — that we'd like to include on the back of the menu. The picture is a bit grainy and has some damage, though, and we'd like you to clean it up as much as possible. We also want to include a picture of the current executive chef, who is Paul and Gina's great-grandniece, in the same section. The only picture we have of her is very dark though, and we're hoping you can make it look better.

In addition, we've taken several pictures of different meals that Suzanne created. We want you to make sure they will look as good as possible when printed. You're the expert, so we trust that you know what needs to be done.

art director comments

Digital images come from a wide variety of sources: scanned photographs and digital cameras are the two most common, as is the case for the client's images for this project. Some images can be used as is, or at least with only minor correction. Realistically, most professional photographers reshoot an image until they have one that doesn't need your help.

Unfortunately, however, not every project involves a professional photographer. Consumer-level cameras have come down in price and gone up in quality to the point where many non-professionals shoot their own photos without proper skill or knowledge. That means many of those images require a bit of help — and some require a lot.

Even when a professional photographer is involved, not every image comes from a perfectly lit studio. Location shots — where a subject is photographed in a "real-world" setting — can't always be captured perfectly. Those images usually need work as well. Fortunately, Photoshop provides a powerful toolset for solving most image problems, or at least improving the worst of them.

project objectives

To complete this project, you will:

- ❑ Remove grain with blur and sharpen techniques
- ❑ Heal severe scratches
- ❑ Clone out major damage
- ❑ Correct minor problems with the Brightness/Contrast adjustment
- ❑ Correct tonal range with the Levels adjustment
- ❑ Correct lighting problems with the Exposure adjustment
- ❑ Correct overall color problems with the Color Balance adjustment
- ❑ Correct precise color values with the Curves adjustment
- ❑ Correct an RGB image to CMYK gamut limits
- ❑ Embed color profile information in a file
- ❑ Combine multiple exposures with the Merge to HDR Pro utility

Stage 1 Retouching Damaged Images

Image repair is the process of fixing scratches, removing dust, making tears disappear, and generally putting broken or damaged pictures back together again. **Retouching**, on the other hand, is the technique of changing an image by adding something that wasn't there or removing something that was there. Damage can come from a wide range of sources: creases, scratches from any number of abrasive objects, water spots, and tape marks to name just a few. Other image problems such as photographic grain are a natural part of photographs (especially old ones), and dust is common (if not inevitable) whenever photographs are scanned.

There are many different ways to approach image repairs. As you complete the exercises in this stage of the project, you will use several tools — from basic to complex — to clean up damage in the client's family portrait from the early 1940s.

Remove Grain with Blur and Sharpen Techniques

Photographic film is made up of microscopic grains of light-sensitive material. These grains capture the image information, which is eventually processed into a print or transparency. While not usually apparent in a standard photographic print, the grain in a photograph can become pronounced when scanned with a high-resolution scanner. Enlarging an image during scanning further enhances any grain that already exists.

When grain is evident in a digital image, the grain pattern can destroy fine detail and create a mottled appearance in areas of solid color or subtle tone variation. Slower-rated film typically has the smallest and least-evident grain, while faster film can produce significant graininess.

Sharpening and blurring techniques are the best methods for removing photographic grain. The techniques you use in this exercise work for any image with grain. Older images — such as the one your client wants to use — almost always have obvious grain problems that can be fixed to some degree; antique images can be fixed only just so much. The techniques you learn in this project produce very good results if you need to remove grain from modern scanned images.

1. **Download `Print5_RF_Project6.zip` from the Student Files Web page.**

2. **Expand the ZIP archive in your WIP folder (Macintosh) or copy the archive contents into your WIP folder (Windows).**

   This results in a folder named **Menu**, which contains the files you need for this project. You should also use this folder to save the files you create in this project.

3. **Open the file `rosemans.jpg` from your WIP>Menu folder.**

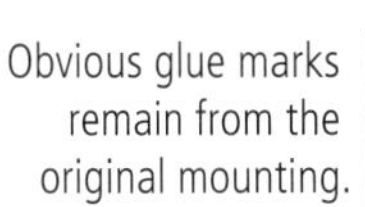

Obvious glue marks remain from the original mounting.

Scratches mar several areas of the image.
A sharp crease cuts into the Rosemans' daughter.
The corner has been torn off.

4. **Choose View>Actual Pixels to view the image at 100%.**

rosemans.jpg @ 100% (RGB/8)

Grain is most obvious in large areas of solid (or nearly solid) color.

Grain in lighter areas can produce a sickly appearance in a person's face.

Note:

Press Command-Opt-Zero/Control-Alt-Zero to view the image at 100%, or double-click the Zoom tool in the Tools panel.

5. **Choose Filter>Blur>Gaussian Blur.**

All Photoshop blur filters work in essentially the same way: they average the brightness values of contiguous pixels to soften the image.

The Noise Filters

PHOTOSHOP FOUNDATIONS

Noise is defined as random pixels that stand out from the surrounding pixels, either hurting the overall appearance of the image (as in the case of visible grains in an old photograph) or helping to prevent printing problems (as in the case of a gradient that extends across a large area). Photoshop includes several filters (Filters>Noise) that can add or remove noise.

The **Add Noise filter** applies random pixels to the image. Uniform distributes color values of noise between 0 and the defined amount. Gaussian distributes color values of noise along a bell-shaped curve. Monochromatic adds random pixels without affecting the colors in the image.

The **Despeckle** filter detects the edges in an image and blurs everything except those edges.

The **Dust & Scratches filter** reduces noise by comparing the contrast of pixels within the defined radius; pixels outside the defined threshold are adjusted.

The **Median filter** reduces noise by blending the brightness of pixels within a selection. The filter compares the brightness of pixels within the defined radius, and replaces pixels that differ too much from surrounding pixels with the median brightness value of the compared pixels.

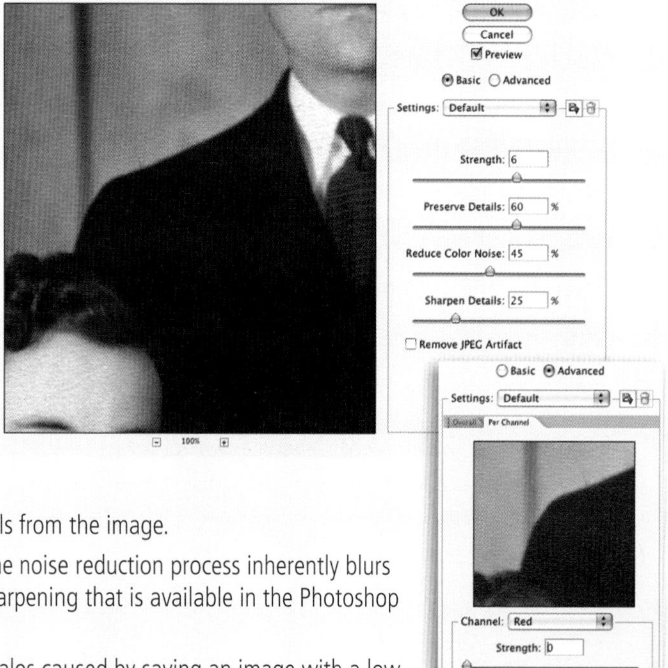

The **Reduce Noise** filter provides far greater control over different aspects of noise correction. In Basic mode, you can remove luminance noise and color noise in the composite image.

In Advanced mode, you can remove noise from individual color channels. (**Luminance noise**, also called grayscale noise, makes an image appear grainy; **color noise** usually appears as color artifacts in the image.)

- **Strength** controls the amount of luminance noise reduction.
- **Preserve Details** controls how carefully the filter compares the difference in luminance between adjacent pixels. Lower values remove more noise but result in less detail.
- **Reduce Color Noise** removes random color pixels from the image.
- **Sharpen Details** sharpens the image. Because the noise reduction process inherently blurs the image, this option applies the same kind of sharpening that is available in the Photoshop Sharpen filters.
- **Remove JPEG Artifacts** removes artifacts and halos caused by saving an image with a low JPEG quality setting (in other words, using a high lossy compression scheme).

6. Make sure Preview is checked and change the Radius field to 1.5 pixels.

The **Radius** field defines (in pixels) the amount of blurring that will be applied. Photoshop uses this value to average the brightness of a pixel with that of surrounding pixels. A radius value near 1 can soften an image and remove most photographic grain.

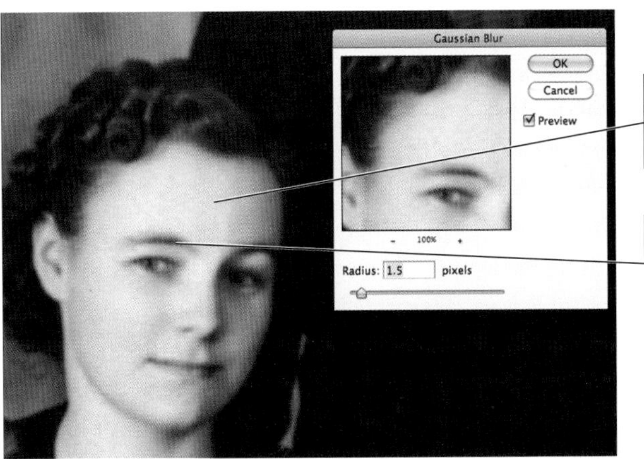

A small amount of Gaussian blur removes most of the photographic grain.

Areas of fine detail are also slightly blurred by the Gaussian Blur filter.

7. Click OK to apply the Gaussian Blur to the image.

To remove the photographic grain, you had to blur the entire image; this means that areas of fine detail were also blurred. You can use a second technique — unsharp masking — to restore some of the lost edge detail.

PHOTOSHOP FOUNDATIONS

The Blur Filters

The Filter>Blur menu includes a number of choices for applying corrective or artistic blurs to an image or selection.

Average finds the average color of an image or selection, and then fills the image or selection with that color to create a smooth appearance.

Blur and **Blur More** smooth transitions by averaging the pixels next to the hard edges of defined lines and shaded areas. When you apply these filters, you have no additional control: Blur is roughly equivalent to a 0.3-pixel radius blur, and Blur More uses approximately a 0.7-pixel radius.

Box Blur averages the color value of neighboring pixels. You can adjust the size of the area used to calculate the average value; a larger radius value results in more blurring.

Gaussian Blur blurs the selection by a specific amount.

Lens Blur adds blur to an image to create the effect of a narrower depth of field so some objects in the image remain in focus, while others areas are blurred.

Motion Blur includes an option for changing the blur angle, as well as a Distance value that defines the number of pixels to blur.

Radial Blur either spins the pixel around the center point of the image, or zooms the pixel around a center point based on the Amount setting. The farther a pixel is from the center point, the more the pixel is blurred. You can drag in the Blur Center window to move the center point of the blur.

Shape Blur uses a specific shape (**kernel**) to create the blur. Radius determines the size of the kernel; the larger the kernel, the greater the blur.

Smart Blur allows you to blur tones closely related in value without affecting edge quality. Threshold determines how closely pixels must be related in tone before being blurred. You can also specify a Quality level, and change the Mode setting. Using Edge Only mode, edges are outlined in white and the image is forced to black. Using Overlay Edges mode, the color image is blurred and edges are outlined in white.

Surface Blur blurs an image while trying to preserve edges. The Radius option specifies the size of the blur in whole numbers. The Threshold option controls how much the tonal values of neighboring pixels must differ before being blurred. (You can only apply whole-number radius blurs.)

8. **Choose Filter>Sharpen>Unsharp Mask and make sure the Preview check box is active in the dialog box.**

   Unsharp masking sharpens an image by increasing contrast along the edges in an image. **Amount** determines how much the contrast in edges will increase; typically, 150–200% creates good results in high-resolution images. **Radius** determines how many pixels will be included in the edge comparison; higher radius values result in more pronounced edge effects. **Threshold** defines the difference that is required for Photoshop to identify an edge. A threshold of 15 means that colors must be more than 15 levels different; using a higher Threshold protects the smooth tones in the faces, while still allowing detail in the faces (the eyes, for example) to be sharpened.

> *Note:*
>
> *Using Gaussian Blur and Unsharp Masking in tandem is a common technique for cleaning up grainy images.*

9. **Change the Amount to 150%, the Radius to 3.0 pixels, and the Threshold to 15 levels.**

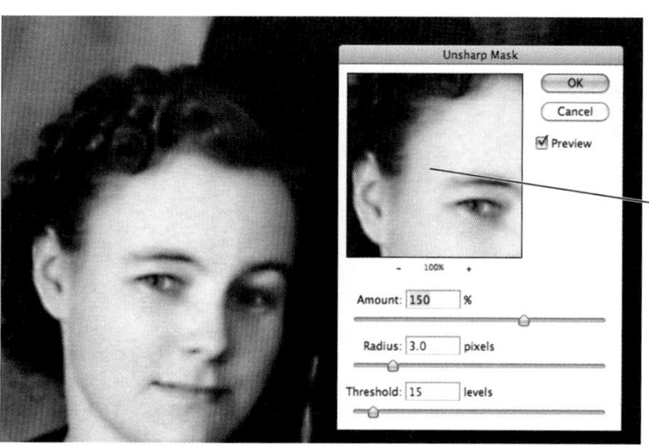

Drag here or click in the document window to change the visible area in the preview window.

> *Note:*
>
> *The degree of sharpening applied to an image is often a matter of personal choice; however, oversharpening an image produces a halo effect around the edges.*

> *Note:*
>
> *The Sharpen, Sharpen More, and Sharpen Edges filters apply sharpening with no user control.*

10. **Click OK to apply the Unsharp Mask filter.**

11. **Choose File>Save As. Save the file as a native Photoshop file named** rosemans_working.psd **in your WIP>Menu folder. Continue to the next exercise.**

The Smart Sharpen Filter

PHOTOSHOP FOUNDATIONS

The Smart Sharpen filter allows you to control the amount of sharpening that occurs in shadow and highlight areas.

Remove defines the algorithm used to sharpen the image. Gaussian Blur is the method used by the Unsharp Mask filter. Lens Blur detects edges and detail, and provides finer detail and fewer halos. Motion Blur tries to reduce the effects of blur due to movement at a defined angle.

The **More Accurate** check box processes the file more slowly for a more accurate blur removal.

In Advanced mode, you can use the Shadow and Highlight tabs to adjust sharpening of only those areas.

Fade Amount adjusts the amount of sharpening.

Tonal Width controls the range of tones that will be modified. Smaller values restrict the adjustments to only darker regions for shadows and only lighter regions for highlights.

Radius defines the size of the area around each pixel used to determine whether a pixel is in the shadows or highlights.

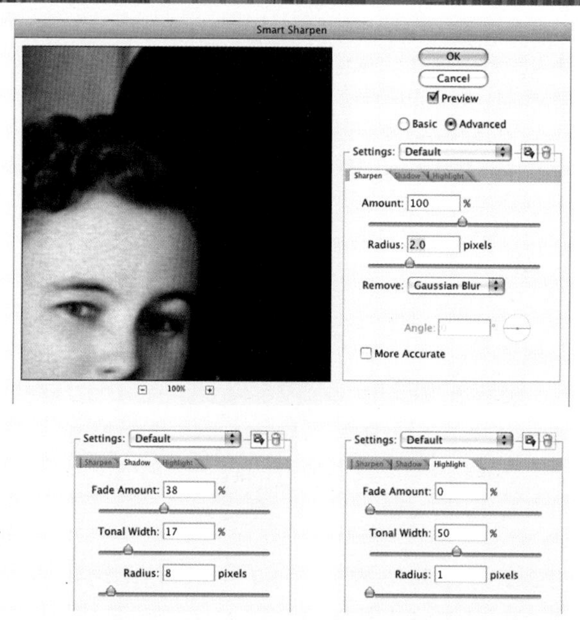

Heal Severe Scratches

The blur and sharpen routine from the previous exercise improved the client's image — the obvious grain is gone. Even though the edges are slightly less sharp than the original scan, they are sharp enough to produce good results when the image is printed. If you're working with images that aren't 70 years old, you will be able to produce far sharper edges using these same techniques.

There are still a number of problems in the image that require intervention. Photoshop includes several tools for changing the pixels in an image — from painting with a brush to nudging selections on a layer to using repair tools specifically designed for adjusting pixels based on other pixels in the image.

The **Spot Healing Brush tool** allows you to remove imperfections by blending the surrounding pixels. The **Healing Brush tool** has a similar function, except you can define the source pixels that will be used to heal a specific area. The **Patch tool** allows you to repair a selected area with pixels from another area of the image by dragging the selection area.

> *Note:*
>
> *Throughout this project, you are going to clean up blemishes on images and make other adjustments that require looking at very small areas. It can be very helpful to clean your monitor so you don't mistake on-screen dust and smudges with flaws in the images you are adjusting.*

1. **With rosemans_working.psd open, view the image at 100%. Set up the image window so you can see the lower half of the image.**

2. **Select the Spot Healing Brush tool in the Tools panel.**

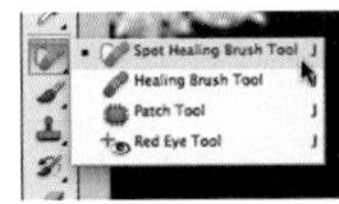

3. **In the Control panel, choose a 20-pixel hard-edge brush.**

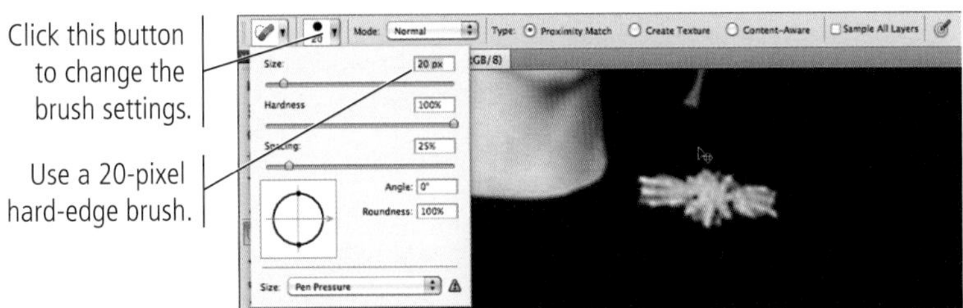

Click this button to change the brush settings.

Use a 20-pixel hard-edge brush.

Proximity Match is the default setting; this method uses the pixels around the edge of the selection to find an image area to use as a patch for the selected area. The **Create Texture** method uses all the pixels in the selection to create a texture for repairing the area. The **Content Aware** mode attempts to match the detail in surrounding areas while healing pixels (this method does not work well for areas with hard edges or sharp contrast). If you select **Sample All Layers**, the tool pulls pixel data from all visible layers.

> *Note:*
>
> *You will work extensively with brushes and brush settings in Project 7.*

4. **Place the cursor over the small white spot in the bottom-left corner of the image. Click immediately over the white spot to heal it.**

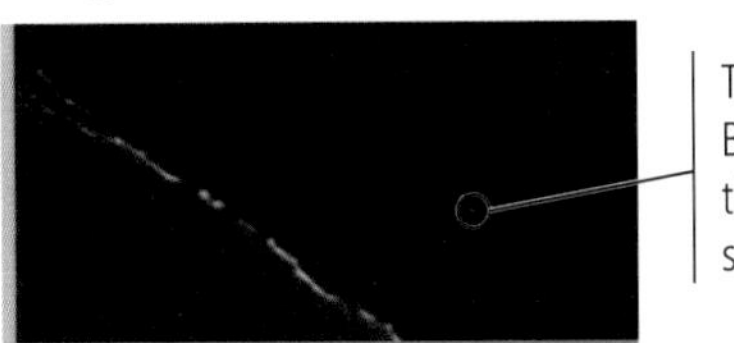

The Spot Healing Brush tool shows the size of the selected brush.

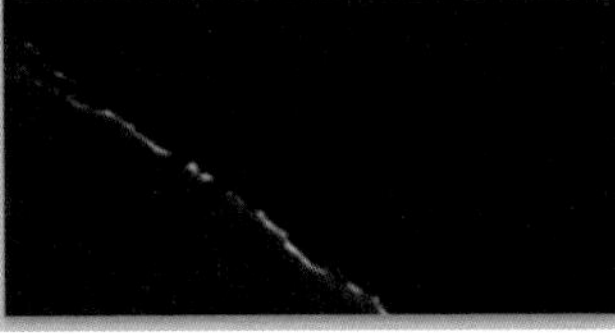

> *Note:*
>
> *Because this image is very dark, it might be difficult to see the cursor over the black image areas. To check the size of the brush, try moving it outside the image area.*

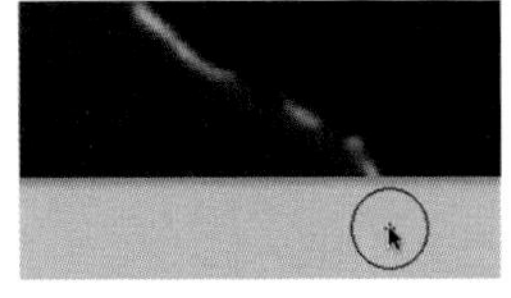

5. **Using the same technique, remove the remaining white spots from the dark areas of the Rosemans' clothing.**

6. **Place the Spot Healing Brush cursor over the white spot on the younger woman's chin, and then click to heal the spot.**

   The Spot Healing Brush tool is not effective in every situation. As you can see in this case, the tool actually makes the spot larger and more obvious instead of removing it.

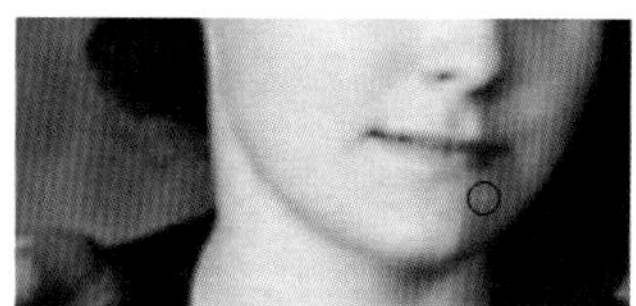
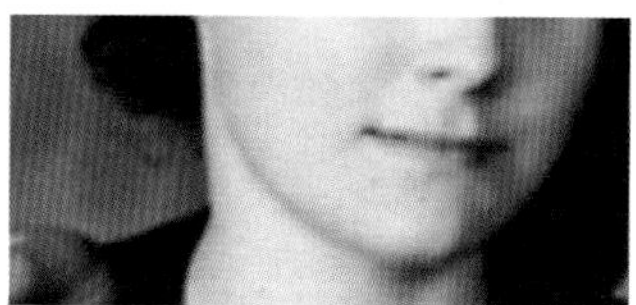

7. **Press Command/Control-Z to undo the previous step.**

8. **Choose the Healing Brush tool (nested under the Spot Healing Brush tool).**

Healing Brush tool

9. **In the Control panel, choose a small brush size that's slightly larger than the white spot on the girl's chin (we used 9 pixels).**

   When using the Healing Brush tool, the Mode menu determines the blending mode used to heal an area. The default option (Normal) samples the source color and transparency to blend the new pixels smoothly into the area being healed. The Replace mode preserves texture in the healed area when you used a soft-edge brush.

Note:

Multiple, Screen, Darken, Lighten, Color, and Luminosity modes have the same function as the blending modes for specific layers and brushes (refer to Project 2 for an explanation of each blending mode).

Note:

You can use the bracket keys to enlarge (]) or reduce ([) the Healing Brush tool brush size.

Aligning the Healing Source

PHOTOSHOP FOUNDATIONS

When you work with the Healing Brush and Clone Stamp tools, you have the option to align the source to the cursor. If the Align option is turned off, the source starting point will be relative to the image. If the Align option is turned on, the source starting point will be relative to the cursor. The following images illustrate this idea.

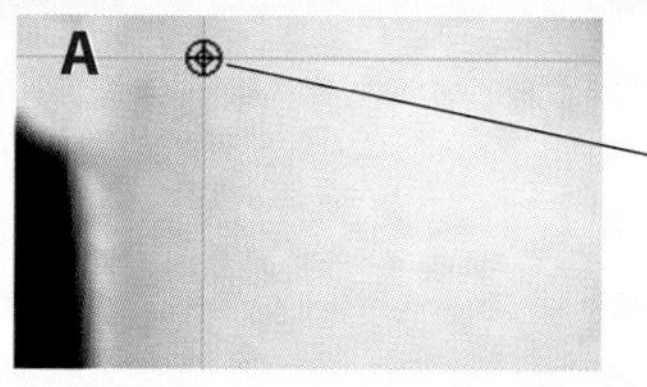

We first Option/Alt-clicked at the guide intersection to define the healing source.

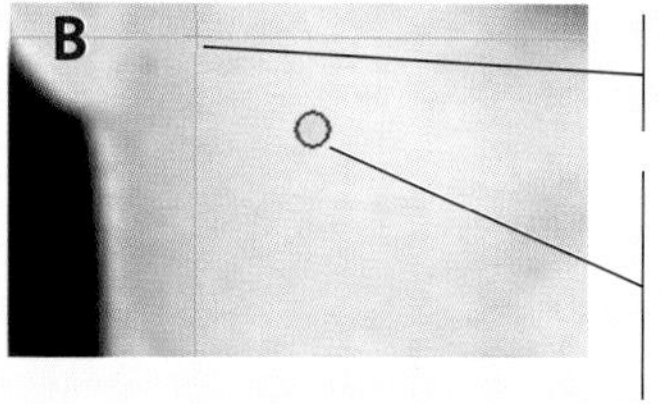

The crosshair shows the source of the healing.

This circle shows the cursor location where we clicked with the Healing Brush tool.

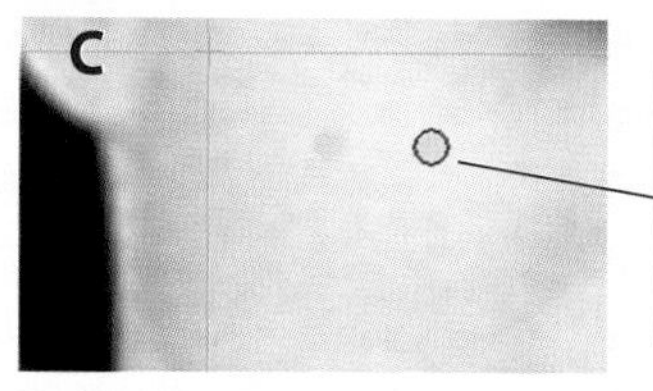

When the Aligned option is turned off, the source remains in the same position even when the Healing Brush tool is clicked farther to the right.

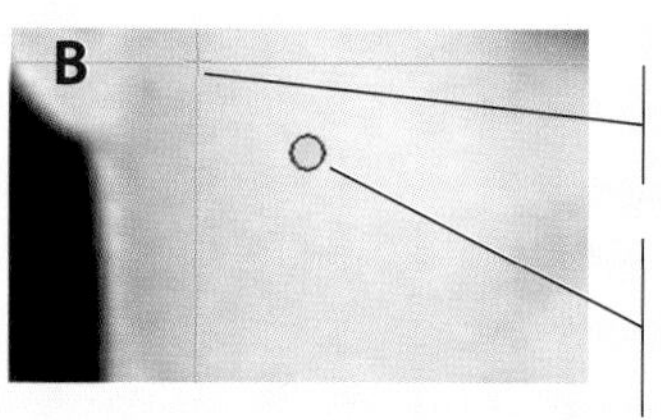

The crosshair shows the original defined source.

This is the first "healed" spot where we clicked after defining the source.

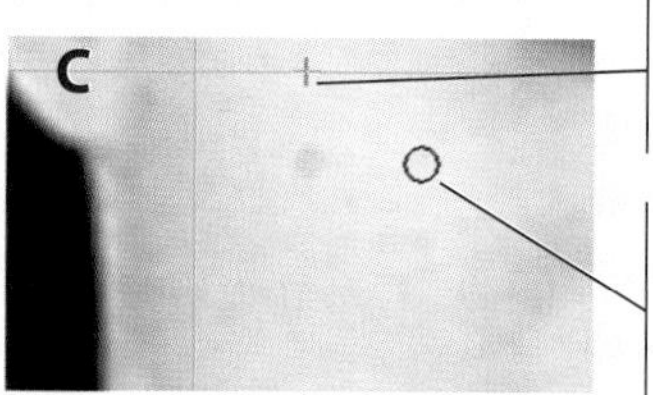

When the Aligned option is turned on, the source moves relative to the tool cursor.

Clicking farther to the right moves the source the same distance from its defined origin.

10. **Place the cursor directly below the spot you want to heal. Press Option/Alt and click to define the healing source.**

    Pressing Option/Alt with the Healing Brush tool allows you to select the source of the brush or the pixels that will be used to heal the spot where you next click.

    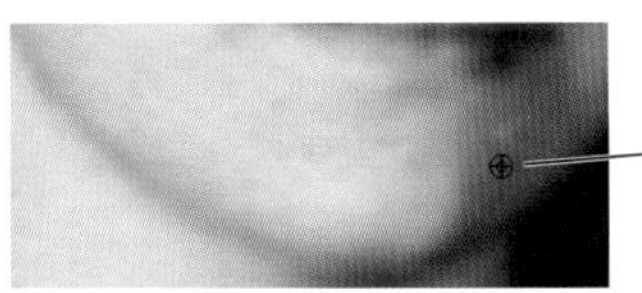
    Pressing Option/Alt allows you to define the source pixels that will be used to heal the next spot you click.

11. **Place the cursor over the blemish on the girl's chin and click.**

    Unlike the Spot Healing Brush tool, the Healing Brush tool allows you to define the source of the healing. By choosing nearby pixels as the healing source, the blemish on the girl's chin disappears, and that spot blends nicely into the surrounding pixels.

    The Healing Brush tool blends colors from the source pixels (which you defined in Step 10) with colors in the area where you click. You can also change the source from Sampled (the pixels you defined by Option/Alt-clicking) to Pattern, which uses pixels from a defined pattern to heal the area. The Pattern option is a good choice for creating artistic effects, rather than healing blemishes in an existing photo.

    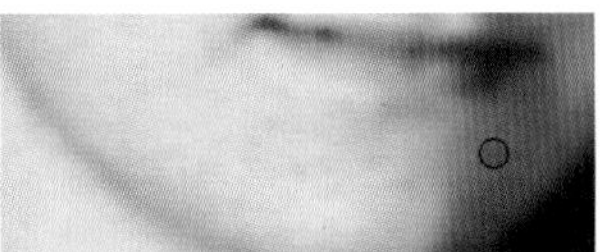 
    After clicking, the spot is healed using the source pixels.

12. **Save the file and continue to the next exercise.**

> *Note:*
>
> *Using the Sample menu in the Control panel, you can sample source pixels from the current layer, from all layers including and below the current layer, or from all visible layers.*

> *Note:*
>
> *It might help to zoom in when you want to heal small areas such as this spot on the girl's chin. We are working at 200% in these screen shots.*

 Clone out Major Damage

The client's image has definitely been improved by removing the grain and healing the small blemishes, but four major areas of damage still need to be fixed. These larger areas require more control over the healing process, which the Clone Stamp tool provides.

The Clone Stamp tool paints one part of an image over another part, which is useful for duplicating objects or removing defects in an image. As with the Healing Brush tool, you can define the source that will be cloned when you click with the tool; the difference is that whole pixels are copied, not just their color value.

> *Note:*
>
> *Be careful when you use the Clone Stamp tool, however, because depending on the brush you choose, you can actually create more damage than you fix.*

1. **With the file rosemans_working.psd open, zoom into the bottom-left corner (where the crease marks the image) and select the Clone Stamp tool.**

2. **In the Control panel, choose a soft-edge brush large enough to cover the crease.**

    When you are using the Clone Stamp tool, the Control panel combines brush options (brush size, blending mode, opacity, and flow) with healing options (alignment and sample source, which you used in the previous exercise).

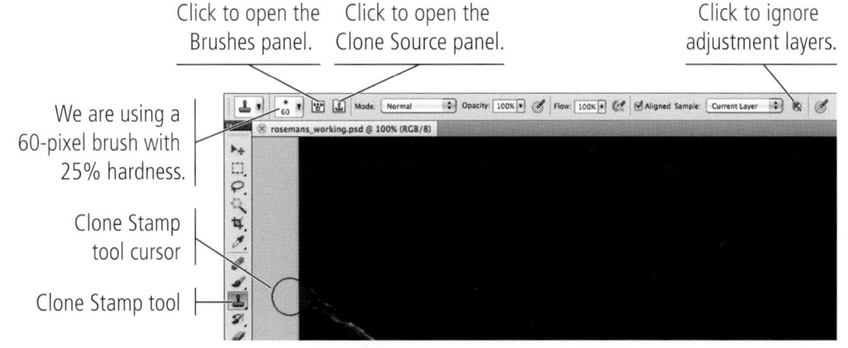

Click to open the Brushes panel.
Click to open the Clone Source panel.
Click to ignore adjustment layers.
We are using a 60-pixel brush with 25% hardness.
Clone Stamp tool cursor
Clone Stamp tool

3. **In the Control panel, make sure the Align option is turned on.**

   In this case, you want the cloning source to remain relative to the cursor, even if you stop and start several times. If you clone a large area relative to the same source origin (in other words, with the Align option turned off), you could end up with an unwanted pattern in the area you clone.

4. **Place the cursor directly above and to the right of the crease. Option/Alt-click to define the cloning source.**

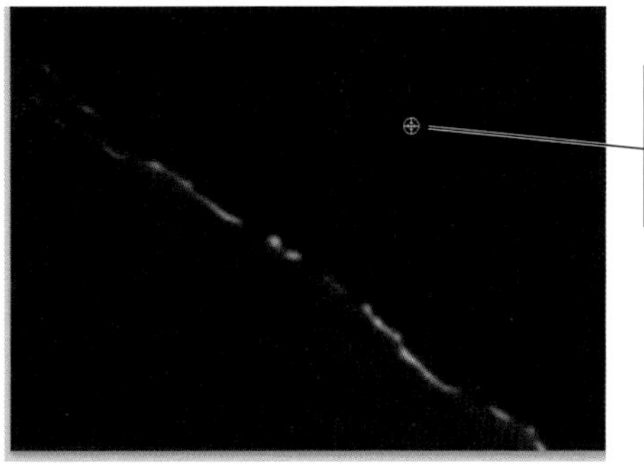

Option/Alt-click to define the cloning source, just as you did with the Healing Brush tool.

5. **Click over an area of the crease and drag to clone out the crease.**

   As you drag, notice that the source crosshairs move in relation to the Clone Stamp cursor. Because you turned on the Align option in Step 3, you can stop and restart cloning, and the source will retain the same relative position to the tool cursor.

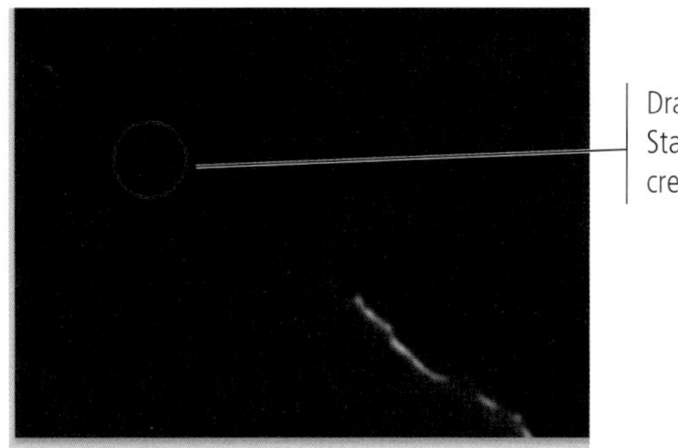

Drag with the Clone Stamp tool until the crease is no longer visible.

6. **Use the same process to fill in the torn area in the bottom-right corner of the image.**

7. **Zoom into the scratch on the man's left shoulder.**

   Cloning out damage in areas of solid color is fairly simple. This area presents a more difficult problem since the area you need to fix has an edge that must be maintained.

8. **In the Control panel, select a brush that just barely covers the edge of the man's jacket, and make sure the Align option is off.**

   To prevent cloning a hard edge, we used a 30-pixel brush with a 50% Hardness value.

Note:

When using the Clone Stamp tool, hard-edge brushes can result in harsh lines where you clone pixels; soft-edge brushes can help prevent harsh lines from appearing.

Note:

You can use the bracket keys to enlarge (]) or reduce ([) the Clone Stamp brush size.

Note:

When you are cloning — especially large areas — it's usually a good idea to clone in small strokes or even single clicks. This method can help you avoid cloning in patterns or "railroad tracks" that do as much damage as good. When cloning large areas, it's also a good idea to frequently resample the clone source to avoid cloning the same pixels into a new noticeable pattern.

9. **Place the cursor over the edge you want to reproduce and Option/Alt-click to define the source.**

   Because the Align option is turned off, each successive click uses the same source point.

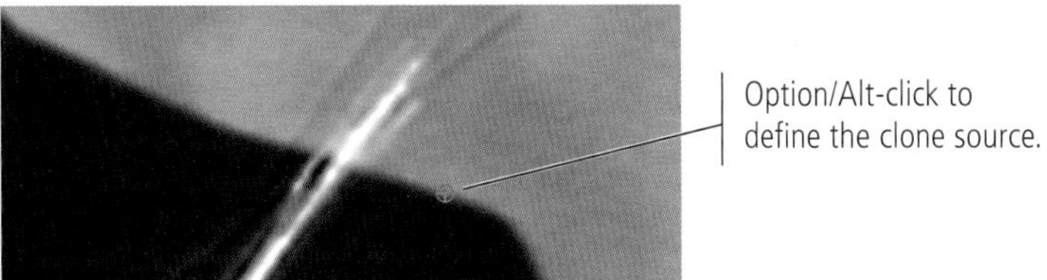

Option/Alt-click to define the clone source.

10. **Place the cursor over the scratched pixels on the man's shoulder.**

    As you move the Clone Stamp tool cursor, the source pixels move along with the tool cursor to give you a preview of what will happen when you click.

11. **Click without dragging when the cloned pixels appear to align properly with the area behind the scratch.**

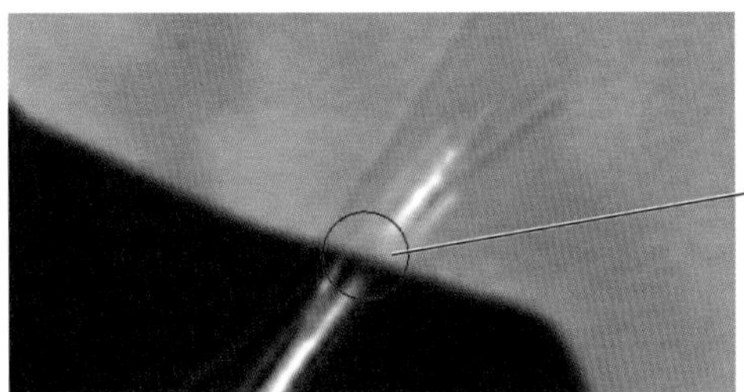

Clicking without dragging clones a 30-pixel area. Because the brush we chose has 50% hardness, the center (where the shoulder edge is) is clear, but the outside parts of the brush are feathered into the surrounding area.

12. **Move the cursor slightly to the left, again centering the cursor preview over the would-be edge, and click without dragging.**

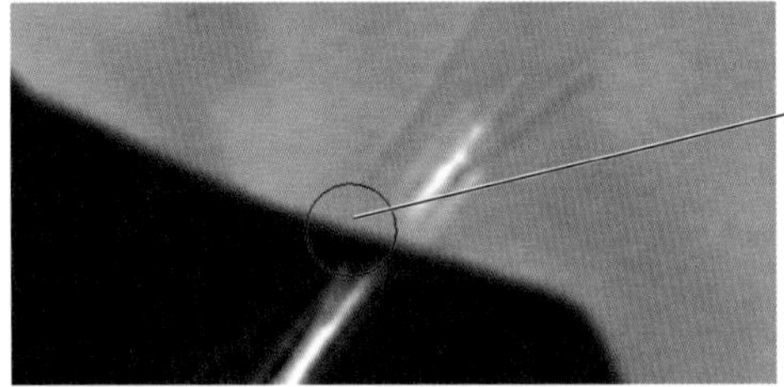

With the Align option turned off, you again clone from the same source point.

13. **Repeat this process as necessary to clone out the remaining scratch along the man's shoulder.**

    We clicked two more times to completely remove the scratch along the shoulder line.

14. **Using the Clone Stamp tool, clean up the rest of the scratch around the man's shoulder.**

    We used a 30-pixel brush size with a 25% Hardness value. In the area of the backdrop, we defined an aligned source that was very close to the scratched areas. By clicking and dragging in small swaths, and by clicking numerous times without dragging, we were able to maintain the mottled appearance of the backdrop without creating pattern-like railroad tracks with the cloning tool.

Note:

If you're not happy with the result of a clone, simply undo the action (Command/Control-Z, or using the History panel) and try again. Cloning — especially edges — often takes more than one try to achieve the desired result.

Note:

As we stated earlier, it's also a good idea to frequently resample the clone source to avoid cloning in unwanted patterns.

15. **Using any method you prefer, clean up the scratches and glue residue on the left side of the photo.**

As with the mottled background above the man's shoulder, it's best to use a small, soft-edge brush and clone out the damage in short strokes or single clicks. Experiment with frequently moving the clone source so you can avoid creating an unwanted pattern while removing the damage.

16. **Choose File>Save As and choose TIFF in the Format menu. Change the file name to rosemans_fixed.tif and save it with the default TIFF options in your WIP>Menu folder.**

The Clone Source Panel in Depth

PHOTOSHOP FOUNDATIONS

The Clone Source panel (Window>Clone Source) allows you to store up to five sources for the Clone Stamp or Healing Brush tool. These sources can be from any layer of any open image, which allows you to create unique blended effects by combining pixels from multiple layers or multiple files.

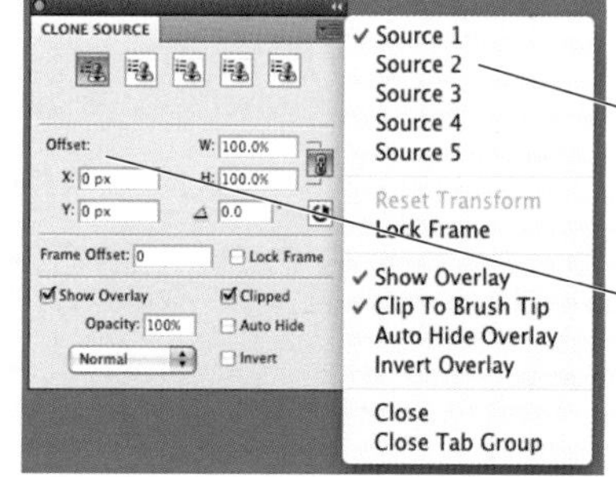

Store and access up to five sources from any layer of any open image.

Transform the offset, size, and angle of the clone source.

The Show Overlay options allow you to show (at the defined opacity) the source pixels on top of the area where you are cloning. For example, let's say you want to clone the gorilla into the giraffe photo. You would first define a clone source in the gorilla image, and then make the giraffe image active.

With the Show Overlay option checked, placing the Clone Stamp cursor over the giraffe image shows the gorilla on top of the giraffe. When you click in the giraffe image with the Clone Stamp tool, that area of the gorilla image will be cloned into the giraffe image; the overlay allows you to preview the areas of the source that will be cloned into the giraffe image.

If the Auto Hide option is checked, the overlay is only visible when the mouse button is not clicked. The Invert option reverses the overlay into a negative representation of the source image. You can also change the blending mode of the overlay from the default Normal to Darken, Lighten, or Difference.

We defined a clone source here.

When the Clipped option is checked, the clone source appears within the tool cursor area.

Using the overlay, you can see the Clone Stamp cursor in relation to the clone source. Clicking will clone this spot from the gorilla image into the giraffe image.

We defined a clone source here.

Stage 2 Correcting Lighting Problems

Before you start correcting problems with lighting and color, you should understand the different parts of an image, as well as the terms used to describe these areas.

- **Highlights** are defined as the lightest areas of the image that include detail. Direct sources of light such as a light bulb or reflected sunlight on water are called **specular highlights**; they should not be considered the highlights of an image.
- **Shadows** are the darkest areas of the image that still contain some detail; areas of solid black are not considered shadow tones.
- The shades between the highlights and shadows are the **midtones** (or **gamma**) of the image.

Contrast and saturation play an integral role in reproducing high-quality images. **Contrast** refers to the tonal variation within an image; an image primarily composed of highlights and shadows is a high-contrast image, while an image with more detail in the midtones is a low-contrast image.

Contrast is closely linked to **saturation**, which refers to the intensity of a color or its variation away from gray. The saturation of individual colors in an image, and the correct saturation of different colors in relation to one another, affects the overall contrast of the image. If an image is under- or oversaturated, the contrast suffers — detail is lost and colors appear either muted or too bright.

Note:

Image adjustments can be applied directly to the image pixels or as non-destructive adjustment layers using the Adjustments panel. In this project, you edit the actual image pixels; you use the adjustment layer method in Project 6.

Correct Problems with Brightness/Contrast

Depending on the image, several tools are available for correcting problems related to images that are either too dark or too light. The most basic adjustment option — Brightness/Contrast — can fix images that need overall adjustment to brightness, contrast, or both. If an image requires more sophisticated adjustment, you should use one of the other adjustment options.

1. **Open the file buffalo.jpg from your WIP>Menu folder.**

   This image has an overall dark feel, probably caused by poor lighting or underexposure. The Brightness/Contrast adjustment can correct this problem.

2. **Choose Image>Adjustments>Brightness/Contrast and make sure the Preview option is checked.**

3. **Drag the Brightness slider to +50.**

Increasing the overall brightness creates an immediate improvement in this image, although some areas of detail are still muddy.

4. **Drag the Contrast slider to +15.**

Increasing the contrast brings out more detail in the food texture, which is the focal point of the image (pay particular attention to the meat).

5. **Click OK to apply the change.**

6. **Use any of the techniques you learned earlier to fix the white spot on the front edge of the steak.**

We used the Spot Healing Brush tool to remove the white spot.

7. **Save the file in your WIP>Menu folder as a TIFF file named `buffalo_fixed.tif` using the default TIFF options.**

8. **Close the file and continue to the next exercise.**

Note:

Remember, you have to choose File> Save As to save the file with a different name or format.

Correct Contrast and Tonal Range with Levels

The **tonal range** of an image is the amount of variation between the lightest highlight and the darkest shadow in a particular image. A grayscale image can contain 256 possible shades of gray. Each channel of a color image can also contain 256 possible shades of gray. To achieve the best contrast in an image, the tonal range of the image should include as many levels of gray as are available.

While the Brightness/Contrast option is a good choice for making basic adjustments, the Levels adjustment is the best approach for enhancing image detail throughout the entire tonal range. Using Levels, adjusting contrast is a three-step process:

- Determine the image's highlight areas (the lightest areas that contain detail).
- Determine the image's shadow areas (the darkest areas that contain detail).
- Adjust the gamma (the contrast in midtones of an image) to determine the proportion of darker tones to lighter tones.

1. **Open the file `chef.jpg` from the WIP>Menu folder.**

2. **Display the Histogram panel (Window>Histogram), and then choose Expanded View from the panel Options menu.**

   The Histogram panel can help you identify problems that need to be corrected. When you first display the panel, it probably appears in Compact view, which shows only the graphs for the individual color channels and the composite image.

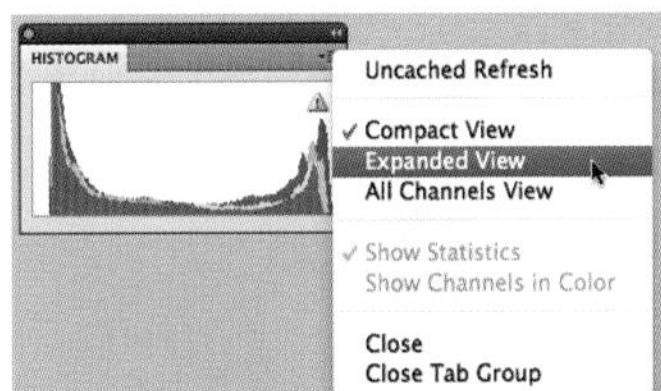

Histogram Statistics

PHOTOSHOP FOUNDATIONS

The histogram shows the distribution of pixels — or more accurately the tonal values of those pixels — from the darkest to the lightest portions of an image, for the entire image or for individual color channels. The Histogram panel can help identify problems that need to be corrected, while also showing the overall effect of a correction you might be considering.

In Expanded view, you can see more information about how pixels are distributed in the image (from shadows on the left to midtones in the center to highlights on the right).

- The **Mean** value is an average point of the brightness values. A Mean of 128 usually identifies a well-balanced image. Images with a Mean of 170 to 255 are light; images with a Mean lower than 90 are very dark.
- The **Standard Deviation** (Std Dev) value represents how widely the brightness values vary.
- The **Median** value shows the middle value in the range of color values.
- The **Pixels** value displays the total number of pixels used for the graphic displayed on the histogram.
- The **Level** statistic displays the intensity level of the pixels below the mouse cursor.
- **Count** shows the number of pixels in the area below the cursor.
- Values displayed as a **Percentile** represent the percentage of pixels **below or to the left** of the cursor location. Zero represents the left edge of the image and 100% is the right edge.
- The **Cache Level** is determined by the Performance preferences and is related to the Cache Refresh icon (and Warning icon). The larger your cache, the more you can do before the image and the disk cache don't match. On the other hand, a larger cache requires more RAM for the application to run smoothly.

3. **In the Histogram panel, change the Channel menu to RGB.**

   The histogram — the chart that shows the distribution of tones — can display a single graph for the entire composite image (all channels combined) or for individual channels.

   In Expanded view, the panel shows the distribution of pixels from the darkest to the lightest portion of the image, for the entire image or for individual color channels.

> *Note:*
>
> *If you see the Warning icon in the Histogram panel, click the icon to match the disk cache with what's happening in the live image.*

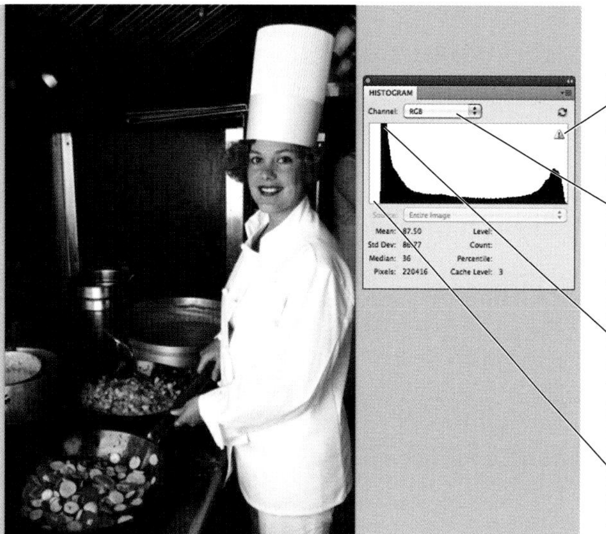

If you see a warning icon, click it to reset the cache.

Choose from this menu to view and modify the histogram for individual channels.

These shadow values are pushing out of the histogram "container," which shows that there is a problem in the shadow tones.

The white space at the left of the histogram indicates that some tones in the available range are not being used.

The Gradient Map Adjustment

PHOTOSHOP FOUNDATIONS

The **Gradient Map adjustment** (Image>Adjustments>Gradient Map) enables you to create interesting artistic effects by mapping the tones of an image to the shades in a defined gradient.

In the Gradient Map dialog box, you can apply any defined gradient by clicking the arrow to the right of the gradient sample and choosing from the pop-up menu, or you can edit the selected gradient by clicking the sample gradient ramp. The **Dither** option adds random noise to the effect. If you check the **Reverse** option, image highlights map to the left end of the gradient, and image shadows map to the right end of the gradient, effectively reversing the gradient map.

The composite histogram of an RGB image starts at the darkest point and ends at the lightest point with 256 total possible tonal values. If you think of the gradient as having 256 steps from one end to the other, then you can see how the shades of the selected gradient map to the tones of the original image.

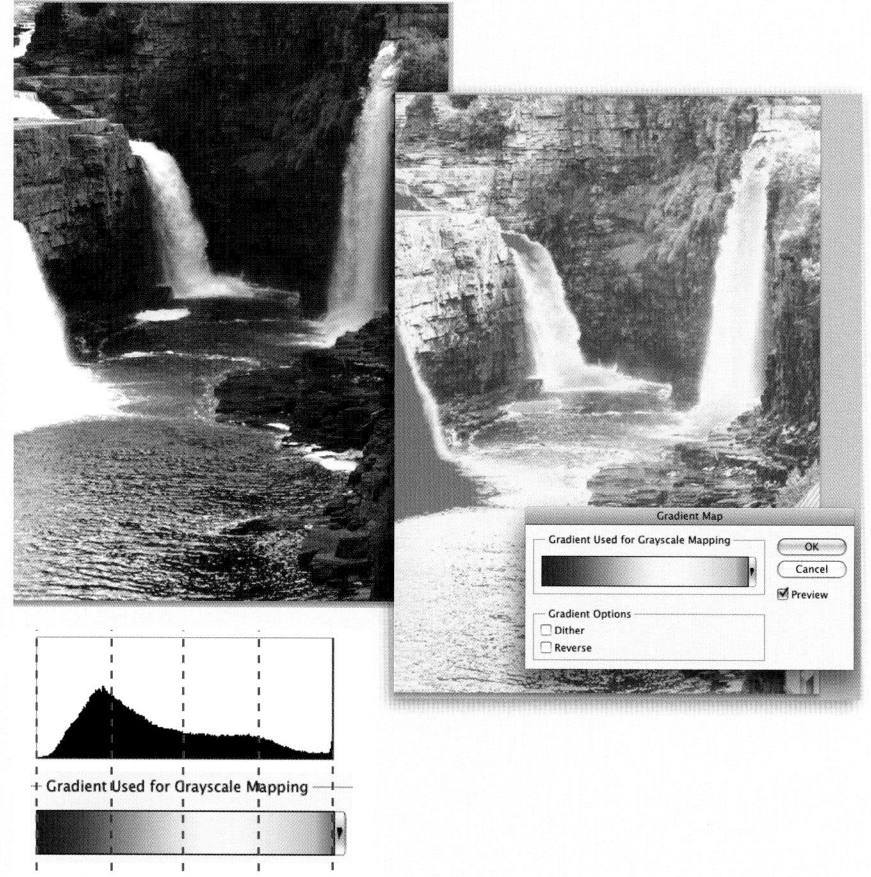

4. **If you see one, click the Warning icon in the upper-right corner of the panel to reset the cache.**

Every time you zoom in or out of an image, Photoshop stores the results of the display in a **cache** (a drive location that keeps track of what you're doing). The image you're looking at on the Histogram often doesn't match the results on the drive. The Warning icon shows there's a problem; clicking the icon resets the image and rereads the cache.

Note:

You can change input and output levels by moving the sliders, entering actual values in the boxes below the slider sets, or by using the eyedroppers to select the brightest and darkest points in the image.

5. **Choose Image>Adjustments>Levels and make sure Preview is checked.**

The Levels dialog box shows a histogram like the one shown in the Histogram panel.

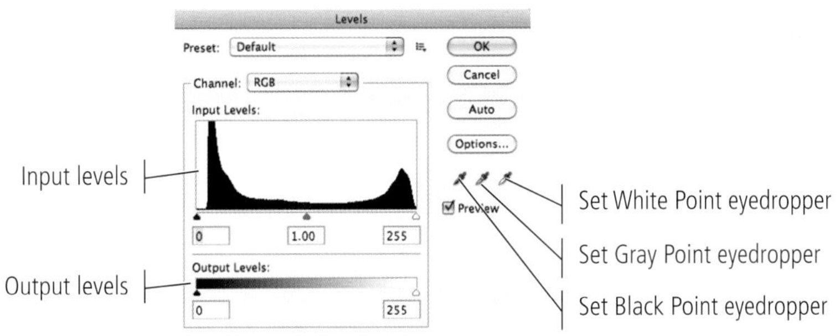

The Levels dialog box has two sets of sliders to control input levels and output levels. Each set has a black slider for adjusting the shadows in an image and a white slider to adjust highlights. The Input Levels slider also has a gray triangle in the center of the slider bar for adjusting gamma or midtones.

The Input sliders in the Levels dialog box correspond to the tonal range of the image. Any pixels that exist to the left of the Input Shadow slider are reproduced as solid black, and they have no detail; any pixels that exist to the right of the Input Highlight slider are reproduced as pure white.

6. **Move the Input Shadow slider to the right until it touches the left edge of the curve.**

This simple adjustment extends the colors in the image to take advantage of all 256 possible tones. This adjustment has a small effect on the shadow area of the image, but the majority of the colors in the image are still clustered near the shadow point (as you can see by the spike in the histogram).

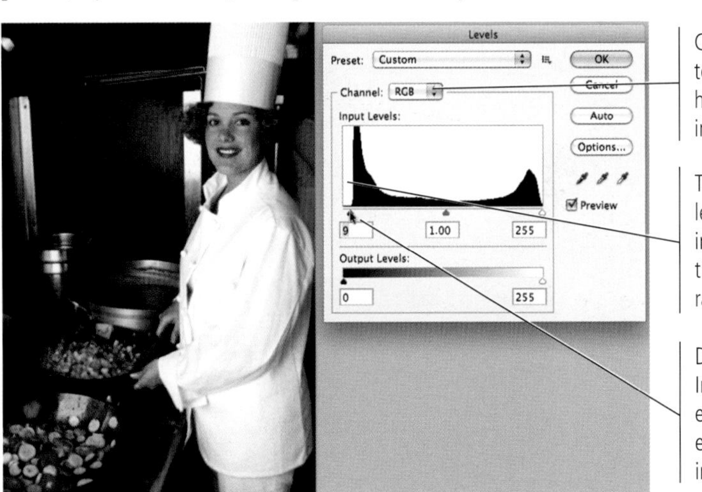

Note:

To decrease contrast in an image, you can adjust the Output sliders. This method effectively compresses the range of possible tones that can be reproduced, forcing all areas of the image into a smaller tonal range. Areas originally set to 0 are reproduced at the value of the Output Shadow slider; areas originally set to 255 are output at the value of the Output Highlight slider.

7. **Move the Input Gamma slider to the left until the middle box below the slider shows approximately 1.75.**

   The Input Gamma slider controls the proportion of darker tones to lighter tones in the midtones of an image. If you increase gamma, you increase the proportion of lighter grays in the image; this effectively increases contrast in lighter shades and lightens the entire image. If you decrease gamma, you extend the tonal range of darker shades; this allows those areas of the image to be reproduced with a larger range of shades, which increases the contrast in darker shades.

> *Note:*
>
> *The entire image is lightened by increasing gamma.*

Levels
Preset: Custom
OK
Cancel
Auto
Options...
Channel: RGB
Input Levels:
Preview
9
1.75
255
Output Levels:
0
255

Dragging the Gamma Input slider extends the range between the midtone and the highlights, creating greater contrast and showing more detail throughout the image.

8. **Click OK to close the Levels dialog box.**
9. **Save the file in your WIP>Menu folder as a TIFF file named `chef_fixed.tif`.**
10. **Close the file and then continue to the next exercise.**

Identifying Shadows and Highlights

PHOTOSHOP FOUNDATIONS

When you move the Shadow and Highlight sliders in the Levels dialog box, you change the **black point** and **white point** of the image — the points at which pixels become black or white. The goal is to find highlight and shadow points that maintain detail. Choosing a point that has no detail causes the area to turn totally white (highlight) or black (shadow) with no detail reproduced. In some images, it can be difficult to visually identify the black and white points in an image; in these cases you can use the Levels dialog box to help you find those areas.

If you press Option/Alt while dragging the Input Shadow or Input Highlight slider, the image turns entirely white or black (respectively). As you drag, the first pixels that become visible are the darkest shadow and the lightest highlight.

Once you identify the highlight and shadow points in the image, select the White Point eyedropper and click the highlight, and then select the Black Point eyedropper and click the shadow to define those two areas of the image.

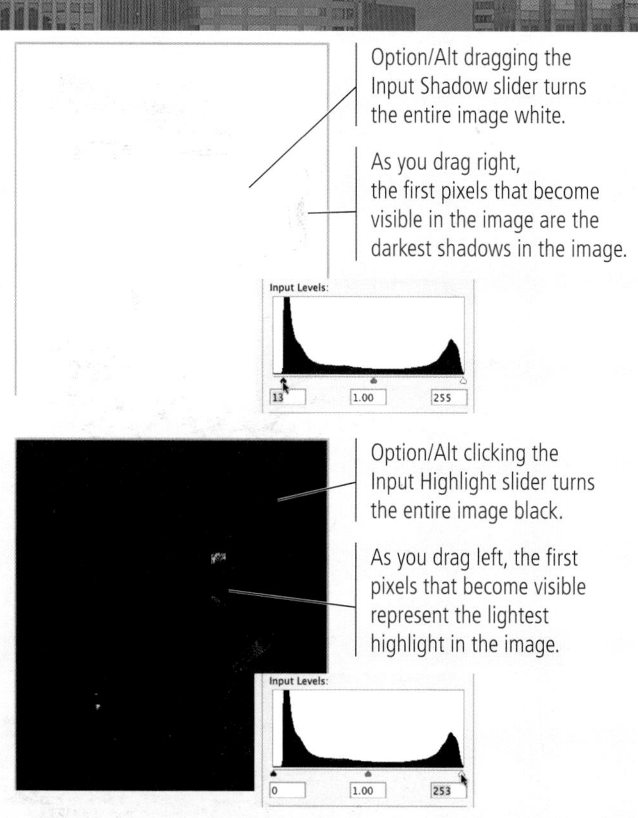

Option/Alt dragging the Input Shadow slider turns the entire image white.
As you drag right, the first pixels that become visible in the image are the darkest shadows in the image.
Input Levels:
13
1.00
255
Option/Alt clicking the Input Highlight slider turns the entire image black.
As you drag left, the first pixels that become visible represent the lightest highlight in the image.
Input Levels:
0
1.00
253

Correct Lighting Problems with the Exposure Adjustment

Many images are either over- or underexposed when photographed. If an image is underexposed, it appears dark and lacks detail in the shadows. If an image is overexposed, it appears too light and lacks detail in the highlights. You can use the Exposure adjustment to correct exposure — and thus, the overall detail and contrast in the image.

Keep in mind, however, that Photoshop cannot create information that doesn't exist. If you have an underexposed image with no detail in the shadow areas, Photoshop cannot generate that detail for you. Some problems are simply beyond fixing.

The Exposure dialog box is designed to make tonal adjustments to 32- and 64-bit HDR (high dynamic range) images, but it also works with 8-bit and 16-bit images. The Exposure adjustment works by performing calculations in a linear color space (gamma 1.0) rather than the image's current color space.

> *Note:*
>
> *HDR refers to high-density range (32- or 64-bit) images.*

1. **Open chicken.jpg from your WIP>Menu folder.**

2. **Choose Image>Adjustments>Exposure and make sure Preview is checked.**

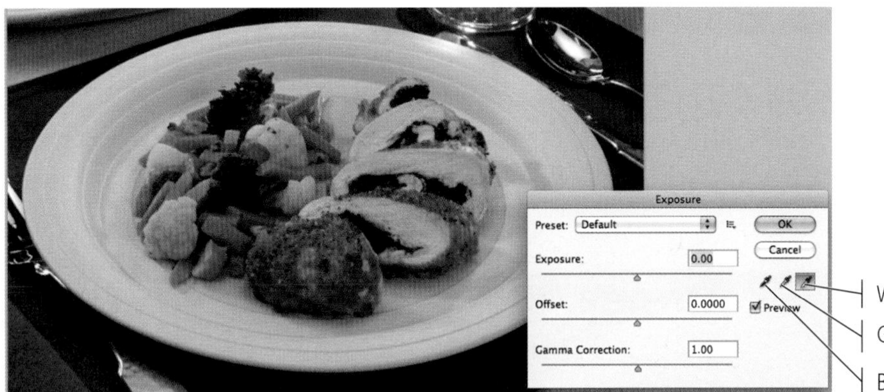

White Point eyedropper

Gray Point eyedropper

Black Point eyedropper

3. **Click the White Point eyedropper, and then click the white area on the top edge of the plate.**

   The eyedroppers in the Exposure dialog box adjust the image's luminance (or the degree of lightness, from white to black). By adjusting the luminance only, you can change the lightness of the image without affecting the color.

   - Clicking with the Black Point eyedropper shifts the point you click to black (0 luminance).
   - Clicking with the White Point eyedropper shifts the point you click to white (100 luminance).
   - Clicking with the Gray Point eyedropper shifts the point you click to gray (50 luminance).

> *Note:*
>
> *The White Point and Gray Point eyedroppers affect the Exposure value. The Black Point eyedropper affects the Offset value.*

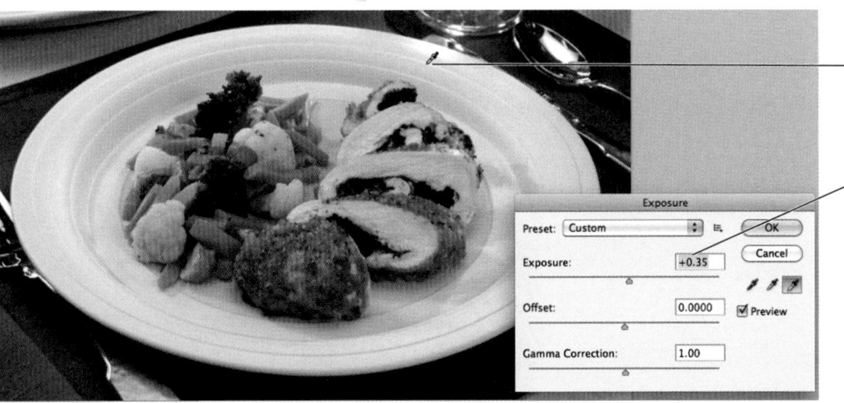

Click here with the White Point eyedropper to define the white area of the image.

Clicking with the White Point eyedropper changes the Exposure setting.

4. **Drag the Gamma Correction slider left to extend the midtone range, which increases contrast and brings out detail in the image. (We used a setting of 1.25.)**

The Gamma slider adjusts the image midtones. Dragging the slider left lightens the image, improving contrast and detail in the midtones and highlights. Dragging the slider right darkens the image, extending the range and increasing detail in the shadows.

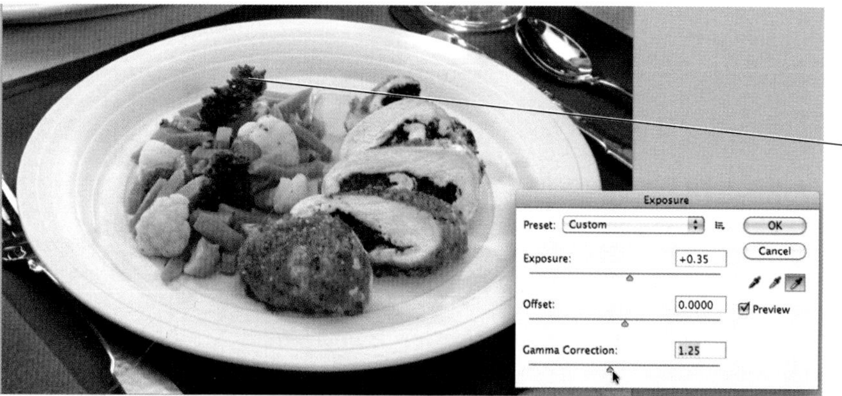

Extending the Gamma Correction value into the shadow range brings out more detail in the midtones.

5. **Click the Offset slider and drag very slightly left to add detail back into the midtones and shadows.**

The Offset slider lightens (dragged to the right) or darkens (dragged to the left) the shadows and midtones of the image. The white point (highlight) remains unaffected, but all other pixels are affected.

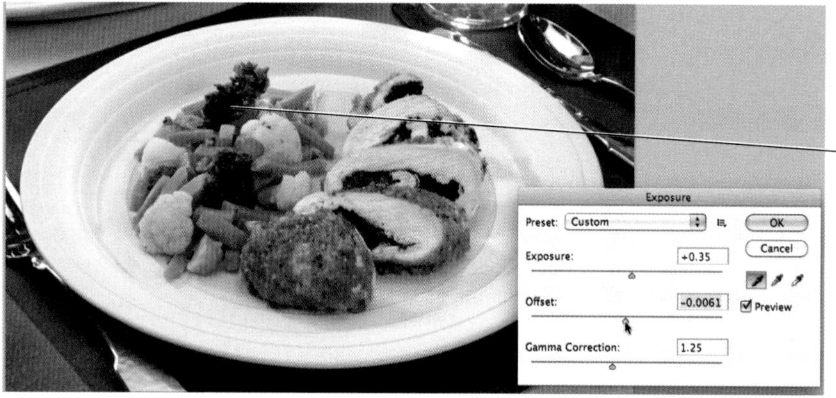

Decreasing the Offset value adds detail back into the shadows.

6. **Click OK to finalize the adjustment.**

7. **Save the file as a TIFF file named `chicken_fixed.tif` in your WIP>Menu folder.**

8. **Close the file and continue to the next stage of the project.**

Stage 3 Correcting Color Problems

Before starting to color-correct an image, you need to understand how different colors interact with one another. There are two primary color models — RGB and CMYK — used to output digital images. (Other models such as LAB and HSL have their own purposes in color conversion and correction, but they are not typically output models.)

Although the RGB and CMYK models handle color in different ways, these two color models are definitely linked. RGB colors are directly inverse (opposite) to CMY colors, referring to the position of each color on a color wheel. The relationship between primary colors is the basis for all color correction.

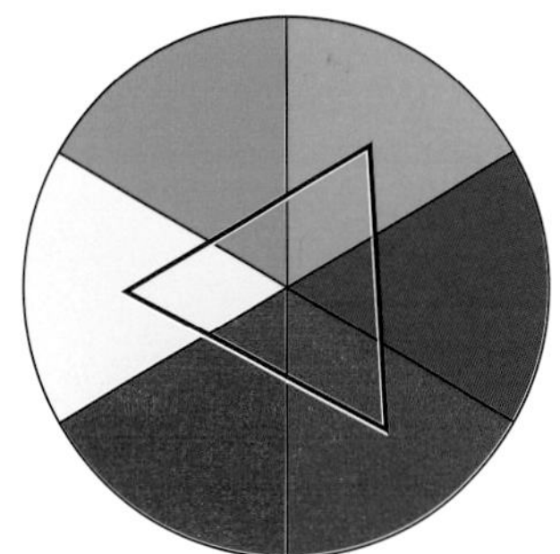

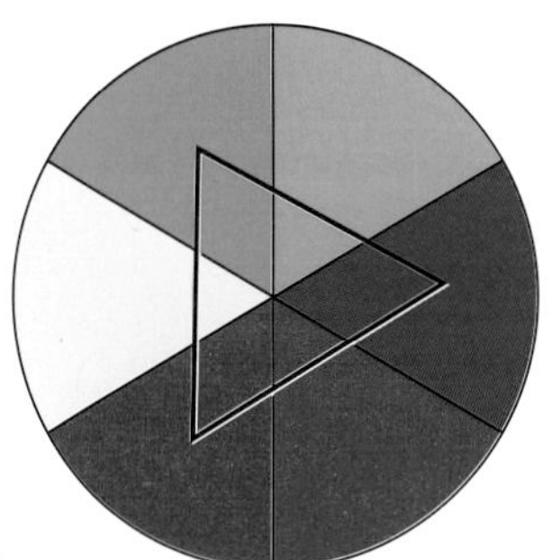

Referencing a basic color wheel can help you understand how RGB colors relate to CMY colors. If you center an equilateral triangle over the color wheel, the points of the triangle touch either the RGB primaries or the CMY primaries. Adding together two points of the triangle results in the color between the two points. Red and blue combine to form magenta, yellow and cyan combine to form green, and so on.

Opposite colors on the color wheel are called **color complements**. Using subtractive color theory, a color's complement absorbs or subtracts that color from visible white light. For example, cyan is opposite red on the color wheel; cyan absorbs red light and reflects green and blue. If you know green and blue light combine to create cyan, you can begin to understand how the two theories are related.

How does all this apply to color correction?

If you want to add a specific color to an image, you have three options: add the color, add equal parts of its constituent colors, or remove some of its complement color. For example, to add red to an image, you can add red, add yellow and magenta, or remove cyan. Conversely, this means that to remove a color from an image, you can remove the color itself, remove equal parts of its constituents, or add its complement. To remove cyan from an image, for example, you can remove cyan, remove blue and green, or add red.

Make sure you understand the relationships between complementary colors:

- To add red, add yellow and magenta or remove cyan.
- To add blue, add cyan and magenta or remove yellow.
- To add green, add cyan and yellow or remove magenta.
- To remove cyan, remove blue and green or add red.
- To remove yellow, remove green and red or add blue.
- To remove magenta, remove blue and red or add green.

Note:

It might seem easiest to simply add or subtract the color in question, but a better result might be achieved by adding one color and subtracting another. For example, if an image needs less blue, simply removing cyan can cause reds to appear pink or cyan to appear green. Adding magenta and yellow to balance the existing cyan creates a better result than simply removing cyan.

Note:

An important point to remember is that any color correction requires compromise. If you add or remove a color to correct a certain area, you also affect other areas of the image.

Understanding Gray Balance

Understanding the concept of neutral gray is also fundamental to effective color correction. Once you correct the contrast (tonal range) of an image, many of the remaining problems can be at least partially (if not entirely) corrected by correcting the **gray balance**, or the component elements of neutral grays within an image.

In the RGB color model, equal parts of red, green, and blue light combine to create a shade of gray that is equal to the percentage of each component — R=0 G=0 B=0 creates pure black, while R=255 G=255 B=255 creates pure white. To correct an image in RGB mode, you should evaluate and correct the neutral grays so they contain equal percentages of the three primary colors.

Using the CMYK color model, equal percentages of cyan, magenta, and yellow theoretically combine to produce an equal shade of gray — C=0 M=0 Y=0 creates pure white, while C=100

Understanding Color Terms

Many vague and technical-sounding terms are mentioned when discussing color. Is hue the same as color? The same as value? As tone? What's the difference between lightness and brightness? What is chroma? And where does saturation fit in?

This problem has resulted in several attempts to normalize color communication. A number of systems have been developed to define color according to specific criteria, including Hue, Saturation, and Brightness (HSB); Hue, Saturation, and Lightness (HSL); Hue, Saturation, and Value (HSV); and Lightness, Chroma, and Hue (LCH). Each of these models or systems plots color on a three-dimensional diagram, based on the elements of human color perception — hue, colorfulness, and brightness.

Hue is what most people think of as color — red, green, purple, and so on. Hue is defined according to a color's position on a color wheel, beginning from red (0°) and traveling counterclockwise around the wheel.

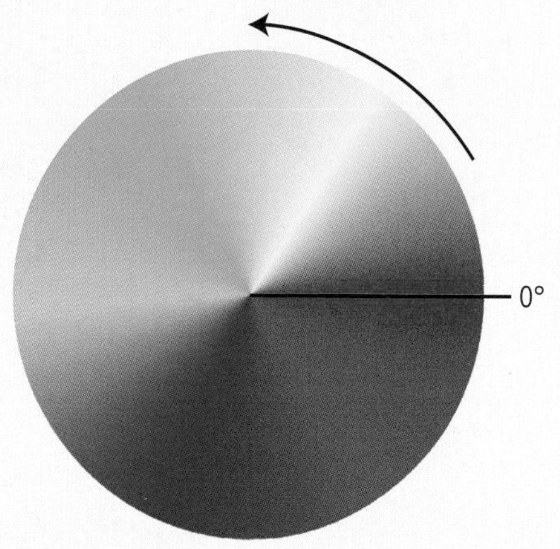

Saturation (also called "intensity") refers to the color's difference from neutral gray. Highly saturated colors are more vivid than those with low saturation. Saturation is plotted from the center of the color wheel. Color at the center is neutral gray and has a saturation value of 0; color at the edge of the wheel is the most intense value of the corresponding hue and has a saturation value of 100.

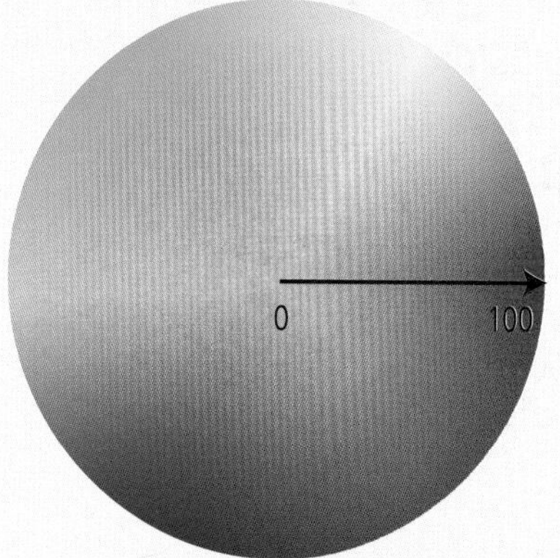

If you bisect the color wheel with a straight line, the line creates a saturation axis for two complementary colors. A color is dulled by the introduction of its complement. Red, for example, is neutralized by the addition of cyan (blue and green). Near the center of the axis, the result is neutral gray.

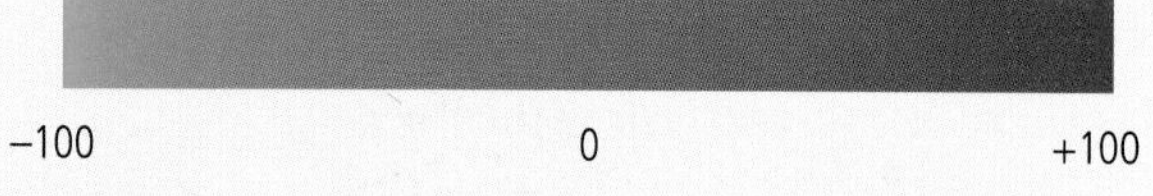

Chroma is similar to saturation, but chroma factors in a reference white. In any viewing situation, colors appear less vivid as the light source dims. The process of chromatic adaptation, however, allows the human visual system to adjust to changes in light and still differentiate colors according to the relative saturation.

Brightness is the amount of light reflected off an object. As an element of color reproduction, brightness is typically judged by comparing the color to the lightest nearby object (such as an unprinted area of white paper).

Lightness is the amount of white or black added to the pure color. Lightness (also called "luminance" or "value") is the relative brightness based purely on the black-white value of a color. A lightness value of 0 means there is no addition of white or black. Lightness of +100 is pure white; lightness of –100 is pure black.

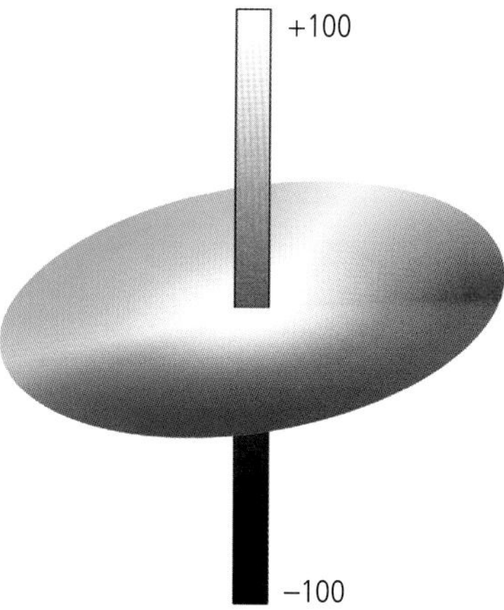

All hues are affected equally by changes in lightness.

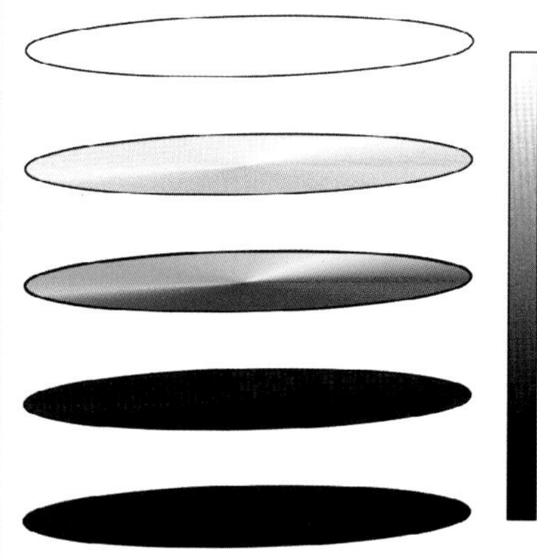

M=100 Y=100 theoretically creates pure black. As you learned earlier, however, the impurities of ink pigments — specifically cyan — do not live up to this theory. When you print an area of equal parts cyan, magenta, and yellow, the result is a muddy brown because the cyan pigments are impure. To compensate for the impurities of cyan, neutral grays must be adjusted to contain equal parts of magenta and yellow, and a slightly higher percentage of cyan.

Correct Color Cast with the Color Balance Adjustment

Color cast is the result of improper gray balance, when one channel is significantly stronger or weaker than the others. An image with improper gray balance has an overall predominance of one color, which is most visible in the highlight areas. The image that you will correct in this exercise has a strong green cast that needs to be removed.

Note:

This exercise relies purely on numbers to correct gray balance. To see an accurate preview of image color on screen, you should calibrate your monitor and create a monitor profile that you can load into Photoshop.

1. **Open the file salmon.jpg from your WIP>Menu folder.**
2. **Display the Info panel (Window>Info).**
3. **If you don't see both RGB and CMYK color modes in the Info panel, choose Panel Options in the Info panel Options menu. Use the Info Panel Options dialog box to choose Actual Color for the First Color Readout and CMYK Color for the Second Color Readout, then click OK.**

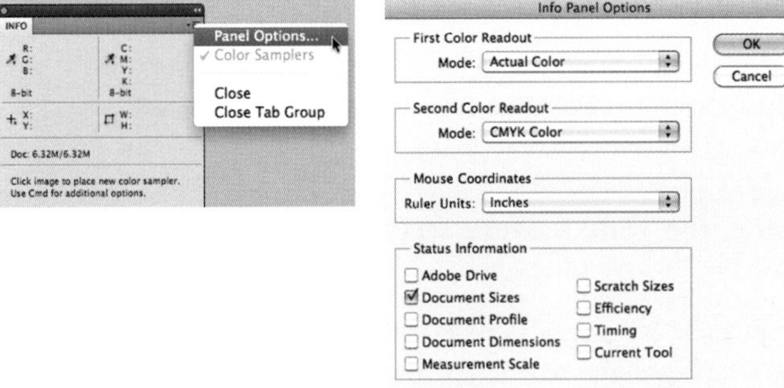

4. **Choose the Color Sampler tool (nested under the Eyedropper tool).**
5. **In the Control panel, choose 3 by 3 Average in the Sample Size menu.**

   Instead of correcting based on individual pixel values, you can average a group of contiguous pixels as the sample value. Doing so prevents accidentally correcting an image based on a single anomalous pixel (a dust spot, for example).

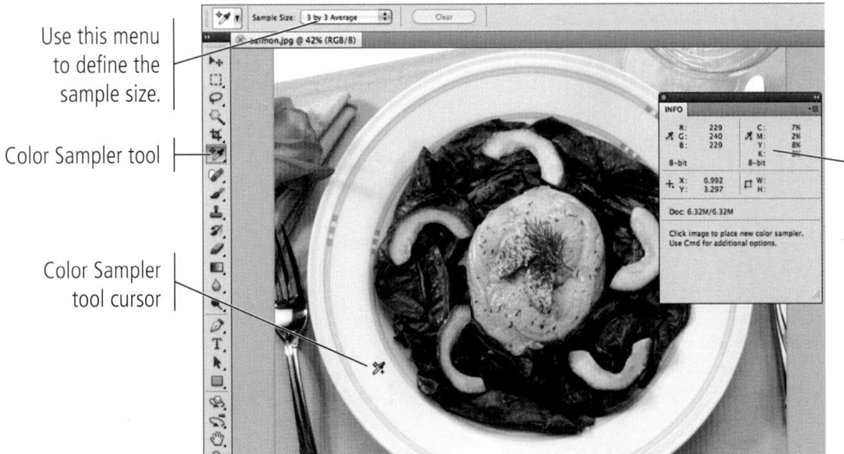

The Info panel shows color values for the current cursor location, in both RGB and CMYK modes.

6. **Click the cursor on the lower-left plate lip to place a color sample.**

7. **Click to add a second sample point to the top-right plate lip.**

   The two samples show a strong predominance of green; the numbers in the Info panel reflect the visible color cast in the image.

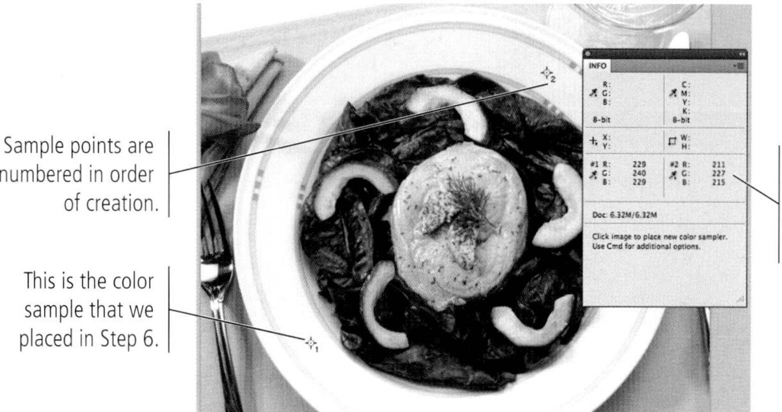

Sample points are numbered in order of creation.

This is the color sample that we placed in Step 6.

The Info panel shows the values associated with each of the sample points you created.

Note:

The Color Sampler tool can place up to four sample points per image.

8. **Choose Image>Adjustments>Color Balance.**

   Color Balance is a basic correction tool that can effectively remove overall color cast. The Color Balance dialog box presents a separate slider for each pair of complementary colors. You can adjust the highlights, shadows, or midtones of an image by selecting the appropriate radio button; the Preserve Luminosity check box ensures that only the colors shift, leaving the tonal balance of the image unchanged.

Note:

To delete an existing sample point, make the Color Sampler tool active, press Option/Alt, and click a point when the cursor icon changes to a pair of scissors.

9. **Click the Highlights radio button in the Tone Balance section at the bottom of the Color Balance dialog box.**

   The focal point of this image is green spinach, which you don't want to affect. Instead, you need to remove the green cast from the highlight, where it is most obvious.

10. **Drag the Magenta/Green slider left until the middle field shows –10.**

    Remember, adding a color's complement is one method for neutralizing that color. Increasing magenta in the highlight areas neutralizes the green color cast.

Note:

Some people find it helpful to work in Full Screen mode when correcting color to eliminate distracting color from other windows or applications that are open behind Photoshop.

The values after the "/" show the result of the changes; these will become the actual sample values if you click OK.

Changing the color balance brings the three values much closer to equal (called "in balance").

These fields correspond to the three color sliders. The middle field shows the Magenta/Green adjustment.

11. **Click OK to apply the adjustment.**

12. **Save the file in your WIP>Menu folder as a TIFF file named** `salmon_fixed.tif`**.**

13. **Close the file and continue to the next exercise.**

Correct Gray Balance with Curves

The Curves adjustment is the most powerful color-correction tool in Photoshop. If you understand the ideas behind curves, you can use this tool to remove color cast, enhance overall contrast, and even modify color values in individual channels.

The diagram in the Curves dialog box is the heart of the Curves adjustment. When you open the Curves dialog box, a straight diagonal line in the graph represents the existing color in the image.

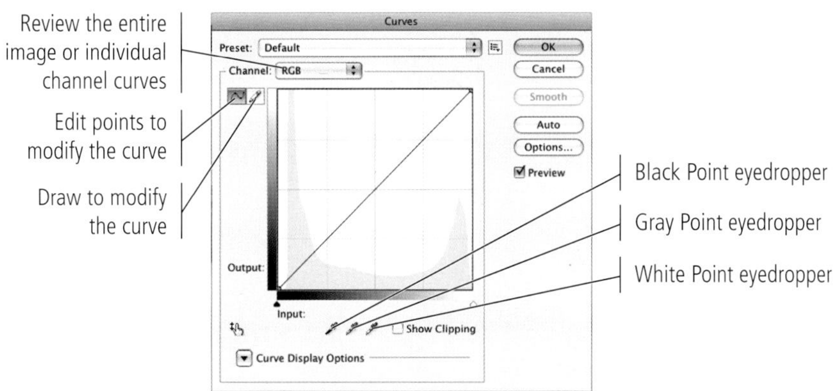

The horizontal axis represents the input color value, and the vertical axis represents the output color value. The upper-right point is the maximum value for that color mode (255 for RGB images and 100 for CMYK images). The bottom-left corner of the curves grid is the zero point.

The color mode of the image determines the direction of the input and output scales. In both CMYK and RGB, 0 means "none of that color." However, remember the difference between the two different color modes:

- The additive RGB color model starts at black and adds values of each channel to produce different colors, so 0, 0, 0 in RGB equals black.
- The subtractive CMYK model starts with white (paper) and adds percentages of each ink (channel) to produce different colors, so 0, 0, 0, 0 in CMYK equals white.

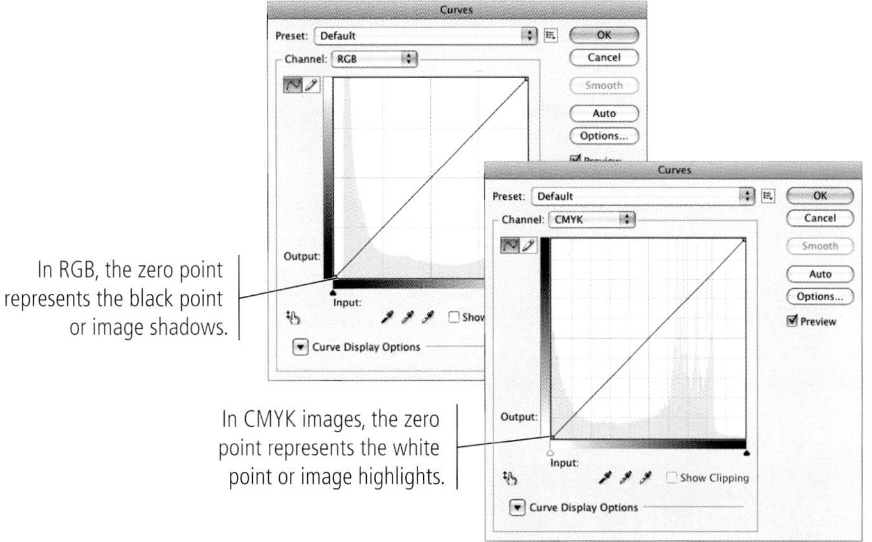

> **Note:**
>
> *Remember, the additive colors (RGB) at full strength combine to create pure white, while the subtractive colors (CMYK) at full strength combine to create pure black.*

Every curve is automatically anchored by a black point and a white point. (For RGB, the black point is at the bottom left and the white point is at the top right.) You can add points along the curve by simply clicking the curve. You can also move any point on the curve by clicking and dragging.

When you move points on the curve of an image (whether for the whole image or for an individual channel), you are telling Photoshop to, "Map every pixel that was [this] input value to [that] output value." In other words, using the following image as an example, a pixel that was 128 (the input value) will now be 114 (the output value). Because curves are just that — curves, and not individual points — adjusting one point on a curve changes the shape of the curve as necessary.

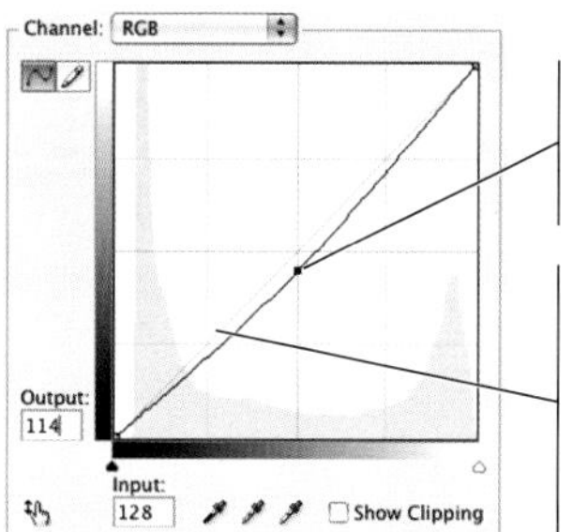

This point changes the input value of 128 to an output value of 114.

On either side of the adjusted point, the curve is adjusted to smoothly meet the other points on the curve (in this case, the black and white points).

1. **Open the file flan.jpg from the WIP>Menu folder.**

2. **Using the Color Sampler tool, place a sample point on the left plate lip.**

   This image has a strong red cast that needs to be neutralized. You can correct cast by removing the cast color or adding the other two primaries; the goal is equal (or nearly equal) parts of red, green, and blue in the neutral areas such as the plate lip.

The sample shows a strong red cast in what should be neutral areas.

   In the Info panel, the sample values show that the red channel has a value of 232, the green channel has a value of 213, and the blue channel has a value of 215. To fix the cast in this image, you will use the middle of these values (the blue channel) as the target and adjust the other two curves.

3. **Choose Image>Adjustments>Curves and make sure the Preview option is checked in the Curves dialog box.**

4. **Choose Red in the Channel menu to display the curve for only the Red channel, and then click the line on the graph to place a point near the three-quarter grid intersection.**

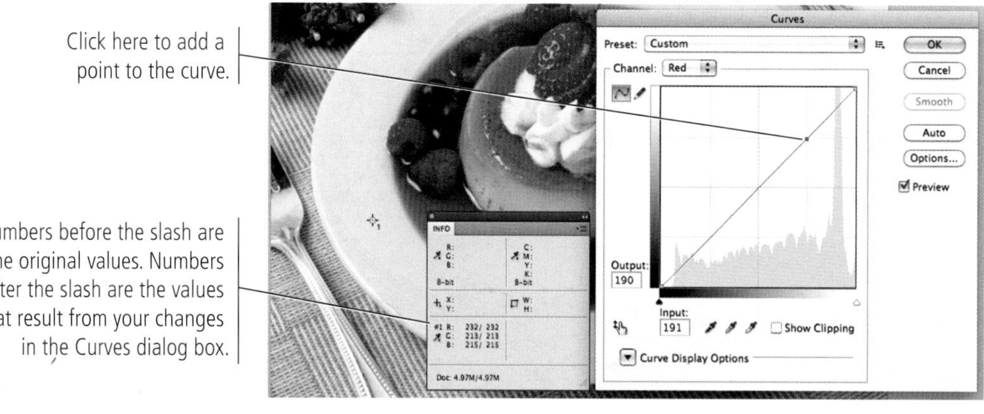

Click here to add a point to the curve.

Numbers before the slash are the original values. Numbers after the slash are the values that result from your changes in the Curves dialog box.

Note:

Easily recognizable "neutral" areas — such as the white plate in this image — are the best places to look for global color problems; fixing these will also fix many problem areas that you might not immediately recognize.

Note:

Your sample might be in a slightly different place, showing slightly different values. Use the values you see on your screen, rather than the numbers in our screen shots, to complete the following steps.

5. **With the new point selected on the curve, type the original Red value in the Input field (ours is 232).**

6. **Type the target value (ours is the original Blue value of 215) in the Output field.**

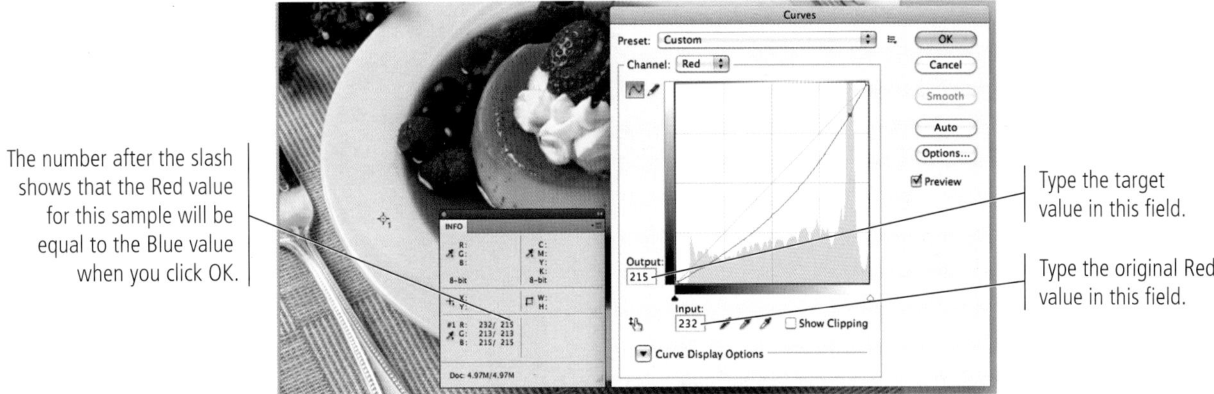

7. **In the Channel menu, choose Green (the other channel that you need to adjust). Add a point to the curve, and then adjust the input value to match your target output value (the original Blue value). Using our sample point, we adjusted the 213 Input value to a 215 Output value.**

   You can add the point anywhere along the curve; when you change the Input value to 215, the point automatically moves to that location along the curve.

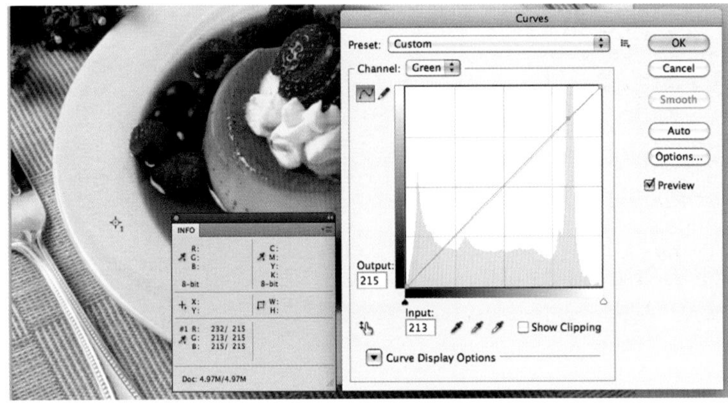

8. **Click OK to apply the change and close the Curves dialog box.**

   You can see how simply correcting gray balance has a significant impact on the image:

9. **Save the file in your WIP>Menu folder as a TIFF file named flan_fixed.tif.**

10. **Close the file and continue to the next exercise.**

Curve Display Options

The Curve Display options allow you to control what is visible in the graph. (If you can't see the Curve Display options, click the button to the left of the heading.) The Show Amount Of radio buttons reverse the input and output tone scales. Light is the default setting for RGB images; Pigment/Ink % is the default setting for CMYK images.

The On-Image adjustment tool lets you click and/or drag directly on an image to determine where the point should appear on the curve. You can add 14 points on a curve, and delete points by pressing Command/Control-delete.

Click this button to show or hide the Curve Display options.

By default, the lightest point for an RGB image is in the top right.

The darkest point for an RGB image is in the bottom left.

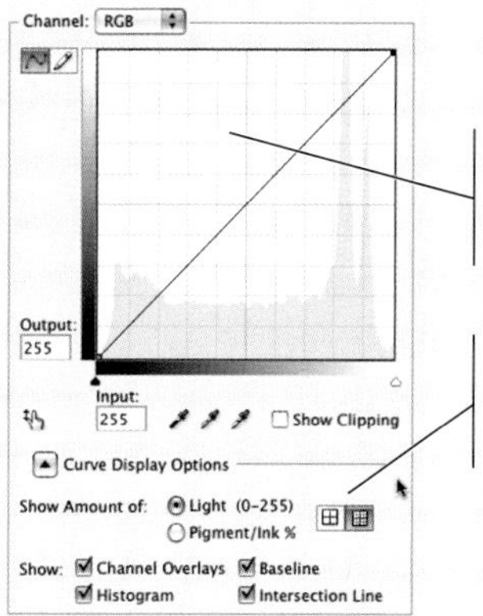

Gridlines in the graph can help you more precisely position curve points.

Use these buttons to show a four-by-four grid or a ten-by-ten grid.

By choosing Show Amount of Pigment/Ink %, the tone scales are reversed. For this RGB image, the lightest point moves to the bottom left and the darkest point moves to the top right.

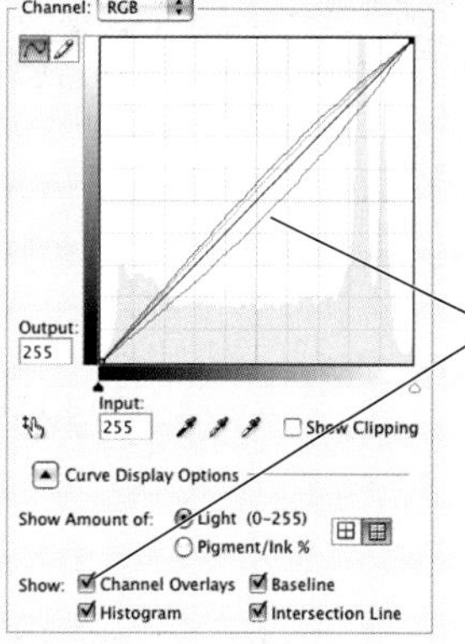

When the Channel Overlays option is checked, each channel is represented on the graph by a separate line.

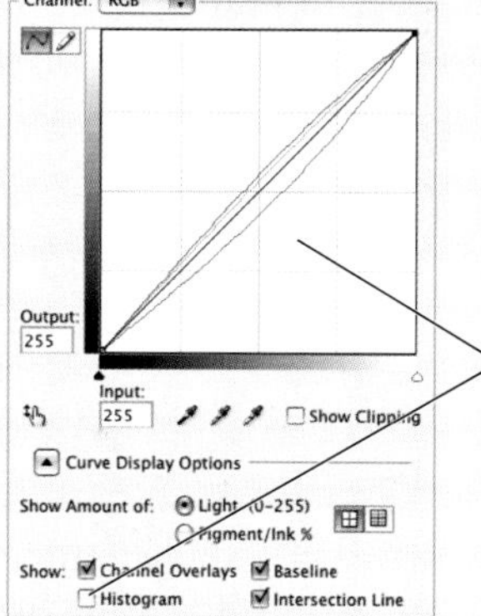

When the Histogram option is turned off, the graph does not show the representative histogram.

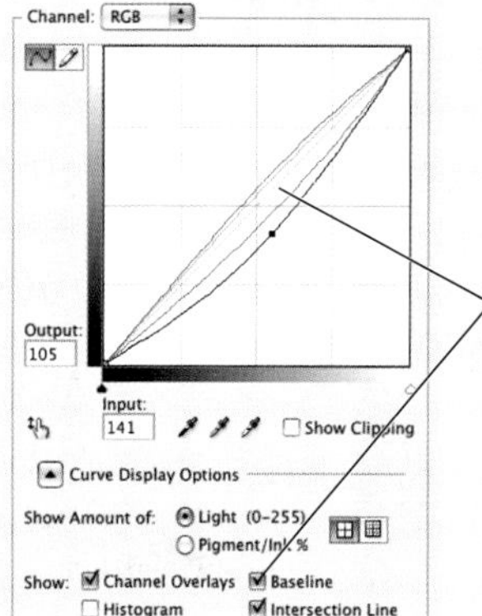

When the Baseline option is active, the original curve is represented by a gray line.

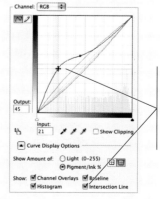

When the Intersection Line option is active, crosshairs appear when you drag a point in the graph, which can help you more precisely adjust curve points.

Correct Contrast with Curves

Remember, contrast is essentially the difference between the values in an image. By adjusting the points on the curve, you increase the tonal range between those points — which means you also increase the contrast in that same range.

In the following image, Point A has an Input value of 167 and an Output value of 182. Point B has an Input value of 87 and an Output value of 62. Mathematically:

- Original tonal range (Input values): 167 to 87 = 80 available tones
- New tonal range (Output values): 182 to 62 = 120 available tones

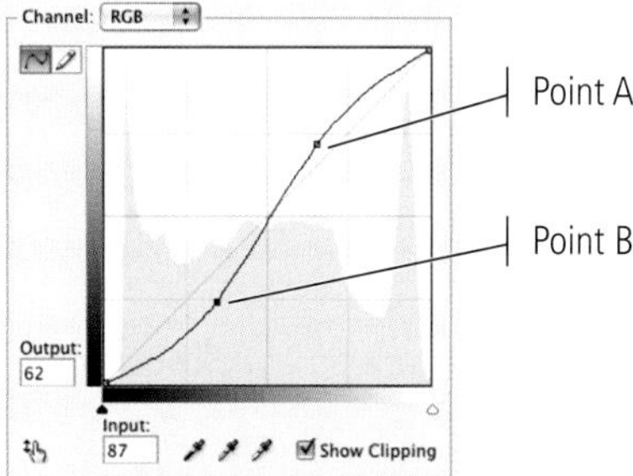

By making these two curve adjustments, we significantly increased the tonal range available for the image's midtones, which means we also significantly increased the contrast in the midtones. A steeper curve indicates increased tonal range and increased contrast. Notice, however, that the curves before Point B and after Point A are much shallower than the original curves, which means this change also significantly reduces the contrast in the shadow and highlight areas.

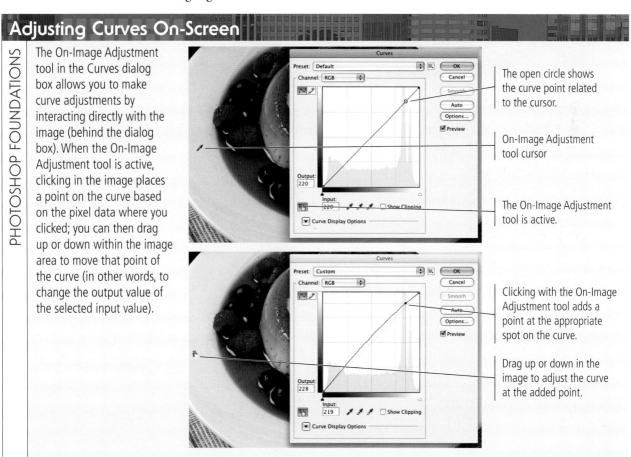

Adjusting Curves On-Screen

PHOTOSHOP FOUNDATIONS

The On-Image Adjustment tool in the Curves dialog box allows you to make curve adjustments by interacting directly with the image (behind the dialog box). When the On-Image Adjustment tool is active, clicking in the image places a point on the curve based on the pixel data where you clicked; you can then drag up or down within the image area to move that point of the curve (in other words, to change the output value of the selected input value).

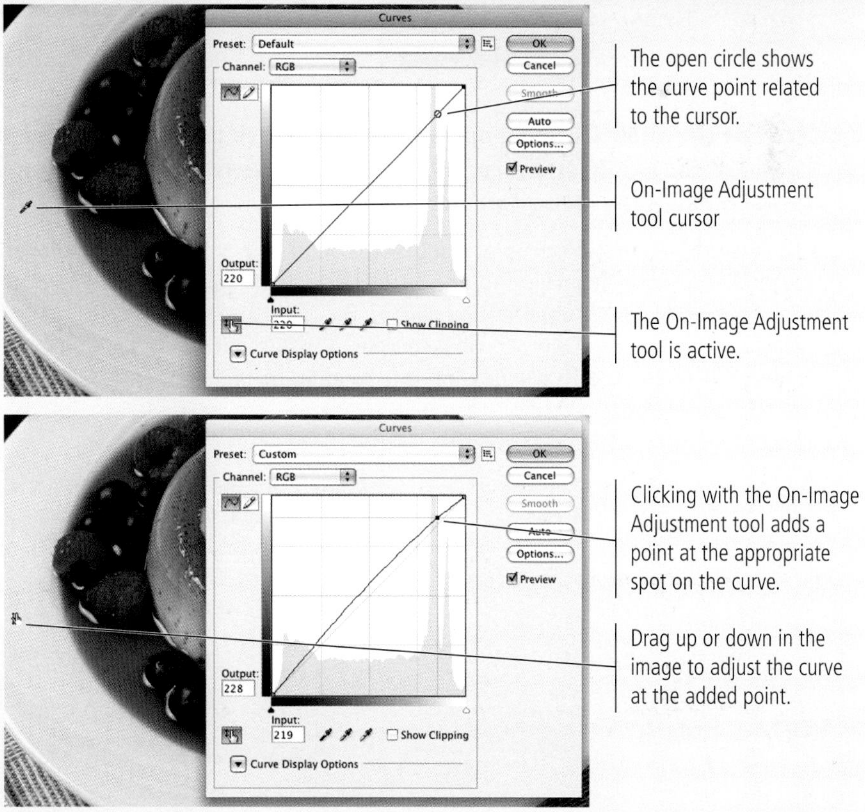

The open circle shows the curve point related to the cursor.

On-Image Adjustment tool cursor

The On-Image Adjustment tool is active.

Clicking with the On-Image Adjustment tool adds a point at the appropriate spot on the curve.

Drag up or down in the image to adjust the curve at the added point.

Points to Remember about Curves

Curves are very powerful tools, and they can be intimidating. To simplify the process and make it less daunting, keep these points in mind:

- Aim for neutral grays.
- You can adjust the curve for an entire image, or you can adjust the individual curves for each channel of the image.
- The horizontal tone scale shows the Input value, and the vertical tone scale shows the Output value.
- Changes made to one area of a curve affect all other areas of the image.
- The steeper the curve, the greater the contrast.
- Increasing contrast in one area inherently decreases contrast in other areas.

1. **Open the file `pasta.jpg` from the WIP>Menu folder.**

2. **Choose Image>Adjustments>Curves and make sure Preview is checked.**

The empty area at the left of the histogram shows that the image does not use the entire available tonal range.

3. **Activate the Show Clipping option, click the black point on the bottom-left corner of the graph, and then drag until some pixels start to appear in the image (behind the dialog box).**

   We dragged the Input Black point just past the point where the histogram shows the darkest shadows in the image. (You performed this same action in the Levels dialog box when you adjusted the Input Shadow slider.) The Input and Output fields show that any pixels with an Input value of 13 will be output as 0; in other words, anything with an Input value lower than 13 will be clipped to solid black.

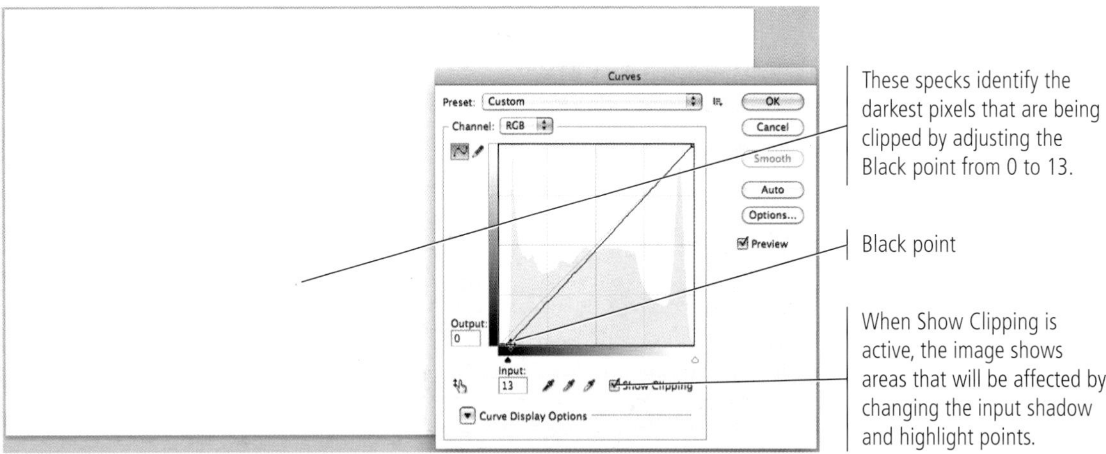

These specks identify the darkest pixels that are being clipped by adjusting the Black point from 0 to 13.

Black point

When Show Clipping is active, the image shows areas that will be affected by changing the input shadow and highlight points.

4. **Repeat Step 3, dragging the White point left until the lightest areas of the image start to appear behind the dialog box.**

5. **Turn off the Show Clipping option so you can see the actual image behind the dialog box.**

   Even this small change improved the image, but the midtones — especially in the pasta, which is the focal area of the image — need some additional contrast. To accomplish that change, you need to steepen the curve in the middle of the graph.

6. **Click the curve to create a point at the quartertone gridline and drag it slightly to the right.**

   We adjusted the curve point from an Input value of 81 to an Output value of 62.

7. **Click the curve at the three-quartertone gridline and drag the point to the left.**

We adjusted the 175 Input value to a 190 Output value.

The adjusted points steepen the curve, increasing contrast between the two points.

8. **Click OK to apply the changes and close the dialog box.**

Adjusting the contrast with curves improved the detail in the image and enhanced the overall image color.

9. **Save the file in your WIP>Menu folder as a TIFF file named pasta_fixed.tif.**

10. **Close the file and continue to the next stage of the project.**

Note:

Contrast adjustments can have a major impact on color as well as on sharpness. Take particular note of the green basil leaves; no direct color adjustment was done to these two images, but the leaves are noticeably greener and brighter after you adjust the curves.

Automatic Color Correction

PHOTOSHOP FOUNDATIONS

Clicking Options in the right side of the Curves dialog box opens the Auto Color Correction Options dialog box. These settings will apply if you click the Auto button in the Levels or Curves dialog box, or if you choose one of the automatic adjustments in the Image>Adjustments menu (Auto Tone, Auto Contrast, or Auto Color). The Algorithms options determine how Photoshop will adjust the image's tonal range.

- **Enhance Monochromatic Contrast** is applied if you choose Auto Contrast. This option clips all channels identically, preserving overall color while making highlights appear lighter and shadows darker.
- **Enhance Per Channel Contrast** is applied if you choose Auto Levels. This option maximizes the tonal range in each channel by moving the darkest shadow to 0 (or 100 for CMYK images) and the lightest highlight to 255 (or 0 for CMYK images). The overall color relationship is not maintained, which might result in color cast in the adjusted image.
- **Find Dark & Light Colors** is applied if you choose Auto Color. This option uses the average lightest and darkest pixels to maximize contrast and minimize clipping. **Snap Neutral Midtones** also relates to the Auto Color adjustment; this option finds an average neutral color in an image, and then adjusts midtone (gamma) values to make that color neutral.

In the Target Colors & Clipping options, you can define the target shadow, midtone, and highlight values by clicking the appropriate color swatch. The Clip fields determine how much of the darkest shadow and lightest highlight will be clipped when you apply an automatic adjustment. In other words, a Shadow Clip setting of 1% means Photoshop will ignore the first 1% of the darkest pixels when adjusting the image. If you change the Target Colors & Clipping settings, you can check the Save As Defaults option; you can then apply those settings by clicking the Auto button in the Levels or Curves dialog box.

Stage 4 Preparing Images for Print

As you learned in Project 2 (page 107), different color models have different ranges or **gamuts** of possible colors. This difference in gamut is one of the biggest problems graphic designers face when working with color images. Digital image-capture devices (including scanners and digital cameras) work in the RGB space, which, with its larger gamut, can more closely mirror the range of colors in the original scene. Printing, however, requires images to first be converted or **separated** into the CMYK color space.

You might have noticed that all the images for this project are in the RGB color mode. Printing, however, relies on the CMYK mode to output color images. The CMYK mode has a much smaller gamut than the RGB mode — which means some colors might be lost when RGB values are converted to CMYK values for output; this is called **color compression** or **color shift**.

This problem leads to two different schools of thought about when to correct colors — in the original RGB image (before converting to CMYK) or in the converted CMYK image (after color shift has already occurred). Most experts lean toward the first option since images are often used for multiple media, some of which require the RGB model. By correcting in RGB, you can do your color corrections once and use the same corrected file for different types of output.

When you correct images that will be printed, however, colors outside the CMYK gamut might shift based on the selected rendering intent (see Project 10). It simply doesn't make sense to blindly allow Photoshop to shift the colors you so painstakingly corrected.

Identify Out-of-Gamut Colors

Fortunately, Photoshop contains the necessary tools for previewing out-of-gamut colors, which means you can correct colors *before* converting an image. If you have no out-of-gamut colors, then there is nothing to shift, and you can be fairly confident that your color images will be reproduced as you intended.

1. **Open the file salad.jpg from the WIP>Menu folder.**

2. **Choose Edit>Assign Profile.**

   Color management and translation relies on **color profiles** to accurately translate color from one model to another. (Color profiles are simply data sets that define the reproduction characteristics of a specific device. A profile is essentially a recipe that contains the ingredients for reproducing a specific color in a given color space. The color recipes in profiles are known as **look-up tables** (LUTs), which are essentially cross-reference systems for finding matching color values in different color spaces.)

   This dialog box shows you the starting point — the embedded image profile. You can use the dialog box to change the profile you're using for this image. If an image has an embedded profile, the third radio button is selected and the embedded profile appears in the list. You can choose to not color manage the image, change to your working profile, or choose any other available profile from the Profile menu.

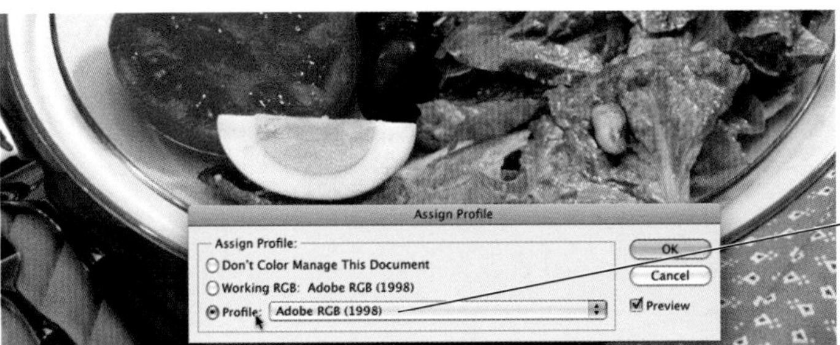

This image uses the Adobe RGB (1998) profile.

Note:

Photoshop CS5 ships with a large collection of common profiles, which are meant to meet the needs of diverse manufacturing environments in which Photoshop is used for what's commonly called ***prepress*** *(the process of getting images ready to print).*

3. **Click OK to close the Assign Profile dialog box.**

4. **Choose Edit>Color Settings. In the Color Settings dialog box, choose U.S. Sheetfed Coated v2 in the Working Spaces CMYK menu, and then click OK.**

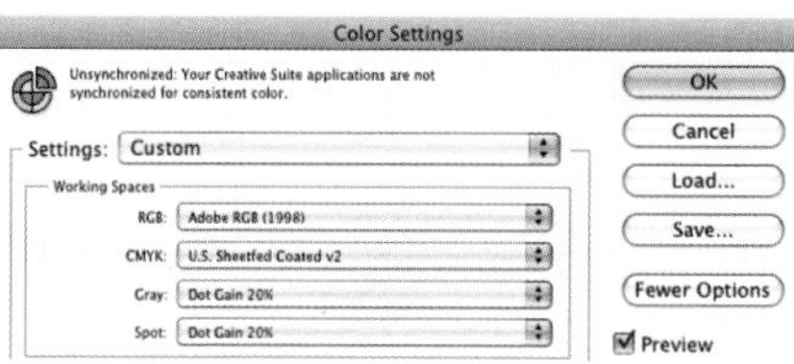

> *Note:*
>
> *Color profiles are sometimes also called "ICC profiles," named after the International Color Consortium (ICC), which developed the standard for creating color profiles.*

5. **Choose View>Proof Colors to toggle that option on.**

   This toggle provides a quick preview of what will happen when the image is converted to the CMYK working-space profile — without affecting the actual file data.

> *Note:*
>
> *We assume this restaurant menu will be printed on a sheetfed press. However, always ask your output provider what profile to use for a specific job.*

View>Proof Colors shows that converting this image will result in a color shift, especially in the red areas.

6. **Choose View>Proof Colors again to display the actual RGB image.**

   The Proof Colors and Gamut Warning displays are toggles; when you select them, they turn on if they were off or turn off if they were on.

> *Note:*
>
> *Command/Control-Y toggles the Proof Colors view on or off.*
>
> *Shift-Command/Control-Y toggles the Gamut Warning View.*

7. **Choose View>Gamut Warning.**

   The areas that shifted are now highlighted with a gray overlay. This overlay shows you exactly what you need to correct; when this image is printed on a commercial sheetfed press, those regions will not reproduce as expected.

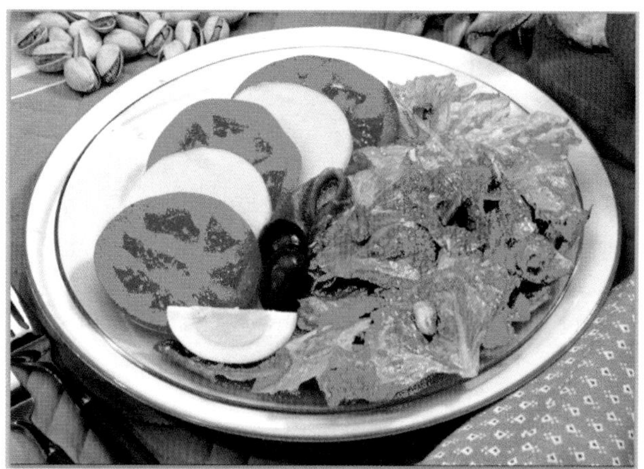

> *Note:*
>
> *You can change the color of the gamut warning overlay in the Transparency & Gamut pane of the Preferences dialog box.*

8. **Save the file as `salad.psd`, and continue to the next exercise.**

Adjust Highlight and Shadow Points for Print

For images that will be commercially printed, some allowance must be made in the highlight and shadow areas for the mechanics of the printing process. In CMYK images, shades of gray are reproduced using combinations of four printing inks. In theory, a solid black would be printed as 100% of all four inks, and pure white would be 0% of all four inks. This, however, does not take into consideration the limitations of mechanical printing.

To accurately reproduce highlights and shadows on a commercial printing press, you need to understand the concept of minimum printable dot and maximum printable dot.

Images are printed as a pattern of closely spaced dots called a **halftone**. When viewed on the page, the dots create the illusion of continuous color. Different sizes of dots create different shades of color — larger dots create darker shades and smaller dots create lighter shades.

There is a limit to the smallest size dot that can be faithfully and consistently reproduced. A 1% dot is so small that the mechanical aspect of the printing process causes anything specified as a 1% dot to drop out, resulting in highlights that lack detail and contrast. The **minimum printable dot**, then, is the smallest printable dot, and should be specified for highlights in a CMYK image. There is some debate over the appropriate highlight setting because different presses and imaging equipment have varying capabilities. To be sure your highlights will work on most printing equipment, you should define the highlight as C=5 M=3 Y=3 K=0.

Maximum printable dot is the opposite of minimum printable dot. The paper's absorption rate, speed of the printing press, and other mechanical factors limit the amount of ink that can be placed on the same area of a page. If too much ink is printed, the result is a dark blob with no visible detail; heavy layers of ink also result in drying problems, smearing, and a number of other issues.

Total ink coverage is the largest percentage of ink that can be safely printed on a single area, and therefore dictates the shadow dot you define in Photoshop. This number, similar to minimum printable dot, varies according to the ink/paper/press combination being used for a given job. The Specifications for Web Offset Publications (SWOP, www.swop.org) indicates a 300% maximum value. Many sheetfed printers require 280% maximum, while the number for newspapers is usually around 240% because the lower-quality paper absorbs more ink.

Unless your images will be printed in a newspaper, 290% is an acceptable shadow for most applications. You can safely define shadows as C=80 M=70 Y=70 K=70. If you need to adjust a lower or higher number for specific projects, you can do so at any time.

1. **With salad.psd open and the gamut warning visible, choose Image>Adjustments>Curves.**

2. **Double-click the White Point eyedropper.**

3. **In the Select Target Highlight Color dialog box, change the CMYK values to C=5 M=3 Y=3 K=0 and click OK.**

Note:

Even though you are working on an RGB image, you can still correct it to target CMYK white and black values.

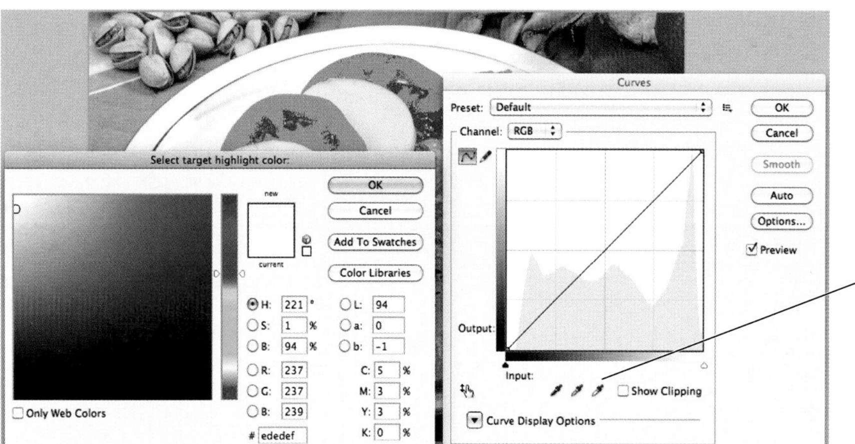

Double-click the White Point eyedropper to open the Select Target Highlight Color dialog box.

4. **With the White Point eyedropper selected, click the lightest highlight in the image where you want to maintain detail.**

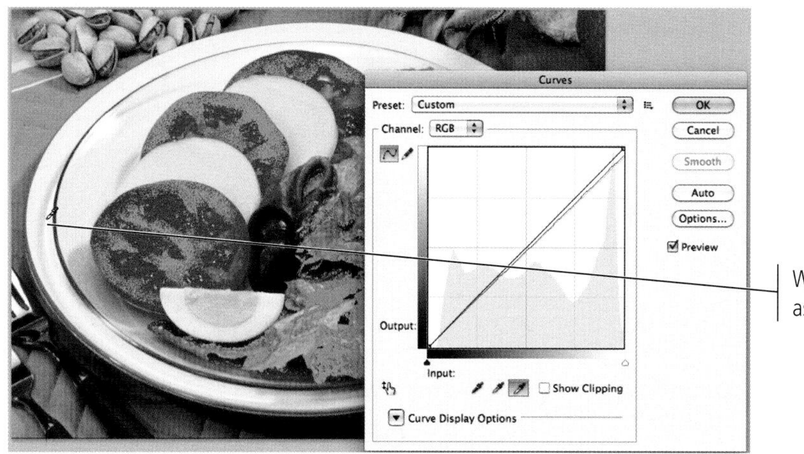

We used this plate edge as the white point.

5. **Double-click the Black Point eyedropper. Change the target CMYK values to C=80 M=70 Y=70 K=70, and then click OK.**

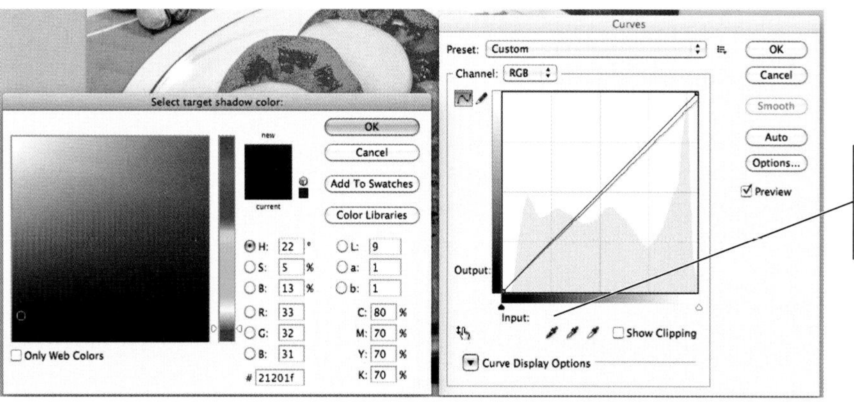

Double-click the Black Point eyedropper to open the Select Target Shadow Color dialog box.

6. **With the Black Point eyedropper selected, click the darkest area of the image where you want to maintain shadow detail.**

   By defining the target highlight and shadow points in the image, you can see that the gray gamut warning is nearly gone from the green areas, and it's significantly reduced in the red areas.

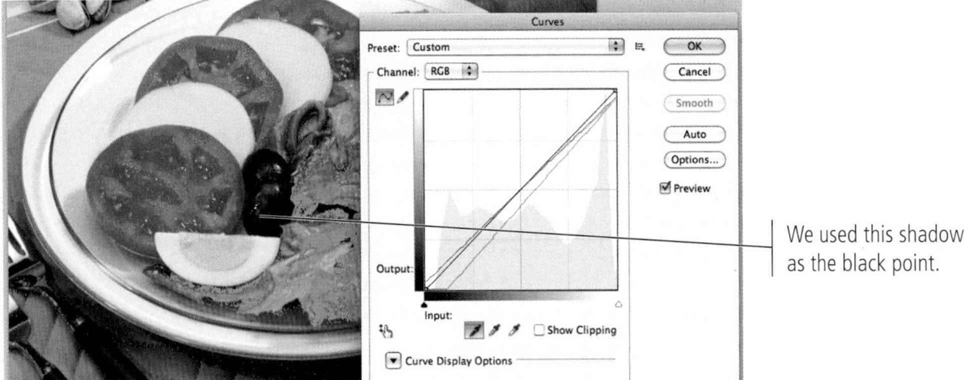

We used this shadow as the black point.

7. **Display the curve for the Red channel only.**

8. **Add a point near the midpoint, and then drag the point down to steepen the overall Red curve.**

   Just a slight adjustment, from 160 Input to 130 Output, removes nearly all the gamut warning from the tomatoes.

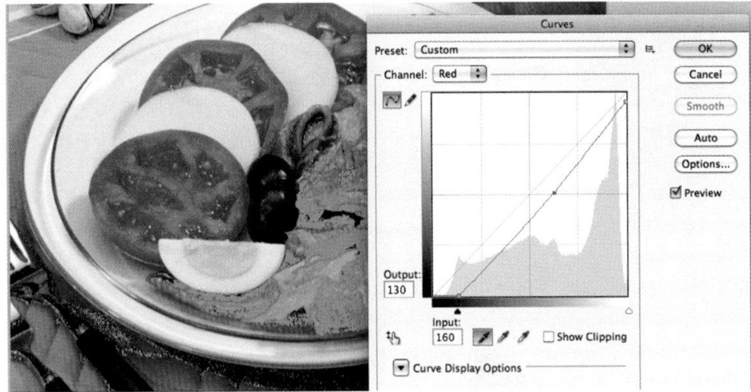

9. **Display the curve for the Green channel and make adjustments until most or all of the gamut warning is gone.**

   Experiment with points along the curve until you are satisfied with the result.

Converting Images to Grayscale

An RGB image has three channels and a CMYK image has four channels; each channel is a grayscale representation of the tones of that color throughout the image. A grayscale image has only one channel; the grayscale tones in that channel are the tones in the entire image. Choosing Image>Mode>Grayscale simply flattens the component color channels, throwing away the color information to create the gray channel.

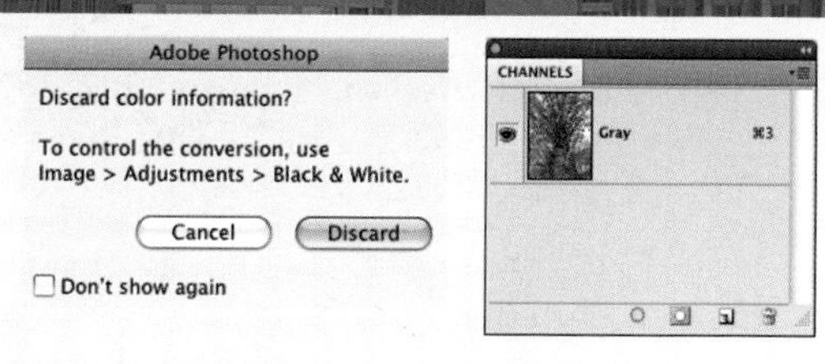

The Desaturate adjustment (Image>Adjustments>Desaturate) has a similar effect, but maintains the same number of channels as the original image. This adjustment averages the individual channel values for each pixel and applies the average value in each channel. (Remember, equal values of red, green, and blue combine to create a neutral gray value.)

If you need to convert a color image to grayscale, you might want to carefully consider which data to use for generating the gray channel. The Black & White adjustment (Image>Adjustments>Black & White) enables you to control the conversion process. In the Black and White dialog box, you can either choose one of the built-in presets, or you can drag the individual color sliders to determine how dark that color component will be in the resulting image.

When you move the mouse cursor over the image, it changes to an eyedropper icon. You can click an area in the image to highlight the predominant color in that area. Click within the image and drag to dynamically change the slider associated with that area of the image.

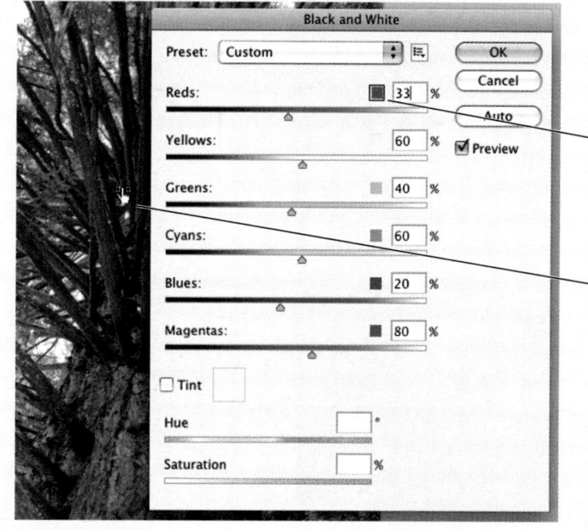

The Reds slider is highlighted, indicating that red is the predominant color where you clicked in the image.

Clicking here and dragging left or right changes the associated Reds slider.

Remember, equals parts red, green and blue combine to create a neutral gray. Applying the Black & White filter maintains the existing color channels, with the exact same data in all three channels. Because the adjusted image is still technically in a color mode (not Grayscale), you can also use the Tint options in the Black & White dialog box to apply a hue or saturation tint to the grayscale image. After using the Black & White dialog box to control the conversion of colors to grayscale, you can safely discard the color data by choosing Image>Mode>Grayscale.

10. **Click OK to apply your changes.**

11. **Click No in the warning message.**

    If you change the target Black Point, Gray Point, or White Point eyedropper values, Photoshop asks if you want to save the new target values as the default settings when you click OK to close the Curves dialog box.

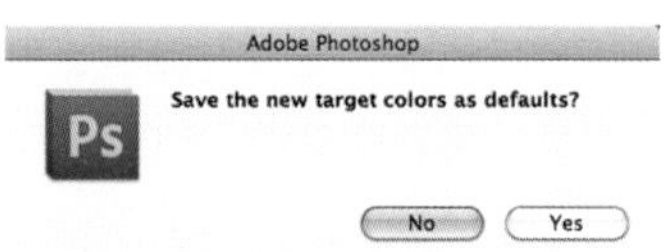

Note:

You can turn the gamut warning off and on while the Curves dialog box is open. Simply choose the option from the View menu and toggle the gray overlay off and on.

12. **Choose View>Gamut Warning to toggle that option off.**

13. **Save the file and continue to the next exercise.**

    Because the RGB gamut is so much larger than the CMYK gamut, you can expect colors to be far less brilliant (especially in the outer ranges of saturation) when corrected to the CMYK gamut. It's better to know this will happen and control it, rather than simply allowing the color management engine to shift colors where it deems best.

Converting Image Color Modes

Although many modern workflows convert RGB images to CMYK during the output process (called "on-the-fly" or "in-RIP conversion"), there are times when you need to manually convert RGB images to CMYK. This is a fairly simple process, especially if you have corrected your images to meet the requirements of the printing process.

1. **With the corrected salad image open from the previous exercise, choose Image>Mode>CMYK Color.**

   This menu option converts the image to the CMYK color mode using the current working space profile. Since you intentionally defined the working profile and corrected the image to that profile, you can safely use this menu option to convert the RGB image to CMYK.

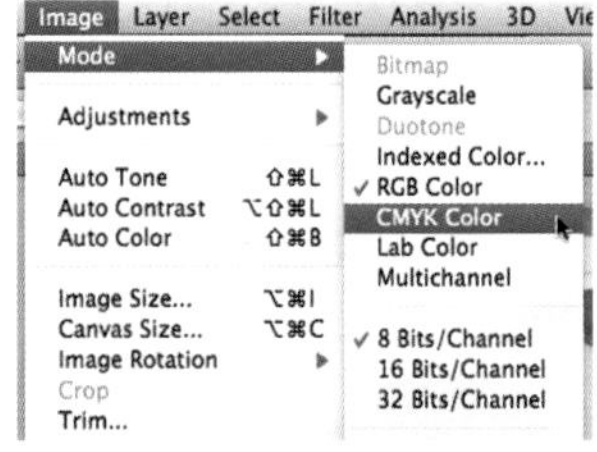

2. **Click OK in the resulting warning dialog box.**

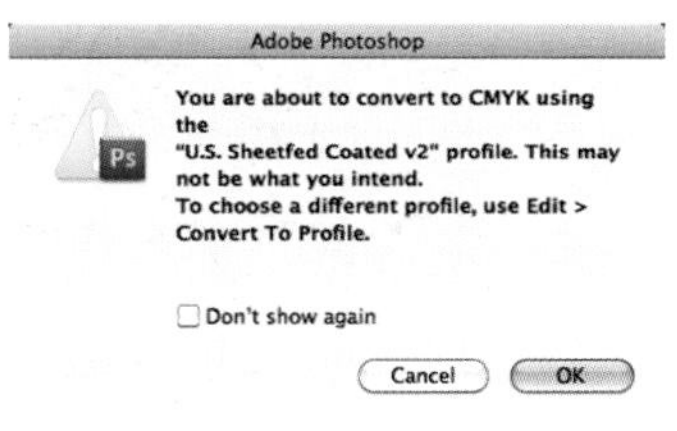

If you had not completed the process in the previous series of exercises, you shouldn't convert the image color mode. Color mode is not something that should be simply switched on a whim; rather, it is the final stage of a specific process.

If you didn't precisely follow this workflow, but you are certain the image colors are correct, you can convert an image to a different model by choosing Edit>Convert to Profile and choosing any available profile in the Destination Space Profile menu.

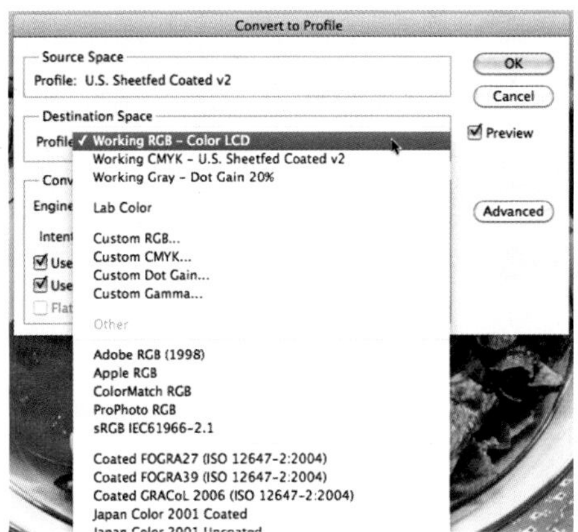

3. **Choose File>Save As. If necessary, navigate to your WIP>Menu folder as the target location.**

4. **Change the Format menu to TIFF, and then add _CMYK to the end of the existing file name (before the extension).**

5. **Macintosh users: In the bottom half of the Save As dialog box, make sure the Embed Color Profile:U.S. Sheetfed Coated v2 option is checked.**

   Windows users: In the bottom half of the Save As dialog box, make sure the ICC Profile: U.S. Sheetfed Coated v2 option is checked.

   This image has been corrected and converted to the U.S. Sheetfed Coated v2 color profile. By embedding the profile into the TIFF file, other applications and devices with color management capabilities will be able to correctly process the image color data in the file, based on the embedded profile.

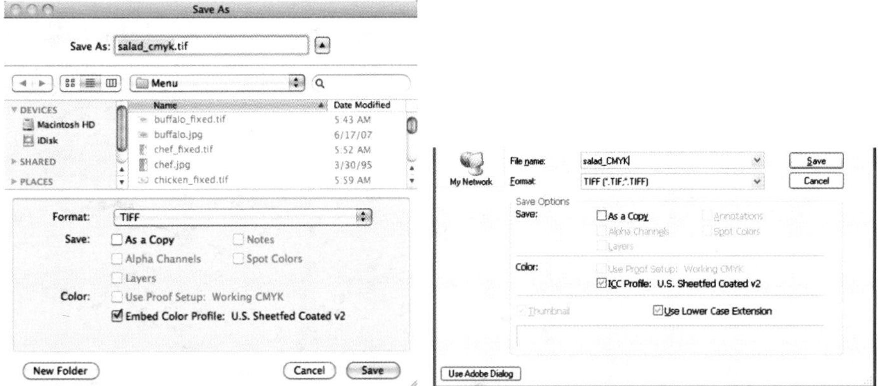

6. **Click Save, and then click OK to accept the default TIFF options.**

7. **Close the file, then continue to the next stage of the project.**

Stage 5 Working with HDR Images

The human eye is extremely sensitive to subtle changes in light. In general, we can perceive detail in both light and dark areas — and areas in between — with a single glance. Camera sensors, on the other hand, are not so sensitive. If you look at most photographs, they typically have sharp detail in one of the ranges — highlights, midtones, or shadows, depending on the exposure and other settings used to capture the image. If a photograph favors highlights, details in shadow areas are lost (and vice versa).

To solve this problem, the concept of HDR (**high dynamic range**) images combines multiple photographs of different exposures into a single image to enhance the detail throughout the entire image — combining highlight, shadow, and midtone detail from various exposures to create an image more like what the human eye is capable of observing, rather than the more limited range that characterizes a digital camera's sensors.

The phrase "dynamic range" refers to the difference between the darkest shadow and the lightest highlight in an image.

- A regular 8-bit RGB photo has a dynamic range of 0–255 for each color channel (2^8 or 256 possible values). In other words, each pixel can have one of 256 possible values to describe the lightness of that color in that specific location.
- A 16-bit RGB photo allows 16 bits of information to describe the information in each pixel, allowing a dynamic range of 2^{16} or 65,536 possible values in each color channel.
- A 32-bit or HDR image allows 2^{32} possible values — more than 4 billion, which is signficantly larger than the visible spectrum of 16.7 million colors (thus, 32-bit dynamic range is sometimes referred to as "infinite").

Use Merge to HDR Pro

The final piece required to complete this project is an image of the antique waterwheel that is one of the hallmarks of the restaurant's exterior. Its location makes it very difficult to capture because the surrounding trees cast shadows even when the sun is at the best lighting angle. The photographer suggested using high dynamic range (HDR) photo techniques to capture the most possible detail in the scene, and has provided you with five photos taken at the same time, using different exposure settings.

1. **With no file open, choose File>Automate>Merge to HDR Pro.**

2. **In the resulting dialog box, click the Browse button.**
3. **Navigate to WIP>Menu>Mill Photos. Shift-click to select all five images in the folder and click Open.**

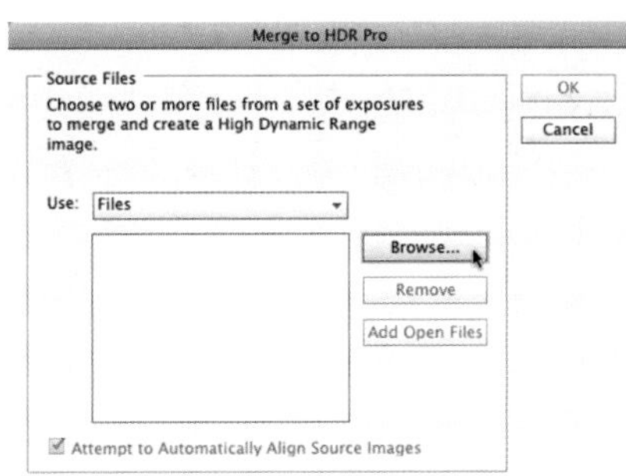

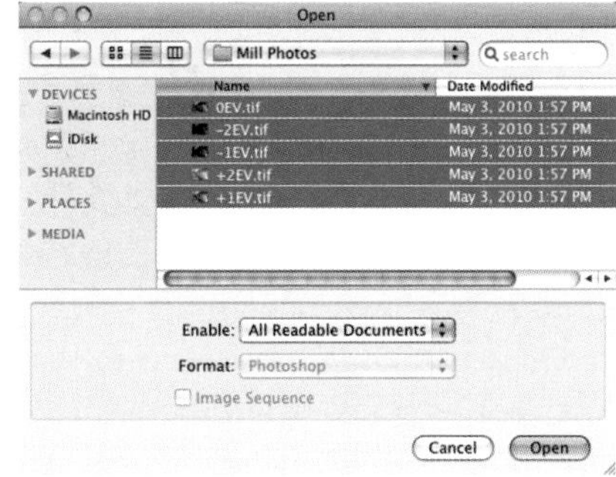

4. **Make sure the Attempt to Automatically Align Source Images box at the bottom of the dialog box is checked, then click OK.**

Because you are merging multiple images into a single one, there is a chance that one or more images might be slightly misaligned. (Even using a tripod, a stiff breeze can affect the camera just enough to make the different exposures slightly different.) When Attempt to Automatically Align Source Images is checked, Photoshop compares details in each image and adjusts them as necessary to create the resulting merged image.

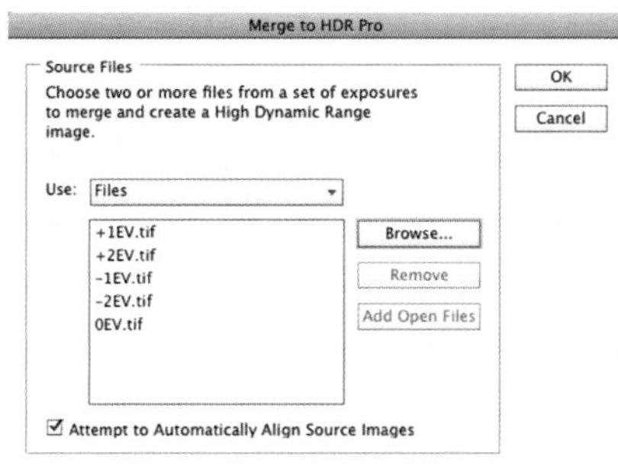

5. **Read the resulting message, then click OK.**

HDR images are best created from Camera RAW files, which can maintain significantly more data than the TIFF or JPEG formats. In many cases, however, you will have to use non-RAW files because that is what your photographer or client will provide to you. The merge process still works very well with JPEG and TIFF files.

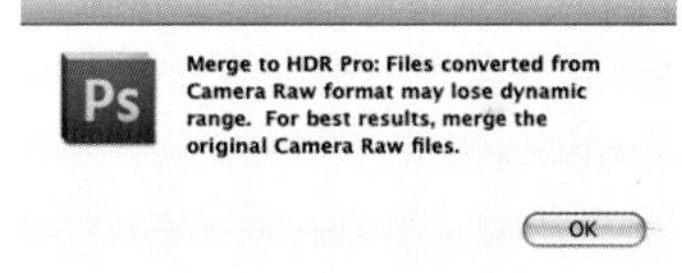

Note:

You can merge up to seven images with the Merge to HDR Pro utility.

6. **If you don't see a histogram on the right side of the dialog box, open the Mode menu and choose 32 Bit.**

   The resulting dialog box shows each selected image as a thumbnail at the bottom. By default, all selected images are included in the merge. You can exclude specific exposures by unchecking the box for that image.

   If you work with HDR, you need to realize that most computer monitors are not capable of displaying 32-bit image depth. When you merge to a 32-bit image, you can use the White Point Preview slider to change the dynamic range that is visible on your screen, but this has no effect on the actual data in the file — it affects only the current display of the image data.

Note:

The merge process might take a minute or two to complete, so be patient.

7. **Check the Remove Ghosts option on the right side of the dialog box.**

   When an HDR image contains movement, merging the individual exposures can blur the areas where that movement occurs — such as the water dripping off the wheel in this image. When you check Remove Ghosts, the software uses one of the exposures (highlighted in green) to define detail in the area of motion; you can change the key exposure by simply clicking a different image in the lower pane.

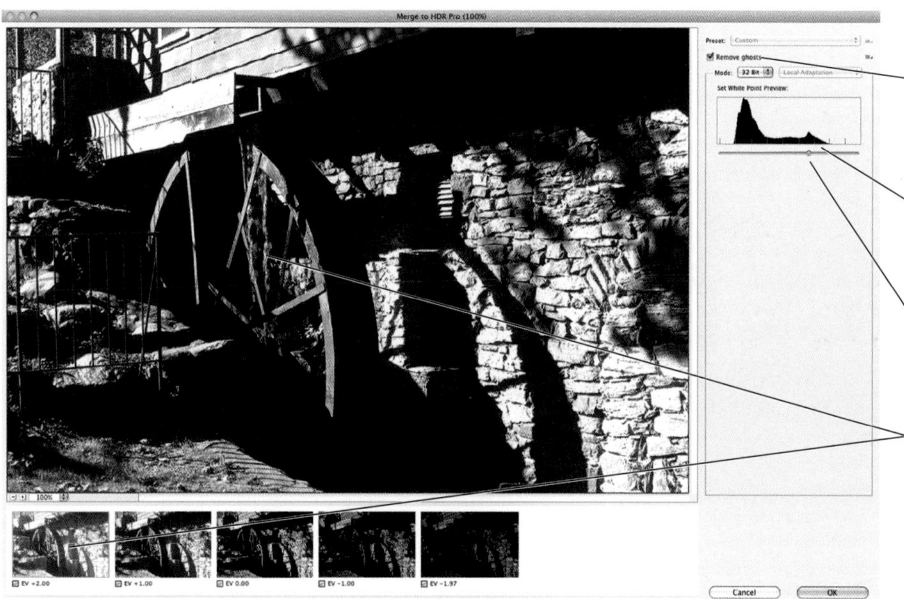

Check Remove Ghosts to eliminate blurring in areas that differ from one exposure to another.

Tones to the right of the white point will be displayed as white.

Drag this slider to change the white point for the active display.

When Remove Ghosts is checked, detail in areas of movement are defined by the selected exposure.

8. **Open the Mode menu and choose 8 Bit.**

   32 bit images can store a tremendous amount of information, which creates images with far more detail than you see in a conventional 8-bit photograph. However, one significant disadvantage of such images is that they cannot be separated for commercial printing. If you're going to use an HDR image in a print application — such as the cover of this menu — you need to apply the process of **tone mapping** to define how the high dynamic range will be compressed into the lower dynamic range that is required by the output process.

9. **Leave the secondary menu set to Local Adaptation.**

   You can use the other options to apply less specific tone mapping to the image. Equalize Histogram and Highlight Compression have no further options. The Exposure and Gamma option allows you to define specific values for only those two settings.

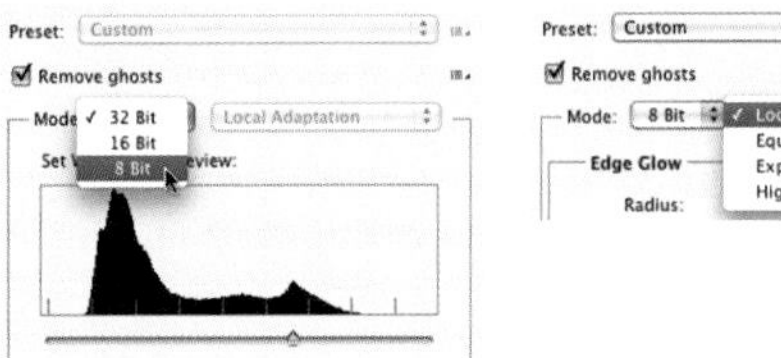

   When the Local Adaptation method is selected, you can change the values for a number of specific options to map the tones in the HDR image to a lower dynamic range.

Note:

You can create your own presets by clicking the button to the right of the Preset menu and choosing Save Preset in the resulting menu.

10. **Open the Preset menu and choose Photorealistic.**

    The application includes a number of standard settings, including several variations of monochromatic, photorealistic, and surrealistic. Each preset changes the values of the Local Adaptation sliders to create the desired effect.

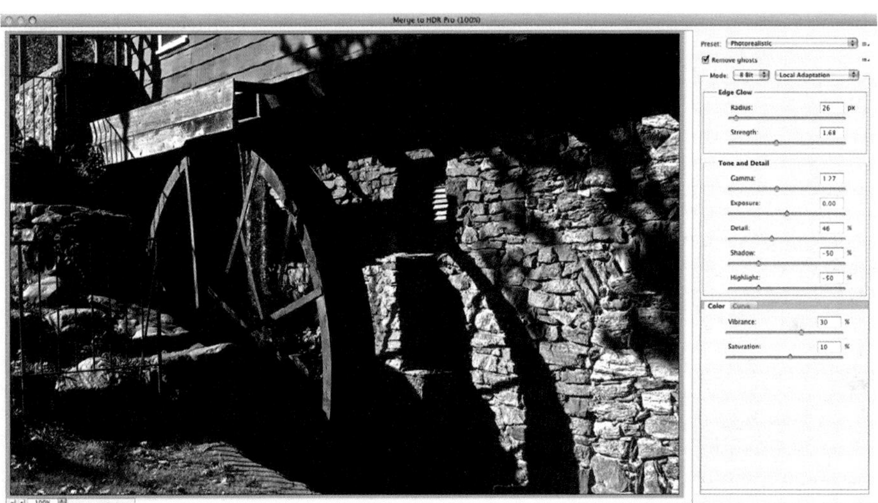

Reducing Dynamic Range for Output

PHOTOSHOP FOUNDATIONS

If you choose 32 Bit mode in the Merge to HDR Pro dialog box, you can simply click OK and save the file as a 32-bit HDR image.

If you need to create a 16- or 8-bit image later for a specific application, you can change the image bit depth in the Image>Mode submenu. The HDR Toning dialog box opens with the same options that are available in the Merge to HDR Pro dialog box using the Local Adaptation method. You can define the settings that will be applied to create the smaller-bit-depth image.

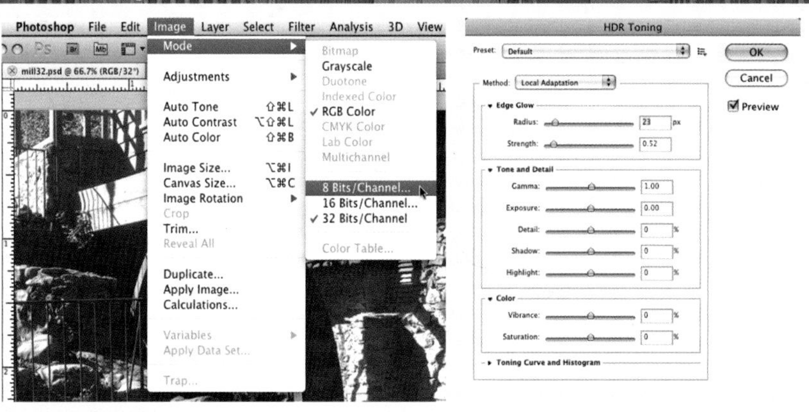

11. **Experiment with the different sliders until you are satisfied with the result.**

Tone mapping is a largely subjective process, and different end uses can influence the settings that you apply to a specific image. You should understand the following information as you experiment with the various settings:

- **Radius** defines the size of the glowing effect in areas of localized brightness.
- **Strength** determines the required tolerance between tonal values before pixels are no longer considered part of the same brightness region.
- **Gamma** values lower than 1.0 increase details in the midtones, while higher values emphasize details in the highlights and shadows.
- **Exposure** affects the overall lightness or darkness of the image.
- **Detail** increases or decreases the overall sharpness of the image.
- **Shadow** and **Highlight** affect the amount of detail in those areas of the image. Higher values increase detail and lower values reduce detail.
- **Vibrance** affects the intensity of subtle colors, while minimizing clipping of highly saturated colors.
- **Saturation** affects the intensity of all colors from –100 (monochrome) to +100 (double saturation).

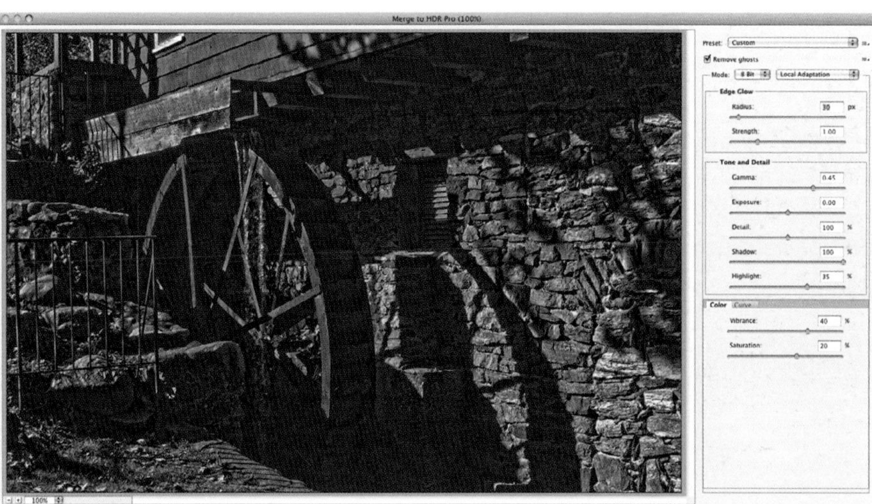

12. **Click OK to finalize the process.**

Because you chose 8 Bit in the Mode menu of the Merge to HDR Pro dialog box, the resulting image is an 8-bit RGB image (as you can see in the document tab).

13. **Save the file in your WIP>Menu>Mill Images folder as a native Photoshop file named mill_merged.psd, then close it.**

Project Review

fill in the blank

1. The ______________ filter locates pixels that differ in value from surrounding pixels by the threshold you specify; it sharpens an image by increasing contrast along the edges in an image.

2. ______________ is defined as random pixels that stand out from the surrounding pixels.

3. The ______________ blends colors from user-defined source pixels with colors in the area where you click.

4. The ______________ paints one part of an image over another part, which is useful for duplicating specific objects or removing defects in an image.

5. ______________ are direct sources of light such as a light bulb or reflected sunlight on water; they should not be considered the highlights of an image.

6. ______________ refers to the tonal variation within an image.

7. A ______________ is a visual depiction of the distribution of colors in an image.

8. ______________ is defined according to a color's position on a color wheel, beginning from red (0°) and traveling counterclockwise around the wheel.

9. ______________ (also called "intensity") refers to the color's difference from neutral gray.

10. ______________ (also called "luminance" or "value") is the amount of white or black added to the pure color.

short answer

1. Explain the concept of neutral gray.

2. List three important points to remember when working with curves.

3. Briefly explain the concepts of minimum printable dot and maximum ink coverage.

Portfolio Builder Project

Use what you learned in this project to complete the following freeform exercise.
Carefully read the art director and client comments, then create your design to meet the needs of the project.
Use the space below to sketch ideas; when finished, write a brief explanation of the reasoning behind your design.

art director comments

The tourism board director dined at The Chateau recently. In a conversation with the restaurant owner, he mentioned a new project about local architecture. Mr. Roseman, pleased with your work on the menu images, recommended you for the job.

To complete this project, you should:

- ❑ Find at least 10 photos of different architectural styles throughout the Los Angeles metropolitan area.
- ❑ Use photo retouching techniques to clean up any graffiti and trash that is visible in the images.
- ❑ Use correction techniques to adjust the tonal range and gray balance of the images.
- ❑ Correct and convert all images based on the U.S. Sheetfed Coated v2 CMYK destination profile.

client comments

Over the next year, we're planning on publishing a series of promotional booklets to show tourists that L.A. is more than just Hollywood.

Each booklet in the series will focus on an 'interest area' such as fine art or — for the first one — architecture. The city has a diverse architectural mix, from eighteenth-century Spanish missions to 1920s bungalows to the Walt Disney Concert Hall designed by Frank Gehry in the 1990s.

We'd like at least ten pictures of different landmarks or architectural styles, corrected and optimized for printing on a sheetfed press. If possible, we'd also like some historical images to include in a 'building a metropolis' section on the first couple of pages.

Of course, Los Angeles is a large city, and cities have their problems — not the least of which are graffiti and garbage. We are trying to attract tourists, not turn them away. Make sure none of the images show any graffiti or blatant litter; if these problems are visible in the images you select, give them a good digital cleaning.

project justification

Project Summary

As with many other skills, it takes time and practice to master image correction techniques. Understanding the relationship between brightness and contrast, and how these two values affect the quality of reproduction in digital images, is the first and possibly most critical factor in creating a high-quality image. An image that has too much contrast (a "sharp" image) or not enough contrast (a "flat" image) translates to an unsatisfactory print.

A basic understanding of color theory (specifically complementary color) is the foundation of accurate color correction. Effective color correction relies on the numbers, rather than what you think you see on your monitor. As you gain experience in correcting images, you will be better able to predict the corrections required to achieve the best possible output.

Remove photographic grain with blur and sharpen techniques

Use the Healing Brush and Spot Healing Brush tools to correct scratches

Use the Clone Stamp tool to remove major damage

Correct contrast and tonal range using the Levels adjustment

Use Merge to HDR Pro to find detail in multiple exposures

Correct minor color problems using the Brightness/Contrast adjustment

Correct gray balance using the Curves adjustment

Correct lighting problems with the Exposure adjustment

Correct overall color cast using the Color Balance adjustment

Correct contrast with the Curves adjustment

Correct and convert the image using the defined destination CMYK profile

project 7

Letterhead Design

Your client, Amelia Crowe, is a local photographer. She hired you to create a letterhead design that incorporates her personal logo and a set of images representing the kind of work she does. She is going to have the letterhead printed commercially so she can use it to print letters, invoices, and other business correspondence.

This project incorporates the following skills:

- ❑ Creating a new file to meet defined project requirements
- ❑ Using the basic InDesign drawing tools to develop visual interest
- ❑ Selecting objects and object contents
- ❑ Creating and formatting basic text attributes
- ❑ Placing and manipulating external graphics files
- ❑ Printing a desktop proof sample

Project Meeting

client comments

Until now, I've just added my logo and address at the top of a Word document whenever I sent out correspondence. My business has been growing lately, and I want something more professional and more indicative of my work in photographing urban architecture and natural landscapes.

I sent you my logo, which was created in Adobe Illustrator. I also selected a bunch of images that I really like; I want to include at least a few of those on the letterhead to give people an idea of my work.

Can you get my contact information from my email sig file, or do I need to send that to you as a separate document?

art director comments

I've looked over the client's images, and I think we should use all of them. Since she's a photographer, a filmstrip across the bottom of the page will make a nice container; InDesign has everything you need to create the necessary graphics directly on the page layout. I already sized the photos down to thumbnails that should be close to the right size, so you won't have to manipulate the actual image files.

I also copied the client's contact info into a file for you. Since she specifically mentioned two areas of photographic specialty, I want you to include the words "urban architecture & natural landscapes" as a tag line.

It might feel like there's a lot involved in creating this piece, but it's not too complicated; and the client liked the initial sketch, so it will be worth it.

project objectives

To complete this project, you will:

- ❑ Create a new document based on the requirements of a commercial printer.
- ❑ Place ruler guides to define "safe" areas of the page.
- ❑ Draw basic shapes using native InDesign tools
- ❑ Edit shapes using the Pathfinder and Align panels
- ❑ Work with anchor points and handles to create a complex shape
- ❑ Apply color to fills and strokes
- ❑ Create and format basic text elements
- ❑ Import external text and graphics files
- ❑ Print a desktop proof

Stage 1 Setting up the Workspace

The best way to start any new project is to prepare your workspace. As you learned in the Interface chapter, InDesign gives you extensive control over your workspace — you can choose where to place panels, whether to collapse or expand open panels, and even to save workspaces with sets of panels in specific locations. Because workspace issues are largely a matter a personal preference, we tell you what tools to use but we don't tell you where to keep the various panels. Many of our screen captures show floating panels so we can maximize the available space and clearly focus on a specific issue. Likewise, we typically don't tell you what view percentage to use; you should use whatever you are comfortable with to accomplish the specific goal of an exercise.

Define a New Layout File

Some production-related concerns will dictate how you design a letterhead. In general, there are two ways to print letterhead: one-offs on a desktop laser or inkjet printer, or commercially in large quantities. (The first method typically involves creating a letterhead template, which you then use to write and print letters from directly within InDesign — a fairly common practice among graphic designers.)

If letterhead is being printed commercially, it's probably being printed with multiple copies on a large press sheet, from which the individual letterhead sheets will be cut. Most commercial printing happens this way. This type of printing typically means that design elements can run right off the edge of the sheet, called **bleeding**.

Note:

Older desktop printers typically have a minimum margin at the page edges; you're usually safe with 3/8". Many newer inkjet printers have the capability to print 8.5 × 11" with full bleed. Consult your printer documentation to be sure.

If you're designing for a printer that can only run letter-size paper, you have to allow enough of a margin area for your printer to hold the paper as it moves through the device (called the **gripper margin**); in this case, you can't design with bleeds.

The most basic process in designing a layout is creating a new InDesign file. The New Document dialog box has a large number of options, and the following exercise explains all of those. Don't be overwhelmed by the length of this process; in later projects, we simply tell you what settings to define without re-explaining every field.

1. **Download Print5_RF_Project7.zip from the Student Files web page.**

2. **Expand the ZIP archive in your WIP folder (Macintosh) or copy the archive contents into your WIP folder (Windows).**

   This results in a folder named **Crowe**, which contains all of the files you need for this project. You should also use this folder to save the files you create in this project.

   If necessary, refer to Page 1 of the Interface chapter for specific information on expanding or accessing the required resource files.

3. **In InDesign, choose File>New>Document.**

   The New Document dialog box always defaults to the last-used document preset; if no presets exist, the dialog box opens with the settings that are stored in the Default preset. Some of the options we define in the following steps might already be reflected in the dialog box, but we can't be sure because someone might have modified the default settings on your computer. If something is already set to the value we define, simply leave that value as is.

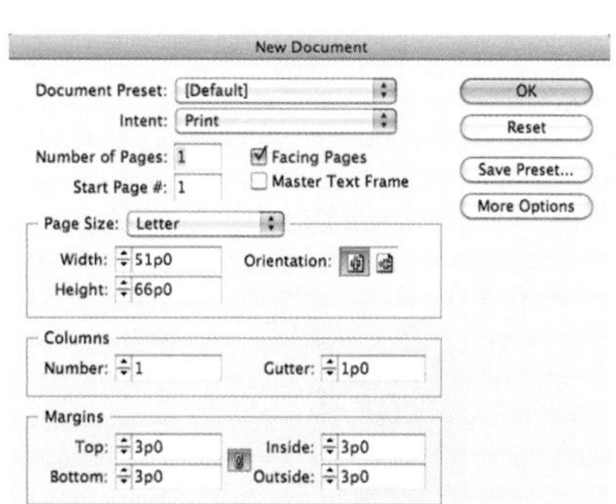

Note:

You can create a new file by pressing Command/Control-N.

4. **Choose Print in the Intent menu.**

InDesign uses picas as the default unit of measurement for print documents; measurements in this dialog box are shown in picas and points, using the "ApB" notation (for A picas and B points). Colors in a print-intent document default to the CMYK color model (see Page 56 in this project).

If you choose Web, InDesign changes the default unit of measurement to pixels, which is more appropriate for Web design. Colors in a Web-intent document default to the RGB color model.

Note:

Picas are the measuring units traditionally used in typography; they are still used by many people in the graphic communications industry.

1 point = 1/72 inch

12 points = 1 pica

1 pica = 1/6 inch

6 picas = 1 inch

5. **Set the Number of Pages field to 1.**

A letterhead is a single page, usually printed on only one side. A one-sided, one-page document needs only a single layout page in the InDesign file.

6. **Set the Start Page # field to 1.**

This option is useful when you work with multi-page files. Odd-numbered pages always appear on the right, as you see in any book or magazine; you can define an even-numbered starting page number to force the first page of a layout to the left.

7. **Uncheck the Facing Pages check box.**

Facing pages are used when a printed job will be read left to right like a book — with Page 1 starting on the right, then Page 2 facing Page 3, and so on. Facing-page layouts are based on **spreads**, which are pairs of left-right pages as you flip through a book (e.g., Page 6 facing Page 7).

8. **Uncheck the Master Text Frame option.**

When this option is checked, InDesign creates a text frame that automatically fills the area created by the defined page margins. A letterhead design primarily focuses on the area outside of the margins, so you don't need to add a master text frame to this file.

9. **Choose Letter in the Page Size menu.**

This menu includes a number of common sizes based on the selected intent. Choosing any of these options automatically changes the width and height fields to match the selected size.

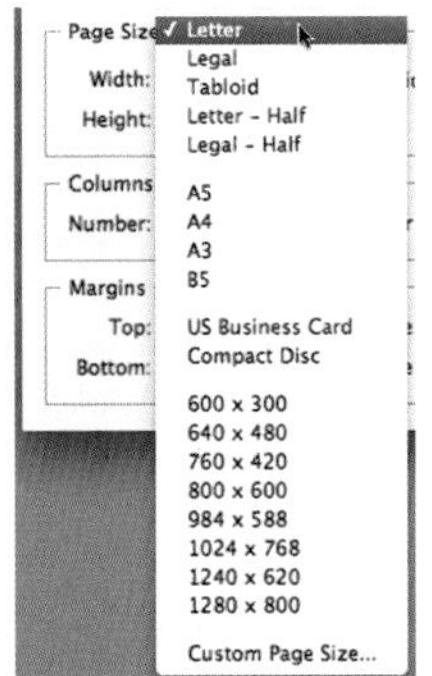

Note:

Choosing Custom in the Page Size menu has no real effect. This setting is automatically reflected as soon as you change the Width or Height field from the standard measurements.

10. **Choose the Portrait Orientation option.**

Portrait documents are higher than they are wide; **landscape** documents are wider than they are high. If you click the orientation option that is not currently selected, the Width and Height values are automatically reversed.

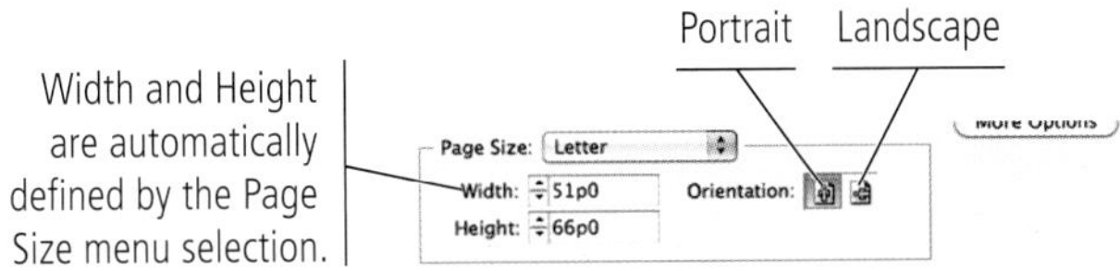
Portrait
Landscape
Width and Height are automatically defined by the Page Size menu selection.
Page Size: Letter
Width: 51p0
Height: 66p0
Orientation:

11. If the chain icon between the Margin fields shows two connected links, click the icon to break the link between the fields.

When the chain icon is active (connected links or highlighted dark gray), all four margin fields will be the same; changing one field changes all margin values to the same value. For this project, you need to define different values for the top and bottom than for the left and right, so you need to unlink (unconstrain) the margin fields if they are currently linked.

> *Note:*
>
> *When you work with non-facing pages, the Inside and Outside margin fields change to Left and Right respectively. Technically, non-facing pages do not have an inside (spine edge) or outside (face or trim edge), so there are only left and right sides.*

12. Highlight the first Margins field (Top) and type 1.25".

Even though the default measurement is picas, you can type values in any unit as long as you type the appropriate unit along with the value; InDesign makes the necessary conversion for you so the values will still bedisplayed in the default units.

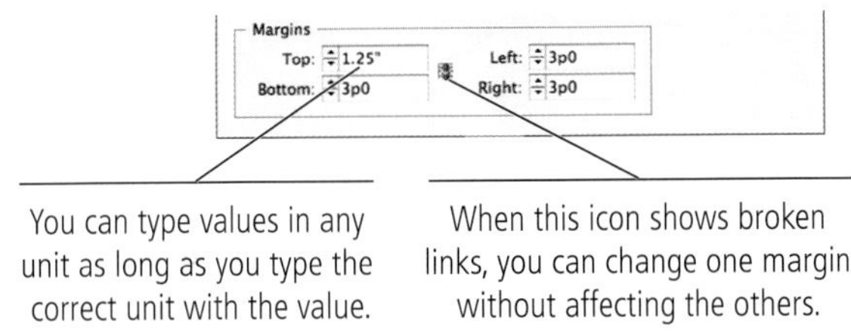
Margins
Top: 1.25"
Bottom: 3p0
Left: 3p0
Right: 3p0
You can type values in any unit as long as you type the correct unit with the value.
When this icon shows broken links, you can change one margin without affecting the others.

> *Note:*
>
> *If you enter a value in a unit other than the default, you have to include the alternate unit. This technique works in dialog boxes and panels — anywhere that you can enter a measurement.*

13. Press Tab to move to the Bottom field.

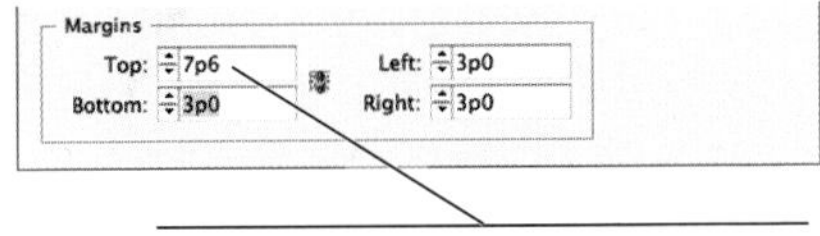
Margins
Top: 7p6
Bottom: 3p0
Left: 3p0
Right: 3p0
When you move to the next field, InDesign converts the Top value to the default unit of measurement (picas).

14. Change the Bottom field to 2", then press Tab two times.

The first time you press Tab from the Bottom field highlights the chain icon. You have to press Tab a second time to highlight the Left field.

> *Note:*
>
> *You can tab through the fields of most dialog boxes and panels in InDesign. Press Shift-Tab to move the highlight to the previous field in the tab order.*

15. Change the Left field to 1", then press Tab.

16. Change the Right field to 1".

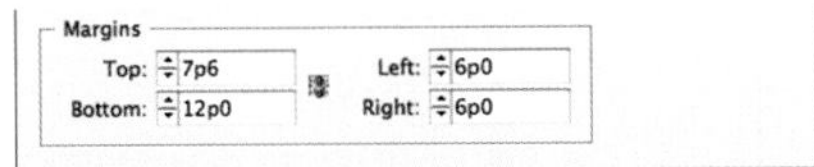
Margins
Top: 7p6
Bottom: 12p0
Left: 6p0
Right: 6p0

17. Click the More Options button to show the Bleed and Slug fields.

If this button reads "Fewer Options", the Bleed and Slug fields are already showing.

18. **Make sure the chain icon to the right of the Bleed fields is active (unbroken links), then change the first Bleed field to `0.125"` (the decimal equivalent of 1/8). Press Tab to apply the new Bleed value to all four sides.**

The letterhead for this project will be printed commercially; the printer said the design can safely bleed on all four sides, and their equipment requires a 1/8" bleed allowance. In this case, you want all four edges to have the same bleed, so the chain icon should be active to constrain all four Bleed fields to the same value.

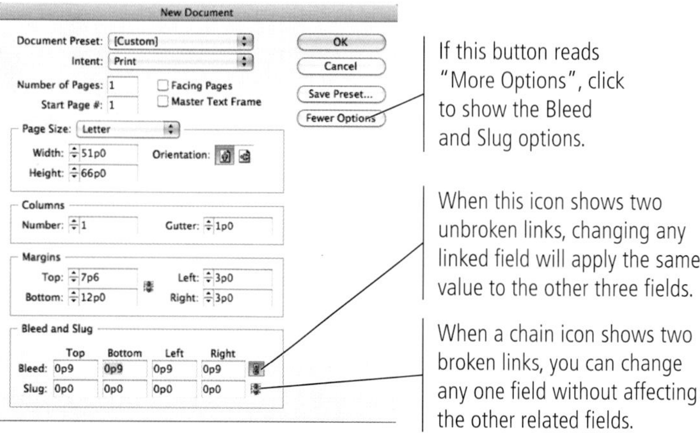

19. **Make sure the chain icon to the right of the Slug fields is active, and then change the first Slug field to `0`.**

A **slug** is an area outside of the bleed, where designers typically add job information that will not appear in the final printed piece.

You don't need to type the full "0p0" notation when you change measurements using the default units. Zero pica is still zero, so you don't need to worry about converting units.

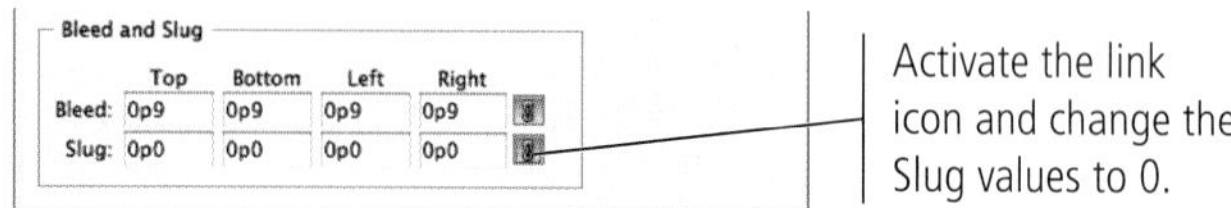

> *Note:*
>
> *A **slug** is an element entirely outside the page area, but included in the final output. The slug area can be used for file/plate information, special registration marks, color bars, and/or other elements that need to be printed on the press sheet, but do not appear within the job area.*

20. **Click OK to create the new document.**

The document appears, filling the available space in the document window. Your view percentage might appear different than what you see in our images.

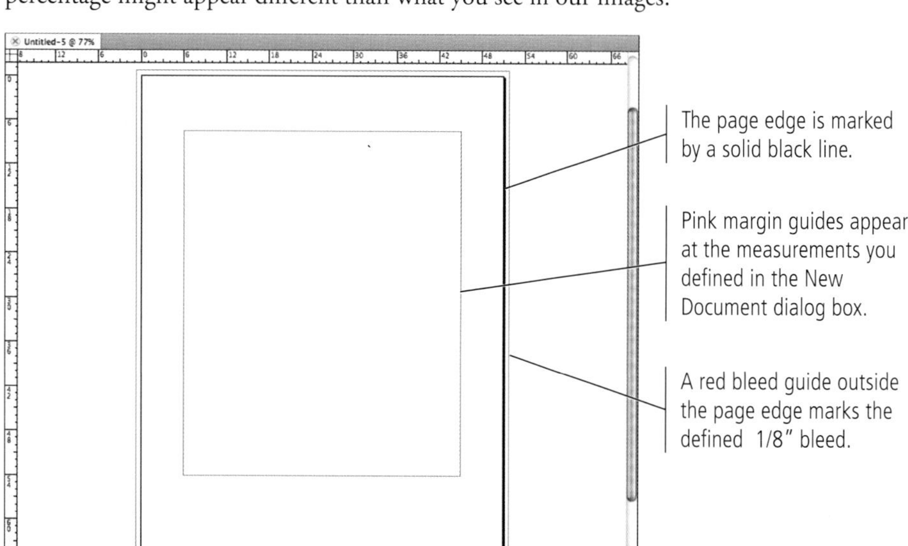

21. **Choose File>Save As. In the Save As dialog box, navigate to your WIP>Crowe folder as the target location for saving the file.**

The Save As dialog box follows a system-standard format. Macintosh and Windows users see slightly different options, but the basic InDesign functionality is the same.

22. **Change the file name (in the Save As field) to identity.indd and click Save.**

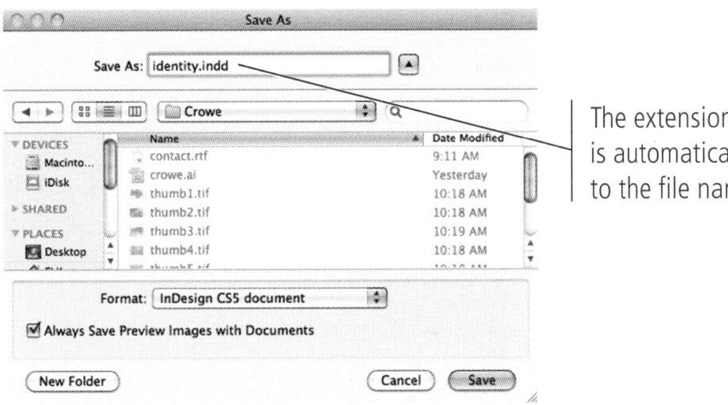

The extension ".indd" is automatically added to the file name.

Note:

The first time you save a file, the Save command opens the same dialog box as the File>Save As command. After saving the file once, you can use Save to save changes to the existing file, or use Save As to create an additional file under a new file name.

23. **Continue to the next exercise.**

Understanding Document Presets

INDESIGN FOUNDATIONS

A **preset** stores groups of common settings; you define a preset once, and then you can access the same group of settings later with a single click. You'll often use this concept while building InDesign documents — when you use text style, table styles, object styles, and output documents for printing.

If you frequently define the same document settings, you can save those choices as a preset so you can create the same document settings with minimal repetition. Clicking the Save Preset button in the New Document dialog box opens a secondary dialog box where you can name the preset. When you return to the New Document dialog box, your new preset appears as the selection in the Document Preset menu. Any time you need to create a file with the same settings, you can choose the saved preset from this menu.

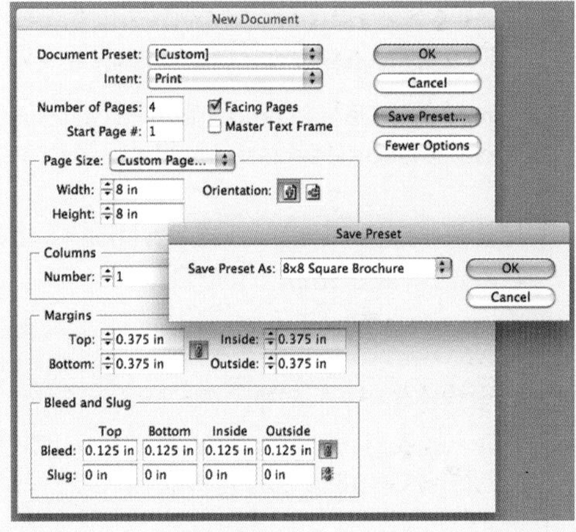

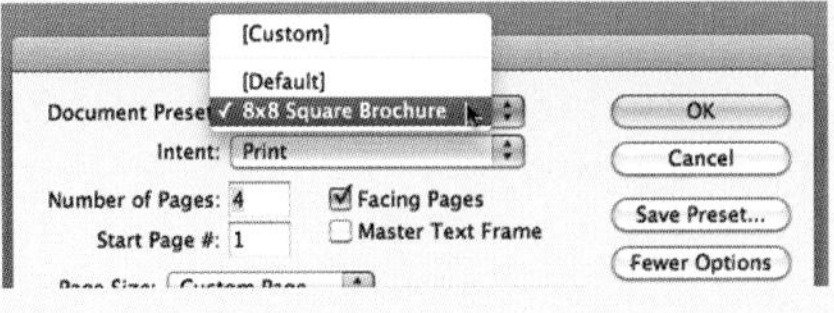

You can access and manage document presets in the File menu. If you choose one of the existing presets in the menu, the New Document dialog box opens, defaulting to the values in the preset that you called (instead of defaulting to the application-default letter-size page). All the settings you saved in the preset automatically reflect in the dialog box. You can also create, edit, and manage presets by choosing Define in the Document Presets submenu; this opens a dialog box that lists the existing presets.

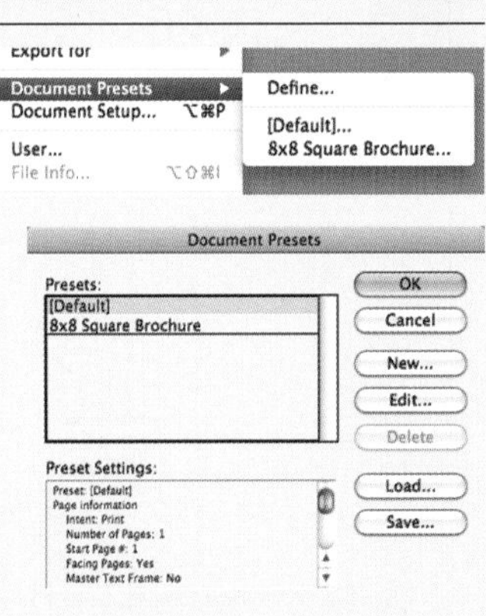

- Click New to open the New Document Preset dialog box, which is basically the same as the New Document dialog box, except the Preset menu is replaced with a field where you can type the preset name instead of clicking the Save Preset button.
- Select a preset and click Edit to change the preset's associated options.
- Select a preset and click Delete to remove the preset from the application.
- Click Load to import presets created on another computer.
- Click Save to save a preset (with the extension ".dcst") so it can be sent to and used on another computer.

Create Ruler Guides

In addition to the margin and bleed guides that you defined when you created the document, you can also place ruler guides to mark whatever other positions you need to identify in your layout.

The **live area** is the "safe" area inside the page edge, where important design elements should reside. Because printing and trimming are mechanical processes, there will always be some variation — however slight. Elements placed too close to the page edge run the risk of being accidentally trimmed off. The printer for this job recommended a 1/8″ live-area margin. You defined the margins for this file to describe the area that would typically occupy the content of a letter; in this exercise you will create ruler guides to mark the live area.

Note:

You should become familiar with the common fraction-to-decimal equivalents:

1/8 = 0.125

1/4 = 0.25

3/8 = 0.375

1/2 = 0.5

5/8 = 0.625

3/4 = 0.75

7/8 = 0.875

1. **With identity.indd open, choose View>Show Rulers if you don't see rulers at the top and left edges of the document window.**

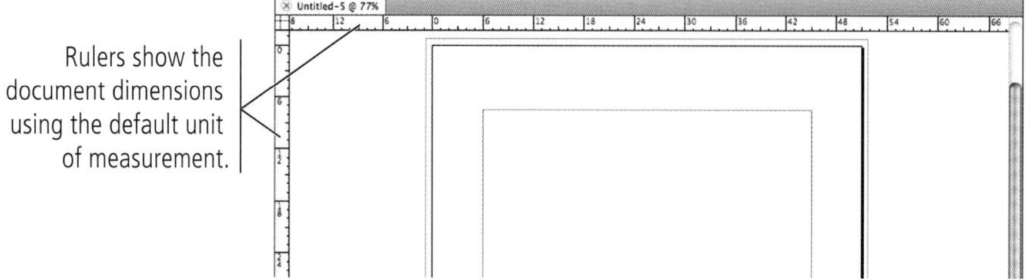

2. **Open the Units & Increments pane of the Preferences dialog box (from the InDesign menu on Macintosh or the Edit menu on Windows).**

   Since most people (in the United States, at least) think in terms of inches, we use inches throughout the projects in this book.

3. **In the Ruler Units area, choose Inches in both the Horizontal and Vertical menus, and then click OK.**

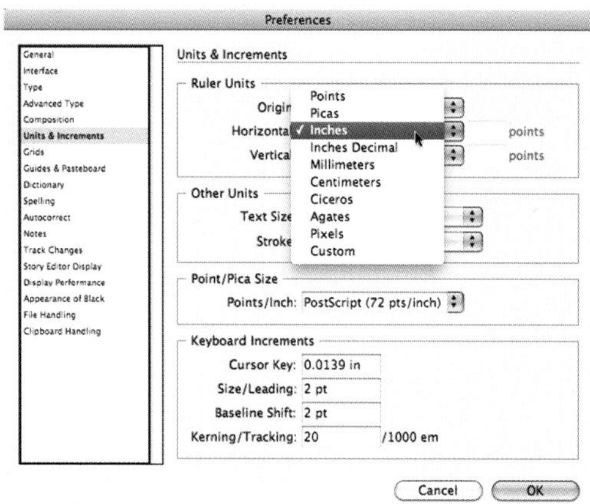

When you return to the document window, the rulers now display in inches.

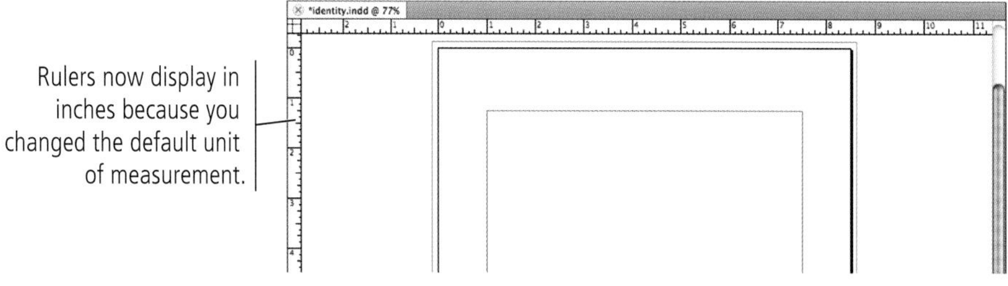

4. **Click the horizontal page ruler (at the top of the document window) and drag down until the cursor feedback indicates that the guide is positioned at Y: 0.125″. With the cursor inside the page area, release the mouse button.**

   As you drag, cursor feedback shows the current position of the guide you are placing; this makes it very easy to precisely position guides.

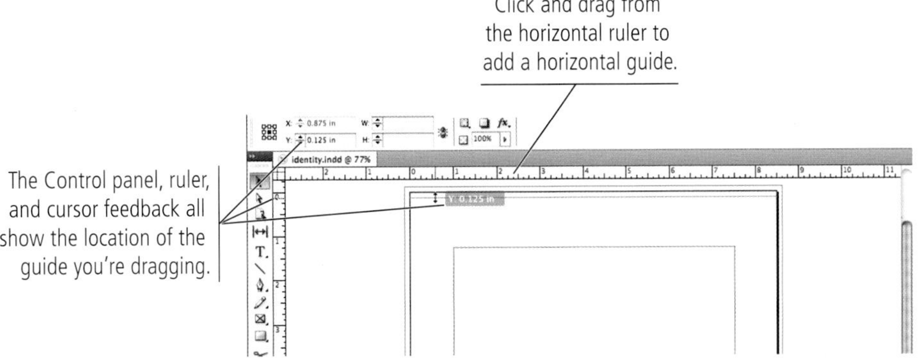

5. **Click the horizontal page ruler again and drag a guide to Y: 10.875″.**

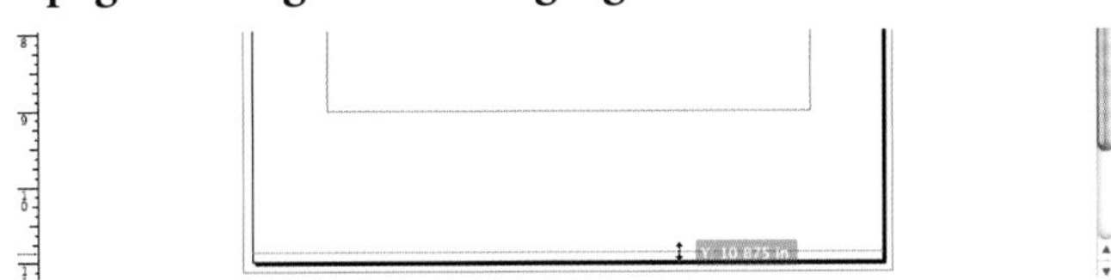

6. **Click the vertical ruler and drag a guide to X: 0.125″.**

   Watch the marker on the horizontal ruler to judge the guide's position.

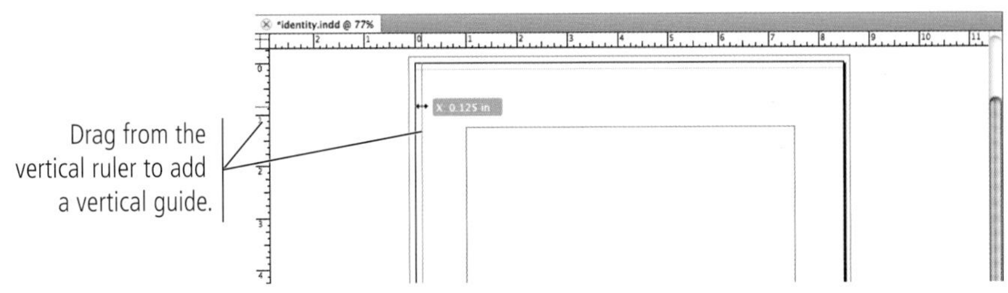

Drag from the vertical ruler to add a vertical guide.

7. **Click the vertical ruler again and drag a second vertical guide to X: 8.375″.**

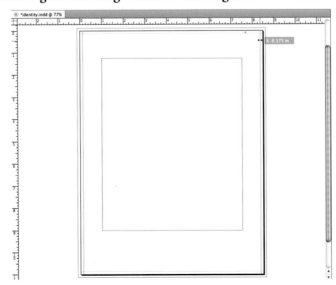

8. **Save the file and continue to the next stage of the project.**

Note:

Y values define vertical (top-to-bottom) position; X values define horizontal (left-to-right) position.

Note:

If you drag a guide outside of the page edge, the guide will extend across the entire pasteboard. You can also press Command/Control while dragging a guide onto the page to extend the guide the entire width of the pasteboard.

Note:

If the Control panel is not visible, you can show it by choosing Window>Control.

Note:

You can click the intersection of the rulers and drag to reposition the zero point away from the top-left corner of the page. If you do reposition the zero point, you can double-click the ruler intersection to reset the original zero point.

Stage 2 Creating Basic Page Elements

Based on the approved sketch, the client's letterhead includes several elements:

- A "filmstrip" graphic to frame a number of thumbnails of the client's work
- A logo that was created in Adobe Illustrator
- A tag line, separated from the logo with a curved line
- Contact information, which was provided to you as a rich-text file
- Actual thumbnails of the client's photographs, which were supplied to you as ready-to-print TIFF files.

Other than the logo and the supplied photos, you need to create these elements directly in the InDesign file.

Create Basic Frames

Although much drawing and illustration work is done in a dedicated illustration program such as Adobe Illustrator, you can use the drawing tools in InDesign to create vector artwork. In fact, the drawing tools in InDesign are actually a limited subset of the more comprehensive Illustrator toolset, which means you can create fairly sophisticated artwork entirely within the layout application. In this exercise, you are going to use the basic InDesign drawing tools to create a filmstrip graphic, which will serve as the background for the client's image samples.

1. **With identity.indd open, choose View>Grids & Guides>Smart Guides to make sure this option is toggled on. If the option is already checked, move the cursor away from the menu and click to dismiss it.**

   Smart guides are a useful function of the application, making it easy to create and precisely align objects. Smart guides show the dimensions of an object when you create it; the position of an object when you drag it; the edge and center position of nearby objects; and the distance between nearby similar objects.

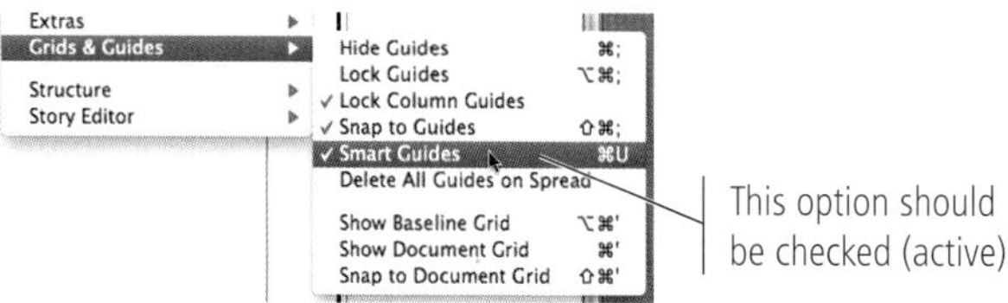

This option should be checked (active).

Note:

You can turn off specific Smart Guide functions in the Guides & Pasteboard pane of the Preferences dialog box.

2. **Click the button at the right end of the Control panel to open the panel Options menu.**

3. **If the Dimensions Include Stroke Weight option is checked, choose that item to toggle the option off.**

   When this option is active, the size of an object's stroke is factored as part of the overall object size. Consider, for example, a frame that is 72 points wide by 72 points high with a 1-point stroke. If you remove the stroke from the frame, the frame would then be only 70 points by 70 points.

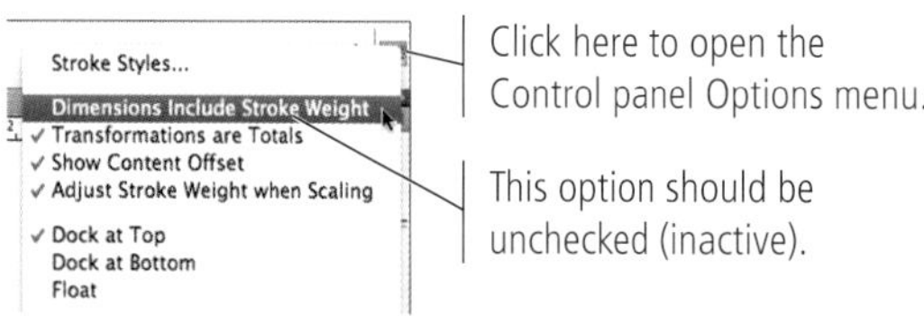

Click here to open the Control panel Options menu.

This option should be unchecked (inactive).

Note:

This option remembers the last-used setting. In many cases, you actually want the stroke weight to scale proportionally, so make sure you confirm the setting of this option if something looks wrong.

4. **Choose the Rectangle tool in the Tools panel.**

   If you don't see the Rectangle tool, click and hold the default shape tool until the nested tools appear; slide over and down to select the Rectangle tool.

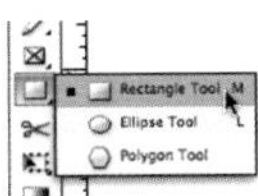

Note:

Tools with nested options default to show the last-used variation in the main Tools panel.

5. **Click the Default Fill and Stroke button at the bottom of the Tools panel.**

   In InDesign, the default fill is None, and the default stroke is 1-pt black.

6. **Click anywhere on the page, and drag down and right to draw a rectangle that is about 1″ high and 2″ wide.**

   As you draw, cursor feedback shows the size of the shape you are creating.

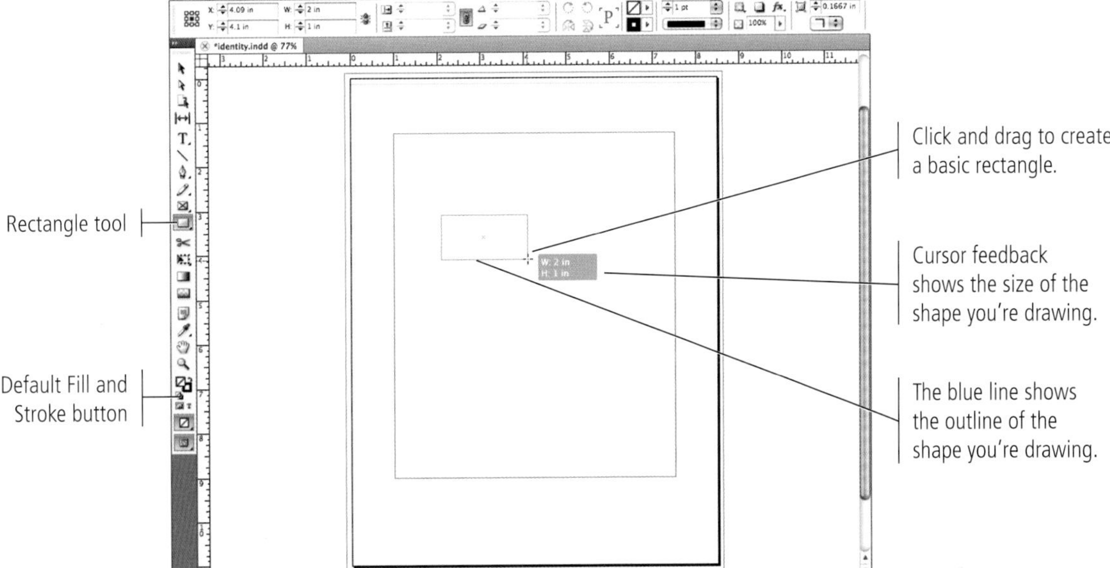

The blue line shows the outline of the shape you're drawing.

7. **Release the mouse button to create the rectangle.**

   Every shape you create in an InDesign document has a **bounding box**, which is a non-printing rectangle that marks the outer dimensions of the shape. (Even a circle has a square bounding box, marking the largest height and width of the object.) The bounding box has eight handles, which you can drag to change the size of the rectangle. If you can see an object's bounding box handles, that object is selected.

Note:

Press Shift while drawing a frame to constrain the horizontal and vertical dimensions of the shape (in other words, to create a perfect square or circle).

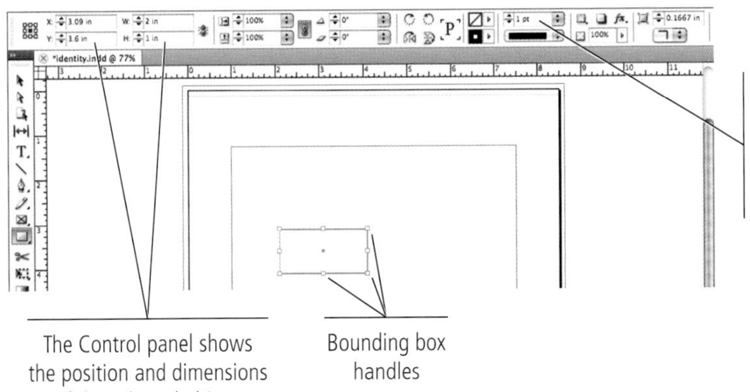

The shape has a 1-pt black stroke because you recalled the default fill and stroke values before creating the shape.
The Control panel shows the position and dimensions of the selected object.
Bounding box handles

The Control Panel in Depth

The Control panel is one of the most versatile, productive tools in the InDesign workspace, combining all of the most common formatting options into a single, compact format across the top of the workspace. It is context sensitive, which means different options are available depending on what is selected in the layout. Finally, it is customizable, which means you can change the options that are available in the panel.

It is also important to note that the options available in the Control panel might be limited by the active workspace, as well as by the width of your monitor or Application frame.

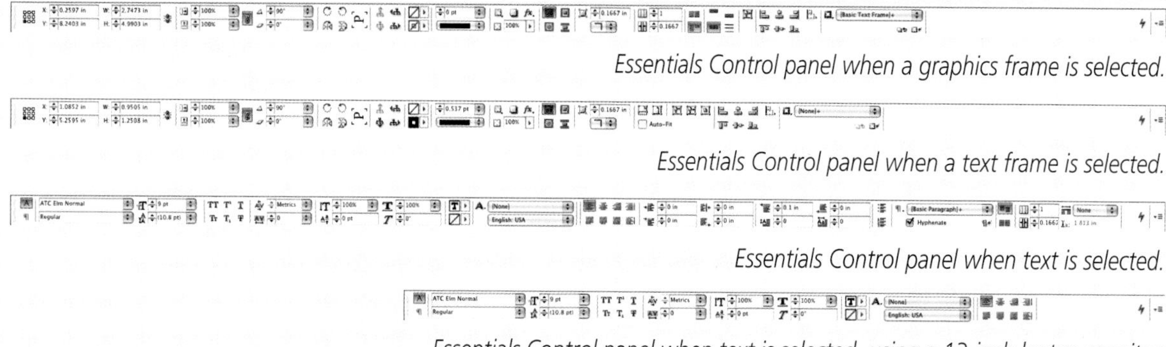

Essentials Control panel when a graphics frame is selected.

Essentials Control panel when a text frame is selected.

Essentials Control panel when text is selected.

Essentials Control panel when text is selected, using a 13-inch laptop monitor.

The panel Options menu includes options for controlling the position of the panel (top, bottom, or floating), as well as how transformations affect selected objects:

Quick Apply button

Click here to open the panel Options menu.

Stroke Styles...
Clear Transformations
✓ Dimensions Include Stroke Weight
✓ Transformations are Totals
✓ Show Content Offset
✓ Adjust Stroke Weight when Scaling
✓ Dock at Top
Dock at Bottom
Float
Customize...

- **Stroke Styles.** This opens a dialog box where you can edit or define custom styles for lines and object strokes.
- **Clear Transformations.** Choosing this option resets an object to its original position (including rotation).
- **Dimensions Include Stroke Weight.** When checked, width and height values include the object width as well as the defined stroke width. For example, if this option is checked, a square that is 72 points wide with a 1-pt stroke would be 73 points wide (using the default stroke position that aligns the stroke on the center of the object edge).
- **Transformations are Totals.** When checked, transformations to an object's contents reflect the object's transformations plus transformations applied to the content within the frame. For example, if an object is rotated 10°, and the graphic within the object is rotated 5°, the object's rotation displays as 15° when this option is checked.
- **Show Content Offset.** When checked, the Control panel shows X+ and Y+ values for a graphic placed within a frame when the actual graphic (not the frame) is selected.
- **Adjust Stroke Weight when Scaling.** When checked, resizing an object changes the stroke weight proportionally. For example, resizing an object with a 1-pt stroke to 50% results in a 0.5-pt stroke.

Choosing **Customize** in the panel Options menu opens a dialog box where you can define the available options in the panel; anything with a checkmark will be available when it's relevant to the selection in the document.

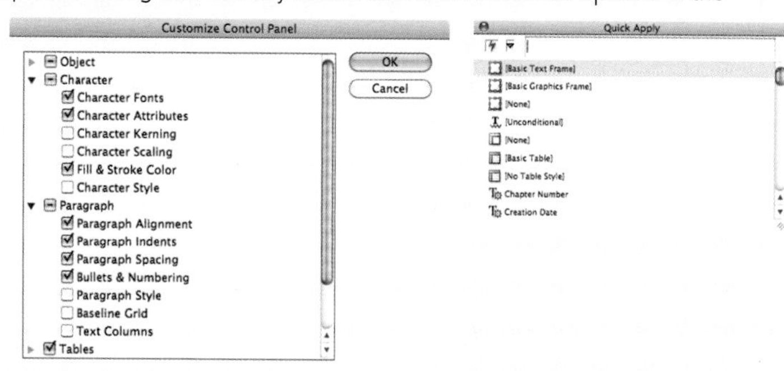

Clicking the Quick Apply button (to the left of the panel Options button) opens a special navigation dialog box. This feature enables you to easily find and apply what you want (menu commands, user-defined styles, and so on) by typing a few characters in the text entry field, and then clicking the related item in the list.

8. **At the bottom of the Tools panel, click the Swap Fill and Stroke button.**

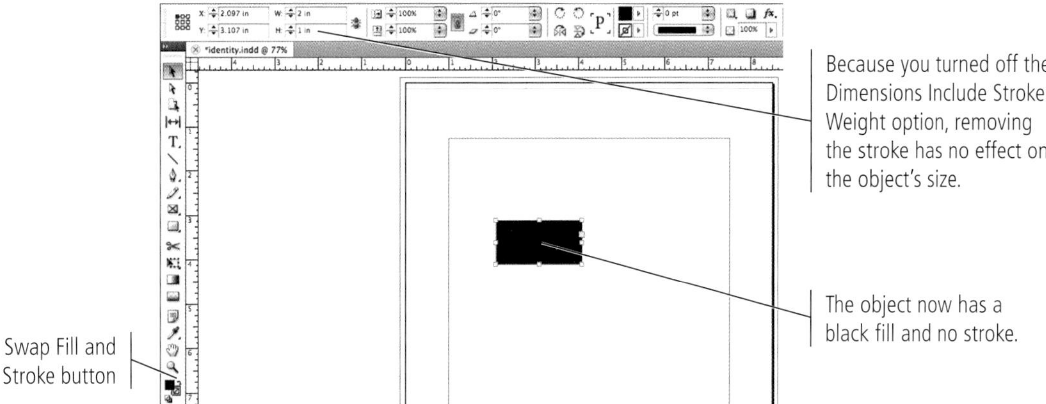

Because you turned off the Dimensions Include Stroke Weight option, removing the stroke has no effect on the object's size.
The object now has a black fill and no stroke.
Swap Fill and Stroke button

9. **At the left end of the Control panel, select the top-left reference point.**

The Control panel is context-sensitive, which means different options are available depending on what is selected in the document. This panel consolidates the most common options from multiple InDesign panels.

The **reference point** determines how transformations will occur (in other words, which point of the object will remain in place if you change one of the position or dimension values). These points correspond to the object's bounding box handles, as well as to the object's exact center point.

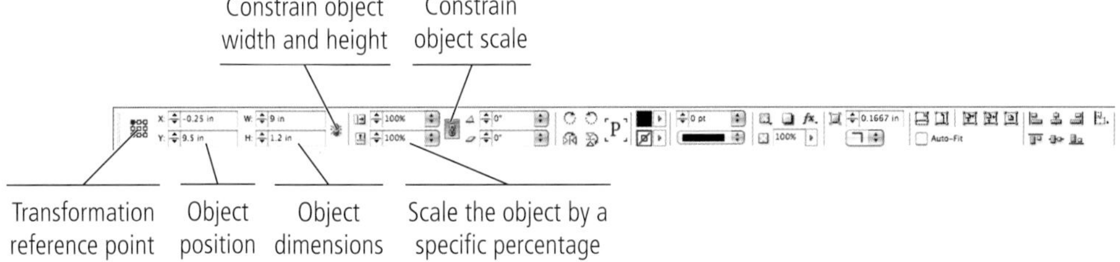

Constrain object width and height
Constrain object scale
Transformation reference point
Object position
Object dimensions
Scale the object by a specific percentage

10. **Highlight the X field in the Control panel and type `-0.25`, then press Tab to move the highlight to the Y field.**

As in dialog boxes, you can use the Tab key to move through the fields in the Control panel. The X and Y fields determine the position of the selected object. X defines the horizontal (left-to-right) position and Y defines the vertical (top-to-bottom) position.

Note:

Because inches are now the default unit of measurement for this file, you don't need to type the unit in the field.

11. **With the Y field highlighted, type 9.5 and then press Return/Enter.**

Pressing Return/Enter applies your changes in the Control panel. You can also simply click away from the object to apply the changes, but then you would have to reselect the object to make further changes.

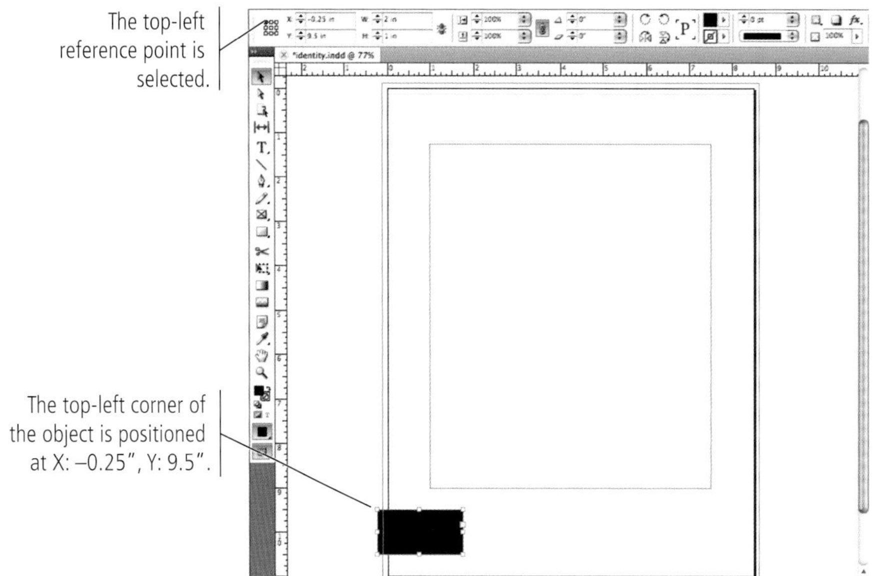

Note:

You can use math operators to add (+), subtract (-), divide (/), or multiply (*) existing values in the Control panel. This is useful when you want to move or change a value by a specific amount.

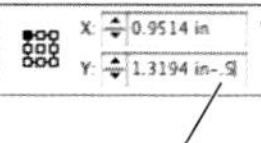

Type –.5 after the value to move the object up half an inch.

12. **In the Control panel, make sure the chain icon for the W and H fields is inactive (not linked). Change the W (width) field to 9", change the H (height) field to 1.2", and then press Return/Enter to apply the change.**

Remember, you don't need to type the units if you are working with the default units.

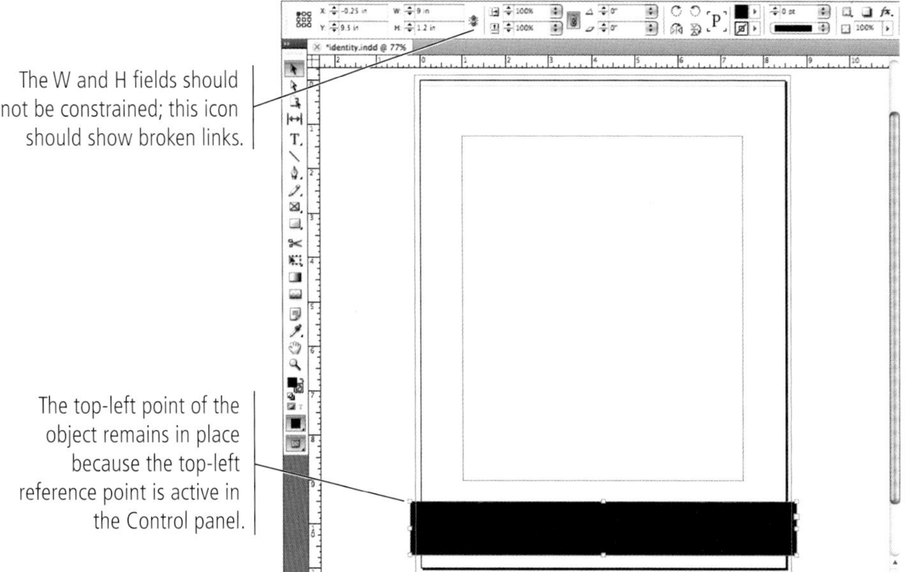

The W and H fields should not be constrained; this icon should show broken links.
The top-left point of the object remains in place because the top-left reference point is active in the Control panel.

Note:

The Transform panel (Window>Object & Layout>Transform) includes the same options that are available in the Control panel when an object is selected with the Selection tool. You can change an object's position or dimensions, scale an object to a specific percentage, and apply rotation or shear to the selected object. The Transform panel Options menu includes the same options that are available in the Control panel Options menu, as well as commands to rotate and flip the selected object.

13. **Save the file and continue to the next exercise.**

Create a Rounded Rectangle

In addition to basic rectangles, you can create frames with a number of special corner treatments. The Rounded Rectangle tool automatically creates frames with special corners, but you can also easily modify the corners of an existing frame to create the effect you want.

1. **With identity.indd open, zoom into the left end of the black rectangle.**

2. **Click away from the existing shape to deselect it (if necessary).**

   If you don't deselect the existing shape, the changes you make in the next step would affect the selected object.

3. **Make sure the Rectangle tool is active.**

4. **In the Control panel, click the arrow button to the right of the Fill swatch to open the attached Swatches panel. Choose Paper from the pop-up panel.**

   There is a difference between no fill and 0% of a color. Using 0% of a color — or using the Paper color — effectively creates a solid "white" fill. (In printing, solid white areas **knock out** or hide underlying shapes.)

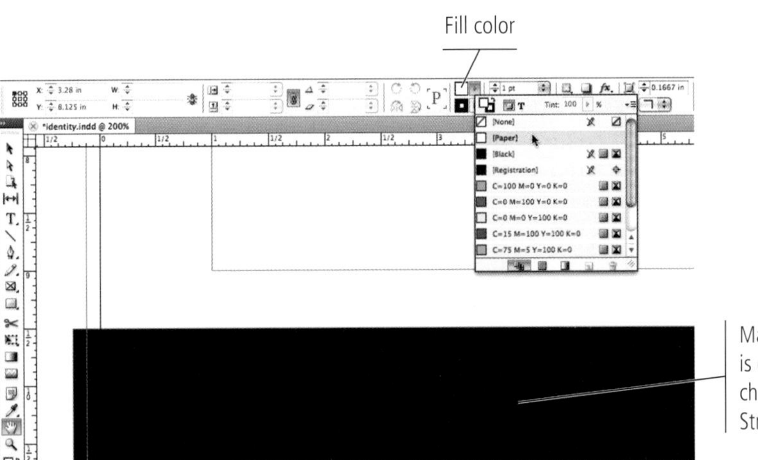

Fill color
Make sure this shape is deselected before changing the Fill and Stroke colors.

5. **In the Control panel, click the arrow button to the right of the Stroke swatch and choose None from the pop-up panel.**

   The "None" color option essentially removes color from that attribute. Underlying objects will be visible in areas where None is applied.

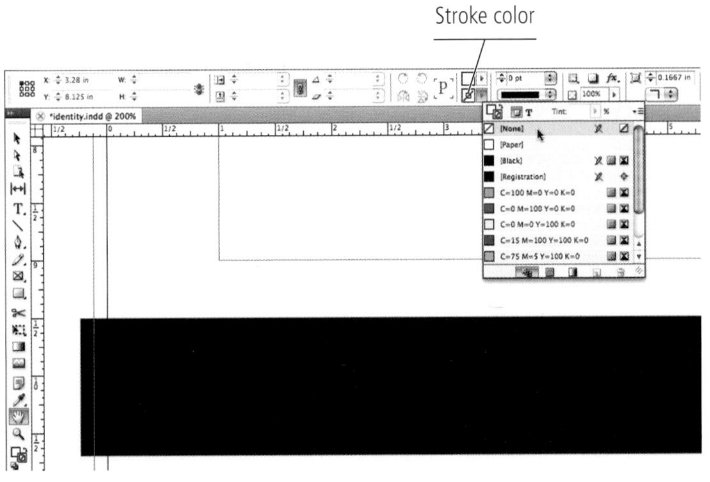

Stroke color

Note:

When an object is selected, changing the fill and stroke values changes those attributes for the selected object. If you change the fill or stroke color value with no object selected, you define the values for the next object you create.

Note:

Paper is basically white, but more accurately named because the paper for a specific job might not be white.

Note:

Changing a fill or stroke attribute when a group is selected affects all objects in the selected group.

6. **Click once on the page to open the Rectangle dialog box.**

   Single-clicking with a shape tool opens a dialog box where you can define specific measurements for the new shape.

7. **In the Rectangle dialog box, set the Width to `0.125"` and the Height to `0.08"`, and then click OK.**

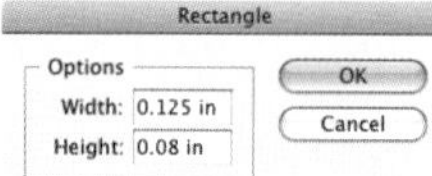

   The new rectangle is placed with the selected reference point where you clicked.

8. **Zoom in so you can more clearly see the small rectangle you just created.**

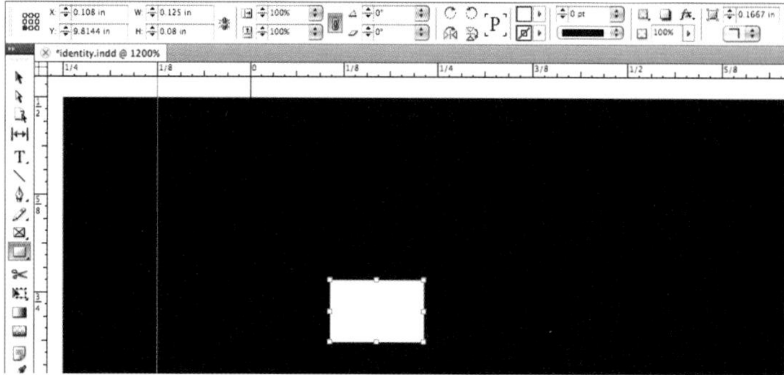

9. **With the new rectangle selected, open the Corner Shape menu in the Control panel and choose the rounded option.**

   Even though the object now has rounded corners, the **bounding box** still marks the outermost corners of the shape. (You might need to zoom in to see the effect of the new corner shape.)

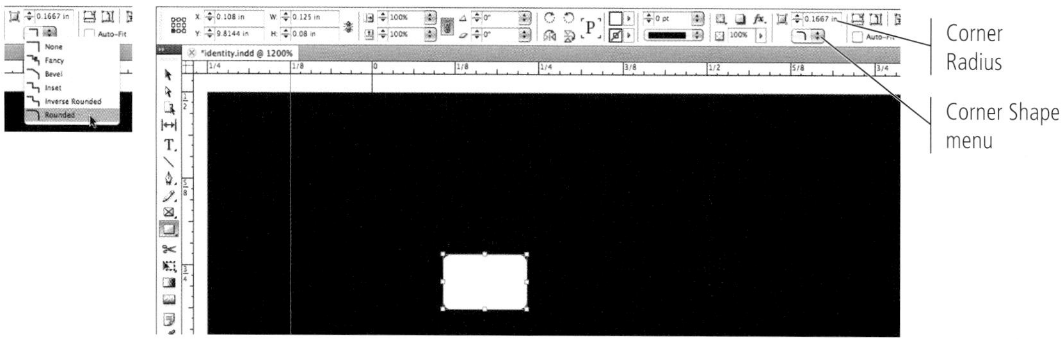

   A rounded-corner rectangle is simply a rectangle with the corners cut at a specific distance from the end (the corner radius). The two sides are connected with one-fourth of a circle, which has a radius equal to the amount of the rounding.

   Radius

10. **Save the file and continue to the next exercise.**

Editing Object Corners

When a rectangular frame is selected in the layout, a small yellow square appears on the right edge of the shape's bounding box. You can click this button to enter Live Corner Effects edit mode, where you can dynamically adjust the appearance of corner effects for all corners (by simply clicking a corner diamond) or for one corner at a time (by pressing the Shift key when you click). Simply clicking away from the object exits the edit mode.

Option/Alt-click this icon to open the Corner Options dialog box.

Click this yellow square to enter Live Corner Effects edit mode.

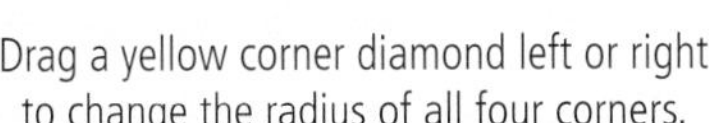

Drag a yellow corner diamond left or right to change the radius of all four corners.

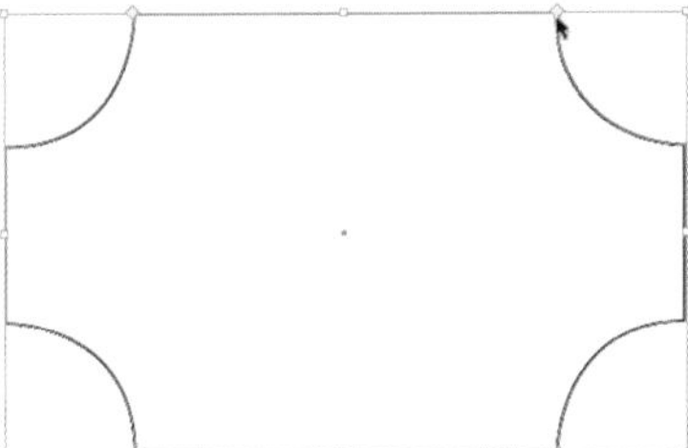

Option/Alt-click a yellow diamond to change the shape of corner effects.

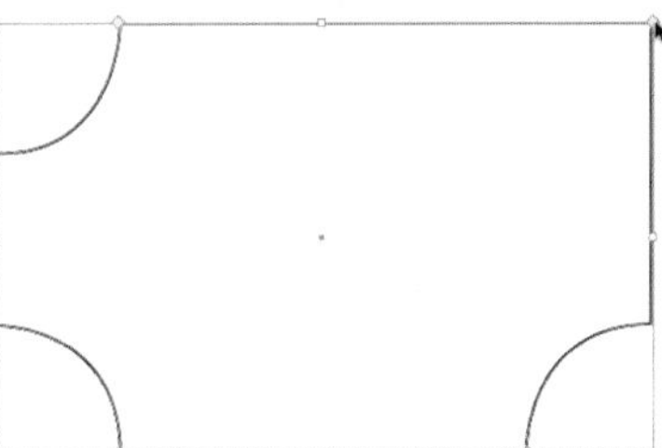

Shift-click a yellow diamond to change the radius of only one corner (or Option/Alt-Shift-click to change the shape of only one corner).

Clone, Align, and Distribute Multiple Objects

As you should have already noticed, there is often more than one way to accomplish the same task in InDesign. Aligning multiple objects on a page is no exception. In fact, InDesign offers a number of methods for aligning objects, both to the page and to each other. In this exercise you will explore a number of those options as you create sprocket-hole shapes that will turn the black rectangle into a strip of film.

1. **With identity.indd open, choose the Selection tool in the Tools panel.**

   The Selection tool is used to select entire objects; the Direct Selection tool is used to select parts of objects or the contents of a frame.

2. **Click inside the area of the rounded rectangle, press the Option/Alt key, and drag right. Release the mouse button when the preview shows a small space between the two objects.**

   Pressing Option/Alt as you drag moves a copy of the selected object (called **cloning**). As you drag, a series of green lines mark the top, center, and bottom of the original object. These green lines are a function of InDesign's Smart Guides, which make it easy to align objects to each other by simply dragging.

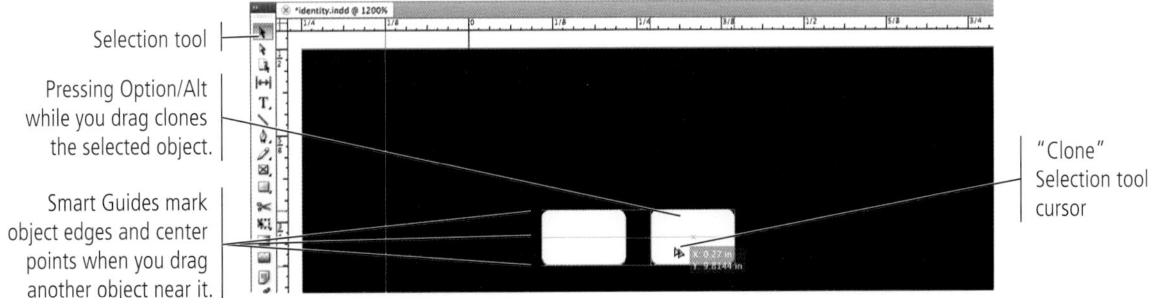

Selection tool
Pressing Option/Alt while you drag clones the selected object.
Smart Guides mark object edges and center points when you drag another object near it.
"Clone" Selection tool cursor

3. **Click the second shape, press Option/Alt, and drag right. Release the mouse button when you see opposing arrows below/between the first and second pair, and the second and third pair of shapes.**

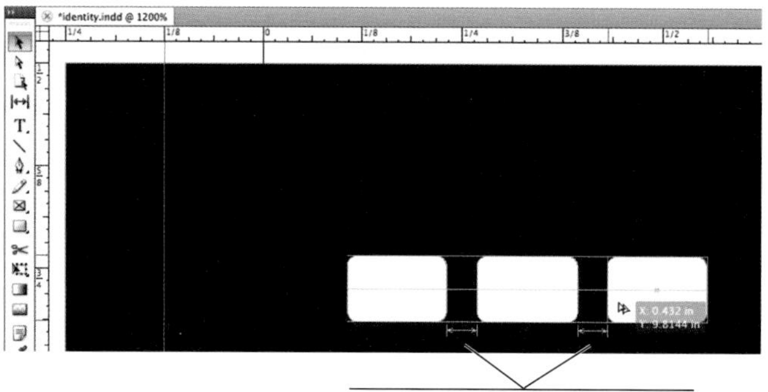

Smart Guides identify equal spacing between multiple objects.

> *Note:*
>
> *Smart Guides also identify equal dimensions when you create a new object near an existing one.*

4. **Press Shift and then click the first and second shapes to add them to the current selection.**

   You can Shift-click an object to select it in addition to the previously selected object(s), or Shift-click an already selected object to deselect it without deselecting other objects.

5. **Click inside the area of any of the selected shapes. Using the following image as a guide, drag the selected objects to the top-left corner of the black rectangle.**

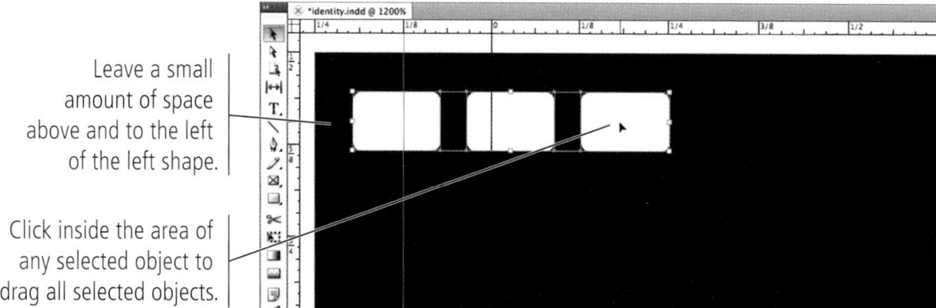
Leave a small amount of space above and to the left of the left shape.
Click inside the area of any selected object to drag all selected objects.

6. **Click away from the active objects to deselect them, then click only the third rounded rectangle. Option/Alt-click and drag right; release the mouse button when the fourth object is evenly spaced with the first three.**

   This step re-establishes the cloning movement as the last-applied transformation.

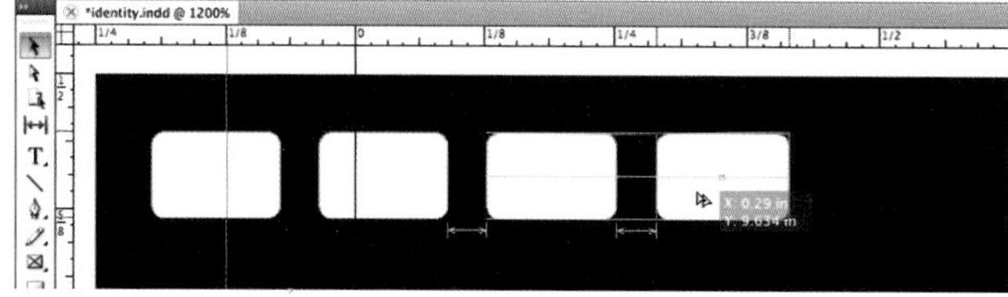

7. **With the fourth object still selected, choose Object>Transform Again> Transform Again.**

   This command applies the last-used transformation to the selected object. Because you used the cloning movement in the previous step, the result is a fifth copy that is spaced at the same distance you moved the copy in Step 6. (The Transform Again command can be used to re-apply rotation, scaling, sizing, and other transformations.)

> *Note:*
>
> *You could also choose Edit>Duplicate, which makes a copy of the selected object using the last-applied movement distance.*

8. **With the new fifth object selected, choose Edit>Step and Repeat.**

9. **Activate the Preview option in the resulting dialog box, and type 45 in the Count field.**

   The Step and Repeat dialog box makes a defined number of copies, spaced according to the defined Offset values. By default, these values are set to the last-used movement that you applied in the layout. As you can see, the 50 copies (the original 5 and the 45 that will result from the Step and Repeat process) are all equally spaced, but not enough to fill the filmstrip.

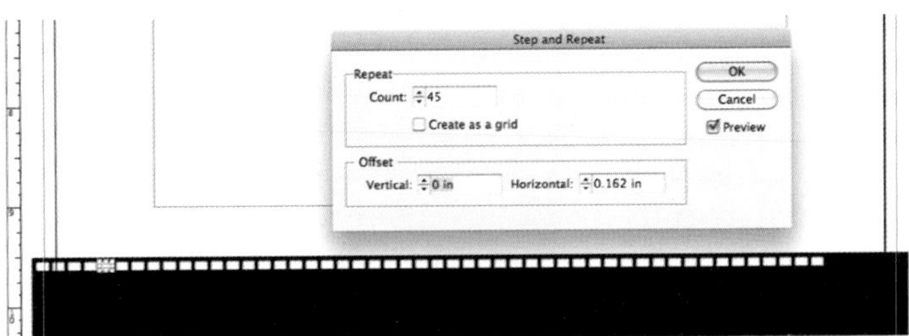

10. **Click OK to make the copies, then click away from the resulting shapes to deselect them.**

11. **Zoom in to the right end of the black rectangle, and select only the right-most rounded rectangle.**

12. **Press Shift, then drag to the right until the center of the object snaps to the bleed guide.**

    Because this object ends up entirely outside the page edge, the Smart Guides no longer appear to mark exact horizontal movement. Pressing Shift while dragging constrains the movement to 45° angles.

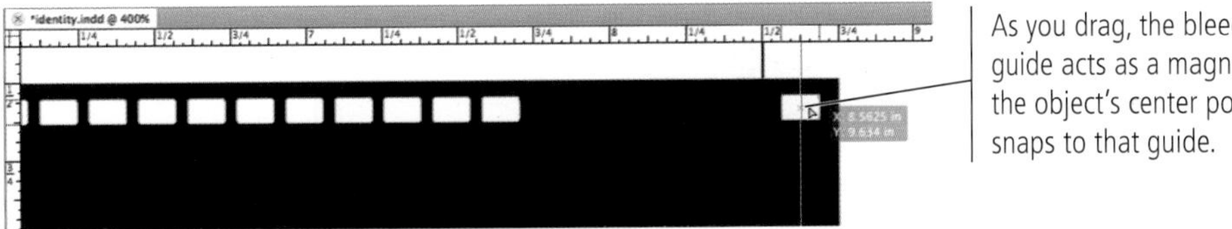

As you drag, the bleed guide acts as a magnet; the object's center point snaps to that guide.

13. **Zoom out so you can see the entire page width, then choose Edit>Select All.**

14. **Press Shift and click the black rectangle to deselect only that object.**

    When you are working with a large number of objects, it is often easier to deselect what you don't want than to select the ones you do want. Steps 13 and 14 show a very easy way to select most, but not all, of the objects on a page.

All of the rounded rectangles should be selected.

The black rectangle should not be selected.

15. **Open the Align panel (Window>Object & Layout>Align).**

Aligning and Distributing Objects

In addition to aligning objects with the assistance of Smart Guides, you can also use the Align panel to align multiple objects relative to one another, to the page margins, to the page, or to the spread.

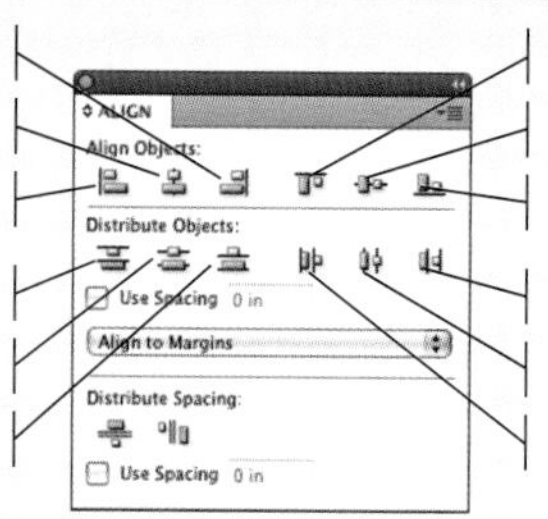

The Align Objects options are fairly self explanatory; when multiple objects are selected, the objects align based on the edge(s) or center(s) you click.

The Distribute Objects options enable you to control the positions of multiple objects relative to each other. By default, objects are equally distributed within the dimensions of the overall selection; you can check the Use Spacing option to space edges or centers by a specific amount.

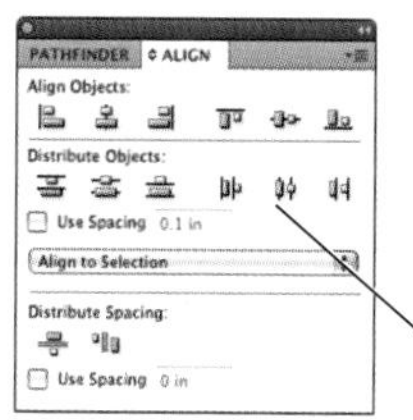

By default, the Distribute Objects options equally space the selected objects within the outermost dimensions of the selection.

The Distribute Spacing options place equal space between the overall selected objects. You can also check the Use Spacing option to add a specific amount of space between the selected objects.

Below the Distribute Objects option, you can choose from the menu to determine how objects will align. (Because you can align objects relative to the document, the align buttons are also available when only one object is selected, allowing you to align any single object to a precise location on the page or spread.)

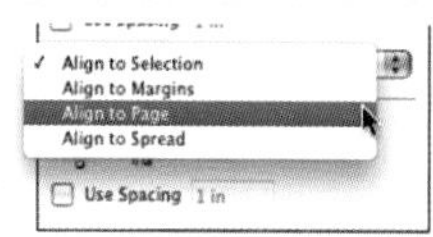

The Use Spacing option places a specific amount of space between the selected edges (or centers) of selected objects.

Many of the options from the Align panel are also available in the Control panel; the Align options are also available in all of the built-in workspaces. If you are using the Essentials workspace, the Distribute options are not available in the Control panel; you can turn them on by customizing the panel or by choosing the Advanced workspace option.

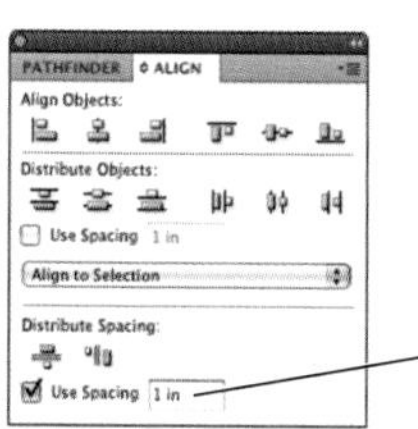

The Distribute Spacing options place a specific amount of space between selected objects.

16. **With all of the rounded rectangles selected, click the Distribute Horizontal Centers button in the Align panel.**

This button places an equal amount of space between the center points of each selected object. The two outer shapes in the selection act as the anchors; all other objects between the outer objects are repositioned.

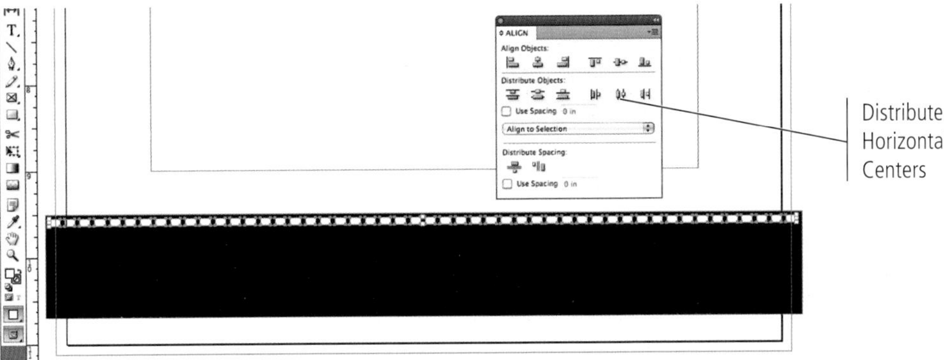

17. **Click any of the selected shapes, press Option/Alt-Shift, and drag down.**

This creates a second row of rounded rectangles that is automatically aligned below the top row.

18. **Save the file and continue to the next exercise.**

Create a Compound Path

Many shapes are composed of more than one path. The letter "O", for example, requires two separate paths — the outside shape and an inner shape to remove the area inside of the letter; without either path, the shape would be incomplete — just a circle instead of a recognizable letter. In this project, you will combine all of the existing shapes so the filmstrip is treated as a single object rather than 101 separate shapes.

1. **With identity.indd open, deselect all objects on the page and then click to select only the black rectangle.**

2. **In the Control panel, click the Drop Shadow button.**

This button applies a drop shadow to the selected object using the default effect settings. As you can see, the shadow is not visible through the sprocket holes because you filled them with the Paper color — which knocks out all underlying color (including the applied shadow). To make the graphic work properly, you have to remove the areas of the rounded rectangles from the black rectangle.

> *Note:*
>
> *You will learn how to change these effect settings in Project 8.*

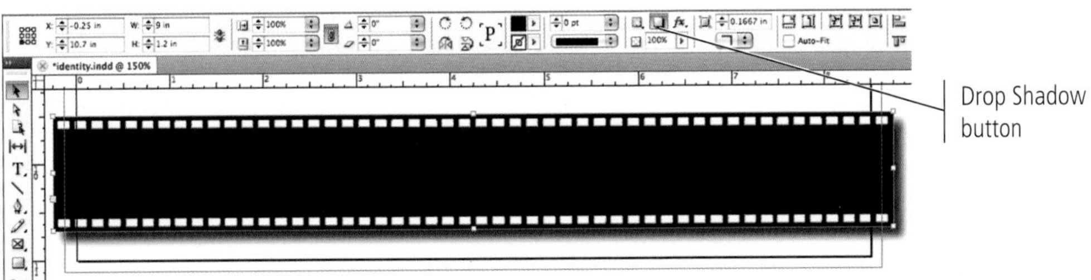

3. **Using the Selection tool, click and drag a marquee that touches all objects that make up the filmstrip graphic.**

   Using the Selection tool, any object that is at least partially surrounded by the selection marquee will be included in the resulting selection.

The gray line identifies the selection area.
Objects even partially selected by the marquee are selected.

4. **Open the Pathfinder panel (Window>Object & Layout>Pathfinder).**

The Pathfinder Panel in Depth

INDESIGN FOUNDATIONS

You can apply a number of transformations to objects using the Pathfinder panel. (The options in the Pathfinder panel are the same as those in the Object>Paths, Object>Pathfinder, Object>Convert Shape, and Object>Convert Point submenus.)

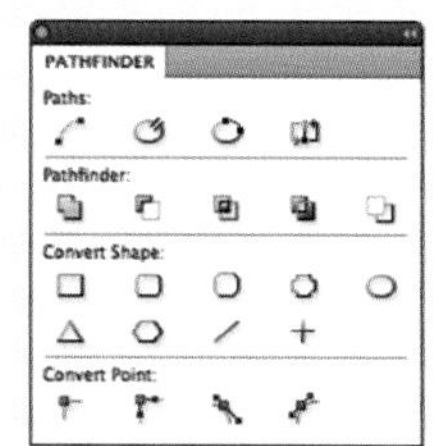

Paths	Pathfinder	Convert Shape	Convert Point
Join Path	Add	Rectangle	Plain Point
Open Path	Subtract	Rounded Rectangle	Corner Point
Close Path	Intersect	Beveled Rectangle	Smooth Point
Reverse Path	Exclude Overlap	Inverse Rounded Rectangle	Symmetrical Point
	Minus Back	Ellipse	
		Triangle	
		Polygon	
		Line	
		Horizontal/Vertical Line	

Path options break (open) a closed path, connect (close) the endpoints of an open path, or reverse a path's direction (start becomes end and vice versa, which is relevant if you use stylized end treatments).

Pathfinder options create complex objects by combining multiple existing objects. When you use the Pathfinder options (other than Subtract), the attributes of the front object are applied to the resulting shape; the Subtract function maintains the attributes of the back object.

- **Add** results in the combined shapes of all selected objects.
- **Subtract** returns the shape of the back object minus any overlapping area of the front object.
- **Intersect** results in the shape of only the overlapping areas of selected objects.
- **Exclude Overlap** results in the shape of all selected objects minus any overlapping areas.
- **Minus Back** results in the shape of the front object minus any area where it overlaps other selected objects.

Convert Shape options change the overall appearance of an object using one of the six defined basic shapes, or using the default polygon settings; you can also convert any existing shape to a basic line or an orthogonal (horizontal or vertical) line.

Convert Point options affect the position of direction handles when a specific anchor point is selected.

- **Plain** creates a point with no direction handles.
- **Corner** creates a point that produces a sharp corner; changing the direction handle on one side of the point does not affect the position or length of the handle on the other side of the point.
- **Smooth** creates a point with opposing direction handles that are exactly 180° from one another; the two handles can have different lengths.
- **Symmetrical** creates a smooth point with equal-length opposing direction handles; changing the length or position of one handle applies the same change to the opposing handle.

5. **Click the Subtract button in the Pathfinder panel.**

   This button removes the area of front objects from the area of the backmost object. The result is a **compound path**, which is a single shape that is made up of multiple paths; interior paths are removed from the background shape, allowing underlying elements to show through.

> *Note:*
>
> *It might take a while for the process to complete because InDesign has a lot of information to process to create a compound shape from 101 different paths.*

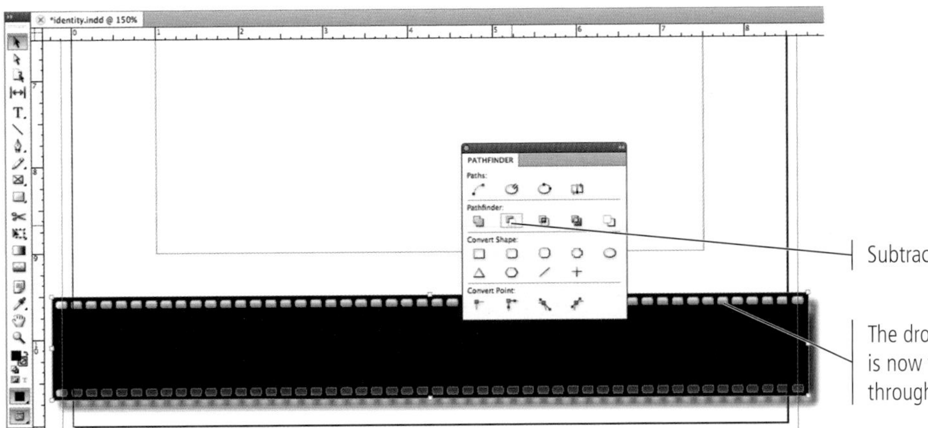

Subtract
The drop shadow is now visible through the holes.

6. **Save the file and continue to the next exercise.**

Create and Transform Multiple Frames

Many layouts have defined space requirements for various elements. This letterhead layout, for example, requires eight thumbnail images across the filmstrip graphic, evenly spaced and equally sized — just as you would see on a traditional piece of photographic film. Rather than simply placing the images and resizing the resulting frames for all eight images, you can speed up the process by first creating empty graphics frames that will contain the images when you place them.

1. **With identity.indd open, arrange your document window and view percentage so you can see the entire filmstrip at the bottom of the page.**

2. **Choose the Rectangle Frame tool in the Tools panel.**

   The frame tools work the same as the basic shape tools; the only difference is that the resulting shape automatically becomes a container for imported graphics or images.

3. **Click the left edge of the filmstrip graphic just below the top row of holes, then drag down and right until cursor feedback shows W: 9", H: 0.8".**

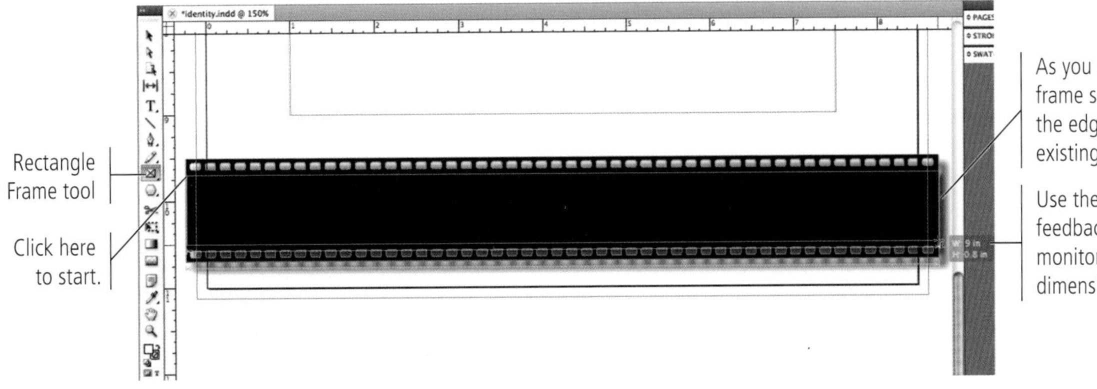

Rectangle Frame tool
Click here to start.
As you drag, the frame snaps to the edges of the existing object.
Use the cursor feedback to monitor the frame dimensions.

4. **While still holding down the mouse button, press the Right Arrow key.**

If you press the arrow keys while creating a frame, you can create a grid of frames within the area that you drag.

- Press the Right Arrow key to add columns.
- Press the Left Arrow key to remove columns.
- Press the Up Arrow key to add rows.
- Press the Down Arrow key to remove rows.

Note:

*This method of creating multiple frames, called **gridified tools**, works with any of the frame or basic shape tools.*

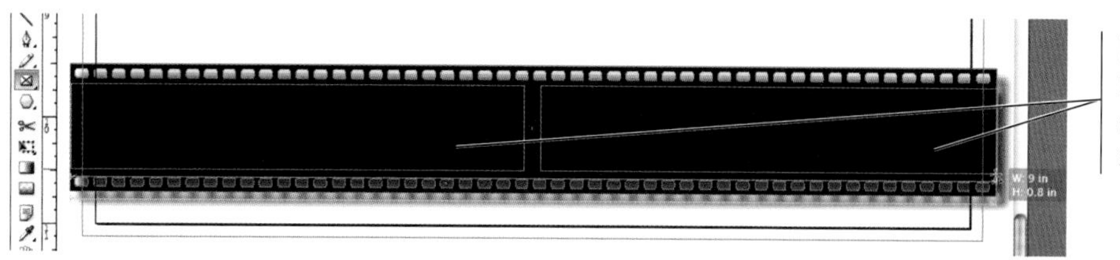

Pressing the Right Arrow key splits the area you draw into two equal-sized frames.

5. **Press the Right Arrow key six more times to create a total of eight frames, then release the mouse button.**

The resulting frames are equal in size, and have the same amount of space between each.

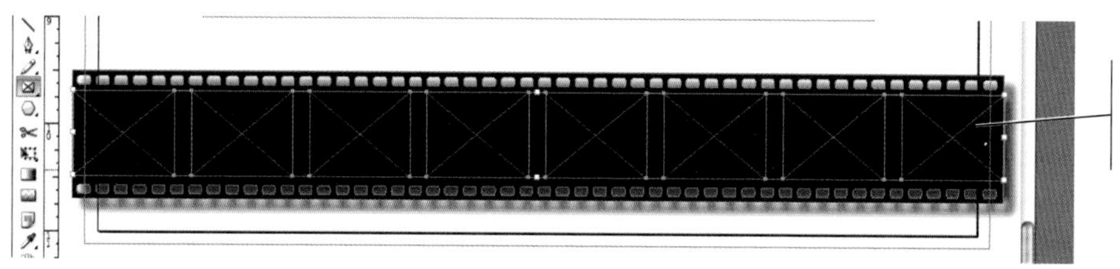

Crossed diagonal lines indicate that these are empty graphics frames.

6. **With the eight resulting frames selected, choose the Selection tool.**

As we stated previously, the Selection tool is used to access and manipulate entire objects. Using the Selection tool, you can:

- Click and drag a handle to resize selected objects.
- Shift-click and drag to resize objects proportionally.
- Command/Control-click and drag to scale selected objects.
- Command/Control-Shift-click and drag to scale selected objects proportionally.
- Press Option/Alt with any of these to apply the transformation around the selection's center point.

Note:

In previous versions of InDesign, you had to group multiple objects before you could transform them as a single unit. In CS5, you can resize, rotate, or scale multiple objects at once without first grouping them.

7. **Click the right-center bounding box handle of the active selection. Press and hold the Spacebar, then drag left.**

As you drag, the space between the selected objects changes; the size of the actual objects is not affected. This method is called **live distribution**; to work properly, you must click the handle before pressing the Spacebar.

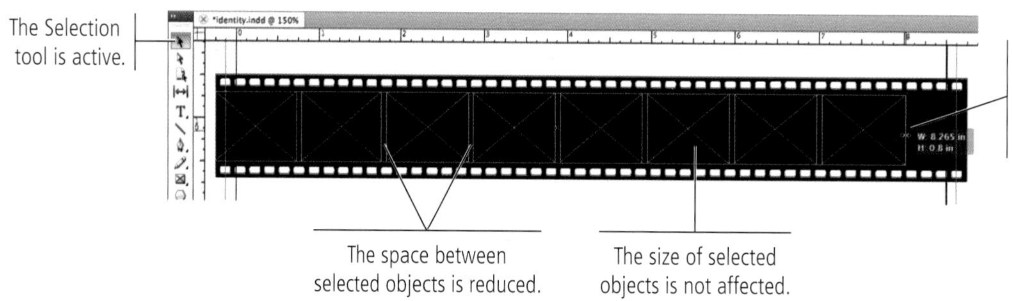

The Selection tool is active.

Click the center handle, then press the Spacebar and drag left.

The space between selected objects is reduced.

The size of selected objects is not affected.

8. **Click the right-center handle again. Without pressing the Spacebar, drag right until the handle snaps to the right edge of the filmstrip.**

   Simply dragging the handle resizes the entire selection; the spacing and position of various selected objects relative to one another is not affected.

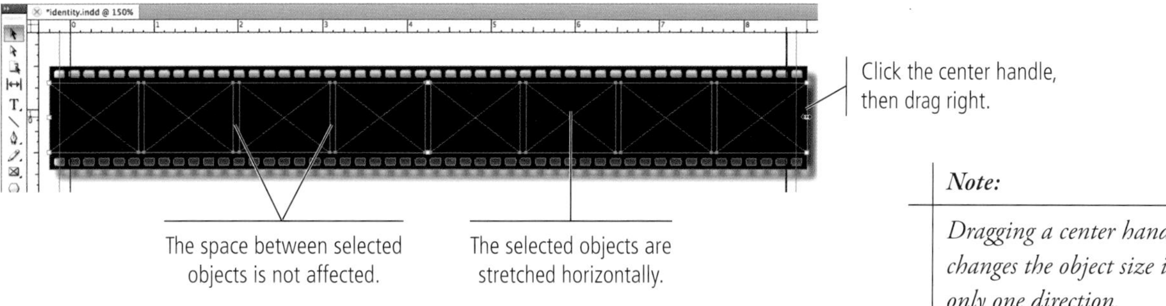

> *Note:*
>
> *Dragging a center handle changes the object size in only one direction.*

9. **With the eight empty frames selected, choose Object>Group.**

   Grouping multiple objects means you can treat them as a single unit. This is necessary when you want to use the align options to position the group of frames relative to other objects without affecting the positioning of the placeholder frames relative to one another.

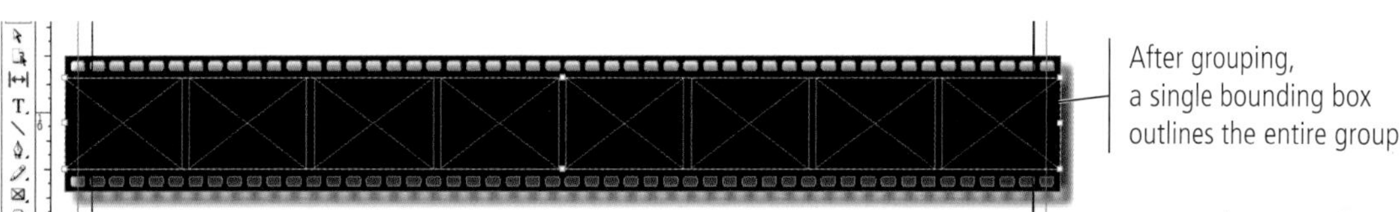

After grouping, a single bounding box outlines the entire group.

> *Note:*
>
> *Group objects by pressing Command/Control-G.*
>
> *Ungroup objects by pressing Command/Control-Shift-G.*

10. **Press Shift, and click the filmstrip graphic to add it to the active selection.**

11. **Using the Align panel or the Control panel, click the Align Horizontal Centers and Align Vertical Centers buttons.**

    Depending on how precisely you created and transformed the frames, this might have a very noticeable effect; it ensures that the frames are centered to the filmstrip graphic.

12. **In the Control panel, choose the center reference point.**

13. **Place the Selection tool cursor just outside the top-right handle of the selection. When you see the Rotate cursor, click and drag up until the cursor feedback shows 3°.**

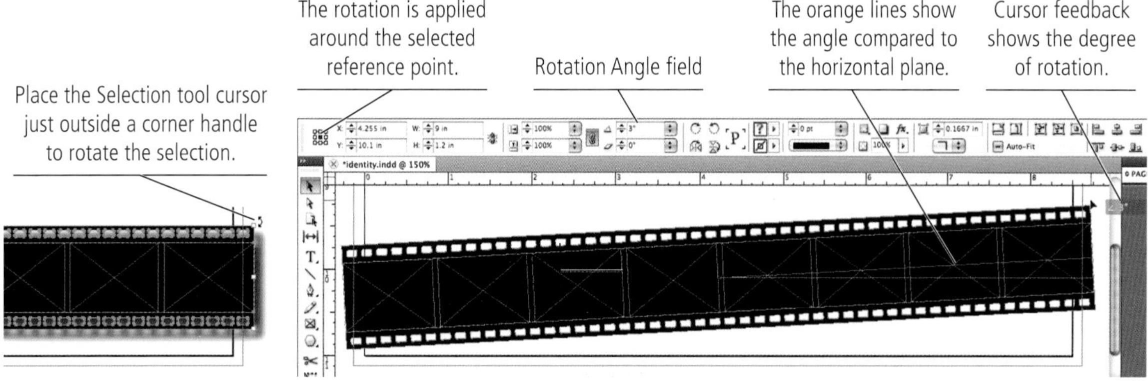

Rotation Angle field
The orange lines show the angle compared to the horizontal plane.

14. **Save the file and continue to the next exercise.**

Create a Simple Line

The InDesign Pen tool works in exactly the same way as the Pen tool in Illustrator and Photoshop. If necessary, refer to Page 91 (Illustrator) or Page 246 (Photoshop) to review the behavior of anchor points and handles. In this exercise, you create the most basic element possible: a straight line; you then add anchor points to the line to create a multi-segment path.

Remember: Every line is composed of anchor points and line segments that connect those points. Even a simple straight line has two points, one at each end. More sophisticated shapes can be created by adding anchor points, and manipulating the direction handles of those points to control the shape of segments that connect the different points.

Note:

Bézier curves can be difficult to master without a relatively deep understanding of geometry or trigonometry. The best training is to practice until you can recognize and predict how moving a point or handle will affect the connected segments.

1. **With identity.indd open, choose the Line tool in the Tools panel.**

2. **Click the Default Fill and Stroke button at the bottom of the Tools panel.**

   The default options for the Line tool are a 1-pt black stroke with no fill.

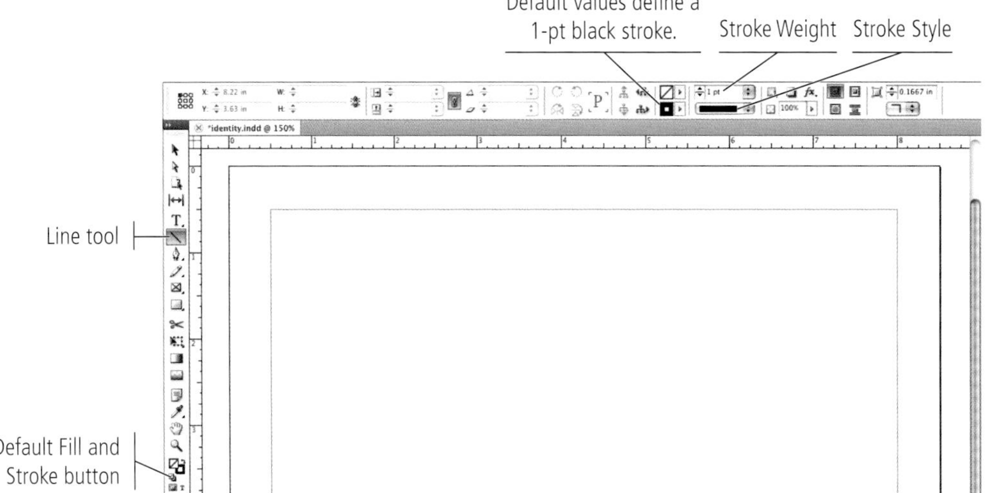
Default values define a 1-pt black stroke.
Stroke Weight
Stroke Style
Line tool
Default Fill and Stroke button

3. **At the top of the page, click at the left bleed guide and drag to the right bleed guide. Press Shift, and then release the mouse button.**

   As you drag, the cursor feedback shows the length of the line you are drawing. The blue line previews what will appear when you release the mouse button. Pressing Shift as you draw forces or constrains the line to exactly 45° angles — including exactly horizontal.

Note:

When drawing lines, cursor feedback shows the length of the segment you are drawing.

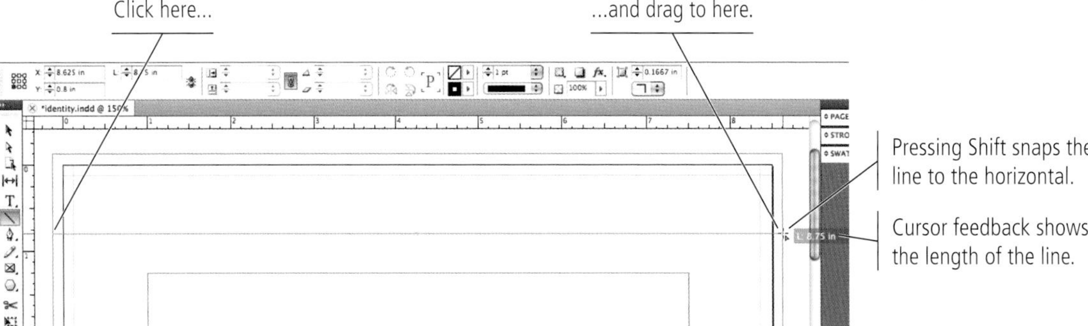
Click here...
...and drag to here.
Pressing Shift snaps the line to the horizontal.
Cursor feedback shows the length of the line.

4. **In the Control panel, open the Stroke Weight menu and choose 2 pt.**

   You can choose one of the stroke weight presets from this menu, or simply type any value in the field.

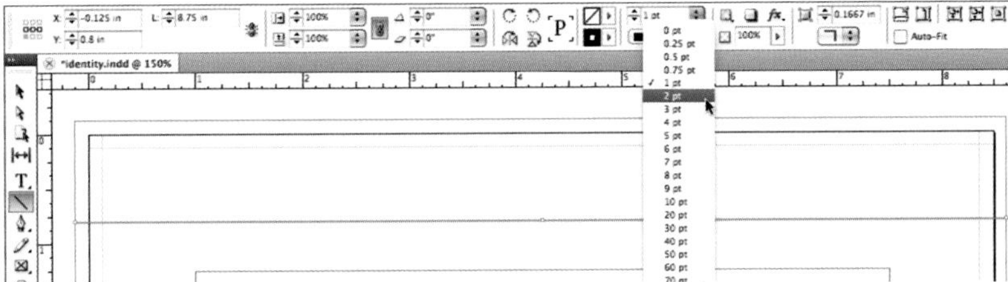

5. **At the left end of the Control panel, change the Y field to 1″ and press Return/Enter to apply the change.**

   Because you constrained this line, changing the Y field moves the entire line.

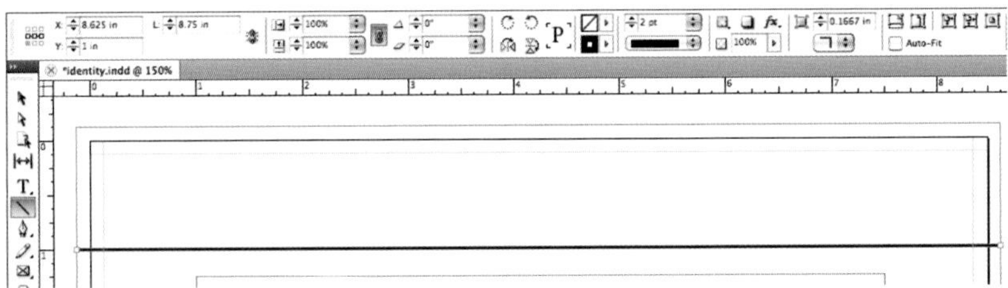

Note:

Remember, you do not need to type the units if you are entering a measurement in the default unit of measurement. We include the units in our steps for the sake of clarity.

6. **Choose the Pen tool in the Tools panel.**

7. **Move the cursor over the line you just created.**

   When the Pen tool is over an existing selected line, it automatically switches to the Add Anchor Point tool cursor; clicking adds a new point to the selected line.

   If the Pen tool is over a specific point on a selected line, it automatically switches to the Delete Anchor Point tool cursor; clicking removes that point from the line.

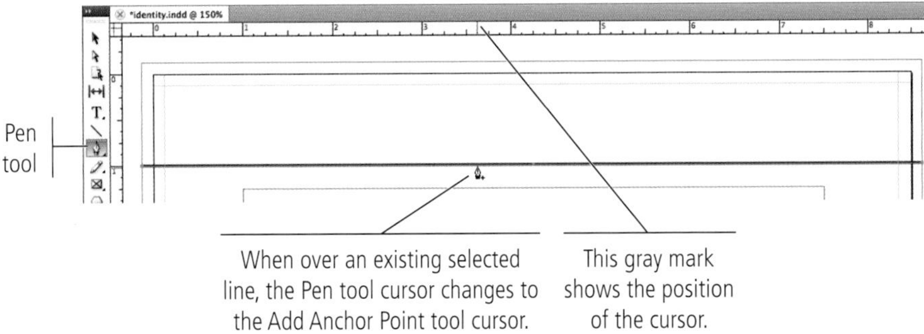
Pen tool
When over an existing selected line, the Pen tool cursor changes to the Add Anchor Point tool cursor.
This gray mark shows the position of the cursor.

8. **When the cursor is at the 3.625″ mark of the horizontal page ruler, click to add a point to the line.**

   The visible center point of the selected line is a bit deceptive. This simply marks the center of the shape (a line, in this case); it is not an actual point on the line.

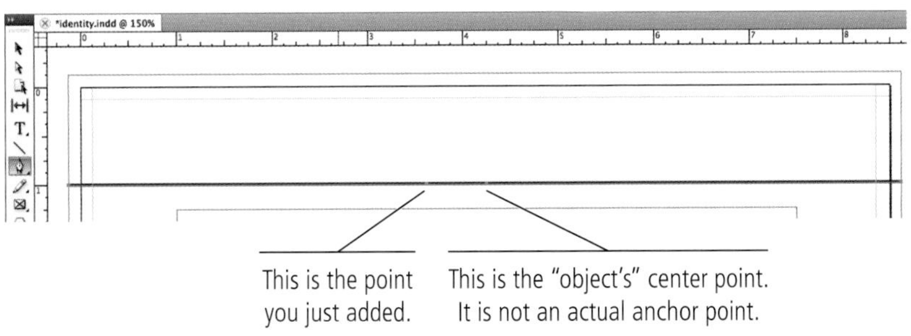
This is the point you just added.
This is the "object's" center point. It is not an actual anchor point.

9. **Move the cursor right to the 4.375″ mark and click to add another point.**

All vector objects are composed of anchor points and connecting line segments, even if you don't create each point manually. The original line had two regular points, one at each end, and a straight connecting segment. You added two new points, for a total of four points and three connecting segments.

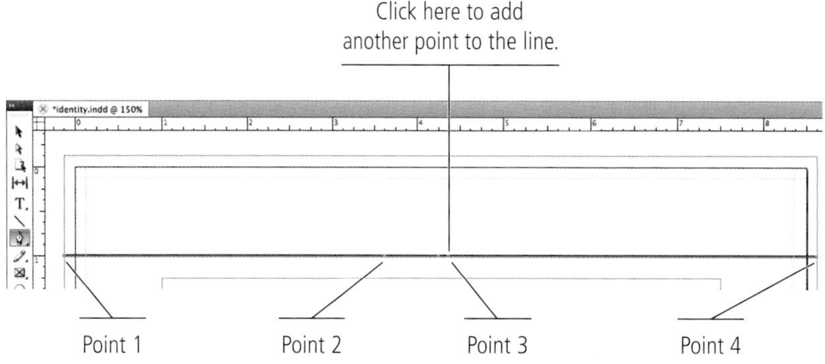

10. **Choose the Direct Selection tool in the Tools panel, and click away from the line to deselect it.**

The Direct Selection tool is used to select individual pieces of objects, such as a specific point on a line, or a specific line segment between two points. However, you have to first deselect the entire line before you can select only part of it.

11. **Move the cursor over the left part of the line.**

When the Direct Selection tool cursor shows a small line in the icon, clicking will select the specific segment under the cursor.

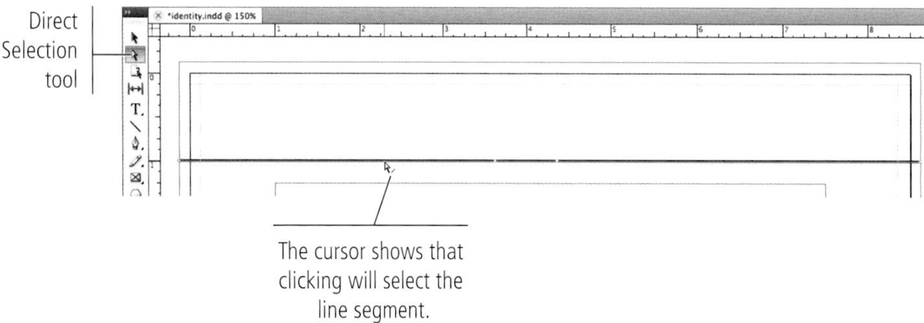

12. **Click anywhere between the first and second points on the line. Press Shift, and drag up until the cursor feedback shows the Y position of 0.19″.**

The segment you selected moves, and the segment between points 2 and 3 adjusts as necessary to remain connected. The segment between points 3 and 4 is not affected.

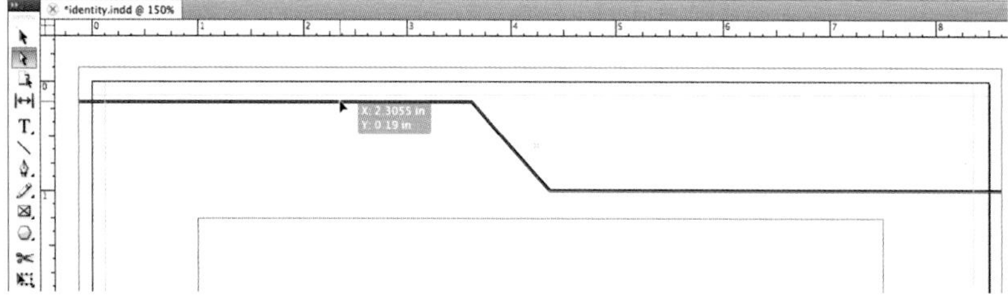

13. **Using the Direct Selection tool, click the second point from the left (Point 2).**

When the Direct Selection tool cursor shows a small circle in the icon, clicking will select the specific point under the cursor.

> *Note:*
>
> *If you add points to a curved line segment, the new points automatically adopt the necessary direction handles to maintain the original curve shapes.*

14. **In the Control panel, change the X position of the selected point 3.625".**

As you can see, you can control the precise position of every point in a shape.

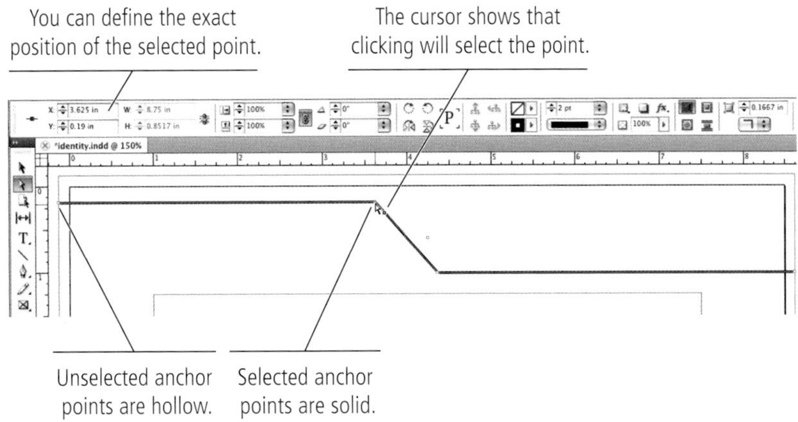
You can define the exact position of the selected point.
The cursor shows that clicking will select the point.
Unselected anchor points are hollow.
Selected anchor points are solid.

15. **Save the file and continue to the next exercise.**

Create Bézier Curves

In this exercise you will make very simple manipulations to the straight line you just created. In Project 8, you will use the Pen tool to create a new curved line. We also encourage you to practice as much as possible using the Pen tool until you are more proficient; for example, try copying the outlines of various shapes in photographs.

1. **With identity.indd open, make sure the line at the top of the page is selected.**

2. **Choose the Convert Direction Point tool nested under the Pen tool.**

   The Convert Direction Point tool changes a corner point to a smooth point. **Smooth points** have handles that control the size and shape of curves connected to that point. You can use the Direct Selection tool to drag handles for a selected anchor point.

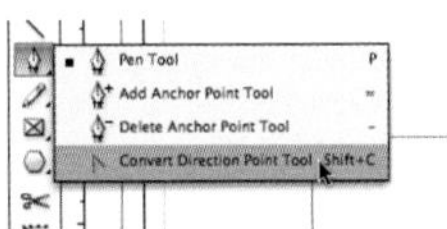
Pen Tool
P
Add Anchor Point Tool
Delete Anchor Point Tool
Convert Direction Point Tool
Shift+C

Note:

Using the Convert Direction Point tool, you can click an existing point and drag to add handles to the point, converting the point to a smooth point.

3. **Click the second point on the line, press Shift, and drag right until the ruler shows that the cursor is at 4.125".**

   When you click a point with the Convert Direction Point tool and immediately drag, you add direction handles to the point. Those direction handles define the shape of the line segments that are connected to the point. As you drag farther away from the point, the affected segment's curve increases.

Pressing Shift constrains the new direction handles to 45° angles — in this case, exactly horizontal. If you look closely, you can see that the direction handle on the left side of the point is exactly on top of the line.

By default, clicking and dragging creates a smooth, symmetrical point, in which equal-length handles are added to each side of the point directly opposite each other. As long as a point is symmetrical, changing the angle of one handle also affects the handle on the other side of the point.

> *Note:*
>
> *The lines that connect anchor points based on the angle and length of the control handles are called Bézier curves.*

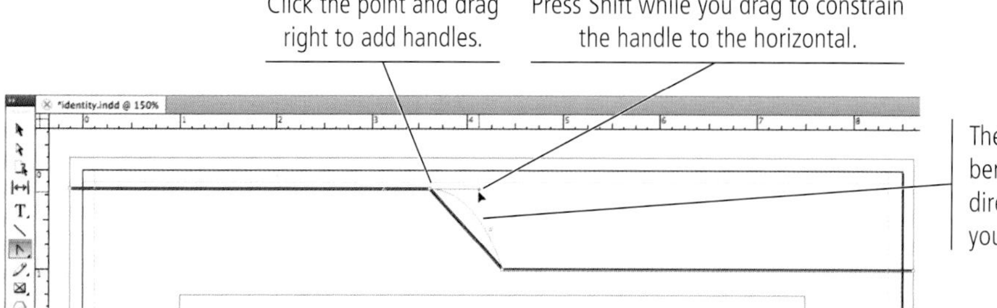

Click the point and drag right to add handles.
Press Shift while you drag to constrain the handle to the horizontal.
*identity.indd @ 150%
The connected line bends in the direction in which you pull the handle.

4. **Click the third point, press Shift, and drag right until the ruler shows that the cursor is at 4.875″.**

   As we just explained, the affected curve gets larger as you drag farther away from the point. Because you're dragging exactly horizontally, the horizontal segment on the right is not curving.

   On the left side of the point, however, you can see the effect of converting Point 3 to a symmetrical point. Dragging to the right side of the point adds direction handles on *both sides* of the point; the length and position of the left handle defines the shape of the curve on the left side of the point — which is the one you want to affect in this step.

> *Note:*
>
> *When you drag direction handles, the blue lines preview the effects of your changes.*

Converting a point creates symmetrical handles on both sides of the point.

The opposite handle affects the shape of the connected curve.

> *Note:*
>
> *If you move an anchor point that has direction handles, the handles don't change angle or length. The related curves change shape based on the new position of the point.*

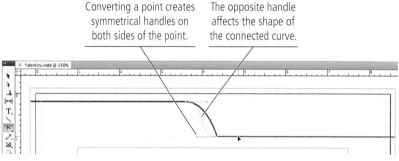

5. **Choose the Pen tool in the Tools panel. (It is now nested under the Convert Direction Point tool.)**

   When you choose a nested tool variation, the nested tool becomes the default option in that position on the Tools panel.

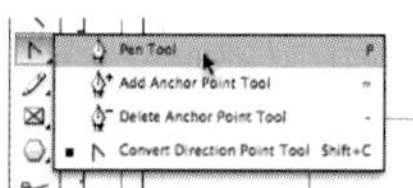

Pen Tool
Add Anchor Point Tool
Delete Anchor Point Tool
Convert Direction Point Tool Shift+C

6. **Move the cursor over the left endpoint of the line. When you see a diagonal line in the cursor icon, click to connect to the existing endpoint.**

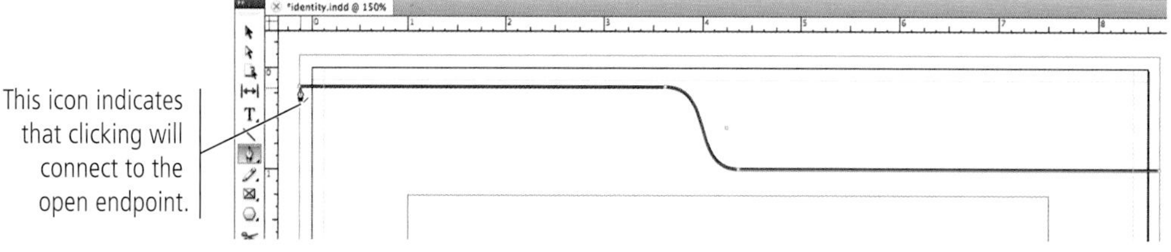

*identity.indd @ 150%
This icon indicates that clicking will connect to the open endpoint.

7. **Press Shift, then click at the top-left bleed guide.**

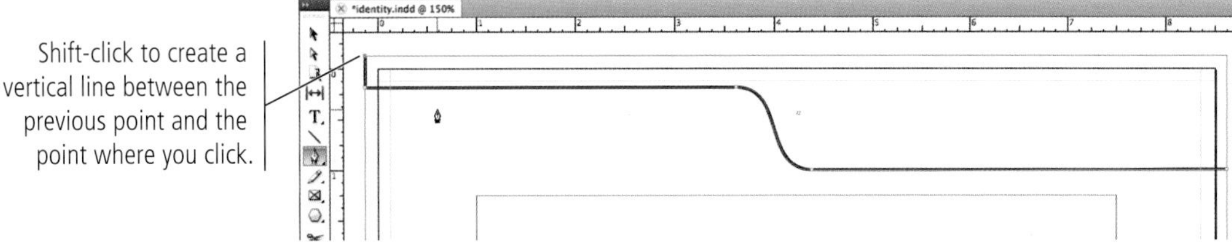
Shift-click to create a vertical line between the previous point and the point where you click.
*identity.indd @ 150%

8. **Press Shift, then click the top-right bleed guide.**

*identity.indd @ 150%
Shift-click to create a horizontal line between the previous point and the point where you click.

9. **Move the cursor over the open endpoint at the right end of the original line. When you see a small circle in the cursor icon, click to close the shape.**

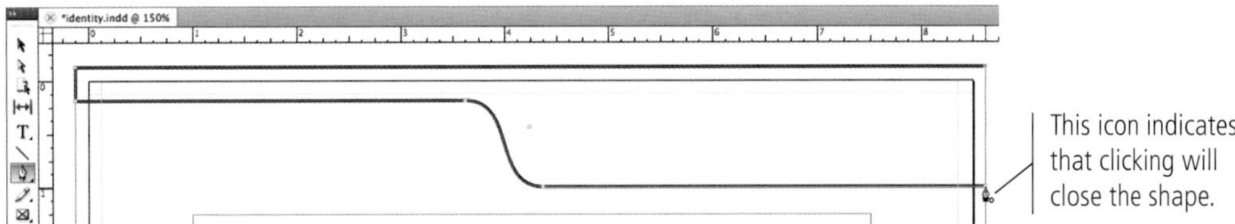
*identity.indd @ 150%
This icon indicates that clicking will close the shape.

You could have created this shape as a regular rectangle and then modified the bottom line with the Pen tool. However, our goal was to teach you how to create a basic line, and then how to perform some basic tasks with the Pen tool and its nested variations.

It's important to realize that there is almost always more than one way to accomplish a specific goal in InDesign. As you gain experience, you will develop personal preferences for the most effective and efficient methods of doing what you need to do.

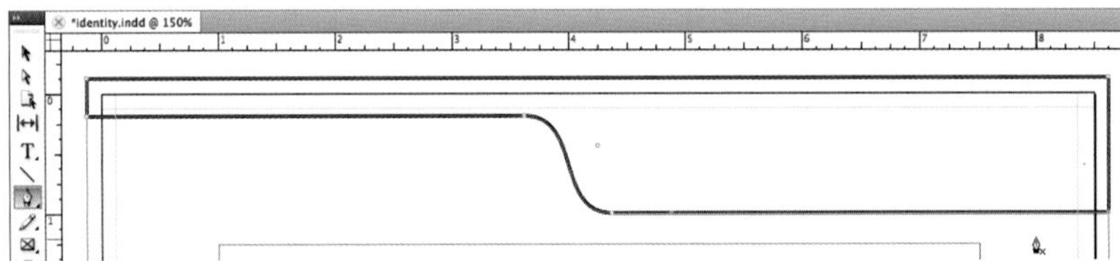
*identity.indd @ 150%

10. **Save the file and continue to the next exercise.**

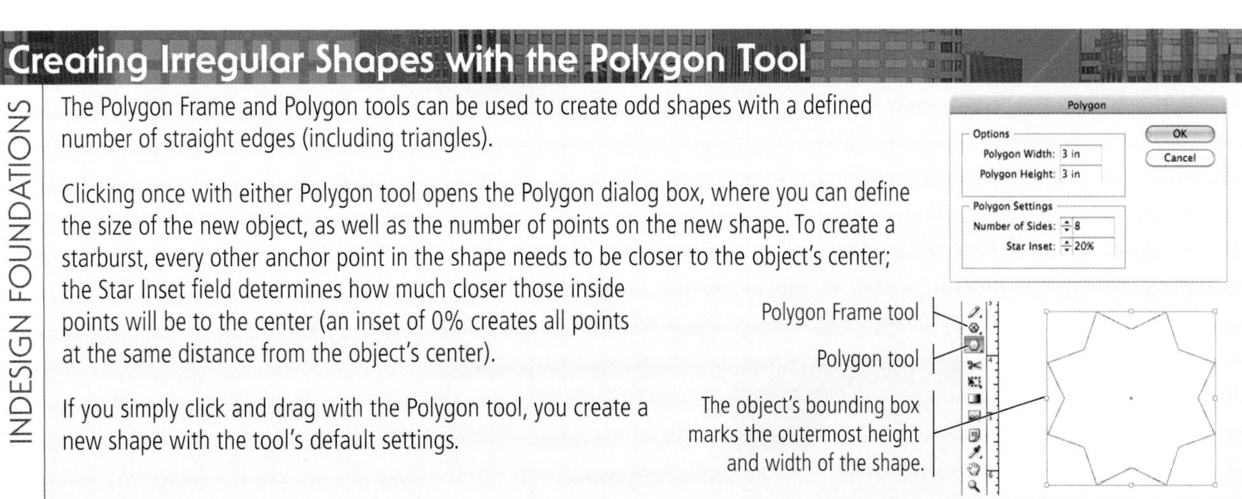
Polygon
Options
Polygon Width: 3 in
Polygon Height: 3 in
Polygon Settings
Number of Sides: 8
Star Inset: 20%
OK
Cancel
Polygon Frame tool
Polygon tool
The object's bounding box marks the outermost height and width of the shape.

Creating Irregular Shapes with the Polygon Tool

INDESIGN FOUNDATIONS

The Polygon Frame and Polygon tools can be used to create odd shapes with a defined number of straight edges (including triangles).

Clicking once with either Polygon tool opens the Polygon dialog box, where you can define the size of the new object, as well as the number of points on the new shape. To create a starburst, every other anchor point in the shape needs to be closer to the object's center; the Star Inset field determines how much closer those inside points will be to the center (an inset of 0% creates all points at the same distance from the object's center).

If you simply click and drag with the Polygon tool, you create a new shape with the tool's default settings.

Change Color Values

Although there are several default color choices built into the Swatches panel of every InDesign file, you are not limited to these few options. You can define virtually any color based on specific values of component colors. Keep in mind, of course, that when you are building a page to be printed, you should use CMYK colors.

1. **With identity.indd open, use the Selection tool to make sure the shape at the top of the page is selected.**

2. **At the bottom of the Tools panel, click the Swap Fill and Stroke button.**

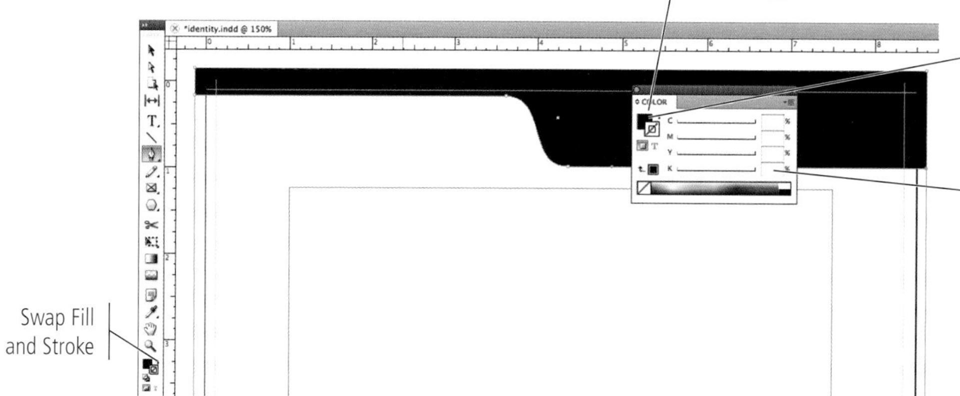

The swatch on top indicates which attribute you can change (in this case, Stroke).

Click the back swatch to review or adjust that attribute.

The panel shows the ink percentages of the fill or stroke color (depending on which is active) of the selected object.

Swap Fill and Stroke

3. **Open the Color panel.**

   Remember, all panels can be accessed in the Window menu. Because workspace arrangement is a matter of personal preference, we won't tell you where to place or keep panels. If the Color panel is not in your panel dock, simply choose Window>Color>Color to display that panel.

4. **Click the Fill swatch to bring it to the front (if it isn't already).**

   When you apply color from any of the Swatches panels (including the ones in the Control panel), the Color panel shows a swatch of that color as a single slider. You can use this slider to easily apply a percentage of the selected swatch. (You'll work more with color swatches in Project 8.)

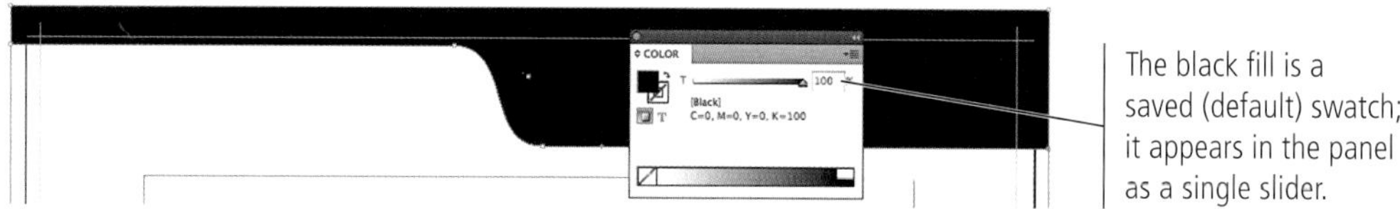

The black fill is a saved (default) swatch; it appears in the panel as a single slider.

5. **Click the Options button in the top-right corner of the panel and choose CMYK from the Options menu.**

   This option converts the single swatch slider to the four process-color sliders. You can change any ink percentage to change the object's fill color.

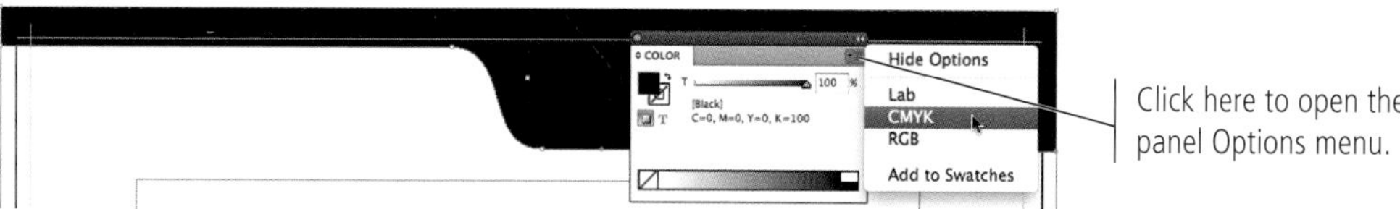

Click here to open the panel Options menu.

6. **Click the M slider and drag until the field shows 40%.**

This color, 100% black with some percentage of another ink, is called a **rich black** or **super black**. By itself, plain black ink often lacks density. Rich blacks are commonly used to add density or "temperature" to flat black; adding magenta results in "warmer" blacks, and adding cyan results in "cooler" blacks.

Note:

You can change the color by typing a specific value or by dragging the slider below the color gradient.

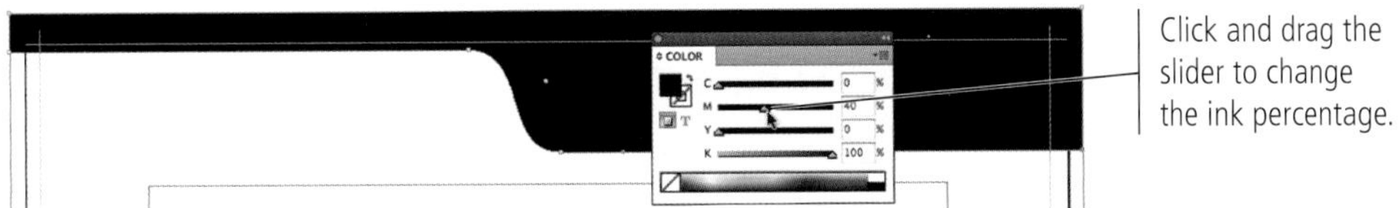

Click and drag the slider to change the ink percentage.

7. **Save the file and continue to the next stage of the project.**

Stage 3 Placing External Images

As you saw in the first stage of this project, InDesign incorporates a number of tools for building graphics directly in a layout. Of course, most page-layout projects will include files from other sources — logos created in Adobe Illustrator, raster-based images created in Adobe Photoshop, digital photographs and scans, stock images and illustrations, and many other types of files can be incorporated into a larger project.

Place an External Graphics File

Every image in a layout exists in a frame. You can either create the frame first and place a file into it, or you can simply place an image and create the containing frame at the same time. In this exercise, you are going to place the client's logo, and transform the file to fit into the space to the left of the curved line at the top of the layout.

1. **With identity.indd open, make sure nothing is selected in the layout.**

   To deselect objects, you can choose Edit>Deselect All, or simply click an empty area of the workspace. If you do click the workspace, though, be careful that you don't accidentally click a white-filled object instead of the empty page or pasteboard area.

2. **Choose File>Place. Navigate to the WIP>Crowe folder and select crowe.ai. At the bottom of the dialog box, make sure none of the options are checked.**

   You will learn about these options in later projects. For now, you simply want to place the logo file into the letterhead.

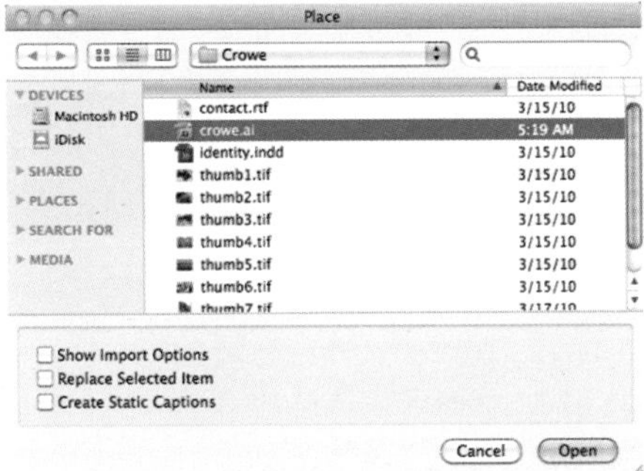

3. **Click Open to load the cursor with the placed file.**

   You still have to place the loaded image into the document.

By default, the loaded Place cursor shows a small thumbnail of the file you're placing.
photography

> *Note:*
>
> *You can turn off the thumbnail preview feature by unchecking the Show Thumbnails on Place option in the Interface pane of the Preferences dialog box.*

4. **Click near the top-left corner of the page to place the image.**

   Every image in an InDesign layout exists in a frame. When you click an empty area of the page to place an image, the containing frame is automatically created for you.

5. **Click the placed image with the Selection tool to select the frame. Using the Control panel, choose the top-left reference point and then change the frame position to X: 0.25″, Y: 0.3″.**

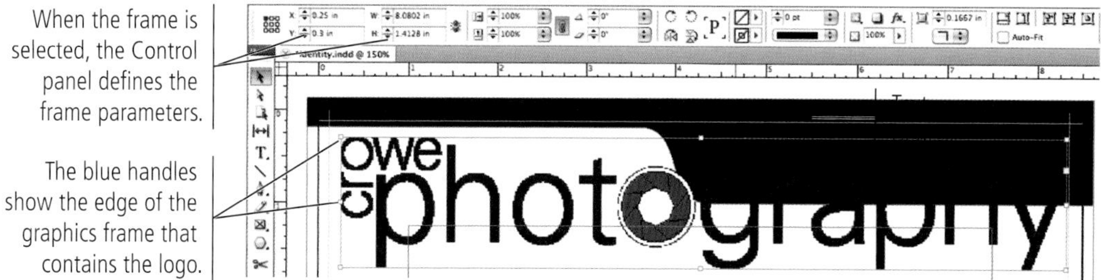

When the frame is selected, the Control panel defines the frame parameters.
The blue handles show the edge of the graphics frame that contains the logo.

6. **With the frame selected, check the Auto-Fit option in the Control panel.**

   By default, the image contained within the frame remains unaffected when you edit the dimensions of a graphics frame. When the Auto-Fit option is checked, however, resizing the frame automatically resizes the contained image to fit the new frame size.

7. **Click the bottom-right handle of the frame. Drag up and left until the cursor feedback shows W: 3.6″. Don't release the mouse button.**

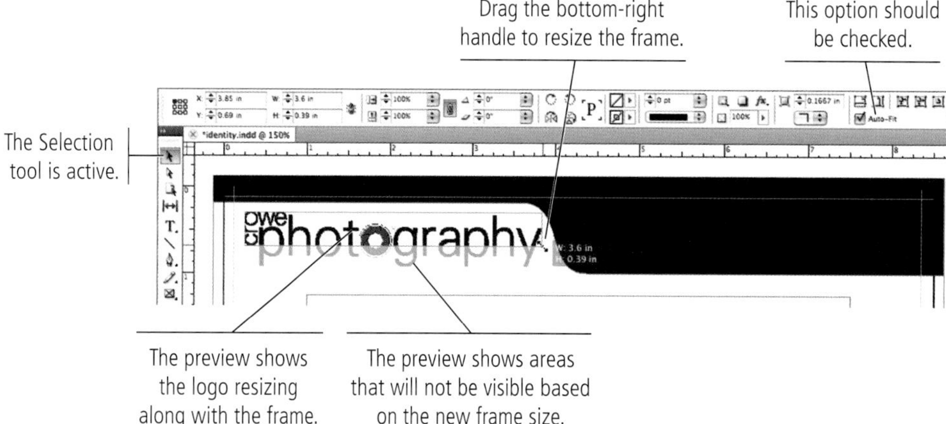

Drag the bottom-right handle to resize the frame.
This option should be checked.
The Selection tool is active.
The preview shows the logo resizing along with the frame.
The preview shows areas that will not be visible based on the new frame size.

8. **Press Shift to constrain the proportions of the resized frame.**

   Pressing Shift maintains the original height-to-width aspect ratio in the resized frame. This means the resized frame will be large enough to show the entire (resized) logo.

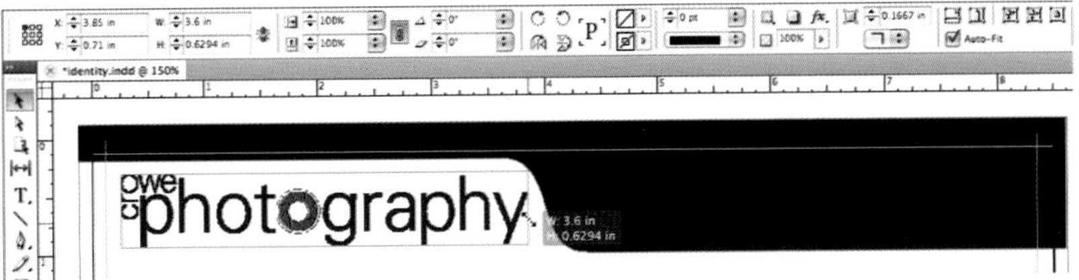

> *Note:*
>
> *When the Auto-Fit option is not selected, you can press the Command key while resizing a frame to scale the content at the same time.*

> *Note:*
>
> *Unlike raster images, vector graphics can be resized without losing quality.*

9. **With the Selection tool active, move the cursor inside the resized frame.**

   This reveals the Content Indicator icon, which you can use to access and manipulate the frame's content without the need to switch tools.

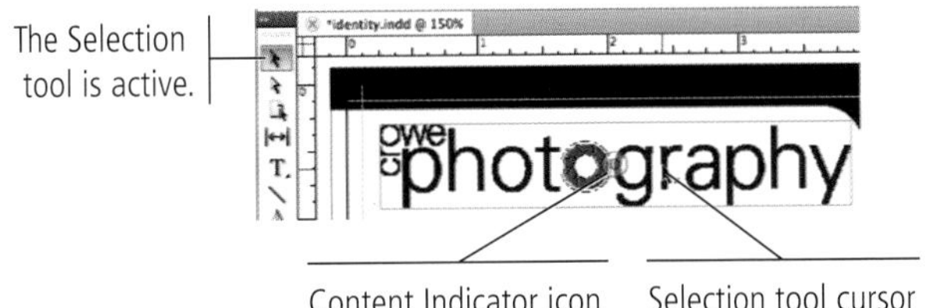
The Selection tool is active.
Content Indicator icon
Selection tool cursor

10. **Click the Content Indicator icon in the logo frame.**

    When the frame's content is selected, options in the Control panel relate to the placed object and not the containing frame. The X+ and Y+ fields define the position of the image *within the frame*. As you can see, InDesign remembers the placed file's original size; the Scale X and Scale Y fields show the file's current size as a percentage of the original.

> *Note:*
>
> *You can also use the Direct Selection tool to access and edit the content inside a graphics frame.*

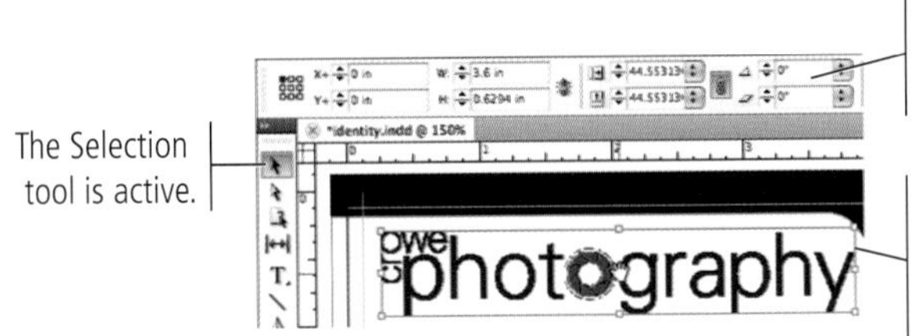
The Selection tool is active.

The Control panel now show the parameters of the content in the frame.

The red frame indicates that you are now editing the frame's content instead of the containing frame.

11. **Press Esc to return to the frame of the selected object.**

    The graphics frame is again selected, and the Selection tool is still active.

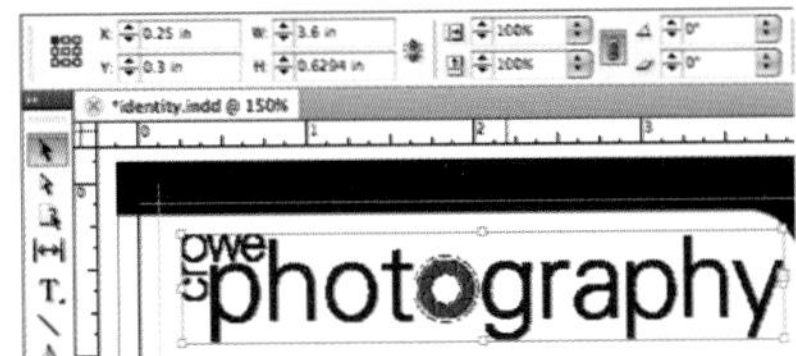

12. **Save the file and continue to the next exercise.**

Place Images into Existing Frames

In many cases, you will need to place an image or graphic into an existing frame and then manipulate the placed file to suit the available space. In the previous stage of this project, you created eight empty graphics frames across the filmstrip graphic; in this exercise, you will place the client's thumbnail photos into those frames.

1. **With identity.indd open, make the filmstrip graphic at the bottom of the page visible in your document window.**

2. **Using the Selection tool, click one of the empty graphics frames.**

   When objects are grouped, the Selection tool selects the entire group.

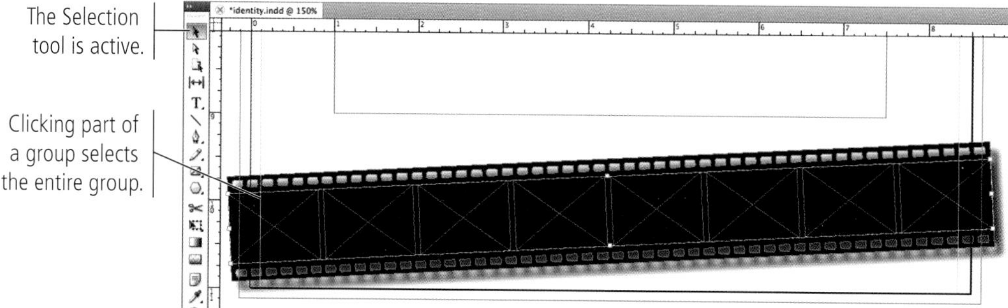

The Selection tool is active.
Clicking part of a group selects the entire group.
*identity.indd @ 150%

3. **Open the Layers panel (Window>Layers), then click the arrow to the left of Layer 1 to expand the layer.**

   Every file has a default layer named "Layer 1", where any objects that you create exist by default. (You will use multiple layers in a later project to create multiple versions of a document.)

   The Layers panel in InDesign CS5 also serves another purpose. Every object on a layer is listed in the panel, nested under the appropriate layer name. Groups, which you created in an earlier exercise, can be expanded so you can access and manage the individual components of the group.

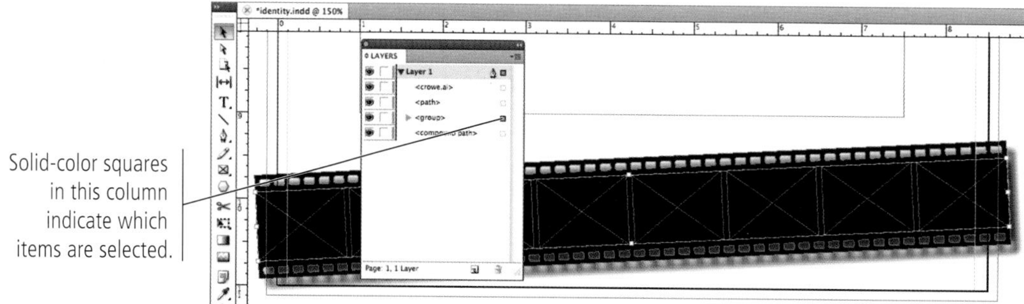

Solid-color squares in this column indicate which items are selected.
*identity.indd @ 150%
LAYERS
Layer 1
<crowe.ai>
<path>
<group>
Page: 1, 1 Layer

4. **Click the arrow to the left of the <group> item to expand the group.**

5. **Click the Select Item button for the first <rectangle> item in the group.**

This method makes it easy to work with individual items in a group, without first breaking apart the group.

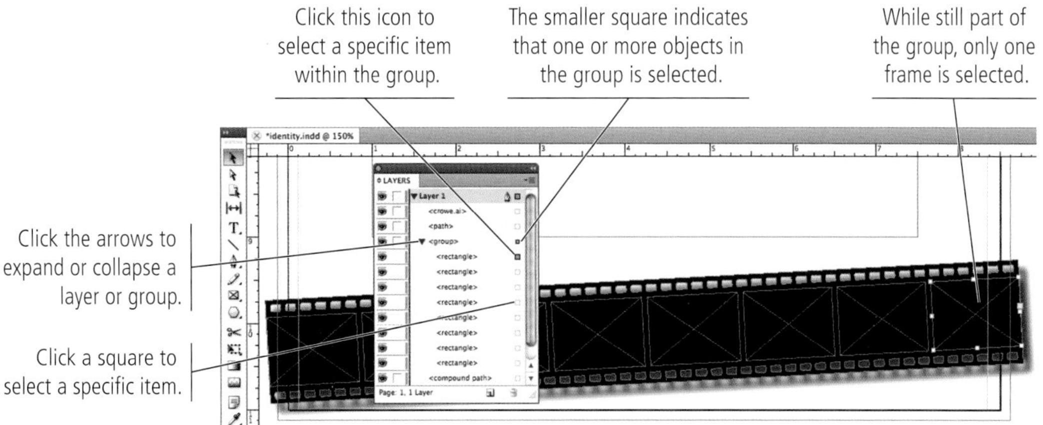

Click this icon to select a specific item within the group.
The smaller square indicates that one or more objects in the group is selected.
While still part of the group, only one frame is selected.
Click the arrows to expand or collapse a layer or group.
Click a square to select a specific item.

6. **In the Control panel, check the Auto-Fit option.**

When this option is checked, the image you place into the frame will automatically be scaled proportionally to fit the available space in the frame.

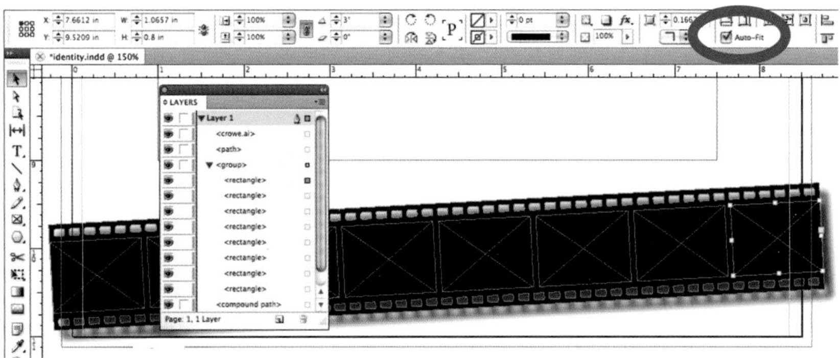

Note:

You can also use the Direct Selection tool to select individual objects within a group.

7. **Repeat Steps 5–6 for the remaining seven placeholder frames.**

8. **Choose File>Place. If necessary, navigate to the WIP>Crowe folder.**

9. **In the Place dialog box, click thumb1.tif to select it. Press Shift and click thumb8.tif to select it and all in-between files.**

In many cases, you will need to place more than one image from the same location into an InDesign layout. Rather than placing images one at a time, you can streamline the process by loading multiple images into the cursor at once, and then clicking to place each image in the correct location.

Note:

You could also have set the Auto-Fit option before copying the frame. The point of this exercise is simply to show how to use the Layers panel to select individual objects within a group.

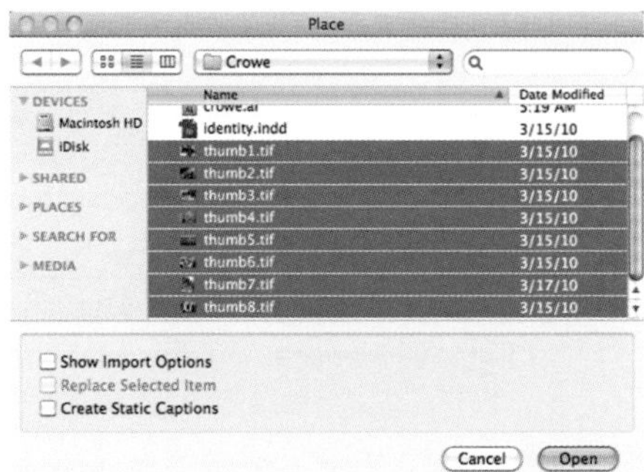

Note:

Press Shift to select multiple contiguous files in a dialog box.

Press Command/Control to select multiple non-contiguous files.

10. **Click Open to load the selected files into the Place cursor.**

When you select multiple files in the Place dialog box, the cursor is loaded with all of the selected pictures; a number in the cursor shows the number of files that are loaded.

You can use the Left Arrow and Right Arrow keys to navigate through the loaded images, watching the cursor thumbnails to find the one you want to place.

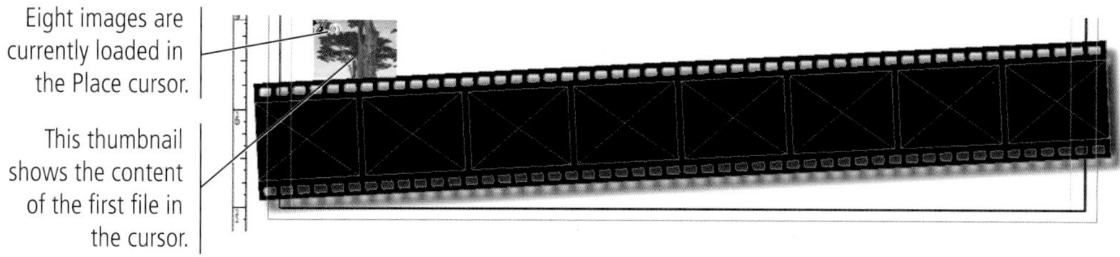

Eight images are currently loaded in the Place cursor.
This thumbnail shows the content of the first file in the cursor.

11. **Click inside the left placeholder frame to place the first image.**

As soon as you place the first file, the next loaded image appears as the cursor thumbnail.

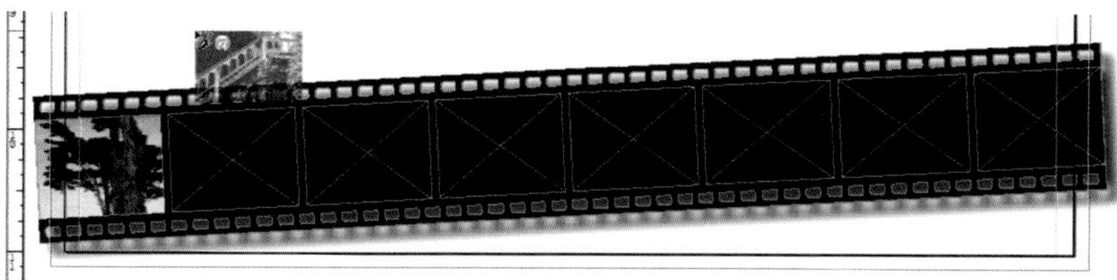

12. **Click inside each empty frame to place the remaining loaded images.**

13. **Choose the Direct Selection tool, and then click the fifth image thumbnail.**

As already mentioned, the Direct Selection tool can be used to access and manipulate the contents inside a frame. This tool does not require ungrouping. (You could also double-click a grouped item with the Selection tool to aceess only one item in a group, and then use the Content Indicator icon to access the frame content.)

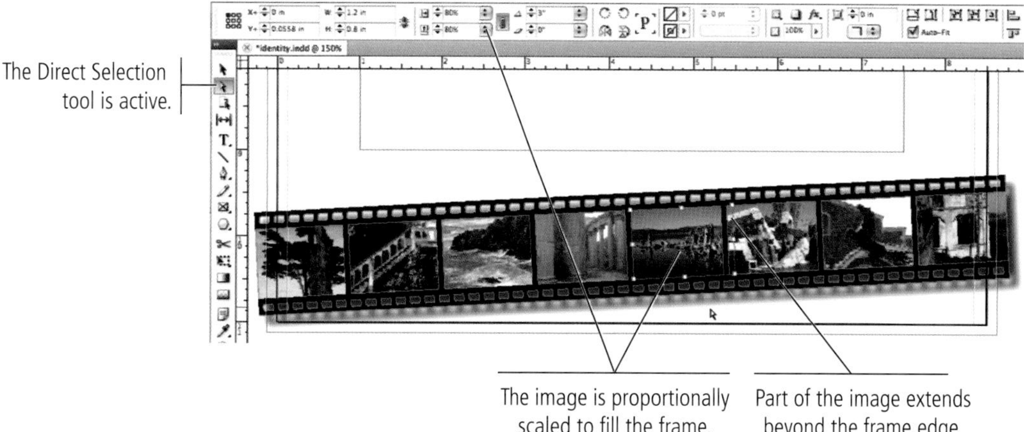

The Direct Selection tool is active.
The image is proportionally scaled to fill the frame.
Part of the image extends beyond the frame edge.

14. **In the Control panel, make sure the link icon for the scaling fields is active (unbroken links). Type `100` in the Scale X field and press Return/Enter to apply the change.**

Because you used the Auto-Fit option, these thumbnail images have all been placed at 80% proportionally. The images are already small, and reducing the percentage makes the detail in the fifth image *too* small. You can always change the image scaling after it has been scaled by the Auto-Fit option.

15. **Click inside the frame area and drag until the right edge of the image is approximately aligned to the right edge of the frame.**

When you drag an image within the frame, the entire image becomes visible; this makes it easy to find the area of the image that you want to be visible.

Note:

Even though you can't see the entire image, InDesign still has to process the hidden data when you output the file. Whenever possible, it's a good idea to crop the image in Photoshop, and then place the cropped version into your InDesign layout.

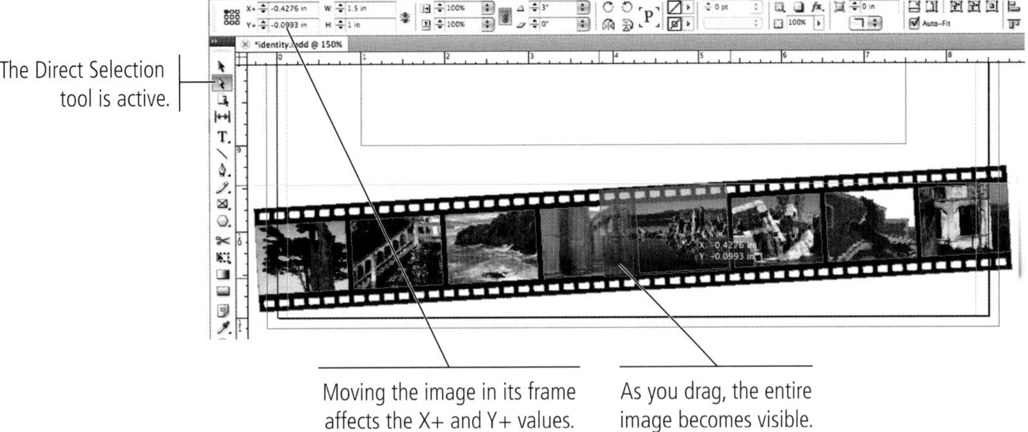
The Direct Selection tool is active.
Moving the image in its frame affects the X+ and Y+ values.
As you drag, the entire image becomes visible.

16. **Save the file and continue to the next stage of the project.**

Stage 4 Creating and Formatting Basic Text

InDesign is ultimately a page-layout application, not an illustration program. **Page layout** means combining text and graphic elements in a meaningful way to convey a message. Text can be a single word (as in the logo used in this project) or thousands of pages of consecutive copy (as in a dictionary). Virtually every project you build in InDesign will involve text in one way or another; this letterhead is no exception.

Create a Simple Text Frame

Adding text to a page is a relatively simple process: draw a frame, and then type. In this exercise, you'll create a new text frame and add the client's tag line, then apply some basic formatting options to style the text.

Keep in mind that this project is an introduction to creating elements on a layout page; there is far more to professional typesetting than the few options you use here. InDesign provides extremely precise control over virtually every aspect of every letter and word on the page. In the following projects, you will learn about the vast number of options that are available for setting and controlling type, from formatting a single paragraph to an entire multi-page booklet.

Note:

Remember from the Getting Started section at the beginning of this book: to complete the projects in this book, you should install and activate the ATC fonts that are provided with the book resource files.

1. **With identity.indd open, select the Type tool in the Tools panel.**

2. **Click in the empty space below the placed logo and drag to create a frame.**

To type text into a layout, you must first create a frame with the Type tool; when you release the mouse button, you see a flashing bar (called the **insertion point**) where you first clicked to create the text frame.

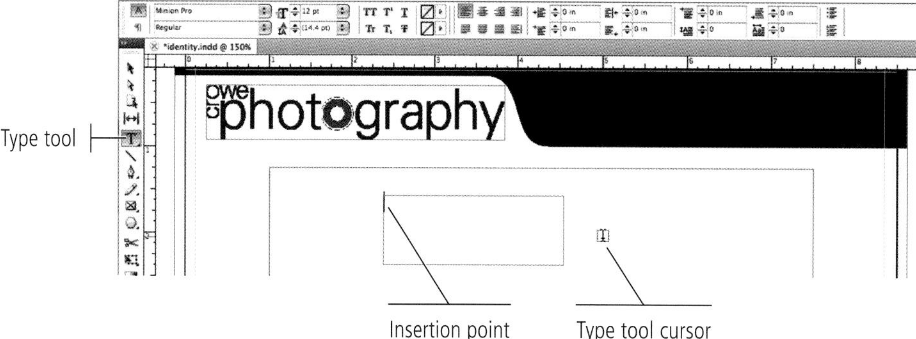

The tag line for the letterhead is supposed to appear in the black area to the right of the logo. However, if you click inside that area with the Type tool, it will convert the existing shape to a type area. In this case you want a simple rectangular text frame, so you are creating it in an empty area, and then moving it into place.

3. **Review the options in the Control panel.**

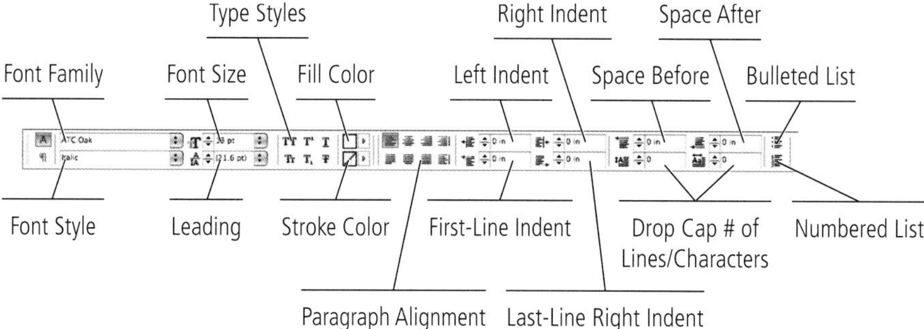

4. **Type urban architecture & natural landscapes.**

The text appears, beginning at the flashing insertion point. Depending on the size of your frame, the text might automatically wrap to a second line within the frame.

New text in InDesign is automatically set in black 12-pt Minion Pro. This font is installed along with the application, so it should be available on your computer unless someone has modified your system fonts. Don't worry if your type appears in some other font; you will change it shortly.

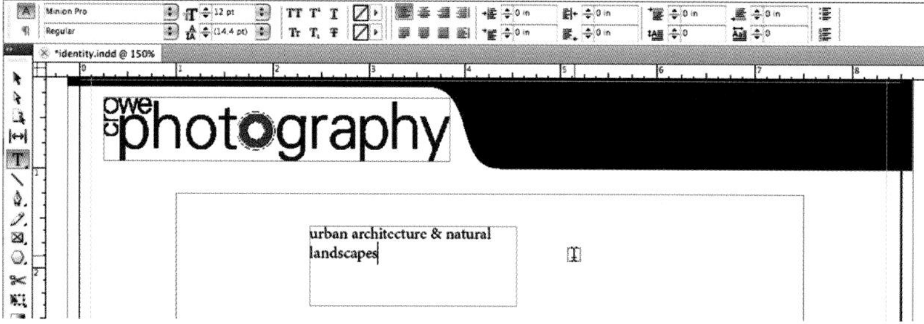

5. **Choose the Selection tool in the Tools panel.**

You must use the Selection tool to change the position and size of a text frame. You can either drag the handles to manually change the frame, or use the Control panel options to define specific parameters.

6. **In the Control panel, choose the bottom-right reference point and then change the frame's dimensions to:**

   X: 8.25″ W: 4.1″

   Y: 0.8″ H: 0.25″

   Some attributes of a type frame are no different than a graphics frame. You can change the position and size (based on the selected reference point) using the fields on the left end of the Control panel.

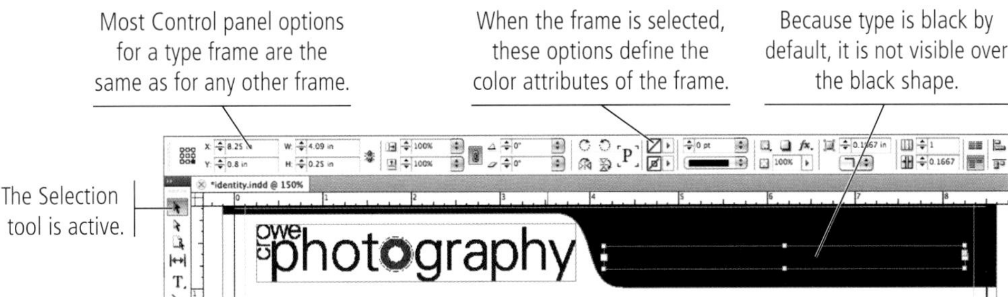

Most Control panel options for a type frame are the same as for any other frame.
When the frame is selected, these options define the color attributes of the frame.
Because type is black by default, it is not visible over the black shape.
The Selection tool is active.
photography

7. **Choose the Type tool, and click inside the repositioned text frame to place the insertion point.**

   Because the default type format is black, you can't see the characters on the black background. Because you know they are there, you can still select them.

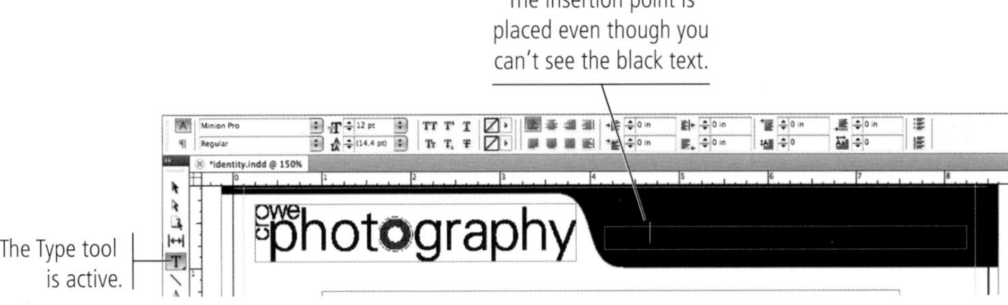

The insertion point is placed even though you can't see the black text.
The Type tool is active.
photography

8. **Choose Edit>Select All to select all of the text in the frame.**

   Character formatting such as the font, style, and size apply only to selected characters. You will learn about all of the available character formatting options in Project 8.

9. **In the Control panel, open the Fill swatch panel and click the Paper color.**

   The white-filled text now appears over the black background. (It is still highlighted, so it currently appears in reverse.)

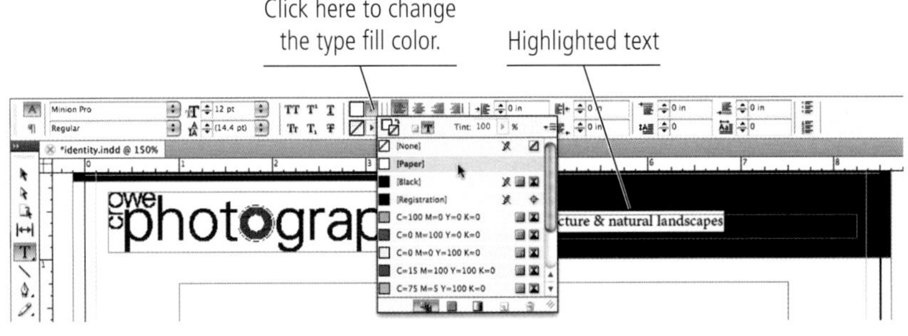

Note:

Type defaults to a 100% black fill with no stroke. (You can apply a stroke to type, but you should be very careful when you do to avoid destroying the letter shapes.)

10. **Macintosh: With the text still selected, open the Font menu in the Control panel and choose ATC Oak>Italic.**

Different styles of the same font appear as submenus to the main font list; the primary font is listed in the menu, and variations are listed in the attached submenu.

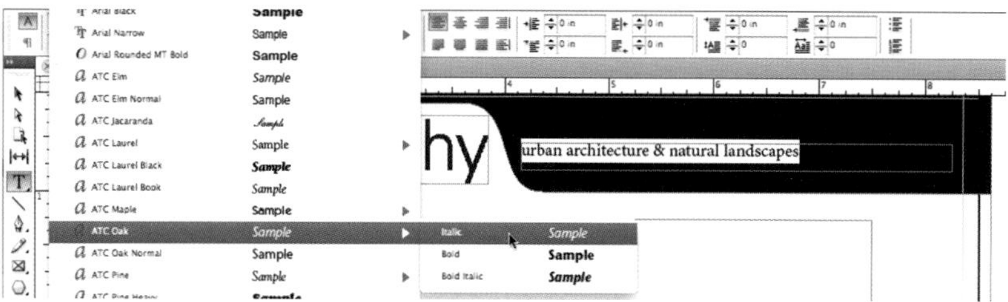

Windows: Open the Font Family menu and choose ATC Oak, and then open the Font Style menu and choose Italic.

Windows does not display different font styles in submenus. You have to choose the font first, and then use the secondary menu to choose the appropriate style.

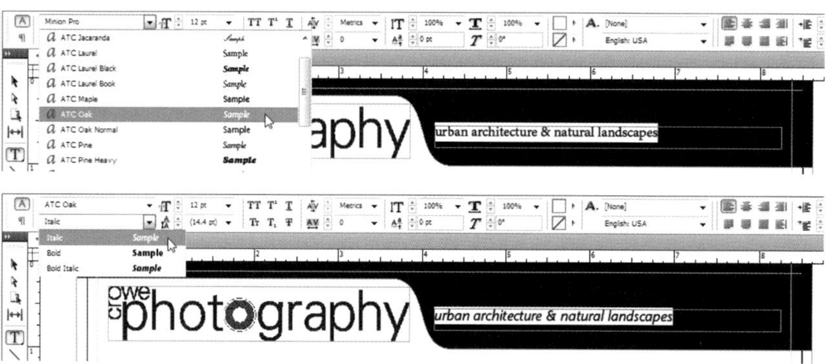

11. **Click the Up-Arrow button for the Font Size field until you see a red icon on the right edge of the frame.**

Each time you click, you increase the type size by one point. The red X is the **overset text icon**; it indicates that more text exists than will fit into the frame.

Click these buttons to change the type size by 1 point.

overset text icon

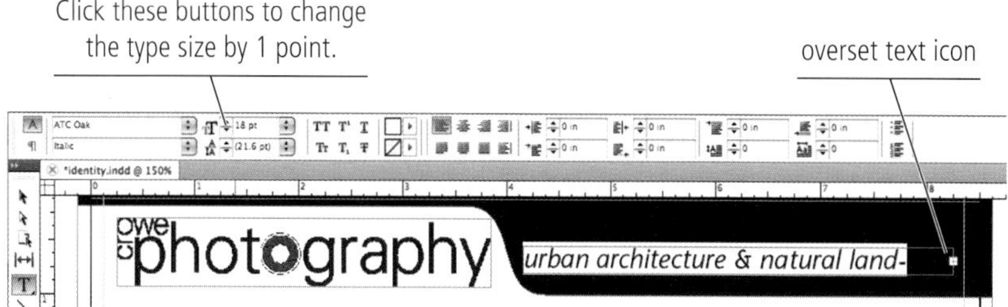

When you see an overset text icon, you can:

- Edit the text to fit the available space, which is usually not allowable for a graphic designer.
- Make the frame larger to fit the text, which is not always possible.
- Add more frames to the story and thread the text into the extra frames, which is also not always possible.
- Reduce the type size or adjust other formatting options to make the type fit into the available space, which can make text unreadable (depending on how small you have to make it).

Note:

There are three primary types of fonts:

***PostScript (Type 1) fonts** have two file components (outline and printer) that must both be available for output.*

***TrueType fonts** have a single file, but (until recently) were primarily used on the Windows platform.*

***OpenType fonts** are contained in a single file that can include more than 60,000 glyphs (characters) in a single font. OpenType fonts are cross-platform; the same font file can be used on both Macintosh and Windows systems.*

InDesign identifies the font types with different icons in the Font menu.

TrueType font

OpenType font

PostScript font

There are other types of fonts, including PostScript Type 3 and Multiple Master, but these should generally be avoided.

12. Click the Down-Arrow button once to reduce the type size by 1 point.

This allows all the type to fit in the frame.

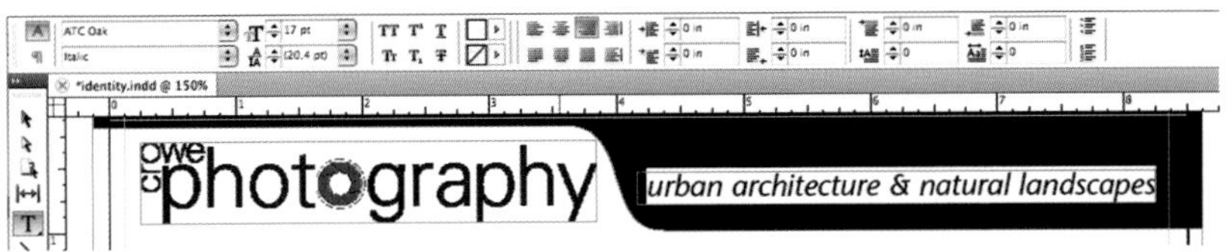

13. Click anywhere in the selected text to place the insertion point.

This removes the highlight, indicating that the characters are now deselected.

14. In the Control panel, click the [Paragraph] Align Right option.

Paragraph formatting — including alignment — applies to the entire paragraph where the insertion point is placed. You don't have to first select the entire paragraph. (You will learn about the available paragraph formatting options in Project 8.)

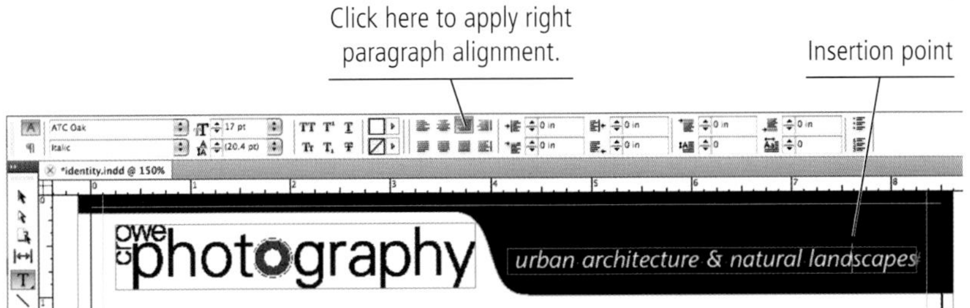

15. Save the file and continue to the next exercise.

Note:

You can also choose from the common preset type sizes in the menu, or type a specific size in the field.

If you type in the Font Size field, you don't need to type the unit "pt" for the type size; InDesign automatically applies the measurement for you.

Note:

Press Command/Control-Shift-> to increase the type size by 2 points, or Command/Control-Shift-< to decrease the type size by 2 points.

Selecting Text

INDESIGN FOUNDATIONS

You have a number of options for selecting type characters in a frame.

- Select specific characters by clicking with the Type tool and dragging.
- Double-click a word to select the entire word.
- Triple-click a word to select the entire line that contains the word.
- Quadruple-click a word to select the entire paragraph that contains the word.
- Place the insertion point and press Shift-Right Arrow or Shift-Left Arrow to select the character to the immediate right or left of the insertion point, respectively.
- Place the insertion point and press Shift-Up Arrow or Shift-Down Arrow to select all characters up to the same position as the insertion point in the previous or next line, respectively.
- Place the insertion point and press Command/Control-Shift-Right Arrow or Command/Control-Shift-Left Arrow to select the entire word immediately to the right or left of the insertion point, respectively.
- Place the insertion point and press Command/Control-Shift-Up Arrow or Command/Control-Shift-Down Arrow to select the rest of paragraph immediately before or after the insertion point, respectively.

Place an External Text File

You just learned how to create a text frame and create new text. You can also import text that was created in an external word-processing application, which is a common situation when creating page-layout jobs (more common, perhaps, than manually typing text in a frame). In this exercise, you import text that was saved in a rich-text format (RTF) file, which can store type-formatting options as well as the actual text.

1. **With identity.indd open, make sure nothing is selected in the layout and then choose File>Place.**

   Remember, you can choose Edit>Deselect All, or simply click in an empty area of the workspace to deselect any selected objects.

2. **Navigate to contact.rtf in the WIP>Crowe folder. Make sure none of the options are checked at the bottom of the dialog box and click Open.**

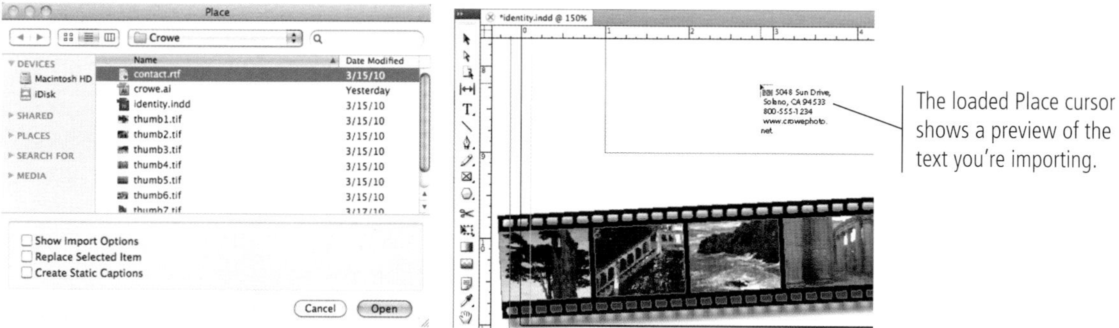

The loaded Place cursor shows a preview of the text you're importing.

3. **Click the loaded Place cursor near the bottom of the page, above the filmstrip graphic but within the margin guides.**

   The resulting text frame is automatically created as wide as the defined margin guides, and extending down to the bottom margin guide on the page.

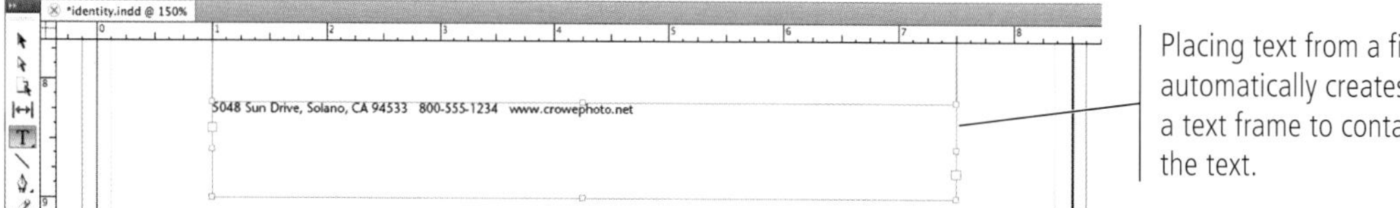

Placing text from a file automatically creates a text frame to contain the text.

4. **Using the Selection tool, click the bottom-right handle of the frame and drag until the frame is just large enough to contain the text.**

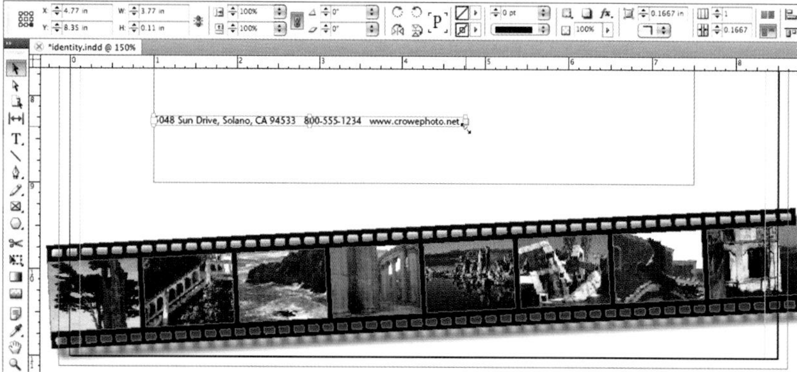

5. **Click the bottom-right bounding box handle of the frame. Press Command/Control-Shift, and then drag to the right.**

   As you drag the frame handle, pressing Command/Control allows you to resize the type along with the frame. Pressing Shift constrains the scaling to maintain the original height-to-width ratio.

6. **When the Scale X and Scale Y fields in the Control panel show approximately 125%, release the mouse button.**

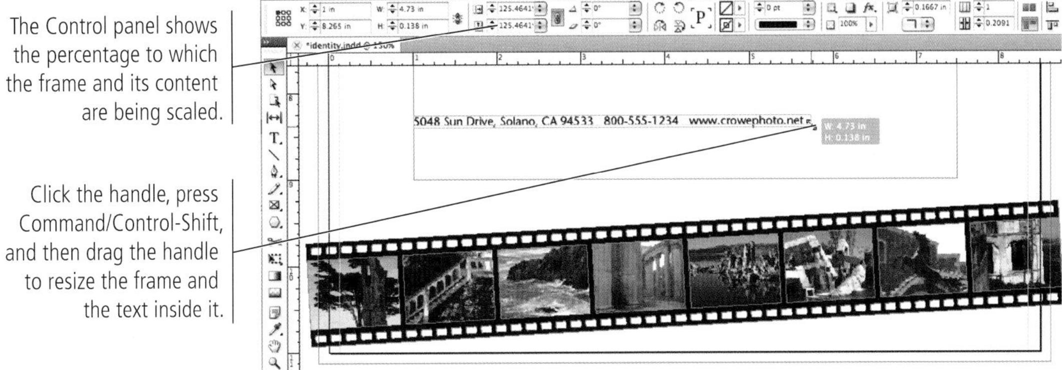

The Control panel shows the percentage to which the frame and its content are being scaled.
Click the handle, press Command/Control-Shift, and then drag the handle to resize the frame and the text inside it.
5048 Sun Drive, Solano, CA 94533 800-555-1234 www.crowephoto.net

7. **With the Selection tool active, double-click inside the text frame.**

   This automatically switches to the Type tool and places the insertion point in the text in the frame where you double-clicked.

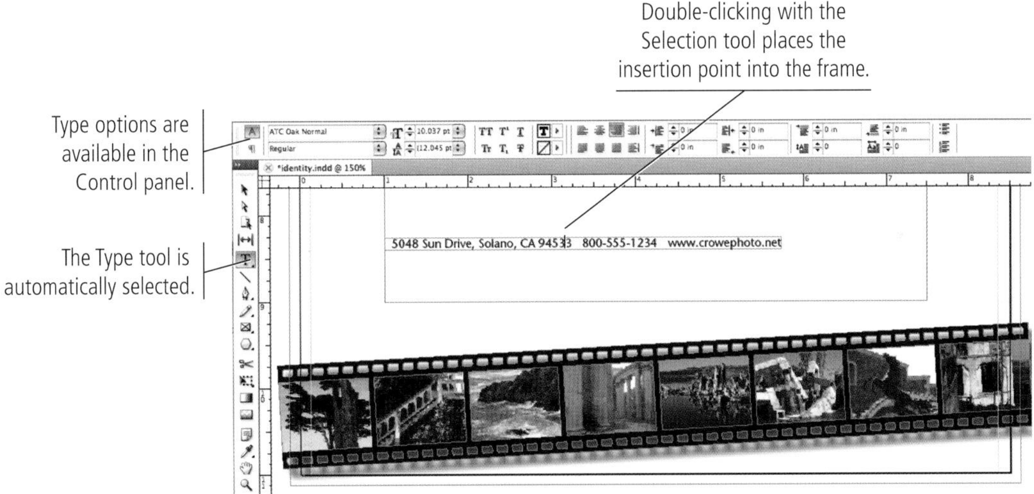

8. **Click the Selection tool to activate it again. Move the cursor outside the top-right corner handle until you see the rotation cursor. Click and drag up until you have rotated the frame by 3°.**

   This is the same angle that you used for the filmstrip graphic.

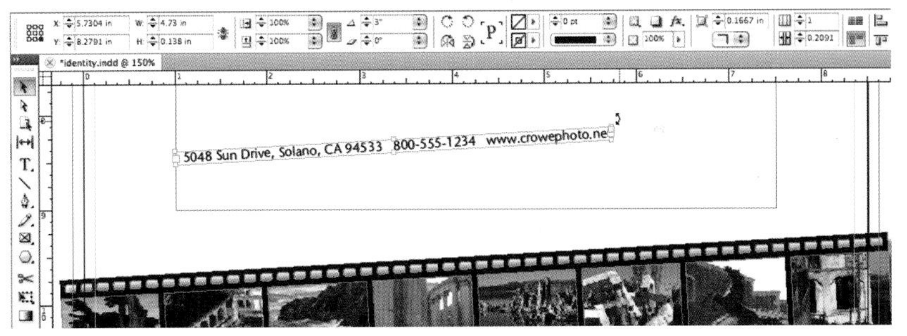

> ***Note:***
>
> *You can also use the Free Transform tool to rotate an object, but changing tools is not necessary since the same rotation functionality can be accessed with the Selection tool.*

9. **Using the Selection tool, move the rotated text frame into place just above the filmstrip, with the right edge at 8.25″.**

   Use the following image as a guide for placing the frame.

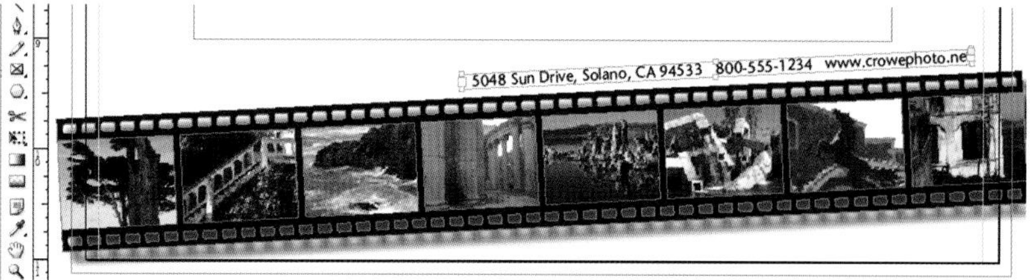

10. **Choose View>Extras>Hide Frame Edges.**

    This command turns off the blue borders that surround every frame. Frame edges can be very valuable when you're working with some objects, but they can be distracting in other cases. Always remember that you can toggle the frame edges on and off in the View>Extras submenu.

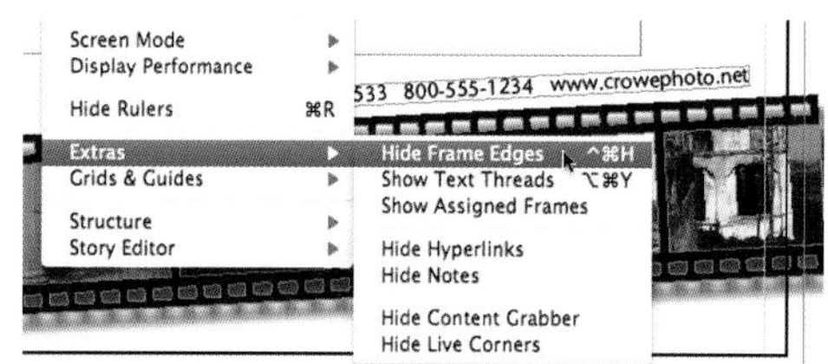

    When frame edges are hidden, moving the Selection tool cursor over a frame reveals its edges. This frame highlighting can make it easier to find exactly the object you want, especially when working in an area with a number of overlapping or nearby objects.

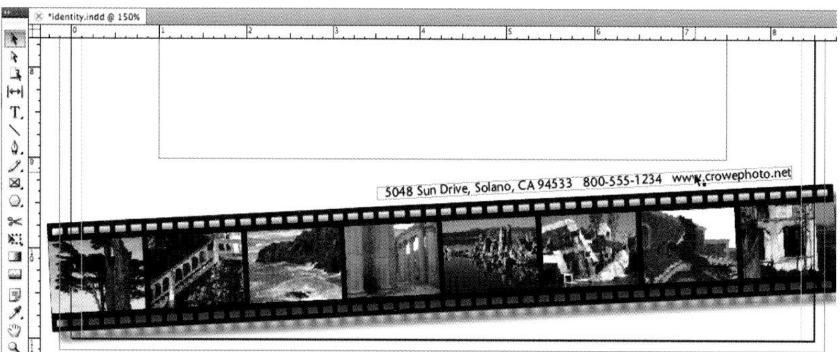

11. **Save the file and continue to the final stage of the project.**

> *Note:*
>
> *If a menu command is not visible, choose Show All Menu Items at the bottom of the menu.*

Tips and Tricks for Working with Layout Elements

Copying and Pasting

The standard Cut, Copy, and Paste options are available in InDesign, just as they are in most applications. Whatever you have selected will be copied or cut to the Clipboard, and whatever is in the Clipboard will be pasted. InDesign has a number of special pasting options in the Edit menu:

Edit Layout Type Object Table
Undo Send Backward ⌘Z
Redo ⇧⌘Z
Cut ⌘X
Copy ⌘C
Paste ⌘V
Paste without Formatting ⇧⌘V
Paste Into ⌥⌘V
Paste in Place ⌥⇧⌘V
Clear ⌫

Paste. If you are pasting an object (frame, etc.), the object will be pasted in the center of the document window. If you are pasting text, it will be pasted at the location of the current insertion point; if the insertion point is not currently placed, the text is placed in a new basic text frame in the middle of the document window.

Paste without Formatting. This command is available when text is in the Clipboard; the text is pasted using the default type formatting options (12-pt black Minion Pro, if it hasn't been changed on your system).

Paste Into. This command is available when an object is in the Clipboard and another object is selected. The pasted object becomes the contents of the object that is selected when you choose this command.

Paste in Place. This command pastes an object at the exact position as the original. If you paste on the same page as the original, you create a second object exactly on top of the first. You can also use this command to place a copy in the exact position as the original, but on a different page in the layout.

Managing Stacking Order

The top-to-bottom order of objects is called **stacking order**; each object you create is stacked on top of existing objects. When you have multiple stacked objects — especially ones that are closely spaced — it can be difficult to select exactly what you want. Fortunately, the application provides a number of options to make it easier.

When you move the Selection tool cursor over an object, the edges of the object are highlighted. This lets you know what will be selected if you click.

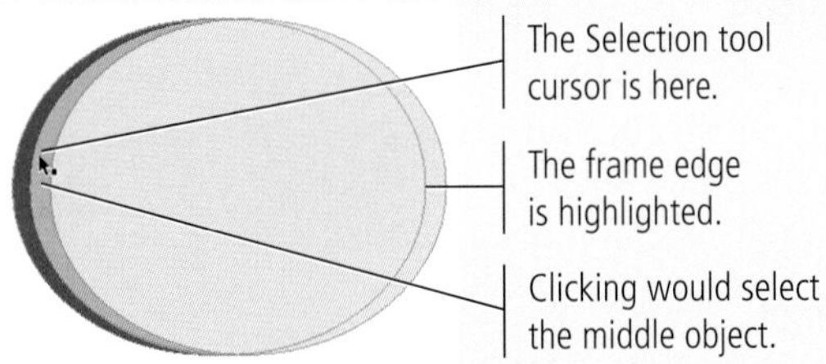

When an object is already selected, InDesign CS5 favors the already selected object. This prevents you from accidentally selecting an object higher in the stacking order (for example, if you want to drag only the middle object); but this also means you have to be careful if you do want to select a different object.

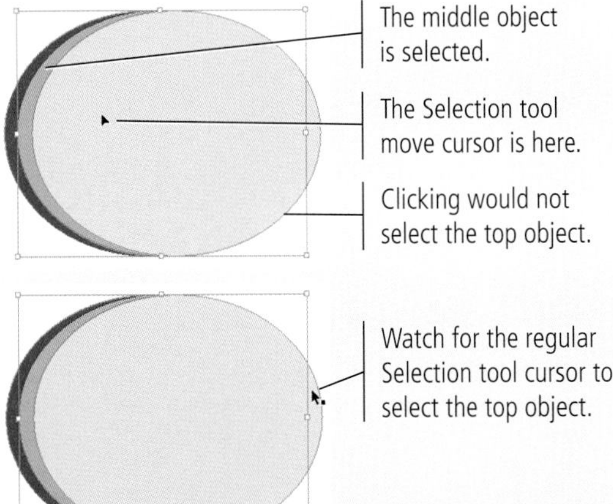

The middle object is selected.
The Selection tool move cursor is here.
Clicking would not select the top object.
Watch for the regular Selection tool cursor to select the top object.

You can use the Object>Select submenu commands (or their related keyboard shortcuts) to access objects relative to their order in the stack.

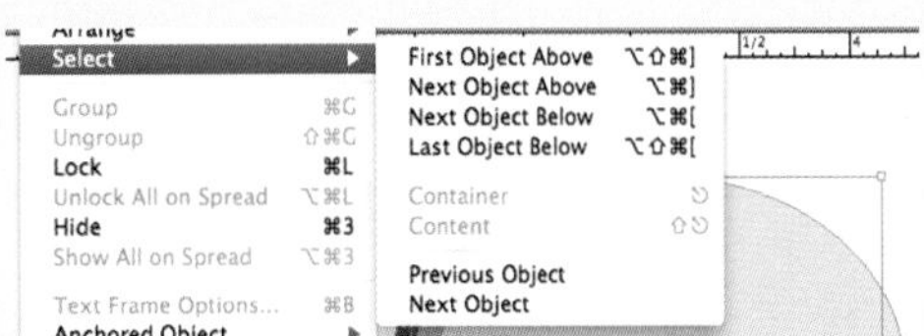

You can use the Object>Arrange submenu commands (or their related keyboard shortcuts) to change the stacking-order position of objects.

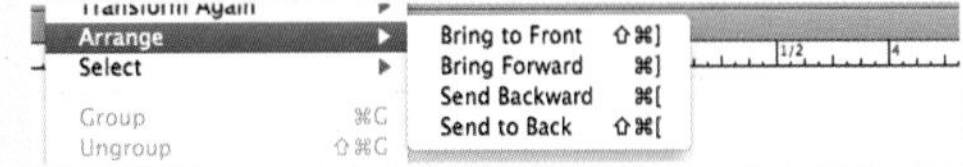

Finally, you can use the individual item listings in the Layers panel to select exactly the object you want, or to rearrange objects in the layer stack.

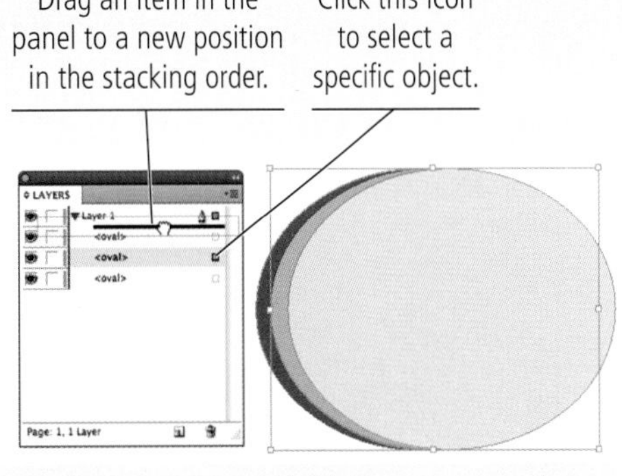

Drag an item in the panel to a new position in the stacking order.
Click this icon to select a specific object.

Stage 5 Printing InDesign Files

For a printer to output high-quality pages from Adobe InDesign, some method of defining the page and its elements is required. These definitions are provided by Page Description Languages (PDLs), the most widely used of which is Adobe PostScript 3.

When a file is output to a PostScript-enabled device, the raster image processor (RIP) creates a file that includes mathematical descriptions detailing the construction and placement of the various page elements; the print file precisely maps the location of each pixel on the page. In the printer, the RIP then interprets the description of each element into a matrix of ones (black) and zeros (white). The output device uses this matrix to reconstruct the element as a series of individual dots or spots that form a high-resolution bitmap image on film or paper.

> *Note:*
>
> *If you do not have a PostScript output device, you can work around the problem by first exporting your InDesign files to PDF (see Project 8) and then opening the PDFs in Acrobat to print a proof. This is a common workflow solution in the current graphic design industry.*

Not every printer on the market is capable of interpreting PostScript information. Low-cost, consumer-level inkjet printers, common in the modern graphic design market, are generally not PostScript compatible. (Some desktop printers can handle PostScript, at least with an additional purchase; consult the technical documentation that came with your printer to make certain it can print PostScript information.) If your printer is non-PostScript compatible, some features in the InDesign Print dialog box will be unavailable and some page elements (particularly EPS files) might not output as expected.

Print a Sample Proof

Not too long ago, every job sent to a commercial printer required a hardcopy proof to accompany the disk as an example of the layout content. As digital file submission continues to gain ground, however, physical printer proofs are becoming less common.

In general, every job you create will be printed at some point in the workflow — whether for your own review, as a client comp, or as a final proof that accompanies a file to the commercial printer. So, whether you need a basic proof or a final job proof, you should still understand what is possible in the InDesign Print dialog box.

> *Note:*
>
> *It is also important to realize that desktop inkjet and laser printers typically do not accurately represent color.*

Composite proofs print all colors on the same sheet, which allows you to judge page geometry and the overall positioning of elements. Final composite proofs that are provided to the printer should include **registration marks** (special printer's marks used to check the alignment of individual inks when the job is printed), and they should always be output at 100% size.

1. **With identity.indd open, choose File>Print.**

   The Print dialog box includes dozens of options in eight different categories.

   The most important options you'll select are the Printer and PPD (PostScript printer description) at the top of the dialog box. InDesign reads the information in the PPD to determine which of the specific print options are available for the current output.

2. **Choose the printer you want to use in the Printer menu, and choose the PPD for that printer in the PPD menu (if possible).**

3. **Review the options in the General pane.**

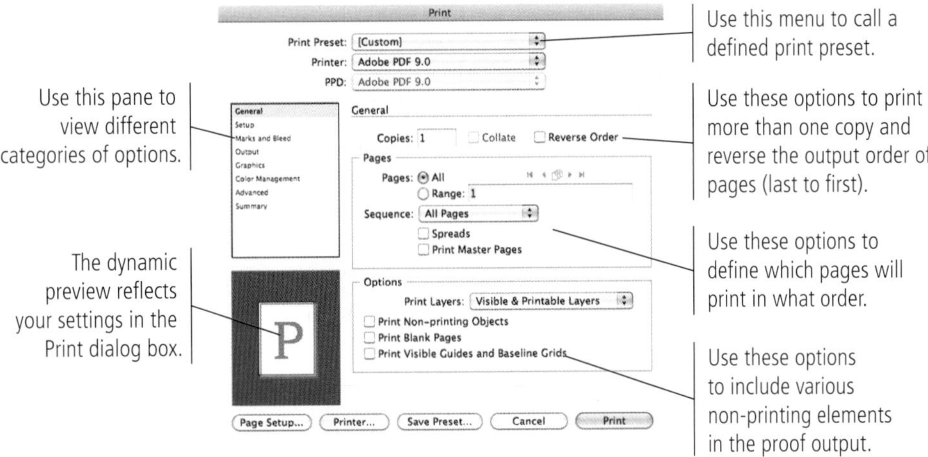

Use this menu to call a defined print preset.
Use this pane to view different categories of options.
Use these options to print more than one copy and reverse the output order of pages (last to first).
Use these options to define which pages will print in what order.
The dynamic preview reflects your settings in the Print dialog box.
Use these options to include various non-printing elements in the proof output.

If you frequently use the same options for printing proofs, simply click the Save Preset button at the bottom of the dialog box after defining those settings. You can then call all of those same settings by choosing the saved preset in the Print Preset menu.

4. **Click the Setup option in the list of categories.**

These options determine the paper size that will be used for the output (not to be confused with the page size), the paper orientation, and page scaling and positioning options relative to the paper size.

5. **If your printer can print to tabloid-size paper, choose Tabloid in the Paper Size menu.**

If you can only print to letter-size paper, choose the landscape paper orientation option, and then activate the Tile check box.

To output a letter-size page at 100% on letter-size paper, you have to tile to multiple sheets of paper; using the landscape paper orientation allows you to tile to two sheets instead of four (as shown in the preview area).

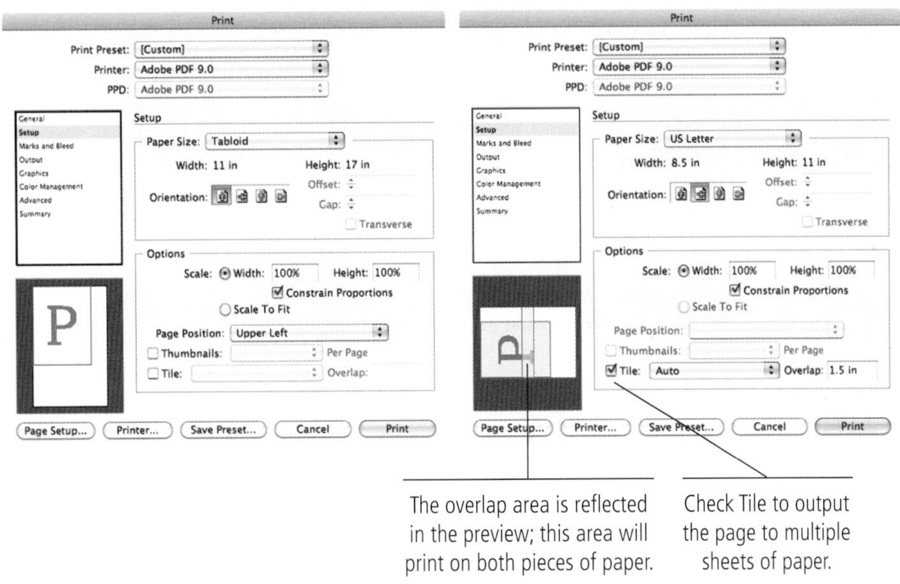

The overlap area is reflected in the preview; this area will print on both pieces of paper.
Check Tile to output the page to multiple sheets of paper.

The Offset and Gap fields should only be used when a job is output to an imagesetter or high-end proofing device. They define page placement on a piece of oversized film or on a printing plate.

6. **Click the Marks and Bleed option in the list of categories. Activate the All Printer's Marks option and change the Offset field to 0.125″. Make sure the Use Document Bleed Settings option is checked.**

You can specify individual printer's marks, or simply print them all. For proofing purposes, the crop and bleed marks are the most important options to include.

The Offset value determines how far from the page edge printer's marks will be placed; some printers require printer's marks to stay outside the bleed area, which means the offset should be at least the same as than the defined bleed area.

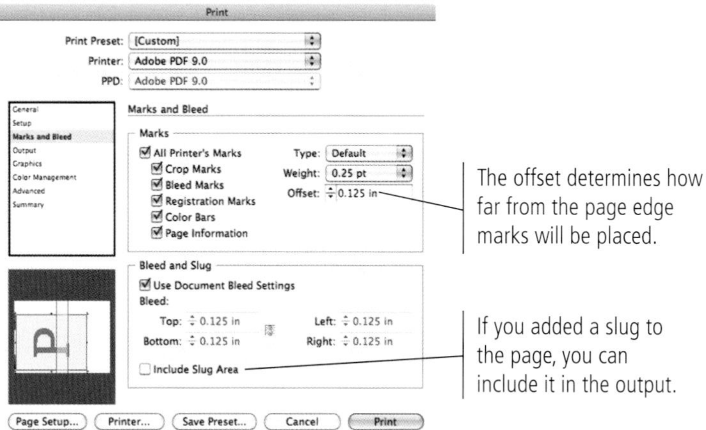

7. **Click the Output option in the list of categories. If you can print color, choose Composite CMYK or Composite RGB in the Color menu; otherwise, choose Composite Gray.**

In the Color menu, you can choose the color model you want to use. (If you only have a black-and-white printer, this menu will default to Composite Gray.) The composite options output all colors to a single page, which is appropriate for a desktop proof. If you choose either Separations option in the menu, the Inks list shows which inks (separations) will be included in the output.

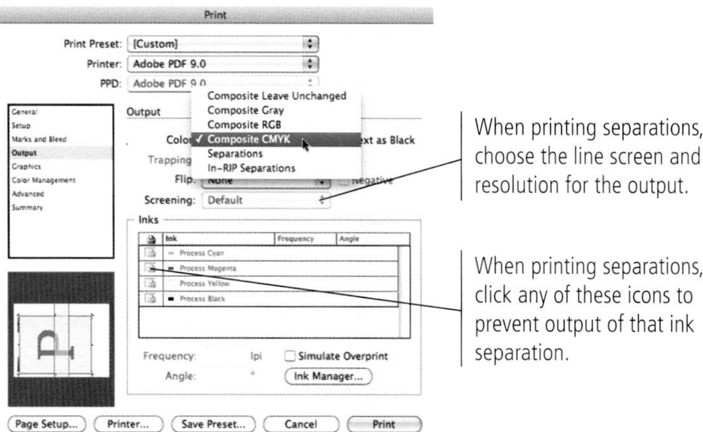

The Trapping, Flip, Negative, Screening, Frequency, and Angle options should only be used by the output service provider; these options relate to the way separations are imaged on a printing plate for commercial print output.

8. **Click Graphics in the list of categories.**

9. **Choose Optimized Subsampling in the Images Send Data menu.**

   This menu determines how much data is sent to the output device for placed images.

   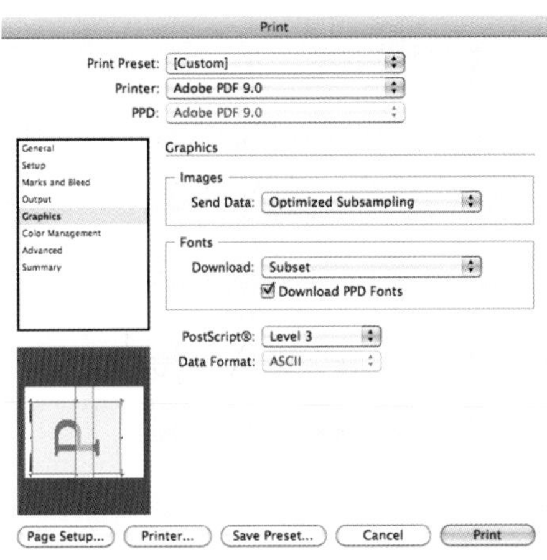

   - All, the default option, sends full-resolution image data.
   - Optimized Subsampling sends only the necessary data to output the best possible resolution on the printer you are using.
   - Proxy outputs low-resolution screen previews, which reduces the time required for output.
   - None outputs all placed images as gray frames with crossed diagonal lines. This is useful for reviewing overall placement when developing an initial layout comp.

10. **Choose Subset in the Fonts Download menu.**

    This menu determines how much font data is downloaded to the printer. (Font data is required by the output device to print the job correctly.)

    - None sends no font information to the printer. (This can cause output problems, especially if you use TrueType fonts.)
    - Complete sends the entire font file for every font that is used in the document.
    - Subset sends font information only for the characters that are used in the document.

11. **Check the Download PPD Fonts option.**

    Professional-quality output devices include a number of resident fonts, from just a few to the entire Adobe type library. If this option is checked, InDesign sends data for all fonts in the document, even if those fonts are installed on the output device. (This can be important because different fonts of the same name might have different font metrics, which can cause text to reflow and appear different in the print than in the file that you created.)

12. **Leave the PostScript and Data Format menus at their default values.**

    The PostScript menu defines which level of PostScript to use. Some older devices cannot process PostScript 3. You should generally leave this menu at the default value.

    The Data Format menu defines how image data is transferred. ASCII is compatible with older devices, and is useful for cross-platform applications. Binary is smaller than ASCII, but might not work on all platforms.

13. **Click Print to output the page.**

14. **When the document comes back into focus, save and close it.**

15. **Close the layout files when you're finished.**

Note:

We're intentionally skipping the Color Management and Advanced panes in the Print dialog box. We explain them in later projects when they are relevant to the project content.

Project Review

fill in the blank

1. ______________ is the area of an object that extends past the edge of a page to compensate for variations in the output process.

2. ______________ is a special kind of raster image that has only two possible color values, black or white.

3. The ______________ defines the outermost dimensions of an object; it is always a rectangle, regardless of the object's specific shape.

4. ______________ are based on the concept of anchor points and their defining control handles.

5. ________________________________ are the four primary colors used in process-color printing.

6. The ______________ tool is used to select entire frames or other objects.

7. The ______________ tool can be used to select the image contained within a specific frame when the frame is part of a group.

8. The ______________ panel can be used to create complex shapes by combining multiple objects.

9. The ______________ can be used to access a frame's content when the Selection tool is active.

10. The ______________ is context sensitive, reflecting different options depending on what is selected in the document.

short answer

1. Briefly explain the difference between a vector graphic and a raster image.

2. Briefly explain how resolution affects a page laid out in InDesign.

3. Briefly explain the concept of process color.

Portfolio Builder Project

Use what you learned in this project to complete the following freeform exercise.
Carefully read the art director and client comments, then create your own design to meet the needs of the project.
Use the space below to sketch ideas; when finished, write a brief explanation of your reasoning behind your final design.

art director comments

The owner of your agency is pleased with your work on behalf of your client. She has decided to create more formal branding for your design agency, and wants you to create a new logo and the accompanying collateral pieces with the new logo.

To complete this project, you should:

- ❑ Develop a compelling logo that suggests the agency's purpose (graphic design). Incorporate the agency's name — Creative Concepts — in the logo.
- ❑ Build a letterhead using the same specifications that you used to design the Crowe letterhead.
- ❑ Build a business card that is 3.5″ wide by 2″ high, with 1/8″ bleeds.
- ❑ Build an envelope layout for #10 business-size envelopes (9.5″ × 4.125″).

client comments

For the logo, I want something that really says 'graphic design' — how can we convince clients that we can design their logos if we don't have a good design for our own? Find or create some kind of imagery that people will immediately recognize as graphics- or art-related.

The letterhead should have the company's mailing address, phone number, and Web site. The business card needs to include a name, title, mailing address, email, and phone number. The envelope should only have the mailing address and the Web site. Use your own contact information as placeholder text for everything.

For the envelope, we're going to print pre-folded envelopes so you can't use bleeds. In fact, you need to keep all objects at least 0.25″ from the edges.

Keep in mind that you're building a complete identity package, so all pieces should have a consistent look. Whatever you do on the letterhead, you should use similar visual elements on all three pieces.

project justification

Project Summary

We designed this project to introduce you to the basics of page layout with InDesign; you will expand on these skills throughout this book. Creating a new document to meet specific project needs — including page size, margins, and the printer's stated bleed requirements — is one of the most important tasks you will complete in InDesign.

After the page structure is created, InDesign has many tools for creating objects — basic shapes, lines and Bézier curves, placeholder frames, and text frames. The built-in drawing tools can create sophisticated artwork directly on the page, such as the filmstrip in this letterhead layout (although InDesign should not be considered an alternative to Adobe Illustrator for creating all vector artwork). You can also place external image and text files, and then transform those files to meet the specific needs of a given project.

There are many different methods for managing objects and their content. The Selection and Direct Selection tools, the Content Indicator icon, frame edge highlighting, and the Layers panel all provide ways to access only — and exactly — what you want to edit.

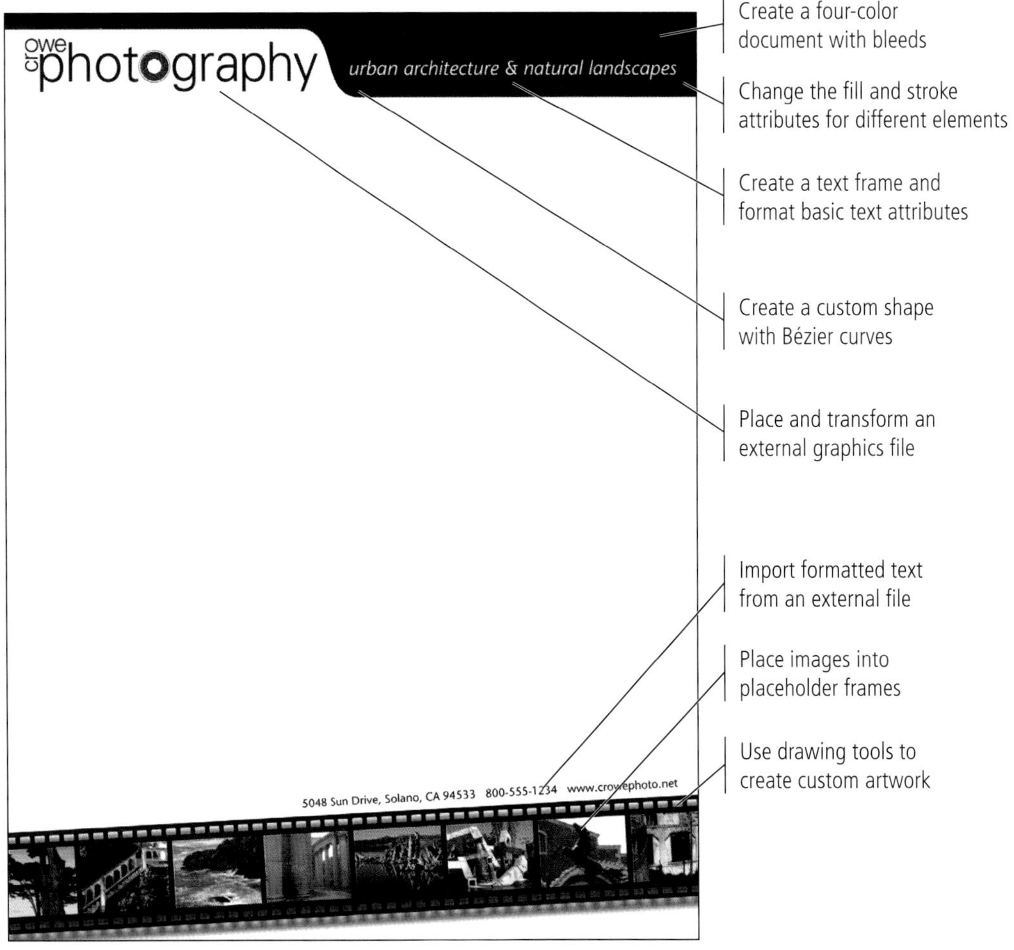
crowe photography
urban architecture & natural landscapes
5048 Sun Drive, Solano, CA 94533 800-555-1234 www.crowephoto.net
Create a four-color document with bleeds
Change the fill and stroke attributes for different elements
Create a text frame and format basic text attributes
Create a custom shape with Bézier curves
Place and transform an external graphics file
Import formatted text from an external file
Place images into placeholder frames
Use drawing tools to create custom artwork

project 8

Festival Poster

Your client is the promoter for the Miami Beach Jazz Festival, which is held annually at several locations throughout the South Beach area. The client wants to create posters that will be plastered all over the city, from local restaurants and clubs to bus stops and construction sites that don't say "Post No Bills." This type of poster should use very little text set in a large, easy-to-read font, and it needs to be eye-catching from a distance, with large, vivid graphics.

This project incorporates the following skills:

- ❑ Creating a file with the appropriate settings for a four-color, commercially printed poster
- ❑ Using gradients, graphics, and image effects to attract the viewer's attention
- ❑ Adding text elements and applying formatting as appropriate for a poster
- ❑ Threading a single text story across multiple text frames
- ❑ Understanding the various options for formatting characters and paragraphs
- ❑ Using inline graphics to highlight important text elements
- ❑ Creating a PDF file that meets the printer's requirements

Project Meeting

client comments

The poster to promote this festival is basically the "play bill," and we will plaster it all over the city. We want the poster to be very attractive, colorful, and vivid, so the main focus — and most of the poster real estate — should be on the graphics. But the text also has to be readable; I emailed the text I want you to place at the bottom of the poster this morning. Our posters for past years' festivals have always been 11 × 17″, and we want to stick with that size.

This year's festival tag line is "Move Your Feet to the Beat." I found an excellent illustration of a saxophone player that we'd like to use as the main image, and we hope you can make the tag line look like it's coming out of the end of the sax. I also found some nice beach images that might make good backgrounds, so we emailed those to you as well.

art director comments

The client has provided all the pieces you need, so you can get started composing the layout. Most of this job is going to involve compositing multiple images and formatting text, but I want you to go beyond basic image placement. InDesign includes many tools for manipulating images; use some of those to make sure this poster consists of more than just plain pictures.

Finally, I want you to use a special metallic ink for the festival's tag line. That should give the poster just a bit more visual impact than regular flat colors. I think the gold 8660 in Pantone's metallic collection will work well with the other visual elements.

You already know the page size, and according to the printer the poster needs a 1/4″ bleed allowance just to be safe. The final poster should be saved as a PDF using the printer's specs, which I'll email to you.

project objectives

To complete this project, you will:

- ❑ Create a print layout using a master text frame
- ❑ Convert the content type of frames
- ❑ Create a custom gradient to add visual impact
- ❑ Create a custom frame using an image clipping path
- ❑ Apply visual effects to unify various graphic elements
- ❑ Thread the flow of text through multiple text frames
- ❑ Format text characters and paragraphs to effectively convey a message
- ❑ Place inline graphics to highlight important textual elements
- ❑ Place text on a path
- ❑ Apply a spot color
- ❑ Create a PDF file for commercial output

Stage 1 Building Graphic Interest

In Project 7, you learned the basics of placing graphics into a layout and drawing shapes using the built-in InDesign tools. You know that graphics and text are contained in frames, and that objects (including graphics frames) can have stroke and fill attributes. You can use those foundational skills to build virtually any InDesign layout.

InDesign also includes a number of options for extending your artistic options beyond simply compositing text and graphics that were finalized in other applications. The first stage of this project incorporates a number of these creative tools to accomplish your client's stated goal of grabbing the viewer's attention with vivid, attractive graphics.

Set Up the Workspace

1. **Download `Print5_RF_Project8.zip` from the Student Files Web page.**

2. **Expand the ZIP archive in your WIP folder (Macintosh) or copy the archive contents into your WIP folder (Windows).**

   This results in a folder named **Jazz**, which contains the files you need for this project. You should also use this folder to save the files you create in this project.

3. **With no file open in InDesign, open the Units & Increments pane of the Preferences dialog box (in the InDesign menu on Macintosh or the Edit menu on Windows).**

4. **Change both Ruler Units menus to Inches and click OK.**

   In Project 7 you changed the default units of measurement for an open file. By changing the preferences with no file open, you're changing the application default preferences; the settings that you define will be applied in any new file you create, but not to already-existing files.

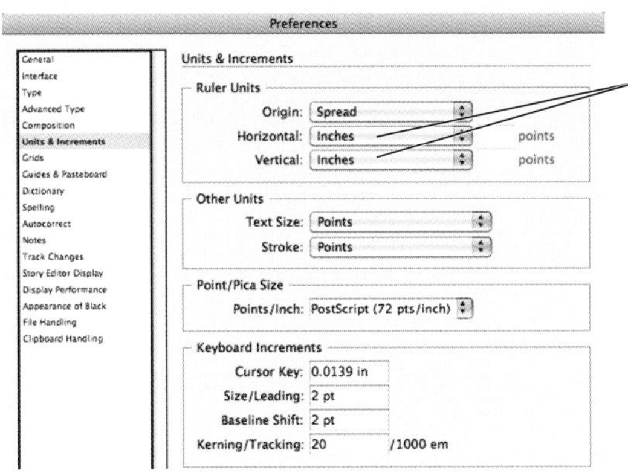

With no file open, change both of these menus to Inches.

5. **Choose File>New>Document.**

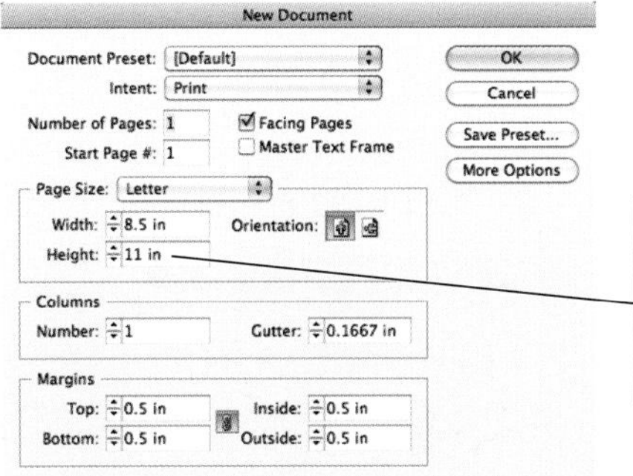

By changing the default units to inches, the measurements in all dialog boxes (including this one) are now shown in inches.

6. **Create a new one-page print document that is 11″ wide by 17″ high (Tabloid-size) with 1″ margins and 0.25″ bleeds on all four sides. Create the file with no master text frame and without facing pages.**

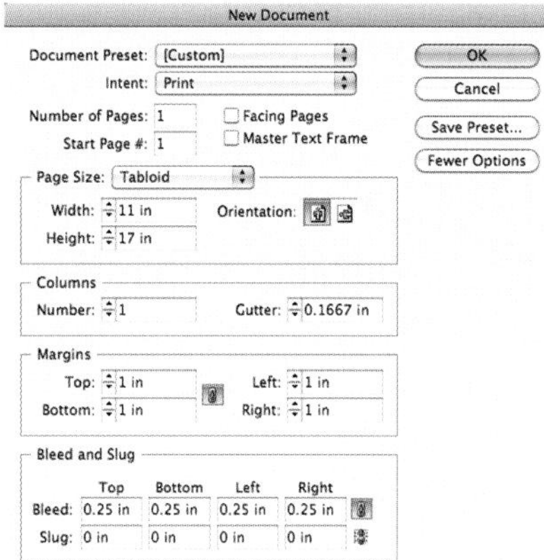

Note:

Industry standards typically call for a 0.125″ bleed, but in this case the printer specifically requested 0.25″ bleed allowance.

7. **Save the file as poster.indd in your WIP>Jazz folder and then continue to the next exercise.**

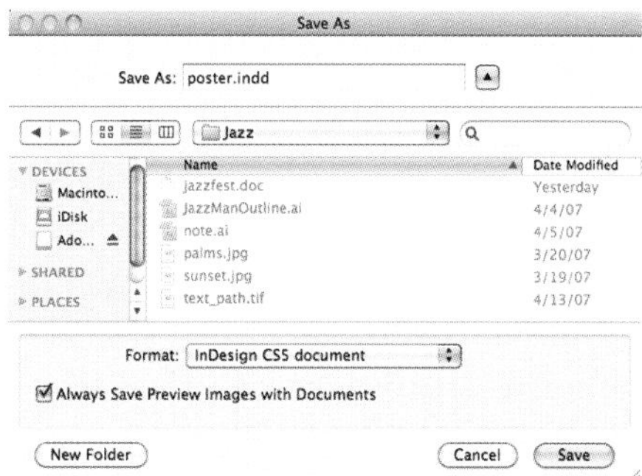

Define Color Swatches

The Swatches panel is used to apply predefined colors to any element in a layout. Six CMYK color swatches are included in the default set for print documents, as well as three special colors (Paper, Black, and Registration) and a None swatch that removes color from the selected attribute.

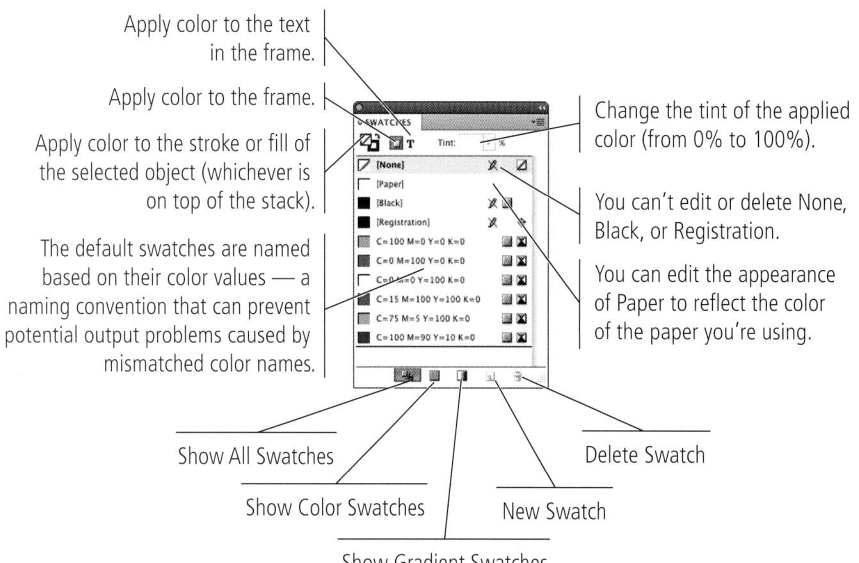

Note:

Using the Fill and Stroke swatches at the top of the Swatches panel, you can apply different colors to the fill and stroke of selected text.

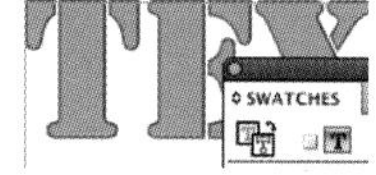

Note:

Editing the appearance of the Paper swatch only affects the on-screen preview. It does not appear in the print output.

You can define colors based on one of three color models (CMYK, RGB, or LAB), or you can call spot colors from built-in libraries of special inks. Each different mode and type of color has an identifying icon in the Swatches panel.

Note:

Anything colored with the Registration swatch will appear on every separation in a job. This color should only be used for special marks or other information placed outside the trim area.

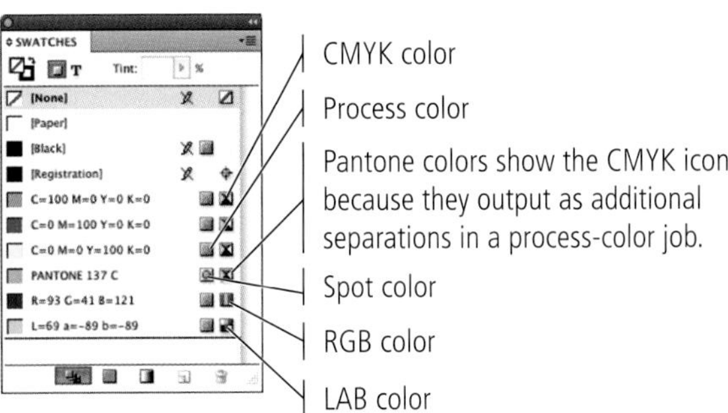

1. **With poster.indd open, open the Swatches panel (Window>Color>Swatches).**

2. **Open the Swatches panel Options menu.**

   This menu has options for creating four types of color swatches: Color, Tint, Gradient, and Mixed Ink.

   - **Color** swatches store specific colors based on defined percentages of each component ink.
   - **Gradient** swatches store specific transitions from one color to another.
   - A **Tint** swatch is a specific stored percentage of another swatch, which is useful if you frequently use (for example) a 30% tint of C=100 M=42 Y=0 K=73. You can apply that tint with a single click instead of applying the color, and then changing the tint of the applied color. Every click you save is a boost in productivity, especially if you're building layouts with multiple elements.
   - **Mixed Ink** swatches allow you to combine percentages of spot and process colors, or of multiple spot colors; this option is only available when at least one spot color exists in the file. The **Mixed Ink Group** option allows you to build multiple swatches at once, based on specific incremental percentages of inks. Be very careful if you use mixed ink swatches; they can be a source of unpredictable color reproduction and potential output problems.

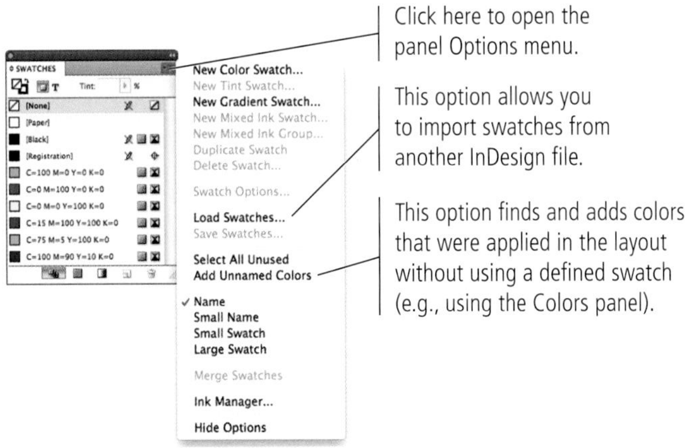

3. **Choose New Color Swatch in the panel Options menu.**

4. **Leave the Name with Color Value option checked. Make sure the Color Type is set to Process and the Color Mode is set to CMYK.**

There is no industry standard for naming colors, but InDesign comes close with the Name with Color Value option. This type of naming convention — basing names on the color components — serves several purposes:

- You know exactly what components the color contains, so you can easily see if you are duplicating colors.
- You can immediately tell that the color should be a process build rather than a special ink or spot color.
- You avoid mismatched color names and duplicated spot colors, which are potential disasters in the commercial printing production process.

Mismatched color names occur when a defined color name has two different values — one defined in the page layout and one defined in an image file that you placed into your layout. When the files are output, the output device might be confused by different definitions for the same color name; the imported value might replace the project's value for that particular color name (or vice versa). The change could be subtle, or it could be drastic.

A similar problem occurs when the same spot color is assigned different names in different applications. For example, you might define a spot color in InDesign as "Border Color"; another designer might define the same spot color in Illustrator as "Spec Blue." When the illustration is placed into the InDesign layout, two different spot-color separations exist, even though the different color names have the same values.

Color by Numbers

INDESIGN FOUNDATIONS

If you base your color choices solely on what you see on your monitor, what appears to be a perfect blue sky will probably not look quite right when it's printed with process-color inks. Even if you have calibrated your monitor, no monitor is 100% effective at simulating printed color. As long as monitors display color in RGB, there will always be some discrepancies.

Every designer should have some sort of process-color chart, available from commercial publishers (some printers might provide the charts produced by the exact press on which your job will be printed). These charts contain small squares of process ink builds so you can see, for example, what a process build of C=10 M=70 Y=30 K=20 will look like when printed. These guides usually show samples in steps of 5% or 10%, printed on both coated and uncoated paper (because the type of paper or substrate can dramatically affect the final result).

When you define process colors in an InDesign project, you should enter specific numbers in the CMYK fields to designate your color choices, rather than relying on your screen preview. As you gain experience defining colors, you will become better able to predict the outcome for a given process-ink build. Rely on what you know to be true rather than what you hope will be true.

The same concept also applies when using special ink libraries. You should have — and use — swatch books that show printed samples of the special inks. You cannot rely on the monitor preview to choose a special ink color. Rather, you should find the color in a printed swatch book, and then enter the appropriate number in the Pantone field (for example) below the color swatches.

Total Area Coverage

When defining the ink values of a process-color build, you must usually limit your **total area coverage** (TAC, also called **total ink coverage** or **total ink density**), or the amount of ink used in a given color.

This might sound complex, but it can be easily calculated by adding the percentages of each ink used to create the color. If a color is defined as C=45 M=60 Y=90 K=0, the total area coverage is 195% (45 + 60 + 90 + 0).

Maximum TAC limits are between 240% and 320% for offset lithography, depending on the paper being used. If you exceed the TAC limits for a given paper-ink-press combination, your printed job might end up with excess ink bleed, smearing, smudging, show-through, or a number of other printing errors because the paper cannot absorb all of the ink.

5. **Define the color with 0% Cyan, 70% Magenta, 95% Yellow, and 0% Black, and then click Add.**

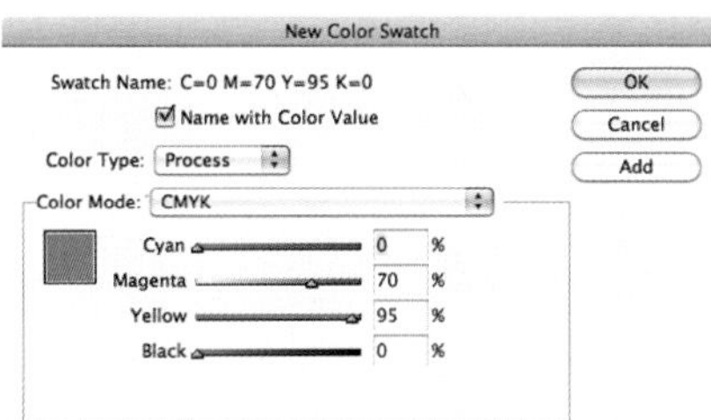

6. **Create two more process-color swatches using the following ink values. Click Done after adding the third color to close the dialog box.**

Color 1: C=0 M=10 Y=75 K=0

Color 2: C=0 M=40 Y=0 K=100

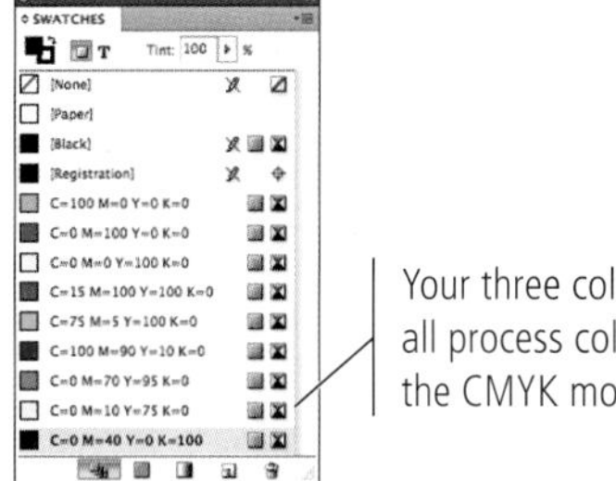

Your three colors are all process colors using the CMYK model.

The third swatch — 100% black and some percent of another color — is called **rich black** or **super black**. Remember, when the inks are printed, adding another ink to solid black enhances the richness of the solid black. Adding magenta typically creates a warmer black, while adding cyan typically creates a cooler black.

7. **Open the Swatches panel Options menu and choose New Color Swatch.**

8. **In the New Color Swatch dialog box, choose Spot in the Color Type menu.**

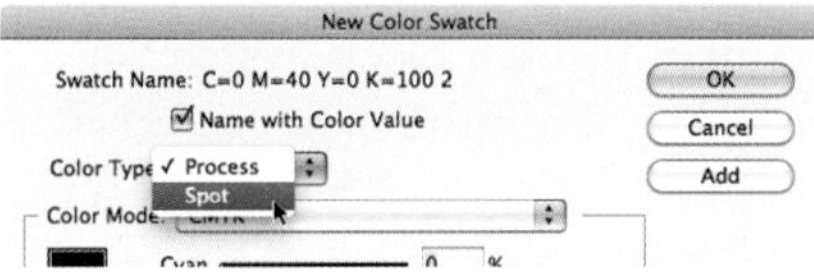

9. **Choose Pantone metallic coated in the Color Mode menu.**

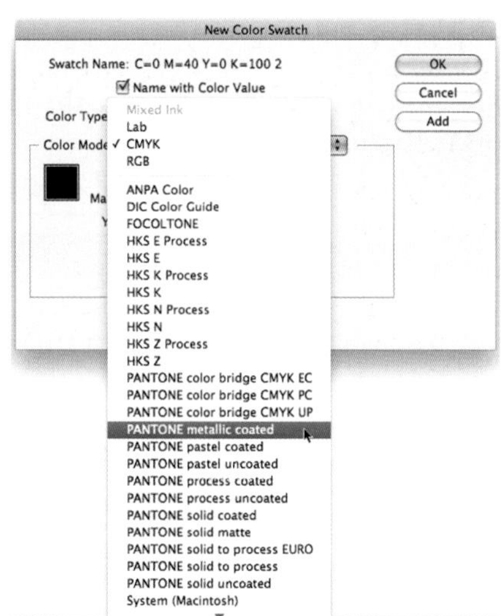

Spot colors are created with special premixed inks to produce a certain color with one ink layer; they are not built from the standard process inks used in CMYK printing. When you output a job with spot colors, each spot color appears on its own separation.

Spot-color inks are commonly used when a special color, such as a corporate color, is required. InDesign includes a number of built-in color libraries, including spot-color systems such as Pantone, Toyo, and DIC. In the United States, the most popular collections of spot colors are the Pantone Matching System (PMS) libraries. TruMatch and Focoltone are also used in the United States; Toyo and DICColor (Dainippon Ink & Chemicals) are used primarily in Japan.

Even though you can choose a color directly from the library on your screen, you should look at a swatch book to verify that you're using the color you intend. Special inks exist because many of the colors cannot be reproduced with process inks, nor can they be accurately represented on a computer monitor. If you specify special colors and then convert them to process colors later, your job probably won't look exactly as you expect.

10. Place the insertion point in the Pantone field and type `8660`.

You can also scroll through the list and simply click a color to select it.

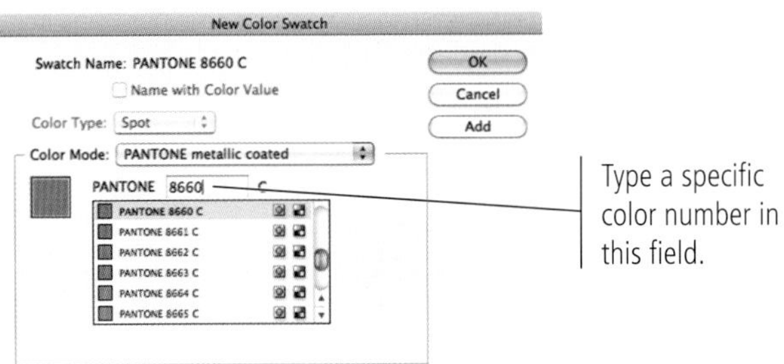

Type a specific color number in this field.

11. Click OK to return to the document window.

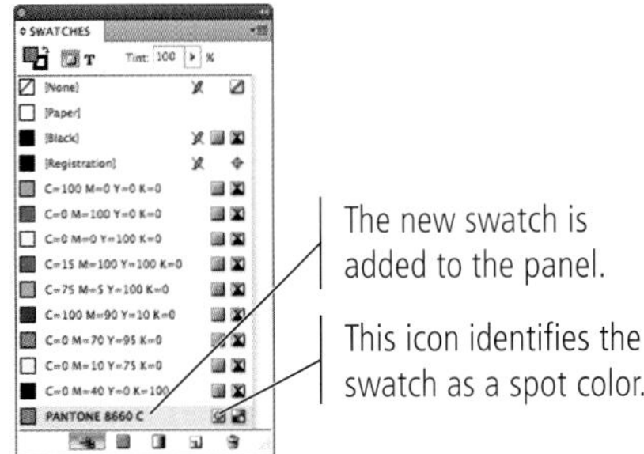

SWATCHES
The new swatch is added to the panel.
This icon identifies the swatch as a spot color.

12. Save the file and continue to the next exercise.

Create the Poster Background

The background of this poster is going to be a solid fill of the rich black swatch you defined in the previous exercise. However, an object filling the entire page can cause certain problems. For example, if you try to create a text frame inside the area, you end up converting the frame to a text frame. In this exercise, you use the Layers panel to prevent problems that could be caused by the background shape.

1. With `poster.indd` open, choose the Rectangle tool in the Tools panel.

2. In the Swatches panel, make sure the Fill swatch is on top and click the C=0 M=40 Y=0 K=100 swatch.

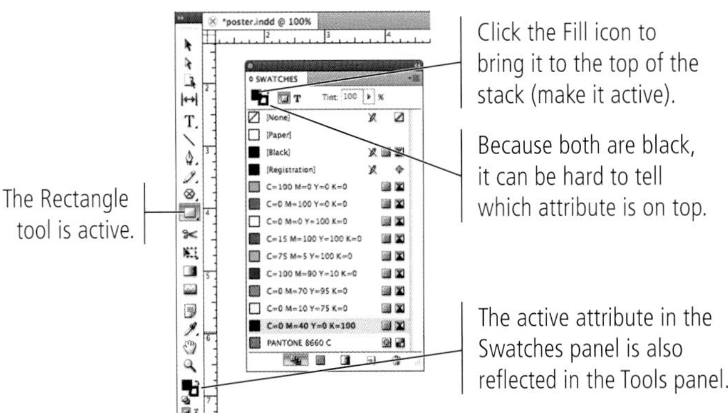

Because both are black, it can be hard to tell which attribute is on top.

3. Click the Stroke icon at the top of the panel to activate that attribute, then click the None swatch.

By changing the fill and stroke attributes when no object is selected, you define those attributes for the next object you create.

Note:

Spot colors are safely chosen from a swatch book — a book of colors printed with different inks, similar to the paint chip cards used in home decorating.

When choosing spot colors, ask your printer which ink system they support. If you designate TruMatch, but they use Pantone inks, you won't get the colors you expect.

Note:

Remember, all panels (whether docked or not) can be accessed from the Window menu. If you don't see a specific menu command, choose Edit>Show All Menu Items.

4. **Using the Rectangle tool, create a rectangle that covers the entire page and extends to the defined bleed guides.**

   You can single-click to define the rectangle size, and then drag it into position with the Selection tool. Alternatively, you can simply click and drag with the Rectangle tool, using the Bleed guides to snap the edges of the shape.

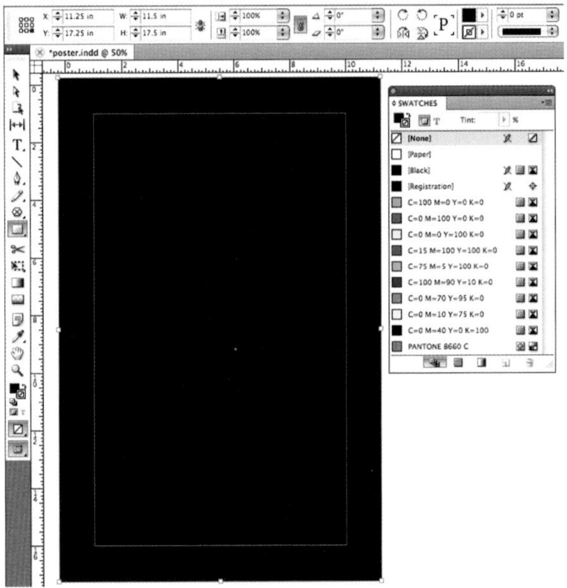

5. **In the Layers panel (Window>Layers), click the arrow to expand Layer 1.**

6. **Click the empty space to the right of the eye icon for the <rectangle> item.**

   The second column in the Layers panel can be used to lock individual items or entire layers. (If you lock a whole layer, all items on that layer are automatically locked.)

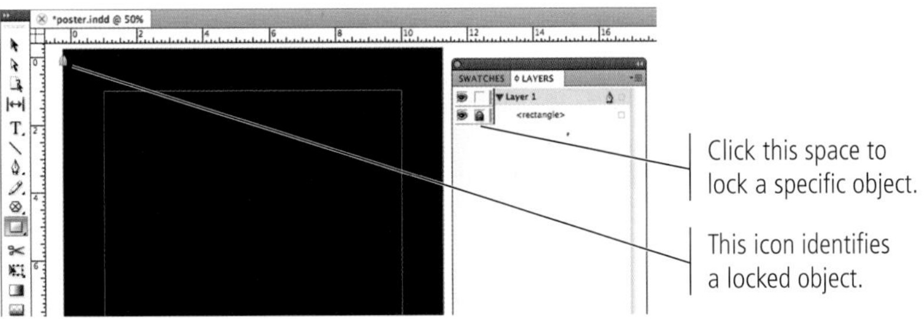

Click this space to lock a specific object.
This icon identifies a locked object.

Note:

You can click an existing lock icon in the Layers panel to unlock an object or layer.

You can also click a lock icon on the page to unlock a specific object.

7. **With the Rectangle tool still selected, change the stroke color to the custom orange swatch. Using the Control panel, change the stroke weight to 6 pt.**

   When you locked the rectangle in Step 6, it was automatically deselected. This means that changing the stroke and fill attributes does not affect the existing object.

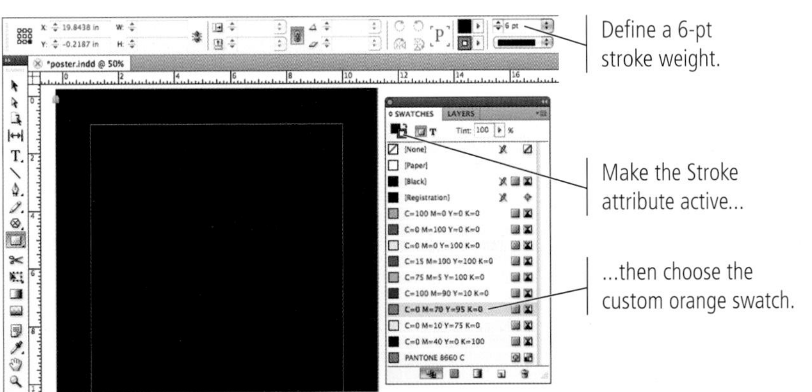

8. **Click and drag to draw a rectangle that fills the area within the defined margin guides.**

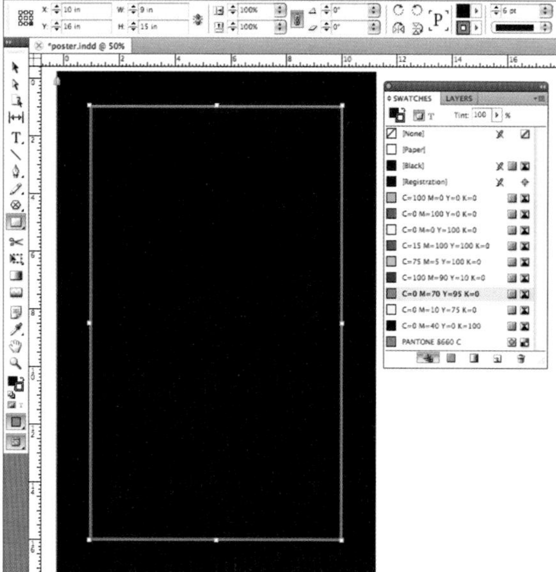

9. **In the Layers panel, click the eye icon to the left of the locked <rectangle>.**

   The visible rectangle has the same fill color as the background shape (which is now hidden). To make it easier to see and work with only specific objects, you can use the Layers panel to toggle the visibility of individual objects or entire layers. (If you hide an entire layer, all objects on that layer are hidden.)

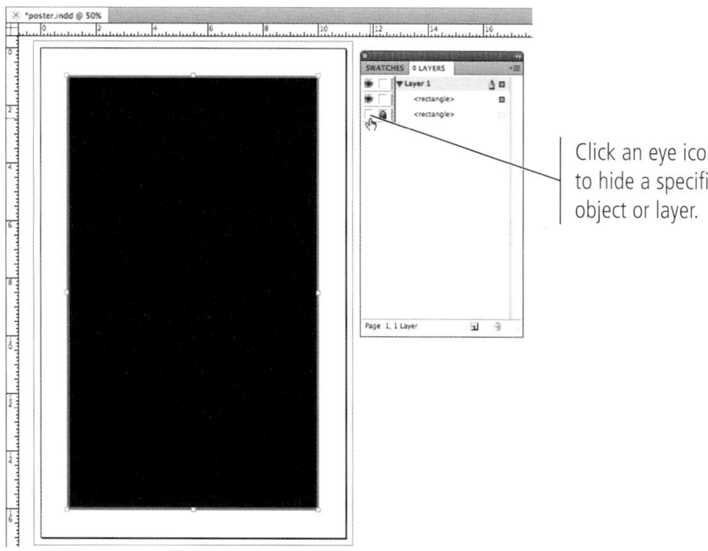

Click an eye icon
to hide a specific
object or layer.

10. **Save the file and continue to the next exercise.**

Define and Apply a Gradient

A **gradient**, also called a **blend**, can be used to create a smooth transition from one color to another. You can apply a gradient to any object using the Gradient panel, or you can save a gradient swatch if you plan to use it more than once.

The Gradient panel controls the type and position of applied gradients. You can apply either linear or radial gradients, change the angle of linear gradients, and change the color and location for individual stops along the gradient ramp.

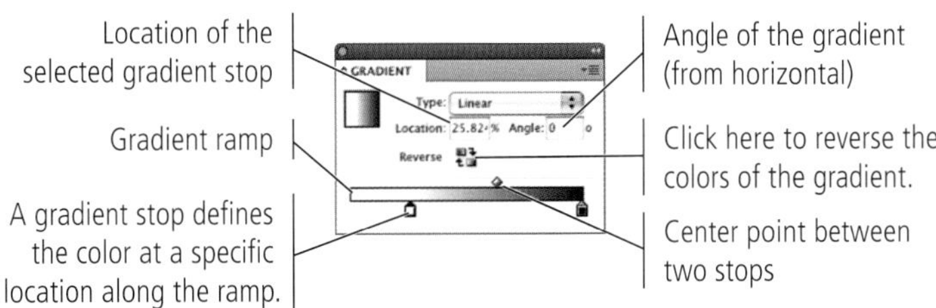

1. **With poster.indd open, click outside the area of the visible rectangle to deselect it.**

2. **Choose New Gradient Swatch from the Swatches panel Options menu.**

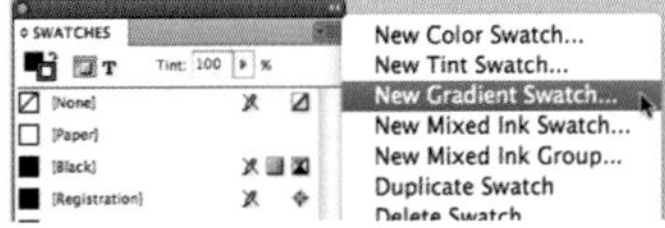

3. **Click the gradient stop on the left end of the gradient ramp to select it.**

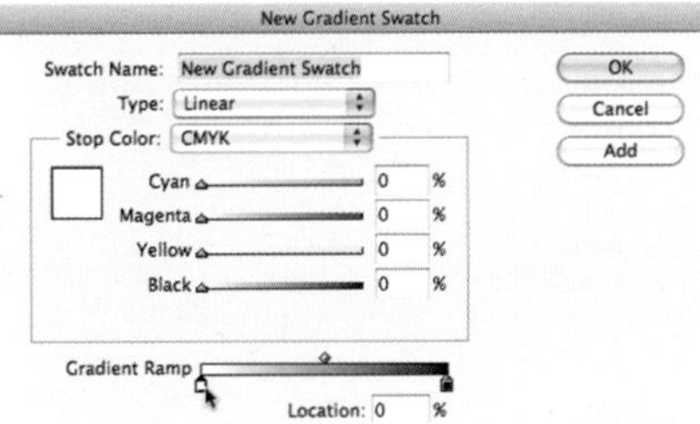

4. **Make sure Linear is selected in the Type menu, and then choose Swatches in the Stop Color menu.**

   You can define gradients using LAB values, CMYK percentages, RGB values, or existing color swatches.

5. **With the first stop selected, click the custom yellow CMYK swatch.**

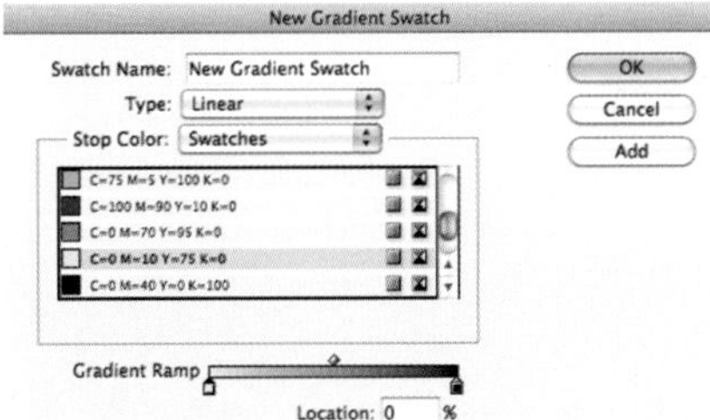

6. **Select the second gradient stop (on the right end of the ramp), and then click the custom orange swatch.**

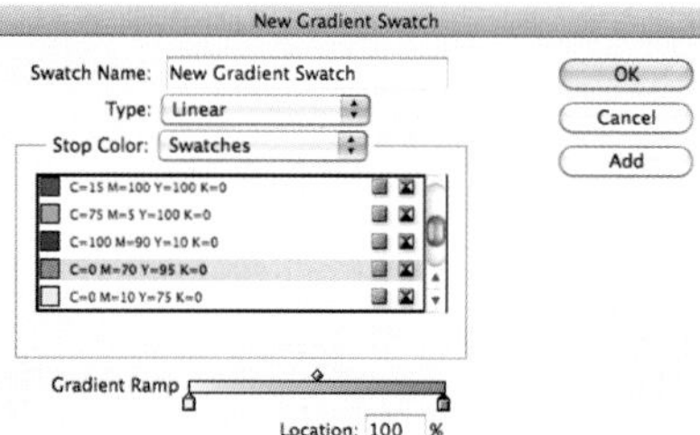

7. **Type** `Yellow to Orange` **in the Swatch Name field and then click OK.**

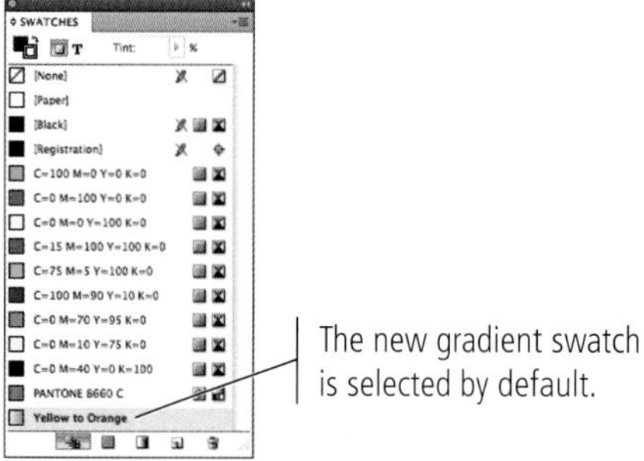

The new gradient swatch is selected by default.

8. **Using the Selection tool, click the visible rectangle on the page to select it.**

9. **Make the Fill icon active in the Swatches panel, and then click the Yellow to Orange gradient swatch.**

   It is important to remember but easy to forget: make sure the correct attribute (fill or stroke) is active when you change a color.

The fill icon is active.

10. **Make the Stroke icon active in the Swatches panel, and then click the Yellow to Orange gradient swatch.**

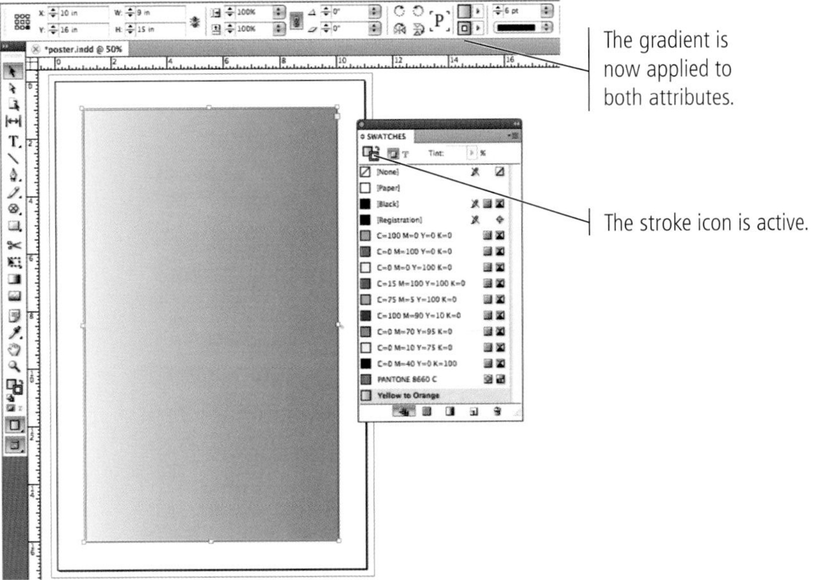

The gradient is now applied to both attributes.
The stroke icon is active.

11. **Save the file and continue to the next exercise.**

Modify Gradient Attributes

As you just saw, it is fairly easy to create and apply a gradient. Once the gradient is in place, you can also modify the specific attributes of a gradient, including its angle and the positioning of specific color stops along its length.

1. **With poster.indd open, make sure the gradient-filled rectangle is selected.**

2. **Using either the Tools or Swatches panel, click to activate the Fill icon.**

3. **Using the Gradient panel (Window>Color>Gradient), change the Angle field to 90° to rotate the gradient.**

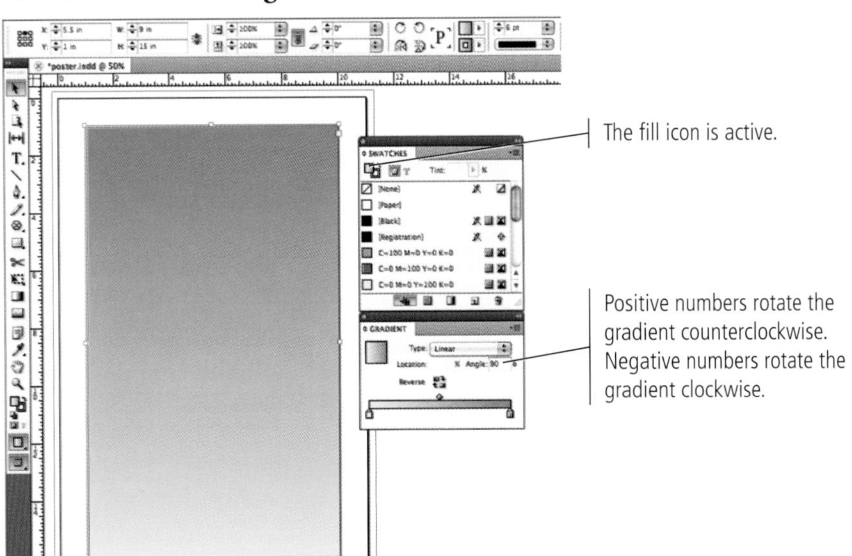

The fill icon is active.
Positive numbers rotate the gradient counterclockwise. Negative numbers rotate the gradient clockwise.

Note:

Remember, all panels can be accessed in the Window menu.

Note:

You can drag a swatch from the Swatches panel to the gradient ramp in the Gradient panel to add a new color stop, or to change the color of an existing stop.

4. **Using the Control panel, change the object height to 10″ based on the top-center reference point.**

   When you change the shape dimensions, the applied gradients are adjusted so the end stops still align to the edges of the object.

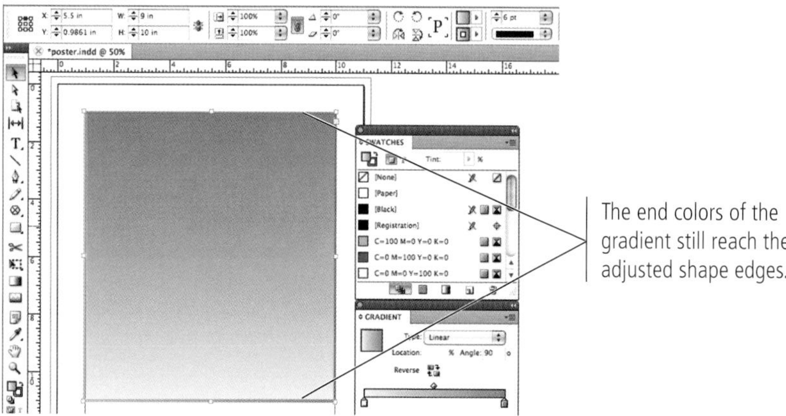

The end colors of the gradient still reach the adjusted shape edges.

5. **With the object still selected, make the Stroke icon active in the Swatches panel.**

   Remember that the attribute on top of the stack is the one you are currently changing. If the wrong attribute is on top of the stack, you will not get the results you are hoping for.

The Gradient Tools

INDESIGN FOUNDATIONS

Clicking a gradient swatch adds a gradient to the selected object, beginning at the left edge and ending at the right edge (for linear gradients), or beginning at the object's center and ending at the object's outermost edge (for radial gradients). When you drag with the Gradient tool, you define the length of the gradient without regard to the object you're filling.

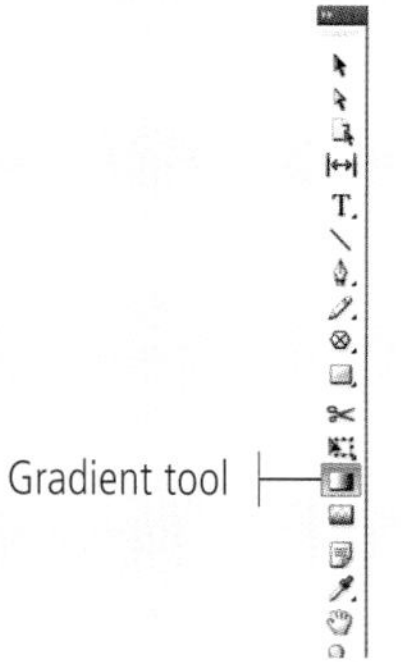

Gradient tool

This box is filled with a gradient that has green at the left end and purple at the right end.

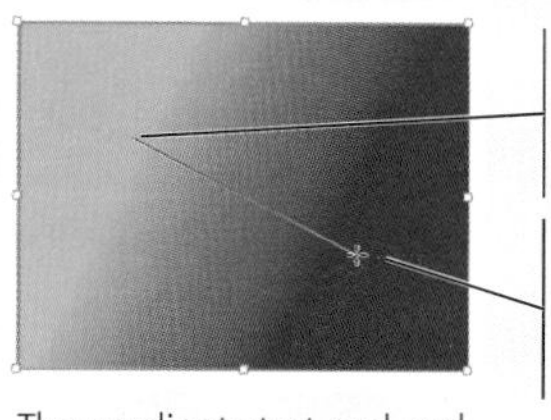

The gradient start and end colors now appear where we first clicked and where we stopped dragging.

We clicked and dragged from here to define the gradient starting point.

Dragging with the Gradient tool changes the length and angle of the gradient.

The Gradient Feather tool has a similar function but produces different results. Rather than creating a specific-colored gradient, the Gradient Feather tool applies a transparency gradient, blending the object from solid to transparent.

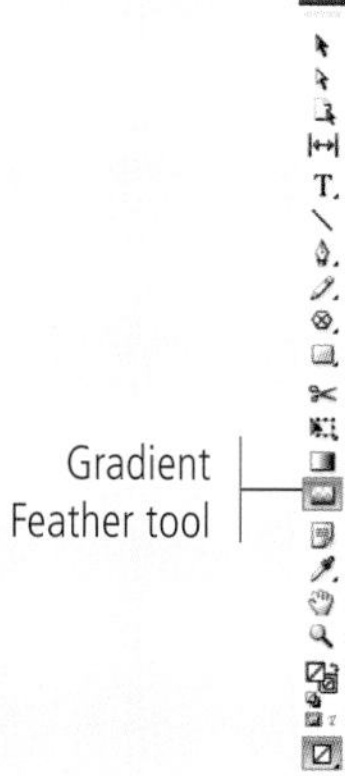

Gradient Feather tool

We placed this image over a blue-filled shape.

The resulting effect blends the image from solid to transparent, allowing the background object to show.

Dragging to here defines the end point of the gradient feather (the area that will be entirely transparent).

We clicked and dragged from here to define the starting point of the feather effect (the area that will be entirely solid).

6. **In the Gradient panel, change the gradient angle to –90° so the stroke goes from yellow at the top to orange at the bottom (the reverse of the fill).**

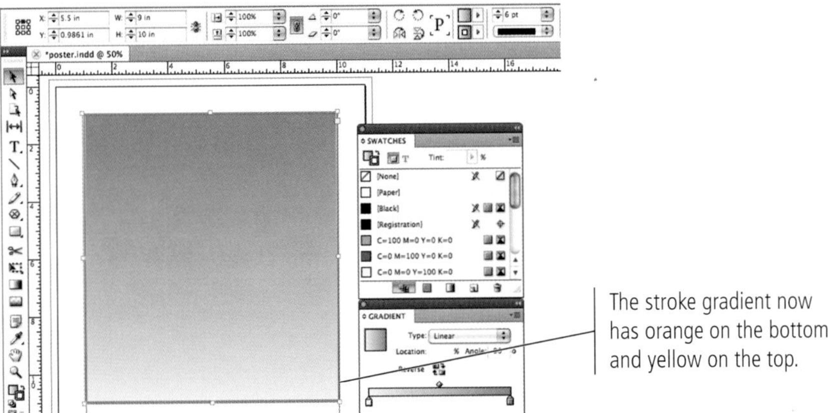

The stroke gradient now has orange on the bottom and yellow on the top.

7. **Click away from the rectangle to deselect it.**

8. **Use the Screen Mode button on the Tools panel or the Application/Menu bar to display the layout in Preview mode.**

   This option hides all guides and frame edges, which makes it easier to see the subtle effect created by the opposing gradients. (We also zoomed in to better show the result.)

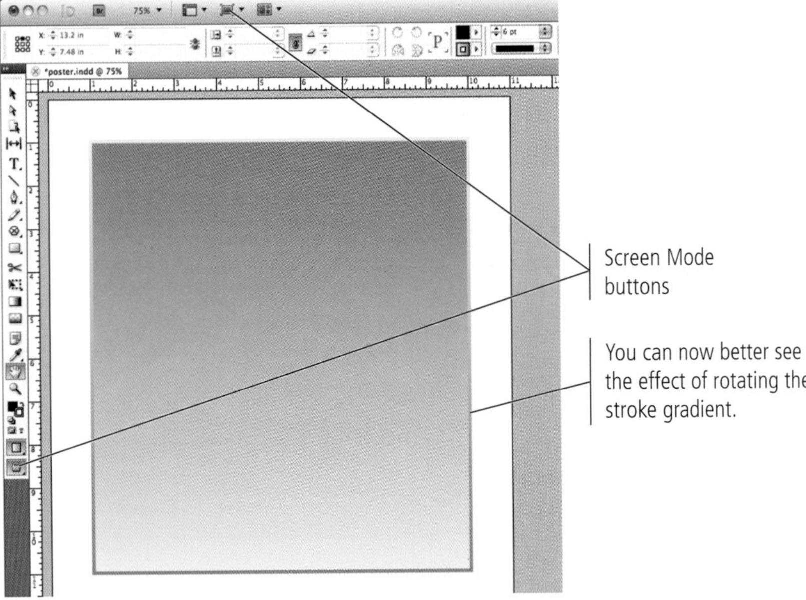

Screen Mode buttons
You can now better see the effect of rotating the stroke gradient.

9. **Choose Normal in the Screen Mode menu to restore the guides and frame edges on screen.**

10. **Save the file and continue to the next exercise.**

Create Visual Impact with Transparency

The image effects and transparency controls in InDesign provide options for adding dimension and depth, allowing unprecedented creative control directly in the page layout. You can change the transparency of any object (or individual object attributes), apply different blending modes so objects blend smoothly into underlying objects, and apply creative effects such as drop shadows and beveling.

Transparency and effects are controlled in the Effects panel. You can change these options for an entire object (fill and stroke), only the stroke, only the fill, the text (if you're working with a text frame), the graphic (if you're working with a graphics frame), or all objects in a group.

> ***Note:***
>
> *The Graphic option is only available when a placed graphic (within a frame) is selected. Group replaces Object in the list only when a group is selected with the Selection tool.*

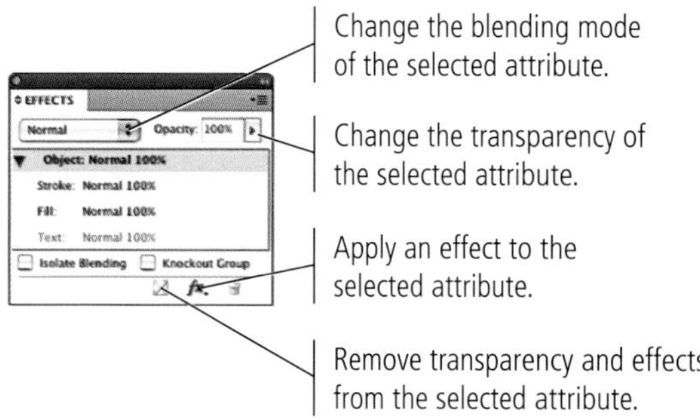
EFFECTS
Normal
Opacity: 100%
Object: Normal 100%
Stroke: Normal 100%
Fill: Normal 100%
Text: Normal 100%
Isolate Blending
Knockout Group
Change the blending mode of the selected attribute.
Change the transparency of the selected attribute.
Apply an effect to the selected attribute.
Remove transparency and effects from the selected attribute.

> ***Note:***
>
> *Effects applied to text apply to all text in the frame; you can't apply effects to individual characters.*

Technical Issues of Transparency

Because all of these features and options are related in some way to transparency, you should understand what transparency is and how it affects your output. **Transparency** is the degree to which light passes through an object so objects in the background are visible. In terms of page layout, transparency means being able to "see through" objects in the front of the stacking order to objects lower in the stacking order.

Because of the way printing works, applying transparency in print graphic design is a bit of a contradiction. Commercial printing is, by definition, accomplished by overlapping a mixture of (usually) four semi-transparent inks in different percentages to reproduce a range of colors (the printable gamut). In that sense, all print graphic design requires transparency.

> ***Note:***
>
> *Transparency is essentially the inverse of opacity. If an object is 20% transparent, it is also 80% opaque.*

But *design* transparency refers to the objects on the page. The trouble is, when a halftone dot is printed, it's either there or it's not. There is no "50% opaque" setting on a printing press. This means that a transformation needs to take place behind the scenes, translating what we create on screen into what a printing press produces.

When transparent objects are output, overlapping areas of transparent elements are actually broken into individual elements (where necessary) to produce the best possible results. Ink values in the overlap areas are calculated by the application, based on the capabilities of the mechanical printing process; the software converts what we create on screen into the elements that are necessary to print.

When you get to the final stage of this project, you'll learn how to preview and control the output process for transparent objects.

1. **In the open poster.indd file, use the Selection tool to select the gradient-filled rectangle.**

2. **Choose Object>Content>Graphic.**

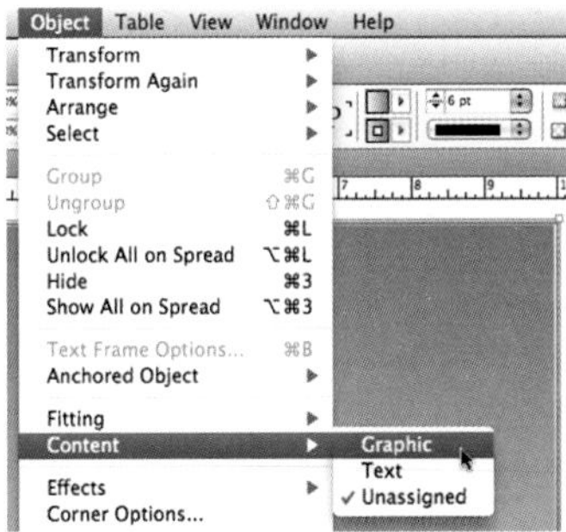

Note:

You can also Control/right-click an object and change its content type in the contextual menu.

When you create a frame with one of the basic shape tools, it is considered "unassigned" because it is neither a text frame nor a graphics frame. You can convert any type of frame (graphics, text, or unassigned) to another type using this menu.

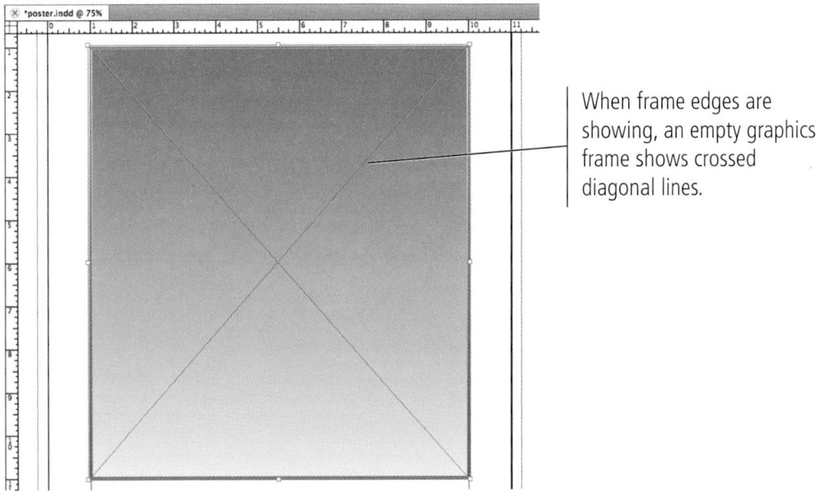

When frame edges are showing, an empty graphics frame shows crossed diagonal lines.

3. **With the gradient-filled rectangle still selected on the page, choose File>Place. Navigate to the WIP>Jazz folder and choose sunset.jpg.**

4. **Check the Replace Selected Item option at the bottom of the dialog box.**

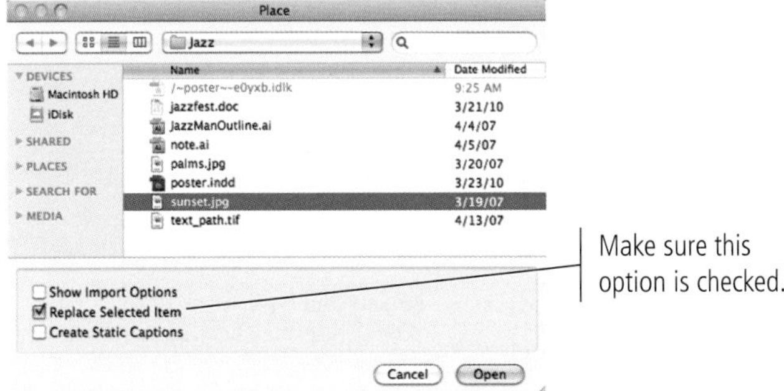

Make sure this option is checked.

5. **Click Open to place the image into the frame.**

   Because you chose the Replace Selected Item option, the image is automatically placed in the selected frame. If another image had already been placed in the frame, the sunset image would replace the existing image (hence the name of the command).

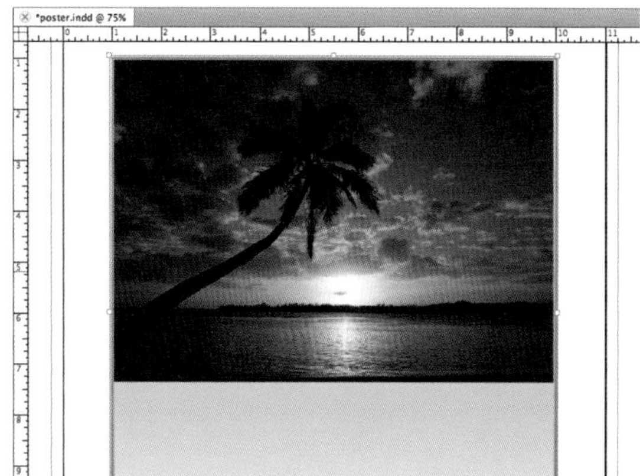

> *Note:*
>
> *If Replace Selected Item was not checked in the Place dialog box, the image would be loaded into the cursor.*

6. **Open the Effects panel (Window>Effects).**

   When you select an object with the Selection tool, you can apply various effects to the entire object, or to the object fill only, the object stroke only, or any text within the object.

7. **Move the Selection tool cursor over the image frame to reveal the Content Indicator.**

The Selection tool is active.
The frame is selected.
Content Indicator
The Effects panel has options for various attributes of the frame.

> *Note:*
>
> *Effects in InDesign are non-destructive, which means they have no effect on the physical file data.*

8. **Click the Content Indicator icon to access the image in the frame.**

   When you select only the placed image, you can apply effects to the image itself, independent of the frame.

The Selection tool is still active.
The image is selected.
The Effects panel has options for the graphic in the frame.

9. **With the Graphic option selected in the Effects panel, choose the Screen option in the Blending Mode menu.**

The image now blends into the gradient background, but there is still a hard line marking the bottom edge of the placed image.

The Screen blending mode merges the image colors into the object's gradient fill.

Blending Modes

INDESIGN FOUNDATIONS

Blending modes control how colors in an object interact with colors in underlying objects. Objects are set to Normal by default, which simply overlays the top object's color onto underlying objects. (If the top object is entirely opaque, there is no effect on underlying objects.)

- **Multiply** multiplies (hence the name) the base color by the blend color, resulting in a darker color. Multiplying any color with black produces black; multiplying any color with white leaves the color unchanged.
- **Screen** is basically the inverse of Multiply, always returning a lighter color. Screening with black has no effect; screening with white produces white.
- **Overlay** multiplies or screens the blend color to preserve the original lightness or darkness of the base.
- **Soft Light** darkens or lightens base colors depending on the blend color. Blend colors lighter than 50% lighten the base color (as if dodged); blend colors darker than 50% darken the base color (as if burned).
- **Hard Light** combines the Multiply and Screen modes. Blend colors darker than 50% are multiplied, and blend colors lighter than 50% are screened.
- **Color Dodge** brightens the base color. Blend colors lighter than 50% significantly increase brightness; blending with black has no effect.
- **Color Burn** darkens the base color by increasing the contrast. Blend colors darker than 50% significantly darken the base color by increasing saturation and reducing brightness; blending with white has no effect.
- **Darken** returns the darker of the blend or base color. Base pixels that are lighter than the blend color are replaced; base pixels that are darker than the blend color do not change.
- **Lighten** returns whichever is the lighter color (base or blend). Base pixels that are darker than the blend color are replaced; base pixels that are lighter than the blend color do not change.
- **Difference*** inverts base color values according to the brightness value in the blend layer. Lower brightness values in the blend layer have less of an effect on the result; blending with black has no effect.
- **Exclusion*** is similar to Difference, except that midtone values in the base color are completely desaturated.
- **Hue*** results in a color with the luminance and saturation of the base color and the hue of the blend color.
- **Saturation*** results in a color with the luminance and hue of the base and the saturation of the blend color.
- **Color*** results in a color with the luminance of the base color and the hue and saturation of the blend color.
- **Luminosity*** results in a color with the hue and saturation of the base color and the luminance of the blend color (basically the opposite of the Color mode

**Avoid applying the Difference, Exclusion, Hue, Saturation, Color, and Luminosity modes to objects with spot colors. It c create unpredictable results (at best) when the file is separated for commercial print requirements.*

10. Click the *fx* button at the bottom of the Effects panel, and choose Gradient Feather.

The Effects dialog box opens to show the Gradient Feather options.

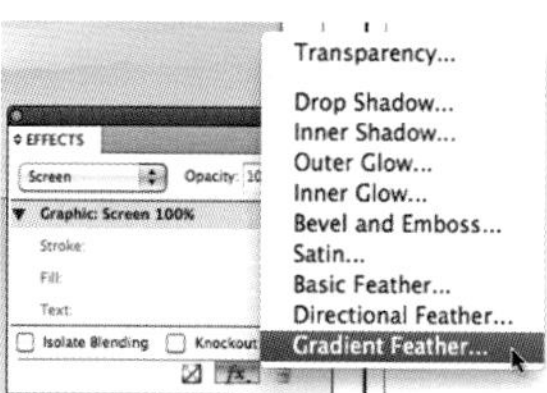

Note:

If you use the Gradient Feather tool, the Gradient Feather effect is automatically applied.

11. In the Effects dialog box, click the Preview check box so you can preview your results before accepting/applying them.

The Gradient Feather effect creates a transparency gradient so an object blends into underlying objects instead of leaving a hard edge. The effect is created using a gradient that shifts from 100% opacity to 0% opacity. The levels of opacity in the gradient determine the opacity of the object to which the feather effect is applied.

12. Click in the Angle circle and drag until the field shows –90° (the line should point straight down).

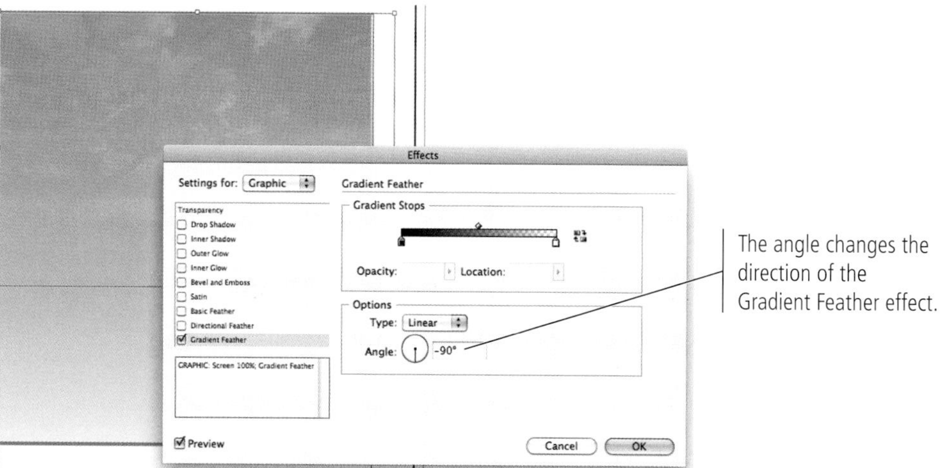

The angle changes the direction of the Gradient Feather effect.

13. Drag the left gradient stop until the Location field shows 75%.

By extending the solid black part of the gradient to the 75% location, the top three-quarters of the affected image remain entirely visible; only the bottom quarter of the image blends into the background.

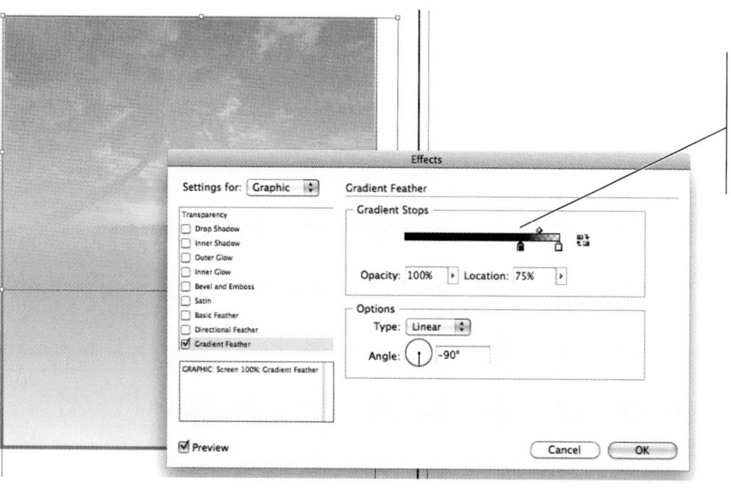

Moving the first stop extends the black area of the gradient, which extends the part of the image that is entirely opaque.

14. **Click OK to close the Effects dialog box and apply your choices.**

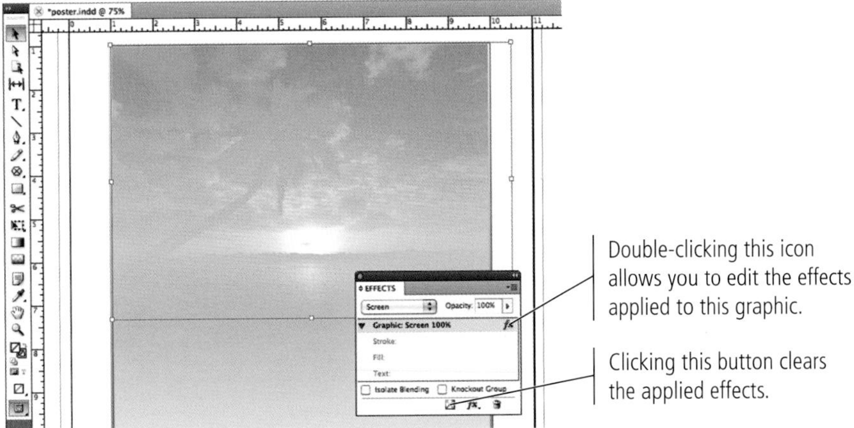

Double-clicking this icon allows you to edit the effects applied to this graphic.
Clicking this button clears the applied effects.

15. **Save the file and continue to the next exercise.**

Create an Irregular Graphics Frame

You can create basic graphics frames using the Rectangle, Ellipse, and Polygon Frame tools. You can also create a Bézier shape with the Pen tool, and then convert the shape to a graphics frame — which means you can create a frame in virtually any shape. However, it requires a lot of work to trace complex graphics with the Pen tool; fortunately, you can use other options to create complex frames from objects in placed graphics.

1. **In the open poster.indd file, choose File>Place. Navigate to the file JazzManOutline.ai in the WIP>Jazz folder.**

2. **Make sure the Replace Selected Item option is not selected, then click Open.**

   If the Replace Selected Item option were turned on, the new image would replace the sunset image from the previous exercise (if the gradient rectangle was still selected) instead of being loaded into the cursor.

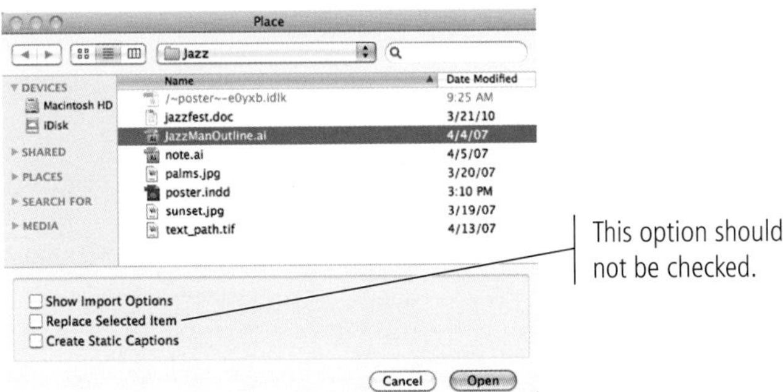

This option should not be checked.

Applying Effects

InDesign offers nine different effects options, which you can apply individually or in combinations to create unique flat and dimensional effects for any object. The effects can be applied by clicking the *fx* button at the bottom of the Effects panel, by clicking the *fx* button in the Control panel, or by choosing from the Object>Effects menu.

Drop Shadow and Inner Shadow

Drop Shadow adds a shadow behind the object. **Inner Shadow** adds a shadow inside the edges of the object. For both types, you can define the blending mode, color, opacity, angle, distance, offset, and size of the shadow.

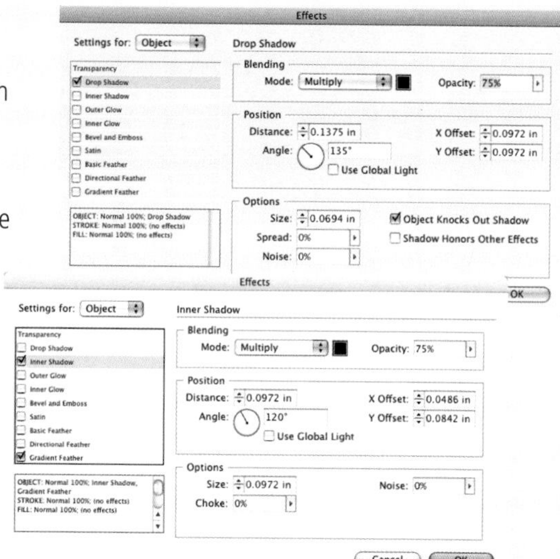

- **Distance** is the overall offset of the shadow, or how far away the shadow will be from the original object. The Offset fields allow you to define different horizontal and vertical distances.
- **Size** is the blur amount applied to the shadow.
- **Spread** (for Drop Shadows) is the percentage that the shadow expands beyond the original object.
- **Choke** (for Inner Shadows) is the percentage that the shadow shrinks into the original object.
- **Noise** controls the amount of random pixels added to the effect.

The **Object Knocks Out Shadow** option for drop shadows allows you to knock out (remove) or maintain the shadow underneath the object area. This option is particularly important if the original object is semi-transparent above its shadow.

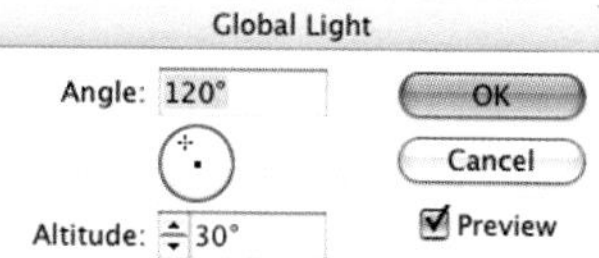

The **Use Global Light** check box is available for the Drop Shadow, Inner Shadow, and Bevel and Emboss effects. When this option is checked, the style is linked to the "master" light source angle for the entire file. Changing the global light setting affects any linked shadow or bevel effect applied to any object in the entire file. (If Use Global Light is checked for an effect, changing the angle for that effect also changes the Global Light angle. You can also change the Global Light settings by choosing Object>Effects>Global Light.)

Outer Glow and Inner Glow

Outer Glow and **Inner Glow** add glow effects to the outside and inside edges (respectively) of the original object. For either kind of glow, you can define the blending mode, opacity, noise, and size values.

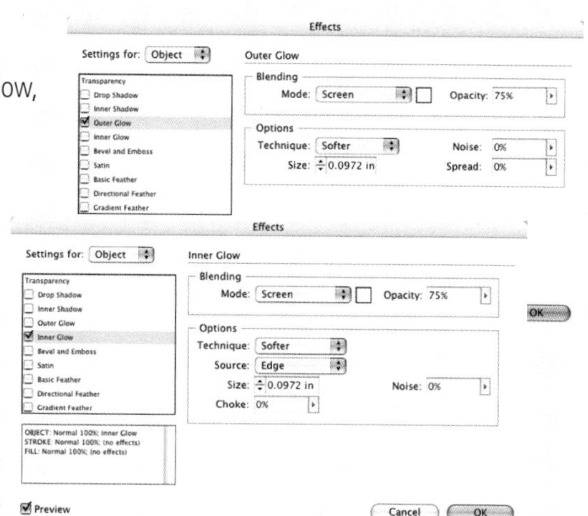

- For either Outer or Inner glows, you can define the **Technique** as Precise or Softer. **Precise** creates a glow at a specific distance; **Softer** creates a blurred glow and does not preserve detail as well as Precise.
- For Inner Glows, you can also define the **Source** of the glow (Center or Edge). **Center** applies a glow starting from the center of the object; **Edge** applies the glow starting from the inside edges of the object.
- The **Spread** and **Choke** sliders affect the percentages of the glow effects.

Applying Effects (continued)

Bevel and Emboss

This effect has five variations or styles:

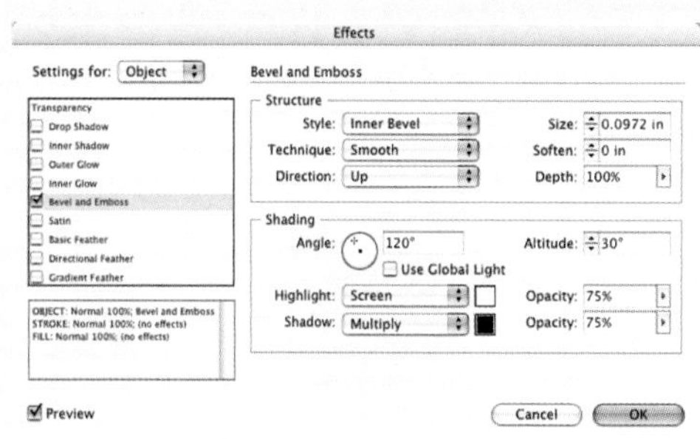

- **Inner Bevel** creates a bevel on the inside edges of the object.
- **Outer Bevel** creates a bevel on the outside edges of the object.
- **Emboss** creates the effect of embossing the object against the underlying layers.
- **Pillow Emboss** creates the effect of stamping the edges of the object into the underlying layers.

Any of these styles can be applied as **Smooth** (blurs the edges of the effect), **Chisel Hard** (creates a distinct edge to the effect), or **Chisel Soft** (creates a distinct, but slightly blurred edge to the effect).

You can change the **Direction** of the bevel effect. **Up** creates the appearance of the layer coming out of the image; **Down** creates the appearance of something stamped into the image. The **Size** field makes the effect smaller or larger, and the **Soften** option blurs the edges of the effect. **Depth** increases or decreases the three-dimensional effect of the bevel.

In the **Shading** area, you can control the light source's **Angle** and **Altitude** (think of how shadows differ as the sun moves across the sky). Finally, you can change the blending mode, opacity, and color of both highlights and shadows created with the Bevel or Emboss effect.

Satin

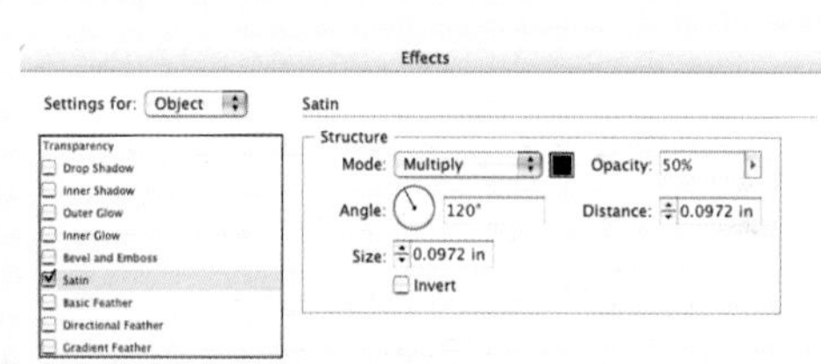

Satin applies interior shading to create a satiny appearance. You can change the blending mode, color, and opacity of the effect, as well as the angle, distance, and size.

Basic Feather, Directional Feather, and Gradient Feather

These three effects soften the edges of an object:

- **Basic Feather** equally fades all edges of the selected object (or attribute) by a specific width. The **Choke** option determines how much of the softened edge is opaque (high settings increase opacity and low settings decrease opacity). **Corners** can be **Sharp** (following the outer edge of the shape), **Rounded** (corners are rounded according to the Feather Width), or **Diffused** (fades from opaque to transparent). **Noise** adds random pixels to the softened area.
- **Directional Feather** allows you to apply different feather widths to individual edges of an object. The **Shape** option defines the object's original shape (First Edge Only, Leading Edges, or All Edges). The **Angle** field allows you to rotate the feathering effect; if you use any angle other than a 90° increment (i.e., 90, 180, 270, 360), the feathering will be skewed.
- **Gradient Feather** creates a transparency gradient that blends from solid to transparent. This effect underlies the Gradient Feather tool. You can move the start and end stops to different locations along the ramp, or add stops to define specific transparencies at specific locations. You can also choose from a Linear or Radial Gradient Feather effect, and change the angle of a Linear Gradient Feather effect.

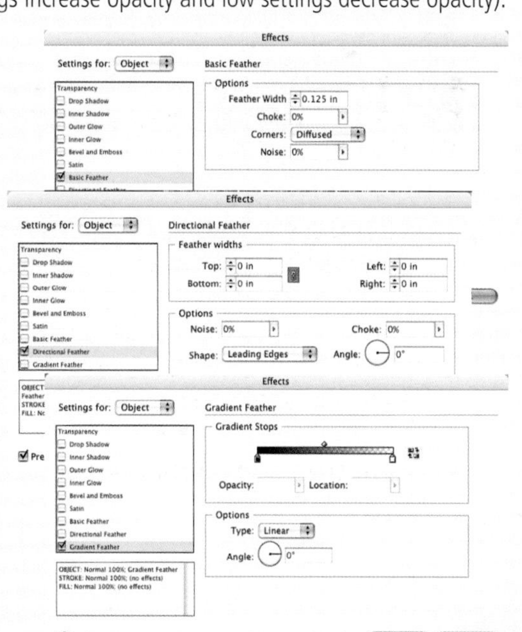

3. **Click the loaded cursor anywhere on the page to place the graphic. Using the Control panel, position the bottom-left corner of the resulting frame at X: 1″, Y: 11″.**

Use the bottom-left reference point to position the graphics frame.

4. **Using the Selection tool, click the Content Indicator icon to access the image inside the frame. Choose Object>Clipping Path>Options.**

A **clipping path** is a hard-edged outline that masks an image. Areas inside the path are visible; areas outside the path are hidden.

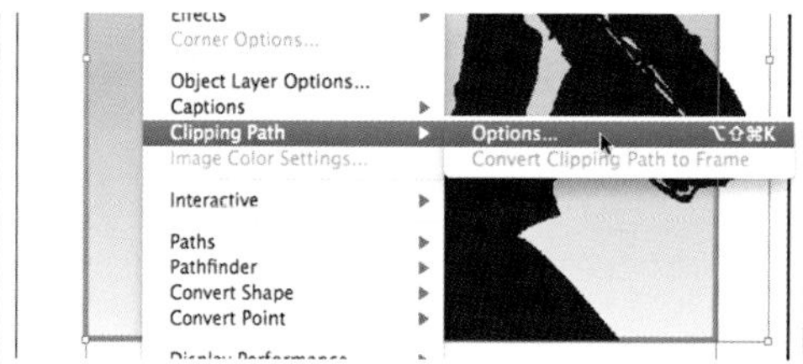

5. **In the resulting dialog box, choose Detect Edges in the Type menu.**

InDesign can access Alpha channels and clipping paths that are saved in an image, or you can create a clipping path based on the image content. Because this graphic is a vector graphic with well-defined edges filled with a solid color, InDesign can create a very precise clipping path based on the information in the file.

Clipping Path Options

INDESIGN FOUNDATIONS

Threshold specifies the darkest pixel value that will define the resulting clipping path. In this exercise, the placed image is filled with solid black, so you can set a very high Tolerance value to refine the clipping path. In images with greater tone variation (such as a photograph), increasing the Tolerance value removes lighter areas from the clipped area.

Tolerance specifies how similar a pixel must be to the Threshold value before it is hidden by the clipping path. Increasing the Tolerance value results in fewer points along the clipping path, generating a smoother path. Lowering the Tolerance value results in more anchor points and a potentially rougher path.

Inset Frame shrinks the clipping path by a specific number of pixels. You can also enter a negative value to enlarge the clipping path.

Invert reverses the clipping path, making hidden areas visible and vice versa.

Include Inside Edges creates a compound clipping path, removing inner areas of the object if they are within the Threshold and Tolerance ranges.

Restrict to Frame creates a clipping path that stops at the visible edge of the graphic. You can include the entire object — including areas beyond the frame edges — by unchecking this option.

Use High Resolution Image generates the clipping path based on the actual file data instead of the preview image.

6. **Check the Include Inside Edges option.**

   When this option is not checked, InDesign generates a clipping path based only on the outside edges of the image. The Include Inside Edges option generates a compound clipping path that removes holes in the middle of the outside path.

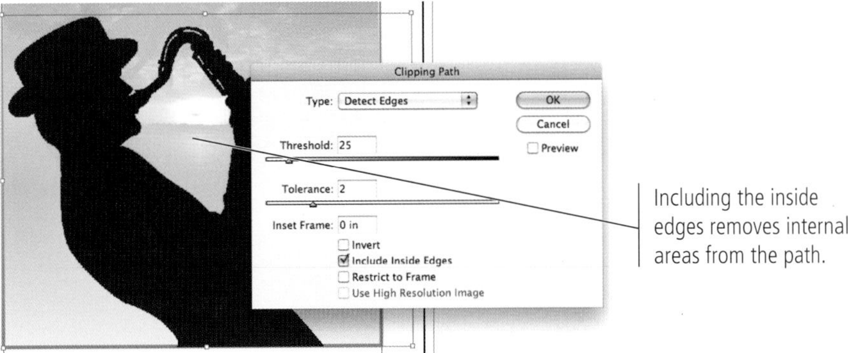

Including the inside edges removes internal areas from the path.

7. **Click OK to close the dialog box and create the clipping path.**

8. **Choose Object>Clipping Path>Convert Clipping Path to Frame.**

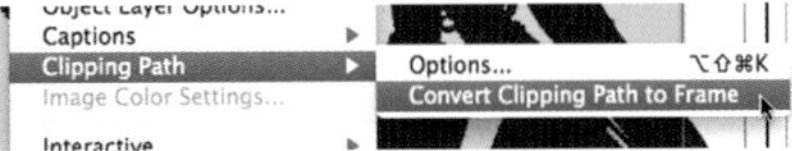

9. **With the frame content still selected, press Delete/Backspace to delete the placed file but leave the frame you created.**

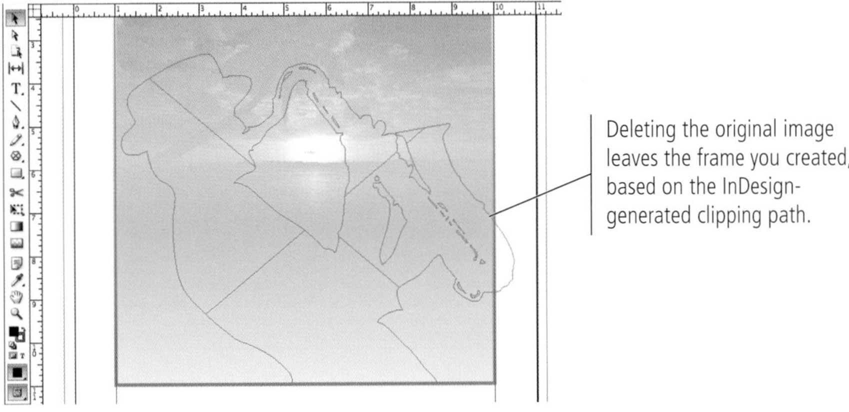

Deleting the original image leaves the frame you created, based on the InDesign-generated clipping path.

10. **Choose File>Place and navigate to palms.jpg in the WIP>Jazz folder. Make sure the Replace Selected Item option is not checked, and click Open. Click inside the empty frame with the loaded cursor to place the image inside the frame.**

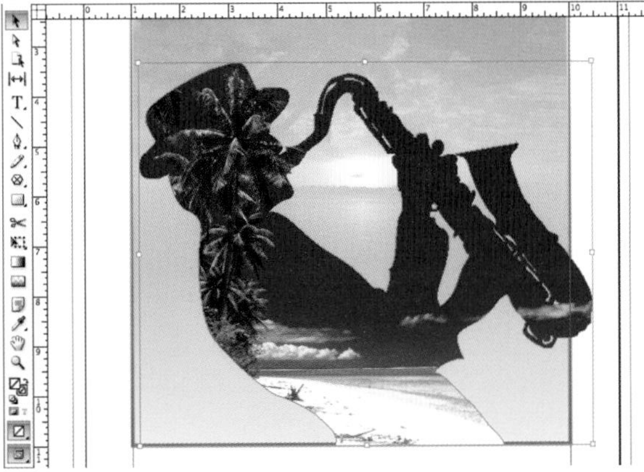

11. **Click the Content Indicator icon to access the placed image inside the frame.**

12. **Using the Control panel, change the top-left corner position of the placed image within the frame to X: –0.25″, Y: –0.25″.**

    When you select an image within a frame (using either the Content Indicator or the Direct Selection tool), the Control panel fields define the position of the graphic *relative to* its containing frame. Negative numbers move the graphic up and to the left from the frame edge; positive numbers move the graphic down and to the right.

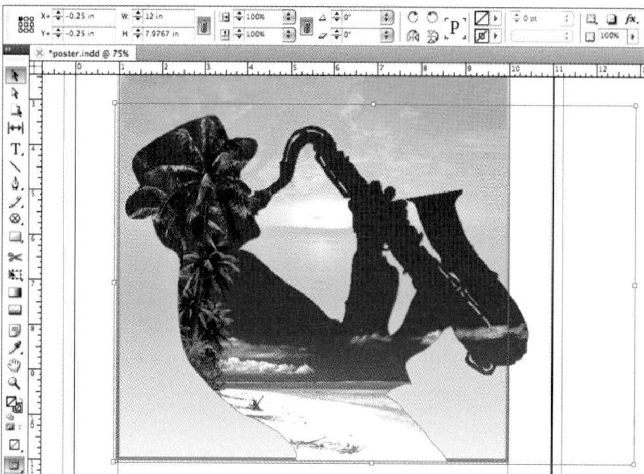

13. **Click the edge of the frame with the Selection tool to re-select the frame (not the placed graphic).**

14. **With the frame selected, press the Up Arrow key until the bottom edge of the frame approximately aligns to the top of the gradient-filled stroke (as in the following image).**

    You can use the Arrow keys to nudge the selected object based on the keyboard increment that is defined in the Units & Increments pane of the Preferences dialog box. The default distance is 0.0139″.

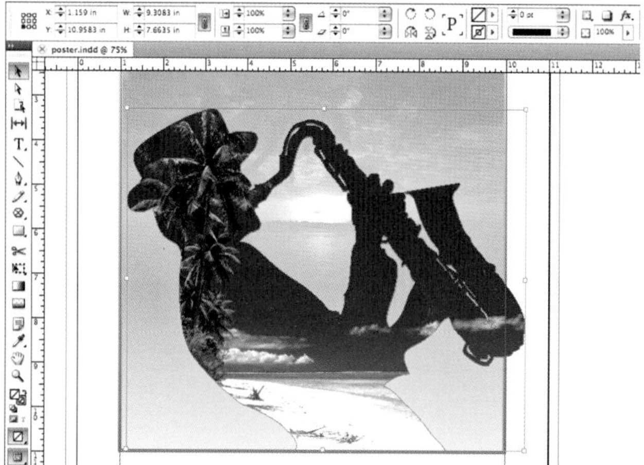

15. **Save the file and continue to the next stage of the project.**

Stage 2 Importing and Formatting Text

Placing text is one of the most critical functions of page-layout software, whether you create the text directly within InDesign or import it from an external file. InDesign provides all the tools you need to format text, from choosing a font to automatically creating hanging punctuation.

Control Text Threading

Some layouts require only a few bits of text, while others include numerous pages. Depending on how much text you have to work with, you might place all the layout text in a single frame, or you might cut and paste different pieces of a single story into separate text frames. In other cases, you might thread text across multiple frames — maintaining the text as a single story but allowing flexibility in frame size and position.

1. **With poster.indd open, zoom into the empty area below the placed images.**
2. **Use the Type tool to create a text frame that is 1″ high and 9″ wide (filling the width between the margin guides).**
3. **Select the frame with the Selection tool, and then use the Control panel to make sure the top edge of the text frame is positioned at Y: 11.25″.**

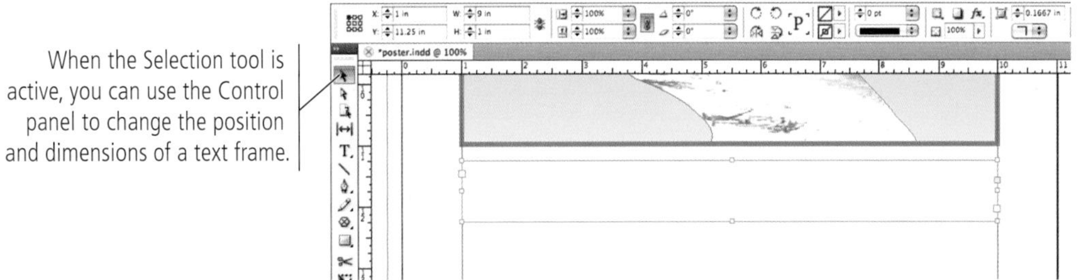

When the Selection tool is active, you can use the Control panel to change the position and dimensions of a text frame.

4. **Create three more text frames using the following parameters:**

Frame 2	**X: 1″**	**W: 3.2″**
	Y: 12.45″	**H: 3.55″**
Frame 3	**X: 5″**	**W: 5″**
	Y: 12.45″	**H: 3.55″**
Frame 4	**X: 1″**	**W: 9″**
	Y: 16.1″	**H: 0.5″**

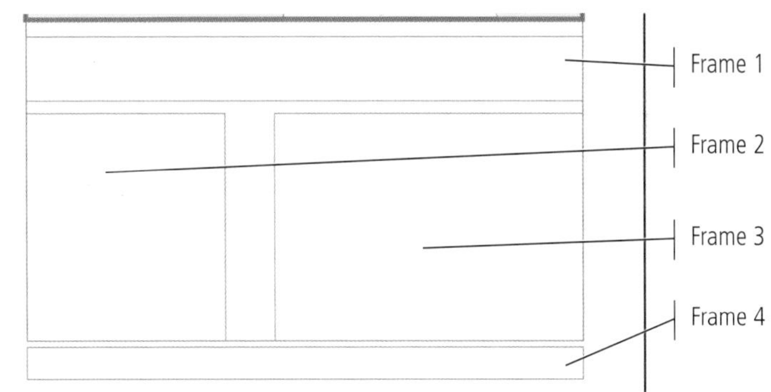

5. **Choose the Type tool, and click inside the first text frame to place the insertion point.**

   When you click in a text frame with the Type tool, you see a flashing insertion point where you click (or in the top-left corner if there is no text in the frame). This insertion point marks the location where text will appear when you type, paste, or import it into the document.

6. **Choose File>Place. Navigate to the file named jazzfest.doc in the WIP>Jazz folder.**

7. **Make sure the Replace Selected Item option is checked and then click Open.**

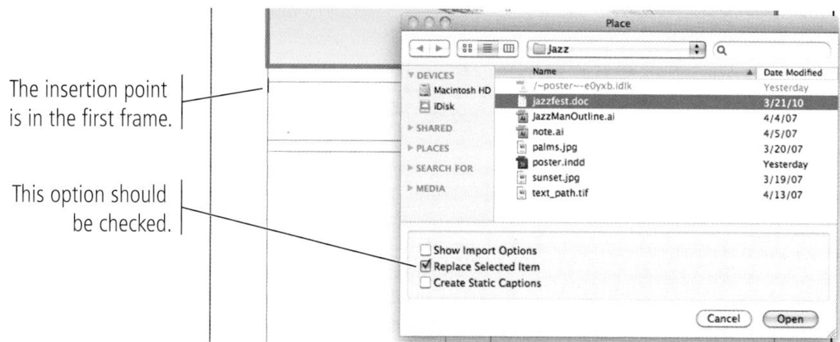

When Replace Selected Item is checked, the imported text file is automatically imported at the location of the insertion point. (If this option is not checked, the text is imported into the cursor.)

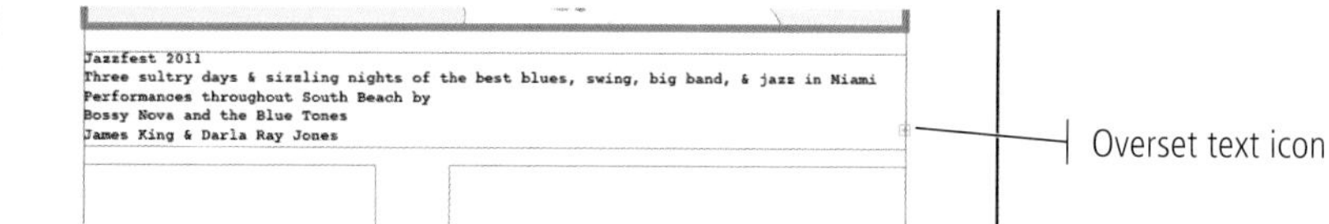

8. **Choose the Selection tool in the Tools panel.**

When a text frame is selected, you can see the In and Out ports that allow you to link one text frame to another. In this case, the Out port shows the **overset text icon**, indicating that the placed file has more text than can fit within the frame.

Note:

The overset text icon is visible even when the In and Out ports are not.

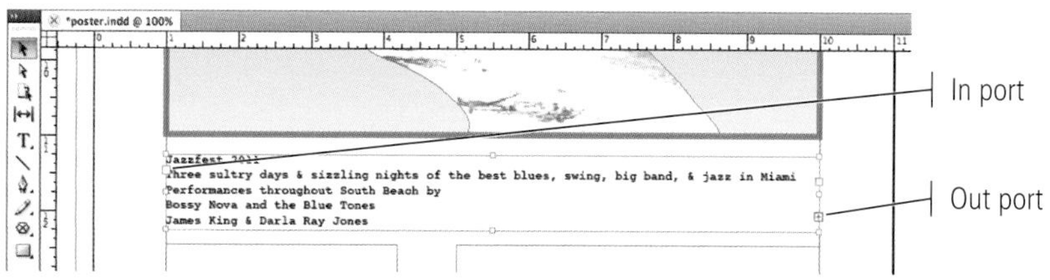

Note:

If you see the overset text icon (the red plus sign), the story does not fit in the current frame (or series of frames). You should always correct overset text.

9. **Click the Out port of the first text frame.**

Clicking the Out port loads the cursor with the rest of the text in the story. When the loaded cursor is over an existing frame, you can click to place the next part of the story in that frame. When the cursor is not over a frame, you can click and drag to create a frame that will contain the next part of the story. You can do this with the Selection tool (as you just did) or the Direct Selection tool.

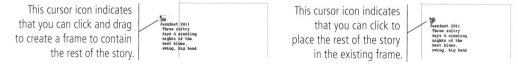

10. **Click inside the second frame to link it to the first frame.**

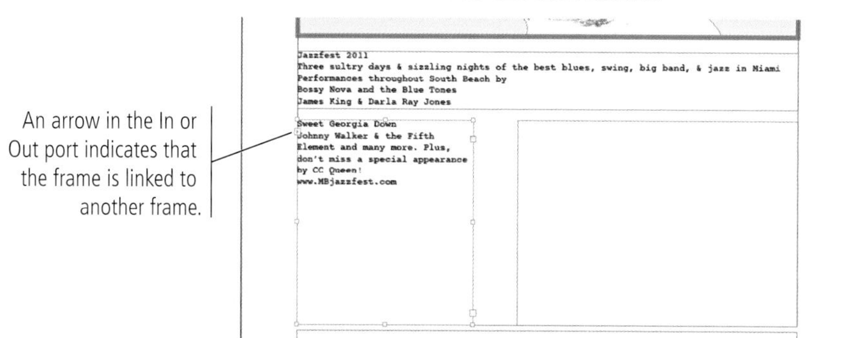

11. **Repeat this process to link from the second frame to the third, and then from the third frame to the fourth.**

You can define the thread of text frames even when there is no text to fill those frames. Simply use the Selection or Direct Selection tool to click the Out port of one frame, and then click anywhere within the next frame you want to add to the thread.

12. **Choose View>Extras>Show Text Threads.**

When this option is toggled on (and you are in Normal viewing mode), you can see all of the threading arrows whenever any of the text frames in the thread is selected.

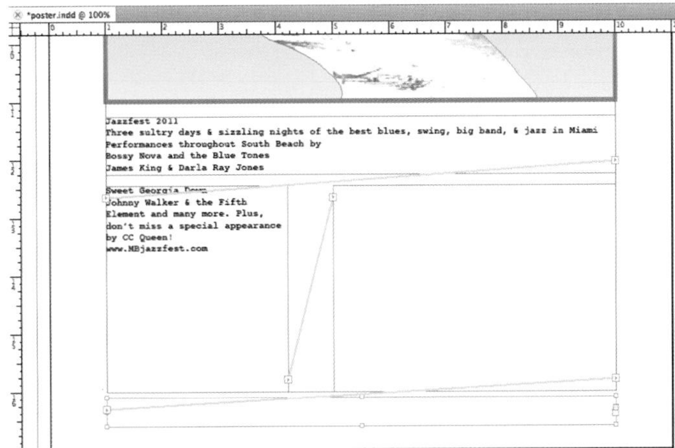

13. **Save the file and continue to the next exercise.**

Note:

You can also press Command/Control while the Type tool is active to click a text frame Out port and thread the frames.

Note:

When you load the cursor with overset text, the loaded cursor shows the text from the beginning of the story — even though the beginning is already placed. This is a quirk of the software; when you click with the loaded cursor, the text will flow into the new frame at the proper place in the story.

Define Manual Frame Breaks

When you thread text from one frame to another (or to multiple columns in the same frame), you often need to control exactly where a story breaks from frame to frame. InDesign includes a number of commands for breaking text in precise locations.

1. **In the open poster.indd file, use the Type tool to click at the end of the first line (after "Jazzfest 2011") to place the insertion point.**

As you complete the following exercises, feel free to zoom in as you think necessary to work with specific areas of your layout.

2. **Choose Type>Insert Break Character>Frame Break.**

InDesign provides several special break characters that allow you to control the flow of text from line to line, from column to column, and from frame to frame. The Frame Break character forces all following text into the next frame in the thread.

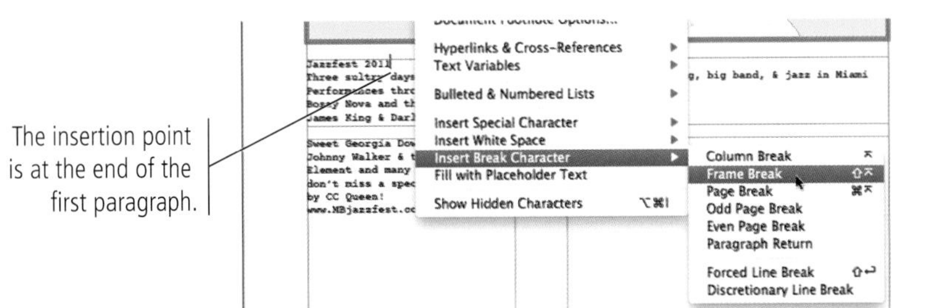

The insertion point is at the end of the first paragraph.

Note:

*Text that appears as a series of gray bars is called **greeked text**. By default, text smaller than 7 pt (at 100%) is greeked to improve screen redraw time. You can change the greeking threshold in the Display Performance pane of the Preferences dialog box.*

View percentage is part of the determination for greeking text; in other words, if your view percentage is 50%, 12-pt text appears as 6-pt text on screen, so it would be greeked using the default preferences.

3. **Choose Type>Show Hidden Characters.**

Each paragraph is separated by a paragraph return character (¶). A paragraph can consist of only one or two words or multiple lines. The important thing is to realize that a paragraph is technically any copy between two paragraph returns (or other break characters).

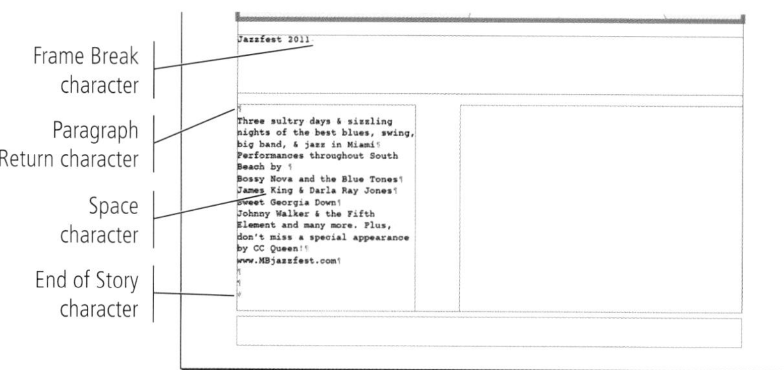

When you placed the Frame Break character in Step 2, everything following the insertion point was pushed to the next frame — including the paragraph return character that had been at the end of the first line. This created an "empty" paragraph that should be deleted.

4. **With the insertion point flashing at the beginning of the second frame, press Forward Delete to remove the extra paragraph return.**

If you don't have a Forward Delete key (if, for example, you're working on a laptop), move the insertion point to the beginning of the next line and press Delete/Backspace.

5. **With hidden characters visible, highlight the paragraph return character at the end of the first sentence in the second frame.**

6. **Choose Type>Insert Break Character>Frame Break to replace the highlighted paragraph return with a frame break character.**

When text is highlighted — including hidden formatting characters — anything you type, paste, or enter using a menu command replaces the highlighted text.

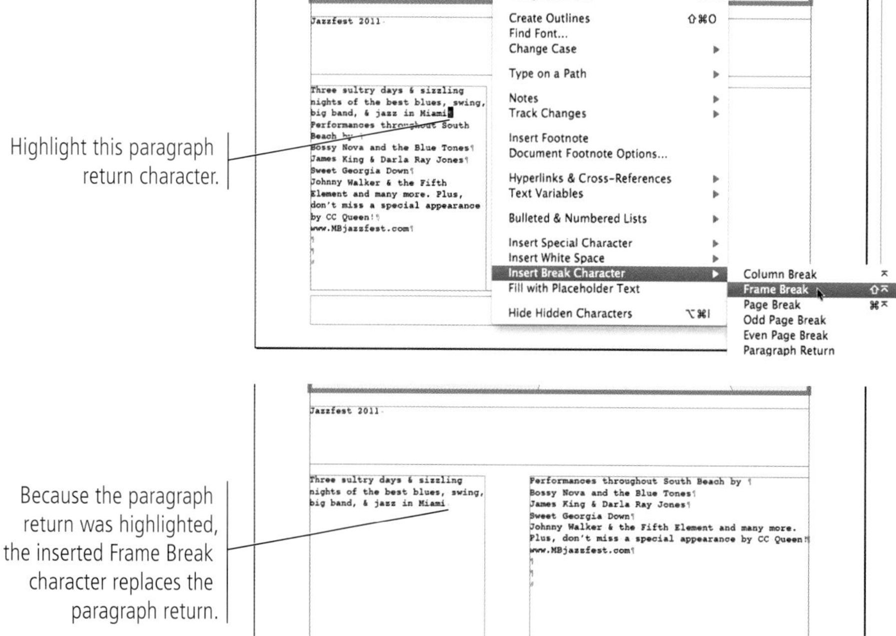

Note:

You can also toggle the visibility of hidden characters using the View Options button in the Application/Menu bar.

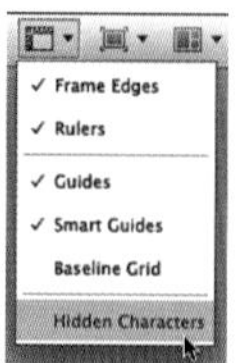

Note:

The Forward Delete key is the one directly below the Help key on most standard keyboards. If you are using a laptop, place the insertion point at the beginning of the first sentence in the second frame ("Three sultry days…") and press Delete/Backspace.

7. **Use the same technique to move only the last paragraph (the Web address) into the fourth text frame.**

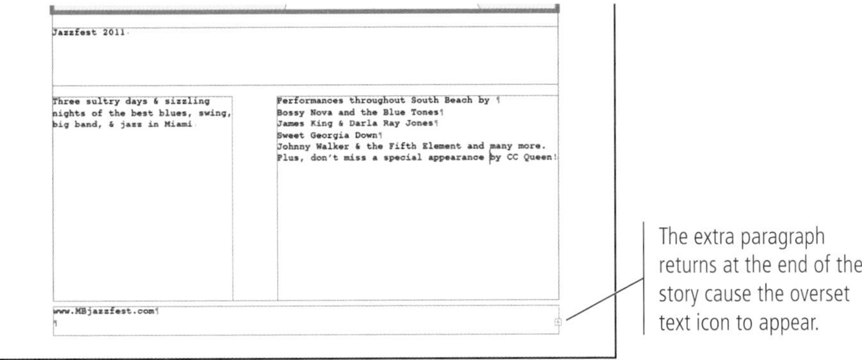

The extra paragraph returns at the end of the story cause the overset text icon to appear.

> *Note:*
>
> *Press Enter (numeric keypad) to add a Column Break.*
>
> *Press Shift-Enter (numeric keypad) to add a Frame Break.*
>
> *Press Command/Control-Enter (numeric keypad) to add a Page Break, which pushes all text to the first threaded frame on the next page.*
>
> *Press Shift-Return/Enter to add a Line Break, which starts a new line without starting a new paragraph.*

8. **Delete the extra paragraph return characters from the end of the story (after the Web address).**

   It is not uncommon to have multiple extra paragraph returns at the end of imported text. InDesign thinks there is still more text than will fit, even though the extra text is just more empty paragraphs. These serve no purpose and cause an overset text icon (and can cause other problems when master pages are involved), so you should delete them.

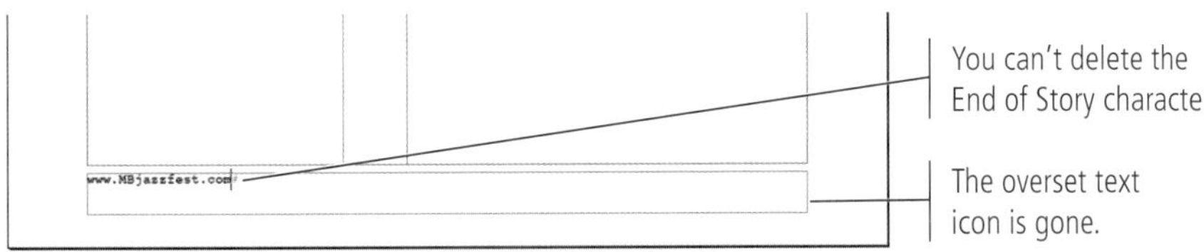

You can't delete the End of Story character.

The overset text icon is gone.

9. **Save the file and continue to the next exercise.**

Apply Character Formatting

Once text is in a frame, you can use character formatting attributes to determine the appearance of individual letters, such as the font and type size. These attributes can be controlled in the Character panel (Window>Type & Tables>Character) or the Control panel (depending on which options are visible in the Control panel).

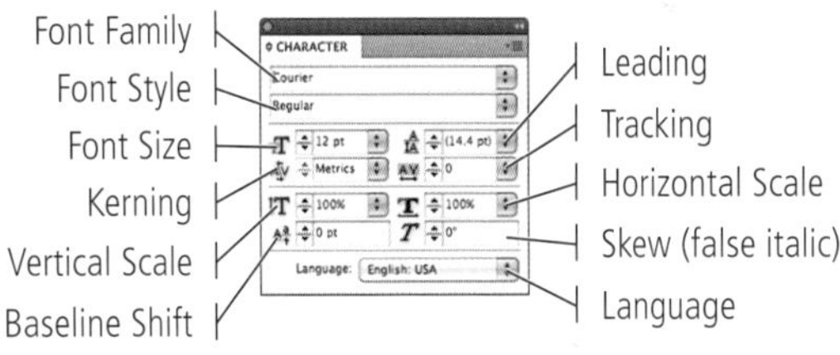

- A **font** contains all of the characters (**glyphs**) that make up a typeface, including upper- and lowercase letters, numbers, special characters, etc. (Fonts must be installed and activated on your computer to be accessible in InDesign.) The **font style** is a specific variation of the selected font, such as bold or condensed.
- **Size** is the height of a typeface measured in points.
- **Leading** is the distance from one baseline to the next. InDesign treats leading as a character attribute, even though leading controls the space between lines of an individual paragraph. (Space between paragraphs is controlled using the Space Before/After options in the Paragraph panel.) To change leading for an entire paragraph, you must first select the entire paragraph. This approach means you can change the leading for a single line of a paragraph by selecting any character(s) in that line; however, changing the leading for any character in a line applies the same change to the entire line that contains those characters.

> *Note:*
>
> *You can change th behavior by ch the Apply I Entire P in th P*

- **Vertical Scale** and **Horizontal Scale** artificially stretch or contract the selected characters. This type of scaling is a quick way of achieving condensed or expanded type if those variations of a font don't exist. Type that has been artificially scaled in this fashion tends to look bad because the scaling destroys the type's metrics; if possible, you should always use a condensed or expanded version of a typeface before resorting to horizontal or vertical scaling.
- **Kerning** increases or decreases the space between pairs of letters. Kerning is used in cases where particular letters in specific fonts need to be manually adjusted to eliminate a too-tight or too-spread-out appearance; manual kerning is usually necessary in headlines or other large type. (Many commercial fonts have built-in kerning pairs, so you won't need to apply too much hands-on intervention with kerning. InDesign defaults to use the kerning values stored in the font metrics.)

Note:

Tracking and kerning are applied in thousandths of an ***em*** *(an em is technically defined as width that equals the type size).*

- **Tracking**, also known as "range kerning," refers to the overall tightness or looseness across a range of characters.
- **Baseline Shift** moves the selected type above or below the baseline by a specific number of points. Positive numbers move the characters up; negative values move the text down.
- **Skew** artificially slants the selected text, creating a false italic appearance. This option distorts the look of the type and should be used sparingly (if ever).

In addition to the options in the basic Character panel, several styling options are also available in the panel Options menu.

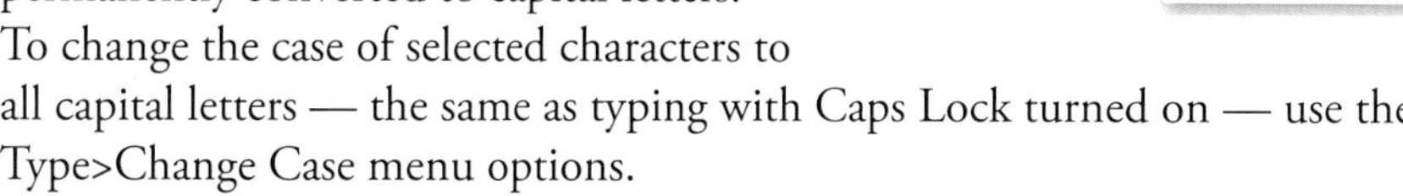

- **All Caps** changes all the characters to capital letters. This option only changes the appearance of the characters; they are not permanently converted to capital letters. To change the case of selected characters to all capital letters — the same as typing with Caps Lock turned on — use the Type>Change Case menu options.
- **Small Caps** artificially reduces the point size of a regular capital letter to a set percentage of that point size. If the font is an Open Type font that contains true small caps, InDesign uses the true small caps.
- **Superscript** and **Subscript** artificially reduce the selected character(s) to a specific percentage of the point size; these options raise (for superscript) or lower (for subscript) the character from the baseline to a position that is a certain percentage of the leading. (The size and position of Superscript, Subscript, and Small Caps are controlled in the Advanced Type Preferences dialog box.)
- **Underline** places a line below the selected characters.
- **Strikethrough** places a line through the middle of selected characters.
- **Ligatures** are substitutes for certain pairs of letters, most commonly fi, fl, ff, ffi, and ffl. (Other pairs such as ct and st are common for historical typesetting, and ae and oe are used in some non-English-language typesetting.)

Note:

Choosing Underline Options or Strikethrough Options in the Character panel Options menu allows you to change the weight, offset, style, and color of the line for those styles.

1. **With poster.indd open, choose the Type tool in the Tools panel. Triple-click the first line of text in the story to select it.**

   Character formatting options apply only to selected characters.

2. **In the Character panel (Window>Type & Tables>Character), highlight the existing font name and type ATC M. Press Return/Enter to apply the new font.**

   As you type, InDesign automatically scrolls to the first font that matches what you type. In this case, the software finds the ATC Maple font.

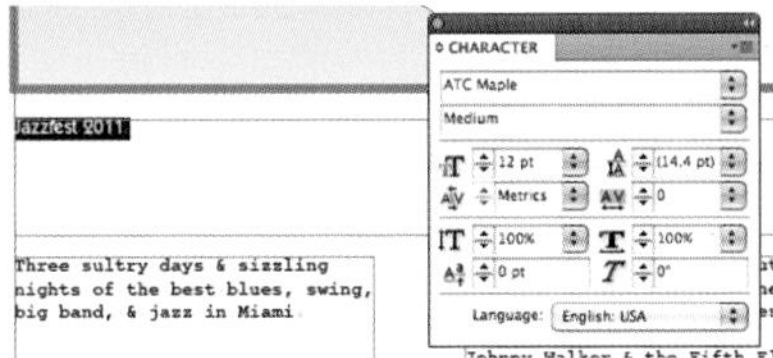

3. **Open the Font Style menu in the Character panel and choose Ultra.**

   You don't need to press Return/Enter when you choose a specific option from the menu.

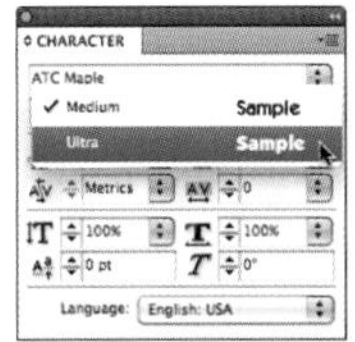

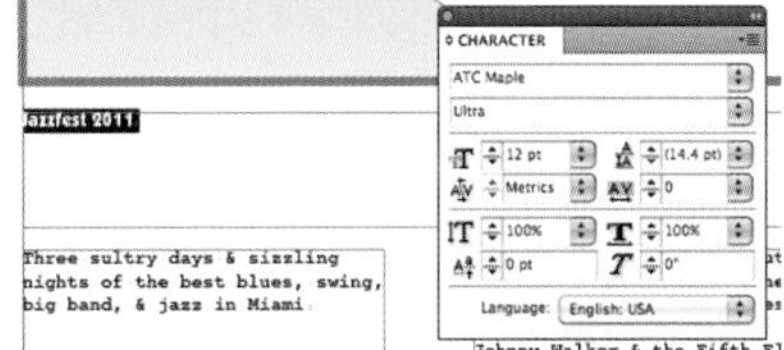

4. **Open the Font Size menu and choose 72.**

   You can choose one of the built-in font sizes, type a specific value in the field, or click the arrow buttons to change the font size by 1 point.

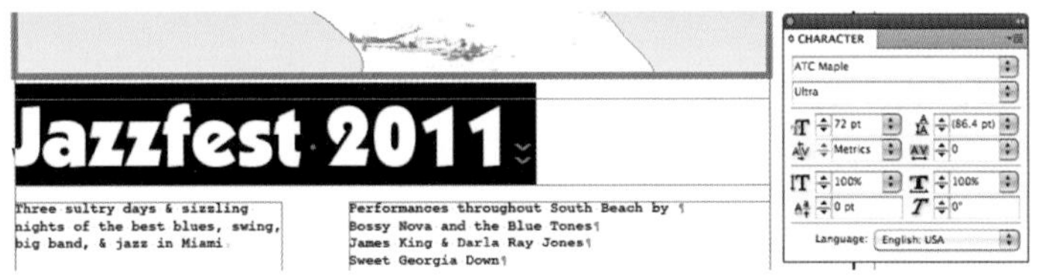

Note:

You can use the Up and Down Arrow keys to nudge paragraph and character style values when the insertion point is in a panel field.

5. **Open the Character panel Options menu and choose the All Caps option.**

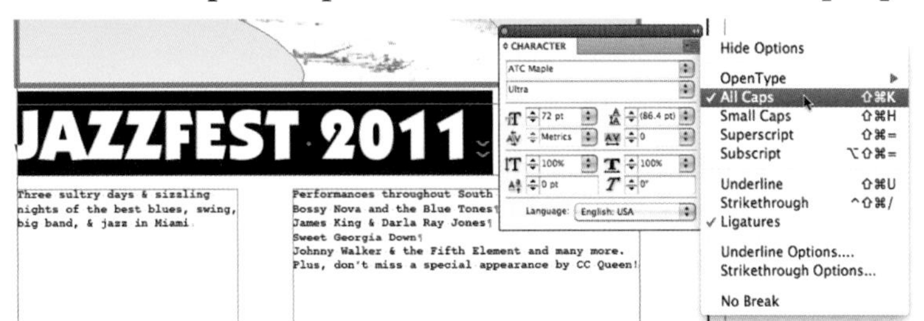

Note:

Most of these character formatting options are also available in the Control panel.

6. **In the Character panel, type 200 in the Tracking field and press Return/Enter.**

7. **Click four times on the paragraph in the second frame to select the entire paragraph.**

   Clicking twice selects an entire *word*, clicking three times selects an entire *line*, and clicking four times selects the entire *paragraph*.

8. **Change the selected text to 34-pt ATC Pine Bold Italic.**

   Using these settings, the paragraph doesn't entirely fit within the available space (or at least, not yet). Because the frame is threaded, the paragraph flows into the third frame, and the rest of the text reflows accordingly.

   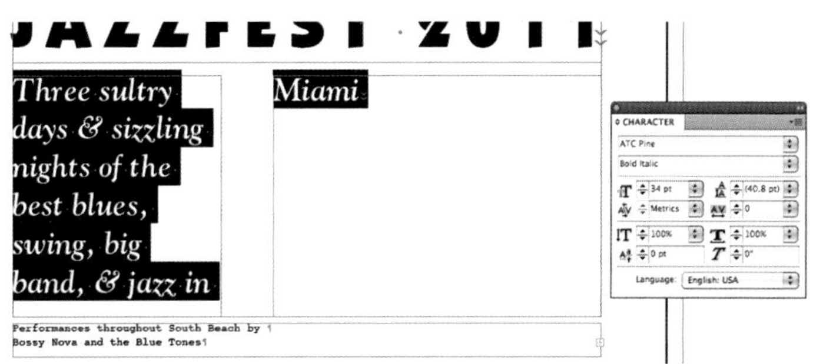

> *Note:*
>
> *Leave the Leading value at the automatic setting. By default, InDesign automatically applies leading as 120% of the type size.*

9. **With the same text selected, change the Horizontal Scale field to 90%.**

   Horizontal and vertical scaling are useful for artificially stretching or contracting fonts that do not have a condensed or extended version. Be careful using these options, though, because the artificial scaling alters the character shapes and can make some fonts very difficult to read (especially at smaller sizes).

   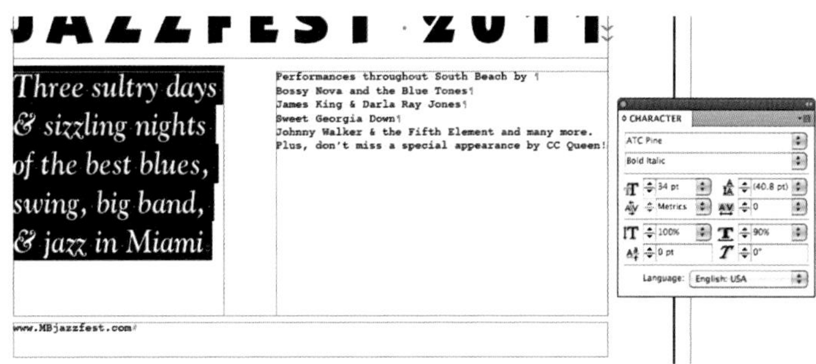

10. **Click three times to select the first line in the third frame, hold down the mouse button, and then drag down to select the other lines in the same frame.**

    When you triple-click to select an entire line, dragging up or down selects entire lines above or below the one you first clicked.

11. **With all of the text in the third frame selected, apply 22-pt ATC Pine Bold with 90% horizontal scaling.**

    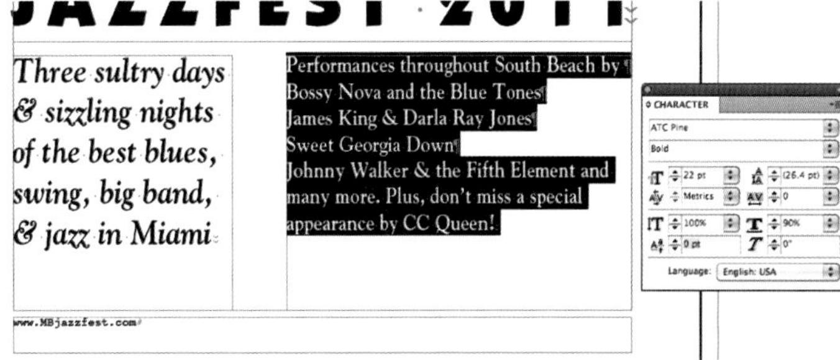

12. **Change the Web address in the fourth text frame to 26-pt ATC Maple Medium.**

13. **Save the file and continue to the next exercise.**

Apply Paragraph Formatting

Character formatting includes any option that affects the appearance of selected characters, such as font, size, horizontal scale, and a host of others. Paragraph formatting options, on the other hand, affect an entire paragraph (everything between two paragraph return characters). Paragraph formatting can control everything from indents to the space between paragraphs to lines above and below paragraphs.

Note:

In InDesign, a paragraph is defined as all text between two paragraph return characters (¶), even if the paragraph exists on a single line.

Paragraph formatting can be controlled in the Paragraph panel (Window>Type & Tables>Paragraph) or the Control panel (depending on which options are available).

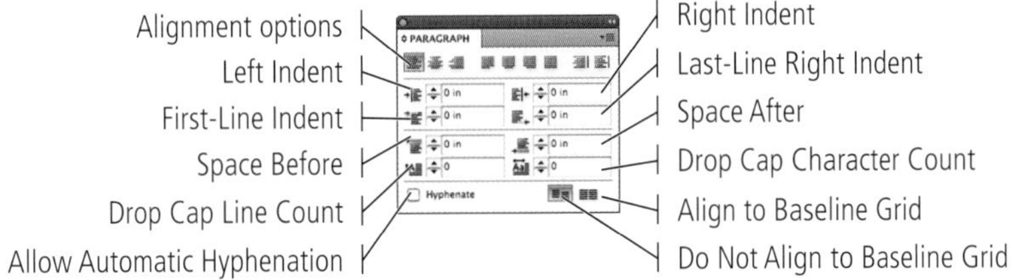

1. **In the open poster.indd file, place the cursor anywhere in the paragraph in the second frame.**

2. **In the Paragraph panel, click the Align Right button.**

   Paragraph formatting applies to the entire paragraph where the insertion point is placed, or to any paragraph that is entirely or partially selected. A paragraph does not have to be entirely selected to change its paragraph formatting attributes.

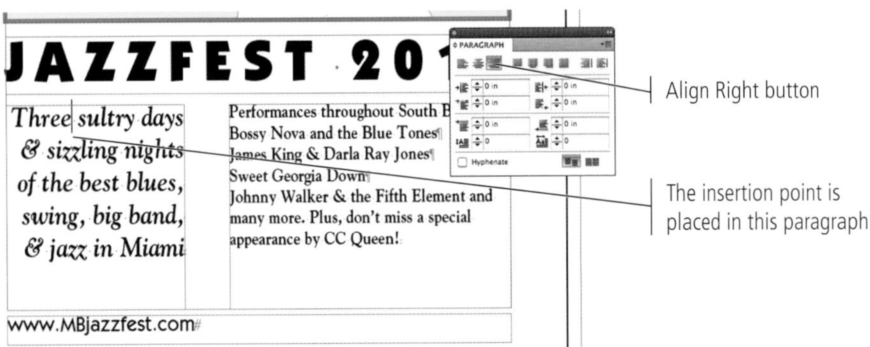

3. **Place the insertion point in the last paragraph of the third frame (Johnny Walker...) and apply centered paragraph alignment.**

4. **Place the insertion point anywhere in the fourth frame (with the Web address) and apply centered paragraph alignment.**

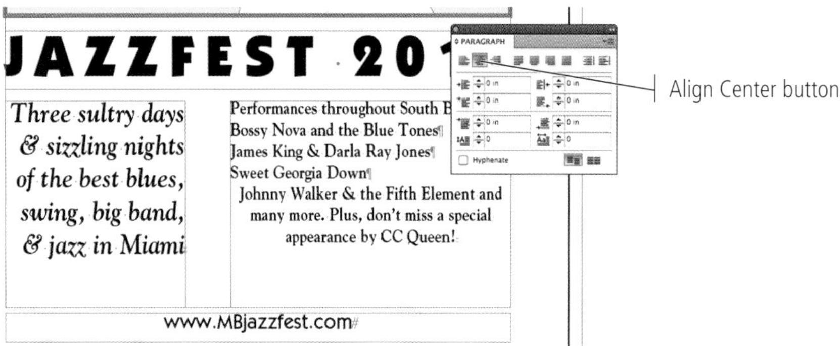

5. **Select any part of the first through fifth lines in the third frame.**

6. **In the Paragraph panel, change the Space Before field to 0.09″.**

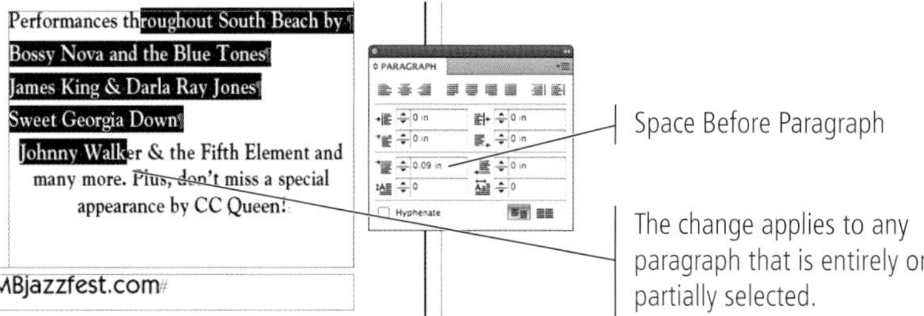

Note:

The arrow buttons for paragraph formatting options step through values in increments of 0.0625″.

7. **Select any part of the second through fifth lines in the same frame and change the Left Indent field to 0.5″.**

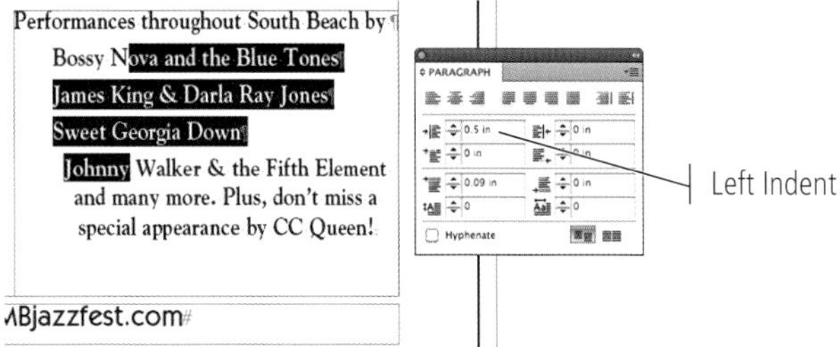

Note:

If you want to apply the same formatting to more than one consecutive paragraph, you can drag to select any part of the target paragraphs. Any paragraph that's even partially selected will be affected.

8. **Place the insertion point at the beginning of the sixth line (before the word "and") and press Return/Enter.**

When you break an existing paragraph into a new paragraph, the attributes of the original paragraph are applied to the new paragraph.

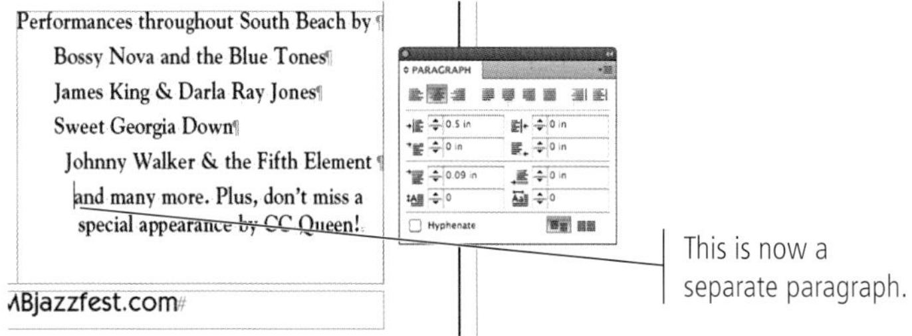

9. **Place the insertion point at the beginning of the fifth line (before "Johnny") and press Delete/Backspace.**

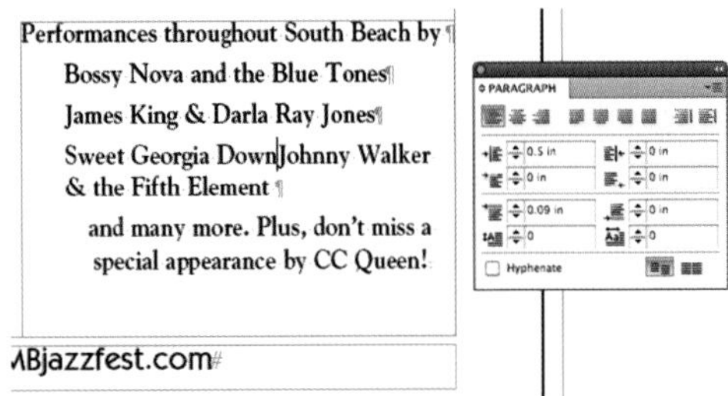

10. **Press Return/Enter to separate the two paragraphs again.**

This is an easy way to copy paragraph formatting from one paragraph to the next. When you re-separate the two paragraphs, the "Johnny" paragraph adopts the paragraph formatting attributes of the "Sweet Georgia Down" paragraph.

11. **Save the file and continue to the next exercise.**

Copying Type Attributes with the Eyedropper Tool

INDESIGN FOUNDATIONS

You can use the Eyedropper tool to copy character and paragraph attributes (including text color), and then apply those attributes to other sections of text.

To copy formatting from one piece of text to another, click with the Eyedropper tool on the formatting you want to copy. If any text is selected when you click the Eyedropper tool, the selected text is automatically re-formatted. If nothing is selected, the Eyedropper tool "loads" with the formatting attributes — the tool icon reverses directions and shows a small i-beam icon in the cursor.

The Eyedropper tool cursor when it is "loaded" with text formatting attributes

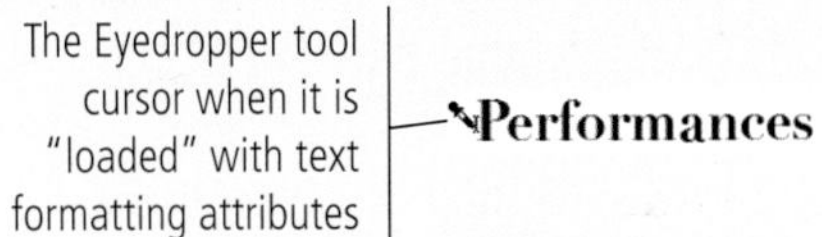

You can click the loaded Eyedropper tool on any text to change its formatting, or you can click and drag to format multiple paragraphs at once. As long as the Eyedropper tool remains selected, you can continue to select text to apply the same formatting. You can also change the formatting in the Eyedropper tool by pressing Option/Alt and clicking text with the new formatting attributes you want to copy.

By default, the Eyedropper tool copies all formatting attributes. You can change that behavior by double-clicking the tool in the Tools panel to access the Eyedropper Options dialog box. Simply uncheck the options you don't want to copy (including individual options in each category), and then click OK.

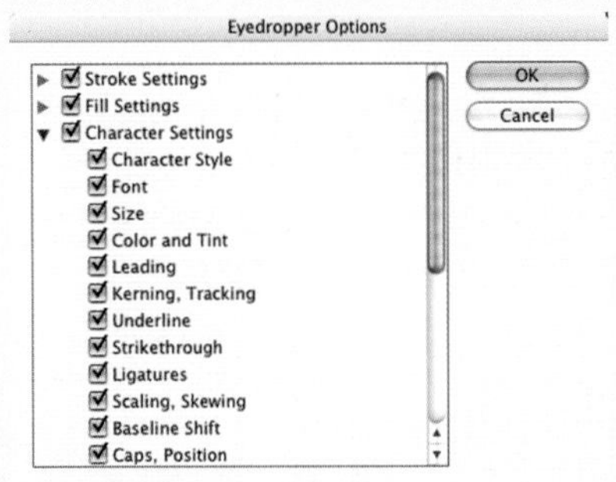

Use Optical Margin Alignment

At times, specific arrangements of text can cause a paragraph to appear out of alignment, even though it's technically aligned properly. Punctuation at the beginning or end of a line — such as quotation marks at the beginning of a line or the commas in lines three and four of the second text frame — often cause this kind of optical problem. InDesign includes a feature called **Optical Margin Alignment** to fix this type of problem.

1. **With poster.indd open, choose Type>Hide Hidden Characters.**

   Although the paragraph in the second frame is technically correctly right-aligned, the text might appear misaligned because of the commas at the ends of lines three and four.

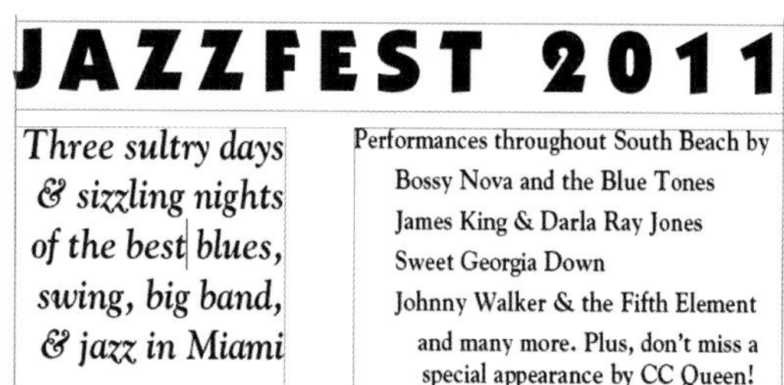

2. **Place the insertion point anywhere in the second text frame.**

3. **Open the Story panel (Window>Type & Tables>Story) and check the Optical Margin Alignment option. Change the Size field to 34 pt.**

   When Optical Margin Alignment is turned on, punctuation marks move outside the text margins (either to the left for left-aligned text or right for right-aligned text). Moving punctuation outside the margins is often referred to as **hanging punctuation.**

   The field in the Story panel tells InDesign what size type needs to be adjusted. The best effect is usually created by defining the size of the type that needs adjustment.

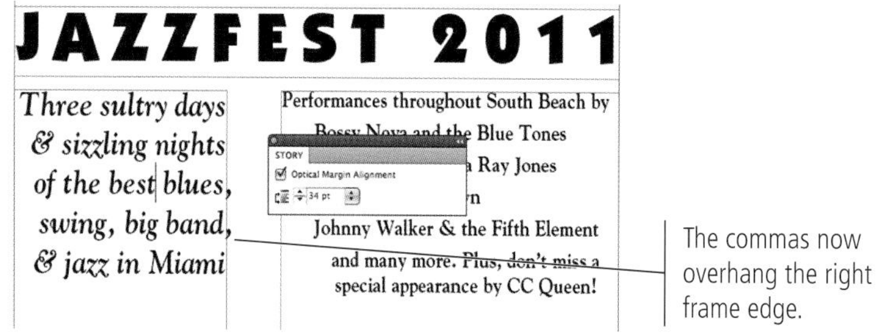

The commas now overhang the right frame edge.

4. **Place the insertion point in the first frame, then choose Ignore Optical Margin in the Paragraph panel Options menu.**

   The Optical Margin Alignment option applies to an entire story (including all text frames in the same thread), not just the selected paragraph. If necessary, you can toggle this option on for individual paragraphs so the selected paragraph is not affected by optical margin alignment that is applied to the overall story.

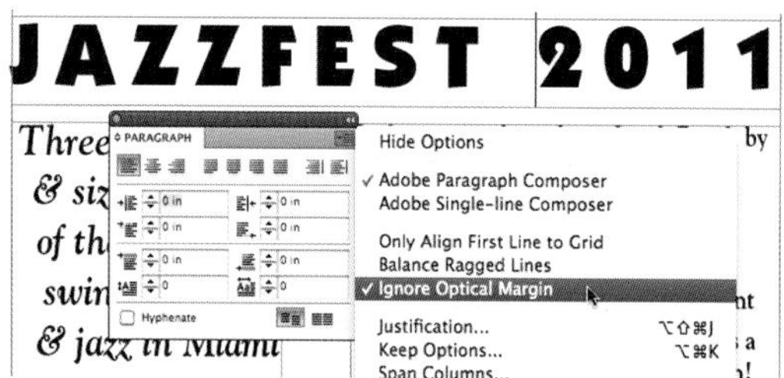

5. **In the Layers panel, click the empty space to the left of the <rectangle> item to make that object visible again.**

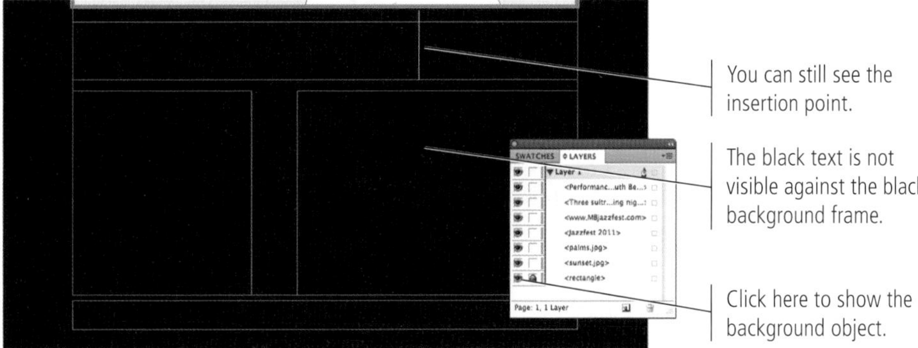

You can still see the insertion point.
The black text is not visible against the black background frame.
Click here to show the background object.

6. **With the insertion point still flashing in the now-obscured text, choose Edit>Select All to select all text in the series of linked frames.**

   The Select All command selects all text in the story, whether that story exists in a single frame or threads across multiple frames. This command also selects overset text that doesn't fit into the current frame (or thread of frames).

7. **In the Swatches panel, make sure the Text icon is selected at the top of the panel, and then click the Paper swatch.**

   In four-color (process) printing, there is no white ink. To achieve white, you have to remove the colors where you want white areas, which is called a **knockout**. By removing or knocking out underlying colors, the paper shows through — regardless of whether it is white or some other color (e.g., if you print on yellow paper, knockout areas will show the yellow color; this is why InDesign refers to this swatch as "Paper" instead of "White").

This "T" icon means you are changing the text color instead of the object color.

8. **Click away from the text to deselect it and review the results.**

9. **Save the file and continue to the next stage of the project.**

Stage 3 Graphics as Text and Text as Graphics

Now that you're familiar with the basic options for formatting characters and paragraphs, you can begin to add style to a layout using two techniques — flowing text along a path, and placing graphics inline with text. (There is, of course, much more to learn about working with text than this project covers; you'll learn much more as you complete the rest of the projects in this book.)

Place Inline Graphics

Any graphics frame that you create on a page float over the other elements in the layout. You can position graphics frames over other objects to hide underlying elements, or you can apply a **runaround** so text will wrap around a picture box.

You can also place images as inline graphics, which means they will be anchored to the text in the position in which they are placed. If text reflows, inline objects reflow with the text and maintain their correct positioning. This feature can be very useful for placing custom bullets (which you will do in this exercise), or for a variety of other purposes, such as where sidebar text needs to remain in proximity to the main body copy.

There are two methods for creating inline objects. For simple applications, such as a graphic bullet, you can simply place the graphic and format it as a text character. (An inline graphic is treated as a single text character in the story; it is affected by many of the paragraph-formatting commands, such as space before and after, tab settings, leading, and baseline position.) For more complex applications, you can use the options in the Object>Anchored Object menu.

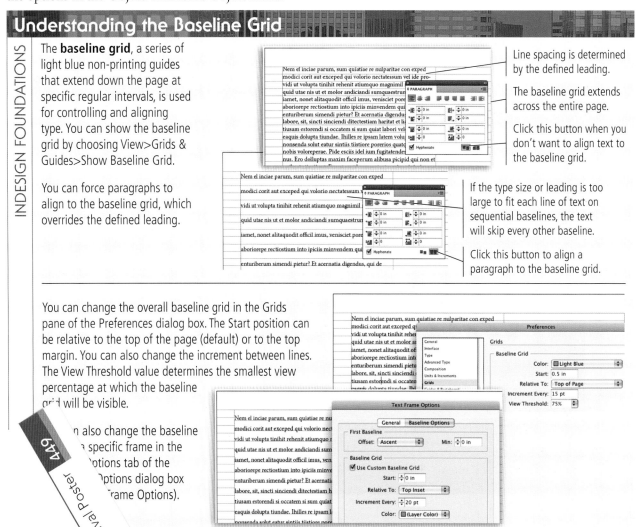

Understanding the Baseline Grid

INDESIGN FOUNDATIONS

The **baseline grid**, a series of light blue non-printing guides that extend down the page at specific regular intervals, is used for controlling and aligning type. You can show the baseline grid by choosing View>Grids & Guides>Show Baseline Grid.

You can force paragraphs to align to the baseline grid, which overrides the defined leading.

Line spacing is determined by the defined leading.

The baseline grid extends across the entire page.

Click this button when you don't want to align text to the baseline grid.

If the type size or leading is too large to fit each line of text on sequential baselines, the text will skip every other baseline.

Click this button to align a paragraph to the baseline grid.

You can change the overall baseline grid in the Grids pane of the Preferences dialog box. The Start position can be relative to the top of the page (default) or to the top margin. You can also change the increment between lines. The View Threshold value determines the smallest view percentage at which the baseline gr·d will be visible.

…n also change the baseline …specific frame in the …ptions tab of the …ptions dialog box …rame Options).

1. **With `poster.indd` open, place the insertion point at the beginning of the second line in the third frame (before the word "Bossy").**

2. **Choose File>Place and navigate to `note.ai` in the `WIP>Jazz` folder.**

Note:

You can also select an existing object, cut or copy it, place the insertion point, and then paste the object inline where the insertion point flashes.

3. **Make sure the Replace Selected Item option is checked, and then click Open.**

If the insertion point is flashing in a story when you place a graphic using the Replace Selected Item option, the graphic is automatically placed as an inline object.

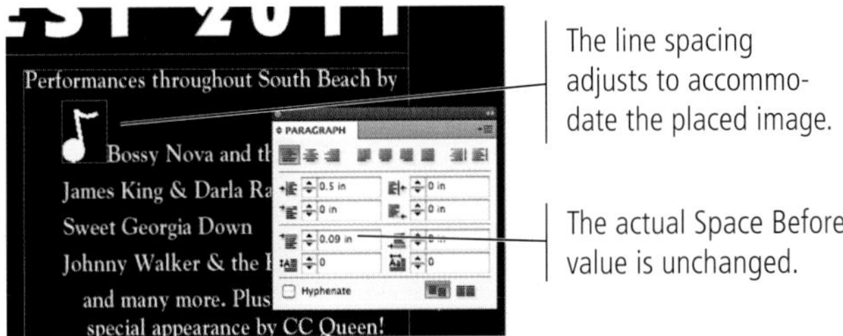

Working with Anchored Objects

INDESIGN FOUNDATIONS

The Anchored Object Options dialog box controls the position of an anchored object relative to the frame in which it is placed. Anchored objects can be aligned inline (such as the music-note bullets you created in this project) or above the line.

When an object is anchored using the Above Line option, the object can be anchored to the left, right, or center of the frame. If you're using facing pages, you can also choose Toward Spine or Away from Spine so the anchored object will be placed in the appropriate position relative to the spread center (for example, you might specify that all sidebars have to be on the inside edge, close to the spine).

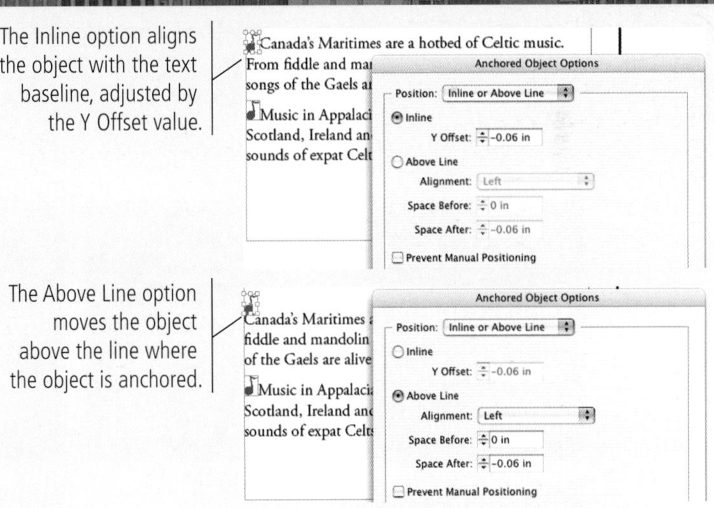

When you use the Above Line option, you can also define the space before and after the anchored object. Space Before defines the position of the object relative to the bottom of the previous line of text. Space After defines the position of the object relative to the first character in the line below the object.

When you work with anchored objects, you can use the Selection tool to drag the object up or down (in other words, change its position relative to the text to which it is anchored). If the Prevent Manual Positioning option is checked, you can't drag the anchored object in the layout.

4. **Select the inline graphic with the Selection tool, and then scale the graphic and frame to 50% horizontally and vertically.**

   Although inline graphics are anchored to the text, they are still graphics contained in graphics frames. You can apply the same transformations to inline graphics that you could apply to any other placed graphics.

Use these fields to scale the placed graphic and the containing frame.

After you finalize the scaling, the fields show 100% when the frame is selected with the Selection tool.

Note:

When you select the frame with the Selection tool, resizing the frame also resizes the frame content.

5. **Choose Object>Anchored Object>Options. Check the Preview option at the bottom of the dialog box.**

6. **Make sure the Inline option is selected, and change the Y Offset to –`0.07`″.**

   A negative number moves the anchored object down; a positive number moves it up.

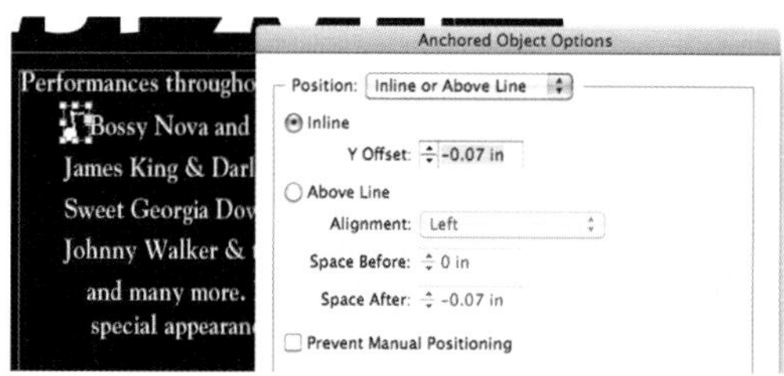

Anchored Object Size and Text Position

INDESIGN FOUNDATIONS

When an anchored object is larger than the defined leading for the text in which it is placed, it might appear that changing the Y Offset values moves the text instead of the anchored object. In a way, this is true, because the text will move until it reaches the defined leading value; after that, greater changes will move the object and not the text.

Default text position without the anchored object

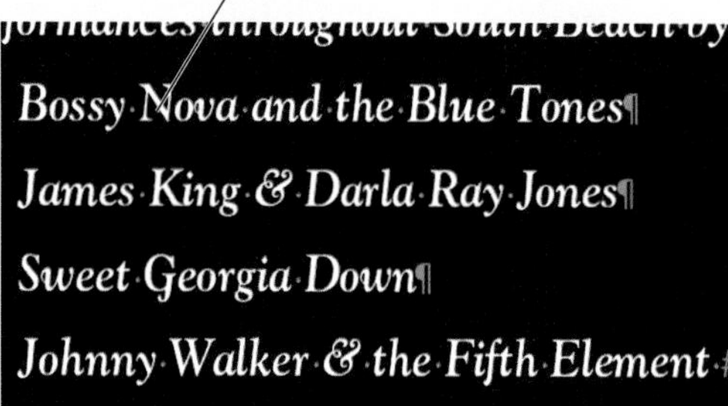

Text position after placing the anchored object

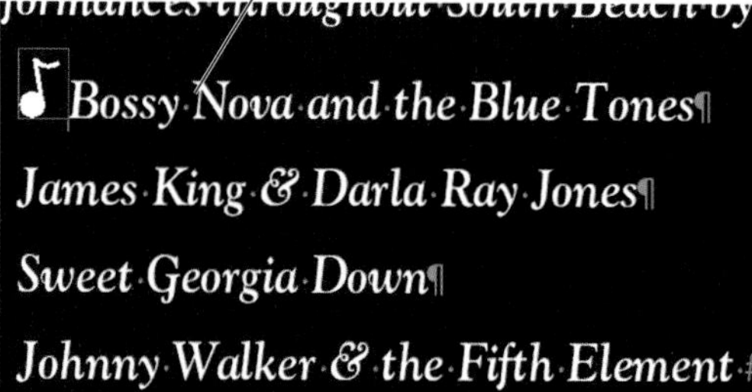

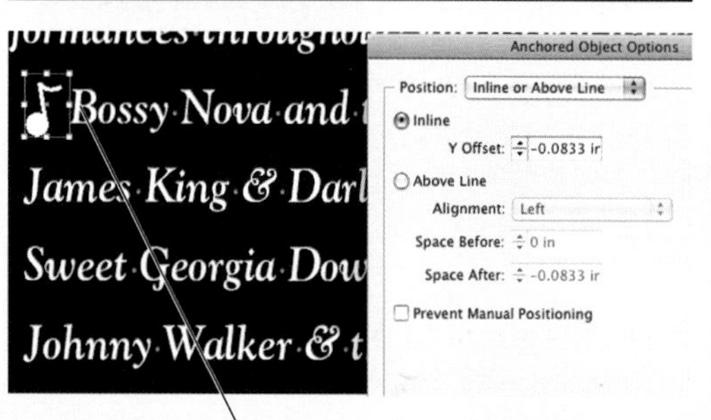

Adjusting the object position allows text to move back to its original place based on defined paragraph formatting.

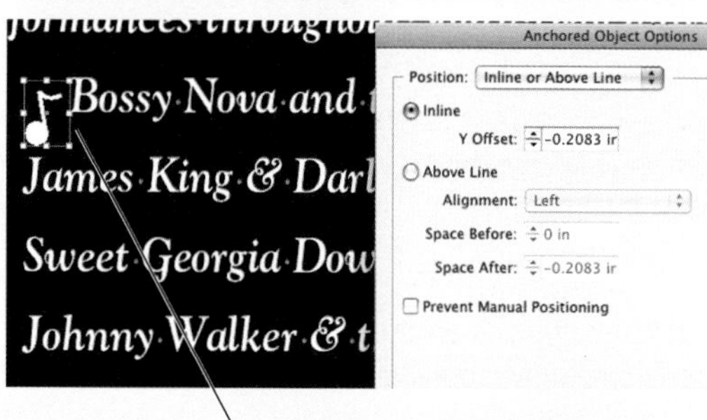

Further adjustments to the anchored object move the actual object by the specified amount.

7. **Click OK, and then place the insertion point between the anchored object and the letter "B."**

8. **Press Shift-Left Arrow to select the anchored object, and then copy the highlighted object/character.**

   You can select an inline graphic just as you would any other text character. Copying text in InDesign is the same as copying text in other applications: choose Edit>Copy, or press Command/Control-C.

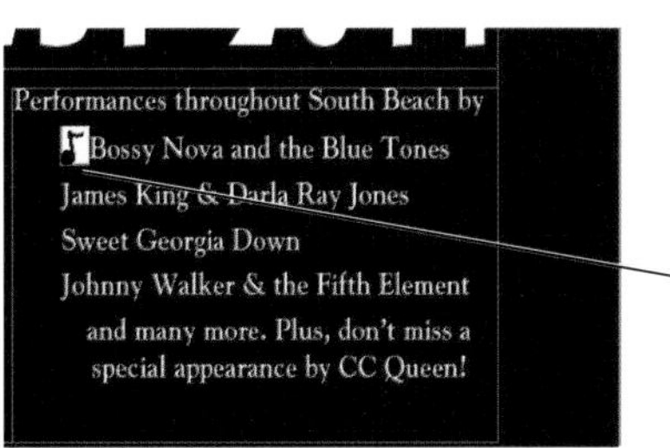

An anchored graphic can be selected just as you would select any other text character.

Custom Anchor Options

INDESIGN FOUNDATIONS

For complex applications — such as moving an anchored object outside a text frame — you can choose Custom in the Anchored Object Options Position menu.

The anchored object is outside the text frame; it is positioned with custom values.

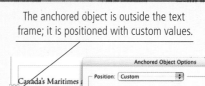

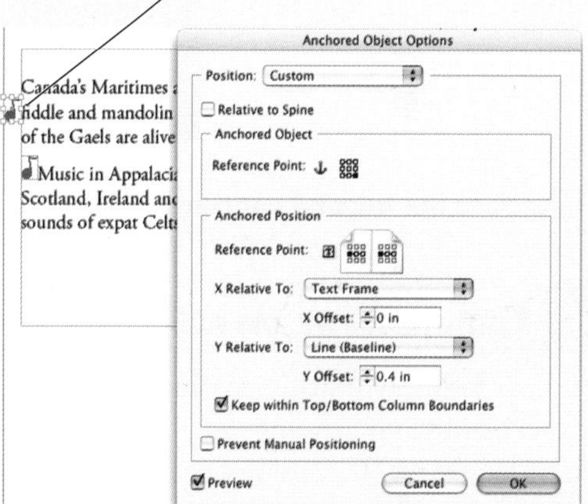

The **Relative to Spine** option, which aligns objects based on the center spread line, is only available if your layout has facing pages. When selected, objects on one side of a spread (such as a sidebar in the outside margin) remain on the outside margin even if the text reflows to a facing page.

The **Anchored Object Reference Point** defines the location on the object that you want to align to the location on the page.

The **Anchored Position Reference Point** defines the page location where you want to anchor an object.

The **X Relative To** field defines what you want to use as the basis for horizontal alignment — Anchor Marker, Column Edge, Text Frame, Page Margin, or Page Edge. The **X Offset** setting moves the object left or right.

The **Y Relative To** field specifies how the object aligns vertically — Line (Baseline), Line (Cap Height), Line (Top of Leading), Column Edge, Text Frame, Page Margin, or Page Edge. The **Y Offset** setting moves the object up or down.

When **Keep Within Top/Bottom Column Boundaries** is checked, the anchored object stays inside the text column if reflowing the text would otherwise cause the object to move outside the boundaries (for example, outside the top edge of the frame if the anchoring text is the first line in a column). This option is only available when you select a line option such as Line (Baseline) in the Y Relative To menu.

When text threads are showing, a dashed blue line indicates the position of anchored objects.

You can manually reposition a custom-anchored object by simply dragging the anchored object with the Selection tool. You can also review the anchored position by choosing View>Show Text Threads.

Creating Anchored Placeholders

If you want to create an anchored object but don't yet have the content, you can use the Object>Anchored Object>Insert option to define the placeholder object. This dialog box allows you to create a frame (unassigned, graphics, or text) of a specific size, and even apply object and paragraph styles (if those exist). The Position options are the same as those in the Anchored Object Options dialog box. (You can always resize and reposition the

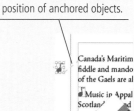

9. **Place the insertion point at the beginning of the next paragraph and paste the copied object.**

   As with copying, pasting text — including inline graphics — in InDesign is the same as in other applications: choose Edit>Paste, or press Command/Control-V.

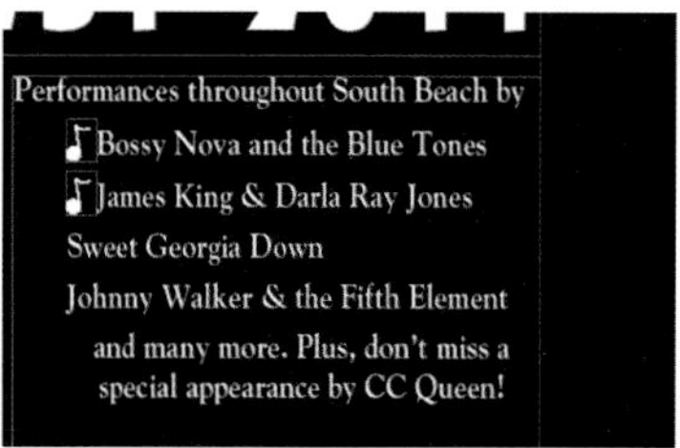

10. **Paste the anchored graphic again at the beginning of the next two paragraphs.**

11. **Apply right paragraph alignment to the last paragraph in the third frame.**

    This simply provides better overall balance to the text in the frame.

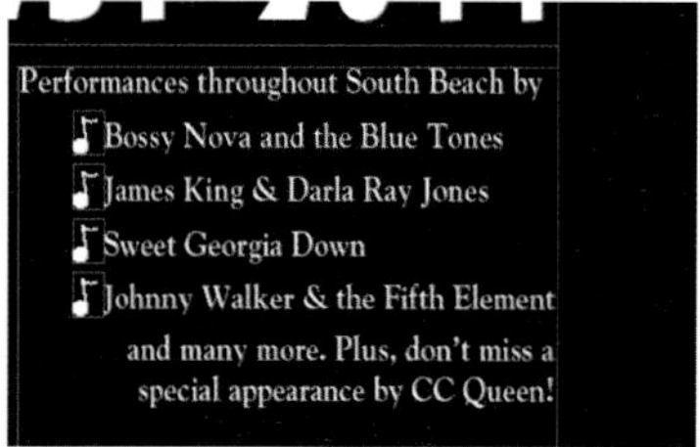

12. **Save the file and continue to the next exercise.**

Create Type on a Path

Instead of simply flowing text into a frame, you can also create unique typographic effects by flowing text onto a path. A text path can be any shape that you can create in InDesign, whether using one of the basic shape tools, a complex graphic you drew with the Pen tool, or a path created by converting a clipping path to a frame.

1. **With poster.indd open, deselect all objects in the layout.**

   As we explained previously, you can choose Edit>Deselect All, or use the Selection tool to click an empty area of the workspace. If you use the click method, make sure you don't click a white-filled object instead of an empty area.

2. **Choose File>Place. Select text_path.tif in the WIP>Jazz folder in the layout and click Open. Position the top-left corner of the placed graphic at X: 0″, Y: 0″.**

   When this image is loaded into the cursor, click outside the defined bleed area to place the image and not replace the content in one of the existing frames. Then use the Control panel to position the image correctly. (The image that you are placing is simply a guide that you will use to create the shape of the text path for this exercise.)

3. **Choose the Pen tool. Change the stroke value to 1-pt Magenta (C=0 M=100 Y=0 K=0) and change the fill value to None.**

   Because the line in the placed image is black, you're using magenta so you can differentiate your line from the one in the image. The solid white background in the TIF file makes it easy to focus on the line instead of the elements you have already [illegible] on the poster.

4. **Using the Pen tool, click once on the left end of the line in the placed image.**

   This first click establishes the first point of the path you're drawing.

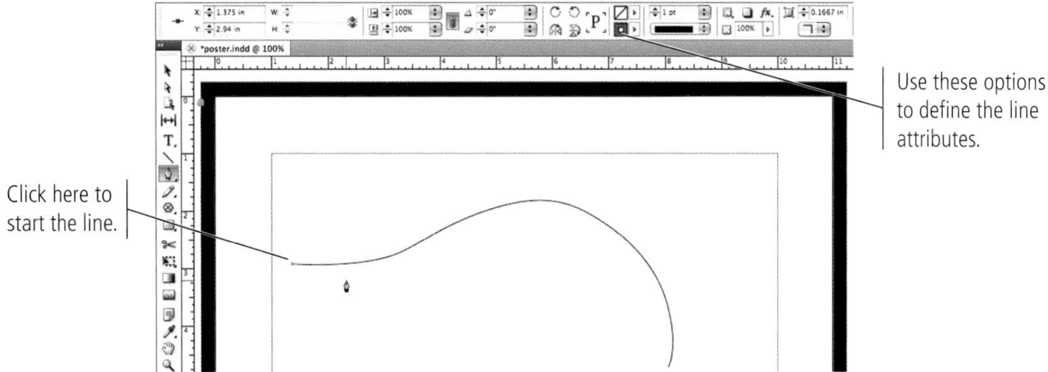

Click here to
start the line.
Use these options
to define the line
attributes.

5. **Click about half way between the point you just set and the topmost arc of the curve, and then drag right to create handles for the second anchor point.**

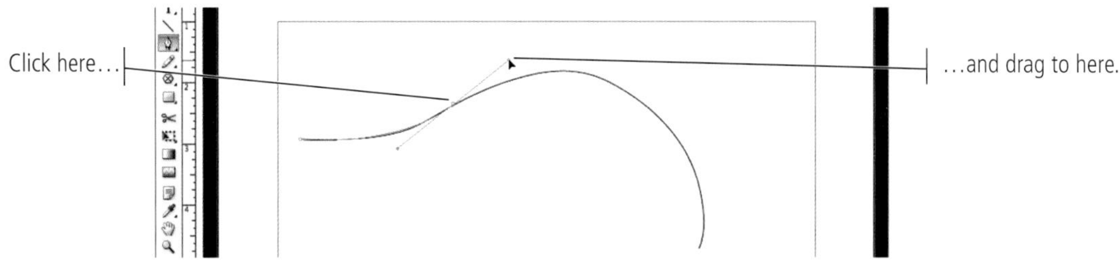

6. **Click again near the middle of the arc on the right, and then drag to create handles for the point.**

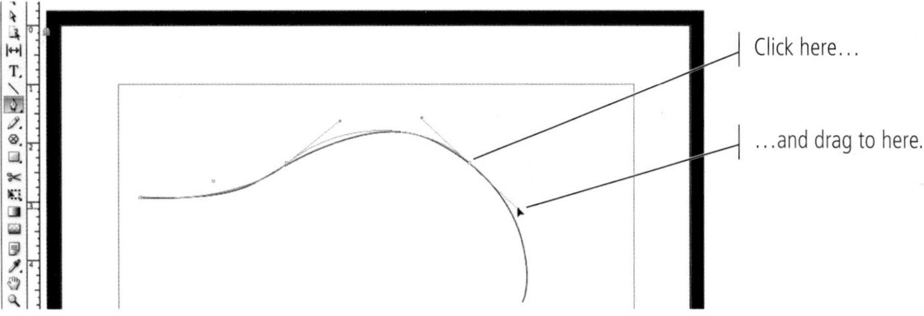

7. **Click a final time on the right end of the line.**

   Don't worry if your path isn't perfect the first time; you can always edit the anchor points and handles with the Direct Selection tool.

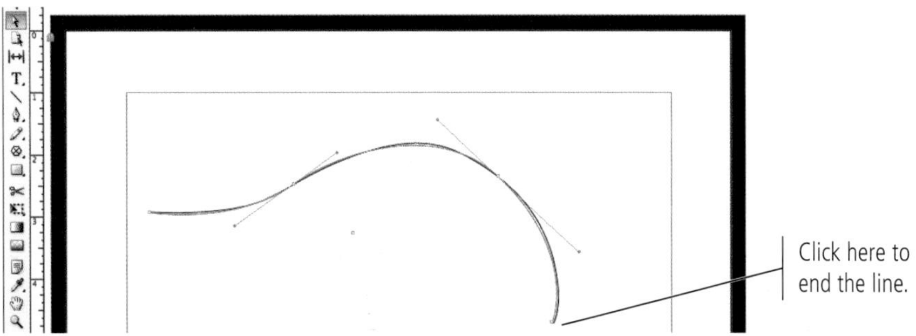

Click here to
end the line.

8. **Using the Direct Selection tool, adjust the points and handles until your line closely resembles the one in the placed image.**

9. **Choose the Type on a Path tool. Move the cursor near the path until the cursor shows a small plus sign in the icon, and then click the path.**

   This action converts the line from a regular path to a type path.

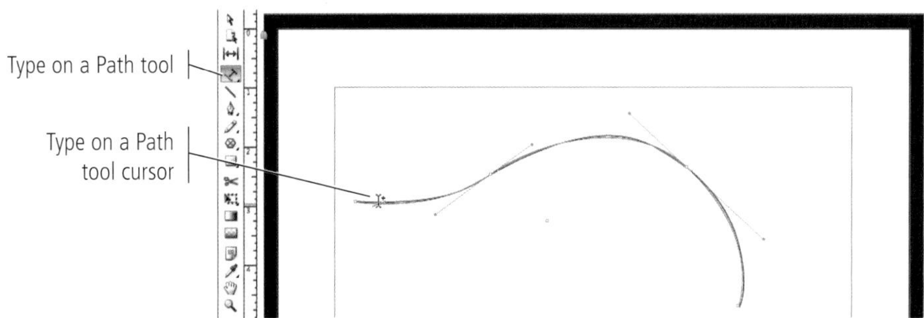

10. **Type** Move your feet to the beat!**, then format the type as 49-pt ATC Maple Ultra.**

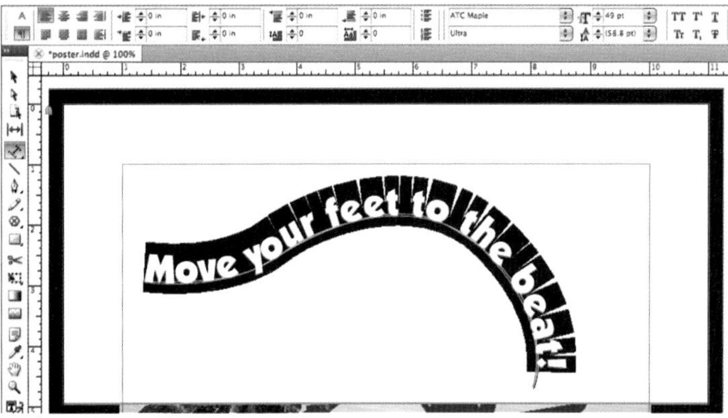

Type on a Path Options

INDESIGN FOUNDATIONS

You can control the appearance of type on a path by choosing Type>Type on a Path>Options. You can apply one of five effects, change the alignment of the text to the path, flip the text to the other side of the path, and adjust the character spacing around curves (higher Spacing values remove more space around sharp curves).

- The **Rainbow** (default) effect keeps each character's baseline parallel to the path.
- The **Skew** effect maintains the vertical edges of type while skewing horizontal edges around the path.
- The **3D Ribbon** effect maintains the horizontal edges of type while rotating the vertical edges to be perpendicular to the path.
- The **Stair Step** effect aligns the left edge of each character's baseline to the path.
- The **Gravity** effect aligns the center of each character's baseline to the path, keeping vertical edges in line with the path's center.

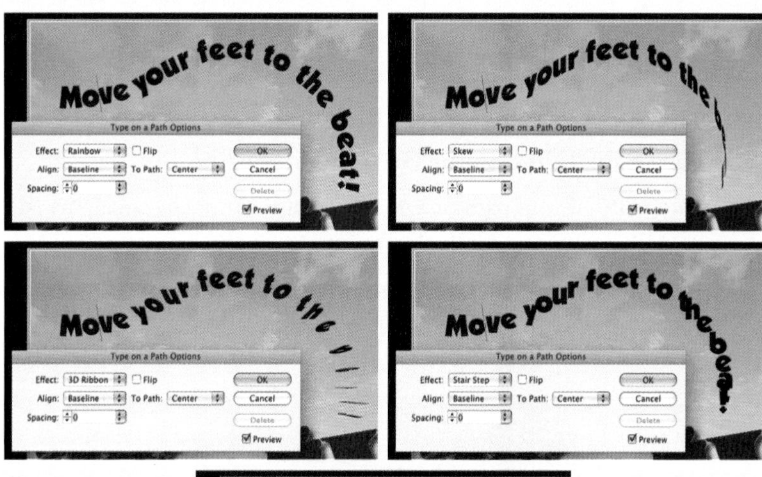

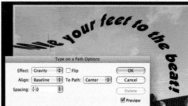

The **Align options** determine which part of the text (Baseline, Ascender, Descender, or Center) aligns to which part of the path (Top, Bottom, or Center).

11. **Using the Selection tool, click the text_path.tif image that you used as a guide. Press Delete/Backspace to remove it from the layout.**

12. **Click the text path with the Selection tool to select the actual line. In the Swatches panel, change the object's stroke color to None.**

    A text path can have a fill and stroke value just like any other path.

Note:

When a text path has no stroke color, you can still view the path by choosing View>Extras>Show Frame Edges.

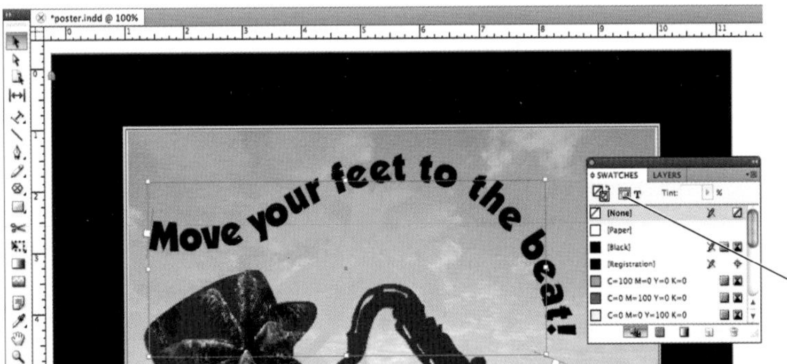

When the actual path is selected, the Swatches panel defaults to show attributes of the path (not the type).

13. **Click the Text Color button at the top of the Swatches panel, and then click the Pantone 8660 C swatch to change the text color.**

    You don't have to select the actual text on a path to change its color. You can use the buttons at the top of the Swatches panel to change the color attributes of either the path or the text.

Note:

The screen preview of the metallic ink is not especially pleasing; in this case, you simply have to rely on the printed ink swatch to know what the text will look like when printed.

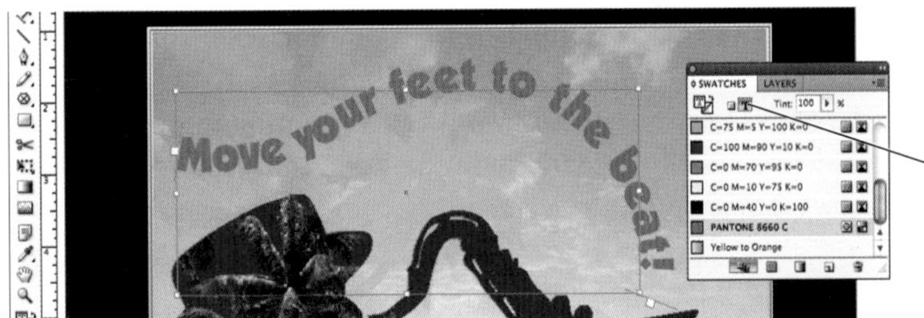

Click here to change the type fill and stroke colors.

14. **Click the bar at the left edge of the text path and drag to the right about 1/4".**

    When you release the mouse button, the left edge of the text moves to the point where you dragged the line. This marks the orientation point of the text on the path.

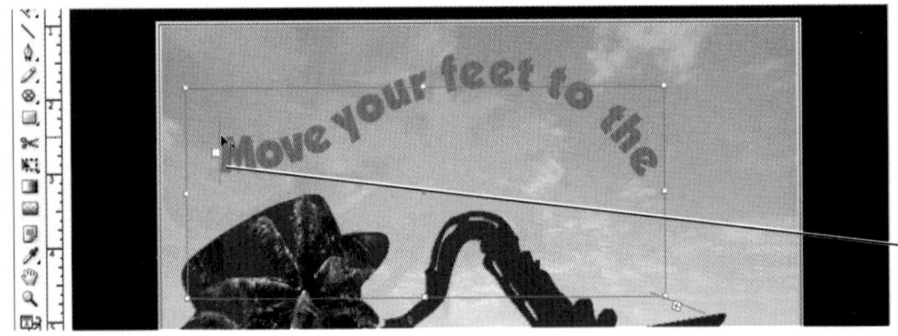

Drag this line to move the starting point of the text along the path.

15. **Choose Edit>Undo (Command/Control-Z) to return the orientation point to the left end of the line.**

16. **Place the insertion point in the text path and apply right paragraph alignment.**

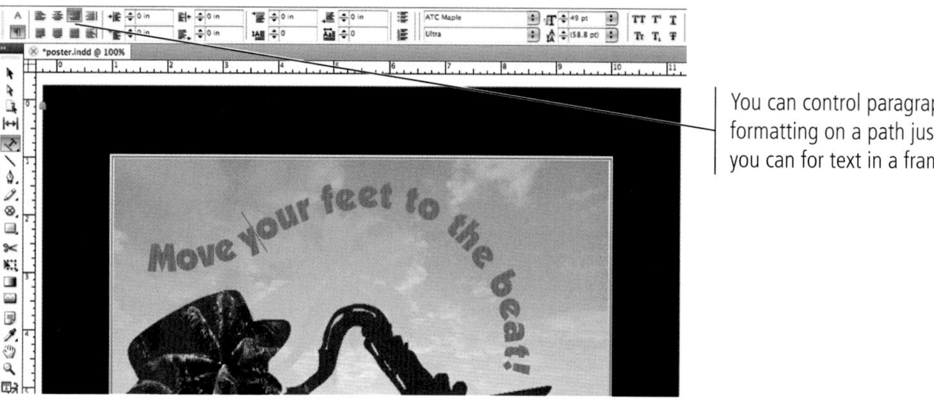

You can control paragraph formatting on a path just as you can for text in a frame.

17. **Save the file and continue to the final stage of the project.**

Stage 4 Outputting the File

If your layout contains transparency or effects, those transparent areas will typically need to be flattened for output. **Flattening** divides transparent artwork into the necessary vector and raster objects. Transparent objects are flattened according to the settings in the selected flattener preset, which you choose in the Advanced options of the Print dialog box (or in the dialog box that appears when you export as PDF, EPS, or another format).

When you work with transparency, InDesign converts affected objects to a common color space (either CMYK or RGB) so transparent objects of different color spaces can blend properly. To avoid color mismatches between different areas of the objects on screen and in print, the blending space is applied for screen and in the flattener. You can define which space to use in the Edit>Transparency Blend Space menu; for print jobs, make sure the CMYK option is selected.

Using the Flattener Preview Panel

INDESIGN FOUNDATIONS

Because of the potential problems that can arise when transparent elements are flattened, you can use the Flattener Preview panel (Window>Output>Flattener Preview) to highlight areas that will be affected by flattening. If you are working on a layout with multiple pages or spreads, you can apply different flattener settings to individual spreads by choosing Spread Flattening in the Pages panel Options menu.

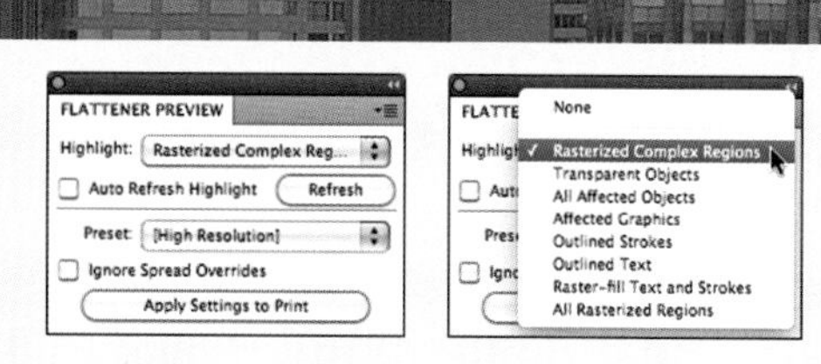

You can highlight different kinds of areas and determine which flattener preset to use for each. Clicking Refresh displays a new preview based on your settings. You can also choose Auto Refresh Highlight.

- **None** displays the normal layout.
- **Rasterized Complex Regions** highlights areas that will be rasterized based on the Raster/Vector Balance defined in the applied preset.
- **Transparent Objects** highlights objects with opacity of less than 100%, objects with blending modes, objects with transparent effects (such as drop shadows), and objects with feathering.
- **All Affected Objects** highlights all objects affected by transparency, including the transparent objects and the objects overlapped by transparent objects. All of these objects will be affected by flattening.
- **Affected Graphics** highlights all placed image files affected by transparency.
- **Outlined Strokes** highlights all strokes that will be converted to filled objects when flattened.
- **Outlined Text** highlights all text that will be converted to outlines when flattened.
- **Raster-Fill Text and Strokes** highlights text and strokes that will have rasterized fills as a result of flattening.
- **All Rasterized Regions** highlights objects (and parts of objects) that will be rasterized when flattened.

Export a PDF File for Print

1. **With poster.indd open, choose File>Export.**

2. **In the Export dialog box, navigate to your WIP>Jazz folder as the target destination and choose Adobe PDF (Print) in the Format/Save As Type menu.**

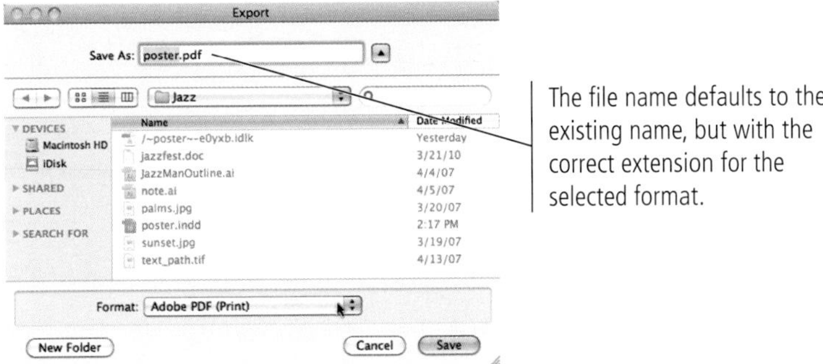

The file name defaults to the existing name, but with the correct extension for the selected format.

3. **Click Save.**

Before the PDF is saved, you have to define the settings that will be used to generate the PDF file.

4. **Choose High Quality Print in the Adobe PDF Preset menu.**

The Adobe PDF Preset menu includes six PDF presets that meet common industry output requirements.

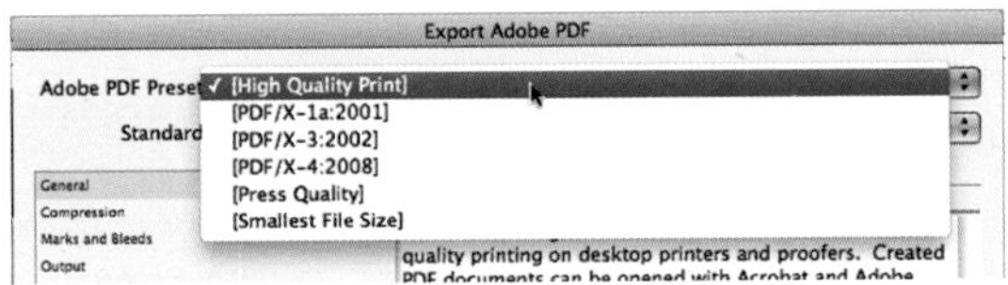

Because there are so many ways to create a PDF — and not all of those ways are optimized for the needs of commercial printing — the potential benefits of the file format are often undermined. The PDF/X specification was created to help solve some of the problems associated with bad PDF files entering the prepress workflow. PDF/X is a subset of PDF that is specifically designed to ensure that files have the information necessary for the digital prepress output process. Ask your output provider whether you should apply a PDF/X standard to your files, and if so, which version to use.

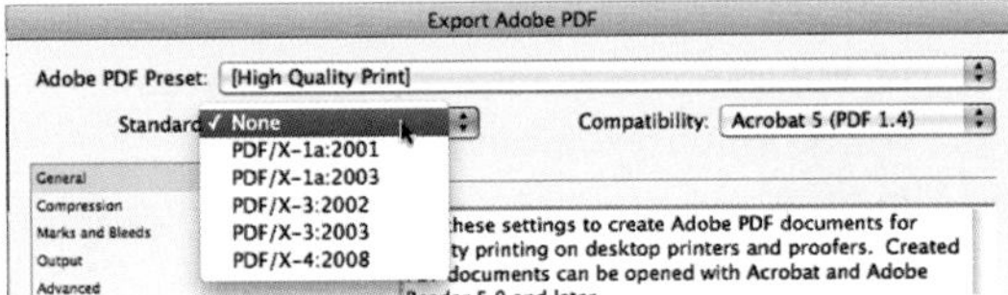

The Compatibility menu determines which version of the PDF format you will create. This is particularly important if your layout uses transparency. PDF 1.3 does not support transparency, so the file will require flattening. If you save the file to be compatible with PDF 1.4 or later, transparency information will be maintained in the PDF file.

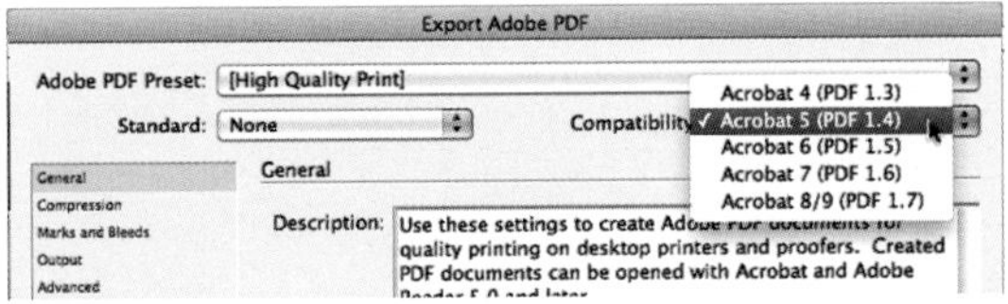

5. **Review the options in the General pane.**

- **Pages** options determine which pages to output, and whether to output facing pages on a single page.
- **Embed Page Thumbnails** creates a thumbnail for each page being exported, or one thumbnail for each spread if the Spreads option is selected.
- **Optimize for Fast Web View** optimizes the PDF file for faster viewing in a Web browser by allowing the file to download one page at a time.
- **Create Tagged PDF** automatically tags elements based on a subset of Acrobat tags (including basic formatting, lists, and more).
- **View PDF after Exporting** opens the PDF file after it has been created.
- **Create Acrobat Layers** saves each InDesign layer as an Acrobat layer within the PDF. Printer's marks are exported to a separate "marks and bleeds" layer. Create Acrobat Layers is available only when Compatibility is set to Acrobat 6 (PDF 1.5) or later.
- **Export Layers** determines whether you are outputting All Layers (including hidden and non-printing layers), Visible Layers (including non-printing layers), or Visible & Printable Layers.
- **Include** options can be used to include specific non-printing elements.

6. **Review the Compression options.**

The compression options determine what and how much data will be included in the PDF file. This set of options is one of the most important when creating PDFs, since too-low resolution results in bad-quality printing, and too-high resolution results in extremely long download times.

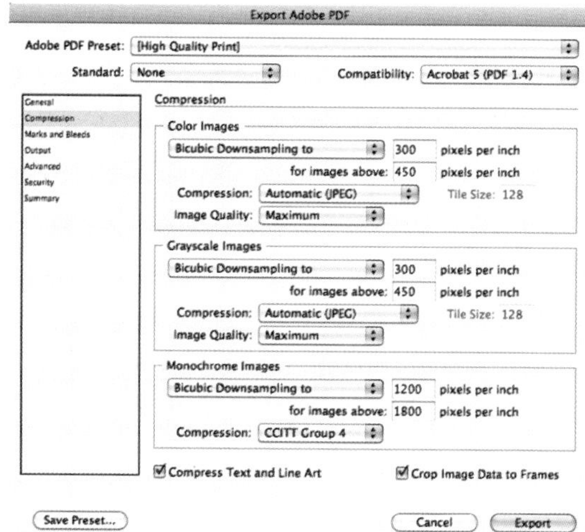

Before you choose compression settings, you need to consider your final goal. If you're creating a file for commercial printing, resolution is more important than file size. If your goal is a PDF that will be posted on the Web, file size is at least equally important as pristine image quality.

You can define a specific compression scheme for color, grayscale, and monochrome images. Different options are available depending on the image type:

- **JPEG compression** options are lossy, which means data is thrown away to create a smaller file. When you use one of the JPEG options, you can also define an Image Quality option (from Low to Maximum).
- **ZIP compression** is lossless, which means all file data is maintained in the compressed file.
- **CCITT compression** was initially developed for fax transmission. Group 3 supports two specific resolution settings (203 × 98 dpi and 203 × 196 dpi). Group 4 supports resolution up to 400 dpi.
- **Run Length Encoding** (RLE) is a lossless compression scheme that abbreviates sequences of adjacent pixels. If four pixels in a row are black, RLE saves that segment as "four black" instead of "black-black-black-black."

Note:

Since you chose the High Quality Print preset, these options default to settings that will produce the best results for most commercial printing applications.

Resolution Options for PDF

When you resize an image in the layout, you are changing its effective resolution. The **effective resolution** of an image is the resolution calculated after any scaling has been taken into account. This number is actually more important than the original image resolution. The effective resolution can be calculated with a fairly simple equation:

$$\text{original resolution} \div \frac{\%\text{ magnification}}{100} = \text{effective resolution}$$

If a 300-ppi image is magnified 150%, the effective resolution is:

300 ppi / 1.5 = 200 ppi

If you reduce the same 300-ppi image to 50%, the effective resolution is:

300 ppi / 0.5 = 600 ppi

In other words, the more you enlarge a raster image, the lower its effective resolution becomes. Reducing an image results in higher effective resolution, which can result in unnecessarily large PDF files.

When you create a PDF file, you also specify the resolution that will be maintained in the resulting PDF file. The Resolution option is useful if you want to throw away excess resolution for print files, or if you want to create low-resolution files for proofing or Web distribution.

- **Do Not Downsample** maintains all the image data from the linked files in the PDF file.
- **Average Downsampling To** reduces the number of pixels in an area by averaging areas of adjacent pixels. Apply this method to achieve user-defined resolution (72 or 96 dpi for Web-based files or 300 dpi for print).
- **Subsampling To** applies the center pixel value to surrounding pixels. If you think of a 3 × 3-block grid, subsampling enlarges the center pixel — and thus, its value — in place of the surrounding eight blocks.
- **Bicubic Downsampling To** creates the most accurate pixel information for continuous-tone images. This option also takes the longest to process, and it produces a softer image. To understand how this option works, think of a 2 × 2-block grid — bicubic downsampling averages the value of all four of those blocks (pixels) to interpolate the new information.

7. In the Marks and Bleeds options, check the Crop Marks option and change the Offset field to 0.25". Check the Use Document Bleed Settings option.

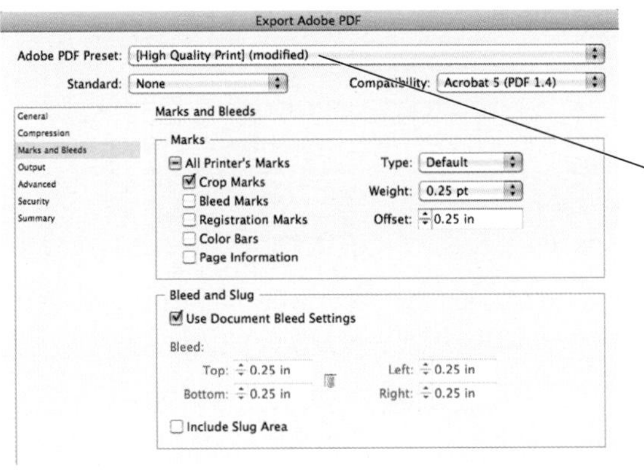

As soon as you choose a setting that is not part of the preset, the preset name shows "(modified)".

8. In the Compatibility menu, choose Acrobat 4 (PDF 1.3).

9. In the Advanced options, choose High Resolution in the Transparency Flattener Preset menu.

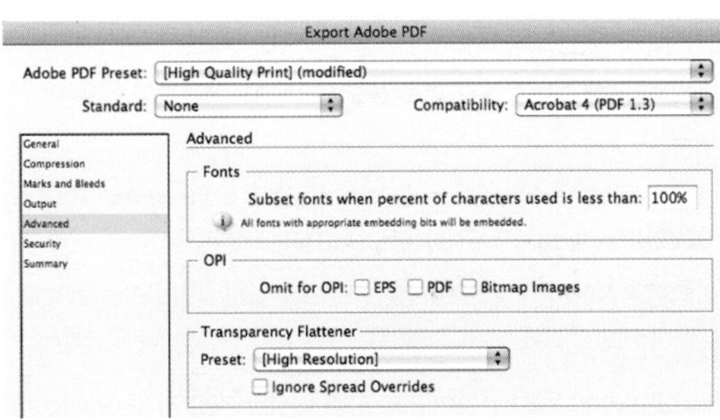

Note:

You can manage PDF Presets by choosing File>Adobe PDF Presets>Define. The dialog box that appears lists the built-in presets, as well as any presets you have created. You can also import presets from other users or export presets to send to other users.

10. **Click Export to create your PDF file. If you see a warning message, click OK.**

Your PDF file will be flattened, so some features (hyperlinks, bookmarks, etc.) will be unavailable. You didn't use those features in this project, however, so you don't have to worry about this warning.

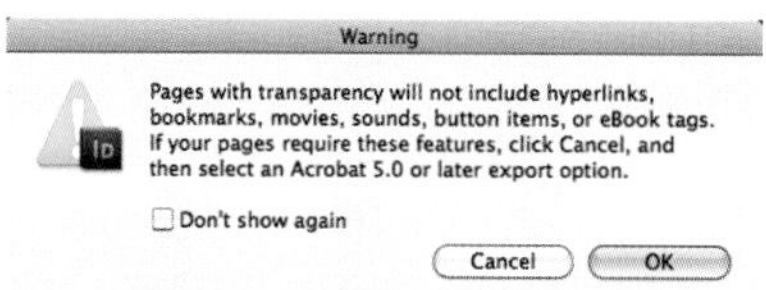

11. **Choose Window>Utilities>Background Tasks.**

The PDF export process happens in the background. This panel shows how much of the process has been completed (as a percentage), and will list any errors that occur. When the PDF file is finished, the export process is no longer listed in the panel.

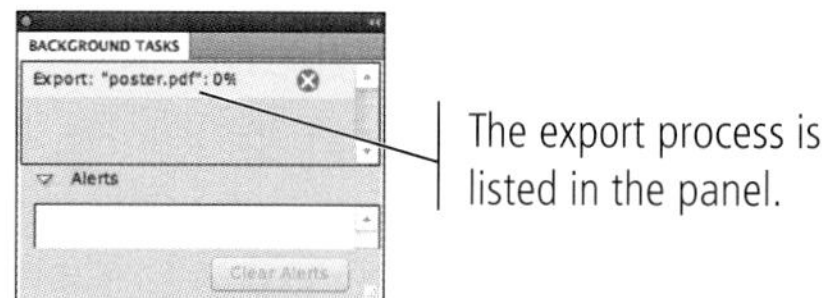

The export process is listed in the panel.

12. **Save the InDesign file and close it.**

INDESIGN FOUNDATIONS

Flattener Presets

InDesign includes three default flattener presets:

- **Low Resolution** works for desktop proofs that will be printed on low-end black-and-white printers and for documents that will be published on the Web.
- **Medium Resolution** works for desktop proofs and print-on-demand documents that will be printed on PostScript-compatible color printers.
- **High Resolution** works for commercial output on a printing press and for high-quality color proofs.

You can create your own flattener presets by choosing Edit>Transparency Flattener Presets and clicking New in the dialog box. You can also use the Transparency Flattener Presets dialog box to load flattener presets created on another machine — such as one your service provider created for their specific output device and/or workflow.

- The preset **Name** will be listed in the related output menus. You should use names that suggest the preset's use, such as "PDF for XL Printing Company." (Using meaningful names is a good idea for any asset that can have a name — from color swatches to output presets. "My Preset 12" is meaningless, possibly even to you after a few days, while "Preset for HP Indigo" tells you exactly when to use those settings.)
- **Raster/Vector Balance** determines how much vector information will be preserved when artwork is flattened. This slider ranges from 0 (all information is flattened as rasters) to 100 (maintains all vector information).
- **Line Art and Text Resolution** defines the resulting resolution of vector elements that will be rasterized, up to 9600 ppi. For good results in commercial printing applications, this option should be at least 600–1200 ppi (ask your output provider what settings they prefer you to use).
- **Gradient and Mesh Resolution** defines the resolution for gradients that will be rasterized, up to 1200 ppi. This option should typically be set to 300 ppi for most commercial printing applications.
- **Convert All Text to Outlines** converts all type to outline shapes; the text will not be editable in a PDF file.
- **Convert All Strokes to Outlines** converts all strokes to filled paths.
- **Clip Complex Regions** forces boundaries between vector objects and rasterized artwork to fall along object paths, reducing potential problems that can result when only part of an object is rasterized.

Project Review

fill in the blank

1. The gradient ______ tool can be used to draw the direction and position of a gradient within a frame.

2. The Type ______ menu command reveals characters such as paragraph returns and tabs.

3. Kerning ______ is the space between specific pairs of letters. To change this value, you have to place the insertion point between two characters.

4. The Baseline ______ is the theoretical line on which the bottoms of letters rest.

5. The Outport ______ indicates that more text exists in the story than will fit into the available frame (or series of linked frames).
   overset text icon

6. The ______ can be used to copy type formatting from one type element to another.

7. The ______ panel is used to apply optical margin alignment.

8. ______ are objects that are attached to specific areas of text.

9. effective Resolution ______ is the resolution of an image after its scaling in the layout has been taken into account.

10. Jpeg ______ compression for raster images is lossy, which means data is thrown away to reduce the file size.

short answer

1. Briefly explain how transparency is applied to objects in an InDesign page layout.

2. Briefly define a clipping path; provide at least two examples of how they might be useful.

3. Briefly explain the difference between character formatting and paragraph formatting.

Portfolio Builder Project

Use what you learned in this project to complete the following freeform exercise.
Carefully read the art director and client comments, then create your own design to meet the needs of the project.
Use the space below to sketch ideas; when finished, write a brief explanation of your reasoning behind your final design.

art director comments

The former marketing director for the Miami Jazz Festival recently moved to California to be the director of the Laguna Beach Sawdust Festival. She was pleased with your work on the jazz festival project, and would like to hire you to create the advertising for next year's art festival event.

To complete this project, you should:

- ❑ Download the **Print5_PB_Project8.zip** archive from the Student Files Web page to access the client-supplied text file.
- ❑ Develop some compelling visual element that will be the central focus of the ads.
- ❑ Create an ad that fits on a tabloid-size newspaper page (9 1/2 × 11 1/2″ with no bleeds).
- ❑ Create a second version of the same ad to fit a standard magazine trim size (8 1/4 × 10 7/8″ with 1/8″ bleeds).

client comments

The Sawdust Festival is one of the longest running and well-known art shows in California, maybe even the entire United States. We're planning our advertising campaign for the 2010 summer.

You might want to poke around our Web site to get some ideas. There's information about the festival's history, as well as images from previous shows.

We need an ad that will be placed in the pull-out sections of regional newspapers, and another version of the same ad that can go into magazines for travel/tourism audiences (like the WestWays magazine from AAA). Both ads should be four-color, although you should keep in mind the basic color scheme that we use on our Web site.

The ads need to have all the relevant text. But just as important, we want the ad to be art in its own right; the visual element you create will actually be repurposed for festival souvenirs like shirts, posters, and so on.

project justification

Project Summary

This project combined form and function — presenting the client's information in a clear, easy-to-read manner, while using large graphic elements to grab the viewer's attention and reinforce the message of the piece. As the client requested, the main focus is on the graphics in the top two-thirds of the piece while the relevant text is large enough to be visible but isn't the primary visual element.

Completing this poster involved adjusting a number of different text formatting options, including paragraph settings and the flow of text across multiple frames. You should now understand the difference between character and paragraph formatting, and know where to find the different options when you need them.

The graphics options in InDesign give you significant creative control over virtually every element of your layouts. Custom colors and gradients add visual interest to any piece, while more sophisticated tools like non-destructive transparency and other effects allow you to experiment entirely within your page layout until you find exactly the look you want to communicate your intended message.

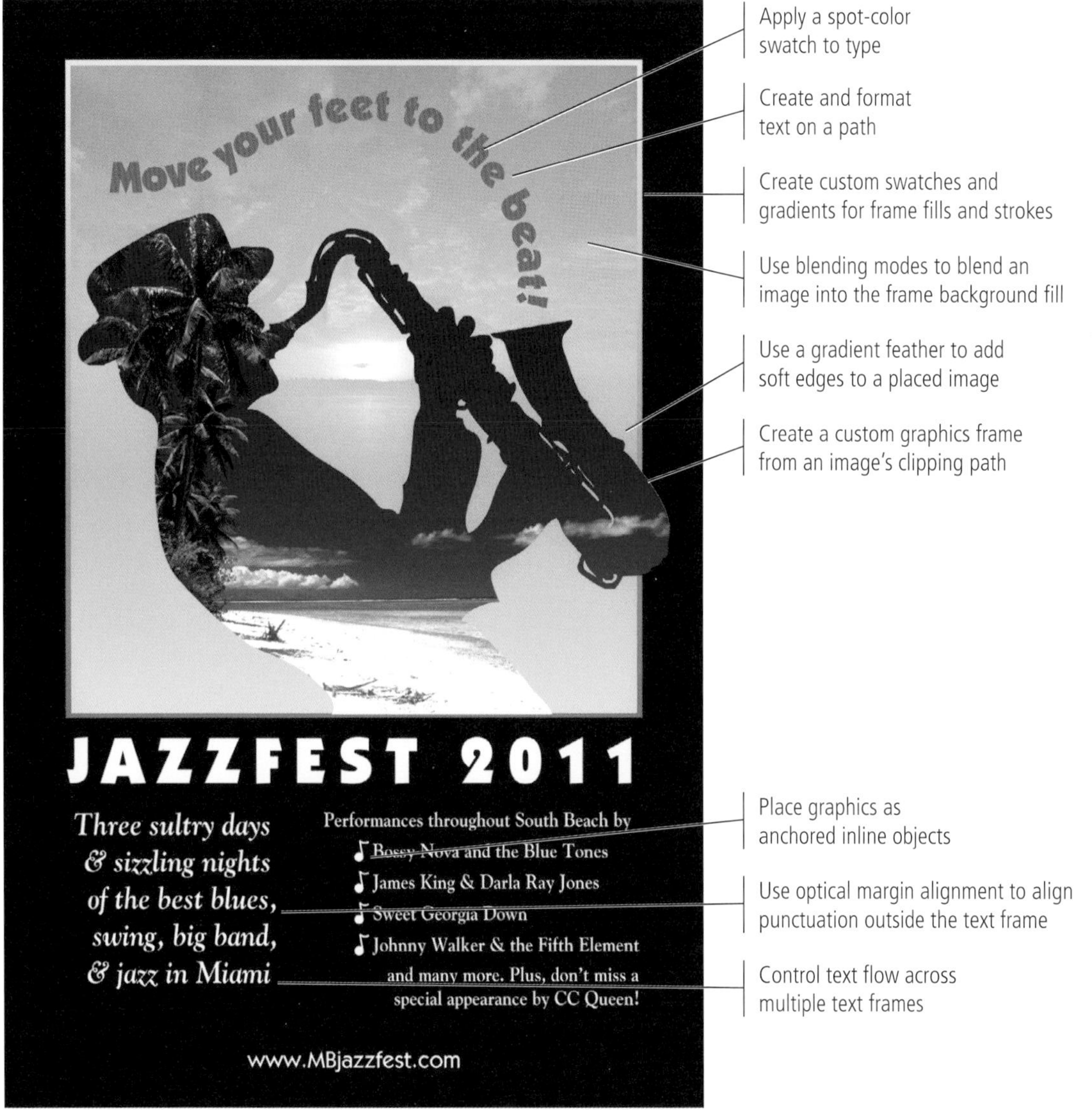

Move your feet to the beat!
JAZZFEST 2011
Three sultry days
& sizzling nights
of the best blues,
swing, big band,
& jazz in Miami
Performances throughout South Beach by
Bossy Nova and the Blue Tones
James King & Darla Ray Jones
Sweet Georgia Down
Johnny Walker & the Fifth Element
and many more. Plus, don't miss a
special appearance by CC Queen!
www.MBjazzfest.com
Apply a spot-color swatch to type
Create and format text on a path
Create custom swatches and gradients for frame fills and strokes
Use blending modes to blend an image into the frame background fill
Use a gradient feather to add soft edges to a placed image
Create a custom graphics frame from an image's clipping path
Place graphics as anchored inline objects
Use optical margin alignment to align punctuation outside the text frame
Control text flow across multiple text frames

project 9

HeartSmart Newsletter

Your client is a non-profit foundation that focuses on health education and public awareness. It publishes a monthly newsletter for people on various mailing lists, which are purchased from a list-management vendor. The editor wants to change the existing newsletter template, and wants you to take over the layout once the template has been revised.

This project incorporates the following skills:

- ❑ Opening and modifying an existing layout template
- ❑ Managing missing font and link requests
- ❑ Replacing graphics files to meet specific color output needs
- ❑ Formatting text with template styles
- ❑ Controlling text-frame inset, alignment, and wrap attributes
- ❑ Creating a table with data from a Microsoft Excel worksheet
- ❑ Preflighting the final layout and creating a job package

Project Meeting

client comments

In the past our newsletter was printed as a two-color job on a duplicator. However, the printer just told us that we can go to four-color printing and pay virtually the same per piece as we used to pay.

We need some other changes too. We want to go from four columns to three on the front, and from three columns to two on the back. The checkerboard area on the front usually has four random pictures, and the bar at the top of the back has a single image. Those all used to be grayscale photos, but now you can use color.

We'd like you to make modifications to the template, and then use the template to create the current issue. We sent you the pictures we want to use for this issue, as well as the three text pieces (the main article, a sidebar for the front, and the story for the back). There's also a table in Microsoft Excel format that we want to include on the back.

art director comments

Whenever you work with a file that someone else created, there is always the potential for problems. When you first open the template, you'll have to check the fonts and images and make whatever adjustments are necessary. Make sure you save the file as a template again before you build the new issue.

Moving from two-color to four-color isn't too big a deal — it's actually easier than going from color to grayscale since color adds possibilities instead of limiting them. You have the opportunity to add color to common design elements (including styles), and you should also use the color version of the nameplate instead of the grayscale one.

The printer said they prefer to work with native application files instead of PDF, so when you're finished implementing the layout, you'll need to check the various elements, and then create a final job package.

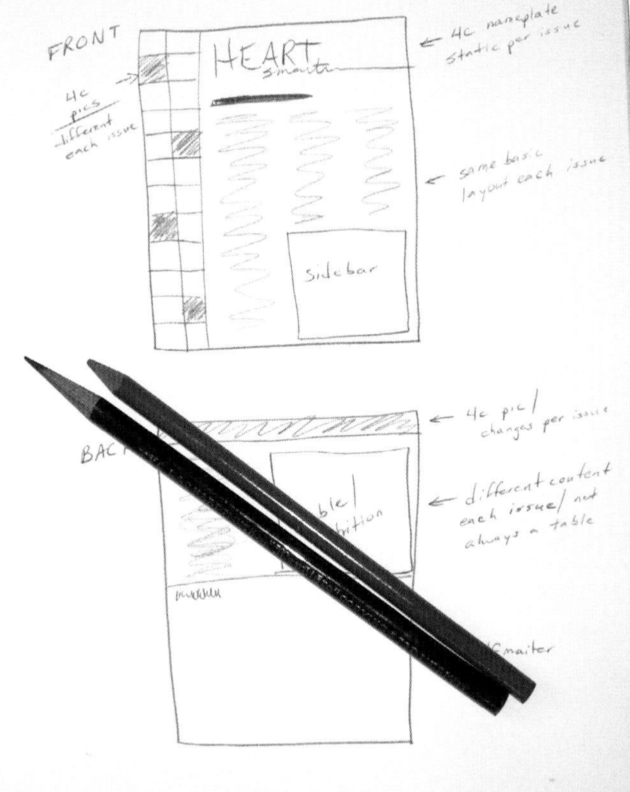

project objectives

To complete this project, you will:

- ❑ Handle requests for missing fonts and images
- ❑ Edit master page elements to meet new requirements
- ❑ Save a layout file as a template
- ❑ Access master page elements on the layout pages
- ❑ Format imported text using template styles
- ❑ Build and format a table using data from a Microsoft Excel spreadsheet
- ❑ Create a final job package for the output provider

Stage 1 Working with Templates

Templates are commonly used whenever you have a basic layout that will be implemented more than once — for example, the structure of a newsletter remains the same, but the content for each issue changes. InDesign templates are special types of files that store the basic structure of a project. Well-planned templates can store layout elements such as nonprinting guides that mark various areas of the job; placeholder frames that will contain different stories or images in each revision; elements that remain the same in every revision, such as the nameplate; and even formatting information that will be applied to different elements so the elements can be consistent from one issue to the next.

Manage Missing Fonts

When you work with digital page layouts — whether in a template or in a regular layout file — it's important to understand that fonts are external files of data that describe the font for on-screen display and for the output device. The fonts you use in a layout need to be available on any computer that will be used to open the file. InDesign stores a reference to used fonts, but it does not store the actual font data.

Note:

Missing fonts are one of the most common problems in the digital graphics output process. This is one of the primary advantages of using PDF files for output — PDF can store actual font data so you don't need to include the separate font files in your job package. (However, PDF can't solve the problem of missing fonts used in a layout template.)

1. **Download Print5_RF_Project9.zip from the Student Files Web page.**

2. **Expand the ZIP archive in your WIP folder (Macintosh) or copy the archive contents into your WIP folder (Windows).**

   This creates a folder named **HeartSmart**, which contains the files you need for this project. You should also use this folder to save the files you create in this project.

3. **Select the file heartsmart.indt in the WIP>HeartSmart folder. Choose the Open Original option at the bottom of the dialog box.**

   You have several options when you open an existing template file:

   - If you choose **Open Normal** to open a regular InDesign file (INDD), the selected file appears in a new document window or tab. When you use this option to open a template file (INDT), InDesign creates and opens a new untitled file that is based on the template.
   - When you choose the **Open Original** option, you open the actual InDesign template file so you can make and save changes to the template.
   - You can use the **Open Copy** option to open a regular InDesign file as if it were a template; the result is a new untitled document based on the file you selected.

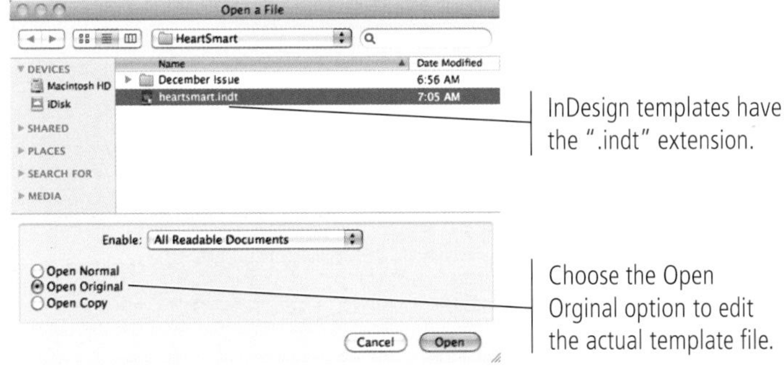

4. **Click Open, then review the warning message.**

   InDesign stores links to images placed in a layout; the actual placed-file data is not stored in the InDesign file. If placed files are not available in the same location as when they were originally placed, you'll see a warning message when you open the file. You'll correct this problem in the next exercise.

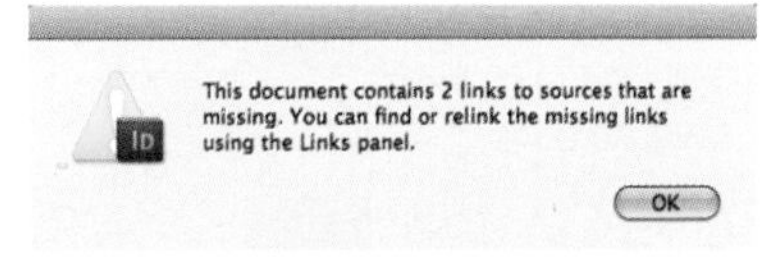

5. **Click OK in the warning, and then review the information in the resulting Missing Fonts dialog box.**

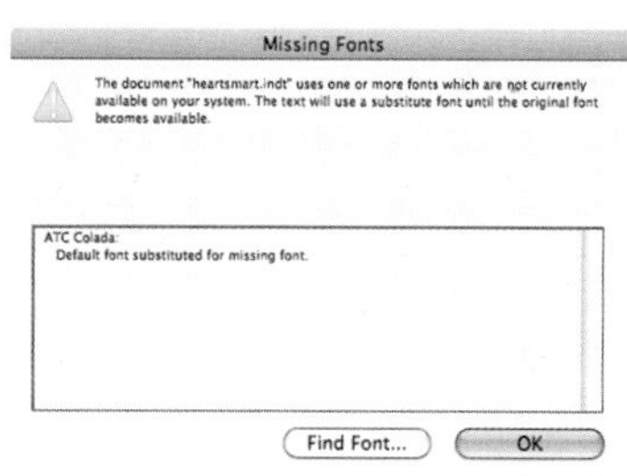

Missing Fonts
The document "heartsmart.indt" uses one or more fonts which are not currently available on your system. The text will use a substitute font until the original font becomes available.
ATC Colada:
Default font substituted for missing font.
Find Font...
OK

Any time you open a file that calls for fonts that are not installed on your computer system, you see this warning. You could blindly fix the problem now (without knowing what will be affected), but we prefer to review problem areas before making changes.

6. **Click OK to dismiss the Missing Fonts dialog box.**

7. **Open the Pages panel (Window>Pages).**

The Pages panel is the easiest way to navigate through the pages in a layout, including master pages. You can navigate to any page by simply double-clicking the page's icon, or navigate to a spread by double-clicking the spread page numbers (below the page icons).

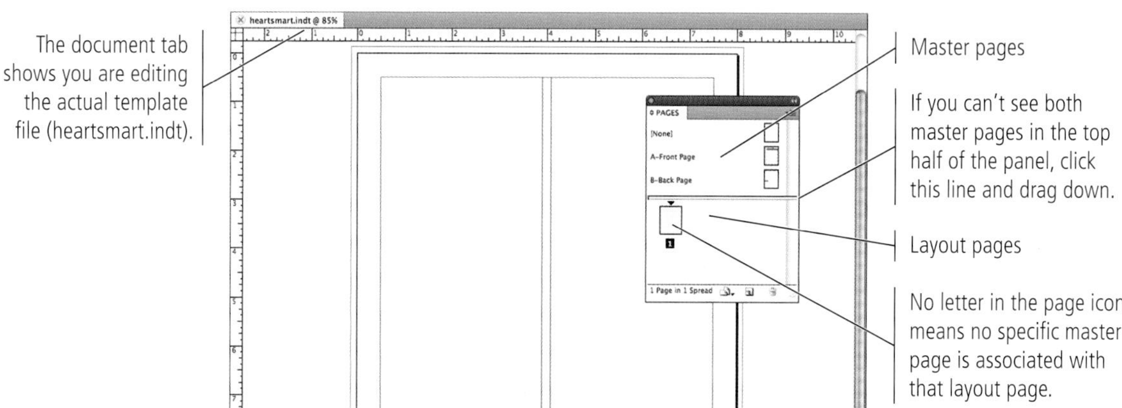

The document tab shows you are editing the actual template file (heartsmart.indt).
Master pages
If you can't see both master pages in the top half of the panel, click this line and drag down.
Layout pages
No letter in the page icon means no specific master page is associated with that layout page.

Think of master pages as templates for different pages in the layout. This file, for example, has two master pages: Front Page and Back Page. The letters preceding each master page name are automatically added and used to identify which layout pages are associated with which master page. (This will become clear as you continue through this project.)

8. **Double-click the A-Front Page icon to display that layout.**

The top area of the newsletter (the **nameplate** area) includes the newsletter logotype, as well as the "Published by…" line and the issue date. A pink highlight around the type shows that the font used in this area is not available.

Note:

The Missing Font highlighting is only a visual indicator on your screen. It is not included when the job is output.

9. **Using the Type tool, click the frame with the missing font to place the insertion point.**

The Control panel shows the missing font name in brackets. Any time you see a font name in brackets, you know you have a potential problem.

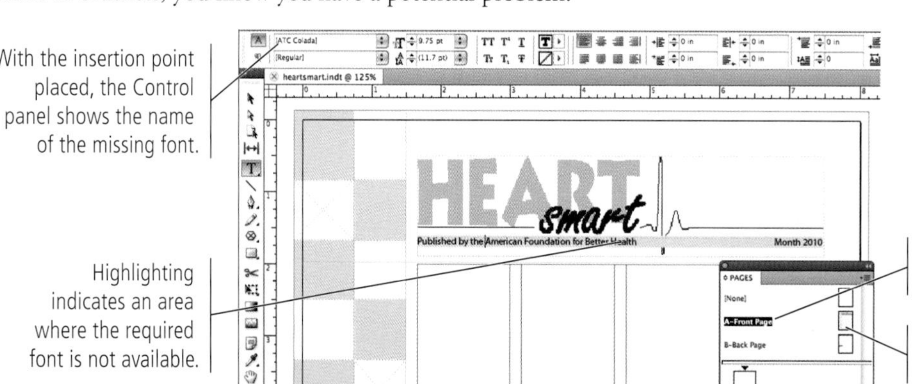

With the insertion point placed, the Control panel shows the name of the missing font.
Highlighting indicates an area where the required font is not available.
HEART smart
Published by the American Foundation for Better Health
Month 2010
The name or number of the active page is highlighted.
The icon of the selected page is highlighted.

10. **Choose Type>Find Font.**

The Find Font dialog box lists every font used in the layout — including missing ones (with a warning icon). You can use this dialog box to replace any font — including missing ones — with another font that is available on your system.

Note:

If the nameplate information is not highlighted, open the Composition pane of the Preferences dialog box and make sure the Highlight Substituted Fonts option is checked.

The highlighting only appears if you are in the Normal viewing mode.

11. **Highlight ATC Colada in the Fonts in Document list and click the More Info button.**

The bottom section of the dialog box shows information about the selected font, including the places where it's used (in this case, 66 characters on A-Front Page).

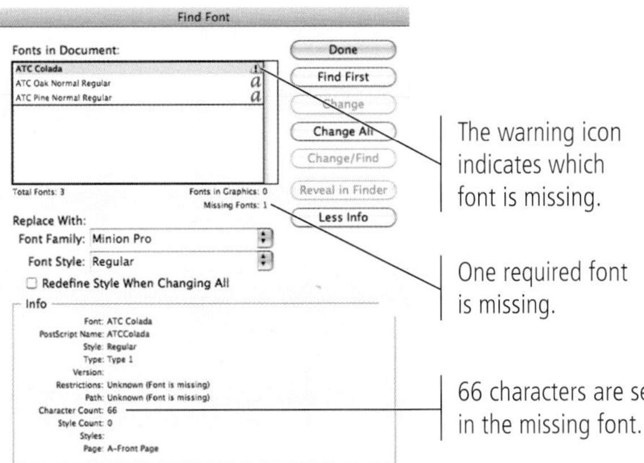

The warning icon indicates which font is missing.
One required font is missing.
66 characters are set in the missing font.

12. **In the Replace With area, choose ATC Oak Normal in the Font Family menu.**

13. **Click Change All to replace all instances of ATC Colada with ATC Oak Normal.**

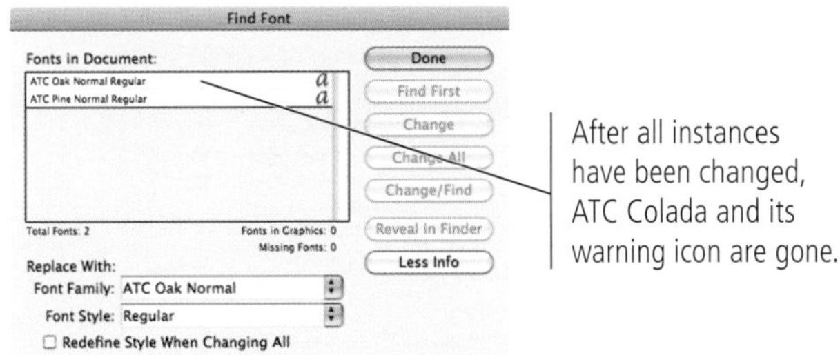

After all instances have been changed, ATC Colada and its warning icon are gone.

Note:

If a font is used in styles, you can apply your font replacement choices to style definitions by checking the Redefine Style When Changing All option.

14. **Click Done to close the Find Font dialog box.**

Once you have replaced the missing font, the pink highlighting disappears.

Note:

You can click the Find Next button to review individual instances of a missing font, or you can click the Change or Change/Find button to replace and review individual instances of the selected font.

15. **Choose File>Save to save your changes to the template file, and then continue to the next exercise.**

Because you used the Open Original option, you are editing the actual template file; this means you can simply use the regular Save command to save your changes to the template. If you used the Open Normal option to open and edit a template file, you would have to use the Save As command and save the edited file with the same name and extension as the original template to overwrite the original.

Replace Missing Graphics

Placed graphics can cause problems if those files aren't where they're supposed to be (or at least where InDesign thinks they should be). Placed graphics files can be either **missing** (they were moved from the location from which they were originally placed in the layout, or the name of the file was changed) or **modified** (they were resaved after being placed into the layout, changing the linked file's "time stamp" but not its location or file name). In either case, you need to correct these problems before the file can be successfully output.

1. **With heartsmart.indt open, display the Links panel (Window>Links).**

   The Links panel lists every file that is placed in your layout. Missing images show a red stop-sign icon; modified images show a yellow yield sign.

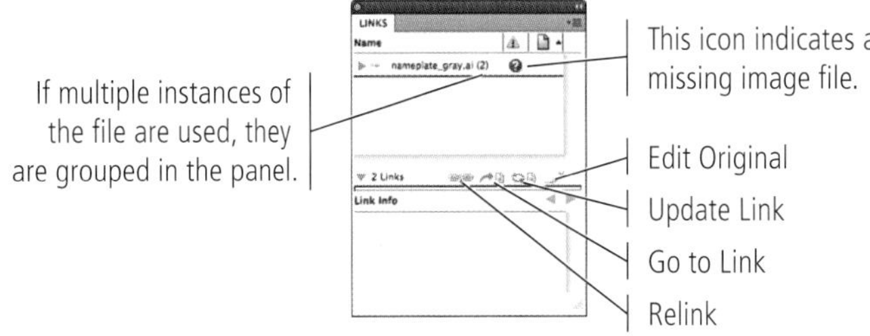

If multiple instances of the file are used, they are grouped in the panel.
This icon indicates a missing image file.
Edit Original
Update Link
Go to Link
Relink

2. **Click the arrow to the left of the nameplate_gray.ai file to show the two instances.**

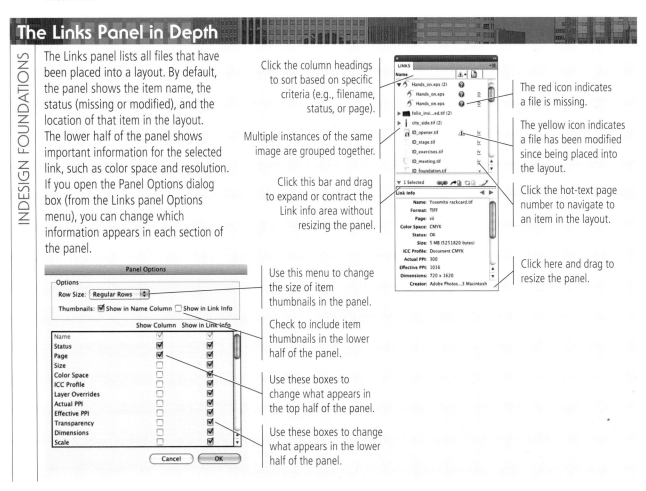

The Links Panel in Depth

INDESIGN FOUNDATIONS

The Links panel lists all files that have been placed into a layout. By default, the panel shows the item name, the status (missing or modified), and the location of that item in the layout. The lower half of the panel shows important information for the selected link, such as color space and resolution. If you open the Panel Options dialog box (from the Links panel Options menu), you can change which information appears in each section of the panel.

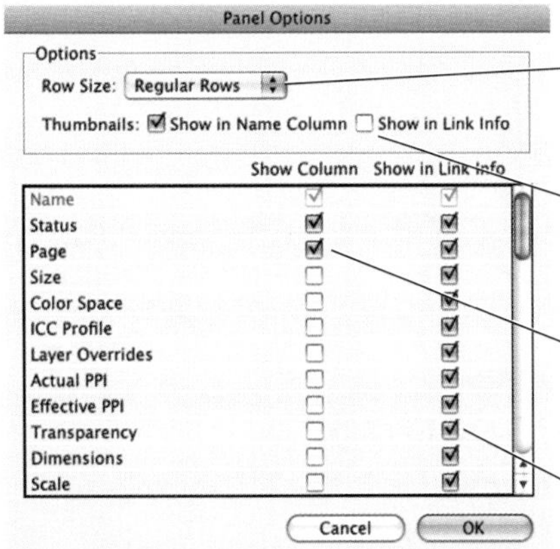

Click the column headings to sort based on specific criteria (e.g., filename, status, or page).

Multiple instances of the same image are grouped together.

Click this bar and drag to expand or contract the Link info area without resizing the panel.

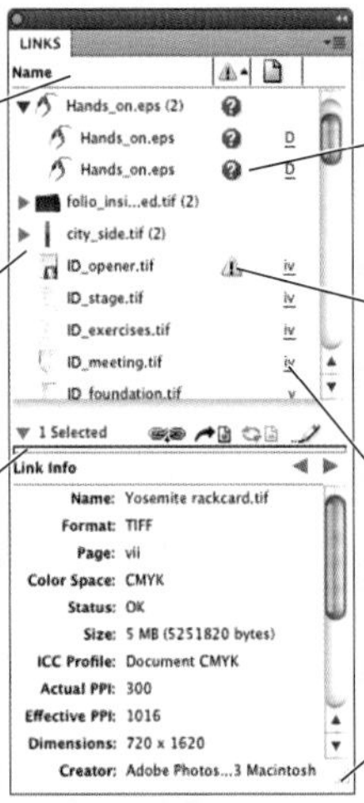

The red icon indicates a file is missing.

The yellow icon indicates a file has been modified since being placed into the layout.

Click the hot-text page number to navigate to an item in the layout.

Click here and drag to resize the panel.

Use this menu to change the size of item thumbnails in the panel.

Check to include item thumbnails in the lower half of the panel.

Use these boxes to change what appears in the top half of the panel.

Use these boxes to change what appears in the lower half of the panel.

3. **Click the first listed instance to select it, and then click the Go to Link button in the middle of the panel.**

   You can also use the hot-text link to the right of an image name to navigate to a specific placed image. The Pages panel shows that the B-Back Page master layout is now active because that is where the selected instance exists.

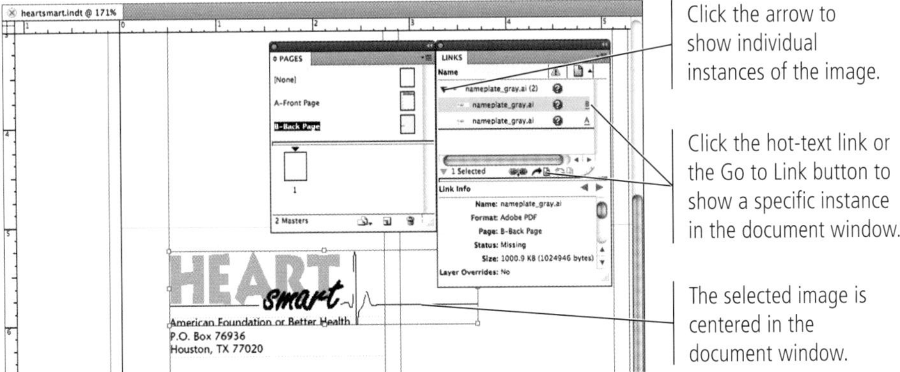

4. **With the file still selected in the panel, click the Relink button.**

5. **Navigate to nameplate_color.ai in the WIP>HeartSmart>December Issue folder and click Open.**

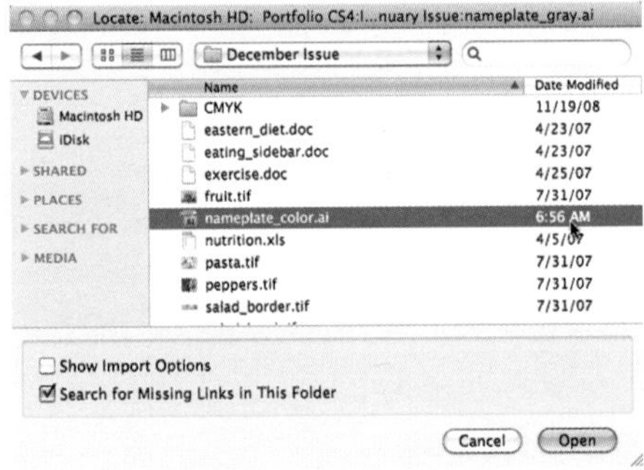

Note:

If the Search for Missing Links option is checked, InDesign will scan the selected folder to find other missing image files.

The selected instance is replaced with the new image. Because this link is a different image than the original, the Links panel now shows two separate items rather than the group of two instances for the same image. The other instance of the original image, listed in the Links panel, is still missing.

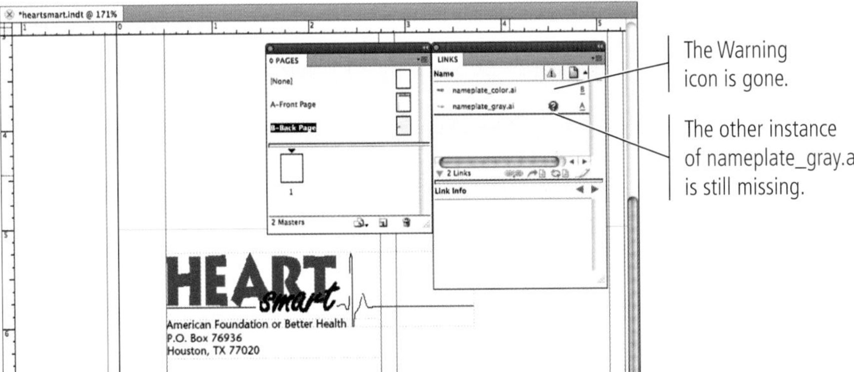

The Warning icon is gone.
The other instance of nameplate_gray.ai is still missing.

6. **Select the remaining missing image in the Links panel and click Go to Link.**

7. **With the file still selected in the panel, click the Relink button.**

8. **Navigate to nameplate_color.ai in the WIP>HeartSmart>December Issue folder and click Open.**

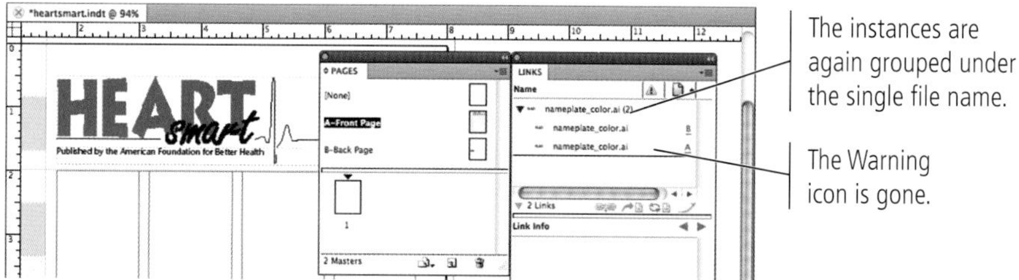

The instances are again grouped under the single file name.
The Warning icon is gone.

9. **Save the file and continue to the next exercise.**

Edit Margin and Column Guides

Your client wants to make several changes to the layout, including fewer columns and incorporating color into various elements. These changes will recur from one issue to the next, so you should change the template instead of simply changing the elements in each individual issue.

1. **With heartsmart.indt open, double-click the A-Front Page icon to show that layout in the document window.**

2. **Choose Layout>Margins and Columns. In the resulting dialog box, change the Columns field to 3 and the Gutter field to 0.2", and then click OK.**

   Every layout has a default setup, which you define when you create the file. Master pages have their own margin and column settings that can be different than the default document settings.

   Changing the column guides has no effect on the text frame; you have to change the text frame independently.

Note:

You can change the default margins and columns for a layout by choosing File>Document Setup.

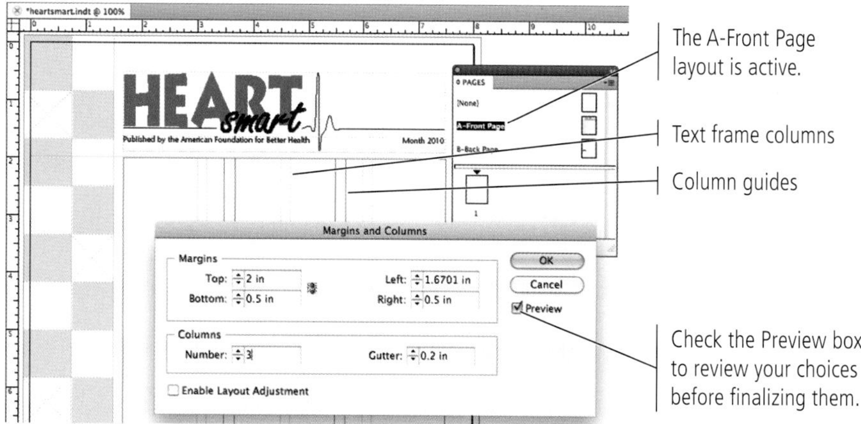

The A-Front Page layout is active.
Text frame columns
Column guides
Check the Preview box to review your choices before finalizing them.

3. **Using the Selection tool, click to select the 4-column text frame, and then Control/right-click the frame and choose Text Frame Options from the contextual menu.**

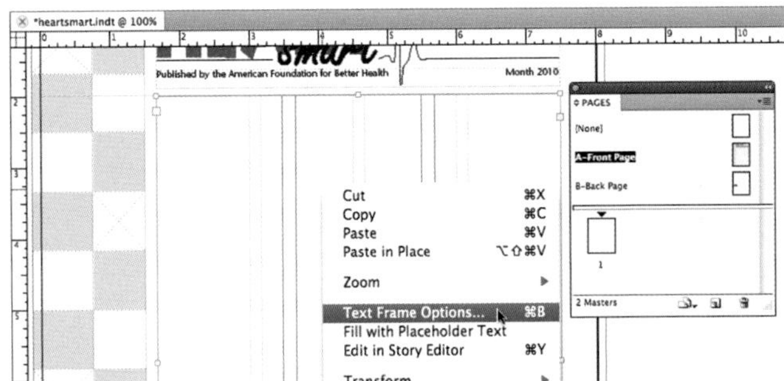

Note:

You can also access the Text Frame Options dialog box from the Object menu.

4. **Change the Number of Columns field to 3 and the Gutter field to 0.2" to match the changes you made to the column guides. Click OK to close the dialog box.**

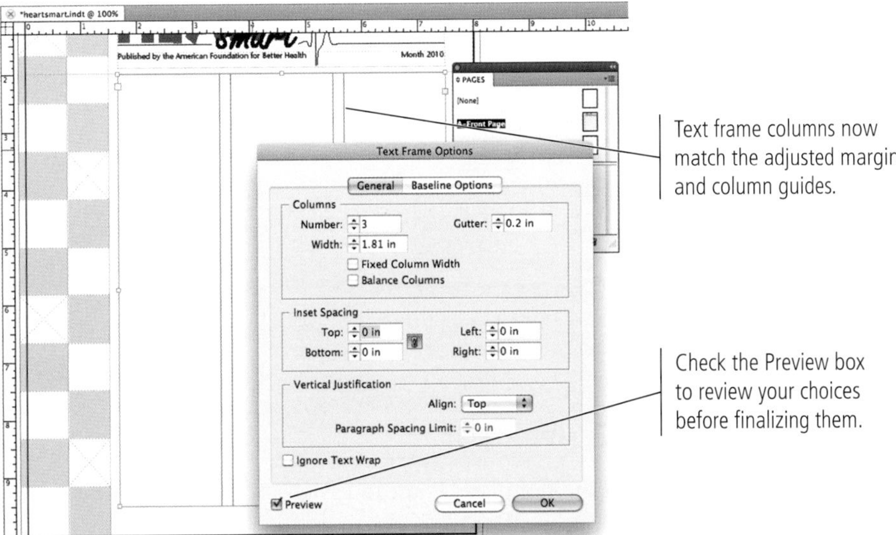

5. **In the Pages panel, double-click the B-Back Page icon to display that layout in the document window.**

6. **Choose Layout>Margins and Columns. Change the Bottom Margin setting to 5.25", change the Columns field to 2, change the Gutter to 0.2", and then click OK.**

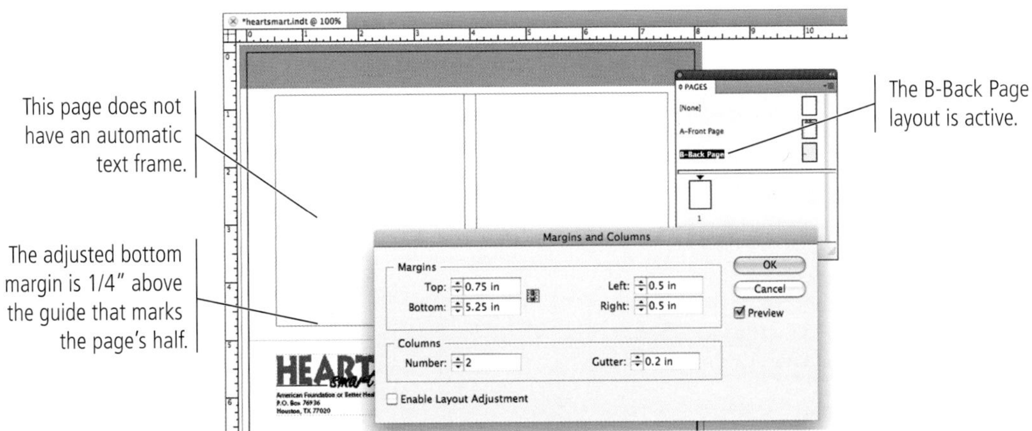

This page does not have an automatic text frame.
The adjusted bottom margin is 1/4" above the guide that marks the page's half.
The B-Back Page layout is active.

7. **Using the Type tool, create a text frame that fills the adjusted margins on the B-Back Page layout.**

8. **Control/right-click the text frame and choose Text Frame Options from the contextual menu. Change the frame to 2 columns with a 0.2″ gutter, and then click OK.**

   One of the advantages to using a template is eliminating repetitive tasks. Since every issue of the newsletter has a story in this area of the back, it makes sense to create the text frame as part of the master page (and template).

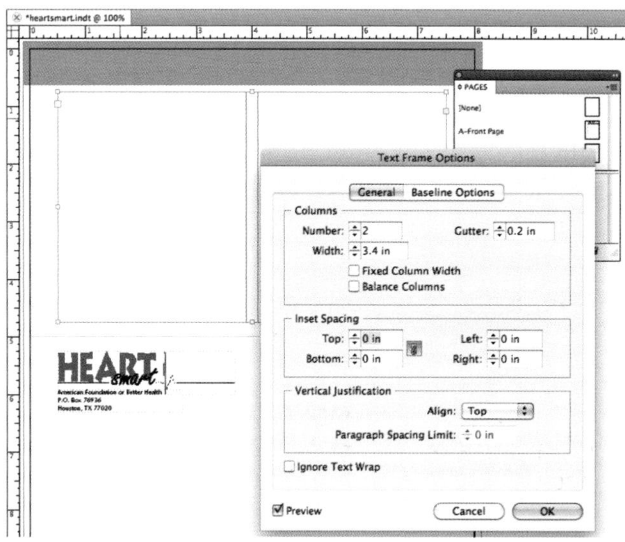

9. **Save the file and close it.**

 Create a New File Based on the Template

Once you have made the client's requested changes in the template, you can easily begin each new issue by simply opening the template. Only a few more things need to be addressed before you're ready to work on the current issue of the newsletter.

Every issue of the newsletter has the same structure — one front page and one back page. These layouts are already prepared as master pages, but you have to apply those master pages to the layout pages for individual issues. Since this occurs for every issue, it will remove a few more clicks from the process if you set up the layout pages as part of the template.

1. **Choose File>Open and navigate to your WIP>HeartSmart folder. Select the heartsmart.indt template file and choose the Open Normal option at the bottom of the dialog box.**

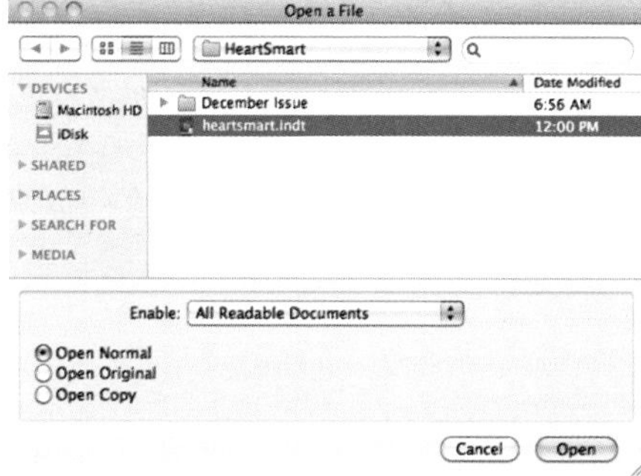

Understanding Master Pages

There are two kinds of pages in InDesign:

- **Layout pages** are the pages on which you place text and images.
- **Master pages** are the pages on which you place recurring information, such as running heads (information at the top of the page) and running footers (information at the bottom of the page).

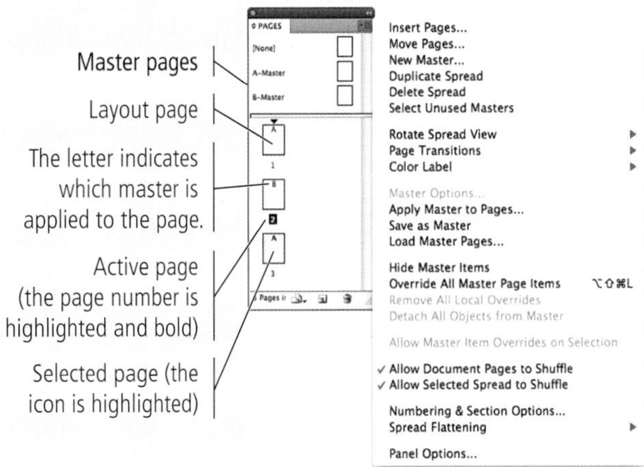

Master pages are one of the most powerful features in professional layout software. Think of a master page as a template for individual pages; anything on the master appears on the related layout page(s). Changing something on a master layout applies the same changes to the object on related layout pages (unless you already changed the object on the layout page, or detached the object from the master).

Master pages are accessed and controlled in the top half of the Pages panel. Layout pages, in the lower half of the panel, show the letter that corresponds to the master applied to that page. The Pages panel Options menu has a number of indispensable options for working with master pages:

- **New Master** opens a dialog box where you can assign a custom prefix, a meaningful name, whether the master will be based on another master page, and the number of pages (from 1 to 10) to include in the master layout.

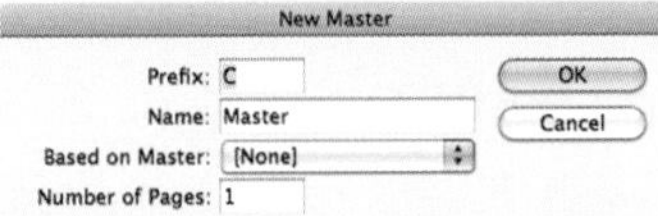

- **Select Unused Masters** highlights all master pages not associated with at least one layout page (and not used as the basis of another master page). This option can be useful if you want to clean up your layout and remove extraneous elements.
- **Master Options** opens a dialog box with the same options you defined when you created a new master.

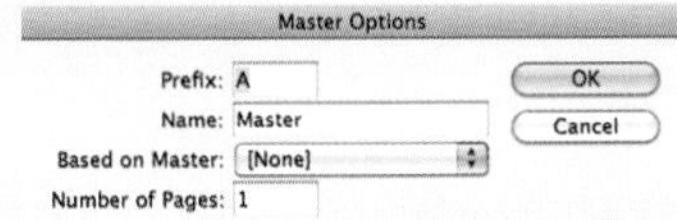

- **Apply Master to Pages** allows you to apply a specific master to selected pages. You can also apply a specific master to a layout by dragging the master icon onto the layout page icon in the lower half of the panel.
- **Save as Master** is useful if you've built a layout on a layout page and want to convert that layout to a master. Instead of copying and pasting the page contents, you can simply activate the page and choose Save as Master.
- **Load Master Pages** allows you to import entire master pages from one InDesign file to another. Assets such as colors and styles used on the imported masters will also be imported into the current InDesign file.
- **Hide/Show Master Items** toggles the visibility of master page items on layout pages.
- **Override All Master Page Items** allows you to access and change master items on a specific layout page. (It's important to realize that this command functions on a page-by-page basis.) You can also override individual objects by pressing Command/Control-Shift and clicking the object you want to override.
- **Remove All Local Overrides** reapplies the settings from the master items to related items on the layout page. (This option toggles to **Remove Selected Local Overrides** if you have a specific object selected on the layout page.)
- **Detach All Objects from Master** breaks the link between objects on a layout page and objects on the related master; in this case, changing items on the master has no effect on related layout page items. (This selection toggles to **Detach Selection from Master** if you have a specific object selected on the layout page.)
- **Allow Master Item Overrides on Selection**, active by default, allows objects to be overridden on layout pages. You can protect specific objects by selecting them on the master layout and toggling this option off.

2. **Click Open to create a new file based on the template.**

Opening a template using the Open Normal option creates a new untitled document that is based on the template.

3. **Double-click the Page 1 icon in the Pages panel.**

4. **In the Pages panel, drag the A-Front Page master icon onto the Page 1 icon in the lower half of the Pages panel.**

When a master page is applied to a layout page, everything on the master page is placed on the layout page.

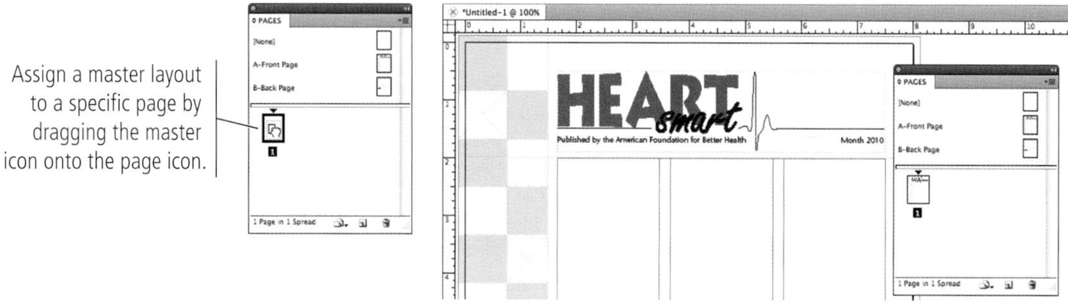

Assign a master layout to a specific page by dragging the master icon onto the page icon.

5. **Using the Selection tool, try to select the empty text frame on the page.**

This step will have no effect, and nothing will be selected. By default, you can't select master page items on a layout page; changes have to be made on the master page.

When you change an object on a master page, the same changes reflect on associated layout pages. For example, if you change the red box to blue on A-Front Page, the red box will turn blue on Page 1 as well.

In many cases, however, you might need to change a master page item for only a single page in the layout — a common occurrence when you use placeholder text or graphics frames on a master page. In this case, you have to override the master page layout for the specific layout page (or for a specific item by Command/Control-Shift-clicking that item), so you can select and change the overridden master page items.

> *Note:*
>
> *You can change the size of page icons in the Pages panel by choosing Panel Options at the bottom of the panel's Options menu.*

6. **Control/right-click the Page 1 icon and choose Override All Master Page Items from the contextual menu.**

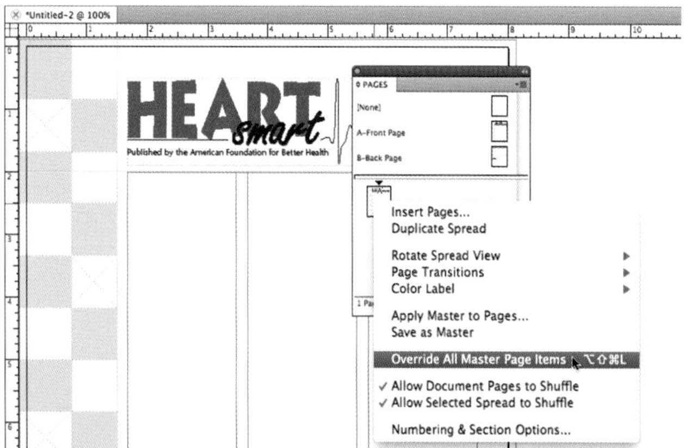

7. **Click to select the empty text frame.**

   By overriding the master page layout for this page, you make it possible to select and change master page items — including the text frame — on the layout page.

8. **Click the B-Back Page icon and drag it into the bottom half of the Pages panel (below the Page 1 icon).**

   You can add new pages to your layout by dragging any of the master page icons into the lower half of the panel.

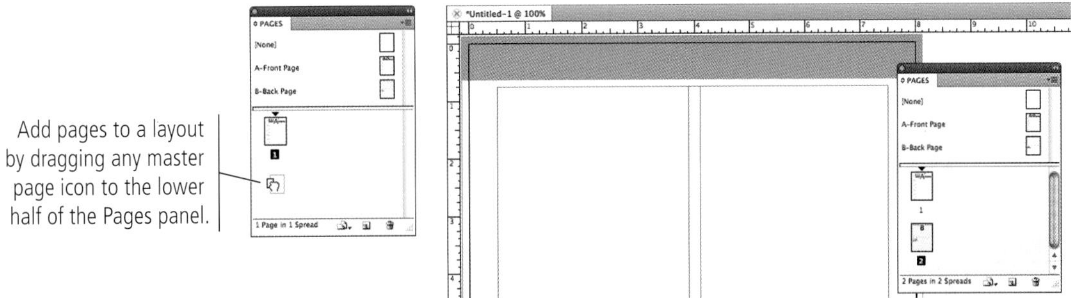

Add pages to a layout
by dragging any master
page icon to the lower
half of the Pages panel.

9. **Control/right-click the Page 2 icon and choose Override All Master Page Items from the contextual menu.**

   You can now select and change the text frame on Page 2, as well as the other objects from the B-Back Page master.

> *Note:*
>
> *Command/Control-Shift-click an object to detach individual objects from the master page.*

10. **Choose File>Save As. Navigate to your WIP>HeartSmart folder as the location for saving the template.**

    Because you opened the template to create a normal layout file, you have to use the Save As command to overwrite the edited template file.

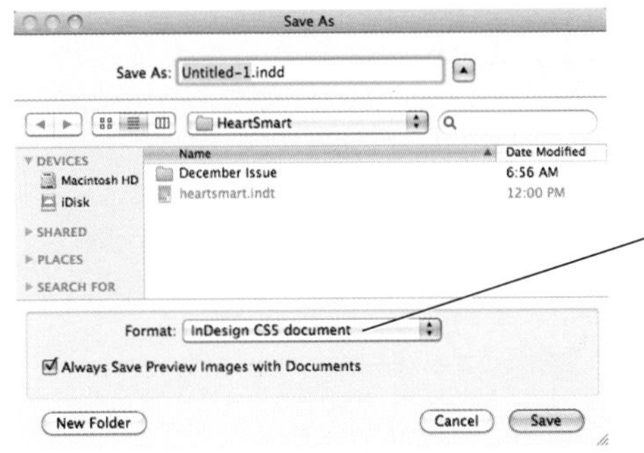

Because you created a new layout file from the template, the Format/Save As Type menu defaults to InDesign CS5 Document.

11. **Change the file name to heartsmart.**

12. **In the Format/Save As Type menu, choose InDesign CS5 Template.**

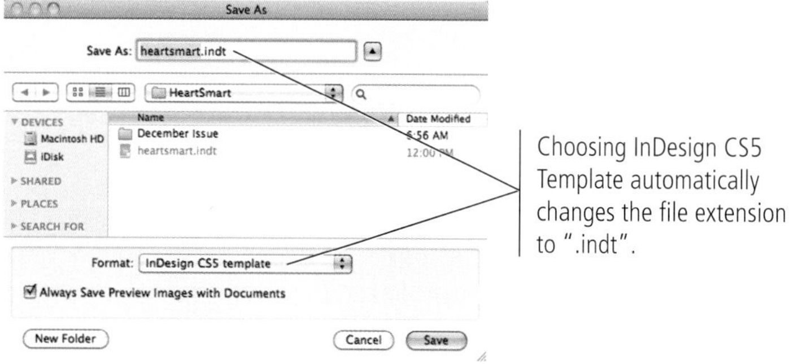

Choosing InDesign CS5 Template automatically changes the file extension to ".indt".

13. **Click Save, then read the resulting message.**

    Because you defined the same name as the original template, you have to confirm that you want to overwrite the template file with the new version.

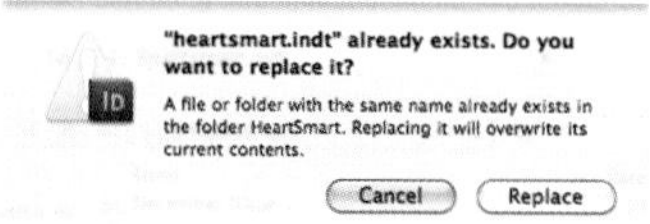

14. **Click Replace. When the save is complete, close the template file.**

Implement the Newsletter Template

By saving your work as a template, you have eliminated a significant amount of repetitive work that would otherwise need to be redone for every issue. There are still some tasks that will need to be done for each issue, such as changing the issue date and adding images to the front and back pages. These elements will change in each issue, so they can't be entirely "templated." But if you review the layout as it is now, you'll see that the template includes placeholders for these elements, so adding these elements is greatly simplified.

1. **Choose File>Open and navigate to your WIP>HeartSmart folder. Select the heartsmart.indt template file, choose the Open Normal option at the bottom of the dialog box, and click Open.**

   As in the previous exercise, opening the template file creates a new untitled document that is based on the template.

2. **Immediately choose File>Save As and navigate to your WIP>HeartSmart folder. Change the file name to newsletter_dec.indd and click Save.**

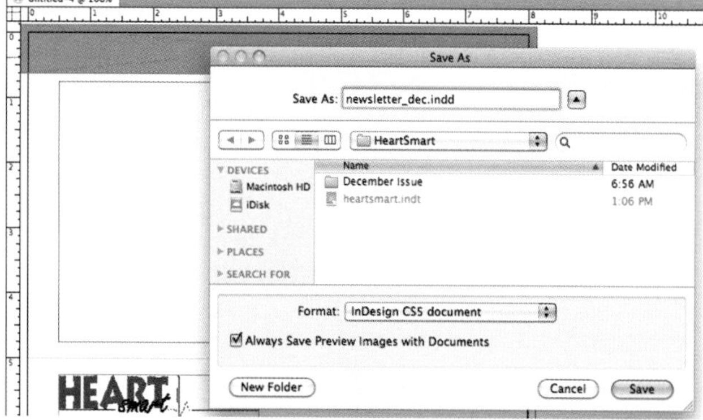

3. **Navigate to Page 1 of the file. Using the Type tool, highlight "Month 2010" in the nameplate area and type** `December 2010`**.**

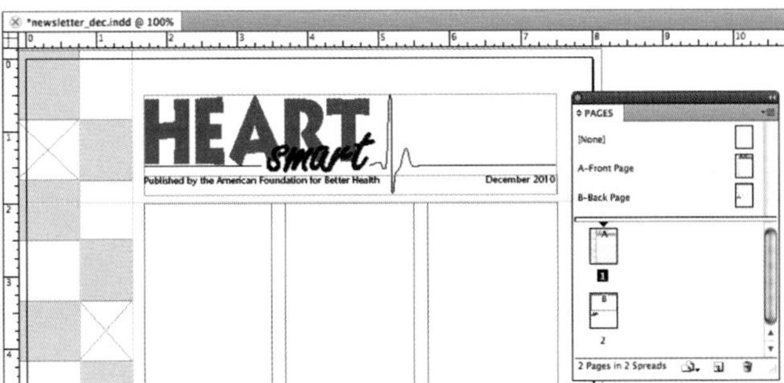

4. **Save the file and continue to the next exercise.**

Use Mini Bridge to Place Images

Mini Bridge, which is available in both Photoshop and InDesign, provides access to certain file-management operations of the full Bridge application, directly from a panel within InDesign. Specifically, it makes it very easy to place files into a layout by simply dragging and dropping. (Refer to Page 211 for an in depth explanation of the Mini Bridge panel.)

1. **With** `newsletter_dec.indd` **open, Shift-click the Go to Bridge button in the Application/Menu bar to open the Mini Bridge panel.**

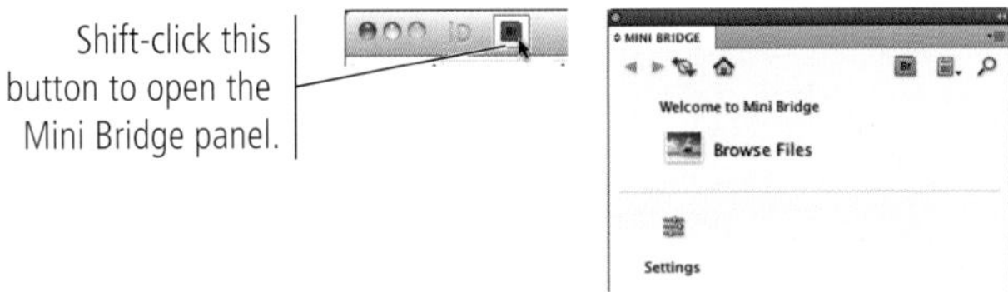

2. **In the Mini Bridge panel, click the Browse Files button.**

3. **Use the panel's Content pod to navigate to the WIP>HeartSmart>December Issue folder.**

   Navigating in the panel is very similar to the basic operating system navigation; simply double-click a folder icon to open it and show the folder's contents. (We can't be sure where your WIP folder is stored; you need to navigate through the correct path on your system.)

4. **Click the View button at the bottom of the panel and choose As Thumbnails.**

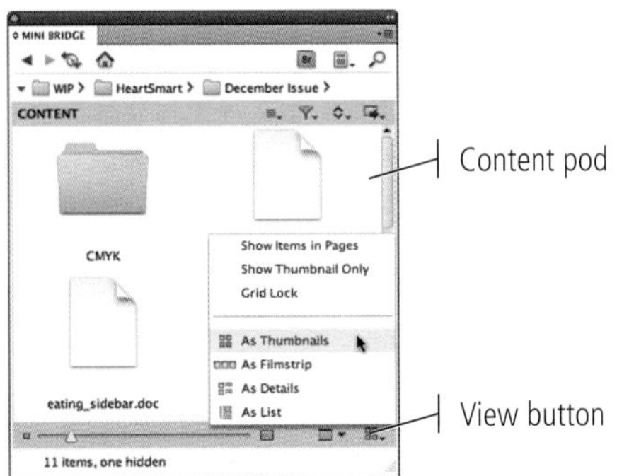

> ***Note:***
>
> *If Bridge is not already running on your computer, it might take a while for the Mini Bridge panel to show anything.*

5. **Scroll through the thumbnails to find fruit.tif. Click the fruit.tif thumbnail in the panel, and then drag it to the first empty graphics frame on the left side of Page 1.**

When you release the mouse button, the selected image is automatically placed into the frame where you drag.

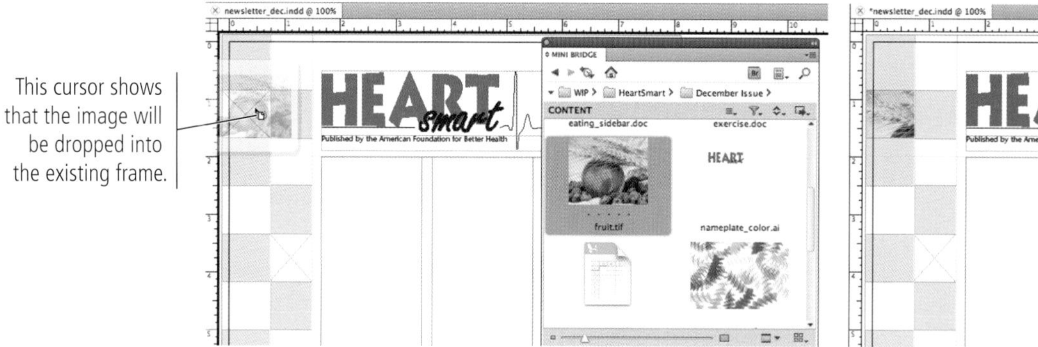

This cursor shows that the image will be dropped into the existing frame.

6. **In the Mini Bridge panel, click the pasta.tif thumbnail to select it. Press Command/Control and then click the peppers.tif and salad_bowl.tif thumbnails to add them to the active selection.**

Press Shift to select multiple contiguous files, or press Command/Control to select multiple non-contiguous files.

Note:

If the cursor is not over an existing frame when you release the mouse button, the selected file is loaded into the cursor; you can then click and drag to create a frame that will contain the loaded image.

7. **Click any of the selected thumbnails, drag into the document window, and then release the mouse button.**

Even if you release the mouse button over an existing frame, InDesign stores all three in the loaded place cursor; nothing is automatically placed in the file.

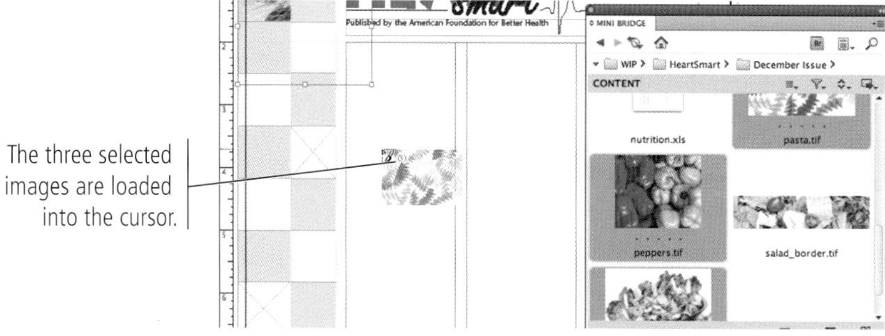

The three selected images are loaded into the cursor.

8. **Click the loaded cursor on the second graphics frame to place the first loaded image.**

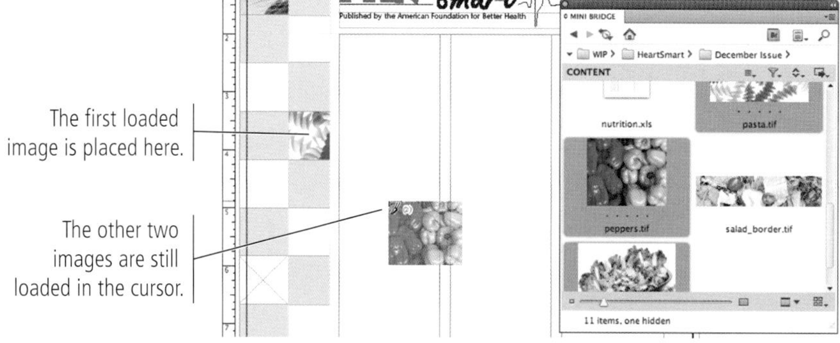

The first loaded image is placed here.
The other two images are still loaded in the cursor.

9. **Click to place the remaining images in the other two empty graphics frames.**

10. **Using the Direct Selection tool or the Content Indicator, click to select the image within the top frame. Control/right-click the selected image and choose Fitting>Fill Frame Proportionally from the contextual menu.**

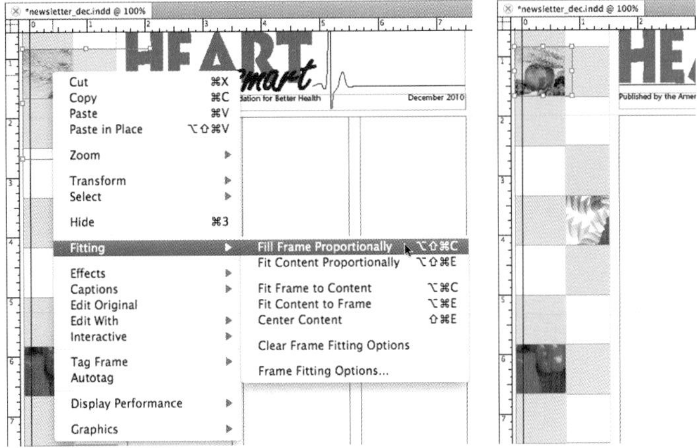

> ***Note:***
>
> *The same Fitting options are available in the Object>Fitting menu.*

> ***Note:***
>
> *Fitting options are available when either the frame or the frame content are selected. When the content is selected, however, you can see the red bounding box that marks the edge of the placed image (rather than only the frame bounding box).*

11. **Repeat Step 10 for the other three images on the left side of the page.**

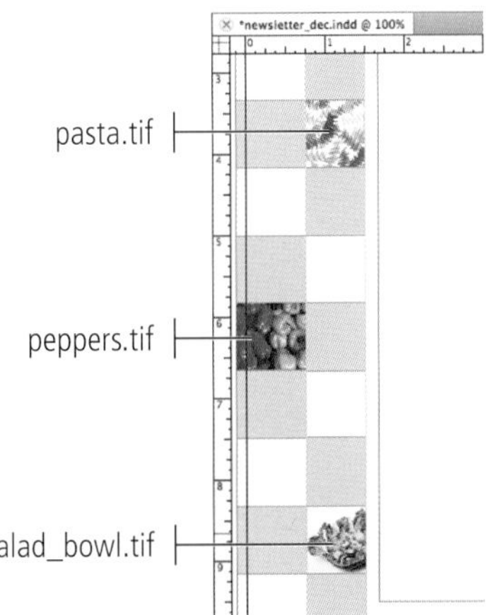

Content Fitting Options

INDESIGN FOUNDATIONS

The Fitting options resize content relative to the containing frame, or resize the containing frame to match the placed content.

- **Fill Frame Proportionally** resizes content to fill the entire frame while preserving the content's proportions.
- **Fit Content Proportionally** resizes content to fit entirely within its containing frame, maintaining the current aspect ratio of the image. Some empty space might result along one dimension of the frame.
- **Fit Frame to Content** resizes the frame to the dimensions of the placed content.
- **Fit Content to Frame** resizes content to fit the dimensions of the containing frame, even if that means scaling the content out of proportion (stretched in one direction or another).
- **Center Content** centers content within its containing frame, but neither the frame nor the content is resized.

Filling proportionally fills the frame; some areas of the image might be cropped.

Fitting proportionally places the entire image into the frame; some areas of the frame might be empty.

12. **Control/right-click the fourth image and choose Fitting>Center Content.**

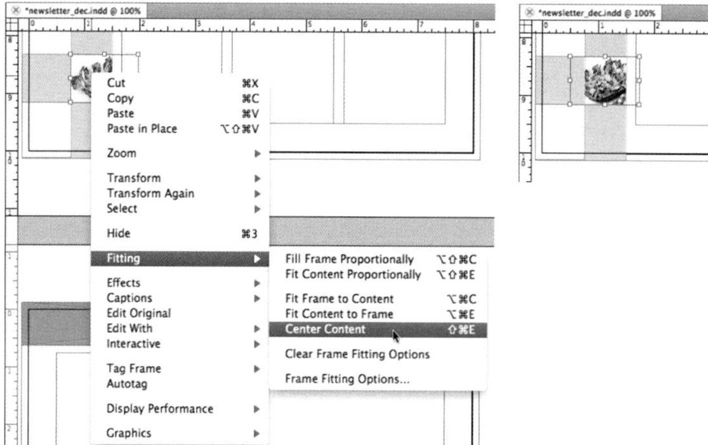

13. **Navigate to Page 2 of the layout. Using the Mini Bridge panel, drag the salad_border.tif thumbnail into the graphics frame at the top of the page.**

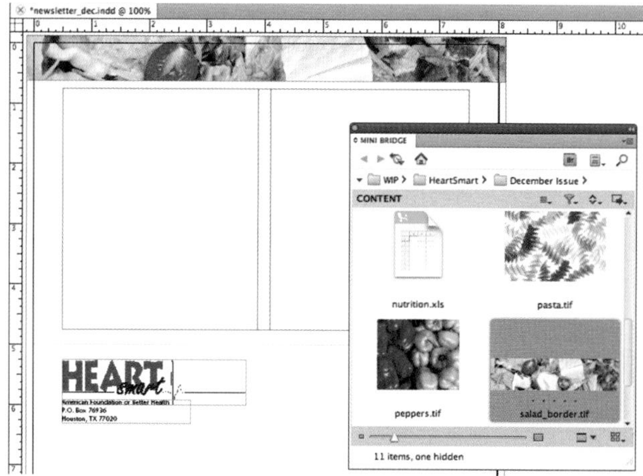

14. **Save the file and continue to the next stage of the project.**

Stage 2 Working with Styles

The principles of good design state that headings, subheadings, body copy, and other editorial elements should generally look the same throughout a single job — in other words, editorial elements should be consistent from one page to another, whether the job is two pages or two hundred.

In Project 8 you learned about the various text formatting options that can be applied in an InDesign layout. For any bit of text, there are dozens of character- and paragraph-formatting options, from the font and type size to the space above and below paragraphs. Whenever you work with longer blocks of copy, you'll apply the same group of formatting options to multiple pieces of text.

If you were to change each editorial element manually, you would have to make hundreds of clicks to create a two-page newsletter. Fortunately, InDesign makes it easy to store groups of text-formatting options as **styles**, which can be applied to any text with a single click.

The major advantages of using styles are ease of use and enhanced efficiency. Changes can be made instantly to all text defined as a particular style. For example, you might easily modify leading in the Body Copy style or change the font in the Subhead style from Helvetica to ATC Oak Bold. When a style definition changes, any text that uses that style automatically changes too.

InDesign supports both character styles and paragraph styles. **Character styles** apply only to selected words; this type of style is useful for setting off a few words in a paragraph without affecting the entire paragraph. **Paragraph styles** apply to the entire body of text between two ¶ symbols; this type of style defines the appearance of the paragraph, combining the character style used in the paragraph with line spacing, indents, tabs, and other paragraph attributes.

In this project, the client's original INDT template included a number of styles for formatting the text in each issue. Because the text frames already exist in the template layout, you only need to import the client's text and apply the existing styles.

Note:

Styles ensure consistency in text and paragraph formatting throughout a publication. Rather than trying to remember how you formatted a sidebar 45 pages ago, you can simply apply a predefined Sidebar style.

Note:

Paragraph styles define character attributes and paragraph attributes; character styles define only the character attributes. In other words, a paragraph style can be used to format text entirely — including font information, line spacing, tabs, and so on.

Apply Template Styles

Most InDesign jobs incorporate some amount of client-supplied text, which might be sent to you in the body of an email or saved in any number of text file formats. Many text files will be supplied from Microsoft Word, the most popular word-processing application in the United States market.

Microsoft Word includes fairly extensive options for formatting text (although not quite as robust or sophisticated as what you can do with InDesign). Many Microsoft Word users apply **local formatting** (selecting specific text and applying character and/or paragraph attributes); more sophisticated Microsoft Word users build text formatting styles similar to those used in InDesign.

Styles are most advantageous when working with text-intensive documents that have recurring editorial elements, such as headlines, subheads, and captions; when working with several people concurrently on the same project; and when creating projects with specific style requirements, such as catalogs or magazines.

1. **With Page 1 of newsletter_dec.indd active in the document window, choose File>Place and navigate to the file exercise.doc.**

   All text files for this project are in the WIP> HeartSmart>December Issue folder.

2. **Check the Show Import Options box at the bottom of the dialog box, and make sure Replace Selected Item is not checked.**

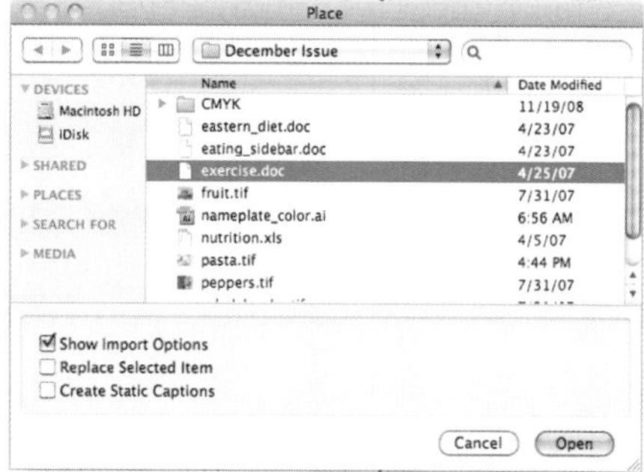

3. **Click Open. In the resulting dialog box, review the options in the Formatting section.**

When you import a Microsoft Word file into InDesign, you can either preserve or remove formatting saved in the Microsoft Word file (including styles defined in Microsoft Word).

4. **Make sure the Preserve Styles and Formatting option is selected and the Import Styles Automatically radio button is selected. Choose Auto Rename in both conflict menus, and then click OK.**

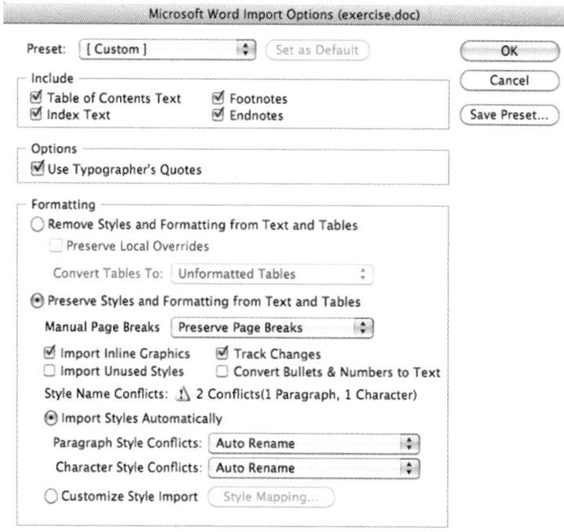

5. **If you see a Missing Fonts warning, click OK.**

You're going to replace the Microsoft Word formatting with InDesign styles, which should correct this problem.

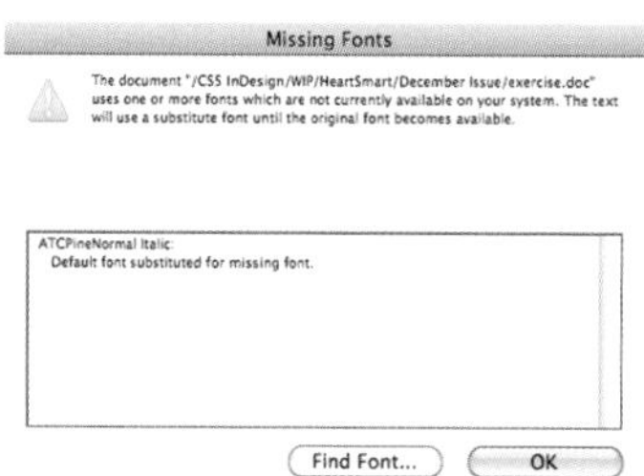

6. **Click the loaded cursor in the empty three-column text frame.**

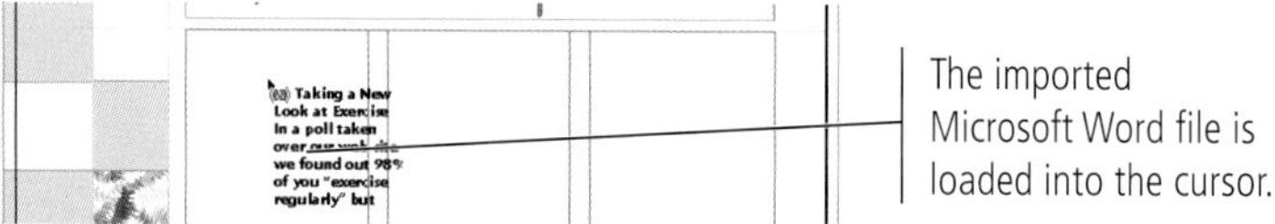

The imported Microsoft Word file is loaded into the cursor.

Working with Microsoft Word Files

Microsoft Word files can include a fairly sophisticated level of formatting attributes, from basic text formatting to defined paragraph and character styles to automatically generated tables of contents. When you import a Word file into InDesign, you can determine whether to include these elements in the imported text, as well as how to handle conflicts between imported elements and elements that already exist in your InDesign layout.

If these elements exist in the Microsoft Word file, checking the associated boxes imports those elements into your InDesign file.

Choose this option to convert straight quote marks to typographer's or "curly" quotes.

Choose this option to strip out all formatting applied in the file and import the file as plain text.

Choose this option to import the Microsoft Word file, including formatting.

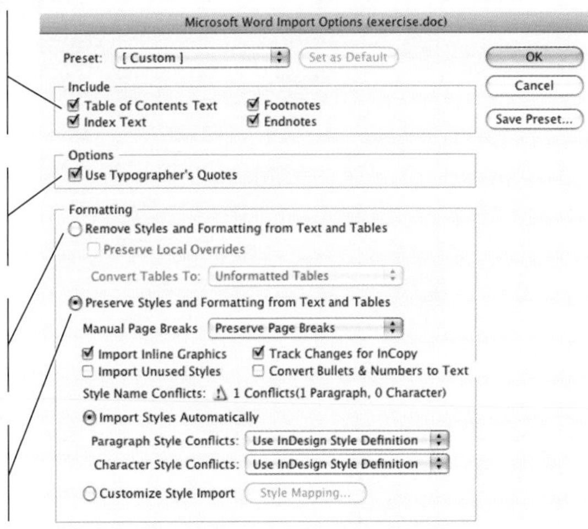

The **Manual Page Breaks** menu determines how page breaks in Word translate to InDesign. You can preserve manual breaks, convert them to column breaks, or ignore them. This option is important because Word users tend to force breaks where appropriate in the file — which rarely translates to a properly formatted InDesign layout. More often than not, you'll end up removing these page breaks, but it might be a good idea to include them in the import and remove them after you've reviewed the imported text.

If graphics have been placed into a Word file, the **Import Inline Graphics** option allows you to include those graphics as anchored objects in the InDesign story. If you choose to include graphics, it is extremely important to understand that the graphics might be embedded into the story instead of linked to the original data file (depending on how the graphic was placed into the Word file).

If you choose **Import Unused Styles**, all styles in the Word file will be imported into the InDesign layout. The most significant issue here is that styles might require fonts that you have not installed.

Word includes a powerful collaboration tool call Track Changes, which allows one person to review another person's changes to a file. (As publishers, we use this feature every day so editors and authors can review each other's changes before permanently changing the text.) If you check the **Track Changes** option, any tracked changes from the Word file will be included in your InDesign layout. This might cause a lot of items to show up in your text that aren't supposed to be there (typos, errors, or, for example, something the general counsel office removed from the original text for a specific legal reason).

Convert Bullets & Numbers to Text allows you to convert automatically generated numbering and bullet characters into actual text characters. This option is extremely useful if the text includes lists; if you don't check this option, you'll have to manually re-enter the bullets or line numbers into the imported text.

The **Style Name Conflicts** area warns you if styles in the Word file conflict with styles in the InDesign file (in other words, they have the same style names but different definitions in the two locations). If you are importing styles from the Word file, you have to determine how to resolve these conflicts.

Import Styles Automatically allows you to choose how to handle conflicts in paragraph and character styles. **Use InDesign Style Definition** preserves the style as you defined it; text in the Word file that uses that style will be reformatted with the InDesign definition of the style. **Redefine InDesign Style** replaces the layout definition with the definition from the Word file. **Auto Rename** adds the Word file to the InDesign file with "_wrd_1" at the end of the style name.

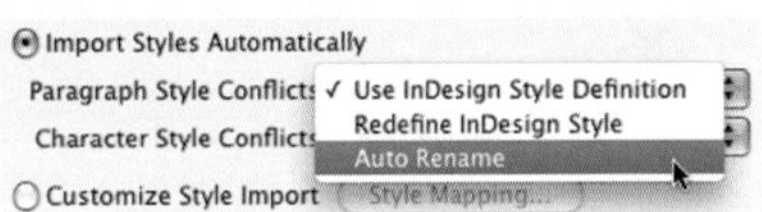

If you choose **Customize Style Import**, the Style Mapping button opens a dialog box where you can review and control specific style conflicts. Click an option in the InDesign Style column to access a menu, where you can choose which InDesign style to use in place of a specific Word style.

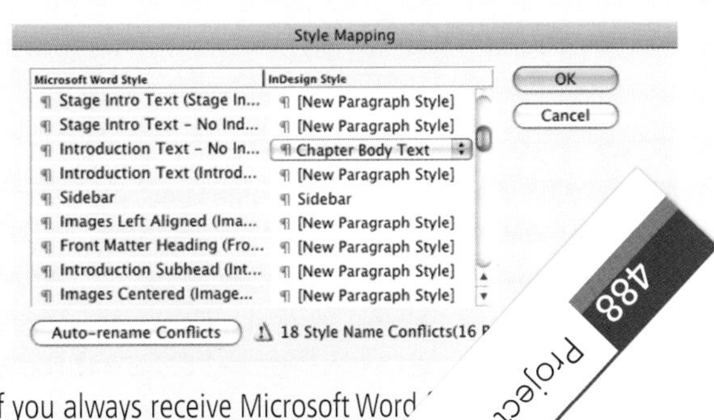

If you always receive Microsoft Word ... source, you can save your choices ... options) as a preset, or even cl... in the Import Options dialo...

At this point, the story does not fit into the frame because you haven't yet applied the appropriate styles to the imported text.

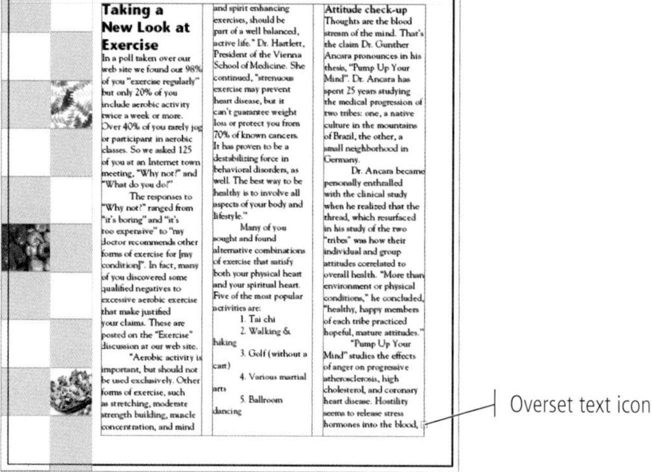

7. **Open the Paragraph Styles panel (Window>Styles>Paragraph Styles).**

8. **Place the insertion point in the first paragraph of the imported story (the main heading) and look at the Paragraph Styles panel.**

   The imported text appears to be preformatted, but the Paragraph Styles panel tells a different story. This paragraph is formatted as "Normal+." When you see a plus sign next to a style name, the selected text includes some formatting other than what is defined in the style.

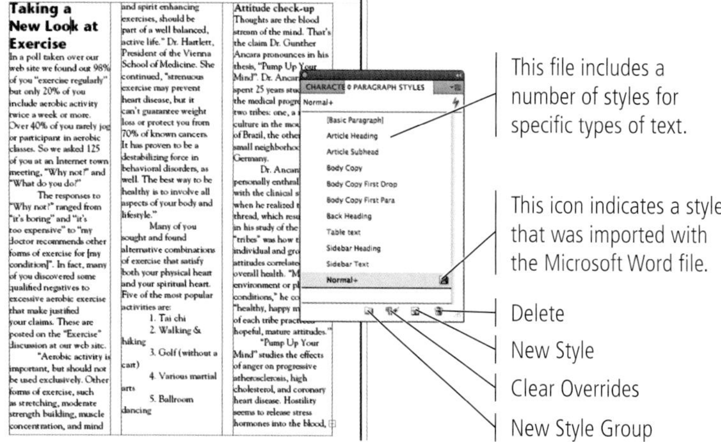

This file includes a number of styles for specific types of text.
This icon indicates a style that was imported with the Microsoft Word file.
Delete
New Style
Clear Overrides
New Style Group

> *Note:*
>
> *You should be able to guess the purpose of these styles from their names. It's always a good idea to use indicative names when you create styles or other user-defined assets.*

When you imported the Microsoft Word file, you preserved the formatting in the file; this is usually a good idea so you can see what the writer intended. Now that the text is imported into your layout, however, you want to apply the template styles to make the text in this issue consistent with other issues.

When you import text into InDesign, any number of new styles might appear in the Styles panels; the most common imported style is Normal. Text in a Microsoft Word file is typically formatted with the Normal style — even if you don't realize it; user-applied formatting is commonly local (meaning it is applied directly to selected text instead of with a defined style).

9. **With the insertion point still in place, click the Article Heading style in the Paragraph Styles panel.**

   Using styles, you can change all formatting attributes of selected text with a single click. Because you are working with paragraph styles, the style definition applies to the entire paragraph where the insertion point is placed.

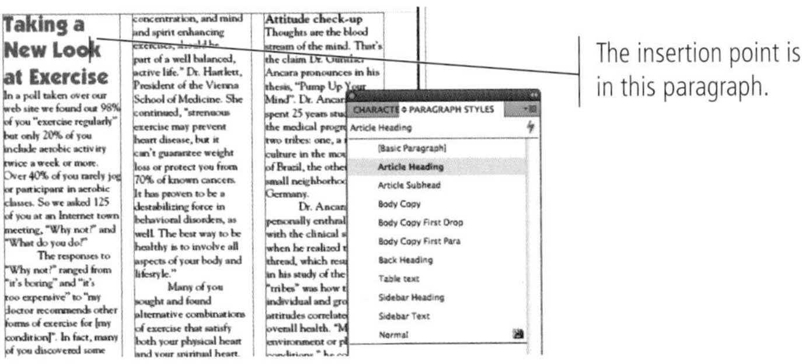
The insertion point is in this paragraph.

> *Note:*
>
> *You can reapply the basic style definition to selected text by clicking the Clear Overrides button at the bottom of the Paragraph Styles panel, or by Option/Alt clicking the applied style name.*

> *Note:*
>
> *Paragraph styles can include character attributes as well as paragraph attributes; character styles can only define character-formatting attributes.*

10. **Click and drag to select any part of the remaining paragraphs in the story, and then click the Body Copy style in the Paragraph Styles panel.**

    Paragraph styles apply to any paragraph that is partially or entirely selected. You don't have to select an entire paragraph before applying a paragraph style.

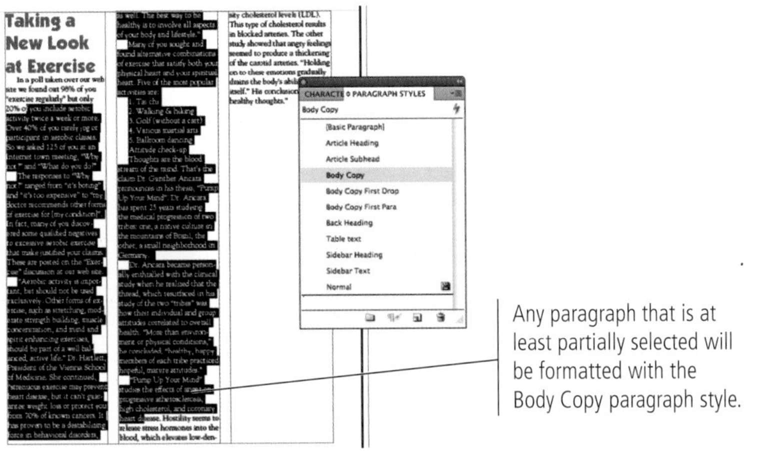
Any paragraph that is at least partially selected will be formatted with the Body Copy paragraph style.

11. **Format the first paragraph after the heading using the Body Copy First Drop style.**

12. **In the second column, format the subheading ("Attitude Checkup", after the numbered list) with the Article Subhead style.**

13. **Format the next paragraph (after the subhead) with the Body Copy First Para style.**

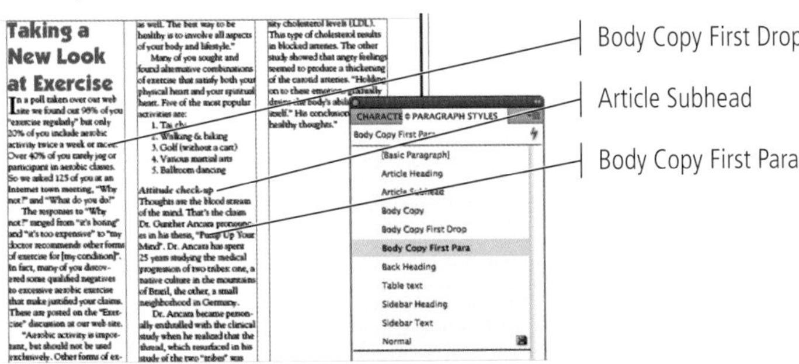
Body Copy First Drop
Article Subhead
Body Copy First Para

14. **Save the file and continue to the next exercise.**

Use Mini Bridge to Place Text

You already saw that you can use the Mini Bridge panel to easily place images into an InDesign layout. The same concept is true for text files: simply drag a text file from the panel into the layout. If you release the mouse button over an existing empty frame, the text is placed inside that frame. If you release the mouse button over an empty area, or over a frame that already has content, the text is loaded into the cursor.

1. **With `newsletter_dec.indd` open, navigate to Page 2 of the layout.**

2. **Open the Mini Bridge panel (if necessary) and navigate to the WIP>HeartSmart>December Issue folder.**

3. **Click the eastern_diet.doc file and drag it into the two-column frame on the top of Page 2.**

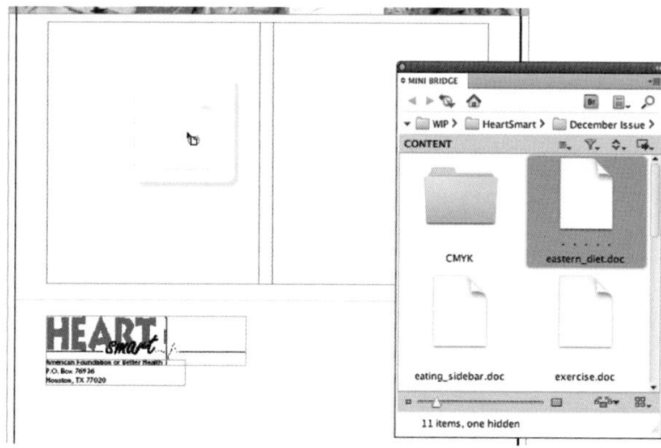

This imports the file using the default import options. In this case, the formatting is maintained, styles are imported, and conflicting styles are automatically renamed — resulting in the new Normal_wrd_1 style, which conflicts with the previously imported Normal style.

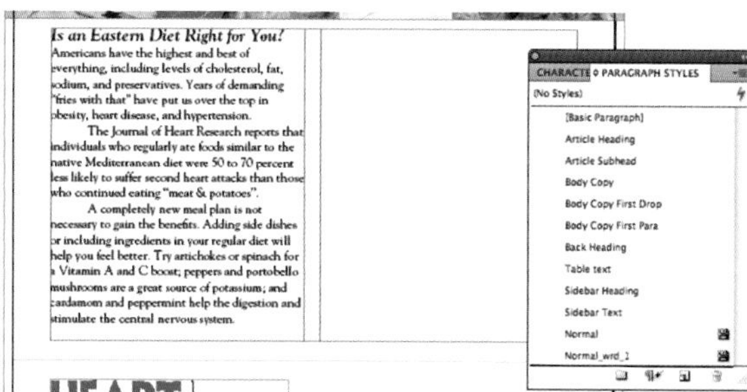

4. **Format the first paragraph with the Back Heading style.**
   Format the second paragraph with the Body Copy First Para style.
   Format the rest of the story with the Body Copy style.

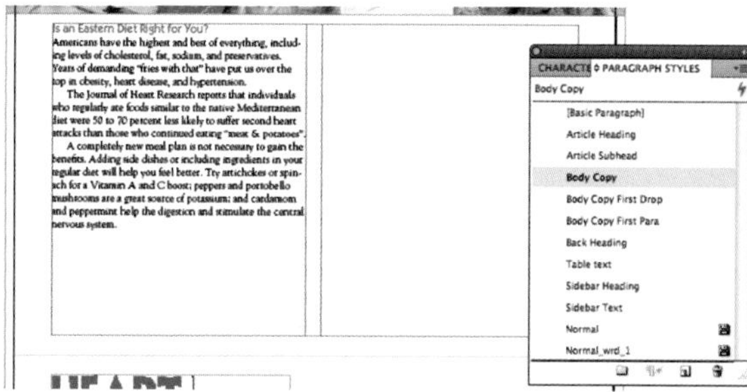

5. **Save the file and continue to the next exercise.**

Edit a Paragraph Style to Span Columns

As a general rule, headlines in newsletters and newspapers extend across the top of the entire related story. In previous versions of the software, this required a separate frame that spanned the width of the multi-column body frame. InDesign CS5 includes a paragraph formatting option that makes it easy to span a paragraph across multiple columns *without* the need for a separate frame. This can be applied to individual paragraphs, or defined as part of a paragraph style.

1. **With newsletter_dec.indd open, navigate to Page 1.**

2. **Control/right-click the Article Heading style in the panel and choose Edit "Article Heading" in the contextual menu.**

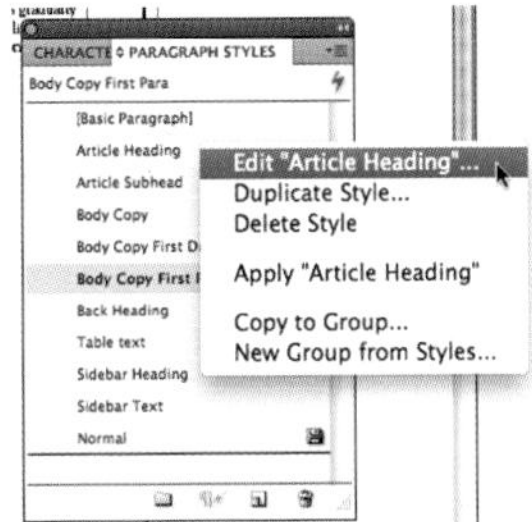

3. **Click the Preview option in the bottom-left corner of the dialog box.**

   When the Preview option is active, you can see the result of your choices before you finalize them.

4. **Select Span Columns in the list of options on the left side of the dialog box.**

5. **Choose Span Columns in the Paragraph Layout menu.**

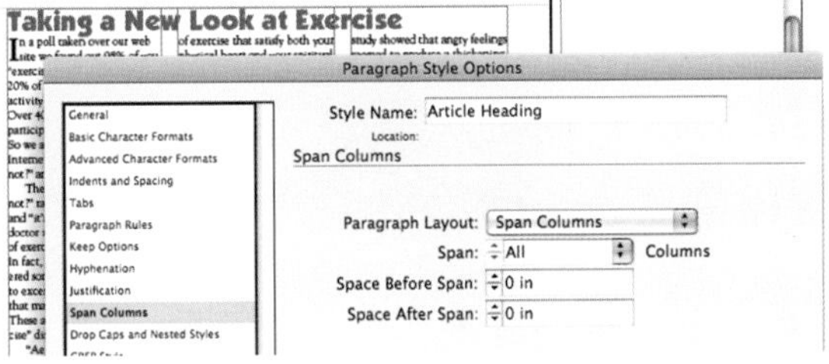

Note:

The Split Column option can be used to divide a specific paragraph into multiple columns within a frame's defined column.

6. **Make sure the Span field is set to All.**

   You can use the Span field to extend a paragraph over only a certain number of columns.

7. **Click the Up Arrow button for the Space After Span field.**

   The Space Before and Space After fields determine how much space is placed between the span paragraph and the paragraphs above or below. (This is the same concept used in the Space Above and Space Below options for regular paragraph formatting.)

Note:

The arrow buttons increase or decrease the related values by 0.0625".

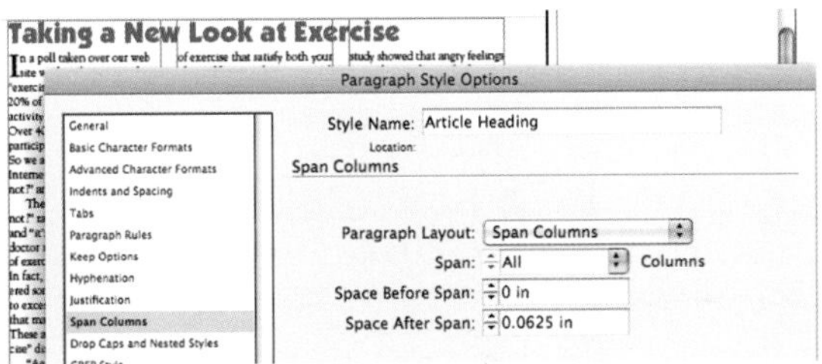

8. **Click OK to finalize the new style definition.**

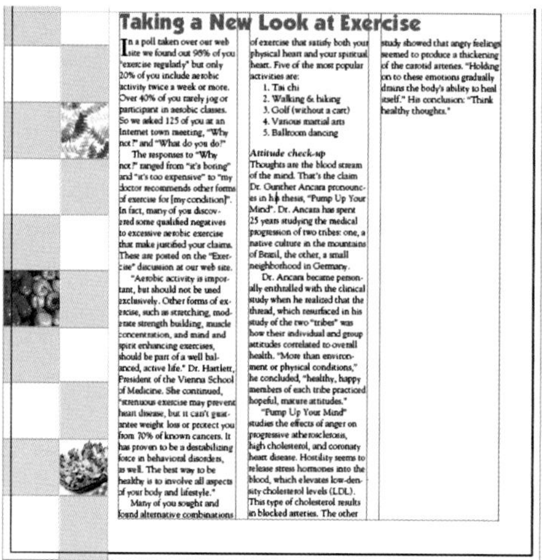

9. **Save the file and continue to the next exercise.**

Create a Sidebar Box

Many page layouts have a primary story (which might flow across multiple pages), as well as related-but-not-connected stories called **sidebars**. These elements are usually not linked to the main story, and they are often placed in their own boxes with some unique formatting to draw attention to the box. Amateur designers often create three separate elements to achieve this effect — an unnecessary degree of complexity when you can change multiple text frame options to create the effect with a single object.

1. **On Page 1 of newsletter_dec.indd, create a text frame with the following dimensions (based on the top-left reference point):**

   X: 3.67″ W: 3.95″
   Y: 6.6″ H: 3″

2. **Fill the text frame with a 20% tint of Pantone 1945 C.**

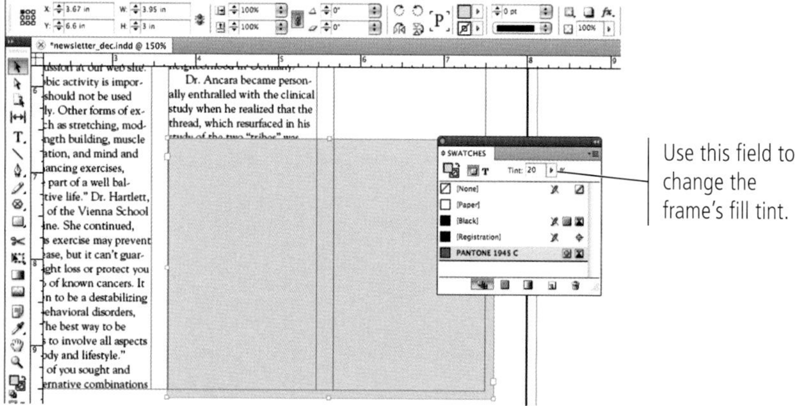

Use this field to change the frame's fill tint.

3. **Place the file `eating_sidebar.doc` into the new frame, preserving the formatting in the imported file.**

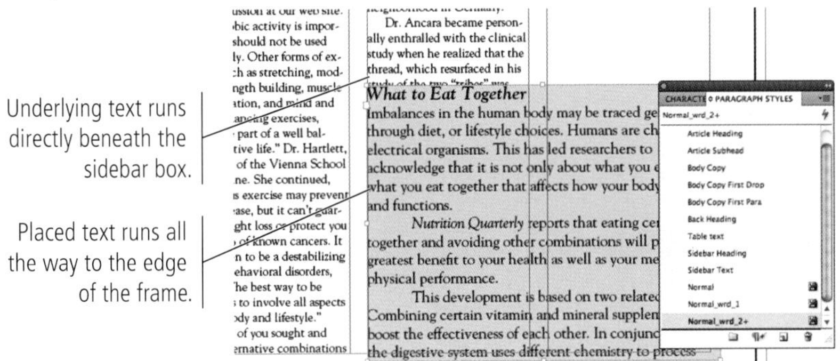

4. **Format the first line of the sidebar with the Sidebar Heading style.**

5. **Format the rest of the text in this frame using the Sidebar Text style.**

   If a paragraph includes local formatting, simply clicking a new style name might not work perfectly. As you can see in this example, the first two words in the second body paragraph are italicized; in the Paragraph Styles panel, the Sidebar Text style shows a plus sign — indicating that some formatting other than the style definition has been applied.

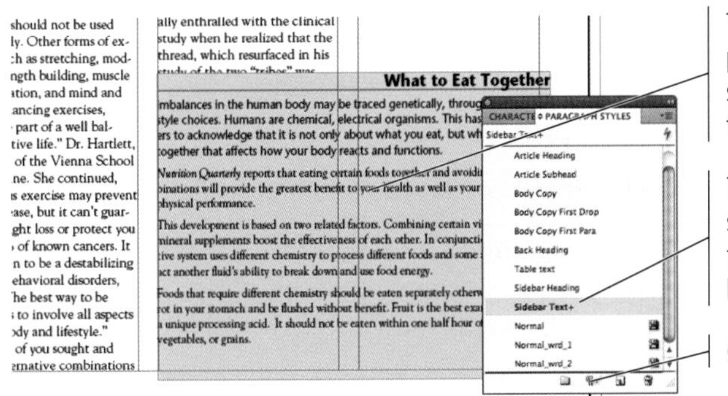

6. **Select the three incorrectly formatted paragraphs of body copy in the sidebar box.**

   You can click and drag to select the paragraphs, or click four times on the first paragraph you want to select and then drag to the last paragraph you want to select.

7. **Click the Clear Overrides button at the bottom of the Paragraph Styles panel.**

   In this case, you do have to select the entire paragraphs; if not, the overrides will be cleared only from the selected characters.

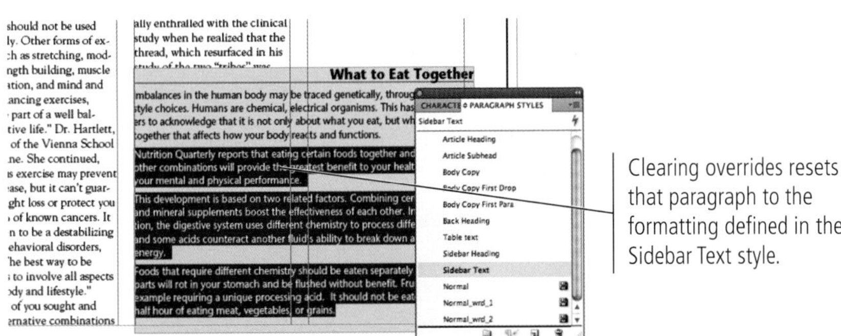

Clearing overrides resets that paragraph to the formatting defined in the Sidebar Text style.
Underlying text runs directly beneath the sidebar box.
Placed text runs all the way to the edge of the frame.
What to Eat Together

Note:

Sometimes there is no apparent reason why text imported from Microsoft Word is not properly formatted when you apply a style in InDesign, as in the case on the third and fourth body paragraphs in this sidebar box. This is usually caused by formatting options in Microsoft that are not supported in InDesign. You should simply be aware that you often need to clear overrides in the imported text before the InDesign style is properly applied.

8. **Select the first two words of the second sidebar paragraph. Change the font to ATC Oak and choose Italic in the Font Style menu.**

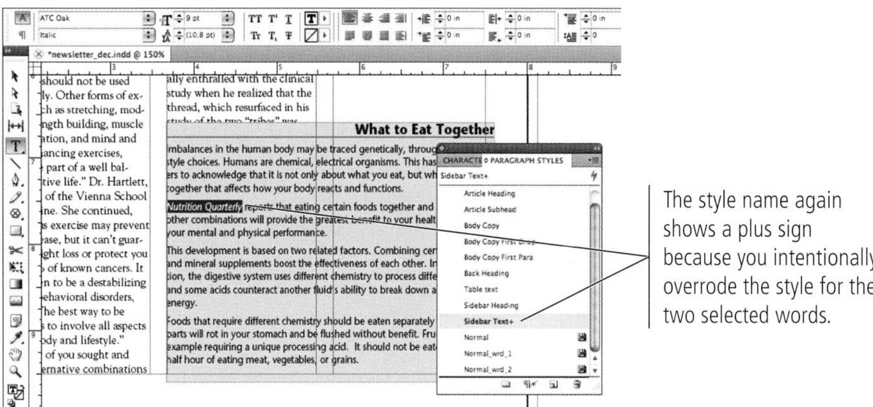

The style name again shows a plus sign because you intentionally overrode the style for the two selected words.

9. **Save the file and continue to the next exercise.**

Edit Text Inset and Wrap Settings

A number of frame attributes can affect the appearance of text both within and around a text frame. In this exercise, you adjust the text inset and text wrap to force text into the proper position.

1. **With newsletter_dec.indd open, Control/right-click the sidebar box and choose Text Frame Options from the contextual menu.**

2. **In the resulting dialog box, make sure the Preview option is checked.**

3. **Make sure the chain icon for the Inset Spacing fields is active.**

   Like the same chain icon in other dialog boxes, this forces all four inset values to the same value.

Text Frame Options

INDESIGN FOUNDATIONS

You can change numerous text frame attributes using the Text Frame Options dialog box (Object>Text Frame Options, or choose Text Frame Options in the object's contextual menu).

A text frame can have up to 40 columns, with a gutter (the space between columns) between 0 and 120". If **Fixed Column Width** is selected, changing the number of columns changes the width of the frame to accommodate the defined number of columns. (For example, 3 columns at 2" each with a 0.25" gutter would require the frame to be 6.5" wide.) If Fixed Column Width is not checked, the number of columns is evenly divided in the existing frame width.

Inset Spacing is the distance at which text is moved in from frame edges. You can define different values for each edge, or you can constrain all four edges to a single value.

If you check the **Ignore Text Wrap** option, the frame is not affected by wrap attributes of overlapping objects.

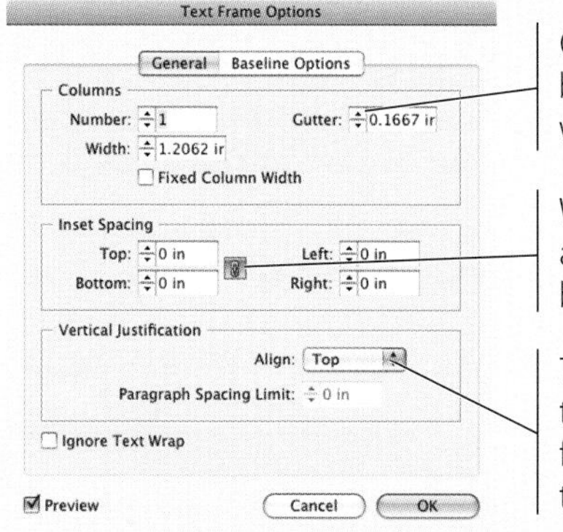

Clicking any of the arrow buttons changes the field value by 0.0625".

When this button is active, all four inset values will be the same.

Text can be aligned to the top, center, or bottom of a frame, or justified (stretched) to fill the frame height.

Some of these options are also available in the right side of the Advanced Workspace Control panel (or if you manually edit the panel options) when a frame is selected with one of the selection tools. It is important to note that some changes to text frames also affect the text inside the frame; scaling, flipping, rotating, or skewing a frame also scales, flips, rotates, or skews the text inside that frame.

4. **Change the Top Inset field to `0.1`", and then press Tab to move the highlight and apply the new Inset Spacing value to all four fields.**

Text inset is the distance text is moved from the inside edge of its containing frame.

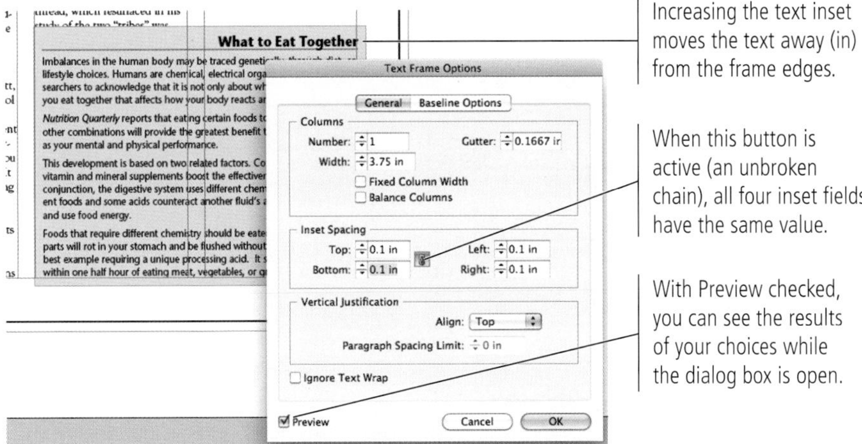

Increasing the text inset moves the text away (in) from the frame edges.
When this button is active (an unbroken chain), all four inset fields have the same value.
With Preview checked, you can see the results of your choices while the dialog box is open.

5. **In the Vertical Justification Align menu, choose Justify.**

Text can be vertically aligned to the top, bottom, or center of its containing frame, or it can be justified — stretched to extend the entire height of the containing frame.

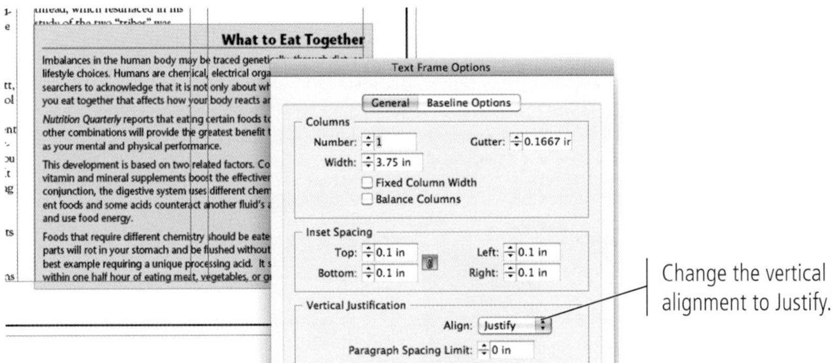

Change the vertical alignment to Justify.

Note:

When you vertically justify type, the Paragraph Spacing Limit field defines the maximum space that can be added between paragraphs to fill the frame.

6. **Click OK to close the dialog box and apply your choices.**

7. **Open the Text Wrap panel (Window>Text Wrap).**

Text wrap is the distance around the edge of an object where surrounding text will flow.

8. **Click the sidebar frame with the Selection tool, and then click the second button from the left in the Text Wrap panel.**

9. **Make sure the chain icon is active so all four offset values are the same. Change the Top Wrap field to `0.1`" and then press Tab to apply the value to all four fields.**

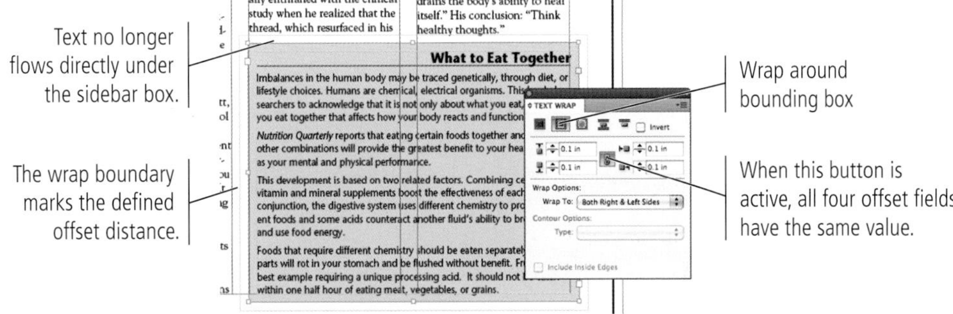

The wrap boundary marks the defined offset distance.

10. **Select the 3-column text box and open the Text Frame Options dialog box. Choose Justify in the Vertical Justification Align menu and click OK.**

This command aligns the bottom lines in the two right columns.

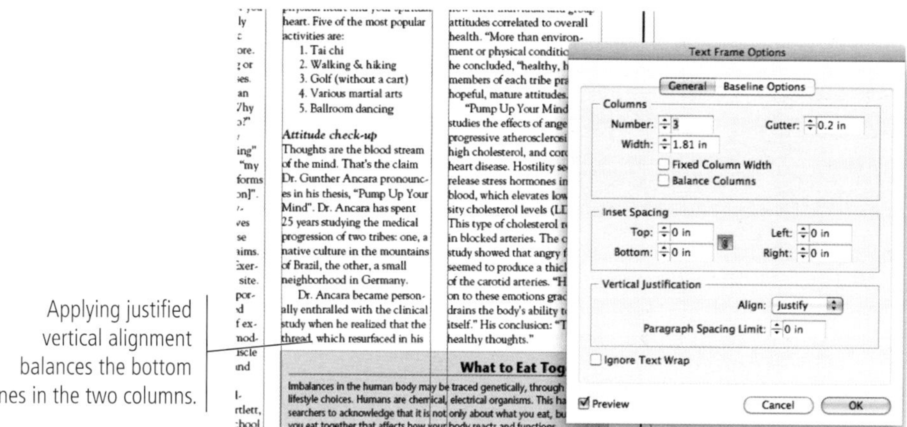

Applying justified vertical alignment balances the bottom lines in the two columns.

11. **Save the file and continue to the next stage of the project.**

Text Wrap Options

INDESIGN FOUNDATIONS

By default, text wrap attributes affect all overlapping objects, regardless of stacking order; you can turn this behavior off by checking the Text Wrap Only Affects Text Beneath option in the Composition pane of the Preferences dialog box. InDesign provides five options for wrapping text around an object; specific wrap attributes are controlled in the Text Wrap panel (Window>Text Wrap)

- **No Text Wrap** allows text to run directly under the object.
- **Wrap Around Bounding Box** creates a straight-edged wrap around all four sides of the object's bounding box.
- **Wrap Around Object Shape** creates a wrap in the shape of the object. In this case, you can also define which contour to use:
  - **Bounding Box** creates the boundary based on the object's bounding box.
  - **Detect Edges** creates the boundary using the same detection options you use to create a clipping path.
  - **Alpha Channel** creates the boundary from an Alpha channel saved in the placed image.
  - **Photoshop Path** creates the boundary from a path saved in the placed image.
  - **Graphic Frame** creates the boundary from the containing frame.
  - **Same as Clipping** creates the boundary from a clipping path saved in the placed image.
  - **User-Modified Path** appears by default if you drag the anchor points of the text wrap boundary.
- **Jump Object** keeps text from appearing to the right or left of the frame.
- **Jump to Next Column** forces surrounding text to the top of the next column or frame.

No Text Wrap | Wrap Around Bounding Box | Wrap Around Object Shape | Jump Object | Jump to Next Column

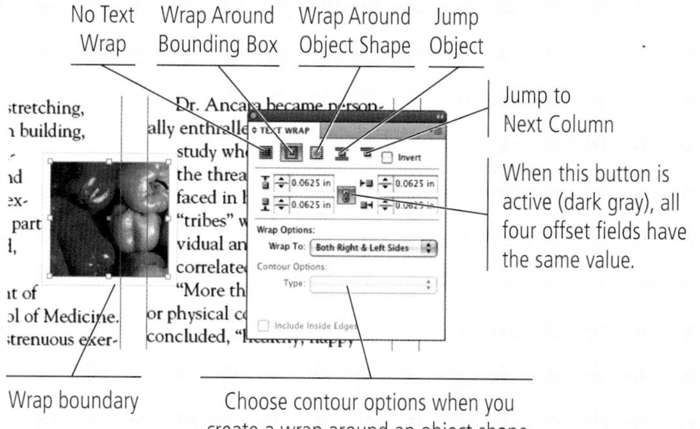

When this button is active (dark gray), all four offset fields have the same value.

Wrap boundary

Choose contour options when you create a wrap around an object shape.

Regardless of which wrap you apply, you can define the offset value, the distance that any surrounding text will remain away from the object. (If you use the Object Shape wrap option, you can define only a single offset value; for the other types, you can define a different offset value for each edge.

If you use the Bounding Box or Object Shape wrap option, you can also define the Wrap To options — whether the wrap is applied to a specific side (right, left, right and left, or the largest side), or toward or away from the spine.

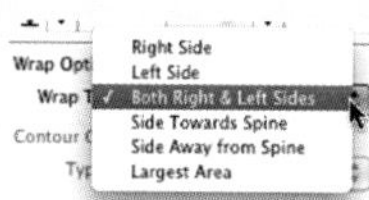

Stage 3 Working with Tables

Many page layouts incorporate tables of information, from basic tables with a few rows and columns to multi-page catalog spreadsheets with thousands of product numbers and prices. InDesign includes a number of options for building tables, each having advantages and disadvantages depending on what you need to accomplish. Regardless of which method you use to create a table, the same options are available for formatting the table, the cells in the table, and the content in the cells.

When you place an insertion point in an existing text frame, you can create a new table from scratch by choosing Table>Insert Table. This method allows you to define your own table parameters, including the number of rows and columns, the number of header and footer rows (top and bottom rows that appear in every instance of the table if the table breaks across multiple columns or frames), and even a defined style for the new table (table styles store formatting options such as gridline weight and color, cell inset, and other attributes that will you learn about in this stage of the project).

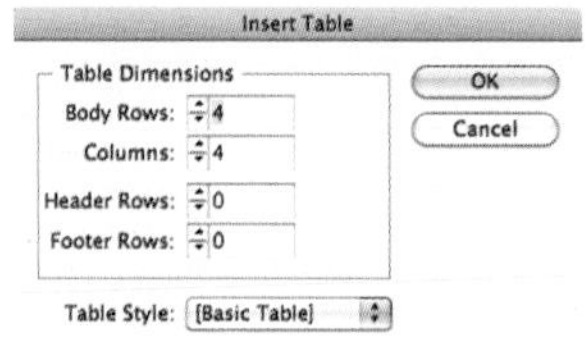

You can also create a table by selecting a series of tab-delimited text in the layout and choosing Table>Convert Text to Table. (Tab-delimited means that the content of each column is separated by a tab character.) Using this method, the new table becomes an inline object in the text frame that contained the original tabbed text.

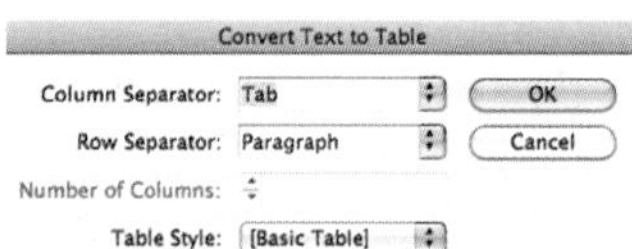

Finally, you can create a new table in InDesign by placing a Microsoft Excel file (Microsoft Excel is the most common application for creating spreadsheets). You'll use this method to complete this stage of the HeartSmart newsletter project.

 Place a Microsoft Excel Table

Microsoft Excel spreadsheets can be short tables of text or complex, multi-page spreadsheets of data. In either case, Microsoft Excel users tend to spend hours formatting their spreadsheets for business applications. Those formatting options are typically not appropriate for commercial printing applications, but they give you a better starting point in your InDesign file than working from plain tabbed text.

1. **With newsletter_dec.indd open, navigate to Page 2. Click the Pasteboard area to make sure nothing is selected.**

2. **Choose File>Place and navigate to the file nutrition.xls in the WIP>HeartSmart>December Issue folder.**

3. **Uncheck the Replace Selected Item option, make sure Show Import Options is checked, and click Open.**

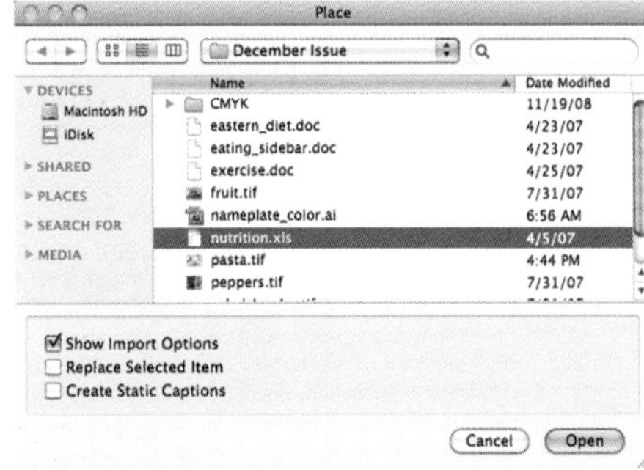

4. **Review the options in the resulting dialog box. Make sure your options match what is shown in the following image, and then click OK.**

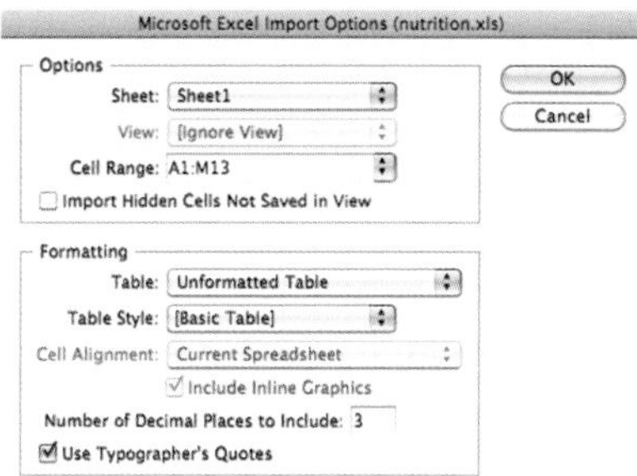

> **Note:**
>
> *If you see a warning about missing fonts, click OK; you're going to reformat the table text in the next exercise, so missing fonts won't be a problem.*

5. **With the table loaded into the cursor, click in the empty area of the right column (in the top half of the page).**

The new table is placed into the layout; a text frame is automatically created to contain the table. (The table currently extends beyond the right edge of the text frame, and the overset text icon in the frame's Out port indicates that the frame is not high enough to fit all the rows of the table).

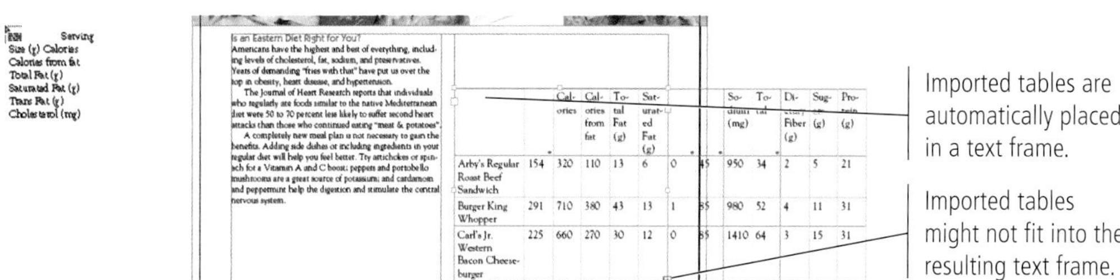

Imported tables are automatically placed in a text frame.
Imported tables might not fit into the resulting text frame.

Obviously this table still needs some significant modification to make it a cohesive part of the newsletter layout. Some placed tables require more work than others, but be prepared to do at least some clean-up work whenever you place a spreadsheet/table.

6. **Drag the text frame with the table to the top edge of the right column.**

7. **Control/right-click the table and choose Fitting>Fit Frame to Content.**

This is the same command you can use to resize a graphics frame; in this case, you're making the text frame big enough to show the entire table width. You should now be able to see the bottom row of the table.

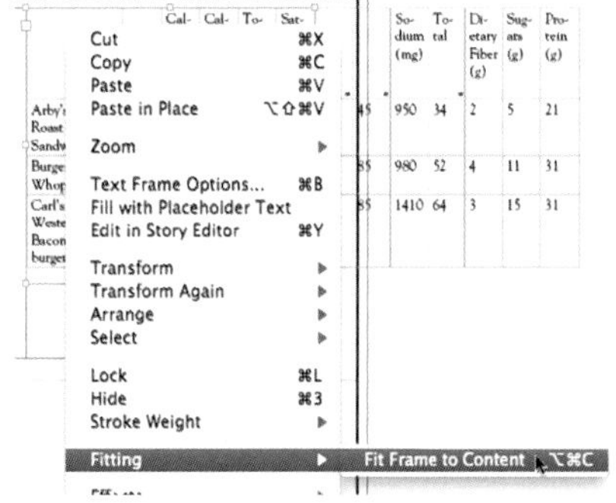

		Calories	Calories from fat	Total Fat (g)	Saturated Fat (g)			Sodium (mg)	Total	Dietary Fiber (g)	Sugars (g)	Protein (g)
Arby's Regular Roast Beef Sandwich	154	320	110	13	6	0	45	950	34	2	5	21
Burger King Whopper	291	710	380	43	13	1	85	980	52	4	11	31
Carl's Jr. Western Bacon Cheeseburger	225	660	270	30	12	0	85	1410	64	3	15	31
Dairy Queen Double Cheeseburger	219	540	280	31	16	0	115	1130	30	2	5	35
Del Taco Del Beef Burrito	227	550	270	30	17	0	90	1090	42	3	2	31
Domino's Hand-Tossed Cheese Pizza (2 pieces)	159	374	101	11	5	0	23	784	54	3	5	15
In-N-Out Double-Double	330	670	370	41	18	0	120	1440	39	3	10	37
KFC Original Recipe Drumstick & Thigh	185	500	290	33	9	0	240	1500	16	0	0	36
McDonald's Big Mac	216	590	310	34	11	0	85	1070	47	3	8	24
Taco Bell Beef Burrito Supreme	247	440	160	18	7	0	35	1220	52	8	5	17
Wendy's Big Bacon Classic	282	570	260	29	12	0	100	1460	46	3	11	34
RDA (based on a 2000-calorie diet)				65	20		300	2400	300	25		

8. **Save the file and continue to the next exercise.**

Format Cell Contents

When you work with tables in InDesign, think of the table cells as a series of text frames. Text in a table cell is no different than text in any other text frame; it can be formatted using the same options you've already learned, including with paragraph and character styles.

> *Note:*
>
> *When working with tables in InDesign, pressing Tab moves the insertion point from one table cell to the next (from left to right, top to bottom). This means you can't press Tab to insert a tab character into text in an InDesign table; you have to choose Type>Insert Special Character>Other>Tab.*

1. **With `newsletter_dec.indd` open, select the Type tool and click in the top-left cell of the table.**

2. **Click and drag to the bottom-right table cell to highlight all cells in the table.**

3. **Click Table Text in the Paragraph Styles panel to format all the text in the selected table cells.**

4. **If a plus sign appears next to the Table Text style name (in the Paragraph Styles panel), click the Clear Overrides button at the bottom of the panel to apply only the base style definition to the text.**

   As with files from Microsoft Word, some options in Microsoft Excel spreadsheets might require this two-step process to apply your style definitions to the selected text.

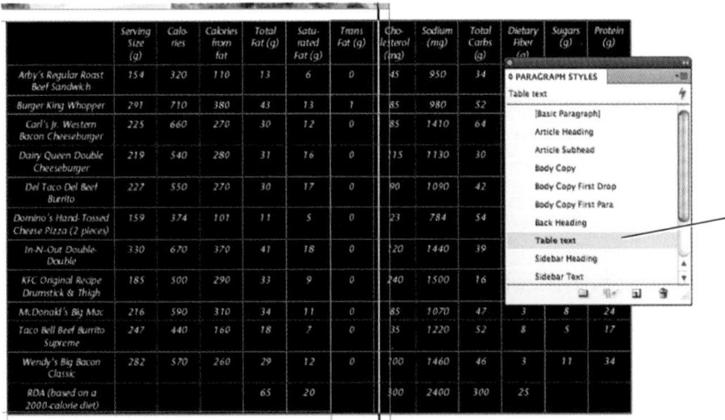

Styles can be used to format table text just as you would format any other text in the layout.

> *Note:*
>
> *You have to use the Type tool to select table cells, either individually, or as entire rows/columns.*

5. **Click in any cell to deselect all table cells.**

6. **Place the cursor over the top edge of the first column of the table. When you see a down-pointing arrow, click to select the entire column.**

   You can also select rows by placing the cursor immediately to the left of a row and clicking when the cursor changes to a right-facing arrow.

The down-pointing arrow means you can click to select the entire column.

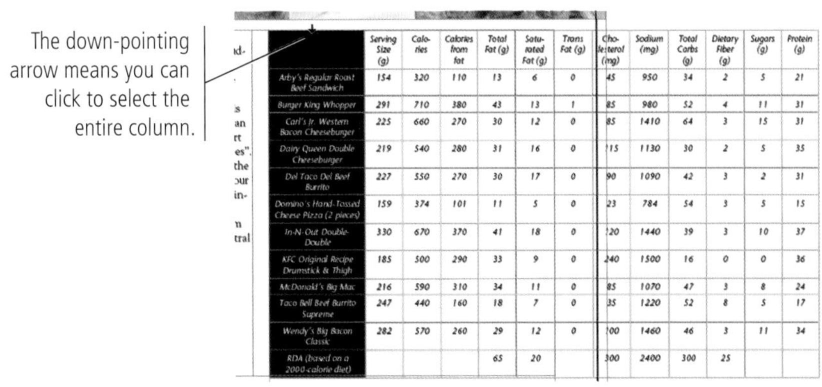

7. **Change the selected column to left paragraph alignment.**

   You can use the Control panel or Paragraph panel, or simply press Command/Control-L to change the alignment of the text within the table cell.

> *Note:*
>
> *Text is still text, even though it's placed inside a table cell. You can apply all of the same text-formatting options to table text that you can apply to text in a regular text frame.*

8. **Save the file and continue to the next exercise.**

Format Cell Attributes

As we mentioned in the previous exercise, table cells are very similar to regular text frames. Individual cells can have different attributes such as height and width, text inset, vertical positioning, and text orientation. These options can be controlled in the Table panel, the Control panel, and the Cell Options dialog box.

1. **With newsletter_dec.indd open, click in the second cell of the first row, and then drag right to select all cells in the row except the first cell.**

2. **In the Table panel (Window>Type & Tables>Table), choose Exactly in the Row Height menu, and then change the field to 0.875".**

3. **Change the Column Width field to 0.2785".**

4. **Click the Rotate Text 270° button so the left edge of the text aligns to the bottom edge of the cell.**

5. **Click the Align Center button so the text in each cell is centered vertically.**

   Because the text is rotated, this button actually aligns the text between the left and right cell edges. It's important to remember that the vertical align options are based on the orientation of the text.

6. **Apply left paragraph alignment to the selected text.**

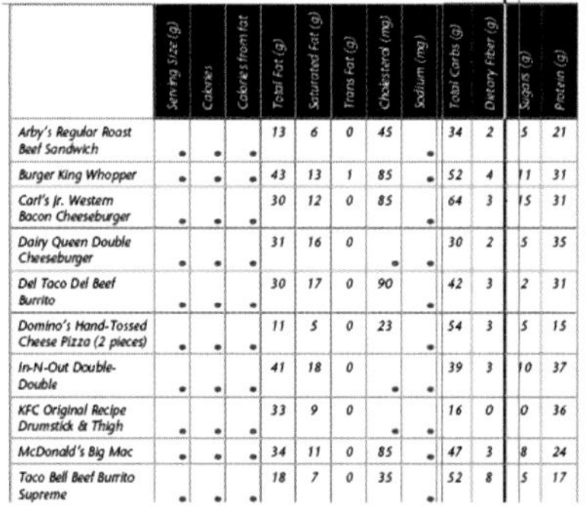

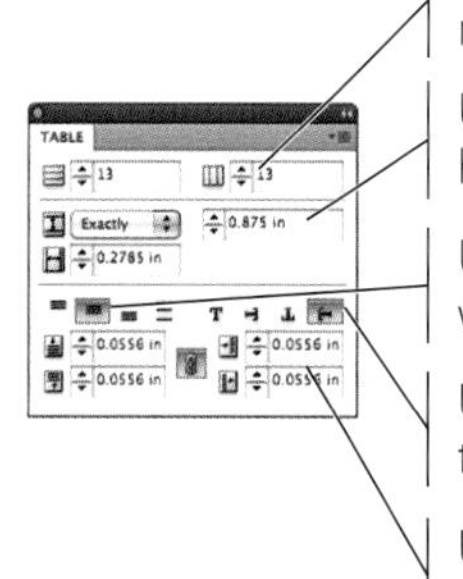

Use these fields to change the number of rows and columns.

Use these fields to control the height and width of cells.

Use these buttons to change the vertical alignment of text within cells.

Use these buttons to rotate text within the cells.

Use these fields to define inset values for cells.

7. **Click the second cell in the second row, and drag down and right to select all the cells that contain numeric data.**

8. **Apply centered vertical alignment to the selected cells.**

9. **Make sure the chain icon for the cell inset fields is active. Change the Top Cell Inset field to 0 and then press Tab to apply the same value to all four fields.**

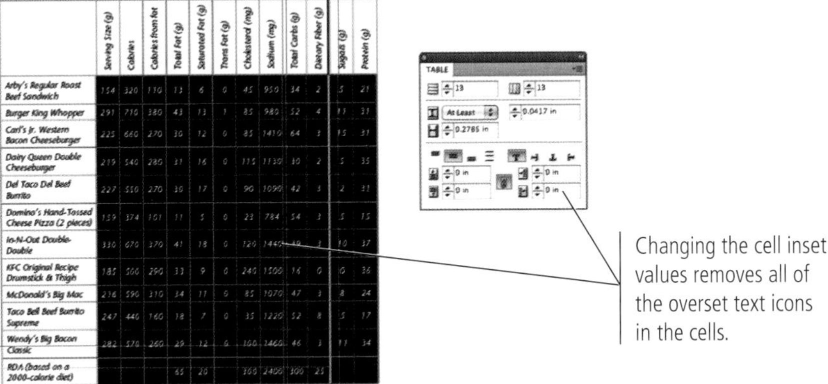

Changing the cell inset values removes all of the overset text icons in the cells.

10. **Select the first four cells in the last row and choose Table>Merge Cells.**

    This function extends the contents of a single cell across multiple cells. (You can also open the Table panel Options menu and choose Merge Cells.)

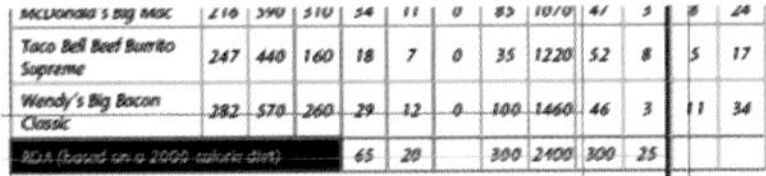

11. **Select the entire first column of the table and change only the Left Cell Inset value to `0.0625"`.**

    To change only one value, you have to make sure the chain icon is not active.

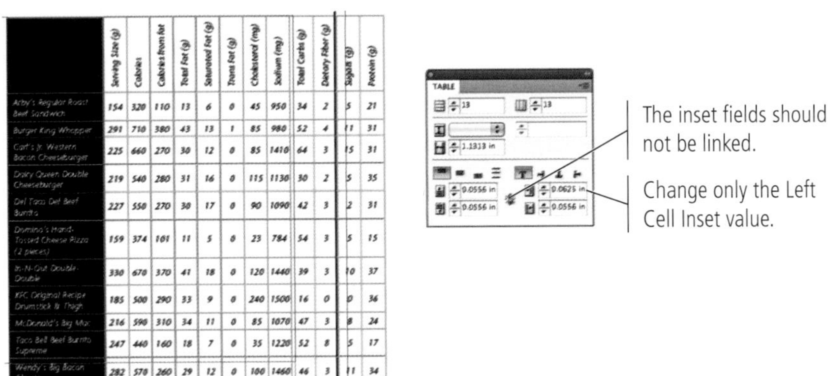

The inset fields should not be linked.

Change only the Left Cell Inset value.

12. **Place the cursor over the right edge of the first column until the cursor becomes a two-headed arrow.**

    When you see this cursor, you can drag the gridline to resize a column or row.

13. **Click and drag right until the column is wide enough to allow the Wendy's Big Bacon Classic to fit on one line.**

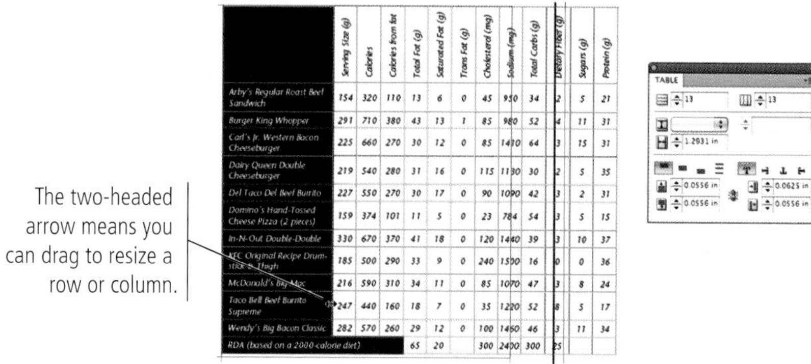

> *Note:*
>
> *Resizing the width of a cell resizes the entire column; resizing the height of a cell resizes the entire row.*
>
> *You can press the Shift key while dragging a gridline to resize a row or column without affecting the overall table size; only the rows or columns next to the gridline you drag are resized.*

14. **Place the insertion point in the cell with the Wendy's product name.**

    When you make the column wide enough to fit the text, the row automatically shrinks to one row. In the Table panel, you can see that the Row Height menu is set to At Least; this option allows cells to shrink to fit the height of cell contents, down to the defined minimum height.

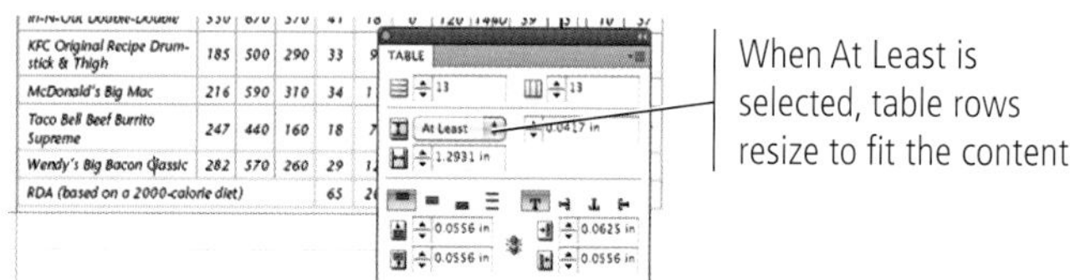

When At Least is selected, table rows resize to fit the content.

15. **Save the file and continue to the next exercise.**

Define Table Fills and Strokes

Like text frames, table cells can also have fill and stroke attributes. InDesign includes a number of options for adding color to tables, from changing the stroke and fill of an individual cell to defining patterns that repeat every certain number of rows and/or columns.

1. **With newsletter_dec.indd open, make sure the table on Page 2 is selected. Open the Table panel Options menu and choose Table Options>Table Setup.**

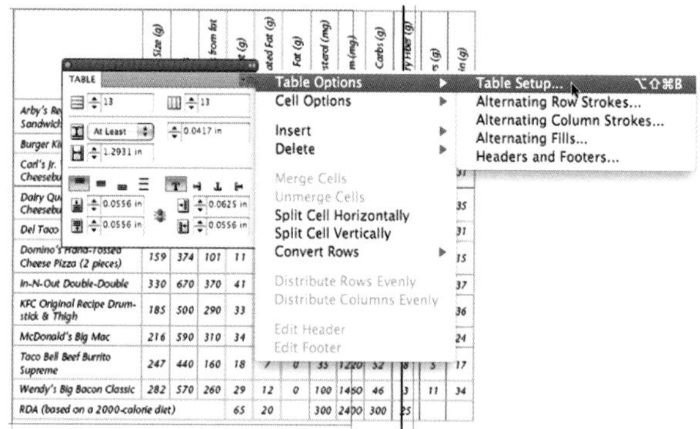

> *Note:*
>
> *You can also choose Table>Table Options>Table Setup to access the dialog box.*

2. **In the Table Setup tab, apply a 0.5-pt solid border of 100% Pantone 1945 C.**

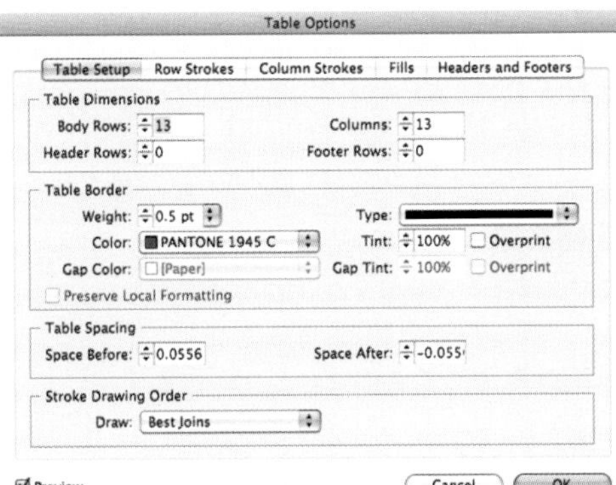

3. **In the Fills tab, choose Every Other Row in the Alternating Pattern menu. Set the First field to 1 row and apply 20% Pantone 1945 C. Set the Next field to 1 row and apply None as the color.**

When frame edges are visible, it's difficult (if not impossible) to see the table border and cell strokes.

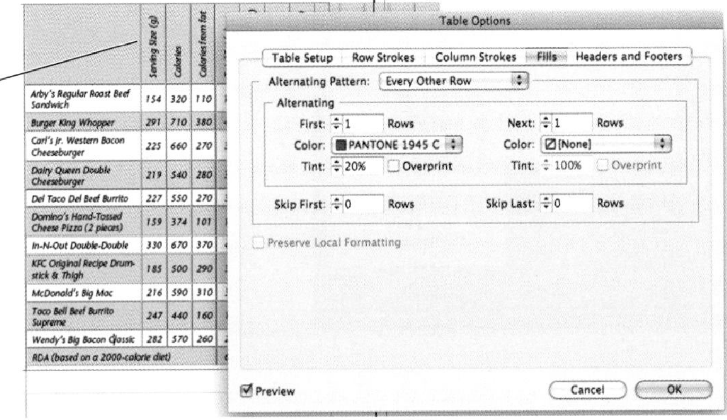

4. **Click OK to apply your choices.**

Note:

In the Table Options dialog box, you can use the Row Strokes and Column Strokes tabs to define patterns based on a sequence you choose in the Alternating Pattern menus. Alternating rows can have different stroke styles, weights, colors, and tints; you can also skip a specific number of rows at the top and bottom of a table.

Managing Table Setup

INDESIGN FOUNDATIONS

The Table Setup tab of the Table Options dialog box defines the table dimensions, table border, spacing above and below the table, and how strokes are applied to the table.

The **Stroke Drawing Order** allows you to control the appearance where gridlines of different styles or colors meet. If Best Joins is selected, styled strokes such as double lines result in joined strokes and gaps.

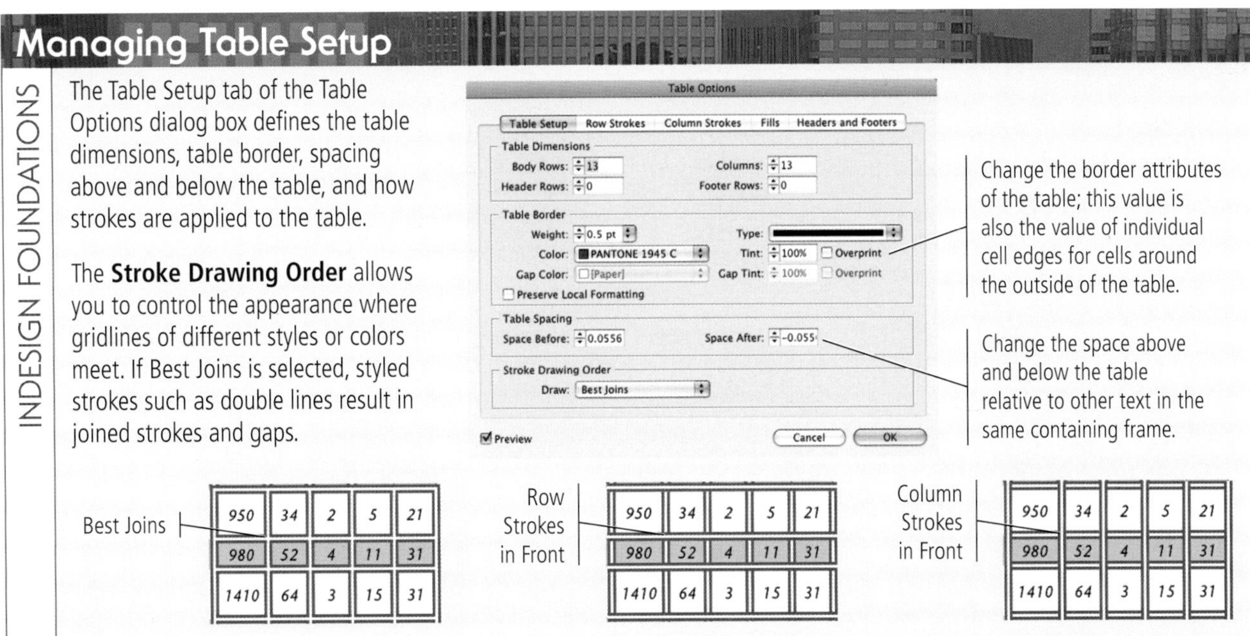

Change the border attributes of the table; this value is also the value of individual cell edges for cells around the outside of the table.

Change the space above and below the table relative to other text in the same containing frame.

5. **Select the last row in the table. Using the Swatches panel, change the cell fill tint to 50%.**

   Remember, table cells are very similar to individual text frames. You can change the color of cell fills and strokes using the Swatches panel, and you can change the cell stroke attributes using the Stroke panel.

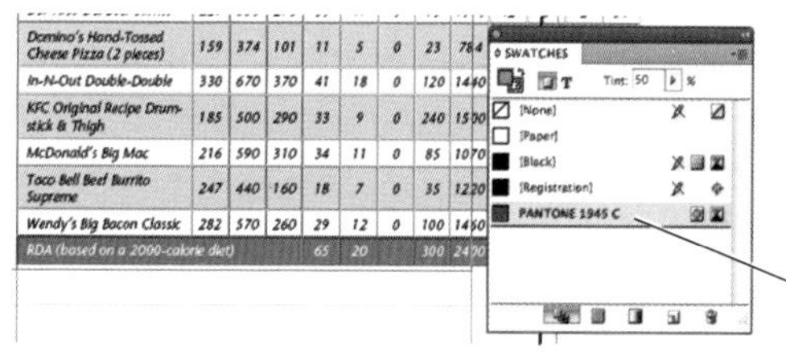

Cell fills can be changed in the Swatches panel, just as you would change the fill of a text frame.

> *Note:*
>
> *When the insertion point is placed in a table cell, press the Escape key to select the active cell.*

6. **Select all cells in the table. Open the Table panel Options menu and choose Cell Options>Strokes and Fills.**

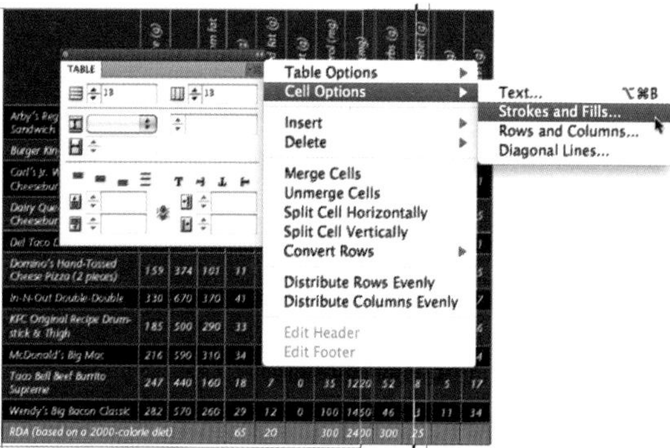

> *Note:*
>
> *If you place the cursor at the top-left corner of the table, it changes to a diagonal arrow icon. Clicking with this cursor selects all cells in the table.*

7. **In the preview area of the dialog box, click all three horizontal lines to remove the strokes from the tops and bottoms of the cells.**

8. **Apply a 0.5-pt, 100% Pantone 1945 C stroke value, using the Solid stroke type.**

   These settings change the attributes of the vertical gridlines for all selected cells.

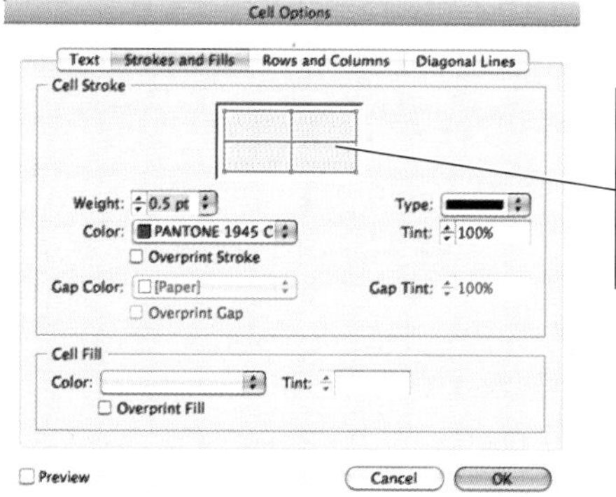

By deselecting the horizontal lines before defining the stroke, you can change the appearance of only the vertical gridlines.

> *Note:*
>
> *You can apply different stroke values to every cell in a table (although you probably wouldn't want to).*

9. **Click OK to apply the stroke values to your table.**

10. **Click away from the table to deselect it, and then choose View>Extras> Hide Frame Edges to review the table formatting.**

	Serving Size (g)	Calories	Calories from fat	Total Fat (g)	Saturated Fat (g)	Trans Fat (g)	Cholesterol (mg)	Sodium (mg)	Total Carbs (g)	Dietary Fiber (g)	Sugars (g)	Protein (g)
Arby's Regular Roast Beef Sandwich	154	320	110	13	6	0	45	950	34	2	5	21
Burger King Whopper	291	710	380	43	13	1	85	980	52	4	11	31
Carl's Jr. Western Bacon Cheeseburger	225	660	270	30	12	0	85	1410	64	3	15	31
Dairy Queen Double Cheeseburger	219	540	280	31	16	0	115	1130	30	2	5	35
Del Taco Del Beef Burrito	227	550	270	30	17	0	90	1090	42	3	2	31
Domino's Hand-Tossed Cheese Pizza (2 pieces)	159	374	101	11	5	0	23	784	54	3	5	15
In-N-Out Double-Double	330	670	370	41	18	0	120	1440	39	3	10	37
KFC Original Recipe Drumstick & Thigh	185	500	290	33	9	0	240	1500	16	0	0	36
McDonald's Big Mac	216	590	310	34	11	0	85	1070	47	3	8	24
Taco Bell Beef Burrito Supreme	247	440	160	18	7	0	35	1220	52	8	5	17
Wendy's Big Bacon Classic	282	570	260	29	12	0	100	1450	46	3	11	34
RDA (based on a 2000-calorie diet)				65	20		300	2400	300	25		

> ***Note:***
>
> *If you can't see the borders and strokes, try hiding frame edges (View>Extras>Hide Frame Edges) while you experiment with these options.*

11. **Using the Selection tool, Control/right-click the table and choose Fitting>Fit Frame to Content from the contextual menu.**

Controlling Cell Attributes

Basic attributes of table cells can be defined in the Text tab of the Cell Options dialog box (Table>Cell Options). Most table cell options are exactly the same as for regular text frames; the only choice unique to tables is **Clip Contents to Cell**. If you set a fixed row height that's too small for the cell content, an overset text icon appears in the lower-right corner of the cell. (You can't flow text from one table cell to another.) If you check the Clip Contents to Cell option, any content that doesn't fit in the cell will be clipped.

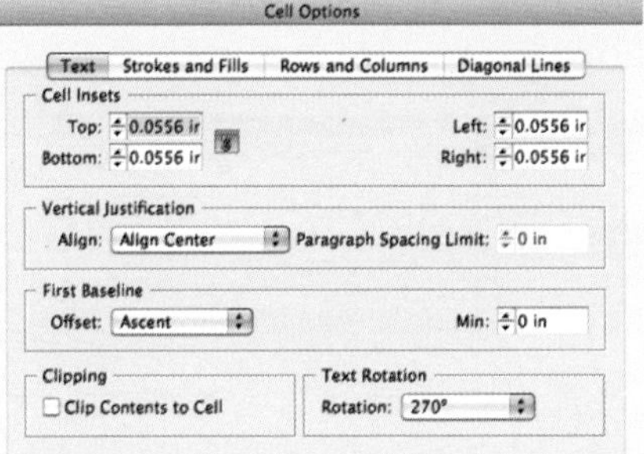

As with any text frame, a table cell can have its own fill and stroke attributes. These attributes can be defined in the Strokes and Fills tab (or using the Swatches and Stroke panels). You can turn individual cell edges (strokes) on or off by clicking specific lines in the preview.

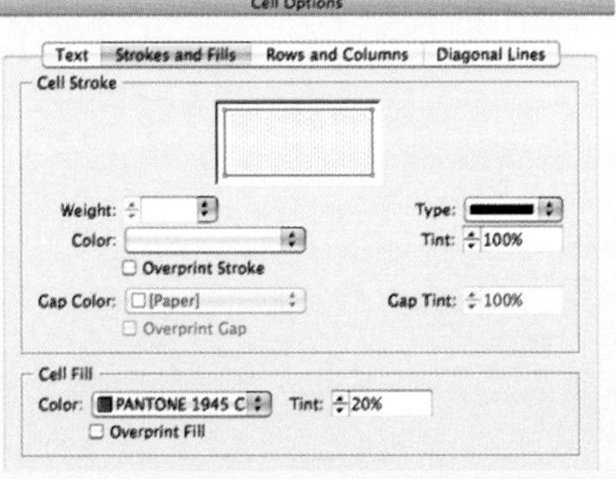

The Rows and Columns tab controls row height and column width. If **At Least** is selected in the Row Height menu, you can define the minimum and maximum possible row height; rows change height if you add or remove text, or if you change the text formatting in a way that requires more or less space. If **Exactly** is selected, you can define the exact height of the cell.

If you're working with an extremely long table, you can break the table across multiple frames by threading (as you would for any long block of text). The **Keep Options** can be used to keep specific (selected) rows together after a break, and they determine where those rows will go, based on your choice in the Start Row menu.

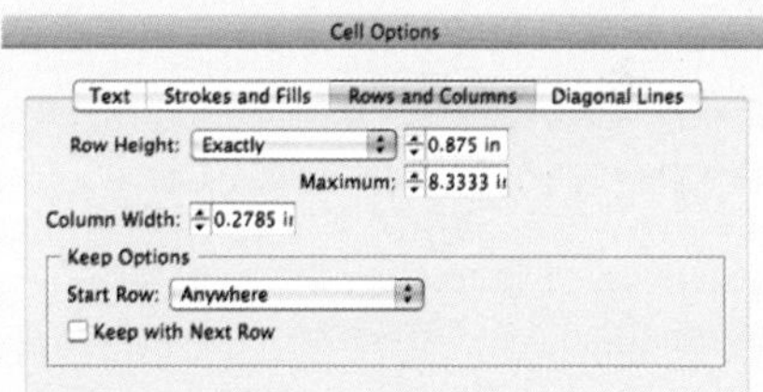

You can add diagonal lines to specific cells using the Diagonal Lines tab. You can apply lines in either direction (or both) and choose a specific stroke weight, color, style, and tint. The Draw menu determines whether the line is created in front of or behind the cell's contents.

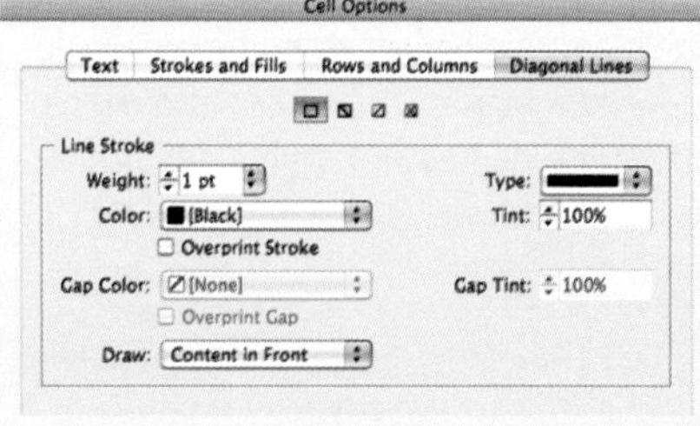

12. Drag the table until the top-right corner of the frame snaps to the top-right margin guide on Page 2.

Text runs right under the table, and is visible where cells have a fill of None.

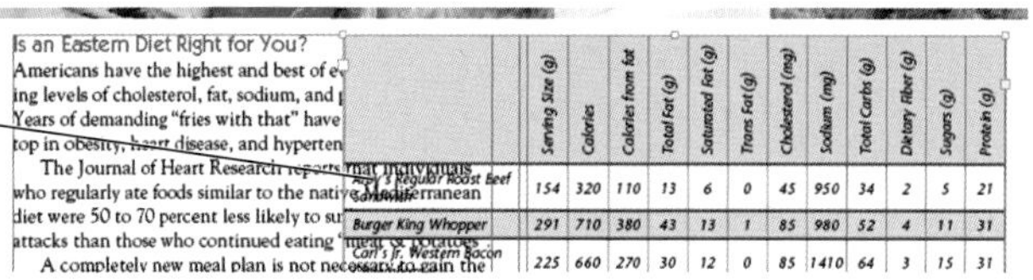

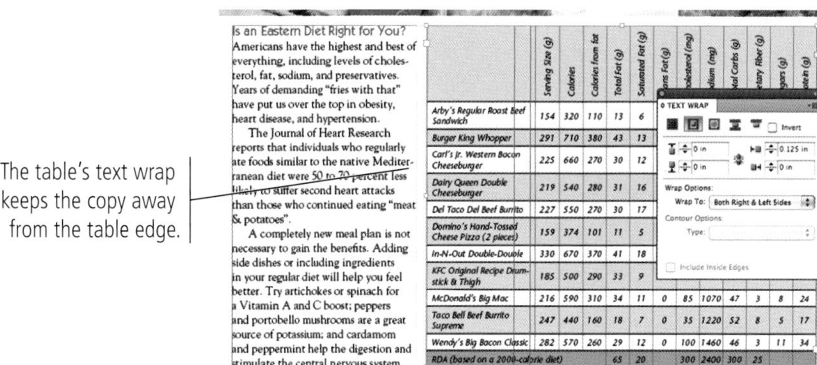

13. With the frame still selected, click the second button in the Text Wrap panel (Window>Text Wrap) so the Eastern Diet story wraps around the frame that contains the table. Change the Left Wrap field to `0.125"`.

A table is always contained inside a text frame. To control the wrap around a table, you have to actually apply the wrap attributes to the frame that contains the table.

The table's text wrap keeps the copy away from the table edge.

> ***Note:***
>
> *Remember, you can turn off the Link button in the Text Wrap panel to apply different wrap values to each side of the frame.*

14. Save the file and continue to the final stage of the project.

Understanding Table Styles

INDESIGN FOUNDATIONS

If you've spent any amount of time refining the appearance of a table, and you think you might want to use the same format again, you can save your formatting choices as a style. InDesign supports both table styles and cell styles, which are controlled in the Table Styles panel and Cell Styles panel.

Table and cell styles use the same concept as text-formatting styles. You can apply a cell style by selecting the cells and clicking the style name in the Cell Styles panel. Clicking a style in the Table Styles panel applies the style to the entire selected table.

The Clear Overrides button clears text-formatting options; the Clear Attributes button clears cell attributes.

Table styles store all options that can be defined in the Table Setup dialog box (except the options for header and footer rows). You can also define cell styles (called **nesting styles**) for specific types of rows, as well as the left and right columns in the table.

Cell styles store all options that can be defined in the Cell Options dialog box, including the paragraph style that is applied to cells where that style is applied.

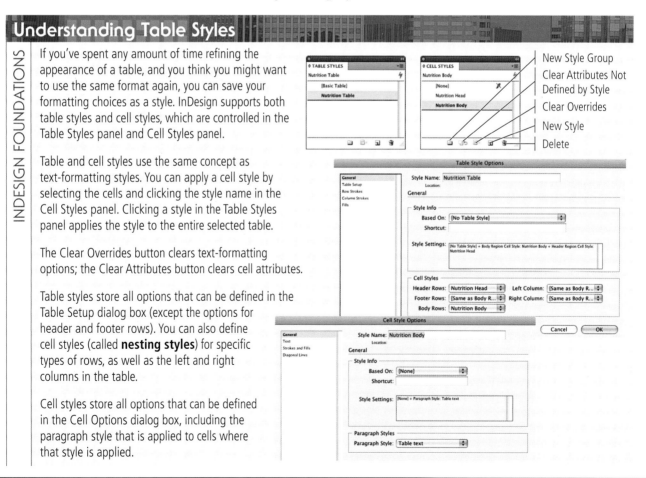

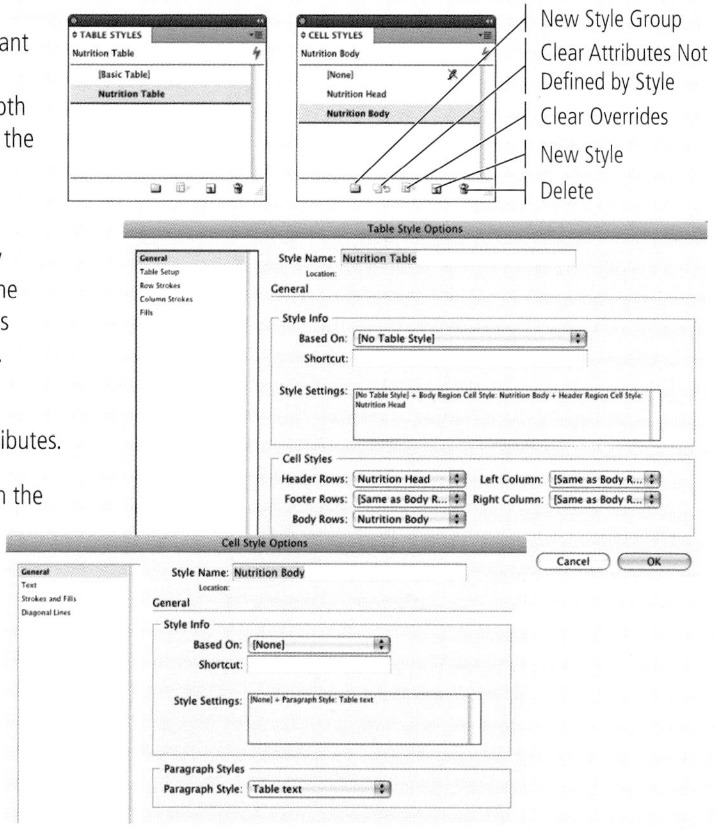

New Style Group
Clear Attributes Not Defined by Style
Clear Overrides
New Style
Delete

Creating Table Headers and Footers

Long tables of data often require more than one text frame (or column, depending on the table). In this case, you can break a table across multiple frames and use repeating headers and footers for information that needs to be part of each instance of the table (for example, column headings). Repeating headers and footers eliminate the need to manually insert the repeating information in each instance of the table.

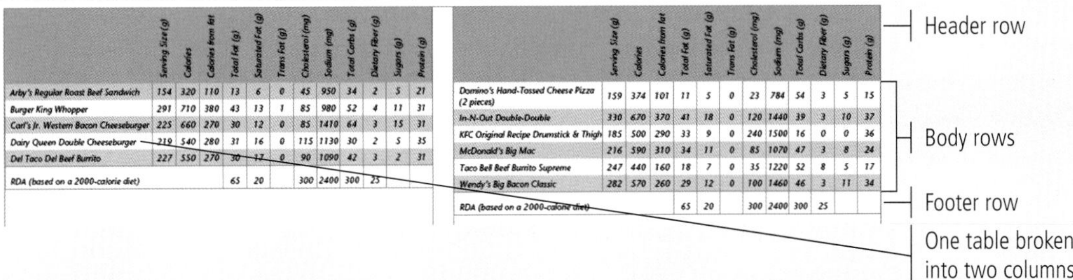

One table broken into two columns

Repeating header and footer rows are dynamically linked; this means that changing one instance of a header or footer changes all instances of the same header or footer.

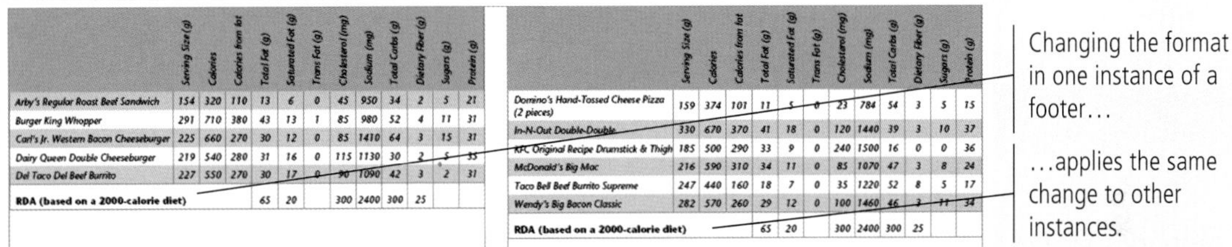

Changing the format in one instance of a footer…
…applies the same change to other instances.

Finally, this capability also means the headers and footers remain at the top and bottom of each instance, even if other body rows move to a different instance.

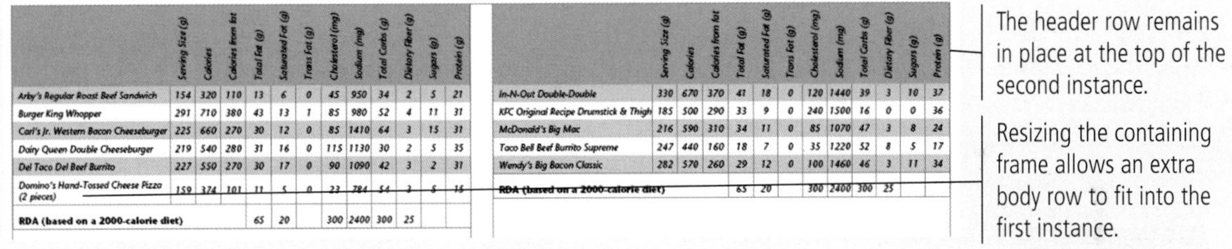

The header row remains in place at the top of the second instance.
Resizing the containing frame allows an extra body row to fit into the first instance.

You can add new header and footer rows to a table when you create the table, or by changing the options in the Headers and Footers tab of the Table Options dialog box. You can also convert existing rows to headers or footers by selecting one or more rows and choosing Table>Convert Rows>To Header or To Footer. You can also control these elements in the Headers and Footers dialog box.

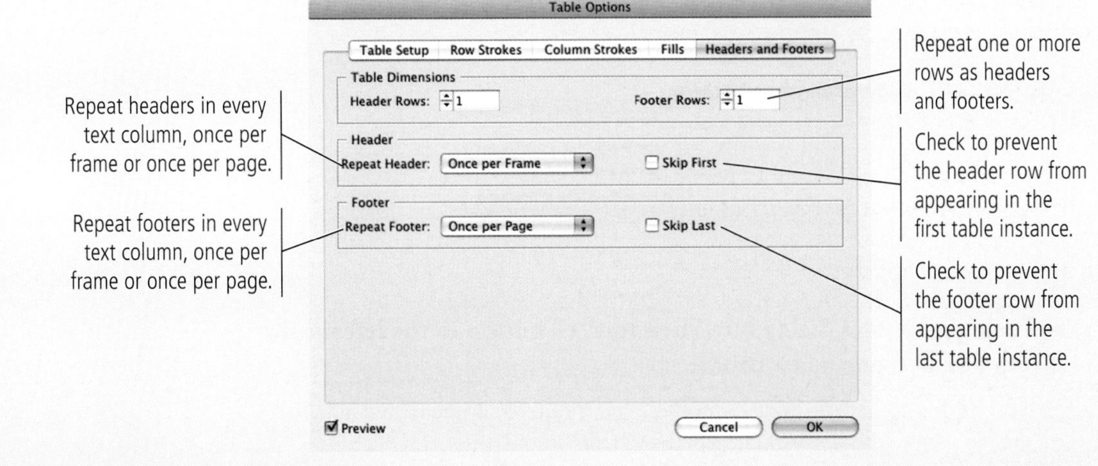

Repeat headers in every text column, once per frame or once per page.
Repeat footers in every text column, once per frame or once per page.

Check to prevent the header row from appearing in the first table instance.
Check to prevent the footer row from appearing in the last table instance.

Stage 4 Preflighting and Packaging the Job

When you submit an InDesign layout to a commercial output provider, you need to send all of the necessary pieces of the job — the layout file, any placed (linked) graphics or other files, and the fonts used in the layout. Before you copy everything to a disk and send it out, however, you should check your work to make sure the file is ready for commercial printing.

When you opened the original template at the beginning of this project, you replaced missing fonts and graphics — two of the most common problems with digital layout files. However, successful output on a commercial press has a number of other technical requirements that, if you ignore them, can cause a file to output incorrectly or not at all. InDesign includes a preflighting utility that makes it easy to check for potential errors, as well as a packaging utility that gathers all of the necessary bits for the printer.

Define a Preflight Profile

InDesign includes a dynamic, built-in preflighting utility that can check for common errors as you build a file. If you introduce a problem while building a file, the bottom-left corner of the document window shows a red light and the number of potential errors. In the following exercise, you define a profile to check for errors based on the information you have. This is certainly not an exhaustive check for all possible output problems. You should always work closely with your output provider to build responsible files that will cause no problems in the output workflow.

Note:

Ask your output provider if they have defined an InDesign preflight profile that you can load into your application to check for the problems that will interrupt their specific workflows.

1. **With newsletter_dec.indd open, look at the bottom-left corner of the document window.**

2. **Click the arrow to the right of the No Errors message and choose Preflight Panel from the menu.**

   The message currently shows no errors, but at this point you don't know exactly what is being checked. The Preflight panel provides an interface for defining preflight profiles, as well as reviewing the specific issues identified as errors.

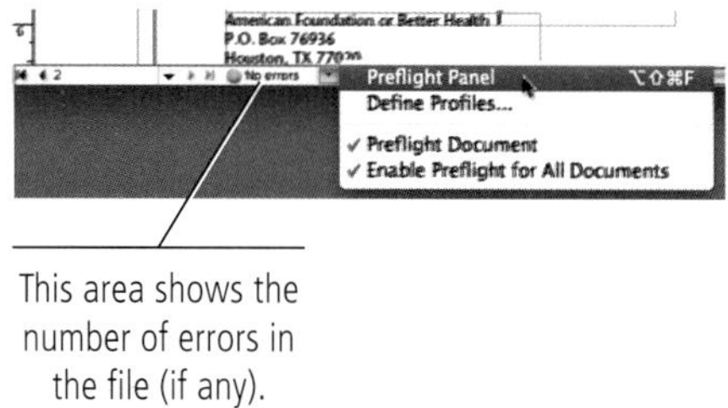

This area shows the number of errors in the file (if any).

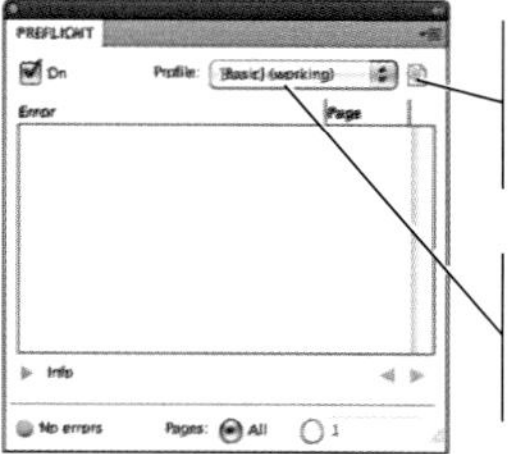

Click this button to embed the current profile into the active document.

The Preflight panel shows which profile is being used to check for errors.

3. **Open the Preflight panel Options menu and choose Define Profiles.**

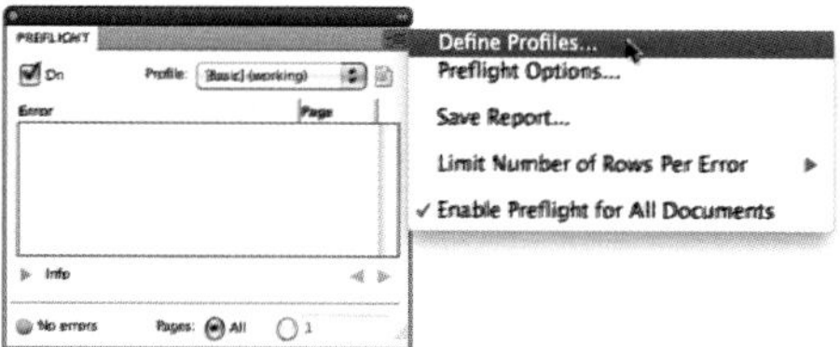

4. **In the Preflight Profiles dialog box, click the "+" button in the left side of the dialog box to create a new profile.**

   Rather than relying on generic built-in profiles, you should be aware of and able to control exactly what is (and is not) flagged as an error.

5. **Type HeartSmart Check in the Profile Name field, then click the empty area below the list of profiles to finalize the new name.**

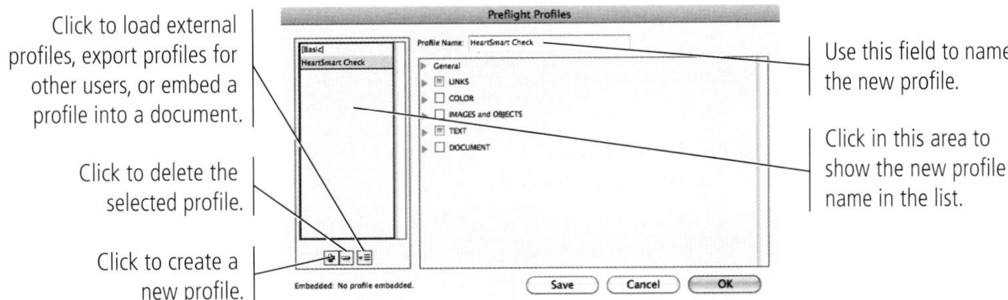

6. **With the HeartSmart Check profile selected on the left side of the dialog box, expand the General category on the right. Highlight the existing text in the Description field, and then type Verify newsletter for 4c press.**

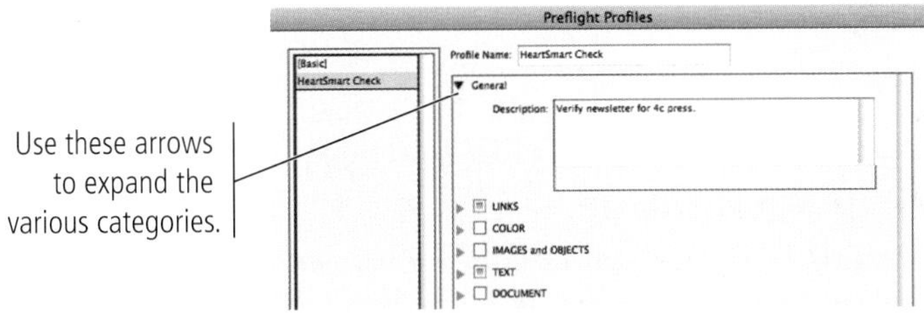

Note:

This description is simply a reminder of the profile's intent.

7. **Collapse the General category and expand the Links category. Check the Links Missing or Modified option.**

Image files placed in a layout need to be available when the job is output. By checking this option, you are warned if any placed image has been moved or modified since it was placed into the layout.

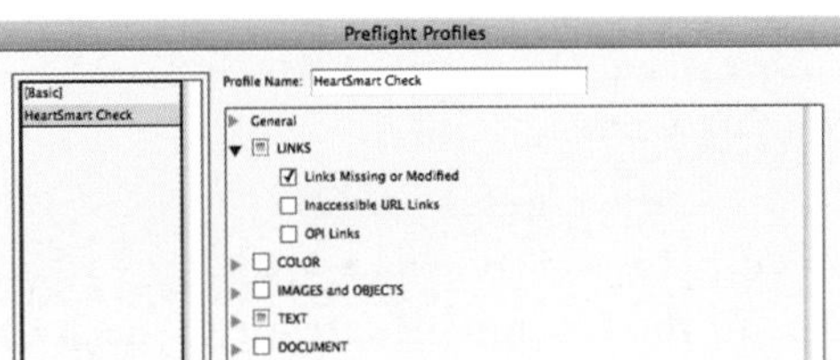

8. **Collapse the Links category and expand the Color category. Check and expand the Color Spaces and Modes Not Allowed option, and then check the RGB and Spot Color options.**

You know this newsletter is going to be output as a 4-color job. Spot colors will create an extra separation, which can be a very costly error. By setting these options, you will receive a warning if you create a spot color in a job that should be output as 4-color.

To achieve the best-quality, predictable output, it's a good idea to check for RGB images and control the conversion process in an image-editing application (i.e., Photoshop).

Note:

Some output processes use a method called in-RIP separation to convert RGB images to CMYK during the output process. However, the conversion process can cause significant color shift if it is not controlled.

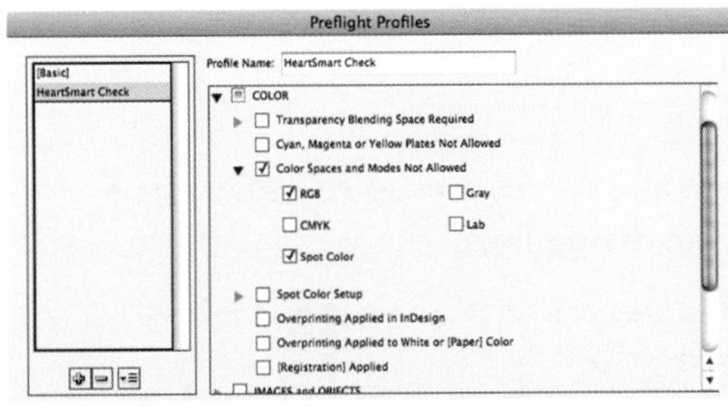

9. **Collapse the Color category and expand the Images and Objects category. Check and expand the Image Resolution option. Check the three Minimum Resolution options. Change the Color and Grayscale minimums to `300` and change the 1-bit option to `1200`.**

   Commercial output devices typically require at least 300 ppi to output raster images at good quality. By setting these minimum restrictions, you will receive a warning if your (or your client's) images do not have enough resolution to output at good quality using most commercial printing processes.

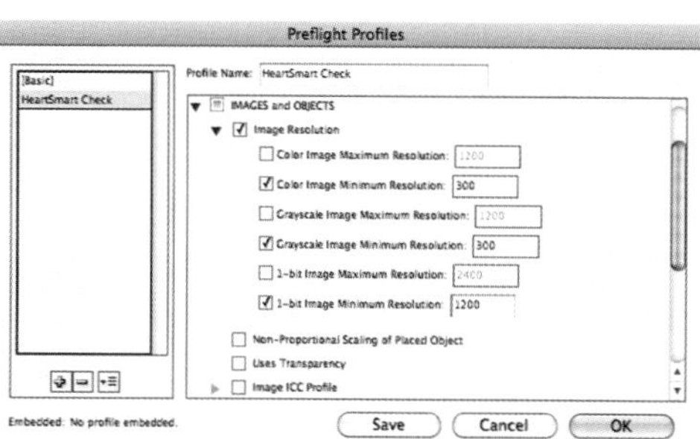

Note:

Remember: required resolution is actually two times the line screen (lpi) used for a specific job. If possible, always ask your service provider what resolution to use for your job. If you don't know the lpi (and can't find out in advance), 300 ppi resolution is a safe choice for most printing.

10. **Collapse the Images and Objects category and expand the Text category. Check the Overset Text and Font Missing options.**

    Overset text could simply be the result of extra paragraph returns at the end of a story. However, you should always check these issues to be sure that some of the client's text has not been accidentally overset.

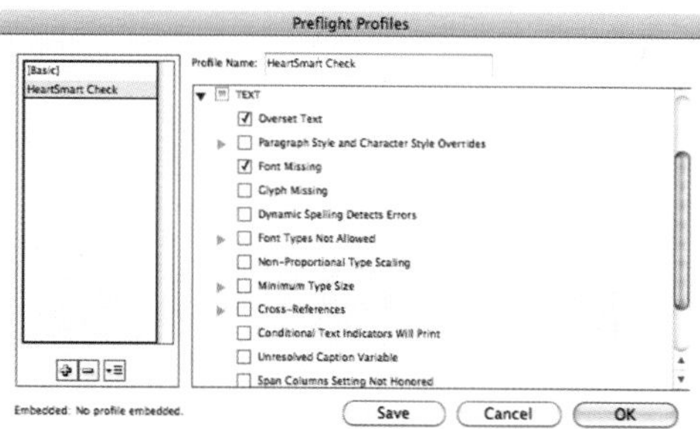

11. **Collapse the Text category and expand the Document category. Check the Number of Pages Required option. Expand that option, choose Exactly in the menu, and type `2` in the field.**

    You know that every issue of the newsletter should be exactly 2 pages. If your file has more or less than 2 pages, you will receive an error message.

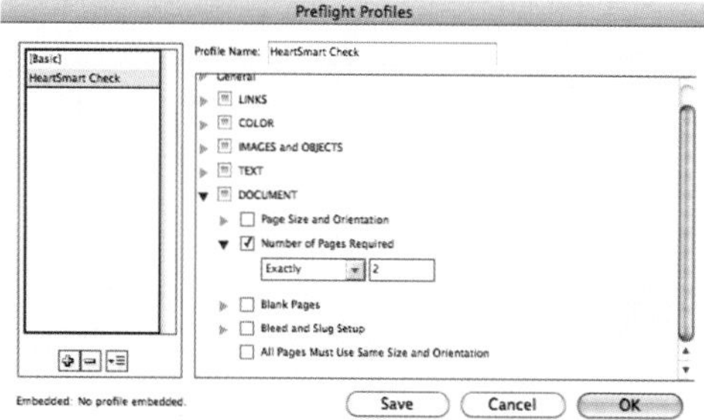

12. **Click OK to save the profile and close the dialog box.**

13. **Continue to the next exercise.**

What's in a Preflight Profile?

The Preflight Profiles dialog box includes a number of options for identifying potential errors. If you are going to build responsible files, you should have a basic understanding of what these options mean.

This is by no means an exhaustive list of all potential problems in digital page-layout files; it's a list of the problems Adobe included in the Preflight Profile dialog box. Other problems are beyond the scope of most graphic designers and are better left to prepress professionals to correct, given the specific equipment conditions in their workflows.

It should also be noted that some of these issues are not necessarily errors, but nonetheless should be reviewed before a job is output. For example, blank pages might be intentionally placed into a document to force a chapter opener onto a right-facing page; in this case, the blank page is not an error. In other cases, a blank page might be left over after text is edited; in this case, the blank page would be an error. You can use the Preflight panel to find definite errors, but also use it to verify that what you have is exactly what you want.

Links

- **Links Missing or Modified.** Use this option to receive a warning if a placed file has been moved (missing) or changed (modified) since it was placed into a layout. If a placed file is missing, the output will use only the low-resolution preview that you see on screen. If a placed file has been modified, the output will reflect the most up-to-date version of the placed file — which could be drastically different than the original, potentially destroying your overall layout.
- **Inaccessible URL Links.** Use this option to find hyperlinks that might cause problems if you are creating an interactive PDF document.
- **OPI Links.** OPI is a workflow tool that allows designers to use low-resolution FPO (for placement only) files during the design stage. When the job is processed for output, the high-resolution versions are swapped out in place of the FPO images. Although not terribly common anymore, some larger agencies still use OPI workflows.

Document

- **Page Size and Orientation.** Use this option to cause an error if the document size is not a specific size; you can also cause an error if the current document is oriented other than the defined page size (i.e., portrait instead of landscape or vice versa).
- **Number of Pages Required.** Use this option to define a specific number of pages, the smallest number of pages that can be in the document, or whether the document must have pages in multiples of a specific number (for example, multiples of 16 for 16-page signature output).
- **Blank Pages.** Use this option to find blank pages in the document.
- **Bleed and Slug Setup.** Use this option to verify the document's bleed and slug sizes against values required by a specific output process.
- **All Pages Must Use Same Size and Orientation.** Because InDesign CS5 supports multiple page sizes in the same document, you can check this option to verify that all pages in the file have the same size.

Color

- **Transparency Blending Space Required.** Use this option to define whether CMYK or RGB should be used to flatten transparent objects for output. (Refer to Project 8 for more on transparency flattening.)
- **Cyan, Magenta, or Yellow Plates Not Allowed.** Use this option to verify layouts that will be output with only spot colors, or with black and spot colors.
- **Color Spaces and Modes Not Allowed.** Use this option to create errors if the layout uses RGB, CMYK, Spot Color, Gray, or LAB color models. (Different jobs have different defined color spaces. The option to flag CMYK as an error can be useful, for example, if you are building a layout that will be output in black only.)
- **Spot Color Setup.** Use this option to define the number of spot colors a job should include, as well as the specific color model that should be used (LAB or CMYK) when converting unwanted spot colors for process printing.
- **Overprinting Applied in InDesign.** Use this option to create an error if an element is set to overprint instead of trap.
- **Overprinting Applied to White or [Paper] Color.** By definition, White or [Paper] is technically the absence of other inks. Unless you are printing white toner or opaque spot ink, white cannot, by definition, overprint. Use this option to produce an error if White or [Paper] elements are set to overprint.
- **[Registration] Applied.** The [Registration] color swatch is a special swatch used for elements such as crop and registration marks. Any element that uses the [Registration] color will output on all separations in the job. Use this option to find elements that are incorrectly colored with the [Registration] color instead of (probably) black.

What's in a Preflight Profile? (continued)

Images and Objects

- **Image Resolution.** Use this option to identify placed files with too little or too much resolution. As you know, commercial output devices typically require 300 ppi to output properly. The maximum resolution options can be used to find objects that, typically through scaling, result in unnecessarily high resolutions that might take considerable time for the output device to process.
- **Non-Proportional Scaling of Placed Object.** Use this option to find placed files that have been scaled with different X and Y percentages.
- **Uses Transparency.** Use this option to find any element affected by transparency. As you learned in Project 8, you should carefully preview transparency flattening before outputting the job.
- **Image ICC Profile.** Use this option to find placed images that have embedded ICC profiles. Typically used in color-managed workflows, placed images often store information — in the form of profiles — about the way a particular device captured or created the color in that image. You can cause errors if the image profile results in CMYK conversion, or if the embedded image profile has been overridden in the layout.
- **Layer Visibility Overrides.** Use this option to find layered Photoshop files in which the visibility of specific layers has been changed within InDesign.
- **Minimum Stroke Weight.** There is a limit to the smallest visible line that can be produced by any given output device. Use this option to find objects with a stroke weight smaller than a specific point size.
- **Interactive Elements.** Use this option to find elements with interactive properties.
- **Bleed/Trim Hazard.** Use this option to find elements that fall within a defined distance of the page edge, or spine for facing-page layouts (i.e., outside the live area).
- **Hidden Page Items.** Use this option to create an error if any objects on a page are not currently visible.

Text

- **Overset Text.** Use this option to find any frames with overset text.
- **Paragraph Style and Character Style Overrides.** Use this option to find instances where an applied style has been overridden with local formatting.
- **Font Missing.** Use this option to create an error if any required font is not available on the computer.
- **Glyph Missing.** Use this option to identify glyphs that aren't available.
- **Dynamic Spelling Detects Errors.** Use this option to cause an error if InDesign's dynamic spelling utility identifies any errors in the document.
- **Font Types Not Allowed.** Use this option to prohibit specific font types that can cause problems in modern output workflows.
- **Non-Proportional Type Scaling.** Use this option to identify type that has been artificially stretched or compressed in one direction (i.e., where horizontal or vertical scaling has been applied).
- **Minimum Type Size.** Use this option to identify any type set smaller than a defined point size. You can also identify small type that requires more than one ink to reproduce (a potential registration problem on commercial output devices).
- **Cross-References.** Use this option to identify dynamic links from one location in a file to another. You can cause errors if a cross reference is out of date or unresolved.
- **Conditional Text Indicators Will Print.** Use this option to create an error if certain visual indicators will appear in the final output.
- **Unresolved Caption Variable.** Use this option to find dynamic caption variables for which there is no defined metadata.
- **Span Columns Setting Not Honored.** Use this option to find paragraphs with a defined column-span setting that is prevented by other objects on the page.
- **Tracked Change.** Use this option to find instances of text that have been changed but not accepted when Track Changes is enabled. (You will explore this utility in Project 10.)

Evaluate the Layout

Now that you have defined the issues that you know are errors, you can check your file for those issues and make the necessary corrections.

1. **With `newsletter_dec.indd` open, click the Profile menu in the Preflight panel and choose HeartSmart Check as the profile to use.**

Note:

Preflight profiles become part of the application, but are not linked to or saved in a specific document unless you intentionally embed the profile.

2. **In the bottom of the panel, make sure the All radio button is checked.**

   When the All option is active, the entire document is checked. You can use the other radio button to define a specific page or range of pages to preflight.

   As soon as you call the HeartSmart Check profile, the panel reports 8 errors.

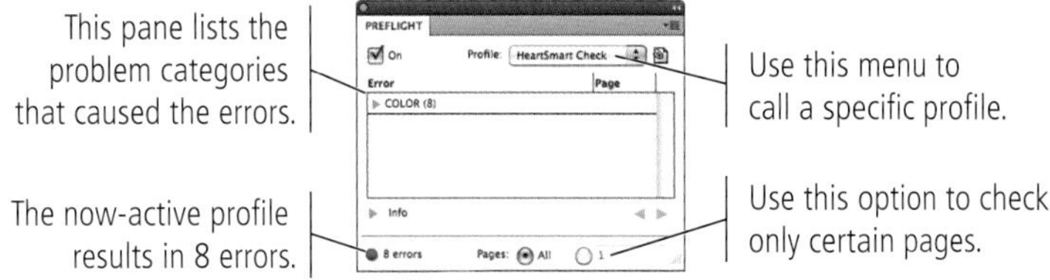

3. **Expand the Info section of the Preflight panel.**

   This area offers information about a specific error, and offers suggestions for fixing the problem.

4. **Click the arrow to expand the Color list, and then click the arrow to expand the Color Space Not Allowed list.**

5. **Click the rectangle listing to select it, and then click the hot-text page number for that item.**

   The hot-text link on the right side of the Preflight panel changes the document window to show the specific item that caused the error.

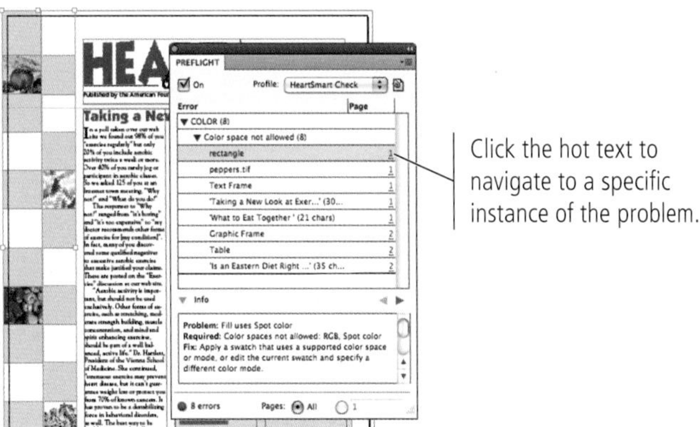

6. **In the Swatches panel, Control/right-click the Pantone 1945 C swatch and choose Swatch Options from the contextual menu.**

7. **In the Swatch Options dialog box, change the Color Mode menu to CMYK, change the Color Type menu to Process, and check the Name with Color Value option.**

You have to change the mode before you can change the type or naming convention.

By changing the color name, you can tell by a quick glance at the Swatches panel that the color is now a CMYK build.

> *Note:*
>
> *Spot colors are not always errors. Check the project's specifications carefully before you convert spot colors to process. Also, be aware that spot colors are often outside the CMYK gamut; converting a spot color to process can result in drastic color shift.*

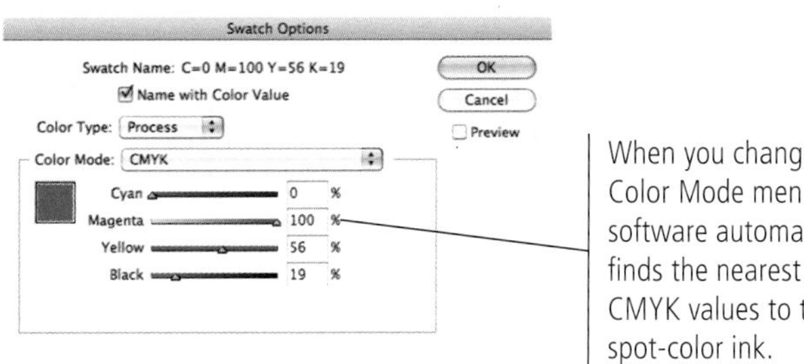

When you change the Color Mode menu, the software automatically finds the nearest possible CMYK values to the spot-color ink.

8. **Click OK to apply the new swatch options.**

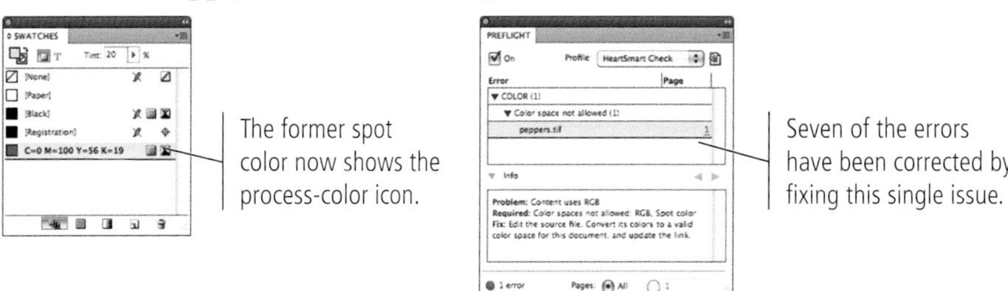

The former spot color now shows the process-color icon.

Seven of the errors have been corrected by fixing this single issue.

9. **Select the remaining problem instance in the Preflight panel and click the hot-text link to show that element in the layout.**

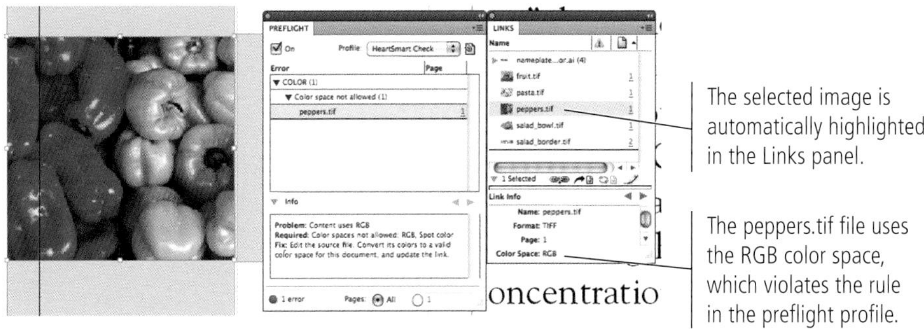

The selected image is automatically highlighted in the Links panel.

The peppers.tif file uses the RGB color space, which violates the rule in the preflight profile.

10. **In the Links panel, click the Relink button. Navigate to peppers_cmyk.tif in the WIP>HeartSmart>December Issue>CMYK folder and click Open. If you see the Image Import Options dialog box, click OK to accept the default options.**

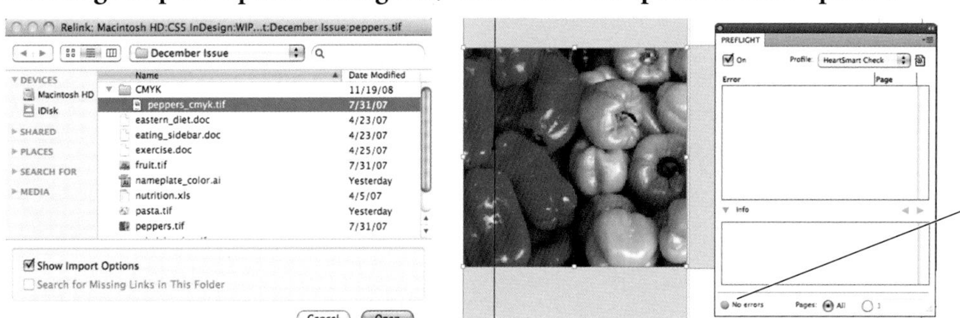

After linking to the CMYK version of the image, the file shows no errors (based on the profile you defined).

11. **Save the file and continue to the next exercise.**

Create the Job Package

Now that your file is error-free, you can package it for the output provider. As we have already stated, the images and fonts used in a layout must be available on the computer used to output the job. When you send the layout file to the printer, you must also send the necessary components. InDesign includes a Package utility that makes this process very easy.

1. **With newsletter_dec.indd open, choose File>Package.**

2. **Review the information in the Package dialog box, and then click Package.**

   If you had not preflighted the file before opening the Package dialog box, you would see warning icons identifying problems with image color space or missing fonts. Because you completed the previous exercise, however, potential errors have been fixed, so this dialog box simply shows a summary list of information about the file you are packaging.

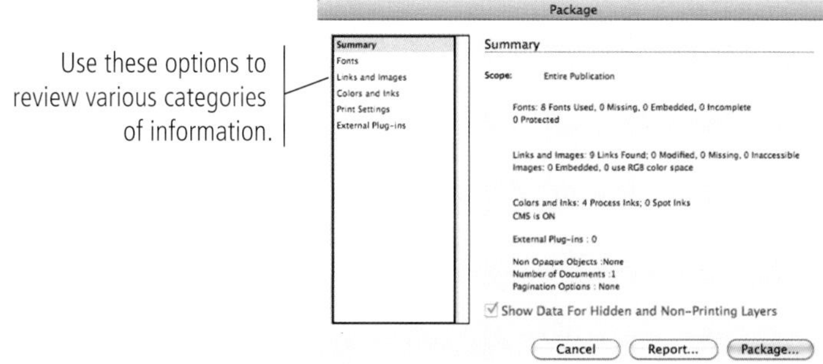

3. **If you see a message asking you to save, click Save.**

4. **In the Printing Instructions dialog box, add your contact information, and then click Continue.**

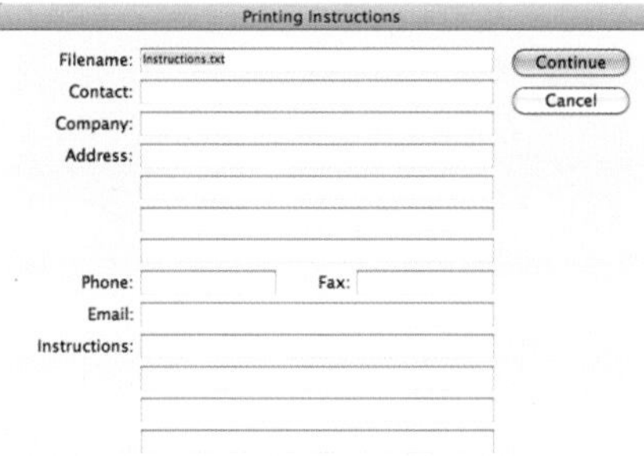

5. **Navigate to your WIP>HeartSmart folder as the target location. Make sure the Copy Fonts, Copy Linked Graphics, and Update Graphic Links options are checked, and then click Package.**

When you create a job package, InDesign automatically creates a new folder for the job.

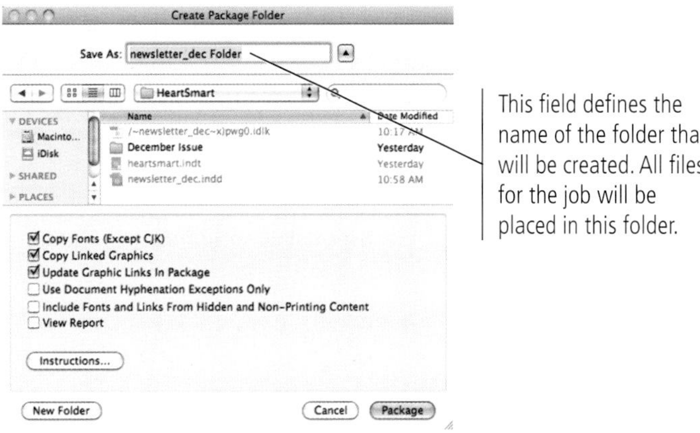

This field defines the name of the folder that will be created. All files for the job will be placed in this folder.

6. **Read the resulting warning and click OK.**

As with any software, you purchase a license to use a font — you do not own the actual font. It is illegal to distribute fonts freely, as it is illegal to distribute copies of your software. Most (but not all) font licenses allow you to send your copy of a font to a service provider, as long as the service provider also owns a copy of the font. Always verify that you are not violating font copyright before submitting a job.

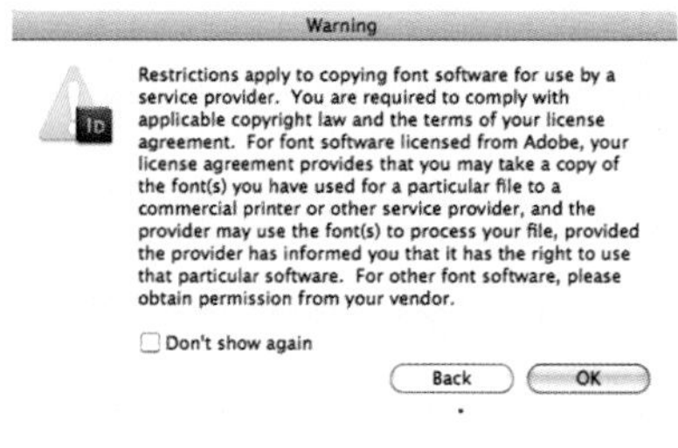

When the process is complete, the necessary job elements appear in the job folder (in your WIP>HeartSmart folder).

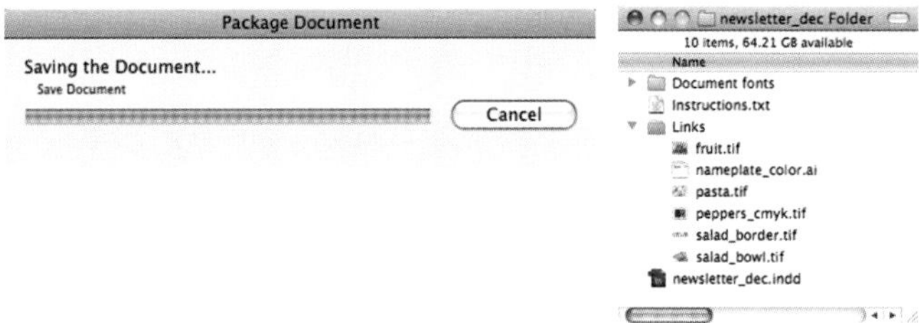

If you hand off the job package folder to another user (or if someone sends you a job package), the fonts in the collected Document Fonts folder will be available in InDesign when you open the packaged INDD file — even if those fonts are not installed at the computer's system level.

Document-installed fonts are installed when the related document is opened and uninstalled when you close that file. These fonts supersede any existing font of the same PostScript name within the document. Document-installed fonts are not available to other documents, or in other applications.

7. **Close the InDesign file.**

Project Review

fill in the blank

1. An image file that has been renamed since it was placed into an InDesign layout shows the status of ______________.

2. The ______________ is used to monitor the status of images that are placed into a layout.

3. ______________ is the distance between the edge of a frame and the text contained within that frame.

4. ______________ is the distance between the edge of an object and text in other overlapping frames.

5. ______________ apply only to selected text characters; this is useful for setting off a few words in a paragraph without affecting the entire paragraph.

6. ______________ apply to the entire body of text between two ¶ symbols.

7. While working in a table, the ______________ key has a special function; pressing it does not insert the associated character.

8. When the ______________ row height method is selected, table rows change height if you add or remove text from the table cells, or if you change the text formatting in a way that requires more or less space.

9. A(n) ______________ is a special kind of table row that repeats at the top of every instance of the same table.

10. ______________ is the process of checking a layout for errors before it goes to print.

short answer

1. Briefly explain the significance of a Missing Font warning.

2. List three advantages of using templates.

3. Briefly define "styles" in relation to text formatting.

Portfolio Builder Project

Use what you learned in this project to complete the following freeform exercise.
Carefully read the art director and client comments, then create your own design to meet the needs of the project.
Use the space below to sketch ideas; when finished, write a brief explanation of your reasoning behind your final design.

art director comments

The Humane Society wants to create a wall calendar to give away as a part of its annual fundraising drive. Each month will be on one sheet, which can be flipped when the month is over.

To complete this project, you should:

- ❑ Design a layout that incorporates the month grid, as well as space for an image and four coupons.
- ❑ Use whatever page size you think is most appropriate for the job.
- ❑ Use the master page to build the basic structure of each page (month) in the calendar.
- ❑ Find images or illustrations for each month; make sure you choose ones that don't require a licensing fee.

client comments

As a not-for-profit organization, we try to dedicate most of our finances to caring for our furry (and feathery, and leathery) friends. The printer has donated the resources to print the job, and your agency has donated your time as well — for which we're extremely grateful.

We want each month to have a different picture of cute, cuddly, happy pets with their people; we want to encourage adoption. Make sure you include different kinds of animals; the Humane Society isn't just for dogs and cats. Can you find images that won't cost anything to use?

Each month will also include a set of three coupons for local pet-related businesses. When you build the layout, plan space for those; when the layout's done, we'll let our donor companies know how much space they have for the coupons.

One final thing: we thought it might be fun to include a monthly 'fun fact' about animals. Can you find some little text snippets to include each month?

project justification

Project Summary

This project introduced a number of concepts and tools that will be very important as you work on more complex page-layout jobs. Importing text content from other applications — specifically, Microsoft Word and Microsoft Excel — is a foundational skill that you will use in most projects; this newsletter showed you how to control that content on import, and then re-format it as appropriate in the InDesign layout.

Templates, master pages, and styles are all designed to let you do the majority of work once and then apply it as many times as necessary; virtually any InDesign project can benefit from these tools, and you will use them extensively in your career as a graphic designer. This project provided a basic introduction to these productivity tools; you will build on these foundations as you complete the remaining five projects of this book.

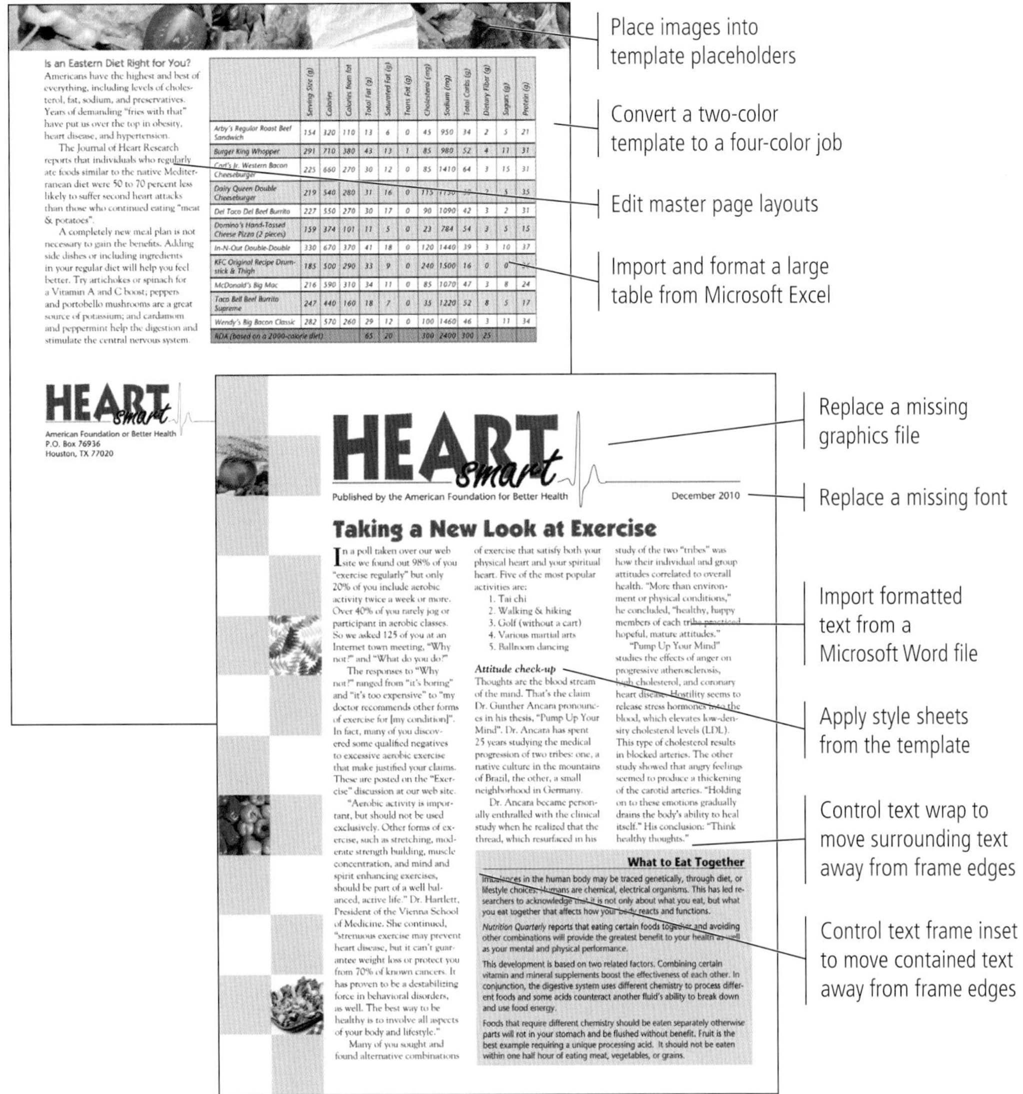

Is an Eastern Diet Right for You?
HEART smart
American Foundation or Better Health
P.O. Box 76936
Houston, TX 77020
HEART smart
Published by the American Foundation for Better Health
December 2010
Taking a New Look at Exercise
Attitude check-up
What to Eat Together
Place images into template placeholders
Convert a two-color template to a four-color job
Edit master page layouts
Import and format a large table from Microsoft Excel
Replace a missing graphics file
Replace a missing font
Import formatted text from a Microsoft Word file
Apply style sheets from the template
Control text wrap to move surrounding text away from frame edges
Control text frame inset to move contained text away from frame edges

project 10

Combined Brochure

Your client produces a monthly brochure that is mailed to consumers throughout the eastern United States and Canada. As the production artist, your job is to complete the brochure layout, verify that everything is correct, and create final files for print and Web distribution.

This project incorporates the following skills:

- ❑ Managing color in placed images and layout files
- ❑ Controlling import options for a variety of image file types
- ❑ Searching and replacing text and special characters
- ❑ Searching and changing object attributes
- ❑ Controlling the language and checking the spelling in layout text
- ❑ Outputting a color-managed PDF file
- ❑ Outputting a PDF file for digital distribution

Project Meeting

client comments

We print a new brochure every month with a few featured products and sale information. The brochures drive a lot of traffic to our Web store, where we close the sales without needing to maintain a brick-and-mortar storefront.

After two years, we're starting to broaden our market. Our original name was VermontKids, but we changed it to ToyTrends so the company doesn't seem so regional. This decision was only finalized yesterday, so you might need to make some adjustments in the files that were already sent to you.

We're going to print the final file, but we also want a version that we can use with digital marketing campaigns.

art director comments

We build each issue of the brochure from a standard template to maintain the brand consistency the client prefers. Every issue of the brochure is printed in five-color — CMYK plus one of the three spot colors in the logo; this issue should use the blue spot color.

The text has already been placed into the template for this issue, but the original designer had to move on to a different project. As the production artist, your job is to assemble the rest of the pieces, and check the text and images for errors or technical problems.

The client said the company's name just changed, so you'll need to make changes in both the text and in some of the graphics.

When everything is in place and verified, you will export two PDF files — one using high-quality settings for the commercial printer, and one that the client can use as an email attachment or Web download.

project objectives

To complete this project, you will:

- ❑ Define file color settings
- ❑ Place and control a variety of file types, including native Illustrator, native Photoshop, EPS, TIFF, PDF, JPEG, and native InDesign layouts
- ❑ Use paragraph and character styles to control the appearance of text
- ❑ Check and correct spelling in the document and linked files
- ❑ Search and replace basic text and special characters, text formatting, and object attributes
- ❑ Proof colors and separations on-screen
- ❑ Export a color-managed PDF file
- ❑ Export a PDF file with settings appropriate for digital distribution

Stage 1 Controlling Color for Output

You can't accurately reproduce color without some understanding of color theory, so we present a very basic introduction in the following pages. We highly recommend that you read this information. Be aware that there are entire, weighty books written about color science; we're providing the condensed version of what you absolutely must know to work effectively with color.

While it's true that color management science can be extremely complex and beyond the needs of most graphic designers, applying color management in InDesign is more intimidating than difficult. We believe this foundational knowledge of color management will make you a more effective and practically grounded designer.

Additive vs. Subtractive Color Models

The most important thing to remember about color theory is that color is light, and light is color. You can easily demonstrate this by walking through your house at midnight; you will notice that what little you can see appears as dark shadows. Without light, you can't see — and without light, there is no color.

Note:

Additive color theory is practically applied when a reproduction method uses light to reproduce color. A television screen or computer monitor is black when turned off. When the power is turned on, light in the monitor illuminates at different intensities to create the range of colors that you see.

The **additive color** model (RGB) is based on the idea that all colors can be reproduced by combining pure red, green, and blue light in varying intensities. These three colors are considered the additive primaries. Combining any two additive primaries at full strength produces one of the additive secondaries — red and blue light combine to produce magenta, red and green combine to produce yellow, and blue and green combine to produce cyan. Although usually considered a "color," black is the absence of light (and, therefore, of color). White is the sum of all colors, produced when all three additive primaries are combined at full strength.

Printing pigmented inks on a substrate is a very different method of reproducing color. Reproducing color on paper requires **subtractive color** theory, which is essentially the inverse of additive color theory. Instead of adding red, green, and blue light to create the range of colors, subtractive color begins with a white surface that reflects red, green, and blue light at equal and full strength. To reflect (reproduce) a specific color, you add pigments that subtract or absorb only certain wavelengths from the white light. To reflect only red, for example, the surface must subtract (or absorb) the green and blue light.

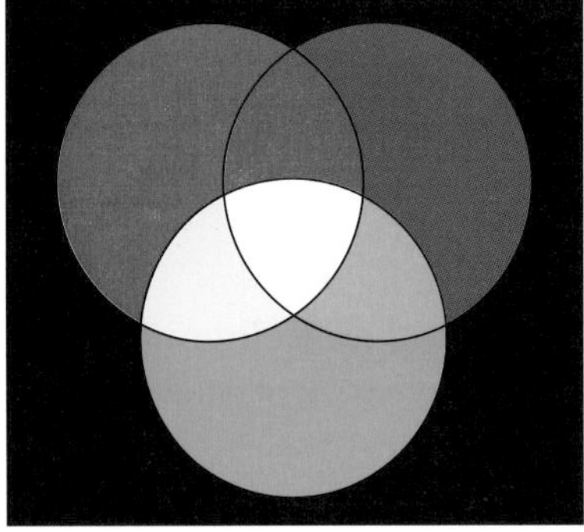

Additive color model

Remember that the additive primaries (red, green, and blue) combine to create the additive secondaries (cyan, magenta, and yellow). Those additive secondaries are also called the subtractive primaries because each subtracts one-third of the light spectrum and reflects the other two-thirds:

- Cyan absorbs red light, reflecting only blue and green light.
- Magenta absorbs green light, reflecting only red and blue light.
- Yellow absorbs blue light, reflecting only red and green light.

A combination of two subtractive primaries, then, absorbs two-thirds of the light spectrum and reflects only one-third. As an example, a combination of yellow and magenta absorbs both blue and green light, reflecting only red.

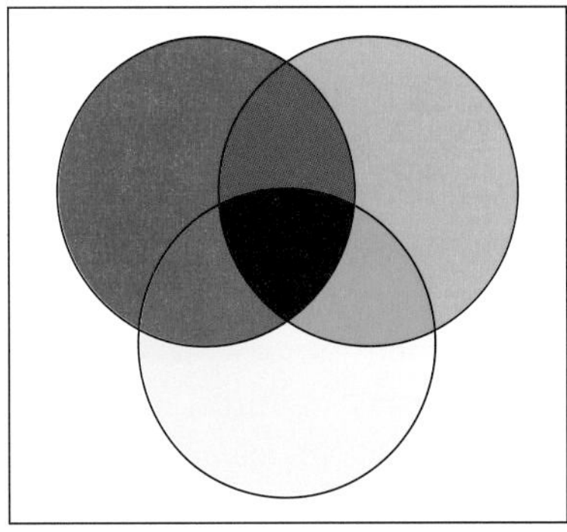

Subtractive color model

Color printing is a practical application of subtractive color theory. The pigments in the cyan, magenta, yellow, and black inks are combined to absorb different wavelengths of light. To create the appearance of red, the green and blue light must be subtracted or absorbed, thus reflecting only red. Magenta absorbs green light, and yellow absorbs blue light; combining magenta and yellow inks on white paper reflects only the red light. By combining different amounts of the subtractive primaries, it's possible to produce a large range (or gamut) of colors.

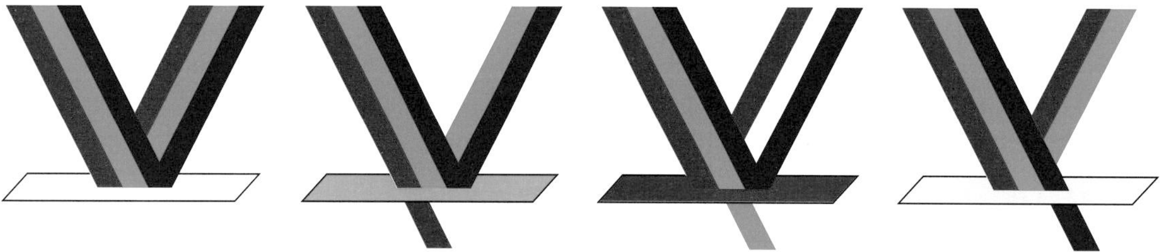

Because white is a combination of all colors, white paper should theoretically reflect equal percentages of all light wavelengths. However, different papers absorb or reflect varying percentages of some wavelengths, thus defining the paper's apparent color. The paper's color affects the appearance of ink colors printed on that paper.

Understanding Gamut

Different color models have different ranges or **gamuts** of possible colors. A normal human visual system is capable of distinguishing approximately 16.7 million different colors. Color reproduction systems, however, are far more limited. The RGB model has the largest gamut of the output models. The CMYK gamut is far more limited; many of the brightest and most saturated colors that can be reproduced using light cannot be reproduced using pigmented inks.

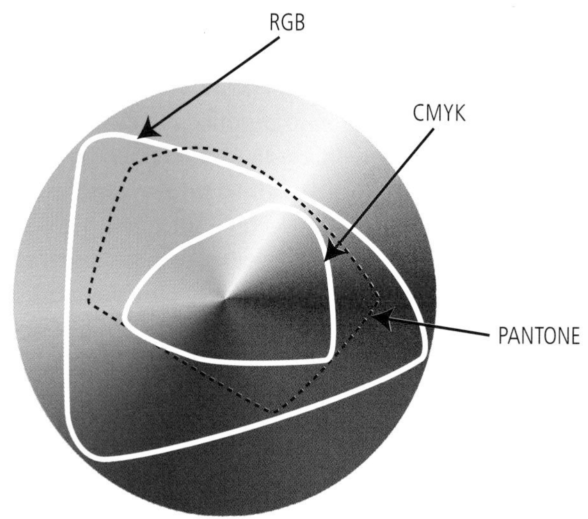

This difference in gamut is one of the biggest problems graphic designers face when working with color images. Digital image-capture devices (including scanners and digital cameras) work in the RGB space, which, with its larger gamut, can more closely mirror the range of colors in the original scene. Printing, however, requires images to be first converted or separated into the CMYK color space.

The usual goal in color reproduction is to achieve a color appearance equivalent to the original. Depending on the images, it is likely that at least some colors in the RGB model cannot be reproduced in the more limited gamut of the CMYK color model. These out-of-gamut colors pose a challenge to faithfully reproducing the original image. If the conversion from RGB to CMYK is not carefully controlled, color shift can result in drastic differences between the original and the printed images.

> ***Note:***
>
> *Color shift can also result when converting from one CMYK profile to another (e.g., a sheetfed press profile to a web press profile), or (though less likely) from one version of RGB to another. Whatever models are being used, color management gives you better control over the conversion process.*

Color Management in Brief

Color management is intended to preserve color predictability and consistency as a file is moved from one color mode to another throughout the reproduction process. Color management can also eliminate ambiguity when a color is only specified by some numbers. For example, you might create a royal purple in the Swatches panel; but without color management, that same set of RGB numbers might look more lilac (or even gray) when converted to CMYK for printing. A well-tuned color management system can translate the numbers that define a color in one space to numbers that can better represent that same color in another space.

It's important to have realistic expectations of color management, and to realize that color management isn't a replacement for a thorough understanding of the color-reproduction process. Even at its best, color management can't fix bad scans or bad photos — all it can do is provide consistency and predictability to a process that otherwise rarely has either.

Color management relies on color profiles, which are simply data sets that define the reproduction characteristics of a specific device. A profile is essentially a recipe that contains the ingredients for reproducing a specific color in a given color space. The color recipes in profiles are known as look-up tables (LUTs), which are essentially cross-reference systems for finding matching color values in different color spaces.

Source profiles are the profiles of the devices (scanners, digital cameras, etc.) used to capture an image. **Destination profiles** are the profiles of output devices. LAB (or L*a*b*, or CIELAB) is a device-independent, theoretical color space that represents the entire visible spectrum. The color management engine uses LAB as an intermediate space to translate colors from one device-dependent space to another.

The mechanics of color-managed conversions are quite simple. Regardless of the specific input and output spaces in question, the same basic process is followed for every pixel in the image:

1. The color-management engine looks up the color values of a pixel in the source (input-space) profile to find a matching set of LAB values.
2. The color-management engine looks up the LAB values in the destination (output-space) profile to find the matching set of color values that will display the color of that pixel as accurately as possible in the output space.

Note:

Color profiles are sometimes called "ICC profiles," named after the International Color Consortium (ICC), which developed the standard for creating color profiles.

Note:

Most professional-level devices come with profiles you can install when you install the hardware; a number of generic and industry-specific destination profiles are also built into InDesign.

Color Management in Theory and Practice

INDESIGN FOUNDATIONS

RGB and CMYK are very different entities. The two color models have distinct capabilities, advantages, and limitations. There is no way to exactly reproduce RGB color using the CMYK gamut because many of the colors in the RGB gamut are simply too bright or too saturated. Rather than claiming to produce an exact (but impossible) match from your monitor to a printed page, the true goal of color management is to produce the best possible representation of the color using the gamut of the chosen output device.

A theoretically ideal color-managed workflow looks like this:

- Image-capture devices (scanners and digital cameras) are profiled to create a look-up table that defines the device's color-capturing characteristics.
- Images are acquired using a profiled device. The profile of the capturing device is tagged to every image captured.
- You define a destination (CMYK) profile for the calibrated output device that will be used for your final job.
- InDesign translates the document and embedded image profiles to the defined destination profiles.

This ideal workflow mentions the word "calibrate," which means to check and correct the device's characteristics. Calibration is an essential element in a color-managed workflow; it is fundamentally important to consistent and predictable output.

Taking this definition a step further, you cannot check or correct the color characteristics of a device without having something to compare the device against. To calibrate a device, a known target — usually a sequence of distinct and varying color patches — is reproduced using the device. The color values of the reproduction are measured and compared to the values of the known target. Precise calibration requires adjusting the device until the reproduction matches the original.

As long as your devices are accurately calibrated to the same target values, the color acquired by your RGB scanner will match the colors displayed on your RGB monitor and the colors printed by your CMYK desktop printer. Of course, most devices (especially consumer-level desktop devices, which are gaining a larger market share in the commercial graphics world) are not accurately calibrated, and very few are calibrated to the same set of known target values.

Keeping in mind these ideals and realities, the true goals of color management are to:

- Compensate for color variations in the different devices
- Accurately translate one color space to another
- Compensate for limitations in the output process
- Better predict the final outcome when a file is reproduced

Define Application Color Settings

InDesign's color management options allow you to integrate InDesign into a color-managed workflow. This includes managing the color profiles of placed images, as well as previewing potential color problems on screen before the job is actually output.

There are two primary purposes for managing color in InDesign: previewing colors based on the intended output device, and converting colors to the appropriate space when a file is output (whether to PDF or an imagesetter for commercial printing).

1. **With no file open in InDesign, choose Edit>Color Settings.**

   The Color Settings dialog box defines default working spaces for RGB and CMYK colors, as well as general color management policies.

   The RGB working space defines the default profile for RGB colors and images that do not have embedded profiles. The CMYK working space defines the profile for the device or process that will be used to output the job.

2. **Choose North America Prepress 2 in the Settings menu.**

   InDesign includes a number of common option groups, which you can access in the Settings menu. You can also make your own choices and save those settings as a new preset by clicking Save, or you can import settings files created by another user by clicking Load.

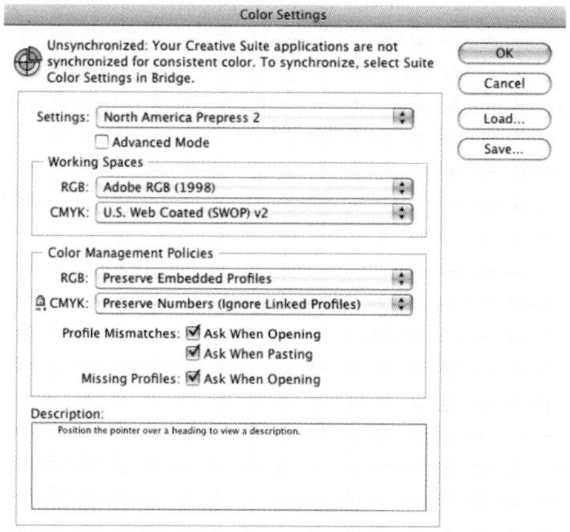

   A working space is a specific profile that defines color values in the associated mode. Using Adobe RGB (1998), for example, means new RGB colors in the InDesign file and imported RGB images without embedded profiles will be described by the values in the Adobe RGB (1998) space.

Note:

The Adobe RGB (1998) space is a neutral color space that isn't related to a specific monitor's display capabilities. Using this space assumes you are making color decisions on numeric values, not by what you see on your monitor.

Note:

The Working Spaces menus identify exactly which version of each space defines color within that space.

3. **In the CMYK menu, choose U.S. Sheetfed Coated v2.**

   There are many CMYK profiles; each output device has a gamut unique to that individual device. U.S. Sheetfed Coated v2 is an industry-standard profile for a common type of printing (sheetfed printing on coated paper). In a truly color-managed workflow, you would actually use a profile for the specific press/paper combination being used for the job. (We're using one of the default profiles to show you how the process works.)

4. **In the Color Management Policies, make sure Preserve Embedded Profiles is selected for RGB, and Preserve Numbers (Ignore Linked Profiles) is selected for CMYK.**

   These options tell InDesign what to do when you open existing files, or if you copy elements from one file to another.

   - When an option is turned off, color is not managed for objects or files in that color mode.
   - **Preserve Embedded Profiles** maintains the profile information saved in the file; files with no profile use the current working space.
   - If you choose **Convert to Working Space**, files automatically convert to the working space defined at the top of the Color Settings dialog box.
   - For CMYK colors, you can choose **Preserve Numbers (Ignore Linked Profiles)** to maintain raw CMYK numbers (ink percentages) rather than adjusting the colors based on an embedded profile.

5. **Check all three options under the Color Management Policies menus.**

The check boxes control InDesign's behavior when you open an existing file or paste an element from a document with a profile other than the defined working space (called a **profile mismatch**), or when you open a file that does not have an embedded profile (called a **missing profile**).

6. **If it is not already checked, activate the Advanced Mode check box (below the Settings menu).**

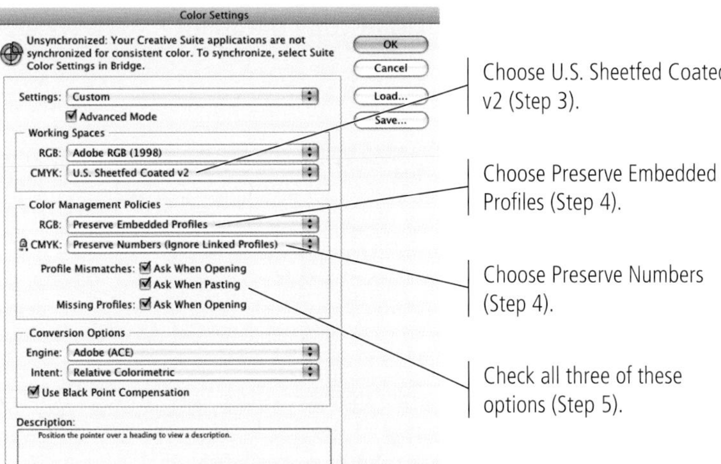

The Engine option determines the system and color-matching method for converting between color spaces:

- **Adobe (ACE)**, the default, stands for Adobe Color Engine.
- **Apple CMM** (Macintosh only) uses the Apple ColorSync engine.
- **Microsoft ICM** (Windows only) uses the Microsoft ICM engine.

The **Intent** menu defines how the engine translates source colors outside the gamut of the destination profile.

When the **Use Black Point Compensation** option is selected, the full range of the source space is mapped into the full-color range of the destination space. This method can result in blocked or grayed-out shadows, but it is very useful when the black point of the source is darker than that of the destination.

7. **Click OK to apply your settings, then continue to the next exercise.**

Understanding Rendering Intents

INDESIGN FOUNDATIONS

LAB color has the largest gamut, RGB the next largest, and CMYK the smallest. If you need to convert an image from an RGB space to a more limited CMYK space, you need to tell the CMS how to handle any colors that exist outside the CMYK space. You can do this by specifying the **rendering intent** that will be used when you convert colors.

- **Perceptual** presents a visually pleasing representation of the image, preserving visual relationships between colors. All colors in the image — including those available in the destination gamut — are shifted to maintain the proportional relationship within the image.
- **Saturation** compares the saturation of colors in the source profile and shifts them to the nearest-possible saturated color in the destination profile. The focus is on saturation instead of actual color value, which means this method can produce drastic color shift.
- **Relative Colorimetric** maintains any colors in both the source and destination profiles; source colors outside the destination gamut are shifted to fit. This method adjusts for the whiteness of the media, and is a good choice when most source colors are in-gamut.
- **Absolute Colorimetric** maintains colors in both the source and destination profiles. Colors outside the destination gamut are shifted to a color within the destination gamut, without considering the white point of the media.

Assign Color Settings to an Existing File

This project requires working on a file that has already been started, so some work has been completed before the file was handed off to you. To manage the process throughout the rest of this project, you need to make sure the existing file has the same color settings that you just defined.

1. **Download Print5_RF_Project10.zip from the Student Files Web page.**

2. **Expand the ZIP archive in your WIP folder (Macintosh) or copy the archive contents into your WIP folder (Windows).**

   This results in a folder named **Toys**, which contains the files you need for this project.

3. **Open the file toys_fall.indd from the WIP>Toys folder.**

   The existing file has neither a defined RGB nor a CMYK profile. Because you activated the Ask When Opening option in the Color Settings dialog box, InDesign asks how you want to handle RGB color in the file.

4. **Read the resulting warning message and click OK.**

   As you know, InDesign remembers the location of files from when they were placed in the layout file. Those files need to be in the same location as when they were placed for the job to output properly. If a file is not in the same location, or the name has been changed, InDesign warns you when you open the file.

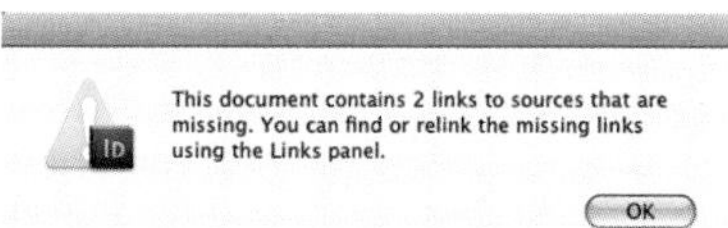

5. **In the Profile or Policy Mismatch dialog box, select the second option (Adjust the document to match current color settings).**

   This option assigns the existing RGB color settings (which you defined in the previous exercise) to the existing file.

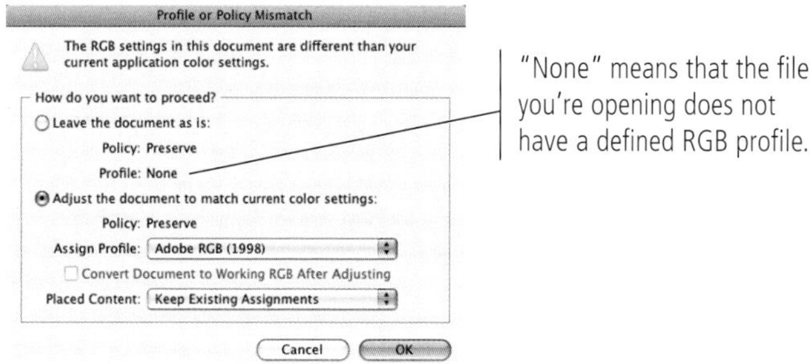

"None" means that the file you're opening does not have a defined RGB profile.

6. **Leave the remaining options at their default values and click OK.**

   Again, your choice in the Color Settings dialog box was to Ask When Opening if a file was missing a CMYK profile. Because the file does not have a defined CMYK profile, you see that warning now.

7. **In the second warning message, choose the second radio button (Adjust the document to match current color settings).**

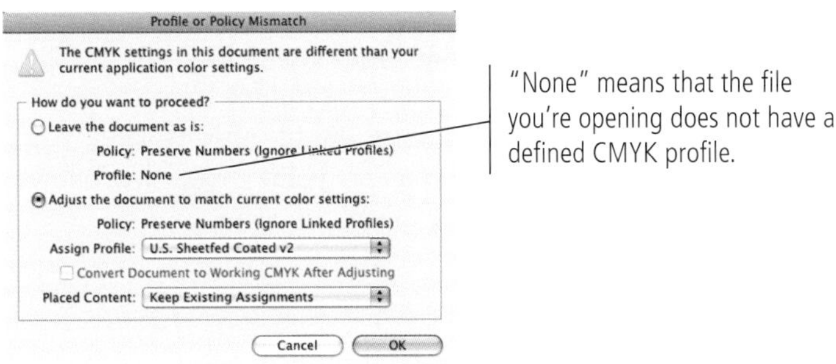

8. **Click OK to open the file.**

This file contains the layout for a four-page folded brochure. The layout is designed with a 17 × 11″ page size; the flat size is 8.5 × 11″ when folded in the middle.

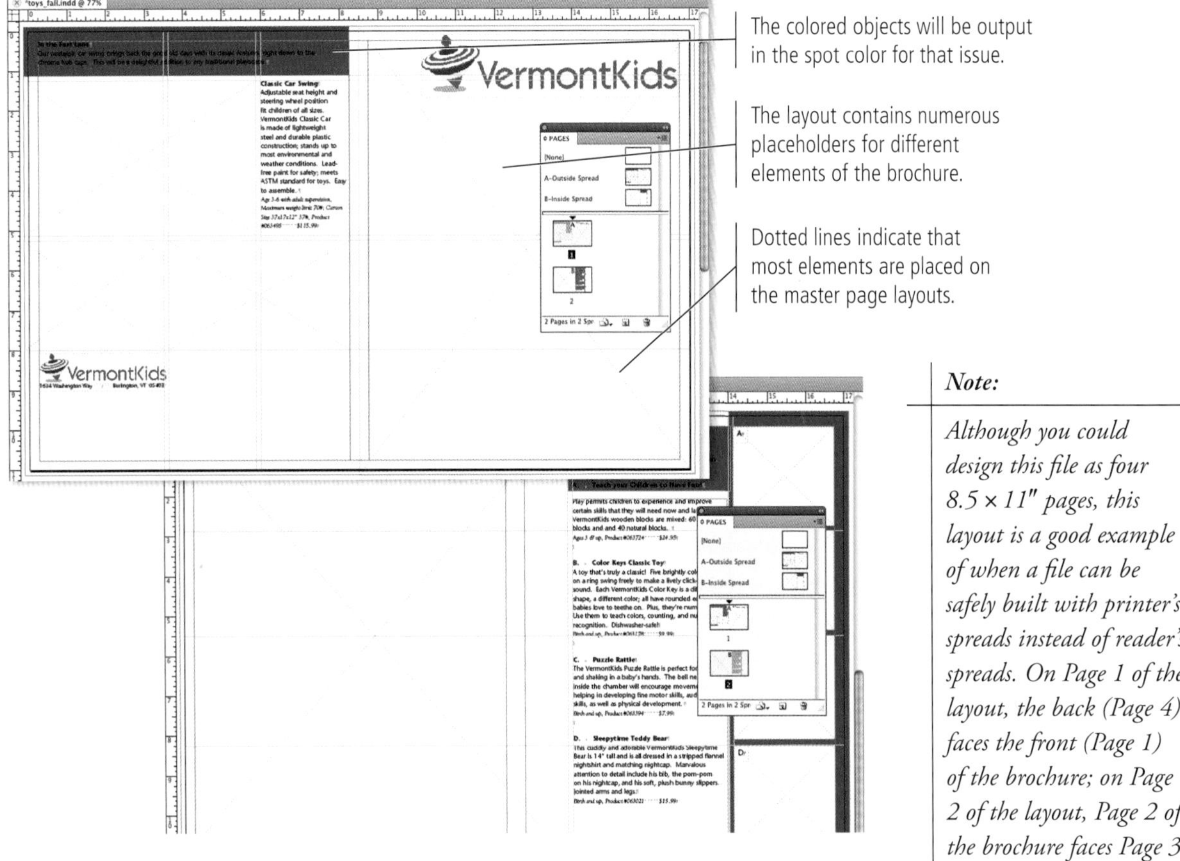

Note:

Although you could design this file as four 8.5 × 11″ pages, this layout is a good example of when a file can be safely built with printer's spreads instead of reader's spreads. On Page 1 of the layout, the back (Page 4) faces the front (Page 1) of the brochure; on Page 2 of the layout, Page 2 of the brochure faces Page 3.

9. **Save the file and continue to the next stage of the project.**

Stage 2 Placing and Controlling Images

Adobe InDesign supports a variety of graphics formats. The specific type of graphics you use depends on your ultimate output goal. For print applications such as the brochure you're building in this project, you should use high-resolution raster image files or vector-based graphics files.

Depending on what type of file you are importing, you have a number of options when you place a file. This stage of the project explores the most common file formats for print design workflows.

Replace a Native Illustrator File

As part of the Adobe Creative Suite, InDesign supports native Adobe Illustrator files (with the ".ai" extension) that have been saved to be compatible with the PDF format. Illustrator files can include both raster and vector information (including type and embedded fonts), as well as objects on multiple layers in a variety of color modes (including spot colors, which are added to the InDesign Swatches panel when the Illustrator file is imported).

Note:

Artwork in an Illustrator file must be entirely within the bounds of the artboard (page) edge. Anything outside the artboard edge will not be included when you place the file into InDesign.

1. **With toys_fall.indd open, double-click the A-Outside Spread icon in the master pages section of the Pages panel to show that layout.**

   Your client sent a new logo, which you need to use in the layout and template.

2. **Using the Direct Selection tool, click the logo on the left side of the page.**

3. **Open the Transform panel (Window>Object & Layout>Transform).**

   The options in the Transform panel are the same as those on the left side of the Control panel. As you can see, the selected graphic is scaled to 50% proportionally.

VermontKids
1634 Washington Way
Burlington, VT 05403
TRANSFORM

4. **Open the Links panel, and click the arrow to the left of the vtk_logo item to show the individual instances of that file.**

   The InDesign Links panel provides valuable information about the status of placed files. It is more than just an informational tool, however; you can also use the Links panel to navigate to and edit selected images, as well as locate links.

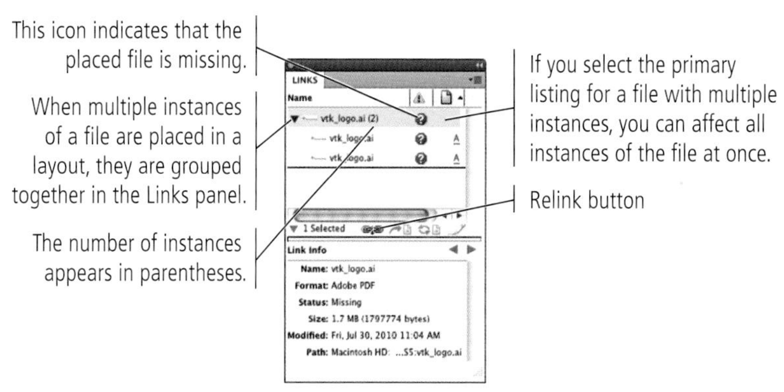

This icon indicates that the placed file is missing.
When multiple instances of a file are placed in a layout, they are grouped together in the Links panel.
The number of instances appears in parentheses.
If you select the primary listing for a file with multiple instances, you can affect all instances of the file at once.
Relink button
LINKS
Link Info

Note:

Make sure you use the Direct Selection tool to select the logo. If you use the Selection tool, the Transform panel shows the values for the frame instead of the graphic placed in the frame.

5. **In the Links panel, click the main listing for the vtk_logo.ai file and then click the Relink button.**

6. **In the resulting navigation dialog box, select the file logo.ai in the WIP>Toys folder.**

7. **At the bottom of the dialog box, check the Show Import Options box.**

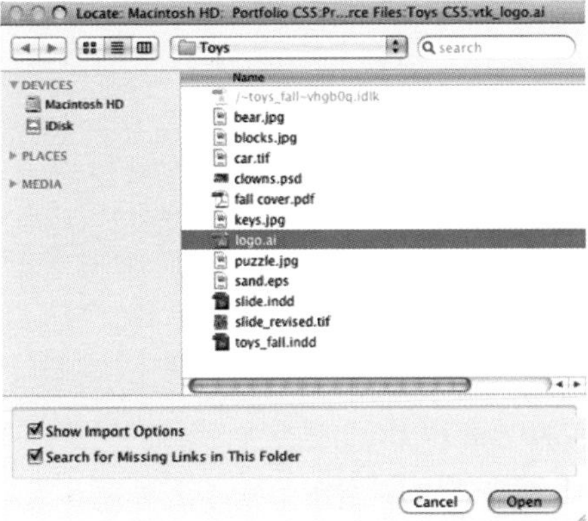

8. **Click Open.**

When Show Import Options is checked, the Place [Format] dialog box opens with the options for the relevant file format. Every file format has different available options.

When you place a native Illustrator file, the dialog box shows the Place PDF options because the PDF format is the basis of Illustrator files that can be placed into InDesign. (For an Illustrator file to be placed into InDesign, it must be saved from Illustrator with the Create PDF Compatible File option checked in the Illustrator Options dialog box.)

9. **In the General tab of the Place PDF dialog box, choose Art in the Crop To menu.**

The Crop To menu determines what part of the file will import:

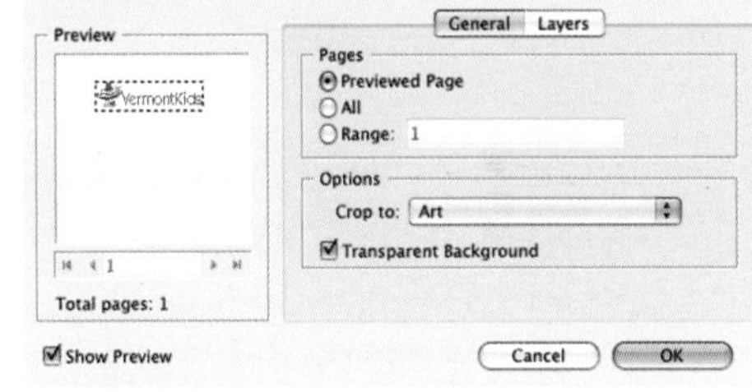

- **Bounding Box** places the file based on the minimum area that encloses the objects on the page. (You can also choose whether to include all layers or only visible layers in the bounding box calculation.)
- **Art** places the file based on the outermost dimensions of artwork in the file.
- **Crop** places the file based on the crop area defined in the file. If no crop area is defined, the file is placed based on the defined artboard dimensions.
- **Trim** places the file based on trim marks defined in the placed file. If no trim marks are defined, the file is placed based on the defined artboard size.
- **Bleed** places the file based on the defined bleed area. If no bleed area is defined, the file is placed based on the defined artboard size.
- **Media** places the file based on the physical paper size (including printer's marks) on which the PDF file was created. This option is not relevant for native Illustrator files.

When the Transparent Background option is checked, background objects in the layout show through empty areas of the placed file. If this option is not checked, empty areas of the placed file knock out underlying objects.

Note:

In the General tab, you can also define the specific PDF page or Illustrator artboard of the file to place.

10. **Click the Layers tab to display those options.**

PDF and native Illustrator files can include multiple layers. You can determine which layers to display in the placed file by toggling the eye icons on or off in the Show Layers list. In the Update Link Options menu, you can determine what happens when/if you update the link to the placed file.

- **Keep Layer Visibility Overrides** maintains your choices regarding which layers are visible in the InDesign layout.
- **Use PDF's Layer Visibility** restores the layer status as saved in the placed file.

11. **Click OK to place the file.**

12. **In the second Place PDF dialog box, choose Art in the Crop To menu of the General options and then click OK.**

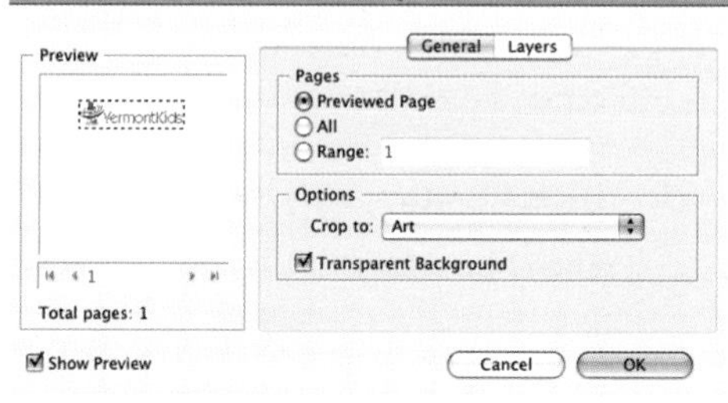

Because there are two instances of the selected file, you are asked to define the placement options for each instance. After clicking OK in the second dialog box, you return to the layout; both instances of the selected file are updated to point to the new file.

In both placed instances, the new file maintains the same transformations that were applied to the original. Because the file was simply renamed and not changed, nothing in the layout appears to change (for example, the replaced file on the left side of the page is also scaled to 50%).

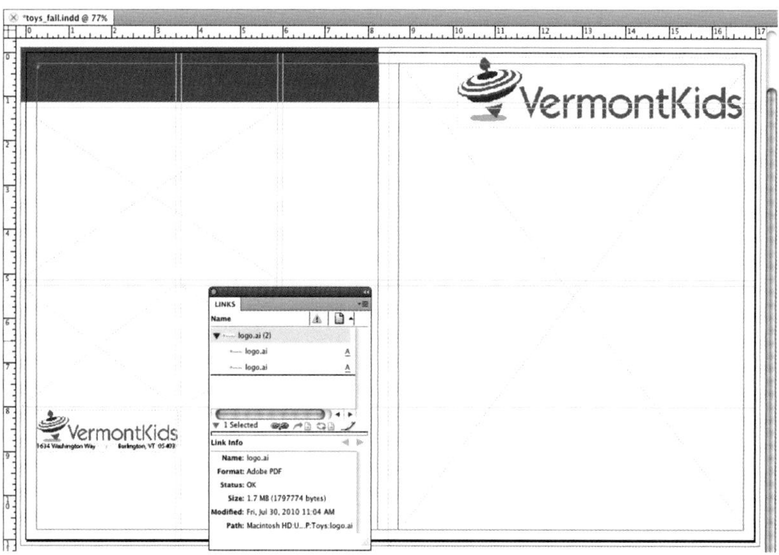

13. **Save the file and continue to the next exercise.**

PLACE A NATIVE PHOTOSHOP FILE

Because Adobe Photoshop is also part of the Adobe Creative Suite, you can easily place native Photoshop files (with the extension ".psd") into an InDesign layout. You can control the visibility of Photoshop layers and layer comps, as well as access embedded paths and Alpha channels in the placed file. If a Photoshop file includes spot-color channels, the spot colors are added to the InDesign Swatches panel.

1. **With toys_fall.indd open, make Page 1 of the layout visible and make sure nothing is selected in the layout.**

2. **Choose File>Place. Select the file clowns.psd (in the WIP>Toys folder), and make sure the Show Import Options and Replace Selected Item options are checked.**

   When Replace Selected Item is checked, the file you choose replaces the selected item in the layout; if nothing is selected in the layout, the file is simply loaded into the cursor so you can click to place it. The Place dialog box defaults to the last-used location, and the check boxes at the bottom of the dialog box also default to the last-used settings.

   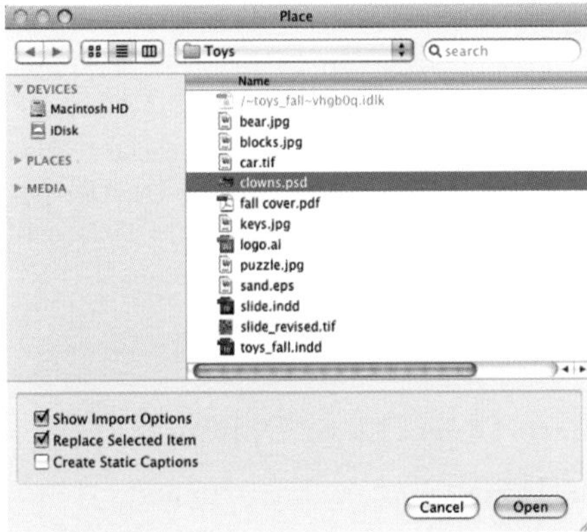

3. **Click Open. In the resulting Image Import Options dialog box, click the Image tab and review the options.**

   If the Photoshop file includes clipping path or Alpha channel information, you can activate those options when you place the file.

   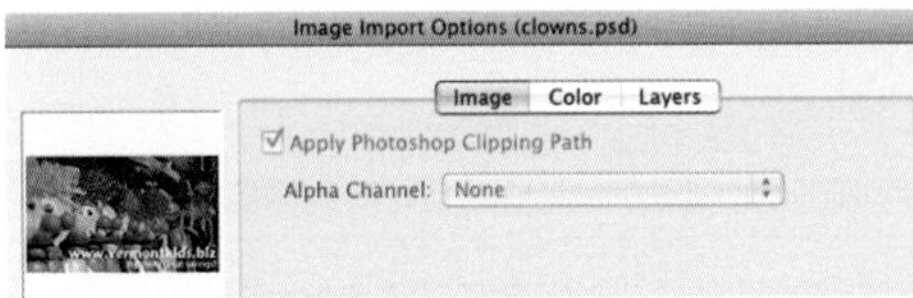

4. **Click the Color tab and review the options.**

   The Profile menu defaults to the profile embedded in the file. If the file was saved without an embedded profile, the menu defaults to Use Document Default. You can use the Profile menu to change the embedded profile (not recommended) or assign a specific profile if one was not embedded.

   The Rendering Intent menu defaults to Use Document Image Intent; you can also choose one of the four built-in options for this specific image.

   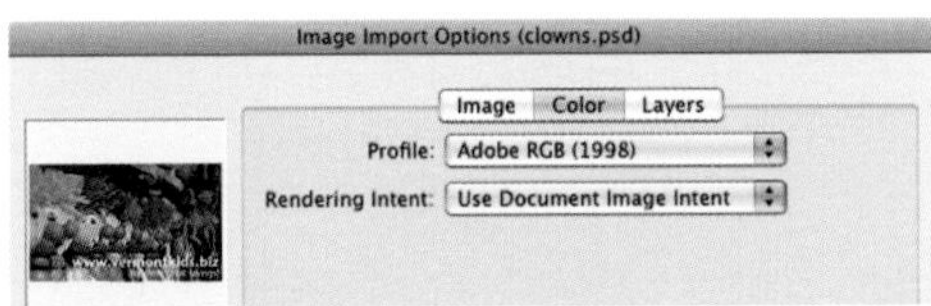

> *Note:*
>
> *You can review and change the profile associated with a specific image by selecting the image in the layout and choosing Object>Image Color Settings. Keep in mind, however, that just because you can change the profile doesn't mean you should change it. If an image has an embedded profile, you should assume that the embedded profile is the correct one; don't make random profile changes in InDesign.*

> *Note:*
>
> *When you export the finished layout to PDF, you will use the PDF engine to convert the RGB images to CMYK. This profile tells InDesign how the RGB color is described in the file so it can be properly translated to the destination (CMYK) profile.*

5. **Click the Layers tab and review the options.**

   Photoshop files can include multiple layers and layer comps (saved versions of specific layer position and visibility). You can turn off specific layers by clicking the eye (visibility) icon for that layer. If the file includes layer comps, you can use the Layer Comp menu to determine which comp to place.

   The Update Link Options you see here are the same as those in the Place PDF dialog box.

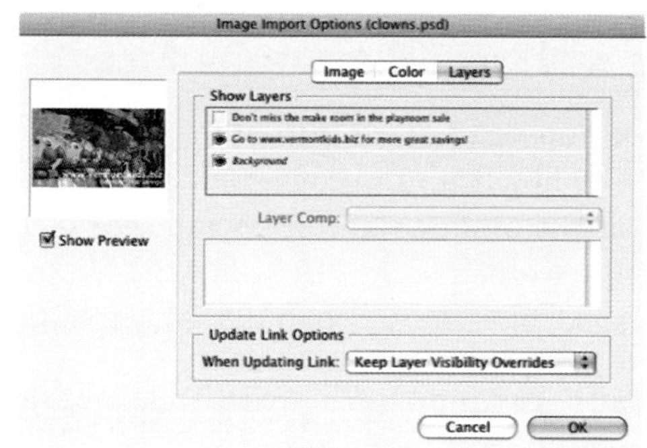

6. **Click OK to load the image into the cursor.**

   Even though you checked the Replace Selected Item option in the Place dialog box, the image is loaded into the cursor because nothing was selected in the layout (in other words, there is nothing to replace).

Note:

Unless you know what the different layers contain, it is difficult to decide what you want to place based solely on the very small preview image.

7. **Click the loaded cursor in the middle frame on the left side of the page to place the image (as shown in the following screen shot).**

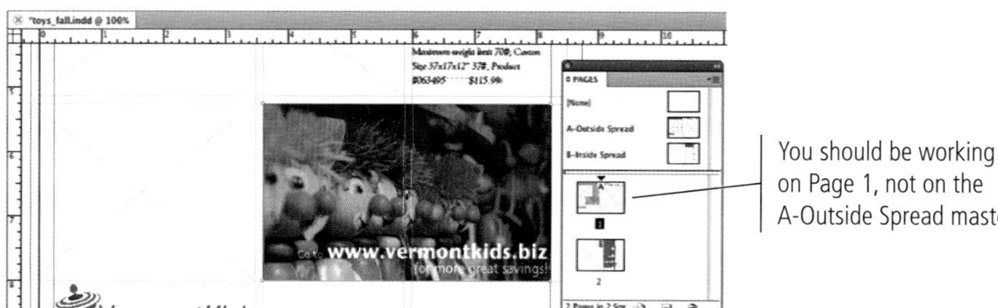

8. **With the placed file selected, choose Object>Object Layer Options.**

   This dialog box contains the same options as the Layers tab in the Image Import Options dialog box.

9. **Activate the Preview option, and then click the space to the left of the top layer ("Don't miss...") to turn on that layer. (If necessary, drag the dialog box out of the way so you can see the placed picture behind the dialog box.)**

   When the Preview option is checked, your changes in the dialog box reflect in the placed image (behind the dialog box). This method makes it easy to experiment with different layer visibility options before finalizing your choices.

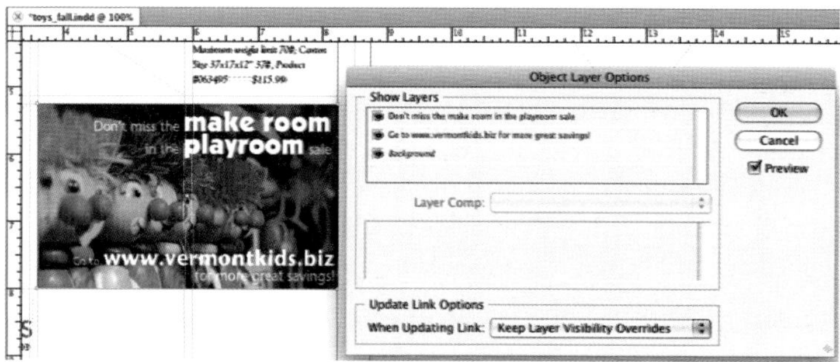

10. **Click OK to close the Object Layer Options dialog box.**

11. **Save the file and continue to the next exercise.**

Place an EPS File

The EPS (Encapsulated PostScript) format is commonly used for exporting vector graphics from Adobe Illustrator or other vector-based applications (although it is becoming less common now that native Illustrator files are supported by most other applications).

The EPS format uses an adaptation of the PostScript page-description language to produce a "placeable" file for PostScript-based artwork. Many vector graphics are saved as EPS files, but not all EPS files are vector graphics; the format supports both vector and raster information. Some Photoshop files — specifically, those with embedded clipping paths or spot-color channels — also use the EPS format.

Because InDesign supports native Illustrator and Photoshop files, as well as PDF files, the EPS format is slowly disappearing from the graphics workflow.

> *Note:*
>
> *If you print a page with an EPS file to a non-PostScript printer, only the screen-resolution preview prints.*

> *Note:*
>
> *Photoshop files with spot-color information might also be saved using the DCS (Desktop Color Separation) format, which is a modification of the EPS format. DCS files are no longer common in modern design and print workflows.*

1. **With toys_fall.indd open, select the placed clowns image on Page 1.**
2. **Choose File>Place and select the file sand.eps (in the WIP>Toys folder).**
3. **With the Show Import Options and Replace Selected Item options checked, click Open.**

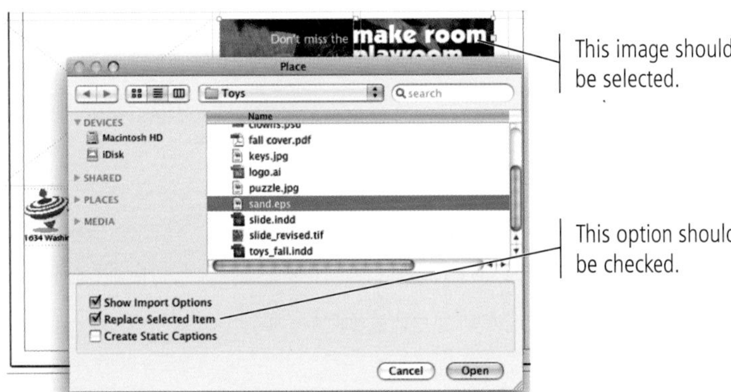

4. **Review the options in the EPS Import Options dialog box.**

The **Read Embedded OPI Image Links** option tells InDesign to read links from OPI comments for images included in the graphic. (OPI is a workflow that allows designers to work with low-resolution placement-only images in the layout; when the file is output, high-resolution versions are merged into the output stream, in place of the low-resolution proxies.)

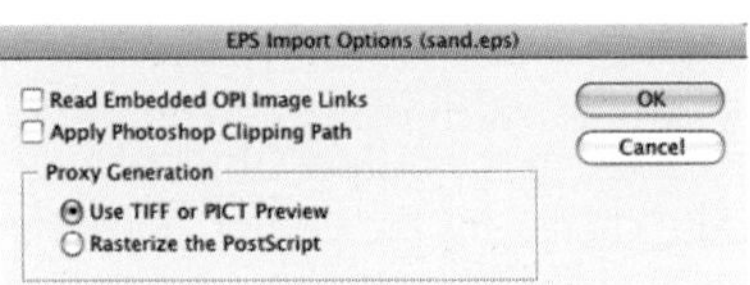

The **Apply Photoshop Clipping Path** option applies a defined clipping path in a Photoshop EPS file. (If you turn off this option, you can later apply the clipping path by choosing Object>Clipping Path>Options.)

The **Proxy Generation** options determine how the placed file will be viewed in the layout:

- **Use TIFF or PICT Preview** shows the preview embedded in the file. If the file has no embedded preview, InDesign generates a low-resolution bitmap after rasterizing the PostScript data.
- **Rasterize the PostScript** discards the embedded preview.

5. **Activate the Use TIFF or PICT Preview option and click OK to place the file.**

   Because the clowns image was selected and the Replace Selected Item option was checked, the sand image automatically appears in the selected frame.

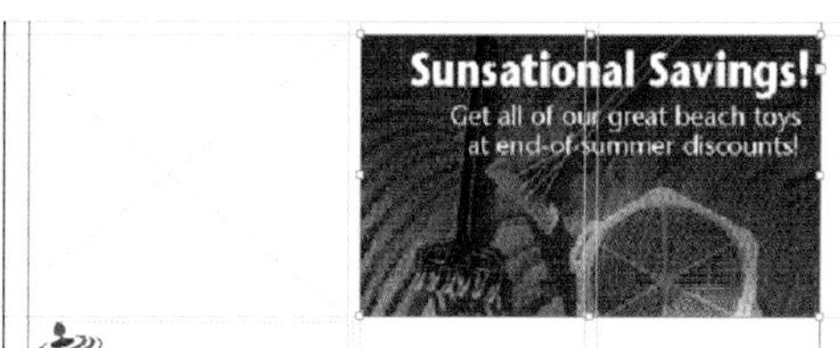

6. **Choose Edit>Undo Replace.**

   If you accidentally replace a selected item, undoing the placement loads the last-placed image into the cursor.

Note:

The Undo command undoes the single last action. In this case, placing the image into the frame — even though it happened automatically — was the last single action.

Controlling Display Performance

INDESIGN FOUNDATIONS

By default, files display in the document window using the Typical display performance settings. In the Display Performance pane of the Preferences dialog box, you can change the default view settings (Fast, Typical, or High Quality), as well as change the definition of these settings. In the Adjust View Settings section, individual sliders control the display of raster images, vector graphics, and objects with transparency.

Choose Fast, Typical, or High Quality view as the default.

Use this menu to review and change the settings for Fast, Typical, and High Quality display.

In the layout, you can change the document display performance using the View>Display Performance menu. If **Allow Object-Level Display Settings** is checked, you can also change the preview for a single image in the layout (in the Object>Display Performance menu, or using the object's contextual menu). To remove object-level settings, choose **Clear Object-Level Display Settings**.

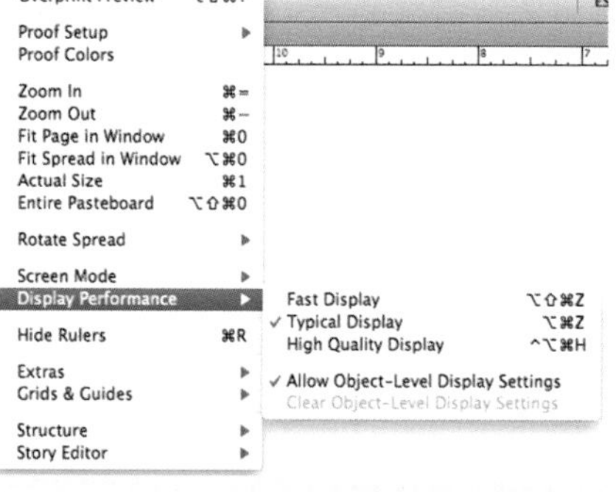

Object-level display settings are maintained only while the file remains open; if you want to save the file with specific object-level display settings, check the **Preserve Object-Level Display Settings** option in the Display Performance pane of the Preferences dialog box.

Fast displays gray boxes in place of images and graphics.

Typical shows the low-resolution proxy images.

High Quality shows the full resolution of placed files.

7. **Click the loaded cursor in the empty frame to the left of the clowns image.**

   This is an easy fix if you accidentally replace an image — simply choose Edit>Undo Replace, and then click to place the loaded image in the correct location.

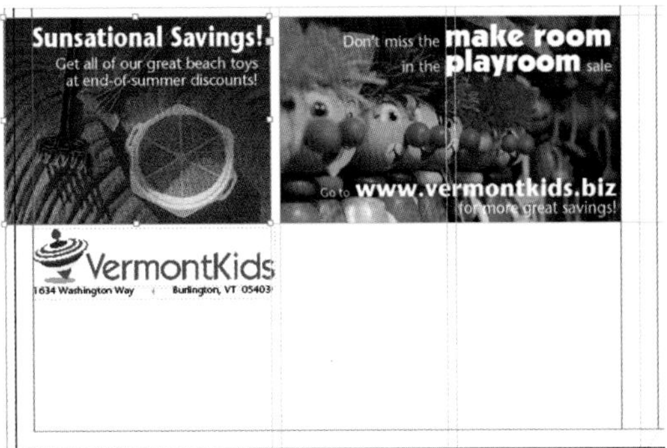

8. **Save the file and continue to the next exercise.**

Place a TIFF File

The TIFF format is used only for raster images such as those from a scanner or digital camera. These files can be one-color (bitmap or monochrome), grayscale, or continuous-tone images.

1. **With toys_fall.indd open, make sure the placed sand image is selected in the layout and choose File>Place.**

2. **In the Place dialog box, select the file car.tif (in the WIP>Toys folder) and uncheck the Replace Selected Item option.**

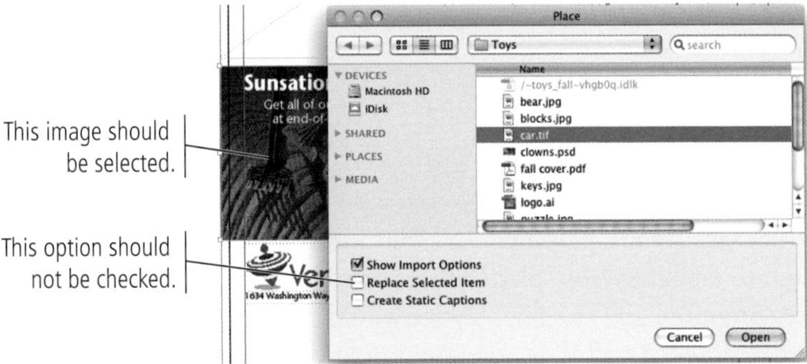

3. **Make sure the Show Import Options box is checked and click Open.**

   In the Image Import Options dialog box, the Image and Color options for placing TIFF files are the same as the related options for placing native Photoshop files.

   When you place a TIFF file into InDesign, you can access the clipping paths and Alpha channels saved in the files. InDesign does not allow access to the layers in a TIFF file; all layers are flattened in the placed file.

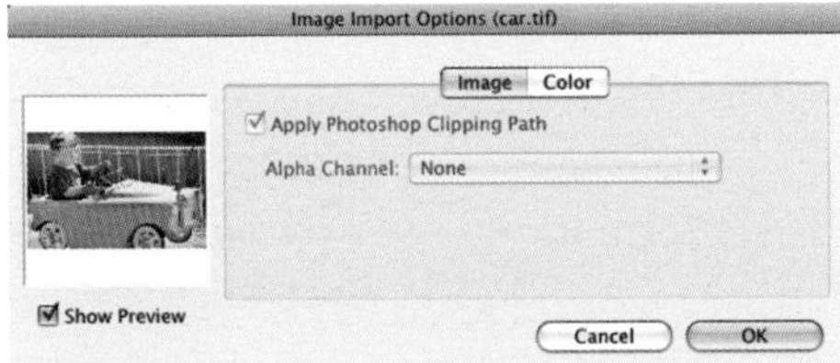

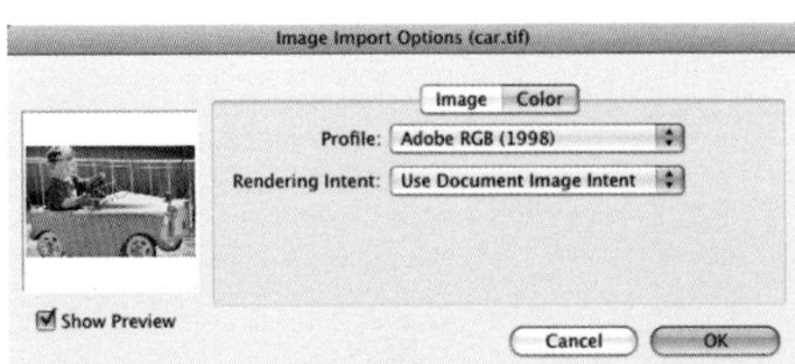

4. **Click OK.**

Although the placed sand image was selected when you reopened the Place dialog box, the car image is loaded into the cursor because you unchecked the Replace Selected Item option.

5. **Click the loaded cursor in the empty frame above the sand image to place the car file.**

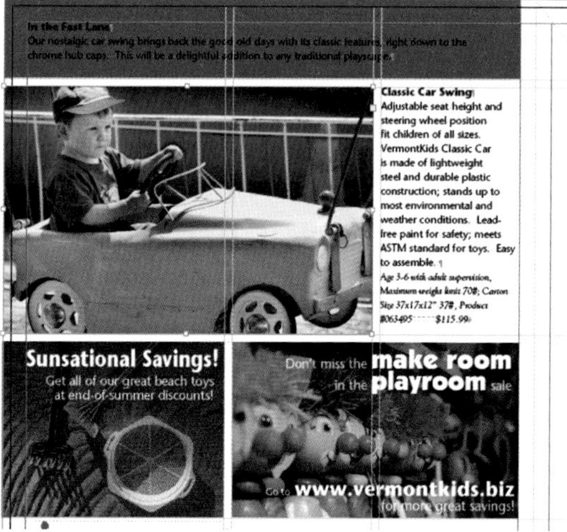

6. **Save the file and continue to the next exercise.**

 Place a PDF File

PDF (Portable Document Format) files save layout, graphics, and font information in a single file. The format was created to facilitate cross-platform file-sharing so one file could be transferred to any other computer, and the final layout would print as intended. While originally meant for Internet use, PDF is now the standard in the graphics industry, used for submitting advertisements, artwork, and completed jobs to a service provider.

You can place a PDF file into an InDesign layout, just as you would place any other image. You can determine which page to place (if the file contains more than one page), which layers are visible (if the file has more than one layer), and the specific file dimensions (bounding box) to use when placing the file.

1. **With toys_fall.indd open, choose File>Place.**

2. **In the Place dialog box, select fall_cover.pdf (in the WIP>Toys folder).**

> *Note:*
>
> *Before placing a PDF file in an InDesign job, make absolutely sure it was created and optimized for commercial printing. Internet-optimized PDF files do not have sufficient resolution to print cleanly on a high-resolution output device; if these are used, they could ruin an otherwise perfect InDesign job.*

3. **Make sure Show Import Options is checked and Replace Selected Item is not checked, and then click Open.**

   The options in the Place PDF dialog box are exactly the same as the options you saw when you placed the native Illustrator file. However, the options in the General tab are typically more important for PDF files than for Illustrator files.

   PDF files can contain multiple pages; you can review the various pages using the buttons below the preview image. You can place multiple pages at once by choosing the All option, or you can select specific pages using the Range option.

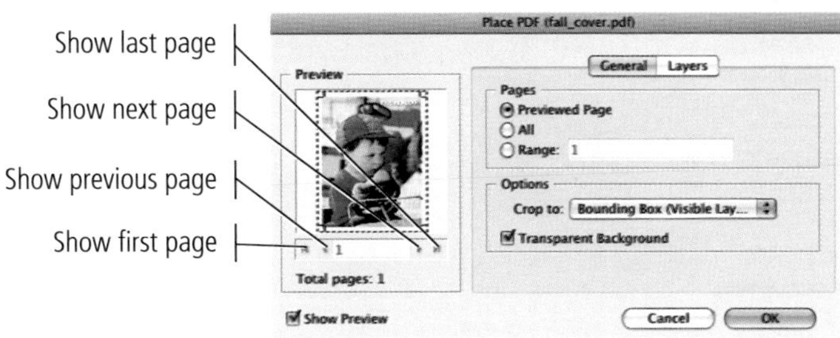

   The Crop To options are also significant when placing PDF files. If the file was created properly, it should include a defined bleed of at least 1/8 inch and trim marks to identify the intended trim size.

4. **Choose Bleed in the Crop To menu and click OK.**

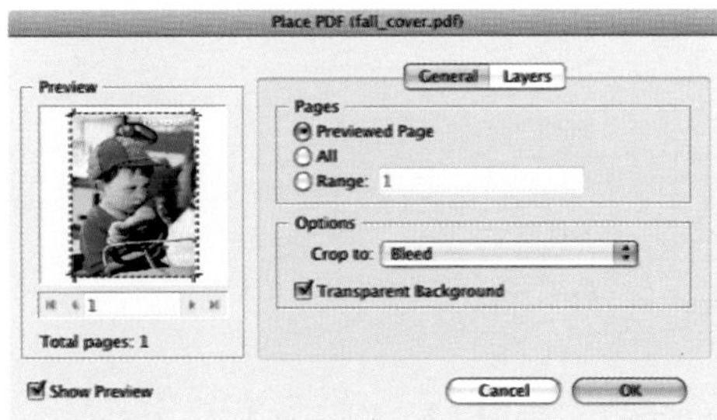

5. **Click the loaded cursor in the empty frame on the right side of Page 1 to place the loaded file.**

6. **In the Pages panel, Control/right-click the Page 1 icon and choose Override All Master Page Items from the contextual menu.**

   When you place an image into a frame from the master page, the frame is automatically detached from the master page, which moves it in front of the logo frame that is still attached to the master page.

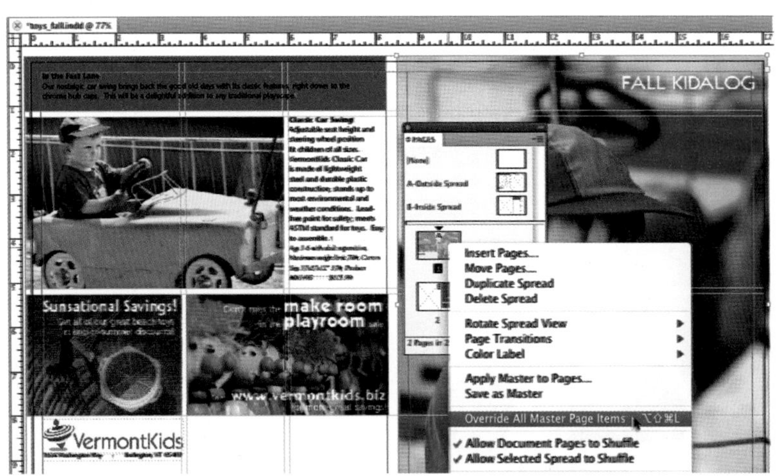

> ***Note:***
>
> *If you place multiple pages of a PDF file, each page is loaded into the cursor as a separate object.*

> ***Note:***
>
> *Import continuous pages by defining a page range, using a hyphen to separate the first page and last pages in the range. Import non-continuous pages by typing page numbers separated by commas.*

> ***Note:***
>
> *If you place an Illustrator file that contains multiple artboards, you have the same options for choosing which artboard (page) to place.*

7. **Select the placed PDF with the Selection tool and then choose Object>Arrange>Send to Back.**

   To change an object's position in the stacking order (top-to-bottom arrangement), you must use the Selection tool to select the actual object (not the object's content).

   After sending the placed PDF to the back of the stacking order, the logo on the right side of the page is now visible.

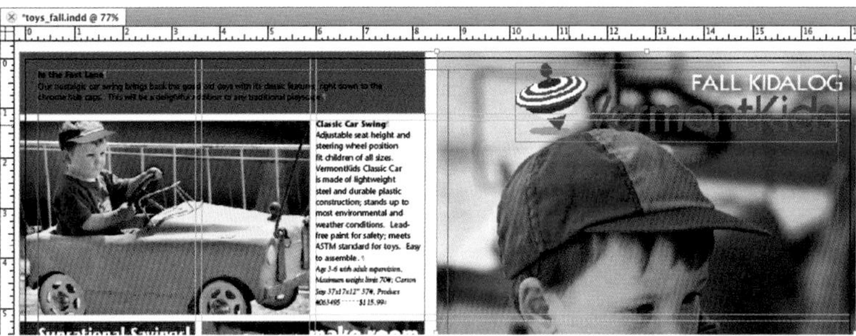

8. **Look at the Links panel.**

   When you detached Page 1 from the master page layout, objects from the master page — including the two placed logo instances — are copied onto the layout page. In the Links panel, you can now see four placed instances of the logo.ai file (two on the master page and two on the layout Page 1).

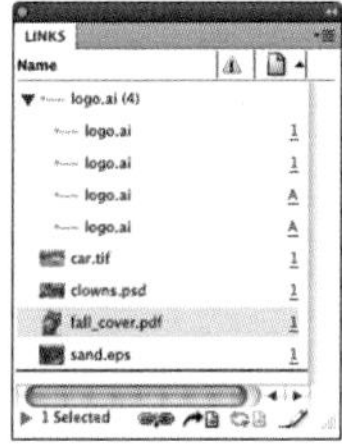

9. **Select the placed PDF file by clicking the image with the Direct Selection tool or by clicking the Content Indicator icon with the Selection tool.**

   This file was created with 1/8" bleeds on all four sides. In this layout, however, the left bleed allowance is not necessary. When you place the image into the frame, the bleed area on the left side causes the image to appear farther to the right than it should.

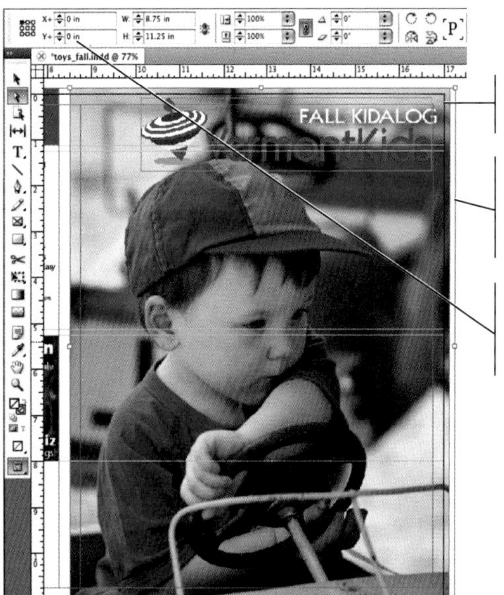

This is the placed PDF file.

When the content is selected, you can see the image edge beyond the frame edge.

The image is placed at X:0, Y:0 (based on the top-left reference point) in relation to the frame.

10. **With the placed file still selected, make sure the top-left reference point is selected, and then change the picture position (within the frame) to X+: –0.125".**

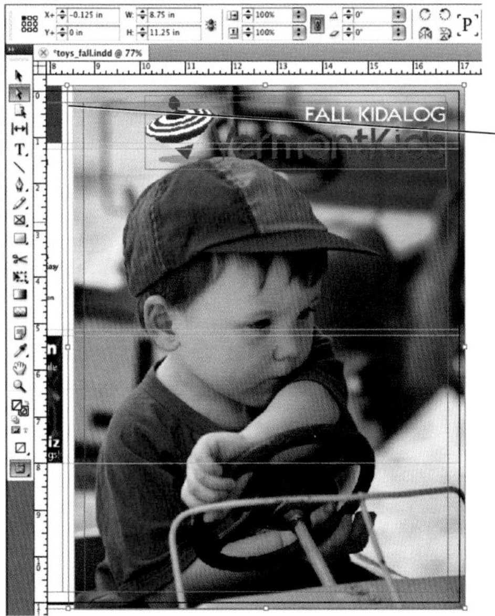

The image bounding box now shows the extra bleed allowance extending beyond the left edge of the frame.

11. **Save the file and continue to the next exercise.**

Place Multiple JPEG Images

The JPEG format is commonly used for raster images, especially images that come from consumer-level digital cameras. Originally used for Web applications only, the JPEG format is now supported by most commercial print-design applications (including InDesign).

The JPEG format can be problematic, especially in print jobs, because it applies a lossy compression scheme to reduce the image file size. If a high-resolution JPEG file was saved with a high level of compression, you might notice blockiness or other artifacts (flaws) in the printed image. If you must use JPEG files in your work, save them with the lowest compression possible.

1. **With toys_fall.indd open, navigate to Page 2 of the layout.**

2. **Choose File>Place. Navigate to the WIP>Toys folder and click the file bear.jpg to select it.**

3. **Press Command/Control and click blocks.jpg, keys.jpg, and puzzle.jpg to add those files to the selection.**

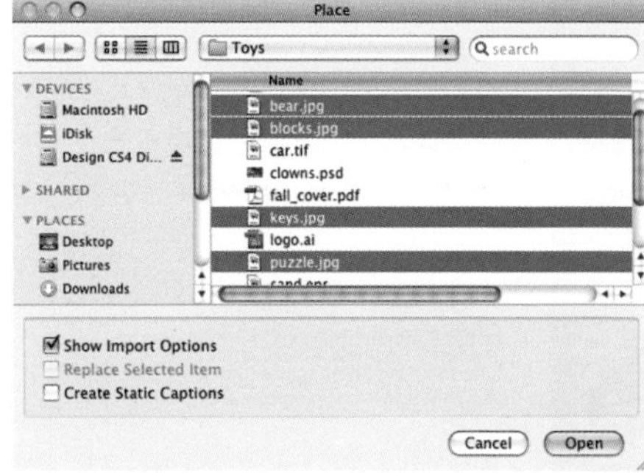

4. **With the Show Import Options box checked, click Open.**

   When multiple images are selected, you will see the Image Import Options dialog box for each selected image. For JPEG images, the options are the same as for TIFF files.

5. **Click OK in each of the four Image Import Options dialog boxes.**

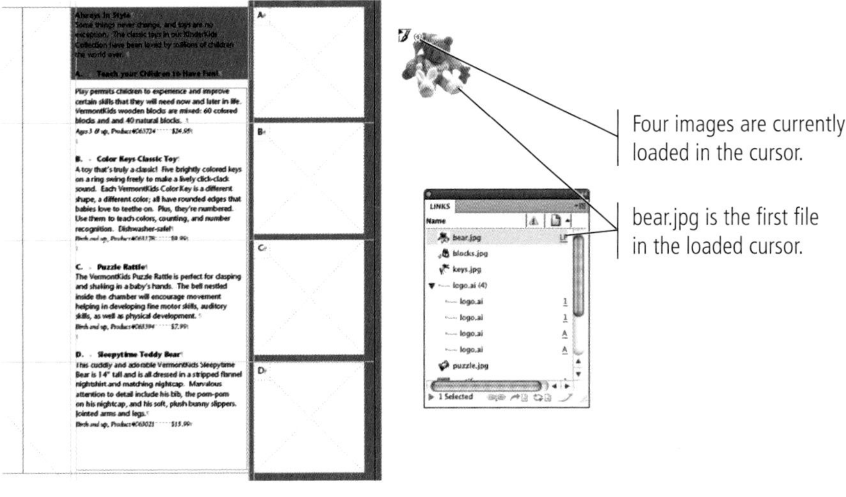

6. **Click in the empty frames to place the images in the appropriate spots.**

   Use the cursor preview to verify which image is currently loaded, and use the brochure copy to match the products to the letters.

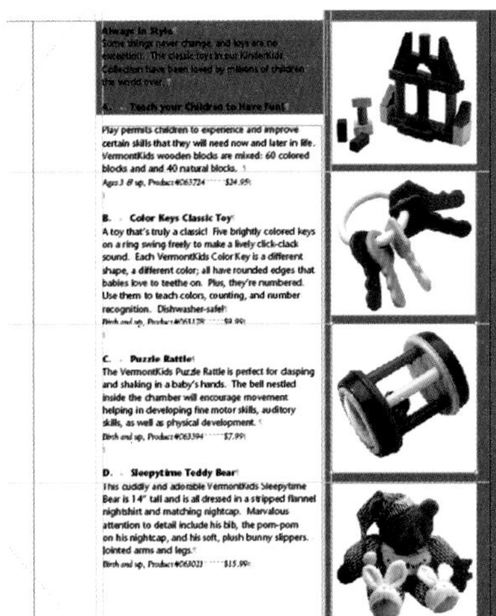

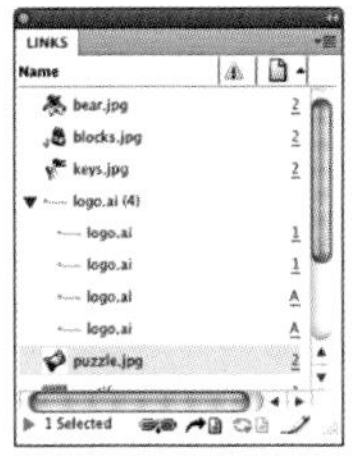

7. **Save the file and continue to the next exercise.**

> ***Note:***
>
> *When multiple images are loaded into the Place cursor, you can use the Left Arrow and Right Arrow keys to change which image will be placed by clicking.*

Place an InDesign File

In addition to the different types of image files, you can also place one InDesign layout directly into another InDesign file. As with PDF files, you can determine which page is placed (if the file contains more than one page), which layers are visible (if the file has more than one layer), and the specific file dimensions (bounding box) to use when the file is placed. Placed InDesign pages are managed as individual objects in the file where they are placed.

1. **With toys_fall.indd open, make sure Page 2 is visible in the document window.**

2. **Choose File>Place. In the Place dialog box, select slide.indd (in the WIP>Toys folder).**

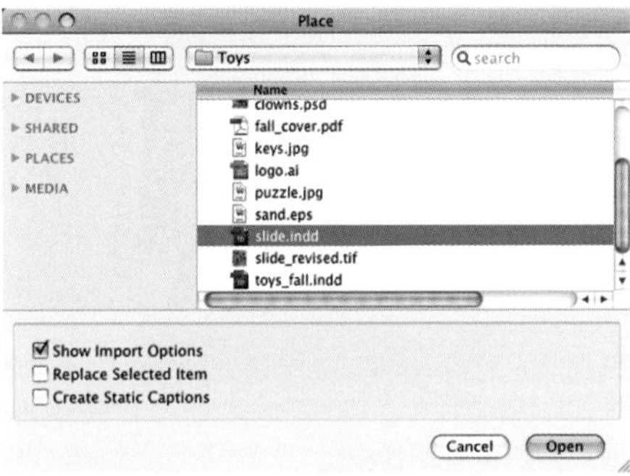

3. **With the Show Import Options box checked, click Open.**

4. **In the General tab of the Place InDesign Document dialog box, choose Bleed Bounding Box in the Crop To menu.**

   The options for placing an InDesign file are mostly the same as for placing PDF files; the only exception is the Crop To menu. When you place an InDesign file into another InDesign file, you can place the page(s) based on the defined page, bleed, or slug, as described in the Document Setup dialog box.

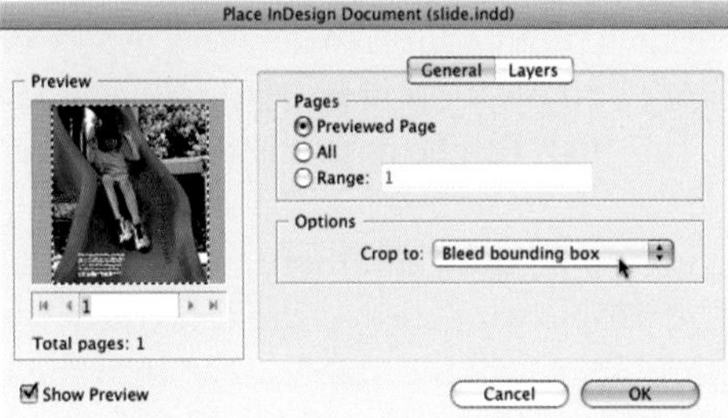

5. **Click OK. Read the resulting warning message and click OK.**

   To output properly, image links need to be present and up to date. Images placed in nested InDesign layouts are still links, so the link requirements apply in those files.

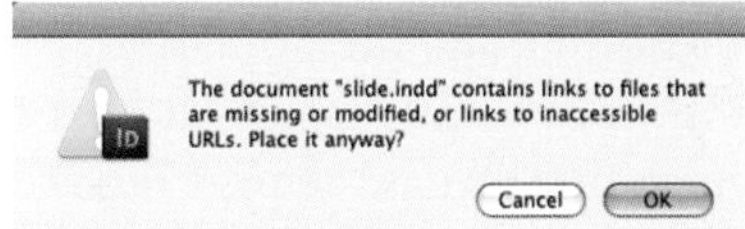

6. **Click the loaded cursor in the empty frame on the left side of Page 2 to place the file.**

   When you place one InDesign file into another, the Links panel lists images placed in the InDesign file (indented immediately below the placed InDesign file). You might need to expand the slide.indd item in the panel to see the nested files.

> *Note:*
>
> *You will fix this problem later in this project.*

7. **Save the file and continue to the next stage of the project.**

Stage 3 Working with Text

Now that all of the images are in place, you can begin the fine-tuning process for the layout text. As your art director informed you during the project meeting, some of the text work had already been completed before the original designer had to move onto a different project. Your assignment in this stage of the project is to complete the text formatting process, and then verify that all text in the document is correct.

As you already know, InDesign gives you extremely tight control over every aspect of the text elements in a layout. You can control the appearance and position of every single character, enabling you to create high-quality typographic elements. This high degree of precision is what separates the amateur from the professional designer.

Some text issues, however, have little to do with typography and more to do with "user malfunction" — common errors introduced by the people who created the text (most often, your clients). Regardless of how careful you are, some problems will inevitably creep into the text elements of your layouts. Fortunately, InDesign has the tools you need to correct those issues as well.

Delete and Create Paragraph Styles

As you can see in the current layout, the first two paragraphs on each page are black text on a dark background, which makes the text difficult to read. The primary heading on each page is set at the same size as the product descriptions, which does not provide enough visual weight to identify and distinguish that text as the page heading instead of a product heading. In this exercise, you will use paragraph styles to correct these issues.

1. **With Page 1 of toys_fall.indd showing, click the Type tool in the first paragraph (In the Fast Lane).**

2. **Look at the Paragraph Styles panel (Window>Styles>Paragraph Styles).**

The first paragraph is formatted with the Main Head style. You can assume that other text with the same basic appearance is also a section head.

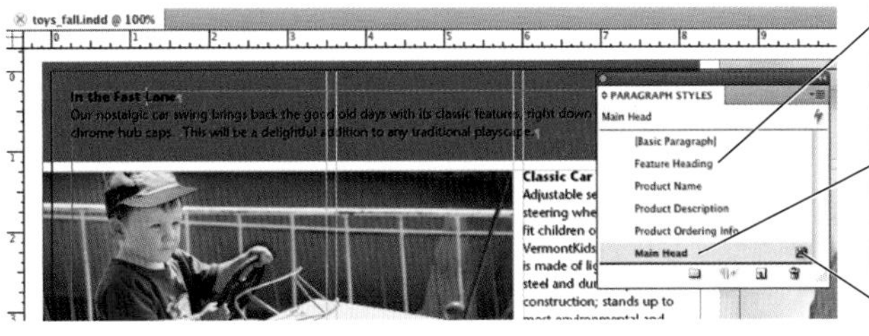

The Feature Heading style is part of the original layout template.

The highlighted style is applied to the selected text (insertion point).

The disk icon identifies styles that were imported with the text file.

3. **Click the Delete button at the bottom of the Paragraph Styles panel to delete the selected style (Main Head).**

Note:

Dragging a style to the panel's Delete button is the same as clicking the Delete button with a style selected.

4. **In the resulting Delete Paragraph Style dialog box, choose Feature Heading in the Replace With menu and click OK.**

If you delete a style sheet that's being used, you have to determine what to do with text that uses the style you want to delete. If you want to maintain the formatting of that text without applying a different style, you can choose [No Paragraph Style].

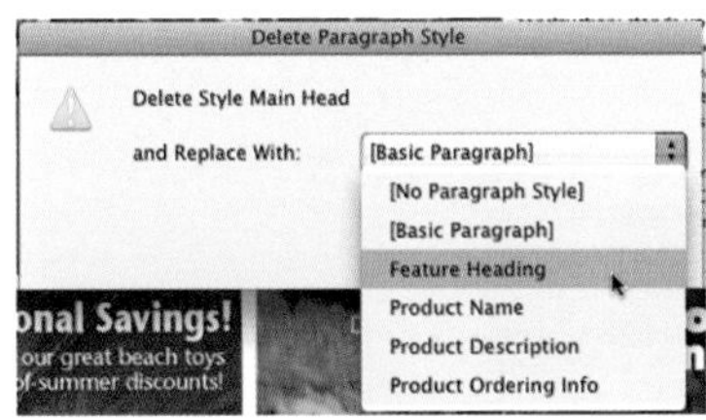

Note:

Any time you choose [No Paragraph Style] in the Replace With menu, the Preserve Formatting option becomes available in the Delete Paragraph Style dialog box.

After the Main Head style has been replaced with the Feature Heading style, the associated headings in the layout change in appearance to match the new style definition.

Text that was formatted with the Main Head style is now formatted with the Feature Heading style.

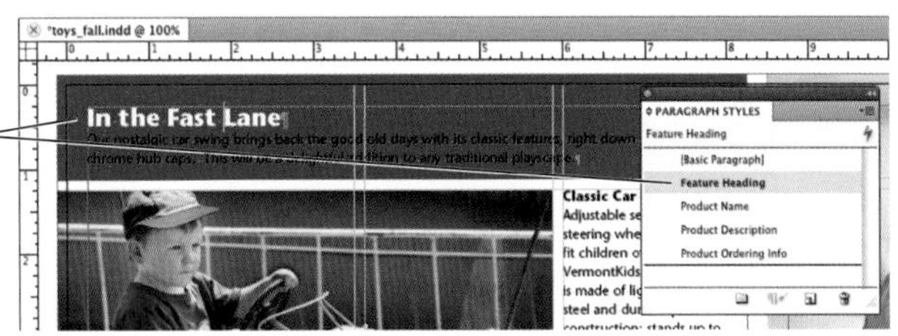

5. **Select the entire second paragraph on Page 1 of the layout.**

The second paragraph is currently formatted with the Product Description style. You are going to change the formatting of this text, but you can't edit the style definition because that would change the appearance of all the descriptive copy in the lower frame. Instead, you will create a new style so you can also apply the same formatting to the intro copy on the second page of the layout.

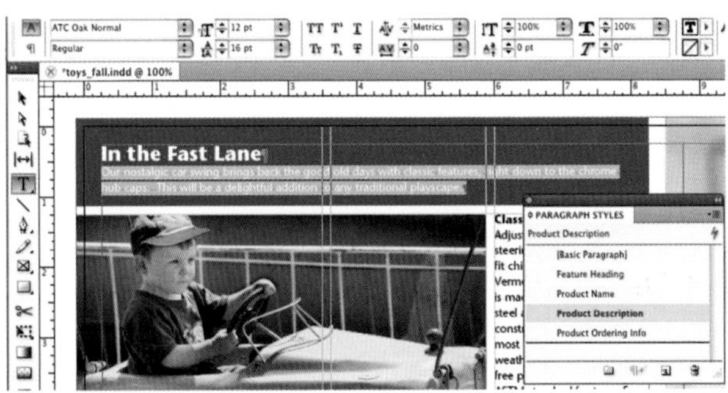

6. **Using the Control panel, change the selected type size to 14-pt with 18-pt leading, and change the type color to Paper.**

   Remember, a plus sign next to the style name (in the Paragraph Styles panel) indicates that some local formatting has been applied to override the style definition.

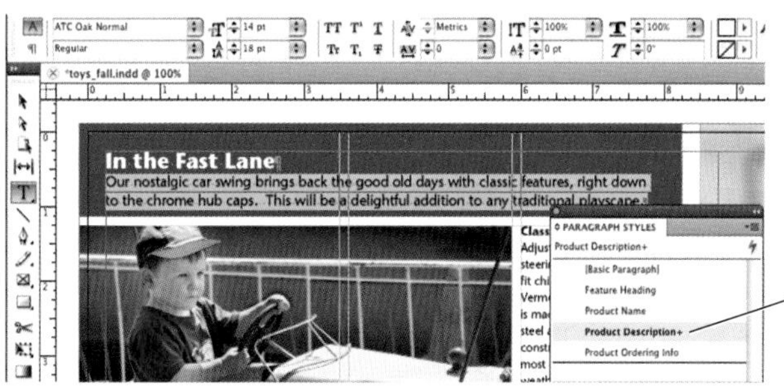

The plus sign shows that formatting other than the style definition has been applied to the selected text.

   White text on a colored background is called **knockout text**. Anything "white" is actually removed from the colored areas because you typically don't print white ink. (Adobe appropriately names the color "Paper" because the actual paper color of the job will be visible in these areas.)

Note:

Knocking out small text (especially serif fonts) can cause output problems. To help minimize potential problems on press, use larger type sizes and (preferrably) sans-serif fonts for knockout text.

7. **With the same text selected, click the Create New Style button at the bottom of the Paragraph Styles panel.**

   When you create a new style, the style automatically adopts the formatting of the selected text (or current insertion point). However, the new style is not automatically applied to the selected text.

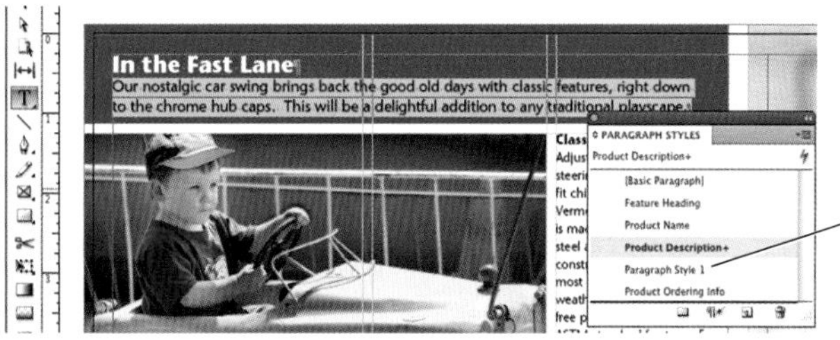

The new style is not highlighted, which means it is not yet applied to the selected text.

8. **Double-click the new Paragraph Style 1 option in the Paragraph Styles panel.**

9. **In the resulting Paragraph Style Options dialog box, change the style name to `Feature Copy`.**

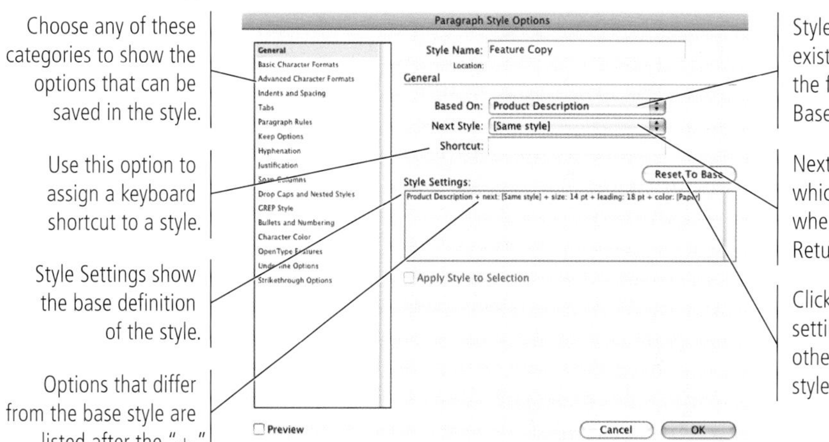

Choose any of these categories to show the options that can be saved in the style.

Use this option to assign a keyboard shortcut to a style.

Style Settings show the base definition of the style.

Options that differ from the base style are listed after the "+."

Styles can be based on existing styles, adopting the formatting in the Based On style.

Next Style determines which style will be applied when you press Return/Enter while typing.

Click to restore the base settings, removing all other options from the style definition.

10. Click OK to return to the layout.

To apply a style to a paragraph, you simply select the paragraph and click the style name. When you double-click the style name, the first click applies the style to the selected text.

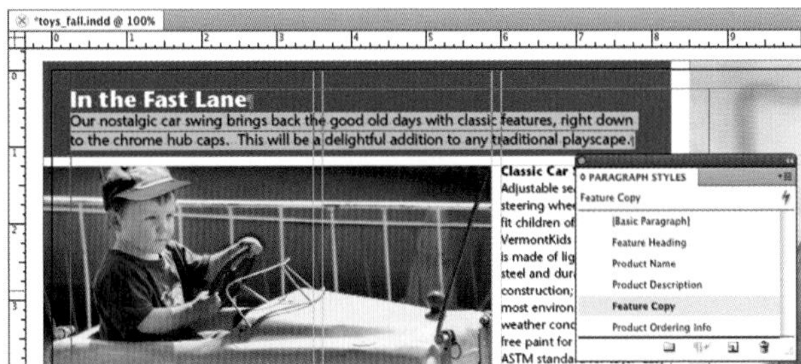

To edit a style without changing the formatting of the selected text, you can Control/right-click a style name in the panel and choose Edit [Style] in the contextual menu. This is a very important distinction — Control/right-clicking allows you to edit the style without applying the style. Double-clicking allows you to edit the style and applies the style to the selected text as well. Each method is useful in different circumstances; be certain that you use the correct method, based on what you are trying to accomplish.

11. In the Paragraph Styles panel, click the Feature Copy style and drag up. When a heavy black line appears below the Feature Heading style, release the mouse button.

When you create a new style, the new style is automatically placed below the previously selected style. You can drag styles in the panel to reorganize them, which helps to keep related styles in proximity.

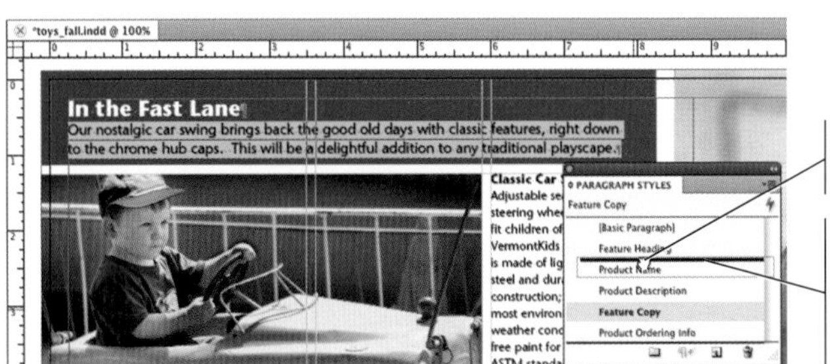

Drag styles in the panel to reorganize them.

Release the mouse button when the black line appears below the Feature Heading style.

Note:

You can click the Create New Style Group button (the folder icon) at the bottom of the Paragraph Styles panel to create a folder in the panel, and then drag related styles into the folder to organize related styles in folders within the panel.

12. Navigate to Page 2 of the layout. Place the insertion point in the second paragraph and click the Feature Copy style to apply it to the paragraph.

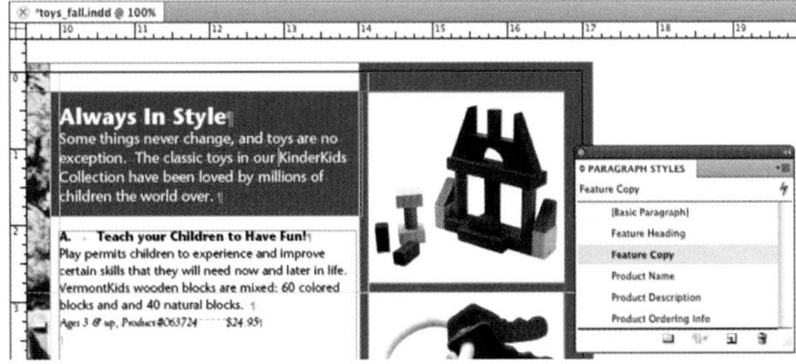

13. Save the file and continue to the next exercise.

INDESIGN FOUNDATIONS

What's in a Paragraph Style?

By completing the InDesign projects in this book, you've already learned about a considerable number of options for formatting text — both character and paragraph attributes — but there's still more to learn. Use the following chart as a reminder of exactly what can be stored in a paragraph style definition, as well as where to find the equivalent in the application interface for selected text. (Character styles include a subset of these same options: General, Basic Character Formats, Advanced Character Formats, Character Color, OpenType Features, Underline Options, and Strikethrough Options.)

Category	Options			Application Equivalent
General	Based On Style Settings	Next Style Reset to Base	Shortcut Apply Style to Selection	N/A
Basic Character Formats	Font Family Leading	Style Kerning	Size Tracking	Character panel
	Case	Position	Styles	Character panel Options menu
Advanced Character Formats	Horizontal Scale Skew	Vertical Scale Language	Baseline Shift	Character panel
Indents and Spacing	Alignment Left & Right Indent Space Before	Balance Ragged Lines First Line Indent Space After	Ignore Optical Margin Last Line Indent Align to Grid	Paragraph panel
Tabs	X position	Leader	Align On	Tabs panel
Paragraph Rules	Rule Above On Width Rule attributes (Weight, Type, Color, etc.)	Rule Below On Offset	 Left & Right Indents Gap attributes	Paragraph panel Options menu
Keep Options	Keep with Next [N] Lines Start Paragraph		Keep Lines Together	
Hyphenation	Hyphenate On/Off (and all related options)			
Justification	Word Spacing Auto Leading	Letter Spacing Single Word Justification	Glyph Scaling Composer	
Span Columns	Paragraph Layout Single Column	 Span Columns	 Split Column	
Drop Caps and Nested Styles	Number of Lines	Number of Characters		Paragraph panel
	Character Style for Drop Characters Scale for Descenders	 Nested Styles	Align Left Edge Nested Line Styles	Paragraph panel Options menu
GREP Style	New GREP Style	Apply [Style]	To Text Pattern	
Bullets and Numbering	List Type Text After Bullet	List Style Character Style	Bullet Character Bullet/Number Position	
Character Color	Fill Color, Tint, Overprint attributes Stroke Color, Tint, Weight, Overprint attributes			Swatches panel/ Control panel
OpenType Features	Titling, Contextual, & Swash Alternates Ordinals, Fractions, Discretionary Ligatures, Slashed Zero, Figure Style, Positional Form Stylistic Sets			Character panel Options menu
Underline Options	Underline On	Stroke attributes	Gap attributes	
Strikethrough Options	Strikethrough On	Stroke attributes	Gap attributes	

Edit Style Definitions

In the current layout, the product names appear in bold, black text. To take better advantage of the layout color, and to make the product names more prominent, you are going to change the product names to use the same red color that is used behind the feature copy at the top of each page.

1. **With Page 2 of `toys_fall.indd` visible in the document window, place the insertion point in the third paragraph of copy.**

   This paragraph is formatted with the Product Name style.

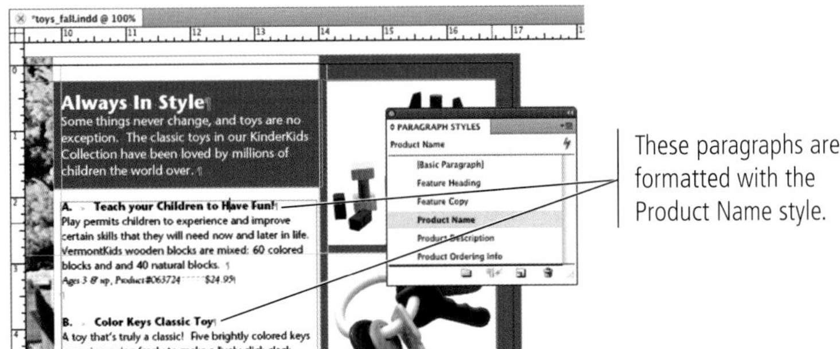

2. **Control/right-click the Product Name style and choose Edit "Product Name" in the contextual menu.**

3. **In the resulting Paragraph Style Options dialog box, click Character Color in the left pane.**

4. **In the Character Color options, make sure the Fill icon is active and then click Pantone 186 C to change the type fill color.**

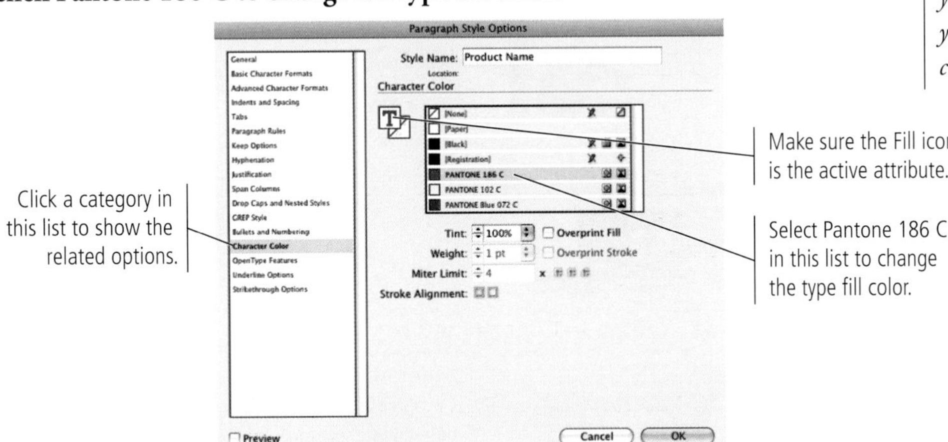

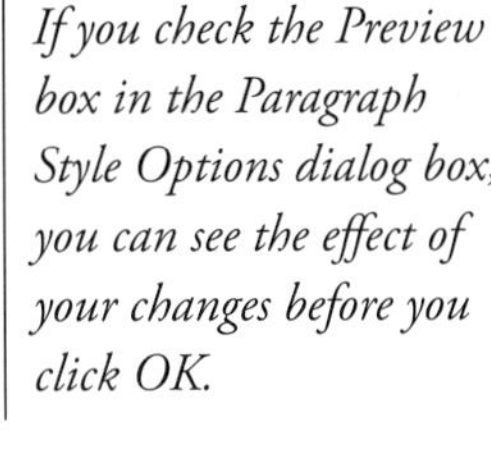

Note:

If you check the Preview box in the Paragraph Style Options dialog box, you can see the effect of your changes before you click OK.

5. **Click OK to change the style definition.**

Editing styles is both easy and efficient. When you change the options in a style definition, any text formatted with that style reformats with the changed definition.

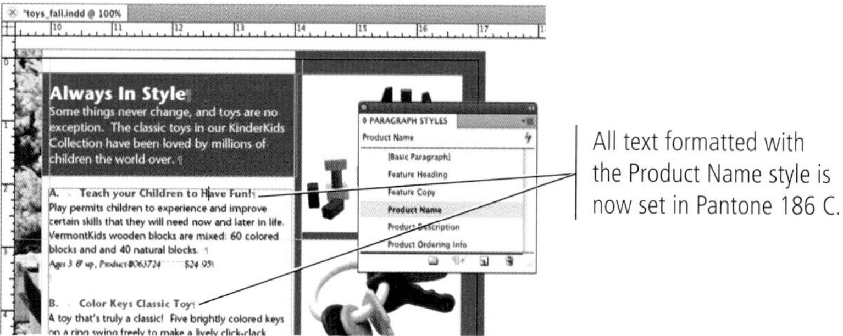

6. **Select the entire third paragraph in the white frame on Page 2 of the layout.**

7. **Using the Control panel, change the font to ATC Oak and choose the Italic font style.**

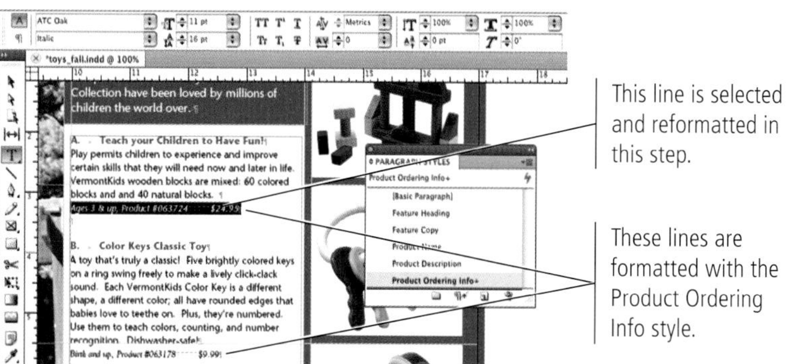

This line is selected and reformatted in this step.
These lines are formatted with the Product Ordering Info style.

8. **Control/right-click the Product Ordering Info style and choose Redefine Style from the contextual menu.**

This option makes it easy to experiment with formatting within the context of the layout, and then change a style definition to match what you created with local formatting. As with editing a style in the Paragraph Style Options dialog box, all text formatted with the redefined style adopts the new style definition.

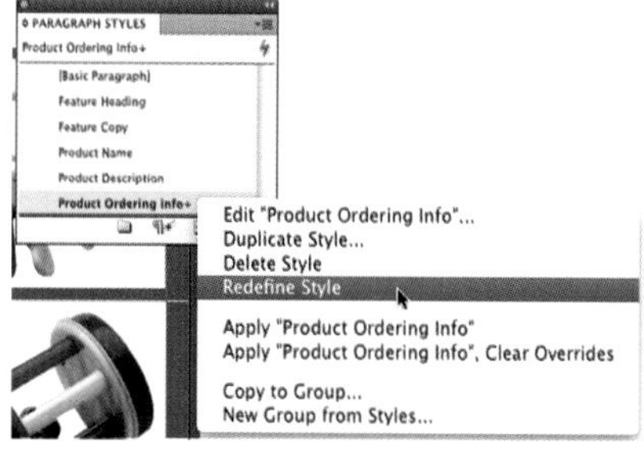

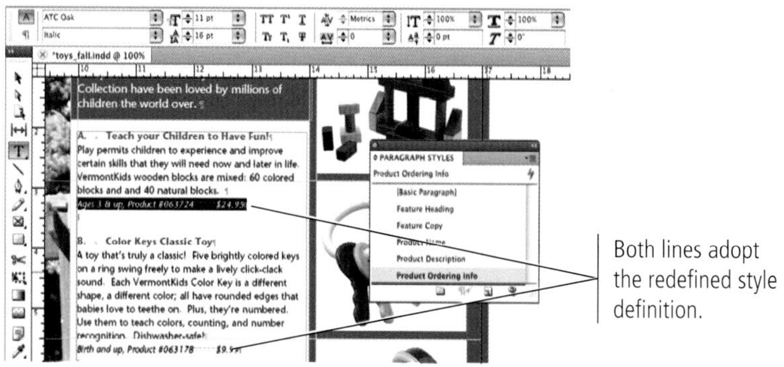

Both lines adopt the redefined style definition.

9. **Save the file and continue to the next exercise.**

Enable Track Changes

Now that the text is formatted, you can evaluate the layout to verify that everything is correct. In many cases, multiple users collaborate on a single document — designers, editors, content providers, and clients all go back and forth throughout the design process. Because the words in a design are a vital part of communicating the client's message, tracking text changes throughout the process can be useful to make sure that all changes are accurate and approved before the job is finalized.

1. **With toys_fall.indd open, place the insertion point in any story.**

2. **Choose Type>Track Changes>Enable Tracking in All Stories.**

   The Track Changes feature can be activated to monitor text editing during development. This allows multiple users to edit the text without permanently altering that text until the changes have been reviewed and approved or rejected. (After you have made all the changes in this stage of the project, you will review and finalize those changes.)

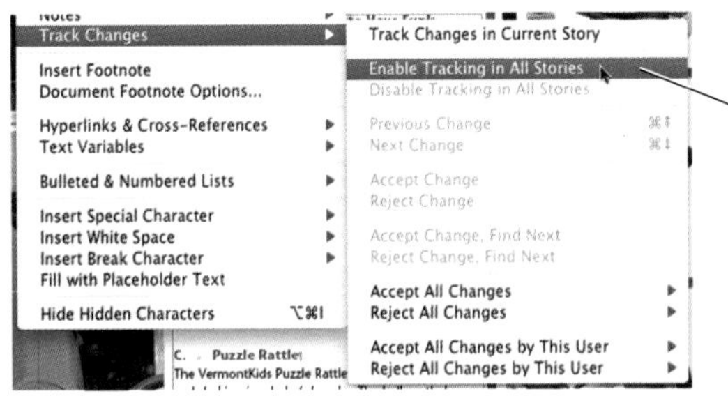

These options are not available unless the insertion point is currently placed.

3. **Open the Track Changes pane of the Preferences dialog box.**

4. **Make sure the Added Text, Deleted Text, and Moved Text options are checked.**

5. **Choose Red in the Deleted Text Background Color menu.**

   The Text Color options define the color of highlighting that will identify each type of change. All three options default to the same color; changing the color for Deleted Text will make it easier to identify this type of change when you review the corrections at the end of this stage of the project.

Note:

Remember, preferences are accessed in the InDesign menu on Macintosh or in the Edit menu on Windows.

6. **Check the option to Include Deleted Text When Spellchecking.**

   It is very easy to make a mistake when spellchecking, so it's a good idea to include those changes in the tracking.

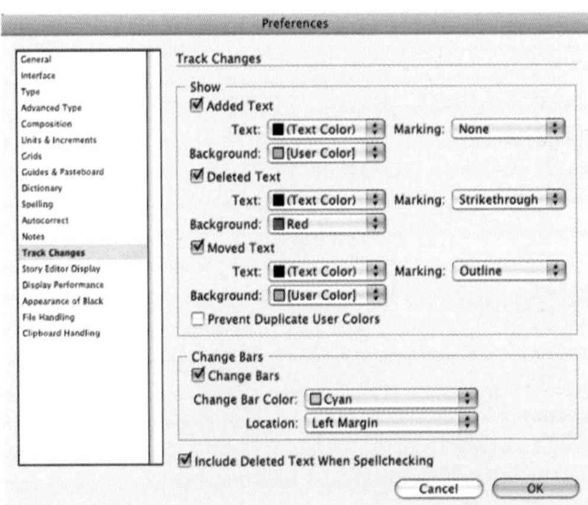

7. **Click OK to return to the document, then save the file and continue to the next exercise.**

Find and Change Text

You will often need to search for and replace specific elements in a layout — a word, a phrase, a formatting attribute, or even a specific kind of object. InDesign's Find/Change dialog box allows you to easily locate exactly what you need, whether your layout is two pages or two hundred. For this brochure, you can use the Find/Change dialog box to correct the client's typing errors.

1. **With toys_fall.indd open, choose Edit>Find/Change.**

2. **Place the insertion point in the Find What field and press the Spacebar twice.**

3. **Press Tab to highlight the Change To field and press the Spacebar once.**

4. **In the Search menu, choose Document.**

   When the insertion point is placed, you can choose to search the entire Document, All [open] Documents, only the active Story, or only text following the insertion point in the selected story (To End of Story).

Note:

If the insertion point is not currently placed, you can only choose to search the active Document or All Documents.

5. **Click Change All. When you see the message that 16 replacements were made, click OK.**

   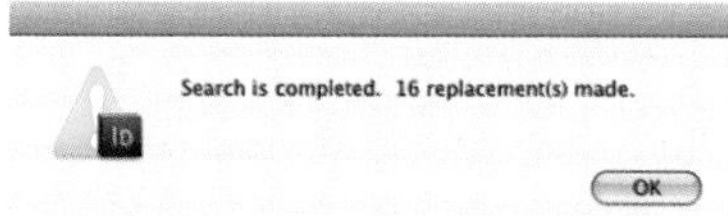

6. **Highlight the content of the Find What field (the two space characters).**

   Because you can't see the space characters in the field, it can be easy to forget about them. If you forget to highlight the space characters, the new content will be added to the space characters instead of replacing them.

7. **Choose End of Paragraph in the menu to the right of the Find What field.**

   Use this menu to place common special characters in the dialog box fields. When you choose a special character in the menu, the code for that character is entered in the field.

   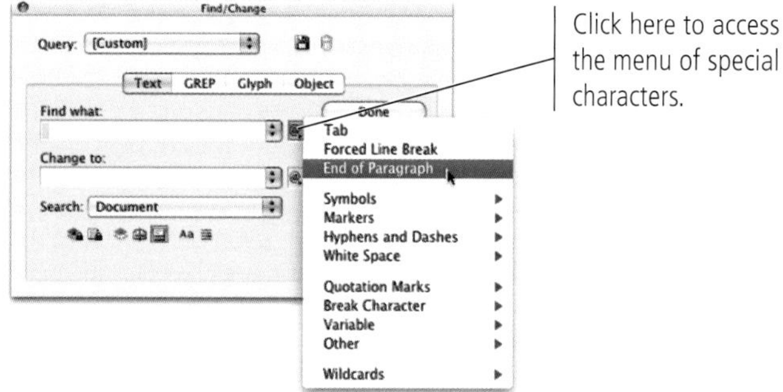

Click here to access the menu of special characters.

The Find/Change Dialog Box in Depth

In addition to the tools you use in this project, the Find/Change dialog box has a number of options for narrowing or extending a search beyond the basic options. The buttons below the Search menu are toggles for specific types of searches:

- When **Include Locked Layers and Locked Objects** is active, the search locates instances on locked layers or individual objects that have been locked; you can't replace locked objects unless you first unlock them.
- When **Include Locked Stories** is active, the search locates text that is locked; you can't replace locked text unless you first unlock it.
- When **Include Hidden Layers** is active, the search includes frames on layers that are not visible.
- When **Include Master Pages** is active, the search includes frames on master pages.
- When **Include Footnotes** is active, the search identifies instances within footnote text.
- When **Case Sensitive** is active, the search only finds text with the same capitalization as the text in the Find What field. For example, a search for "InDesign" will not identify instances of "Indesign," "indesign," or "INDESIGN."
- When **Whole Word** is active, the search only finds instances where the search text is an entire word (not part of another word). For example, if you search for "old" as a whole word, InDesign will not include the words "gold," "mold," or "embolden."

As you have seen, the Text tab allows you to search for and change specific character strings, with or without specific formatting options. The Object tab identifies specific combinations of object formatting attributes, such as fill color or applied object effects.

The GREP tab is used for pattern-based search techniques, such as finding phone numbers in one format (e.g., 800.555.1234) and changing them to the same phone number with a different format (e.g., 800/555-1234). Adobe's video-based help system (www.adobe.com) provides some assistance in setting up an advanced query.

The Glyph tab allows you to search for and change glyphs using Unicode or GID/CID values. This is useful for identifying foreign and pictographic characters, as well as characters from extended sets of OpenType fonts.

You can also save specific searches as queries, and you can call those queries again using the Query menu at the top of the Find/Change dialog box. This option is useful if you commonly make the same modifications, such as changing Multiple Return to Single Return (this particular search and replacement is so common that the query is built into the application).

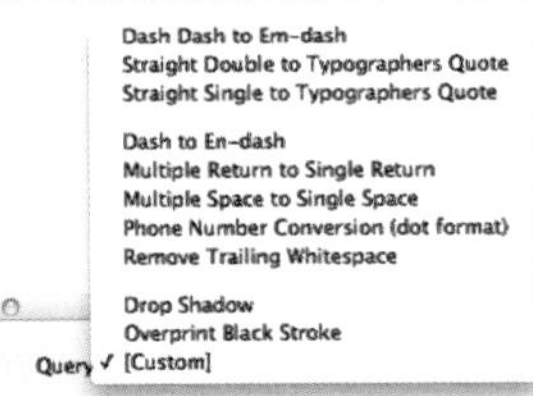

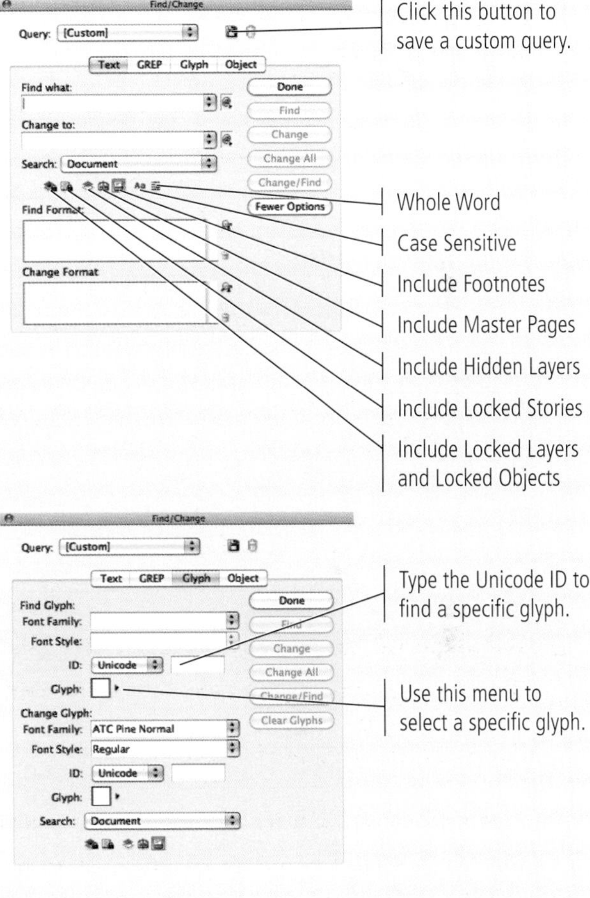

Entering Special Characters in Dialog Boxes

You can enter special characters in InDesign dialog boxes using the following special codes, called metacharacters. (Note that these metacharacters are case specific; for example, "^n" and "^N" refer to different special characters.)

Character	Code (Metacharacters)
Symbols	
Bullet (•)	^8
Caret (^)	^^
Copyright (©)	^2
Ellipsis (…)	^e
Paragraph (¶)	^7
Registered Trademark (®)	^r
Section (§)	^6
Trademark (™)	^d
Dashes and Hyphens	
Em Dash (—)	^_
En Dash (–)	^=
Discretionary hyphen	^-
Nonbreaking hyphen	^~
White Space Characters	
Em space	^m
En space	^>
Third space	^3
Quarter space	^4
Sixth space	^%
Flush space	^f
Hair space	^| (pipe)
Nonbreaking space	^s
Thin space	^<
Figure space	^/
Punctuation space	^.
Quotation Marks	
Double left quotation mark	^{
Double right quotation mark	^}
Single left quotation mark	^[
Single right quotation mark	^]
Straight double quotation mark	^"
Straight single quotation mark	^'
Page Number Characters	
Any page number character	^#
Current page number character	^N
Next page number character	^X
Previous page number character	^V

Character	Code (Metacharacters)
Break Characters	
Paragraph return	^p
Forced line break (soft return)	^n
Column break	^M
Frame break	^R
Page break	^P
Odd page break	^L
Even page break	^E
Discretionary line break	^j
Formatting Options	
Tab character	^t
Right indent tab character	^y
Indent to here character	^i
End nested style here character	^h
Nonjoiner character	^k
Variables	
Running header (paragraph style)	^Y
Running header (character style)	^Z
Custom text	^u
Last page number	^T
Chapter number	^H
Creation date	^S
Modification date	^o
Output date	^D
File name	^l (lowercase L)
Markers	
Section marker	^x
Anchored object marker	^a
Footnote reference marker	^F
Index marker	^I
Wildcards	
Any digit	^9
Any letter	^$
Any character	^?
White space (any space or tab)	^w
Any variable	^v

8. **Choose End of Paragraph from the menu again to search for all instances of two consecutive paragraph returns.**

9. **Highlight the Change To field and choose End of Paragraph from the associated menu.**

   You are replacing all instances of two paragraph returns with a single paragraph return.

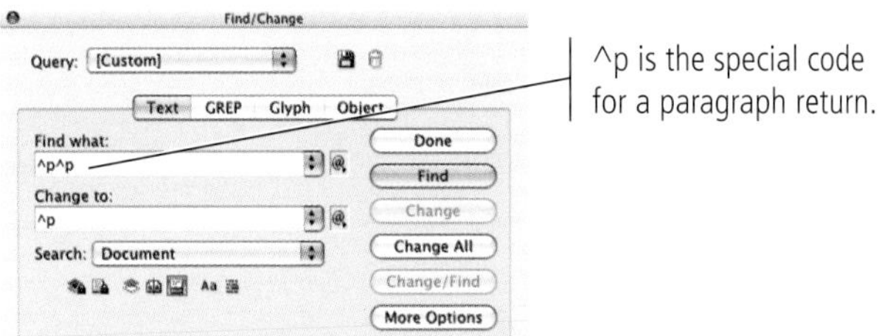

^p is the special code for a paragraph return.

Note:

In professional situations, you might need to do these replacements several times to remove all double spaces and paragraph returns from text received from clients.

10. **Click Change All, and then click OK to close the message box.**

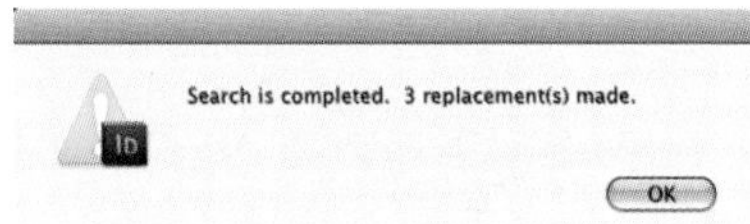

11. **Change all instances of the word "VermontKids" to ToyTrends.**

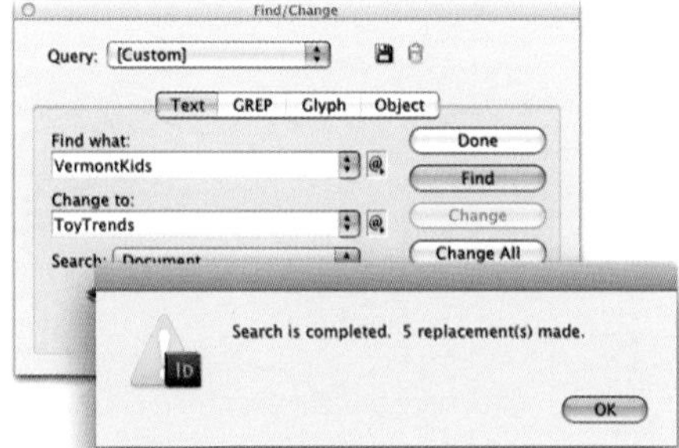

12. **Click OK to dismiss the message about the number of changes, then click Done to close the Find/Change dialog box.**

13. **Save the file and continue to the next exercise.**

 Find and Change Text Formatting Attributes

In addition to finding and replacing specific text or characters, you can also find and replace formatting attributes for both text and objects. For this project, you need to use the blue spot color as the accent, replacing the red spot color from the template. You can't simply delete the red spot color from the Swatches panel, however, because that color is used in the placed logo file. The Find/Change dialog box makes this kind of replacement a relatively simple process.

1. **With toys_fall.indd open, choose Edit>Find/Change. Delete all characters from the Find What and Change To fields.**

   You only want to change the formatting, not the text that is formatted. To accomplish this result, you have to delete all characters from both fields.

2. **Highlight the Find What field. Click the associated menu and choose Any Character from the Wildcards submenu.**

   Wildcards allow you to search for formatting attributes, regardless of the actual text. In addition to searching for Any Character, you can also narrow the search to Any Digit, Any Letter, or Any White Space characters.

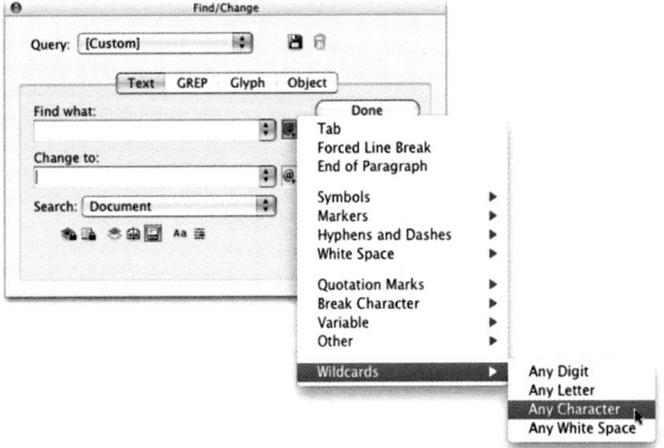

3. **Click the More Options button to show the expanded Find/Change dialog box.**

   When more options are visible, you can find and replace specific formatting attributes of the selected text.

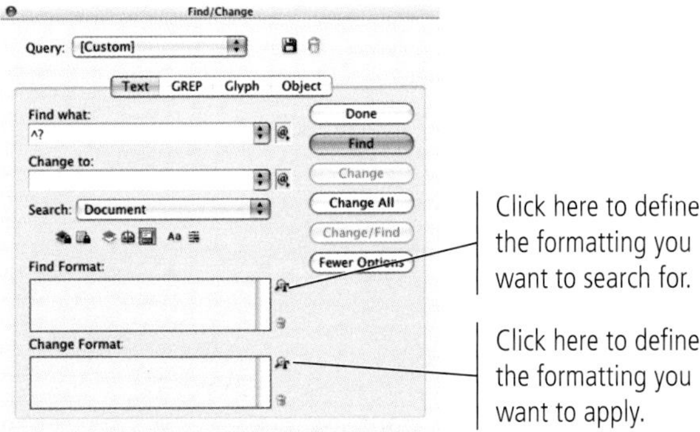

4. **Click the button for the Find Format field to open the Find Format Settings dialog box.**

   You can search for and replace any character formatting option (or combination of options) that can be applied in the layout.

5. **Show the Character Color options and click the Pantone 186 C swatch.**

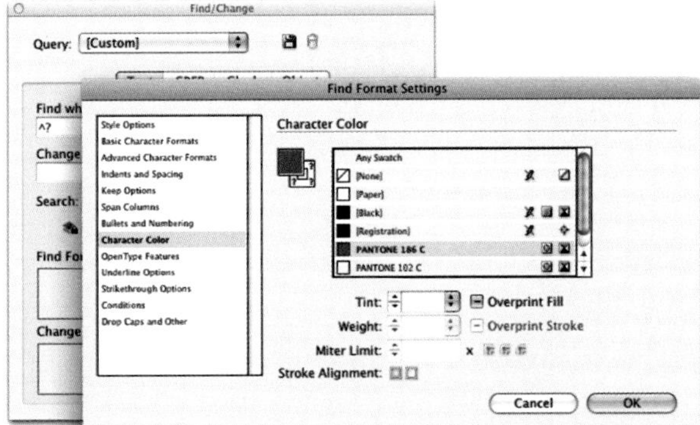

6. **Click OK to return to the Find/Change dialog box.**

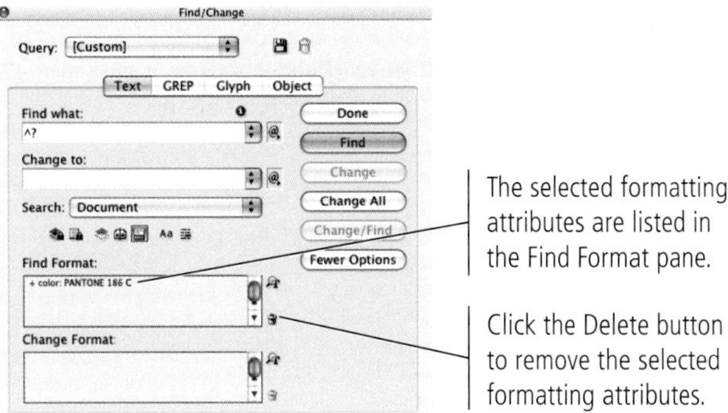

7. **Click the button for the Change Format field to open the Change Format Settings dialog box.**

8. **Show the Character Color options and click the Pantone Blue 072 C swatch.**

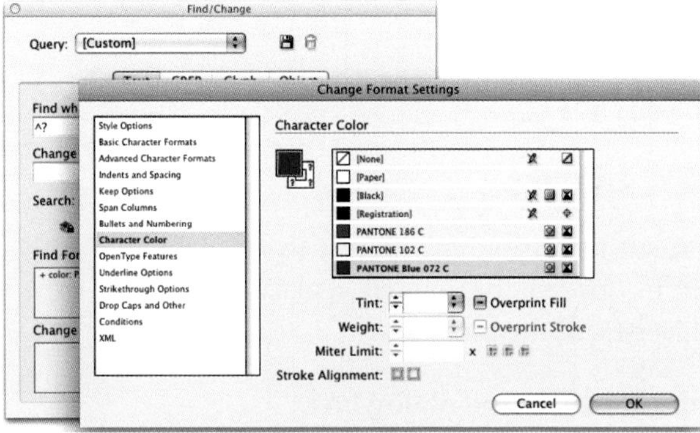

9. **Click OK to return to the Find/Change dialog box.**

10. **Make sure Document is selected in the Search menu and click Change All. Click OK to close the message about the number of replacements.**

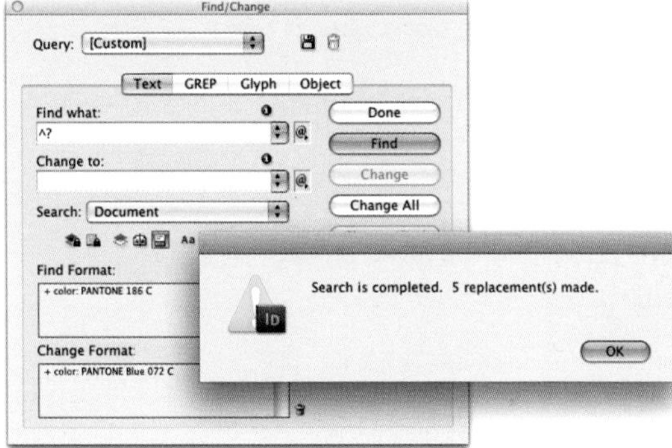

11. **In the Find/Change dialog box, click the Delete buttons to remove the formatting options from the Find Format and Change Format fields.**

It can be easy to forget to remove these formatting choices, and if you leave them in place, your next search will only find the Find What text with the selected formatting. To prevent this problem, it's a good idea to clear these formatting choices as soon as you're done with them.

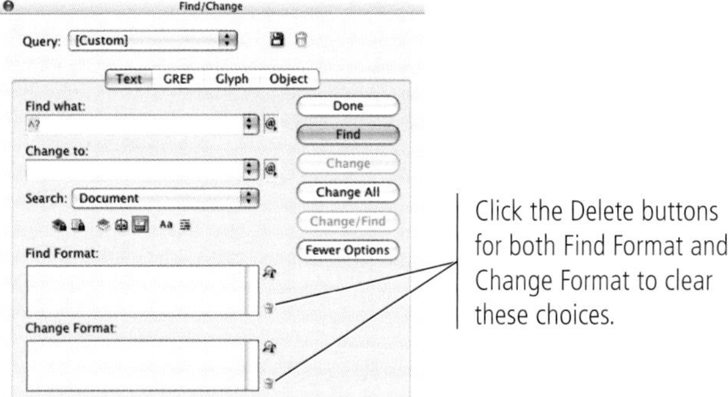

Click the Delete buttons for both Find Format and Change Format to clear these choices.

12. **Save the file and continue to the next exercise.**

Find and Change Object Attributes

In addition to searching for specific text formatting attributes, you can also find and replace specific object formatting attributes. In this exercise you will replace all red-filled frames with the blue spot color for this issue of the brochure.

1. **With `toys_fall.indd` open, open the Find/Change dialog box.**

2. **Click the Object tab to display those options, and make sure Document is selected in the Search menu.**

   When you search objects, you can search the current document, all documents, or the current selection.

3. **In the Type menu, choose All Frames.**

   You can limit your search to specific kinds of frames, or search all frames.

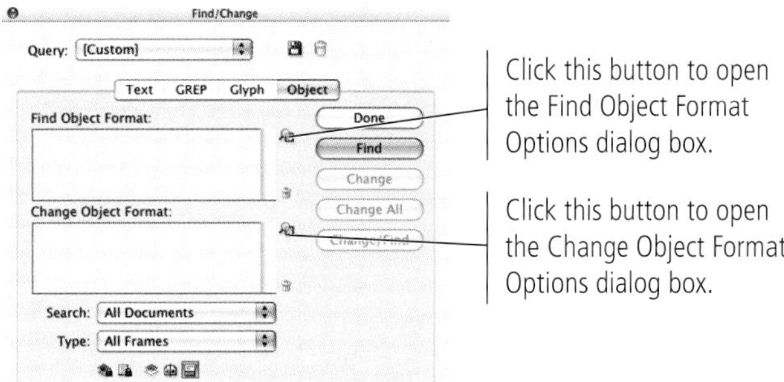

Click this button to open the Find Object Format Options dialog box.

Click this button to open the Change Object Format Options dialog box.

4. **Click the button to open the Find Object Format Options dialog box.**

   You can find and change any formatting attributes that can be applied to a frame.

5. **Display the Fill options and click the Pantone 186 C swatch.**

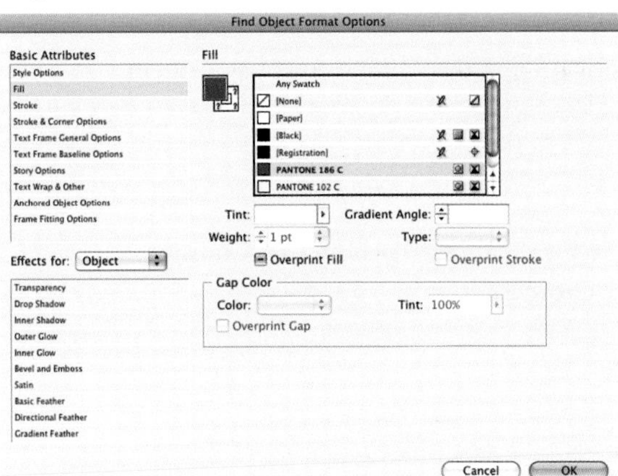

Note:

Selected formatting options are cumulative. If you added the stroke color to the Find options, the search would only identify objects that have a red fill ***and*** *a red stroke. To find* ***either*** *of these options, you have to perform two separate searches.*

6. **Click OK to return to the Find/Change dialog box.**

7. **Open the Change Object Format Options dialog box and choose the Pantone Blue 072 C swatch in the Fill options.**

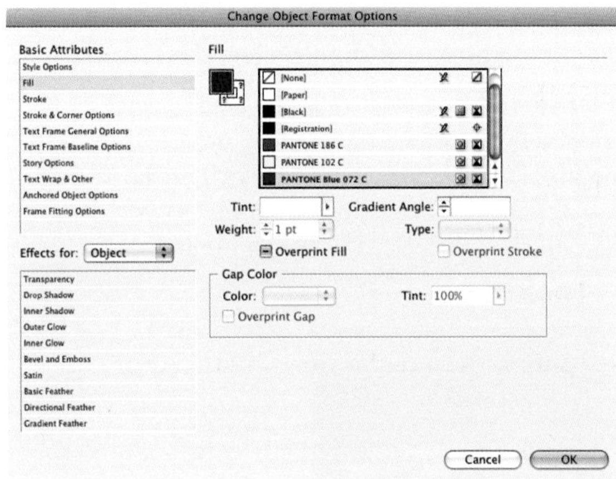

8. **Click OK to return to the Find/Change dialog box.**

9. **Click the Include Master Pages icon to activate that option.**

Because some frames exist only on the master pages for this file, you need to activate the Include Master Pages option to successfully replace the fill color in all frames.

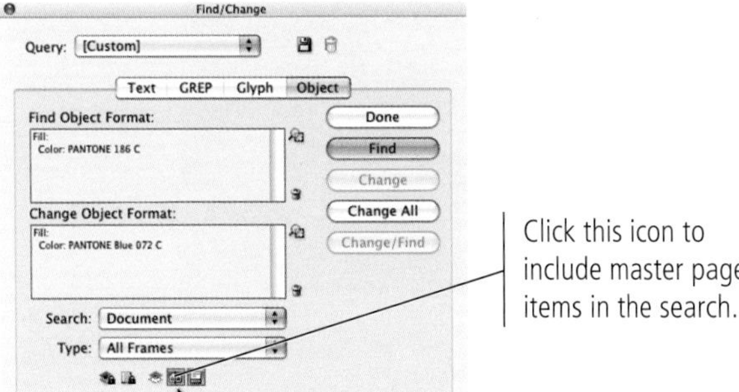

Click this icon to include master page items in the search.

10. **Click Change All, then click OK to dismiss the message about the number of changes.**

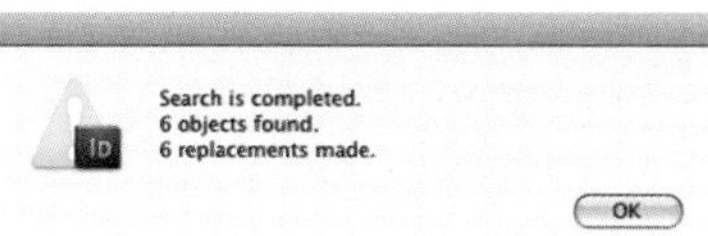

11. **Click the Delete buttons for both the Find Object Format and Change Object Format options to clear your choices.**

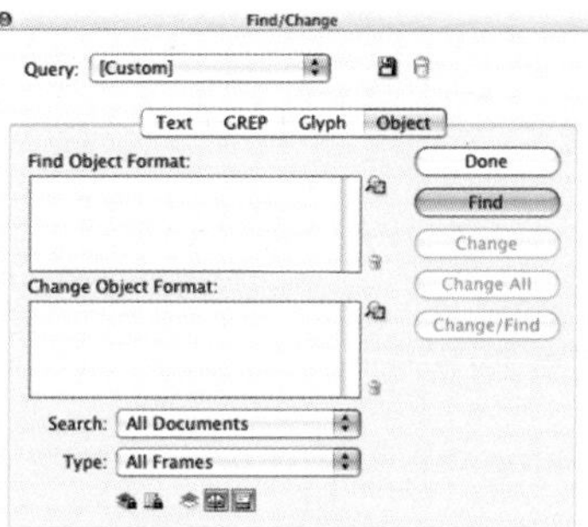

12. **Click Done to close the Find/Change dialog box, and then review the layout.**

    Elements of placed Illustrator, EPS, and PDF files are not affected by the Find/Change function. Placed InDesign files are only affected by the search if those files are also open when you initiate the search and if you specified All Documents in the Search menu. Because the slide.indd file was not already open, the red spot-color text in the placed InDesign file was not affected; you now have to open the placed InDesign file and manually change the red text.

13. **Save toys_fall.indd and continue to the next exercise.**

CHECK DOCUMENT SPELLING

In Project 9 you learned about preflighting and how to verify that required elements (graphics and fonts) are available. This simple process prevents potential output disasters such as font replacement or low-resolution preview images in the final print.

Many designers understand these issues and carefully monitor the technical aspects of a job. It is all too common, however, to skip another important check — for spelling errors. Misspellings and typos creep into virtually every job despite numerous rounds of content proofs. These errors can ruin an otherwise perfect print job.

Note:

You might not (and probably won't) create the text for most design jobs, and you aren't technically responsible for the words your client supplies. However, you can be a hero if you find and fix typographical errors before a job goes to press; if you don't, you will almost certainly hear about it after it's too late to fix. Remember the cardinal rule of business: the customer is always right. You simply can't brush off a problem by saying, "That's not my job" — at least, not if you want to work with that client in the future.

1. **With toys_fall.indd open, open the Dictionary pane of the Preferences dialog box.**

   InDesign checks spelling based on the defined language dictionary — by default, English: USA. You can choose a different language dictionary in the Language menu.

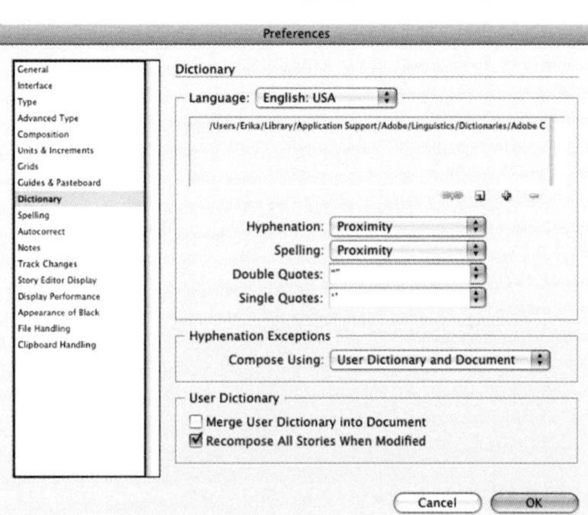

2. **Make sure English: USA is selected in the Language menu and click OK.**

3. **Choose Edit>Spelling>Dictionary.**

   When you check spelling, you are likely to find words that, although spelled correctly, are not in the selected dictionary. Proper names, scientific terms, corporate trademarks, and other custom words are commonly flagged even though they are correct. Rather than flagging these terms every time you recheck spelling, you can add them to a custom user dictionary so InDesign will recognize them the next time you check spelling.

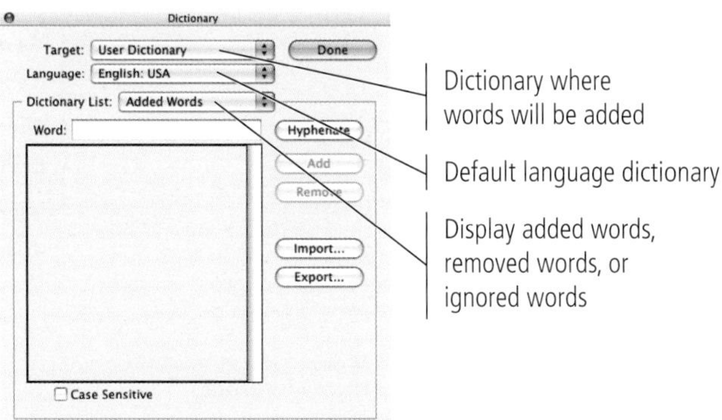

4. **In the Target menu, choose toys_fall.indd.**

   By default, the user dictionary is associated with all documents. You can define custom words for a specific file using the Target menu; when you change the user dictionary for a specific file, words you add for that file will still be flagged in other files.

5. **In the Word field, type ToyTrends.**

Your client's company name is not a real word (even though it is a combination of two real words). If you know that certain words will be flagged, you can manually add those words to the user dictionary at any time.

By adding this word to the file's dictionary (not the language dictionary), you prevent potential errors that might arise if you work on a project that uses the term in a more generic sense. For example, a magazine article about "Toy Trends in Middle America" should result in an error if the first two words are not separated by a space.

6. **Check the Case Sensitive option at the bottom of the dialog box, and then click Add.**

If Case Sensitive is not checked, InDesign will not distinguish between ToyTrends (which is correct) and toytrends (which is incorrect).

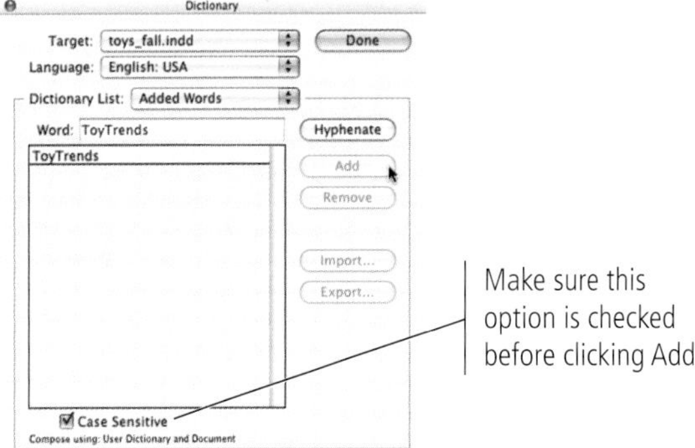

Make sure this option is checked before clicking Add.

7. **Click Done to close the Dictionary dialog box.**

8. **With nothing selected in the layout, choose Edit>Spelling>Check Spelling.**

As soon as you open the Check Spelling dialog box, the first flagged word is highlighted in the layout. The same word appears in the first field of the Check Spelling dialog box.

The first flagged word is the sole capital letter "B." Many single letters will be flagged when you check spelling.

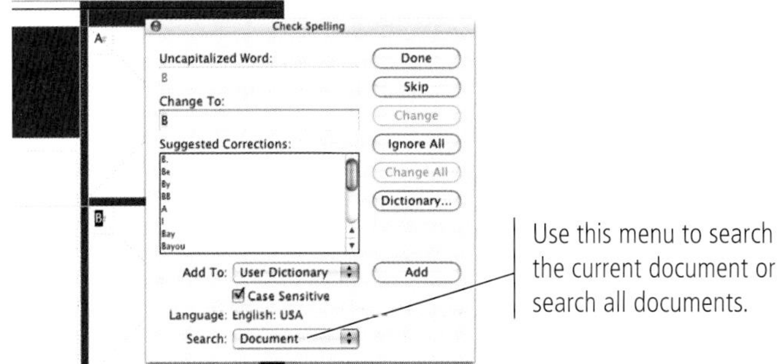

Use this menu to search the current document or search all documents.

> ***Note:***
>
> *If the insertion point is currently placed in a story, the Search menu also includes options to search the selected story or the selected story after the insertion point.*

9. **Click Skip.**

In context, this single letter is used as an identifier, so it is correct. However, other instances of the single letter B might be errors. Clicking Skip moves to the next flagged word without adding the word to the user dictionary.

10. **Review the next flagged word ("playscape").**

The word "playscape" is the name of a product, and it is spelled correctly according to your client.

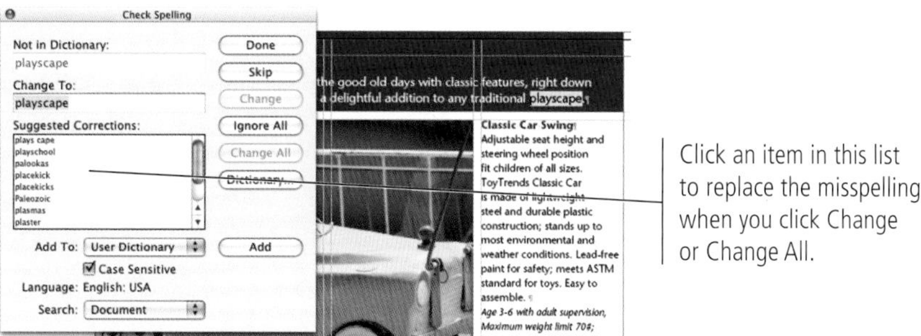

Click an item in this list to replace the misspelling when you click Change or Change All.

11. **Click the Dictionary button in the Check Spelling dialog box. Choose toys_fall.indd in the Target menu and click Add.**

When you add words in the Check Spelling dialog box, the words are added to the default user dictionary. When you open the Dictionary dialog box from the Check Spelling dialog box, you can choose the file-specific dictionary in the Target menu and click Add to add the word to the dictionary for the selected file only.

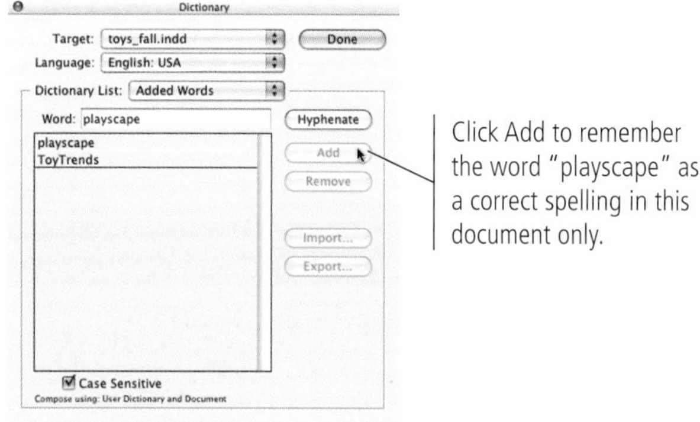

Click Add to remember the word "playscape" as a correct spelling in this document only.

Note:

Never simply click Change when checking spelling. Review each flagged word carefully and make the correct choices within the context of the layout.

12. **Click Done to close the Dictionary dialog box and return to the Check Spelling dialog box. Click Skip.**

When you return to the Check Spelling dialog box, playscape still appears in the Word field. You have to click Skip to find the next suspect word.

13. **With ASTM highlighted, click Ignore All.**

When you click Ignore All, the word is added to a special list in the user dictionary so it will not be flagged again.

Note:

InDesign checks spelling based on the defined language dictionary. In addition to misspellings, however, InDesign also identifies repeated words (such as "the the"), uncapitalized words, and uncapitalized sentences. These options can be turned off in the Spelling pane of the Preferences dialog box.

14. **Continue checking the spelling in the document. Make the following choices when prompted:**

37x17x12	**Skip**
KinderKids	**Add to toys_fall.indd dictionary (as in Step 11)**
and and	**Click "and" in the Suggested Corrections list and click Change**
Sleepytime	**Add to toys_fall.indd dictionary**
Marvalous	**Click "Marvelous" in the Suggested Corrections list and click Change**

15. When you get to the word "Burlington", click Add to add the word "Burlington" to the default user dictionary.

Spellings added to the default user dictionary apply to all InDesign files; if you want to define a spelling for only a specific file, you have to add it to the dictionary for the active file (as you have done for "playscape", "KinderKids", and other product names in this layout).

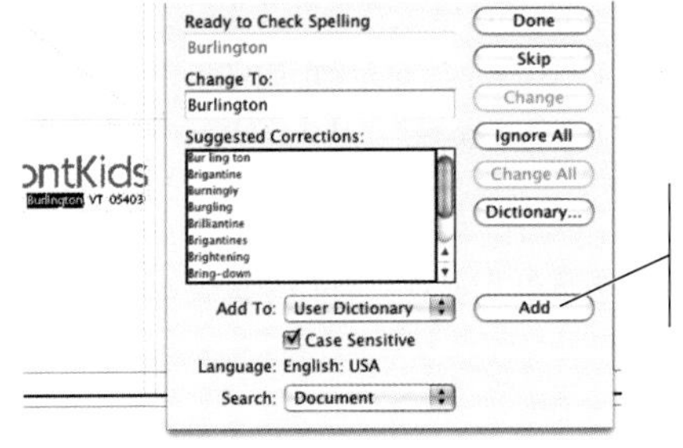

Click Add to add the flagged word to the default user dictionary.

Note:

If you are using a shared computer, it is possible that another user might have already added this word to the user dictionary (not the current file's dictionary). If this is the case, this word will not be flagged for your file.

16. When you see the green checkmark at the top of the dialog box, click Done to close the Check Spelling dialog box.

Note:

As with the Find/Change function, the Check Spelling function only interacts with nested files if those files are already open and the All Documents option is selected in the Search menu.

17. Save toys_fall.indd and continue to the next exercise.

Using Dynamic Spelling

INDESIGN FOUNDATIONS

You can turn on dynamic spelling (Edit>Spelling>Dynamic Spelling) to underline potential spelling and capitalization errors in a document without opening the Check Spelling dialog box. You can use the Spelling pane of the Preferences dialog box to assign a different-color underline for each of the four potential problems.

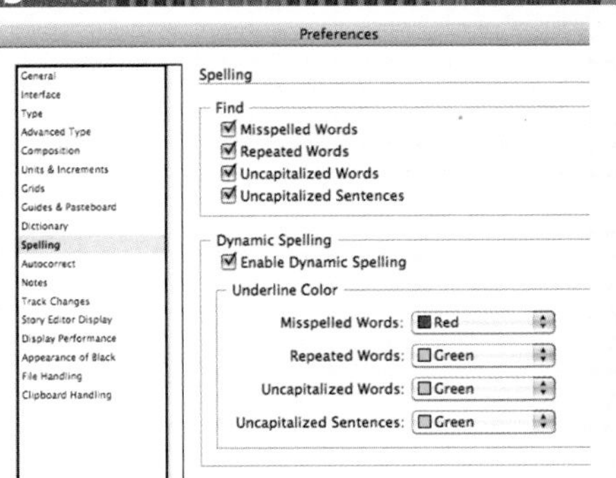

Midevil document give us many very sophisticated examples of this type of visual communication. Illuminations, or the the beautiful color illustrations we find in documents that survive from the Middle Ages, were added by artistically talented monks to embellish the hand-written pages.

The misspelled word is underlined in red.

The repeated word is underlined in green.

If you type directly into InDesign, you can turn on the Autocorrect feature (Edit>Spelling>Autocorrect) to correct misspelled words as you type. Of course, automatic corrections are not always correct; software can't always select the correct word within the context of the layout, and it might produce some very strange results for words that aren't in the active dictionary (technical or corporate terms, for example). To avoid the potential for fixing "errors" that aren't really errors, you can define what misspellings to replace and what spelling should replace those specific errors.

In the Autocorrect pane of the Preferences dialog box, you can click Add to define a specific misspelling, as well as the correct spelling to use. The Autocorrect List is maintained for the specified language dictionary.

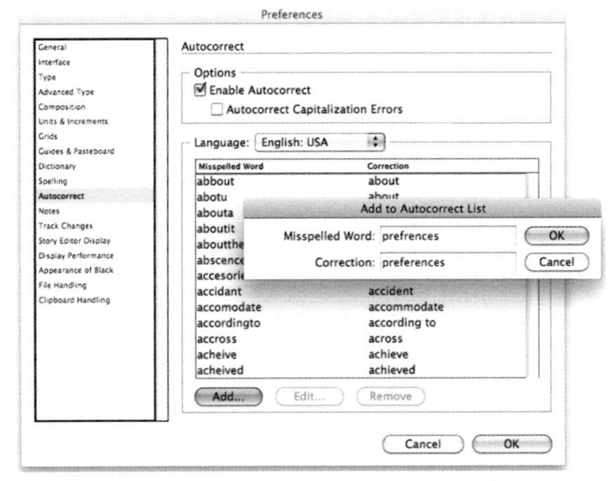

Review Tracked Changes

At the beginning of this stage of the project, you enabled the Track Changes feature for all stories in this document. You might have noticed, however, that there is no visual indication of those changes in the layout. Tracking editorial changes is useful for monitoring changes in the text, but displaying those changes in the layout would make it impossible to fit copy and accurately format the text in a layout. To avoid this confusion, changes are tracked in a special utility called the Story Editor, which more closely resembles a word-processor screen.

1. **With toys_fall.indd open, place the insertion point in the text frame of the right half of Page 2.**

2. **Choose Edit>Edit in Story Editor.**

   The Story Editor opens in a separate window, showing only the current story. (A **story** in InDesign is the entire body of text in a single frame or string of linked frames.)

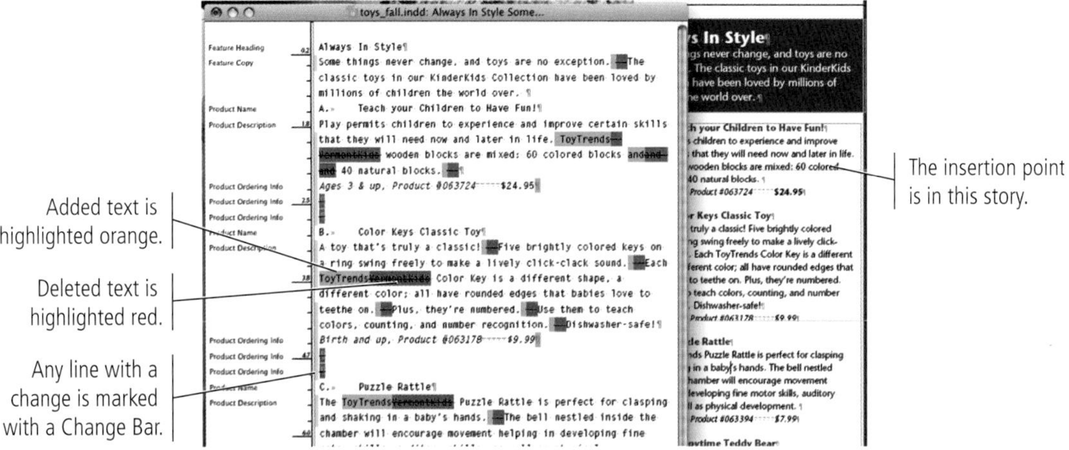

3. **Click at the top of the story editor to place the insertion point anywhere above the first marked change.**

4. **Choose Type>Track Changes>Next Change.**

   The first change — a single space added at the end of the first sentence — is highlighted after you choose the menu command. Although you replaced double spaces with single spaces using a single action in the Find/Change dialog box, adding and deleting are technically two separate changes that are highlighted and reviewed individually.

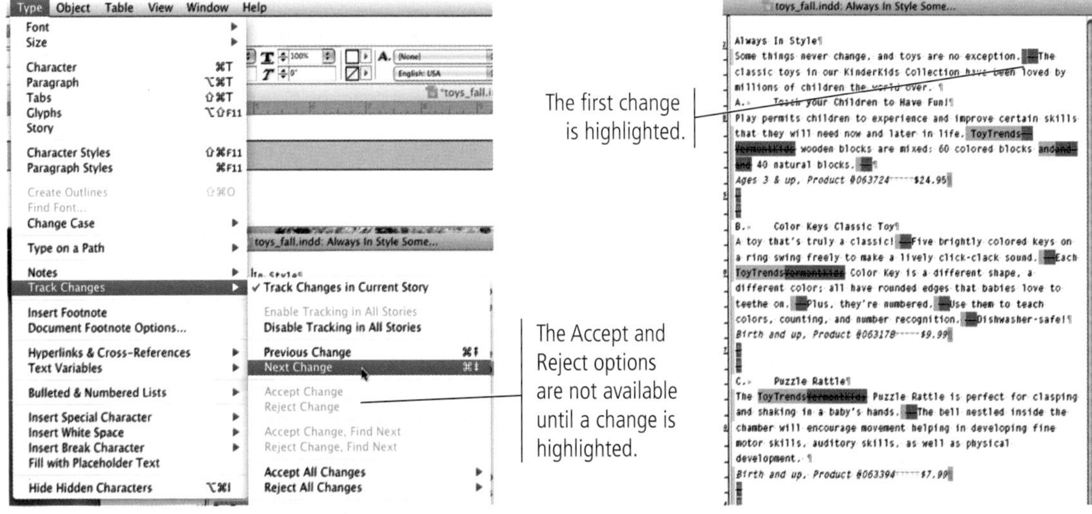

5. **Choose Type>Track Changes>Accept Change, Find Next.**

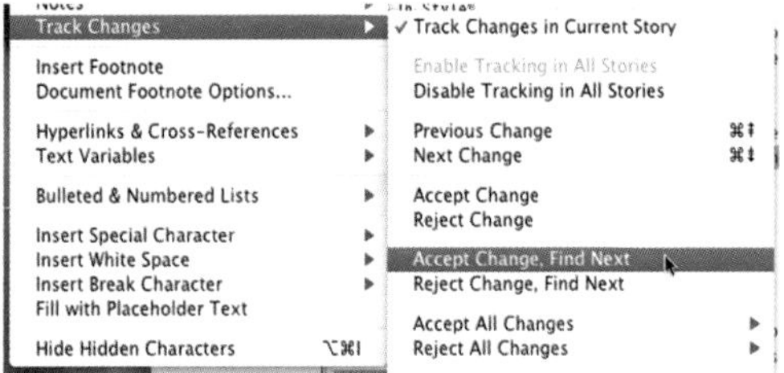

After implementing this command, the added single space is no longer highlighted; the deleted double space is the next change in the story, so it becomes highlighted.

6. **Choose Type>Track Changes>Accept All Changes>In This Story.**

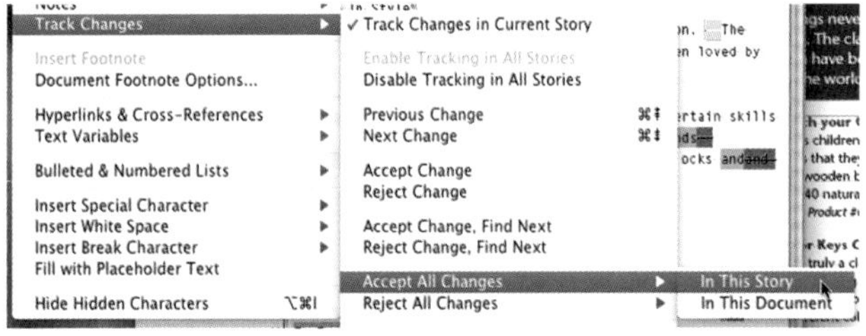

Note:

If your deleted text is not highlighted red, you missed a step in the earlier exercise where you enabled the Track Changes feature (see page 551). You can open the Track Changes pane of the Preferences dialog box and change the highlight options now.

7. **Click OK to dismiss the Warning dialog box and accept the changes.**

Accepting all changes without reviewing them essentially defeats the purpose of tracking changes. However, you were conscientious in making these changes through this project; we are telling you that, in this case, it is safe to simply accept all the changes. In a real-world workflow — and especially if more than one person has been working on the same document — you should be sure to carefully review all tracked changes before finalizing the job.

After accepting all changes in the story, all highlighting is gone.

8. **Close the Story Editor window.**

9. **Choose Type>Track Changes>Accept All Changes>In This Document.**

In Step 7 you only accepted the changes in the active story; other stories in the layout still have tracked changes that should be reviewed. Again, we are telling you it is safe to simply accept those changes. In a professional environment, you should open each story and review the changes carefully.

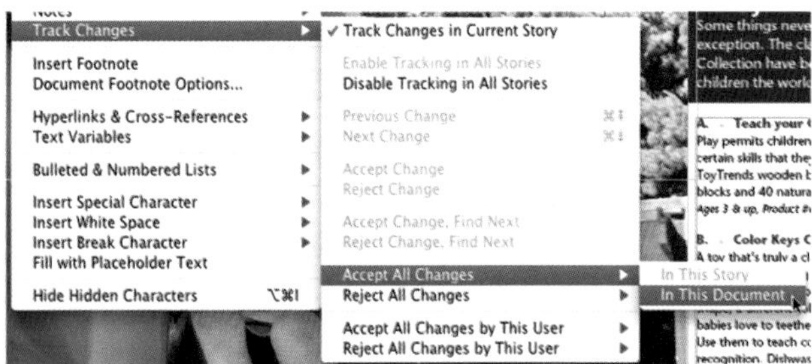

10. **Click OK to dismiss the Warning dialog box and accept the changes.**

11. **Save the file and continue to the next stage of the project.**

Stage 4 Editing Linked Files

The interaction between applications is one of the true benefits to working with the entire Adobe Creative Suite. Using the Links panel, you can easily manage linked files — including opening them in their native applications to make any necessary changes. In this stage of the project, you will navigate between InDesign, Illustrator, and Photoshop to correct several problems with the placed files in this brochure.

Edit a Linked InDesign File

As you have already learned, the Links panel provides valuable information about the status of placed files. It is more than just an informational tool, however; you can also use the Links panel to navigate to and edit selected images.

> *Note:*
>
> *The Edit Original option works for any type of placed file (as long as your computer recognizes the file type), including native Illustrator and Photoshop files, TIFF files, JPEG files, EPS files, and so on.*

1. **With toys_fall.indd open, open the Links panel and click the arrow to the left of slide.indd to show the nested images.**

   You should become familiar with the options at the bottom of the Links panel.

   - The **Relink** button opens a navigation dialog box, where you can locate a missing file or link to a different file.
   - The **Go to Link** button selects and centers the file in the document window.
   - The **Update Link** button updates modified links. If the selected image is missing, this button opens a navigation dialog box so you can locate the missing file.
   - The **Edit Original** button opens the selected file in its native application. When you save the file and return to the InDesign layout, the placed file is automatically updated.

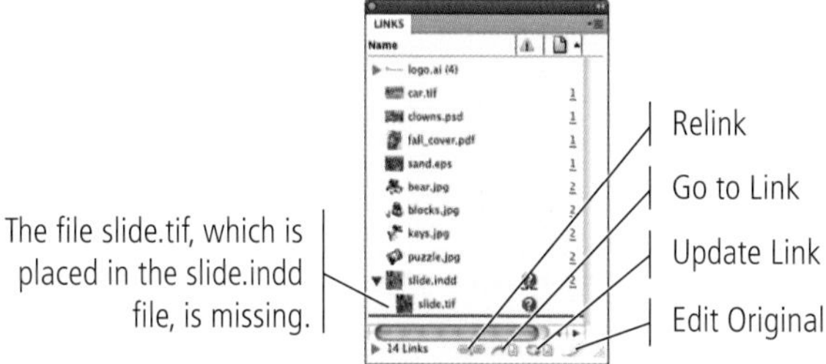

2. **Click slide.indd in the Links panel, and then click the Edit Original button.**

   The Edit Original option opens the file selected in the Links panel. Because slide.indd is a placed InDesign file, that document opens in a new document window in front of toys_fall.indd.

   When you open any InDesign file, of course, you are first warned if any necessary source file is missing (which you already knew from the Links panel of the toys_fall.indd file).

> *Note:*
>
> *You can also Control/right-click a specific image in the layout and choose Edit Original from the contextual menu.*

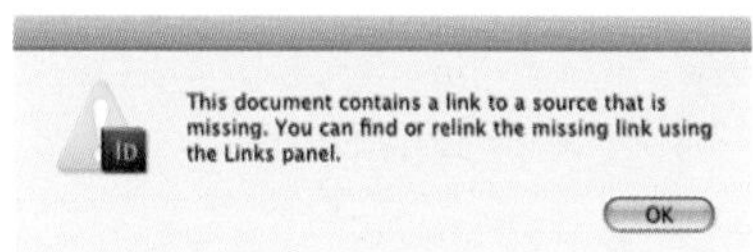

This document contains a link to a source that is missing. You can find or relink the missing link using the Links panel.
OK

3. **Click OK to dismiss the warning message.**

4. **In the resulting Profile or Policy Mismatch dialog box, choose the Adjust option and click OK.**

Again, when you open any file, InDesign verifies the file's color based on your choices in the Color Settings dialog box.

This file (slide.indd) was created with the U.S. Web Coated (SWOP) v2 CMYK working space, as you can see from the profile listed in the Leave Document As Is section. You are working with the U.S. Sheetfed Coated v2 working space, however, so you need to convert this file to the same CMYK working space as the main brochure file.

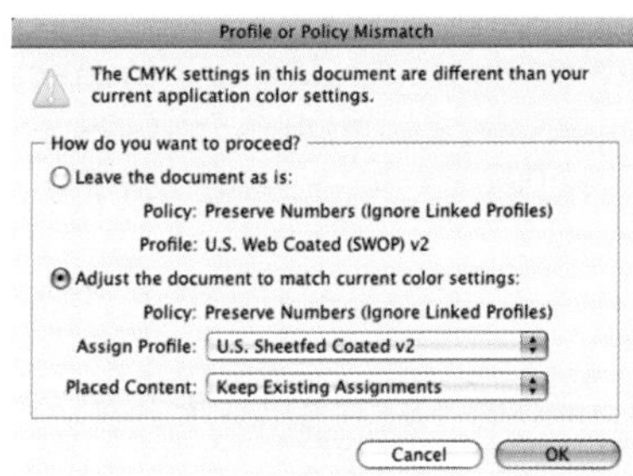

When the file opens, you see the missing image link in the Links panel — the reason you are editing the file.

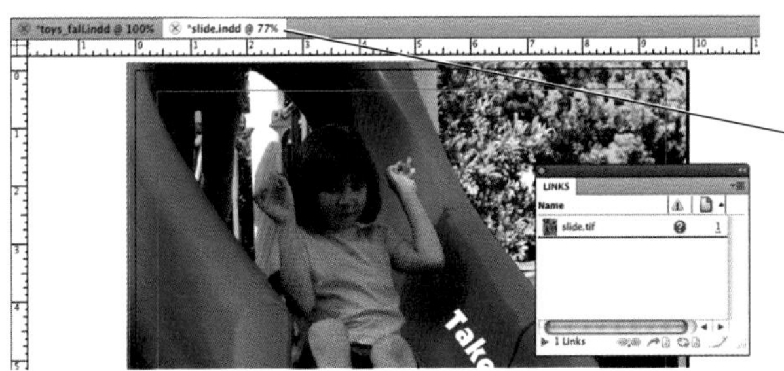

The document tab shows which file is active.

5. **In the Links panel for slide.indd, click the missing file to select it, and then click the Relink button at the bottom of the panel.**

6. **Navigate to `slide_revised.tif` in the WIP>Toys folder and click Open.**

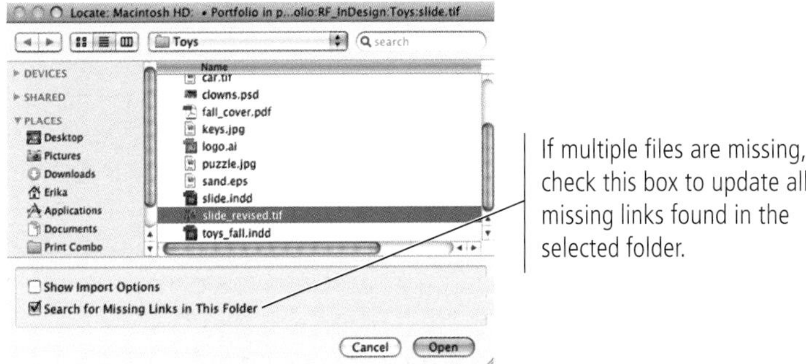

If multiple files are missing, check this box to update all missing links found in the selected folder.

7. **If the Image Import Options dialog box opens, click OK.**

8. **Save the `slide.indd` file and close it.**

When you save and close the slide.indd file, the Links panel for toys_fall.indd automatically reflects the new placed file.

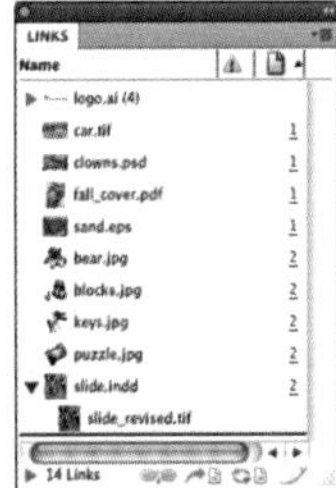

Note:

If you change a placed file without using the Edit Original option, the Links panel shows a Modified icon. In this case, you have to manually update the link.

9. **Save toys_fall.indd and continue to the next exercise.**

Edit a Placed Illustrator File

You might have noticed that the Find/Change function changed the old company name throughout the InDesign layout. However, this function did not affect text in the placed graphics. The Edit Original function works equally well for Illustrator files as it does for placed InDesign layouts.

1. **With toys_fall.indd open, navigate to Page 1 of the layout.**
2. **Select the logo.ai file in the Links panel and click the Edit Original button.**

   If Adobe Illustrator is not already running on your computer, it might take a few moments for the application to launch.

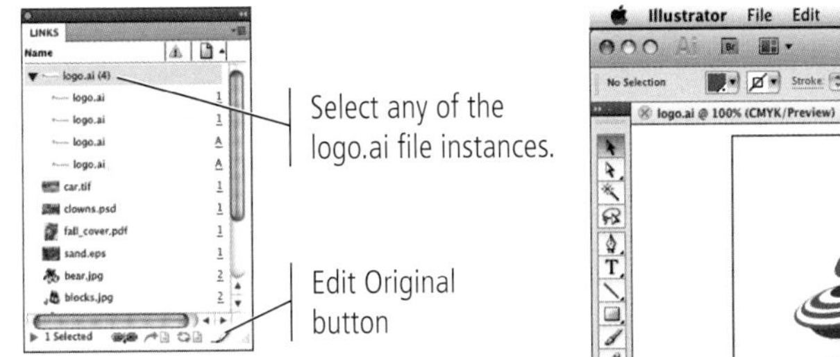

3. **When the logo.ai file opens in Illustrator, use the Type tool to highlight the word "VermontKids" and then type ToyTrends.**
4. **Using the Character panel, adjust the kerning for the new company name until you are satisfied with the letter spacing.**

5. **Save the file (File>Save) and close it, and then return to InDesign.**

   All instances of the edited file are automatically updated to reflect the new file content. When you replace one file with another, the new file is automatically scaled proportionally to fill the existing frame dimensions. Because the word "ToyTrends" is much shorter than the original "VermontKids", the revised logo is scaled larger to fill the horizontal dimensions of the frame; the logo no longer fits into the vertical dimensions of either frame.

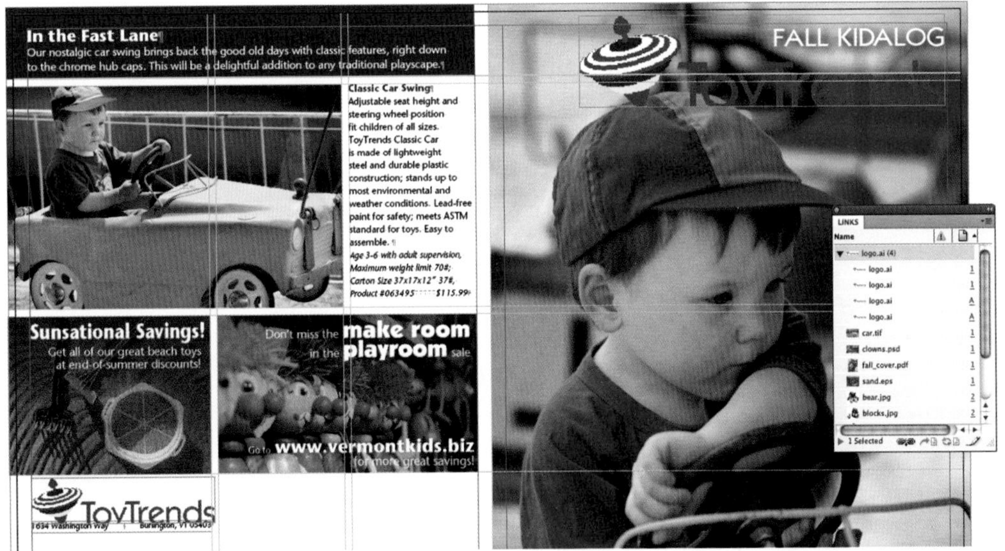

6. **Using the Direct Selection tool, select the logo instance on the right side of Page 1.**

The edited image is scaled to fit the current frame dimensions.

7. **Using the Control panel, change the image scale to 100% horizontally and vertically.**

   The original logo was placed at 100%, so the revised logo now fits into the vertical frame dimension. The difference in width, however, requires a few extra steps to correctly position the adjusted logo.

8. **With the logo selected on the right side of the page, Control/right-click the image and choose Fitting>Fit Frame to Content.**

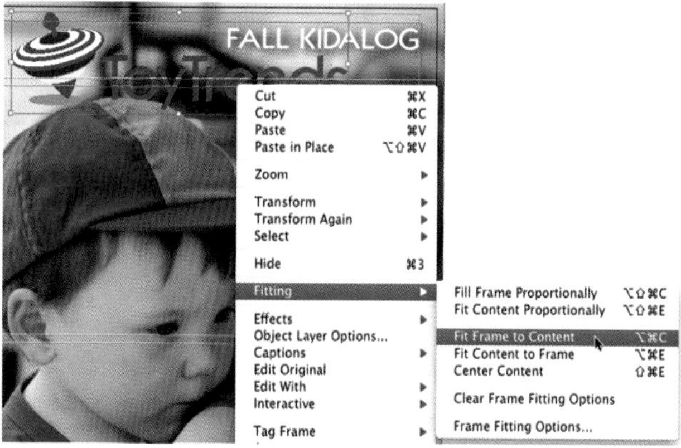

9. **Choose the Selection tool, click the logo frame, press Shift and drag right until the right edge of the frame snaps to the right margin guide.**

10. **Using the Direct Selection tool, select the logo instance on the left side of the page. In the Control panel, change the image scale to 50% (the same as the original logo, which you saw at the beginning of this project).**

11. **With the logo selected on the left side of the page, Control/right-click the image and choose Fitting>Fit Frame to Content.**

12. **Save the file and continue to the next exercise.**

Edit a Placed Photoshop File

In the previous exercise you used the Edit Original function to make required changes in placed graphics. When you returned to the layout, placed instances of the edited files were automatically updated in the layout. The workflow presents obvious advantages because the layout always reflects the most current version of a placed file.

In many cases, placed files are edited outside the context of the layout — other people who provide files make revisions and resubmit, another artist opens a file on a server and makes changes, etc. When changes are made without using the Edit Original option, the InDesign Links panel warns you that a placed file has been modified. For the layout to output properly, you need to update the linked file to the most current version.

1. **Launch Photoshop (if it is not already running).**

2. **Choose File>Open. Navigate to the file clowns.psd in your WIP>Toys folder and click Open.**

3. **Review the Layers panel (Window>Layers).**

   Type formatting options in Photoshop are essentially the same as those available in Illustrator. The primary difference, however, is that each type "object" (to relate it to Illustrator's type treatment) in Photoshop is managed on separate, special type layers. In other words, when you click with the Type tool in a Photoshop file, a new type layer is automatically created to contain the type that you enter.

4. **In the Layers panel, select the "Go to www.vermontkids.biz..." layer and then choose the Type tool.**

5. **Double-click the word "vermontkids" (in the Web address) to highlight it, and then type `toytrends`.**

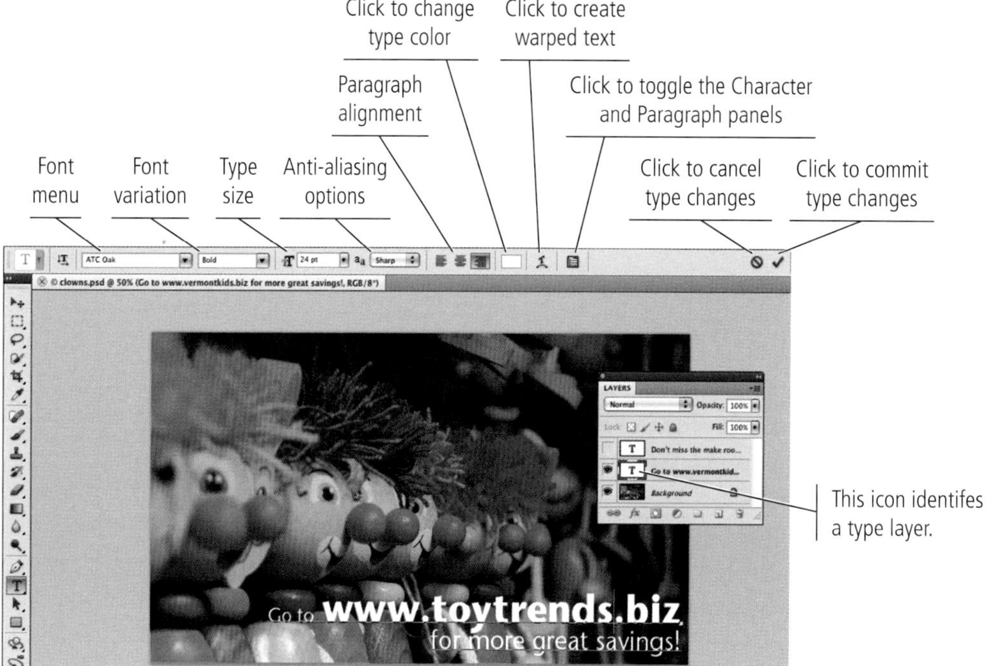

6. **Click the Commit button in the Control panel to finalize the new type.**

Type layers are automatically named using the text that exists on the layer.

> ***Note:***
>
> *You can also simply click the layer name to finalize the new type.*

7. **Save the file, close it, and then return to the `toys_fall.indd` file in InDesign.**

8. **In the Links panel, click the clowns.psd file to select it and then click the Go To Link button.**

When you click the Go To Link button, the selected object is enlarged and centered in the document window.

9. **With clowns.psd still selected in the Links panel, click the Update Link button.**

10. **Return the document to 100% (or smaller to fit into your document window), then save the file and continue to the next exercise.**

Preview Separations

To be entirely confident in color output, you should check the separations that will be created when your file is output to an imagesetter. InDesign's Separations Preview panel makes this easy to accomplish from directly within the application workspace.

1. **With toys_fall.indd open, choose Window>Output>Separations Preview.**

2. **In the View menu of the Separations Preview panel, choose Separations.**

   When Separations is selected in the View menu, all separations in the active file are listed in the panel. You can turn individual separations on or off to preview the different ink separations that will be created:

   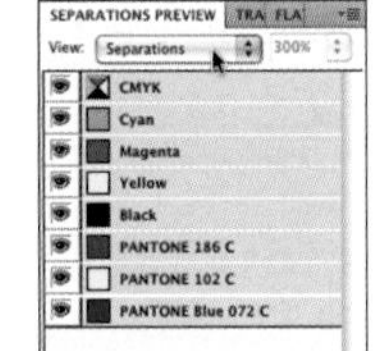

   - To view only a single separation, click the name of the separation you want to view. By default, areas of coverage appear in black; you can preview separations in color by toggling off the Show Single Plates in Black command in the panel Options menu.
   - To view more than one separation at the same time, click the empty space to the left of the separation name. When viewing multiple separations, each separation is shown in color.
   - To hide a separation, click the eye icon to the left of the separation name.
   - To view all process plates at once, click the CMYK option at the top of the panel.

3. **Click Pantone 186 C in the Separations Preview panel, and then click the empty space to the left of Pantone 102 C to review where those two colors are used in the layout.**

   The placed logos on Page 1 use both selected Pantone colors.

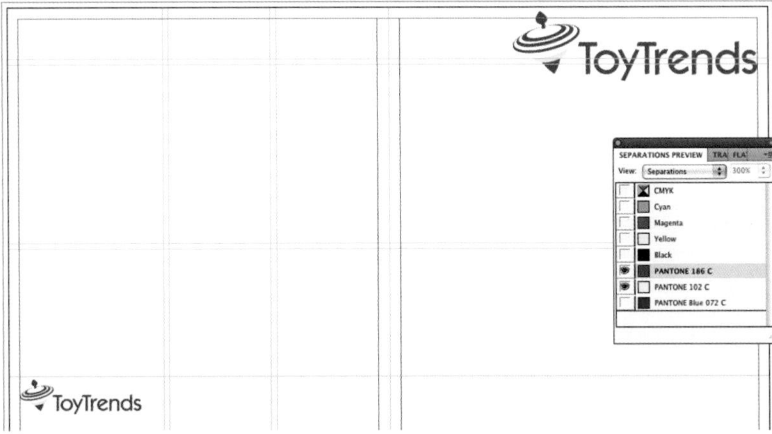

4. **Click Pantone Blue 072 C in the Separations Preview panel to see where that color is used.**

   As your client stated, the brochure should use a single spot color — for this issue, the blue spot color in the logo. By reviewing the separation, you can see that the blue from the logo is also used for the accent elements on both pages of the layout.

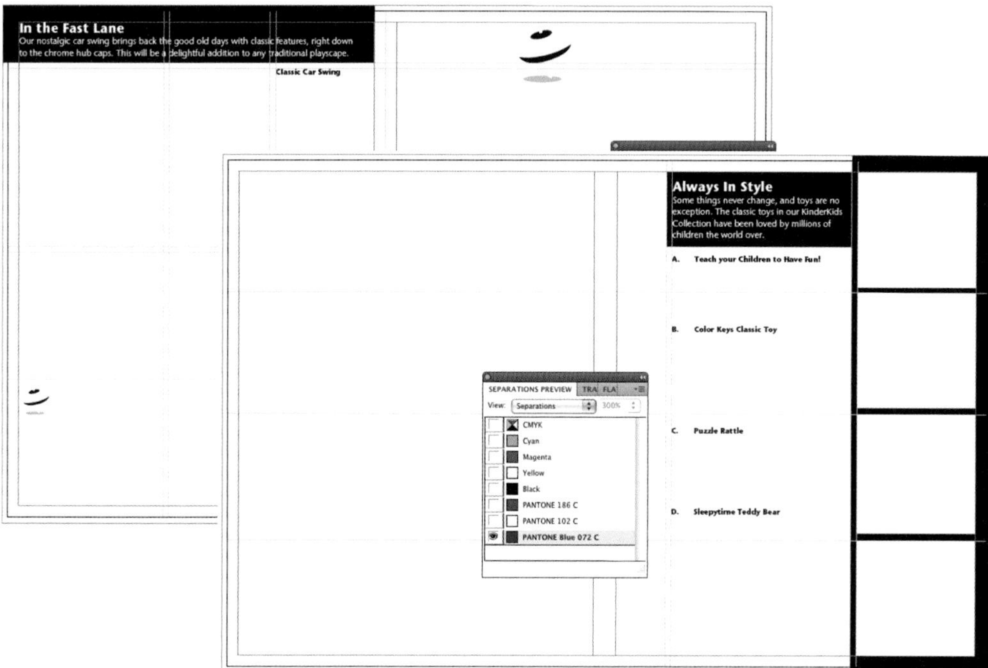

5. **Click the empty space left of CMYK in the Separations Preview panel to view the CMYK separations in addition to the Pantone Blue 072 C separation.**

   You can't simply delete the spot colors because they are used elsewhere in the document. You could convert them for output only, but if you need to output more than once you would have to convert the colors again each time you output the file. In this case, the most efficient option is to convert the unwanted spot colors to process colors before you output the file.

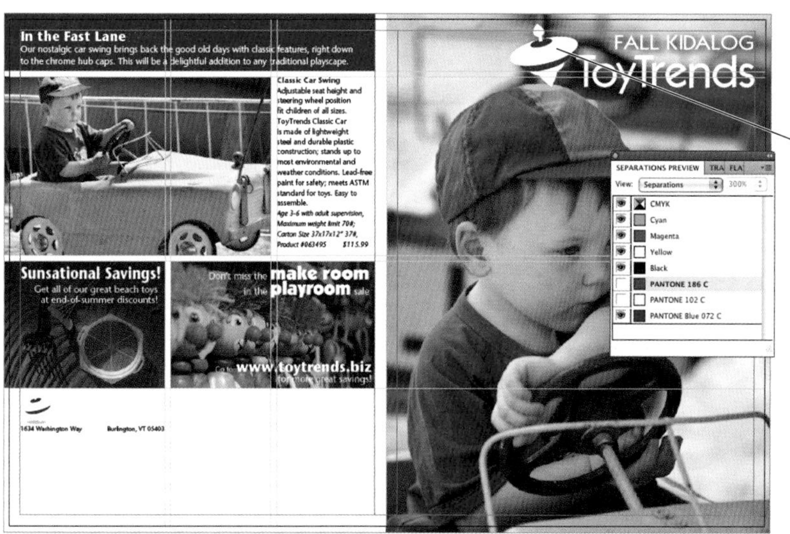

The red and yellow elements from the two hidden spot separations are not visible.

6. **In the Swatches panel, Control/right-click Pantone 186 C and choose Swatch Options from the contextual menu.**

7. **Change the Color Type menu to Process and click OK.**

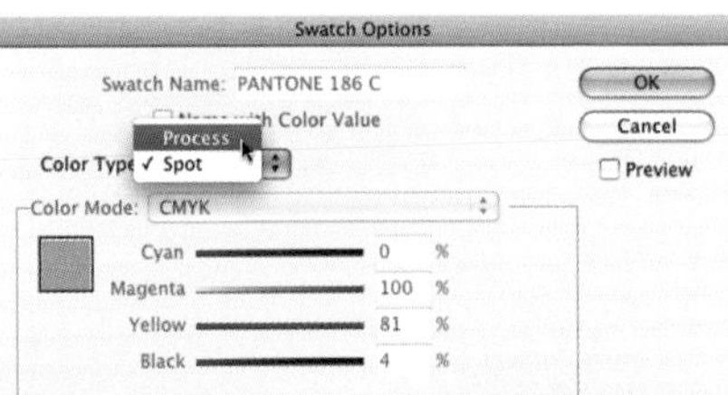

Note:

Be very careful when changing spot colors to process. One reason for using spot colors is to reproduce colors that are outside the CMYK gamut; when spot colors are converted to their nearest possible CMYK equivalents, some (possibly drastic) color shift will occur.

The missing red elements now appear because they are CMYK builds instead of spot colors.

After converting the Pantone 186 C swatch to process color, the separation is removed from the Separations Preview panel.

8. **Repeat Steps 6–7 for the Pantone 102 C swatch.**

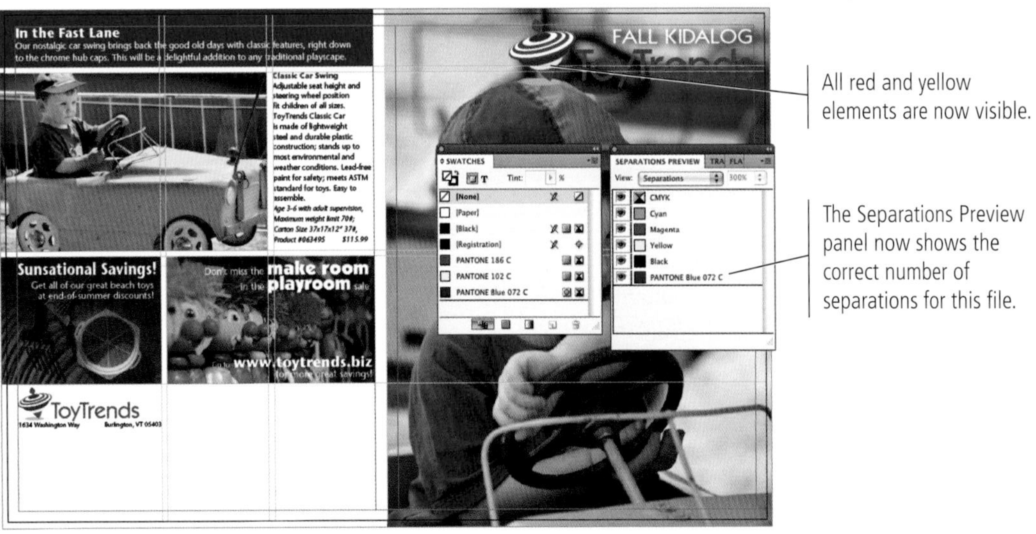

All red and yellow elements are now visible.

The Separations Preview panel now shows the correct number of separations for this file.

9. **Save the file and continue to the next exercise.**

Export Color-Managed PDF Files

1. **With toys_fall.indd open, choose File>Export. In the Save As field, change the file name to toys_fall_print.pdf.**

2. **Navigate to your WIP>Toys folder as the destination and choose Adobe PDF (Print) in the Format/Save As Type menu.**

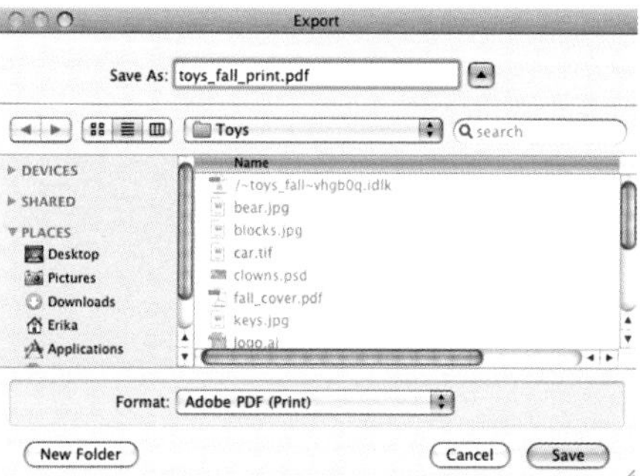

3. **Click Save. In the Export Adobe PDF dialog box, choose [High Quality Print] in the Preset menu.**

4. **In the Marks and Bleed pane, turn on Crop Marks and change the Offset value to 0.125". In the Bleed and Slug section, activate the Use Document Bleed Settings option.**

5. **In the Output pane, choose Convert to Destination in the Color Conversion menu.**

You have several options for converting colors when you output a file:

- **No Color Conversion** maintains all color data (including placed images) in its current space.
- **Convert to Destination** converts colors to the profile selected in the Destination menu.
- **Convert to Destination (Preserve Numbers)** converts colors to the destination profile if the applied profile does not match the defined destination profile. Objects without color profiles are not converted.

The Destination menu defines the gamut for the output device that will be used. (This menu defaults to the active destination working space.) Color information in the file (and placed images) is converted to the selected Destination profile.

6. **Choose Include Destination Profile in the Profile Inclusion Policy menu.**

   The **Profile Inclusion Policy** menu determines whether color profiles are embedded in the resulting PDF file. (Different options are available, depending on what you selected in the Color Conversion menu.)

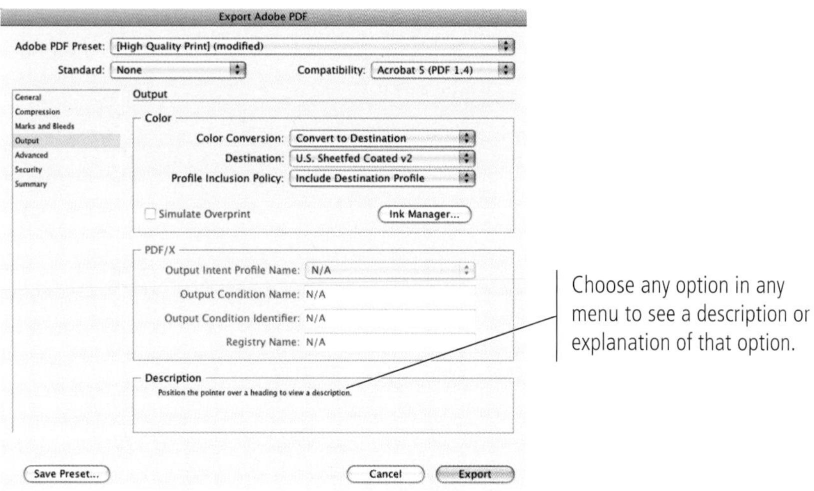

Choose any option in any menu to see a description or explanation of that option.

Note:

Spot-color information is preserved when colors are converted to the destination space.

Note:

These options are also available in the Print dialog box.

7. **Click Export to create the PDF file.**

8. **When the layout file comes back into focus, save it and then continue to the final exercise.**

Create a PDF for Digital Distribution

In addition to the printed job, your client requested a low-resolution PDF file that can be posted on the company's Web site.

1. **With toys_fall.indd open, open the Page Transitions panel (Window>Interactive>Page Transitions).**

2. **In the Pages panel, double-click the Page 1 page number (below the page icon) to select the page.**

   Remember, there can be a difference between the active and selected pages. Double-clicking the targeted page or spread ensures that the spread you want is the one selected.

3. **Open the Page Transitions panel Options menu and select Choose.**

The Page 1 spread is selected and active.

4. **In the resulting Page Transitions dialog box, roll your mouse cursor over the icons to preview the general effect of each.**

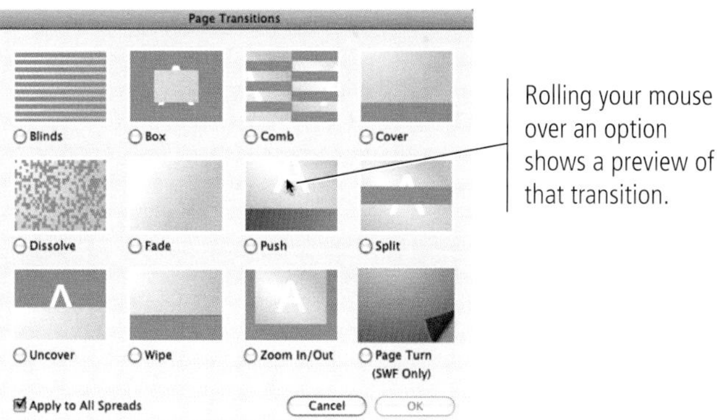

5. **Make sure the Apply to All Spreads option is checked, then activate the Wipe radio button and click OK.**

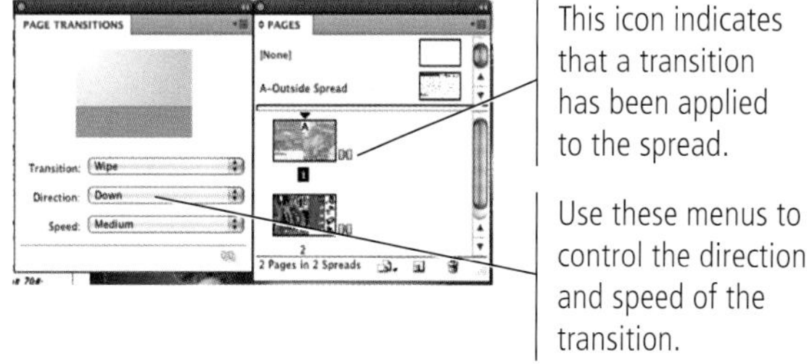

6. **Choose File>Export. In the Save As field, change the file name to** `toys_fall_web.pdf`**.**

7. **Choose Adobe PDF (Interactive) in the Format/Save As Type menu and then click Save.**

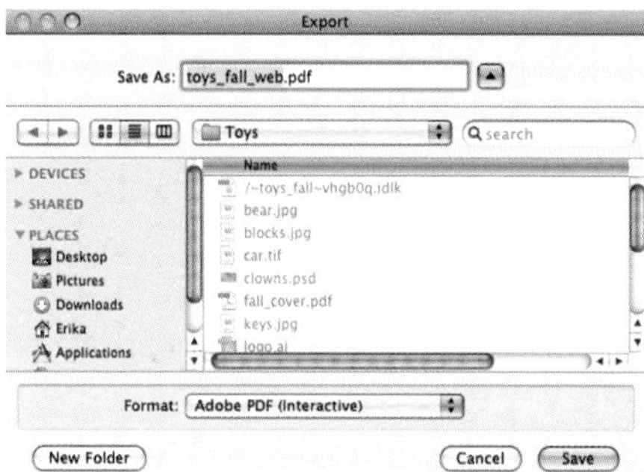

8. **Review the options in the resulting Export to Interactive PDF dialog box.**

The Adobe PDF (Interactive) option opens a simplified dialog box with only the settings that are relevant to PDF files intended for digital distribution.

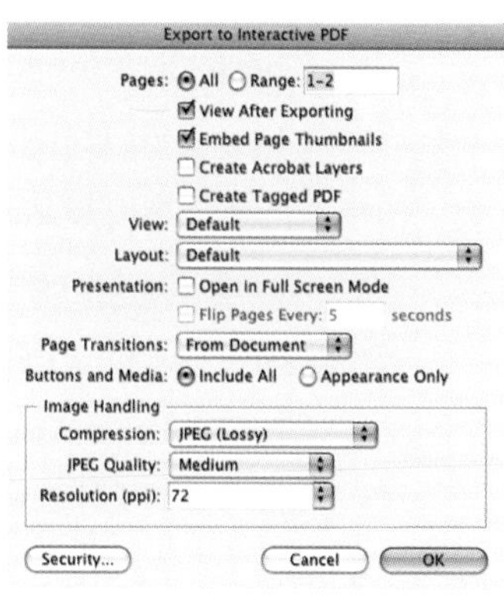

- **Pages** determines which pages will be included in the resulting PDF file. It is important to understand that the Interactive PDF export treats every *spread* as a page in the resulting file. If you design with facing pages, as in this document, every facing-page spread in the Pages panel will result in a single page in the PDF file.
- **View After Exporting**, when active, automatically opens the file in your system's default PDF application.
- **Embed Page Thumbnails** creates a thumbnail preview for every page that is exported.
- **Create Acrobat Layers** maintains any InDesign layers as Acrobat layers in the resulting PDF file. (If you have Acrobat 6.0 or later, you can access those layers to create multiple versions from the same PDF file.)
- **Create Tagged PDF** automatically tags elements in the story based on a subset of the Acrobat tags that InDesign supports (basic text formatting, lists, tables, etc.).
- **View** determines the default view percentage of the exported PDF file. You can cause the file to open at actual size, fit the page into the Acrobat window based on a number of dimensions, or choose a specific percentage (25, 50, 75, or 100).
- **Layout** determines how spreads appear in the resulting PDF file.
  - The **Single Page** options export each spread separately.
  - The **Continuous** options export files so that users can scroll through the document and view parts of successive pages at the same time. Using the non-continuous options, scrolling has the same effect as turning a page; you can't view successive spreads at once.
  - The **Two-Up Facing** options exports two spreads side-by-side.
  - The **Two-Up Cover Page** options export the first spread as a single page, and then the remaining spreads two at a time side-by-side. This allows the pages to appear as they would in a book, with even-numbered pages on the left and odd-numbered pages on the right.

Note:

The default view and layout options open the file based on the reader application's default options.

- **Presentation Opens In Full Screen Mode** opens the resulting PDF without showing Acrobat's menus or panels. You can then use the Flip Pages Every field to automatically change pages after a defined interval.
- **Page Transitions** defaults to the From Document option, which maintains the settings that you define in the Transitions panel. You can choose None to export the PDF without page transitions, or choose one of the available methods in the attached menu to override any settings that exist in the document.
- **Buttons and Media** options can be used to include movies, sounds, and buttons that are created or placed in the InDesign file. If you choose Appearance Only, the PDF will show only the static version of those interactive objects.
- **Compression** determines how images in the resulting PDF are managed to reduce file size for digital distribution. JPEG (Lossy) removes data, and can result in poor image quality. JPEG 2000 (Lossless) reduces file size without discarding image data, but can result in larger file size than JPEG (Lossy). Automatic allows the software to determine the best quality for images.
- **JPEG Quality** defines how much compression is applied if you choose JPEG (Lossy) or Automatic compression. Higher quality settings result in larger files.
- **Resolution** defines the resolution of raster images in the exported PDF. High resolution is important if you want users to be able to zoom in close to an image, but higher resolution settings mean larger file sizes.

9. Define the following settings:
   - Make sure the All [Pages] radio button is selected.
   - Check the View After Exporting option.
   - Check the Embed Page Thumbnails option.
   - Choose Fit Height in the View menu.
   - Choose Single Page in the Layout menu.
   - Check the Open in Full Screen Mode option.
   - Leave the Flip Pages Every option unchecked.
   - Choose From Document in the Page Transitions menu.
   - Choose JPEG 2000 (Lossless) in the Compression menu.
   - Define the target Resolution as 72 ppi.

10. Click OK to create the PDF file.
    If you get a Full Screen warning message when Acrobat opens, click Yes to allow the file to switch to Full Screen mode.

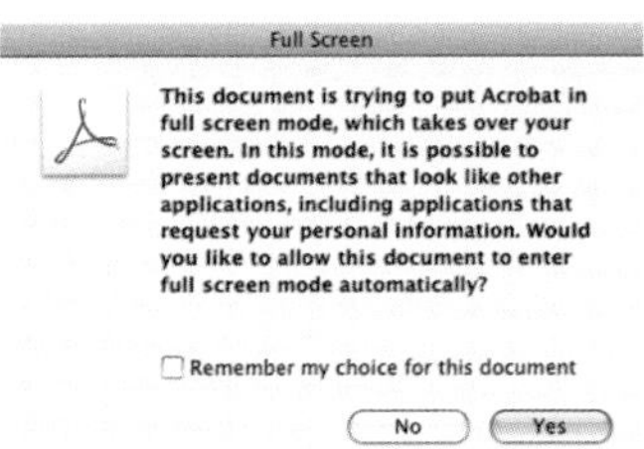

11. When the PDF file opens, press the Down Arrow button to see the interactive page transition.

You have to view the file in Full-Screen mode to see the page transitions.

12. Press the Escape key to exit Full-Screen mode, then close the PDF file. Return to InDesign and then save and close the InDesign file.

Project Review

fill in the blank

1. A(n) _______________ describes the color reproduction characteristics of a particular input or output device.

2. _______________ is the range of possible colors within a specific color model.

3. _______________________________________ are the four component colors in process-color output.

4. When importing an Adobe Illustrator file, the Crop To _______________ option places the file based on the defined artboard size.

5. When placing a native Photoshop file, you can check the _______________ option in the Place dialog box to be able to control layer visibility before the file is placed.

6. When you place a PDF file, the _______________ option in the Place PDF dialog box determines which area of the file (trim, bleed, etc.) is imported.

7. When placing images into a layout, press _______________ to select multiple, non-contiguous files in the Place dialog box.

8. The _______________ lists all files that are placed in a layout, including the location and status of each placed file.

9. A local formatting override is indicated by _______________ next to the style name in the Paragraph Styles panel.

10. The _______________ can be used to review tracked changes.

short answer

1. Briefly explain the difference between additive and subtractive color.

2. Briefly explain the concept of color management, as it relates to building a layout in InDesign.

3. Briefly explain how spot colors relate to print separations.

Portfolio Builder Project

Use what you learned in this project to complete the following freeform exercise.
Carefully read the art director and client comments, then create your own design to meet the needs of the project.
Use the space below to sketch ideas; when finished, write a brief explanation of your reasoning behind your final design.

art director comments

Every professional designer needs a portfolio of their work. If you have completed the projects in this book, you should now have a number of different examples to show off your skills using Illustrator, Photoshop, and InDesign CS5.

The projects in this book were specifically designed to include a broad range of *types* of projects; your portfolio should use the same principle.

client comments

Using the following suggestions, gather your best work and create printed and digital versions of your portfolio:

- ❏ Include as many different types of work as possible, including illustration, photographic manipulation, and page layout.
- ❏ Print clean copies of each finished piece that you want to include.
- ❏ For each example in your portfolio, write a brief (one or two paragraph) synopsis of the project. Explain the purpose of the piece, as well as your role in the creative and production process.
- ❏ Design a personal promotion brochure — create a layout that highlights your technical skills and reflects your personal style.
- ❏ Create a PDF version of your portfolio so you can send your portfolio via email, post it on job sites, and keep it with you on a CD at all times — you never know when you might meet a potential employer.

project justification

Project Summary

As you have seen, placing pictures into an InDesign layout is a relatively easy task, whether you place them one at a time or load multiple images at once and then simply click to place the loaded images into the appropriate spots. InDesign allows you to work with all of the common image formats (including PDF), as well as placing one InDesign layout directly into another. The Links panel is a valuable tool for managing images, from updating file status, to replacing one image with another, to opening an external file in its native application so you can easily make changes in placed files. Fine-tuning a layout requires checking for common errors — both technical (such as low-resolution images) and practical (such as spelling errors).

Place and control a PDF file
Place and control a TIFF file
Place and control a layered Photoshop file
Place and control an EPS file
Place and control a native Illustrator file
Place and control a native InDesign file
Load and place multiple images at one time
Edit placed images using the Links panel
Find and replace elements with specific formatting attributes
Find and replace text strings, with and without specific formatting attributes
Check for and correct spelling errors
In the Fast Lane
FALL KIDALOG
ToyTrends
Sunsational Savings!
make room
playroom
www.toytrends.biz
Always In Style
Take a Ride on a Slide!

D

E

T